Masterplots

Fourth Edition

Masterplots

Fourth Edition

Volume 11
Thebaid—When Rain Clouds Gather

Editor

Laurence W. Mazzeno
Alvernia College

SALEM PRESS
Pasadena, California   Hackensack, New Jersey

Editor in Chief: Dawn P. Dawson

Editorial Director: Christina J. Moose	*Editorial Assistant:* Brett S. Weisberg
Development Editor: Tracy Irons-Georges	*Research Supervisor:* Jeffry Jensen
Project Editor: Desiree Dreeuws	*Research Assistant:* Keli Trousdale
Manuscript Editors: Constance Pollock,	*Production Editor:* Joyce I. Buchea
Judy Selhorst, Andy Perry	*Design and Graphics:* James Hutson
Acquisitions Editor: Mark Rehn	*Layout:* William Zimmerman

Cover photo: William Shakespeare (The Granger Collection, New York)

Library of Congress Cataloging-in-Publication Data

Masterplots / editor, Laurence W. Mazzeno. — 4th ed.
    v. cm.
  Includes bibliographical references and indexes.
  ISBN 978-1-58765-568-5 (set : alk. paper) — ISBN 978-1-58765-579-1 (v. 11: alk. paper)
  1. Literature—Stories, plots, etc. 2. Literature—History and criticism. I. Mazzeno, Laurence W.
  PN44.M33 2010
  809—dc22

2010033931

Fourth Edition
First Printing

Contents

Contents

Complete List of Titles

Volume 1

Volume 2

Volume 3

Volume 4

Volume 5

Volume 6

Volume 7

Contents ccxlvii
Complete List of Titles ccli

Volume 8

Volume 9

Contents cccxxiii

Complete List of Titles cccxxvii

Volume 10

Volume 11

Contents. cccxcix
Complete List of Titles. . . . . cdiii

Volume 12

Contents . . . . cdxxxvii

Complete List of Titles. . . . . cdxxxix

Masterplots

Fourth Edition

Thebaid

Author: Statius (Between 40/45-c. 96 C.E.)
First transcribed: Thebais, c. 90 C E. (English
translation, 1767)
Type of work: Poetry
Type of plot: Epic
Time of plot: Antiquity
Locale: Argos, Nemea, and Thebes

Principal characters:
OEDIPUS, the deposed king of Thebes
JOCASTA, his wife and mother
ETEOCLES,
POLYNICES,
ANTIGONE, and
ISMENE, their children
CREON, Jocasta's brother
MENOECEUS, his son
ADRASTUS, the king of Argos
ARGIA, his daughter, Polynices' wife
TYDEUS,
CAPANEUS,
AMPHIARAUS,
HIPPOMEDON, and
PARTHENOPAEUS, Argive heroes of the march against
    Thebes
HYPSIPYLE, the former queen of Lemnos, a slave

The Poem:

After the fall of Oedipus, Eteocles and Polynices, the two sons of Oedipus and Jocasta, are to alternate as rulers. The plan is doomed to failure because Oedipus calls down the wrath of the Furies upon his unnatural sons. The first year of the kingship falling to Eteocles, Polynices goes into temporary exile in Argos. There he quarrels with Tydeus, a great warrior and hero, but King Adrastus, obeying the prompting of an oracle, settles the dispute by betrothing one of his daughters to each of the young men.

At the end of a year, however, Eteocles refuses to step aside in favor of Polynices, according to the agreement between them. Argia, the wife of Polynices, then persuades her father to aid the prince in asserting his right to the Theban throne. Tydeus is first dispatched as an envoy to the city. Jealous of the fame of the young warrior, Eteocles sets an ambush for Tydeus, who kills all of his attackers except one. The survivor, Maeon, returns to tell Eteocles what happened and then kills himself.

The march against Thebes begins. At Nemea the army is halted by a great drought, but the Argives are saved from their distress when Hypsipyle, the one-time queen of Lemnos before the great massacre there and reduced to a slave entrusted with the care of King Lycurgus's small son, guides them to a stream that still flows. When a snake bites her infant charge, the Argives protect her from the king's anger and, in observance of the boy's funeral, institute the Nemean games. On the arrival of the army before the walls of Thebes, Jocasta and her daughters appear to plead with Polynices in an effort to prevent bloodshed. The battle is joined, however, when two tigers attack the driver of Amphiaraus's chariot; Amphiaraus himself disappears into the underworld when the earth suddenly opens and swallows him alive. In an engagement with the Thebans, Tydeus falls mortally wounded; he dies while gnawing the skull of his foe. The Argive heroes are killed one by one, fighting valiantly but powerless against the might of the gods. Capaneus, who rested from battle to challenge the justice of the gods, is struck by one of Jove's own thunderbolts as he attempts to scale the wall of the city. In a hand-to-hand combat, Eteocles and Polynices kill each other. Only King Adrastus survives. The war ends with the intervention of King Theseus of Athens, who was moved by the prayers of the Argive women. Creon dies at the hands of King Theseus; his son, Menoeceus, previously listens to the words of the oracle and throws himself from the city wall.

Critical Evaluation:

The *Thebaid* of Statius, a retelling in epic form of *Hepta epi Thēbas* (467 B.C.E.; *Seven Against Thebes*, 1777) by Aeschylus, draws extensively on the general body of material dealing with the ill-fated family of Oedipus. Statius's version of the tale of the contending brothers, Eteocles and Polynices, extends to twelve books. Written over a period of twelve years, this narrative of bloody and tragic conflict is a product of the so-called Silver Age of Latin literature. Statius's epic, produced during the reign of the Emperor Domitian, represents a falling off from that of great works such as Vergil's *Aeneid* (29-19 B.C.E.; English translation, 1553), the model for this lesser and more melodramatic poem.

The *Thebaid* is usually mentioned in conjunction with Lucan's *Pharsalia Bellum civile* (60-65 C.E.; *Pharsalia*, 1614). Both epic works grew up under the shadow of the *Aeneid*, and both are responses to it. Lucan attempts to escape the mold, Statius to fill it. Lucan is militantly topical and innovative; Statius is unapologetically derivative. He misses few of the situations and mannerisms that have become the epic stock-in-trade—extended simile, scenes in the underworld, funeral games, catalog of forces, single combats, interference by the gods, and so on. In fact, Statius's greatest contribution to literature, for better or worse, has been to turn all that Vergil borrowed from Homer into an expected element of all future literary epics.

As a writer of verse Statius has few breathtaking passages but considerable flexibility of language, ranging from the softly pathetic to the grandly rhetorical. Statius boasts of the polishing the work received and claims that it required twelve years of labor. This latter claim may be exaggerated, but clearly the language of the *Thebaid* has been worked over carefully.

Statius appears to have taken Aristotle's stricture against loose, episodic epics to heart. Rather than telling the whole story of Thebes, he centers on the conflict between the two sons of Oedipus, climaxing with their mutual destruction in book 11. Book 12 is an appropriate epilogue dealing with the dispute over the burial of Polynices and the Argive invaders and ending with a general reconciliation. The frame is narrow enough for unity but provides room for numerous digressions. One of the most conspicuous features of the epic is the dense texture of legendary and mythological allusion along with the creation of pseudomythological incidents. Such detail can seem distracting, pedantic, and artificial, but Statius generally manages to incorporate such material smoothly and economically.

The sons of Oedipus work better as a structural device than as subject matter. An epic is a large, demanding form. It is dense and ceremonious. For such a work the reader should have some stake in the material. Statius's story, written for a Roman audience, is set in Greece in a city with little historical importance to Rome. In fact, the Roman poet, Juvenal, in his first satire, includes the Thebes among the overworked

and outdated themes poets too often choose. The material was already well worked over about two millennia before, and there is nothing particularly new or involving in Statius's treatment of it. The two brothers are not sympathetic or even particularly interesting characters traditionally, and Statius does little to make them so.

If a story's theme is not of vital interest, then at least the characters should be. By comparison, *Odyssey* (c. 725 B.C.E.; English translation, 1614) is a compelling story, though it makes little difference to the big picture whether Odysseus arrives home or not. In *Thebaid*, however, there is nothing like Homer's wonderful gallery of distinct and fascinating individuals. Characters in Homer may give long and formal speeches, but no two characters talk quite alike, and the language is always convincing as dialogue. Speeches in Statius are usually rhetorical set pieces, grand and melodramatic, but too little bound to the character and the context.

There is no truly engaging character in *Thebaid*. The central figures, Eteocles and Polynices, are not developed in depth, and neither engages the readers' interest nor their sympathy. The character who most stands out is Tydeus, who is small and ferocious, but these two words sum up most of his character. There are few women; Oedipus's wife Jocasta has only a few scenes. The other notable female character, Hypsipyle, is little more than the standard pathetic victim.

Statius is better with the gods, although his characterization echoes Vergil's closely. The authoritarian Jupiter and the softly manipulative Venus are more memorable than any of the humans. Statius also follows Vergil's tendency to summarize rather than to dramatize as Homer does. In Vergil, however, there is always the sense of a context far vaster than whatever is happening at any one time. In the *Thebaid* the context, the fate of the faded city of Thebes, is of rather limited significance.

In following the epic pattern established by Vergil, but largely derived from Homer, Statius seems more dedicated to the epic tradition than to telling a story with its own inner dynamics. Book 5 interrupts the action for a long narrative of past events. There is a similar interruption in books 2 and 3 of the *Aeneid* and in books 9 through 12 of the *Odyssey*. The fall of Troy and the previous adventures of Odysseus, however, are essential to the larger story; Statius's narrative of Hypsipyle is simply an unconnected interlude.

During Hypsipyle's narration, a young prince left in her charge is killed by a huge snake, and book 6 is devoted to funeral games for the child. The *Iliad* (c. 750 B.C.E.; English translation, 1611) and the *Aeneid* establish funeral games as a standard epic feature. The bustle, petty quarrels, and rough humor of Homer's games seem a brilliant counterpart to the grim deaths of Patroclos and Hector, while Vergil's games for Anchises seem at least appropriate. One has to doubt the probability of such contests for the funeral of an infant and to doubt the structural logic of devoting one whole book to the funeral of someone who never appears alive in the story.

In the late classical world and in the Renaissance, when the Vergilian epic was the supreme literary form, Statius's adherence to form, along with his rich tapestry of allusion and incident, made the *Thebaid* widely admired and influential. To the modern world, the epic has lost much of its mystique, and readers are likely to find the characterization, dialogue, and structure of the *Thebaid* less than completely satisfying.

"Critical Evaluation" by Jack Hart

Further Reading

Bernstein, Neil W. *In the Image of the Ancestors: Narratives of Kinship in Flavian Epic.* Toronto, Ont.: University of Toronto Press, 2008. Statius's *Thebaid* and *Achilleid* are two of only four extant epics from the Flavian period, 69-96 C.E. Bernstein examines how the depictions of kinship in these four works differs from earlier epics, placing the epics in the context of social, political, and aesthetic changes during the early Roman Empire. Chapter 3 discusses kinship as destiny and as gender in the *Thebaid*.

Ganiban, Randall T. *Statius and Virgil: "The Thebaid" and the Reinterpretation of the "Aeneid."* New York: Cambridge University Press, 2007. Examines the relationship of Vergil's *Aeneid* to *Thebaid*. Argues that in *Thebaid*, Statius adapted themes, scenes, and ideas from Vergil's epic in order to show that the *Aeneid* inadequately depicted monarchy. Maintains that the horror, spectacle, and violence in *Thebaid* is Statius's critique of the moral and political virtues in the *Aeneid*.

Lovatt, Helen. *Statius and Epic Games: Sport, Politics, and Poetics in "The Thebaid."* New York: Cambridge University Press, 2005. Focuses on Statius's use of athletic games in book 6 of the epic. Argues that each event in the games depicts a theme, such as cosmic disruption, national identity, masculinity, war, and kingship.

Mendell, C. W. *Latin Poetry: The Age of Rhetoric and Satire.* Hamden, Conn.: Archon Books, 1967. Establishes the context and explains the aesthetic values of the era in which Statius lived.

Smolenaars, Johannes J. L., Harm-Jan van Dam, and Ruurd R. Nauta, eds. *The Poetry of Statius.* Boston: Brill, 2008. Several of the essays in this collection examine *Thebaid*, including discussions of the battle narrative, the character of Jupiter in book 1, rituals of succession in the poem, and how Statius adapts the tradition of Jocasta's suicide in Greek and Roman drama.

Statius. *Thebaid.* Translated by A. D. Melville. New York: Oxford University Press, 1992. This very accurate translation is written in a graceful and formal blank verse that preserves the poetic quality of the original. An introduction explains and justifies *Thebaid* with enthusiasm.

Tillyard, E. M. W. *The English Epic and Its Background.* 1954. Reprint. New York: Oxford University Press, 1966. Deals with a number of epics from the ancient world and the Renaissance. Places *Thebaid* in the broad context of a tradition extending more than two thousand years.

Vessey, David. *Statius and "The Thebaid."* New York: Cambridge University Press, 1973. One of the largest and most comprehensive studies of *Thebaid* by an enthusiast of the poem.

Their Eyes Were Watching God

Author: Zora Neale Hurston (1891-1960)
First published: 1937
Type of work: Novel
Type of plot: Bildungsroman
Time of plot: Around 1900
Locale: Florida

Principal characters:
JANIE CRAWFORD KILLICKS STARKS WOODS, the thrice-married, twice-widowed protagonist
PHEOBY WATSON, her friend
NANNY, her grandmother
LOGAN KILLICKS, her first husband
JOE STARKS, her second husband
TEA CAKE WOODS, her third husband

The Story:

Janie Starks returns to town. One sundown, the Eatonville inhabitants watch and gossip as Janie walks the street toward her house, dressed in overalls, with her long braid hanging down her back. Only her friend Pheoby has the kindness to greet her. Pheoby sits down to hear her friend's story.

As a little girl, Janie assumed she was white. She lived with her grandmother and played constantly with the children of the Washburns, for whom Nanny worked. Only when a photographer took the children's picture did Janie realize that she was the black girl in the photo. Nanny was protective of her and worried when she became a teenager. To Nanny, the easiest way to protect Janie from the attentions of useless men was to marry her off young to a good one.

So Janie found herself married early to Logan Killicks, an older man with a house and land. No affection existed between them; Logan seemed to want someone to share the work. Janie could hardly stand to be around him. She complained to Nanny about his big belly, his mule-foot toenails, and the fact that he refused to wash his feet before coming to bed: "Ah'd ruther be shot wid tacks than tuh turn over in de bed and stir up de air whilst he is in dere."

One day Janie met a stranger on the road, a handsome, charming man named Joe "Jody" Starks. He was on his way to make a place for himself in a new all-black town, Eatonville. After sneaking off to meet Jody in the scrub oaks for several days and getting him to promise to marry her, Janie ran away with him.

Jody did make himself a place in the new town, becoming the mayor and opening the first store. Janie found herself the most envied woman in town, with the most important husband and the biggest house. She spent her days working in the store but soon found that life with Jody was not all wonderful. He was given to jealousy and insisted that she wear a kerchief over her beautiful long hair so that the men who came into the shop would not admire or touch it. To keep her in her place, he frequently criticized her work and refused to let her express her opinions to their acquaintances and friends who visited with them on the porch of the house in front of the store. Over the years this treatment drained the life from Janie: "She was a rut in the road. Plenty of life beneath the surface but it was kept beaten down by the wheels."

One night Joe became angry when Janie miscut a plug of tobacco. Although she knew it was better to keep silent, she talked back and he, fearing to lose face in front of his friends, struck her. From then on, Jody slept downstairs. Soon after, he became sick, but he still refused to let Janie come near him again. Even on the night of his death, when she came into his room to speak with him, he could not forgive her.

After Joe's death, Janie tended the store. Joy came back into her life with Tea Cake Woods, a young man of questionable reputation who found his way to the store one day and entertained her with checker games and his guitar. Before Jody was dead nine months, Janie started spending all of her time with Tea Cake, wearing colorful dresses and showing off her hair. When Janie left town to marry Tea Cake, the town was sure she was being taken for her money. The townsfolk were wrong, though. Despite the difference in their ages—Janie was close to forty by this time—and the difference in their former lives, Janie found that her new husband loved and appreciated her. He took her to the Everglades, where they went "on de muck" picking beans. Here, Janie found herself in the center of a community of lively, happy, hardworking folk. Janie and Tea Cake's house became the center of activity after a day's work, and the main activities were making music and gambling, both of which Tea Cake did well. For the first time, Janie found happiness in a marriage.

After two good seasons, disaster came when a hurricane struck, broke the dam, and flooded the area. Most of the residents anticipated the storm and left early enough, but Tea Cake and Janie stayed. By the time they finally tried to make it to high ground, the dam burst and they found themselves swimming to safety. Janie almost died in the rush of water but managed to grab a swimming cow's tail to be carried along. When a dog riding on the cow's back tried to bite Janie and force her away, Tea Cake rose up and killed the dog, but not before the dog bit him in the face. Finally, exhausted, Janie and Tea Cake reached safety.

Their relief was short-lived, however, for Tea Cake began to suffer from terrible headaches and became ill-tempered. Janie finally arranged for a doctor to see him, who informed her that the dog that bit him was rabid and that it was not too late for treatment. The doctor warned Janie to be careful around the ill man. When Tea Cake, in the middle of one of his attacks, came at Janie with a gun, she shot him in self-defense. She was brought to trial but found not guilty, and Tea Cake's death was ruled an accident. After a few weeks with Tea Cake's friends in the Everglades, she headed back to Eatonville, where her life began.

Critical Evaluation:

Upon its publication, *Their Eyes Were Watching God* received rather harsh judgment from such African American writers as Richard Wright and Ralph Ellison, who called the book "quaint." Above all, they criticized Zora Neale Hurston for presenting a romantic view of the African American community and for not writing in the Harlem Renaissance protest tradition. Others reviewed the book more favorably, but it was soon out of print and became forgotten.

In 1965, *Their Eyes Were Watching God* was republished, after which it began to receive a great deal of attention and to be reevaluated by many as a staple of the American literary canon. The book was lauded in particular for its calling on the black folkloric tradition, for its language, and for its female hero. Janie is light colored and beautiful, and as a child she does not even realize she is black. When she is in her forties, her neighbor, Mrs. Turner, admires her for her coffee-and-cream complexion and her luxurious hair. However, Janie's road to self-knowledge takes her deeper into blackness. She moves from her home among white folks through two black husbands to the blackest of them all, Tea Cake, and the blackest community of all, that of the seasonal workers in the Everglades.

African American lore was passed down not in writing but in speech. *Their Eyes Were Watching God* documents the oral tradition in two ways. The book actually describes the community passing on its lore, first on the porch of Joe Starks's store and later at the evening get-togethers at the house on the muck. In one of the most memorable and comic scenes of the book, the Eatonville inhabitants hold a ceremonious mock funeral for Matt Bonner's yellow mule, an occasion that elicits delighted participation from the entire town. A subtler device by which Hurston documents the oral tradition is in her method of narration when Janie tells her story not to the audience by the printed word but orally to her friend Pheoby. Readers get the spoken narrative, what Henry Louis Gates, Jr., called "a speakerly text."

The novel is richly packed with direct speech in poetic black dialect. Nanny, warning Janie not to give her heartache, tells her, "Put me down easy, Janie. Ah'm a cracked plate." When Janie frets to Tea Cake about being older than he, he says, " . . . don't say you'se ole. You'se uh lil girl baby all de time. God made it so you spent yo' ole age first wid somebody else, and saved up yo' young girl days to spend wid me." Even the third-person narrative is presented to the reader in Janie's dialect. After Joe's death, Janie "starched and ironed her face and came set in the funeral behind her veil. . . . She sent her face to Joe's funeral, and herself went rollicking with the springtime across the world."

The richest element of the novel is Janie herself. She becomes powerful and self-reliant as she moves from being controlled by men to being self-assertive and independent. Janie is ultimately never beaten down because she learns to separate her private self from her public life until she finally gets the opportunity to combine the two. Janie provides a positive image of the black woman who is able to reject con-

formity and security at the same time that she controls her life on her own terms. Her choice—to trust love—invigorates her; upon her return from the muck, she tells Pheoby, "Ah been a delegate to do big 'ssociation of life. Yessuh! De Grand Lodge, de big convention of livin' is just where Ah been."

Janie's experiences reflect the difficulties of being black and female in the South in the early twentieth century. Hurston shows her both as a part of a community and as an outsider in that community by virtue of her gender and her choices. She rises above her circumstances. Saddened but not defeated at the end of her tale, Janie tells her old friend Pheoby not to judge harshly the neighbors who gossiped so cruelly upon her return to Eatonville: "Two things everybody's got tuh do fuh theyselves. They got tuh go tuh God, and they got tuh find out about livin' fuh theyselves." Janie finds out about livin', and she is at peace.

Janine Rider

Further Reading

Awkward, Michael. *New Essays on "Their Eyes Were Watching God."* New York: Cambridge University Press, 1990. In five essays, the author presents various interpretations of the novel.

Bloom, Harold, ed. *Zora Neale Hurston's "Their Eyes Were Watching God."* New ed. New York: Bloom's Literary Criticism, 2008. Collection of essays providing critical analyses of the novel, including character analyses and discussions of the novel's language, speech, narrative structure, voice, and vision.

Boyd, Valerie. *Wrapped in Rainbows: The Life of Zora Neale Hurston.* New York: Scribner, 2002. A comprehensive, meticulously researched account of Hurston the woman and the writer, based in part on information available within the past twenty years. Includes a discussion of the Hurston "resurrection," a list of her published works, selected bibliography, and index.

Callahan, John F. "'Mah Tongue Is in Mah Friend's Mouf': The Rhetoric of Intimacy and Immensity in *Their Eyes Were Watching God.*" In *In the African-American Grain: The Pursuit of Voice in Twentieth-Century Black Fiction.* Urbana: University of Illinois Press, 1988. Callahan's essay examines the most controversial aspect of Hurston's novel—the role of narrative voice in the telling of Janie's story. He emphasizes the novel's use of African American folk forms of storytelling, which promote a democratic conception of culture.

Campbell, Josie P. *Student Companion to Zora Neale Hurs-*

ton. Westport, Conn.: Greenwood Press, 2001. Includes a brief biography, an overview of Hurston's fiction, and separate chapters discussing each of her four novels. Designed for students and general readers.

Cooke, Michael G. "Solitude: The Beginnings of Self-Realization in Zora Neale Hurston, Richard Wright, and Ralph Ellison." In *Afro-American Literature in the Twentieth Century: The Achievement of Intimacy.* New Haven, Conn.: Yale University Press, 1984. Cooke highlights the movement from materialism to self-fulfillment in the work of three very different African American writers.

Gates, Henry Louis, Jr., and K. A. Appiah, eds. *Zora Neale Hurston: Critical Perspectives Past and Present.* New York: Amistad, 1993. Includes the original, rather harsh reviews of *Their Eyes Were Watching God,* along with positive later essays. Includes Gates's important essay, "*Their Eyes Were Watching God:* Hurston and the Speakerly Text."

Lowe, John. *Jump at the Sun: Zora Neale Hurston's Cosmic Comedy.* Chicago: University of Illinois Press, 1994. A study of humor in Hurston's work, including a fifty-page chapter on *Their Eyes Were Watching God.*

Plant, Deborah G. *Zora Neale Hurston: A Biography of the Spirit.* Westport, Conn.: Praeger, 2007. A biography of Hurston that portrays her strength and tenacity of spirit. Her literary achievements, including *Their Eyes Were Watching God,* are also discussed here. This work draws on Hurston's 1942 autobiography, *Dust Tracks on a Road,* as well as newly discovered sources.

West, Margaret Genevieve. *Zora Neale Hurston and American Literary Culture.* Gainesville: University Press of Florida, 2005. A chronicle of Hurston's literary career, describing how her work was marketed and reviewed in her lifetime and why her writing did not gain popularity until long after her death.

them

Author: Joyce Carol Oates (1938-   )
First published: 1969
Type of work: Novel
Type of plot: Psychological realism
Time of plot: August, 1937-1967
Locale: Detroit, Michigan

Principal characters:
LORETTA BOTSFORD WENDALL, a wife and mother
BROCK BOTSFORD, her brother
RITA, her childhood friend
HOWARD WENDALL, her first husband, a police officer
JULES WENDALL, her son
MAUREEN WENDALL and BETTY WENDALL, her daughters
NADINE, Jules's lover
PAT FURLONG, Loretta's second husband

The Story:

In August, 1937, sixteen-year-old Loretta Botsford looks into her bedroom mirror and assesses herself, giddy in the belief that she is in love. Annoyed with her brother, Brock, whom she sees as shifty and malicious, she grudgingly makes supper for him before going out for the evening. In the course of arguing with him about the shiftlessness of their father, recently fired, Loretta notices that Brock has a gun.

The next morning, Brock finds a boy in Loretta's bedroom and shoots and kills him. After realizing what her brother has done, Loretta runs to her friend Rita's house in desperation, with Rita attempting to calm Loretta but offer-

ing no solution. Loretta leaves Rita's house and sees a police officer watching her at the end of the street. She wonders if he knows what has happened and if he is waiting for her to confess. She takes him to the scene of the crime. He tells her that everyone will know what she had done with the boy before he died, and that he will do the same to her. The officer's name is Howard Wendall.

Now married to Howard, and pregnant, Loretta begins living with him on the south side of Detroit, glad to be away from the home that she considers a dump and the family she considers hopeless. Just when Loretta believes that she will have a settled, normal life, Howard is suspended from the police force because of his illegal activities, and the Wendalls move to the country with Mama Wendall, her husband, and their daughter, Connie; this is the worst possible scenario, as far as Loretta is concerned.

With her domineering mother and a sullen, broken-spirited husband, the one bright spot in Loretta's life is her son, Jules, who seems different from the rest of the family—lively and joyful and always involved in a new activity, sometimes creative and sometimes destructive. With his sister, Maureen, he is playing in the barn one day. He lights a match and drops it into a pile of hay, burning down the barn and receiving a whipping from his grandmother.

In the meantime, while Howard is in Europe, fighting in the war, Loretta receives letters from her friend Rita, wondering how she is and when she will visit. Longing for city life and to be away from her mother-in-law, Loretta announces that she and the children are moving to Detroit. After a long night of name-calling and threats from Mama Wendall, Loretta, Jules, and Maureen leave, taking a bus to Detroit. Although Jules is confused and intimidated by big-city life, Loretta feels as if she is finally home again and resumes her routine of visiting friends and going out at night, narrowly avoiding being arrested for soliciting one evening.

Jules attends Catholic school, and at the age of twelve develops a crush on a nun, mainly because of her passionate piano playing. From this point on, he seems to realize that he is different from other boys his age, more sensitive and attuned to the special, hidden qualities that others, especially women, keep to themselves. Throughout his life he openly approaches girls and women who appeal to him, sometimes with tragic consequences, as in the passion he develops for Nadine, the niece of an employer. Nadine wants to run away, so they travel to the Southwest, staying in cheap motels. One day, Jules feels deathly ill and is in and out of consciousness. He wakes up to find himself alone; Nadine had left him, driving his car.

After spending some time in the West doing odd jobs, serving a stint in the military, and even being a subject in a research study, Jules returns to Detroit. He sees Nadine in a restaurant. Although she is married, they start a passionate affair that ends with Nadine shooting Jules while they are taking a walk; she then turns the gun on herself. They both survive, but do not see each other again.

Meanwhile, Loretta has remarried following the death of Howard in an accident at work. Daughters Maureen and Betty have to adjust to a new man in the house, Pat Furlong. Maureen is an overachiever, and is proud to be home-room secretary at school. She spends much of her time in the li-brary, which she finds peaceful and civilized compared to her home life. She is traumatized when she loses her secretarial notebook, and feels she let down not only herself but also the nuns who gave her the secretarial position. She seems to be giving up her dream of having a career and living in her own apartment, finding that there is an easy way for her to make money after she accepts a ride from a man and receives money for her services to him. This leads to money from other men as well. Furlong spots her one day in a strange man's car, then beats her so badly when she gets home that it takes Maureen thirteen months to recover; Furlong is sent to prison.

After her recovery, Maureen attends night school and realizes that she wants a house and a husband more than anything. She decides that she will marry her English composition instructor, who is already married with children. They begin an affair when he offers to drive her home, and they eventually marry. Jules visits her in the aftermath of the fires, looting, and killings of the 1967 Detroit riots, but Maureen closes the door on him and the rest of the family when she realizes that she has the normalcy that she had always wanted and that she will soon have the baby to complete the picture. Jules, in the brief conversation they have at the door, says that he loves Loretta and will always think of her.

Critical Evaluation:

Joyce Carol Oates is a prolific writer, publishing more than fifty novels as well as dozens of short stories, poems, dramatic works, essays, and books for children and young adults. She has won numerous awards for her novels and short stories, including a National Book Award for *them*, as well as awards for lifetime achievement, such as the National Arts Club Medal of Honor in Literature, the Humanist of the Year Award, the *Chicago Tribune* Literary Prize for Lifetime Achievement, the Fairfax Prize for Lifetime Achievement in the Literary Arts, the Carl Sandburg Literary Award for Lifetime Achievement, the F. Scott Fitzgerald Award for Lifetime Achievement in American Literature, and the PEN/Malamud Award for Lifetime Achievement in the Short Story. Oates also has received seven honorary doctorates. She is a Distinguished Professor of Humanities at Princeton University, where she began teaching in 1978.

In *them*, Oates presents the story of the Wendalls, the prototypical dysfunctional family living in Detroit. Loretta, the mother, is trying to raise her children and eke out a living when she does not have a man to support her, and her children—Jules, Maureen, and Betty—get themselves into some compromising situations but manage to emerge from these situations undefeated, although not unscathed.

Although narrated in the third person, the novel focuses on the perspectives of Jules and Maureen as they navigate the development of their identities and the discovery that they are different from others. Through following Jules on his wanderings around town and his job changes after he drops out of school, readers learn that he is a romantic, always drawn to young women who seem somewhat inaccessible to him, yet also a cynic in his sometimes settling for women and jobs that are good enough for the time being. Maureen shares some of her older brother's idealism in her love of books and libraries, especially British novels, yet she also becomes cynical when she finds she can get money for the time she spends with men who pick her up for sex. This illusion of easy money is ruined when she is severely beaten by her stepfather.

Oates presents the lives of these siblings and their mother through a realistic lens. Readers get a sense of urban grit in Detroit from the 1940's to the 1960's, where inhabitants lead lives of desperation. Racial tension is constant, as is violence, both on the street and in the home; relationships fail and jobs are lost. Loretta, depending on a man to validate her existence and financially support her, seems to make the wrong choices, expecting her children to unconditionally accept the men that she brings into their home, even to see them as fathers, all the while thinking that she is destined for greater things. Maureen escapes to the civilized quiet of the library, and Jules escapes to the streets, always searching for adventure and love, dabbling in crime but never getting caught. Nearly sixteen years old at the time of his father's funeral, he realizes that he cannot remember his father's face or anything he said: Jules feels "depressed and lifeless," with "no music anywhere around him or the promise of music."

Similarly, fourteen-year-old Maureen loses the notebook with which she has been entrusted as home-room secretary, and feels as if "her life was coming undone. The world was opening up to trap her, she was losing her mind, she was coming undone, unfastened," with "no way out, no escape, no help." No matter how much she strived, she would always be Loretta's daughter, destined for the same fate as her mother. In fact, Maureen does end up taking a similar path. Longing for a house and a husband, she decides that she will achieve these with her married English instructor. Disregarding the children he already has, she sets her sights on a child of her own with him, and when she is married at the end of the novel, readers see her turning Jules away from her door after a brief conversation with him. She has decided that she is a different person and does not wish to see her family anymore. When Jules kisses her hand and says goodbye, Maureen realizes that she loves him for "going away, saying good-by, leaving her forever."

Through realistic and sometimes surrealistic portrayals of urban and psychological breakdown, along with the desperation to keep living despite all the threats to one's well-being, Oates has created a world in which her characters are desperate to keep living. Having based *them* on a letter from one of her former students describing this desperation to survive and achieve some semblance of normalcy in her life, Oates has depicted a world that she has described as "remote"; this world may be remote, but in *them*, it is accessible.

Holly L. Norton

Further Reading

Cologne-Brookes, Gavin. *Dark Eyes on America: The Novels of Joyce Carol Oates*. Baton Rouge: Louisiana State University Press, 2005. An analysis of selected significant works by Oates, with a focus on exposing her philosophical and cultural worldviews. A valuable addition to studies of Oates's wide-ranging work.

Johnson, Greg. *Invisible Writer: A Biography of Joyce Carol Oates*. New York: Plume, 1998. A biography of Oates that draws on private letters, journals, and interviews to reveal the details of her development as a writer in her formative years, her study of writing and publication in her university years, and her career as a writer and professor in her later years.

Milazzo, Lee, ed. *Conversations with Joyce Carol Oates*. Jackson: University Press of Mississippi, 1989. A collection of pieces by various interviewers from early in Oates's career on subjects such as her prolific output, the gothic nature of much of her work, depictions of love and violence in her stories and novels, her writing process, and her writings on boxing.

Oates, Joyce Carol. *The Faith of a Writer: Life, Craft, Art*. New York: HarperCollins, 2003. Oates describes her reading and writing experiences in school, discusses her favorite poems from childhood and the craft of writing, and offers self-criticism.

_____. *The Journal of Joyce Carol Oates, 1973-1982*, edited by Greg Johnson. New York: Ecco, 2007. A wide-ranging collection of entries that traces Oates's life from her time as a professor at the University of Windsor through her move to Princeton. She describes the joys and frustrations of writing as well as spending time with friends and family. Includes Oates's philosophical explorations and musings on the human condition as well as a record of her productivity as a writer.

_____. *Joyce Carol Oates: Conversation*, edited by Greg Johnson. Princeton, N.J.: Ontario Review Press, 2006.

This collection of interviews with Oates from 1970 to 2006 in publications such as *Atlantic Monthly, Newsweek, Paris Review,* and *The New York Times Magazine* includes her thoughts on the art of fiction, her "lighter" side, and Marilyn Monroe, the subject of her novel *Blonde* (2000). The volume also includes a brief chronology of her life.

Wesley, Marilyn. *Refusal and Transgression in Joyce Carol Oates's Fiction.* Westport, Conn.: Greenwood Press, 1993. A feminist analysis that focuses on the family as portrayed in Oates's fiction. Contends that the young protagonists of many of her stories and novels commit acts of transgression that serve as critiques of the American family.

Thesmophoriazusae

Author: Aristophanes (c. 450-c. 385 B.C.E.)
First produced: *Thesmophoriazousai,* 411 B.C.E.; first published, 1650, in *Silex Scintillans* (English translation, 1837)
Type of work: Drama
Type of plot: Satire
Time of plot: Fifth century B.C.E.
Locale: Athens

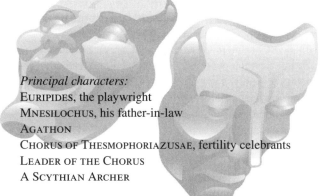

Principal characters:
EURIPIDES, the playwright
MNESILOCHUS, his father-in-law
AGATHON
CHORUS OF THESMOPHORIAZUSAE, fertility celebrants
LEADER OF THE CHORUS
A SCYTHIAN ARCHER

The Story:

On the way to the house of Agathon, Euripides, the celebrated dramatist, explains to his aged but lusty father-in-law, Mnesilochus, that he is in great danger. The Thesmophoriazusae are gathered at the temple of Demeter to decide on an appropriate punishment for the playwright—Euripides—who so consistently and so bitterly insults their sex in his plays. Agathon will surely be able to help him. At the door of Agathon's house a servant appears and orders the people and the winds to be quiet because his master is seized with poetical inspiration. Mnesilochus knows at once that no real help can come from such a man.

When Agathon appears, reposing on a bed, dressed in a saffron tunic, and surrounded by feminine toilet articles, Mnesilochus insults him roundly for his lack of manhood. As expected, Agathon refuses to aid Euripides by dressing as a woman in order to mix with the fertility celebrants and plead Euripides' cause; the plan is simply too risky. Mnesilochus then offers himself and is promptly and painfully shaved, undressed, and depilated. Disguised as a woman, the old man is suddenly very reluctant to go to the temple until Euripides swears by all the gods to come to his aid if anything goes wrong.

Striving to act as womanly as possible and giving his voice a feminine lilt, the old man enters the temple with a

prayer to Demeter and Persephone that he will not be recognized. After certain preliminaries the women within begin their deliberations concerning Euripides' fate. The First Woman, after spitting as orators do, opens with the charge that Euripides presents women in his plays as adulterous, lecherous, bibulous, treacherous, and garrulous; he causes husbands, especially old ones, to be suspicious of their wives; and he provokes them into keeping the keys to the storerooms and sealing doors upon their wives. She declares that the playwright deserves any form of death, but preferably by poison. The Second Woman explains that she, a widow with five children, supported herself by selling religious chaplets until Euripides convinced spectators of his plays that there are no gods. Mnesilochus, unable to restrain himself upon hearing his son-in-law so defamed, agrees that Euripides indeed committed two or three such indiscretions, but he urges the women to consider all their horrendous faults that Euripides has not attacked. Mnesilochus then proceeds to present a detailed catalog of feminine failings.

The outraged women turn upon Mnesilochus in furious wrath, but before the face-slapping leads to hair-pulling Clisthenes arrives with the warning that a man disguised as a woman is in their midst. Unmasked, the desperate Mnesilochus seizes what he thinks is a woman's child and threatens to slit its throat if he is not allowed to go free. The "child," however, turns out to be a wineskin and the enraged women begin to gather faggots in order to roast Mnesilochus alive.

Euripides, summoned by messages scratched on wooden idols that Mnesilochus throws out of the temple, enters, declaiming Menelaus's lines from his play *Helenē* (412 B.C.E.; *Helen*, 1782). Mnesilochus responds with Helen's lines, but before a rescue can be effected a magistrate accompanied by a hefty Scythian archer arrives and Euripides flees. The magistrate, after ordering Mnesilochus to be lashed to a post, leaves him under the guard of the Scythian. As the women begin their ceremonies, Euripides, playing Echo of his drama on Perseus and Andromeda, begins to echo Mnesilochus's laments as he enters the temple in the dress of Perseus. The illiterate Scythian, however, refuses to believe that old Mnesilochus is really Andromeda, as Euripides insists.

During the ceremonies the guard falls asleep. Euripides proceeds to disguise himself as a procuress. He then offers the women a proposal of peace: If they will release his father-in-law, he will no longer insult them in his plays. The women agree, but there remains the Scythian to be outwitted. Still disguised as a procuress, Euripides offers the Scythian a good time with the little flute girl whom the barbarian eagerly purchases. While the two are away, Euripides releases his father-in-law and they both escape. His lust satisfied, the Scythian returns to find his prisoner gone; the obliging Thesmophoriazusae send him off in hot pursuit—in the wrong direction.

Critical Evaluation:

Among the extant plays of Aristophanes, *Thesmophoriazusae* is easily the poet's best marriage of literary parody with comic farce. The actual date of production is not precisely known; the play was probably presented in 411 B.C.E., notably the same year in which *Lysistratē* (411 B.C.E.; *Lysistrata*, 1837) was performed. Both plays deal in different ways with the tension between the sexes and depend for their comic effect on a temporary inversion of sexual roles, which were very clearly defined in classical Athens. Through the device of farcical transvestism and elaborate imitation of the elevated tragic diction of Euripidean drama, Aristophanes achieves in *Thesmophoriazusae* a masterpiece that satirizes sexual politics and literary pretension.

The play's title might be translated as "Women Celebrating the Thesmophoria," referring to an Athenian fertility festival that rigorously excluded men from its celebration. A central element of the plot, a man, disguised as a woman, trying to spy on the festival, is not entirely far-fetched. Women's festivals at Athens naturally aroused the curiosity and suspi-

cion of the men who were obliged to support them financially but who were often excluded from participation. Few details are known about what happened at such festivities, but it is clear that they gave women a temporary autonomy and allowed them to conduct sacred fertility rites. Stories from legend and history refer to attempts made by men to infiltrate these all-female rites, often with such dire results as death or castration on discovery. Male anxiety that women secretly indulged in wine or sex or (worse yet) plotted to subvert male domination is the realistic background of the comic fantasy of *Thesmophoriazusae*.

In the play, as the women gather for the festival, they begin to debate a proposal to prosecute the tragic poet Euripides for his slanders against women. Euripides is perfectly suited to be the focus of their hatred. His reputation for misogyny, whether deserved or not, is frequently mentioned in ancient sources. The reputation seems to have arisen from a (superficial) reading of the characterization of women in his tragedies. Euripides is satirized in other surviving plays of Aristophanes, but in this play he is a principal target. Nowhere else is the criticism of his style and his material more elaborate than in *Thesmophoriazusae*. In this play Aristophanes produces astonishingly close imitations of Euripides' style and diction, suggesting that he and his audience were intimately familiar with the tragedian's work. As is often the case in parody, there is a sense that Aristophanes held some grudging respect for Euripides' skill as a tragic poet.

The opening scene shows Euripides attempting to send a spy to infiltrate the meeting of the women. The transvestism is inherently comic, the stuff of farce throughout Western culture. The transvestism underscores the extraordinary separation of the sexes in ancient Athens, where women lived most of their lives apart from men, as well as the mutual ignorance that must have arisen from these circumstances. From repeated jokes that are made in the play, it appears that Athenian women were supposed to be excessively fond of drink, eager to deceive their husbands at every turn, and always ready to conspire against men, who controlled the city. These accusations represent male anxiety about the subordinate and cloistered role of women that was a fact of Athenian life. Humor at the expense of Agathon, an effeminate poet, and Clisthenes, who is homosexual and is unhesitatingly welcomed by the women celebrating the festival, suggests a tension within the Athenian conception of masculinity that Aristophanes exploits for his comic purposes.

Aristophanes next presents the assembly of women, who debate the proposal to try Euripides. Such a formal meeting is, in and of itself, supposed to be comic, since Athenian women were excluded from all political life of the city. During their own private festival where no man is permitted, it is supposed that, as it were, an alternative state is created, with its own laws and customs. As Euripides' spy, Mnesilochus attempts to speak in defense of the poet but only manages to insult the women more. When he is discovered, he is seized and bound. The rest of the play involves attempts to rescue him. The humor of this remaining part of the play depends on knowledge of Euripides' work, which contains many such scenes of rescue. Aristophanes is indulging in a peculiar species of literary criticism. He parodies such plays as Euripides' *Helen*, which was recently presented, and implies that *Helen* is something less than a real tragedy. Scholars admit that some of Euripides' later works, such as *Helen*, are closer to what might properly be called melodrama than to traditional tragedy.

Thesmophoriazusae is different from most other surviving plays of Aristophanes in not representing riotous celebration when the protagonist finally overcomes opposition and achieves his or her goal. Through a ritual celebrating heterosexual love, this traditional element of older Greek comedy—called the marriage or *gamos*, after the Greek, because it supposedly reenacts a sacred marriage of Dionysus—usually signals closure and reconciliation at the end of an Aristophanic play. In *Thesmophoriazusae* the brief dalliance of the Scythian archer with the flute girl may have been included to substitute for this traditional motif, and there is reconciliation of a kind at the end when Euripides agrees to stop insulting the women. The parody of Euripidean schemes of rescue continues right to the end of the play. It is likely that Aristophanes' delight in his elaborate literary spoof caused him to stretch the limits that were typically imposed on the comic genre.

"Critical Evaluation" by John M. Lawless

Further Reading

Aristophanes. *Thesmophoriazusae*. Edited and translated by Alan H. Sommerstein. Warminster, England: Aris & Phillips, 1994. Provides scholarly introduction, bibliography, Greek text, facing English translation, and commentary keyed to the translation. Sommerstein's translation supersedes most earlier versions.

Dover, K. J. *Aristophanic Comedy*. Berkeley: University of California Press, 1972. Useful and authoritative study of the plays of Aristophanes. Chapter 13 provides a synopsis of the play, a discussion of the characters, and notes on the topicality of the play. An essential starting point for study of the play.

Harriott, Rosemary M. *Aristophanes: Poet and Dramatist*. Baltimore: Johns Hopkins University Press, 1986. The plays are discussed not in individual chapters but as each illustrates the central themes and techniques of Aristophanes' work.

Platter, Charles. "The Return of Telephus: *Acharnians, Thesmophoriazusae*, and the Dialogic Background." In *Aristophanes and the Carnival of Genres*. Baltimore: Johns Hopkins University Press, 2007. Platter interprets Aristophanes' plays according to the theories of literary critic Mikhail Bakhtin, focusing on how the Greek playwright used multiple genres and styles of speech to create different forms of dialogue and characterization. Includes discussions on several plays, including this chapter about *Thesmophoriazusae*.

Silk, M. S. *Aristophanes and the Definition of Comedy*. New York: Oxford University Press, 2002. Silk looks at Aristophanes not merely as an ancient Greek dramatist but as one of the world's great poets. He analyzes *Thesmophoriazusae* and the other plays to examine their language, style, lyric poetry, character, and structure.

Spatz, Lois. *Aristophanes*. Boston: Twayne, 1978. A reliable introduction to Aristophanes for the general reader. Chapter 7 provides a summary of the problems of the play and offers several approaches to the theme of tension between the sexes and to the role of literary parody.

Whitman, Cedric. *Aristophanes and the Comic Hero*. Cambridge, Mass.: Harvard University Press, 1964. A standard work on the characterization of the Aristophanic protagonist. Chapter 6, "The War Between the Sexes," provides excellent discussion of the issue in the play.

A Theory of Justice

Author: John Rawls (1921-2002)
First published: 1971
Type of work: Political and social philosophy

John Rawls, a philosopher who held the James Bryant Conant University Professorship at Harvard University, published several books and many articles. He is chiefly known, however, for his book *A Theory of Justice*, an effort to define social justice. The work has greatly influenced modern political thought.

Rawls was dissatisfied with the traditional philosophical arguments about what makes a social institution just and about what justifies political or social actions and policies. The utilitarian argument holds that societies should pursue the greatest good for the greatest number. This argument has a number of problems, including, especially, that it seems to be consistent with the idea of the tyranny of majorities over minorities. The intuitionist argument holds that humans intuit what is right or wrong by some innate moral sense. This is also problematic because it simply explains away justice by saying that people "know it when they see it," and it fails to deal with the many conflicting human intuitions.

Rawls attempts to establish a reasoned account of social justice through the social contract approach. This approach holds that a society is in some sense an agreement among all those within that society. If a society were an agreement, Rawls asks, what kind of arrangement would everyone agree to? He states that the contract is a purely hypothetical one: He does not argue that people had existed outside the social state or had made agreements to establish a particular type of society.

Rawls begins his work with the idea of justice as fairness. He identifies the basic structure of society as the primary subject of justice and identifies justice as the first virtue of social institutions. He considers justice a matter of the organization and internal divisions of a society. The main idea of a theory of justice asks, What kind of organization of society would rational persons choose if they were in an initial position of independence and equality and were setting up a system of cooperation? This is what Rawls sees as a hypothetical original position: the state in which no one knows what place he or she would occupy in the society to be created.

After considering the main characteristics of justice as fairness and the theoretical superiority of this approach to utilitarianism, intuitionism, or other perspectives, Rawls looks at the principles of justice. He identifies two principles: One, that each person should have equal rights to the most extensive liberties consistent with other people enjoying the same liberties; and two, that inequalities should be arranged so that they would be to everyone's advantage and arranged so that no one person would be blocked from occupying any position. From these two principles Rawls derives an egalitarian conception of justice that would allow the inequality of conditions implied by equality of opportunity but would also give more attention to those born with fewer assets and into less favorable social positions.

Rawls concludes the first part of his book by looking at the idea of the original position outside society. This hypothetical original position can be approximated by using the thought experiment of the veil of ignorance. If no one could know what place he or she would occupy in the society being formed, what arrangement of the society would a rational person choose? Rawls maintains that the choice would be for a social structure that would best benefit the unknowing chooser if she or he happened to end up in the least desirable position.

In the second part of the work, Rawls considers the implications of his view of justice for social institutions. He discusses in detail equal liberty, economic distribution, and duties and obligations as well as the main characteristics of each that would make up a just society. He does not, however, identify any particular type of social or political system that would be consistent with his theory. He deals only with the demands that his version of justice places on institutions.

In the third and final section, Rawls deals with ends or ultimate goals of thinking about social justice. He argues for the need to have a theory of goodness, and he makes a case for seeing goodness as rationality. Then, he turns to moral psychology and considers how people acquire a sentiment of justice. Finally, he examines the good of justice, or how justice is connected to goodness. Rawls argues that in a well-ordered society, ideas of goodness and justice must be consistent with each other.

A Theory of Justice is widely recognized as an essential contribution to thought about the nature of justice. However, even supporters of Rawls acknowledge that his work raises many questions. One of the earliest major responses to the book came from his Harvard colleague, philosopher Robert Nozick. In *Anarchy, State, and Utopia* (1974) Nozick offers a libertarian response to Rawls. The assumptions behind *A Theory of Justice* are essentially redistributive: That is, Rawls posits equal distribution of resources as the desirable state and then argues that inequality can be justified only by benefits for the least advantaged. Nozick points out that resources are produced by people and that people have rights to the things they produce. Thus, attempts to improve the condition of the least advantaged through redistribution are unjust because they make some people work involuntarily for others and deprive people of the goods and opportunities they have created through time and effort.

Other critics have focused on the idea of the original state and the veil of ignorance used as a thought experiment to approximate the original state. The claim that rational individuals behind a veil of ignorance would choose the greatest possible equality has been challenged as arbitrary and unverifiable. Rational individuals might well choose a social structure with large rewards for the majority of people and small rewards for the minority on the grounds that one is more likely to end up as part of a majority than a minority. Moreover, the veil of ignorance of where one will be in a society also takes away all knowledge of what one will do. Legal justice is generally considered a matter of appropriate responses to actions: In the version offered by Rawls, justice is detached from anything that anyone has done and thus may have nothing to do with any idea of what people deserve.

The reluctance of Rawls to identify any particular type of society as just, especially in the second part of the book dealing with institutions, may leave Rawls open to the charge that he offers no guidance for the actual content of justice. For example, proponents of a highly unequal and competitive market economy may argue that the abundance of wealth produced by their preferred system contributes to the absolute standard of living of the poorest people in society. On the other hand, advocates of a highly redistributionist economy can maintain that radical redistribution of wealth will provide the greatest support for the poorest. Because no one can know—behind a veil of ignorance—which system would lead to the best possible lives for the poor, there can be no way of deciding what kind of society should be preferred.

The fundamental idea that justice is a matter of the basic structure of society is also open to question. To say that the basic structure of society can be made just or fair is to say that it can be designed both hypothetically and actually. Some social thinkers argue that societies are not designed per se; they are produced through history and by complex webs of inter-action among individuals and institutions. From this perspective, justice is a characteristic of specific acts or processes within social systems, such as legal actions or political mechanisms, and it is misleading to extend the concept of justice to a society as a whole.

Supporters of Rawls often look to revise parts of his argument, while opponents suggest alternatives. Still, most political thinkers acknowledge that *A Theory of Justice* introduced a new conceptual basis for debates about the core principles of social policy and action.

Carl L. Bankston III

Further Reading

Audard, Catherine. *John Rawls*. Montreal: McGill-Queen's University Press, 2007. An introduction to Rawls's central ideas, with a discussion of his contributions to contemporary political thinking. A good text for beginning any study of this major political and social philosopher.

Freeman, Samuel R. *Justice and the Social Contract: Essays on Rawlsian Political Philosophy*. New York: Oxford University Press, 2007. A series of essays on the major works of Rawls. The five essays in the first part deal with specific issues in *A Theory of Justice*.

_____. *Rawls*. New York: Routledge, 2007. An extensive study of the philosopher's thinking on distributive justice and political liberalism.

_____, ed. *The Cambridge Companion to John Rawls*. New York: Cambridge University Press, 2003. Articles on topics in the philosophy of Rawls, with contributions by political and social philosophers, including Thomas Nagel and Martha Nussbaum. The editor, the foremost contemporary authority on Rawls, provides an introductory overview and a chapter on the idea of the good of justice.

Schaefer, David Lewis. *Illiberal Justice: John Rawls Versus the American Political Tradition*. Columbia: University of Missouri Press, 2007. A critique of Rawls that argues that his thinking moves away from the fundamental traditions of American constitutional liberalism and toward libertarianism.

Sen, Amartya. *The Idea of Justice*. Cambridge, Mass.: Belknap Press, 2009. A theory of justice that is influenced by Rawls but critical of the concept of the veil of ignorance. Sen is skeptical of all arguments that attempt to identify the just society in the abstract, arguing instead that judgments need to be based on comparing social arrangements to make decisions on what is more or less just.

The Theory of the Leisure Class
An Economic Study in the Evolution of Institutions

Author: Thorstein Veblen (1857-1929)
First published: 1899
Type of work: Social criticism and economics

The Theory of the Leisure Class is Thorstein Veblen's first and best-known book. In all his writings, he offers an approach to social commentary that tends to invert much of the conventional economic wisdom of his day. On the surface, his style of writing is flat and unemotional, and often pedantic. However, the cumulative effect results in powerful social criticism. He often casts his writings (certainly *The Theory of the Leisure Class*) in the mode of anthropological commentaries, drawing on illustrations from many times and places beyond his own (but without explicit source references). He also stresses the evolutionary character of social institutions, in a somewhat Darwinian mode.

Veblen does not directly identify the leisure class with the rich, but the overlap is substantial. Where class distinctions have been strongly observed, he argues, the upper classes do not engage in "industrial occupations"—the most basic types of useful work. Instead, their occupations—which include government employ, warfare, religion, and sports—are considered highly honorable. The most honorable activities tend to involve what Veblen calls exploit—physical prowess, as in hunting or warfare or sports, or exercising authority over others, as in civic leadership. Traditionally, these honorable activities have been associated with men. Contrasting activities—drudgery—tend to be associated with women.

Conventional economics regards consumption as the goal of productive effort, particularly in accumulating wealth. For most people, though, the goal is to achieve "the invidious distinction attaching to wealth." Each person is in competition with others. Although one individual may gain self-esteem by rising on the social scale, it is not possible for everyone to do so simultaneously. To rise socially requires not merely possessing wealth and power but also making this condition known to the others by displaying it. Here, leisure enters the analysis. Engagement in productive labor marks a person as less wealthy, thus less worthy.

The leisure that serves as a marker in social competition does not connote idleness, merely the lack of productivity. Appropriate leisure activities include an exaggerated attention to styles of clothing, furniture, food, and social events. Veblen's scorn for practitioners of social snobbery rises close to the surface in these passages.

Interwoven through the text are Veblen's many observations about the status of women. He notes that marriage can involve "ownership" by the man, and "conspicuous leisure," a term Veblen coined, is often demonstrated by the role and activities of the wife. Beyond the wife's role is a hierarchical range of domestic servants. Needless to say, for the wife to have a productive job outside the home would contradict a family's efforts to project a leisure-class existence. In Veblen's time, the prejudice against women's employment extended far down the socioeconomic scale, including much of "keeping house," which was considered unproductive, even by Veblen. Also, his exposition lacks perspective on child raising.

At this point in the book, Veblen introduces his most celebrated concept: conspicuous consumption (he also coined the phrase). A large part of consumption reflects the social goal of impressing others, particularly with one's wealth, power, and superiority. Economist Robert Frank has elaborated on this with abundant descriptive detail. He refers to "positional goods"—the luxury car, the "McMansion"—which have become particularly eligible markers in competition for social status and for self-regard. Lavish spending on such items, financed by borrowing, played a major role in creating the economic depression that began in 2007.

Veblen also believes, in seeming contrast to the competitive drive for status, that people have an "instinct of workmanship"—that is, a wish for effective work, serviceability, and efficiency—as well as a distaste for waste, futility, and ineptitude. Because of this "instinct," people are impelled to activity. The leisure class may indulge in much busy work, perhaps involving ceremonial social activities and organizations, but these efforts do not serve human life or human well-being on the whole.

Veblen constantly stressed the importance of peer pressure on consumption decisions. Often people have internalized the customs and conventions that dictate choices concerning what one should eat, wear, or drive. Once these standards have been internalized, maintaining them becomes a matter of self-regard, perhaps as much as conscious rivalry. The wealthy leisure class plays the role of tastemakers, helping to shape the social and cultural standards to which others aspire.

In Veblen's view, the propensity for emulation is one of the most powerful economic motives, and the varieties of conspicuous waste he identifies absorb a large part of the products of economic growth. To keep up appearances, most people spend almost all of their income. The pressure on their income shows up in the low birthrate of the leisure class. Since Veblen's time, too, expenditure of money and effort on children's schooling, talents, and skills has become a huge outlet for positional rivalry. One consequence of this rivalry is the corruption of extracurricular activities, in which parents compel their children to try to become "stars," resulting in a lack of enrichment for "ordinary" children.

In Veblen's view, houses of worship often embody the goal of conspicuous waste. He cites as examples of this waste the often grand, ornate, and expensive trappings of religion and the wasteful physical "emptiness" of places of worship, which are often used only a few hours a week. He marks the priestly class, too, for conspicuous waste for its relative exemption from doing laborious work.

For consumers, the perception of what is beautiful may be strongly influenced by what is expensive. The appeal of a custom-tailored wedding dress or ball gown may lie as much in the cost and exclusivity as in the design. Consumers believe that a product carrying a higher price must be of superior quality. To Veblen, clothing styles are chosen to display their relative high costs and to signal that the wearer does not or cannot engage in productive physical activity—for example, high heels and wasp waists certainly limit one's physical activity. A measure of the rights of women since Veblen's time has been their greater freedom to dress comfortably.

Midway through *The Theory of the Leisure Class*, Veblen offers more, and comprehensive, observations about the leisure class and economic life. One clear characteristic is that the leisure class tends to be conservative in politics and lifestyle. In particular, it stands against institutional changes that might benefit those outside the class at the expense of the leisure class. Another observation concerns economic life, which Veblen divides into two categories: one related to business (bad) and the other to industry (good). Later commentators would differentiate between making money (business) and making goods (industry). To Veblen, the upper classes are parasites, associated with business rather than industry. This caricature, however, ignores the productive functions of entrepreneurship and finance. By implication, Veblen envisions the obsolescence of the innovative, risk-taking entrepreneur in the wake of the emergence of giant corporations.

Veblen was writing at a time when wealthy entrepreneurs such as J. P. Morgan and John D. Rockefeller were under fire from muckrakers such as Ida M. Tarbell and Henry Demarest Lloyd. Veblen's own remarks are more restrained; he names no names, whether of persons or businesses. Instead, he suggests that economic evolution has favored personality types geared to unscrupulous competition and struggle, to the detriment of "sympathy, honesty, and regard for life." In Veblen's opinion, the favored personality traits are not those conducive to economic efficiency and productivity. In the hierarchy of occupations, the highest esteem is attached to ownership, finance, banking, and law. Veblen casually remarks that "there is no hereditary leisure class of any consequence in the American community, except in the South." This statement is clearly false. The prototypes of the American leisure class were the Vanderbilts and the Astors, inheritors of wealth from vigorous and creative entrepreneurs. Inherited wealth, especially landed property, figures in most discussions of social class in the United States.

Indeed, Veblen's characterization of the leisure class in and of itself is of little scholarly value. One would never know that, in the same decade *The Theory of the Leisure Class* was published, the United States was witnessing the miraculous age of electricity, which was spreading from the Columbian Exposition of 1893 to the electrification of the American household. Veblen's characterization of the business world lacks any sense of the dramatic increase in productivity, the upgrading of jobs, or the successful annual absorption of millions of immigrants.

The lasting contribution of *The Theory of the Leisure Class* lies in its examination of the dimensions of conspicuous consumption. The American leisure class of the twenty-first century consists mainly of retirees who compete with each other not so much in conspicuous consumption but in showing off their physical and mental vigor. The extremes of conspicuous consumption are found in working-age families whose "McMansions," lavish weddings, and expensive college educations have many of the negative dimensions cited by Veblen. However, these extremes now are associated with overwork, not leisure.

Paul B. Trescott

Further Reading

Adil, Mouhammed H. *An Introduction to Thorstein Veblen's Economic Theory*. Lewiston, N.Y.: Edwin Mellen Press, 2003. Examines Veblen's theories of business cycles and growth, and his other ideas about economics.

Dorfman, Joseph. *Thorstein Veblen and His America*. 1934. 7th ed. Clifton, N.J.: A. M. Kelley, 1972. The definitive study of Veblen's life and work by an economist-historian. Includes a valuable discussion of the historical context of Veblen's writing. Also includes corrections and updated appendixes.

Edgell, Stephen. *Veblen In Perspective: His Life and Thought*. Armonk, N.Y.: M. E. Sharpe, 2001. Focuses on Veblen's ideas about marginality, ethnicity, the culture of the leisure class, and other subjects. A good place to start.

Harris, Abram L. "Veblen and the Social Phenomenon of Capitalism." *American Economic Review* 61, no. 2 (May, 1951). A succinct critique of Veblen's naive remarks on anthropology and his neglect of the contributions of business toward achieving high productivity. A dated but still helpful article.

Heilbroner, Robert L. *The Worldly Philosophers: The Lives, Times, and Ideas of the Great Economic Thinkers*. 7th ed. New York: Simon & Schuster, 1999. In this justly popular history of economic thought, chapter 8, "The Savage Society of Thorstein Veblen," gives high praise to its subject.

Lerner, Max, ed. *The Portable Veblen*. 1948. Reprint. New York: Viking Press, 1968. This classic collection includes a variety of Veblen's writings and an enthusiastic review of his ideas by the editor, Max Lerner. This comprehensive introduction is considered one of the most perceptive analyses of Veblen in print.

Reisman, David. *Thorstein Veblen: A Critical Interpretation*. 1953. Reprint. New York: Seabury Press, 1975. Sociologist Reisman, who was much influenced by Veblen's emphasis on peer pressure and "other-directedness," elaborates on these and other issues in this critical study of Veblen's work.

Spindler, Michael. *Veblen and Modern America: Revolution Iconoclast*. Sterling, Va.: Pluto Press, 2002. Describes Veblen's major ideas and examines his influence as an economist, a sociologist, and an analyst and critic of modern American culture.

Thérèse

Author: François Mauriac (1885-1970)
First published: Thérèse Desqueyroux, 1927 (English translation, 1928)
Type of work: Novel
Type of plot: Psychological realism
Time of plot: Early twentieth century
Locale: France

Principal characters:
BERNARD DESQUEYROUX, a petty landowner
THÉRÈSE DESQUEYROUX, his wife
MARIE DESQUEYROUX, their daughter
GEORGES FILHOT, a law student and Marie's lover
ANNE DE LA TRAVE, Bernard's half sister
JEAN AZÉVÉDO, a young intellectual

The Story:

In the little French town of Argelouse, where she has spent the first part of her life, Thérèse Desqueyroux is known not so much for her beauty as for her charm. Her wit and independence of mind make her conspicuous in the stifling and inbred atmosphere of her native province, and she inspires in her friends and relatives as much disapproval as admiration. Left to her own devices by a father more intent on his political career than on the problems of fatherhood, Thérèse spent her girlhood in isolated brooding. Her one friend has been Anne de la Trave, the half sister of Bernard Desqueyroux, to whom Thérèse is now married.

Thérèse can remember little of her youth and the days before her marriage. For the most part, her memories are clouded by the confusion in her own mind caused by her intense love of life and desire for experience joined to provincial willingness to sacrifice self to tradition. She sees her marriage to Bernard Desqueyroux as the natural culmination of a social cycle, but her honeymoon is not yet over before Thérèse begins to feel acutely the loss to herself that her marriage represents. She discovers in Bernard all that is worst in the provincial character: a fanatical pride of family and material possessions. To a fatal degree, he lacks the insight and imagination to understand his wife. For her part, Thérèse is disgusted by the marriage.

During the honeymoon, Bernard receives a letter from his family informing him that his half sister, Anne, has fallen in love with a penniless young man named Jean Azévédo. To preserve the family name and honor, Bernard prevails on

Thérèse to try to help stop the affair. Thérèse returns to Argelouse and persuades Anne to go on a trip. After Anne has gone, Thérèse meets Azévédo and discovers in him that intensity and individualism she misses in her own life. Azévédo admits that he is not really in love with Anne, and he readily agrees to write to her to tell her his true feelings. He and Thérèse meet from time to time and are drawn to each other. When Azévédo leaves Argelouse, he promises that he will return in a year.

After Azévédo has gone, Thérèse settles into the routine of a farmer's wife. Even the birth of a child, Marie, fails to give her life meaning, for motherhood only further intensifies her frustration. Almost involuntarily, Thérèse decides to poison Bernard.

The attempted murder is quickly discovered, and Thérèse is brought to trial. At the last moment, however, Bernard offers a trumped-up explanation and saves her from conviction. Thérèse returns home to learn that Bernard has lied only to save the family from scandal. After telling her that divorce is impossible, he forces her, under threat of disclosing the truth, to live a life of semi-imprisonment in her bedroom. Thérèse regains her freedom, however, when Bernard allows her to go to Paris. Alone in the city, Thérèse tries to make a new life for herself, but without success—the sense of sin she carries with her perverted all her attempts to find happiness. As the years pass, she retreats more and more into herself.

Fifteen years after her banishment from Argelouse, Thérèse is found living in an apartment in Paris by her daughter, Marie, now seventeen years old. Marie, who explains that she has come to Paris because of a young law student from her native province, is shocked to find Thérèse in poor health and looking years older than her age. Thérèse, hoping to extirpate the sense of her own sinfulness, decides to help Marie win the love of the student, Georges Filhot. To persuade Filhot to marry Marie and to mitigate his parents' disapproval, Thérèse tells her daughter, she will turn over to Marie all her own landholdings in Argelouse. The next day, Thérèse visits Filhot and invites him to dinner. At the conclusion of the evening, Marie returns to Argelouse with the promise of a final reunion with Filhot in three months.

In the next few days, it becomes painfully and thrillingly evident to Thérèse that Filhot is in love with her and not with her daughter. In a violently emotional scene, she confesses to the student not only her past crime but a whole series of crimes of which she believes herself guilty but that are not recognized as criminal by the law. Then she sends Filhot away. Rather than insist that he sacrifice himself to her daughter, however, she urges him to write to Marie to tell her that he does not love her.

A short time later, Marie returns to Paris to confront her mother, who by this time is living in a confused and paranoid world in which she believes all of her acquaintances are engaged in a plot to bring her to justice for her sins, real and imaginary. Marie's anger is softened when she realizes her mother's state, and she takes Thérèse with her when she returns to Argelouse.

In her birthplace, Thérèse slowly regains her sanity; the doctor predicts, however, that she will soon die. She is nursed during her last days by her daughter and Bernard—for whom, by this time, she feels neither pity nor disgust. During this time, Thérèse tries to put her mind in order. She awaits death with hope, seeing it as the final deliverance from self.

Critical Evaluation:

François Mauriac's literary career was launched in 1909 when he submitted his first volume of poems, *Les Mains jointes*, to Maurice Barrès, who was so impressed that he predicted a glorious future for the young writer. It was, however, in the writing of novels that Mauriac's talents flourished. In his first novels he dealt with those themes that preoccupied him throughout his life: the opposition between the flesh and the spirit, between sin and grace, and between godliness and godlessness. In addition to his many novels, Mauriac also wrote philosophical essays, a few biographies, and some plays. In 1952, he received the Nobel Prize in Literature. He died in 1970 at the age of eighty-four.

The story and meaning of the life of Thérèse Desqueyroux preoccupied Mauriac's mind over a long period. The book is not a novel in the conventional sense; rather, it is a series of four stories connected by the mind of the major character rather than by incident. Nevertheless, it is a powerful and dramatic revelation of the human condition and its relation to sin. Although Mauriac did at one time rebel against the religious practices of his family and did ultimately reject Jansenism, he never rejected the Catholic faith. Such is the primacy that he gave to his religious beliefs that he wished to be considered a Catholic who wrote novels rather than a Catholic novelist. In *Thérèse*, Mauriac catches the complex movement of guilt as it exists in everyone.

Most of Mauriac's novels take place in Bordeaux and its surrounding countryside, with Paris appearing only incidentally. The estate of the writer's grandmother, for example, becomes the home of Thérèse Desqueyroux, which he locates in a village he names Argelouse. Beyond the very important fact that he was deeply attached to his native region, the pastoral setting is featured prominently in his novels because, for Mauriac, the contrast between the physical world and the world of the spirit is more intense in the country, where nature bombards people with sensual stimuli that draw them into a preoccupation with physical things, with pleasures of the eye and ear, and ultimately with pleasures of the flesh. There the allure of physical things is much greater than in the city. In *Thérèse*, the descriptions of natural scenes are suffused with an almost erotic atmosphere.

Throughout the novel, Thérèse is strongly identified with elemental things. She thrives on the odors, colors, and shapes of nature. She yearns, in fact, to become one with nature. She says at one point that she has the pine trees in her blood. During her confrontation with Bernard, she wants to ask him to let her disappear into the night, into the forest, for she is not afraid of the trees—they know her, and she knows them. The illusory character of this union with nature is exposed a few paragraphs later, when Bernard tells Thérèse that she will be confined in Argelouse for the rest of her life. Suddenly, the beloved pine trees become the bars of Thérèse's prison. For Mauriac, the human tragedy is that while individuals are of this world, they can never be really united with it. It is no coincidence that the key generic symbols used by Mauriac are earth, fire, and water. Whatever their immediate significance might be—and they are used in a variety of ways—the underlying sense is the dichotomy between human beings and nature.

All the characters in *Thérèse*, as in most of Mauriac's novels, are identifiable types from the social milieu of traditional provincial life. Bernard Desqueyroux, Madame de la Trave, Monsieur Larroque, Anne de la Trave, and Aunt Clara are all representative of the various shades of bourgeois aspirations, ideals, opinions, and standards. The servants have the values of their employers. When he was criticized for making literary use of friends and acquaintances as characters, Mauriac retorted that it is impossible to create something that does not already exist.

As a young man, Mauriac had witnessed the trial of a woman accused of poisoning her husband. The image of that woman, "pale and biting her lip" (as Mauriac describes Thérèse in the prologue), was the source of inspiration for the novel. All the rest is Mauriac's invention. The real woman's motivation for murder was her desire to be with another man; Thérèse's motive is not nearly so simple. The probing analysis of motivation in the novel comes, according to Mauriac, from the uncovering of the potential for evil found in his own nature. He could say, as Gustave Flaubert did of Madame Bovary, "Thérèse Desqueyroux, c'est moi."

Influenced, like most other writers of the twentieth century, by Sigmund Freud's studies of the human unconscious, Mauriac's great contribution to French letters is the integration of psychological insights with the teachings of Christianity. As a novelist writing after Marcel Proust's great probing of the inner life, Mauriac felt it was his duty to give these investigations a dimension lacking in Proust's works.

Thérèse is the study of a tormented woman's soul. Endowed with great emotional depth and intellectual curiosity, the heroine is from the beginning set apart from others. Her great affection for Anne de la Trave is, for example, tempered by Thérèse's awareness of the incongruities between them. Anne's simplicity and naïveté form a contrast to Thérèse's intelligence and subtle sensitivity. Thérèse feels superior to Anne, but this superiority is part of the reason for her alienation, and at times she almost seems to regret it.

Thérèse's marriage represents an unconscious attempt by the heroine to overcome her differentness. To be sure, the marriage is prearranged on the basis of all the proper bourgeois concerns: status, wealth, family name. Without ever questioning the marriage or examining her own feelings, she behaves according to what is expected of her and plays the role of the enamored fiancé. In retrospect, however, she realizes that she married Bernard out of a desperate hope that he would save her from a vague danger that haunts her. Although this danger is never named, it is in fact alienation itself.

During her engagement, she feels for the first time in her life that she belongs, that she is integrated into her milieu, that she fits in. She hopes that by doing what all other young women do, she will become more like them. As it turns out, however, the marriage intensifies her alienation to an unbearable degree and sets in motion the chain of events that brings about her final downfall.

As Azévédo points out in one of his conversations with Thérèse, the penalty for differentness in her society is annihilation. Either one behaves as everyone else does or one is destroyed. Thérèse's grandmother, Julie Bellade, serves as an example of this rule, for she was totally obliterated by the family in reaction to an undisclosed scandal.

There is an implication that Thérèse may be cursed by this past, a possibility of inherited evil that recurs throughout the novel, and Thérèse herself is preoccupied with the legacy of shame she will bequeath to her daughter. Mauriac's concern with the inheritance of evil can be interpreted as a holdover from his Jansenist beliefs, which emphasize predestination. Thérèse can never determine at which point her crime had its inception; it was always there. Mauriac reinforces this impression by, for example, describing Thérèse's peace at the time of her engagement as the temporary "quietness of the serpent in her bosom."

Thérèse's differentness is not in itself sinful, but it is apparently what causes her to sin. Mauriac sympathizes with her refusal to conform to the hypocrisy and mediocrity around her, but as a Christian he can only denounce the final turn her refusal takes. If Thérèse has a basic flaw, it is her lack of self-awareness. She never consciously decides to murder Bernard; circumstances suggest it, and she slips into it. The narrator points out that Thérèse has never thought anything out, never premeditated anything, in her entire life. She has no positive goals, only a retrospective awareness of what she has sought to escape. She never knows what she wants, only what she does not want. The crime with which she is charged seems totally alien to her, and she cannot satisfactorily explain, even to herself or to Bernard, why she did it.

Once freed from her marriage, she attempts to give meaning to her life by engaging in a series of love affairs. That she fails should not be surprising in view of Mauriac's concept of human love: that it is destined to failure, being physical and therefore prey to time, corruption, and decay. The only way to transcend one's mortality and finitude is through union with God. Thérèse is dimly aware that human love is not something on which to base one's hope. In the farewell scene at the Café de la Paix, she considers for a moment going back to Argelouse, there to embark on the only meaningful quest, the search for God. A few moments later, however, she reaffirms her intention to look for fulfillment among men.

Thérèse's lack of awareness is compounded, if not generated, by intense self-involvement and self-indulgence. Anne's pain never evokes any sympathy in Thérèse, only self-pity. Thérèse is indignant that Anne, unlike herself, has been given the joy of knowing love. She always absolves herself of responsibility in shaping her own destiny. To be sure, this may be a flaw in Mauriac, not Thérèse; according to Jean-Paul Sartre, Thérèse is doomed beforehand by a flaw in her character on one hand and a divine malediction on the other. Many other critics have denounced what they consider the lack of free will in Mauriac's characters. The line separating free will from predestination is at best nebulous in Mauriac's vision of human behavior. Regardless of whether the novel is flawed by this predisposition, it is unquestionably a profound, moving study of a woman lost in the contradictions between her own psychology and the realities of her society.

"Critical Evaluation" by Vera Lucia de Araujo Haugse

Further Reading

Flower, John E. *Intention and Achievement: An Essay on the Novels of François Mauriac.* Oxford, England: Claren-don Press, 1969. Includes analysis of *Thérèse* that links it to other novels by Mauriac with characters who seem increasingly saturnine and enigmatic. Contends that *Thérèse* is a powerful figure of alienation who stands out as an unconventional literary heroine.

Flower, John E., and Bernard C. Swift, eds. *François Mauriac: Visions and Reappraisals.* Providence, R.I.: Berg, 1991. Collection of essays provides a lucid presentation of Mauriac's life and works. One essay evaluates *Thérèse* as an approximation of a Colette figure.

Landry, Anne G. *Represented Discourse in the Novels of François Mauriac.* New York: AMS Press, 1970. The section on *Thérèse* emphasizes the austerity of Mauriac's language and examines the dramatic flow of the novel's structure between central action and flashback.

Moloney, Michael F. *François Mauriac: A Critical Study.* 1958. Reprint. Whitefish, Mont.: Kessinger, 2006. Presents an excellent treatment of Mauriac's use of poetic imagery in his fiction.

O'Connell, David. *François Mauriac Revisited.* New York: Twayne, 1995. Provides a useful introduction to Mauriac, with information about the author's life and analyses of his novels and other works. Includes discussion of *Thérèse*.

Smith, Maxwell A. *François Mauriac.* New York: Twayne, 1970. Connects *Thérèse* with Mauriac's other literary achievements and offers many perceptive observations about the novel based on Smith's interview with the author. Mauriac defends himself against critical reactions that are overly pessimistic about *Thérèse*'s destiny and insists that he has merely presented an isolated study of oppression and confinement.

Speaight, Robert. *François Mauriac: A Study of the Writer and the Man.* London: Chatto & Windus, 1976. Provides an overview of Mauriac's career, including discussion of *Thérèse* in which the work is described as a poetic tour de force.

Wansink, Susan. *Female Victims and Oppressors in Novels by Theodor Fontane and François Mauriac.* New York: Peter Lang, 1998. Compares the depictions of female characters and society in the works of Mauriac and Fontane, focusing on Mauriac's novels *Thérèse* and *Genitrix* (1923; English translation, 1950) and Fontane's novels *Effi Briest* (1895; English translation, 1914, 1962) and *Frau Jenny Treibel* (1893; *Jenny Treibel*, 1976).

Welch, Edward. *François Mauriac: The Making of an Intellectual.* New York: Rodopi, 2006. Examines Mauriac's career, tracing his evolution from a novelist in the 1920's and 1930's to a major French intellectual and journalist in the years following World War II. Describes how the arc of Mauriac's career reflected broader changes in French culture.

Williams, Timothy J. *Desire and Persecution in "Thérèse Desqueyroux" and Other Selected Novels of François Mauriac*. Lewiston, N.Y.: Edwin Mellen Press, 2007.

Uses French literary critic René Girard's concept of scapegoating to analyze Mauriac's novel, arguing that Thérèse is both oppressor and victim. Compares *Thérèse* to other novels by Mauriac, including *L'Agneau* (1954; *The Lamb*, 1955), to describe how scapegoating and persecution are common themes in the author's fiction.

Thérèse Raquin

Author: Émile Zola (1840-1902)
First published: 1867, serial, as *Un Mariage d'amour*; 1867, book (English translation, 1881)
Type of work: Novel
Type of plot: Naturalism
Time of plot: Early 1860's
Locale: Paris

Principal characters:
MADAME RAQUIN, a widow and the owner of a dry-goods shop
CAMILLE, the only son of Madame Raquin
THÉRÈSE, the niece of Madame Raquin
LAURENT, a childhood friend of Camille
MICHAUD, a retired police commissioner and the friend of Madame Raquin

The Story:

A dramatic story of murder and adultery takes place in Paris among a small group of people from the same town in Normandy, Vernon, northwest of Paris. The group's unifying link is Madame Raquin, a widow about sixty years old, who owns a small dry-goods shop on a dark, narrow street in Paris. She previously owned a dry-goods shop in Vernon, but, after her husband dies, she sells the business and retires. At the demand of her frail, sickly, but ambitious son, Camille, then twenty-two years old and married to his cousin Thérèse, Madame Raquin is compelled to move the family to Paris. She finds a tiny shop that she can afford with family living quarters above it. Madame Raquin and Thérèse run the shop together, while Camille finds employment in a railroad company office, where he hopes to rise to a high administrative post.

Thérèse is the child of Madame Raquin's brother, a French army captain, serving in Algeria. One day, the brother, Captain Degans, appears in Vernon and presents his sister with a two-year-old baby girl, saying that the child's mother, a native Algerian of great beauty, died and that he is unable to care for the child himself. Captain Degans leaves with his sister a certificate affirming that he is the father of this child born out of wedlock and that she bears his name. Her African heritage gives Thérèse a high-strung, emotionally intense nature, but growing up in Vernon with her aunt and her cousin,

she develops a self-protective mask of reserved docility. She shows little emotion but willingly does whatever is asked of her to guarantee acceptance from her aunt. Two years younger than Camille, she is raised as his sibling, and when Madame Raquin announces her hope that the two will marry, Thérèse makes no objection, though she has no real affection—or even respect—for this small, delicate, insecure young man who is to become her husband.

The emotional dynamics among the Raquin threesome has to lead to trouble, even though they are, at first, isolated in Paris, living on an obscure little street seldom used except as a convenient shortcut from one lively Paris thoroughfare to another. To remedy this isolated feeling, the Raquins begin inviting company to their home every Thursday evening. Madame Raquin runs into an old acquaintance from Vernon, a retired commissioner of police named Michaud. Michaud comes to the Thursday evenings, accompanied by his son and daughter-in-law. Camille invites an older man, Camille's superior at the railroad office, whose job Camille hopes one day to inherit. The Thursday evenings are mostly spent in playing dominoes, but Thérèse finds the company boring and often spends much of the evening by herself in the shop downstairs.

One Thursday, Camille brings a new guest home, triumphantly declaring that this is Laurent, a schoolmate and friend of his youth in Vernon, whom he recognized, even though Laurent grew into a tall, robust, and darkly handsome young man. Thérèse shows immediate interest in the new Thursday guest but quickly resumes her mask of indifference before the other guests. Laurent, however, notices her momentary reaction. The inevitable result follows in a matter of weeks: They become lovers. The fateful drama then begins to unfold.

The lovers are quickly thwarted by the lack of opportunities to meet. Laurent first comes to the dry-goods shop in the middle of the day, at Thérèse's suggestion, but that proves impossible as a regular arrangement. Madame Raquin is always there, and Laurent cannot regularly absent himself from work. They cannot meet in the evenings at Laurent's place, since Thérèse has no plausible pretext for going out alone. This frustration soon tempts the lovers to consider eliminating Camille. Because Camille fears water and cannot swim, Laurent devises a scheme to throw Camille out of a boat during a Sunday excursion. At a suitable moment, Laurent seizes the frail Camille. To Laurent's surprise, however, Camille fights back savagely and manages to sink his teeth into Laurent's neck, leaving a horrible wound, before Camille is thrown into the water. Laurent then capsizes the boat to make it look like an accident, and he and Thérèse are soon rescued. Laurent then shrewdly persuades Michaud, the retired police commissioner, to report the "accident" properly and to tell Madame Raquin what happened. As a result, no suspicions are ever raised that a murder occurred.

After Camille is duly buried, life resumes its normal course, including the usual Thursday evenings. Laurent and Thérèse carefully regulate their public behavior to show no trace of their passion for each other and bide their time as agreed. Eventually, Michaud persuades Madame Raquin that the best remedy for Thérèse's constant melancholy is to marry Laurent. For Michaud, this is merely a device by which he can guarantee for himself the continuation of the Thursday evenings. For Thérèse and Laurent, however, it is the opportunity they need, and the marriage is quickly arranged.

Unhappily, the marriage solves nothing for them. To their mutual shock and dismay, Thérèse and Laurent find that they cannot make love, because the "ghost" of Camille is always present and visible in the bed between them, and they cannot rid themselves of his spectral presence. Their relationship becomes so strained that the lovers take to quarreling bitterly, each accusing the other of bad faith. To add to the horror, Madame Raquin suffers a stroke that leaves her paralyzed and unable to speak, but she overhears the quarrels, learns unmistakably of Camille's murder, and fervently seeks the means,

in her helpless state, of denouncing the culprits. She fails, but Thérèse and Laurent can tell by her demeanor that she now knows the truth. That causes the relationship between Thérèse and Laurent to become irretrievably poisoned. Each plots the murder of the other, seeking liberation from the bond of guilt. Abruptly recognizing their own madness, the lovers tacitly agree to a suicide pact, sharing the poison Laurent prepared for the murder of Thérèse. As the lovers collapse and die, Madame Raquin watches their fall with grimly avid satisfaction.

Critical Evaluation:

Thérèse Raquin, completed in 1867 when Émile Zola was only twenty-seven years old, was actually his fourth novel. The previous three novels, however, were plainly immature work, awkwardly composed and sensationalistic, written solely for money. *Thérèse Raquin*, on the other hand, embodied Zola's serious ideas about the art of the novel and was his first real critical success, not merely because it was a daring story of a wife and her lover who conspire to murder her inconvenient husband, but because it was well written, constructed with a sense of form, and filled with powerfully unforgettable scenes and images. Perhaps because, in it, Zola also succeeded so well in conveying the gritty feel of daily life among the urban poor, *Thérèse Raquin* became the first of Zola's books to attract substantial sales. That makes *Thérèse Raquin* a milestone, marking the start of Zola's distinguished career as a novelist of realism—or, as he would later call it, naturalism, the literary movement in France that Zola founded.

The significant sense of form exhibited in this novel can be seen in its unusual organization into thirty-two very short chapters, each of which advances the narrative in a terse and dramatic way. This structure imparts a feeling of rapid movement and suspense to the novel, which compels the reader's excited attention. Viewing the novel as a whole, one also recognizes a symmetrical division into three approximately equal parts, like the three acts of a play, each part ending on a note of high drama: part one, the adultery, culminating in the murder of Camille; part two, the marriage of the criminals, apparent proof that they got away with their crime; part three, the horror of their haunted marriage, ending in a double suicide. By confining the plot to just a few characters and presenting their story in three relentlessly fast-paced parts leading inexorably to the fatal outcome, Zola manages to give his novel the power and the inevitability of a classical tragedy. Zola also shows instinctive skill in modifying the real event that inspired his novel (in which the criminal lovers were brought to justice and executed), allowing his criminals to escape detection, only to find themselves condemned to death by their own guilty consciences and their inescapable feelings of remorse.

Zola insists, in his preface to the second edition of *Thérèse Raquin* in 1868, that his intention is to study temperaments and not characters, showing that individuals whose temperaments are conditioned directly by their nerves and blood, rather than their intellect, will display the beast that is in every human and will invariably act according to the force of their physical drives. That is why, Zola argues, his presentation of the criminal lovers, Thérèse and Laurent, includes no moral judgment of their conduct. His purpose is simply to portray truthfully the behavior of certain human types in order to understand the physical bases of their actions. Even their remorse, Zola maintains, arises from physiological causes.

Most readers will recognize Zola's effort to emphasize the physical in *Thérèse Raquin*. Thérèse is a creature of violent passion, long suppressed by the necessity of survival but suddenly released by a chance encounter. Laurent is lazy, unambitious, and fond of sensual pleasures. Camille is a weakling and a physical coward, viewed with contempt by both Thérèse and Laurent. Nevertheless, Zola is clearly less dispassionate than he claims in this early novel. His description of the wound Camille inflicts on Laurent as a vivid, red stigma that can never heal makes it a symbolic representation of Laurent's guilt, less physical than emotional. The same is true of the several different portraits Laurent paints—in the last part of the novel—each hauntingly expressive, but each, Laurent finally recognizes, an unconscious variation on his guilty recollection of Camille's face as he sees it in the morgue. The symbolic role of the family cat, François, is another example of Zola's indirect moralizing in spite of himself. Thérèse has a fantasy that the cat, which witnesses her adultery, will one day tell all to the authorities, and Laurent believes that the cat is somehow possessed by the soul of Camille, which leads him to hurl the cat against a wall, killing it. Such details, which pervade the novel, mark Zola's need to show that conscience exacts a price even from the most amoral and bestial of humans. Indeed, the role, however indirect, that Zola assigns to conscience is perhaps the secret of *Thérèse Raquin*'s power as a psychological novel. The entire third part is a sustained demonstration of how much more cruelly the human conscience can punish criminals than can the law. In spite of

Zola's conscious intentions, *Thérèse Raquin* is an eminently moral work of fiction.

Murray Sachs

Further Reading

Brooks, Peter. "Zola's Combustion Chamber." In *Realist Vision*. New Haven, Conn.: Yale University Press, 2005. Zola's novels are among the works of literature and art examined in this study of the realist tradition in France and England during the nineteenth and twentieth centuries.

Brown, Frederick. *Zola: A Life*. New York: Farrar, Straus and Giroux, 1995. A detailed and extensive biography of Zola that discusses his fiction and the intellectual life of France, of which he was an important part. Shows how Zola's naturalism was developed out of the intellectual and political ferment of his time; argues that this naturalism was a highly studied and artificial approach to reality.

Grant, Elliott M. *Émile Zola*. New York: Twayne, 1966. A solidly researched account of Zola's life and works, including excellent pages on *Thérèse Raquin*.

Hemmings, F. W. J. *Émile Zola*. 2d ed. New York: Oxford University Press, 1970. One of the best critical studies of Zola's literary career. The section devoted to *Thérèse Raquin* is especially insightful.

Lapp, J. C. *Zola Before the "Rougon-Macquart."* Toronto, Ont.: University of Toronto Press, 1964. Offers the most detailed study of *Thérèse Raquin*, written from the perspective of its place in the early development of Zola's literary career, before he became famous.

Nelson, Brian, ed. *The Cambridge Companion to Émile Zola*. New York: Cambridge University Press, 2007. Collection of essays, including discussions of Zola and the nineteenth century; his depiction of society, sex, and gender; and "*Thérèse Raquin*: Animal Passion and the Brutality of Reading" by Susan Harrow. Includes a summary of Zola's novels, a family tree of the Rougon-Macquarts, a bibliography, and an index.

Walker, Phillip. *Zola*. London: Routledge & Kegan Paul, 1985. Well-written general study of Zola's writings, especially perceptive about his use of symbols and myths.

Wilson, Angus. *Émile Zola: An Introductory Study of His Novels*. Rev. ed. London: Secker and Warburg, 1965. Readable analytical study, written by a practicing novelist.

These Jaundiced Loves

Author: Tristan Corbière (1845-1875)
First published: Les Amours jaunes, 1873 (English translation, 1995)
Type of work: Poetry

Tristan Corbière was born in Brittany in 1845 and died there thirty years later. He knew illness throughout his life, and it prevented him from completing his formal education. In a land of seafarers, he was acutely conscious of his physical debility. Corbière's exacerbated sensibility is a major part of his outstanding originality. In his poems, the image that he presents of himself is never flattering. Indeed, Corbière seems greatly to have exaggerated his unattractive appearance.

Most of Corbière's poetic production is grouped in the collection titled, in the original, *Les Amours jaunes*—literally, "yellow loves" or "off-color loves." This collection, first published in 1873, went almost unnoticed. The title can scarcely be fully explained, for it seems to involve a characteristic, deliberate attempt at obfuscating originality on the part of the poet. The title may seem appropriate, however, after a reading of the pieces it covers; in fact many of the poems in the collection might be considered the product of a sickly or jaundiced view of the world.

"That," the title of the first section of *These Jaundiced Loves*, offers little help to those seeking a thematic unity within the group. The title is also that of the first piece in the section. The poet frames a negative answer to the questions put to him about his art by an interlocutor. The dialogue is brought to a close by the poet, who says, "Art does not know me, and I don't know Art." This should not be interpreted as a declaration of ignorance on the part of an unlettered provincial. Corbière seems to have been sufficiently aware of France's nineteenth century poets to have borrowed from some—Charles Baudelaire in particular—where it suited him, and to castigate others, notably Alphonse de Lamartine and Alfred de Musset. Rather, it might be useful to evoke the idea of an opposition between literature and art on one hand and poetry and life on the other, for what Corbière's originality causes his poetry to lose in technical value it causes it to gain in vitality, color, relief, and strength. If Corbière's poems seem to step outside any framework of definition, so, one is tempted to add, does life.

Corbière lived for some time in Paris, and the first section of his collection contains a sonnet sequence describing the impressions made upon him by the city. The number of writers who have contributed to the evolution of the myth of the French capital as a tentacular city seizing and devouring its unfortunate victims is great. Corbière adds his name to this company.

A poem that is on occasion included with the eight Parisian sonnets in the first chapter is titled "Paris at Night." Certain aspects of the poem recall the "Parisian Tableaux" in Baudelaire's *Les Fleurs du mal* (1857, 1861, 1868; *Flowers of Evil*, 1931). Like Baudelaire, Corbière evokes sinister scenes and characters and frenetic activity, while sickness and death seem to hover over the poem. "Paris at Night" and others like it remain strikingly original. In the metropolis, the Breton is reminded of home, of the sea he knows well; the comparison of the city to the sea is strange, but not forced: "It's the sea,—a flat calm.—And the great tide/ With a far-off roar has withdrawn." Even where the poem moves from general description to closer perspectives, Corbière's sustained use of maritime imagery remains peculiarly appropriate: "The waves will soon come rumbling back in./ Can you hear the crabs scratching about in the dark?" "Paris at Night" illustrates some of the finer aspects of Corbière's technique. As is the case in many others of his poems, the imagery is powerful, even shocking. There is, moreover, an element of deliberate ambiguity that leaves questions in readers' minds. Above all, the poem becomes for readers a form of adventure on which they embark with the poet; readers are involved in the discovery of a world that unfolds before them while retaining its mystery.

Corbière's use of irony has been much discussed. Irony generally implies the presentation of two points of view or more, the offering of landmarks, as it were, from which readers may establish proper perspective. Corbière's approaches to irony are numerous, but they are closely related to one another. At the most basic level, the poet makes considerable use of puns and plays on words. In many places, he closely intertwines the sublime with the grossly vulgar, or the divine with the familiar. His purpose in each case seems to be to bring the lofty down to a level where it may be more easily viewed. The purposes and forms of Corbière's irony seem to be manifold in *These Jaundiced Loves*. If his irony is frequently corrosive and negative or even simply facetious, it is also occasionally used with serious intent to goad readers into revising their opinions, or into thinking deeply. Often the prime target of the poet's irony is himself. He uses it to prevent himself from falling into a fixed pose or attitude or identity. One example is his description of his situation in Paris: "Five-hundred-thousandth Prometheus/ Chained to the rock of painted cardboard." Corbière is equally capable of using irony to deflate the posturing of others. Often, too, the irony seems to take the form of a defense reaction; the poet, in the teeth of adversity, rather than give way to a hysterical lamentation, manages to raise a smile.

"These Jaundiced Loves" is also the title of a section within the collection of poems. The unity of the section is not clear at first. The poems in it deal with love and women, although in a somewhat bizarre and indirect fashion. It would seem unlikely that these strange pieces would ever help win over a coy mistress. This group of poems is uneven, but one or two outstanding ones are to be found, and the section does help shed light on Corbière's technique as a poet.

One of the most effective, trenchant pieces in *These Jaundiced Loves* is "A Young Man Dying." Corbière has a young poet present the question, To die or not to die? Corbière reveals in the young man an alternating appetite for and aversion to life. Corbière scathingly mocks the line of consumptive Romantic poets who seemed to spend their lives setting down their protracted death throes in writing. Avoiding the obvious, as he generally does, Corbière writes: "How many of them have I *read* die away." Corbière's refusal to identify with these poets seems doubly significant when one recalls his constant ill health and his early death.

Perhaps the most significant of the poems in this section is a long work titled "The Contumacious Poet." It is a description of a poet's taking up residence in an old ruined building, once a convent, in Brittany. The poem involves a characteristic mingling of tones humorous and nostalgic. The poet, for example, after fervently praying that his absent loved one might come to him, and even vividly imagining her to be there, hears a knock at the door of his tumbledown dwelling. He is of course disappointed when he goes to answer: "Show yourself with a dagger in your heart!.../ —There's a knock... oh! it's someone.... Alas! Yes, it's a rat."

The one section of *These Jaundiced Loves* in which Corbière is truly consistent in form, theme, and mood is titled "Armorica." The name refers to Brittany. It is obvious that the poet's sensibility is permeated with the atmosphere and folklore of his native province, and he communicates his feeling for it beautifully. In this section there is little of the frenetic pursuit of originality at all costs that detracts from several pieces in other sections. The first poem of "Armorica" could easily stand as one of the better short Surrealist poems of a

later period. It is an irregular sonnet titled "Evil Landscape." It succeeds in communicating an intense impression not only of gloom but also of a spectral world from which humanity seems excluded, or in which a person would be an intruder. The starkness of the landscape, captured in Corbière's harsh alliteration, and the whole uncanny atmosphere would surely strike a receptive chord in the heart of any Celt.

"Seamen" is probably the most vitally alive, if not the most consistent, of the sections in *These Jaundiced Loves*. As the title suggests, it deals with the sea, seamen, and seaports, viewed realistically and sometimes ribaldly, from close up. The finest of these wild, undisciplined pieces is probably "Bitor the Hunchback," the tale of a deformed ship's watchman who, on his annual spree ashore, heads for a brothel, eager to know love and with money to burn. The pace of the poem is such that the reader seems to be following hard on Bitor's heels. With Bitor, the reader sees the interior of the brothel displayed: its selection of women who are paid according to their "tonnage," the sailors of many different nationalities, for each of whom Corbière does a remarkable thumbnail sketch:

> Tall Yankees, blind-drunk as always,
> Sitting in pairs, shooting at the wall
> Their stream of tobacco-juice aiming at a target,
> Always hitting the mark.

From a joyously bawdy atmosphere, however, the mood changes to become frightening. The reader experiences the impression of mounting apprehension as all the people in the brothel turn their attention to Bitor. He is stripped naked and tossed up and down in a blanket. He is finally badly bruised. Later, Bitor's body turns up in the harbor, but the reader is left with no explanation of his death. It might be that Bitor, having known the full pleasures of the flesh, had nothing more to live for:

> What was left by the crabs now served as material
> For the jests of the public; and the street-urchins,
> Playing alongside the black water beneath the
>   sunny sky
> Beat on his hump as you would on a drum ...
> A burst drum ...
> —That poor body had known love.

Paul Verlaine was one of the first writers in France to comment enthusiastically on the originality of Tristan Corbière. Since Verlaine, other talents have pointed to the unique qualities of the Breton poet. Nonetheless, Corbière's work has attracted relatively little attention. It is perhaps worth noting that the poet's best critics have themselves been original, creative writers. This is understandable given the fact that Corbière's work does not fit neatly into any real literary tradition. It may be argued, however, that Corbière belongs to an excellent tradition—one that he started. Many poets have followed him.

Further Reading

Burch, Francis F. "The Iconography of Tristan Corbière." In *International Perspectives in Comparative Literature: Essays in Honor of Charles Dedeyan*, edited by Virginia M. Shaddy. Lewiston, N.Y.: Edwin Mellen Press, 1991. Compares the image that Corbière presents in his pictorial self-portraits with the image that he presents in the self-portrait that is *These Jaundiced Loves.*

Corbière, Tristan. *Selections from "Les Amours jaunes."* Translated with an introduction and notes by C. F. MacIntyre. Berkeley: University of California Press, 1954. Includes a sketch of the poet's life along with short appraisals by his contemporaries and by later critics. The notes provide valuable, detailed information about each of the poems included.

_____. *The Centenary Corbière: Poems and Prose of Tristan Corbière.* Translated and with an introduction by Val Warner. Chester Springs, Pa.: Dufour, 1975. Collection includes a translator's introduction that offers a complete, concise appraisal of *These Jaundiced Loves* and its effect on later writers.

_____. *These Jaundiced Loves: A Translation of Tristan Corbière's "Les Amours jaunes."* Translated by Christopher Pilling. Calstock, England: Peterloo Poets, 1995. An excellent resource for students of Corbière's work. Both English translations and the original French are provided.

_____. *Wry-Blue Loves = "Les Amours jaunes," and Other Poems.* Translated and introduced by Peter Dale. London: Anvil Press Poetry, 2005. Collection includes *Les Amours jaunes* in its entirety, plus some of Corbière's previously uncollected poems.

Lunn-Rockliffe, Katherine. *Tristan Corbière and the Poetics of Irony.* New York: Oxford University Press, 2006. Analysis of *These Jaundiced Loves* focuses on Corbière's innovative use of language and irony and demonstrates how the poet contributed to the changes in French poetry that were taking place in the 1870's.

Mitchell, Robert L. *Corbière, Mallarmé, Valéry: Preservations and Commentary.* Saratoga, Calif.: Anma Libri, 1981. Discusses *These Jaundiced Loves* in terms of the difficulty that it presents to translators. Includes extremely close analyses of ten of Corbière's poems.

_____. *Tristan Corbière.* Boston: Twayne, 1979. Places *These Jaundiced Loves* in the contexts of Corbière's life and the poetic movements of his time. Includes extremely detailed analyses of the poems.

The Thin Man

Author: Dashiell Hammett (1894-1961)
First published: 1934
Type of work: Novel
Type of plot: Detective and mystery
Time of plot: 1930's
Locale: New York

Principal characters:
MIMI JORGENSEN, Clyde Wynant's former wife
DOROTHY WYNANT, her daughter
GILBERT WYNANT, her son
CHRISTIAN JORGENSEN, her present husband and Wynant's former associate
NICK CHARLES, a detective
NORA CHARLES, his wife
HERBERT MACAULAY, Wynant's attorney
MORELLI, a gangster
ARTHUR NUNHEIM, a former convict

The Story:

Nick Charles, a onetime detective and now a California lumberman, arrives in New York with his wife, Nora, for the Christmas holidays. He is drawn into investigating the murder of Julia Wolf, who was the secretary of Nick's old client Clyde Wynant, a lunatic-fringe inventor whose wife, Mimi, divorced him in order to marry a man named Christian

Jorgensen. Wynant is reported to be out of town, working on a new project, and Herbert Macaulay, Wynant's attorney, has told police that he has not seen him since October, when Wynant gave him power of attorney.

The police suspect a number of people in Julia's murder, including Mimi Jorgensen, her husband, a gangster named Morelli, Gil Wynant, and Clyde Wynant himself. Mimi had just returned from Europe and had gone to see Julia to get her former husband's address because she needed more money to support their two children, twenty-year-old Dorothy and eighteen-year-old Gilbert; her new husband, Christian Jorgensen, had spent the large settlement Wynant had made at the time of their divorce. Mimi had arrived just in time for Julia to die in her arms.

Jorgensen had worked with Wynant several years earlier (at the time he was using a different name), and he believed that Wynant had not treated him fairly. In the course of the murder investigation, it is discovered that Jorgensen has a wife living in Boston and that he has married Mimi only to get Wynant's money.

Morelli, the gangster, had once been fond of Julia. When he learns that Nick is on the case, Morelli goes to Nick and Nora's apartment and, just as the police arrive, shoots Nick in the chest, a glancing shot that does not produce a serious wound. Nick refuses to press charges because the man is apparently in enough trouble already. The police beat Morelli but, not having a reason to hold him, release him the same day.

The members of the Wynant family do not have much love for one another. Gil is an odd young man who asks Nick about bizarre subjects such as incest and cannibalism. He is frequently found at keyholes, listening to private conversations.

The police also suspect Arthur Nunheim, who identified Julia Wolf's body. When Nick goes with a detective named Guild to see Nunheim, they find him living in an extremely untidy apartment with a big, frowsy blond woman. In the presence of their callers, Nunheim and the woman insult each other until the woman leaves. Nunheim escapes from Nick through a back window, and he is reported murdered a little while later.

Macaulay reports that Wynant had made an appointment with him on the day the murder was committed, but he failed to appear. During the course of the investigation, several people receive communications from Wynant that seem to throw suspicion on Mimi and Jorgensen. One day, there is a false report that Wynant has tried to commit suicide in Allentown, Pennsylvania.

Wynant has maintained a shop on First Avenue that the police have examined cursorily. Nick insists that they return and tear it apart, if necessary, for he is convinced that the place holds some clues. When the police do as he recommends, they notice that one section of the cement floor of the shop is newer than the rest; they tear it up and find the bones of a dead man, a cane, clothes that apparently would fit a larger man than Wynant, and a key chain with the initials D. W. Q.

Eventually, Nick accuses Macaulay of murdering Wynant, Julia, and Nunheim. He believes that Macaulay and Julia joined forces to get Wynant's money, that Wynant went to Macaulay's house in Scarsdale to accuse Macaulay of the plot, and that Macaulay killed his client there. Then, Nick reasons, Macaulay dismembered the body and brought it back to the workshop, where he buried it in the floor, covering it with new cement. The cane, the large-size clothes, and the key chain were intended to prevent the correct identification of the body.

Macaulay, according to Nick, renewed the lease on the shop and kept it vacant while, with a forged power of attorney and Julia's help, he began to transfer Wynant's fortune to his own accounts. Mimi's return from Europe and her search for Wynant had precipitated matters, and when Nick arrived for the Christmas holiday and agreed to help Mimi find the missing inventor, Macaulay felt he would be safer with Julia dead. He himself had written the letters that seemed to be from Wynant. Nick theorizes that Macaulay killed Nunheim because the former convict had been near Julia's apartment and might have heard the shots that killed her. When Nunheim demanded hush money from Macaulay, the lawyer murdered him to keep him quiet permanently.

So Nick outlines his case, but on that very day, Gilbert Wynant receives a letter that seems to be from his father, telling him to use an enclosed key to go to Julia's apartment and look for an important paper between the pages of a certain book. Following the instructions in the letter, Gilbert enters the apartment, where a plainclothes policeman strikes him and handcuffs him before taking him to police headquarters. The boy shows the officials and Nick the letter he received, but the book and the paper it describes are fictitious. When Nick takes Gilbert home, he learns from Mimi that Wynant had just been there to give Mimi ten thousand dollars in bonds.

As it turns out, Macaulay, knowing the police would be in Julia's apartment, had sent the letter to Gilbert in an attempt to shift the suspicion back to Wynant. Macaulay himself brought Wynant's bonds to Mimi, making her promise to say that Wynant had brought them and thus give credence to his own story that Wynant is in town. Nick forces Mimi to admit the truth by explaining that Macaulay now has possession of Wynant's fortune and that, if she continues to support him, she will never get more than occasional small sums, whereas if she stops shielding Macaulay she will get control of her former husband's entire fortune. Jorgensen has meanwhile gone back to his legal wife in Boston. When Nick finishes explaining the case to Nora, she cannot help feeling that the business of a detective, based as it is on so much speculation, is at best unsatisfactory.

Critical Evaluation:

Dashiell Hammett's *The Thin Man* presents a picture of sophisticated New York life at the end of the Prohibition era. The plot itself follows the pattern set by Edgar Allan Poe in "The Murders in the Rue Morgue" (1841) and by Arthur Conan Doyle in his Sherlock Holmes stories. Hammett, too, pits an astute detective against a questioning companion and the somewhat obtuse and distrustful police, and he, too, drops clues to give the reader a chance to solve the mystery before allowing his detective to provide the final explanation.

The Thin Man was the last and most popular of Hammett's novels. It is the most briskly paced of his books, and its intricate plot is ingenious and deceptive as well as logical and believable. The action takes place among members of New York café society during the Prohibition era, a frenzied, colorful world of money, corruption, sex, booze, and violence that Hammett portrays with accuracy and energy. The book did very well commercially, and it also spawned a radio program, a television series, and an extremely successful sequence of films in the 1930's and 1940's starring William Powell and Myrna Loy.

With the characters Nick and Nora Charles, Hammett created one of the most distinctive detective couples in the entire genre. They give the novel the kind of verbal wit and situational humor seen only occasionally in Hammett's earlier works. As a former detective of obvious skill and experience, Nick is adroit enough in dealing with crime solving, but he is no aggressive, hard-boiled Continental Op, Sam Spade, or Ned Beaumont. He has retired from the business to manage Nora's not inconsiderable lumber interests and—at least until his curiosity is aroused—has no desire to return to his former occupation. Nick reluctantly becomes involved because Nora coaxes and dares him. Nick is a witty, cocky, charming man who would rather socialize than fight, and Nora, too, loves fun. The mystery is an exciting game to her—until it gets dangerous. The best scenes in the novel are not, as in previous Hammett books, those of action and violence but those featuring witty banter and sexual byplay between Nick and

Nora. Nick sums up the mood at the end of the novel: "Let's stick around for a while. This excitement has put us behind in our drinking."

Despite its ingenuity and charm, however, *The Thin Man* is one of Hammett's weaker novels and shows a clear decline in his powers. The picture of New York in the 1930's is realistic and vivid but also superficial and cliché-ridden. The plot is clever and facile but has no implications beyond that of an interesting puzzle. The character of Nick Charles, while witty and charming, is relatively shallow and frivolous as well as morally questionable. He is content to live off of Nora's money, indulge her whims, and drift from party to party and city to city. The intense personal morality of Hammett's earlier works gives way to a kind of lazy, benevolent hedonism in which nothing is more important than a 3:00 A.M. whiskey and soda. The vital ethical and intellectual center of Hammett's previous works is replaced by slick, though enormously entertaining, superficiality.

Further Reading

Bruccoli, Matthew J., and Richard Layman. *Hardboiled Mystery Writers: Raymond Chandler, Dashiell Hammett, Ross MacDonald*. New York: Carroll & Graf, 2002. Handy reference volume includes interviews with the three mystery authors as well as some of their letters and previously published studies of their work. Illustrated.

Dooley, Dennis. *Dashiell Hammett*. New York: Frederick Ungar, 1984. Basic survey of Hammett's work and life is specifically aimed at the general reader. Chapter 9, "Time's Shadow," provides an introduction to an interpretive reading of *The Thin Man*, which Dooley finds Hammett's least successful novel.

Gale, Robert L. *A Dashiell Hammett Companion*. Westport, Conn.: Greenwood Press, 2000. Encyclopedia-style resource includes a chronology of the major events in Hammett's life along with alphabetically arranged entries that cover his works, characters, family, and acquaintances.

Gregory, Sinda. *Private Investigations: The Novels of Dashiell Hammett*. Carbondale: Southern Illinois University Press, 1985. Study of Hammett's five major novels includes a chapter titled "*The Thin Man*: The Detective Novel and the Comedy of Manners," which argues that the novel successfully merges the two genres and constitutes a serious and artistically unified work.

Layman, Richard. *Shadow Man: The Life of Dashiell Hammett*. New York: Harcourt Brace Jovanovich, 1981. Objective, readable, and carefully researched work is one of the most scholarly and reliable of the various biographies of Hammett. Provides a plot synopsis as well as valuable historical and biographical context for each of his novels.

Marling, William. *Dashiell Hammett*. Boston: Twayne, 1983. Concise and well-informed introductory survey is intended for the general reader. Provides a unified overview of all of Hammett's novels. Brief chapter on *The Thin Man* gives a plot summary and some biographical context.

Mellen, Joan. *Hellman and Hammett: The Legendary Passion of Lillian Hellman and Dashiell Hammett*. New York: HarperCollins, 1996. Although primarily a biographical study of the relationship of the two writers, this scrupulously researched work provides insight into the background of Hammett's fiction.

Metress, Christopher, ed. *The Critical Response to Dashiell Hammett*. Westport, Conn.: Greenwood Press, 1994. Collection of essays begins with an introduction that surveys the history of Hammett criticism and then presents a series of excerpts from reviews, commentaries, and critical discussions of each novel as well as a section dealing more generally with Hammett's work. The section on *The Thin Man* reprints a journal article on the novel by George J. Thompson.

Things Fall Apart

Author: Chinua Achebe (1930-   )
First published: 1958
Type of work: Novel
Type of plot: Tragedy
Time of plot: Late nineteenth century
Locale: Umuofia, along the lower Niger River

Principal characters:
OKONKWO, warrior and leader
OBEREIKA, Okonkwo's close friend
NWOYE, Okonkwo's eldest son
IKEMEFUNA, boy held for a kinsman's crime

The Story:

Okonkwo's father is cowardly, foolish, and poor in his life, an outcast at his death. When his father dies, Okonkwo, on the other hand, though still a young man, has three wives, two barns full of yams, two of his people's titles, and a reputation as the strongest wrestler and the bravest warrior in the nine villages of Umuofia. Okonkwo takes great pride in these accomplishments, sometimes forgetting the assistance of his personal god, or *chi*, and of the man from whom he borrowed yams to start his own farm.

Despite his accomplishments, Okonkwo fears being seen as like his father. One of his great disappointments is his eldest son, Nwoye, who seems to inherit Okonkwo's father's weakness. Nwoye dislikes the men's stories of war, preferring his mother's childish stories. Okonkwo, who has a quick temper, often tries to beat these behaviors out of Nwoye.

A change happens when the village leaders put under Okonkwo's care a Mbaino boy named Ikemefuna. Ikemefuna comes to Okonkwo's village because the Mbainos killed a Umuofian woman; eventually the boy is to be killed in retribution. While living in Okonkwo's compound, Ikemefuna exerts a good influence on Nwoye and wins the affection of everyone, including Okonkwo.

During Ikemefuna's stay, the village observes the sacred Week of Peace that always precedes planting season. Violence is strictly forbidden for that week. Nonetheless, Okonkwo, in a fit of anger, severely beats his youngest wife. This angers the earth goddess. As punishment Okonkwo pays a fine. He repents inwardly but does not admit his error outwardly, and so it is said that he lacks respect for the clan gods.

Three years after Ikemefuna's arrival, the village council decides it is time for him to be killed. The oldest man in the village warns Okonkwo not to take part, because Ikemefuna is like a son to Okonkwo. Okonkwo, fearful of appearing weak, not only attends Ikemefuna's killing but also deals his death blow. This act disturbs Okonkwo afterward, which puzzles him, because he followed his people's practice. Nwoye, who greatly loved Ikemefuna, resents his father's action bitterly. Later, Okonkwo confronts his friend Obereika, who did not take part in the killing. Obereika says that although the oracle said the boy had to die, it did not compel a man to take part.

Shortly, the elder who advised Okonkwo to stay away from Ikemefuna's execution dies. At his funeral rites, as the cannons and guns sound, there is a sudden silence in the dancing crowd. Okonkwo's gun mysteriously explodes and kills the dead man's son. Guilty of another crime against the earth goddess, Okonkwo and his family are banished to his motherland for seven years. No longer can he hope to become a lord of the clan of his fathers, Okonkwo laments. His *chi* does not affirm his plans.

While exiled, Okonkwo maintains his material wealth with the assistance of his kinsmen and Obereika. Changes are happening, chief among them the arrival of white missionaries and governing officials. After some initial confusion and severe punishment for violence against the newcomers, there comes a time of peaceful coexistence. Some Umuofians are converted by the missionaries, and among them is Nwoye. He is attracted by the new religion's criticism of such Umuofian practices as killing an innocent boy like Ikemefuna and throwing newborn twins into the Evil Forest to die. Learning of Nwoye's conversion, Okonkwo beats him and banishes him from the family compound.

After seven years, Okonkwo returns to his fatherland with plans for regaining his former status and for leading his people in a war against the newcomers before they destroy Umuofia. Obereika says that by converting native people and employing them in government posts, the newcomers already inserted a "knife" into their community. The people have already fallen "part."

Okonkwo's opportunity to incite his people comes when a native convert desecrates a Umuofian ceremony. Okonkwo rejoices as his people take revenge by tearing down the missionaries' church building. Government officials, however, soon capture Okonkwo and the other leaders, punishing them cruelly.

Once their leaders are released, the people gather to determine whether to respond with conciliation or with war. A Umuofian who works for the new government arrives and orders the meeting stopped. Angered, Okonkwo kills him, and, fearful, the people disband. The officials who come to arrest Okonkwo are led to the place where he hung himself. Suicide is against the Umuofian tradition; Okonkwo is buried as an outcast.

Critical Evaluation:

Chinua Achebe was born in the colony of Niger in 1930, to Ibo parents who were Christian converts. He attended British-style schools in Nigeria, including University College, Ibadeen, and graduated from London University in 1953.

Achebe's first novel, *Things Fall Apart*, is a classic of African literature. Among all the colonial governments in Africa, the British in Nigeria fostered first education in its territory. As a result, Nigerian writers preceded those in other areas of Africa. *Things Fall Apart* is noted as the first African

novel. Achebe, a master of his craft, also wrote *No Longer at Ease* (1960), *Arrow of God* (1964), *A Man of the People* (1966), and *Anthills of the Savannah* (1987). Achebe also published poetry, short stories, and essays.

In *Things Fall Apart* and in his later novels, Achebe wanted to counter demeaning and incorrect stereotypes of his people and Eurocentric presentations of the confrontation between the Ibo of Nigeria and the British intruders. In his novels, Achebe admits, he strives for artistic excellence but also wants to give a message. Just as the oral tradition of the Ibo people served their society by sustaining its values, so the modern Ibo, writing in English, should serve Ibo society.

In *Things Fall Apart*, Achebe combines the Ibo oral tradition's narrative style with the Western world's traditional novel form. In novel form Achebe narrates an African tale in African style. The novel's narrative voice could be Achebe's or it could be the voice of a village elder. In either case, the voice is connected to the world of the novel. Though the voice is objective, it is also a part of the scene depicted.

To achieve an African voice, Achebe uses plain, short, declarative sentences. Also, throughout the novel, characters narrate or listen to traditional stories from the society's past and stories that illustrate and teach the culture's values. The novel opens with the retelling of Okonkwo's exploits in a traditional wrestling match, the ritual by which young men proved themselves worthy of a high place in their clan.

Achebe weaves Ibo proverbs into the novel's dialogue, to clarify a point, to teach a lesson, and, usually, to provide humor. Also, many Ibo words are used in the text without translation. Some of these can be understood by the reader through context, but others remain mysterious and create a distance between the non-Ibo reader and the Ibo world of *Things Fall Apart*. Taken together, sentence structure, Umuofian stories, proverbs, and language create a memorable colloquial narrative voice.

The novel's structure, on the other hand, is formal. There are twenty-five chapters: thirteen in book 1, six in book 2, and six in book 3. The pivotal chapter about Okonkwo's accidental shooting of a young boy and his subsequent banishment is at the book's center, in chapter 13. Achebe establishes the nature of the Umuofian society and Okonkwo's character in book 1. In book 2 tension heightens as the outsiders appear. In book 3 the conflict comes to a head when Okonkwo kills the clerk and his people retreat before the power of the new government. The novel's last page has the required unexpected yet inevitable ending. The novel is a very orderly work.

To return to character, *Things Fall Apart* presents Okonkwo as a tragic hero who struggles against internal and external forces and meets a tragic end. Obereika calls his fallen friend a "great man." The hero is a complex man with both strengths and weaknesses. At the novel's start Okonkwo's deep shame about his father's failure motivates him to become a respected man, an exemplar of all that is valued in his society. His accomplishments feed his pride and cause his rigidity. His pride, rigidity, and short temper lead to sins against the gods of his people and criticism from his *chi*. Finally, Okonkwo is banned from his fatherland for seven years and, when he returns home, kills in anger. Okonkwo then takes his own life, the greatest sin against the gods of his people. His is a tragic end.

The plot line of Okonkwo's struggle and fall reveals not only his complex character but also the strong social fabric of the Umuofian people. Like Okonkwo's character, this society is complex, having both strengths and weaknesses. Its traditions create a stable community in which each individual finds meaning. The oral storytelling and rituals for planting, harvesting, and human passage sustain an orderly society. Some of the harsher customs, such as killing the innocent Ikemefuna, exiling Okonkwo for an accidental killing, and banishing some persons to live their entire lives as outcasts, raise doubts about the ultimate wisdom of Umuofian customs. Some, like Nwoye and Obereika, question what was always done and suggest that change is necessary. Others, like Okonkwo, stand fast in defense of the tradition. When the newcomers come with a new religion and laws, the fabric of Umuofian society weakens.

The newcomers also have strengths and weaknesses. They offer a gentler religion and different laws. Their excessive zeal and righteousness, however, provoke the anger of the people the newcomers want to win over. Finally, the Umuofian people and the newcomers share a common weakness. Few attempt to learn each other's language, customs, or beliefs. Conflict is inevitable. The situation and characters that Achebe draws in his novel are fraught with complexity. It is this complexity, as well as Achebe's masterful writing style, that make *Things Fall Apart* a classic novel.

Francine Dempsey

Further Reading

Carroll, David. *Chinua Achebe.* New York: Twayne, 1970. A general introduction to Achebe's first four novels.

Gikandi, Simon. *Reading Chinua Achebe: Language and Ideology in Fiction.* Portsmouth, N.H.: J. Currey, 1991. Study of the interplay of the creative process and the political situation in Achebe's novels. Devotes a chapter to an analysis of *Things Fall Apart*.

Iyasere, Solomon O., ed. *Understanding "Things Fall Apart": Selected Essays and Criticism.* Troy, N.Y.: Whitston, 1998. Nine essays interpret the novel from a variety of perspectives. They include a reading of Okonkwo as a tragic hero, a discussion of the rhythm of the novel's prose as it echoes African oral tradition, and a discussion of how Achebe successfully transformed the colonizers' language to tell the story of the colonized

Ogede, Ode. *Achebe's "Things Fall Apart."* New York: Continuum, 2007. A reader's guide to the novel with information about its literary and historical context, language, style, form, critical reception, and interpretations.

Okpewho, Isidore, ed. *Chinua Achebe's "Things Fall Apart": A Casebook.* New York: Oxford University Press, 2003. Collection of essays analyzing the novel. Includes Achebe's essays "The African Writer and the English Language," as well as discussion of Igbo cosmology in the novel and the problems of gender and history in teaching the book.

Lindfors, Bernth, ed. *Approaches to Teaching "Things Fall Apart."* New York: Modern Language Association of America, 1991. Suitable for students and teachers. Contains Achebe's only essay on the novel, as well as articles of literary and cultural analysis and an excellent bibliographical essay.

Wren, Robert M. *Achebe's World: The Historical and Cultural Context of the Novels of Chinua Achebe.* Washington, D.C.: Three Continents Press, 1980. Study of the historical and cultural setting of Achebe's novels. Compares Achebe's presentation of the Igbo world with archaeological and sociological research.

The Thirty-nine Steps

Author: John Buchan (1875-1940)
First published: 1915
Type of work: Novel
Type of plot: Espionage
Time of plot: 1914
Locale: England and Scotland

Principal characters:
RICHARD HANNAY, a retired mining engineer
FRANKLIN SCUDDER, a private investigator
SIR WALTER, a government official
THE BLACK STONE, espionage agents

The Story:

Richard Hannay, a mining engineer, has returned to England after having made a modest fortune in South Africa. Before long, he finds that he is very bored with the conversations and actions of the English people he meets. He has almost decided to return to South Africa when a strange series of events begins. One day, as he is unlocking the door of his flat, he is startled by the sudden appearance of Franklin Scudder, another tenant in the building. Scudder, obviously badly frightened, begs Hannay to give him refuge in his flat. Hannay lets him in, and after the two men are settled comfortably, Scudder tells Hannay a fantastic tale. He says that a plot to start a war between England and Germany is under way. The Greek premier, Constantine Karolides, the only really strong leader in Europe, is scheduled to visit London on June 15. The assassination of Karolides during the visit will suffice as an excuse for the declaration of war.

Scudder tells Hannay that the members of a group called the Black Stone are the agents arranging for the assassination. They know that Scudder has learned of their plot, and they have tried several times to kill him. He has planted a body in his flat, hoping that the murderers will think the body his. He asks Hannay to let him stay with him until plans can be made to prevent the assassination.

Impressed by the sincerity with which Scudder tells his story, Hannay gives him sanctuary. Soon after, he returns to his flat one day to find Scudder there dead, a knife through his heart. Hannay knows then that the Black Stone found Scudder and that his own life is in danger. Presumably, the police, too, will want to question Hannay.

When Hannay sees two men strolling back and forth in front of his building, he suspects that they are part of the enemy group. By a ruse, he exchanges clothes with the milkman and leaves his flat, taking with him a little black book in which he had seen Scudder making notes. He is afraid to go to any government office with his fantastic story. His plan is to disappear for the three weeks remaining before June 15 and then, at the last minute, try to get someone in authority to listen to him.

He travels to Scotland, thinking he might be able to hide more easily there. Because the London newspapers have carried the story of Scudder's murder and a description of Hannay has been circulated, he has several narrow escapes from local Scottish police. The Black Stone has traced him as well. When an airplane, obviously on the lookout for him, flies low over the spot where he has taken refuge, he finds shelter at an inn. The Black Stone finds him there, too, and he is forced to flee again.

In every spare moment, Hannay studies Scudder's little black book. He deciphers the code that Scudder used and learns that the murder of Karolides is only a small part of the plot. The main plan involves an invasion of England. Airfields are already laid out, and mines have been placed to line the shores at a given signal. The time for invasion is to be determined once the Black Stone has intercepted the French envoy who is coming to London to secure plans for the arrangement of the British fleet. Once the enemy agents know where the ships are, they can see to it that mines are laid in strategic positions to destroy a great portion of the fleet. The only clues Hannay can find in Scudder's book about the time and place of the enemy operation are references to thirty-nine steps and a high tide at 10:17 P.M.

By luck, Hannay meets a man who has an uncle in an influential position in the government. This man believes Hannay's story and promises to write to his uncle to ask him to talk to Hannay and help thwart the plot. Hannay travels carefully, for the police and the Black Stone are still pursuing him. Once he is captured by a member of the Black Stone, but he manages to blow up the building in which he is being held and escapes. At last, he reaches his friend's uncle, Sir Walter, who listens carefully to Hannay's report. At first Sir Walter is disposed to dismiss Scudder's story as that of a loyal but overly anxious young man, but when he receives a call informing him that Karolides has been killed, he knows that the information Hannay has given him is correct, and he promises to take the information to the proper authorities.

Although Hannay is not to be allowed to attend the secret conference of government officials, he has the uneasy feeling that his presence there is of the utmost importance and that only he can find out how the highly confidential information about the French envoy's visit leaked out to the enemy. Against Sir Walter's orders, Hannay goes to the house where the officials are meeting. As he sits in the hall waiting to be admitted to the meeting room, one of the officials comes out of the room. Hannay realizes that he has seen the man elsewhere, and that the man has recognized him. He bursts into the meeting room and tells the astonished officials that the man who just left is an impostor. They think Hannay mad, for the man who just left is the First Lord of the Admiralty, and everyone knows him well. Then they remember that the man had scanned the drawings and figures carefully and could have memorized them. If he were to leave the country, the whole plan of defense could be in the hands of the enemy. The only hope is to capture him.

There are hundreds of small ports from which a small boat can leave England, but by checking isolated spots along the coast, Hannay finds a small cove where high tide is at 10:17 P.M., and he surmises that there is a house nearby with thirty-nine steps leading down to the cove. Accompanied by police, Hannay locates just such a house, which is occupied by three Englishmen on vacation. Their actions are so natural that he doubts they could be spies. The presence of a fast yacht in the water close to the cove seems suspicious, however, and when Hannay notices the unconscious habit one of the vacationers has of tapping his fingers, he recognizes the man as the enemy agent who had captured him. Hannay and the police are able to capture two of the men. The third escapes to the ship, but as it has already been boarded by English police, he also is caught.

The murder charge that had been brought against Hannay is dropped, and he is safe for the first time in many weeks. Three weeks later, war is declared between England and Germany. The war is not, however, fought on English soil, and no surprise invasion takes place. Hannay enlists in the army, but he knows that he has done his greatest service for his country even before he put on a uniform. The Black Stone is no more, and Scudder's murder has been avenged.

Critical Evaluation:

The Thirty-nine Steps is generally recognized as the first authentic spy novel. Although elements of the form are evident in earlier works—adventure tales, chase-and-capture narratives, detective stories, mystery stories, and gothic horror tales—it was John Buchan who established the patterns that became basic to the genre, which developed and flourished in the twentieth century. In an essay on Buchan, novelist Graham Greene singled out the first ingredient in his formula for what Buchan himself called the "shocker"—a formula Greene was to use with considerable success in his own spy novels: "John Buchan was the first to realize the enormous dramatic value of adventure in familiar surroundings happening to unadventurous men." The average-person-caught-in-a-web-of-intrigue formula proved to be fertile.

Buchan once stated that his own object was to write "romance where the ingredients defy the probabilities and march just inside the borders of the possible." *The Thirty-nine Steps* effectively follows that dictum. The hero, Richard Hannay, is believable, and the settings are vivid and realistic, but the situations do "march" very close to the impossible.

Although not deeply characterized, Hannay is colorful and convincing. He is bright, cultured, eager, and resourceful. Once his boredom and curiosity lead him to accept the challenge of strange events and become involved in an intrigue, his patriotism and optimism ensure that he commits himself totally to the cause and that he believes steadfastly in final victory. Furthermore, his experience as a mining engineer on the African veldt realistically accounts for his endurance and adroitness in evading capture as well as his skill in exploding his way out of danger.

The settings, too, are scrupulously accurate. Buchan used locations he knew personally, and many of the sites, including the real thirty-nine steps, were important to him. Not only is Hannay's escape route geographically possible but, more important, Buchan also creates a realistic atmosphere that gives the adventure immediacy.

Although the characters and settings of *The Thirty-nine Steps* are realistic, the plot moves perilously between the possible and the fantastic. The essence of the thriller is the chase, and while the heroes or heroines of thrillers may not begin as hunters, they soon become the hunted, frequently with both the established authorities and the villains in pursuit. Hannay is chased almost from the beginning and, despite several close calls, avoids capture by using several devices that were to become the stock-in-trade of the genre: disguise (a milkman, a political speaker, a rural "road-man"), physical concealment, and plain good luck (one does not look too closely at "coincidence" in the thriller).

In *The Thirty-nine Steps*, Buchan also introduces the false rescue scene, an element that later became central to many intrigue novels: When the hero has apparently reached a sanctuary and is safe from his pursuers, he is suddenly thrust into an even more dangerous situation, which then leads to his most impressive escape. Hannay is rescued from the police by a kindly bald archaeologist who turns out to be his archenemy. To get out of this perilous predicament, Hannay must demonstrate the most extreme physical courage and mental agility.

In Buchan's shockers, the hero usually clears himself with the authorities, whereupon together they defeat the conspiracy. Other thriller writers leave all the responsibility to their protagonists, but either way, it is up to the hero to direct the destruction of the villains. Hannay does so by deciphering Scudder's coded notebook (another common thriller gimmick) and exposing the criminals personally. The central motif of the thriller is that of the isolated individual who is, either by choice or by circumstance, outside the established system and pitted against an implacable and immensely powerful criminal. Often, civilization itself may be at stake.

Written during the first months of World War I, *The Thirty-nine Steps* reflects a logical world. The changes to the genre since Buchan—whether in "superman" intrigues such as Ian Fleming's James Bond series or in the grimy realism of books by writers such as Eric Ambler and John le Carré—are the result of more complex and ambiguous attitudes toward the world; they are not alterations in the basic formulas first established by Buchan in *The Thirty-nine Steps*.

Further Reading

Cawelti, John G., and Bruce A. Rosenberg. *The Spy Story*. Chicago: University of Chicago Press, 1987. Offers one of the best overall analyses of Buchan's spy novels. Praises *The Thirty-nine Steps* as Buchan's most completely successful book and examines its connections to John Bunyan's *The Pilgrim's Progress* (1678, 1684).

Daniell, David. *The Interpreter's House: A Critical Assessment of John Buchan*. London: Thomas Nelson, 1975. Presents an assessment of all of Buchan's writing, both nonfiction and fiction. Focuses on the earlier, lesser-known works, but also contains a fine analysis of his spy and adventure fiction.

Kestner, Joseph A. *The Edwardian Detective, 1901-1915*. Brookfield, Vt.: Ashgate, 2000. Examines *The Thirty-nine Steps* and other British detective fiction as cultural history, focusing on such issues as legal reform, surveillance, international diplomacy, Germanophobia, masculinity and femininity, and the concept of popular literature.

Lownie, Andrew. *John Buchan: The Presbyterian Cavalier*. Rev. ed. Boston: David R. Godine, 2003. Interesting biography focuses on the Scottish roots of Buchan's writing. Includes a chronology of the major events of the author's life.

MacGlone, James M. "The Printed Texts of John Buchan's *The Thirty-nine Steps*, 1915-1940." *Bibliotheck* 13 (1986): 9-24. Exhaustive study of the printed texts of *The Thirty-nine Steps* traces the varying stages of the novel's development.

Panek, LeRoy L. *The Special Branch: The British Spy Novel, 1890-1980*. Bowling Green, Ohio: Bowling Green State University Popular Press, 1981. Traces the origins of Buchan's spy novels to the earlier books of Edgar Wallace, E. Phillips Oppenheim, and William Le Queux and to the development of espionage fiction during the late nineteenth century.

Winks, Robin. "John Buchan: Stalking the Wilder Game." In *The Four Adventures of Richard Hannay*, by John Buchan. Boston: David R. Godine, 1988. Places Buchan's spy novels within the context of the times in which they were written to explain and dispel concerns about the racism, sexism, jingoism, and anti-Semitism these works contain.

This Side of Paradise

Author: F. Scott Fitzgerald (1896-1940)
First published: 1920
Type of work: Novel
Type of plot: Bildungsroman
Time of plot: 1896-1920
Locale: Minneapolis; Princeton and Atlantic City, New Jersey; New York City

Principal characters:
AMORY BLAINE, a well-to-do youth
BEATRICE O'HARA BLAINE, his mother
MONSIGNOR DARCY, a family friend and Amory's confidant
KERRY and BURNE HOLIDAY,
THOMAS (TOM) PARKE D'INVILLIERS,
JESSE FERRENBY,
FRED SLOANE, and
ALEC CONNAGE, Amory's Princeton University classmates
ISABELLE BORGÉ, Amory's first romance
CLARA PAGE, a widow who infatuates Amory
ROSALIND CONNAGE, Amory's great love
ELEANOR SAVAGE, Amory's last fling

The Story:

Amory Blaine is the only child of an alcoholic mother and an absent father. As his mother's companion, he spends his early childhood traveling and living in hotels. When Beatrice's alcoholism results in a breakdown, Amory goes to live with an aunt and uncle in Minneapolis, where he resides for nearly two years. These years are encapsulated in the description of a party and first kiss shared with Myra St. Claire, and the pattern of Amory's subsequent life is established as one of anticipation and disappointment. His fledgling character also emerges, as Amory assumes an aristocratic posture.

Amory is reunited with Beatrice at the family estate in Lake Geneva, Wisconsin, before traveling east to attend prep school at St. Regis's. After taking his entrance examinations, Amory visits his mother's friend Monsignor Darcy in New York City. Darcy becomes a mentor and confidant of Amory. At St. Regis's, where he spends two years from ages fifteen to seventeen, Amory begins badly but eventually distinguishes himself as a star quarterback, actor, and editor of the school paper, though when later he recalls his prep school years he remembers his failures more than his successes.

In 1913 at age seventeen, Amory enters Princeton University. In his freshman year, he lives with Kerry Holiday and Tom D'Invilliers and he begins a friendship with Alec Connage. Amory begins to write poetry and vows to make more of his abilities in his sophomore year. Most concerned with his own accomplishment, Amory is unaffected by outside events such as the beginning of World War I. He achieves success as a writer and actor in the fall of his sophomore year. In Minneapolis between terms, he begins a romance with

Isabelle Borgé. At the end of his sophomore year, Amory and his classmates travel to New York City. On the return trip to Princeton, a car accident caused by drunken driving kills Dick Humbird.

Amory ends his relationship with Isabelle, and before his junior year he fails an important mathematics examination. When his father dies, he learns of the family's fading financial fortunes. He discovers the poetry of Rupert Brooke and begins to publish his own poems. On a drunken outing in New York City, he sees an apparition of a man in a brown suit wearing slippers that curl upward at the toes. Unnerved, Amory is convinced he has seen the devil.

In his last year at Princeton, Amory reads seriously and disdains the certainties of the Victorians. For a brief time, he thinks he is in love with Clara Page, a widowed third cousin who lives in Philadelphia. He has solemn conversations with Burne Holiday, who has renounced the social victories of college to become a socialist and pacifist. Amory leaves Princeton for a post as a second lieutenant in the infantry.

When he is twenty-three and has been discharged from the Army, Amory falls deeply in love with nineteen-year-old Rosalind Connage, Alec's sister. Amory's job writing advertising copy pays modestly, however, so, with deep regret on both sides, Rosalind ends their relationship and eventually becomes engaged to a wealthier man. Amory then embarks on a three-week alcoholic binge, during which he quits his job and is beaten up. This spree ends with the passing of Prohibition. In Maryland, Amory meets Eleanor Savage, a literate, sharp-witted, and reckless eighteen-year-old. Their three-week affair ends with Eleanor riding a horse off a cliff, though she jumps to safety.

In Atlantic City with Alec Connage, Amory chooses to sacrifice himself by pretending to detectives that he is with the underage woman Alec brought across the state line in violation of the Mann Act. During this episode, Amory sees an aura of evil that his sacrifice dispels. His family's finances worsen, and Monsignor Darcy dies. Feeling more on his own than ever, Amory takes realistic stock of his character, deciding that the antidote to his ingrained vanity and selfishness is helping others feel more secure.

Restless and down to his last twenty-four dollars, Amory sets off on a long walk toward Princeton. He is picked up by a limousine, and as Amory talks to the car's owner, he tries out a number of ideas on the pace of modern life, the barriers to progress, and the advantages of socialism. The rich man turns out to be the father of Jesse Ferrenby, a Princeton classmate who was killed in the war. The novel ends with a disillusioned Amory admitting that he knows himself but nothing more.

Critical Evaluation:

Though he was in dire financial straits and critically neglected when he died, F. Scott Fitzgerald is now considered one of the great American writers of fiction. That reputation rests largely on *The Great Gatsby* (1925) and *Tender Is the Night* (1934), as well as a number of masterful short stories including "The Rich Boy" (1926), "May Day"(1920), and "Winter Dreams" (1922). Sometimes mistakenly viewed as a mere chronicler of the Roaring Twenties—an era evocative of flappers in bobbed hair and short skirts, easy Wall Street riches, and parties soaked with wild jazz and prohibited alcohol—Fitzgerald most rewards readers with graceful prose, psychological acumen, and a heartrending awareness of the fragility within American dreams. Critics also admire Fitzgerald's fiction for its serious moral and philosophical insights.

His debut novel, *This Side of Paradise* launched Fitzgerald's fame in the 1920's. Widely reviewed, the book was praised by most critics for its fresh depiction of America's youth, with the hard-to-impress H. L. Mencken going far and calling it "a truly amazing first novel." Other reviewers, however, were disturbed by the characters' seemingly dissolute behavior. A review in the Springfield, Massachusetts, *Union* complained that "the leading persons are of a nature disgusting to the average taste." Matthew J. Bruccoli observes that, served well by his good looks and even by negative reviews, the twenty-three-year-old Fitzgerald became almost instantly famous. Selling out its first printing in three days,

This Side of Paradise earned for Fitzgerald the large sum of sixty-two hundred dollars in 1920 alone.

The novel documents a national youth culture, vividly capturing its mores, attitudes, and tastes. While today the behavior of the young characters may not scandalize, Fitzgerald rather boldly depicts the "petting" of the time—the casual kissing of more than one partner—as well as the excessive imbibing of alcohol both before and after Prohibition. He describes a new kind of young woman, the Popular Daughter, or P.D., who becomes engaged often before shrewdly marrying a financially secure man.

Along with practicality, traditional morality is not abandoned. Although late in the novel it is clear that Alec Connage has had sex with the underage woman he brought to Atlantic City for that purpose, earlier it is suggested that, though in love, Amory and Rosalind have not slept together. A chronic waster of his talent, Amory is not immoral or even amoral. He believes in evil so palpably that he has visions of it as a man in brown suit and in the atmosphere that hovers over the illicit scene in the Atlantic City hotel room. In addition, Amory's discussions with his classmates about literature and society reflect a spiritual questing that undergirds his development. In an era of rapid social and cultural change, Amory seeks a way of being and of being better.

Much of Amory's maturation occurs as a series of poses that he half-knowingly adopts. Chief among these is a romantic self-conception that is reinforced through purposeful or perceived failure, as if he is deliberately playing and replaying the role of the tragic character. When Amory refuses to study for an important mathematics examination and inevitably fails, he blames his failure on fate and not his own indolence. Amory's identity often appears as a conscious construction, but Fitzgerald presents the instability of selfhood more as a condition of youthful development than as a social malaise. Near the novel's end, as he rides atop a bus, Amory engages in an inner conversation with himself that signals the consolidation of his identity. Ultimately, he scornfully accepts his essential personality, his vanity and easily hurt feelings.

Constructed in part from sketches, poetry, episodes in stream-of-consciousness, and playlets, *This Side of Paradise* presents an example of modernist experimentation in narrative. The novel's fragmentary structure is also emblematic of Amory's fitful maturation and of a postwar period rife with moral and social discontinuities. As Amory seeks a coherent sense of himself, so the novel's form seeks to knit disparate literary modes into a whole.

Titled "The Romantic Egotist" in early versions, *This Side of Paradise* recognizes its own romantic yearnings, as Amory twice says, "the sentimental person thinks things will last—the romantic person has a desperate confidence that they won't." The novel dramatizes Fitzgerald's sympathy with young people who learn painfully that time flees swiftly, that youth and pleasure are transitory, and that beauty and self-confidence offer no protection against the world. Even as it helped register the tenor of a new age for readers at the time and even as it reanimates the American 1920's for readers today, *This Side of Paradise* thrums like the bass in a jazz combo, sounding the somber note that all roaring eras must inevitably end.

Scott D. Emmert

Further Reading

Bruccoli, Matthew J. *Some Sort of Epic Grandeur: The Life of F. Scott Fitzgerald.* 2d rev. ed. Columbia: University of South Carolina Press, 2002. This authoritative biography was first published in 1981 by Harcourt Brace Jovanovich. Includes a genealogical afterword by Scottie Fitzgerald Smith.

Bryer, Jackson R. *The Critical Reputation of F. Scott Fitzgerald: A Bibliographical Study.* Hamden, Conn.: Archon Books, 1967. An especially useful annotated list of reviews of Fitzgerald's books and of articles about him published in his lifetime. Annotations of critical works chart directions in scholarship during the twenty-five years after Fitzgerald's death. A supplement published in 1984 covers scholarship through 1981.

_____, ed. *F. Scott Fitzgerald: The Critical Reception.* New York: Burt Franklin, 1978. Reprints contemporary reviews of Fitzgerald's novels and story collections.

Bryer, Jackson R., Ruth Prigozy, and Milton R Stern, eds. *Scott Fitzgerald in the Twenty-first Century.* Tuscaloosa: University of Alabama Press, 2003. Collects nineteen essays, most of which were first presented at the 1996 International F. Scott Fitzgerald Conference held at Princeton University. Individual essays consider *This Side of Paradise* in detail, focusing on philosophical, moral, and social issues that influenced the novel.

Curnutt, Kirk, ed. *A Historical Guide to F. Scott Fitzgerald.* New York: Oxford University Press, 2004. Informative essays on Fitzgerald's life and times. Coverage of World War I and of the intellectual, commercial, and cultural background of the early twentieth century carefully places Fitzgerald's fiction in a context of influences.

Prigozy, Ruth, ed. *The Cambridge Companion to F. Scott Fitzgerald.* New York: Cambridge University Press, 2002. Eleven essays by prominent scholars discuss aspects of Fitzgerald's life and work, including celebrity and youth culture in the 1920's and the treatment of women in his fiction.

West, James L. W., III. *The Making of "This Side of Paradise."* Philadelphia: University of Pennsylvania Press, 1983. Details the composition of the novel from its beginnings as "The Romantic Egotist" through efforts to correct errors in the first printing.

This Sporting Life

Author: David Storey (1933-   )
First published: 1960
Type of work: Novel
Type of plot: Naturalism
Time of plot: 1950's
Locale: Industrial town in Northern England

Principal characters:
ARTHUR MACHIN, a rugby player for a team called The City
MRS. VALERIE HAMMOND, Machin's landlady and lover
MR. WEAVER, a factory owner and member of The City's governing committee
MRS. WEAVER, his wife
MR. SLOMER, the town's crippled patriarch
MAURICE, Machin's teammate
ED PHILIPS, a local journalist

The Story:

Rugby player for a team called The City, Arthur Machin gets hit in a scrum and loses six teeth. He is taken to a dentist to have his teeth fixed. He is given anesthesia and passes out. While unconscious, he recalls a time before he entered the ranks of professional rugby.

As a novice seeking a position, Machin convinces a man

named Johnson to give him a tryout with a professional team. Machin has been living with a Mrs. Hammond since leaving his parents. Mrs. Hammond charges less rent than other landladies, the prime reason he had chosen to live with her. She has two children, is a widow, and is emotionally distant. When Machin tells Mrs. Hammond about his trial, she does not care. She tells Machin that her deceased husband meant everything to her; she still keeps his boots next to the hearth and regularly polishes them.

Machin learns he will be signed with the team but must negotiate a fee for himself. Advised by his teammate Maurice to ask for five hundred pounds plus bonuses, Machin waits nervously in a bar to hear from Weaver and the rest of the committee. Ed Philips, a journalist for the *City Guardian*, tells Machin not to take his situation too seriously, insisting rugby is only a game. Machin is signed at the salary he wanted.

Weaver drives Machin home in his Bentley and tells him about Mrs. Hammond's husband dying at Weaver's factory. While Mr. Hammond was working on a lathe, a file pierced his abdomen, killing him. Mrs. Hammond did not receive any compensation, because the death was ruled a suicide.

Machin tells Mrs. Hammond about the money and discusses how Weaver talked about her husband. Trying to sleep, he hears her crying downstairs. A little later, she comes to his door and asks if he will leave. He says he will stay.

In the narrative present, Machin comes out of anesthesia in the dentist's office. He is taken in Weaver's car to Weaver's Christmas party. Groggy from the anesthesia, Machin tries to find a place to sleep it off and returns to his unconscious reminiscences.

In the past again, Machin buys a Jaguar. Mrs. Weaver refuses to sit in it for five weeks because the money came from Weaver. When they do get in the car, people in the neighborhood watch them. Machin drives Hammond and her children, Lynda and Ian, to Markham Abbey and Howton's Hall for dinner.

At home, while Mrs. Hammond is making his bed, Machin makes a pass at her, but Mrs. Hammond fights him off. Hammond leaves to continue cleaning, but later Machin and Mrs. Hammond begin an affair. Mr. Hammond's boots disappear from the hearth.

Later, Machin visits his parents, who reprimand him for losing his ideals. They cite his hanging around with disreputable sorts such as Mr. Weaver, gambling on dog races, and living large with his money, buying cars and clothes.

At the Christmas party in the present, Machin finds himself locked in a bedroom by a teammate. He climbs onto the roof and jumps to the ground. Machin returns to the party and

enters a room where Mr. and Mrs. Weaver and Mr. Slomer are talking. Slomer suggests that there is a relationship between Machin and Mrs. Weaver. Machin sees Slomer off and denies the relationship. He staggers home with Christmas presents for Mrs. Hammond and her two children.

Later, Machin is having lunch in the stockyards when he is joined by Mr. Weaver. Mr. Weaver implies that, because of Machin's relationship with Mrs. Weaver, he tried to have him benched. However, Mr. Slomer overruled that idea.

Mrs. Hammond seems to be adjusting to her role as Machin's kept woman. She enjoys the car, wears a fur coat, and brings up the idea of getting a television. All the while, neighbors watch, and the pressure of appearances starts to affect her. During a car trip, she tells Machin she feels "dirty" as his kept woman. Soon after, she starts letting herself go, starts smoking, and starts running down physically.

Feeling the emptiness of his relationship with Mrs. Hammond and the strain of being a rugby player, Machin starts thinking of himself as merely an ape performing for others. He visits Mr. Weaver's home for a talk but finds only Mrs. Weaver at home. He discusses his problems with her. Mrs. Weaver proves insightful, suggesting that Mrs. Hammond probably measures herself against Machin—the successful rugby player—and feels that she suffers in the comparison.

Mrs. Hammond and Machin have a confrontation in her home. She says he does not work. He says he does. He says she does not appreciate all he has done for her. She kicks him out, and he sullies the memory of her husband by mentioning his suicide and saying she must have driven him to it.

Machin goes to the team's rugby pitch, Primstone, to find he has been left off the team roster. He returns to Mrs. Hammond to pack his things and moves to a rooming house. He moves out of his rooming house and goes to his parents' house, where, to his surprise, he discovers Mrs. Hammond. When Mrs. Hammond leaves, his mother insists he let her go, saying she is no good for him. After an exchange of harsh words with his parents, his father slaps him. Machin is now living with his parents.

Machin meets Mrs. Hammond twice more. First, he visits her and finds her worn out and sick. Next, he meets her on the street near his new apartment, but she wants nothing to do with him.

Machin receives a letter informing him that Mrs. Hammond has been hospitalized for a blood clot in the brain. He has not seen her for over a year, but he visits her and arranges a private room. He goes to her every night. One night, he sees an insect with two eyes approaching Mrs. Hammond. Machin attempts to kill it, but it skitters away. Mrs. Hammond's blood clot bursts, sending blood out of her nose. After an operation, she is awake but does not remember the past clearly. She enjoys the flowers Machin sends, holding Machin's hand, and the sight of her children, whom she vaguely remembers. A week later, she dies. After Mrs. Hammond's death, Machin continues playing rugby. He grows older and finds the game tougher as his body begins to betray him and as his position on the team is challenged by younger athletes.

Critical Evaluation:

David Storey, a poet, playwright, and novelist, was born in Wakefield, England. A rugby player for Leeds, he bought himself out of his contract before beginning his career as a writer. He has become a noted writer. In 1960, he won the Macmillan prize for *This Sporting Life*, and he won the 1976 Booker Prize for his novel *Saville*. He has published many plays, collections of poetry, and dramas. He has also won recognition for his screenplay adaptation of *This Sporting Life*.

In his novels, Storey places quiet, tough men in opposition to their environments. He comes from the tradition of Kingsley Amis, John Osborne, and others of the Angry Young Man movement in British literature; these writers challenged the class structure of society in their writing.

This Sporting Life is the first of three successive novels that explore the relationship between body and soul with an eventual synthesis of the two. *This Sporting Life* deals with the body; *Flight into Camden* (1961) deals with the soul; *Radcliffe* (1963) synthesizes the duality. The protagonist of *This Sporting Life* can express himself physically on the rugby pitch, breaking opposition and returning to the fray even after serious injury. He is, however, incapable of expressing his gentler feelings, especially his love for Mrs. Hammond. Instead, he cajoles, screams, and bullies. Machin cannot express his soul. As loud as he is, when expressing affection and care he is a mute.

This Sporting Life gives an unflinching view of life on a rugby team in a small mill city in Northern England. The play on the rugby pitch is vicious, full of blood, broken bones, and broken men. The setting is bleak, with mills and their emitted smoke making up most of the landscape. Men eat lunch overlooking mill works, and people populate dirty, small housing. In a world of such physicality, communication between people is difficult, and attempts to make one's feelings heard can lead to tragedy.

The main theme of *This Sporting Life* is the individual trying to break out of the rut of the common men in his environment. Forced to live a life of unrelenting toil in the mills and the mines, the men of the town can only find escape by sacrificing their bodies as rugby players. Even with the fame and money that comes with success on the pitch, most are still stuck in their class. The hero of the novel, Machin, battles with his parents, who spout philosophical idealism about keeping one's place in society and is provoked by his lover Mrs. Hammond, a woman who constantly undermines his attempts to make their life more physically comfortable. For all his success on the rugby pitch, Machin remains mired in his class, and the upper-crust owners of the team and town patriarchs such as Slomer and Weaver remain distant and mysterious, signing a new rugby player or cutting an old or unwanted one on a whim, as if he were a piece of meat or a commodity.

The novel is divided into two parts, with the first part using flashbacks to establish the background of the protagonist, Machin. Part 1 ends with Machin finally seeming to have achieved a relationship with Mrs. Hammond, giving Christmas presents to the kids, and at last having her spend the night in his bed. Part 2, though, shows the end of their relationship and the decline of Mrs. Hammond. Mrs. Hammond's time in the hospital, especially her time spent with Machin after brain surgery, shows the hopelessness of her position in society. Meant for drudgery in life, she can find happiness only when she is near death. The tragedy of this situation is particularly poignant given the love Machin has for her.

The novel achieves depth through the characters Machin meets throughout the novel. These include Johnson, the man who Machin befriends to help him get a spot on the rugby team but then ditches; Maurice, the fun-loving teammate of Machin who shows affection for others only when he needs something; the mysterious town patriarch, Slomer, crippled but all-powerful; Weaver and Mrs. Weaver, the true status of their marriage never really revealed to leave open the possibility that Weaver is gay; the captain of the rugby squad, who is holding on to his job year by year in hope of sinking back into the pits, which, for a rugby star, would mean oblivion; and the jaded newspaperman, Philip, who understands rugby as nothing more than a game played on the pitch by players and off the pitch by the group of men who own the players.

Brett Conway

Further Reading

Bradbury, Malcolm. Review of *This Sporting Life*, by David Storey. *The New York Times Book Review*, September 18, 1960, p. 68. Initial reception of the novel by an internationally renowned literary scholar.

Gindin, James. *Postwar British Fiction: New Accents and Attitudes*, Berkeley: University of California Press, 1962. Details the differences between British fiction produced before and after World War II; places *This Sporting Life* in the context of the literary concerns of its moment.

Gray, Nigel. *The Silent Majority: A Study of the Working Class in Post-War British Fiction*. New York: Barnes & Noble, 1973. Examines the representation of labor and laborers in British fiction produced after 1945.

Klaus, H. Gustav, and Stephen Knight, eds. *British Industrial Fictions*. Cardiff: University of Wales Press, 2000. Collection of essays surveying the representation of industrialization and industrialized labor in British literature.

Taylor, John Russell. *David Storey*. London: Longman, 1974. An account of the author's life and work.

Thomas and Beulah

Author: Rita Dove (1952-   )
First published: 1986
Type of work: Poetry

Rita Dove's third collection of poems, *Thomas and Beulah*, presents a fictionalized version of the author's maternal grandparents' lives in Akron, Ohio. Dove explains that she likes to show many sides of an event or experience. Accordingly, the book is divided into two almost-equal sections. The first section, "Mandolin," contains twenty-three poems from Grandfather Thomas's point of view, and the second section, "Canary in Bloom," contains twenty-one poems telling the story according to Grandmother Beulah.

The book, which won the Pulitzer Prize in poetry in 1987, explores the changing lives of a middle-class African American family set against the background of American history in the first half of the twentieth century. Dove includes a chronology at the end of the book that starts in 1900 with Thomas's birth in Wartrace, Tennessee, and ends in 1969 with Beulah's death. Events listed in the chronology include both personal events, such as the couple's wedding in December, 1924, and birth of their first child, Rose, in 1926, and public events, such as the building of the Goodyear Zeppelin Airdock in 1929 and the 1963 March on Washington for civil rights. The events of history and the cultural changes remain in the background. Dove wished to convey the meaning of her grandparents' lives rather than be strictly factual.

In both Tennessee and Ohio, the couple faces discrimination in various forms. For example, in "Nothing Down," Thomas remembers having to hide from rampaging white men. In "Roast Possum," Thomas tells his grandchildren stories, but omits the passage from an encyclopedia that claims that "Negro" children become lazy at puberty. After Thomas's death ("Wingfoot Lake"), Beulah attends a company picnic on Independence Day, 1964, in which the families of whites and the families of African Americans sit on opposite sides at the picnic, yet unpacking similar food items.

Musical imagery, as the section titles indicate, is a structural link among the poems, starting with the mandolin that Thomas's friend Lem plays and echoing through the sequence as Thomas joins a gospel chorus and Beulah gets a pet canary and a musical jewelry box. Poem titles include "Jiving," "Refrain," and "Lightnin' Blues." Both the rhythms of many of the poems and the book's themes of love and loss suggest blues songs.

A chain of images revolves around the colors yellow and blue. Thomas gives Beulah a yellow scarf when they are courting. In "Dusting," Beulah remembers having a goldfish, and she later gets a pet canary. Thomas gets a blue car (which gets repossessed during the Depression) and shows Beulah her first swimming pool when she is thirty-six years old.

Another recurring image is that of river and water. The book grew from a story that Dove learned about her grandfather after his death. In "The Event," Thomas and his friend Lem, a musical duo, are traveling on a riverboat. One night, Thomas dares Lem to swim, but he drowns, leaving Thomas to grieve the rest of his life. In fact, Lem appears in several poems by name or by reference as a kind of guide for Thomas ("Variation on Pain," "The Charm," "The Stroke," and "Thomas at the Wheel"). As Thomas dies in his car in the parking lot of a pharmacy, where he had driven for his medication, he thinks about how he, too, must now swim the river, as did Lem years ago.

Thomas starts out as a young dandy but becomes a family man. He is disappointed that he fathers only daughters and is happy when he gains a son-in-law. The Depression finds him struggling to support his family. He would like to join the

U.S. Army during World War II ("Aircraft"), but is deemed too frail to serve. Instead, he gets a job as a riveter at Goodyear Aircraft.

In a 2005 interview in the journal *Callaloo*, Dove explains that she had written the poem "Dusting" for inclusion in an earlier book, *Museum*, published in 1983. She began working on a series of poems after this, about her grandfather, and realized that "Dusting" represented her grandmother speaking to her: "Wake up Girl! I'm here too! I wanna talk!" Beulah wanted to be part of the evolving book, along with her husband—and so the Beulah sequence derived from this start. For the book, Dove changed her grandmother's name from Georgianna to Beulah because she wanted the biblical allusions and because it was more effective rhythmically to use a shorter name in the poems. The name Beulah is derived from the Hebrew word that means "married," and it refers to the land of Israel in the book of Isaiah. Dove asserts that Beulah also means "desert in peace."

In *Thomas and Beulah*, the mother of the young Beulah wishes to protect her from her father: In "Taking in Wash," her mother warns her husband not to "touch that child." The poem "Promises," about the wedding of Thomas and Beulah, deals as much with Beulah's father as it does with her new husband. After her marriage to Thomas, Beulah's life revolves around her family and housekeeping. As the mother of four daughters, she still finds space to indulge her private fantasies ("Daystar") and has dreams of Paris and travel, which she never fulfills. Poems such as "Taking in Wash," "Dusting," "A Hill of Beans," and "Sunday Greens" refer to the women's work of housekeeping and cooking. When she is forty-two years old, Beulah gets a part-time job pressing clothes and making alterations in a dress shop.

The marriage is a comfortable one, although Dove treats the couple realistically rather than romantically. In "Company," as Thomas is suffering his last illness, Beulah reminds him of the following: "listen: we were good,/ though we never believed it." In an interview, the poet said that she had wished to honor her grandmother as a curious and imaginative person, "a very strong woman, who still has no way of showing how strong she could be."

Dove's intent in writing the book was to combine the "grandness" and "sweep of time" that narrative poems achieve with the immediacy of lyric poetry. In another interview, Dove said she wanted the book to embody the best features of both lyric and narrative, "to string moments as beads on a necklace." In writing the book, she said, she believed she was returning to her family background and honoring her grandparents.

Karen F. Stein

Further Reading

Dove, Rita. "Rita Dove." Interview by Camille Dungy. *Callaloo* 28, no. 4 (2005): 1027-1040. This discussion ranges over several books and examines Dove's participation in an African American poetic tradition. Dove sees this tradition as moving in many directions and encompassing a variety of forms, both formal and loose.

Ingersoll, Earl G., ed. *Conversations with Rita Dove*. Jackson: University Press of Mississippi, 2003. A collection of interviews with Dove, in which she discusses *Thomas and Beulah* and describes the origin of the poems, her background research, and her techniques and themes. Includes an index that points to specific poems.

Pereira, Malin. *Rita Dove's Cosmopolitanism*. Urbana: University of Illinois Press, 2003. This book explores Dove as part of an African American poetic tradition. Chapter 5 discusses *Thomas and Beulah* in terms of blues music. The appendix contains an interview between Pereira and Dove.

Righelato, Pat. *Understanding Rita Dove*. Columbia: University of South Carolina Press, 2006. Chapter 4 discusses *Thomas and Beulah* in terms of "the changing landscape of the American Dream highlighted in the personal moment." Part of the Understanding Contemporary American Literature series.

Schneider, Steven, "Writing for Those Moments of Discovery." In *Conversations with Rita Dove*, edited by Earl G. Ingersoll. Jackson: University Press of Mississippi, 2003. This informative interview is chiefly focused on *Thomas and Beulah* and on Dove's reactions to winning the Pulitzer Prize.

Shoptaw, John, "Segregated Lives: Rita Dove's *Thomas and Beulah*." In *Reading Black, Reading Feminist*, edited by Henry Louis Gates, Jr. New York: Meridian, 1990. Shoptaw focuses on the disjunction among the lives of the protagonists and on this disjunction as a stylistic device in the poems.

Steffen, Therese. *Crossing Color: Transcultural Space and Place in Rita Dove's Poetry, Fiction, and Drama*. New York: Oxford University Press, 2001. Chapter 3 focuses on *Thomas and Beulah*. Explains that the book counteracts negative stereotypes of African American families. Places the book in the context of African American history and also discusses Dove's artistry.

Vendler, Helen. "Rita Dove: Identity Markers." In *The Given and the Made: Strategies of Poetic Redefinition*. Cambridge, Mass.: Harvard University Press, 1995. Vendler terms the poems brief "snapshots" and small "vignettes." She explicates the poem "Aircraft" in terms of theme, language, and poetic structure.

A Thousand Acres

Author: Jane Smiley (1949-   )
First published: 1991
Type of work: Novel
Type of plot: Psychological realism
Time of plot: 1979
Locale: Zebulon County, Iowa

Principal characters:
VIRGINIA "GINNY" COOK SMITH, the narrator
LARRY COOK, her father
ROSE COOK LEWIS and CAROLINE COOK RASMUSSEN, her
    sisters
TYLER "TY" SMITH, her husband
PETER "PETE" LEWIS, Rose's husband
PAMMY and LINDA, Rose and Pete's daughters
HAROLD CLARK, Larry's neighbor and old friend
JESS and LOREN, his sons

The Story:

The grandparents of Virginia "Ginny" Cook Smith had settled Zebulon County when the land there was fertile but full of standing water and abundant wildlife. They had used tiles to drain the excess water into cisterns and wells; when the land was cultivated, the ponds, plants, and animal life became marginalized; the fertilizer and chemicals used on the land then drained into the wells and cisterns.

Ginny, along with sisters Rose and Caroline, spend part of their childhood being raised by their father, Larry Cook, after the death of their mother. Larry often beats and sometimes rapes the older girls, Rose and Ginny. The daughters marry young—Ginny at the age of nineteen to Tyler "Ty" Smith, who brings his father's acreage into the family. By 1979, after a series of miscarriages, Ginny still has no children. Rose also marries at a young age. With her husband, Pete Lewis, they have two daughters, Pammy and Linda. Pete, a frustrated musician who is stuck farming and hates it, gets drunk and breaks Rose's arm, but he stops harming her even further when she puts him on notice. Rose is diagnosed with breast cancer at the age of thirty-four; Ginny nurses her through the surgery and becomes a loving aunt to Pammy and Linda, sometimes envying Rose for having children and wishing that the girls could come home from boarding school.

In the spring of 1979, their neighbor Harold Clark holds a hog roast to welcome back his son Jess, who went to Canada to evade the draft during the Vietnam War. During the hog roast, Larry announces that he is turning the family farm into a corporation, with shares going to each of the daughters and their husbands. In fact, he is turning over control of the property—a farm of now one thousand acres—to the younger generation.

Everyone seems to give their assent to Larry's idea, everyone except Caroline. Larry angrily tells her that she will therefore not receive a share. Caroline leaves the party and drives away without another word.

Ginny anxiously tries to make peace during the next few days, mainly by arguing with Caroline to change her mind. Soon the family gathers to sign the papers, with Marv Carson, from the bank, and Ken Lasalle, the family lawyer, present. Caroline drives up and approaches the screen door, but Larry gets to the door first and slams it in Caroline's face. Now alienated from the family, she stays away, working at her law practice in Mason City and commuting to New York frequently. When she marries Frank Rasmussen, another lawyer, the family receives only an announcement, and no invitations to the wedding.

Ginny's husband, Ty, is happy about the arrangement. He borrows money from Marv's bank to set up a large hog-confinement operation, which involves putting up new buildings and buying equipment and breeding sows. The farm is already the most successful farm in Zebulon County, and among the largest.

Larry no longer works on the farm and begins some erratic behavior that worries Rose and Ginny. When Ginny, who continues to cook for him, tries to reason with him about his actions, he becomes angry and tells Ginny to stop giving him orders. Later, Ginny drives by Larry's house and sees him sitting immobile in the window, but when she asks if he is okay, he becomes angry. It is apparent that he is watching Ty prepare one of the fields for planting, and disapproving of Ty's actions.

The younger generation of Clarks and Cooks start spending evenings together playing the board game Monopoly. As they play, some tell stories about their lives—Pete about his attempts to start a career in music and Jess a little bit about the years he was away in Canada. Jess and Ginny become more acquainted, and Jess and Ty become friends. Jess often visits Ginny, and the two of them talk about their lives, their hopes, their dreams—Jess telling Ginny about his fiancé, who had died in a crash, and Ginny tells Jess about the miscarriages she has had, the last few she has kept secret from Ty. Jess is more environmentally aware than the men of Larry and Harold's generation, and he tells Ginny that the well water, contaminated by fertilizer and chemicals that can reach the well through the tile drainage system, probably had caused her miscarriages and also Rose's cancer.

Ginny and Jess's closeness leads to one sexual encounter, but after Ginny tells Jess that she loves him, he becomes more distant. Meanwhile, Larry, consumed by anger, is eventually arrested for driving while intoxicated. He refuses to discuss this with Ginny, and he becomes more critical of her treatment of him and of everyone's way of running the farm. Rose and Ginny argue over what to do about their father, and Rose finally tells Ginny that she hates him because he had raped her repeatedly years ago. Rose thinks the same thing had happened to Ginny, but Ginny remembers nothing of it. Rose keeps Pammy and Linda in boarding school because she fears Larry will rape them, too.

Harold Clark sympathizes with Larry and urges Ginny, Rose, and their families to attend a church supper, where he plans to help them make peace with each other. Instead, Harold uses the occasion to denounce Ginny, Rose, and Jess publicly, and he does so using foul language.

One night during a violent storm Larry confronts daughters Ginny and Rose, making outlandish accusations and calling them names. Then he disappears into the rain. Caroline makes contact with her sisters again, but despite Larry's own bad treatment of her, she now blames them for Larry's disappearance during the storm. Ginny and Rose finally learn that Larry plans to sue them to regain control of the farm, with Caroline a party to the suit on their father's side. Before the case goes to court, Pete, Rose's husband, sets up an accident that leads to Harold's blindness, then drunkenly threatens to kill Harold and Larry. Later, Pete drowns after driving his truck into a flooded quarry.

During the time of Pete's death and funeral, Rose reveals to Ginny that she is having an affair with Jess. In shock, Ginny begins to remember her own times when Larry had raped her, but her anger is at Rose, and she jealously plans to kill Rose by poisoning her.

The lawsuit finally goes to court, but the judge dismisses Larry's suit after a short session. Larry seems to have advanced dementia. After returning from court, Ty and Ginny argue, and Ty believes, as he always has, that Ginny and Rose had treated their father badly. Ginny asks Ty for one thousand dollars cash, takes it, and drives to Minneapolis, leaving him for good; Ty and Rose are the only surviving family on the farm.

Ginny settles into a contented, although somewhat lonely, life in Minneapolis. Eventually, Ty visits and tells her he is giving up the farm and going to Texas to start over and that Larry is dead. Later, Rose calls and tells Ginny that her cancer has returned, and this time it is terminal. She asks Ginny to take care of Pammy and Linda after she dies. Rose and Ginny make peace, and Ginny is relieved that Rose never took her poison. After Rose dies, Ginny takes the girls to Minneapolis. No one is left on the farm, which is bought out and taken over by a corporation.

Critical Evaluation:

A Thousand Acres led to critical acclaim for Jane Smiley, including the 1992 Pulitzer Prize for fiction, a National Book Critics' Circle Award, and a *Chicago Tribune* Heartland Prize. Smiley grew up in the Midwest at Webster Groves, Missouri, and after receiving a bachelor's degree from Vassar College returned to the heartland for advanced degrees, including a doctorate, at the University of Iowa. While she has seen and written about much of the world—she spent a year in Iceland on a Fulbright Fellowship before finishing at Iowa—life in the Midwest remains a frequent theme for her.

Smiley's historical novel, *The All-True Travels and Adventures of Lidie Newton* (1998), for example, is set in Kansas just before the American Civil War, during the battle between pro- and antislavery supporters. Her work includes a critical work on Charles Dickens and *Thirteen Ways of Looking at the Novel* (2005), which reveals her to be an even more prolific reader than writer, one who takes so much pleasure in reading that it improves her health.

Smiley's narrative technique has the simultaneous effect of immersing the reader in place (Zebulon County, Iowa), introducing the major characters, creating a sense of suspense by hinting at hidden tensions, and revealing the anxieties of Ginny Cook Smith, the narrator. A view of the endless flat prairie of the Cook farm, looking toward the farms of the Clarks and the Ericsons, immediately exposes the corrupt value system that creates the huge farms: For example, Larry Cook and Harold Clark argue over who will get the Ericsons' farm when its mortgage is foreclosed.

Next begins the account of Harold's hog roast to welcome his son Jess back from his disappearance to avoid the Vietnam War. This welcome-home party, ironically, begins the principle conflict that will later divide families and generations: Larry's proposal to divide his farm among his daughters and their husbands. The first ties are broken as Caroline rejects the idea, and Larry almost disowns her. Another source of conflict is introduced in Jess, who will later become the lover of both Rose and Ginny and, in part, the cause of their distancing from one another. Meanwhile, Harold, who is throwing the party to welcome Jess home, will later reject Jess's newfangled ideas and publicly denounce him as a draft dodger.

Much critical attention has focused on the similarities between Smiley's novel and William Shakespeare's play *King Lear* (pr. c. 1605-1606, pb. 1608). However, while the plot may parallel Shakespeare's work—Lear, an aging king, proposes to divide his kingdom among his three daughters just as Larry does with his farm—the themes and tensions arising in the stories are different. Lear's tragedy arises when two of his daughters lie about their love for him and later betray him, but Larry's suffering is of his own making. His abuse of the land, once a watery home to a rich variety of wildlife, poisons his daughters, while his sexual abuse of them destroys his family, and his legacy.

Timothy C. Frazer

Further Reading

Carden, Mary Paniccia. "Remembering/Engendering the Heartland: Sexed Language, Embodied Space, and America's Foundational Fictions in Jane Smiley's *A Thousand Acres*." *Frontiers: A Journal of Women's Studies* 18, no. 2 (1997): 181-202. Examines how Smiley, in *A Thousand Acres*, challenges agrarian ideologies that serve to silence women.

Farrell, Susan Elizabeth. *Jane Smiley's "A Thousand Acres": A Reader's Guide*. New York: Continuum, 2001. Provides a close look at Smiley's award-winning novel. Addresses such subjects as father-daughter relationships, King Lear as a legendary character, and rural families and farm life. Includes bibliographical references.

Leslie, Marina. "Incest, Incorporation, and King Lear in Jane Smiley's *A Thousand Acres*." *College English* 60, no. 1 (January, 1998): 31-50. Presents a scholarly comparison of *King Lear* and *A Thousand Acres*, with an emphasis on Shakespearean criticism that recognizes incest themes in *King Lear*.

Nakadate, Neil. *Understanding Jane Smiley*. Columbia: University of South Carolina Press, 1999. An academic book that is helpful for general readers and students new to Smiley's work. Includes a bibliography and an index.

Rozga, Margaret. "Sisters in Quest: *Sister Carrie* and *A Thousand Acres*—Search for Identity in Gendered Territory." *Midwestern Miscellany* 22 (1994): 18-29. Rozga examines the ways in which the heroines of both novels seek authenticity in a world of male value.

Sheldon, Barbara H. *Daughters and Fathers in Feminist Novels*. New York: Peter Lang, 1997. Feminist literary criticism has long focused on Freudian and other views of father-daughter relationships, including sexual tensions. This study employs this tool to examine *A Thousand Acres* and other works.

Walker, Nancy A. *The Disobedient Writer: Women and Narrative Tradition*. Austin: University of Texas Press, 1995. Walker argues that Smiley, in writing *A Thousand Acres*, reformulates William Shakespeare's *King Lear* to give authority to women's voices.

Thousand Cranes

Author: Yasunari Kawabata (1899-1972)
First published: Sembazuru, 1949-1951, serial; 1952, book (English translation, 1958)
Type of work: Novel
Type of plot: Psychological realism
Time of plot: Mid-twentieth century
Locale: Tokyo and Kamakura, Japan

The Story:

Kikuji Mitani is on his way to a tea ceremony that will be performed at the inner cottage of Engakuji Temple in Kamakura, Japan. When Kikuji received an invitation to this ceremony from Kurimoto Chikako, his deceased father's for-

Principal characters:
KIKUJI MITANI, a Tokyo office worker in his mid-twenties
KURIMOTO CHIKAKO, a tea ceremony teacher and a former mistress of Kikuji's father
MRS. OTA, the last mistress of Kikuji's father
FUMIKO OTA, her daughter
YURIKO INAMURA, a young woman whom Chikako wants Kikuji to marry

mer mistress, he initially thought it was being conducted in memory of his deceased father, but a postscript mentioned that she wanted him to meet Yuriko Inamura, her student. As he again reads the note, Kikuji remembers that, when he was taken by his father to visit Chikako, he accidentally viewed the large birthmark that covers half of her left breast. Kikuji has been haunted by this image since then.

After Kikuji enters the temple's grounds, he spots two young women, one of whom is carrying a bundle wrapped with a kerchief with a beautiful thousand-crane pattern. When Kikuji arrives at the cottage, he notices that the girl with the kerchief is there as well. Chikako tells Kikuji that the girl's father was a friend of his father. She then takes him aside and apologetically informs him that Mrs. Ota, his father's last mistress, is also attending the ceremony, along with her daughter Fumiko. Kikuji is puzzled because he knows that Chikako hates Mrs. Ota. In order to show Yuriko off to Kikuji, Chikako has her perform the tea ceremony using a bowl that originally belonged to Mrs. Ota's husband and that was later given to Kikuji's father.

After the ceremony is completed, Kikuji leaves. He runs into Mrs. Ota, who tells him that the ring that Fumiko is wearing was given to her by his father as a reward for helping him in an air raid during the war. Kikuji begins to feel that Mrs. Ota is treating him as if he were his father. They have dinner and spend the night together. He talks to her about Chikako's birthmark, and she is disgusted. Two weeks later, Fumiko visits Kikuji and apologizes for her mother's behavior. He tells her that her mother is a good person.

Chikako calls Kikuji at his office, telling him that she has cleaned his tea cottage and will cook for him. She also says that she will invite Yuriko for dinner. He returns home and tells a surprised Yuriko how much he dislikes Chikako's meddling ways. The next day, a very sick, tearful Mrs. Ota visits and discloses her overwhelming guilt over her past actions. Kikuji accuses her of thinking that he and his father are the same person. She asks for his forgiveness, declares that she does not understand herself and wants to die, and begs him to take care of Fumiko and quickly marry Yuriko. At 2:00 A.M. the next day, Fumiko calls to inform Kikuji that her mother has taken her own life.

Eight days after Mrs. Ota's memorial service, Kikuji visits Fumiko. He notices that a fine, white, glazed Shino tea ceremony water jar is being used to hold flowers. He speculates about whether it was guilt or love that killed Mrs. Ota and says that he made her die. Fumiko retorts that she died because of herself and that perhaps she was asking for forgiveness. Fumiko serves tea using red and black Raku "man and wife" ceremonial bowls. Kikuji is surprised but believes Fumiko is not being malicious. They speak about death and the importance of taking care of the dead. She gives the water jar to Kikuji.

Kikuji starts to feel that he is in love with Mrs. Ota. He

calls Fumiko and invites her to visit. She refuses and says she is going to sell her house. Meanwhile, Chikako visits him, announcing that she knows Mrs. Ota committed suicide and that it was good that she did so, for she was interfering with his plan to marry Yukio. Kikuji is shocked by her remarks, and suddenly an image of Fumiko comes to him. Later that day, he becomes very angry at his maid when she erroneously claims that gourds and morning glories are both vines. Several days later, Fumiko presents him with an old, small, white, cylindrical Shino tea bowl that has the faint red mark of Mrs. Ota's lipstick on it. Chikako appears, makes tea, and insults Fumiko, who remains impassive. Kikuji fails to defend Fumiko.

Chikako falsely tells Kikuji that Fumiko and Yuriko have both married, but he does not believe her. She informs him that she has a buyer for his father's tea-vessel collection. Fumiko drops in, and they make a deal: If the tea bowl in his father's tea chest is of better quality than her mother's white female Shino bowl, then she will break the Shino bowl. It turns out that Mr. Mitani's bowl is a beautiful, undecorated, greenish Korean Karatsu bowl with a touch of carmine and saffron. They carefully compare the bowls and conclude that Mr. Mitani's is the best. They then use the bowls, and Fumiko symbolically breaks the Shino. Later, she gives herself up to Kikuji and then disappears. He feels that she has brought him back to life and tries, unsuccessfully, to find her.

Critical Evaluation:

Winner of the Nobel Prize in Literature in 1968 for the significance of his novels *Yukiguni* (1935-1937, serial; 1947, book; *Snow Country*, 1956), *Thousand Cranes*, and *Kyoto* (1962; *The Old Capital*, 1987), Yasunari Kawabata is generally considered one of the greatest Japanese novelists of the twentieth century. Kawabata was the first modern Japanese writer to be extensively translated into English. Born in Osaka, Japan, in 1899, he was educated at Tokyo Imperial University; he committed suicide in 1972.

Kawabata began to write professionally in the mid-1920's and was a member of the lyrical New Sensationalist school, which revolted against the realism of the naturalist and proletarian schools of writing that were then popular in Japan. The New Sensationalists stressed the importance of purely artistic values and used mixed sensory impressions, striking images, and sudden transitions in their writings. They were influenced by both traditional Japanese haiku poetry and such varied European sources as Surrealism, Futurism, Dadaism, and expressionism. Kawabata went on to develop a style that was deeply rooted in traditional Japanese literature but that also contained non-Japanese elements.

Thousand Cranes was initially serialized in a magazine from 1949 to 1951; it was published in book form in 1952. The short work consists of five chapters and is 147 pages long. Kawabata's writing style in this novel is classical Japanese in temperament: It is loosely structured, sparse, frequently episodic, and impressionistic, and it displays a delicacy of sentiment. Dialogues between characters are highly suggestive, and what is not said is often just as important as what is said; nuances are just as revealing as direct statements. Kawabata's sentences are simple in vocabulary and syntax, have a haiku-like precision, and are often highly sensory. Consequently, his paragraphs are very short and succinct.

Kawabata also uses non-Japanese elements in his writing. He seems constantly to be looking for fresh, nontraditional impressions. The images and situations he constructs are at times surrealistic, and they create an odd, dream-like atmosphere. In addition, Kawabata randomly jumps from association to association in order to capture the quickly changing, immediate consciousness of his characters in a manner that is clearly influenced by the Western writing technique of stream of consciousness.

Thousand Cranes is a psychological exploration of feelings about death and the haunting ties that past events exert on the present. The dominating theme is retribution for sins committed in the past. Kikuji and Fumiko's attempt to understand and overcome the guilt associated with his father's and her mother's behavior is resolved at the end of the story by Fumiko's symbolic breaking of the female Shino bowl and by her giving herself to Kikuji the night before she disappears. Through these acts, dark emotions of the past are purged, and the reincarnations of love (Kikuji as his father, Fumiko as her mother) are made to end. This sense of resolution is captured in the final chapter, when it is noted that "There had been no resistance from Fumiko, only from the cleanness itself." One might think that this lack of resistance could indicate that Kikuji has sunk deeply into the meshes of the curse of his father's actions. Instead, Kikuji feels the reverse, that he has escaped the curse and its accompanying paralysis.

Many readers of the novel assume that it ultimately defends and evokes traditional Japanese values, as exemplified by the tea ceremony. In his 1967 Nobel lecture, "Japan, the Beautiful, and Myself," Kawabata warned readers against drawing this conclusion. He described the novel as a negative work and said that it was intended to serve as a warning that the ceremony had become commercialized and vulgarized in Japan. Kawabata was no simple traditionalist. His genius lay in his ability to take a traditional Japanese symbol, remake it

while keeping its essence, and use it to provide commentary on a modern problem, thereby providing new and original meanings.

The image of the tea ceremony that centers the story serves four extremely important roles. First, it helps further define the novel's characters. Tea utensils reflect the Zen values of refinement, constraint, and simplicity. For example, Chikako's uncouth and meddling nature is demonstrated by the casual way in which she lets personal interests override aesthetic values when she performs the tea ceremony. In contrast, Yuriko, who embodies the beauty of traditional Japan (symbolized by her kerchief with the thousand-crane pattern), has the correct attitude toward the ceremony and performs the ritual flawlessly in the first chapter. The abject passivity of Kikuji, whose main function is to permit the story's female figures to disclose their characters, is further underscored by his lackadaisical approach to the ceremony.

Second, the tea ceremony helps highlight the theme of mortality. The first tea ceremony in the novel occurs in the mausoleum of the founder of Engaku-ji Temple, one of the most famous Zen Buddhist temples in Japan, which was founded in 1282. Many of the china bowls and cups used in the ceremony are old, frequently connected with famous past tea masters, and described in loving detail. For instance, the red and black "man and wife" Raku bowls in which Fumiko serves tea for Kikuji were first produced in the sixteenth century. The timelessness of the tea rituals, which date back to Japan's Nara period (710-794); the old tea vessels used; and the locations in which the ceremony is performed provide a sharp contrast to the temporality of the present.

Third, the utensils used in the ceremony reflect emotional states and feelings and also serve as intermediaries for communication between individuals. The revealing but suggestive face-to-face conversations between Fumiko and Kikuji in chapters three, four, and five occur while they are drinking tea or discussing tea utensils. Fumiko's gifts of tea vessels communicate her true feelings.

Finally, the tea ceremony is used to demonstrate how this tradition has become commercialized and coarsened in modern Japan. The rules governing the performance of the ceremony and the handling of objects are very strict and highly stylized. The intention is to cleanse the senses and clear the mind. Throughout the novel, these rules are observed carelessly or not at all. Chikako, who teaches the tea ceremony, constantly violates its key tenets. For example, in chapter 4, she carelessly brings tea to Kikuji "like a waitress filling an order." Fumiko and Kikuji use ceremonial bowls as ordinary teacups and a three-hundred-year-old tea-ceremony water jar as a flower vase for occidental flowers. In the second chapter, Mrs. Ota lets a tear fall on the tea kettle and leaves her lipstick on an old Shino cylindrical tea bowl. Kikuji neglects the garden next to his tea cottage, which is considered to be an important part of the teahouse. Kawabata's *Thousand Cranes* is like the traditional tea bowls that pervade the novel: seemingly simple but in reality enigmatic, evocative, and intricate, requiring close and thoughtful scrutiny.

Ronald Gray

Further Reading

Cornyetz, Nina. *The Ethics of Aesthetics in Japanese Cinema and Literature: Polygraphic Desire*. New York: Routledge, 2007. Discusses the moral dimension of Kawabata's poetics and the relationship between aesthetic strategies and morality generally.

Keene, David. *Dawn of the West: Japanese Literature of the Modern Era*. Vol. 1. New York: Holt, Reinhart and Winston, 1984. Written by the most famous American scholar of Japanese literature, this massive book includes a long chapter on Kawabata and presents a detailed introduction to modern Japanese literature.

_____. *Five Modern Japanese Novelists*. New York: Columbia University Press, 2003. Kawabata is one of the five novelists whom Keene knew personally that he profiles and discusses at length in this study that combines memoir with literary biography.

Petersen, Gwenn Boardmen. *The Moon in the Water: Understanding Tanizaki, Kawabata, and Mishima*. Honolulu: University of Hawaii Press, 1979. An excellent overview of Kawabata's writings. Discusses *Thousand Cranes* in detail.

Starrs, Roy. *Soundings in Time: The Fictive Art of Yasunari Kawabata*. New York: RoutledgeCurzon, 1998. A book-length study devoted entirely to Kawabata's writings. Accessible and interesting.

Ueda, Markoto. *Japanese Writers and the Nature of Literature*. Stanford, Calif.: Stanford University Press, 1976. Presents an insightful discussion of Kawabata's writing style and themes.

Washburn, Dennis C. *The Dilemma of the Modern in Japanese Fiction*. New Haven, Conn.: Yale University Press, 1995. Includes an excellent chapter on the topic of Kawabata and the problem of cultural amnesia.

A Thousand Splendid Suns

Author: Khaled Hosseini (1965-   )
First published: 2007
Type of work: Novel
Type of plot: Social realism
Time of plot: 1964-2003
Locale: Afghanistan and Pakistan

Principal characters:
MARIAM, an illegitimate child
NANA, her mother
JALIL, her father
RASHEED, her husband
FARIBA, her neighbor
HAKIM, Fariba's husband
LAILA, their daughter
TARIQ, Laila's friend and lover
AZIZA, Laila and Tariq's daughter
ZALMAI, Laila and Rasheed's daughter

The Story:

Mariam and her mother, Nana, a former housekeeper for Mariam's wealthy father, Jalil, have been banished to a hut near a small Afghan village to avoid humiliating Jalil's three wives and nine children in Herat. Nana bitterly disparages both Mariam and Jalil, who visits his daughter weekly. Even though the village mullah urges Nana to send the girl to school, she refuses, insisting that the only skill a woman needs is endurance.

To celebrate her fifteenth birthday, Mariam begs Jalil to take her to a cinema in Herat, but both parents strenuously object. When Jalil fails to meet her, Mariam walks alone to the city, only to be told that her father is not at home. On her return she discovers that Nana has killed herself.

Reluctantly, Jalil takes Mariam into his home. The three wives, who wish to get rid of her permanently, inform her that they have found a suitor, Rasheed, a forty-five-year-old shoemaker from Kabul, whom she will marry tomorrow. At the wedding, she is ignored by her father. She mopes in Kabul until Rasheed instructs her to behave like a wife. His only son had drowned, and he wants another son. Waiting at the communal oven, Mariam encounters Fariba, a politically and socially liberal neighbor, whose husband, Hakim, is a teacher.

Conservative Rasheed buys Mariam a burka, a floor-length garment that covers her completely; he orders her to wear the garment in public. He also thoroughly disapproves of Fariba, who merely covers her hair with a scarf. Rasheed takes Mariam to a restaurant, buys her a beautiful shawl, and shares her bed that night, but when she miscarries in the public bathhouse, his attitude changes. After four years of marriage and six more miscarriages, which he regards as personal insults, he believes Mariam is a useless nineteen year old; he frequently beats her.

Meanwhile, Hakim and Fariba have a daughter, Laila. Fariba is full of fire until their two sons go on jihad against the invading Soviets. Then, blaming Hakim for permitting them to leave, she retreats to her bed. After the brothers are killed, Laila becomes a caregiver for her parents, preparing her father's dinner while he helps her with schoolwork. A calm and patient scholar, Hakim urges her to get an education before marrying.

When the Soviets are finally driven from Afghanistan, unrest returns to Kabul, as local warlords turn against each other. Fariba supports the Mujahideen, the Islamic militia that her sons had joined, but Hakim fears them and wants to leave Kabul. As ethnic violence continues, Laila is forced to drop out of school after a fellow student is blown to bits in the street.

Laila's closest friend, the neighbor boy Tariq, has an artificial leg because of a Soviet land mine. Tariq and Laila become intimate after Tariq announces that his family is going to a refugee camp in Pakistan. Although he begs Laila to come with them, she cannot leave her father, who seems lost without Fariba's support. Hakim and Fariba are killed when their home is shelled, and Rasheed finds Laila injured in the rubble. Mariam reluctantly tends her as she recovers. Later, Laila is informed that Tariq has died in a Pakistani hospital. Observing her husband with Laila, Mariam realizes that Rasheed, now sixty years old, is courting the fourteen-year-old girl. Mariam attempts to dissuade him, but she is at his mercy, as is Laila, who accepts his marriage offer because she is pregnant with Tariq's baby. She hopes to deceive Rasheed.

Rasheed keeps his new bride at home, and Mariam serves them both. The two women resent each other until Laila's baby girl, Aziza, brings them together. In time, Mariam be-

comes another mother to Laila and a grandmother to the child. Laila begs her to escape with them to Pakistan. They prepare to flee but cannot travel without a male relative. A young husband offers to help but betrays them, keeping their money. They are questioned by police and returned to Rasheed, who hurls Aziza across the room and imprisons the women for three days.

The fundamentalist Taliban seizes Kabul, leading Rasheed to view them as liberators. They distribute strict rules: All men must have beards; no school for girls; no jobs for women, who must stay in their homes unless with a male relative. The university is closed, books other than the Qurʾān are burned, and musicians are imprisoned. Rasheed threatens to send Aziza away or to lie about Laila's behavior to the authorities. Then Laila discovers she is pregnant with Rasheed's child.

In labor, Laila goes to the former women's hospital and is turned away because the hospital now accepts male patients only. She is sent to a small hospital without medicine, clean water, or electricity. She requires a caesarean section and must suffer through the surgery without anesthetics. Her female doctor, who is required to perform her duties while wearing a burka, is unable to properly see through the garment, so a nurse guards the door to warn of any approaching Taliban. Laila gives birth to a boy, Zalmai.

Two-year-old Zalmai loves both parents but favors Rasheed, who is gentle with him while holding his wives in contempt. Although in debt, Rasheed brings home a television for his son, but decides that daughter Aziza, who is six years old, will beg on the streets. Laila objects, and Rasheed slaps her. They struggle, then he shoves a gun barrel in her mouth. Mariam ends up digging a hole to hide the forbidden television.

Rasheed's shop burns, and he must sell nearly everything. He steals food, but the family begins to starve. Finally, Aziza is sent to an orphanage so she will get some food. The director seems kind and comforts Laila, who is weeping, but Aziza panics when her mother leaves. Laila is permitted to visit her daughter but cannot travel without Rasheed, who often deliberately stops and turns back, forcing her to do the same. Without him, she risks a beating from the Taliban, but she quickly learns to use padding to cushion the potential blows.

Tariq suddenly appears at Laila's home; the story of his death was false. Son Zalmai, although still an innocent, throws a tantrum, luring his mother away from Tariq. Furious, Rasheed beats her with his belt, but she retaliates. He begins to choke her. Mariam, realizing he will murder both of them if he can, hits him with a shovel. Laila revives from the beating, horrified, but Mariam is very calm. Together they dispose of Rasheed's body, and Laila tells Zalmai his father has gone away. While Laila, Aziza, and Zalmai disappear, Mariam refuses to escape; she will accept the blame. She is sent to a women's prison and publicly executed for murdering her husband.

Arriving with the children in Pakistan, Laila and Tariq marry. Once the Taliban are driven from Afghanistan, the family returns to contribute to the rebuilding. Kabul has changed—a seeming normalcy—although the local warlords responsible for so many deaths have also returned. Laila teaches at the orphanage where Aziza once lived, and she is once again pregnant.

Critical Evaluation:

Khaled Hosseini, the son of an Afghan diplomat and a teacher, was born in Kabul, where he spent his first eight years. When he was fifteen years old, his family sought political refuge in the United States, where he attended California schools and earned a medical degree before he turned to writing. Many critics invariably compare *A Thousand Splendid Suns* with Hosseini's well-received first novel, *The Kite Runner* (2003), but the general consensus is that the newer book is more fully realized.

The novel is divided into four parts, the first tracing Mariam's life through four years of marriage. Part 2 spans Laila's early years until the death of her parents. In alternating chapters, part 3 brings the two women together in their relationship to Rasheed and to each other. Hosseini effectively builds tension in the scene in which the supposedly dead Tariq appears to Laila. Their quiet conversation is interspersed with Rasheed's angry questions later that evening after little Zalmai informs him that his mother has had a visitor. Part 4 forms an epilogue for the living.

Hosseini's characters seem to represent contradictory aspects of Afghanistan. Rasheed, although a fundamentalist, is not even a good Muslim. He drinks liquor, enjoys pornography, and does not fast during Ramadan. Although it is difficult to read of Rasheed's abuses, his intense pride in and love of his son contrast with his appalling insensitivity to girls and women. Hakim, Laila's father, is his opposite: a husband who considers his wife and a gentle intellectual who has sacrificed much. Hakim's warning to his daughter, "A society has no chance of success if its women are uneducated," is the antithesis of Rasheed's terse comment to Mariam, "A woman's face is her husband's business only."

The leading female characters form another contrast. Mariam is a poor, traditional woman, and Laila is a more modern and educated woman, but both are in conflict with their rigid patriarchal society. Mariam, who grows up unloved and alone, submits until she reaches the breaking point and must act; Laila, who is cherished by her father, never really gives up. Both become surprisingly strong.

Hosseini attempts to deliver a brief history of Afghanistan, including dates, as a necessary foundation for the Western reader. His novel encompasses some forty years of political struggle, with dominance shifting among feuding warlords, Soviets, Mujahideen, Taliban, and Americans. Kabul itself is the target of territorial leaders; fighting in the streets is rampant, and civilians are raped, tortured, and murdered. Although some critics attack the author's "taste for melodramatic plotlines," the violence of war is real.

The novel's title is taken from a well-known seventeenth century poem by Persian poet Sā'ib of Tabriz, written about the city of Kabul: "One could not count the moons that shimmer on her roofs,/ Or the thousand splendid suns that hide behind her walls." Ironically, this is neither the modern Kabul the reader discovers nor the one Hosseini's characters inhabit; it is an idealized city—a dream, a memory, a sorrowful reminder of what long ago might have been. The lines also form an elegy for Laila's dead companion-wife: "mostly, Mariam is in Laila's own heart, where she shines with the bursting radiance of a thousand suns." Perhaps the lines also serves as a promise of what someday might come again.

A Thousand Splendid Suns is a chronicle of political upheaval and the dreadful toll it takes, as well as an examination of the limited role of women in Afghan society. Many of its details were inspired by Hosseini's visit to Afghanistan in 2003 and by the stories he heard there. As a physician, he saw firsthand the deprivations of the women's hospital where Zalmai is born. His novel offers insights into an ancient, undeveloped country that has become a crucial concern of world politics; it provides an awareness of the cultural clashes that still exist there; and it offers a greater understanding of its people.

Joanne McCarthy

Further Reading

Foley, Dylan. "Two Afghan Wives Salvage Joy Amid Strife." *Denver Post*, July 15, 2007. In this interview, Hosseini discusses sources of the novel, which resulted from his 2003 visit to Afghanistan and a widely distributed local video of one woman's public execution.

Hosseini, Khaled. "Kabul's Splendid Son: Interview with Khaled Hosseini." *Mother Jones* 34, no. 3 (2009): 74-75. This magazine article includes a brief biographical sketch of Hosseini. In the interview, Hosseini deplores the impoverished condition of Afghans living in a war-torn country.

Kakutani, Michiko. "A Woman's Lot in Kabul, Lower than a House Cat's." *The New York Times*, May 29, 2007. An initially harsh review ("soap-opera-ish events") of *A Thousand Splendid Suns* that grows more forgiving as the novel unfolds into scenes of daily Afghan life and "genuinely heart-wrenching" moments.

Null, Linda, and Suellen Alfred. "A Thousand Splintered Hopes." *English Journal* 97, no. 6 (July, 2008): 123-125. Exploring the irony of Hosseini's title in such a dark novel, the authors compare Jalil, Rasheed, and Hakim and note parallels with Nathaniel Hawthorne's *The Scarlet Letter* (1850).

Reed, Cheryl L. "Afghanistan's True Darkness." *Chicago Sun-Times*, June 10, 2007. Compares Hosseini's novel *The Kite Runner*, which views Afghanistan "from a distance," with the intimacy of *A Thousand Splendid Suns*. Praises the emotional power of this novel, which allows readers to experience, for example, the difference "between imagining the depravity of war and actually smelling the orphans left in its wake."

Scharper, Diane. "Two Afghan Women Fight to Endure Decades of Oppression." *Denver Post*, May 20, 2007. Compares Mariam to a Charles Dickens heroine—poor but plucky—but argues that Hosseini is hesitant to get close to his female characters, thereby allowing them to seem flat.

Three Lives

Author: Gertrude Stein (1874-1946)
First published: 1909
Type of work: Novel
Type of plot: Psychological realism
Time of plot: Late nineteenth and early twentieth centuries
Locale: Bridgepoint, eastern United States

Principal characters:
ANNA FEDERNER, a household servant
MISS MATHILDA, her employer
MISS MARY WADSMITH, Anna's former employer
MRS. LEHNTMAN, Anna's dearest friend
MELANCTHA HERBERT, an African American woman
ROSE JOHNSON, Melanctha's friend
JANE HARDEN, Melanctha's mentor
JEFFERSON CAMPBELL, a physician Melanctha loves
LENA MAINZ, a young German woman
MATHILDA HAYDON, Lena's aunt
HERMAN KREDER, the tailor Lena marries

The Story:

The Good Anna. For five years, Anna Federner, a small German woman of about forty, has managed Miss Mathilda's full household of both women, an underservant, three regular dogs (old Baby, young Peter, and fluffy Rags), and various strays. Anna manages the household well but becomes flustered when her mistress spends money frivolously. Miss Mathilda, on the other hand, tries to curb Anna's lending to friends.

Anna's story begins when she is a young woman; a servant since she was seventeen years old, she travels from Germany to the United States with her mother. After her mother dies, Anna moves from the Deep South to Bridgepoint, in the Northeast, where her half brother lives. In Bridgepoint, Anna first goes to work as a servant to Miss Mary Wadsmith and her orphaned niece and nephew. Anna likes working for the large, helpless woman, who lets Anna manage all her affairs, but Anna does not care much for children. She prefers the spoiled Edgar to the obstinate Jane. One day, Jane gives Anna an order that she says comes from Miss Mary. Anna angrily tells Miss Mary about the incident, and her employer faints. Jane and Anna make no more trouble after that.

When Anna begins having severe headaches, Jane Wadsmith and Mrs. Lehntman, a widowed friend who works as a midwife, convince her to let Dr. Shonjen operate. She improves some, but she is never really well again.

When Jane marries, Miss Mary goes to live with her. Anna does not believe that she can work in a household with Jane as mistress; therefore, she begins working for Dr. Shonjen. She loves working for men, who enjoy eating and let her manage the home. Anna continues helping the midwife, Mrs. Lehntman, who adopts a baby boy. Anna is concerned that her friend cannot afford another child, but Mrs. Lehntman is resolved to keep the baby.

Anna often helps another poor family, the Drehtens, whom her sister-in-law despises. Her best friend is Mrs. Lehntman, and when her friend wants money to start a lying-in home, Anna lends it to her, despite reservations about the venture. Anna's troubles are compounded by Mrs. Lehntman's interest in a man and by her employer's marriage. Dr. Shonjen's new wife and Anna do not get along, so Anna looks for a new place. She learns of Miss Mathilda, who has recently moved to Bridgepoint. Anna is reluctant to work for a woman again, but Mrs. Lehntman urges her to consult a medium, who encourage her to take the job. Anna enjoys working for Miss Mathilda, who lets Anna manage everything and keep her dogs. However, Anna loses her friendship with Mrs. Lehntman after Mrs. Lehntman fails to pay back another loan and continues her involvement with an unscrupulous physician.

Anna continues to befriend stray animals and needy people, including Mrs. Lehntman's foolish newly married daughter. She also nurses Mrs. Drehten through an operation. Anna experiences some sadness when her old dog Baby, who had been a gift from Mrs. Lehntman, dies, and Miss Mathilda moves to another country.

Anna takes in boarders at Miss Mathilda's house, and the boarders love her, but she charges too little to make a profit. She works so hard that she wears herself out and dies during an operation. Mrs. Drehten writes to Miss Mathilda to tell her about Anna's death.

Melanctha. Melanctha Herbert, a young African American woman with some white blood, has recently befriended Rose Johnson, a black woman reared by white people. When Rose and Sam Johnson's baby is born, Melanctha helps her friend with the child. Rose is so lazy that she fails to take care of the child when Melanctha is not there, and the baby dies. Melanctha reflects that she did not really love her black father or her light-skinned mother. Her father once fought a man who he thought was too interested in Melanctha.

Melanctha's story begins when she is an adolescent, wandering the streets and talking with men. She becomes friends with Jane Harden, who tells her much about men and the world but drinks far too much. Melanctha's mother becomes ill, and Dr. Jefferson Campbell arrives at their home to treat her. As he and Melanctha talk, she becomes so fond of him that she ceases to wander. They discuss his beliefs about African American people. Melanctha's mother dies, her father disappears, and she focuses all her attention on Jeff Campbell.

Jeff is uncertain about his feelings for her, however. Just as he is beginning to feel love for Melanctha, Jane tells him of Melanctha's earlier interest in men. This information makes him angry, and he fears that he will quarrel with Melanctha. He also doubts her love for him. Jeff's mistrust of Melanctha drives them apart, and she begins to love him less. She surrounds herself with friends, including Rose Johnson.

After several breakups and reunions with Jeff, Melanctha explains to him that she loves him, but not with her former passion. At that point he realizes that he truly loves her. After she and Jeff end their relationship, Melanctha casually dates white men. Jeff, having been schooled in love, finds that he is now a better doctor.

Melanctha begins dating Jem Richards, who, like her, loves horses. He gets into trouble betting at the racetrack. Melanctha becomes more dependent on Rose and Sam Johnson, but Rose becomes increasingly cold toward her. Jem breaks up with her, leaving Melanctha quite alone in the world. She thinks about killing herself, but she does not. After an illness and brief recovery, she dies.

The Gentle Lena. Lena Mainz came from Germany with her aunt, Mrs. Haydon, to Bridgepoint, where Lena has worked for the same family for four years. Lena is gentle and finds the family agreeable. She had been quite ill on the voyage to America but recovered upon arrival.

Lena's aunt decides to find a husband for Lena, and she settles on Herman Kreder, a tailor. Neither Lena nor Herman wants to marry, however. On the day they are supposed to wed, Herman cannot be found, and the wedding must be postponed. Eventually, Herman's father finds him at his married sister's house in New York and brings him back to Bridgepoint.

Lena and Herman get married and move into his parents' house. The Kreders are sloppy, and the usually neat Lena adopts their ways. Mrs. Kreder scolds, but Herman takes Lena's side. Lena becomes withdrawn.

Lena gets pregnant and has a healthy baby, and after the child is born she becomes even more careless about her life. She has two more babies, whom Herman adores. Lena's fourth child is stillborn, and Lena dies soon after. Herman happily cares for his children.

Critical Evaluation:

Gertrude Stein's *Three Lives*, a trilogy of character sketches, is remarkable for its experimental style, its lower-class characters, and its naturalistic themes. Stein uses a deceptively simple, repetitive style, sometimes reminding the reader of previously made points. For example, in the section of the novel titled "The Good Anna," Stein writes, "Anna never liked her brother's wife." Two lines later, she writes, "Anna never liked her half brother's wife." After describing Anna's nieces, Stein writes, "Our good Anna loved them not, nor their mother." The reader begins to realize that Stein means more than she says; Anna's half brother's wife does not deserve to be liked. Each repetition gets the reader closer to this truth. The repetitions also mirror the thinking of Anna, whose dislike for her sister-in-law is constant and annoying.

Stein also eschews most punctuation because, in her opinion, it interrupts the flow of language. The sparsity of punctuation marks makes Stein's writing read more like thought than like written ideas.

The simple language of *Three Lives* reflects the simplicity of the women whose lives the novel portrays. Anna Federner and Lena Mainz are German American servants. Melanctha Herbert is a young, relatively uneducated African American woman. The language in the first and third parts of the book, the ones about the servants, is less sophisticated than that of the middle piece, partly because "Melanctha" includes conversations between a physician and the young woman, who is fairly intelligent. In the second character sketch, paragraphs are longer and more fully developed. The characters use simple words and repeat their ideas, however, a hallmark of Gertrude Stein's style. For example, Dr. Jefferson Campbell says, "You see Miss Melanctha I am a very quiet kind of fellow, and I believe in a quiet life for all the colored people." Melanctha replies, "Yes I certainly do see that very clear Dr. Campbell. . . . I see that's certainly what it is always made me not know right about you and that's certainly what it is that makes you really mean what you was always saying."

Many critics have remarked that Stein treats lower-class characters with the same regard with which Henry James and other authors treat upper-class characters. She illustrates the importance of the lives of servants and other members of the underprivileged classes and makes the pains, joys, and loves of lower-class characters real to the reader. She shows the value of their emotional and intellectual lives.

Stein's theme in *Three Lives* is naturalistic. No matter how hard Anna, Melanctha, and Lena try, they are defeated in their efforts by a society that does not sufficiently value them. Anna, possibly based on a woman who worked for Stein in France, is the best servant anyone can be, always trying to make her employers' lives happy and easy. In the end, her generosity is her downfall; others take advantage of her friendship, borrowing money and never paying it back, eating her good food at her boardinghouse while paying little for it, and letting her work herself to death for them. Most of them are not bad people, but Anna's goodness cannot stand up to the harsh reality of her life.

Melanctha befriends weak people, and their weakness interferes with a love that could have made her very happy. Jane Harden tells Jeff Campbell about Melanctha's youthful wanderings and interest in men, and he doubts Melanctha's love for him. His doubt destroys their love. Her sorrow and loneliness leave her vulnerable to illness and death.

Lena's gentleness destroys her. She resigns herself to being ruled by her aunt, who believes that marriage is best for all girls. Lena lets herself be married to a man who does not love her, lets herself have children, lets her husband ignore her, and finally dies bearing a fourth child. Her gentleness, like Anna's goodness, cannot stand up to a world that is not gentle.

Gertrude Stein was a well-educated, intelligent, upper-class woman who surrounded herself with artists and writers. In *Three Lives* she displays interest in and affection for people not like herself, treating them with sympathy but not pity, with respect, not condescension. Even their flaws are admirable. Her keen eye and ear and her generous heart are evident on every page.

M. Katherine Grimes

Further Reading

Bloom, Harold, ed. *Gertrude Stein.* New York: Chelsea House, 1986. Collection of essays discusses Stein's writings. Donald Sutherland's essay on *Three Lives* and Richard Bridgman's on *Things as They Are* and *Three Lives* are informative.

Bridgman, Richard. *Gertrude Stein in Pieces.* New York: Oxford University Press, 1970. Argues that all three women in *Three Lives* are "victimized by fate" and that Stein is concerned more with thoughts than with actions.

Curnutt, Kirk, ed. *The Critical Response to Gertrude Stein.* Westport, Conn.: Greenwood Press, 2000. Collection of contemporary and modern reviews and essays addresses Stein's works as well as her persona. Includes quintessential pieces on Stein by Carl Van Vechten, William Carlos Williams, and Katherine Anne Porter along with previously obscure estimations from contemporaries, such as H. L. Mencken, Mina Loy, and Conrad Aiken.

Doane, Janice L. *Silence and Narrative: The Early Novels of Gertrude Stein.* Westport, Conn.: Greenwood Press, 1986. Discusses the artists who influenced Stein, explaining that she was not constrained by convention. Some of Doane's arguments, such as the assertion that in *Three Lives* Stein shows that marriage destroys women and uplifts men, are provocative but not always easily supported.

Hoffman, Michael J. *Gertrude Stein.* Boston: Twayne, 1976.

Compares *Three Lives* with Stein's roman à clef *Things as They Are* (1950; later *Quod Erat Demonstrandum*, or *Q.E.D.*). Provides good discussions of Stein's "wise-child" style and of the narrator of *Three Lives*.

Malcolm, Janet. *Two Lives: Gertrude and Alice*. New Haven, Conn.: Yale University Press, 2007. Account of Stein's relationship with Alice B. Toklas provides previously unavailable information about the couple's lives during the German occupation of France.

Mellow, James R. *Charmed Circle: Gertrude Stein and Company*. New York: Praeger, 1974. Thorough treatment of Stein's literary and artistic circle includes an examination of the autobiographical undertones of *Three Lives* and the circumstances of its publication.

Souhami, Diana. *Gertrude and Alice*. New York: Harper-Collins, 1991. One of the most thorough accounts available of Stein's longtime lesbian relationship with Alice B. Toklas. Shows how strong Toklas was and how she dominated many aspects of her forty-year association with Stein.

_____. Introduction to *Three Lives*. New York: Bantam Books, 1992. Informative introduction offers a strong feminist reading of *Three Lives*.

Stein, Gertrude. *"Three Lives" and "Q.E.D.": Authoritative Texts, Contexts, Criticism*. Edited by Marianne DeKoven. New York: W. W. Norton, 2006. In addition to the texts of the two novels, this edition contains a discussion of their intellectual backgrounds and a biography of Stein. Nineteen essays, arranged chronologically, provide numerous interpretations of the novels, including examinations from the perspectives of feminism, queer studies, and African American studies.

The Three Musketeers

Author: Alexandre Dumas, *père* (1802-1870)
First published: Les Trois Mousquetaires, 1844 (English translation, 1846)
Type of work: Novel
Type of plot: Historical
Time of plot: 1626
Locale: France

Principal characters:
D'ARTAGNAN, a Gascon adventurer
ATHOS,
PORTHOS, and
ARAMIS, the three musketeers
CONSTANCE BONANCIEUX, the queen's seamstress
CARDINAL RICHELIEU, the minister of state
LADY DE WINTER, Cardinal Richelieu's agent

The Story:

In the spring of 1625, a young Gascon named D'Artagnan, on his way to Paris to join the musketeers, proudly rides up to an inn in Meung. He is mounted on an old pony that his father gave him along with some good advice and a letter of introduction to the captain of the musketeers. In Meung he shows his fighting spirit by fiercely challenging to a duel a stranger who seems to be laughing at his orange horse. Before continuing his journey to Paris he has another encounter with the stranger, identified by a scar on his face, and the stranger's companion, a young and beautiful woman.

Athos, Porthos, and Aramis are the three best blades in the ranks of the musketeers of the guard, in the service of King Louis XIII. D'Artagnan becomes the fourth member of the group within three months of his arrival in Paris. He has earned the love and respect of the other men by challenging each in turn to a duel and then helping them to drive off Cardinal Richelieu's guards, who wish to arrest them for brawling.

D'Artagnan is not made a musketeer at once; he has to serve an apprenticeship as a cadet in a lesser company of guards before being admitted to the musketeer ranks. Athos, Porthos, and Aramis look forward to the day when he will become their true comrade in arms, and the three take turns accompanying him when he is on guard duty. D'Artagnan is curious about his friends but can learn nothing about them. Athos looks like a nobleman. He is reserved, he never mentions women, and it is said that a great treachery has poisoned his life. Porthos is a squire of dames, bragging incessantly of his loves. Aramis, who always dresses in black, insists that he is a musketeer only temporarily, that he is a churchman at heart and soon will enter a monastery and exchange his plumed hat for a monk's cowl.

The three musketeers were earlier rewarded in gold by the timid king for their bravery against the cardinal's guards, but they have since spent all of their money. They are trying to figure a way out of their financial difficulties when Bonancieux, D'Artagnan's landlord, comes to D'Artagnan because he has heard that his tenant is a brave man. Bonancieux says that his wife, Constance, has been abducted; Constance is a seamstress for the royal court, and her devotion to the queen is well known. The landlord suggests that D'Artagnan find and rescue Constance in payment for long-overdue rent and for financial compensation.

When Bonancieux describes Constance's abductor, D'Artagnan realizes that he is the man he had challenged at Meung. On these two scores, the Gascon is willing to help the stricken husband, but he becomes even more eager when he discovers that the purpose of the abduction is to force Constance to tell what she knows of a rumored romance between the queen and the duke of Buckingham.

Constance escapes her captors and returns to her home, where the cardinal's men again try to seize her, only to be attacked and scattered by D'Artagnan, who has overheard the struggle. Later that evening D'Artagnan meets Constance as she is hurrying along alone on the streets at a late hour. He questions her, but she will not say where she is going. He tells her that he loves her, but she gives him no encouragement. Still later that evening he encounters her again as she is leading the duke of Buckingham, in disguise, to the queen.

The queen has sent for Buckingham to beg him to leave the city, where his life is in danger. As they talk she confesses her love for him and gives him as a memento a small rosewood casket containing twelve diamond studs that the king has given her. Buckingham then departs for London. Richelieu, through his spies, learns of the gift, and soon he suggests to the king that he should give a fete and ask the queen to wear her diamond studs. The cardinal then orders Lady de Winter, who is in London, to snip two of the studs from Buckingham's clothing. This deed gives him a chance to strike at the king, the queen, and also Buckingham. Learning of this scheme, Constance goes to D'Artagnan. D'Artagnan loves Constance, and he wants to serve his queen, so he undertakes to recover the jewels. With his three comrades he starts out for London, but only D'Artagnan arrives there because the group is ambushed by the cardinal's agents, and the three musketeers are wounded and left behind. D'Artagnan reaches the duke in time to recover the studs and return to Paris with them. Richelieu's plot is foiled.

After D'Artagnan has received the thanks of the queen, he is to meet Constance that evening, but Constance is again seized and imprisoned by the cardinal's spies, one of whom is identified as the man from Meung. D'Artagnan decides that he needs the help of his three friends, and, accompanied by his servant Planchet, he sets out to find them. First he calls at the inn where he had left Porthos and finds him still there, recovering from his wounds. Later, he finds Aramis talking with some doctors of theology and about to renounce the world. Athos has barricaded himself in a wine cellar. In his drunken state, Athos relates a story about a friend of his, a count, who, when he was young, had married a beautiful woman and had made her the first lady in his province. Later, however, he had discovered that she was branded on the shoulder with the fleur-de-lis, the mark of a convicted criminal, and he had hanged her on a tree, leaving her for dead.

Once again the four friends are together. Then D'Artagnan, who has followed Porthos into a church, sees a beautiful woman whom he recognizes as the companion of the man he had met at Meung. He follows her out of the church and sees her get into her coach. Later he and his friends take the same road her coach had taken, and they encounter the coach by the side of the road. The lady is talking to a young man who, D'Artagnan discovers, is her brother-in-law, Lord de Winter. D'Artagnan had earlier become a friend of Lord de Winter after sparing his life in a duel; the lord introduces him to his sister-in-law. D'Artagnan falls in love with Lady de Winter, but she loves another, Monsieur de Wardes, who, unknown to her, has been killed.

D'Artagnan deceives Lady de Winter one night into believing she has an assignation with de Wardes. D'Artagnan presents himself to her disguised as de Wardes that night, and she gives him a magnificent sapphire ring. When D'Artagnan shows the ring to Athos, he recognizes it as one that had belonged to his mother and that he had given to his wife. Athos begins to suspect that his wife is not dead; he suspects that Lady de Winter is his wife.

D'Artagnan overhears Lady de Winter making insulting remarks about him because he spared the life of her brother-in-law. She is Lord de Winter's heir. D'Artagnan also realizes that Lady de Winter is the cardinal's spy. At his next meeting with her, D'Artagnan, as himself, confesses his duplicity to her, and she angrily strikes him, causing him to step on the hem of her dress. The material of the dress pulls away from her shoulder, exposing the brand of the fleur-de-lis. As D'Artagnan realizes the truth, Lady de Winter attacks him with a knife and screams that she will get revenge. D'Artagnan flees to Athos.

The war between England and France is reaching a climax, and the siege of La Rochelle is of particular political importance. The four friends prepare to go to La Rochelle. Before they leave, D'Artagnan is called for an interview with the cardinal. Richelieu tries to bribe D'Artagnan to enter his own guards, but D'Artagnan refuses; he departs with the knowledge that his refusal might mean his death. In La Rochelle two young soldiers try to kill D'Artagnan. He learns from them that Lady de Winter had hired them to kill him, and he also learns that she is responsible for the imprisonment of Constance.

The musketeers do not have much to do with the siege, and they lead a carefree life in La Rochelle. One evening, on a lonely road, they encounter two horsemen, one of whom is the cardinal. He is on his way to a nearby inn, and he orders the musketeers to go with him. Lady de Winter is at the inn, and the musketeers overhear the cardinal instructing her to go to London, where she is to tell Buckingham that unless he ends the war, his affair with the queen will be exposed. If he refuses, Lady de Winter is to poison him. As her reward for doing as the cardinal asks, Lady de Winter requests that two of her enemies be killed. These two are Constance, who has been conveyed to a convent by an order the queen obtained from the king, and D'Artagnan. Richelieu then writes out a letter of safe conduct for Lady de Winter.

A few minutes later, Athos is in Lady de Winter's room; he has recognized her voice. He reveals himself as the count de la Fere, her husband. She is terrified, for she had thought him dead as well. Athos takes the cardinal's letter of safe conduct from her and orders her to leave France at once under threats of exposure.

The four friends return to the siege of La Rochelle, where they conduct themselves with such bravery that they again draw notice from the cardinal. When the cardinal speaks of them to their captain, the captain tells him that D'Artagnan is not in the service of the musketeers. The cardinal then gives orders that D'Artagnan is to be made a musketeer, and this news, when relayed to D'Artagnan, makes him very happy. The friends write out a message to warn Lord de Winter against his sister-in-law and send Planchet to deliver it. They also send a message to a cousin of Aramis and learn from her the name of the convent in which Constance is confined.

When Lady de Winter arrives in England, she is held prisoner by Lord de Winter. Her pretense of religious fervor and her beauty, however, convince her young Puritan jailer of her innocence. After she tells him a fantastic tale to the effect that her downfall has been caused by Buckingham, he helps her to escape. To avenge her, he then goes to Buckingham and stabs him. Having discovered his sister-in-law's escape, Lord de Winter also hurries to Buckingham, but he arrives too late to save his life. Before Buckingham dies, a messenger from Paris brings him word from the queen of her faithful love.

Lady de Winter escapes to the convent in France where Constance is staying, and there she manages to poison Constance and flee again before the four companions arrive to rescue the queen's faithful servant. Lord de Winter, also in pursuit of Lady de Winter, arrives a few minutes after they have discovered Constance. Continuing their pursuit of Lady de Winter, they overtake her and hold a trial. They condemn her to die, and she is executed by the public executioner of Lille, who had branded her for her crimes many years before.

On his return to La Rochelle, D'Artagnan is arrested and taken to the cardinal. The man who takes him prisoner is the stranger D'Artagnan had met at Meung, identified now as the Chevalier de Rochefort. The cardinal charges D'Artagnan with treason, but D'Artagnan interrupts and recites the long list of crimes of the woman who has accused him. Then he informs the cardinal of her death and produces the safe-conduct pass, signed by the cardinal, that Athos had taken from the woman. D'Artagnan tells Richelieu that as bearer of the pass he should be allowed to go free. The cardinal is so pleased by the Gascon's cleverness that he cannot be angry. Instead, he offers D'Artagnan a commission in the musketeers. D'Artagnan offers it to his friends, but each refuses it, insisting that he deserves the rank, an honor that great nobles often seek in vain.

La Rochelle surrenders to the French, and the faithful four disband. Athos returns to his estate, Porthos marries a rich widow, and Aramis becomes an abbé. D'Artagnan becomes a famous soldier. He and de Rochefort, his old enemy, fight three times but finally become good friends.

Critical Evaluation:

The Three Musketeers was the most popular novel written by Alexandre Dumas, *père*, and the one he considered his best. It has retained a great deal of popularity in spite of some weaknesses. The characterization is sketchy. The dialogue, by modern, realistic standards, is often long-winded and full of preposterous declarations of adoration, fidelity, patriotism, and other noble sentiments. Dumas's dialogue shows the influence of that early genius of the historical novel, Sir Walter Scott. That *The Three Musketeers* has survived with so many generations of readers is testament to Dumas's talent for describing violent action and tempestuous love affairs while maintaining suspense for nearly eight hundred pages.

An example of Dumas's craftsmanship can be seen in chapter 47, "The Council of the Musketeers." In this chapter, D'Artagnan consults with Athos, Porthos, and Aramis about how to foil the insidious schemes of Cardinal Richelieu. This could be a dull, static scene, but Dumas dramatizes it by placing his devil-may-care heroes in a bastion where they are under attack by waves of enemy soldiers. From masterful scenes such as this, professional writers of many lands have learned how to maintain suspense and avoid stretches of dreary exposition. The scene furnishes an excellent example of what American novelist Henry James meant when he advised fiction writers, "Dramatize, dramatize, dramatize!"

What made *The Three Musketeers* the best and most successful of Dumas's five or six hundred volumes was the sinister character of Cardinal Richelieu. The machinations of this seventeenth century political genius are like the mainspring in a clock that keeps the entire mechanism running. All the other characters in the book are either acting under Richelieu's orders or reacting to foil a scheme he has set in motion.

The main plot running throughout *The Three Musketeers* has to do with D'Artagnan and his three friends trying to prevent Richelieu from exposing Queen Anne's love affair with the duke of Buckingham. Richelieu is like Professor Moriarty, the archvillain created by Arthur Conan Doyle for his Sherlock Holmes stories. Whether he is present or absent in a particular story, his influence can be felt. Richelieu comes to admire his resourceful, courageous opponent D'Artagnan and is forced to capitulate.

Dumas, one of the most successful writers of all time, had a strong influence over novelists for decades to come. He had a genius for plotting and understood that the most important element in a plot is a strongly motivated protagonist who will not stop until he or she has either achieved the goal or gone down in defeat. Richelieu is the protagonist in *The Three Musketeers*, and the queen of France is his antagonist. D'Artagnan and his comrades are major characters in the novel but only minor figures in the historical context of the enormously complicated military, political, and religious conflict that embroiled most of Europe in bloodshed and destruction during the Thirty Years' War. In the novel, Richelieu is trying to undermine Queen Anne's influence over her husband, King Louis XIII, because she is a member of the powerful Habsburg family, rulers of both Austria and Spain and Richelieu's unrelenting enemies.

Dumas started his career as a dramatist and continued to write plays all his life. This valuable experience had a strong influence on his success as a novelist, because he filled his novels with dramatic scenes and impassioned dialogue. Fortunately, not all his dialogue is flowery and unrealistic: He acquired a reputation for writing whole pages of one-line verbal exchanges full of tension and information. This kind of dialogue writing is realistic and engrossing.

Dumas's action-packed plots, colorful scenes, and dramatic dialogue make his novels good candidates for motion-picture adaptation. Many film versions of *The Three Muske-* teers have been made. The flamboyant costuming of the musketeers, with their enormous plumed hats, is one of the more interesting visual features that filmmakers find appealing. Another surefire ingredient is the many scenes in which the musketeers ride galloping thoroughbreds along dark roads infested with the cardinal's soldiers and spies. A third ingredient that has great film-audience appeal is the abundance of armed clashes, sometimes involving as many as a dozen skillful swordsmen. A fourth ingredient is the many love scenes the story provides.

Dumas knew how to please an audience, and his works have taught succeeding generations of authors how to do the same. He was not the best writer of his time, but he was probably the most popular. He was admired by such writers as the great Victor Hugo, who was a far more polished and serious craftsman. Dumas earned a fortune from his writings and squandered the money on women and dissipation until his fantastic energy and inspiration ran out, and he died in poverty. He was not unlike his most famous characters, D'Artagnan, Athos, Porthos, and Aramis, who lived with gusto, fought many duels, drank a dozen bottles of wine at a sitting, and scattered gold coins to innkeepers and servants with regal liberality.

"Critical Evaluation" by Bill Delaney

Further Reading

Hemmings, F. W. J. *Alexandre Dumas: The King of Romance.* New York: Charles Scribner's Sons, 1979. Chapter 9, "The Novelist," discusses *The Three Musketeers* at length and describes Dumas's transition from playwright to novelist. Includes illustrations.

Maund, Kari, and Phil Nanson. *The Four Musketeers: The True Story of D'Artagnan, Porthos, Aramis, and Athos.* Stroud, England: Tempus, 2005. Chronicles the lives and times of the men on whom the characters in Dumas's novel are based: four men who were members of the elite Black Musketeers in the 1640's.

Maurois, André. *Alexandre Dumas: A Great Life in Brief.* Translated by Jack Palmer White. 1955. Reprint. New York: Alfred A. Knopf, 1971. Dramatic biography by one of the most widely recognized authorities on Dumas includes several chapters that discuss aspects of *The Three Musketeers.*

_____. *The Titans: A Three-Generation Biography of the Dumas.* Translated by Gerard Hopkins. 1957. Reprint. Westport, Conn.: Greenwood Press, 1971. Definitive biography of Dumas, his swashbuckling father, and his son (Dumas, *fils*) includes a section that discusses Dumas's most famous novel, *The Three Musketeers*, and its sequels.

Poulosky, Laura J. *Severed Heads and Martyred Souls: Crime and Capital Punishment in French Romantic Literature*. New York: Peter Lang, 2003. Examines the depiction of capital punishment in the works of Dumas and other French Romantic authors.

Ross, Michael. *Alexandre Dumas*. North Pomfret, Vt.: David & Charles, 1981. Excellent biography highlights Dumas's collaboration with anonymous writers to produce his prodigious output of five to six hundred novels, plays, travel books, and miscellaneous works. Discusses Dumas's colorful reputation and the truth about his character.

Schopp, Claude. *Alexandre Dumas: Genius of Life*. Translated by A. J. Koch. New York: Franklin Watts, 1988. Biography focuses on Dumas's personal life, which was full of romance and adventure, with many love affairs and duels. Describes how Dumas earned and squandered fortunes and died in poverty. Includes discussion of his writing of *The Three Musketeers*.

Severson, Marilyn S. *Masterpieces of French Literature*. Westport, Conn.: Greenwood Press, 2004. Includes an analysis of *The Three Musketeers* that covers its plot, character development, style, and themes and places the novel in its biographical and historical context. Designed for students.

The Three Sisters

Author: Anton Chekhov (1860-1904)
First produced: *Tri sestry*, 1901; first published, 1901 (English translation, 1920)
Type of work: Drama
Type of plot: Impressionistic realism
Time of plot: Nineteenth century
Locale: Russia

Principal characters:
ANDREY PROZOROV, a student
NATASHA, his fiancé, later his wife
OLGA,
MASHA, and
IRINA, his three sisters
FYODOR KULIGIN, Masha's husband
ALEXANDR VERSHININ, a battery commander
BARON TUSENBACH, a lieutenant
VASSILY SOLYONY, a captain
IVAN TCHEBUTYKIN, an army doctor

The Story:

On Irina's name-day, her friends and family call to wish her happiness. It is exactly one year since the death of her father, who was sent from Moscow eleven years before to this provincial town at the head of a brigade. Irina and her sister Olga long to go back to Moscow, and Masha would like to go, too, except that she married Kuligin, whom she once thought the cleverest of men. They all pin their hopes on their brother Andrey now, who is studying to become a professor.

An old army doctor, Tchebutykin, brings Irina a samovar because he loved her mother. Masha's husband gives her a copy of the history of the high school in which he teaches; he says he wrote it when he had nothing better to do. When Irina tells him that he already gave her a copy for Easter, he merrily hands it over to one of the army men who is calling. Tusenbach and Solyony quarrel half-heartedly because Tusenbach and Irina decided that what they need for happiness is work.

Tusenbach never did anything but go to cadet school, and Irina's father prepared his children only in languages. Both have a desire to labor hard at something.

When Vershinin, the new battery commander, comes to call, he reminds the girls that he lived on the same street with them in Moscow. He praises their town, but they say they would rather go to Moscow. They believe that they are oppressed with an education that is useless in a dull provincial town. Vershinin thinks that for every intelligent person then living, there will be many more later on, and that the whole earth will be unimaginably beautiful two or three hundred years hence. He thinks it might be interesting to relive one's life to see if one can improve on the first version.

Natasha comes in while they are still sitting at the dinner table. Olga criticizes her dress, and the men begin to tease her about an engagement. Andrey, who cannot stand having her teased, follows her out of the room and begs her to marry him. She accepts.

After their marriage, Andrey loses any ambition he ever had to become a professor; he spends much of his time gambling, trying to forget how ill-bred, rude, and selfish Natasha is. Irina, meanwhile, takes a job in the telegraph office, and Olga teaches in the high school. Tired when they come home at night, they let Natasha run the house as she pleases, even to moving Irina out of her own bedroom so that Natasha and Andrey's baby can have it.

Vershinin falls in love with Masha, though he feels bound to his neurotic wife because of his two daughters. Kuligin realizes what is going on but cheerfully hopes Masha still loves him. Tusenbach, afraid that life will always be difficult, decides to give up his commission and seek happiness in a workingman's life. Vershinin is convinced that, by living, working, and struggling, people can create a better life. Because his wife periodically tries to commit suicide, he looks for happiness not for himself but for his descendants.

Andrey asks Tchebutykin to prescribe for his shortness of breath, but the old doctor swears he forgot all the medical knowledge he ever knew. Solyony falls in love with Irina, who will have nothing to do with him. He declares that he will have no happy rivals.

One night, all gather to have a party with mummers who are to come in. Natasha decides that the baby is not well and calls off the party at the last minute. Then Protopopov, the chairman of the rural board, comes by with his carriage to take Natasha riding while Andrey sits reading in his room.

A short time later, fire destroys part of the town. Olga gives most of her clothes to those whose homes were burned and, after the fire, invites the army people to sleep at the house. Natasha berates Olga for letting her old servant sit in her presence and finally suggests that Olga herself move out of the house. The old doctor becomes drunk because he prescribed incorrectly for a woman who died. After the fire, people want him to help them, but he cannot. In disgust, he picks up a clock and smashes it.

Masha, more bored than before, gives up playing the piano. She is disgusted, too, because Andrey mortgages the house in order to give money to Natasha. Everyone but he knows that Natasha is having an affair with Protopopov, to whose rural board Andrey was recently elected.

Irina, at twenty-four, cannot find work to suit her, and she believes she is forgetting everything she ever knew. Olga persuades her to consider marrying Tusenbach, even if he is ugly; with him Irina might get to Moscow. Masha confesses that she is in love with Vershinin and that he loves her, though he is unable to leave his children.

Andrey berates his sisters for treating his wife so badly and then confesses that he mortgaged the house that belongs to all four of them. He so hoped they could all be happy together. Irina hears a report that the brigade will move out of town. If that happens, they will have to go to Moscow because no one worth speaking to will be left.

On the day the first battery is to leave, the officers come to say their farewells to the sisters. Kuligin tells Masha that Tusenbach and Solyony had words because both of them were in love with her and she promised to marry Tusenbach. Kuligin eagerly anticipates the departure of the brigade because he hopes Masha will then turn back to him. Masha is bored and spiteful. She feels that she is losing, bit by bit, whatever small happiness she has.

Andrey wonders how he can love Natasha when he knows she is so vulgar. The old doctor claims that he is tired of their troubles, and he advises Andrey to walk off and to never look back. Nevertheless, the doctor himself, who is to be retired from the army in a year, plans to come back to live with them because he really loves them all.

Irina hopes to go off with Tusenbach. Olga intends to live at the school of which she is now headmistress. Natasha, expecting to be left in sole charge of the house, plans all sorts of changes to wipe away the memory of the sisters' being there. Andrey wonders how his children can possibly overcome the influence of their mother's vulgarity.

Tusenbach fights a duel with Solyony, and Tchebutykin returns to tell them that Tusenbach was killed. The sisters are left alone with their misery, each thinking that she must go on with her life merely to find out why people suffer so much in a world that has the potential to be beautiful.

Critical Evaluation:

The Three Sisters, which premiered in January, 1901, is the first play Anton Chekhov wrote specifically for the Moscow Art Theatre. The play was directed by cofounder Konstantin Stanislavsky, the great teacher and originator of a technique of acting, and the cast included Olga Knipper, Chekhov's future wife, in the role of Masha. Although it was not immediately successful with the critics, *The Three Sisters* has become the most frequently performed of the Chekhov canon.

Ill with tuberculosis and therefore forced to remain in the warm climate of Yalta, Chekhov instilled much of his own frustration and longing for culture and civilization into the sisters' dream of returning to Moscow. Olga, Masha, and Irina feel overwhelmed and smothered by the banality of their provincial backwater town. They were educated for a society in which people have an appreciation of language and conversation and perfected a graceful style of living, but that society is fast becoming obsolete. Confused and lacking resources, the sisters search for a fulfilling existence, represented by the dream of returning to Moscow. There, they believe, they can be engaged in activities commensurate with their talents, and life will be meaningful.

The Moscow existence is no more than an idealization of the past, however. Vershinin's entrance in the first act revivifies the time and environment of their Moscow girlhood, but, as a friend of the sisters' father, he is a remnant of a past time. The sisters must somehow learn to exist in the changing world of the present. That present is represented by Natasha, who comes from a new middle class and is less educated, less sensitive, and less humane. In fact, she is downright greedy and grasping, one of the few unpleasant characters that Chekhov ever created.

As the skeptical doctor Tchebutykin says, "life is ugly and petty, happiness an illusion, and the only cure for despair is work." The ideal of work, which in the eyes of Tusenbach and Irina, is the means to fulfillment and the solution to boredom, replaces the dream of Moscow. Irina's position in the telegraph office is not satisfying, however, and Tusenbach's management of the brick factory never reaches fruition. The others encounter equal disillusion: Olga's elevation to headmistress only represents more work, Masha's love relationship is doomed, and Andrey's ambitions to become a professor are fantasy. Vershinin's optimistic claim that life will be better in the future suggests a present of compromise and resignation. Throughout the play, the tension increases between the hope of fulfillment and the disappointment of reality, underscoring Chekhov's themes of the absurdity of the human condition and the futility of the quest for meaning in life.

The external action of the play concerns the Prozorov sisters' gradual physical dispossession at the hands of Natasha. Chekhov's descriptions of the settings, the seasons of the year, and the times of day contribute to this development. Irina's pleasant name-day party of the first act occurs on the fifth of May; spring and hope are in the atmosphere, although, as Olga remarks, the birches are not yet budding. It is a bright, sunny noontime, and the clock is striking twelve. The action sprawls through the living and dining rooms. The second act occurs on a winter evening. The same setting is now darkened and constricted by the presence of Natasha and her vulgar taste. It is Shrovetide, but the carnival maskers are not permitted in the house. In the third act, Natasha successfully usurps even more space and consigns Olga and Irina to a small bedroom. The time is even later, between two and three in the morning, and outside a fire rages in the town.

In the fourth act, autumn arrives, the cranes are migrating, and the leaves falling, creating a sense of farewell and resignation. Although it is noon again, Chekhov ironically contrasts the scene with the first act by setting it outside, visually conveying that the sisters have been ousted from their home by Natasha and her progeny.

Chekhov's use of sound effects is particularly notable. Seemingly insignificant by themselves, various mundane sounds echo through the play, not only creating an atmosphere but also commenting ironically on the characters and their situation. In the first production, Chekhov strenuously objected to Stanislavsky's attempts to add to the effects that were so carefully inserted in the text. There are bells—sleighbells on Protopopov's troika, chiming bells on the clock, and the anxious alarm bell of the fire—footsteps, tappings, and musical instruments. among them, piano, violin, accordion, and a band. In the first moments of the play, Olga remembers how the band played at their father's funeral. In the final moments, the band plays more and more softly, as the brigade leaves town and the Prozorovs' new lives begin. The clock strikes twelve as Olga speaks in the first act, Tchebutykin breaks the clock in the third act just as the dream of Moscow shatters. Masha whistles somberly before meeting Vershinin; afterward they communicate their love through musical phrases. Tusenbach plays the piano in the first scene, and offstage Andrey plays the violin. In the last act, someone plays "The Maiden's Prayer" on the piano as the hope of Irina's marriage dies.

Some critics view the sisters as passive victims of social conditions, who lack the aggression and the ingenuity necessary to realize their dreams and to better their lives. Others claim that the sisters strive to resist banality and consider that Masha's great love, Irina's decision to marry the baron, and Olga's acceptance of the headmistress position represent that active resistance.

The Three Sisters is a cleverly crafted, realistic play with neither heroes nor villains and without startling theatrical effects (both the fire and the duel occur offstage). Chekhov creates a group of ordinary people, existing in a particular time and place, whose dreams of a better life are shared by all in any time and place.

"Critical Evaluation" by Joyce E. Henry

Further Reading

Barricelli, Jean-Pierre, ed. *Chekhov's Great Plays: A Critical Anthology.* New York: New York University Press, 1981. An excellent collection of critical essays, of which four directly pertain to the play. One deals with the love theme, another discusses Vershinin, the third analyzes cyclical patterns and triads, and the fourth compares the women characters of the four major plays.

Bunin, Ivan. *About Chekhov: The Unfinished Symphony*. Edited and translated by Thomas Gaiton Marullo. Evanston, Ill.: Northwestern University Press, 2007. Bunin, a writer and Nobel laureate, began a biography of Chekhov but did not complete it before he died in 1953. Although incomplete, the book provides intimate details of Chekhov at work, in love, and in relationships with other Russian writers.

Clyman, Toby W., ed. *A Chekhov Companion*. Westport, Conn.: Greenwood Press, 1985. An eclectic book examining many aspects of the plays and the stories. Specific essays focus on Chekhov's craftsmanship, his impact in the theater, and performance on stage and in film. Includes a good bibliography.

Gottlieb, Vera, and Paul Allain, eds. *The Cambridge Companion to Chekhov*. New York: Cambridge University Press, 2000. Collection of essays on Chekhov, including a biography, an essay placing his life and work within the context of Russia, and a discussion of the playwright at the Moscow Art Theatre. Also includes director Trevor Nunn's notes about staging *The Three Sisters*.

Kataev, Vladimir. *If Only We Could Know: An Interpretation of Chekhov*. Edited and translated by Harvey Pitcher. Chicago: Ivan R. Dee, 2002. Kataev, a Russian scholar, offers interpretations of Chekhov's works, emphasizing the uniqueness and the specificity of each character and incident. Includes the essay "'If Only We Could Know': *Three Sisters*."

McVay, Gordon. *Chekhov's "Three Sisters."* London: Bristol Classical Press, 1995. Analyzes the plot, themes, and characters in the play as well as its reception by Russian- and English-language critics.

Pennington, Michael. *Anton Chekhov's "Three Sisters": A Study-Guide*. London: Nick Hern, 2007. Provides a scene-by-scene analysis of the plot and describes how the play's staging affects an audience's understanding of the drama. Offers information about Chekhov's life and playwriting techniques, the play's themes, and an individual study of each character.

Rayfield, Donald. *Anton Chekhov: A Life*. New York: Henry Holt, 1998. Comprehensive biography, providing a wealth of detail about Chekhov's life and work.

Troyat, Henri. *Chekhov*. Translated by Michael Henry Heim. New York: E. P. Dutton, 1986. A readable biography with rare photographs of the author. Includes an interesting description of the writing of *The Three Sisters* and the reception of the first production.

Wellek, René, and Nonna D. Wellek, eds. *Chekhov: New Perspectives*. Englewood Cliffs, N.J.: Prentice Hall, 1984. A brief collection of eight essays with a good discussion of *The Three Sisters* as well as a historical review of criticism, typical dramatic structure, and Chekhov's artistic development.

Three Soldiers

Author: John Dos Passos (1896-1970)
First published: 1921
Type of work: Novel
Type of plot: Social realism
Time of plot: 1917-1919
Locale: France

Principal characters:
DAN FUSELLI, a U.S. soldier from San Francisco
CHRISFIELD, a U.S. soldier from Indiana
JOHN ANDREWS (ANDY), a U.S. soldier from Virginia
GENEVIÈVE ROD, a friend of Andrews

The Story:

Private First Class Dan Fuselli is anxious to become Corporal Dan Fuselli. He has seen motion pictures of Huns impaling Belgian babies on their bayonets and then being chased like rabbits by heroic Yankee soldiers who are later rewarded with embraces by pretty Belgian milkmaids. He looks forward to the time when his girl, Mabe, writing from San Francisco, his hometown, addresses her letters to Corporal Dan Fuselli.

Fuselli, of the Medical Corps, hates the U.S. Army and everything about it, but he knows that to become a corporal he must keep clean, keep his mouth shut, obey the brass, and continually cajole the sergeant. He is infuriated one night when he goes into town to see a young woman named Yvonne and learns that the sergeant has taken her over. Then, when he returns to camp, he hears that the consumptive corporal is back, the one in whose absence Fuselli had been made acting corporal. Fuselli, however, keeps his mouth shut. Someday he will be a corporal, perhaps even a sergeant, but for the time being he keeps his mouth shut. Finally, after a setback doing endless kitchen police duty and following his recovery from a venereal disease, and after the armistice, he does become Corporal Dan Fuselli; by that time, his girl has married a naval officer.

Matters work out differently for Chrisfield. He finds that Army life is not as easygoing as life in the Indiana farm country that is his home. The officers shout at the men and then make them do things they hate, but these things must be withstood. One night, Chrisfield becomes so furious that he pulls a knife on a sergeant named Anderson, but his friends hold him back and nothing happens. In Europe, life is not much better. Occasionally, Chrisfield has a talk about the stars and the fields with his educated buddy John Andrews, known as Andy. Mostly, however, the war is awful.

The marches are endless, and Chrisfield's shoulders ache from his heavy pack. When bombardments come, the marchers scatter facedown in a field. Once Chrisfield asks Andrews to speak French for him to a French girl at an inn, but nothing comes of it. One day, walking alone through a wood near the front, Chrisfield finds the body of a dead German. When he kicks the body over, he sees that it has no face, only a multicolored, pulpy mass with green flies hovering around it. In the man's hand is a revolver—he was a suicide. Chrisfield runs off, panting.

Chrisfield is high-strung. One time, as he is sitting and thinking, another soldier prods him and asks him what he is dreaming about, and Chrisfield punches the fellow in the nose. He and Andy hate the YMCA men who are always telling the men at the front what brutes the Huns are and urging them in the name of Old Glory to kill Germans. Chrisfield is court-martialed when he announces that he intends to kill Sergeant Anderson after the war is over.

One day, Chrisfield goes wandering and makes his way silently into the kitchen of a house near the front. Looking into the next room, he sees a man in a German uniform. He reaches into his pocket for a hand grenade, presses the spring on the grenade, and tosses it into the room. Not long afterward he comes across Anderson, now a lieutenant, seated in a deserted section of the wood; Anderson is wounded. Chrisfield has two more grenades in his pocket, and he throws them at the man he hates. After the armistice, the rumor that he killed Anderson somehow leaks out. Afraid, Chrisfield

deserts the Army and becomes a refugee in France, eternally on the move.

John Andrews is a Harvard graduate and a would-be composer. An idea for a musical composition comes to him as he washes the barracks windows. He curses the Army for slowly stamping him into its iron mold. Overseas, he sees action and becomes more convinced than ever that war is needless butchery. He feels happiest when he is away from the regiment. One day, he walks away from his company in order to be alone. He is looking at little frogs in a pool when a shell bursts near him. He awakes on a stretcher. For a while, he finds the hospital a relief from the endless orders and general mechanization of Army routine. Lying in his bed, he begins to realize that he has respect for himself only when he thinks of rebelling against the Army system. Soon the tedium of the hospital begins to gall him. After his wounds heal, he rejoins his company reluctantly, full of rebellion. The armistice agreement has been signed. When he hears that he can go to a French university through a school detachment being set up, he lies to secure some recommendations and finds himself in Paris.

In Paris, he meets Geneviève Rod, a young Frenchwoman who admires his piano playing and his artistic tastes. She thinks of artists as men who, because of their special sensitivity, should be exempt from the horrors of war. Andrews disagrees—he believes that one worker is like another, and the whole of humanity should be exempt. One day, he leaves Paris without official permission to take a country trip with Geneviève. He is picked up for being absent without leave and is taken to a local office, where he is beaten by the military police officers on a lieutenant's orders. He is then transferred to a labor battalion that is loading concrete for a stadium being presented by the Americans to the French. It is crushing work. Convinced that Army life is a menace to human freedom, Andrews decides to desert, reasoning that one man less in the system makes it weaker by that much.

One night, he leaps from a plank and swims out to a barge in the Seine. The family living on the barge cares for him for a few days. They dispose of his uniform in the river, buy him new clothes, and, as anarchists, proclaim their solidarity with him. He eventually goes back to Paris to find Geneviève, and he stays there for a while with Chrisfield and a group of other concealed deserters. He learns that Geneviève is at her country place, and he joins her there. At first, he does not tell her of his desertion. He lives in an inn nearby and begins composing music about John Brown, liberator of slaves, using the musical ideas that had first come to him while he was washing windows at the barracks. When he finally confesses to Geneviève that he has deserted the Army, a noticeable reserve creeps into her attitude toward him. She cannot comprehend the motive for his rebellion. Perhaps, she suggests, he should give himself up. She and her family depart for the seashore, leaving him behind.

One day, Andrews hears the voice of an American officer at the door of the inn below his window. He thinks of the prison sentence he must face. Too late, he discovers that the landlady, who has betrayed him to the military police, has stolen his revolver. As the MPs take him away, the wind blows in through the window of his room, and the music papers on which he has been working flutter one by one to the floor.

Critical Evaluation:

Having served in France during World War I as an ambulance driver and then as a private in the Medical Corps, Dos Passos was thoroughly conversant with the military life of an enlisted man and was able to portray that life vividly and realistically in his writing. He was the first American novelist since Stephen Crane (1871-1900) to use war as a theme for fiction, but he went far beyond his predecessors in showing the immorality and brutality of the military machine, not toward the enemy but toward its own individual atoms, the soldiers.

The analogy with the machine is clearly seen in the titles of the six parts of *Three Soldiers*: "Making the Mould," "The Metal Cools," "Machines," "Rust," "The World Outside," and "Under the Wheels." In counterpoint to this structure are the narratives of the three soldiers who represent the diverse American experience. Fuselli, the urban ethnic who tries to get ahead by obsequiously cooperating with the machine's agents, dominates the first two sections. Chrisfield, the Indiana farm boy, is the principal figure in the third part. Andrews, the Virginia-born aristocratic aesthete, is the central figure of the final three sections. All three of the soldiers appear in all of the sections, but toward the end Fuselli is referred to by one of the deserters only as a way of the author's concluding Fuselli's narrative. Andrews increasingly becomes the dominant figure of the novel as a whole, first as the intellectual who interprets the actions that occur and finally as the personage with whom readers may identify.

Andrews's portrait is the most complex. He is gradually revealed first as a composer and aesthete, then as a music critic in civilian life, and finally as a Harvard graduate. The musical context associated with the character is not always accurate and has been even disparaged by some critics as name-dropping. Thoroughly authentic, however, is Andrews's outrage at the mindless and petty indignities and harassments to which he is subjected, culminating in a beating by the military police because he has failed to salute an officer and his subsequent ordeal in the labor battalion.

Although *Three Soldiers* does not incorporate the stylistic devices (such as the "Camera Eye," "Newsreel," and biographical snippets) of such later Dos Passos works as the *U.S.A.* trilogy (1937), the author's use of alternating narrative segments anticipates the more complex structure of his later works. Elements that appear in Dos Passos's later works do appear, although in a more conventional novelistic structure, in *Three Soldiers*; these include the use of contrast and juxtaposition to achieve an effect of irony, dreams, and the equivalent of cinematic still images.

Although *Three Soldiers* has often been called an anarchistic novel, ideology as such, like combat, appears in the background: The bargeman who saves and shelters Andrews after his escape from the labor battalion is an anarchist. The reader meets a similar type in Eisenstein, the older man who is drafted and is mysteriously taken away from Fuselli's company because of his subversive ideas. Much of Andrews's rage, however, is aesthetic rather than ideological.

The language of the novel is straightforward, more like that of Crane than of Dos Passos's later *U.S.A.* trilogy. Snatches of popular songs are often used to capture fleeting moods. Although in the dialogue profanity is frequent, Dos Passos does not employ the pervasive obscenity that many subsequent writers have used to lend realism to novels of World War II and other conflicts. Some readers may be repelled by the characters' casual use of racial and ethnic slurs, but it is important to note that such terms were in common use in the early years of the twentieth century, especially among the uneducated.

One common theme affects each of the novel's three protagonists: Although each has a goal, his difficulties with the Army prevent him from achieving a sense of order in his life. Fuselli is constantly thwarted despite his compliant behavior and acceptance of the system. He finally achieves his dream of becoming a corporal, but readers are left to infer that he has achieved it at the cost of everything else. Readers last see him as one of the lowest specimens of Army life, a member of the permanent "kitchen police." Chrisfield's conflict with Anderson is not really clarified for readers, but in life many conflicts that end in murder are all but impossible to clarify. Some critics have asserted that the portrayal of Andrews is unrealistic because of the overripe prose of his speech and of his interior monologues, but one must remember that Andrews is an aesthete of the early twentieth century.

The subordinate characters are unevenly portrayed. The two groups disdained the most by the author, the officers and the "Y men" (agents of the Young Men's Christian Association, or YMCA, who seek to inculcate in the soldiers a hatred of the enemy) are referred to only by rank or occupation, very rarely by name. Andrews's relationship with his love interest, Geneviève, is not consummated; Andrews avoids opportunities to enhance the relationship, often by refusing to play his compositions or those of others for her.

The central thesis of the novel is the essential mindlessness and cruelty of the mass organization as shown by the fates of the three characters who are crushed by it. Throughout his career, Dos Passos displayed a fear and hatred of bureaucratic power and its agents, whether in the anarchism of his early works, in his disillusionment with communism, or in his turning to political conservatism in his later years.

Three Soldiers had a mixed reception on its appearance. The old American literary establishment had been strongly supportive of the Allied Powers, and at first many resented the young novelists who had served in World War I and later exposed it as a sham. Although F. Scott Fitzgerald and H. L. Mencken praised Dos Passos's novel highly, Ernest Hemingway was later to consider its dialogue false and the combat scene unconvincing. Dos Passos's first major novel will always resonate, however, with those who have ever served in the armed forces as enlisted personnel, and its influence can be seen in at least one major novel of World War II, Norman Mailer's *The Naked and the Dead* (1948).

"Critical Evaluation" by R. M. Longyear

Further Reading

Brantley, John. *The Fiction of John Dos Passos*. The Hague, the Netherlands: Mouton, 1968. Surveys the novels chronologically, discussing the structure of *Three Soldiers* as well conceived but less successfully executed. Shows how each of the three soldiers is destroyed by the military machine.

Casey, Janet Galligani. *Dos Passos and the Ideology of the Feminine*. New York: Cambridge University Press, 1998. Discusses Dos Passos's female characters, placing them within the context of the gender representations and ideas about gender that were prevalent in the 1920's and 1930's. Includes discussion of *Three Soldiers*.

Clark, Michael. *Dos Passos's Early Fiction*. Selinsgrove, Pa.: Susquehanna University Press, 1987. Considers Walt Whitman's poetry and William James's psychology as the main influences on *Three Soldiers* and gives a psychological interpretation of the principal characters.

Cooperman, Stanley. "John Dos Passos' *Three Soldiers*." In *The First World War in Fiction*, edited by Holger Klein. London: Macmillan, 1978. Still the standard and most extensive reading of the novel, emphasizing its foreshadowing of the *U.S.A.* trilogy. This volume's excellent introductory essay provides a context for novels about the Great War.

Ludington, Townsend. *John Dos Passos: A Twentieth-Century Odyssey*. Rev. ed. New York: Carroll & Graf, 1998. Standard biography comprehensively chronicles Dos Passos's artistic endeavors and political leanings. Includes analysis of *Three Soldiers* and the writer's other novels.

Nanney, Lisa. *John Dos Passos Revisited*. New York: Twayne, 1998. Excellent introductory study of Dos Passos's life and works draws on previously untapped sources to describe how Dos Passos's own paintings, his interest in the visual arts, and his friendships with artists affected his development as a modernist.

Sanders, David. *John Dos Passos: A Comprehensive Bibliography*. New York: Garland, 1987. Valuable resource includes informative brief annotations. A section devoted to *Three Soldiers* includes a listing of the reviews the novel received when it first appeared.

Three Tall Women

Author: Edward Albee (1928-   )
First produced: 1991; first published, 1994
Type of work: Drama
Type of plot: Existential
Time of plot: 1980's
Locale: The elegant bedroom of an elderly woman

Principal characters:
A, a wealthy, autocratic woman in her nineties
B, her fifty-two-year-old caretaker
C, a twenty-six-year-old representative of A's law firm
THE BOY, A's twenty-three-year-old son

The Story:

Three women sit in an elegant bedroom that is tastefully furnished in pastel colors and silks. The bedroom belongs to the eldest woman, A, who announces that she is ninety-one years old. The middle-aged woman, B, is her paid caregiver, who clearly has long experience helping A with her daily routine, escorting her to the bathroom, placing her pillows, and humoring her mood swings. The young woman, C, appears to be a newcomer, unfamiliar with A's personal habits and her autocratic attitudes. She comes with papers, and eventually it emerges that she has come from the law firm that handles A's affairs to try to sort out some missing bills.

As C tries to get a sense of her elderly client, A tries to impress her new audience with her power. When C tries to argue, A rebuffs her with total contradiction and condescension. Her authority dissolves into confused tears, however, and C begins to understand the extent of A's physical and mental deterioration. B explains to C that A is often incontinent and is suffering from osteoporosis and an atrophying arm that she refuses to have amputated. C begins to sympathize, but B sneers at her "softness," insisting that people should look directly at their mortality.

A's thoughts turn to memories of the past. She describes her guarded childhood under her mother, who warned A that everyone would want something from her. Her defensiveness continued through her prosperous marriage, in which she enjoyed riding horses but found herself confronting hostile in-laws, an unfaithful husband, and the increasing burden of her alcoholic sister. A recalls nursing her husband through a gruesome infection and bringing her abusive elderly mother to live with her. In her memories, A is constantly embattled: "I think they all hated me, because I was strong, because I *had* to be." C is repulsed by A's casual anti-Semitic and racist remarks, although B explains more tolerantly that these are simply the words that she learned early in life.

In the present, too, A is certain that everyone is out to take advantage of her. She accuses B of stealing from her and insists that she will handle her own financial affairs, despite C's offer of additional assistance. A becomes confused and weeps that she cannot remember anything anymore. B reassures her that all her memories are "somewhere in there." Exhausted by retelling a humiliating sexual anecdote about her husband, A retreats to bed. She complains about her son, who brings her flowers but does not love her. Act 1 ends as A shudders and falls silent; B checks her pulse and announces that A has had a stroke.

Act 2 appears to continue in the same setting, with B and C watching A lying in bed. It gradually emerges, however, that the dramatic situation has changed entirely. B and C, in different costumes from those of act 1, now represent two earlier stages in A's life: B represents A at the age of fifty-two, and C represents her at the age of twenty-six. A herself reenters the scene in a new costume, now entirely rational and free from pain. The figure lying in the bed is a dummy. The three selves of A are watching their body approach death. "I wonder how long *this'll* go on. I hope it's quick."

During the death-bed vigil, the three women compare notes about their life. C, the youngest, is curious to hear about her future. C's recent memories of flirtation and sexual awakening are very fresh, and she hopes her future husband will be the man of her dreams; she is appalled by B's and A's funny, cynical descriptions of marriage and infidelity. She says angrily that she refuses to become A, or even B, although they laugh at her presumption. B, in middle age, is more curious to hear from A about endings: She asks when her husband will die and what will happen to her mother.

The women's conversation is interrupted by the appearance of the Boy, their son, who enters silently and seats himself by the sleeping A. C is fascinated to see the handsome young man, but B is instantly enraged and tries to throw him out, although he is impervious. The Boy never speaks but sits silently by the dying woman.

In a harsh monologue, B explains to C how she buried some of her rage at her husband in an affair with a stable groom. Bitterly disappointed in her homosexual son, she threatened to throw him out, but he insulted her over her affair and left without saying good-bye. A informs B that the Boy will return twenty years later but that they will never forgive each other. Sitting on the bed next to her dying body, A speaks directly to the Boy, who is able to hear her. A describes a premonition of watching her own death and watching her son fake the motions of mourning without any actual feeling. The Boy weeps silently onstage.

In the wake of these deep disappointments, in the last section of the play each woman searches for her happiest moment. C hopes that her best, happiest moments are all ahead; surely, she thinks, her life has not peaked already at twenty-six. B says that middle age is the happiest time, comparing it to a mountain view of all directions, past and future. A, in the final speech, says that the happiest moment is coming to an end of life. She takes B and C by the hands for the final line of the play: "When it's all done. When we stop. When we can stop."

Critical Evaluation:

With its unflinching look at mortality and its masterly control of theatricality, *Three Tall Women* would be a triumph for any playwright. For Edward Albee, the play marked a return to the critical and popular success that had eluded him for fifteen years. Albee established his name as a daring provocateur in 1960 with the New York premiere of *The Zoo Story* (pr., pb. 1959). He solidified his reputation with *Who's Afraid of Virginia Woolf?* (pr., pb. 1962), winner of the Tony Award, and *A Delicate Balance* (pr., pb. 1966), winner of the Pulitzer Prize in drama. With scathing wit and passionate rage, Albee's early plays decried the emptiness and terror inside the American Dream (he produced and published a play called *The American Dream* in 1961).

Albee continued to write steadily through the 1970's and 1980's, winning a second Pulitzer Prize for *Seascape* (pr., pb. 1975), but critics and audiences became increasingly indifferent, even hostile, to Albee's dramaturgy. *Three Tall Women* premiered in Vienna's English Theatre in 1991, and few American theaters were interested in producing the play. Lawrence Sacharow directed a successful production at River Arts Repertory in Woodstock, New York, in 1992, but it took over a year to find a New York City venue for the piece. Opening Off-Off-Broadway at the Vineyard Theatre in 1994, the production transferred to the Promenade Theatre, where it ran for over a year. *Three Tall Women* won the Pulitzer Prize and the New York Drama Critics' Circle Award in 1994. Albee's stature in the American theater was reaffirmed with the Obie Award for Sustained Achievement in 1994 and the National Medal of Arts in 1996.

Three Tall Women uses a bifurcated structure to bring its audience to a profound catharsis. Act 1 observes the conventions of realism with its bedroom setting and naturalistic dialogue. The first act allows the audience to judge A, the old lady, externally, much as C gets to know her elderly client. A is strong-willed, arrogant, and volatile; her vanity and selfishness are inextricably tied to her independence and dignity, yet her physical deterioration and frustration are pathetic. While A's command of her present circumstances seems flimsy, her memories of the past are vivid, and the audience begins to see the pattern of choices and consequences that have made A who she is.

In act 2, Albee radically shifts the theatrical mode. The realist character of a woman embodied by a single actor is fractured into an internal dialogue among A's three distinct selves, embodied by three actors in a strategy reminiscent of Luigi Pirandello. The audience now listens to A's interior consciousness, and the character of A becomes fractious and disintegrated as her selves argue with one another about their life, which looks different from each vantage point. A's young self is horrified by the bitter, compromised woman she will become, while her older selves are cynically amused by

her youthful hopes and illusions. Albee's strategy turns the passive act of remembering into active drama, as the selves accuse and betray one another. Their self-loathing finally gives way to self-acceptance as the three tall women join hands in the final moment of the play.

Albee readily admitted that the main character, A, was based on his own adoptive mother, Frances Cotter Albee, who died in 1989, and many incidents in *Three Tall Women* recall the family history. The playwright's relationship with his mother was painful and did involve a twenty-year separation, followed by a chilly reconciliation in later life. The character of the Boy in *Three Tall Women* is, in a sense, autobiographical, yet that character is notably silent. He does not speak in judgment of his mother, although her disappointment in him is clearly articulated, but he weeps.

An audience need not know the story of Albee's family to appreciate *Three Tall Women*. The play looks unflinchingly at aging and dying, the profound mysteries of any human life. Audiences have been deeply moved by the old woman's acceptance of "coming to the end of it." In its contemplation of mortality, *Three Tall Women* recalls Samuel Beckett, one of Albee's great influences, yet Albee's voice is distinctly his own, with a venomous wit and an intense, unforgiving eye. *Three Tall Women* marks the return to power of a masterful American dramatist.

Julia Matthews

Further Reading

Adler, Thomas P. "Albee's 3½: The Pulitzer Plays." In *The Cambridge Companion to Edward Albee*, edited by Stephen Bottoms. New York: Cambridge University Press, 2005. Compares *Three Tall Women* to Samuel Beckett's *Krapp's Last Tape* (pr., pb. 1958): While both plays explore the disjunctions among split selves, Albee's play ends with an integrative image of a unified subject.

Gussow, Mel. *Edward Albee: A Singular Journey.* New York: Simon & Schuster, 1999. Provides a lengthy analysis of Albee's relationship with his adoptive mother and a detailed account of the writing and production of *Three Tall Women*.

Jenckes, Norma. "Postmodernist Tensions in Albee's Recent Plays." In *Edward Albee: A Casebook*, edited by Bruce J. Mann. New York: Routledge, 2003. Argues that, despite the play's postmodern staging of a discontinuous, fragmented self, *Three Tall Women* continues Albee's modernist search for truth and hope for meaning, even in a valueless universe.

Lahr, John. "Sons and Mothers." *The New Yorker* 70 (May

16, 1994): 102-105. Describes Albee's approach to the play as cubist and reflects on the autobiographical fuel stoking the dramaturgical energy of the play.

Mann, Bruce J. "*Three Tall Women*: Return to the Muses." In *Edward Albee: A Casebook*, edited by Mann. New York: Routledge, 2003. Reads the play as an autobiographical psychological drama inspired by the aging Albee's need to revisit his mother-muse.

Murphy, Brenda. "Albee's Threnodies: *Box-Mao-Box, All Over, The Lady from Dubuque*, and *Three Tall Women*." In *The Cambridge Companion to Edward Albee*, edited by Stephen Bottoms. New York: Cambridge University Press, 2005. Contrasts the external and seemingly realist portrayal of death in act 1 of *Three Tall Women* with the three internal perspectives of the dying woman in act 2.

Sacharow, Lawrence. "Directing *Three Tall Women*." In *Edward Albee: A Casebook*, edited by Bruce J. Mann. New York: Routledge, 2003. Director Lawrence Sacharow describes his rehearsal process for the first American production of *Three Tall Women* at River Arts Repertory (1992) and for the play's subsequent productions in New York City (1994-1995).

Staub, August. "Public and Private Thought: The Enthymeme of Death in Albee's *Three Tall Women*." *Journal of Dramatic Theory and Criticism* 12, no. 1 (Fall, 1997): 149-158. Staub compares the theatrical effect of *Three Tall Women*, in bringing a totally private consciousness into the public sphere for collective witnessing, to that of ancient Greek drama.

Zinman, Toby. *Edward Albee*. Ann Arbor: University of Michigan Press, 2008. Provides thoughtful overviews of each of Albee's plays. The discussion of *Three Tall Women* emphasizes its connections to Samuel Beckett's plays, particularly *Rockaby* (pr., pb. 1981) and *Fin de partie* (pr., pb. 1957; *Endgame: A Play in One Act*, 1958).

The Threepenny Opera

Author: Bertolt Brecht (1898-1956)
First produced: Die Dreigroschenoper, 1928; first published, 1929 (English translation, 1949)
Type of work: Drama
Type of plot: Social satire
Time of plot: 1837
Locale: London

Principal characters:
MACHEATH, a master criminal
JONATHAN JEREMIAH PEACHUM, proprietor of the firm "The Beggar's Friend"
CELIA PEACHUM, his wife
POLLY PEACHUM, their daughter
TIGER BROWN, the police chief of London
LUCY BROWN, his daughter
GINNY JENNY, the owner of a brothel
FILCH, an aspiring beggar

The Story:

The criminal elements of London's Soho district (thieves, beggars, and harlots) ply their various occupations while the balladeer sings about crime increases in the area, because of the reappearance of master criminal Captain James MacHeath ("Mack" or "Mackie the Knife"). The song concludes as Mack strolls down the street, causing occupants to quit their businesses and draw aside.

Jonathan Jeremiah Peachum, as notorious as Mack, heads a beggars' organization that plays on the sympathies of wealthier citizens. Filch, an aspiring beggar, applies to Peachum for protection and a suitable costume and pays his fee under protest. Mrs. Celia Peachum ages the costume by staining it. Polly Peachum, their daughter, is out with a man she met a few days earlier. When Celia describes the man, Peachum realizes he is Mack the Knife. Celia tries to calm him, and they sing about how young love's magic sours when the novelty wears off.

Mack escorts Polly to their wedding site, an empty stable that his bumbling henchmen, formally dressed for the wedding, ready for celebration by stealing furniture and even food for the banquet. Unfortunately, the henchmen have no taste and everything is wrong, even the dirge they sing as a wedding hymn to honor the couple. A minister comes to perform the ceremony, and Polly entertains everyone with a song about the revenge of the downtrodden on their social superiors. Mack's best friend, Tiger Brown, chief of the London police, appears, and after reassuring Mack that his police record is wiped clean, the chief joins Mack in singing about being army buddies.

To her parents, Polly explains her marriage to Mack by saying that a "proper" man is not, necessarily, the "right" man. Peachum's scolding is interrupted by the beggars, but he decides to bribe Mack's harlots to turn on Mack. Polly boasts about the relationship between Tiger and Mack, but the Peachums reproach her by singing that "the world is poor and men are bad."

Polly runs to the stable and warns Mack of plans for his arrest. He agrees to leave town, provided Polly will agree to collect his share from his thieves, send the money to his banker, and then turn the thieves over to the police. She agrees, and the newly arrived thieves swear their allegiance to her. She sings of her heartbreak at losing Mack.

Celia bribes Ginny Jenny to turn in Mack, and they plot his betrayal while singing "The Ballad of Sexual Submissiveness." Mack hides out in Jenny's brothel, where Jenny entertains him, and they sing about the days when they lived together. When the police raid the establishment, Mack attempts to escape through the window, but Celia and more police are waiting for him.

In prison, Mack refuses to acknowledge Tiger's apologies for arresting him. After Tiger leaves, Mack attempts to bribe the jailer, singing about the "luxurious" life. Lucy Brown, Tiger's daughter, visits Mack to tell him she is pregnant with his child. When Polly arrives, Mack pretends to scorn her so that Lucy will not tell her father about her pregnancy. Polly and Lucy bait each other in "The Jealousy Duet." After Celia appears and drags Polly away, Mack persuades Lucy to help him escape. Tiger and Peachum discover Mack's escape, and Peachum blackmails Tiger into rearresting him. Meanwhile, Jenny and Mack sing about how human beings live off one another.

At Peachum's establishment, while the beggars prepare to work the crowds lining the streets for Queen Victoria's coronation, Jenny and her girls come by to claim their reward, but Celia refuses to give it until Mack is reincarcerated. Tiger bursts in and attempts to arrest everyone, but Peachum outwits him and sends him to Sulky Tawdry's to find Mack. Peachum sings about life's futility, while Jenny sings about life's absurdities. Polly visits Lucy and they become friendly, with Lucy admitting she is not actually pregnant. Celia brings Polly news of Mack's impending execution and a widow's veil.

Back in prison, Mack sings of his despair as he tries to

borrow money from his henchmen to bribe his jailer. Polly arrives, but she has no money either. The only salvation for Mack is a queen's pardon. Tiger comes with Mack's last meal. Mack pays Tiger the protection money he owes, and all of Mack's friends enter to say good-bye. There is such a crowd for his execution that no one is attending the coronation. Mack is standing on the gallows when, at the last moment, the queen's messenger appears with a full pardon, which also gives Mack a castle and a pension. Peachum sermonizes the moral of the piece: "Life was hard, and pardons seldom came." Everyone sings a reinforcement of the moral.

Critical Evaluation:

Bertolt Brecht was one of the greatest innovators of theatrical productions and dramatic theory of the twentieth century. His approach to theater emerged from the German expressionist school, which reflected the alienation from society caused by expanding technological industrialism as well as the discontent and disorientation that followed World War I. His first theatrical success, *The Threepenny Opera*, which received its premiere on August 28, 1928, took Berlin by storm. Jarring, jangling, irreverent, amusing, scintillating, cynical, exciting, and unnerving, the play brought international fame to Brecht.

To some extent, however, the play confirmed critics in their uneasy feelings about Brecht the creative artist: Was Bertolt Brecht a genius or a plagiarist? A joke, current in Berlin at the time, went to the heart of their uneasiness: "Who wrote it?"—"Brecht."—"All right. Who wrote it?"

The Threepenny Opera was perfect fodder for a charge of plagiarism. It was an adaptation of *The Beggar's Opera*, a 1728 ballad opera by the English playwright John Gay. Brecht's secretary translated the first few scenes into German, but when the play was accepted for production, Brecht rushed the preparation of the script, lifting entire scenes, characters, and dialogue from the original. Rather than using the original songs and score, Brecht drew on a file of his own song lyrics and poems based on translations of the medieval French poet François Villon and the English Victorian poet-novelist Rudyard Kipling. To this mix, he added a heavy sprinkling of Bible verses. Even the most famous line from the play, "Food comes first, and then morality," originated with the German Romantic playwright Friedrich von Schiller. If Brecht escaped the accusation of plagiarism, it was because he blended the many borrowings to make a uniquely original concoction.

While *The Threepenny Opera* presented a criticism of society during the 1920's, Brecht chose to date the action at the time of Queen Victoria's coronation (1837) and to place it in London's Soho area. Berliners, who were enthralled by American gangsterism, nevertheless saw past the time and place into the references to their age. A part of Brecht's genius was that he anticipated the audience's recognition.

It was a tribute to Brecht's theatrical sense that he secured the services of the young composer Kurt Weill to provide the score for the production. Weill's music was in large part responsible for making the production the success that it became, for his compositions were as avant-garde as Brecht's lyrics and theories. Influenced by such diverse sources as a classical training and American jazz, Weill provided music that was perfect for the play: a pastiche of jazz, cabaret, operetta, and vaudeville. It was fresh, irreverent, new, and startling, and it satirized opera and traditional serious music with a jangling sound akin to a berserk hurdy-gurdy that, while it grated on the ears, excited and stimulated listeners.

Oddly enough, what made Brecht's presentational style engrossing was not stylistic consistency but the element of the anachronistic, which was subtle enough not to call attention to itself. In *The Threepenny Opera*, for example, Brecht drew on Chicago gangsters, modern music, and a Roaring Twenties atmosphere in an eighteenth century play set in nineteenth century England.

Eventually Brecht's ideas coalesced into his credo for epic theater. Even at the time of *The Threepenny Opera*, Brecht was reading Aristotle. The term epic theater was not original with Brecht; like so much of his work, it was borrowed from the German playwright and impresario Erwin Piscator, who used the term to describe his presentational style of theater. Brecht used Piscator's term and theories and elaborated and enlarged on them.

In Aristotle's *De poetica* (c. 334-323 B.C.E.; *Poetics*, 1705), epic and tragic poetry are contrasted. Tragic poetry was represented by the classical Greek dramas and demanded emotional involvement that reached its climax in catharsis. The epic, on the other hand, was a saga without emotional identification by the audience and was didactic in nature.

For Brecht, the social and political critic-commentator, the epic was the ideal method of communication, and he used devices in *The Threepenny Opera* that he would later incorporate into epic theater. The term most often associated with Brecht is the effect of alienation (*Verfremdungseffekt*). He believed that distancing was necessary if the spectators were to take the social message of the play to heart. To this end, Brecht developed his play in short, concise vignettes that were connected by theme rather than by chronology; he in-

terrupted the action of the play with songs that, instead of furthering the plot, reinforced the message; he used the machinery of the theater (lights, setting, the stage itself, properties, placards, slogans, signs, and later, projections) to call attention to the fact that the play was theater and not reality; and he recommended that his actors stay emotionally distant from their characters. All of these concepts can be seen in *The Threepenny Opera*. Brecht's influence on other writers, producers, and theorists is tremendous and indelible. In many ways, Brecht is synonymous with modern theater.

H. Alan Pickrell

Further Reading

Brecht, Bertolt. *The Threepenny Opera*. Translated by Ralph Manheim and John Willett. New York: Arcade, 1995. In addition to an English translation of the play, this edition includes Brecht's own notes on how the play should be produced, discarded songs, and extensive editorial commentary on the play's genesis.

Ewen, Frederic. *Bertolt Brecht: His Life, His Art, and His Times*. New York: Citadel Press, 1967. Exhaustive examination of Brecht's total oeuvre in chronological sequence. Examines people and theories that influenced Brecht's work.

Hayman, Ronald. *Bertolt Brecht*. Totowa, N.J.: Barnes & Noble, 1984. Contains an excellent analysis of major themes and sources for Brecht's plays.

Morley, Michael. *Brecht: A Study*. Totowa, N.J.: Rowman & Littlefield, 1977. Contains a complete discussion of *The Threepenny Opera*, detailing how the play was written and analyzing its themes.

Speirs, Ronald. *Bertolt Brecht*. New York: St. Martin's Press, 1987. Contains an analysis of Brecht's evolution as a playwright and charts the evolution of epic theater.

Thomson, Peter, and Glendyr Sacks, eds. *The Cambridge Companion to Brecht*. 2d ed. New York: Cambridge University Press, 2006. Collection of essays offering numerous interpretations of Brecht's work, including examinations of Brecht and cabaret, music, and stage design; his work with the Berliner Ensemble; and key words in his theory and practice of theater. Chapter 5 discusses *The Threepenny Opera*.

Unwin, Stephen. *A Guide to the Plays of Bertolt Brecht*. London: Methuen, 2005. Contains analyses of many of Brecht's plays and discusses his theories of drama, his impact, and his legacy. Designed as an accessible introduction to Brecht for students, teachers, and other readers.

Through the Looking-Glass and What Alice Found There

Author: Lewis Carroll (1832-1898)
First published: 1871
Type of work: Novel
Type of plot: Fantasy
Time of plot: Nineteenth century
Locale: A dreamworld

Principal characters:
ALICE, a fanciful child
DINAH, a cat
THE BLACK KITTEN
THE WHITE KITTEN
THE WHITE KING and THE WHITE QUEEN
THE RED KING and THE RED QUEEN
GNAT
TWEEDLEDUM and TWEEDLEDEE
HUMPTY DUMPTY
THE LION and THE UNICORN
THE WHITE KNIGHT and THE RED KNIGHT

The Story:

Alice is sure the whole thing is not the white kitten's fault. It must surely be the fault of the black kitten. Dinah, the mother cat, who has been washing the white kitten's face, certainly has nothing to do with it. The mischievous black kitten, however, has been unwinding Alice's ball of yarn and in all ways acting naughty enough to cause the whole strange affair.

While the black kitten is curled up in Alice's lap, playing with the yarn, Alice tells it to pretend that the two of them can go right through the mirror and into the looking-glass house. As she talks, the glass of the mirror grows misty and soft, and in a moment Alice is through the mirror and in the looking-glass room. The place is very strange; although the room looks just the same as the real room she had seen in the mirror, the clock and the fire and the other things in the room seem to be alive. Even the chessmen (Alice loves to play chess) are alive.

When Alice picks up the White Queen and sets her on the table, the White Queen screams in terror, thinking that a volcano has shaken her about. The White King has the same fear, but he is too astonished to cry out. They do not seem to see or hear Alice, and although she wants to stay and watch them and read the king's rather funny poetry, she feels she must look at the garden before she has to go back through the looking glass. When she starts down the stairs, she seems to float, not even once touching the steps.

In the garden, every path Alice takes leads her straight back to the house. She asks Tiger Lily and Rose and Violet whether there are other people in the garden, hoping they might help her find the right path. The flowers tell her there is only one person, and Alice finds her to be the Red Queen— but a very strange chess figure, for the Red Queen is taller

than Alice herself. As Alice walks toward the Red Queen, she once more finds herself back at the door of the house. Then Alice figures out that in order to get to any place in this queer land, one must walk in the opposite direction. She does so and comes face-to-face with the Red Queen.

The queen takes Alice to the top of a hill. There, spread out below them, is a countryside that looks like a large chessboard. Alice is delighted and says that she would love to play on this board. The Red Queen tells her that they will play; Alice will be the White Queen's pawn, and they will start on the second square. At that moment, however, the Red Queen grabs Alice's hand and they start to run. Alice has never run so fast in her life, but although she is breathless, the things around them never change at all. When they finally stop running, the queen tells Alice that in this land one has to run as fast as one can to stay in the same place and twice as fast as one can to get somewhere else. Then the queen shows Alice the pegs in the second square of the chessboard and tells her how to move. At the last peg, the Red Queen disappears, leaving Alice alone to continue the game.

Alice starts to run down the hill, but the next thing she knows she is on a train filled with insects and having quite an unpleasant time because she does not have a ticket. All the insects talk unkindly to her, and, to add to her discomfort, the train jumps over the brook and takes them all straight up in the air. When Alice comes down, she is sitting under a tree talking to Gnat, who is as big as a chicken and very pleasant. He tells her about the other insects that live in the woods; then he too melts away, and Alice has to go on alone.

Turning a corner, she bumps into two fat little men called Tweedledum and Tweedledee, the funniest little creatures she has ever seen. Everything they say seems to have two meanings. They recite a long poem about a walrus and a carpenter and some oysters. Then, while they are explaining the poem to Alice, she hears a puffing noise, like the sound of a steam engine. Tweedledee tells her that it is the Red King snoring, and, sure enough, they find him asleep. Tweedledee tells Alice that the Red King is dreaming about her and that if he stops dreaming Alice will be gone for good. Alice cries when they tell her she is not real but only a part of the Red King's dream.

As she brushes her tears away, she sees Tweedledum staring in terror at something on the ground. It is an old broken rattle, and the two foolish men get into a terrible fight over it—that is, they talk a terrible fight, but neither seems very eager to have a real battle. The Crow flies over and frightens them, and the funny men run away into the woods. Alice runs too, and as she runs, she sees a shawl blowing about. Looking for the owner of the shawl, Alice sees the White Queen running toward her. The White Queen is a very odd person; she lives backward and remembers things before they happen—for example, she feels pain before she pricks her finger. While the queen is talking, she turns into a sheep, and Alice finds that she and the sheep are in a shop. It is a very curious shop; the shelves are full of things that disappear when Alice looks at them. Sometimes the boxes go right through the ceiling. Then the sheep gives Alice some needles and tells her to knit.

As she starts to knit, the needles become oars, and Alice finds herself and the sheep in a little boat, rowing in a stream. The oars keep sticking in the water, and the sheep explains that the crabs are catching them. Alice picks some beautiful, fragrant rushes that melt away as soon as she picks them. To her surprise, the river and boat soon vanish, and she and the sheep are back in the shop. She buys one egg, although in this shop two are cheaper than one, and the egg begins to grow larger and larger and more and more real, with eyes, a nose, and a mouth. Then Alice can tell as plain as day that the egg is Humpty Dumpty.

She has an odd conversation with Humpty Dumpty, a conversation filled with riddles. They take turns at choosing the topics to discuss, but even though Alice tries to be polite, most of the subjects lead them to arguments. Humpty Dumpty explains to Alice the meaning of the "Jabberwocky" poem, the one she had seen in the White King's book. Then, while reciting another poem, Humpty Dumpty stops right in the middle and says that is all. Alice thinks this very strange, but she does not tell him so. She thinks it is time for her to leave, but as she walks away, a terrible crash shakes the whole forest.

Thousands of soldiers on horseback come rushing toward her, the riders constantly falling off their horses. Frightened,

she escapes from the woods into the open. There she finds the White King, who tells her that he sent the soldiers and horses and that the loud crash she heard was the noise of the Lion and the Unicorn fighting for the crown. She goes with the king to watch the fight, which is indeed a terrible one. It is silly of them to fight for the crown, since it belongs to the White King and he has no intention of giving it away. After the fight, Alice meets the Unicorn and the Lion. At the king's order, she serves them cake, a very strange cake that cuts itself as she carries the dish around.

A great noise interrupts the party. When it stops, Alice thinks she might have dreamed the whole thing until the Red Knight comes along, followed soon by the White Knight. Each claims her as his prisoner. Alice thinks the whole business silly, since neither of them can do anything except fall off his horse and climb back on again, over and over and over. At last, the Red Knight gallops off, and the White Knight tells her that she will be a queen as soon as she crosses the next brook. He is supposed to lead her to the end of the woods, but she spends the whole journey helping him back on his horse each time he falls off. The trip is filled with more queer conversation, but by this time, Alice is used to strange talk from her looking-glass friends. At last, they reach the brook. The knight rides away, and Alice jumps over the brook and into the last square of the chessboard. To her delight, when she reaches that square she feels something tight on her head. It is a crown, and she is a queen.

Soon she finds the Red Queen and the White Queen confronting her; they are very cross because she thinks she is a queen. They give her a test for queens that she apparently passes, for before long they are calling her "Your Majesty" and inviting people to a party that she is to give. After a time, the Red Queen and the White Queen go to sleep, and Alice watches them until they disappear. She then finds herself before a doorway marked "Queen Alice." All of her new friends are there, including the queens who just vanished. The party is the most amazing experience of all. Puddings talk, guests pour wine over their heads, and the White Queen turns into a leg of mutton. Alice is exasperated, so much so that she seizes the tablecloth and jerks it, knocking everything from the table onto the floor. She then grabs the Red Queen and shakes her as she would a kitten. What is this? It is a kitten she is shaking, the black kitten. Alice talks to Dinah and both the kittens about the adventure they have all experienced, but the silly kittens do nothing but purr.

Critical Evaluation:

It is rare for the sequel to a highly creative literary work to surpass the original, but such is the case with *Through the*

Looking-Glass and What Alice Found There, which followed Lewis Carroll's *Alice's Adventures in Wonderland*, published six years earlier. For most readers, the two books are so closely entwined that they are considered a unit. Although joined by a common heroine and themes, the characters in the two books are quite distinct. *Through the Looking-Glass* is perhaps more attractive to adults than to children, for this second fantasy by Carroll (the pen name for the Oxford mathematics lecturer and tutor the Reverend Charles Lutwidge Dodgson) presents an even more sophisticated puzzle about reality and logic than does the earlier story. In *Through the Looking-Glass* there is a conscious suggestion of the cruel questions rather more delicately presented in *Alice's Adventures in Wonderland*.

The books share many characteristics: Each has twelve chapters, and both merge the fairy tale with science. Alice is seven years old in the first book and seven and a half on her second adventure. A slight shift in scene turns the pleasant outdoor summer setting of *Alice's Adventures in Wonderland* into the more somber indoor winter stage of *Through the Looking-Glass*. Corresponding to the card game of the first book is chess in *Through the Looking-Glass*, another game that involves kings and queens. Within the chess-and-mirror framework of the looking-glass world, Carroll has, however, constructed an intricate symbolic plan unlike the seemingly spontaneous movement of Wonderland.

Although medieval and Renaissance sportsmen sometimes enjoyed chess that used human players on a giant field, Carroll seems to have been the first to use the idea in literature. (The science fiction of later ages has often employed this image.) In the game plan, Alice is a white pawn on a giant chessboard of life in which the rows of the board are separated by brooks and the columns by hedges. Alice never speaks to any piece who is not in a square beside her, as is appropriate for the pawn, who never knows what is happening except at its spot on the board. Alice remains in the queen's field except for her last move (by which time she has become a queen), when she captures the Red Queen and shakes her into a kitten; as a result, she checkmates the Red King, who has slept throughout the game. Her behavior complements the personalities assigned to the other pieces, for each assumes the qualities of the figure it represents. As in chess, the queens are the most powerful and active beings, and the kings are impotent. Erratic and stumbling, the White Knight recalls the movement of the chess knight, which moves two squares in any direction, then again one square in a different direction, forming a sort of spastic "L."

Critics have noted inconsistencies in the chess game, charging that the White side makes nine consecutive moves;

that the White King is placed in an unnoticed check, the queen's castle; and that the White Queen misses a chance to take the Red Knight. In a later explanatory note, however, Carroll said that the game is correct in relation to the moves, although the alternation of the sides is not strictly consistent, and that the "castling" of the queen is merely his phrase to indicate that they have entered the palace. Not interested in the game as an example of chess strategy, Carroll conceived of it as a learning experience for a child who was to "be" a pawn warring against all the other pieces controlled by an adult, an idea apparently stimulated by the chess tales Carroll had fashioned for Alice Liddell, who was learning the game. Alice, the daughter of the dean of Christ Church, Oxford, had also been the Alice whom the author had placed in Wonderland.

Arising inevitably from Carroll's use of this structure has been the proposal that Alice is Everyman and that chess is Life. Like human beings, who exists from birth to death only vaguely comprehending the forces directing their moves, Alice never understands her experience. Indeed, none of the pieces really assimilates the total concept of the game. Even the mobile queens do not really grasp the idea that beyond the board there is a room and people who are determining the game. A person's own reality thus becomes very unreal if the individual, like the chess pieces, has such a limited perception of the total environment.

Carroll pursues still another definition of reality when Alice confronts the Red King and is told that she exists merely as part of his dreams, not as an objective being. Upsetting to Alice is the sage advice of Tweedledum and Tweedledee that if the king were to wake, Alice would vanish like the flame of a candle. The incident recalls philosopher George Berkeley's empirical proposal that nothing exists except as it is perceived. Alice, like Samuel Johnson—who refuted Berkeley by painfully kicking a stone—insists that she is "real" because she cries "real" tears. When she leaves the world of the looking glass and supposedly awakens, Carroll mischievously permits her to ask herself: "Which dreamed it?" His final poem apparently provides the answer in the last words: "Life, what is it but a dream?"

In examining the second structural device of the book, the mirror reversal theme (perfectly mated with chess, given that in the game the initial asymmetric arrangement of the pieces means that the opponents are mirror images of one another), readers find that Carroll has achieved another tour de force. The left-right reversals—including, for example, the Tweedle brothers, Alice's attempt to reach the Red Queen by walking backward, memory that occurs before the event, and running to stay in the same place—are not merely mind teasers. Since the book was written, scientists have seriously proposed the existence of antimatter, which is, in effect, a mirror image of matter, just like Alice's looking-glass milk. Again readers wonder: Which is the real matter, the real milk?

Further developing this continuing paradox are Carroll's damaging attacks on ordinary understanding of language. Humpty Dumpty (like the Tweedles, the Lion, the Unicorn, and Wonderland's Jack of Hearts, a nursery-rhyme character) says that ideas are formulated in one's mind; to express them, one may use any word one pleases. Alice and the White Knight debate the difference between the name of the song and the song, between what the name is and what the name is called. The fawn becomes frightened of Alice only when it realizes she is a "child." In these and many more incidents, Carroll explores how language works, directly and indirectly making fun of misconceptions that on one hand see language as part of a totally objective system of reality and on the other forget how language actually helps create that reality. His nonsense words and poems are his final jibe at so-called logical language, for they are no more and no less disorderly than ordinary table talk.

Like *Alice's Adventures in Wonderland*, *Through the Looking-Glass and What Alice Found There* is a sparkling achievement. Both books reflect the incomparable vision of an alienated man who found in the world of fantasy all the delight and horror of the adult environment he was subconsciously attempting to escape.

"Critical Evaluation" by Judith Bolch

Further Reading

Carroll, Lewis. *The Annotated Alice: "Alice's Adventures in Wonderland" and "Through the Looking-Glass."* Definitive ed. Edited by Martin Gardner. New York: W. W. Norton, 2000. Features abundant marginal notes that explain references in the Alice tales, linking them to Carroll's life, events and controversies in Victorian England, and mathematics. Also includes reproductions of the works' original illustrations.

_____. *More Annotated Alice: "Alice's Adventures in Wonderland" and "Through the Looking-Glass."* Edited by Martin Gardner. New York: Random House, 1990.

Based on letters from readers of the first edition of *The Annotated Alice* as well as new research, this sequel supplements rather than revises that book. Reprints for the first time Peter Newell's illustrations and includes Newell's essay on visually interpreting *Alice in Wonderland*.

Guiliano, Edward, ed. *Lewis Carroll: A Celebration.* New York: Clarkson N. Potter, 1982. Collection of essays devoted to Carroll's works includes one of Donald Rackin's existential readings, a surrealist reading, and an analysis of the "hair motif" in *Through the Looking-Glass*.

Jones, Jo Elwyn, and J. Francis Gladstone. *The Alice Companion: A Guide to Lewis Carroll's Alice Books.* New York: New York University Press, 1998. Interesting resource is full of information and commentary on the people and places that made up Carroll's and Alice Liddell's world in mid-nineteenth century Oxford. Good supplement to the extensive existing literature on this period in Carroll's life.

_____. *The Red King's Dream: Or, Lewis Carroll in Wonderland.* London: Jonathan Cape, 1995. Places Carroll within his life and times through the discussion of his literary milieu, friends, and influences.

Kelly, Richard. *Lewis Carroll.* Rev. ed. Boston: Twayne, 1990. Provides an excellent introduction to the works of Carroll, including a section on *Through the Looking-Glass*. Offers a broad critical study of Carroll's life and writings, with special emphasis on his mastery of nonsense.

Phillips, Robert S., ed. *Aspects of Alice: Lewis Carroll's Dreamchild as Seen Through the Critics' Looking-Glasses, 1865-1971.* New York: Vanguard Press, 1971. One of the largest and most important single collections of critical essays on Carroll's work. Analyzes Carroll as an author for adults and for children.

Reichertz, Ronald. *The Making of the Alice Books: Lewis Carroll's Uses of Earlier Children's Literature.* Montreal: McGill-Queen's University Press, 1997. Analyzes children's literature from the seventeenth through nineteenth centuries. Argues that Carroll combined the formality and themes of earlier books with his narrative imagination to create an original form of children's literature.

Thus Spake Zarathustra

Author: Friedrich Nietzsche (1844-1900)
First published: Also sprach Zarathustra: Ein Buch für
    Alle und Keinen, 1883-1885 (English translation, 1896)
Type of work: Philosophy

Friedrich Nietzsche was ignored and misunderstood during his lifetime, but his ideas went on to influence a variety of disciplines, including philosophy, psychology, and literature, and eventually he came to be considered one of the greatest philosophers of all time. Trained as a classical Greek scholar, Nietzsche was a prodigy in his field, appointed associate professor at the University of Basel at the age of twenty-four. Because he suffered from poor health, particularly problems with his vision and his digestion, Nietzsche resigned his post in 1879 and turned his full attention to writing. He used his training in ancient Greek culture to critique traditional philosophy, and his insights into the hidden motives behind the formation of Western morality and ethics formed the basis for much twentieth century thought. Although he never completed an organized summary of his ideas, his revolutionary approach ensured him an important place in intellectual history.

In his early work, Nietzsche probed psychological phenomena and began to describe the function of the unconscious (some of this work foreshadowed his nervous breakdown in 1889, from which he never fully recovered). He analyzed humanity's hidden drives, the human desire to dominate and to be dominated—drives that he would later describe as "the will to power" and that led to the famous skeptical doctrine in which he proclaimed the death of God—as forming the core of Christian virtue.

Nietzsche's thought is best represented by his major work, *Thus Spake Zarathustra*. A long parable, full of sentimentality and satire, the work exhorts readers to abandon their conditioning and embrace a new mode of living: that of the *Übermensch*, or Overman, a being free from the constraints of society in general and of Christianity in particular. For Nietzsche, the Overman possessed a reason or a will that enabled him to master his passions and thus freed him to discover "truth," or what Nietzsche called "the eternal recurrence of the same."

Nietzsche declared that he chose the name Zarathustra because he was inspired by the Persian prophet, who had created the first moral vision of the world and transposed morality into the metaphysical realm so that, far from being a simple code of conduct, morality became an end in itself as both a force and a cause shaping the human universe. Consequently, Nietzsche's book *Thus Spake Zarathustra* begins with the acknowledgment of its relevance to human life. As Zarathustra abandons his mountain solitude, he proclaims that he is going to travel in the world "once again to be a man." Using metaphor, Nietzsche presents the mountain as the solitude of the soul, while the lowlands symbolize the plain inhabited by ordinary human beings. A similar symbolic contrast occurs with the appearance of Zarathustra's pagan attendants, or animal familiars, the serpent and the eagle. The serpent is bound to the earth, while the eagle rules the sky, and Zarathustra, the bridge between the two, is the future healer of humanity's split personality, tending on one hand toward the body and on the other toward the spirit.

Zarathustra contemplates the mystery of the sun, which sets and is reborn the next morning as a new and burning god. Nietzsche thus opens his book with metaphors for rebirth and resurrection, the theme underlying the entire work. After the stultifying effect of centuries of Christianity and of the kind of dogmatic moral beliefs that had led to the Crusades and the Inquisition, Nietzsche wonders how humanity can be reborn.

Nietzsche's answer is to send his prophet Zarathustra, murderer of God, on a journey where he will preach the enlightened doctrine of daylight as a metaphor for consciousness and the limitations of human perception: "the drunken happiness of dying at midnight, that sings: the world is deep, *deeper than day had been aware.*" When humanity becomes "aware," it is faced with a contradiction: How can those who have denied God find the strength to become creators themselves?

Nietzsche discusses humanity's dilemma in being forced to learn to live without God's comfort and in coming to terms with the numbing indifference of the cosmos without being paralyzed by it. To avoid destruction, members of humanity must become the *Übermensch*, capable of embracing misery with enthusiasm, even delight.

Nietzsche explores ways to reach this inner peace, which requires both perfect self-knowledge and self-transcendence. For Nietzsche, the Overman is the symbol of the robust health he himself lacked. The Overman is the individual who has learned to live without belief and without truth, yet who superhumanly accepts life as it comes to him—this individual accepts the "eternal recurrence of the same." Indeed, to embrace the prospect of repeating one's life, exactly as it occurs, day by day, complete with all of its pain and disappointment, is for Nietzsche the highest achievement and the greatest display of courage. The individual's personal goal, according to Nietzsche, ought to be the cultivation of "perfect moments."

Having attained this existence—which is to be enjoyed if repeated endlessly—the Overman despises his former self, that weak creature who had desired that not only law and order but also his own personal morality be imposed from outside himself. Through this concept of the Overman, Nietzsche becomes the great philosophical liberator who anticipates the decline of morality in civilization by sending forth the Overman as a secular savior. Nietzsche saw that Christianity was losing its hold on the world, for with the death of God (a phenomenon Nietzsche described without necessarily welcoming it), humanity found itself exposed to itself, its own most dangerous predator. God the protector was gone, killed by science. Therefore, lest humanity destroy itself in its infancy, Nietzsche created the Overman as the model of what humanity could become if people showed courage and lived every moment as if that moment were to be repeated for all eternity.

With God dead, assassinated by skepticism and rationality, Nietzsche acknowledges that humanity, deprived of this potent ally, will, metaphysically speaking, shrink. Deprived of God and therefore of significance, human beings fall from grace and becomes no more than animals. Yet Nietzsche does not accept humanity's decline in status simply because people lack the superstition to regard themselves as divine creations. Instead, Nietzsche counters the "shrinkage" that humanity experiences when deprived of a god by substituting the Overman, an ideal created by human beings for human beings, a thoroughly human creation that acknowledges itself as human and not divine in its origin.

The Overman, the apotheosis of the human and the apex of becoming, thus represents a kind of salvation. The eternal recurrence of salvation in turn guarantees his reappearance, and thus a kind of secular afterlife. Nietzsche sees God, then, as the ultimate form of human self-aggrandizement, as a comforting delusion, and yet he acknowledges humanity's need for something beyond itself, humanity's fundamental yearning, which, if it is not to be exploited by organized religion or unchecked nationalism, must be given an outlet. Nietzsche considers the ideal Overman humanity's only true savior.

In *Thus Spake Zarathustra*, the Overman has conquered his cloying need for God's approval. Like a child, he has had to learn to take care of himself, an important skill when the school bully appears. Even more important, the Overman has traveled beyond his lust for meaning outside himself, finding sufficient glory in what remains behind. Nietzsche writes, "Those who cannot bear the sentence, 'There is no salvation,' *ought* to perish!" Nietzsche argues that the old, simple, God-fearing people ought to fade into extinction like some ill-adapted hominid ancestor, making way for the *Übermensch*, bearer of the torchlight of knowledge and freedom.

Nietzsche addresses and explores the problems and pain at the heart of nineteenth and twentieth century consciousness. Raised on illusion, on exorbitant expectations and wild dreams, the mind loves life but can find no meaning in it. It despairs of ever finding fundamental purpose or of discovering the emotional riches promised in childhood. Nietzsche dares his readers to approach the abyss with him. Indeed, he subtitles *Thus Spake Zarathustra* "a book for all and none," which is a warning that only the stout of heart should approach the edge with him, for to confront the implications of the absence of God is to be utterly alone. Nietzsche writes of the end of the journey toward truth, of "the Don Juan of the Mind"—the lover of all things, cursed with the inability to enjoy them—and of the final bleak candor with which the honest or "authentic" individual views existence: "And in the very end he craves for Hell . . . perhaps it too will disappoint. . . . And if so, he will have to stand transfixed through all eternity, nailed to disillusion, having himself become the Guest of Stone, longing for a last supper of knowledge that he will never receive."

Nietzsche's importance lies precisely in the fact that he was finally not pessimistic. Squinting through the mist of an intellectual dark age, he sparked a light and had the courage to focus on what he saw as the truth, without turning away or softening his description. Nietzsche's tool for philosophizing, as he said himself, was a hammer. Accordingly, it was his driving ambition to crack open the truth, even at great personal sacrifice: "Oh grant madness, you heavenly powers! . . . I am consumed by doubts, for I have killed the Law. . . . If I am not more than the Law, then I am the most abject of all men." That he survived as long as he did, and even managed to relate the tale of his extraordinary journey off the mountaintop, is Zarathustra's, and Nietzsche's, final triumph.

David Johansson

Further Reading
Berkowitz, Peter. *Nietzsche: The Ethics of an Immoralist.* Cambridge, Mass.: Harvard University Press, 1995. Shows

how Nietzsche's attacks on conventional and traditional morality entail a distinctive ethical outlook.

Hayman, Ronald. *Nietzsche.* New York: Routledge, 1999. Provides an excellent biographical introduction to the thoughts of the philosopher, clearly presented and requiring no special background.

Higgins, Kathleen. *Nietzsche's "Zarathustra."* Philadelphia: Temple University Press, 1987. Clearly written and accessible work explores in depth the themes and issues raised in *Thus Spake Zarathustra.*

Kaufmann, Walter. *Nietzsche: Philosopher, Psychologist, Antichrist.* 4th ed. Princeton, N.J.: Princeton University Press, 1974. Standard and important study by one of Nietzsche's most respected translators provides comprehensive discussion of the philosopher's life and thought.

Klein, Wayne. *Nietzsche and the Promise of Philosophy.* Albany: State University of New York Press, 1997. Discusses Nietzsche's vision of what philosophy should and should not be and traces the implications of his analysis.

Luchte, James, ed. *Nietzsche's "Thus Spoke Zarathustra": Before Sunrise.* London: Continuum, 2008. Collection of essays by fifteen Nietzsche scholars includes discussion of *Thus Spake Zarathustra* as Nietzsche's autobiography and examinations of the book's concepts of time, freedom, and justice.

Magnus, Bernd. *Nietzsche's Existential Imperative.* Bloomington: Indiana University Press, 1978. Interpretation of Nietzsche's philosophy focuses on his doctrine of eternal recurrence and takes *Thus Spake Zarathustra* as a principal source.

Magnus, Bernd, and Kathleen M. Higgins, eds. *The Cambridge Companion to Nietzsche.* New York: Cambridge University Press, 1996. Collection of insightful essays examines diverse aspects of Nietzsche's philosophy.

Seung, T. K. *Nietzsche's Epic of the Soul: "Thus Spoke Zarathustra."* Lanham, Md.: Lexington Books, 2005. Provides a unified reading of the entire text to unravel its thematic contradictions. Approaches the work as a baffling series of riddles and puzzles and as Zarathustra's journey to find spiritual values in a secular world.

Waite, Geoff. *Nietzsche's Corpse: Aesthetics, Politics, Prophecy—Or, The Spectacular Technoculture of Everyday Life.* Durham, N.C.: Duke University Press, 1996. Offers an assessment of the significance and impact of Nietzsche's work on the development of culture, politics, and technology in the twentieth century and beyond.

Thyestes

Author: Seneca the Younger (c. 4 B.C.E.-c. 65 C.E.)
First produced: c. 40-55 C.E. (English translation, 1581)
Type of work: Drama
Type of plot: Tragedy
Time of plot: Antiquity
Locale: Greece

Principal characters:
ATREUS, the king of Argos
THYESTES, his brother
THYESTES' THREE SONS

The Story:

Megaera, one of the Furies, summons the ghost of Tantalus to return from Hades to Argos, where Tantalus in life had been king, to watch revenge, hate, and havoc spread across that kingdom. Tantalus does not want to be reminded of the part he played in the story of his royal house, but Megaera forces him to witness the fate of his descendants.

The grandsons of Tantalus, the sons of Pelops, whom Tantalus sacrificed to the gods, are at war with each other. The elder of Pelops's sons, Atreus, is the rightful ruler of Argos, but his brother, Thyestes, has seduced Atreus's wife and carried her away. With them they have taken the golden ram, the symbol of power held by the ruler of the kingdom.

Civil war breaks out, and Thyestes is defeated. After his defeat, he is exiled by Atreus.

Exile is not sufficient punishment for Thyestes. The fierce hatred of Atreus, burning over his brother's crimes and his own misfortune in the loss of his wife, demands greater revenge. A tyrant who believes that death is a comfort to his subjects, Atreus broods over fierce and final vengeance upon his younger brother. He feels that no act of revenge can be a crime when committed against a man who has worked against him as his brother has. Moreover, he feels that he, as a king, can do as he wishes; private virtues are not for rulers. When an attendant suggests that Atreus put Thyestes to the sword, Atreus says that death is only an end. He wants Thyestes to suffer torture. Atreus finally decides on a punishment: He will feed Thyestes' own children to him at a banquet.

Atreus takes the first step toward accomplishing his revenge. He sends his own sons, Agamemnon and Menelaus, as emissaries of goodwill to Thyestes and asks the exile, through them, to return to a place of honor at his brother's side. Fearing that if his sons know his plans they might lack the discretion they need to act as friendly ambassadors, he does not tell them the part they are playing in his scheme of revenge.

Thyestes, trusting the king, returns to Argos with his three sons, including one named Tantalus, for his great-grandfather of famous memory. When Thyestes looks again on familiar landscapes, he feels a sense of foreboding. His footsteps falter, and his sons note his apparent unwillingness to return. The offer of peace and half the kingdom seems to Thyestes unlike his brother's earlier hatred and fury. He fears that there has been too much hate and bloodshed between them for real peace to be possible. His sons, silencing his doubts, lead him on to the court of Atreus. Atreus, seeing his brother and nephews in his power, apparently unmindful of the revenge plotted against them, is overjoyed and acts as such, concealing his hatred and welcoming them to the kingdom once again.

Atreus announces a great feast to celebrate his brother's homecoming. Then, taking the three sons of Thyestes aside, he leads them to a grove behind the palace, where he slays them with all the ceremony of a sacrifice to the gods. The first he stabs in the neck, the second he decapitates, and the third he kills with a blade thrust through the body. Thyestes' sons, knowing that appeals are useless, suffer death in silence. Atreus draws off their blood and prepares the carcasses like so much beef. The limbs he quarters and places upon spits to roast; the bodies he hacks into small pieces and places in pots to boil.

The fire seems reluctant to burn as an accomplice to his deed, but Atreus stands by and acts as cook until the ghastly banquet is ready. As he cooks, the sky grows dark, and an unnatural night settles across the face of the earth. When at last the banquet is prepared, Atreus feels that he is the equal of the gods themselves.

The feast begins. After the banquet has progressed to the point that the guests are glutted by all they have eaten, Atreus prepares for Thyestes a drink of wine and blood drained from the bodies of Thyestes' sons. All the while, a premonition of evil has hung like a cloud in the back of Thyestes' mind. Try as he might, he cannot be happy and enjoy the feast, for vague

terrors strike at his heart. When Atreus gives him the cup of blood and wine, he cannot lift it to drink at first, and when he does try to drink, the wine seems to roll around the brim of the cup rather than pass through his lips. Filled with sudden fears, Thyestes demands that Atreus produce his sons.

Atreus leaves and then shortly returns with the heads of Thyestes' three sons on a platter. Thyestes, chilled with horror at the sight, asks where the bodies are. He fears that Atreus has refused them honorable burial and has left them for the dogs to eat. Atreus tells Thyestes that he has eaten his own children. Then Thyestes realizes why unnatural night has darkened the skies. Still Atreus is not satisfied. He is disappointed that he did not plan to force Thyestes to drink some of his children's blood while they were yet alive.

The king brags of what he has done and describes how he himself committed the murders and spitted the meat before the fires. Atreus, enjoying his revenge, can never believe that the greatest weight on Thyestes' mind is his regret that he did not think of such revenge and cause Atreus to eat his own children.

Critical Evaluation:

The most fiendish revenge play in the history of drama, this gruesome story of a banquet at which the father partakes of his own children is a landmark in dramatic history. *Thyestes* is the model for many revenge plays that appeared in the sixteenth and seventeenth centuries in English drama. Seneca the Younger was not the first ancient author to make use of the Thyestes legend, but his version of the story had the most direct influence on the tragedians of the Renaissance. Versions of the story by Sophocles, Euripides, Ennius, and Accius have not survived the years; scholars do not even have enough information about the other ancient versions of the drama to compare the treatments by those authors with that of Seneca. As a result of both Seneca's influence on Renaissance playwrights and historical accident, Seneca's name is foremost in discussions of the type of play he wrote, called the revenge tragedy or the tragedy of blood.

Seneca's *Thyestes* is spectacle rather than true drama. Whereas genuine tragedy arises from character conflicts or internal divisions within characters, spectacle relies on sensational events carried out by characters who exist merely for the sake of the events and who have no actual existence of their own. This is certainly the case with every character in Thyestes. Each exists simply to point up the horror of Atreus's revenge on his brother, Thyestes.

Another important point of difference between true drama and spectacle lies in the use of language. The speech of authentic tragedy approximates, in a formal way, the devices of normal conversation to reveal passions. The language of spectacle, however, being florid and highly artificial, tends toward bombast. Spectacle operates by set pieces, rhetorical essays that develop simple ideas at great length, by tedious and lush descriptive passages, and by moralizing epigrams. Seneca uses all three, and the result is that his characters speak in a highly unnatural way. Instead of communicating, they attitudinize, talking largely to the audience or soliloquizing.

This characteristic of Senecan drama has led many scholars to believe that Seneca wrote his plays for private recitation rather than for public performance. This idea gives no reason for assuming they were not produced. Spectacle, rhetorical overindulgence, and horrors were all part of public entertainment under the Roman emperors Caligula, Claudius, and Nero, who ruled during Seneca's maturity. Scholars know for a fact that Seneca's tragedies were staged in the Elizabethan period and that they had immense influence on the dramas of Thomas Kyd, Christopher Marlowe, William Shakespeare, John Webster, and others.

Thyestes derives from Greek legend and is based on an incident that occurred in the tragic family descended from Tantalus. Seneca's treatment of the myth has some interest in its own right, but it also serves to illuminate his own biography. He handles the figure of Thyestes rather sympathetically, making him the victim of Atreus's lunatic lust for revenge. Seneca plays down the fact that Thyestes seduced Atreus's wife, stole his symbol of power, and caused a civil war. When Thyestes appears onstage, he assumes the role of the Stoic hero, determined to bear whatever fate has in store for him, and he frankly prefers the hardships of exile to the pomp of power that Atreus has treacherously extended to him. Exile has tempered his character.

It is worth noting that Seneca underwent eight years of exile on Corsica after he was accused of an intrigue with Emperor Claudius's niece, Julia. The parallel is striking, but it extends even further. Like Thyestes, Seneca was recalled from exile with the promise of power. He was to tutor and guide Nero in the art of statesmanship. When Nero became emperor in 54 C.E., Seneca was able to exercise some control over him for the first five years of his reign, but then Nero began acting on his own, and Seneca retired from public life. *Thyestes* is Seneca's personal testament on the instability of power and the helplessness of those who incur the wrath of an absolute and maniacal ruler. The only solution Seneca finds in this play is the same one he found in life—to bear one's misfortune with Stoic dignity. Eventually Nero ordered Seneca to commit suicide as punishment for his part in an alleged conspiracy. Seneca met his death bravely.

Through the murky rhetoric of *Thyestes* two important themes emerge: the nature of kingship and the necessity of maintaining a Stoic endurance in the face of a murderous, disintegrating cosmos. The appearance of Tantalus and Megaera the Fury at the beginning of the play is not accidental. Tantalus served his son, Pelops, as food for the gods, and as part of his eternal torment he must not only witness the kin murders of his descendants but also abet them. Presumably, he inspires the idea of cannibalistic revenge in Atreus's mind, but Atreus carries his scheme out with gloating satisfaction. Atreus is an unrelieved monster, raging with paranoid pride.

Against him Seneca sets the idea of kingship founded on morality and restraint. The aphoristic conversation between Atreus and the attendant in act 2, scene 1, is a debate on whether kings should serve the people or the people should be utterly subservient to the king. In the first case morality is the main law; in the second, the will of the tyrant. The point is made that morality creates a stable kingdom, whereas tyranny is supremely unstable. Later, the chorus says that true kingship lies in self-control, not in wealth, power, or pomp.

Unfortunately, these observations make no impression whatever on Atreus, who is intent on proving his godlike power over human life, much like the Roman emperors Seneca knew. In striving to become like a god in his pride, Atreus becomes loathsomely bestial. Seneca constantly generalizes from the concrete situation of Atreus and Thyestes to the universe. When kings are corrupt, society is corrupted, and the rot extends throughout the cosmos. Nature mirrors human conditions in Seneca: The fire hesitates to broil the slain sons of Thyestes; an unnatural night falls upon the banquet. The play is full of hyperbole about the disintegrating universe, rendered in purple poetry. Against this profusion of rhetoric stand the pithy epigrams, like a Stoic element trying to bear up tightly against the frenetic declamations. The Stoic attitude can never prevail in a world full of crime, but it can enable one to endure great stress with courage. Seneca, in *Thyestes*, embodies the shame of Rome and his own valor in a style eminently suited to his subject.

"Critical Evaluation" by James Weigel, Jr.

Further Reading

Davis, P. J. *Seneca: "Thyestes."* London: Duckworth, 2003. Argues that the savage violence and human bestiality in the drama are Seneca's response to Nero's tyrannical rule. Discusses the drama's context, performance history, themes, reception, and impact on subsequent playwrights, including William Shakespeare and Ben Jonson.

Griffin, Miriam T. *Seneca: A Philosopher in Politics*. Rev. ed. Oxford, England: Clarendon Press, 1991. Definitive study of Seneca evaluates the man who had so many lofty ideals and whose life was so full of less-than-lofty facts. Dramatizes the problem of public service in a corrupt state.

Harrison, George W. M., ed. *Seneca in Performance*. London: Duckworth, with the Classical Press of Wales, 2000. Collection of twelve essays examines ancient and more modern productions of Seneca's plays. Includes discussions of the acting, characterization, and physical settings of his drama.

Henry, Denis, and Elisabeth Henry. *The Mask of Power: Seneca's Tragedies and Imperial Power*. Chicago: Bolchazy-Carducci, 1985. Examines Seneca's tragedies and places them within the context of the times in which they were written.

Holland, Francis. *Seneca*. 1920. Reprint. New York: Books for Libraries Press, 1969. Thorough, readable, and still authoritative biography explores the events of Seneca's life.

Littlewood, C. A. J. "Images of a Flawed Technical Genesis: *Thyestes*." In *Self-Representation and Illusion in Senecan Tragedy*. New York: Oxford University Press, 2004. Chapter devoted to *Thyestes* is part of a larger examination of Seneca's dramas as works of Neronian literature. Traces the influence of Greek and other Roman literature, and of Stoic philosophy, on Seneca's plays.

Motto, Anna Lydia. *Seneca*. New York: Twayne, 1973. Offers a clear presentation of Seneca's life and work. A good starting place.

Rosenmeyer, Thomas G. *Senecan Drama and Stoic Cosmology*. Berkeley: University of California Press, 1989. Argues that one must study Seneca's Stoicism, as expressed in his philosophical works, to understand his plays fully.

Schiesaro, Alessandro. *The Passions in Play: "Thyestes" and the Dynamics of Senecan Drama*. New York: Cambridge University Press, 2003. Uses modern critical approaches and psychoanalytic theory to analyze the play. Points out common themes and stylistic characteristics in *Thyestes* and other Senecan tragedies.

Sutton, Dana Ferrin. *Seneca on the Stage*. New York: Brill, 1986. Argues against the long-held idea that Seneca's tragedies were written to be read rather than performed. Supports this claim by showing how the playwright included stage directions in the form of clues in the characters' speeches.

Thyrsis
A Monody, to Commemorate the Author's Friend, Arthur Hugh Clough, Who Died at Florence, 1861

Author: Matthew Arnold (1822-1888)
First published: 1866
Type of work: Poetry

Thyrsis is a pastoral elegy written by Matthew Arnold to honor his friend Arthur Hugh Clough, who died in 1861. It is one of the greatest elegies in English literature, equal in stature to John Milton's "Lycidas" (1638) and Percy Bysshe Shelley's *Adonais* (1821). *Thyrsis* is 240 lines long, divided into twenty-four ten-line stanzas. All the lines are in iambic pentameter, except the sixth line of each stanza, which is in iambic trimeter. The rhyme scheme for each stanza is *abcbcadeed*. The stanzaic form of *Thyrsis* is thus a slight variation on the ten-line stanza John Keats developed for his odes ("Ode to a Nightingale," 1820, for example). Keats's slightly different rhyme scheme is *ababcdecde*. The lines of Keats's stanzas are in iambic pentameter, except for the eighth line, which like Arnold's tenth is in iambic trimeter.

Clough and Arnold attended both Rugby School and Oxford University together, but while Clough was acknowledged as a bright star, Arnold was perceived as a dandy. It was not until his first volume of poems was published—a collection with a definite elegiac tone—that Arnold's friends and family realized his extravagant style of dress was a mask he wore to face the alien Victorian world outside academia and to cope with having a famous father, the headmaster of Rugby. Clough did not do as well at Balliol College, Oxford, as at Rugby. He graduated with second-class honors, telling Arnold's father that he had failed. However, he was awarded a fellowship at Oriel College. Several years later, he resigned his position, partly over reservations about accepting the Thirty-nine Articles of the Anglican Church.

Clough traveled on the Continent for a time, returned to England, and accepted a rather dull position in the Education Office. Clough died in Florence in 1861. Arnold began his elegy shortly thereafter, but he did not complete and publish it until 1866.

Thyrsis is set in the countryside around Oxford, where Arnold and Clough had taken many walks in happier days. An elm tree on a hill came to have meaning for both of them. They agreed that, as long as the tree stood, the "Scholar-Gypsy" was still alive, roaming the Cumnor Hills near Oxford. The Scholar-Gypsy was a legendary seventeenth century Oxford scholar who, growing impatient with the learning of his day, was said to have left Oxford to live among the gypsies and learn their lore. According to the story, the scholar said that he would return once he had mastered the gypsies' lore, but he never did, and he passed out of time into the realm of myth: From the seventeenth century into the nineteenth century, people would claim to have seen the Scholar-Gypsy wandering about the region. He would appear without warning and just as suddenly be gone. He became for Arnold and Clough a symbol of a sacred search for an unattainable truth. Arnold wrote a poem relating this tale around 1851, and it forms a kind of companion piece to *Thyrsis*. Arnold felt that Clough, in leaving Oxford, had impatiently abandoned the search for truth, and this feeling came to have a dominant effect on his elegy to Clough.

In 1861, Arnold returned to Oxford and the countryside he had known so well to think through Clough's life and their relationship. This visit became the basis for the walking tour described in *Thyrsis*. The first four stanzas of the poem provide the setting. The poet is alarmed at the changes that have occurred since he was an undergraduate. He has come to see if the "signal elm" is still there, which would mean that the Scholar-Gypsy still continues his search for truth. However, all the changes he witnesses cast that possibility in doubt. Stanza 4 explicitly introduces the pastoral element in the poem: There is talk of shepherds and the "pipes" Arnold and Clough used to play. At the stanza's end, Thyrsis's name is introduced, but not Thyrsis himself. He has gone away.

Stanza 5 makes explicit that this elegy will have more to do with criticizing the deceased than with honoring his memory. Thyrsis was impatient in this pastoral setting. A shadow grew over his head as he thought of "Some life of men unblest." Outside the pastoral world, his piping took on a tone of anger and protest, and he could not wait out the "storms." As a result, now, "he is dead." In stanzas 6 through 8, Thyrsis's actions are compared to those of the cuckoo who foolishly fled, not waiting for the return of spring. In one of Vergil's eclogues, the shepherd Thyrsis loses a singing contest to Corydon. Arnold's Thyrsis met a different fate: "Time, not Corydon, hath conquered thee!"

In a traditional pastoral elegy such as "Lycidas," one of the conventions is to ask why the gods did not prevent the loss of the deceased. The poet, instead of questioning the gods, blames Thyrsis himself for his demise. Stanzas 9 and 10 draw heavily on pastoral tradition. The poet recalls that in Sicily during the classical period, when a shepherd died, one of his fellows would take his pipe and play a "ditty sad," so that in Hades Proserpine would see to it that the dead shepherd was returned to life. Unfortunately, the poet laments, Proserpine was never in England, so calling on her to return Thyrsis would be "in vain."

What follows, in stanzas 11 through 15, is the lament that the poet is now forced to sing since Thyrsis will not be returning. Though his words will be "wind-dispersed and vain," the poet still must have his time to grieve and find "our tree-topped hill." However, he is thwarted by the thought that perhaps he does not have the power to create his song, though he knows the countryside well. In stanzas 11 through 13, the speaker's poetic power is revealed through his detailed and lyrical description of the flowers that grow in the region and of people he knew who worked along the Thames. He laments, however, "They all are gone, and thou art gone as well!" Time has taken them all, and now the night, "In ever-nearing circle weaves her shade" about him in his dejection. Almost swooning, the poet feels the night's "slowly chilling breath invade/ The cheek grown thin, the brown hair sprent with grey." His footsteps and his heart slow; hope is not as quick to recover; and the challenges he must face seem stronger and larger than ever, for "long the way appears, which seemed so short/ To the less practiced eye of sanguine youth." Because the world's problems seem insurmountable now, "near and real" becomes the "charm" of night's "repose."

Fortunately, in stanzas 16 and 17, the silence is interrupted by a group of hunters riding back to town, "jovial and talking." Their presence draws the poet away from his darkening thoughts, and at last he is able to see the signal elm. Though he cannot get to it this night, it is definitely there. The quest is still alive. From stanza 18 to the end of the poem, the poet attempts to recoup the image of Thyrsis whom he has up until now disparaged. Though Thyrsis is not buried in England, he lies in a "boon southern country" (Italy) and is "now in happier air." He rests where he can hear the ancient pastoral shepherds sing their ditties. The poet, though, is in England, where the Scholar-Gypsy still seeks the truth, having outlived Thyrsis.

The poet's final consolation is a reversal of what he says earlier. According to the final lines, after Thyrsis left the

Cumnor Hills, he was still following the Scholar-Gypsy's vision, but in the world outside he was forced to become a wanderer. What does it matter now, the poet asks, if Thyrsis's poetry turned from pastoral to angry protest? He had the vision, but now he is gone. The poet, admitting that he rarely visits Oxford any more, asks that Thyrsis's voice will be there for him in the future as a reminder of the quest: "Why faintest thou? I wandered till I died./ Roam on!" After all, the tree is still there and the Scholar-Gypsy still wanders the hills.

George F. Horneker

Further Reading

Allott, Miriam, ed. *The Poems of Matthew Arnold.* 2d ed. London: Longman, 1979. This edition of Arnold's poems is in the respected Longman Annotated English Poets series. It contains an accurate edition of the poems, with variants, and is fully annotated.

Connolly, Patrick Carill. *Matthew Arnold and "Thyrsis."* London: Greenwich Exchange, 2004. This study of Arnold's intellectual and poetic development includes a full analysis of *Thyrsis*, with an emphasis on its mythic, literary, and philosophical backgrounds.

Culler, A. Dwight. *Imaginative Reason: The Poetry of Matthew Arnold.* New Haven, Conn.: Yale University Press, 1966. A study focused on Arnold's poetic development, Culler's book contains close readings of the major poems and their relations to Arnold's life and to each other. The treatment of *Thyrsis* combines a full analysis of the poem with a discussion of its relation to the friendship of Arnold and Clough.

Hamilton, Ian. *A Gift Imprisoned: The Poetic Life of Matthew Arnold.* New York: Basic Books, 1999. Hamilton's critical biography attempts to show how a young poet lost his battle over the years against the social and literary critic he later became. The discussion of *Thyrsis* examines the friendship and rivalry between the two friends. In the poem, Arnold seems determined to prove that Clough may have failed, but he did not.

Honan, Park. *Matthew Arnold: A Life.* New York: McGraw-Hill, 1981. The first fully detailed biography of Arnold. Covers his childhood, his school years, his travels in Europe, his marriage, and his later life. Deals with Arnold's literary and social ideas and provides detailed portraits of some of the key literary figures of the day whom Arnold knew. The friendship with Clough is fully covered and explicitly related to *Thyrsis*.

Roper, Alan. *Arnold's Poetic Landscapes.* Baltimore: Johns Hopkins University Press, 1969. Examines the way the landscape functions in Arnold's poetry. In the chapter "The Cumnor Hills," Roper details the landscape that is the background for both *Thyrsis* and "The Scholar-Gypsy." He thoroughly presents both the similarities the two poems share and their significant differences.

Tiger at the Gates

Author: Jean Giraudoux (1882-1944)
First produced: La Guerre de Troie n'aura pas lieu, 1935; first published, 1935 (English translation, 1955)
Type of work: Drama
Type of plot: Mythic
Time of plot: Trojan War era
Locale: Troy

Principal characters:
HECTOR, the Trojan hero and a man of goodwill, the son of Priam
ANDROMACHE, his wife
PARIS, his younger brother
HELEN, beloved of Paris
PRIAM, king of Troy
HECUBA, his wife
CASSANDRA, the daughter of Hecuba and Priam, whose predictions, always true, are never heeded
ULYSSES, the Greek ambassador
AJAX, a Greek warrior
DEMOKOS, a poet
A MATHEMATICIAN
TROJAN PATRIOTS
TROILUS, a Trojan youth

The Story:

Hector's wife, Andromache, joyfully tells Cassandra, his sister, that there will be no Trojan war because Hector, as soon as he comes home, will assuage the feelings of the Greek ambassador. Cassandra, true to her reputation, claims that she knows destiny will provoke a war. She knows this not as a result of her ability to prophesy but because she always takes into account the stupidity and the folly of men. Since Andromache cannot understand destiny in the abstract, Cassandra offers her the picture of a tiger prowling at the palace gates and waiting for the moment to enter.

Hector, home from war, is delighted to hear that Andromache will soon bear a child that she expects to be a son. Andromache fears that the child will have the father's love of battle, but Hector assures her that he and his soldiers return this time disabused of their former ideas of war as a glorious adventure. They are all ready for peace, and he intends to get from his father, Priam, permission to shut the gates of war permanently.

Cassandra brings the younger brother Paris to Hector to give his version of his abduction of Helen. He tells Hector that he happened to sail past Helen while she was bathing in the sea. While Menelaus was busy removing a crab from his toe, Paris casually took her into his ship and sailed on. He likes her because she—unlike Trojan women, who tend to cling—seems always to be at a distance, even while in his arms. This is not the first time Hector took Paris away from a woman, but Paris resists obeying Hector, promising instead to obey Priam, their father.

Cassandra realizes that destiny is already lurking like a tiger because Priam would rather give up his own daughters than let Helen leave the kingdom. Priam and all the other old men in Troy spend their days admiring Helen as she takes a daily walk around Troy, to be greeted by toothless shouts whenever she appears. To the old men Helen is a symbol; she is Beauty. Hecuba, Priam's wife, suggests that the old men would do well to find a symbol among their own Trojan women, and not a blond one such as Helen, because blond beauty fades fast. The men, however, are intoxicated by Helen. The poet gets his inspiration from her. The mathematician finds all measurements related to Helen—the weight of her footfall, the length of her arm, the range of her look. They argue the justification of war for Helen's sake. Paris says he is willing to let Hector handle the situation because Paris feels humiliated to be cast as the seducer, a role that he does not want to play within his large family. He brings Helen to Hector.

While Hector speaks with her in his attempt to avoid conflict between the Greeks and the Trojans, he finds that Helen is completely unpredictable. It is hard to tell whether she has any sense at all or whether she depends completely on fate to do what it would with her. She agrees to leave Troy because she can no longer see Paris plainly. She claims also that she never saw Menelaus plainly and supposes she often walked over him without realizing it. She warns that she sees a battle raging, a city burning, and a figure in the dust that she recognizes as Paris only by his ring. She admits that the things she sees do not always come to pass, and she promises to leave Troy with Ulysses. Left with Cassandra, Helen begs Cassandra to make Peace appear but cannot see the figure until Peace paints herself outrageously. By that time Trojan patriots are shouting that the gods are insulted and have struck down the temple. Peace becomes sick. As Hector prepares to shut the gates of war, Helen turns her blandishments on the young Troilus, who refuses to kiss her. She promises him that her chance will come later. The poet, the mathematician, and others prepare for war by agreeing on a war song and by discussing the usefulness to soldiers of insulting epithets.

In spite of the opposition of the poet, the mathematician, and the others, and in spite of dire forebodings by a traveling expert on the rights of nations, Hector makes an ironic Oration for the Dead and closes the gates of war just before the Greeks come ashore. Ajax is the first Greek to reach Hector. He approaches in an insulting manner and strikes Hector on the cheek, but Hector refuses to rise to the insult. When the poet calls shame on him, Hector strikes the poet, who vows revenge. Ajax, amused, admiring Hector's courage, swears he will not fight against Hector.

Hector promises Ajax and Ulysses that he will give Helen back to them. To Ulysses' questioning as to whether there is cause for reprisals, Paris's crew tells of Paris and Helen's apparent delight in each other on the trip to Troy. Ulysses senses that war is inevitable but, talking to Hector as soldier to soldier, he regrets it, particularly since the cause of it is Helen, a woman of shallow brain, hard heart, and narrow understanding. Still trying to defy destiny, Ulysses attempts to get back to his ship. Ajax is a little slower and is caught by the mob when the poet, struck down by Hector, calls for war and cries out that Ajax mortally wounded him. The crowd kills Ajax as the gates of war open to show Helen kissing Troilus.

Critical Evaluation:

Beginning with the production of his first play, *Siegfried*, in 1928, Jean Giraudoux dominated the French stage for the next three decades. *Tiger at the Gates*, with its witty, sparkling debate, illustrates the reason for his prominence. It presents a subject long of great importance to Giraudoux, not only as a writer but also as a career diplomat: the relationship between France and Germany. In an early novel, later made into his first play, *Siegfried*, he dramatized the necessity to reconcile the German and French peoples after World War I.

Unfortunately by 1935, when Giraudoux wrote *Tiger at the Gates*, such a reconciliation seemed increasingly impossible. As does Hector, he felt that it was vital to make every effort toward peace to avoid the devastation and destruction of another war. This play, like most of his dramas, centers on one main issue: in this case, war versus peace. Despite its single-mindedness in theme, the play operates on many different levels. As he frequently did, Giraudoux turned to the classics for his plot. It is first a retelling of the *Iliad* (c. 750 B.C.E.; English translation, 1611). It is also a comment on the political situation in Europe in 1935. Finally, it is an abstract philosophical discussion about the nature of war and peace and about those qualities in human nature that direct persons and nations to choose one or the other.

Unlike the *Iliad*, which opens in the tenth year of the Trojan War, *Tiger at the Gates* is set immediately before the war begins. The conflict in the play is not the war but the issues that cause war. The prowar and antiwar positions are clearly and quickly drawn. On one side is Andromache and most of the female characters in the play. The women are antiwar. They would not lose their husbands and sons for the sake of Helen. Hecuba vividly describes her vision of war: "When the baboon is up in a tree with its hind end facing us, there is the face of war exactly: scarlet, scaley, glazed, framed in a clotted, filthy wig." Hector, just returned from war, joins their side. He experienced the bloodshed of war. The opposing view is presented by the poet, Demokos. He finds war an inspiration. King Priam adds that only by fighting death are men truly alive; even Hector reluctantly agrees with them on this count. Demokos insists that war must be flattered and adored in order to gain its goodwill. To ensure this, he plans a war song comparing the face of war with the face of Helen. He is joined by all the old men of Troy who would sacrifice anything for another glimpse of Helen.

The play uses minimal action to develop this debate; it is primarily composed of dialogues between the representatives of war and of peace. While Hecuba and Demokos may provide the most vivid definitions of war, each new dialogue brings another insight into the causes of war or the reasons for peace. In the opening scene, Andromache, who is pregnant, insists there must be peace to protect her husband and unborn child. Her faith in Hector's ability to solve the problem is countered by Cassandra's warning that Troy is too complacent; its arrogant self-confidence antagonizes fate. The crowd of Trojans is willing to accept war for national

honor. If Ulysses returns Helen, swearing her virtue is intact, this will be a terrible blow to Trojan masculinity.

Ulysses, while agreeing to work for peace, presents the economic reasons why wars occur. The cunning diplomat shocks Hector when he tells him of the dangerous message Troy's golden fields and temples send to the Greeks trapped on rockier soil. When Hector insists Greece will be ashamed forever for using Helen as a pretext to take Troy's wealth, Ulysses simply responds that the Greeks will lie, denying all responsibility. However, he is willing to try peace because Andromache's eyelashes dance like Penelope's do. Peace and the future of Troy may rest on as slender a thread as an eyelash.

Giraudoux's use of language has often been compared to Impressionism in art. Although his staging may be static, his words dance. *Tiger at the Gates* is filled with brilliant images, such as Helen's description of men as being "as pleasant as soap and a sponge and water." He often makes serious points with witty epigrams. Ulysses notes that "one of the privileges of the great is to witness catastrophe from a terrace."

Giraudoux blends this wit with irony throughout the play, building toward the tragedy. The French title, *La Guerre de Troie n'aura pas lieu* (the Trojan War will not take place), provides an example. While Hector and Andromache work desperately to ensure peace, the audience and almost all of the other characters know that these two will fail. For readers familiar with the *Iliad*, many lines have extra poignancy. When Hector asks Helen to visualize the body of Paris dragged behind a chariot, this portends Hector's death in the *Iliad*. In an ironic twist Giraudoux never planned, it also foreshadows the Nazi occupation of Paris. The final irony is that it is the peace-loving Hector himself who causes the war with one foolish act of violence. Alive, Demokos can never match Hector's influence, but in killing Demokos, Hector destroys Troy. Cassandra predicts this in the first scene. When she shouts that the tiger arrives, Hector enters. Critics debate whether the play implies that war is inevitable. Peace, however, nearly wins in the play; Giraudoux believed that everyone must work unceasingly toward peace. In the end, Hector proves able to control everyone except himself.

"Critical Evaluation" by Mary Mahony

Further Reading

Anspach, Mark R. "Trying to Stop the Trojan War: Prophesying Violence, Seeing Peace." *Western Humanities Review* 62, no. 3 (Fall, 2008): 86-97. Using the Trojan War as an example, Anspach examines the predictability of violence, noting that prophecies of violence and war tend to be self-fulfilling. Includes an analysis of *Tiger at the Gates*, Giraudoux's commentary on the Trojan War.

Clurman, Harold. Introduction to *Judith, Tiger at the Gates, Duel of Angels*. Vol. 1 in *Jean Giraudoux: Plays*, translated by Christopher Fry. New York: Oxford University Press, 1963. Provides a clear overview of French theatrical history, placing Giraudoux as a transitional figure between classic and modern French drama. Includes discussion of Fry's translation.

Cohen, Robert. *Giraudoux: Three Faces of Destiny*. Chicago: University of Chicago Press, 1968. Examines Giraudoux's background and the intellectual system underlying his writing. Uses charts and diagrams to analyze the dialogue between war and peace, emphasizing language, imagery, and use of symbol.

Jacobs, Gabriel. "'Cassandre à la propagande': *La Guerre de Troie* and the Phoney War." In *Aspects of Twentieth-Century Theatre in French*, edited by Michael Cardy and Derek Connon. New York: Peter Lang, 2000. Jacobs's analysis of the play is included in this collection of essays about twentieth century French drama.

Korzeniowska, Victoria B. *"La Guerre de Troie n'aura pas lieu."* London: Grant & Cutler, 2003. A concise introductory overview and survey of the drama's critical reception.

_____. *The Heroine as Social Redeemer in the Plays of Jean Giraudoux*. New York: Peter Lang, 2001. Focuses on Giraudoux's female characters, describing the gender politics in his plays and his heroine's roles in both the domestic and public spheres. Places his heroines within the context of the French idealization of women during the interwar years.

Lemaitre, George. *Jean Giraudoux: The Writer and His Work*. New York: Frederick Ungar, 1971. Clear general introduction to Giraudoux. Discusses the play's portrayal of the dualism of human nature and the play's relation to Greek tragedy.

Mankin, Paul A. *Precious Irony: The Theatre of Jean Giraudoux*. The Hague, the Netherlands: Mouton, 1971. Provides a clear, precise literary explanation of the different types of irony, including examples from *Tiger at the Gates*. Presents Cassandra, Helen, and Ulysses as outsiders who function as the chorus, helping to emphasize the importance of fate.

Reilly, John R. *Jean Giraudoux*. Boston: Twayne, 1978. Divides Giraudoux's work into three periods, with *Tiger at the Gates* signaling the entrance into the final period, in which fate appears as a hostile presence and the themes of war, love, and politics predominate. Includes biographical details and an annotated bibliography.

The Time Machine
An Invention

Author: H. G. Wells (1866-1946)
First published: 1895
Type of work: Novel
Type of plot: Fantasy
Time of plot: Late nineteenth century
Locale: England

Principal characters:
THE TIME TRAVELER
WEENA, a woman the Time Traveler meets in the future

The Story:

One evening after dinner with friends at his home, the Time Traveler leads the discussion to the subject of the relationship between time and space. It is his theory that time is a fourth dimension, and he believes that this concept can be proved. To the astonishment of his guests, he exhibits a small model of his Time Machine and declares that it can travel backward or forward in time. One of the guests is invited to touch a lever on the model, and, to the amazement of all, the machine disappears. The Time Traveler explains that the instrument is no longer visible because it is traveling into the past at such great speed that it is below the threshold of visibility.

The following week, the Time Traveler is not at home to greet his dinner guests when they arrive, but he has left word that they are to proceed without him. Everyone is at the table when their host comes in, dirty from head to toe, limping, and with a cut on his chin. After he has changed his clothes and dined, he tells his friends this story of his day's adventures.

In the morning, he seats himself in his Time Machine and activates the mechanism. As he reels through space in the machine, he sees days shoot past him like minutes, and the rapid alternation of light and darkness as the sun rises and sets hurts the Time Traveler's eyes. Falling from his machine when he brakes too suddenly, he finds himself on the side of a hill. In the misty light, he can see the figure of a winged sphinx on a bronze pedestal. As the sun comes out, the Time Traveler sees enormous buildings on the slope. Some figures are coming toward him, one of them a little man about four feet tall. Regaining his confidence, the Time Traveler waits to meet this citizen of the future.

Soon a group of these creatures gather around the voyager. Without a common language, he and his new acquaintances have to communicate with signs. After they have examined the Time Machine, from which the traveler has had the presence of mind to remove the levers, one of them asks him through gestures if he has come from the sun.

The creatures lead the Time Traveler to one of the large buildings. There he is seated on a cushion and given fruit to eat. Everyone in this civilization is a vegetarian, as animals have become extinct. When the Time Traveler has eaten, he unsuccessfully tries to learn his new friends' language. These people, who call themselves the Eloi, are not able to concentrate for long without tiring.

Free to wander about, the Time Traveler climbs a hill, and from the crest he sees the ruins of an enormous granite structure. Looking at some of the Eloi who are following him, he realizes that they all wear similar garb and have the same soft, rounded figures. Children can be distinguished from adults only by their size. The Time Traveler realizes that he is seeing the sunset of humanity. In the society of the future, there is no need for physical or mental strength. The world is secure and at peace, and the strong of body and mind would only feel frustrated.

As he looks around to find a place to sleep, he discovers that his Time Machine has disappeared. He tries to wake the people in the building in which he had dined, but he succeeds only in frightening them. At last, he goes back to the lawn where his machine had been and there, greatly worried about his plight, falls asleep.

The next morning, he manages to trace the path the Time Machine made when it was dragged away from where he had left it. The path leads to the huge pedestal base of the sphinx, but the bronze doors in the pedestal are closed. The Time Traveler tries to communicate to some of the Eloi that he wishes to open the doors, but they answer him with looks of insult and reproach. He attempts to hammer in the doors with a stone, but he soon must stop from weariness.

Weena, a young woman the Time Traveler has rescued from drowning, becomes his friend and guide. On the fourth morning, while he is exploring one of the ruins, he sees eyes staring at him from the dark. Curious, he follows a small, apelike figure to a well-like opening, down which the strange figure retreats. The Time Traveler theorizes that this creature is also a descendant of humanity, a member of a subterranean species that works belowground to support the dwellers in the upper world.

Convinced that the subterranean dwellers—which, the Time Traveler learns, are called the Morlocks—are responsible for the disappearance of his Time Machine, and hoping to learn more about them, he climbs down into one of the wells. At its bottom, he discovers a tunnel that leads into a cavern, where he sees a table set with a joint of meat. The Morlocks are carnivorous. The Time Traveler is also able to distinguish some enormous machinery in the cavern.

The next day, the Time Traveler and Weena visit a green porcelain museum containing animal skeletons, books, and machinery. Because they have walked a long distance to reach the museum, the Time Traveler plans that he and Weena will sleep in the woods that night after building fire to keep the dark-loving Morlocks away. When he sees three crouching figures in the brush, however, he changes his mind and decides that he and Weena will be safer on a hill beyond the forest. He starts a fire in the woods to keep the Morlocks at a distance.

When they reach the hill, the Time Traveler starts another fire before he and Weena fall asleep. When he awakes, the fire has gone out, his matches are missing, and Weena has vanished. The fire he had started earlier is still burning, and while he has been sleeping, it has set the forest on fire. Between thirty and forty Morlocks perish in that blaze while the Time Traveler watches.

When daylight returns, the Time Traveler retraces his steps to the sphinx. He sleeps all day, and then in the evening he prepares to pry open the doors in the pedestal with a lever he found in the porcelain museum. He finds the doors open, however, and his machine is in plain view. He climbs into it and, as a group of Morlocks spring at him, takes off again through time.

The Time Traveler's encounter with the Morlocks and the Eloi had taken place in the year 802,701. On his next journey, he moves through millions of years toward that time when the earth will cease rotating. He lands on a deserted beach, empty except for a flying animal, which looks like a huge white butterfly, and some crablike monsters. He travels on, finally halting thirty million years after the time he left his laboratory. In that distant age, the sun is dying. It is bitter cold, and it begins to snow. All around is deathly stillness. Horrified, the Time Traveler starts back toward his present.

As he tells his story in the evening, his guests grow skeptical. In fact, the Time Traveler himself has to visit his laboratory to make sure his machine exists. The next day, however, all doubts cease, for one of his friends watches him depart in his vehicle. It is this friend who writes the story of the Time Traveler's experiences three years later. The Time Traveler has not reappeared during that time, and his friends speculate on what kind of mishap has made him a lost wanderer in space and time.

Critical Evaluation:

H. G. Wells's first novel, *The Time Machine*, enjoyed instant popularity and rescued its author from obscurity and poverty. *The Time Machine* was the first of Wells's classic "scientific romances," which, along with some of Jules Verne's "extraordinary voyages," provided the foundation of the modern genre of science fiction. Previous visions of the future in fiction had been exactly that: dreams, which were implicitly banished to the realms of mere possibility when the dreamers awoke. Wells wanted to solidify his vision of the future, to give it the status of reality, so he invented a machine capable of traveling through time.

Such a machine was thought impossible, as Wells knew perfectly well, but he also knew that its invocation would provide his story with a new kind of plausibility and narrative force. To this end, he was careful to provide a clever "explanation" of the manner of the machine's functioning, invoking the idea of duration as a fourth dimension comparable to the three dimensions of space.

Although Wells once referred to his story, in a moment of excitement, as "the new Delphic Oracle," *The Time Machine* ought not to be seen as an attempt at prophecy. In its later phases the story does try to come to grips with what Wells considered to be inevitable—the extinction of humanity when the sun runs out of fuel—but in its more interesting phase it is best construed as a warning. Wells extrapolated to a horrific extreme the division of English society into a leisured aristocracy and a mass of downtrodden workers, the lovely but effete Eloi having degenerated to the point where they have become the prey of the monstrous Morlocks.

Readers can now see, after the passage of a mere hundred years, that no part of this vision will come to pass. What seemed inevitable to Wells no longer seems inevitable to readers today. Modern scientists know that the sun gives out heat by virtue of nuclear fusion, not because it is on fire, and that it will not burn out nearly as quickly as Wells imagined. The seemingly fundamental division of society that Wells magnified in his vision of eight hundred thousand years has already been rendered less than fundamental.

It should be noted, however, that *The Time Machine* seems rather old-fashioned to modern readers to some extent because of the novel's own success, both as a literary landmark and as an example of how to imagine the future. Wells's time machine became the archetype of a vast range of imaginary machines the uses of which have opened limitless imaginative territories. Unlike the far more modest machines employed by Verne's voyagers, which were careful extrapolations of existing vehicles, the time machines, spaceships, and dimensional gateways of genre science fiction became devices that can transport characters into an infinite number of hypothetical worlds. While they do so, they stoutly maintain the pretense that these are no mere fairylands; rather, they are worlds that could and actually might exist.

The fact that this is a pretense—in other words, a fiction—does not detract from the seriousness that the best of such imaginative work can devote to the description of hypothetical worlds. It is at least arguable that one of the most encouraging lessons learned from this serious contemplation is that the extinction of humanity need not be inevitable, even though the sun is not eternal, because the universe beyond the solar system is not inaccessible in any absolute sense.

Wells's depiction of the society of the Eloi and the Morlocks was not the unprecedented leap that his invention of a time machine was. That kind of extrapolation of the familiar to caricaturish extremes has long been a standard method of satire. *The Time Machine*, however, is not a satire; its rhetoric is not calculated to make the extreme seem absurd but rather to make it seem tragic. The novel is science fiction instead of satire, so the argument of this parable is not simply that the divisions in society that it exaggerates are foolish or unjust; rather, it is that they possess an internal dynamic that is ominous and dangerous.

It is difficult for twenty-first century readers to appreciate how unusual it was for a nineteenth century writer to see the world as something essentially in flux, subject to constant and irresistible change. Previously, the great majority of people, and virtually all literary discourse, had seen change in terms of a lurching movement from one potentially stable state to another. Before Wells, before the scientific discoveries regarding evolution, relativity, and uncertainty, and before the popularization of ideas that follow from such discoveries, the world was seen as a place that might achieve stability. Utopian dreaming was a matter of choosing some static ideal that would obviate the need for further change. Wells's early scientific romances constitute a brilliant exploration of the vast spectrum of possibilities implicit in a world where change is constant and insistent.

If readers accept that the future is as yet unmade, and that it is unforeseeable in principle as well as in practice (or, to put it another way, that God plays dice with the universe), then the real function of futuristic visions is to warn of the pitfalls that might lie ahead for humanity. The best of such books are not those that depict changes that come true, even in part, but those that help to prevent the futures they foresee. For this reason, *The Time Machine* should be regarded not as a dated work whose image of the future is obsolete but as an authentic triumph of the nineteenth century imagination.

"Critical Evaluation" by Brian Stableford

Further Reading

Bergonzi, Bernard, ed. *H. G. Wells: A Collection of Critical Essays*. Englewood Cliffs, N.J.: Prentice Hall, 1976. Includes two readable and informative critical essays on *The Time Machine*, one addressing the novel as myth, the other examining it as prophecy.

Costa, Richard Hauer. *H. G. Wells*. Rev. ed. Boston: Twayne, 1985. Provides a sympathetic survey of Wells's career and influence, with an emphasis on his major novels in the context of literary traditions before and after Wells. Includes discussion of *The Time Machine*.

Hammond, J. R. *H. G. Wells and Rebecca West*. New York: St. Martin's Press, 1991. Associates *The Time Machine* with Wells's scientific understanding of the human species and his interest in a fourth dimension. Includes illustrations.

_____. *H. G. Wells and the Modern Novel*. New York: St. Martin's Press, 1988. Argues that Wells is an overlooked, innovative writer. Describes *The Time Machine* as a "watershed in the coming of modernism."

_____. *H. G. Wells's "The Time Machine": A Reference Guide*. Westport, Conn.: Praeger, 2004. Provides an introductory overview of the novel, discussing its textual history, historical and intellectual contexts, themes, literary style, and critical reception. Includes a plot summary and bibliographic essay.

_____. *A Preface to H. G. Wells*. New York: Longman, 2001. Examines Wells's life, his cultural background, important people and places in his life, and his literary reputation. Offers critical commentary on his works, with special attention to *The Time Machine*.

McLean, Steven, ed. *H. G. Wells: Interdisciplinary Essays*. Newcastle, England: Cambridge Scholars, 2008. Collection of essays presents analyses of individual novels and discussions of general characteristics of Wells's work, including the depiction of the natural environment in his futuristic vision. "What the Traveller Saw: Evolution, Romance, and Time Travel," by Sylvia A. Pamboukian, examines *The Time Machine*.

Parrinder, Patrick. *Shadows of the Future: H. G. Wells, Science Fiction, and Prophecy*. Liverpool, England: Liverpool University Press, 1995. Describes how Wells assumed the role of a prophet in *The Time Machine* and some of his other works. Relates this role to Wells's belief in a modern scientific outlook and to the genre of science fiction and utopian writing.

Wagar, W. Warren. *H. G. Wells: Traversing Time*. Middletown, Conn.: Wesleyan University Press, 2004. Analyzes all of Wells's work, focusing on its preoccupation with the unfolding of public time and the history and future of humankind. Demonstrates how Wells's writings remain relevant in the twenty-first century.

The Time of Your Life

Author: William Saroyan (1908-1981)
First produced: 1939; first published, 1939
Type of work: Drama
Type of plot: Psychological realism
Time of plot: 1939
Locale: New York City

Principal characters:
JOE, a young loafer with money and a good heart
TOM, his admirer, disciple, errand boy, and stooge
KITTY DUVAL, a young woman who falls in love with Tom
NICK, owner of Nick's Pacific Street Saloon, Restaurant, and Entertainment Palace
ARAB, an Eastern philosopher and harmonica player
KIT CARSON, an old Indian fighter
MCCARTHY, an intelligent and well-read longshoreman
KRUPP, a policeman who hates his job
HARRY, a dancer whose efforts at comedy do not make people laugh
WESLEY, a talented black pianist
DUDLEY, a young man in love
ELSIE, a nurse, the woman Dudley loves
BLICK, the head of the vice squad in search of streetwalkers at Nick's restaurant

The Story:

At Nick's restaurant and saloon, a motley crew of individuals from all walks of life gathers to pass the time, converse, philosophize, seek employment, and fall in love. These colorful, odd characters all have their histories and idiosyncrasies. Joe, for example, sends Tom on errands to purchase toys—not for a child but for Kitty Duval, a woman who cannot stop crying. Tom grumbles that Joe is always making him do things that end up embarrassing Tom. When Kitty, a streetwalker who formerly performed in burlesque theaters, enters the saloon, Joe buys her a bottle of champagne as if she were royalty—a gesture that makes Nick exclaim that Joe is crazy.

Other strange characters who enter the saloon are Dudley and Harry. Dudley constantly telephones Elsie Mandelspiegel from the restaurant and begs her to marry him; Harry is determined to relieve the world's sorrow by becoming a famous comedian. Another newcomer who arrives on the scene is Wesley, a gifted black musician with a flair for the piano. Nick, the owner of the saloon, is dumbfounded at the eccentric people who frequent his establishment. Joe makes Nick stock expensive champagne although the place is a dive. Kitty expects the others to treat her like an elegant lady.

Comedians and musicians beg to make their debuts at Nick's obscure old honky-tonk. The customers and visitors feel a sense of belonging and experience a sense of home. At Nick's saloon, they feel secure and protected from the hostile outside world. There they encounter the acceptance, friendship, generosity, and goodwill that they do not get from the world at large, a world that appears to them mad and absurd.

A threat to Nick's restaurant, and thus to the modicum of happiness it brings to its customers, comes from Blick, a police detective who suspects the saloon to be a den of prostitution. Nick warns Blick that his moral earnestness for reform is doomed, saying that Blick is "out to change the world from something bad to something worse." In defending his saloon, home and haven to a motley crew of humanity, Nick notes that although the restaurant is in the worst part of town, no one has been murdered, robbed, or cheated on his premises in five years. He refers to his honky-tonk as a humble, honest place, saying that his patrons "bring whatever they've got with them and they say what they must say."

Several of the characters who frequent Nick's saloon explain their thoughts and feelings. Krupp, a disillusioned policeman, is disturbed by the corruption and avarice of the world, the inability of humans to enjoy the simple pleasures of life, such as taking a walk. He comments: "Here we are in this wonderful world, full of all the wonderful things—here we are—all of us, and look at us. . . . We've got everything, but we always feel lousy and dissatisfied just the same." Arab summarizes his whole life as an existence of unending hard work: "Work. All my life, work." He finds life inscrutable and incomprehensible, repeating, "No foundation. All the way down the line." McCarthy, a longshoreman, also has much to say. He believes that each person has a choice to be a "heel" or a "worker," confessing, "I haven't the heart to be a heel, so I'm a worker." A great reader, McCarthy expounds on poetry, William Shakespeare, communism, and writers. He theorizes that all maniacs once aspired to be writers. Failing in their great ambitions, they changed their careers "by becoming important heels." Those who cannot be Shakespeare become senators or communists.

Although these diverse characters come from varied backgrounds and have different ambitions and philosophies, it is clear that a common humanity unites them. At the core of these individuals dwells a simple goodness that transcends the political and economic problems of the world and the chaos of life. Tom expresses his heartfelt gratitude for Joe's kindness, especially the brotherly care Joe gave him in a time of illness: "You made me eat all that chicken soup three years ago when I was sick and hungry." Joe fondly remembers the magic of toys that cured the tearful times of his childhood; thus he urges Tom to take toys to the distressed Kitty in the hope that they will again effect a miraculous cure. Joe also encourages a romance between Kitty and Tom, hiring an automobile for them in which they ride to the ocean, where they watch the sunset and delight in the pleasure of dancing. This time, out of the generous goodness in his heart, Joe goes on an errand for Tom.

The customers in the saloon protect Kitty when she is pursued by Blick and his vice squad. When Blick interrogates her and learns that she was an actress who performed in burlesque theaters, Blick demands that she mount the stage and dance for his pleasure, shouting for her to take off her clothes. Joe, Wesley, Nick, and others rise to her defense and honor her dignity. Their essential decency transforms the lowly saloon into a noble, chivalrous institution. Although Nick warns Blick that he had better leave, the detective is determined to make his arrest and destroy the humane world of the saloon. Suddenly, there is a gunshot. Kit Carson, who tells tall tales in the saloon (for example, he once fought a six-footer with an iron claw for a hand), has fired a gun. The teller of tall tales who boasts about herding cattle on a bicycle states the simple truth: "Killed a man once, in San Francisco, name of Glick or Blick or something." Kit Carson's crazy statement and wild shooting make more sense than a policeman's arrest of a lawbreaker.

Critical Evaluation:

In the preface to *The Time of Your Life*, William Saroyan describes the play's characters as "people you are likely to see any day in almost any part of America, certainly at least in certain kinds of American places." Saroyan announces the theme of the play in his introduction: "In the time of your life, live—so that in that wondrous time you shall not add to the misery and sorrow of the world, but shall smile to the infinite delight and mystery of it." Critics acknowledge the play as Saroyan's appeal to the virtues of compassion and kindness as the antidote to the cruelty of the world and the problems of life.

When it first appeared, *The Time of Your Life* was such an innovative play that critics labeled it experimental, recognizing that it did not conform to the conventions of modern drama, specifically, the theater of ideas, as popularized by Henrik Ibsen and George Bernard Shaw. Saroyan avoids didactic polemics in the play, which was written shortly before the entry of the United States into World War II. Rather, *The Time of Your Life* evokes an atmosphere of respect for the forgotten and the unfortunate. This aspect of Saroyan's play left him vulnerable to charges of vagueness and of failure to think things through. Critics in the intervening years have nevertheless appreciated the well-constructed three-act play.

Some critics have objected to the work's naïve sentiment and simplistic optimism about brotherhood and the goodwill found in common humanity. They have pointed out the unlikelihood of the actual existence of a saloon that is a home for so many different kinds of people: Nick the Italian, Wesley the black man, Arab the Eastern Philosopher, the Assyrian Harry, and others. Other critics have praised Saroyan's play for avoiding the dramatic conventions of American theater of the time it was written. Critics have noted as refreshing Saroyan's ability to write a gentle, optimistic play at a time when Adolf Hitler was in ascendancy and World War II was beginning. In the play, Saroyan uses comedy to deflate the heavy-handed tactics of the determined police detective Blick. Some critics have observed that Saroyan's depiction of the camaraderie and kinship that can develop among outsiders and people of different racial backgrounds is more than an example of wishful thinking—rather, it shows wisdom.

Saroyan wrote of his indebtedness to George Bernard Shaw, and many parallels have been drawn between *The Time of Your Life* and Shaw's dramas. Saroyan stated that "Shaw . . . is the tonic of the Christian peoples of the world. He is health, wisdom, and comedy, and that's what I am too." The characters in Saroyan's play who epitomize health, wisdom, and comedy are Dudley Bostwick, who overcomes the obstacles of his formal learning to realize that what he wants is a woman; the Greek American newsboy, who sings "When Irish Eyes Are Smiling" to the delight of the Italian American Nick; and Krupp the policeman, whose wry commentary on human nature reveals his comic, sardonic understanding. In addition, Wesley's love of piano playing, Arab's harmonica playing, and Willie's enjoyment of the pinball machine all convey the simple exuberance of being alive, a feeling that the tragic outlook suppresses.

The Time of Your Life received the New York Drama Critics' Circle Award and the Pulitzer Prize. Saroyan, however, refused the Pulitzer because he thought that moneyed interests should not influence art or corrupt the integrity of the writer's work.

Mitchell Kalpakgian

Further Reading

Balakian, Nona. *The World of William Saroyan*. Lewisburg, Pa.: Bucknell University Press, 1998. Traces Saroyan's evolution from "ethnic" writer to master of the short story and master of playwriting. Balakian, who knew Saroyan personally in his last years, views it as her mission to resurrect his reputation and restore him to recognition as one of the finest American writers of the twentieth century.

Calonne, David Stephen. *William Saroyan: My Real Work Is Being*. Chapel Hill: University of North Carolina Press, 1983. Provides a thorough account of Saroyan's life and work. Chapter 5 interprets *The Time of Your Life* as a play that views life as chaotic and miraculous and relates the play to vaudeville and to the Theater of the Absurd.

Fletcher, Anne. "Precious Time: An Alternative Reading of Thornton Wilder's *Our Town* and William Saroyan's *The Time of Your Life* as Pre-World War II Dramas." In *Theatre, War, and Propaganda: 1930-2005*, edited by M. Scott Phillips. Tuscaloosa: Southeastern Theatre Conference and the University of Alabama Press, 2005. Describes how the two plays defined and perpetuated national mythologies about the impending world war.

Floan, Howard R. *William Saroyan*. Boston: Twayne, 1966. Discusses the four main periods and genres of Saroyan's writing: short fiction, drama, the novel, and autobiography. Chapter 4 interprets *The Time of Your Life* as a microcosm of America's romanticized past and its harsh economic reality.

Foster, Edward Halsey. *William Saroyan: A Study of the Short Fiction*. New York: Twayne 1991. Valuable work combines literary criticism of Saroyan's short fiction, discussion of his autobiographical writings, and an interview with Saroyan.

Hamalian, Leo, ed. *William Saroyan: The Man and the Writer Remembered*. London: Associated University Presses, 1987. Collection of essays and memoirs by critics, friends, and admirers of Saroyan covers various topics, including Saroyan's experiences in an orphanage and the literary influences that shaped his art.

Keyishian, Harry, ed. *Critical Essays on William Saroyan*. New York: G. K. Hall, 1995. Includes a review of *The Time of Your Life* and essays discussing Saroyan and the "theatre of transformation," the character of Joe as a "Christ-type," and absurdity in the play.

Lee, Lawrence, and Barry Gifford. *Saroyan: A Biography*. New York: Harper & Row, 1984. Biography draws on many interviews with Saroyan's friends, acquaintances, and family members. Provides the background and details of the 1948 film version of *The Time of Your Life*.

Leggett, John. *A Daring Young Man*. New York: Alfred A. Knopf, 2003. Biographical work relies heavily on Saroyan's journals to produce a sustained glimpse of the author that is neither admiring nor forgiving.

The Time Quartet

Author: Madeleine L'Engle (Madeleine Camp, 1918-2007)
First published: 1989; includes *A Wrinkle in Time*, 1962; *A Wind in the Door*, 1973; *A Swiftly Tilting Planet*, 1978; *Many Waters*, 1986
Type of work: Young adult fiction
Type of plot: Science fiction
Time of plot: Twentieth century
Locale: Connecticut

Principal characters:
MARGARET "MEG" MURRY, the protagonist
CHARLES WALLACE MURRY, her brother
SANDY MURRY and DENNYS MURRY, Meg and Charles Wallace's twin brothers
KATE MURRY, their mother
ALEX MURRY, their father
CALVIN O'KEEFE, Meg and Charles Wallace's friend
THE MRS. W's, helpful strangers

The Story:

Meg Murry, Charles Wallace Murry, and Calvin O'Keefe are in a battle of good versus evil. The three find themselves aided by mysterious beings, who are helping them in a battle against the forces of evil, represented by the Black Thing and the Echthroi. Meg and Charles Wallace's twin brothers, Sandy and Dennys, soon have an adventure of their own.

A Wrinkle in Time. A stranger named Mrs. Whatsit, one of the Mrs. W's—Mrs. Whatsit, Mrs. Which, and Mrs. Who—arrives one night at the Murrys' door during a storm and informs Kate Murry, a microbiologist, of the existence of something called a tesseract, a method for moving through time and space. As so happened, scientist Alex Murry—husband and father—had been experimenting with time travel for the government when he had disappeared some time ago.

Meg is fourteen years old and considers herself to be awkward, gangly, and an ugly duckling. She has a bad temper that is made worse when the inhabitants of her small town talk about her father or about her five-year-old brother, Charles Wallace, who exhibits some savant abilities. Charles Wallace had not started to speak until he was four years old, but when he did first talk, he did so in complete sentences. Most of the townspeople do not know this, as he rarely speaks in public.

When Meg and Charles Wallace visit Mrs. Whatsit the next day, they are met by Calvin, a brilliant teenager who goes to school with Meg. He is extremely popular at school, but he is neglected by his own family.

The Mrs. W's inform the Murry family and Calvin a few days later that it is time for them to rescue Alex Murry. They tesser to the planet where the Happy Medium lives, and she shows them the Black Thing, which has taken over planets and shadows Earth, held back only by brilliant artists, scientists, philosophers, and religious leaders like Leonardo da Vinci, William Shakespeare, and Jesus of Nazareth. Then they are shown Camazotz, a planet overtaken by the Black Thing. Camazotz is where Alex is being held captive.

The Mrs. W's transport the searchers to Camazotz but cannot go farther, sending Meg, Charles Wallace, and Calvin into the town. Mrs. Whatsit reminds them of their strengths and weaknesses, and Mrs. Who gives Meg her glasses.

The four searchers go into town, where they see everyone behaving exactly the same. All the children are bouncing balls the same way at the same time. A boy delivering newspapers sends the searchers to Central Intelligence to confront IT, a great pulsating brain that refers to itself as the Happiest Sadist. Everything on Camazotz resonates to the pulsating IT.

Charles Wallace's pride is his downfall, as he believes he can resist IT when IT approaches in the form of a man with red eyes. Charles Wallace lets the man with red eyes into his mind, giving it the opportunity to take him over. IT uses Charles Wallace to lead Meg and Calvin to Alex, who is imprisoned in a glass column. Meg uses Mrs. Who's glasses to enter the column and pull her father out. They are then led to IT, which nearly takes over Meg. Alex tessers Calvin, Meg, and himself from Camazotz, but he has to leave his son Charles Wallace behind in the grasp of IT.

The three tesser through the Black Thing, which freezes Meg from head to toe. Creatures on the planet, including one she refers to as Aunt Beast, care for her. The creatures also are fighting the Black Thing, but they cannot help to rescue Charles Wallace from IT. Meg, angry with her father for leaving her brother behind, cannot figure out what to do until the Mrs. W's arrive.

Meg alone must face IT again, and only with the knowledge supplied by Mrs. Which, giving Meg something that IT does not have. Meg soon realizes that IT can feel hate but not love. Meg's love for her brother frees him from IT's grasp. Charles Wallace runs to Meg, and they find themselves suddenly whisked away, landing in a vegetable garden with Alex and Calvin as well, for a joyous reunion with the Murrys, who had stayed behind.

A Wind in the Door. One year later, Charles Wallace is ill with a disease that is taking his breath, and Meg finds herself angry with the elementary-school principal, Mr. Jenkins, for not adequately protecting her brother. She remains angry despite learning about the good deeds of Mr. Jenkins. Kate Murry, a microbiologist, has discovered that something is wrong within Charles Wallace's mitochondria—parts of his cells.

Charles Wallace tells Meg that he had seen a dragon in the garden; the dragon turns out to be a cherubim, Proginoskes, nicknamed Progo. Meg, Calvin, Charles Wallace, and Progo have all been called to the class of Teacher Blajeny, who tells them of the machinations of the Echthroi, who are trying to destroy the universe by unnaming, or Xing, things. Meg, like Progo, can combat the Echthroi by naming things. Meg's first test is her confrontation with Mr. Jenkins and two Echthroi, who are masquerading as the principal. She has to name Mr. Jenkins, which she can only do through finding something to love in the unlovable man. Naming him will keep him from being Xed by the Echthroi.

As Charles Wallace gets sicker, Meg learns that the Echthroi are attempting to destroy Charles Wallace by keeping the fictional farandolae in his mitochondria from taking root. Meg, Calvin, Mr. Jenkins, and Progo are then miniaturized and transported into one of Charles Wallace's cells to convince an immature farandola named Sporos to take root.

Meg, Calvin, and Charles Wallace learn during this time to communicate telepathically in a manner referred to as kything. As the Echthroi create vacuums in creation, Progo sacrifices himself to fill the void—Xing himself as Sporos takes root—and saving Charles Wallace from death.

A Swiftly Tilting Planet. Charles Wallace is a teenager, and Calvin has earned a doctorate. Meg and Calvin have married, and Meg is expecting her first child. The Murry family has come together on Thanksgiving—without Calvin, who is at a conference in England, but with his antisocial and unlovable mother, Mrs. O'Keefe. Alex Murry receives a call from the White House, informing him that the South American dictator, Mad Dog Branzillo, is threatening nuclear war.

Out of this news, Mrs. O'Keefe begins to speak, teaching Charles Wallace what she knows as Patrick's Rune. When Charles Wallace goes out to the garden and recites the rune, he calls the unicorn Gaudior to him. Gaudior explains that Charles Wallace will have to go "within" people in different times and places, using his kything ability, to change might-have-beens. Meg is able to follow Charles Wallace through her own kything ability.

Meg and Charles Wallace discover that the Echthroi are trying to turn the might-have-beens into something evil, an act that would result in nuclear war. Charles Wallace must turn the might-have-beens toward something good. He inhabits different people in the same family line along the way, a Welsh prince who crossed the Atlantic before Columbus, a Puritan settler, a Civil War-era writer, and Mrs. O'Keefe's brother Chuck, correcting the might-have-beens toward the side of good by reconciling differences between the line of Madoc and the line of Gwydyr. Alex again receives a call from the White House, and this time the news is that the dictator, Branzillo, has become peaceful; Mrs. O'Keefe passes away, so only Charles Wallace and Meg know the truth about what has happened.

Many Waters. Sandy and Dennys Murry, the twin brothers of Meg and Charles Wallace, are on an adventure of their own. The more practical twins are the so-called normal ones of the Murry family. In the middle of a Connecticut winter, they interfere with an experiment their parents are running and wish for someplace warm, with few people.

Soon, the twins are transported to biblical times, before the Flood. They meet Japheth, who takes them to the nearest oasis. Riding unicorns, the boys take the journey but suffer heat exhaustion. The unicorns are "solid" only when the literal-minded twins believe in them, so when Dennys passes out from heat exhaustion, the unicorn he is riding disappears. Dennys is dumped into a trash heap and later found by the family of Noah; they tend to him. Sandy, in the meantime, is now living with Japheth, Noah's son, and Lamech, Noah's father.

Over the course of one year, the boys meet two kinds of angels—seraphim, who are heavenly creatures able to transform into animals, and nephilim, who marry human women and are considered fallen angels, also able to transform into animals. Both boys fall in love with Noah's daughter Yalith. Dennys helps Noah and Lamech reconcile. Both twins help build the Ark, though they worry about the coming Flood and worry that neither Yalith nor they will be on the Ark. Yalith is swept up to Heaven, and the seraphim lead the unicorn-riding boys back home to their own time and place. They have gained a new appreciation for the adventures of Meg and Charles Wallace. According to Teacher Blajeny, the twins will later become Teachers as well, instructing others to fight the greater war against evil and darkness.

Critical Evaluation:

One of the overarching themes of *The Time Quartet*, a work of young adult fiction, is the battle of good versus evil. Madeleine L'Engle demonstrates this battle on both the macrocosmic (outer space) and the microcosmic (cellular) levels, and then back through time. This is a battle that is informed by L'Engle's Christian beliefs; the battle between good and evil is infused with divine implications. Characters often quote or paraphrase biblical verses and imply that those fighting the Dark Thing and the Echthroi are doing so at the behest of a divine power. This is especially true in *A Wrinkle in Time*, *A Wind in the Door*, and *A Swiftly Tilting Planet*. *Many Waters* also deals with Christian beliefs, but does so in a more direct way, simply inserting the twins into a biblical tale.

Another overarching theme in the quartet is the power of love. L'Engle describes love as a sort of weapon for goodness. In *A Wrinkle in Time*, Meg has love, but IT lacks it; her deliberate choice to love the essentially unlovable Mr. Jenkins helps her to save the life of her brother Charles Wallace in *A Wind in the Door*. Charles Wallace is able to influence the might-have-beens in *A Swiftly Tilting Planet* because of his ability to influence the decisions of those he "inhabits." The title *Many Waters* is based upon a verse from the Song of Solomon: "Many waters cannot quench love."

L'Engle also relies heavily upon symbolism in her novels, especially with the names for her more fantastical creatures. In *Many Waters*, she uses names from Jewish and Christian legends to name the seraphim and nephilim that inhabit Noah's prediluvian times. Even the name of the dog, Ananda, who joins the Murry family in *A Swiftly Tilting Planet* has meaning that is discussed in the context of the story.

L'Engle also creates strong female characters. Kate Murry is an educated woman, with a doctorate in microbiology, and she is able to hold her family together in the absence of her husband. Mrs. Whatsit, Mrs. Who, and Mrs. Which are the agents of good who serve as mentors to Meg, Charles Wallace, and Calvin. In *A Wind in the Door*, a Dr. Louise helps Kate diagnose Charles Wallace's mitochondrial disease, providing strength to both Kate and Charles Wallace. Meg herself is a strong character, but she also deals with the common problems of a young woman in her teenage years, such as worrying about the way she looks and about her seeming lack of friends. She also worries about more important concerns, such as her missing father and her ill little brother.

Fantastic creatures, most specifically unicorns, appear as well. Unicorns are the creatures that transport Sandy and Dennys before the Flood in *Many Waters* and that assist them in returning home. The twins' ability to touch a unicorn is dependent on their sexual purity, however. This also falls into line with the Christian morals that L'Engle subtly emphasizes in her writing. The unicorn Gaudior also helps Charles Wallace move through time in *A Swiftly Tilting Planet*. Other supernatural creatures, notably angels—cherubim, seraphim, and nephilim—make appearances that also are intimately connected to L'Engle's Christian background.

Christianity plays a major role in every part of *The Time Quartet*. L'Engle, a member of the Episcopal Church, uses her faith to form the cornerstone of her plots. Though Jesus Christ is referred to as only a combatant in the greater war, L'Engle refers to a greater "He," often in the context of quotations from the Bible, to suggest a greater God waging the war on the side of good. She also relies on Jewish legends and mysticism. The rune she attributes to Saint Patrick in *A Swiftly Tilting Planet* is based on a medieval prayer as well as an Episcopal hymn, also known as "St. Patrick's Breastplate." Her descriptions of Noah's time in *Many Waters* shows common humans experiencing God in a personal way, though in the other novels of the quartet, characters experience simply the goodness that L'Engle believes God represents.

Emily Carroll Shearer

Further Reading

Hammond, Wayne G. "Seraphim, Cherubim, and Virtual Unicorns: Order and Being in Madeleine L'Engle's *Time Quartet*." *Mythlore* 20, no. 4 (Winter, 1995): 41-45. A brief discussion of the angels and other creatures of *The Time Quartet* and their use as both tangible and virtual beings in a differently ordered universe.

L'Engle, Madeleine. "An Interview with Madeleine L'Engle." Interview by James S. Jacobs and Jay Fox. *Literature and Belief* 7 (1987): 1-16. In this revealing interview, Jacobs and Fox discuss writing and personal beliefs with L'Engle and how she interweaves the two in her creations.

_____. *The Rock That Is Higher: Story as Truth*. Colorado Springs, Colo.: Shaw Books, 2002. L'Engle explains her own methods of telling stories and discusses how she brings Christian thought into her fantastic tales.

Oziewicz, Marek. *One Earth, One People: The Mythopoeic Fantasy of Ursula K. Le Guin, Lloyd Alexander, Madeleine L'Engle, and Orson Scott Card*. Jefferson, N.C.: McFarland, 2008. Argues that the works of fantasy authors, including L'Engle, have socially transformative powers, giving expression to a worldview based on the supernatural or spiritual.

Rosenberg, Aaron. *Madeleine L'Engle*. New York: Rosen Press, 2005. Rosenberg gives a good overview of L'Engle's life and writings, including the work and ideas that went into the novels of *The Time Quartet*.

Schneebaum, Katherine. "Finding a Happy Medium: The Design for Womanhood in *A Wrinkle in Time*." *The Lion and the Unicorn: A Critical Journal of Children's Literature* 14, no. 2 (December, 1990): 30-36. Schneebaum discusses the female characters and models in *A Wrinkle in Time* and how L'Engle strikes a balance between traditional and nontraditional female roles.

Shaw, Luci, ed. *The Swiftly Tilting Worlds of Madeleine L'Engle: Essays in Her Honor*. Colorado Springs, Colo.: Shaw Books, 2000. The essays in this book cover a variety of issues in L'Engle's books. Published in honor of her eightieth birthday.

Timon of Athens

Author: William Shakespeare (1564-1616)
First produced: c. 1607-1608; first published, 1623
Type of work: Drama
Type of plot: Tragedy
Time of plot: Fourth century B.C.E.
Locale: Athens and the nearby seacoast

Principal characters:
TIMON, an Athenian nobleman
FLAVIUS, his faithful steward
APEMANTUS, his philosophical and candid friend
ALCIBIADES, an Athenian general

The Story:

The Athens house of Timon, a wealthy lord of the city, is the scene of much coming and going. Poets, artists, artisans, merchants, politicians, and well-wishers in general seek the friendship and favors of a man whose generosity knows no bounds. While waiting to speak to Timon, a poet discloses his vision to an artist: Timon is depicted as the darling of Dame Fortune, and his friends and acquaintances spare no effort in admiring his favored position. The vision continues; Fortune turns and Timon tumbles into penury, his friends doing nothing to comfort him.

Timon joins the crowd of suitors in his reception chamber. When a messenger reports that Ventidius, his friend, was jailed for a debt, Timon promises to pay the debt and to support Ventidius until he becomes solvent again. An old man complains that one of Timon's servants stole the heart of his only daughter. Timon promises to match the girl's dowry with an equal sum. Then he receives the poet and the painter and the jeweler graciously, accepting their shameless flattery. Apemantus, a crudely candid friend, declares broadly that these flatterers and seekers of bounty are a pack of knaves. Alcibiades, a great military leader, comes with a troop of followers to dine with Timon. As all prepare to feast at Timon's bounteous table, Apemantus curses them roundly.

A great feast is served to the accompaniment of music. Ventidius, freed from jail, offers to repay the money spent on his behalf, but Timon declares that friendship will not allow him to accept Ventidius's money. When Apemantus warns Timon that men will readily slay the man whose food and drink they consume, Timon expresses his gratitude at having so many friends with which to share his generosity. He wishes, however, that he might be poorer so that these good friends might know the joy of sharing their largess with him. Timon's eyes fill with tears, so overcome is he by the sentiments of friendship, as a group of costumed Athenian ladies present lavish gifts to him from men of wealth. Timon then presents rich gifts to his departing friends. Flavius, his steward, observes that his master's infinite generosity almost emptied his coffers. Timon tells Apemantus that he will give him gifts, too, if he will cease railing at these felicities of friendship.

Before long Timon is reduced to insolvency and to near beggary. A senator to whom he owes a great sum of money sends his servant to collect. Other servants of Timon's creditors also gather in front of his house. Timon, who never gave Flavius a chance to explain that he, Timon, has no more money, asks the steward the reason for the crowd outside. When Flavius tells him the truth, Timon orders the sale of all of his lands. Flavius discloses that his lands are already sold or mortgaged. Refusing to share Flavius's alarm, Timon declares that he now has a chance to test his friends. He directs his servants to borrow money from Lucius, Lucullus, and Sempronius; the servants are then to go to the senators and borrow more. Flavius discloses that he already tried without success to borrow from these sources. Timon makes excuses for them, however, and suggests that the servants try Ventidius, who recently came into a large fortune.

The servant who goes to Lucullus is told that times are difficult and that Timon's friendship alone is not sufficient security for a loan. When Lucullus offers the servant a bribe to say that he was unable to see Lucullus, the horrified servant throws down the bribe money and departs in disgust. Lucius claims that he, needing money, hoped to borrow from Timon. A third servant goes to Sempronius. Upon learning that Lucullus, Lucius, and even Ventidius deny Timon loans, Sempronius pretends to be hurt that Timon did not send to him first, and he also refuses.

As Timon continues to be importuned by his creditors' servants, he goes out in a rage and bids them cut out of his heart what he owes their masters. Still enraged, he directs Flavius to invite all of his creditors to a feast. Alcibiades, meanwhile, pleads in the senate for the remission of the death sentence on a veteran soldier who committed murder. The senators, deaf to arguments that the man killed in self-defense, persist in their decision. When Alcibiades continues to plea, the senators sentence him, on pain of death, to be banished from Athens.

At Timon's house, tables are arranged as though for a great banquet. Apologizing profusely for being unable to honor his requests for money, Timon's guests appear at his house expecting a lavish banquet. When Timon bids them eat, however, they discover that the covered dishes are filled only with warm water. Timon then curses them, throws the water in their faces, and drives them out of his house.

Now a confirmed misanthrope, Timon leaves Athens. For the moment he focuses all of his hatred on Athens and its citizens, but he predicts that his curses will eventually encompass all humanity. Flavius, meanwhile, announces to his fellow servants that their service in Timon's house comes to an end. After sharing what little money he has with his fellows, Flavius pockets his remaining money and declares his intentions of seeking out his old master.

One day Timon, who is living in a cave near the seashore, digs for roots and discovers gold. As he is cursing the earth for producing this root of all evil, Alcibiades appears, accompanied by his two mistresses. Timon curses the three and tells them to leave him. When Alcibiades discloses that he is on his way to besiege Athens, Timon gives him gold and wishes him every success. He also gives the two women gold, after exhorting them to infect the minds and bodies of all men with whom they come in contact. When Alcibiades and his troops march away, Timon continues to dig roots for his dinner.

Apemantus appears to rail at Timon for going to the opposite extreme from that which caused his downfall. He declares that wild nature is as cruel as men, that Timon, therefore, would do well to return to Athens and flatter men who are still favored by fortune. After Apemantus leaves, a band of cutthroats, having heard that Timon possesses a great store of gold, goes to the cave. When they tell Timon that they are destitute, he throws gold at them and orders them to practice their malign art in Athens. So bitter are Timon's words that they leave him, determined to abandon all violence.

Flavius, finding the cave, weeps at the pitiful state to which his master has fallen. Timon, at first rude to his faithful steward, is almost overcome by Flavius's tears. He gives Flavius gold, wishes him well, and admonishes him to succor only dogs.

After reports of Timon's newly found wealth reaches Athens, the poet and the painter go to his cave. Timon greets them sarcastically, praises them for their honesty, and gives them gold to use in destroying other sycophants and flatterers. Flavius returns, accompanied by two senators, who apologize for the great wrongs done to Timon and offer to lend

him any amount of money he might desire. They also promise him command of the Athenian forces in the struggle against Alcibiades; Timon, however, curses both Athens and Alcibiades. His prescription to the Athenians for ending their troubles is that they come to the shore and hang themselves on a tree near his cave. When he retreats into his cave, the senators, knowing their mission fruitless, return to Athens.

In Athens, the senators beg Alcibiades to spare the city because its importance transcends the petty griefs of an Alcibiades or a Timon. Alcibiades agrees to spare Athens only on the condition that those who offended Timon and him should be punished. As the city gates open to the besiegers, a messenger reports that Timon is dead. Alcibiades reads Timon's epitaph, copied by the messenger. It reaffirms Timon's hatred of humanity and expresses his desire that no one pause at his grave.

Critical Evaluation:

One of William Shakespeare's most neglected plays, *Timon of Athens* has only rarely been performed. The reasons for its unpopularity include its strongly bitter tone and its lack of an emotionally satisfying ending. Further, the play has many elements that are uncharacteristic of Shakespeare's work: clashing themes, irregular verse passages, confused character names, and a shallow central character. For these reasons, scholars long suspected that *Timon of Athens* was a collaborative effort. Modern scholars, however, hold that the play's problems arose because Shakespeare wrote it himself, but never polished it because he left it unfinished. His reasons for abandoning the play are not known, but inferences may be drawn from the play's curious nature.

Timon of Athens defies easy classification. As a bleak tale about a once kind man who dies a bitter misanthrope, the play appears to be a tragedy. What leads to Timon's financial ruin and ultimate destruction is, ironically, the generosity that permits him to rise high in Athenian society. His sudden and deep fall points up the fateful vulnerability of human existence—a nearly universal theme in tragedy. Despite this tragic motif, the play has many characteristics of traditional comedy. Because of its unusual blend of tragedy and comedy, it is now regarded not only as a curious experiment but also as an important transitional phase in Shakespeare's mature writing career.

There are several reasons for regarding *Timon of Athens* as a comedy. The play's savage depiction of greed, hypocrisy, and duplicity among the Athenian nobility constitutes the kind of social satire that became a dramatic staple in seventeenth century England. The immorality of the ruling classes was itself one of Shakespeare's own favorite themes.

The theme is demonstrated here in the actions of the governors of Athens, who ruin Timon by cruelly calling in his debts. When they banish Alcibiades merely for seeking clemency for a deserving veteran, they expose Athens to the threat of his sacking the city. Later, after Timon is known again to have wealth, they hypocritically try to recruit him to defend the city against Alcibiades.

The play's satire is expressed most powerfully through the voice of Timon's friend Apemantus, who frequently utters crude jokes about wealthy men and government leaders. The sheer viciousness of his remarks is in itself often comical. Even more telling, however, is the play's use of a traditional device for ending comedies: reconciliation. However, it is not Timon himself who achieves a reconciliation but Alcibiades—who gives up his plan to sack Athens. In rejecting vengeance, Alcibiades expresses the play's ultimate theme: that mercy is more valuable than justice. This strongly positive conclusion contrasts sharply with the harshly negative manner in which Timon ends his life.

What makes this oddly ambiguous play most significant within Shakespeare's dramatic work is the timing of its composition. Hard evidence for dating the play is lacking, but Shakespeare most likely wrote it around 1606 to 1608. These years immediately followed the period in which he wrote the three dramas that have become known as his "problem plays"—*Troilus and Cressida* (pr. 1601-1602, pb. 1609), *All's Well That Ends Well* (pr. c. 1602-1603, pb. 1623), and *Measure for Measure* (pr. c. 1604, pb. 1623). All three plays are unresolved examinations of psychological and sociological complications of life, sex, and death. *Timon of Athens* resembles them in its own ambiguities and its attention to the issues of atonement and reconciliation.

Shakespeare wrote many plays in the tradition of medieval morality plays, which combined comedy with moral lessons in order to educate audiences. The central lesson of *Timon of Athens* is that one cannot find happiness in leading a materialistic life, such as Timon lives until his downfall. While he is financially able to give great feasts and lavish expensive gifts on friends, he believes himself happy and well loved. Only after his money runs out does he realize the shallowness of his happiness. Even then, however, he still fails to recognize true friendship when it is offered by his faithful steward, Flavius. Thus, in contrast to traditional morality plays, *Timon of Athens* does not end with its hero finding happiness by learning how to appreciate more spiritual values. Instead, Timon declines even deeper into despair and dies miserably. The play thus begins with Timon symbolizing friendship and ends with him symbolizing misanthropy.

Whatever Shakespeare's intentions were when he began *Timon of Athens*, the play served as an experiment in which to work out new themes. After abandoning it, he wrote the plays known as his romances: *Pericles, Prince of Tyre* (pr. c. 1607-1608, pb. 1609), *Cymbeline* (pr. c. 1609-1610, pb. 1623), *The Winter's Tale* (pr. c. 1610-1611, pb. 1623), and *The Tempest* (pr. 1611, pb. 1623). Like *Timon of Athens*, these plays explore such themes as exile and return, the absence of moral absolutes, and the transcendent quality of mercy.

Further Reading

Greenblatt, Stephen. *Will in the World: How Shakespeare Became Shakespeare.* New York: Norton, 2004. Critically acclaimed biography, in which Greenblatt finds new connections between Shakespeare's works and the Bard's life and engagement with Elizabethan society.

Hadfield, Andrew. "*Timon of Athens* and Jacobean Politics." *Shakespeare Survey* 56 (2003): 215-226. Examines the political elements of Shakespeare's plays, including their criticisms of the monarchy, by focusing on *Timon of Athens*. Argues that the play's plot implies that society can learn from its own mistakes.

Höfele, Andreas. "Man, Woman, and Beast in Timon's Athens." *Shakespeare Survey* 56 (2003): 227-235. Analyzes the play's characterization of men, women, and beasts, focusing on the character of Timon. Describes the characters' significance to each other, the likeness of men and beasts, and Timon's misogyny.

Nuttall, A. D. *Timon of Athens.* Hemel Hempstead, England: Harvester Wheatsheaf, 1989. Provides a stage history, an account of the critical reception to the play, and a sustained analysis.

Shakespeare, William. *Timon of Athens.* Edited by Karl Klein. New York: Cambridge University Press, 2001. In addition to the text, this edition contains almost seventy pages of introductory material, including discussions of the play's date, themes, critical approaches, performances, authorship, narrative, and dramatic treatment of the Timon legend.

Shakespeare, William, and Thomas Middleton. *The Life of "Timon of Athens."* Edited by John Jowett. New York: Oxford University Press, 2004. Includes more than one hundred pages of detailed introduction to the text of the play in which Jowett explores numerous aspects of the drama, including its early staging possibilities, sources in Plutarch and Lucian, themes, characters, and Shakespeare's collaboration with Middleton.

Soellner, Rolf. *Timon of Athens.* Columbus: Ohio State University Press, 1979. Critical analysis with reference to dramatic and cultural contexts. Discusses the merits of the play.

Vickers, Brian. *Shakespeare, Co-author: A Historical Study of Five Collaborative Plays*. New York: Oxford University Press, 2002. Seeks to develop a coherent system for identifying Shakespeare's collaborative works. Dis-cusses concepts of authorship in English Renaissance drama and describes methods used to determine author-ship since the nineteenth century. Closely analyzes five collaborative plays, including *Timon of Athens*, which Vickers attributes to Shakespeare and Thomas Mid-dleton.

The Tin Drum

Author: Günter Grass (1927-   )
First published: Die Blechtrommel, 1959 (English translation, 1961)
Type of work: Novel
Type of plot: Social satire
Time of plot: 1899-1954
Locale: Poland and Germany

Principal characters:
OSKAR MATZERATH, the narrator and hero
AGNES MATZERATH, his mother
ALFRED MATZERATH, her husband
JAN BRONSKI, Mrs. Matzerath's cousin and lover and possibly Oskar's father
MR. BEBRA, a circus midget and a universal artist
ROSWITHA RAGUNA, his associate and the most celebrated somnambulist in all Italy
HERBERT TRUCZINSKI, a neighbor of the Matzeraths
MARIA TRUCZINSKI, Herbert's youngest sister
GREFF, a greengrocer
LINA, his wife
SISTER DOROTHEA KÖNGETTER, a trained nurse and a neighbor of Oskar in Düsseldorf
GOTTFRIED VON VITTLAR, a man whose testimony leads to Oskar's arrest and later Oskar's friend

The Story:

In 1899, Oskar's Kashubian grandmother is sitting in a potato field, her wide skirts concealing the fugitive Joseph Koljaiczek from pursuing constables. She thereby conceives Oskar's mother, Agnes. In 1923, in the free city of Danzig, Agnes Koljaiczek marries Alfred Matzerath, a citizen of the German Reich, and introduces him to her Polish cousin and lover, Jan Bronski, with whom Alfred becomes fast friends. When Oskar is born, he soon shows himself to be an infant whose mental development is complete at birth.

Oskar is promised a drum for his third birthday. That drum, in its many atavistic recurrences, allows him mutely to voice his protest against the meaninglessness of a world that formulates its destructive nonsense in empty language. The drum also allows him to re-create the history of his con-sciousness and to recall in the varied music of the drum the rhythms of his mind's apprehensions of the world around him. On his third birthday, Oskar, by a sheer act of will, de-cides to stop growing and to remain with his three-year-old body and his totally conscious mind for the rest of his life. As he later boasts, he remains from then on a precocious three-year-old in a world of adults who tower over him but are nev-ertheless inferior to him. While he is complete both inside and out, free from all necessity to grow, develop, and change as time passes, they continue to move toward old age and the grave.

Oskar's refusal to grow, to measure his shadow by that of older persons, or to compete for the things they desire, is the assertion of his individuality against a world that, miscon-struing him, tries to force him into an alien pattern. He is pleased when he discovers his ability to shatter glass with his voice, a talent that becomes not only a means of destruction, the venting of his hostility and outrage, but also an art whereby he can cut a neat hole in the window of a jewelry shop, through which Bronski—upon whom he heaps the filial affection he does not feel for his actual father—can snatch an expensive necklace for his beloved Agnes.

The later period of Oskar's recorded existence is crammed with outlandish events. His mother, after witnessing a revolting scene of eels being extracted from the head of a dead horse submerged in water, perversely enforces a diet of fish on herself and dies. Oskar becomes fascinated with the hieroglyphic scars on the massive back of his friend Herbert Truczinski, but Herbert, who works as a maritime museum attendant, grows enamored of a ship's wooden figurehead called Niobe. In an attempt to make love to her, he is instead impaled to her by a double-edged ship's axe. Jan Bronski is executed after an SS raid on the Polish post office, where he had gone with Oskar. Oskar is overwhelmed with guilt after the death of his mother and that of the man who was probably his father.

In one of the most superbly preposterous seduction scenes in literature, Oskar becomes the lover of Herbert's youngest sister, Maria, and fathers a child with her. Maria then marries Alfred Matzerath, and Oskar, as prodigious sexually as he is diminutive physically, turns to the ampler comforts of Lina Greff, whose closeted gay husband, upon receiving a summons to appear in court on a morals charge, commits a fantastically elaborate, grotesque suicide. Oskar then joins Bebra's troupe of entertainers and becomes the lover of the timeless Roswitha Raguna. When the Russians invade Danzig, Alfred Matzerath, to conceal his affiliations, swallows a Nazi Party pin, which Oskar has shoved into his hand, and dies. Again Oskar feels responsible for the death of a parent.

Before long, against his will, Oskar begins to grow and to develop a hump. His postwar life takes him to West Germany, where he is at various times a black marketeer, a model, and a nightclub entertainer, and eventually to Düsseldorf, where a destiny not his own catches up with him in the guise of the accusation that he killed Sister Dorothea Köngetter, the woman who had been living in the room next to his. The testimony of Vittlar, meant to save Oskar (although Vittlar earlier thought him guilty), damns him. Oskar submits to being judged insane and atoning for a guilt not strictly his because of his own sense that he is guilty by implication, an emblem of the modern world even in his isolation from it.

Critical Evaluation:

Günter Grass's iconoclastic novel *The Tin Drum* shook the moral complacency of the German people and forced them to acknowledge their responsibility for the triumph of Nazism. Earlier, Grass had won minor acclaim for his poetry, but in 1959 Group 47, a German association of young artists and writers, awarded him its prepublication cash prize for *The Tin Drum*. When the novel appeared, it caused one of the greatest uproars in the history of German literature. Translated into most major languages over the next few years, it won international critical acclaim. Grass himself instantly became the best-known and most controversial figure of postwar German literature.

In addition to Group 47's prepublication prize, *The Tin Drum* won three major international literary awards. In 1965, while Grass was accepting the coveted George Büchner Prize, members of a youth organization in Düsseldorf publicly burned copies of *The Tin Drum*. Despite critical acclaim and many awards, Grass and *The Tin Drum* became the targets of more than forty lawsuits and innumerable denunciations in the letters-to-the editor columns of virtually every publication in Germany. People from all social strata in Germany accused Grass of pornography, blasphemy, sacrilege, slander, defamation, and other heinous crimes. The furor over *The Tin Drum* arose from one central theme, that Grass refused to exculpate himself or any other German from guilt for the Nazi regime. In his novel, Grass identifies Nazi affinities in most of the people and in all of the institutions of German society.

Critics have called Grass's account of the Nazi era wildly satirical, wickedly humorous, and morally chilling. Grass presents a German religious institution only too willing to accommodate itself to Adolf Hitler's regime. Some of his most damning barbs are directed at Grass's own Catholicism, but Protestants are not spared their share of guilt. The picture of the acclaimed German educational institution presented in *The Tin Drum* suggests that its discipline and regimentation prepared the way admirably for Hitler and his movement. In Grass's book, the German political tradition of authoritarianism and antiliberalism almost invited a Hitler to take power. Grass also showed how the Nazis capitalized on and institutionalized a widespread view of women that relegated them to a subordinate status in family relationships and the workforce. In *The Tin Drum*, all economic classes in Germany willingly sacrificed their personal freedom to gain the economic prosperity that Hitler promised and delivered. In short, Grass insisted that Hitler was no accident but the logical development of German history; therefore, all the evil of the Nazi era was the direct responsibility of all Germans living at the time.

After World War II, West Germany's new economic and military partnership with the Western bloc engendered an attempt on the part of many Germans to disassociate themselves from their country's Nazi past. Many German teachers, historians, writers, and government officials argued that Hitler and his movement represented a historical anomaly, not the logical development of German history. Hitler came to power, these apologists maintained, because of a special set of circumstances: the German defeat in World War I and the ensuing Treaty of Versailles, the economic dislocations in Germany during the Weimar Republic, and middle-class Germans' fear of a Communist takeover. The German nation as a whole, they concluded, should not be forced to bear the guilt for atrocities committed by a group of madmen who illegally seized control of their government.

During the period between 1945 and 1959, a body of literature in Germany and elsewhere propounded the thesis that most Germans had deplored Hitler and the Nazis. Accounts of various German resistance groups that had actively sought to overthrow Hitler appeared alongside stories of individual Germans who had helped to rescue Jews from deportation to concentration camps. German artists, writers, and scientists pointed out that many of their number had emigrated shortly after Hitler came to power. Most of those who remained insisted that they had been part of the so-called inner emigration, that though they had remained in Germany they had never cooperated with the regime and had worked in subtle ways to thwart Hitler's purposes.

Grass portrayed those Germans who had engaged in active resistance to Hitler's regime as having been opposed only to Hitler himself and not to the substance of Nazism. He also dismissed those German intellectuals engaged in the "inner emigration" as being nothing more than court jesters for Nazi propaganda minister Joseph Goebbels. Taken in total, the novel condemned all Germans and insisted that they acknowledge the moral and spiritual shortcomings of their institutions—it was little wonder that almost every German reader found something offensive in *The Tin Drum*.

Despite the controversy, *The Tin Drum* was widely read and discussed in Germany, especially by young people (more than half a million copies sold there during the five years following its publication). The West German government began insisting that students be taught the history of the Nazi era, which had been neglected in the immediate postwar era. In the succeeding decades, *The Tin Drum* and Grass's other novels and poetry became the foci for an entire nation as it reinterpreted its past and reexamined the moral foundations of its institutions.

After *The Tin Drum* appeared in translation in the United States in 1961, Grass was acclaimed by many critics as Germany's greatest living writer. Literary critics in France, Den-

mark, and many other countries went so far as to rank Grass as the world's greatest living novelist, and they praised his courage in raising such controversial issues in his own country. A few critics were perceptive enough to point out that the elements of German society that Grass satirized so scathingly—which, according to him, had led directly to Nazism—became present in every industrialized nation in the second half of the twentieth century. Although Grass directed his message to Germans, many of his admirers argued that all humankind must learn from his pages or suffer a resurgence of the tyranny that nearly engulfed the world before 1945.

"Critical Evaluation" by Paul Madden

Further Reading

Arnds, Peter. *Representation, Subversion, and Eugenics in Günter Grass's "The Tin Drum."* Rochester, N.Y.: Camden House, 2004. Focuses on Grass's depiction of "asocials," or the physically disabled, criminals, gays and lesbians, and others whom the Nazis regarded as unfit to live. Demonstrates how the character of Oskar, the dwarf, is a metaphor for and a voice of these asocials, and how Grass created a counterculture that opposed the Nazis' racism and eugenics.

Delaney, Antoinette T. *Metaphors in Grass' "Die Blechtrommel."* New York: Peter Lang, 2004. Focuses on Grass's use of metaphor in the novel, using graphs to depict the book's numerous metaphorical meanings.

Grass, Günter. *Peeling the Onion.* London: Harvill Secker, 2007. Grass recounts the events of his life, including the revelation that he served in a Nazi combat unit during the last months of World War II. He describes how he fictionalized people and events in his life.

Hollington, Michael. *Günter Grass: The Writer in a Pluralist Society.* London: Marion Boyars, 1980. Credits Grass with forcing Germans to look candidly at the Nazi era and with inspiring a younger generation to fight against the complacency of their elders. Devotes a chapter to *The Tin Drum.*

Mews, Siegfried. *Günter Grass and His Critics: From "The Tin Drum" to "Crabwalk."* Rochester, N.Y.: Camden House, 2008. Concisely summarizes how scholars and the popular press reacted to Grass's work between 1959 and 2005. Includes a chapter on *The Tin Drum.*

Miles, Keith. *Günter Grass.* New York: Barnes & Noble, 1975. Offers interpretations of and insights into *The Tin Drum* that are perceptive and very useful to readers trying to understand Grass's often cryptic prose. Although only chapter 2 deals exclusively with *The Tin Drum*, the novel and its impact are discussed in the introduction and throughout the rest of the book.

Shafi, Monika, ed. *Approaches to Teaching Grass's "The Tin Drum."* New York: Modern Language Association, 2008.

Provides numerous materials useful to students as well as to teachers, including essays placing *The Tin Drum* in its historical context, discussing Oskar as an unreliable narrator, and examining the imagery, use of German fairy tales, and gender, sex, and violence in the novel.

The Tin Flute

Author: Gabrielle Roy (1909-1983)
First published: Bonheur d'occasion, 1945 (English translation, 1947)
Type of work: Novel
Type of plot: Social realism
Time of plot: February to June, 1940
Locale: Montreal

Principal characters:
FLORENTINE LACASSE, a waitress
ROSE-ANNA, her mother
AZARIUS, her father
EUGENE, her oldest brother
JEAN LÉVESQUE, a young machinist, and Florentine's lover
EMMANUEL LÉTOURNEAU, a soldier, and Florentine's suitor
DANIEL, Florentine's youngest brother

The Story:

In the late winter of 1940, Canadians are emerging from the effects of the Great Depression and now face the outbreak of World War II. One young woman, Florentine Lacasse, helps support her family by working as a waitress at the lunch counter in a five-and-dime store in Montreal's St. Henri slum district. The lunch area's flashy decor, which appeals to Florentine's shallow taste, stirs her ambition to escape the dreary poverty that entraps her family.

Jean Lévesque, a young machinist, flirts with Florentine while she is working. She, in turn, is captivated by his slick, confident appearance. Although Florentine dislikes Jean's arrogance and offhand manner, she agrees to meet him at the cinema. Later, at his lodgings in the district's bleak warehouse area, Jean analyzes the contradictory nature of his attraction to Florentine's fragile prettiness and vulnerability. After concluding that his drive for success leaves him no time to waste on an affair, Jean avoids his date with Florentine.

Jean visits The Two Records, a neighborhood snack bar. There, he overhears a heated discussion between the store owner and Azarius Lacasse, Florentine's father, concerning the war. Azarius argues for the defense of countries victimized by war, such as Poland. Other bar patrons protest, saying that as French Canadians, they will resist fighting in an "English" conflict. Jean notes the similarities between Azarius and his daughter Florentine.

Emmanuel Létourneau, a soldier, stops by Ma Philbert's restaurant in St. Henri. A former inhabitant of the slum, he is now well educated, gainfully employed, and living in a better neighborhood. He encounters three former school chums—Alphonse, Boisvert, and Pitou—who are unemployed, bored, and disillusioned. They appear surprised and resentful that Emmanuel had joined the military, so Emmanuel gives idealistic reasons for fighting in a war that he believes will change the world, especially its greedy social systems. Feeling despondent, Emmanuel leaves and encounters Jean, his close friend. They discuss women, and Jean invites him to meet Florentine.

In her bleak house, Rose-Anna Lacasse worries about her family's poverty and awaits her husband and two oldest children. Son Eugene comes home wearing an army uniform. He explains to his horrified mother that he had enlisted to be usefully employed, and not for the army pay. Later, Rose-Anna berates her husband for his procrastination in finding the family a cheaper rental home; they face eviction in May. Her house-hunting is described as an annual spring ritual that is shared by many women in the slum.

Jean reconsiders his relationship with Florentine and asks her to dinner. They dine at a classy restaurant, although she remains angry because he missed their first date. Embarrassed by Florentine's gauche behavior at dinner, Jean decides against dating her again. Later in the evening, when he embraces her, she becomes convinced that he has fallen for her. Days later, Jean introduces Emmanuel to Florentine at her job. Confused by Jean's indifference, Florentine attempts to make him jealous by flirting with Emmanuel, who is attracted to her. Jean feels confident that he has dumped Florentine on his best friend. Emmanuel invites everyone to a party at his house. At the party, Florentine is impressed by the middle-class prosperity of the Létourneaus. Still, she is distraught by Jean's absence. She nonetheless dances and flirts with Emmanuel, who is enamored of her.

Azarius takes his family to visit his wife's childhood home in Saint-Denis-de-Richelieu, a rural area outside Montreal. Initially, Rose-Anna is overjoyed, but she becomes despondent when she compares her own sickly children to their robust country cousins. Above all, her mother's negative, critical attitude makes her feel inadequate and discouraged. On their way home, Azarius gets into an accident with the truck he borrowed from his employer. He consequently loses his job. Rose-Anna's dreams of recovering the past collapse, and the family's fortunes further decline. The youngest son, Daniel, is soon hospitalized with leukemia, and Eugene reneges on his promise to help the family with his army pay.

While the family is away, Florentine invites Jean to dinner. To thwart her expectations of romance and marriage with him, he overpowers her sexually and then disappears from her life. When she realizes she is pregnant and that he has abandoned her, her dreams for a better future vanish. After Rose-Anna discovers her daughter's pregnancy, Florentine leaves home to stay with her friend Marguerite. Florentine decides to save her reputation and secure her economic future by accepting Emmanuel's courtship. Confronted by Florentine's disgrace and the family's eviction and removal into dreadful lodgings, Rose-Anna's hopes for her family hit rock bottom.

Emmanuel returns home on furlough and looks for his friends. After visiting The Two Records, he discovers that his old chums have been adversely affected by the war. He ponders their fates and his own future, and he angrily blames the unjust social system for blighting the lives of French Canadians. Burdened by despondency and solitude, he decides to find Florentine. After meeting her at Easter Sunday Mass, he takes her out for dinner and dancing. He further pursues his courtship of her, leading Florentine to push him to propose marriage. He does, and the two are married.

Florentine's marriage to Emmanuel saves her from the shame of unwed motherhood, but it does not mend the tensions between herself and her mother; they part from each other unreconciled. Little Daniel is sustained by care and attention from his English nurse, Jenny. However, he soon dies, surrounded by his toys but not his family. Florentine's younger sister, Yvonne, announces her intention to become a nun. The family's disintegration seems complete when Azarius joins the army, presumably to earn an income; actually, he joins to avoid confronting his failures as a provider. The birth of her newest baby brings Rose-Anna some measure of comfort and hope.

A mixed mood of optimism and despair prevails, as Emmanuel and other soldiers leave for war from Montreal's train station. Florentine, preoccupied by materialistic plans for the future, appears to be unaffected by her husband's departure. Emmanuel is depressed by the false bravado of the mob around him and by the ironic thought of "salvation through war," pondering the future of his world. Nonetheless, his hopes for humankind rebound when, out of the crowd, an old woman—a stranger—gestures to him that someday humanity's conflicts will end.

Critical Evaluation:

The Tin Flute is Gabrielle Roy's first and best-known novel. Considered by many critics to be one of the greatest works of French Canadian literature, it won numerous prizes, including Canada's prestigious Governor-General's Award and France's distinguished Prix Femina. Roy began her writing career as a journalist. Her meticulous description of the St. Henri slum in Montreal is based on her observations for a series of journal articles she wrote about the social and economic crises generated by the city's growing industrialization.

Roy's novel is especially important in the development of French Canadian fiction because it marks a turning point in the depiction of the province of Quebec, which had been portrayed by earlier writers as rural, traditional, and inward-looking. By contrast, *The Tin Flute*, whose English title is taken from the name of a child's toy—symbolizing the repressed longings of deprived people—presents a grittily realistic panorama of urban life with the dilemmas that threaten to overwhelm French Canadians at a transformative time—when Canada was emerging from the economic hardships of the Great Depression and plunging into the global turmoil of World War II. Critics of the work have especially praised Roy for her capturing of the stark contrast between the poor, decaying environment of Montreal's French Canadian slum and the orderly, manicured world of the city's Westmount district—a district inhabited by the affluent Anglophone bankers and industrialists who helped to build the socioeconomic system that has oppressed Quebec's working classes.

The power of Roy's storytelling in *The Tin Flute* springs

chiefly from the direct narrative style used to portray the characters and their environment. The sights, sounds, and smells of the places where the protagonists play out their emotional lives—neighborhood streets, restaurants, stores, bars, houses, and churches—are portrayed with near-clinical detail and with striking, evocative imagery. The narrative follows a conventional linear plot structure that traces the stories of individuals in a chronological progression. The author adheres closely to the viewpoints of her characters and provides no specific transitions between chapters, which appear as independent episodes in cinematic fashion.

Roy also goes beyond the viewpoint of the omniscient narrator and deeply probes the psychology of the major players in her story, especially the psyches of Florentine, Rose-Anna, Emmanuel, and Jean. She reveals their doubts, illusions, and self-analyses through an intensely gripping presentation that borders on stream of consciousness. Even an unsympathetic character like Jean is portrayed with complexity and sensitivity, as he ponders his tragic relationship with Florentine. Through her skillful use of dialogue, Roy individualizes her characters by exactly rendering the nuances of dialect and unique speech patterns. She was one of the first French Canadian writers to capture *joual*, a popular form of Québécois French spoken in Montreal, and employs it extensively in the novel to authentically reproduce the conversations of St. Henri's inhabitants.

The Tin Flute is an innovative work also for its introduction of the theme of social change into French Canadian literature. As Quebec's first major urban novel, *The Tin Flute* has a social realism that undercuts the idealization of rural life that had been the focus of previous French Canadian fiction. The theme of transformation is complexly explored on two levels, within a broad sociohistorical context and within the interrelated stories of individual characters. Thus, Roy juxtaposes the experiences of her two major female protagonists to underscore how differently they react to the stresses of the powerless and harsh existence of Québécois women.

Florentine rejects the patient self-sacrifice that Rose-Anna follows as wife and mother, whose dreams and family disintegrate. Instead, the younger woman acquires an attitude of tough, mercenary practicality and faces her disillusionment with romance and secures her reputation and economic future through a loveless marriage. Many feminists interpret Roy's portrayal of women in her novel as one of the earliest, subversive critiques of the traditional role women played in French Canadian society, when that society was dominated by the patriarchal institutions of church and state.

Roy also uses her deft talent as an ironist in her treatment of the central theme of the novel: the impact of socioeco-nomic changes on French Canada. She describes how global conflict transforms the fortunes of St. Henri as World War II pulls the slum inhabitants out of the trap of insularity and poverty; they enlist in the army and thus acquire income for their families and some freedom from responsibility. Others, like ruthless and selfish Jean, survive at home to become successful war profiteers. Emmanuel, Roy's voice of idealism and Florentine's "rescuer," sacrifices himself to the war because he believes it will eventually destroy a rotten system that exploits the underprivileged. Nonetheless, at the novel's end, he bitterly notes the irony that war is what brings salvation to his community, that is, a form of "secondhand" happiness, as the original French title of novel indicates.

With its complex themes and compelling character portrayals, *The Tin Flute* adds a modern dimension to the development of French Canadian literature. Through sensitive depiction of human foibles and through intelligent exploration of humankind's aspirations, Roy's novel is a masterpiece of fiction that continues to attract universal praise and critical attention.

Diana Arlene Chlebek

Further Reading

Clemente, Linda, and Bill Clemente. *Gabrielle Roy: Creation and Memory.* Toronto, Ont.: ECW Press, 1997. This biographical account focuses on three crucial eras in Roy's early life, when she was honing her craft as a writer. Provides an especially insightful account of the genesis and publication of *The Tin Flute*, including the effects of the work's success on Roy's career and personal life.

Coleman, Patrick. *The Limits of Sympathy: Gabrielle Roy's "The Tin Flute."* Toronto, Ont.: ECW Press, 1993. An extensive and informed study of the novel. Thoroughly analyzes the work's narrative techniques, themes, and methods of character portrayal.

Everett, Jane, ed. *In Translation: The Gabrielle Roy-Joyce Marshall Correspondence.* Toronto, Ont.: University of Toronto Press, 2005. A compilation of the extensive correspondence between the author and her English translator. Of special focus are the musings on the art of translation and the problems involved in rendering French prose into English.

Hess, M. G. *Gabrielle Roy.* Boston: Twayne, 1984. A useful survey volume in the Twayne World Authors series, examining all of Roy's writings. Includes brief commentary and analysis of each of her works.

Knoller, Eva-Marie, ed. *Cambridge Companion to Canadian Literature.* New York: Cambridge University Press,

2004. Helpful, timely essays covering a range of topics, with especially pertinent chapters on Francophone writing and Canadian fiction.

Ricard, François. *Gabrielle Roy: A Life.* Translated by Patricia Claxton. Toronto, Ont.: McClelland & Stewart, 1996. This penetrating and eloquent portrait of Roy was originally published in French in 1975. Written by an award-winning biographer, it remains the definitive account of Roy's life.

Shek, Ben-Zion. *Social Realism in the French-Canadian Novel.* Montreal: Harvest House, 1977. Shek's chapter on *The Tin Flute* examines the novel in relationship to its ideological and socioeconomic context. The critique focuses on the work's narrative technique and emphasizes such themes as social conflict and the search for identity.

Smart, Patricia. "When the Voices of Resistance Become Political: *The Tin Flute* or Realism in the Feminine." In *Writing in the Father's House: The Emergence of the Feminine in the Quebec Literary Tradition.* Toronto, Ont.: University of Toronto Press, 1991. Originally published in French in 1988. Smart's analysis of *The Tin Flute* is presented from a feminist perspective. Underscores the novel's innovative role in bringing to the forefront the political message of women's writing in Quebec.

Tinker, Tailor, Soldier, Spy

Author: John le Carré (1931-   )
First published: 1974
Type of work: Novel
Type of plot: Spy
Time of plot: 1971-1973
Locale: Devon County and London, England; Hong Kong; Czechoslovakia

Principal characters:
GEORGE SMILEY, an intelligence officer who has been forced into retirement from the Secret Intelligence Service (nicknamed the Circus)
BILL HAYDON, a highly placed Circus officer
JIM PRIDEAUX, Bill's friend and former colleague, now a temporary master (teacher) at Thursgood's preparatory school
PETER GUILLAM, a Circus officer who has been sidelined
RICKI TARR, a Circus field officer
CONTROL, the former head of the Circus, now deceased
KARLA, a Russian spymaster
OLIVER LACON, a government official responsible for oversight of the Circus
BILL ROACH, a new student at Thursgood's

The Story:

Jim Prideaux and Bill Roach are both new to the English preparatory school of Thursgood's in Devon. Prideaux is a mysterious character with a crooked back who has taken a temporary appointment, while Roach is a lonely student who is gratified when Prideaux praises his powers of observation.

In London, George Smiley was until recently an officer in the British Secret Intelligence Service known to its members as the Circus. Smiley arrives home one evening to find an old associate, Peter Guillam, waiting for him. Guillam drives Smiley to the residence of Circus adviser and overseer Oliver Lacon in order to hear a story from field officer Ricki Tarr. It seems that Tarr has deserted his post in Hong Kong and secretly made his way back to England after becoming in-volved with the wife of a Soviet trade delegate. Hoping to defect, she had confided that there was a "mole," or double agent, in the Circus and that another agent named Polyakov collected the mole's intelligence for a Soviet spymaster known as Karla. Tarr cabled his superiors about the situation in guarded terms, but when the Circus did nothing and the woman disappeared, Tarr fled.

In talking over Tarr's story, Smiley and Lacon discuss the disaster that led to the forced resignation of Smiley and his superior, the aging director of the Circus known only as Control. The disaster was the botched Operation Testify, in which Control sent Prideaux on a secret mission to Czechoslovakia to interview another potential defector about a spy in the

Circus—apparently the very mole whom Tarr has just told them about. After being shot in the back, Prideaux was taken to the Soviet Union for interrogation. He was released only through the efforts of his old friend and colleague (and perhaps one-time lover) Bill Haydon. In the wake of the disaster, Percy Alleline became head of the Circus, his position bolstered by a new, steady flow of seemingly valuable intelligence (code-named Witchcraft) about the Soviet bloc from a mysterious source (code-named Merlin). Haydon emerged as Alleline's deputy, and about the same time he began an affair with Smiley's chronically unfaithful wife Ann.

Tarr's story makes it clear that Control was right about the mole, and Lacon authorizes Smiley to identify him. Smiley secures a safe house where he can work undisturbed, poring over documents delivered by Lacon and Guillam. At one point, he tells Guillam about his own unnerving encounter with Karla in 1955. He also slips out to interview other retired colleagues: Former Circus head of research Connie Sachs is able to give him more information about Polyakov. Sam Collins, who was at Circus headquarters the night Prideaux was shot, explains that he called Smiley's house in desperation, only to learn from Ann that her husband was out of the country. Haydon showed up at Circus headquarters shortly afterward to take command, suggesting that he had been spending the night with Ann.

In the meantime, Prideaux has been located by Smiley's trusted friend Inspector Mendel, and Smiley sets out to interview him. Roach is finally able to help Prideaux, informing him that a stranger has come looking for him. Prideaux explains to Smiley that Control had narrowed the identity of the mole to one of five officers and that Prideaux was to determine which one it was and relay the information to him using code words based on a children's fortune-telling rhyme: "Tinker, tailor, soldier, sailor, rich man, poor man, beggar man, thief, doctor, lawyer, Indian chief." The five suspects were Alleline (Tinker), Haydon (Tailor), Roy Bland (Soldier), Toby Esterhase (Poor man), and Smiley himself (Beggar man). All but Smiley are still employed at the Circus.

Now Smiley tricks Esterhase into an interrogation and establishes that the Witchcraft intelligence—much of which he suspects is of minor value—is collected by the mole from Merlin (that is, from Polyakov) in a Circus safe house. The mole uses the opportunity to pass Polyakov British secrets of much greater value. Those who know of the Merlin operation think that rumors of a mole in the Circus are merely a cover story—they know the mole meets with Polyakov, but they think that Polyakov is the one providing valuable secrets and the mole is the one trading minor intelligence in return.

With the help of Guillam and Mendel, Smiley sets a trap for the mole: Tarr sends a telegram to Alleline informing him that he has vital information. The mole is guaranteed to hear of the telegram (if he is not Alleline himself); he will assume that the information is about him, and he will be forced to arrange an emergency meeting with Polyakov. The plan works, and the traitor arrives at the safe house. He turns out to be Tailor—Bill Haydon.

In the aftermath of the disclosure, Alleline is given indefinite leave and Smiley is invited back to the Circus to repair the damage done by the mole. Haydon confesses all to Smiley, explaining that Operation Testify was a trap designed to destroy Control and that Witchcraft was intended to install the easily managed Alleline in his place. Haydon knew the details of Testify because Prideaux, who thought Control was going mad, made the mistake of confiding in him before he left for Czechoslovakia. Finally, Haydon admits that he began the affair with Ann in order to cloud Smiley's judgment.

Plans are made to swap Haydon for British agents in the Soviet Union, but Prideaux slips into the compound in which he is being held and breaks his neck. He then returns to Thursgood's to take up his new life, looked over by Roach.

Critical Evaluation:

Tinker, Tailor, Soldier, Spy was inspired by real events involving Harold "Kim" Philby, a talented and charming intelligence officer who had risen to the highest echelons of the British espionage establishment by the middle of the twentieth century. In 1951, however, two of Philby's colleagues were revealed to be Soviet agents of long standing, and in 1963 Philby himself was unmasked as the "Third Man" who had helped the other two escape. Like them, he defected to the Soviet Union, dealing a severe blow to the prestige of the British Secret Intelligence Service (MI6). John le Carré wrote the introduction to a book about the affair, *The Philby Conspiracy* (1969), by Bruce Page, David Leitch, and Phillip Knightley, and he went on to publish his own novelistic treatment in 1974. The same dilemma is posed by both factual and fictional events: As Lacon remarks to Smiley, "'It's the oldest question of all, George. Who can spy on the spies?'"

Readers of the novel might be forgiven for thinking that they have been presented with the pieces of a jigsaw puzzle—a puzzle made doubly difficult by the fact that they cannot guess what the final picture is supposed to look like. A master solver of puzzles himself, George Smiley acts as a surrogate for readers, who watch him carefully assemble the pieces one by one. When the revelation finally comes, Smiley realizes that, like everyone else, he had known all along that the traitor was Haydon. They had "tacitly shared that unexpressed half-knowledge which like an illness they hoped would go away if it was never . . . diagnosed."

The handsome, sexually magnetic, multitalented Bill Haydon is regarded with awe by those who know him. His colleagues think of him as another Lawrence of Arabia (T. E. Lawrence), the English soldier whose exploits in the Near East during World War I captured the British imagination. Guillam imagines him as the "torch-bearer of a certain kind of antiquated romanticism." Thus, it seems that Haydon betrays not only his country and his friends but also his friends' vision of him—a vision in which they had found inspiration and purpose. Smiley sees him somewhat more clearly as an "ambitious man born to the big canvas . . . for whom the reality was a poor island."

The novel balances the duplicitous character of Haydon with that of Smiley himself, who is his opposite in almost every regard. Described as being the kind of adult Bill Roach is likely to become, Smiley is short, plump, and ungainly. He wears expensive clothes poorly. His saving graces are his cool intellect and his humanity. He loves his beautiful wife Ann unreservedly, but by novel's end he has come to see her as she really is, "essentially another man's woman." One of modern fiction's most appealing characters, Smiley had been introduced by le Carré in *Call for the Dead* (1960) and made what would presumably be his last appearance in *The Secret Pilgrim* (1991). His epic struggle with the Soviet spymaster Karla, begun in *Tinker, Tailor, Soldier, Spy*, continues in *The Honourable Schoolboy* (1977) and concludes—with victory of a sort—in *Smiley's People* (1980). The three books have been published together as *The Quest for Karla* (1982).

Fellow writer Graham Greene called le Carré's third book, *The Spy Who Came in from the Cold* (1963), the best spy novel he had ever read. For many readers and critics, however, *Tinker, Tailor, Soldier, Spy* surpasses it. It is in this novel and its two successors that le Carré makes greatest use of the Circus, its personnel, its shadowy procedures, and its arcane vocabulary. The work is dauntingly complex but rewards careful reading and rereading.

A distinguished tradition of British spy fiction lies behind John le Carré's works. One of its earliest practitioners was John Buchan, whose novel *Greenmantle* (1916) features a character inspired by Lawrence of Arabia—the sort of dashing character Haydon's friends and colleagues imagine him to be. Prideaux is reading Buchan to one of the dormitories when Smiley comes to talk to him, but he must leave the boys and the boys' book behind in order to reenter the morally ambiguous world of real espionage, a world in which betrayal is the norm.

Grove Koger

Further Reading

Aronoff, Myron Joel. *The Spy Novels of John le Carré: Balancing Ethics and Politics*. New York: St. Martin's Press, 1999. Addresses such subjects as bureaucratic politics, ethics in espionage, and the similarities between real-life and fictional spies. Includes a dramatis personae, comprehensive notes, and primary and secondary bibliographies.

Beene, LynnDianne. *John le Carré*. New York: Twayne, 1992. A thorough examination of le Carré's career, placing his work within the tradition of espionage fiction. Chronology, substantial bibliography.

Cobbs, John L. *Understanding John le Carré*. Columbia: University of Carolina Press, 1998. Considers le Carré's espionage works, his 1971 mainstream novel *The Naïve and Sentimental Lover*, and his post-Smiley thrillers through *The Tailor of Panama* (1996). Good bibliography.

Le Carré, John. *Conversations with John le Carré*. Edited by Matthew J. Bruccoli and Judith Baughman. Jackson: University of Mississippi Press, 2004. Collection of major interviews in which le Carré comments upon his own work.

Monaghan, David. *Smiley's Circus: A Guide to the Secret World of John le Carré*. New York: Thomas Dunne/St. Martin's Press, 1986. Invaluable handbook to the Circus. Includes chronologies of major operations, an extensive and detailed who's who, short plot summaries, maps, and illustrations.

O'Neill, Philip. "Le Carré: Faith and Dreams." In *The Quest for le Carré*, edited by Alan Bold. New York: St. Martin's Press, 1988. Analysis of *Tinker, Tailor, Soldier, Spy* in terms of its appeal to English readers after the collapse of the British Empire.

'Tis Pity She's a Whore

Author: John Ford (1586-after 1639)
First produced: 1629?; first published, 1633
Type of work: Drama
Type of plot: Tragedy
Time of plot: 1620's
Locale: Parma, Italy

Principal characters:
BONAVENTURA, a friar
SORANZO, a nobleman
FLORIO, a citizen of Parma
DONADO, another citizen
GRIMALDI, a Roman gentleman
GIOVANNI, son of Florio
BERGETTO, nephew of Donado
RICHARDETTO, a supposed physician
VASQUES, servant of Soranzo
ANNABELLA, daughter of Florio
HIPPOLITA, wife of Richardetto
PUTANA, tutor of Annabella

The Story:

Previously recognized as a brilliant young scholar, Giovanni confesses to his tutor, Friar Bonaventura, that his love for his own sister, Annabella, is without limit. The friar warns Giovanni of eternal damnation if he does not forget this sinful lust and exhorts his young pupil to pray. Grimaldi, a Roman gentleman, in Parma to court Annabella, fights with Vasques, the servant of Soranzo, a nobleman. Grimaldi, enraged, proclaims that he will be revenged on Soranzo for Vasques's assault. Putana, Annabella's tutor, tells the girl that she is fortunate to have Grimaldi and Soranzo wooing her; personally, the old nurse prefers Soranzo, a virile and wealthy man of twenty-three. Annabella does not care to hear of the virtues of any suitor, but she has no patience for Bergetto, a tiresome twit.

Giovanni tries prayers and fasting, but nothing alleviates his misery. It is not his lust, he feels, that leads him on, but his fate. He confesses to Annabella his love for her, and she admits that she also loves him. Their father, Florio, worries about his studious son's health and has more hope for descendants from his daughter's marriage; the father says he wants her to marry for love rather than wealth. Florio is receptive, however, when Donado promises large amounts of money if Florio will let Donado's simple-minded nephew, Bergetto, pay court to Annabella. Giovanni and Annabella yield to their desires and become intimate; then they worry about being separated if she is forced to marry.

Hippolita, Soranzo's former mistress, believing she was recently widowed, reminds Soranzo that he promised to marry her when her husband died. In frustration and anger at being rejected, Hippolita promises to revenge herself upon

Soranzo. Vasques promises to assist Hippolita in gaining her revenge. A supposed doctor, recently come to Parma, is really Hippolita's husband, Richardetto. He comes in disguise to spy on his wife. While Richardetto is suspicious of Annabella's indifference to all men, he tells Grimaldi that Soranzo stands between him (Grimaldi) and Annabella's heart; together they plot to kill Soranzo. Thus, Richardetto will have his own revenge on the man who cuckolds him.

Giovanni confesses his relationship with his sister to the friar. The friar is greatly shocked and warns Giovanni of damnation. Giovanni tries by sophistical reasoning to prove that the love he and his sister bear for each other is not wrong. The friar replies that the only thing they can do to save themselves is to have Annabella marry. Bergetto sends a letter and a jewel to Annabella, but she tells Donado that she will never marry his nephew. Donado makes her a gift of the jewel his nephew sent to her, but Bergetto stubbornly decides that he will continue to woo Annabella. When Giovanni sees his sister wearing the ring originally sent by Bergetto, he is tormented with jealousy.

Florio prefers Soranzo to Annabella's other suitors, but Annabella tells Soranzo that he should give up his thought of marrying her. She attempts to console him by promising that if she has to accept any of her suitors, he would be the one to win her favor. Annabella discovers that she is pregnant, and Putana confides the news to her brother. Meanwhile, Florio decides that his daughter has to marry Soranzo and asks the friar to help win her over. Annabella confesses her intimacy with her brother to the friar, and he eloquently warns her of Hell and tells her that the only way to preserve her honor is to marry Soranzo. At last, she yields to his insistence.

At the same time, the plot between Grimaldi and Richardetto to kill Soranzo develops. Grimaldi, mistaking Bergetto for Soranzo, stabs him with a rapier that was coated with poison by the fake doctor. Vasques tells Hippolita that her former lover, his master, is now betrothed to Annabella and that the marriage will take place in two days. Hippolita renews her pledge to have revenge on the man she feels betrayed her. Soon, it is revealed that it is Grimaldi who killed Bergetto. He gives himself up to the cardinal, who grants him protection, in the name of the pope. Grimaldi explains that he intended to kill Soranzo, not the foolish Bergetto. Donado and Florio lament the absence of justice on Earth; none comes, even from churchmen.

After the marriage of Annabella to Soranzo, there is a lavish banquet, but the miserable Giovanni cannot hide his despair. Hippolita appears in a masque, but believing that she will not keep her side of the bargain they made, Vasques gives her the poisoned cup intended for his master; unknowingly, she drinks it. Realizing that she is poisoned by Vasques, Hippolita dies cursing Soranzo and his new bride. Soranzo learns that Annabella is pregnant by another man; she admits that she chose him not for love but to protect her honor. She refuses to tell him the name of her lover. In his rage, he draws his sword but is prevented from killing his young wife by the intervention of Vasques. Nevertheless, Soranzo contemplates revenge upon this woman he so recently loved. Putana unwittingly tells Vasques that Giovanni is the man who made Annabella pregnant. She then is gagged and kidnapped—and blinded—before she can warn Annabella. Vasques tells his master, Soranzo, the full truth.

Annabella, imprisoned in her room, gives the friar a letter for her brother warning him to repent and not to believe Soranzo. Meanwhile, Soranzo and Vasques plot to have revenge upon both Annabella and Giovanni. The friar gives Annabella's letter, written in her own blood, to Giovanni. Soon after, Vasques invites Giovanni to a birthday feast that Soranzo is holding: The feast is merely a ploy to bring Soranzo's revenge to fruition. Giovanni accepts the invitation; he feels that it does not matter what he does because his fate will find him.

Soranzo pays bandits to assist him in his plot. Giovanni, Florio, the cardinal, and other citizens of Parma come to the feast. Giovanni, sent by Soranzo to fetch her, talks passionately and despairingly with Annabella in her bed chamber. Giovanni stabs Annabella as they kiss. Giovanni enters the banquet room with Annabella's heart on his dagger. At first, the assembly is too stunned to take him seriously. Wildly, he

confesses to everyone of his sin with his sister. Vasques goes to Annabella's room and returns to confirm that she is, indeed, murdered. Florio falls dead at the news.

Giovanni stabs Soranzo. Vasques and Giovanni fight, and the bandits rush in and fight Giovanni. Soranzo, realizing that he is mortally stabbed, dies telling Vasques not to let Giovanni survive him. Giovanni soon bleeds to death, however, bidding death welcome.

Critical Evaluation:

While summoning up echoes of Thomas Kyd's *The Spanish Tragedy* (c. 1585-1589) and William Shakespeare's *Romeo and Juliet* (pr. c. 1595-1596, pb. 1597), *'Tis Pity She's a Whore*, by John Ford, the last distinctive playwright in English Renaissance drama, offers new attitudes toward sex, death, and immortality. This play also provides evidence that Elizabethan and Jacobean theater had exhausted itself, even before the theaters were closed in 1642.

Without question, choosing incest between brother and sister was a daring choice of subject matter, one that was not ignored by other playwrights. In John Webster's *The Duchess of Malfi* (pr. 1614, pb. 1623), there is the obsessive, incestuous love of Ferdinand, duke of Calabria, for his twin sister, the duchess of Malfi. There is incest in Thomas Middleton's *The Revenger's Tragedy* (pr. 1606-1607, pb. 1607) between stepmother and stepson, and also between uncle and niece in his *Women Beware Women* (c. 1621-1627), a play directly analogous to *'Tis Pity She's a Whore*. However, nowhere except in Ford's play is there serious examination of the complex emotions that a love between brother and sister may involve. There is little evidence that Ford's plays were popular in his time, but *'Tis Pity She's a Whore* has been produced many times in the twentieth and twenty-first centuries.

The play does not condone a love between brother and sister. Annabella's reputation is sullied from the start, even though it is her brother, not she, who initiates their intimacy. Lest anyone imagine otherwise, note that Ford gives her tutor the name of Putana, or whore. While Annabella confesses that she loves Giovanni, she dare not to say so or even to think it. The friar is immediately aware that Giovanni's love is a heinous sin. Even Vasques, the Spanish servant to Soranzo, who scruples not at murder (Hippolita) or torture (Putana), and who exits the play congratulating himself that he, a Spaniard, outdoes an Italian in revenge, is horrified to discover that Annabella is pregnant by her own brother: "To what height of liberty in damnation hath the devil trained our age. Her brother!" (act 4, scene 3). Finally, the father of this brother and sister drops dead, of a heart attack, when he hears of his children's incest.

Ford's essentially nonmetaphorical dialogue can be very powerful, but too often the language of his characters, who do not have their own distinct modes of speaking, recalls other plays. Ford borrows much from Shakespeare, for example. Ford's comic subplots are virtually pointless. Even so, Ford's characterization of the two lovers is multifaceted, and Giovanni, although he is a criminal, must be seen as a sympathetic character.

The play begins with Giovanni confessing his love for his sister to the friar. By the second scene of the first act, he is confessing his love to Annabella, to whom he lies, maintaining that the church sanctions his love. In the last scene of the play, the audience learns from Giovanni that he and his sister were lovers for nine months. Giovanni becomes increasingly possessive of his sister as the play progresses; Annabella's love for him remains constant. Having confessed her love to her brother, she knows she fell into mortal sin; she simultaneously savors her love and wants to do penance for it. Ford presents her as superior to Putana and to Hippolita, who is guilty of adultery with Soranzo and of plotting to kill her husband. Philoitis, Richardetto's niece, a minor character, serves to remind the audience that taking refuge in a nunnery is always an option for a young woman of the time—Annabella, although less of a hypocrite than other women characters in the play, is still a sinner who has a way to escape her predicament.

Friar Bonaventura is Lawrence in Shakespeare's *Romeo and Juliet*. Friar Lawrence, who should know better, secretly marries Romeo and Juliet in a marriage designed to create harmony between the feuding Capulets and Montagues. His naïveté leads to the deaths of the lovers. Friar Bonaventura is not only naïve but also morally culpable in insisting that Annabella marry Soranzo when she is already pregnant with Giovanni's baby. This action leads only to further degradation for brother and sister. Some other elements of *'Tis Pity She's a Whore* that are also analogous to other plays could be either deliberate or accidental.

For example, there is Annabella's resemblance to Kyd's Bel-Imperia in *The Spanish Tragedy*. Bel-Imperia's brother locks her away when she manages to write a letter in her own blood to Hieronimo, who needs to know who killed his son. Also, Bel-Imperia is supposedly in disgrace over some early intimacy with her lover, but Don, her lover, is not her brother. When Annabella writes a letter to Giovanni in her own blood to warn him that Saranzo knows he is her lover, Giovanni is past caring whether or not anyone knows.

At no point, however, does Annabella manifest the moral and physical courage demonstrated by Bel-Imperia. Annabella is victimized by her brother, who cares less about her being beaten by Soranzo than he cares about whether or not Soranzo is a better lover. Owned by men, Annabella is killed by her brother, as she asks forgiveness for her sins and his. Annabella's love for her brother is unfailing, but she is always aware that this love is wrong.

Giovanni, however, sees their love as in some way natural, no matter what divine law prohibits, and as decreed by Fate. Increasingly insensitive to ethical values, he welcomes death as no earlier protagonists had done. Just before he kills his sister as part of his revenge on Soranzo, Giovanni tells her that if he could believe that water burns, he might be able to believe that Hell or Heaven is real. As he dies, the only grace he desires is to see Annabella's face.

"Critical Evaluation" by Carol Bishop

Further Reading

Bradbrook, M. C. *Themes and Conventions of Elizabethan Tragedy*. New York: Cambridge University Press, 1960. Argues that Ford deals with a single subject, a personal human love, and that T. S. Eliot is quite mistaken in stating that the relationship between Giovanni and Annabella is only carnal.

Bullman, James. "Caroline Drama." In *The Cambridge Companion to English Renaissance Drama*, edited by A. R. Braunmuller and Michael Hattaway. New York: Cambridge University Press, 2003. *'Tis Pity She's a Whore* and Ford's other plays are discussed in this chapter.

Eliot, T. S. *Essays on Elizabethan Drama*. New York: Harcourt, Brace & World, 1960. Eliot asserts that the two lovers have nothing except a physical relationship. Eliot's influential criticism is often a starting point for later critics, and so needs to be read as a reference.

Ellis-Fermor, Una Mary. *The Jacobean Drama: An Interpretation*. New York: Vintage Books, 1964. Ellis-Fermor argues the importance of aristocratic virtues to Ford, including courage, chivalry, and chastity, with chastity being the greatest of those virtues. Includes an index.

Mousley, Andy. *Renaissance Drama and Contemporary Literary Theory*. New York: Macmillan, 2000. Chapter 4 provides a psychoanalytical interpretation of the play.

Ornstein, Robert. *The Moral Vision of Jacobean Tragedy*. Madison: University of Wisconsin Press, 1965. The chapter on Ford's plays is excellent. Ornstein argues that only the most ethically dogmatic should be offended by this play.

Sanders, Julie. *Caroline Drama: The Plays of Massinger, Ford, Shirley, and Brome*. Plymouth, England: Northcote House/British Council, 1999. Examines the works of

Ford and his contemporaries Philip Massinger, James Shirley, and Richard Brome, focusing on their concern with issues of community and humanity.

Simkin, Stevie, ed. *Revenge Tragedy*. New York: Palgrave, 2001. *'Tis Pity She's a Whore* is one of the Renaissance revenge tragedies that is examined from the perspective of modern critical analysis. The specific essays about Ford's play are "*'Tis Pity She's a Whore*: Representing the Incestuous Body" by Susan J. Wiseman and "'What Strange Riddle This?': Deciphering *'Tis Pity She's a Whore*" by Michael Neill.

Wymer, Rowland. *Webster and Ford*. New York: St. Martin's Press, 1995. Describes the careers of Ford and John Webster, placing their work within the contexts of Jacobean and Caroline theater. Provides a detailed analysis of six plays, including *'Tis Pity She's a Whore*.

The Titan

Author: Theodore Dreiser (1871-1945)
First published: 1914
Type of work: Novel
Type of plot: Naturalism
Time of plot: 1870's-1890's
Locale: Chicago

Principal characters:
FRANK ALGERNON COWPERWOOD, a multimillionaire and financial genius
AILEEN COWPERWOOD, his mistress and then his wife
STEPHANIE PLATOW, his mistress
BERENICE FLEMING, his protégé and mistress
PETER LAUGHLIN, his business partner

The Story:

When he is released from a Pennsylvania prison in the 1870's, Frank Algernon Cowperwood is a millionaire but not very young. He goes to Chicago to begin a new life with his mistress, Aileen Butler, and within a short time has made friends among influential businessmen there. Divorced by his first wife, Cowperwood finally marries Aileen. He prepares to increase his fortune, to become a power in the city, and to conquer its society. To this end, he seeks an enterprise that will yield heavy returns on his investment quickly. In his first battle among the financial barons of Chicago, he gains control of the gas companies.

At the same time, the Cowperwoods lay siege to Chicago society, but with little success. Aileen Cowperwood is too high-spirited and lacking in the poise that is required for social success. Then Cowperwood becomes involved in several lawsuits, and his earlier political and economic disgrace in Philadelphia is exposed in the Chicago newspapers. After a long battle, Cowperwood is able to force the rival gas companies to buy out his franchises at a profit to himself. That deal brings social defeat to the Cowperwoods, at least temporarily, for Frank's rivals in finance are also the social powers of Chicago at the time. Cowperwood turns once again to a mistress, but the affair ends when Aileen attempts to kill her rival.

For several years, a cable-car system of street railways claims most of Cowperwood's time. He buys control of the horsecar company that serves the north side of Chicago.

Then his naturally promiscuous temperament asserts itself when he meets the dark, lush Stephanie Platow. Ten years younger than his wife and interested in art, literature, and music, she is able to fill a place in his life that Aileen never could.

While involved in his affair with Stephanie, Cowperwood coerces the street railway company on the west side into giving its franchise to him. His enjoyment of his victory is partially spoiled when he learns that Stephanie is also the lover of another man. Meanwhile, financial forces are at work against Cowperwood. Two city bosses hope to play the city politicians against him, for without the support of the city council to aid him with franchises and grants, the financier will be helpless to merge all the street railways of the city under his control.

The first battle is fought in an election to gain possession of the Chicago city council. Cowperwood finds it far more painful to learn at this time that his wife has been unfaithful to him than to discover that he has arrayed the whole financial and social element of the city against himself. The loss of the election proves no permanent setback to Cowperwood, however, nor does his wife's infidelity. From the latter he recovers, and the former is soon undone by his opponents when they fail to pave the way with favors and money when they try to push bills through the new reform council. Even the new mayor is soon an ally of Cowperwood.

Soon afterward, Cowperwood meets Berenice Fleming; the daughter of a woman who runs a house of ill repute, Berenice is being prepared in a fashionable boarding school for a career in society. Cowperwood takes her and her family under his wing. He also becomes her lover, though with some misgivings, given the fact that Berenice is but seventeen and he is fifty-two.

At about this time, his financial rivals are trying to gain franchises for elevated rail lines powered by electricity. This new development means that his own street railways have to be converted to electricity, and he has to compete for at least a share of the elevated lines to prevent ruin. The South Side's elevated train, or "L," is already a tremendous success because of the World's Fair of 1893, and the whole city is now clamoring for better transportation service. Cowperwood's opponents control the city's banks, so those institutions will not lend him the funds he needs to begin operations. When he attempts to secure funds in the East, Cowperwood discovers that his assets are in question. With one masterstroke, however, the financier wipes out any question of his ability and his credit: He donates three hundred thousand dollars to the local university for a telescope and observatory.

Even with unlimited credit, gaining franchises is not easy. Cowperwood is determined to keep control of the Chicago transportation system, but he begins to realize that neither he nor his wife will ever be accepted socially. He decides to build a mansion in New York to hold his collection of art, hoping to make that his card of entry into society.

Having obtained his franchises in Chicago, he begins work on elevated lines there. Cowperwood's enemies hope that he will overreach, after which they can force him out of Chicago financially as well as socially. With the collapse of the American Match Corporation, however, a failure partially engineered by Cowperwood, a series of runs begin on the Chicago banks controlled by his enemies. When their attempts to recall the enormous loans made to Cowperwood fail, he emerges from the affair stronger than ever.

The final battle, and the climax of Cowperwood's financial career in Chicago, is the one he wages to secure fifty-year franchises for his growing transportation system. This project is doubly difficult because of Cowperwood's latest property, the Union Loop, by which he controls the elevated lines. This loop of elevated track encircling the downtown business district has to be used by all the lines in the city. The moneyed interests oppose Cowperwood because he is not with them; the newspapers oppose him because they want to see better and cheaper facilities. In the face of such opposition, even the most reckless of the city's aldermen fear to grant the franchises Cowperwood wants, regardless of the

money and power he is prepared to give them. Cowperwood's lawyers inform him that the state constitution prevents the city from granting such long-term franchises, even if the city council could be coerced into approving them. Cowperwood's next idea is to use bribery to get a transportation commission set up in the state legislature. The bill that will set up the commission includes a clause extending existing franchises for a period of fifty years. The bill is passed by the legislature, but it is vetoed by the governor.

Meanwhile, Cowperwood's New York mansion has been completed, and Aileen has moved in. She meets with no social success in New York City, except among the bohemian set. Berenice Fleming settles at the same time with her family in a mansion on Park Avenue. Aileen hears of Cowperwood's affair with Berenice, and when he asks her for a divorce, she tries to commit suicide but fails.

Cowperwood again tries to force his bill through the Illinois legislature, but the legislators return it to the Chicago city council. There, as before, Cowperwood loses. The aldermen are so afraid of the people and the newspapers that they dare not grant what the financier wishes, despite his huge bribes. With his hope of controlling the Chicago transportation system gone, Cowperwood sells his interests. Admitting defeat, he goes to Europe with Berenice. The titan's empire has fallen.

Critical Evaluation:

The Titan is the second in Theodore Dreiser's trilogy of novels tracing the career of Frank Algernon Cowperwood, which the author had planned to call "A Trilogy of Desire." *The Financier* (1912, 1927) tells the story of Cowperwood's early successes in the financial world of Philadelphia, the start of his extramarital affair with Aileen, and his conviction and imprisonment for grand larceny. In the final novel, *The Stoic* (1947), Cowperwood is still portrayed as shrewdly energetic and ambitious, now living abroad after his defeat in Chicago, and amassing a large but unneeded fortune in London. Estranged from Berenice, he dies a lonely death while his overextended empire finally crumbles.

Cowperwood's character is based on that of nineteenth century Chicago financier Charles Yerkes (1837-1905). Like Dreiser's Cowperwood, Yerkes was a shrewd schemer in business who made his fortune in Philadelphia public transportation, spent a short time in prison for illegal business manipulations, and then moved to Chicago and gained control of a gas trust. Yerkes later tried to monopolize the city's transportation system through long-term franchises, and when he failed he turned to new business interests in the London Underground. According to Richard Lehan's account in *The-*

odore Dreiser: His World and His Novels* (1969), several even more specific details in *The Titan* are taken directly from Dreiser's own exhaustive research into the life of Yerkes and the activities of the Chicago business world he dominated for a time.

The Titan reflects Dreiser's absorption with the ideas of Herbert Spencer, T. H. Huxley, and other nineteenth century social Darwinists who viewed society as essentially controlled by the law of "survival of the fittest." In Dreiser's view, it is the nature of the universe that "a balance is struck wherein the mass subdues the individual or the individual the mass." Cowperwood's struggle against Hand, Schryhart, and Arneel is one for survival in the financial jungle of Chicago big business.

For Dreiser, such a struggle is wholly amoral. There is no right or wrong because it is the nature as well as the condition of human beings to have to struggle for power and survival. Cowperwood's cause is neither more nor less just than that of his antagonists, nor are his means any less scrupulous than their own. He may be said to be more shrewd than they, or to possess more ruthlessness in certain circumstances, but for Dreiser his struggle is the elemental contest between the impulse-driven energies of the individual and those of others in his society.

The forces underlying Cowperwood's ambitions are actually larger than mere individual desires on his part. Described in the novel as "impelled by some blazing internal force," Cowperwood is driven by instincts beyond his control. Caught up in a natural struggle for survival and for power over others, he is dominated by "the drug of a personality he could not gainsay." He can no more remain satisfied with the money and success he has already attained than he can stay content with one woman. Hence the need to conquer, to dominate and control, characterizes both Cowperwood's financial and his romantic interests. To both, he brings the same shrewd scheming and forcefulness that are needed for success.

The two major plots—Cowperwood's business life and his romantic life—alternate and mirror each other throughout the novel, and they prove to be integrally related. Cowperwood is as direct in his dealings with women as he is in his confrontations with men of business. The frankness with which he first approaches Rita Sohlberg is very similar to the blunt way he attempts to bribe Governor Swanson. In fact, many of Cowperwood's mistresses are related to the very men who, mainly as a consequence of his amorous trespassing, end up opposing him most bitterly in Chicago. His affairs with Butler's, Cochrane's, and Haguenin's daughters—like his interlude with Hand's wife—not only lessen his cir-

cle of friends but also gain him those enemies who eventually pull together to defeat him.

As the title of the novel suggests, Cowperwood is a titan among men, one striving after more and achieving greater victory because he is driven to do so by his very nature. As he has himself come to recognize, the "humdrum conventional world could not brook his daring, his insouciance, his constant desire to call a spade a spade. His genial sufficiency was a taunt and a mockery to many." Yet his is a lonely victory, a fact emphasized by his almost self-imposed alienation from the business community with which his life is so connected and by his being socially ostracized in Chicago despite his wealth.

In a sense, Cowperwood is as much a victim of his will to power as any of those he defeats on the stock exchange. For such men as he, power is the very means of survival, and in the world of Chicago business, power generates money, which in turn generates more power. The cycle, as much as the struggle, is endless. If a balance is ever struck between the power of the individual and that of the group, it is, Dreiser suggests, only temporary, for "without variance, how should the balance be maintained?" For Dreiser, as for Cowperwood, this is the meaning of life, a continual rebalancing, a necessary search on the part of the individual to discover a means of maintaining or acquiring personal desires against those of society. Human beings are but tools of their own private nature, "forever suffering the goad of a restless heart."

For men like Cowperwood, defeat is no more final or settling than triumph. If he has won anything permanent by the novel's end, it is the love of Berenice. She is part, at least, of the whole that Cowperwood has been driven to seek and attain. More than that he will never achieve or understand about life. "Thou hast lived," concludes Dreiser at the end of the novel, as if to say that the struggle and the searching are themselves the whole that human beings seek.

"Critical Evaluation" by Robert Dees

Further Reading

Cassuto, Leonard, and Clare Virginia Eby, eds. *The Cambridge Companion to Theodore Dreiser.* New York: Cambridge University Press, 2004. Collection of twelve essays discusses the novelist's examination of American conflicts between materialistic longings and traditional values. Topics addressed include Dreiser's style, Dreiser and women, and Dreiser and the ideology of upward mobility.

Gogol, Miriam, ed. *Theodore Dreiser: Beyond Naturalism.* New York: New York University Press, 1995. Collection of essays offers interpretations of Dreiser's fiction from the perspectives of new historicism, poststructuralism, psychoanalysis, feminism, and other points of view. Gogol's introduction advances the argument that Dreiser was much more than a naturalist and deserves to be treated as a major author.

Hussman, Lawrence E., Jr. *Dreiser and His Fiction: A Twentieth-Century Quest.* Philadelphia: University of Pennsylvania Press, 1983. Presents an informative discussion of Dreiser's attitudes toward women, marriage, and prostitution as well as his belief in "the giving spirit of women." Also discusses Cowperwood's search for the ideal woman.

Juras, Uwe. *Pleasing to the "I": The Culture of Personality and Its Representations in Theodore Dreiser and F. Scott Fitzgerald.* New York: Peter Lang, 2006. Examines how the two authors depict the concept of personality, defined as the outward presentation of self, in their work. Includes a discussion of *The Titan.*

Lehan, Richard. *Theodore Dreiser: His World and His Novels.* Carbondale: Southern Illinois University Press, 1969. Critical study of Dreiser's novels examines their genesis, evolution, pattern, and meaning. Discusses such influences on the author's imagination as family, city, work,

and politics. Analyzes Cowperwood as a materialist Horatio Alger hero who appreciates beauty and art.

Lingeman, Richard. *An American Journey, 1908-1945.* Vol. 2 in *Theodore Dreiser.* New York: Putnam, 1990. Explores Dreiser's composition of *The Titan* in relation to other aspects of his life. Points out that his research for the book in Chicago in 1912 diverged from his previous procedure in writing *Sister Carrie* (1900) and *Jennie Gerhardt* (1911).

Loving, Jerome. *The Last Titan: A Life of Theodore Dreiser.* Berkeley: University of California Press, 2005. Engrossing survey of the author's life and work is a welcome addition to Dreiser scholarship. Focuses on Dreiser's work, including his journalism, discussing the writers who influenced him and his place within American literature.

Pizer, Donald. *The Novels of Theodore Dreiser: A Critical Study.* Minneapolis: University of Minnesota Press, 1976. Chronicles Dreiser's research of historical sources relating to Charles Yerkes for the character of Cowperwood and examines his creative choices and the novel's publication history. Presents extensive discussion of Cowperwood's sexual life as representing Dreiser's interpretation of public morality in America.

Titus Andronicus

Author: William Shakespeare (1564-1616)
First produced: 1594; first published, 1594
Type of work: Drama
Type of plot: Tragedy
Time of plot: Early Christian era
Locale: Rome and vicinity

Principal characters:
SATURNINUS, the emperor of Rome
BASSIANUS, his brother
TITUS ANDRONICUS, a Roman general
LUCIUS, his son
LAVINIA, his only daughter
MARCUS, his brother, a tribune
TAMORA, the queen of the Goths
AARON, her lover, a Moor
ALARBUS,
DEMETRIUS, and
CHIRON, her sons

The Story:

Early in the Christian era, Saturninus and Bassianus, sons of the late emperor, contend for the crown of the Roman Empire. Both men are leaders of strong factions. Another candidate, a popular one, is Titus Andronicus, a Roman famed for his victories over the barbarian Goths to the north. Marcus Andronicus, brother of Titus, states in the forum that Titus is the popular choice to succeed the late emperor. The sons,

willing to abide by the desires of the populace, dismiss their factions.

As the prominent men of the city go into the senate house, Titus makes his triumphant entry into Rome. He is accompanied by his surviving sons and by a casket containing the bodies of other sons. In his train also are Tamora, the queen of the Goths; her sons, Alarbus, Demetrius, and Chiron; and her lover, Aaron, a Moor. Before the senate house, one of Titus's sons demands that a Gothic prisoner be sacrificed to appease the spirits of his dead brothers in the casket. When Titus offers as sacrifice the oldest son of Tamora, the queen pleads for mercy, reminding Titus that her sons are as precious to her as his are to him. Titus pays her no heed. Alarbus is sacrificed, and the casket is then laid in the tomb of the Andronici. At that moment Lavinia, Titus's only daughter, appears to greet her father and brothers and to pay her respects to her fallen brothers.

Marcus comes out of the senate house, greets Titus, and informs him that he is the choice of the people for the emperorship. Titus, unwilling to take on that responsibility at his age, persuades the people to name Saturninus emperor instead. Saturninus, in gratitude, asks for and receives the hand of Lavinia to become his queen. Bassianus, however, to whom Lavinia gives her heart, seizes the maid with the help of Marcus and the sons of Titus and carries her away. Titus's son, Mutius, who stays behind to cover their flight, is killed by his father.

Saturninus, who begrudges Titus his popularity with the people, disavows all allegiance and debt to the general and plans to take Tamora as his wife. Titus, deserted by his emperor, his brother, and his sons, is deeply shaken.

Marcus and Titus's sons return and express the desire to bury Mutius in the family vault. Titus at first refuses, saying that Mutius was a traitor; then he relents after his brother and his sons argue effectively for proper burial. When Bassianus appears with Lavinia, Saturninus vows that he will avenge the stealing of the maid who was given him by her father. Bassianus speaks in Titus's behalf, but Titus declares that he can plead his own case before the emperor. Tamora openly advises Saturninus to be gracious to Titus, but secretly she advises him to gain Titus's friendship only because Titus is so popular in Rome. She assures Saturninus that she will destroy Titus and his family for their having sacrificed one of her own sons. Saturninus therefore pardons the Andronici and declares his intention of marrying Tamora. Believing their differences reconciled, Titus invites Saturninus to hunt with him the next day.

Aaron, contemplating Tamora's good fortune and the imminent downfall of Saturninus and of Rome as well, comes upon Chiron and Demetrius, disputing and about to draw their swords over their chances of winning the favors of Lavinia. Advising the youths to contain themselves, he tells them that both can enjoy Lavinia by seizing her in the forest during the hunt, which will be attended by the lords and ladies of the court.

Later, while the hunt is under way, Aaron hides a sack of gold at the foot of a large tree in the forest. He previously arranged to have a pit dug near the tree; this pit he covered over with undergrowth. There Tamora finds him and learns that both Bassianus and Lavinia will come to grief that day. Before Aaron leaves Tamora, he gives her a letter with directions that the message should reach the hands of Saturninus. Bassianus and Lavinia approach and, seeing that the Moor and Tamora are together, chafe Tamora and threaten to tell Saturninus of her dalliance in the forest. Chiron and Demetrius come upon the scene. Informed by Tamora that Bassianus and Lavinia insulted her, they stab Bassianus to death. When Tamora urges them to stab Lavinia they refuse, saying that they will enjoy her first. Lavinia then appeals to Tamora to remember that Titus spared her life. Tamora, recalling how Titus ignored her pleas to spare her son from sacrifice, is determined that her sons should have their lustful pleasure. The brothers, after throwing the body of Bassianus into the pit, drag Lavinia away to rape her.

Meanwhile, Aaron, on the pretext that he trapped a panther, brings two of Titus's sons, Quintus and Martius, to the pit and leave them there. Martius falls into the trap, where he recognizes the murdered Bassianus by a ring he wears on his finger. When Quintus tries to pull Martius out of the pit, he loses his balance and tumbles into it. Aaron, returning with Saturninus, claims that Titus's sons murdered Bassianus. Tamora then gives Saturninus the letter that Aaron gave her. The letter, written ostensibly by one of the Andronici, outlines a plot to assassinate Bassianus, to bury him in a pit, and then to collect payment, which is a bag of gold hidden near the pit. When the bag of gold is found where Aaron placed it, Saturninus is convinced of the brothers' guilt. Despite Titus's offer of his own person as security for his sons, Saturninus sentences them to be tortured. Tamora assures Titus that she will speak to Saturninus on his behalf.

In another part of the forest, Chiron and Demetrius, their evil deed accomplished, cut off Lavinia's hands and tongue so that she will be able neither to write nor to tell of what befell her. Alone in the forest, Lavinia is joined at last by her uncle, Marcus, who leads her to her father.

Later, in Rome, Titus recalls his years of faithful military service to the state and begs the tribunes to spare his sons, but they will not listen to him. Another son, Lucius, a great favorite with the people, attempts unsuccessfully to rescue his brothers. He is banished from the city. As Titus pleads in vain, Marcus brings the ravished Lavinia to him. The sight of his daughter leads Titus to wonder to what infinite depths of grief a man can come. Aaron announces to the grieving Andronici that Saturninus will release Martius and Quintus if one of the family will cut off his hand and send it to the court.

Titus agrees to let Lucius and Marcus decide between them; when they go to get an ax, Titus directs Aaron to cut off his hand. Later, a messenger brings Titus his hand and the heads of Martius and Quintus as well. Having suffered as much as a man can suffer, Titus vows revenge. He directs the banished Lucius to raise an invading force among the Goths.

At his home, Titus appears to be demented. Even so, it is clear to him one day that Lavinia is trying desperately to tell him something. She indicates in Ovid's *Metamorphoses* the section in which the story of Tereus's brutal rape of Philomela is recounted. Suddenly, it occurs to Marcus that he can, by holding a staff in his teeth and between his knees, write in the sand on the floor. Lavinia takes the staff thus and writes in the sand that Chiron and Demetrius are her violators.

Titus now sends his grandson with a bundle of weapons to present to Tamora's sons. The youths do not understand the message that Titus attached to the gift, but Aaron quickly sees that Titus knows who Lavinia's ravishers are. As the brothers admire their gift, a blast of trumpets announces the birth of a child to Tamora. A nurse enters with the newborn baby, who is black, and states that Tamora, fearful lest Saturninus see it, should send the child to Aaron. Chiron and Demetrius, aware of their mother's shame, insist that the infant be killed immediately. When they offer to carry out the murder, Aaron, the father, defies them. As a precaution, he kills the nurse, one of three women who know the baby's color. Then he has a fair-skinned baby, newly born, taken to Tamora before he flees to the Goths.

Titus, now reputed to be utterly demented, writes messages to the gods, attaches them to arrows, and, with Marcus and his grandson, shoots the arrows into the court. He persuades a passing farmer to deliver a letter to Saturninus. The emperor is already disturbed because the messages carried by the arrows state Titus's grievances against the state. When Saturninus threatens to execute justice on old Titus, Tamora, feeling her revenge complete, advises him to treat the distracted old soldier gently. The farmer, meanwhile, delivers Titus's letter. Enraged by its mocking message, Saturninus commands that Titus be brought to him to be executed.

A messenger then brings word that the Goths, led by Lucius, threaten to sack Rome. Knowing Lucius's popularity with the Romans, Saturninus is fearful. Tamora, however, confident of her ability to save the city, directs the messenger to arrange a conference with Lucius at the house of Titus.

In the camp of the Goths, Aaron and his child are brought before Lucius. Aaron's captor discloses that he came upon the Moor in a ruined monastery and heard him state aloud that the baby's mother was Tamora. At Lucius's promise to preserve the life of the child, Aaron confesses to his crimes against the Andronici. Lucius decrees that the Moor must die a horrible death.

Tamora, meanwhile, believing that Titus is demented beyond all reason, disguises herself as Revenge and with her sons, also disguised, presents herself to Titus. Although Titus recognizes her, she insists that she is Revenge, his friend. Titus, for his own purposes, pretends to be taken in by the disguises; he tells Rapine and Murder, Revenge's cohorts, to seek out two such as themselves and destroy them. At Tamora's bidding, Titus directs Marcus to invite Lucius to a banquet, to which Saturninus and Tamora and her sons will also come.

Titus persuades Chiron and Demetrius to stay with him while their companion, Revenge, goes to perform other duties. He then calls in his kinsmen, who seize and bind the brothers. Titus tells them that he intends to kill them and feed to their mother a paste made of their bones and blood. Lavinia holds a bowl between the stumps of her arms to catch their blood as Titus cuts their throats.

Lucius, accompanied by a guard of Goths, comes to his father's house, where he puts Aaron in the charge of Marcus. Saturninus and Tamora make their appearance and are ushered to a banquet served by Titus, dressed as a cook. Titus, hearing from Saturninus that Virginius, in the legend, did well to kill his ravished daughter, stabs Lavinia. The startled Saturninus asks if Lavinia was raped and by whom. When Titus discloses that Tamora's sons did the evil deed, Saturninus asks to see the youths at once. Titus, declaring that Tamora is eating their remains, stabs her. Saturninus stabs Titus, and Lucius, in turn, stabs Saturninus. A general fight ensues. Lucius and Marcus, with their followers, retire to a balcony to tell the people of Rome of the manifold evils wrought by Tamora, her sons, and Aaron. After the people choose him as their new emperor, Lucius sentences Aaron to be buried waist deep and left to starve. He also decrees that Tamora's body be fed to wild beasts.

Critical Evaluation:

Titus Andronicus, the first of William Shakespeare's ten tragedies, was written between 1589 and 1592, probably in 1590. The young writer was eager to establish himself as a commercially successful playwright, so he resorted to the traditionally accepted form of revenge tragedy for this play. Revenge tragedy is a particularly violent form of theater and had been used by Thomas Kyd in his spectacularly successful *The Spanish Tragedy* (c. 1585-1589). Shakespeare, no doubt, had Kyd's success in mind as he created a play of unprecedented violence. In *Titus Andronicus*, eleven of the individually named characters are murdered, eight in view of the audience, and several are horribly mutilated. Lavinia's rape and mutilation represent the acme of brutality in the Elizabethan theater, and Shakespeare was unabashedly pandering to the Elizabethan audience's taste for blood and gore in his first attempt at tragedy. It is largely because of this excessive violence that many critics, from Shakespeare's fellow dramatist Ben Jonson to twentieth century poet T. S. Eliot, have censured this play as unworthy of Shakespeare. Some critics have even denied that Shakespeare wrote the play. Such condemnation fails to recognize that it is only when *Titus Andronicus* is considered in the light of Shakespeare's mature tragedies, which are among the greatest in the English language, that it falls short of the mark. It measures up very well when it is compared with *The Spanish Tragedy* or Christopher Marlowe's *The Jew of Malta* (c. 1589), especially in regard to the important areas of characterization, language, and theme.

Although the characters in *Titus Andronicus* are clearly not as rich and subtle as are many of those in Shakespeare's later tragedies, some of them are still quite compelling and foreshadow several of Shakespeare's mature figures. Titus Andronicus is the first of Shakespeare's great Roman warriors who falls from high status because of a fatal flaw of character or intellect. In broad outline, his tragic downfall anticipates the destructive careers of Coriolanus, Julius Caesar, and Mark Antony. Even Othello's monumental rages recall Titus's propensity for impulsive violence. Titus is an outstanding example of Aristotle's conception of the tragic protagonist as a man who is greater than the ordinary and basically good, but who suffers from a deadly defect that destroys him. Titus's terrible suffering is a harrowing dramatic experience, and his character is an altogether remarkable creation for a dramatist in his twenties.

Tamora and Aaron also deserve particular mention. Tamora is the first of a small number of Shakespeare's malevolent women, some others being Goneril and Reagan in *King Lear* (pr. c. 1605-1606, pb. 1608) and Lady Macbeth in *Macbeth* (pr. 1606, pb. 1623). Like them, Tamora is seen in dramatic contrast to a benevolent female character, in this case Lavinia. Like the other villainesses, Tamora is crafty and manipulative, psychopathic and driven by a lust for power, but her animus against the Andronici is understandable in view of the sacrificial execution of her son Alarbus. She is perhaps ultimately less sympathetic than Lady Macbeth, who loses her mind because of her guilt, but she is clearly more human than Goneril and Reagan, who are arguably the most malignant women in all of drama. Aaron is the first of Shakespeare's Machiavellian villains, the others being Richard III in *Richard III* (pr. c. 1592-1593, pb. 1597), Iago in *Othello, the Moor of Venice* (pr. 1604, pb. 1622), and Edmund in *King Lear*. Like the behavior of all villains of this type, Aaron's actions are scheming, sadistic, and psychopathic. He revels in doing evil, and his catalog of his life after his capture recalls the hateful braggadocio of Ithamore in Marlowe's *The Jew of Malta*, upon whom he is partially based.

The sheer excesses of his play run the risk of disgusting the audience, even one as fond of violence as the Elizabethan audience was. The shock of Lavinia's mutilations is reduced by the language which is used to describe her. It is the language of euphemism—"what stern ungentle hands/ Hath lopped and hewed and made thy body bare/ Of her two branches" and "a crimson river of warm blood/ Like to a bubbling fountain stirred with wind/ Doth rise and fall between thy rosed lips"—and it creates a psychic distance between the fact of the violence and the audience's perception of it. References to classical myths involving physical dismemberment provide an imaginative context for the most grotesque outrages. Lavinia's rape and the removal of her tongue and hands to prevent disclosure of her persecutors recall the myth of Procne, Philomela, and Tereus, which is recorded in Ovid's *Metamorphoses* (c. 8) and which every Elizabethan would have known. The feast at which Tamora is served the baked bodies of her evil sons Chiron and Demetrius has a grim precedent in a Roman tragedy of Seneca. The language of euphemism and the language of myth buffer the shock of the most extreme episodes of violence in this play, rendering them more palatable to the audience.

Titus Andronicus is not without moral significance even though it obviously fails to achieve the catharsis of *Hamlet, Prince of Denmark* (pr. c. 1600-1601, pb. 1603) and *King Lear*. Revenge is shown to be unsatisfactory as a moral code of governance. Titus's obstinate sacrifice of Alarbus, a son of the captured Gothic queen Tamora, provides the motive for the subsequent outrages against his family. Avengers and victims become indistinguishable in the course of the play and are alike destroyed in the cruel and ultimately mindless bloodbath that follows Alarbus's execution. Titus, the once majestic leader, is reduced by the final act to a craftily insane murderer, not only of his enemies but also of his own daughter. Rome is in tatters until a semblance of order is restored at the end by the very Goths who were the original enemy. The play, then, is a powerful testament to the irrationality of revenge, or even of justice untempered by mercy, as a moral imperative.

"Critical Evaluation" by Robert G. Blake

Further Reading

Bartels, Emily C. "'Incorporate in Rome': *Titus Andronicus* and the Consequence of Conquest." In *Speaking of the Moor: From Alcazar to Othello*. Philadelphia: University of Pennsylvania Press, 2008. In the late sixteenth and early seventeenth centuries, as England expanded its influence around the globe, the Moor became a central character in *Titus Andronicus* and other English plays. Bartels analyzes the depiction of Moorish characters in these plays, as well as in contemporary historical writings and the letters of Elizabeth I.

Bessen, Alan C. *Shakespeare in Performance: "Titus Andronicus."* New York: Manchester University Press, 1989. Follows the stage history of the play, noting that the watershed performance was the highly successful 1955 production by Peter Brook, starring Laurence Olivier and Vivien Leigh. Addresses the numerous staging problems involved in a production of *Titus Andronicus*.

Bowers, Fredson T. *Elizabethan Revenge Tragedy, 1587-1642*. 1940. Rev. ed. Princeton, N.J.: Princeton University Press, 1966. Although somewhat old, this book is still useful and enjoyable. It traces the origins of the revenge tragedy to the plays of Seneca. Bowers shows how *Titus Andronicus* follows a pattern first formulated in English by Thomas Kyd in *The Spanish Tragedy*.

Leggatt, Alexander. "*Titus Andronicus*: This Was Thy Daughter." In *Shakespeare's Tragedies: Violation and Identity*. New York: Cambridge University Press, 2005. Examines how acts of violence in *Titus Andronicus* and six other tragedies generate questions about the identities of the victims, the perpetrators, and the acts themselves.

Metz, G. Harold. *Shakespeare's Earliest Tragedy: Studies in "Titus Andronicus."* Madison, N.J.: Fairleigh Dickinson University Press, 1996. Discusses the play's authorship, sources, origins, influence, date of composition, and use of music. Provides an overview of twentieth century criticism and of stage productions from 1970 through 1994.

Rozett, Martha Tuck. *The Doctrine of Election and the Emergence of Elizabethan Tragedy*. Princeton, N.J.: Princeton University Press, 1984. Argues that the Calvinistic doctrine of predestination and election was influential upon Elizabethan tragedy.

Vickers, Brian. *Shakespeare, Co-author: A Historical Study of Five Collaborative Plays*. New York: Oxford University Press, 2002. Seeks to develop a coherent system for identifying Shakespeare's collaborative works. Discusses concepts of authorship in English Renaissance drama and describes methods used to determine authorship since the nineteenth century. Closely analyzes five collaborative plays, including *Titus Andronicus*, which Vickers attributes to Shakespeare and George Peele.

Wells, Stanley, ed. *The Cambridge Companion to Shakespeare Studies*. New York: Cambridge University Press, 1986. This is where all studies of Shakespeare should begin. Includes excellent chapters introducing the poet's biography, conventions and beliefs of Elizabethan England, and reviews of scholarship in the field.

To a Skylark

Author: Percy Bysshe Shelley (1792-1822)
First published: 1820
Type of work: Poetry

One evening in June, 1820, while walking in a meadow near Livorno (Leghorn), Italy, Percy Bysshe Shelley and his wife Mary Wollstonecraft Shelley heard skylarks sing. The next day, reflecting upon the experience, he wrote "To a Skylark" and sent it to his London publisher to be added to a forthcoming volume featuring *Prometheus Unbound: A Lyrical Drama in Four Acts* (pb. 1820). A similar story is told about "Ode to a Nightingale" (1820), which John Keats wrote in May, 1819, the morning after hearing the song of a nightingale nesting in a tree outside his window. The opening stanza of William Wordsworth's "To a Cuckoo" (1802) anticipates Shelley's poem in language and theme.

> O blithe newcomer! I have heard,
> I hear thee and rejoice.
> O cuckoo! Shall I call thee bird,
> Or but a wandering voice?

Wordsworth's "The Green Linnet" (1803, 1807), a similar paean to a songbird, includes the following lines:

Hail to Thee, far above the rest
In joy of voice and pinion!
Thou, Linnet! In thy green array,
Presiding Spirit here to-day,
Dost lead the revels of the May;
And this is thy dominion.

Samuel Taylor Coleridge, in his "To the Nightingale" (1796), calls the bird "Sister of love-lorn Poets." In all of these works, the essential reality of a bird is represented as being manifest not in a physical presence, but in a noncorporeal song that suggests to the poet a permanence denied to humankind. In sum, long before Shelley's 1820 walk in the meadow, songbirds had become commonplace muses to Romantic poets.

"To a Skylark" is one of several poems Shelley wrote between 1816 and 1821 that sprang from his contemplation of the natural world. Others include "Ode to the West Wind" (1820), "Mont Blanc" (1817), and "The Cloud" (1820). It is divided into stanzas of four trimeter lines with a concluding alexandrine and has a traditional *ababb* rhyme scheme. This pattern of short lines with frequent enjambment hastens the progress of each stanza, which Shelley then brings to a brisk close with a final hexameter line. In addition, the opening trochaic foot of each line not only provides emphasis but also, combined with other aspects of the metrics, may be Shelley's attempt to replicate in verse the flight of the bird.

The poem effectively breaks into three parts. In the first part (lines 1-30), Shelley describes the flight of an actual skylark, albeit one that already has flown beyond his ability to see. The skylark, unlike most birds, sings only when flying, usually when it is too high to be seen from the ground: "from Heaven, or near it . . . singing still dost soar, and soaring ever singest." Shelley betrays a note of envy in the opening words of the poem—"Hail to thee, blithe Spirit!"—by implying a contrast between the bird and himself. Earthbound, the speaker has suffered emotionally debilitating personal tragedies and is struggling to achieve recognition as a poet, while the unfettered skylark enjoys a joyful freedom that is given expression by the "shrill delight" of its song.

By employing the phrase "blithe Spirit" at the start, Shelley instantly focuses attention not only on the sheer joy the bird exudes but also upon its noncorporeal, symbolic quality. He continues this thought in the second line—"Bird thou never wert"—by suggesting that the skylark differs from other birds, which neither rise as high nor sing as "profusely." "Unpremeditated art," which concludes the stanza, suggests a spontaneity central to Romanticism but that humans, constrained by society's mores, usually are forced to sublimate. The next three stanzas trace the upward flight of the singing

bird with a series of similes that continues to emphasize the creature's freedom from earthly restraints, in part because the object of each simile also is unseen. The most effective simile compares the bird, whose progress the speaker follows by the sound of its song, to Venus, the morning star, "that silver sphere" whose "arrows" (rays of light) fade in "the white dawn clear," but whose presence continues to be felt.

All the earth and air
With thy voice is loud,
As, when night is bare,
From one lonely cloud
The moon rains out her beams,
    and Heaven is overflowed.

In the second section of the poem (lines 31-60), Shelley shifts his style and tone. Rather than invoking heaven, sun, clouds, or star, his imagery focuses upon earthbound things: a poet struggling to find an audience, a lovelorn maiden in a tower, a glowworm whose "aereal hue" is hidden by flowers and grass, and a rose deflowered by winds and obscured by its leaves. All of these earthly things, though beautiful, are unseen and thus unappreciated. By contrast, the skylark's song compensates for the fact that the bird is not seen, so it can still be appreciated. There is a universality to Shelley's several similes, as the images encompass the human, animal, vegetable, and mineral realms. What is more, his imagery in these stanzas (lines 36-60) also evokes all five senses.

Having liberated the skylark with his opening invocation, Shelley the human poet in the third section (lines 61-105) pays tribute to the skylark as natural poet, whom he then asks to teach him and his fellows the secret of its joy. The opening ("Teach us, Sprite or Bird . . .") echoes the start of the poem, though "Spirit" now is "Sprite" and the earlier enthusiastic greeting ("Hail to thee . . .") now is an imploring "Teach us. . . ." (There is a similar pleading in the first line of the last stanza of "Ode to the West Wind," which Shelley wrote a year earlier: "Make me thy lyre, even as the forest is.") The two poems often are compared.) Nothing else he has heard—neither the traditional Greek poems in praise of love or wine, nor a "Chorus Hymeneal" (marriage song), nor even a "triumphal chant" (an army's victory march)—matches the "flood of rapture so divine" that is the skylark's song.

In four questions that compose the next stanza (lines 71-75), Shelley asks what the sources are of the skylark's "happy strain," its "love of thine own kind," and "ignorance of pain," and he again invokes varied aspects of the physical world: fields, waves, mountains, sky, and plain. He proceeds further to highlight differences between the bird and humankind, culminating in the implied contrast to himself personally in line 80: "Thou lovest—but ne'er knew love's sad satiety." In the next stanza, "we mere mortals" also suggests that the poet is speaking both of his situation and of that of humankind generally. Continuing this thought, Shelley further highlights the contrast between the lives of humans and that of the skylark.

> We look before and after,
> And pine for what is not:
> Our sincerest laughter
> With some pain is fraught;
> Our sweetest songs are those that
>   tell of saddest thought.

In the next and final stanza, however, Shelley retreats to a self-serving introverted plaint, asking the skylark to help him attain public recognition as a poet.

> Teach me half the gladness
> That thy brain must know,
> Such harmonious madness
> From my lips would flow
> The world should listen then—
>   as I am listening now.

Because Shelley portrays the skylark as totally happy and not needing to confront mortality, one can conclude that the bird symbolizes ultimate joy, maybe even a Platonic ideal. Like so much Romantic lyric poetry, however, "To a Skylark" ultimately is a personal manifesto: As a poet, Shelley also is a singer and expresses in his poems a yearning for an immortality that he imagines the skylark, through its song, surely has. In the summer of 1816, in "Hymn to Intellectual Beauty" Shelley asked the awe-inspiring but unseen "loveliness" or "Spirit of Beauty" that pervades the material world to endow him with "whate'er these words cannot express." Four years later, in "To a Skylark," a more straightforward lyric, he continued his quest, which was a quintessential aspect of Romanticism.

Gerald H. Strauss

Further Reading

Bieri, James. *Percy Bysshe Shelley: A Biography*. Baltimore: Johns Hopkins University Press, 2008. This massive biography by a psychologist, not a literary scholar, covers all aspects of Shelley's life in great detail and is based on a scrupulous study of available sources.

Chernaik, Judith. *The Lyrics of Shelley*. Cleveland, Ohio: Press of Case Western Reserve University, 1972. Detailed analyses of more than two dozen Shelley lyrics form the centerpiece of this book, which also traces the developmental process of many of the works.

Reiman, Donald H. *Percy Bysshe Shelley*. New York: St. Martin's Press, 1969. Including a brief biography, this book is useful for Reiman's discussions and explications of what he considers Shelley's most important poetry and prose.

Wasserman, Earl R. *Shelley: A Critical Reading*. Baltimore: Johns Hopkins University Press, 1971. An invaluable book by a major Shelley scholar, this volume presents careful analyses and explications of Shelley's major works of poetry and prose.

White, Newman Ivey. *Shelley*. 2 vols. New York: Alfred A. Knopf, 1940. This classic, monumental biography remains the touchstone by which subsequent studies are evaluated.

Wroe, Ann. *Being Shelley: The Poet's Search for Himself*. New York: Pantheon Books, 2007. An unconventional biography, this is a study of Shelley's poetry as it reveals the man, with attention paid to the composition and development of individual works.

To Autumn

Author: John Keats (1795-1821)
First published: 1820
Type of work: Poetry
Type of plot: Ode

John Keats wrote one of his best poems, "To Autumn," on Sunday, September 19, 1819. Its remarkably quick completion exemplifies Keats's accomplishments generally. The poem was written rapidly in a life notable as one of the briefest and most compact of all the great poets' lives. It is the last of the odes that Keats composed from May to September of 1819 and thus one of the last poems he ever wrote. At the beginning of the following year, the signs of his tuberculosis appeared, and on February 23, 1821, he died in Rome at the age of twenty-five. Keats's poetic career lasted only five years, and he wrote intensively for only three of those years.

Keats wrote five poems that he called odes during these middling months of 1819; "To Autumn" is designated by its title as an ode, and its form and manner echo those other poems, so critics generally classify it thus. The ode is a Greco-Roman classical form. Its two greatest early practitioners were the Greek Pindar and the Roman Horace. Keats's odes resemble Horace's more than they resemble Pindar's. They comprise stanzas that incidentally bear some resemblance to the very nonclassical sonnets he had already written. In all the odes except "Ode to Psyche" (1820), the stanzas are of regular length.

For "To Autumn," Keats chose an eleven-line length instead of his more usual ten-line pattern. He always begins his odes with an initial *abab* rhyme scheme, then switches to a different pattern in the second four lines and reuses rhymes from this second set of lines in the two or three following lines. In "To Autumn," the seventh and eleventh lines rhyme. Having established a scheme for one stanza, he repeats it in the others. Many poets do not like rhymes at all, and Keats himself refers to "dull rhymes" in one of his poems, but once he establishes such a pattern, he repeats it precisely, with different rhyming words in each stanza—in as many as ten stanzas in "Ode to Indolence" (1848).

In addition to the end rhymes and the varied iambic movement of the lines, Keats creates many sound effects such as internal rhymes ("reap'd" and "sleep"), alliteration ("mists" and "mellow"), and assonance ("touch" and "stubble"). These patterns, intricate and subtle, may be studied at great length. Most of these effects can be found in an early version of the poem, suggesting that although they are to some extent calculated, they primarily demonstrate an ear innately sensitive to sound.

A more important characteristic of the ode as Keats practiced it is its dedication to a specific theme, well reflected in the titles he chose for his work. However, to say that "Ode on a Grecian Urn" (1820) is only about an urn is to neglect the intense provocativeness of the figures on the urn. The emotional appeal of "To Autumn" is similarly rich. In the first of the poem's three stanzas, Keats develops the "mellow fruitfulness" of autumn; in the second, he considers nature's gifts, both those heaped in a granary and those in the immediate surroundings. The third stanza contrasts autumn's "songs" with those of spring, strongly emphasizing the beauty of the end of the season of natural growth that began months earlier.

The imagery of "To Autumn" is an important resource in conveying its theme. The sensory appeals in the poem are multiple. One particularly important such appeal in the first stanza is the sense of motion reflected in many of the verbs, such as "load," "bind," "run," "fill," "plump," and "swell." The summer sun and the bees have generated a harvest. In the second stanza, nature's store is depicted as "sitting" on the floor of a granary, and the air is full of the smell of flowers. The growing apples in the first stanza give way to a "cyderpress" in the second. The harvest is not depicted as gleaned but as itself a "gleaner," the grain itself personified in the image of a girl with hair swept by the wind.

In the third stanza, aural imagery predominates. Autumn, like spring, has its songs: bleating lambs, crickets, and birds. The scene has shifted away from granary and cider press to the outside world after the harvest, a principal image being the stubble of the harvested grain. Keats, describing one of his walks, also praised the sight of this stubble in a letter to a friend written only two days later. "To Autumn" includes no image of the actual cutting of the grain. Stubble is not for him a mere aftermath, for the stubble is "rosy" under the sun, as significant and admirable as the grain that has been harvested. Perhaps no poet has depicted natural change so brilliantly and yet managed at the same time to sustain the abiding presence of the temporal moment.

The movement of the poem from ripeness, to garnering, to the stubbly field is just one of the processes that unfold in "To Autumn." Autumn represents the culmination of the year's propagating forces, and the poem's imagery also marks a trend from morning, with an image of the sun ready to shine upon and "bless" the fruit that is ripening, to afternoon details of heat and summer listlessness, and finally to the evening scene of crickets and gathering birds. Thus, the poem's movement might also be reckoned as directional: from east to west, the course of the sun as it appears to the human eye. Also implied is movement from the sun's "maturing" to its southward recession in autumn, when the swallows gather to fly in that direction.

Another process pertains to the working life of the poet. In a sonnet written early in the preceding year—"When I have fears that I may cease to be" (1818)—Keats uses much of the same imagery to refer to his own work. He portrays the poet as a gleaner and his poem as comparable to ripe grain. As a former medical student, Keats had considerable insight into his own physical condition, and he sensed that his poetic mission might be aborted. The tubercular disorder that would kill him showed its warning signs only a few months after he wrote "To Autumn." Therefore, although the poem is not overtly metaphorical, any reader familiar with Keats's health and prior poetry is likely to see the poem as pertaining to the autumn of his life. It does not, however, refer in any explicit fashion to his approaching infirmity or death, for he catches and holds in place the splendor of the season at hand. Like a fine painting, it makes an enduring spectacle.

The tone of this poem is quite different from that of "When I have fears." There is nothing negative, nothing morbid in the later work. The stubble is not a ruined field but a beautiful evening sight. The poem is not about an interrupted harvest or the fear of its failure but about its fulfillment. The swallows depicted in the last line of the poem are "gathering." An Englishman lives in a latitude that sees this gathering as an October preparation for a retreat to the south; the swallows will return the following spring. Keats, in an earlier version, used the past tense, saying the swallows "gather'd." The result of the change is an emphasis not on a finished act but on a living, moving one. A phase of nature is retained as indelibly here as the dancers are held in place in "Ode on a Grecian Urn."

Robert P. Ellis

Further Reading

Bloom, Harold, ed. *The Odes of Keats.* New York: Chelsea House, 1987. "To Autumn" is discussed in several essays in this collection of scholarly work, particularly in Geoffrey H. Hartman's "Poem and Ideology: A Study of Keats's 'To Autumn.'"

Bush, Douglas. *John Keats: His Life and Writings.* New York: Collier Books, 1967. This biography by a Keats critic is one of the earliest studies to judge the poem the most mature and flawless of the poet's odes.

Hebron, Stephen. *John Keats: A Poet and His Manuscripts.* London: British Library, 2009. The process by which the poet's shaping imagination and artistic sense effectuate the development of the final poem is here on display.

Hirst, Wolf Z. *John Keats.* Boston: Twayne, 1981. Argues that in "To Autumn" time triumphs over Keats's usual balance between time and eternity.

Stillinger, Jack, ed. *John Keats: Complete Poems.* Cambridge, Mass.: Belknap Press, 1982. This authoritative and handy edition of Keats's poems also has useful commentaries on "To Autumn" and other odes to which it can be usefully compared.

Vendler, Helen. *The Odes of John Keats.* Cambridge, Mass.: Belknap Press, 1983. The final chapter on "To Autumn" shows how the poet's acquaintance with poems by William Shakespeare, John Milton, William Wordsworth, and other poets contributed to this last of Keats's odes.

To His Coy Mistress

Author: Andrew Marvell (1621-1678)
First published: 1681, in *Miscellaneous Poems*
Type of work: Poetry

In "To His Coy Mistress," his most famous poem, Andrew Marvell follows many of the conventions of the carpe diem (Latin for "seize the day") theme in poetry. This type of poem dates from ancient times and was made popular in English in the late sixteenth and early seventeenth centuries by such writers as Sir Walter Ralegh, Christopher Marlowe, and Robert Herrick. In such poems, typically, the speaker is an eager male lover lamenting the brevity of life to persuade his female listener to yield to his sexual advances. Thus a carpe diem complaint is perhaps best understood not as a love poem but as a lust poem.

Marvell adheres to this tradition in several ways, but he dispenses with the pastoral scenery and songlike lyrical quality typical of much carpe diem verse. Marvell cleverly invests this pagan argument (life is short and uncertain, so one must partake of all the pleasures one can) with somewhat melancholy Christian allusions. His poem is more ambitious as art than is the standard shepherd's lament. Marvell frames the familiar urgings of the frustrated lover within three strictly organized verse paragraphs that resemble a three-part syllogism, a formula logicians use to demonstrate the validity of an argument. The argument in the poem concerns sexual gratification. The speaker's premise in the first verse paragraph describes the rate at which he would woo the lady, given time enough to do so properly. In the second verse paragraph, the premise is the blunt fact of human mutability: Time is limited. In his conclusion, Marvell's speaker resolves these conflicts—figuratively, at least.

Marvell's poem's originality of structure has contributed to the work's being ranked as the epitome of carpe diem verse. Everything contributes to the speaker's overall urgency. Marvell's clipped, tetrameter (four-beat) rhymed couplets create a hurried pace. The poem begins, for example, with two closed couplets, or couplets of a single sentence each. This clipped beginning hints at urgency. As the speaker gains confidence, he loosens this form and uses more enjambment, running lines over into the following lines more often. By the third verse paragraph, he seems hardly to pause for breath at all. The variety of allusion, metaphor, and other figures of speech give the poem an exuberance appropriate to its theme.

As if to call attention to the fleetingness of time, the speaker opens with a terse, elliptical statement, not wasting even a syllable in his wooing. "Had we but world enough, and time" saves him from having to utter the only slightly longer "If we had," and "This coyness, lady, were no crime" similarly condenses the more customary and conversational "would be no crime." In this opening couplet, then, the speaker argues that time and distance—not his own impulsiveness or lust—are the primary enemies of love. If men and women had all eternity and all the world to devote to each other, "coyness" (her refusing his amorous suggestions) would hardly bother him. As it is, however, he deems coyness a crime against his emotions and her own—indeed, perhaps a crime against nature. He then offers examples of how, if immortal, they would pass their "long love's day." Part flattery, part display of his own inventiveness, wit, and learning, this catalog of praises follows the classical tradition of a list of charms designed to weaken the woman's resistance and make her admirer's advances more appealing.

Marvell's speaker employs a wide range of such stratagems. He draws on geography, implying that the distance between two of the world's rivers—the Ganges in India and the Humber in England—is somehow equal to the distance he feels lies between them as he makes this traditional lover's complaint. From the tide of the Humber he moves to Noah's flood (near the dawn of time) and then ahead to the "conversion of the Jews," in Marvell's day a proverbial reference to the end of the world. These allusions not only emphasize the infinitely slow "rate" at which his mistress deserves to be praised but also introduce the idea that her coyness is vaguely sacrilegious. The speaker's "vegetable love" in line 11 is botanical (hence natural), historically significant (vaster and more lasting than empires), and personal in its physical, clinging aspect.

By the end of this first verse paragraph, the speaker has achieved an almost geological perspective of love, claiming that hundreds or thousands of years, even entire ages or eras of time, would be necessary to praise adequately his prospective lover's beauty. That Marvell's ardent speaker is careful to conclude that her "heart"—her inner beauty—demands the most attention of all indicates a shrewdness hardly compatible with the inarticulate throes of sincere affection. This is a poem of persuasion, after all. The speaker aims to disarm the lady further with an even more grandiose piece of flattery: "For, lady, you deserve this state;/ Nor would I love at lower rate." This summation allows the speaker to make promises he knows he shall never be forced to keep, since, of course, the couple does not have all the world to range upon and all of time to spend.

Having professed his boundless love for her, the eager lover quickly contrasts what would be with what, unfortunately, must be: the eventual death of them both. Fittingly, this second part of the argument is the briefest, and it employs the starkest imagery found in the poem. This paragraph makes reference to ashes and dust, another subtle religious echo. The first part of the poem emphasizes lasting emotion, but the second turns grimly final before leavening these images with what might be the poem's best couplet: "The grave's a fine and private place,/ But none, I think, do there embrace." The offhandedness of this quip is intentional. It keeps the mood from becoming too somber, as if the speaker knows he runs the risk of going too far. He seems almost to be reading his mistress's expression for clues as he describes the process of bodily decay.

The word "embrace" sets the final section's argument in motion. This argument is couched in the most urgent language of the poem. The section's initial words—"Now, therefore"—provide the tone. The word "now" appears twice more in the following few lines, along with such synonymous terms as "at once." The emphasis is on the fleetingness of the present moment: "while the youthful hue/ Sits on thy skin," "while thy willing soul transpires," "let us sport us while we may."

Marvell chooses metaphors and similes that make the lovers seem almost ferociously passionate. The pores of the skin burn "with instant fires." The lovers should become, he claims, like "amorous birds of prey." They shall "devour" time, roll their combined strength and sweetness "up into one ball," "tear" their pleasures with "rough strife," and so on. Time, still the enemy of their love's consummation, is defeated in the poem's final paradox, as the speaker admits, "Thus, though we cannot make our sun/ Stand still, yet we will make him run." That is, since they have not the power to stop time, they might at least control it in another way; indulging in sexual pleasures will make time seem to pass more quickly. Also, making time run implies that lovers make the universe work.

Love's other enemy, distance, is overcome as well in this last section. The first two parts of the poem deal mainly in "you" and "I" constructions, but Marvell concludes the poem with no fewer than ten first-person plural pronouns, emphasizing with grammatical subtlety the physical union the speaker desires with this lady. (Such pronouns occur only four times in all of the preceding thirty-two lines.) Then, too, the lovers are likened to birds of prey rather than the inert vine-and-wall relationship of the first section or the union of worm and corpse in the second section.

Further thematic shifts should be noted as well, such as the symbolic use of "rubies" and "marble" in the first and second paragraphs, respectively. The precious, deep-red stones denote tokens of affection and befit the early catalog of praises; likewise, the more common but still impressive marble seems in keeping with the mortality theme. Then, in the last section, these find their counterpart in another element, a metal: iron, a humble enough material, yet one that intimates the lovers' earthbound reality. The speaker urges their passage through the "iron gates of life," a telling contrast to the heavenly gates, the promise of which presumably forms the reason for the lady's chastity.

For years, Marvell's poem was taken to be a fairly typical instance of the courtly love poetry popular among English and European poets of this era. Recently, critics have pointed to the poem's complex ambiguities as a hallmark of Marvell's work in general. One need not, however, turn this seventeenth century Metaphysical poet into a mystery in order to appreciate this particular poem's unique gusto and lyrical grace. Although it employs many features of the traditional lover's complaint, "To His Coy Mistress" ranks above nearly all other carpe diem poems because of Marvell's keen sense of irony, reversal, and strategic order. Perhaps the sharpest irony of all rests in the poet's distinctive use of syllogistic structure, for as logically appealing as the speaker's argument may be, Marvell could very well be reminding readers that, in matters of the heart, logic holds little sway.

James Scruton

Further Reading

Brooks, Cleanth. "Andrew Marvell: Puritan Austerity with Classical Grace." In *Poetic Traditions of the English Renaissance*, edited by Maynard Mack and George deForest Lord. New Haven, Conn.: Yale University Press, 1982. Discusses "To His Coy Mistress" and "The Garden" as companion poems that offer complementary points of view.

Eliot, T. S. "Andrew Marvell." In *Selected Essays*. 1932. Reprint. London: Faber, 1999. Famous piece of modern literary criticism is credited with recovering Marvell from his status as a minor Metaphysical poet. Eliot examines the poem's ironic wit and incongruous imagery.

Friedman, Donald M. "Andrew Marvell." In *The Cambridge*

Companion to English Poetry, Donne to Marvell, edited by Thomas N. Corns. New York: Cambridge University Press, 1993. Analysis of Marvell's poetry is part of a collection of essays that discuss topics related to poetry in seventeenth century England, including politics, religion, gender roles, and rhetoric.

Healy, Thomas, ed. *Andrew Marvell*. London: Longman, 1998. Collection of ten essays provides analyses of "To His Coy Mistress" and other Marvell poems.

Legouis, Pierre. *Andrew Marvell: Poet, Puritan, Patriot*. 2d ed. Oxford, England: Clarendon Press, 1968. Presents a clear discussion of "Marvell's most erotic poem," citing not only classical and later examples of carpe diem verse but also Marvell's departures in tone and persona.

Marvell, Andrew. *Andrew Marvell: A Critical Edition of the Major Works*. Edited by Frank Kermode and Keith Walker. New York: Oxford University Press, 1990. Provides textual and manuscript notes to the poem that explain the sources of various images and allusions; also compares specific lines to lines in the works of Marvell's contemporaries and poetic predecessors.

Murray, Nicholas. *World Enough and Time: The Life of Andrew Marvell*. New York: St. Martin's Press, 2000. Comprehensive biography chronicles Marvell's political and literary careers. Describes how Marvell's poetry was relatively unrecognized until it was rediscovered in the 1920's, when it began to attain full recognition.

Ray, Robert H. *An Andrew Marvell Companion*. New York: Garland, 1998. Reference guide features alphabetically arranged entries that discuss the characters, allusions, ideas, words, and phrases in individual Marvell poems as well as other aspects of Marvell's works.

To Kill a Mockingbird

Author: Harper Lee (1926-   )
First published: 1960
Type of work: Novel
Type of plot: Bildungsroman
Time of plot: Three-year span in the mid-1930's
Locale: Alabama

Principal characters:
ATTICUS FINCH, a lawyer
SCOUT (JEAN LOUISE), his daughter
JEM (JEREMY ATTICUS), her older brother
BOO (ARTHUR) RADLEY, a recluse

The Story:

Scout Finch, almost six years old, her brother Jem, four years older, and their little friend Dill (Charles Baker Harris), a visitor to Maycomb, Alabama, spend their summer thinking of ways to lure Boo Radley from his house. The children never have seen the recluse, but a few townspeople saw him some years ago when Boo reportedly stabbed his father in the leg with a pair of scissors, was locked up for a time, and then was returned to his family. No one in Maycomb has seen him since.

Challenged by Dill, Jem, although fearful he will be killed by Boo—who "dined on raw squirrels and any cats he could catch" —runs and touches the Radley house. The children flee home and look back to see what appears to be an inside shutter move.

In the fall, Scout enters school and gets into trouble in class because she can already read and out of class for fighting with boys. During the year, she and Jem find children's treasures in a knothole in an oak tree on the Radley place. Before they can put a thank-you note in the tree for the unknown benefactor, Nathan Radley, Boo's brother, fills the knothole with cement.

The next summer Dill returns. Rolling inside a runaway tire, Scout slams into the Radley porch. She hears laughing inside as she recovers and runs. The three children play Boo Radley games until stopped by Jem and Scout's father, Atticus.

The last night of Dill's visit, the three try to look in a window of the Radley home. Jem raises his head to look in, and the children see a shadow coming toward them. They run and a shotgun roars. Jem catches his pants on a wire fence and has to leave them there. After Nathan tells the neighbors he fired at an intruder, Jem goes back for his pants and finds them not only mended but also neatly folded over the fence.

The next winter it snows in Maycomb, and Scout and Jem make their first snowman. During the cold snap, the house of a neighbor, Miss Maudie Atkinson, burns down. Back home after shivering from the cold with the other onlookers, Scout discovers a blanket placed around her shoulders. The only adult in town not at the fire is Boo Radley. Jem tells his father of the treasures in the tree and about his mended pants, fixed by the strange man who never hurts them even when he has the chance.

Scout and Jem begin hearing their father called a "nigger-lover" around town, because of his appointment to defend a black man, Tom Robinson. Atticus warns them to hold their heads high and to not fight about it, but at Christmas Scout bloodies a boy cousin's nose for repeating the accusation.

The brother and sister receive air rifles for Christmas but are cautioned by their father that to kill a mockingbird is a sin. Their friend Miss Maudie later explains that mockingbirds only make music and sing their hearts out for people.

One day a mad dog comes down the street, and the town's sheriff asks Atticus to shoot it. He dispatches it with one shot. The children are told that their father, whom they think of as old and feeble, was once known as One-Shot Finch, the best shot in Maycomb County.

An old lady, Mrs. Henry Lafayette Dubose, baits Jem by calling Atticus a "nigger-lover." Enraged, Jem knocks the tops off her flowers. His father orders Jem to read to the sick woman every afternoon for two months. After her death, Atticus tells the children Mrs. Dubose, although unpleasant, was the bravest woman he ever knew; she broke a morphine habit rather than die addicted. Real courage, the father says, is not a man with a gun in his hand. "It's when you know you're licked before you begin but you begin anyway and you see it through no matter what."

Scout and Jem go to an African American church with Cal (Calpurnia), their cook, who has raised the children since the death of their mother when Scout was two. A collection is taken for the family of Robinson, the man Atticus is to defend. Aunt Alexandra, Atticus's proper sister, comes to live with them to make a lady out of the tomboy Scout and restore proper southern order to their home.

Before the trial, the sheriff and a group of citizens warn Atticus that death threats were made against the defendant. Atticus stays at the jail and, weaponless, faces a mob come to get the prisoner. Jem, Scout, and Dill arrive, and Scout kicks a man who grabs Jem. She recognizes the father of a schoolmate in the mob and embarrasses him by talking calmly about his son, until the man orders the mob to leave. Atticus says the children made the schoolmate's father stand in his shoes for a minute and turned the animals in the mob back into humans.

At the trial, where Scout, Jem, and Dill sit in the balcony with Calpurnia's minister, Atticus demonstrates the untruth of the charges by Bob (Robert E. Lee) Ewell, a white man who lives on whiskey and welfare down by the dump, that Robinson beat and raped his daughter, Mayella. A doctor was not called to examine and treat the daughter, and the bruises on the right side of her face were caused by a left-handed man. Ewell is left-handed, and Robinson's left arm is withered and useless.

Atticus asks Mayella on the witness stand if her father inflicted the abuse. She denies it, but Robinson testifies that the day of the alleged rape, she invited him in and kissed him. She said she never kissed a grown man—what her father did to her did not count—so she might as well kiss a "nigger." Ewell arrived at that moment.

Jem and Scout believe that Robinson will be acquitted, but he is found guilty by the all-white jury. It is the word of a white person against a black one, and Robinson made the mistake of saying he felt sorry for a white person—Mayella.

After the trial, Ewell threatens Atticus in public. Robinson is killed after allegedly trying to escape from a prison exercise yard, giving up hope of getting justice in the white courts, although Atticus told him they had a chance on appeal.

Near Halloween, Scout and Jem attend a school pageant. On the way home in the dark, the children are attacked. Scout is saved from a knife thrust by the wire-mesh ham costume she is wearing. Jem struggles with the man and is thrown to the ground. A fourth person appears; there is a struggle, and Scout sees Jem being carried to their house by the stranger. Back home, Scout finds that Jem has a broken arm and the "stranger" who rescued him, standing silently in a corner, is Boo Radley.

The sheriff finds Ewell dead where the attack occurred, with a kitchen knife stuck up under his ribs. Atticus says that he believes Jem did it and does not want it covered up. The sheriff insists that Ewell fell on his own knife, and, besides, it would be a sin to drag someone with shy ways into the limelight. Atticus gives in and thanks Boo Radley for his children's lives. Scout says it would be "sort of like shootin' a mockingbird" to expose their rescuer.

Scout escorts Boo Radley home. She never sees him again. Atticus, putting her to bed, says that most people are nice "when you finally see them."

Critical Evaluation:

Harper Lee was awarded the Pulitzer Prize in fiction in 1961 for her only novel, *To Kill a Mockingbird*, based to a large degree on her childhood experiences growing up in Monroeville, Alabama. Her father was a small-town lawyer like Atticus Finch, and an old house in her neighborhood was rumored to have a reclusive owner, rather like Boo Radley. The author stated the character of Dill is based on author Truman Capote, a childhood companion.

The voice narrating the regional story is that of Scout— Jean Louise Finch—revealing the experiences of her childhood from an adult perspective. The novel begins with a discussion of Jem's broken arm (the last event in the actual plot) and a family history of the Finches in the "tired old town" of Maycomb. Lee presents a dual vision throughout *To Kill a Mockingbird*. The two plot lines—the attempt to lure Boo Radley out and the trial of Tom Robinson—reinforce the contrasting dual themes of prejudice, ignorance, hypocrisy, and hate, opposed by courage, kindness, tolerance, calm reason—and humor.

The gradual moral awakening and growth of Scout and Jem are centered on their "education" by their father, Atticus, a man of conscience, who patiently counsels—and demonstrates—how they should walk in the other person's shoes, hold up their heads, and show restraint in the face of hate and ignorance. Atticus suggests the larger theme that the white South of the time would progress when people quit catching "Maycomb's usual disease." Those suffering from the disease are "reasonable people [who] go stark raving mad when anything involving a Negro comes up."

The novel is in part a social history of a small southern town of the Depression period. In the novel, there is much preoccupation of white people with family trees, social class, racial matters, education (the children learn more outside the classroom than in), and superstition. Although the town (and the South) are places of tradition and ingrained habits, where the past often determines the present, the potential for progressive change resides in at least some enlightened people.

The novel is of a genre called bildungsroman, or novel of maturation. In such a novel, the main character journeys through a series of adventures from innocence to experience and mature enlightenment. At the end, the character is prepared for adulthood.

In the three years covered by the novel, Scout and Jem abandon their superstitions about Boo Radley, learn to value townspeople as individuals, develop moral courage in the face of the town's hypocrisy, realize that justice should be administered without regard to race and class, and, Atticus's final lesson, learn that most people are nice when you finally come to understand them. The children develop open minds—unprejudiced and individual.

The words "it's a sin to kill a mockingbird" echo throughout the novel. The songbird is symbolic of innocence and joy allowed to live—or be threatened and destroyed. Robinson and Boo Radley become its human equivalents in the novel.

The editor of Maycomb's newspaper likens the killing of Robinson during his alleged escape attempt to "the senseless slaughter of songbirds," and Scout says that turning Boo Radley over to the police for killing Bob Ewell would be "sort of like shootin' a mockingbird."

M. E. Gandy

Further Reading

Bloom, Harold, ed. *To Kill a Mockingbird*. New York: Chelsea House, 2007. Collection of critical essays about the novel, including discussions of romantic regionalism, Lee's tragic vision, the female voice in the novel, and Lee and the "destabilization of heterosexuality."

Dave, R. A. "*To Kill a Mockingbird*: Harper Lee's Tragic Vision." In *Indian Studies in American Literature*, edited by M. K. Naik et al. Dharwar, India: Karnatak University, 1974. Discusses the history of the mockingbird as a symbol of innocence and joy in American literature. Draws parallels between *To Kill a Mockingbird* and Walt Whitman's poem "Out of the Cradle Endlessly Rocking." Explores how Lee, like Jane Austen, evokes a regional place yet makes it a macrocosm, describing a range of human behavior.

Going, William T. "Store and Mockingbird: Two Pulitzer Novels About Alabama." In *Essays on Alabama Literature*. University: University of Alabama Press, 1975. Discusses Lee's use of point of view to relate the story's themes in a fresh manner. Examines Lee's ties to the other southern writers who emerged in the late 1950's and early 1960's.

Johnson, Claudia Durst. *To Kill a Mockingbird: Threatening Boundaries*. New York: Twayne, 1994. An in-depth analysis of the novel, placing the book within the historical context of southern racism and the Civil Rights movement of the late 1950's. Discusses the book's critical reception and place in American literature.

_____. *Understanding "To Kill a Mockingbird": A Casebook to Issues, Sources and Historical Documents*. Westport, Conn.: Greenwood Press, 1994. An aid to students and other readers seeking a better understanding of the novel. Includes an analysis of unifying themes in the book and features primary documents about the Scottsboro trials in the 1930's and the Civil Rights movement.

Mancini, Candice, ed. *Racism in Harper Lee's "To Kill a Mockingbird."* Detroit, Mich.: Greenhaven Press, 2008. Designed for junior high and high school students, this book is a collection of essays examining the issue of racism as it relates to the novel's author, characters, and situations. Includes a brief biography of Lee and a time line of her life, a bibliography, an index, and illustrations.

O'Neill, Terry, ed. *Readings on "To Kill a Mockingbird."* San Diego, Calif.: Greenhaven Press, 2000. Aimed at high school students, this book contains essays analyzing the novel's literary techniques, its critical reception, social issues, and the character of Atticus Finch. It also includes a brief biography of Lee, a summary of the novel's plot and characters, and a bibliography.

Petry, Alice Hall. *On Harper Lee: Essays and Reflections.* Knoxville: University of Tennessee Press, 2007. Collection of essays, the majority of which provide analyses of *To Kill a Mockingbird*, including discussions of the religious vision, humor, and humanity in the novel and the South African response to the book. The final essay, written by Petry, addresses Lee's literary status as a "one-hit wonder."

Remler, Nancy Lawson, and Hugh Lawson. "Situating Atticus in the Zone: A Lawyer and His Daughter Read Harper Lee's *To Kill a Mockingbird*." In *Literature and Law*, edited by Michael J. Meyer. New York: Rodopi, 2004. Remler and Lawson focus on the treatment of the law and the legal system in Lee's novel.

Rubin, Louis D., Jr., ed. *The History of Southern Literature.* Baton Rouge: Louisiana State University Press, 1985. A brief history of Lee's place among her contemporary southern writers, such as Truman Capote, Eudora Welty, William Styron, and Carson McCullers. Discusses how these writers reflect on the past yet look toward the future, explore the plight of the black man in the South, and focus on portrayals of a new type of southerner—the liberal who is in conflict with his or her environment because of an awareness of racism.

Shields, Carol. *Mockingbird: A Portrait of Harper Lee.* New York: Henry Holt, 2006. Shields's biography recounts the events that led Lee to write *To Kill a Mockingbird* as well as her decision to shun the spotlight after its publication.

To the Lighthouse

Author: Virginia Woolf (1882-1941)
First published: 1927
Type of work: Novel
Type of plot: Stream of consciousness
Time of plot: c. 1910-1920
Locale: Isle of Skye in the Hebrides

Principal characters:
MR. RAMSAY, a professor of philosophy
MRS. RAMSAY, his wife
JAMES, their son
CAMILLA, their daughter
MR. TANSLEY, Mr. Ramsay's guest and friend
LILY BRISCOE, an artist
MR. CARMICHAEL, a poet

The Story:

Mrs. Ramsay promises James, her six-year-old son, that if the next day is fair he will be taken on a visit to the lighthouse they can see from the window of their summer home on the Isle of Skye. James, the youngest of Mrs. Ramsay's eight children, is his mother's favorite. The father of the family is a professor of philosophy whose students believe is inspiring and one of the foremost metaphysicians of the early twentieth century, but his own children, particularly the youngest, do not like him because he makes sarcastic remarks.

Several guests are visiting the Ramsays at the time. There is young Mr. Tansley, Ramsay's student, who also is unpopular with the children because he seems to delight in their dis-comfiture. Tansley is mildly in love with his host, despite her being fifty years old and having eight children. Another guest is Lily Briscoe, who is painting a picture of the cottage with Mrs. Ramsay and little James seated in front of it. There is old Mr. Carmichael, a ne'er-do-well who amuses the Ramsay youngsters with his white beard and a mustache tinged with yellow. Another guest is William Bankes, an aging widower. Prue, the prettiest of the Ramsay daughters, is there too.

The afternoon goes by slowly. Mrs. Ramsay goes to the village to call on a sick woman. She spends several hours knitting stockings for the lighthouse keeper's child, whom they are planning to visit. Many people wonder how the Ramsays, particularly the wife, manages to be so hospitable and charitable, for they are not rich. Mr. Ramsay cannot possibly be making a fortune by expounding English philosophy to students or by publishing books on metaphysics.

Mr. Carmichael, pretending to read, has actually fallen asleep early after lunch. The children, except for James, who is busy cutting pictures out of a catalog, busy themselves in a game of cricket. Mr. Ramsay and Mr. Tansley pass the time in a pointless conversation. Miss Briscoe has made only a daub or two of paint on her canvas. For some reason, the lines of the scene refuse to come clear in her painting. She then goes for a walk with Mr. Bankes along the shore.

Even the dinner goes by slowly. The only occasion of interest to the children, which is one of tension to their mother, comes when Mr. Carmichael asks the maid for a second bowl of soup, thereby angering his host, who likes to have meals dispatched promptly. As soon as the children have finished, their mother sends the younger ones to bed. Mrs. Ramsay hopes that Mr. Bankes will marry Lily Briscoe. Lily always gets seasick, so it is questionable whether she will want to accompany them in the small sailboat if they should go to the lighthouse the following day. Mrs. Ramsay also thinks about the fifty pounds needed to make some necessary repairs on the house.

After dinner, Mrs. Ramsay goes upstairs to the nursery. James has a boar's skull that his sister detests. Whenever Camilla tries to remove it from the wall and her sight, he bursts into a frenzy of screaming. Mrs. Ramsay wraps the boar's skull in her shawl. Afterward, she goes downstairs and joins her husband in the library, where they sit throughout the evening. Mrs. Ramsay knits, while Mr. Ramsay reads. Before they go to bed, they agree that the trip for the next day will have to be canceled. The night has turned stormy.

Night follows night. The trip to the lighthouse is never made that summer, and the Ramsays do not return to their summer home for some years. In the meantime, Mrs. Ramsay dies quietly in her sleep. Her daughter, Prue, gets married and later dies in childbirth. World War I begins. Andrew Ramsay enlists and is sent to France, where he is killed by an exploding shell.

Time passes. The wallpaper in the house comes loose from the walls, and books mildew. In the kitchen, a cup is occasionally knocked down and broken by old Mrs. McNab, who comes to look after the house from time to time. In the garden, the roses and the annual flowers grow wild or die.

Mr. Carmichael publishes a volume of poems during the war. About the time his book appears, daffodils and violets bloom on the Isle of Skye. Mrs. McNab looks longingly at a warm cloak left in a closet. She wishes the cloak belonged to her.

At last, the war ends. Mrs. McNab receives a telegram requesting that the house be put in order. For several days, the housekeeper works, aided by two cleaning women. When the Ramsays arrive, the cottage is in order once more. Several visitors come again to share a summer at the cottage. Lily Briscoe returns for a quiet vacation. Mr. Carmichael, the successful poet, also arrives.

One morning, Lily Briscoe comes down to breakfast and wonders at the quiet that greets her. No one had been down ahead of her, although she expected that Mr. Ramsay and the two youngest children, James and Camilla, would have eaten early and departed for the long-postponed sail to the lighthouse, to which the youngsters had not been looking forward with joyful anticipation. Very shortly, the three straggle down; all had slept past the time they had intended to arise. After a swift breakfast, they disappear toward the shore. Lily Briscoe watches them go. She sets up her canvas with the intention of once again trying to paint her picture of the cottage.

The children never really liked their father; he had taken too little time to understand them. He is short and sharp when they do things that seem foolish to him, although these actions are perfectly comprehensible to his son and daughter. James, especially, expects to be blamed caustically and pointlessly if the crossing is slow or not satisfactory in some other way, for he has been delegated to handle the sheets and the tiller of the boat.

Mr. Ramsay goes down to the beach with his offspring, each carrying a paper parcel to take to the keepers of the lighthouse. They soon set sail and point the prow of the sailboat toward the black-and-white-striped pillar of the lighthouse in the hazy distance. Mr. Ramsay sits in the middle of the boat, along with an old fisherman and his son. They are to take over the boat in case of an emergency, for Mr. Ramsay has little trust in James as a reliable seaman. James himself sits in the stern, nerves tingling lest his father look up from his book and indulge in unnecessary and hateful criticism. His nervous tension, however, is needless, for within a few hours the little party reaches the lighthouse and, wonderful to relate, Mr. Ramsay springs ashore like a youngster, smiles back at his children, and praises his son for his seamanship.

Critical Evaluation:

To the Lighthouse, Virginia Woolf's most autobiographical novel, explores two sets of interlocking issues: perception and creativity. The stream-of-consciousness narrative forces the reader to examine and experience the complexities of individual perception and individual attempts to create coherence from the borderless flow of everyday events. As Woolf writes in her 1919 essay "Modern Fiction," "Life is not a series of gig-lamps symmetrically arranged; life is a luminous halo, a semi-transparent envelope surrounding us from the beginning of consciousness to the end." Woolf takes her exploration of consciousness one step further by demonstrating how perception depends on gender: Men and women perceive the world differently. These contrasting perceptions of the world produce different creative urges. In the end, however, creativity transcends gender.

Woolf's adult male characters, except for the poet Mr. Carmichael, are philosophers or scientists, analytical men. These characters are quantifiers of experience. Mr. Ramsay, the philosopher (who bears a resemblance to Woolf's father, Leslie Stephen) imagines that knowledge is arranged like the alphabet and that each person's intellectual worth lies in how far he or she can progress along that alphabet. He is frustrated because he is stalled at Q, even though he acknowledges that only one person each generation can actually reach Z. Mr. Tansley, a student of Mr. Ramsay's, finds his life in his books, his dissertation, and his acute sense of his own poverty. Mr. Bankes, the botanist, has definite opinions about properly cooking vegetables. He labels the Ramsay children with mock royal names, and he clinically examines Lily's painting. These male characters create order from life by systematizing its disparate elements and reducing them to bitter pronouncements (as Mr. Tansley does), disconnected lines of poetry (as Mr. Ramsay does), or impersonal images (as Andrew Ramsay does when he tells Lily Briscoe to picture Mr. Ramsay's work as a kitchen table).

The adult female characters, on the other hand, view life more intuitively. Mrs. Ramsay (who is based upon Woolf's mother, Julia Stephen) is celebrated for her beauty and her maternal nature. She pours herself into others, nourishing her children and her husband with her love and sympathy. What she values most in life, and what she seeks to create, is union, particularly marriage (she thinks, "they all must marry"). She also manifests her creative energies at her dinner party, where she recognizes that she must bring together the disparate people sitting at the table: "The whole of the effort of merging and flowing and creating rested on her." The artist Lily Briscoe (who perhaps represents Woolf herself) also feels creative pressures as she seeks to transform her private vision into art. Despite her own fears about the value of her work, and despite Mr. Tansley's proclamation that "Women can't write, women can't paint," Lily believes in her artistic vision and uses it to create order for herself from her puzzling, sometimes painful feelings and perceptions.

Woolf's narrative style emphasizes her definition of perception. The narrative drifts from point of view to point of view, entering various characters' minds in an apparently random succession of associations. Woolf also contrasts objective, external time with subjective, internal time. The narrative moves fluidly between past and present, memory and experience, disorienting the reader in the process.

The structure of the novel further emphasizes the contrast between external and internal time. The first section, "The Window," occupies more than half the novel and spans a single afternoon and evening. The middle section of the novel, "Time Passes," compresses the events of ten years into twenty pages of narrative and parenthetically inserts major events into a description of the slow decay of the Ramsays' summer home. The final section, "The Lighthouse," takes approximately seventy pages to describe the events of a single morning.

Woolf uses imagery, particularly the sea and the lighthouse, to reveal the unity and individuality of human perception. The characters are drawn to the sea, often in pairs: Mr. and Mrs. Ramsay, Paul and Minta, Mr. Bankes and Lily. At such moments, the sea creates a sense of unity and constancy of vision. The same sea also represents the isolation of human beings, as when Mr. Ramsay murmurs "we perished, each alone" as he and his children journey to the lighthouse. The lighthouse unifies and isolates as well. It stands at the center of the novel, uniting the several sections. It is a focus for the family as a desired destination. The lighthouse separates them, however, through their own individual visions of it. As James thinks, "nothing was simply one thing."

In the end, it is contingent upon the artists, Mr. Carmichael and Lily Briscoe, to bring together male and female creativity, intellect and emotion, public statement and private vision. They must have, as Woolf writes in *A Room of One's Own* (1929), the clearer vision of androgynous minds, which, unimpeded by gender prejudice, are "naturally creative, incandescent and undivided." The feminized Mr. Carmichael, who sits on the edge of the domestic circle dozing and waiting for the words of his poetry to come to him, brings his deeply felt poems about Andrew Ramsay and World War I into the public sphere. Lily forges ahead with her artistic efforts despite her recognition that her paintings will end up underneath beds or in attics. As she paints, she is preoccupied with thoughts of Mr. and Mrs. Ramsay as she attempts to understand them both. Lily mocks Mrs. Ramsay's sentimentality, but she recognizes the beauty and power of the older woman's love and grieves for her loss. This grief draws Lily into sympathetic union (which she earlier refused) with the coldly intellectual Mr. Ramsay.

The final chapter brings together Mr. Ramsay and the memory of Mrs. Ramsay, as well as the male artist with the female artist, in unspoken communion. The Ramsays reach the lighthouse, Lily has her artistic vision and completes her painting, and Mr. Carmichael silently pronounces a benediction on them all. The novel concludes with a moment that is a culmination and a commencement.

Judith Burdan

Further Reading

Barrett, Eileen, and Patricia Cramer, eds. *Virginia Woolf: Lesbian Readings*. New York: New York University Press, 1997. Part 2 of this collection of conference papers focuses on the novels, interpreting *To the Lighthouse* and six other books by Woolf through the lens of lesbian experience.

Beja, Morris. *Critical Essays on Virginia Woolf*. Boston: G. K. Hall, 1985. Attempts to reconcile disparate schools of Woolf criticism. Includes a review of *To the Lighthouse*, written by Conrad Aiken, which appeared in 1927, the year the novel was published.

Blair, Emily. *Virginia Woolf and the Nineteenth-Century Domestic Novel*. Albany: State University of New York Press, 2007. Describes the influence upon Woolf's writing of nineteenth and early twentieth century literature, particularly its descriptions of femininity. Compares her novels to those of Elizabeth Gaskell and Margaret Oliphant, two popular Victorian novelists.

Briggs, Julia. *Virginia Woolf: An Inner Life*. Orlando, Fla: Harcourt, 2005. Biography focusing on Woolf's work and her fascination with the workings of the mind. Briggs traces the creation of each of Woolf's books, from *The Voyage Out* through *Between the Acts* and including *To the Lighthouse*, combining literary analysis with details of Woolf's life.

Daugherty, Beth Rigel, and Mary Beth Pringle, eds. *Approaches to Teaching Woolf's "To the Lighthouse."* New York: Modern Language Association of America, 2001. Essays discuss *To the Lighthouse*'s narrative theory, diverse rhythms, and "language of fabric"; the novel as both traditional and postmodern; the Ramsays as a dysfunctional family; and a comparison of this novel with Zora Neale Hurston's *Their Eyes Were Watching God*.

De Gay, Jane. "*To the Lighthouse* and the Ghost of Leslie Stephen." In *Virginia Woolf's Novels and the Literary Past*. Edinburgh: Edinburgh University Press, 2006. Examines Woolf's preoccupation with the fiction of her predecessors. Analyzes eight novels and other works to explore her allusions to and revisions of the plots and motifs of earlier fiction.

Goldman, Jane, ed. *Virginia Woolf: "To the Lighthouse," "The Waves."* New York: Columbia University Press, 1998. Surveys the changing critical reception of the two novels from the earliest contemporary reviews through critiques published in the 1990's.

Kelley, Alice van Buren. *"To the Lighthouse": The Marriage of Life and Art*. Boston: Twayne, 1987. Provides a reading of the novel, a wealth of background information, a chronology, and a discussion of critical responses. A good place to begin studies of *To the Lighthouse*.

Marcus, Jane, ed. *New Feminist Essays on Virginia Woolf*. 1981. Reprint. London: Palgrave Macmillan, 1985. An insightful collection of essays that approach Woolf from the perspective of feminist criticism. Includes a chapter by Jane Lilienfeld that features a feminist interpretation of the Ramsays' marriage.

Winston, Janet. *Woolf's "To the Lighthouse": A Reader's Guide*. New York: Continuum, 2009. A concise reading and study guide to the novel. Places *To the Lighthouse* in historical, intellectual, and cultural context, and provides analyses of its style, themes, and structure.

Zwerdling, Alex. *Virginia Woolf and the Real World*. Berkeley: University of California Press, 1986. A study of Woolf's social vision and her response to the historical events and the sociopolitical currents of her age. Includes an enlightening chapter on the domestic politics of *To the Lighthouse*.

To Urania
Selected Poems, 1965-1985

Author: Joseph Brodsky (1940-1996)
First published: Chast'rechi: Stikhotvoreniya, 1964-
    1971, 1977; *Uraniia: Novaya kniga stikhov*, 1987
    (English translation, 1988)
Type of work: Poetry

From the time when the Soviet authorities forced Joseph Brodsky into exile on June 4, 1977, the theme of exile dominated his poetry. Brodsky had tasted the bitterness of exile, however, even prior to his expulsion from his native land. Described by poet Anna Akhmatova as "the most gifted poet of his generation," Brodsky was charged with the crime of being a "social parasite" and was arrested in January of 1964. After a quick trial, he was sentenced to five years of hard labor in internal exile, but, thanks to pressures on the Soviet government at home and abroad, he was released in November, 1965.

After his release from the labor camp, Brodsky returned to his native city of Leningrad. Already one could see the development of the theme of exile in his poetry, for which he was awarded the Nobel Prize in Literature in 1987, along three distinct lines: an effort to convey a sense of what is sacred through images of things borrowed from everyday life, an attempt to convey in words a realm of silence that underlies all poetry, and an affirmation of a home that is forever approached but forever lies in a realm that is elsewhere. The poems in his collection *To Urania*, most of which he translated from Russian to English himself, exemplify these aspects of Brodsky's art.

To Urania is a collection of forty-six poems, including the well-known long poem *Gorbunov and Gorchakov* (1968). The title poem is the twenty-fourth poem in the collection; it uses the metaphor of the body to express the exile of the spirit, particularly in these lines:

> And what is space anyway if not the
> body's absence at every given
> point? That's why Urania's older than sister Clio!

Urania is the muse of the heavens, while Clio is the muse of history. Urania is older because it is the longing for the heavens, which are the abode of the gods, that gives rise to history. Brodsky views history as the tale of the human effort to reach the heavens, since the heavens are the realm of the Great Elsewhere that reveals to humanity its condition of exile.

If Urania is the muse who gives rise to the poetry of exile, she does so from the beginning of Brodsky's work. The collection's first poem, "May 24, 1980," commemorates Brodsky's fortieth birthday, and in it he insists that, even though he has "munched the bread of exile," only gratitude will come "gushing from" his throat. While exile is a condition that may invite despair, the poet struggles to overcome that despair by writing poetry.

The next six poems—"To a Friend: In Memoriam," "October Tune," "A Polar Explorer," "Lithuanian Nocturne," "Twenty Sonnets to Mary, Queen of Scots," and "North Baltic"—examine exile in terms of the separation of one human being from another. Home consists not only of familiar places but also of familiar faces, and in these poems Brodsky explores the pain of separation from loved ones. The return home that brings exile to an end is, above all, a return to loving human relationships.

Because the poems in this collection deal with exile, many of them are set in places all around the world. Examples include "The Berlin Wall Tune," "Dutch Mistress," "Allenby Road" (a famous road in Israel), "Polonaise: A Variation," "Cafe Trieste: San Francisco," "Near Alexandria," "Roman Elegies," "Belfast Tune," and "In Italy." Especially noteworthy among these poems about other places is a passage from "Venetian Stanzas II," a poem about the poet's being out of place.

> I am writing these lines sitting outdoors, in winter,
> on a white iron chair, in my shirtsleeves . . .
> and the coffee grows cold. And the blinding lagoon
>   is lapping
> at the shore as the dim pupil's bright penalty
> for its wish to arrest a landscape quite happy
> here without me.

The poet's distance from a dwelling place is here proclaimed in images of disjuncture: shirtsleeves in winter, cold coffee, and a landscape there without him. Like the eye that would arrest the landscape, the words in the poem try to capture some meaning, but both rush ahead to leave the speaker behind, outdoors in winter.

Just as some of the poems in *To Urania* are about places that are elsewhere, so others are about a time out of joint. These include "The Fifth Anniversary," "The Hawk's Cry in Autumn," "Eclogue IV: Winter," "Eclogue V: Summer," "Letter to an Archaeologist," and "Afterword." Brodsky once described words as "almost palpable vessels of time," and these poems that deal with time often deal also with poetry itself and the words that go into it. At the end of "Eclogue IV: Winter," for example, he writes:

> That's the birth of an eclogue. Instead of the
>   shepherd's signal,
> a lamp's flaring up. Cyrillic, while running witless
> on the pad as though to escape the captor,
> knows more of the future than the famous sybil.

What is perhaps most striking about these lines is the idea that the Cyrillic alphabet (the alphabet used in the Russian language) has a certain life of its own. According to Brodsky, language is not just a tool used by a speaker; rather, language itself speaks. In the voice of language, the voice of the muse can be heard. The task of the poet is to attend to that voice in an effort to join words to the meaning that tries to escape them. For the poet, the exile of the human being from home is the exile of meaning from words.

Another poem worth noting from among these poems about time and poetry is "The Fifth Anniversary." Its title designates the fifth anniversary of Brodsky's exile from his homeland on June 4, 1977. In it he declares that he does not know "what earth will nurse my carcass," but he ends by saying, "Scratch on, my pen: let's mark the white the way it marks us." Brodsky often uses the phrase "the white" to designate the opposite of home. Just as one who travels through a wilderness may "mark" that landscape by building a home, so does the poet mark the white, the blank page, by constructing words. For the poet in exile, words take the place of a dwelling place. Yet marking the white with words is just what makes the white visible, making all the more visible the poet's condition of exile. The greater the sense of exile, the greater the need to write, and the more the poet writes, the more deeply he is entrenched in exile.

If the blank space designated by the white represents a condition of homelessness, it also represents a condition of silence. Here Brodsky understands the task of the poet to include the transformation of silence as emptiness into silence as eloquence. Silence, he maintains, is a kind of other language, and, as a poet, he endeavors to translate silence into words. The struggle between life and death, between exile and homeland, is a struggle between words and silence. Therefore the poet, who is the bearer of signs and images in his poetry, becomes a messenger who bears more than his message can contain. He becomes the messenger of silence.

In Brodsky's poetry, the theme of silence is connected to the theme of time in that silence represents a realm of the future, which is the realm of becoming. As the poet in exile becomes the poet of exile, he is faced, if he is ever to set out for home, with the task of becoming other than who he is. Among the poems in *To Urania* that address this issue are "Minefield Revisited," "The Bust of Tiberius," "Seaward," "Ex Voto," and "At Karel Weilink's Exhibition." In this last poem, Brodsky declares that the sign of true self-mastery lies in the ability to "not take fright at the procedure of nonbeing." With this insight, the poet discovers that not only is he in exile but also he is exile; not only is his home elsewhere but also he is elsewhere. Therefore, if the poet is to move homeward to that other place, then he must become other than who he is—and that other being the poet must become resides in silence.

In *To Urania*, the poem that most thoroughly explores the topic of silence is the final one, *Gorbunov and Gorchakov*, an extended dialogue between two patients in a psychiatric hospital outside Leningrad. One patient says to the other:

> Silence is the future of all days
> that roll toward speech . . .
> Indeed, the future of our words is silence . . .
> And silence is the present fate of those who
> have lived before us; it's a matchmaker
> that manages to bring all men together
> into the speaking presence of today.
> Life is but talk hurled in the face of silence.

Because Brodsky's poetry entails an examination of poetry itself, silence is often its subject matter. Like the exile that accentuates the homeland, silence calls forth the spoken part of the human being to draw him or her into a relation to another human being. Human presence is a speaking presence that harbors a nonspeaking, and the human task in life is to become present as a human being before another human being. In this task, the poet is the teacher.

Poetry is the most ancient of the verbal arts. It is the medium in which humanity first seeks its voice and the place where dwelling in the world first unfolds. It continues to unfold in the poetry of Joseph Brodsky. A poet for whom language is sacred, Brodsky is attuned to the capacity of language to open up a place where a trace of the sacred may show itself. As the poems in *To Urania* indicate, however, the sacred manifests itself as something at a distance. The notion of the sacred, then, includes the idea of drawing nigh. The poet engages in an effort to join word and meaning not in the midst of the sacred, which lies in the homeland, but in a movement toward it. The poet is the one who, in his homelessness, reveals a certain homelessness within the human condition itself. This revelation is the most significant feature of *To Urania*, for it is the most significant to the life of the human soul.

David Patterson

Further Reading

Bethea, David M. *Joseph Brodsky and the Creation of Exile.* Princeton, N.J.: Princeton University Press, 1994. Offers an informative discussion of the development of Brodsky's poetry and its significance for American letters; examines the influence of other major poets on Brodsky. Chapter 6 is particularly helpful for readers seeking to understand the themes addressed in *To Urania.*

Loseff, Lev, and Valentina Polukhina, eds. *Brodsky's Poetics and Aesthetics.* New York: St. Martin's Press, 1990. Collection of essays on Brodsky's poetry also includes Brodsky's 1987 Nobel lecture and an interview with him conducted by Bella Akhmadulina. Of special interest to students of *To Urania* are the essays by George L. Kline and Peter France.

_____. *Joseph Brodsky: The Art of a Poem.* New York: Palgrave, 1999. Collection of essays, two by well-known poets, provides detailed analyses of Brodsky's poetry written between 1970 and 1994. Includes discussion of *To Urania.*

MacFadyen, David. *Joseph Brodsky and the Baroque.* Montreal: McGill-Queen's University Press, 1998. Presents a comprehensive examination of Brodsky's poetry and prose. Defines Brodsky's worldview as baroque and points out how that philosophy was influenced by John Donne and other seventeenth century poets and by post-Soviet aesthetics.

_____. *Joseph Brodsky and the Soviet Muse.* Montreal: McGill-Queen's University Press, 2000. Focuses on Brodsky's early poetry, describing the writers who influenced him and the wide range of American, French, German, and Polish literature that was read by Brodsky and his acquaintances.

Murphy, Michael. *Poetry in Exile: A Study of the Poetry of W. H. Auden, Joseph Brodsky, and George Szirtes.* London: Greenwich Exchange, 2004. Examines the work of Brodsky and two other exiled poets to demonstrate how they were influenced by the experience of exile.

Patterson, David. "Exile in the Diaspora: The Poetry of Joseph Brodsky." In *Exile: The Sense of Alienation in Modern Russian Letters.* Lexington: University Press of Kentucky, 1995. Situates the poetry and the themes from *To Urania* within the larger contexts of Brodsky's general concerns as a poet. Contains a detailed discussion of the concepts of the sacred, silence, and the elsewhere in Brodsky's poetry.

Polukhina, Valentina. *Joseph Brodsky: A Poet for Our Time.* New York: Cambridge University Press, 1989. Offers insightful examinations of the notions of time and space, word and spirit, exile and silence. All of the book's six chapters discuss poems from *To Urania*, and the last three chapters include comments on the collection as a whole.

Rigsbee, David. *Styles of Ruin: Joseph Brodsky and the Postmodernist Elegy.* Westport, Conn.: Greenwood Press, 1999. Analyzes Brodsky's elegiac poetry, demonstrating how these works reflect his efforts to find a source of consolation for the death of family, friends, and the self. Describes *To Urania* as a farewell to W. H. Auden.

Tobacco Road

Author: Erskine Caldwell (1903-1987)
First published: 1932
Type of work: Novel
Type of plot: Naturalism
Time of plot: 1920's
Locale: Georgia

Principal characters:
JEETER LESTER, a poor white man
ADA, his wife
DUDE, his son
ELLIE MAY, his daughter
PEARL, another daughter
LOV BENSEY, Pearl's husband
BESSIE, a backwoods evangelist

The Story:

Lov Bensey, husband of Pearl, the fifteen-year-old daughter of Jeeter Lester, feels low in his mind when he stops by the Lester house on his way home with a bag of turnips. Pearl, he complains, refuses to have anything to do with him; she will neither sleep with him nor talk to him.

The Lesters live in a one-room shack that is falling apart. They have nothing to eat but pork rind soup. Jeeter is trying to patch an inner tube so that the Lester car, a nondescript wreck that was refused even by the junk dealer, can be used to carry firewood to Augusta. Jeeter's harelipped daughter, Ellie May, charms Lov away from his bag of turnips. While she and Lov are flirting in the yard in front of the shack, the other Lesters pounce upon the bag of turnips. Jeeter grabs it and runs into the scrub woods, followed by his worthless son Dude. Jeeter eats his fill of turnips. He gives Dude several and even saves a handful for the rest of the family. They return from the woods to find Lov gone. Sister Bessie, a woman preacher, comes for a visit. Bessie, middle-aged, and Dude, sixteen, are attracted to each other. Bessie, upon leaving, promises to return to elope with Dude.

The Lesters are starving. Jeeter has long been unable to get credit at the local stores in order to buy seed, fertilizer, and food. His land is exhausted, and there is no chance of reclaiming it because of Jeeter's utter laziness. Jeeter and his wife Ada had seventeen children. Twelve of them survived, and all except Ellie May and Dude left home.

Bessie returns and announces that God gave her permission to marry Dude, but Dude refuses to listen until Bessie says that she is planning to buy a new car with some money that her late husband left her. She and Dude go to town and buy a new Ford, the loud horn of which Dude highly approves. At the county courthouse, over the mild protestations of the clerk because of Dude's youth, Bessie gets a marriage license. Back at the Lester shack, Bessie, using her authority as preacher, marries herself to Dude. The newlyweds go for a ride in their new car; they return to the tobacco road at sundown with one fender of the car completely ruined. They ran into a farm wagon on the highway and killed an African American man, whom they left lying by the roadside.

Jeeter, eager to get food and snuff, persuades Bessie and Dude to take him to Augusta with a load of firewood. Their arrival in Augusta is delayed, however, by the breakdown of the car. A gallon and a half of oil poured into the crankcase enables them to get to the city, where Jeeter fails to sell one stick of wood. The trio sells the car's spare tire, for which they can see no use, and buy food. They mistake a brothel for a hotel; Bessie is absent from Jeeter and her young husband most of the night.

During the return trip to the tobacco road, Jeeter unloads the wood beside the highway and sets fire to it. He is about to suggest another trip in the car, but Bessie and Dude ride away before he can stop them. As the car rapidly falls apart, the warmth between Bessie and her young husband cools. In a fight between Bessie and the Lesters over Jeeter's right to ride in the car again, Dude sides with his wife. After all, the car still runs a little.

Meanwhile, Pearl runs away from Lov; she manages to escape after he ties her to their bed. Jeeter advises Lov not to look for Pearl but to take Ellie May in her place. He then tells Ellie May to bring back food and clothes from Lov's house. The grandmother, who was run over by Bessie's Ford, dies in the yard.

Jeeter anticipates seeding time by burning the broomsedge off his land. A wind blows the fire to the house while Jeeter and Ada are asleep. The destitute sharecroppers are burned to death on the land that Jeeter's family once owned as prosperous farmers.

Critical Evaluation:

In *Tobacco Road*, Erskine Caldwell relied on a combination of humor and social consciousness that sometimes created confusion among critics. They wondered if they were to laugh at the impoverished and degraded characters he described or sympathize with them. They questioned whether humor was the best way to inspire social change.

Caldwell was made acquainted with the social conditions of the persons he described by his minister father. Besides helping the poor of every denomination, Ira Caldwell was also an amateur sociologist, who published his observations of the white people who lived in poverty in Georgia in *Eugenics*, a magazine concerned with the devolution of society. Entitled "The Bunglers," Ira's series of articles detailed the nearly hopeless condition of the rural poor. Caldwell, who accompanied his father on his visits to impoverished households, fictionalized many of the same facts mentioned in his father's articles.

The literary movement of naturalism, which served as a vehicle for similar subject matter in the fiction of Theodore Dreiser, Frank Norris, Jack London, and Stephen Crane, was congenial to Caldwell's purpose. Like other naturalistic works, *Tobacco Road* uses stark, realistic detail to establish its characters on the bottom of society, among its poorest and most degraded elements. Caldwell's purposes in choosing characters so remote from middle-class norms are to shock his readers out of their complacency and to call attention to the devastating effects of poverty. The details of the lives he chooses to describe are stripped of any civilized buffer. He prods his audience with Ellie's harelip, Ada's pleurisy, Grandmother's pellagra, Pearl's marriage at a young age, and Jeeter's chronic laziness resulting from malnutrition. He dramatizes a Darwinian struggle for survival over a bag of turnips; the characters are animal-like as they position themselves to steal Lov's food; equally animal-like are their sexual relations. They are controlled by the forces of hunger, sex, and tribal solidarity.

Caldwell uses the technique of fragmentation to create an impression of unremitting social chaos. Characters perform actions that are incongruous with one another. They talk at cross-purposes, which dramatizes the fact that they are essentially uncivilized, motivated by their own individual desires, having no regard for others. The effect created is of a splintered society, each of its members struggling for survival in a hostile environment.

However, besides Caldwell's careful documenting of degrading and tragic social conditions, he also delights his readers with humorous accounts of his characters' antics. He achieves comedy by having those characters act and speak in a manner showing their ignorance of middle-class norms. Bessie and the Lesters virtually destroy a new automobile in one day without seeming concerned about it. In the Augusta episode, Bessie, Jeeter, and Dude are treated as country bumpkins who exit Augusta as impenetrably ignorant of the ways of the urban world as when they entered it. They do not realize that they spent the night in a brothel.

Caldwell also satirizes his characters' religious pretensions. Middle-aged Bessie is a self-styled preacher who seeks to continue her late husband's ministry by marrying, at God's command, the teenage Dude. She invokes God whenever she seeks to justify her own selfish desires. The unregenerate Jeeter, meanwhile, is pleased when Bessie chastises him for his sinfulness, for he believes that there still must be hope for him if a woman of God cares enough to criticize him. Simultaneous with his "reverence" for Bessie's religious authority is Jeeter's frank admiration of her physical presence. Caldwell's characters are unaware of the discrepancy between their spiritual desires and the trap of their animalistic sensory existence. This lack of awareness is another source of humor.

For all its degradation and bawdy humor, *Tobacco Road* approaches tragedy in its depiction of Jeeter. Despite his many flaws, his loyalty to the land stands out as a redeeming characteristic. His spirit and instincts are in harmony with the seasons, and he maintains his hope that one day he will be able to resume the planting rituals that his blood seems to call for each spring. He dies when his feeble attempt to resume his life as a farmer turns disastrous.

Although the novel's mixture of ribaldry and social protest may have puzzled critics, the novel and the play made from it enjoyed tremendous popularity with general readers whose imaginations were easily captured by them. Caldwell, who geared his books for the common reader, was gratified by the popularity of his work. He went on to write other bestselling works, such as *God's Little Acre* (1933), which made him, during the 1940's and 1950's, a most widely read writer.

"Critical Evaluation" by William L. Howard

Further Reading

Arnold, Edwin T., ed. *Erskine Caldwell Reconsidered*. Jackson: University Press of Mississippi, 1990. A series of essays about this generally underappreciated novelist dealing with both biographical and literary topics.

Cook, Sylvia Jenkins. *Erskine Caldwell and the Fiction of Poverty: The Flesh and the Spirit*. Baton Rouge: Louisiana State University Press, 1991. Focuses on the physical and spiritual effects of poverty on Caldwell's characters. For all of their preoccupation with material reality, they aspire also to a higher purpose in life.

Devlin, James E. *Erskine Caldwell*. Boston: Twayne, 1984. An analysis of *Tobacco Road*'s themes and techniques.

Identifies Caldwell as a naturalist and the Lesters as part of a subculture. Tries to account for the novel's seemingly contradictory combination of humor and serious social commentary.

Klevar, Harvey L. *Erskine Caldwell: A Biography.* Knoxville: University of Tennessee Press, 1993. Covers the writing of the novel, Caldwell's relationship with his publishers, and the influence of his father's study of the white southern poor for *Eugenics* magazine.

McDonald, Robert L., ed. *The Critical Response to Erskine Caldwell.* Westport, Conn.: Greenwood Press, 1997. Includes reviews of Caldwell's major works, including *Tobacco Road*, scholarly discussions of his themes and techniques, and academic analyses of the image of the South presented in his fiction.

_____. *Reading Erskine Caldwell: New Essays.* Jefferson, N.C.: McFarland, 2006. Collection of twelve essays examining Caldwell as a novelist, a humorist, an antilynching advocate, and a modernist.

MacDonald, Scott, ed. *Critical Essays on Erskine Caldwell.* Boston: G. K. Hall, 1981. Includes introductions that Caldwell wrote for several of his novels, including *Tobacco Road*, as well as contemporary reviews and scholarly essays.

Miller, Dan B. *Erskine Caldwell: The Journey from Tobacco Road, a Biography.* New York: Alfred A. Knopf, 1995. A biography of Caldwell, focusing on his first forty years; details Caldwell's life and his growing up within the context of southern culture.

Stevens, C. J. *Storyteller: A Life of Erskine Caldwell.* Phillips, Maine: John Wade, 2000. Comprehensive biography, focusing on Erskine's life and "complicated personality." Describes how he wrote his novels and other works, summarizes their contents, and traces their receptions.

The Toilers of the Sea

Author: Victor Hugo (1802-1885)
First published: Les Travailleurs de la mer, 1866 (English translation, 1866)
Type of work: Novel
Type of plot: Mythic
Time of plot: Late 1820's
Locale: Isle of Guernsey, English Channel

Principal characters:
GILLIATT, a young recluse
MESS LETHIERRY, his friend, a ship owner
DÉRUCHETTE, his niece
SIEUR CLUBIN, the captain of Lethierry's steamboat
RANTAINE, Lethierry's former business partner
EBENEZER CAUDRAY, a rector

The Story:

The shy, reclusive Gilliatt and his mother arrive on the Isle of Guernsey. From where they came, no one knows. They settle in an isolated house by the shore. The mother dies when Gilliatt is still a young man, and he remains alone. His superstitious neighbors fear him because of his uncanny skills at fishing, farming, and mechanics, and because of his extensive knowledge of medicinal plants. They believe he can communicate with evil spirits and can cure mysterious illness.

Meanwhile, based on Guernsey, the enterprising businessman Mess Lethierry loses his fortune when his partner, Rantaine, absconds with it. To recoup his losses, Lethierry establishes the first steamboat service in the English Channel. Although the local fishermen think the steam engine is an invention of the Devil, Lethierry nevertheless prospers by transporting passengers and goods and by shore-trading along the northern French coast. He loves two things above all else: the steamboat *La Durande* and Déruchette, the shallow, pretty, orphaned niece who is his ward.

On Christmas Day, Gilliatt sees Déruchette tracing some letters in the snow. When he reaches the spot, he sees his own name. Because she has already publicly defended Gilliatt against the false accusations of his neighbors, he thinks she must care about him, and he falls in love with her. He goes to her garden by night and serenades her with his bagpipes, but he lacks the courage to approach her or her uncle directly.

Meanwhile, a new rector, Ebenezer Caudray, arrives at the local parish. One day, while Gilliatt is fishing from his sloop, he rescues Caudray, who had climbed onto a rock exposed at low tide without realizing he would be trapped and would drown when the tide returned. Caudray then meets Déruchette and falls in love with her.

La Durande's captain, Sieur Clubin, becomes widely respected as a scrupulously honest man, but he has been hiding behind a mask of virtue to await the opportunity to commit, undetected, a crime that will enrich him. Clubin tracks down Rantaine in France and forces him at gunpoint to return the money he stole from Lethierry. As Rantaine departs in a boat, he shouts to Clubin that he will write to tell Lethierry that the captain now has his employer's money. To keep it, Clubin will have to stage an accident, during which he will seem to drown and disappear.

On the return to Guernsey, Clubin surreptitiously tempts his alcoholic helmsman with a bottle of brandy so that the man will become intoxicated and steer the boat onto a reef in a heavy fog. In the confusion, Clubin slips away and hides in a cave with the money. He has hired smugglers to meet him there later and to take him to South America. After the passengers of *La Durande* depart in lifeboats, Clubin looks out to discover that he has accidentally grounded the steamboat on the wrong reef. He still can use his exceptional skills as a swimmer to cover the several miles to Guernsey and hide there until he can escape, but he is confronted by a huge octopus, which seizes him before he can leave the cave. Clubin drowns, with the money box chained to his corpse.

Survivors of the wreck reach Guernsey and tell their story. Clubin is remembered as a hero. Lethierry, however, despairs; his fortune is now gone. The boat itself could be replaced, but the expensive engine must be salvaged and repaired before it is battered to pieces on the isolated, storm-swept reef. Lethierry promises Déruchette as the prize for whoever can rescue the steam engine intact. Motivated by his secret love, Gilliatt is the only person brave and confident enough to accept the challenge.

At the scene of the wreck, Gilliatt labors tirelessly for weeks, despite the high waves, tides, and dangerous storms. He improvises tools and replacement parts. One day he finds the underwater cave where Clubin had drowned, and is confronted by the same octopus. The creature nearly kills Gilliatt before Gilliatt cuts out its eyes. In the depths of the cave he finds a belt around the skeleton containing Clubin's name and a fortune in coins. Later, after much effort, he is able to protect the boat's engine from another violent storm and hoists it onto his sloop. He sails for home.

Once he receives Rantaine's letter, Lethierry begins to suspect Clubin's duplicity. Now, no one believes that Clubin went down with his ship. At last, Lethierry sees Gilliatt's sloop returning to port with the engine aboard. Overjoyed, Lethierry is ready to make good his promise. He also insists that Gilliatt become his new steamboat captain. He feels even deeper gratitude because Gilliatt also found the money re-

covered from Clubin. Déruchette, however, faints with horror when she sees the haggard, filthy, unkempt Gilliatt, who has just returned from his near-fatal ordeal.

Gilliatt later hears Déruchette and Caudray pledging their mutual love in the garden, so he decides to sacrifice himself to ensure the happiness of the one person he loves. Because the rector and Déruchette cannot marry without Lethierry's consent, and because Lethierry is adamant in insisting that Déruchette marry Gilliatt, the latter obtains Lethierry's written consent. Then, Gilliatt secretly convenes the two lovers and a clergyman, produces the letter of consent, and gives the bride away. Caudray and Déruchette are married, too obliviously happy to realize the depth of Gilliatt's self-sacrifice.

As the newlyweds embark to elope to England, Gilliatt presents Déruchette with the trousseau he had inherited from his mother. He then climbs on the rock from which he had once rescued Caudray and watches the newlyweds sail out of sight until the ocean engulfs him.

Critical Evaluation:

Victor Hugo's *The Toilers of the Sea* can be appreciated in many ways: as a regional novel that celebrates the Channel Islands and the beauty and majesty of the open sea that surrounds them; as a crime story (compare Hugo's knowledgeable depiction of the unending struggle between the underworld and the police in *Les Misérables* [1862; English translation, 1862]); as a tragedy of unrequited love; as an allegorical celebration of human material progress; and as the mythic struggle of a hero against the blind natural forces of storms, the raging sea, and a giant octopus.

Most critics are drawn to the novel's mythic and lyrical dimensions, which inspired some of the greatest French symbolist poets, including Arthur Rimbaud in "La Bateau ivre" (1883; "The Drunken Boat," 1941) and Stéphane Mallarmé in *Un Coup de dés jamais n'abolira le hasard* (1897; *A Dice-Throw*, 1958). However, these poets often neglect to explain the political and biographical contexts from which Hugo's inspiration arose.

The Toilers of the Sea mirrors and transposes the three most agonizing personal disasters of Hugo's life. First, at the age of twenty-five, the precocious Hugo became the unquestioned leader of the French Romantic movement, but his very fame isolated him. His beloved wife, Adèle, became estranged from him, and although the couple remained in the same house, she started a lifelong affair with Hugo's best friend. Gilliatt's unrequited love for Déruchette and his flawless, self-sacrificial devotion reflect Hugo's poignant disappointment in his first and greatest love. Second, open water became Hugo's worst enemy when his first child, Léopoldine, happily married and pregnant with Hugo's first grand-child, drowned at the age of nineteen (in 1843) in a sailing accident near the mouth of the Seine River. Finally, Hugo had to flee from the police of Emperor Napoleon III, owing to the poet's principled support of a constitutional republic. He ended up on the British Isle of Guernsey, in the English Channel.

Almost alone among prominent French figures, Hugo remained in exile for nineteen years (1851-1870), until Napoleon III was overthrown. He refused amnesty, but starting in 1861, his wife—who did not risk arrest—began spending the winters in Paris. Lonely, but grateful to the island that sheltered him, he embodied his appreciation for the place and its people in loving descriptions of the local landscape and customs of those who earned their living from the sea. This dimension of the work is concentrated in the forty-page first chapter, which had been withheld from the 1866 edition and was published only in 1883.

In his political role as a humanitarian socialist, not conventionally religious but inspired by Christ's teachings in the Gospels, Hugo wrote *The Toilers of the Sea* to glorify manual labor performed by skilled, dedicated craftspersons and seafarers. (Compare his admiring depiction of the Flemish shoemaker, guild leader, and ambassador in *Notre-Dame de Paris* [1831; *The Hunchback of Notre Dame*, 1833]). After diligent research, Hugo records the details of work or its social meaning and function. At the same time, and unknown to the protagonist Gilliatt himself, Hugo's toil is metaphysical and transcendent. Many critics see Gilliatt as Promethean, a demigod who brings fire—in this instance, the steamboat engine—to humanity.

Finally, with *The Toilers of the Sea*, Hugo completes the novelistic trilogy that depicts humanity's epic struggle against various oppressive external forces. *The Hunchback of Notre Dame* treats individual resistance to metaphysical misfortune arbitrarily inflicted by an apparently cruel god, raising the philosophical puzzle of permissive evil: How can a loving, all-powerful deity allow gratuitous human suffering to exist? What providential purpose could it serve? Hugo leaves those questions unanswered. *Les Misérables* analyzes social fatality rooted in the class system; in wage slavery; in the vicious cycle of poverty, crime, excessive punishment, resentment, and retaliation; and in the unequal distribution of wealth, while driving home the distinction between two forms of *la misère*: extreme poverty and moral degeneration, and while multiplying examples of the innocent child victims of dysfunctional families. *The Toilers of the Sea* drama-tizes the destructive fatality of nature: the elements and wild beasts. In each situation, Hugo affirms, the best recourse for humanity is the divine guidance offered by human conscience and a loving concern for fellow human beings. The most virtuous life, however, provides no protection from loss and pain; God's purposes will be revealed only in the afterlife.

Revised by Laurence M. Porter

Further Reading

Brombert, Victor. "*The Toilers of the Sea*." In *Victor Hugo and the Visionary Novel*. Cambridge, Mass.: Harvard University Press, 1984. Emphasizes the supernatural and the lyrical dimensions in Hugo's epic glorification of skilled craftsmanship coupled with the myth of material progress, derived from the Enlightenment.

Frey, John Andrew. *A Victor Hugo Encyclopedia*. Westport, Conn.: Greenwood Press, 1999. A comprehensive guide to the works of Hugo. Alphabetically arranged entries discuss his works, characters, themes, and persons and places important to him. Includes a foreword, biography, and bibliography.

Grant, Richard B. "The Myth Concentrated: *Les Travailleurs de la mer*." In *The Perilous Quest: Image, Myth, and Prophecy in the Narratives of Victor Hugo*. Durham, N.C.: Duke University Press, 1968. A strong reading of the archetype of heroic self-sacrifice in *The Toilers of the Sea*.

Grossman, Kathryn M. "Trading Places: Public and Private Transport in Hugo's *Les Travailleurs de la mer*." *Nineteenth-Century French Studies* 26, nos. 3-4 (Spring/Summer, 1998): 295-307. Speculates that an anti-imperialist subtext presents an allegory of a France destined to salvage social progress despite human villainy.

Porter, Laurence M. *Victor Hugo*. New York: Twayne, 1999. Analyzes Hugo's major works in the context of his life and times. Includes a critical bibliography and an index.

Robb, Graham. *Victor Hugo*. New York: Norton, 1998. This definitive biography reveals many previously unknown aspects of Hugo's long literary and political career. Impeccable scholarship.

Roche, Isabel. *Character and Meaning in the Novels of Victor Hugo*. West Lafayette, Ind.: Purdue University Press, 2007. Hugo's major novels exemplify the heroic quest archetype. Roche perceptively relates Hugo's major characters to character theory—a relatively neglected area of study.

Tom Brown's School Days

Author: Thomas Hughes (1822-1896)
First published: 1857
Type of work: Novel
Type of plot: Didactic
Time of plot: Early nineteenth century
Locale: Rugby, Warwickshire, England

Principal characters:
THOMAS "TOM" BROWN, a student at Rugby
HARRY EAST, his friend
GEORGE ARTHUR, a boy befriended by Tom
DR. ARNOLD, the headmaster of Rugby
FLASHMAN, a bully

The Story:

Tom Brown is the son of a country squire who believes in letting his children mingle not only with their social equals but also with any children who are honorable. Before Tom left home to attend Rugby School, therefore, he had the advantage of friendship with all types of boys. This training would be of value to him at the famous school. When Tom alights from the coach on his arrival at Rugby, he is met by Harry East, a lower-school boy who has been at the school for a half year. East gives Tom good advice on how to dress and how to take the hazing and bullying that every new boy must endure. The two boys become immediate friends and are to remain so throughout their years at school.

From the first, Tom loves the school. He conducts himself with such bravery, both on the playing field and in dormitory scuffles, that he soon gains popularity among the other boys. One of the sixth-form boys, a leader among the students, makes such an impression on Tom with his talks on sportsmanship and kindness to weaker boys that Tom is almost a model student during his first half year. He does join in some mischief, however, and is once sent to Dr. Arnold, the headmaster. By and large, however, he and East profit by the lessons they learn in classes and in games.

At the beginning of the second half year, Tom is promoted into the lower fourth form, a large and unruly class dominated by bullies and ruffians. Formerly he had liked his masters and tried to please them; now he begins to believe that they are his natural enemies, and he attempts to do everything possible to thwart them. He cheats in his lessons and shirks many of his other duties. He and East disobey many rules of the school and often taunt farmers in the neighborhood by fishing in their waters or killing their fowl. All in all, Tom, East, and their friends behave in very ungentlemanly ways.

Nevertheless, Tom and East also do some good in the school, for they are basically boys of sound character. Both come from good homes and received good early training. They finally decide that something must be done about "fagging," the custom under which the younger boys are ex-

pected to run errands for the older boys. Each older boy is allowed two fags, but some of them make every younger lad in the school wait on them. One particular bully is Flashman. Tom and East decide to go on strike against Flashman's domination; they lock themselves in their room and defy his demands that they let him in. After attempting to break the door down, Flashman retreats temporarily, but he is not through with the rebels. For weeks, he catches them and tortures them at every possible chance, but they hold firm and persuade some of the other lower-school boys to join them in their strike. At last, Flashman's brutality to Tom and East and their friends so disgusts even the bully's best friends that they begin to desert him, and his hold on the school is broken. Tom and East then thrash him soundly, and from that time on, Flashman never lays a hand on them. Not long afterward, Flashman is caught drunk by the headmaster and is sent away from the school.

Tom and East begin to get into trouble in earnest, and Dr. Arnold despairs of their even being allowed to stay in school. The wise headmaster, however, can see the good in the boys, good that they seem to try hard to hide, and he arranges for them to be split up. Tom is given a new roommate, a shy young boy who is new to the school, George Arthur. Arthur is a half orphan, and Tom's better nature responds to the homesick younger boy. Arthur is to be the greatest influence to enter Tom's life during his career at Rugby. He is of slight build, but he has moral courage that makes Tom ashamed. Arthur does what he thinks is right, even when it means that he must endure the taunts of his housemates. Tom cannot let a younger boy appear more courageous than he, so he reverts to his own former good habits, which he had dropped because of fear of hazing. He begins again to kneel in prayer morning and night; he reads his Bible and discusses earnestly the meanings of certain passages. Indeed, as East says, although Tom is seemingly becoming a leader in the school, it is really Arthur who is leading Tom and thus the other boys. East fights the change as hard as he can, but in the end he too follows Tom, and, despite himself, he begins to change for the better.

When fever strikes the school, many of the boys become seriously ill, Arthur among them. One boy dies. Arthur remains very weak after his illness, and his mother decides to take him out of school until he can recover his strength. Before he leaves, Arthur speaks to Tom about cribbing. Although Tom, believing that to fool the masters is a schoolboy's duty, scoffs at his friend's views on cheating, Arthur as usual prevails. Tom finds it hard to do his lessons honestly, but each time he weakens, the memory of Arthur's face and voice sets him straight again. East does not completely change in this respect, but he does try harder on his own before resorting to dishonest means.

Another result of Arthur's influence is that East takes Communion. He has never been confirmed in the Church, but as a result of a conversation with Tom, during which Tom put forth many of Arthur's beliefs, East talks with Dr. Arnold and receives spiritual stimulation. After he begins to receive Communion, East rapidly changes into the good young man he has unknowingly wanted to be.

So the school years pass. East finishes up and goes off to fight in India. Tom becomes the leader of the school, and he and Arthur, who has returned after his illness, influence many changes in the actions and attitudes of the boys. After graduation, Tom goes on to Oxford. While there, he learns of the death of his old headmaster, Dr. Arnold. He returns to Rugby to mourn the man who played such a large part in influencing his life. It is not until Dr. Arnold is gone that Tom and the others realize how much the good man had done for them. Tom's friends are scattered over the earth, but he knows that his heart will always be with them and those wonderful days at Rugby.

Critical Evaluation:

In *Tom Brown's School Days*, Thomas Hughes created what proved to be the archetypal novel of life in a British public school (that is, privately funded boarding school). Written as his own eight-year-old son went off to Rugby School, Hughes's novel was to be an inspiration and a model of what his son might expect. Hughes had entered Rugby School in 1833, five years after Dr. Thomas Arnold had become headmaster, and many of the incidents and much of the atmosphere of the novel reflect Hughes's own years at Rugby. *Tom Brown's School Days* is not, however, merely a fictional recollection of Hughes's experiences. Hughes had a didactic purpose: He produced a moral tract concerning what the public schools and their students might attain.

Some of England's most prestigious public schools had

their origins in the late Middle Ages. By the early nineteenth century, these boarding schools had become the exclusive preserve of the sons of Britain's ruling class. Fees and tuition were charged, and although scholarships were sometimes available, the schools were extremely exclusive. The public schools were producing the next generation's government leaders, politicians, generals, admirals, and diplomats; they were the training ground for the rulers, not the ruled.

The first section of *Tom Brown's School Days* has nothing to do with Rugby. Instead, it portrays Tom's early childhood and where he grew up, a rural area far removed from London and where the traditional gentry still maintained their influence. Hughes was a member of the gentry, and his choice of the common name of Brown suggests that Tom comes from that rural governing class that Hughes claimed formed the backbone of England. In this idyllic setting were young Tom's roots, and there he played with the sons of artisans and workers, people further down the social scale than the Browns. There were no boys from that lower social stratum at Rugby, however, where only those from the middle classes and the aristocracy—the top 10 percent of the population— were brought together.

Arnold's tenure at Rugby marked a milestone in the history of the British public schools. If he was not the first reformer to make a significant impact on the institution of the boarding school, he was the most prominent. The father of the poet, essayist, and critic Matthew Arnold, Thomas Arnold left an indelible mark on the nineteenth century, in part because of Hughes's *Tom Brown's School Days*. Arnold's hopes for Rugby and the Rugby portrayed in Hughes's novel were different. Arnold was committed to turning his charges into Christian gentlemen, to giving them a moral grounding to shape their entire lives. Good form had to be matched, in Arnold's view, by a commitment to performing one's duties to society. Public school students would become the governing class, and their lives must be guided by Christian moral principles. Hughes would not have disagreed with the moral imperative propounded in Arnold's approach. In his novel, in what may be a reflection of Arnold's religious ideology, Hughes creates a climate that is essentially anti-intellectual. Squire Brown, musing to himself about what he wants for Tom at Rugby, notes: "I don't give a straw for Greek particles, or the digamma. . . . If he'll only turn out a brave, helpful, truth-telling Englishman, and a gentleman, and a Christian, that's all I want."

At Hughes's Rugby, games take precedence over scholarship. Tom's first introduction to Rugby is taking part in a football match, the rules of which had yet to be codified into the modern sport of rugby. When the match is over, Tom's house having emerged victorious, one of the senior boys, Brooke, addresses the boys of the house and claims that he is prouder of the house's victory than if he had won a scholarship to Oxford University's prestigious Balliol College. Tom's last activity while still a student is to captain the cricket eleven against the famous Marylebone players. Arnold, who loved and respected the intellectual life, would have opposed this overemphasis on games. As the nineteenth century went on, however, public school life revolved increasingly around games. The change of focus is evident in the stories and novels of schoolboy life that multiplied in the wake of Hughes's success with *Tom Brown's School Days* and in the many new schools that emerged in the latter half of the nineteenth century. The formation of character on the sports field took precedence over the development of the intellect.

Tom Brown's School Days has never been out of print since it first appeared in 1857, and its impacts on succeeding generations have been profound, not only among those who might expect to attend a school such as Rugby but also among schoolboys in the middle class and in the working class. The novel's moral lessons are clear, and its events are often exciting and easily accessible even to those without roots in the public school milieu. The importance of telling the truth, being brave, fighting fair, and doing well at games became the novel's message. Lying is breaking the code, and bullying—endemic in the schools—is condemned. Flashman, who torments Tom and others, has become a lasting symbol of the cowardly bully.

Hughes was himself a Christian gentleman who exhibited his social responsibilities in his commitment to furthering the rights and opportunities of the working class. Less than a generation after his death in 1896, it would largely be former public schoolboys who, as junior officers, died in considerable numbers leading their troops into battle during World War I. It is difficult to imagine, in the different environment of a later era, that the effect of *Tom Brown's School Days* on readers can be as influential as when it first appeared. In the late twentieth century, another British writer, George Mac-Donald Fraser, turned Hughes's Flashman, still the cowardly bully, into a notable success as an antihero in a series of popular novels.

"Critical Evaluation" by Eugene Larson

Further Reading

Allen, Brooke. "A World of Wizards." *New Leader* 82, no. 13 (November 1-15, 1999): 13-14. Critical review of the works of J. K. Rowling compares the world of Hogwarts in her Harry Potter books to the public school as depicted in *Tom Brown's School Days*.

Briggs, Asa. *Victorian People: A Reassessment of Persons and Themes, 1851-1867*. Rev. ed. Chicago: University of Chicago Press, 1990. An eminent British historian discusses the notable figures, ideas, and events of the high Victorian era. Includes a brilliant chapter titled "Thomas Hughes and the Public Schools."

Chandos, John. *Boys Together*. New Haven, Conn.: Yale University Press, 1984. Scholarly analysis of the English public school from 1800 to 1864 includes discussion of the central role played by Dr. Thomas Arnold. Examines the importance of Hughes's *Tom Brown's School Days* in popularizing Arnold's reforms at Rugby.

Mack, Edward C., and W. H. G. Armytage. *Thomas Hughes: The Life of the Author of "Tom Brown's School Days."* London: Ernest Benn, 1952. Standard biography of Hughes, an archetypal Victorian figure, illustrates his many literary, political, and social endeavors. Includes an extensive discussion of *Tom Brown's School Days*.

Quigly, Isabel. *The Heirs of Tom Brown: The English School Story*. London: Chatto & Windus, 1982. Analyzes the development of the numerous stories written about England's public schools, a genre that began with Hughes's *Tom Brown's School Days*.

Stoneley, Peter. "Family Values and the 'Republic of Boys': Tom Brown and Others." *Journal of Victorian Culture* 3, no. 1 (Spring, 1998): 69-92. Examines *Tom Brown's School Days* and *Eric: Or, Little by Little* (1858) by Frederic William Farrar, describing how these novels depict school as a microcosm of Victorian society.

Trory, Ernie. *Truth Against the World: The Life and Times of Thomas Hughes, Author of "Tom Brown's School Days."* Hove, England: Crabtree, 1993. Biography provides information on Hughes's writing as well as on his political career.

Worth, George J. *Thomas Hughes*. Boston: Twayne, 1984. Focuses on Hughes the writer rather than Hughes the politician and public figure. Includes in-depth discussion of *Tom Brown's School Days*.

Tom Jones

Author: Henry Fielding (1707-1754)
First published: 1749, as *The History of Tom Jones, a Foundling*
Type of work: Novel
Type of plot: Picaresque
Time of plot: Early eighteenth century
Locale: England

Principal characters:
TOM JONES, a foundling
SQUIRE ALLWORTHY, his foster father
BRIDGET, Allworthy's sister
MASTER BLIFIL, Bridget's son
MR. PARTRIDGE, the schoolmaster
MR. WESTERN, an English squire
SOPHIA WESTERN, his daughter

The Story:

Squire Allworthy lives in retirement in the country with his sister Bridget. Returning from a visit to London, he is surprised upon entering his room to find an infant lying on his bed. His discovery causes astonishment and consternation in the household. The squire is a childless widower. The next day, Bridget and the squire inquire in the community to discover the baby's mother. Their suspicions are shortly fixed upon Jenny Jones, who spent many hours in the squire's home while nursing Bridget through a long illness. The worthy squire sends for the girl and in his gentle manner reprimands her for her wicked behavior, assuring her, however, that the baby will remain in his home under the best of care. Fearing malicious gossip in the neighborhood, Squire Allworthy sends Jenny away.

Jenny was a servant in the house of a schoolmaster, Mr. Partridge, who educated the young woman during her four years in his house. Jenny's comely face made Mrs. Partridge jealous of her. Neighborhood gossip soon convinced Mrs. Partridge that her husband is the father of Jenny's son, whereupon Squire Allworthy calls the schoolmaster before him and talks to him at great length concerning morality. Mr. Partridge, deprived of his school, his income, and his wife, also leaves the country.

Shortly afterward, Captain Blifil wins the heart of Bridget. Eight months after their marriage, Bridget has a son. The squire thinks it would be advisable to rear the baby and his sister's child together. The boy is named Jones, for his mother.

Squire Allworthy becomes exceedingly fond of the foundling. Captain Blifil dies during his son's infancy, and Master Blifil grows up as Squire Allworthy's acknowledged heir. Otherwise, he remains on even terms with the foundling, so far as opportunities for advancement are concerned. Tom, however, is such a mischievous lad that he has only one friend among the servants, the gamekeeper, Black George, an indolent man with a large family. Mr. Thwackum and Mr.

Square, who consider Tom a wicked soul, are hired to instruct the lads. Tom's many deceptions are always discovered through the combined efforts of Mr. Thwackum, Mr. Square, and Master Blifil, who dislikes Tom more and more as he grows older. It is assumed by all that Mrs. Blifil would dislike Tom, but at times she seems to show greater affection for him than for her own son. In turn, the compassionate squire takes Master Blifil to his heart and becomes censorious of Tom.

Mr. Western, who lives on a neighboring estate, has a daughter whom he loves more than anyone else in the world. Sophia has a tender fondness for Tom because of a deed of kindness he performed for her when they were still children. At the age of twenty, Master Blifil becomes a favorite with the young ladies, while Tom is considered a ruffian by all but Mr. Western, who admires his ability to hunt. Tom spends many evenings at the Western home, with every opportunity to see Sophia, for whom his affections are increasing daily. One afternoon, Tom has the good fortune to be nearby when Sophia's horse runs away. When Tom attempts to rescue her, he breaks his arm. He is removed to Mr. Western's house, where he receives medical care and remains to recover from his hurt. One day, he and Sophia have occasion to be alone in the garden, where they exchange confessions of love.

Squire Allworthy becomes mortally ill. The doctor assumes that he is dying and sends for the squire's relatives. With his servants and family gathered around him, the squire announces the disposal of his wealth, giving generously to Tom. Tom is the only one satisfied with his portion; his only concern is the impending death of his foster father and benefactor. On the way home from London to see the squire, Mrs. Blifil dies suddenly. When the squire is pronounced out of danger, Tom's joy is so great that he becomes drunk through toasting the squire's health, and he quarrels with young Blifil.

Sophia's aunt, Mrs. Western, perceives the interest her

niece shows in Blifil. Wishing to conceal her affection for Tom, Sophia gives Blifil the greater part of her attention when she is with the two young men. Informed by his sister of Sophia's conduct, Mr. Western suggests to Squire Allworthy that a match be arranged between Blifil and Sophia. When Mrs. Western tells the young woman of the proposed match, Sophia thinks that Mrs. Western is referring to Tom, and she immediately discloses her passion for the foundling. It is unthinkable, however, that Mr. Western, much as he likes Tom, would ever allow his daughter to marry a man without a family and a fortune, and Mrs. Western forces Sophia to receive Blifil under the threat of exposing the woman's real affection for Tom. Sophia meets Tom secretly in the garden, and the two lovers vow constancy. Mr. Western discovers them and goes immediately to Squire Allworthy with his knowledge.

Aware of his advantage, Blifil tells the squire that on the day he was near death, Tom was out drinking and singing. The squire feels that he forgave Tom many wrongs, but this show of unconcern for the squire's health infuriates the good man. He sends for Tom, reproaches him, and banishes him from his house.

With the help of Black George, the gamekeeper, and Mrs. Honour, Sophia's maid, Tom and Sophia are able to exchange love letters. When Sophia is confined to her room because she refuses to marry Blifil, she bribes her maid to flee with her from her father's house. Tom, setting out to seek his fortune, goes to an inn with a small company of soldiers. A fight follows in which he is severely injured, and a barber is summoned to treat his wound. When Tom tells the barber his story, the man surprisingly reveals himself to be Partridge, the schoolmaster, banished years before because he was suspected of being Tom's father. When Tom is well enough to travel, the two men set out together on foot.

Before they go far, they hear screams of distress and come upon a woman struggling with a soldier who beguiled her to a lonely spot. Promising to take her to a place of safety, Tom accompanies the unfortunate woman to the nearby village of Upton, where the landlady of the inn refuses to receive them because of the woman's torn and disheveled clothing. When the landlady hears the true story of the woman's misfortune and is assured that the woman is the lady of Captain Waters, a well-known officer, she relents. Mrs. Waters invites Tom to dine with her so that she can thank him properly for her rescue.

Meanwhile, a lady and her maid arrive at the inn and proceed to their rooms. They are followed, several hours later, by an angry gentleman in pursuit of his wife. Learning from the chambermaid that there is a woman resembling his wife in the inn, he bursts into Mrs. Waters's chambers, only to confront Tom. At his intrusion, Mrs. Waters begins to scream. Abashed, the gentleman identifies himself as Mr. Fitzpatrick and retreats with apologies. Shortly after this disturbance subsides, Sophia and Mrs. Honour arrive at the inn. When Partridge unknowingly reveals Tom's relationship with Mrs. Waters and the embarrassing situation that Mr. Fitzpatrick discloses, Sophia, grieved by Tom's fickleness, decides to continue on her way. Before leaving the inn, however, she has Mrs. Honour place on Tom's empty bed a muff that she knows he will recognize as hers.

Soon after setting out, Sophia overtakes Mrs. Fitzpatrick, who arrived at the inn early the previous evening and who fled during the disturbance caused by her husband. Mrs. Fitzpatrick is Sophia's cousin, and they decide to go on to London together. In London, Sophia proceeds to the home of Lady Bellaston, who is known to her through Mrs. Western. Lady Bellaston is sympathetic with Sophia's reasons for running away.

Unable to overtake Sophia, Tom and Partridge follow her to London, where Tom takes lodgings in the home of Mrs. Miller, whom Squire Allworthy patronizes on his visits to the city. The landlady has two daughters, Nancy and Betty, and a lodger, Mr. Nightingale, who is obviously in love with Nancy. Tom finds congenial residence with Mrs. Miller, and he becomes friends with Mr. Nightingale. Partridge is still with Tom in the hope of future advancement. Repeated visits to Lady Bellaston and Mrs. Fitzpatrick finally give Tom the opportunity to meet Sophia during an intermission at a play. There, Tom is able to allay Sophia's doubts as to his love for her. During his stay with the Millers, Tom learns that Mr. Nightingale's father objects to his marrying Nancy. Through the kindness of his heart, Tom persuades the elder Nightingale to permit the marriage, to Mrs. Miller's great delight.

Mr. Western learns of Sophia's whereabouts from Mrs. Fitzpatrick. He comes to London and takes Sophia from Lady Bellaston's house to his own lodgings. When Mrs. Honour brings the news to Tom, he is in despair. Penniless, he cannot hope to marry Sophia, and now his beloved is in the hands of her father once more. Then Partridge brings news that Squire Allworthy is coming to London and is bringing with him Master Blifil to marry Sophia. In his distress, Tom goes to see Mrs. Fitzpatrick but encounters her jealous husband on her doorstep. In the duel that follows, Tom wounds Mr. Fitzpatrick and is carried off to jail.

There he is visited by Partridge, the friends he made in London, and Mrs. Waters, who has been traveling with Mr. Fitzpatrick since their meeting in Upton. When Partridge and Mrs. Waters meet in Tom's cell, Partridge recognizes her as Jenny, Tom's reputed mother. Horrified, he reveals his knowledge to everyone, including Squire Allworthy, who by that time has arrived in London with Blifil.

In Mrs. Miller's lodgings, so many people praise Tom's goodness and kindness that Squire Allworthy almost makes up his mind to relent in his attitude toward the foundling when news of his conduct with Mrs. Waters reaches his ears. Fortunately, however, the cloud is soon dispelled by Mrs. Waters herself, who assures the squire that Tom is no son of hers but the child of his sister Bridget and a student whom the squire befriended. Tom's true father died before his son's birth, and Bridget concealed her shame by putting the baby on her brother's bed upon his return from a long visit to London. Later, she paid Jenny liberally to let suspicion fall upon her former maid.

Squire Allworthy also learns that Bridget claimed Tom as her son in a letter written before her death, a letter Blifil probably destroyed. There is further proof that Blifil plotted to have Tom hanged for murder. Mr. Fitzpatrick, however, did not die, and he recovers sufficiently to acknowledge himself the aggressor in the duel; Tom is released from prison.

Upon these disclosures of Blifil's villainy, Squire Allworthy dismisses Blifil and makes Tom his heir. Once Tom's proper station is revealed, Mr. Western withdraws all objections to his suit. Reunited, Tom and Sophia are married and retire to Mr. Western's estate in the country.

Critical Evaluation:

In a relatively short life span, Henry Fielding was a poet, a playwright, a journalist, a jurist, and a pioneer in the development of the modern novel. The early poetry may be disregarded, but his dramatic works gave Fielding the training that later enabled him to handle adeptly the complex plots of his novels. Although he wrote perhaps a half dozen novels (some attributions are disputed), Fielding is best remembered for *The History of Tom Jones, a Foundling*. This novel contains a strong infusion of autobiographical elements. The character Sophia, for example, was based on Fielding's wife Charlotte, who was his one great love. They eloped in 1734 and had ten years together before she died in 1744. Squire Allworthy combined traits of a former schoolmate from Eton named George Lyttelton (to whom the novel is dedicated) and a generous benefactor of the Fielding family named James Ralph. Moreover, Fielding's origins in a career army family and his rejection of that background shaped his portrayal of various incidental military personnel in this and his other novels; he had an antiarmy bias. Fielding's feelings of revulsion against urban living are reflected in the conclusion of *Tom Jones* (and in his other novels). The happy ending consists of a retreat to the country. Published a scant five years before Fielding's death, *Tom Jones* was a runaway best seller, going through four editions within a twelve-month period.

The structure of the novel is carefully divided into eighteen books in a fashion similar to the epic form that Fielding explicitly praised. Of those eighteen books, the first six are set on the Somersetshire estate of Squire Allworthy. Books 7 through 12 deal with events on the road to London, and the last six books describe events in London. The middle of the novel, books 9 and 10, covers the hilarious hiatus at the inn in Upton. Apparent diversions and digressions are actually intentional exercises in character exposition, and all episodes are deliberately choreographed to advance the plot—sometimes in ways not evident until later. Everything contributes to the overall organic development of the novel.

This kind of coherence was intimately connected with Fielding's concern about the craft of fiction. *Tom Jones* is one of the most carefully and meticulously written novels in the history of English literature. It is, in fact, remarkably free of inconsistencies and casual errors. Fielding saw his task as a novelist to be a "historian" of human nature and human events, and he considered himself obligated to emphasize the moral aspect of his work. More important, Fielding introduced each of his eighteen books with a chapter about the craft of prose fiction. Indeed, the entire novel is dotted with chapters on the craft of the novel and on literary criticism. The remainder of the novel applies the principles enunciated in the chapters on proper construction of prose fiction. The chapters on literature in themselves constitute a substantial work of literary criticism. Fielding amplifies these theories with his own demonstration of their application by writing a novel, *Tom Jones*, according to his own principles. So compelling a union of theory and practice renders Fielding's hypotheses virtually unassailable.

As Fielding made practical application of his theories of craftsmanship, their validity becomes readily apparent in his handling of characterization. Fielding viewed human nature ambivalently, as a combination of good and bad. Whereas the bad person has almost no hope of redemption, the fundamentally good person is somewhat tinged with bad but is nonetheless worthy for all that, according to Fielding. Therefore, the good person may occasionally be unwise (as Allworthy is) or indiscreet (as Jones often was) but still be an estimable human being, for such a person is more credible as a good person, Fielding thought, than one who is without defect. Consequently, the villain Blifil is unreconstructedly wicked, but the hero Tom Jones is essentially good, although flawed. To succeed, Tom has to improve himself—to cultivate "prudence" and "religion," as Squire Allworthy recommends.

Into this dichotomy between evil and good, and villain and hero, a species of determinism creeps—possibly not a factor consciously recognized by Fielding. Blifil and Tom are born and reared in the same environment, but one is wicked and one is good. Only innate qualities can logically explain the difference. Some minor characters are not so fully psychologized; they are essentially allegorical, representing ideas (Thwackum and Square, for example). Overall, however, Fielding's command of characterization in general comprises a series of excellent portraits. These portraits, however, are never allowed to dominate the novel, for all of them are designed to contribute to the development of the story. Such a system of priorities provides insight into Fielding's aesthetic and epistemological predispositions.

Fielding subscribed to a fundamentally classical set of values, ethically and aesthetically. He saw the novel as a mirror of life, not an illumination of life. He valued craftsmanship, he assumed a position of detached objectivity, he esteemed wit, and he followed the classical unity of action. His plot brings Tom full circle from a favored position to disgrace back to the good graces of Squire Allworthy and Sophia. In the course of the novel, Fielding demonstrates his objectivity by commenting critically on the form of the novel. He further reveals his classical commitments by embellishing his novel with historical detail, creating a high degree of verisimilitude. His sense of humor and his sharp wit also testify to his reliance on classical ways of thought. The easygoing development of the plot additionally reveals Fielding's detachment and objectivity, and the great variety in types of characters whom he presents is another indication of his classical inclinations toward universality.

"Critical Evaluation" by Joanne G. Kashdan

Further Reading

Dircks, Richard J. *Henry Fielding.* Boston: Twayne, 1983. Offers a detailed reading of the novel and its moral structures. Examines plot and structure, themes, realism, digressions, the sentimental tradition, and the novel's characterizations.

Irwin, Michael. *Henry Fielding: The Tentative Realist.* Oxford, England: Clarendon Press, 1967. Irwin sees Fielding as a moralist who was intent on creating a new literature. In an analysis of the structure of *Tom Jones,* Irwin notes the didactic content of the novel's themes. He also discusses the limitations of Fielding's characterizations.

Pagliaro, Harold E. *Henry Fielding: A Literary Life.* New York: St. Martin's Press, 1998. An excellent, updated account of Fielding's life and writings, with chapter 3 devoted to his novels and other prose fiction. Includes bibliographical references and an index.

Paulson, Ronald. *The Life of Henry Fielding: A Critical Biography.* Malden, Mass.: Blackwell, 2000. Paulson examines how Fielding's literary works—novels, plays, and essays—all contained autobiographical elements. Each chapter of the book begins with an annotated chronology of the events of Fielding's life; also includes a bibliography and index.

Price, Martin. "The Subversion of Form." In *Henry Fielding's Tom Jones,* edited by Harold Bloom. New York: Chelsea House, 1987. Price sees the joining of the naïve hero and the sophisticated narrator as a source of Fielding's humor; the result is an ironic stance that pleasantly confuses the reader's expectations.

Rawson, Claude, ed. *The Cambridge Companion to Henry Fielding.* New York: Cambridge University Press, 2007. A collection of essays commissioned for this volume, which includes an examination of Fielding's life, major novels, theatrical career, journalism, Fielding and female authority, and Fielding's style, among other topics. Chapter 6 is devoted to an analysis of *Tom Jones.*

_____. *Henry Fielding, 1707-1754: Novelist, Playwright, Journalist, Magistrate, a Double Anniversary Tribute.* Newark: University of Delaware Press, 2008. A collection of essays by Fielding scholars designed as a tribute to the 250th anniversary of his death in 1754 and the tercentenary of his birth in 1707. The essays cover all aspects of Fielding's life and work.

Reilly, Patrick. *"Tom Jones": Adventure and Providence.* Boston: Twayne, 1991. Most of this book is devoted to a reading of *Tom Jones.* Examines the work's Christian comedy and its use of satire. Draws some contrasts with the work of Samuel Richardson and Jonathan Swift.

Stevenson, John Allen. *The Real History of Tom Jones.* New York: Palgrave Macmillan, 2005. Examines the historical sources from which Fielding constructed his novel, including the politics, social class structure, justice system, and other aspects of life in Georgian England.

Watt, Ian. "Fielding as Novelist: *Tom Jones.*" In *Henry Fielding's Tom Jones,* edited by Harold Bloom. New York: Chelsea House, 1987. Draws contrasts between *Tom Jones* and Samuel Richardson's *Clarissa.* Notes Fielding's comparatively superficial characterizations and his somewhat greater interest in plot.

Tono-Bungay

Author: H. G. Wells (1866-1946)
First published: 1908
Type of work: Novel
Type of plot: Social satire
Time of plot: Late nineteenth and early twentieth centuries
Locale: England; West Africa; Bordeaux, France

Principal characters:
GEORGE PONDEREVO, a young scientist and the narrator
THE HONORABLE BEATRICE NORMANDY, an aristocrat
EDWARD PONDEREVO, George's uncle
SUSAN PONDEREVO, George's aunt
MARION RAMBOAT, George's wife

The Story:

George Ponderevo grows up in the shadow of Bladesover House, where his mother is the housekeeper. In that Edwardian atmosphere, the boy soon becomes aware of the wide distinctions between English social classes, for the neighborhood around Bladesover is England in miniature, a small world made up of the quality, the church, the village, the laborers, and the servants. Although George spends most of his time away at school, he returns to Bladesover for his vacations. During one of his vacations, he learns for the first time about the class of which he is a member—the servants.

His lesson comes as the result of the arrival at Bladesover House of the Honorable Beatrice Normandy, an eight-year-old child, and her snobbish young half brother, Archie Garvell. Twelve-year-old George Ponderevo falls in love with the little aristocrat that summer. Two years later, their childish romance ends abruptly when George and Archie fight each other. George is disillusioned because the Honorable Beatrice does not come to his aid. In fact, she betrays him, abandons him, and lies about him, depicting George as an assailant of his social betters.

When George refuses flatly to apologize to Archie Garvell, he is taken to Chatham and put to work in the bakery owned by his mother's brother, Nicodemus Frapp. George finds his uncle's family dull, cloddish, and overreligious. One night, in the room he shares with his two cousins, he tells them in confidence that he does not believe in any form of revealed religion. Traitorously, his cousins report George's blasphemy to their father. As a result, George is called upon in a church meeting to acknowledge his sins. Humiliated and angry, he runs away, going back to his mother at Bladesover House.

Mrs. Ponderevo then sends him to live with another uncle, his father's brother, Edward Ponderevo, at Wimblehurst, in Sussex. There George works in his uncle's chemist's shop, or pharmacy, after school. Edward Ponderevo is a restless, dissatisfied man who wants to expand his business and make money. His wife, Aunt Susan, is a gentle, patient woman who treats George kindly. George's mother dies during his years at Wimblehurst.

George's pleasant life at Wimblehurst is eventually brought to a sudden end. Through foolish investments, Edward Ponderevo loses everything of his own, including the chemist's shop, as well as a small fund he had been holding in trust for George. Edward and Susan Ponderevo are forced to leave Wimblehurst, but George remains behind as an apprentice with Mr. Mantell, the new owner of the shop.

At the age of nineteen, George goes to London to matriculate at the University of London for his bachelor of science degree. On the trip, his uncle, now living in London, shows him the city and first whispers to him the name of Tono-Bungay, an invention on which the older Ponderevo is working. Instead of attending the university at that time, however, George decides to accept a scholarship at the Consolidated Technical Schools at South Kensington. When he finally arrives in London to begin his studies, he is nearly twenty-two years old. One day, he meets an old schoolfellow, Ewart, an artist who exerts a broadening influence on the young man. He also meets Marion Ramboat, who is later to become his wife. Under these influences, George begins to neglect his studies. When he sees a billboard advertising Tono-Bungay, he remembers the hints his uncle had thrown out several years before. A few days later, George's uncle sends him a telegram in which he offers the young man a job paying three hundred pounds per year.

Tono-Bungay is a patent medicine, a stimulant that is very inexpensive to make and only slightly injurious to the persons who take it. After a week of indecision, George joins his uncle's firm. One factor that helps to sway him is the thought that Marion Ramboat might be persuaded to marry him if he were to improve his income. Using new and bold methods of advertising, George and his exuberant uncle make Tono-Bungay a national product. The enterprise is highly successful, and both George and his uncle become wealthy. At last, Marion consents to marry George, but their marriage is unsuccessful. They are divorced after Marion learns that her husband had gone off for the weekend with Effie Rink, one of the secretaries in his office. After his divorce, George devotes himself to science and research, and he also becomes interested in flying.

In the meantime, Edward Ponderevo branches out into many enterprises, partly through the influence of the wealthy Mr. Moggs, with whom he has become associated. His huge corporation, Domestic Utilities, becomes known as Do-Ut, and his steady advancement in wealth can be traced through the homes in which he lives. The first is an elaborate suite of rooms at the Hardingham Hotel. Next comes a villa at Beckenham; next, an elaborate estate at Chiselhurst, followed by the chaste simplicity of a medieval castle, Lady Grove; and finally, the ambitious but uncompleted splendor of the great house at Crest Hill, on which three hundred workmen are at one time employed.

While his uncle is buying houses, George is absorbed in his experiments with gliders and balloons, working in his special workshop with Cothope, his assistant. The Honorable Beatrice Normandy is staying near Lady Grove with Lady Osprey, her stepmother, and she and George become acquainted again. After a glider accident, she nurses him back to health. Although the two fall in love, Beatrice refuses to marry him.

Suddenly all of Edward Ponderevo's world of top-heavy speculation collapses. On the verge of bankruptcy, he clutches at anything he can to save himself from financial ruin and the loss of his great, uncompleted project at Crest Hill. George does his part by undertaking a voyage to Mordet Island in the brig *Maude Mary*, to secure by trickery a cargo of quap, an ore containing two new elements valuable to the Ponderevos largely because they hope to use canadium—one of the ingredients—in making a new and better lamp filament. The long, difficult voyage to West Africa is unpleasant and unsuccessful. After the quap has been stolen and loaded on the ship, the properties of the ore cause the ship to sink in midocean. Rescued at sea, George learns of his uncle's bankruptcy as soon as he arrives ashore at Plymouth.

To avoid arrest, George and his uncle decide to cross the English Channel at night in George's airship and escape the law by posing as tourists in France. The stratagem proves successful, and they land about fifty miles from Bordeaux. Then Edward Ponderevo becomes dangerously ill at a small inn near Bayonne, and a few days later he dies, before his wife can reach his side.

Back in England, George has a twelve-day love affair with Beatrice Normandy, who still refuses to marry him because, she says, she is spoiled by the luxury of her class. George Ponderevo, by this time a severe critic of degeneration in England, becomes a designer of destroyers.

Critical Evaluation:

H. G. Wells's novels, as well as other literary forms, are vehicles for his social analysis and criticism. Some of his early works, such as *The Time Machine: An Invention* (1895), *The Invisible Man: A Grotesque Romance* (1897), and *The War of the Worlds* (1898), reflect an extreme fin de siècle pessimism. In those works, Wells predicts nothing ahead but doom and destruction for humanity. In later writings, however, such as *A Modern Utopia* (1905), he presents at least the possibility of salvation through an elite leadership called the Samurai. If society can produce such an elite out of the morass of democratic mediocrity, survival of the species might become possible. This elitist ideology is present in Wells's writing to the time of his death. In *Tono-Bungay*, Wells seems to take a position somewhere between the two extremes of pessimism and guarded hope, with the emphasis leaning in the direction of the pessimistic. Nevertheless, elements in the character and behavior of George Ponderevo and his aunt Susan suggest real, if qualified, signs of hope.

Tono-Bungay represents Wells at his best, using witty language and clever plotting to dramatize his dire predictions of humanity's fate. It is also his most autobiographical and intensely personal work. Although Wells denied any resemblance, his own experiences remarkably paralleled those of his hero, George Ponderevo. Like George in *Tono-Bungay*, Wells was little influenced by his father, who deferred to his domineering wife, the housekeeper of a large country estate. Wells and Ponderevo both studied science at the Consolidated Technical Schools at South Kensington but dropped out after mediocre academic careers. Both married dull, insipid women and became unfaithful husbands. In fact, the many similarities between Wells's life and Ponderevo's strongly imply that the author wrote *Tono-Bungay* as a statement of his personal beliefs.

As the children of servants, Wells and Ponderevo had opportunities to view English society from the bottom up. The descriptions of life at Bladesover House, particularly the afternoon teas over which George's mother presides, reveal its pomposity and pretension. The incident with Archie Garvell exposes the treachery and deceit of the supposed "better sort." Ponderevo's Bladesover experiences introduce an important theme that runs through the whole novel: the sham, artificiality, and superficiality of the world as Wells saw it.

The history of Tono-Bungay, the patent medicine that brings fame and fortune to Edward Ponderevo and his nephew George, serves as a metaphor for Wells's view of English society. The tonic is an instant success, rising meteorically in the commercial sky. The book contains several allusions to dramatic spurts and rapid rises. Nothing, however, sustains them; Tono-Bungay is a fraud, and the financial empire that it spawns depends on manipulation, chicanery, and, in the end, even forgery. Its spectacular rise is followed by an equally spectacular demise: Like a rocket, it bursts into the sky, only to disintegrate and fall back to earth. The world in which Wells lived was also in a state of degeneration and disintegration.

Pervasive decay provides Wells with another theme, one that follows logically from the sudden success of a venture built on a sham. As Edward Ponderevo's business conglomerate crumbles under the weight of its own inadequacies, the man responsible for it begins to rot away himself. Wells's account of Edward's terminal illness emphasizes its deteriorating impact. Even Beatrice Normandy is affected by the decay. Her involvement with the upper class and her role as mistress to an English nobleman have corrupted her. She finally rejects a relationship with George because she feels herself contaminated by the stench of high society. The ultimate symbol of decay is the quap, the material that, still through manipulation and fraud, is expected to save Edward Ponderevo and his assorted schemes. He looks on quap as a quick and total remedy for his dying empire, but instead it destroys everything it touches. It kills all life in its vicinity in Africa; it provokes George Ponderevo into killing an innocent African; it even rots the ship carrying it back to England, causing the ship to sink to the bottom of the ocean.

Wells's criticisms and accusations of degeneracy are not confined to the upper classes. In his view, all elements of English society are equally at fault. The Ramboat family, for example, represent the proletariat but do not come across as a socialist might have portrayed them. Instead, they are dull, vacuous, and inept, as decayed in their own way as the gentility of Beatrice Normandy and Archie Garvell. No group emerges from Wells's attack unscathed.

Social criticism was hardly new with Wells and *Tono-Bungay*. The uniqueness and superior quality of this novel rest not on the novelty of its format but on the skill with which Wells presents his argument in the context of an amusing story. Despite the somber message, an exuberant humor runs through the dialogue of the characters, and even their names show Wells's wit at work. Strong character development, however, is not an element of *Tono-Bungay*. The personages remain almost stereotypes of their respective classes, caricatures rather than real humans.

Only two exceptions provide relief from Wells's pessimism and criticism. One, Edward's wife, Susan, lives through all of her husband's escapades without losing her sensible good nature or her affection for George. Another very positive element appears in Ponderevo's research first with gliders and then with destroyers. "Sometimes," he says, "I call

this reality Science, sometimes I call it Truth." Nevertheless, Wells fails to explain why or how Susan manages to resist the forces of illusion and decay that surround her, and he does not consider Ponderevo one of the "Samurai" who might save civilization through scientific research. Thus neither exception offers an answer to the question of what might be done to provide humanity salvation from degeneration and destruction. At least Wells, through his alter ego Ponderevo, engages in a search for a solution.

"Critical Evaluation" by R. David Weber

Further Reading

Costa, Richard Hauer. *H. G. Wells*. Rev. ed. Boston: Twayne, 1985. Includes a critical summary of *Tono-Bungay*, which is described as "heralding . . . the new [twentieth] century amidst the debris of the old." Demonstrates how this novel shows Wells as both "mystic visionary" and "storyteller."

Hammond, J. R. *An H. G. Wells Companion: A Guide to the Novels, Romances, and Short Stories*. New York: Barnes & Noble, 1979. Describes *Tono-Bungay* as "a picture of a radically unstable society and an indictment of irresponsible capitalism." Calls the novel Wells's "finest single achievement."

_____. *A Preface to H. G. Wells*. New York: Longman, 2001. Provides information on Wells's life and cultural background as well as the important people and places in his life. Also offers critical commentary on Wells's works, including *Tono-Bungay*, and a discussion of his literary reputation.

Huntington, John, ed. *Critical Essays on H. G. Wells*. Boston: G. K. Hall, 1991. Collection of essays updates critical work on Wells, including the novel *Tono-Bungay*.

Mackenzie, Norman, and Jeanne Mackenzie. *H. G. Wells*. New York: Simon & Schuster, 1973. Discusses the autobiographical aspects of the narrator of *Tono-Bungay*, George Ponderevo; the circumstances of the writing of the novel; and its critical reception. Argues that "with *Tono-Bungay* Wells reached the peak of his career as a novelist."

McLean, Steven, ed. *H. G. Wells: Interdisciplinary Essays*. Newcastle, England: Cambridge Scholars, 2008. Collection of essays analyzes individual novels and discusses general characteristics of Wells's work.

Wagar, W. Warren. *H. G. Wells: Traversing Time*. Middletown, Conn.: Wesleyan University Press, 2004. Analyzes all of Wells's work, focusing on the author's preoccupation with the unfolding of public time and the history and future of humankind. Demonstrates how Wells's writings remain relevant in the twenty-first century.

Top Girls

Author: Caryl Churchill (1938-   )
First produced: 1982; first published, 1982
Type of work: Drama
Type of plot: Social realism
Time of plot: Early 1980's
Locale: England

Principal characters:

MARLENE, the "top girl" who is promoted to managing director of her employment agency

JOYCE, her sister

ANGIE, Marlene's teenage daughter, who believes that Joyce is her mother

KIT, Angie's young friend

ISABELLA BIRD, a nineteenth century Scotswoman famous for her travels

LADY NIJO, a thirteenth century Japanese woman, first an emperor's courtesan, then a Buddhist nun

DULL GRET, the subject of a Breughel painting in which she leads peasant women into hell to battle devils

POPE JOAN, the legendary woman who, disguised as a man, is thought to have been pope in the ninth century

PATIENT GRISELDA, the obedient wife in Chaucer's "Clerk's Tale"

The Story:

Marlene organizes a Saturday-night party in a London restaurant to celebrate her promotion at the Top Girls' Employment Agency. She invites a group of women drawn from history, legend, literature, and art, who tell their stories as Marlene orders food and drink. The stories overlap and compete with one another; the women sometimes listen, sometimes editorialize, and often talk at the same time. Isabella Bird and Lady Nijo are the earliest arrivals. Bird's story is about her problems with illness, which make her unable to deal with the life expected of a clergyman's daughter (Bird does not seem to make this connection). Her problems led to travel, a marriage proposal from mountain man Jim Nugent—"a man any woman might love but none could marry"—and a return to Scotland after her sister Hennie's death. Because of her need to atone, given Hennie's goodness and that of the doctor who cared for her through her last illness, Isabella married the doctor and devoted herself to caring for him through his long last illness. After his death and her own charitable work, she experienced a return of her own nervous illness, the result of trying "very hard to cope with the ordinary drudgery of life."

Interwoven with Bird's story is Lady Nijo's account of being raised to become a courtesan of the emperor. She enjoyed the beautiful clothes and status while she was the emperor's favorite; later she took lovers and lost a daughter to one of these lovers, whose wife raised the girl to follow in

Nijo's footsteps. When she lost favor with the emperor, she became a Buddhist nun and now wanders the countryside.

Pope Joan enters next and tells her tale, which begins when as a precocious fourteen-year-old disguised as a boy she left home and traveled with a male friend who was also her lover. They studied theology together until his death. Her intelligence attracted attention, and she rose rapidly, becoming a cardinal and then pope. As pope, she discreetly took a lover and became pregnant without realizing it. When she interrupted a religious process to deliver her baby on the side of a road, she was stoned to death.

Everyone at Marlene's party is by that time quite drunk and giggling at Joan's description of the pierced chair that subsequent popes are required to sit on to prove that they are men. They are getting ready for dessert when Patient Griselda enters. Marlene tells the others, "Griselda's in Boccaccio and Petrarch and Chaucer because of her extraordinary marriage," which Marlene characterizes as "like a fairy story, except it starts with marrying the prince." Griselda reminds Marlene that her husband is "only a marquis." All the guests listen when Griselda tells how her husband set the wedding day before telling anyone who the bride would be. Griselda, a peasant girl, was surprised when the nobleman came to ask her father for her hand. The only requirement was that if Griselda agreed to the marriage, she would have to obey her husband in everything. When the guests question her willingness to agree to this condition, she replies, "I'd rather obey the Marquis than a boy from the village."

Griselda recounts the things to which she was asked to agree over the years: She had to give up her six-week-old daughter to what she believed was certain death; six years later, she gave up her two-year-old son; she returned to her father twelve years after the loss of her son so that her husband could marry a young girl; she helped her husband prepare for this new marriage because only she knew "how to arrange things the way he liked them." Her reward, the "fairy-tale" ending, was the restoration of her children (her daughter was the supposed new bride). Griselda forgave her husband and stayed with him because he had "suffered so much all those years."

Griselda's tale releases angry emotions in the other guests. Nijo tells the story of the concubines beating the emperor in retaliation for their own beatings at the hands of his attendants during a fertility ceremony. Joan recites a thematically important passage from Lucretius on how sweet it is to observe the struggles of others from a safe remove. At this point, Dull Gret, who says little, tells the story of her march with other peasant women through the mouth of hell, where most of them fought with the devils, although some were distracted by wealth. For Gret, it was going to the source of the evil that cost her two children. The party ends with Nijo crying, Joan vomiting, and Isabella finishing her tale of searching at the age of seventy for a "lasting chance of joy."

At the agency on Monday morning, Marlene interviews a young woman looking for a better job. She emphasizes the necessity for choosing—or appearing to choose—between career and family, as she herself did.

In Joyce's backyard in Suffolk on the previous Sunday afternoon, Kit and Angie's play focused on Angie's attempt to intimidate the younger child. Joyce forced Angie to clean her room; Angie returned in a dress too small for her, saying she put it on to kill her mother.

Back at the agency on Monday morning, Angie shows up, to Marlene's frustration. They are interrupted by Win, the wife of the man who expected to get Marlene's promotion, who now suggests that Marlene give up the new job. Several interviews conclude with Win talking to Angie, who has no skills. Showing no emotion, Marlene tells Win, "She's not going to make it."

In Joyce's kitchen one year earlier, Angie had called Marlene, who had not visited her family for six years, telling her that Joyce wanted to see her. When Marlene arrived, the sisters argued about Marlene abandoning her daughter, the rest of her family, and ultimately the working class from

which she came. Angie, who heard some of the discussion, came to Marlene, calling her "Mum." Marlene insisted, "It's Aunty Marlene." Angie responded, "Frightening."

Critical Evaluation:

Caryl Churchill, a prolific playwright, is considered a major contemporary writer. Although she came from a rather traditional middle-class British background, her social conscience was a significant factor in her development as a playwright. In *Top Girls*, as in many of Churchill's plays, feminism and socialism are necessary and inseparable.

The structure of the play is experimental. The first scene is a fantasy influenced by Bertolt Brecht's concept of the "alienation effect" that was designed to prevent the audience from getting emotionally involved with characters. (Brecht felt such emotion would prevent the audience's developing an active concern for the problems he presented.) Churchill employs effective distancing techniques, such as the overlapping dialogue and the tales of the women guests juxtaposed with Marlene ordering a dinner more typically associated with male preferences—steak, potatoes, and plenty of liquor.

The other scenes are realistic and depict the bleak and petty world of the employment agency and of Marlene's family in Suffolk, who are unable to compete in the capitalistic world of Margaret Thatcher's England. The realistic scenes in the play are also treated experimentally, for Churchill wrenches them out of their linear time sequence. The first scene, the fantasy dinner party, actually is chronologically in the middle of the various events. Chronologically, the first scene is Marlene's visit to Joyce's home, which occurs a year before the fantasy dinner, but the scene is placed at the end of the play. The effect of this is to give the revelation that Marlene abandoned her daughter, Angie, even greater force. The two Monday-morning scenes at the employment agency are interrupted by the Sunday scene in Suffolk, which ends with Angie dressed in the too-small dress Marlene gave her—as the audience will learn in the play's final scene—one year earlier.

Churchill stated that the impetus for writing *Top Girls* came during a 1979 trip to the United States, when American feminists told her that things were going well for women here because more top executives were women. This surprised Churchill, who was used to a different kind of feminism in England, one more closely allied with socialism. This led her to explore the idea that "achieving things isn't necessarily good, it matters *what* you achieve."

In *Top Girls*, Churchill analyzes the relationship between women and work and examines possibilities of the past and present. In the first scene, the women of history and legend start by boasting of accomplishments, then gradually become bitter as they realize what they have lost. The tenuous community shared by these women is based on negative aspects of experience—dead lovers, lost children, and anger at the power that others, usually male, exercised over them.

Churchill, in this play and others, explores the meaning of feminist empowerment. She examines the dichotomy between traditional women's work, which centers on concern for and nurturing of others, and traditional men's work, which is focused on power and competition. She shows that women have been able to compete but that without concern for the powerless, winning such competitions does not constitute a feminist victory.

Churchill does not advance an answer to this problem in *Top Girls*, but she firmly rejects the notion that there is progress by stressing the lack of women who are both successful and fulfilled. Clearly something is missing in the lives of the "top girls" as well as in the lives of those like Joyce and Angie who will not "make it."

Elsie Galbreath Haley

Further Reading

Aston, Elaine. *Caryl Churchill.* 2d ed. Plymouth, England: Northcote House/British Council, 2001. A cultural and feminist study of Churchill's theater, chronicling her development as a playwright, her socialist ideas, and her experimental style.

Cousin, Geraldine. *Churchill the Playwright.* London: Methuen Drama, 1989. Views Churchill's plays in the context of her experimentations with collaborative productions, in which the author, actors, and director research, write, and develop a play together through a prerehearsal workshop period. Cousin examines the way *Top Girls* manipulates traditional time schemes and questions notions of achievement, success, and what Churchill considers "joy."

Fitzsimmons, Linda. *File on Churchill.* London: Methuen Drama, 1989. A comprehensive listing of Churchill's plays, including unperformed ones, and selected reviews and comments from Churchill about her work. The general introduction and brief chronology are helpful. Includes a bibliography with selected play collections, essays, interviews, and secondary sources.

Kritzer, Amelia Howe. *The Plays of Caryl Churchill: Theatre of Empowerment.* New York: St. Martin's Press, 1991. Written from a feminist perspective, this book opens with an overview of theories of theater and drama and of feminist and socialist criticism in relation to Churchill's plays. The chapter "Labour and Capital" analyzes *Top Girls*, *Fen* (1983), and *Serious Money* (1987) as characteristic of Churchill's concern about the socioeconomic effects of Margaret Thatcher's government and its conservative policies.

Randall, Phyllis R., ed. *Caryl Churchill: A Casebook.* New York: Garland, 1988. A collection of essays, including one on *Top Girls* that comments on the challenge this play presents to feminists, asking them to realize that individual solutions are not successful and to confront the need to deal with the "larger contradictions created by a capitalistic patriarchy."

Reinelt, Janelle. "Caryl Churchill and the Politics of Style." In *The Cambridge Companion to Modern British Women Playwrights*, edited by Elaine Aston and Reinelt. New York: Cambridge University Press, 2000. In addition to this essay analyzing Churchill's work, the book contains numerous references to Churchill and *Top Girls* that are listed in the index.

Thomas, Jane. "The Plays of Caryl Churchill: Essays in Refusal." In *The Death of the Playwright?*, edited by Adrian Page. New York: St. Martin's Press, 1992. This essay analyzes *Top Girls* and *Cloud Nine* (1979) in the light of Churchill's acknowledged reading of Michel Foucault's *Surveiller et punir: Naissance de la prison* (1975; *Discipline and Punish: The Birth of the Prison*, 1977).

Tycer, Alicia. *Caryl Churchill's "Top Girls."* London: Continuum, 2008. A student guide to the play, discussing its background, context, and production history and analyzing its structure, style, and characters. Includes annotated guide to further reading.

Topdog/Underdog

Author: Suzan-Lori Parks (1963-   )
First produced: 2001; first published, 2001
Type of work: Drama
Type of plot: Psychological realism
Time of plot: Now
Locale: Here

Principal characters:
LINCOLN (LINK), the topdog
BOOTH (3 CARD), the underdog, his brother

The Story:

Booth, an African American man in his early thirties, sits in a small, ill-conceived boarding-house room, playing three-card monte, a game of hustling and chance. His gaming table is composed of a plank across two mismatched milk crates. His manipulation of the cards is awkward, indicating a lack of skill and experience. Booth is startled by the entrance of his older brother, Lincoln, and he pulls a gun. Lincoln is dressed like his namesake, he wears a fake beard, and his face is whitened by stage makeup.

Link, as he is called by his brother, is employed as an Abraham Lincoln impersonator: He is assassinated in play by persons desiring to reenact history by pulling the trigger. Booth, on the other hand, is unemployed and deeply infatuated with Grace, the woman of his dreams. Because of his strong desire to succeed as a hustler, Booth decides to change his name to "3 Card." Lincoln, prior to his new career as a presidential impersonator, had been a successful three-card monte player; he gave up the game after a close associate, Lonnie, was shot and killed by an irate customer. However, he is nervous about the security of his job reenacting history: It seems that he is about to be replaced by a dummy as a cost-saving move. He practices dying as Abraham Lincoln in an effort to defer his being let go.

The following evening, Booth enters dressed in an oversized coat, from which he extracts the booty he has lifted from various shops. In his cache are such disparate items as two new suits, girlie magazines, and a bottle of whiskey with two glasses. Though not skillful at three-card monte, he seems adept at shoplifting. Lincoln wants to practice dying, but Booth has a rendezvous with his girlfriend, a woman "so sweet she makes my teeth hurt." Upon his brother's departure for his date, Lincoln is left with the whiskey and begins to drink.

Upon his return from a successful date with Grace, Booth finds a drunk Lincoln. Because of his need to win Grace, Booth insists that Lincoln teach him to be a successful three-card monte hustler. In return, Lincoln cajoles his brother into helping him practice dying as the assassinated president.

When Lincoln thinks his brother is asleep, he begins to test himself to see if he still has the chops for three-card monte. According to the stage directions, "He studies [the cards] like an alcoholic would study a drink." Without his knowledge, he is watched intently by Booth.

Some time later, Booth is setting up for a romantic dinner with Grace. It is past two in the morning, and Lincoln comes in from work. Given the extremely late hour, Grace is obviously not coming as Booth had expected, but he refuses to accept this fact. Lincoln reveals that he has lost his job: he has been replaced by a wax dummy. Booth, who has "boosted" all the finery used to set the table, is pleased with the news; his brother is now free to return to the streets as the hustler supreme. It is revealed that the two were deserted when they were teenagers, first by one of their parents and then by the other. Lincoln muses, "Maybe they got 2 new kids. 2 boys. Different than us, though. Better."

With nothing to lose, Lincoln begins to teach Booth three-card monte in earnest. Lincoln allows Booth to win each throw of the cards; after all, they are playing in jest, with no stakes on the table. With his success against his brother, Booth leaves to find his missing date. Lincoln continues to work the cards, faster and faster, as the scene ends.

The next night, Thursday, Lincoln enters with a wad of money he has made on the street by hustling cards. Booth is already in the room; his mood is heavy. Lincoln announces the success he has had; Booth boasts of his success as well, that Grace actually asked him to marry her and she wants to move into the room with him, meaning that Lincoln will need to leave right away. Lincoln reveals he has a new job as a security guard.

The truth slowly begins to be revealed. Booth has not been romantically successful, and he needs success of some sort. He convinces Lincoln to play three-card monte with him for real stakes, his inheritance from his mother, five hundred dollars. The game begins, in earnest this time. Booth announces that he is not getting married after all, that he has actually shot and killed Grace. He loses his inheritance to Lincoln's hustle. Booth stands behind Lincoln, the same way they had practiced before, only this time he has his gun in his hand, pressed against his brother's neck. He pulls the trigger. Lincoln is assassinated one final time. The play ends with Booth, sobbing, hugging his dead brother's body.

Critical Evaluation:

In 2001, Suzan-Lori Parks was recognized by the MacArthur Foundation as a recipient of the prestigious MacArthur Fellowship (the so-called genius award). *Topdog/ Underdog* was awarded the 2002 Pulitzer Prize in drama, making Parks the first African American woman to be so honored. Her work continues to place her at the forefront of the American theater, as she continues to develop haunting plays for the stage.

Parks in *Topdog/Underdog* tells her most linear story in a traditional way. In her earlier work—including *Imperceptible Mutabilities in the Third Kingdom* (pr. 1989, pb. 1995) and *The Death of the Last Black Man in the Whole Entire World* (pr., pb. 1990)—she explodes dramatic traditions. The tradition of providing a play with a beginning, middle, and end makes its way into her later works, such as *In the Blood* (pr. 1999, pb. 2000) and *Fucking A* (pr. 2000, pb. 2001), and is firmly realized in *Topdog/Underdog*. In her essay "Elements of Style" (1995), Parks writes

> I don't explode the form because I find traditional plays "boring"—I don't really. It's just that those structures never could accommodate the figures which take up residence inside me.

Even though Lincoln, the older brother and so-called topdog, bears a connection to The Founding Father in *The America Play* (pr. 1993, pb. 1995), in that both are presidential impersonators at a side show, the resemblance goes no further than the choice of career. Lincoln is a fully realized human being, not a vestige or emblem. By the same token, Booth bears some resemblance to Monster, Hester's illegitimate son in *Fucking A*, but Parks's "underdog" perpetrates evil actions because he is far too human, rather than a monster who defies all humanity. It is logical, then, for *Topdog/ Underdog* to take a more traditional form than Parks's earlier works.

Thus, Parks in this play moved away from her earlier experiments to explore the possibilities of traditional drama. However, in an interview included in the hour-long documentary *The Topdog Diaries* (2002), Parks states that the idea of her play being traditional is an illusion, that in fact the structure of the drama is similar to the card game, three-card

monte: It is never really what it appears to be. In this sense, the hustling that Parks includes inside the drama continues into the audience and beyond: The audience and its reaction are part of the con game that the playwright employs as a dramatic technique.

As in her earlier works, Parks continues in *Topdog/ Underdog* to use preexistent motifs as the root of her storytelling. In *In the Blood* and *Fucking A*, she turns to Nathaniel Hawthorne's classic American novel, *The Scarlet Letter* (1850), using the original as an impulse to explore contemporary matters such as welfare, evangelical religion, and abortion. In *Topdog/Underdog*, she turns to the Bible and the ageless myth of Cain and Abel. She also echoes one of the themes found in Sam Shepard's dramas, such as *True West* (pr. 1980, pb. 1981) and *The Late Henry Moss* (pr. 2000, pb. 2002): two brothers warring over the past, through the present, and into the future.

In each case, Parks makes the subject uniquely her own. Just as Hester Prynne from Hawthorne's nineteenth century American masterpiece is echoed in the aforementioned plays, Cain and Abel and their mythic relationship are mere echoes in *Topdog/Underdog*. More relevant to an analysis of the play are the direct and unrelenting historical references to the assassination of Abraham Lincoln. The irony of having an African American, the progeny of slavery, putting on white-face make-up and reenacting the death of the American president who abolished slavery nearly a hundred and fifty years earlier is not lost on the audiences who witness the play. That Lincoln is unable to escape his fate (Booth must pull the trigger) is reflective of the statement by the topdog in the play that no one can win at three-card monte, the other over-arching metaphor that defines Parks's drama.

A few of the "contemporary matters" that Parks addresses in the play are the inevitability of violence, the destructive impact of unrelenting poverty, the futility such poverty perpetrates, the barrenness of failure, and the fact that history will repeat itself in spite of all efforts to prevent it from doing so. These matters not only define the work but also provide audiences with opportunities for significant personal thought following the final curtain. *Topdog/Underdog*, like Parks's other plays, is not an easy work to experience. It forces audiences to enter a world that most would prefer to avoid and perhaps deny.

Parks does not allow her audiences to take a relaxing journey; instead, she prods them with a mixture of humor and horror. The relationship between the two brothers is such that viewers of the play are provoked to laughter even as they prepare themselves for the disasters that are promised to come. The issues that propel *Topdog/Underdog* forward are found in most if not all of Parks's works for the stage, and, as a consequence, she has created for herself a position in contemporary theatrical studies that carries with it an expectation for moving, thought-provoking experiences.

Kenneth Robbins

Further Reading

Anderson, Lisa M. *Black Feminism in Contemporary Drama.* Urbana: University of Illinois Press, 2008. In her chapter "Battling Images: Suzan-Lori Parks and Black Iconicity," Anderson brings clarity and understanding to the developing art of the playwright.

Green, Amy S. "Whose Voices Are These? The Arts of Language in the Plays of Suzan-Lori Parks, Paula Vogel, and Diana Son." In *Women Writing Plays: Three Decades of the Susan Smith Blackburn Prize.* Austin: University of Texas Press, 2006. Focuses on the works of Parks alongside two other American female playwrights.

Parks, Suzan-Lori. *The America Play, and Other Works.* New York: Theatre Communications Group, 1995. The character of a Lincoln-esque figure at a penny-arcade was introduced by Parks in *The America Play* as The Founding Father. Among her other works collected in this volume are three essays written in 1994 that provide insights into the playwright's methods.

_____. "Tradition and the Individual Talent." In *Stages of Drama: Classical to Contemporary Theater*, edited by Carl H. Klaus, Miriam Gilbert, and Bradford S. Field, Jr. 5th ed. New York: Bedford/St. Martin's Press, 2003. Parks's commentary on the relationship between artistic tradition and artistic creativity responds to the essay of the same name by T. S. Eliot.

Torch Song Trilogy

Author: Harvey Fierstein (1954-   )
First produced: 1978-1979; first published, 1979
Type of work: Drama
Type of plot: Psychological realism
Time of plot: Mid-1970's
Locale: New York City and upstate New York

Principal characters:
ARNOLD BECKOFF, a young gay man
ED REISS, Arnold's lover
LAUREL, Ed's lover
ALAN, Arnold's lover
DAVID, Arnold's foster son
MRS. BECKOFF, Arnold's mother

The Story:

The International Stud. In the first of the play's three one-act segments, Arnold Beckoff, twenty-four years old, prepares for his performance as torch singer Virginia Hamm in a New York City nightclub. As he applies false eyelashes in his dressing room, Arnold complains about the difficulty of establishing successful romantic relationships. Disappointed with the casual nature of many gay encounters, Arnold longs for a committed, domestic relationship. Arnold meets Ed Reiss, a thirty-four-year-old teacher, in the International Stud bar. Arnold makes clear that he is not interested in a backroom sexual encounter, and Ed reveals that he also dates women. The men leave for Arnold's apartment.

Four months later, Arnold waits for Ed to call. Arnold finally phones Ed, who is expecting a new friend—a woman named Laurel. Arnold declares his love for Ed and accuses him of preferring the woman because she will seem more acceptable to Ed's parents. Ed insists that he loves Arnold but wants more than their relationship. Three months after his break-up with Ed, Arnold accompanies his friend, Murray, to the International Stud. Although he protests the impersonal backroom encounters, he finally allows Murray to talk him into venturing there, and another man has sex with him in the dark. Still not jaded, Arnold halfway expects the man to meet him outside the bar. Two months later, Ed comes to Arnold's dressing room after a show. Still feeling rejected, Arnold asks Ed to leave, but Ed pleads for Arnold's friendship. He tells of a good summer with Laurel and his parents at his farm in upstate New York. Despite the fact that he and Laurel are considering commitment, Ed declares that he still loves Arnold and confesses that he sometimes thinks about him during sex. Arnold decides that he loves Ed "enough" to endure the frustrations of their relationship, and the men leave together.

Fugue in a Nursery. One year later, Arnold and his new lover Alan, a handsome eighteen-year-old model and former hustler, spend a few days at the farm with Ed and Laurel. Laurel is excited about the visit, but Ed is jealous of Arnold's solicitousness toward Alan. When Ed and Arnold disappear to review their relationship, Laurel makes a pass at Alan. Pressed by Ed to clarify his relationship with Alan, Arnold admits that he still spends two or three evenings a week in the International Stud's back room. He explains that he stays with Alan because he feels somewhat maternal toward him. Ed recalls that he had once wanted a son. The next day, while Arnold helps Laurel with the dishes, Ed seduces Alan in the barn. Arnold learns that Ed has lied to Laurel about receiving phone calls from him. He and Alan leave a day early.

Ed soon telephones to say he and Laurel are having problems and that Arnold should not cross him off his list. Visiting the city, Laurel talks with Arnold about whether she will leave Ed, and Arnold learns that Alan had sex with Ed but not with Laurel. Despite Arnold's pessimism, Laurel and Ed become engaged, and Arnold and Alan decide to make a commitment—to raising a puppy.

Widows and Children First! Five years pass: Arnold and Alan stay together. Alan is beaten to death by gay bashers. Arnold, partly to assuage his grief, takes in a foster son, David, a fifteen-year-old gay boy, and promptly becomes his overbearing Jewish "mother." Four days later, Ed, who is now separated from Laurel, moves in with Arnold and David. Arnold's mother herself comes for a visit. Although she knew of Arnold's sexual orientation even before he had told her when he was thirteen years old, his mother clings to the hope that he will marry a woman and have children. Arnold's mother arrives confused about his relationships with Ed and David, who she thinks is his "friend," her euphemism for lover.

David, skipping school, arrives when Arnold is in the shower and breaks the news to his foster grandmother about his status in the household. After the initial shock, Mrs. Beckoff returns David to school and spends the rest of the afternoon with him.

Despite her affection for him, she disapproves of Arnold's plans to adopt David because she fears that Arnold will develop a sexual interest in the boy. During the ensuing argument, when Arnold compares his loss of Alan to his mother's widowhood, Mrs. Beckoff becomes outraged. She complains that she is tired of hearing about his sexuality, and she attributes her husband's decline, in part, to the

strain of it. Arnold asks how she would feel if the world were predominately homosexual and she were in the minority as a heterosexual. Confronted by Arnold's insistence that she accept his honesty or leave, Mrs. Beckoff escapes to her room.

Meanwhile, near the place where Alan had been killed, David and Ed discuss Ed's future. David, noting that Arnold lives "like an old Italian widow," encourages Ed to resurrect the relationship. When Arnold shows up and Ed departs, David remarks to Arnold that Arnold is just like Mrs. Beckoff—no more understanding about Ed's bisexuality than she is about Arnold's homosexuality.

The next morning, when Ed asks a very drunk Arnold for another chance, Arnold's bitterness about Ed's bisexuality becomes apparent: Ed can stay with Laurel and have a traditional family, children included. Arnold notes that, ironically, he wants almost exactly the kind of life his mother had had. Ed says that he loves Arnold and thinks that he can find the family he wants with Arnold and David. Mrs. Beckoff, departing for the airport, interrupts, and finally notices the black eye David got in a school fight. Softened, she asks Arnold if he loves Ed, and he says yes, but not like he loves Alan. She cautions him that, although his mourning will get easier, he will never stop missing Alan. Distracted by a song dedication David had phoned in to a radio station to remind Arnold of Alan, Arnold does not notice when his mother slips quietly out the door.

Critical Evaluation:

Harvey Fierstein's *Torch Song Trilogy*, which won the 1983 Tony Award for best play and earned its author a Tony for best actor in his role as Arnold Beckoff, is often cited as the first play with a clear gay theme to be popular with mainstream theater audiences. Although one of its themes is the difficulty of being gay in a heterosexual society, it is not essentially a problem play. The play insists that Arnold's problems are common to all relationships. Fierstein drives home the vulnerability of gay men through Alan's murder and David's fight, but his real interest is in the similarities—not the differences—among gays, heterosexuals, and bisexuals. David says that a person's relationship with his or her mother involves the same difficulties whether that mother is Mrs. Beckoff or Arnold. Although Arnold's mother is initially offended when he compares his mourning to hers, her advice about coping with grief and loneliness establishes her awareness of the similarity between the relationships.

Another central theme of the play is honesty. "Honest" is the first adjective Fierstein uses to describe the characters of *The International Stud.* He wants *Widows and Children*

First! to be performed with "pace" and "honesty." Arnold is troubled that Ed will not acknowledge him to his parents or Laurel. As he asks himself whether he really cares if those who say, "I love you" are truthful, he concludes that his honest answer is yes. In *Widows and Children First!* Arnold's mother protests that she is tired of hearing about his homosexuality. Arnold responds that he is not "flaunting" his sexual orientation but is just being himself. David is the play's best testament to the importance of allowing people to be themselves, having been subjected to therapists who tried to make him heterosexual.

The play advocates a traditional family atmosphere. The set for *Widows and Children First!*, the most domestic of the three segments, is described by Fierstein as "the set of a conventional sit-com," and Arnold's interaction with David, from his reviewing the young man's report card to encouraging him to carry a handkerchief, is vintage television mom. The questions about relationships between lovers that *Torch Song Trilogy* examines are also quite common: What happens when one partner is much more attractive than the other? How are parents to be introduced to the lover? What happens when new lovers meet old ones? How does it feel when the lover says he will call but does not? Does the couple want to raise children? What happens if the lover dies?

Fierstein also has a knack for provoking the new perspective. When his mother complains about how often she hears about homosexuality, Arnold asks her to imagine herself, as a heterosexual, living in a world saturated with images of and norms based on homosexuality. A few pages later, David plays the same card on Arnold, attempting to show him how parents feel when their offspring violate their expectations. David asks, "What would you do if I met a girl, came home and told you I was straight?" Arnold's responses are as pat as his mother's: "If you were happy, I'd be happy." At the end of the scene, Arnold asks David to reassure him that he is not, in fact, heterosexual.

Although Fierstein's themes are ultimately conventional, his staging is often heavily stylized. This is particularly true in *Fugue in a Nursery*, the majority of which is acted by the four principals—Arnold, Alan, Ed, and Laurel—in a huge bed. As lighting focuses on one pair and then the other, Fierstein constructs a polyphony of voices all talking about the same themes. The similarities between the homosexual and heterosexual relationships are underscored by the occasional overlapping of conversations, with a person in one relationship answering a question asked by a person in the other. The trilogy's handling of impersonal sexual encounters between gay men, such as those experienced by Arnold in the back room of the bar, is reminiscent of a time before

HIV and AIDS. *The International Stud*, for example, was first performed in 1978, about five years before HIV and AIDS became household words. Fierstein sees such anonymous sexual encounters as desperate acts; he told *Newsweek*'s Jack Kroll, "Gay liberation should not be a license to be a perpetual adolescent. If you deny yourself commitment then what can you do with your life?"

Perhaps Fierstein's greatest achievement is the character of Arnold, a slightly overweight drag queen, or crossdresser, who is simultaneously drawn to and frightened by romance. "Beckoff," Fierstein has said, is a combination of the words "beckon" and "back off." Arnold is, in many ways, a conventional romantic heroine who, no matter how many Mr. Wrongs he finds, continues to search for Mr. Right. Described by his creator as "a kvetch of great wit and want," Arnold practices quick, sometimes biting, humor. "What's the matter?" he asks Ed, "catch your tongue in the closet door?" Playwright Marsha Norman has said that a playwright nominates characters for preservation in the public mind and then lets audiences do the voting. It seems likely that Fierstein's Arnold Beckoff will be among the elected.

Lana A. Whited

Further Reading

Clarke, Gerald. "No One Opened Doors for Me." *Time*, February 22, 1982. This brief news-magazine article discusses Fierstein's process in getting the play produced and the effect of the work's success on his career.

Dace, Tish. "Fierstein, Harvey (Forbes)." *Contemporary Dramatists*. 6th ed. Edited by K. A. Berney. Detroit, Mich.: St. James Press, 1998. An overview of Fierstein's career, with emphasis on *Torch Song Trilogy*. Discusses the play's themes and Fierstein's styles of presentation, particularly the use of fugue.

DiGaetani, John Louis. "David Mamet and Harvey Fierstein: Gender Roles and Role Playing." In *Stages of Struggle: Modern Playwrights and Their Psychological Inspirations*. Jefferson, N.C.: McFarland, 2008. Examines works by Fierstein that explore his mental struggles and the struggles of the people he loves, and looks at the playwright's elaboration of gender roles through gender "play."

Fierstein, Harvey. "His Heart Is Young and Gay." Interview by Jack Kroll. *Newsweek*, June 20, 1983. Fierstein explains why *Torch Song Trilogy* is not gay propaganda, as some critics argue. Explores the autobiographical nature of the play and the reactions of gays and lesbians against the work.

Furnish, Ben. "From Sholem Aleichem to Harvey Fierstein and Wendy Wasserstein: Love Makes a Family and History in Jewish-American Performance." In *American Judaism in Popular Culture*, edited by Leonard J. Greenspoon and Ronald A. Simkins. Omaha, Nebr.: Creighton University Press, 2006. Compares the themes of love and family in the works of Fierstein, Sholem Aleichem, and Wendy Wasserstein, three Jewish American playwrights.

_____. "Harvey Fierstein." In *Contemporary Jewish-American Dramatists and Poets: A Bio-Critical Sourcebook*, edited by Joel Shatzky and Michael Taub. Westport, Conn.: Greenwood Press, 1999. The entry on Fierstein features a brief biography and a discussion of his plays, their themes, and their critical reception. Also includes bibliographies of Fierstein's works and of secondary sources about him.

Oliver, Edith. "Tripleheader." *The New Yorker*, February 1, 1982. A theater critic explains why *Torch Song Trilogy* deserves the high praise it has received. Excellent analysis of the characters.

Tortilla Flat

Author: John Steinbeck (1902-1968)
First published: 1935
Type of work: Novel
Type of plot: Naturalism
Time of plot: Early 1920's
Locale: Monterey, California

Principal characters:
DANNY, the hero, a free spirit fettered by the inheritance of two houses
PILON,
PABLO,
JESUS MARIA CORCORAN,
THE PIRATE, and
BIG JOE PORTAGEE, his friends and tenants
MRS. MORALES,
SWEETS RAMIREZ, and
SEÑORA TERESINA CORTEZ, three of Danny's short-term loves

The Story:

Danny returns home from serving in World War I to find that his grandfather has bequeathed him two houses on Tortilla Flat. The responsibility of ownership depresses Danny, and a drunken spree of window breaking and the jail sentence it earns him do little to relieve his malaise. Then he runs into his friend Pilon, who moves into the larger of the two houses with him, agreeing to pay fifteen dollars a month in rent. After an argument, Pilon moves into Danny's smaller house. The pair share wine, women, and worry. Ownership plagues Danny.

The rent Pilon that never intended to pay bothers him, but his troubles seem to be over when he strikes a deal with Pablo. Pablo agrees to move in with Pilon for fifteen dollars a month rent—money he never can or will pay.

Danny enjoys a brief affair with his neighbor, Mrs. Morales, who owns her own house and has two hundred dollars in the bank. He wants to give her a present but has no money. The suggestion that he cut squids for a day laborer's wages

incenses him, and he demands rent from Pilon and Pablo, who stalk away in anger. They find Jesus Maria Corcoran lying under a bush with a bottle of wine and learn that he has recently acquired a fortune of seven dollars. Pilon and Pablo agree to rent him space in their house for fifteen dollars a month. Masters at rationalizing self-interest into altruism, they talk Jesus Maria out of his money and buy Mrs. Morales a bottle of wine, which they then drink themselves.

Pilon, Pablo, and Jesus Maria fall into a drunken sleep in Danny's second house, leaving a candle lit. The candle flame ignites a wall calendar, the fire spreads, and the house burns to the ground. The friends escape, dismayed that they have left a bottle of wine inside. Danny is relieved to be free of the property, and his three friends move into the big house with him.

The Pirate, along with his five dogs, lives in what had been a chicken coop. Each day he collects wood from the forest and sells it. He never spends any money, so everyone wonders where he hides his savings. In one of his finest feats of logic, Pilon convinces his friends that finding and spending the Pirate's money for him would serve the man's best interests, but try as they might, they cannot discover his hiding place.

The Pirate moves into Danny's house and comes to trust his new friends so much that he hands his money over to Danny for safekeeping. He explains that he is saving to buy a gold candlestick for the church in honor of Saint Francis of Assisi. He believes a prayer to the saint saved one of his dogs from death. That story ends all the hopes Danny and his friends had for diverting the money to their own uses, but the Pirate and his dogs are good to keep around. They beg food from the restaurants along the waterfront every day and bring it home for all to share.

Big Joe Portagee gets out of jail and, learning that Danny owns a house, sets off to find his friends. He joins Pilon for the traditional Saint Andrew's Eve hunt in the forest, when, legend promises, buried treasure emits a faint phosphorescent glow through the ground. Big Joe moves in with the others, steals Danny's blanket, and trades it for wine in anticipation of the fortune he expects to unearth. That night, he and Pilon dig up a survey marker. They drink wine and sleep on the beach. Pilon awakes first, steals Big Joe's pants as the Portagee is sleeping, and trades the pants for wine in retaliation for Joe's theft of the blanket. Later, they steal back both the pants and the blanket.

Danny succumbs to an infatuation with Sweets Ramirez and buys her a vacuum cleaner, although Tortilla Flat is not wired for electricity. Sweets revels in the elevated social standing the gift brings her. Danny grows listless and pale, perhaps tiring of Sweets's affections. The group of friends resolves to free him. They steal the vacuum cleaner and trade it for wine—probably more than a fair trade since the machine has no motor.

Jesus Maria rescues a Mexican corporal and his baby from the police and brings them home to Tortilla Flat. The corporal wants his baby son to be a general someday, so he can have a better life than his father's. The baby dies, and the corporal returns to Mexico.

Big Joe Portagee seeks shelter from the rain in the house of a woman called Tia Ignacia. Ignoring her charms, he drinks her wine and falls asleep. She hits him and chases him outside, but he embraces her, and the physical closeness arouses passion. A police officer orders the pair out of the street for fear they might get run over. Big Joe steals the Pirate's money from beneath Danny's pillow and buries it by the front gate. The friends beat him, cut him, and rub salt in his wounds. Then they discover that the Pirate has saved enough to buy the golden candlestick. The Pirate goes to church dressed in his friends' clothes to hear the priest's thanks for his gift. Reluctantly, he leaves his dogs at home, but they burst through the church doors to join their master. Later, the Pirate feels sure that the dogs actually saw a vision of Saint Francis. The friends forgive Big Joe and nurse him back to health.

Señora Teresina Cortez feeds eight children on the beans she culls from the chaff after the threshers have cleared the fields. When the bean crop fails, Danny and his friends steal a variety of foods for her family, but the change in diet makes the children sick. All ends well when the friends deliver four hundred pounds of beans to Teresina's home. Teresina, pregnant again, wonders which of Danny's friends is responsible for the gift.

As Danny steps over his sleeping tenants each night, he yearns to return to the days of his freedom, when he slept outdoors and the weight of property was not upon him. He runs away and sets about a binge of drinking, vandalism, and theft. He sells the house for twenty-five dollars, but his friends burn the transfer of ownership.

After a term in jail, Danny returns home a broken man. His friends, determined to dispel his lethargy, throw a party never equaled in Tortilla Flat, so generous is the exchange of food, wine, and love. When Danny, suffused with alcohol and valor, charges out to fight some unnamed enemy, he falls to the bottom of a forty-foot gulch and dies. His friends cannot attend his funeral, for they have no suitable clothes. They lie in the grass to watch his burial. Later, when his house catches fire, they make no attempt to stop the blaze (although they have learned, from the previous fire, to save the wine). Turning away from the smoldering ruins, they go their separate ways.

Critical Evaluation:

Turned down by nine publishers before it was accepted, *Tortilla Flat* earned the California Literature Gold Medal in 1936 and became one of John Steinbeck's most popular and highly acclaimed works, despite the fact that it was denounced by the Monterey Chamber of Commerce. It was the first of Steinbeck's novels to look at life through the eyes of those without homes, possessions, or security, and Danny and his friends foreshadow others of their kind who appear powerfully and poignantly in such distinguished later works as *In Dubious Battle* (1936), *Of Mice and Men* (1937), and *The Grapes of Wrath* (1939).

Steinbeck wrote *Tortilla Flat* as a series of episodes with long subtitles in the style of Sir Thomas Malory's *Le Morte d'Arthur* (1485). In his preface, the author compares the escapades of Danny and his friends with the events of King Arthur's Round Table: the formation of the association, the heroic deeds of its members, the passing of the almost deified king, and the subsequent dissolution of the brotherhood. The imitation is further enhanced by the use of "thee" and "thy" in the speech of the friends. Steinbeck was never a regional writer, but he was a writer of his locale, his inspiration a unique product of California, especially during the years of the Great Depression. As he was a man of place, so too are his characters. Danny and his friends exist in a deep and fundamental relationship with Tortilla Flat. It is so saturated with their spirit and melded with their consciousness that the men and their environment are as one.

Steinbeck won the Nobel Prize in Literature in 1962. Accepting the award, he said that the "writer is delegated to declare and to celebrate man's proven capacity for greatness of heart and spirit—for gallantry in defeat, for courage, compassion and love. In the endless war against weakness and despair, these are the bright rally flags of hope and of emulation." In *Tortilla Flat*, as in many other novels and stories, Steinbeck exalts the natural man, untainted by civilization, unspoiled by either conventional wisdom or conventional morality. Danny, who earns a near-god status on Tortilla Flat, is flawed not by his innate nature but by the greed, conflict, and loneliness property ownership forces upon him. He and his friends are the kinds of characters Steinbeck loves most and paints most vividly. They are human, fallible, earthy, uninhibited, irresponsible, and unspoiled.

For all its irreverence, *Tortilla Flat* is a deeply religious book. Through his characters, Steinbeck develops a naturalistic theology; Danny and his friends are right and good because they are as they are, without artifice and without redemption. When Steinbeck characterizes Danny as "clean of commercialism," he implies a spiritual purity akin to being washed of sin. Still, his moralizing is constrained by a gentle humor, as, for example, when he adds to the observation "the soul capable of the greatest good is also capable of the greatest evil" the offhand qualifier "this, however, may be a matter of appearances." Ever cynical of religious conventions, he observes, "Ah, the prayers of the millions, how they must fight and destroy each other on their way to the throne of God."

Steinbeck lets his characters comment on the search for meaning in stories, perhaps reflecting his intent in relating tales from Tortilla Flat. After Pablo tells of the old man who tried to fake a suicide to win a young girl's love, only to fail

and die, Pilon complains, "It is not a good story. There are too many meanings and too many lessons in it. Some of those lessons are opposite. There is no story to take into your head. It proves nothing." Pablo responds, "I like it because it hasn't any meaning you can see, and still it does seem to mean something, I can't tell what."

Faith Hickman Brynie

Further Reading

Benson, Jackson J., ed. *The Short Novels of John Steinbeck: Critical Essays with a Checklist to Steinbeck Criticism.* Durham, N.C.: Duke University Press, 1990. Comprehensive collection of essays presents investigations into Steinbeck's characters, technique, and motivation in *Tortilla Flat* and his other short novels.

George, Stephen K., and Barbara A. Heavilin, eds. *John Steinbeck and His Contemporaries.* Lanham, Md.: Scarecrow Press, 2007. Collection of essays comes from a 2006 conference about Steinbeck and the writers who influenced or informed his work. Some of the essays discuss Steinbeck's European forebears, particularly Henry Fielding and Sir Thomas Malory, and his American forebears, such as Walt Whitman and Sarah Orne Jewett, while other essays compare his work to that of Ernest Hemingway, William Faulkner, and other twentieth century American writers.

Hughes, R. S. *John Steinbeck: A Study of the Short Fiction.* New York: Macmillan, 1988. Focuses on providing a behind-the-scenes look at the creation of Steinbeck's short fiction. Includes summaries of published literary criticism on the works.

Shillinglaw, Susan, and Kevin Hearle, eds. *Beyond Boundaries: Rereading John Steinbeck.* Tuscaloosa: University of Alabama Press, 2002. Collection features essays by writers from the United States, Japan, France, England, Thailand, and India that examine Steinbeck's work and worldwide cultural influence. One of the essays describes a Thai musical adaptation of *Tortilla Flat*.

Simmonds, Roy S. *A Biographical and Critical Introduction of John Steinbeck.* Lewiston, N.Y.: Edwin Mellen Press, 2000. Charts Steinbeck's evolution as a writer from 1929 through 1968, discussing the themes of his works and the concepts and philosophies that influenced his depictions of human nature and the psyche. Interweaves details about his writings with accounts of his personal life.

The Tower

Author: William Butler Yeats (1865-1939)
First published: 1927
Type of work: Poetry

The 1920's were years of professional and personal achievement for William Butler Yeats. His son, Michael, was born in 1921. He was awarded the Nobel Prize in Literature in 1923, enjoying the worldwide recognition of not only his own work but also the Irish Literary Revival. In 1922, he was appointed to the first senate in the Irish Free State and received an honorary doctorate from Trinity College. Yeats was approaching his sixties and beginning to wonder what would be the impetus for his poetry in old age since so much of it had always been love poetry. As the decade progressed, his health was failing, and he was convinced that his generation was no longer the moving force in Ireland.

The Tower reflects these conflicting forces in Yeats's life. His poetic voice and technique were at the height of their mature intensity and power, and he was excited by his developing philosophical system, yet the content and tone of many of the poems suggest that Yeats was obsessed with his own aging, angry at the violence in Ireland, and desirous of a world more conducive to art. After rereading *The Tower* shortly after its publication, he wrote to Olivia Shakspear that he "was astonished at its bitterness," yet he also recognized that "its bitterness gave the book its power."

The original edition, with a beautiful cover design by T. Sturge Moore depicting Yeats's Norman tower at Thoor Ballylee, contained twenty-one poems, including two sequences ("Meditations in Time of Civil War" and "A Man Young and Old") with their separately numbered and titled shorter poems. "The Gift of Harun Al-Rahsid" was later removed, whereas "Fragments" was added in 1933 and "The Hero, the Girl and the Fool" was cut down to "The Fool by the Roadside." Currently, *The Tower* comprises thirty-six poems in volume 1 of *The Poems* in *The Collected Works of W. B. Yeats* (1989), edited by Richard Finneran. The separately numbered and titled parts of the two sequences are listed as individual poems. Yeats added notes to six of the poems in the original edition (which are reproduced in an appendix to Finneran's edition along with many explanatory notes provided by the editor).

In his *Autobiography* (1916), Yeats expressed hope that a nation could be unified by "a bundle of related images." His own bundle of images was well established, and they appear here repeatedly in images of trees, birds (especially swans),

the sun, the moon, fish, and a dancer. As usual, Maude Gonne MacBride, the woman who was his most consistent symbol of beauty and unrequited love, is alluded to often. Moreover, his obsession with his philosophical system, expressed in *A Vision*, published in its first version in 1925, informs these poems, as it had started to do in his previous volume, *Michael Robartes and the Dancer* (1920).

Yeats's poetic prowess is evident in the range of style and poetic form in this collection. The poems range from very short epigrams to some of Yeats's longest, most obscure modernist lyrics. Concentrated, allusive, imagistically intense poems, such as "Leda and the Swan," alternate with the more discursive and conversational mood of poems such as "All Soul's Night." Like most of Yeats's poetry, the poems in this volume are written in traditional rhymed forms, ranging from many poems with six-line rhymed stanzas, to the eight-line ottava rima stanzas of "Sailing to Byzantium" and "Among School Children," to one of his rare uses of the sonnet form in "Leda and the Swan," to longer poems, such as "The Tower," with different forms juxtaposed to each other in separate sections.

The first poem, "Sailing to Byzantium," suggests that the aging poet, no longer comfortable among the fertile young in Ireland, travels to Byzantium—Yeats's symbol of the integration of aesthetic and practical life—to find "the singing masters of [his] soul" who will teach him to create "the artifice of eternity" in this less transient spiritual context. The volume reads as if Yeats is repeatedly retracing the steps that led him to leave for Byzantium. Three long poems follow in which Yeats continues to explore his fear of loss of creativity as well as his anger at the state of Ireland and the world. He explains some of the historical and poetic allusions in these obscure poems in his notes. After contrasting his aged body and excited imagination in section 1 of the title poem, "The Tower," and then retracing the historical and imaginative ancestry of his home in Thoor Ballylee in section 2, Yeats prepares his will in section 3, invoking images such as his fisherman and swan as well as "memories of love." Leaving all to "upstanding men" who climb the mountain in the dawn, he will make his soul as he waits for death in peaceful indifference. The six poems that make up "Meditations in Time of Civil War" enact a contrast between the classical stasis of art and the volatile brutality of the Irish Civil War in the early 1920's. In the last poem in this sequence as well as in "Nineteen Hundred and Nineteen," he laments his growing difficulty in creating lasting art amid the violent, nightmarish, dismembering images present now as in all eras since classical Greece.

In most of the eight short poems between "Nineteen Hundred and Nineteen" and "Among School Children," Yeats creates a series of contrasts, all of which pit the old against the new: winter and spring, age and youth, old and new faces, Dionysus and Christ, Eden and Lockean science. Yeats interjects "A Prayer for My Son," very different in tone and content from most of the more philosophical poems in this collection, in this part, invoking the angels to protect his infant son, Michael. Though heartfelt, the poem lacks the poetic and philosophical intensity of "A Prayer for My Daughter," written for Anne (born in 1919) and included in *Michael Robartes and the Dancer*.

"Leda and the Swan," which Yeats also included at the beginning of the "Dove and Swan" chapter in *A Vision*, uses the image of the rape of Leda by Zeus to depict the violent cataclysmic upheaval that Yeats, an occultist, believed occurred in 2000 B.C.E. This two-thousand-year reversal, which happened again in 1 C.E., is the basis of the contrasting views of the classical and Christian eras as alluded to in "Two Songs from a Play." Yeats's increasing longing for a return to the art of classical Greece, which in his cyclic system also represents a forward thrust to the kind of art that would prevail again in the two-thousand-year cycle starting in 2000 C.E., is also reflected in the choruses from his adaptations of Sophocles' *Oedipus Tyrannus* (c. 429 B.C.E.; *Oedipus Tyrannus*, 1715) and *Oidipous epi Kolōnōi* (401 B.C.E.; *Oedipus at Colonus*, 1729), which are included in *The Tower*.

In the book, Yeats retraces, as he has in others, his own poetic and love history in connection to the Irish struggle. "Among School Children" starts in a conversational mode with Yeats as a sixty-year-old school inspector (one of his duties as a senator), strolling among the school children and daydreaming of Gonne's "Ledean body" at their age. He uses the classical allusion in a semicomic tone, admitting that her image still has the power to drive him wild while remembering that he himself had "pretty plumage once." His reverie brings him back to his own birth, and he wonders how any mother could think childbirth worth the labor if she could imagine her child at sixty. The phrase "honey of generation" in the fifth stanza, taken, as he explains in a note, from the Neoplatonist Porphry, brings Plato to mind again, and he considers the fixity of Plato's forms in contrast to changing natural bodies. At the end of this poem, as at the end of "The Tower"

and "Sailing to Byzantium," he longs for a source of art that can blossom and dance without splitting and bruising nature.

He continues to focus on his past and present love relationships in the next set of poems. His more recent attractions to Iseult Gonne and to his wife are the basis of "Owen Aherne and His Dancers." He recounts his whole love history in the sequence of poems gathered under the title "A Man Young and Old." In the first edition, there were ten of these very short poems. Later, he moved the chorus entitled "From 'Oedipus at Colonus'" to the end of this sequence. "First Love," "Human Dignity," and "The Mermaid" look back from a cynical viewpoint at a lover who remembers "a heart of stone," a lack of response to his sorrow, and a lad drowning in the "cruel happiness" of a mermaid's embrace. "The Empty Cup" pictures an old man who still finds the cup "dry as bone." "His Memories," the pivotal poem (sixth of eleven in the sequence), recalls in highly allusive language that for a brief moment, "she who brought great Hector down" lay in his arms and found pleasure. This is one of Yeats's few references to the brief physical relationship he had with Gonne (whom he often imaged as Helen of Troy) in the middle of a spiritual pact these two occultists had in the early years of the twentieth century. In the course of this sequence, he refers obliquely to several other women with whom he had relationships as well. At the end, old age dominates, and he longs for the less agonized indifference of "a gay goodnight and quickly turn away."

He concludes the collection with "All Soul's Night," which he identifies in a subtitle as "Epilogue to 'A Vision.'" In this poem, as repeatedly seems true throughout this collection, he appears more comfortable conversing with the dead or absent of his own generation than with the young he leaves behind in "Sailing to Byzantium."

This attitude and focus change drastically in his next collection, *The Winding Stair, and Other Poems* (1933), where he chooses to return to a delight in the physical world. In fact, Yeats continued to produce a prolific and self-renewing output of lyric poetry without interruption until his death. As a separate collection, nevertheless, *The Tower* sounds a consistent note of concern about his own growing old and the violent state of the world. As a poet, he seeks an untroubled indifference and longs for the cyclic change the next great reversal will bring; yet the intensity of the poetry undercuts any suggestion of a placid retirement from writing. *The Tower* remains one of the most intense collections in the entire body of poetry written by one of the finest lyric poets in English in the twentieth century.

Catherine Cavanaugh

Further Reading

Adams, Hazard. *The Book of Yeats's Poems.* Tallahassee: Florida State University Press, 1990. A poem-by-poem reading that takes into consideration the order Yeats intended for the poems. Chapter 5 discusses *The Tower* as a series of returns.

Doggett, Rob. "Discovering a 'New Vintage,' a New Vantage: *The Tower* and Imagined Exile." In *Deep-Rooted Things: Empire and Nation in the Poetry and Drama of William Butler Yeats.* Notre Dame, Ind.: University of Notre Dame Press, 2006. Focuses on selected plays and poems that reflect Yeats's ambivalence toward Irish nationalism in the years when Ireland was making the transition from British colony to partially independent nation. Argues that nationalism for Yeats is a series of masks that he adapts, rejects, and re-creates.

Ellmann, Richard. *Yeats: The Man and the Masks.* New York: Macmillan, 1948. An excellent introductory work by a major literary critic that melds poetic interpretation into biographical context. Provides a brief but insightful chapter on *The Tower.*

Jeffares, A. Norman. *A New Commentary on the Poems of W. B. Yeats.* Stanford, Calif.: Stanford University Press, 1984. An indispensable companion to Yeats's poems. All proper names, place names, and autobiographical references are explicated, and prose passages are included.

Kinsella, Thomas. *Readings in Poetry.* Dublin: Dedalus, 2006. Kinsella, himself a poet, provides a close reading of *The Tower,* analyzing its textual detail, method, and structure.

Unterecker, John. *A Reader's Guide to William Butler Yeats.* New York: Farrar, Straus & Giroux, 1971. The first chapter discusses Yeats's major themes, while a separate chapter on *The Tower* offers a strategy for interpreting Yeats's poems.

Vendler, Helen Hennessy. *Our Secret Discipline: Yeats and Lyric Form.* New York: Oxford University Press, 2007. Vendler, a well-regarded literary critic and Yeats scholar, examines the technical and emotional aspects of his poetry. Describes how he constructs his poems, analyzing their form, proportion, meter, and other elements.

Yeats, William Butler. *The Autobiography of William Butler Yeats.* New York: Collier Books, 1965. Yeats's own commentary on the major influences on his life and his poetry remains one of the best complements to his poetry.

The Tower of London

Author: William Harrison Ainsworth (1805-1882)
First published: 1840
Type of work: Novel
Type of plot: Historical
Time of plot: Sixteenth century
Locale: England

Principal characters:
THE DUKE OF NORTHUMBERLAND
GUILFORD DUDLEY, Northumberland's son
LADY JANE GREY, Dudley's wife
CUTHBERT CHOLMONDELEY, Dudley's squire
CICELY, Cuthbert's beloved
LAWRENCE NIGHTGALL, the jailer
SIMON RENARD, the Spanish ambassador
QUEEN MARY
PRINCESS ELIZABETH, Mary's sister
EDWARD COURTENAY, the earl of Devonshire

The Story:

At the death of King Edward VI, there are several claimants to the English throne, among them Mary, Elizabeth's older sister, and Lady Jane Grey, the wife of Lord Guilford Dudley, who is supported by her father-in-law, the duke of Northumberland. According to custom, Lady Jane is brought to the Tower of London for her coronation. There, the supporters of Mary, while pretending to be in accord with Northumberland, wait to betray Lady Jane.

Among those present is Cuthbert Cholmondeley, Dudley's squire, who has fallen in love with a beautiful young girl he has seen in the Tower. Through inquiries among his servants, Cuthbert learns that the girl, Cicely, is the adopted daughter of Peter the pantler and Dame Potentia Trusbut; the true circumstances of Cicely's birth are unknown. The chief jailer of the Tower, Lawrence Nightgall, also loves Cicely. When Simon Renard, the Spanish ambassador, and Lord

Pembroke, both Mary's supporters, conspire to assassinate Cuthbert because they know him to be Dudley's favorite, Nightgall eagerly agrees to help them.

Nightgall tells Cicely that her new lover has been taken from the Tower and that she will never see him again. Meanwhile, Cuthbert, a prisoner in a dungeon below the Tower, is accosted by a strange woman who cries out that she wants her child to be returned to her. When Nightgall visits Cuthbert, the prisoner asks his jailer about the woman, but Nightgall evades the question by stating that the woman is mad.

At Northumberland's command, Gunnora Broase, an old woman, administered a dose of poison to the late boy-king, Edward VI. She is directed by a strange man to reveal Northumberland's part in the murder and thus to defeat his intention to place Lady Jane on the throne of England.

Simon Renard and Lord Pembroke have instigated a conflict between Lady Jane and Northumberland by convincing Lady Jane that she should not consent to make Dudley a king. Northumberland desires this distinction for his son, but Lady Jane believes that making her husband a king will cause too much dissension in the kingdom. In anger at this slight from his wife, Dudley leaves the Tower. Lady Jane, who is surrounded by intrigue, is convinced that Renard and Lord Pembroke are her friends and that Northumberland is her enemy. Lord Pembroke next persuades Lady Jane to send Northumberland against Mary's forces, which are reportedly advancing on London. With Northumberland separated from Lady Jane, Lord Pembroke and Renard are certain that they can destroy her rule. Lady Jane is easily persuaded because she does not suspect the treachery of her two advisers.

Cuthbert Cholmondeley escapes from his dungeon. Dudley returns to his wife and his queen in time to convince her of the treachery of Lord Pembroke and Renard, whom Lady Jane then orders imprisoned. Cicely comes to Dudley and Lady Jane with the tale of what has happened to Cholmondeley. Soon after Lord Pembroke and Renard are imprisoned, Nightgall helps them to escape from the Tower. Meanwhile, Lady Jane has made Cicely a lady-in-waiting.

Gunnora Broase gains an audience with Lady Jane and declares that Northumberland poisoned Edward and that his purpose in marrying his son to Lady Jane was to elevate Dudley to the throne; Lady Jane will then be poisoned. Meanwhile, Cuthbert has found his way from the lower dungeons, and he and Cicely are reunited. He is present when the duke of Suffolk, Lady Jane's father, urges her to avoid execution by abdicating. Dudley, however, persuades his wife not to surrender the crown. Mary is proclaimed queen, and Lady Jane is placed in prison with Cicely and Cuthbert. Dudley is separately confined. Gunnora Broase sneaks into Lady Jane's cell and helps

her to escape from the prison with the promise that Dudley will follow shortly, but when Northumberland disbands his forces and acknowledges Mary as queen, Lady Jane surrenders herself and returns to her cell in the Tower.

The people acclaim Mary when she enters London. The new queen's first act is to release all Catholic prisoners and replace them with her former enemies. When Northumberland is arrested and condemned to the scaffold, he pleads for mercy for Lady Jane because he was the chief proponent of her pretension to the throne. Although the duke publicly embraces Catholicism in the mistaken belief that his life will be spared, he is executed by Mary's order. Mary puts pressure on Lady Jane and Dudley to embrace Catholicism as Northumberland did in order to save their lives, but Lady Jane is determined to die a Protestant. Cuthbert is released from custody and returns to look for Cicely, but she is nowhere to be found. He does find the strange madwoman again—she is lying in a cell, dead.

Edward Courtenay, the earl of Devonshire, is among the prisoners Mary has released from the Tower. The young nobleman is really in love with Elizabeth, although, covetous of Mary's throne, he pretends to love Mary. Without scruple, he is able to win Mary's promise that she will make him her husband. Renard, however, lurks menacingly in the background. When Courtenay goes to Elizabeth with one last appeal of love, Mary and Renard listen to their conversation from behind a curtain. In anger at his betrayal, Mary commits Courtenay to the Tower and then confines Elizabeth to her room. On Renard's advice, Mary affiances herself to Philip, king of Spain. Later, Mary's counselors persuade her to release Elizabeth.

Moved by compassion for the innocent Lady Jane, Mary issues a pardon for the pretender and her husband. The couple retire to the home of Lady Jane's father, where Dudley begins to organize a new plot to place his wife on the throne. Lady Jane is aware that Dudley is determined to carry out his plans. Faithful to her husband, she consents to follow him in whatever he does. Another revolt is led by Sir Thomas Wyat, a fervent anti-Catholic, supported by those who oppose an alliance between England and Spain. The rebellion is quelled, and Wyat and Dudley are captured. Lady Jane and Cuthbert surrender themselves to Mary, and Lady Jane pleads for the life of her husband in exchange for her surrender. The only condition on which Mary will allow Dudley to live is that Lady Jane must embrace Catholicism. When she refuses, she is sentenced to death along with Dudley. Elizabeth is brought to the Tower, as Mary plans to do away with Courtenay and her sister after she has completed the destruction of Lady Jane and Dudley.

Still suffering from jealousy over Cicely's love for Cuthbert, Nightgall has held the girl in prison since the fall of Lady Jane. Meanwhile, Nightgall has been hired by the French ambassador to assassinate Renard. Renard and Nightgall meet in Cuthbert's cell after the squire has been tortured, and, in the ensuing fight, Cuthbert escapes and runs to find Cicely. Renard succeeds in killing Nightgall, who lives long enough to provide proof of Cicely's noble birth. She is the daughter of the unfortunate madwoman, Lady Grace Mountjoy. Before her execution, Lady Jane requests that Cicely and Cuthbert be allowed to marry. With strange generosity, Mary pardons them and grants their freedom. At the scene of Lady Jane's execution, even her enemies shudder at the sight of so good and fair a woman about to die. On the block, she reaffirms her Christian faith as the ax descends on one of the most ill-fated of English monarchs.

Critical Evaluation:

The Tower of London is a historical novel in the tradition of Sir Walter Scott, yet the author's unique approach to his historical material makes the book stand apart from other novels of the genre. William Harrison Ainsworth makes the Tower itself the protagonist of the story. He was quite explicit about this point, stating that his goal in *The Tower of London* was to write about incidents that would illuminate every corner of the edifice or, in his words, "naturally introduce every relic of the old pile." Unlike a story that deals with a period in the life of a human being or with the unfolding of character development, *The Tower of London* centers on a phase in the history of a complex of buildings. If the reader is willing to accept this premise, he or she must be content to see action and character subordinate to setting and to some preconceived notions concerning plot.

The Tower functions not only as the historical backdrop for the incidents in the novel and the stage on which the action takes place but also as the major structural device of the book. Indeed, the Tower is so thoroughly integrated with the other materials of the novel that it becomes a vital participant in the action and provides the novel's unity by acting as a focal point around which all other elements are organized. The novel has a clearly defined beginning in Lady Jane Grey Dudley's arrival at the Tower on July 10, 1553, and an equally definite end: her execution on Tower Green on February 10, 1559. In between the two events, much of the major action of the book takes place in the Tower's chapels, halls, chambers, and gateways.

The novel can be viewed as two distinct parts joined together by the Tower. During the first half of the book, Lady Jane, the queen for barely a month, is supported in her tenuous claim to the throne by her father-in-law, the duke of Northumberland, and by her husband, Lord Dudley. She is plotted against, however, by those who wish to put Mary on the throne. In the second part, Mary is queen, but she, too, is the object of conspiracies by the champions of both Elizabeth and the deposed Jane. At the novel's conclusion, Lady Jane has been beheaded, Elizabeth is in protective custody, and Mary is committed to a Spanish marriage that pleases no one. All that survives unimpaired is the Tower, having been the scene of yet one more series of events in its long history.

Although one might at first suspect that Lady Jane is the heroine of the novel, given that it chronicles her stay in the Tower, this is not the case. Mary Tudor and her half sister, Elizabeth, play larger roles. Nevertheless, it is obviously the Tower itself that dominates this novel, and the book's best writing is found in the passages describing the structure. Ainsworth spaces his descriptions judiciously throughout in such a way as to heighten their effects. The only apparent exception to this general descriptive practice occurs in the second book, as Ainsworth digresses for more than a dozen pages to relate an account of the Tower's history from the time of William the Conqueror down to the nineteenth century. This interruption, however, is not entirely indefensible, because even the architectural history of the Tower has a decided part in creating mood, establishing motivation, and advancing action in the novel.

In turning his descriptive powers toward his human characters, Ainsworth generally achieves the same effectiveness he does with his descriptions of the Tower; yet his characterizations also exhibit major flaws in technique. He describes in almost minute detail not only the physical appearances of the characters but also their manners of dress and every aspect of the ceremonial occasions in which they participate. Although the quantity of sociohistorical research necessary for Ainsworth to provide such descriptions of ceremonial pomp and costumery is noteworthy, the sheer detail of the descriptions tends to slow down the action of the novel in places and becomes tedious for even the most patient reader. Most readers, however, would admit that they are never left with any uncertainty concerning the appearance of the principal participants in any scene of *The Tower of London*—even regarding such minute details as the texture of the duke of Suffolk's cloak, "flowered with gold and ribanded with nets of silver."

Ainsworth's characters often tend to be mere types, such as the meritorious young man who has to make his way in the world against great odds. He is in love with a chaste maiden who is subjected to a series of threats ranging from the inconvenient to the unspeakable. These types can be seen in *The

Tower of London in the characters of Dudley's squire, Cuthbert, and his beloved, Cicely, who are the victims of imprisonment and conspiracy but escape unscathed to marry at last. A second stock character is the power-hungry schemer personified by Simon Renard, the Spanish ambassador who lurks in the background attempting to manipulate the fortunes of the other characters. His skill in plotting is seen when he effectively ruptures the relationship between Lady Jane and Northumberland by convincing her to deny Dudley the kingship as a part of a larger scheme to weaken Lady Jane's claim to the throne. A final example of Ainsworth's stock characters is the "unmotivated villain," Nightgall the jailer, who seems to perpetrate evil deeds for their own sake and who adds greatly to the misfortunes of Cuthbert and Cicely.

Ainsworth compounds his problems of characterization with the use of the hackneyed device of mistaken identities. The details of Cicely's birth are unknown until the novel's conclusion, when Nightgall confirms that she is the daughter of Lady Grace Mountjoy. This is at best only a slight variation on plots employed by Ainsworth in at least six of his other works. Sometimes these false identities are deliberately assumed, or, as in this novel, they stem from mysteries of parentage of which the main characters are themselves unaware. In any case, the device was overworked long before Ainsworth employed it in *The Tower of London*.

The author's treatment of the nonfictional characters is somewhat more effective because he is dealing with real people about which something is known, but he nevertheless weakens their portraits through his intrusive moral judgments of their actions. He tells readers quite clearly what they should think of the characters. The duke of Northumberland, for example, is "haughty and disdainful," while Queen Mary's "worst fault as a woman and her sole fault as a sovereign was her bigotry." No writer of his age was less reticent than Ainsworth about intruding his own personal views into his writing. These problems of characterization, however, will be overlooked by most readers in their acceptance of the premise of the novel, which is to narrate the history of the Tower.

It is true that *The Tower of London* is an unusual work and not without its flaws, but it is an effective novel in terms of its vivid and ordered chronicling of fascinating historical events. Ainsworth's appeal springs from his sense of structure and his ability to arouse in the reader a sense of being in a crowded, swarming, self-contained world where adventure and intrigue are staples of everyday life.

"Critical Evaluation" by Stephen Hanson

Further Reading

Carver, Stephen James. "Twin-Born Romances: *Guy Fawkes* and *The Tower of London*, 1840." In *The Life and Works of the Lancashire Novelist William Harrison Ainsworth, 1805-1882*. Lewiston, N.Y.: Edwin Mellen Press, 2003. Chapter devoted to discussion of *The Tower of London* and another of Ainsworth's romance novels is part of an extensive analysis of the author's writings.

Ellis, S. M. *William Harrison Ainsworth and His Friends*. 2 vols. 1911. Reprint. New York: Garland, 1979. First complete biography of the author is based on original correspondence and recollections. Includes a detailed discussion of the sources used for *The Tower of London*.

Fleishman, Avrom. *The English Historical Novel: Walter Scott to Virginia Woolf*. Baltimore: Johns Hopkins University Press, 1971. Discusses Ainsworth as a mass producer of historical fiction and judges *The Tower of London* to be filled with grotesque characters, antiquarian digressions, and sentimental emotions.

Mitchell, Rosemary. "The Picturesque Face of the Past: The 1840's Novels of William Harrison Ainsworth." In *Picturing the Past: English History in Text and Image, 1830-1870*. New York: Oxford University Press, 2000. Chapter devoted to Ainsworth is part of a larger examination of nineteenth century history books, history textbooks, and historical novels with the aim of describing Victorian attitudes toward British history. Demonstrates how the text and images in popular and scholarly publications contributed to Victorian cultural identities.

Sanders, Andrew. *The Victorian Historical Novel, 1840-1880*. New York: St. Martin's Press, 1979. One chapter of this comprehensive study presents a harsh evaluation of *The Tower of London*. Argues that the novel is overcrowded with characters, abrupt in its transitions from scene to scene, intellectually slight, and sensationalistic.

Sutherland, J. A. *Victorian Novelists and Publishers*. Chicago: University of Chicago Press, 1976. Offers a well-written, thoughtful, and detailed examination of how business relationships between novelists and publishers affected the shape of novels in the Victorian era. Explains why *The Tower of London* was one of Ainsworth's most popular novels, despite its formulaic qualities.

Worth, George J. *William Harrison Ainsworth*. New York: Twayne, 1972. Presents a critical study of Ainsworth's career. Notes that *The Tower of London*'s focus on setting, rather than on plot and characters, is a departure from Ainsworth's more typical novels and asserts that this approach is interesting, creative, and challenging to received notions about plot.

The Town

Author: William Faulkner (1897-1962)
First published: 1957
Type of work: Novel
Type of plot: Psychological realism
Time of plot: 1909-1927
Locale: Jefferson, Yoknapatawpha County, Mississippi

Principal characters:
FLEM SNOPES, the shrewdest of the Snopes family
EULA VARNER SNOPES, his wife
LINDA SNOPES, their daughter
MANFRED DE SPAIN, the mayor of Jefferson and Eula's lover
GAVIN STEVENS, a county attorney
V. K. RATLIFF, a salesman and friend of Gavin Stevens
CHARLES MALLISON, Stevens's nephew
MONTGOMERY WARD SNOPES,
WALLSTREET PANIC SNOPES,
BYRON SNOPES,
MINK SNOPES,
ECK SNOPES, and
I. O. SNOPES, Flem's cousins

The Story:

The Snopes family, which comes out of nowhere after the Civil War, successfully completes the invasion of Frenchman's Bend. Now Flem Snopes, son of Ab Snopes, a bushwhacker, sharecropper, and horse thief, is ready for the next goal, the domination of Jefferson, the county seat of Yoknapatawpha County. Flem is ruthless, shrewd, uneducated, and possessed of a fanatic belief in the power of money. The townspeople, who saw him when he took over Frenchman's Bend and then left it under the control of other family members, are wondering about Flem's next move. Among those interested are Gavin Stevens, a young lawyer educated in Heidelberg, and V. K. Ratliff, a good-natured sewing machine salesman, who makes up for his lack of education with a great measure of common sense. Stevens feels a moral responsibility to defend the town against the Snopeses, and Ratliff was once the victim of Snopesism when, thinking that it contained a buried treasure, he bought worthless property from Flem for a high price. Another who becomes an assistant in the fight against the Snopes infiltration is Stevens's nephew, Charles Mallison, who watches the Snopes invasion from his childhood through adolescence.

Flem realizes that more subtle methods for conquering Jefferson are necessary than those he used in Frenchman's Bend. The greatest advantage for him is his marriage with Eula Varner, daughter of Will Varner, chief property owner in that community. When Eula is pregnant, impotent Flem marries her after making a profitable deal with Varner, who despises Snopes but wants to save his daughter's honor.

In a small rented house, Flem and his wife make a modest beginning in Jefferson by operating a small restaurant of which Ratliff was a partner before he lost his share in the business deal with Flem. Later, the restaurant is transformed into a hotel. The first hint that Flem is aiming even higher comes when he is appointed superintendent of the local power plant, before the people even know that such a position exists. As the new mayor of Jefferson, Manfred de Spain is not in favor with the town conservatives, but he wins the election in a landslide when he declares himself against an automobile ban imposed by the former mayor. Soon it becomes known in the town that Eula and the new mayor are lovers. No one sees anything, but everybody seems to know about the affair except her husband.

Shortly after the war, during which Gavin serves overseas, the president of Jefferson's oldest bank is killed in an auto accident. De Spain, named president on account of the bank stock he inherits, resigns as mayor. The election of a new president makes necessary a routine check by government auditors, who uncover the theft of a large sum of money by a defaulting clerk, Byron Snopes, who fled to Mexico. An announcement is made that the money was replaced by the new president and that Flem has been made a vice president of the bank. Flem's appointment indicates to his opponents a new phase of Snopesism: The search for money and power is now tinted with Flem's desire for respectability. This new tactic also becomes apparent when he rids himself and Jefferson of some undesirable kinsmen, such as Montgomery

Ward Snopes, who might destroy his efforts to make the name Snopes respectable. Montgomery returns from the war in France with a rich supply of pornographic pictures. A short time later, he opens a photographic studio and gives nightly slide shows for a large part of the male population of Yoknapatawpha County. Flem, not wishing to have his name associated with this shady enterprise, puts bootleg whiskey in Montgomery's studio to ensure his arrest. When another Snopes, Mink, is jailed for murder, Flem fails to give him any assistance. There is also Eck Snopes, who does not fit into the Snopes pattern on account of his weak intelligence. Flem has no need to bring about his removal, for Eck removes himself. He is hired to watch an oil tank. While a search is being made for a lost child, Eck, trying to make sure that the child did not climb into his oil tank, takes a lantern and goes to look inside the tank. After the explosion, only Eck's metal neck brace is available for burial. Meanwhile, the child is found safe somewhere along the road.

Flem's new desire for respectability also makes him forget Wallstreet Panic Snopes, who dared to become a self-made man without his kinsman's help. Wallstreet Panic, a successful grocer, introduces the first self-service store in Jefferson. Flem also dislikes the outcome of one of his family projects with I. O. Snopes, who is trained to tie mules to the railroad track in order to collect money from damage lawsuits against the railroad. When I. O. is killed during one of these operations, Flem hopes to collect the indemnity. I. O.'s stubborn wife, however, keeps all the money, and Flem, in order to avoid complications, is forced to pay off the man who supplied the mules. Flem also tries to live up to his new social standing by letting a professional decorator furnish his house.

In the meantime, Gavin, who was never able to rid himself of the attraction Eula holds for him, concentrates his reform efforts on Linda, Eula's daughter. Linda, now in high school, does not know that Flem is not her real father. The lawyer loves Linda and tries to influence her to attend a northern college far away from Snopesism. Flem, however, needing a front of outwardly solid family life for his show of respectability, is opposed to the possibility of losing his control of Linda, especially since a will exists that gives the girl a great deal of Varner's estate. So Flem disregards the pleas of his daughter because he still has one more step ahead of him to achieve the position he desires in Jefferson: his scheme to replace de Spain as president of the bank. When he fails in his first attempt to ruin the bank by instigating a run on it, he decides that the time comes to use his knowledge of his wife's adultery as a weapon. Acting as if he just learned of the eighteen-year-old affair, and armed with a declaration from

Linda that she will leave her part of her inheritance to her father, he visits Varner. Once more, in order to save the honor of his daughter and in return for Flem's promise to destroy Linda's note about the inheritance, Varner helps Flem to get rid of de Spain, and Flem became president of the bank. Hoping Eula will run away with him, de Spain sells his bank stock, but Eula, hoping to keep her daughter from ever learning of her affairs, remains in Jefferson. She commits suicide after securing from Gavin a promise that he will marry Linda.

Flem, having reached his goal, agrees to let Linda leave Jefferson. For a short interval, the ghost of old Snopesism comes back to Jefferson, when bank thief Byron Snopes sent his four half-Indian children to stay with his kinfolk. After a series of incidents in which the children terrorized Jefferson and Frenchman's Bend, Flem himself makes sure that these last reminders of primitive Snopesism are sent back to Mexico. Meanwhile, he buys the de Spain house, and workers are busy transforming it into a mansion suitable for Flem, president of the Bank of Jefferson.

Critical Evaluation:

It was in the 1920's that William Faulkner first conceived of the Snopes saga: a clan of crude, avaricious, amoral, unfeeling, but energetic and hard-driving individuals who would move into the settled, essentially moral society of the Old South and gradually, but inevitably, usurp the old order. To Faulkner, the Snopeses were not a special Mississippi phenomenon but a characteristic evil of the mechanized, dehumanized twentieth century that filled the void left by the collapse of the agrarian pre-Civil War South. Flem Snopes is the supreme example of the type, and the Snopes trilogy, of which *The Town* is the second part, is primarily a chronicle of his career and its implications.

Faulkner finished *The Hamlet*, the first book in the series, in 1940 (although several short stories appeared earlier), and not until 1959 did he complete the trilogy with *The Mansion*. In the intervening time, Faulkner's vision of human morality and society became more complex and, although the original design remained intact, the quest of the Snopes clan became more devious and complicated, and "Snopesism" took on increasingly ambiguous meanings.

At the beginning of *The Town*, Flem arrives in Jefferson fresh from his triumphs in Frenchman's Bend, but with only a wagon, a new wife, Eula Varner Snopes, and their baby daughter, Linda. The book traces his rise in short order from restaurant owner to hotel owner, to power plant supervisor, to bank vice president, and finally to bank president, church deacon, and appropriately grieving widower. The book also describes the life of his wife, Eula, her lengthy affair with Manfred de Spain, her relations to the community, and her efforts for her daughter—all of which leads her, at last, to suicide.

If Flem is the embodiment of ruthless, aggressive inhumanity and devitalized conformity, Eula is the essence of warmth, emotional involvement, sexuality, and freedom. Although their direct confrontations are muted, *The Town* is basically about the struggle between these two characters and the contrasting approaches to life that they represent. The story is told by three anti-Snopesian citizens: V. K. Ratliff, the sewing machine salesman who previously tangled with Flem in Frenchman's Bend; Gavin Stevens, a Heidelberg- and Harvard-educated county attorney; and Charles Mallison, Stevens's young nephew. Although they confirm the essential facts, each speaker has a separate interpretation of the events. Thus, the reader must sift through their different attitudes and conclusions to arrive at the "truth" of the book. Frequently, it is the ironical distance between the events and the characters' interpretations of them that gives the book its bite and message—as well as its humor.

Mallison, who sees the events as a child but recounts them as an adult, is probably the most detached of the narrators. Ratliff is sardonic and realistic, but his bitter experiences with the Snopeses somewhat color his accounts. Gavin Stevens is the primary narrator and chief enemy of Flem, but the reliability of his statements is jeopardized by his lengthy, emotional, somewhat confused involvements with both Eula and Linda. Gavin is a well-educated, sophisticated modern man who understands the complexities and difficulties of human relationships; but, at the same time, he is an old-fashioned southern gentleman who clings to old attitudes and traditions. When Eula offers herself to him, it is not morality but romanticism coupled with self-doubt that stimulates his refusal. He insists on viewing her through a romantic haze that prevents him from reacting realistically in the most critical situations. "What he was doing was simply defending forever with his blood the principle that chastity and virtue in women shall be defended whether they exist or not."

The same kinds of assumptions determine his relationship to Linda Snopes. Since he is nearly twice her age, he cannot imagine a sexual or marital arrangement between them in spite of the fact that he loves her and is encouraged by her mother. So, in the role of father protector and educator, Gavin reads poetry to Linda over sodas and feeds her dreams with college catalogs. Thus, because of his intense emotions, sense of morality, and traditional assumptions, Gavin is unable to deal either with Eula's simple sensuality or Flem's one-dimensional inhumanity.

In the final conflict between these two forces, Flem's ruthless rationality overcomes Eula's passionate free spirit. Being both physically and spiritually impotent, Flem can coldly and callously manipulate the sexual and emotional drives of others. Not only does he do so to thwart Gavin's anti-Snopes efforts, but more important to his plans, he also uses them to gain control over his primary Jefferson rival, Manfred de Spain.

Flem learns of his wife's affair with de Spain soon after his arrival in Jefferson, but he chooses to ignore it as long as it is profitable. It is even suggested that the two men work out a tacit agreement whereby Flem overlooks the affair in return for an appointment to the newly created job of power plant superintendent. De Spain's influence is later instrumental in securing Flem the vice presidency of the Sartoris Bank. After eighteen years, however, when Flem decides to make his move for the bank presidency, he suddenly becomes the outraged husband. He uses the threat of scandal to provoke Will Varner to action, to drive de Spain from the bank, to push Eula to suicide, and to coerce Gavin into unwilling complicity. Neither integrity nor sensuality can stop Snopesism.

As Flem succeeds in his drive to monetary wealth, another goal becomes predominant—respectability. He learns from de Spain that in Jefferson one can become respectable without being moral—if one has the necessary money. So Flem systematically acquires all the requisite signs of success, and they, in turn, provide him with access to respectability. Only one last obstacle remains between Flem and complete social acceptance—the other Snopeses.

Consequently, it is Flem himself who finally rids Jefferson of the Snopeses. Using the same callous attitude and devious strategy on his kin that he uses on other victims, he eliminates all of the lesser Snopeses who might pose a threat to his new status: Mink, Byron, Montgomery Ward, I. O., and, finally, Byron's brood of wild, half-breed children, "The last and final end of Snopes out-and-out unvarnished behavior in Jefferson."

So Flem becomes respectable. Faulkner's final question to the reader is this: Has Flem's drive to social acceptance weakened and narrowed him to the point where he is vulnerable, if not to the morality of the Ratliffs, Stevenses, and Mallisons, then to the latent vengeance of Snopesism? Faulkner answers that question in *The Mansion*.

"Critical Evaluation" by Keith Neilson

Further Reading

Donaldson, Susan V. *"Faulkner's Snopes Trilogy and Cold War Masculinity."* In *White Masculinity in the Recent*

South, edited by Trent Watts. Baton Rouge: Louisiana State University Press, 2008. Donaldson's essay examining the depiction of the male characters in *The Town*, *The Hamlet*, and *The Mansion* is included in this study of the representation of white southern manhood since World War II.

Kerr, Elizabeth. *William Faulkner's Gothic Domain*. Port Washington, N.Y.: Kennikat Press, 1979. Discusses Flem Snopes, Gavin Stevens, and Mink Snopes in reference to their respective roles in *The Town*. Lists and discusses interconnected themes in the trilogy. Includes a fairly extensive bibliography.

Marcus, Steven. "Snopes Revisited." In *William Faulkner: Three Decades of Criticism*, edited by Frederick J. Hoffman and Olga W. Vickery. East Lansing: Michigan State University Press, 1960. Discusses content, characterization, and criticism of *The Town*. Points out failings but contends that Faulkner intentionally wrote the novel to represent truth, as art must. Contains an extensive bibliography, including periodical sources.

Meriwether, James B., and Michael Millgate, eds. *Lion in the Garden: Interviews with William Faulkner, 1926-1962*.

New York: Random House, 1968. Provides Faulkner's own responses to specific questions about *The Town* and its chief characters and reports Faulkner's views on themes in his fiction. Indexed and coded to specific works and characters.

Millgate, Michael. *The Achievement of William Faulkner*. New York: Random House, 1966. Millgate's readable, discerning text must be included in any credible bibliography of Faulkner's work. Provides insight into Gavin Stevens, a central character of *The Town*. Includes notes and index.

Polk, Noel. "Water, Wanderers, and Snopes Trilogy." In *Faulkner and Welty and the Southern Literary Tradition*. Jackson: University Press of Mississippi, 2008. An analysis of *The Town*, *The Hamlet*, and *The Mansion* by a preeminent scholar of southern literature.

Towner, Theresa M. *The Cambridge Introduction to William Faulkner*. New York: Cambridge University Press, 2008. An accessible book aimed at students and general readers. Focusing on Faulkner's work, the book provides detailed analyses of his nineteen novels, discussion of his other works, and information about the critical reception for his fiction.

The Tragedy of King Christophe

Author: Aimé Césaire (1913-2008)
First produced: La Tragédie du Roi Christophe, 1964; first published, 1963 (English translation, 1969)
Type of work: Drama
Type of plot: Historical
Time of plot: Early nineteenth century
Locale: Haiti

Principal characters:
PÉTION, president of the Haitian Republic
CHRISTOPHE, king of Haiti
CORNEILLE BRELLE, an archbishop
JUAN DE DIOS, an archbishop

The Story:

Stylized Haitian peasants are acting out a cock fight between King Christophe and President Pétion, who are fighting for political power in Haiti. At the same time, French forces under Emperor Napoleon I are threatening to invade Haiti and to destroy the newly independent country that owes its freedom to a successful slave revolt led by François-Dominique Toussaint Louverture. The French later kill him in prison.

Most ominously, the French want to reestablish slavery in Haiti. The external threat weighs heavily, as the vain and rac-

ist megalomaniac Napoleon bitterly resents that black people had driven French soldiers from Haiti. A violent French attack against Haiti is expected at any time.

The incredibly vain King Christophe is to be rewarded for his courageous service as a general to Toussaint Louverture. The Haitian senate offers him the office of president of the republic. He haughtily rejects this honor because the Haitian constitution restricts the president's power so that tyranny can be prevented.

As a representative of the senate, President Pétion tells

Christophe that his desire for unlimited power means that he has rebelled against the state. Because of his vanity, Christophe provokes a civil war in Haiti. Southern Haiti remains a democracy, but Christophe transforms northern Haiti into an absolute monarchy and names himself king. He claims that he grants Haitians dignity by giving them noble titles—such as the duke of Lemonade and Sir Lolo Prettyboy—as artificial as those that can be found at any European royal court such as Versailles in France. The newly crowned king is blissfully oblivious to the simple fact that Haitians had revolted against their slave masters to obtain freedom, and not meaningless titles.

At Pétion's urging, the Haitian senate declares war against traitor Christophe in an attempt to restore national unity. While troops from southern Haiti start to liberate Christophe's monarchy from him, Christophe descends into even more bizarre behavior. He spends precious time discussing why it is important to declare rum, made from Haitian sugar cane, to be the national drink of Haiti.

Christophe continues to say insightful things about the dignity of black people, but he reduces northern Haiti to abject poverty by wasting precious resources. He has built a pretentious royal palace that he calls Sans Souci (meaning "without a care"), an obvious reference to the extravagant royal palace that Frederick the Great had built in Potsdam, just outside Berlin.

Haiti needs effective armed forces to prevent France from reestablishing colonial power over Haiti, more than it needs a palace. The irony in the very name of Christophe's palace is immediately obvious. The danger to Haitian freedom is real, but Christophe does not want reality to interfere with his illusory views on his kingdom. When the aged archbishop Corneille Brelle expresses a desire to spend his final years in France, Christophe has him killed. Without reason, Christophe has others killed as well.

As the forces of democratic Haiti advance farther and farther into northern Haiti, Christophe descends even further into madness. He tells the new archbishop, Juan de Dios, that if the Virgin Mary wants Haitian priests to say mass on August 15, the holy day that honors the assumption of the Virgin Mary, then she should come to Haiti herself and tell Christophe that Haitians should celebrate this day.

As the certainty of his defeat becomes obvious, even to him, Christophe continues to give nice speeches about the importance of Haitians' remaining faithful to their African roots. His words are sensible, but there is a clear distinction between his words and his actions.

Christophe had wanted to be an admired monarch, like King Louis XIV of France and Frederick the Great of Prussia, but such a desire is incompatible with the sound desire of recently liberated slaves to remain faithful to their African identity. The Prussian baroque palace of Sans Souci in Potsdam is an overt imitation of the palace in Versailles and neither Sans Souci nor Versailles has anything to do with Haiti and Africa.

Christophe completes his descent into madness by killing himself. The very survival of Haiti as an independent country had required his death.

Critical Evaluation:

Aimé Césaire's *The Tragedy of King Christophe* has been greeted by struggle, as readers and audiences have difficulty understanding the work, which is based on historical events. Henri Christophe was, in fact, the leading general in the forces of Toussaint Louverture. After the defeat of the French slave masters in Haiti under the command of Christophe and Toussaint Louverture, Christophe became a rebel and revolted against the new Haitian democracy that was then headed by Alexandre Pétion. A city named Pétionville exists in Haiti, but no city in Haiti bears the name of the egotistical Christophe. Traitors deserve no honors.

Christophe had himself named emperor of Haiti, and he governed in an area of northern Haiti that he called the Kingdom of Haiti. Haitians still consider Pétion to be one of the three great early leaders in Haiti, along with the martyred Toussaint Louverture and Jean-Jacques Dessalines, who became the leader of the Haitian Revolution in 1802 after the arrest and deportation to France of Toussaint Louverture. Dessalines declared Haitian independence in 1804 and was assassinated in 1806. Toussaint Louverture died under mysterious circumstances in April, 1804, while he was imprisoned in France.

Interpreting this tragedy is even more complicated because Césaire's unsympathetic title character argues against colonialism in a way that contradicts the arguments developed by Césaire in his *Discours sur le colonialisme* (1950; *Discourse on Colonialism*, 1972). Like many tyrants, Christophe is an effective orator, and he knows how to manipulate people by adapting his arguments so that what he says is what they want to here. There is, however, a contradiction between what Christophe does and what he says.

In his *Discourse on Colonialism*, Césaire argues persuasively that white Europeans are condescending toward people of color and do not respect them as their equals. In addition, he writes that people of color need to reject the racist values of those who seek to dominate them. During Haiti's long colonial period, which began in the seventeenth century and did not end until the 1960's, the French attempted to justify their presence by speaking about their mission to civilize the Haitians.

Until he descends into complete madness in the third act, the self-crowned King Christophe delivers well-structured speeches against racism. Had Césaire made Christophe a sympathetic character with whom readers could identify, readers likely would not have paid careful attention to his words. Readers reject the dangerous behavior of the egotistical Christophe, who endangers the newly acquired independence of Haiti, while, at the same time, agree with the validity of antiracist arguments; readers come to recognize his clear hypocrisy. Toussaint Louverture lost his freedom and then his life so that ordinary Haitians could obtain the basic civil rights to which all people are entitled. Christophe should have understood, as Pétion did, that freedom can be lost if political leaders are more interested in their vanity than in their citizens' basic needs.

France had enriched itself by the slave trade and by slavery. Christophe wants to declare rum the Haitian national drink. Rum is made from the sugar cane that was cut and gathered by slaves. Many people in Haiti and in other former French Caribbean colonies, such as the islands of Martinique and Guadeloupe, refuse to drink rum because of this history.

For more than fifty years after World War II, Césaire served as the mayor of Martinique's capital, Fort-de-France, and represented Martinique as a deputy in France's National Assembly. His solution to the "rum" problem was to have rum distillers on Martinique sell local rum at exorbitant prices. The extra money allowed the distillers to purchase needed farm equipment and, most important, to pay higher wages to their workers. If foreign tourists were willing to pay forty dollars per bottle for Martinican rum, this was fine with Césaire.

King Christophe, however, is an irresponsible brute who does nothing to improve the lives of those whom he is sup-posed to serve. In *Tragedy of King Christophe*, Césaire makes readers and theatergoers think about human dignity, to which all are entitled.

Edmund J. Campion

Further Reading

Davis, Gregson. *Aimé Césaire*. New York: Cambridge University Press, 1997. A thoughtful analysis of levels of meaning in *The Tragedy of King Christophe*. Part of a series on African and Caribbean literature. Includes a bibliography and an index.

Irele, Francis Abiola. "Postcolonial Negritude: Aimé Césaire's Political Plays." *West Africa* (London), January 27, 1968, pp. 100-101. Discusses how the concepts of negritude, or blackness, apply to *The Tragedy of King Christophe*. Césaire created this term, which refers to the positive values of African culture in Africa and in the African diaspora.

Munro, Martin. *Shaping and Reshaping the Caribbean: The Work of Aimé Césaire and René Depestre*. London: Maney, 2000. Describes the central role of Césaire in the development of modern French-language literature in the Caribbean.

Pallister, Janis L. *Aimé Césaire*. New York: Twayne, 1991. A clear overview of Césaire's political career and his importance as a poet, playwright, and essayist.

Suk, Jeannie. *Postcolonial Paradoxes in French Caribbean Writing: Césaire, Glissant, Condé*. Oxford, England: Clarendon Press, 2001. This study of Caribbean writing includes an analysis and discussion of the works of Césaire.

Wilks, Jennifer M. *Race, Gender, and Comparative Black Modernism*. Baton Rouge: Louisiana State University Press, 2008. Describes well the profound influence of Césaire's concept of blackness on many different writers.

The Tragedy of Tragedies
Or, The Life and Death of Tom Thumb the Great

Author: Henry Fielding (1707-1754)
First produced: 1731; first published, 1731
Type of work: Drama
Type of plot: Farce
Time of plot: Age of chivalry
Locale: King Arthur's court

Principal characters:
TOM THUMB THE GREAT, a pocket-size epic hero
KING ARTHUR, Tom Thumb's liege lord
QUEEN DOLLALLOLLA, King Arthur's consort, in love with Tom
PRINCESS HUNCAMUNCA, in love with Tom and Lord Grizzle
LORD GRIZZLE, suitor for Huncamunca's hand
QUEEN GLUMDALCA, a captive giant, in love with Tom

The Story:

According to the legends told in his lifetime, Tom Thumb's peasant father and mother were unable to have any children until Tom's father went to the magician Merlin and received from him a charm that resulted in the wife's giving birth to the valiant but diminutive Tom Thumb. When he reaches manhood, Tom Thumb enters the service of King Arthur, in whose court he accomplishes great deeds and earns a vast reputation. At the court, Queen Dollallolla falls in love with Tom Thumb, loving him, in fact, as much as she loves drinking, but she keeps her love a secret from all. Least of all does she tell King Arthur, who is afraid of no one except his queen.

Tom Thumb's greatest achievement is his victory over the giants who dwell in the land ruled by the amazonian Queen Glumdalca. Tom subdues ten thousand giants and then returns with the surviving foes fastened to his chariot, among them the comely Queen Glumdalca. Because of their size, all the giants except the queen, who is a foot shorter than her subjects, have to be left outside the castle walls. Queen Glumdalca is brought into the castle. As soon as he sees her, King Arthur falls in love with her.

Eager to reward Tom Thumb for his great deeds, the king promises him anything within reason. Tom at first replies that permission to serve his king is sufficient reward. When pressed, however, he asks for the hand of Princess Huncamunca, with whom he has long been in love. The queen is furious that her daughter should become the wife of the man the queen herself loves. She rails at her husband and swears that the marriage should not take place, but the king for once holds his own against his virago queen and tells her to be quiet. The queen, furious also at her husband, goes to Lord Grizzle, a discontented courtier, to secure his aid in preventing the marriage. Lord Grizzle, who is himself in love with Princess Huncamunca, is quite willing to oblige and prom-

ises the queen that he will kill Tom Thumb. Too late, Queen Dollallolla realizes that she does not want Tom killed. She hopes, instead, that King Arthur will die so that she might be free to marry Tom.

When King Arthur tells Princess Huncamunca of his decision to marry her to Tom Thumb, the princess is only too happy to hear of his decision, for she has been in love with Tom for a long time. She has also been afraid that she might die an old maid and, as old superstition would have it, be doomed to lead apes through hell. After the king has gone, Lord Grizzle comes to plead his suit with Princess Huncamunca, who tells him that she loves him, too. Taking her cue from the career of the queen of the giants, who has had twenty husbands, Princess Huncamunca decides that she can love both Tom and Lord Grizzle. She promises to marry Lord Grizzle, and he leaves at once to secure a license for the ceremony.

Shortly after Lord Grizzle has left on his happy errand, Tom Thumb comes to the princess's apartment. Learning of her promise to Lord Grizzle, he pays no attention to it. While he is talking with the princess, Queen Glumdalca comes into the room and offers herself to Tom Thumb, who, she says, would take the place of her twenty former husbands. Tom refuses, saying he prefers the smaller gold coin of Princess Huncamunca to the large dross coin of the giant. Queen Glumdalca leaves in a fury, but her anger abates when she discovers that the king is in love with her.

Tom Thumb hurries Princess Huncamunca off to a parson, who marries them quickly and wishes them at the same time a long life and many children. Lord Grizzle, returning just after the ceremony, finds Princess Huncamunca married to his rival. The princess assures him that there is room in her heart for two husbands and offers to marry him as well. This does not appease Lord Grizzle, who rushes out to create a rebellion and kill Tom Thumb.

That night, the ghost of Tom Thumb's father appears to King Arthur and warns him that Tom's life and the king's rule are both endangered by Lord Grizzle and his rebels. After the ghost's departure, the king sits meditating on what he has been told until the queen, rousing from a drunken slumber, comes to see what is the matter. She is unable to set the king's mind at ease.

The next morning, Tom Thumb, in company with the giant, goes forth to subdue the rebels. On the way to the battlefield, Merlin's magic vouchsafes Tom Thumb a vision in which he sees that he is doomed to be eaten by a red cow. The vision puts him in awe of death, but when Merlin then reveals that Tom will become famous through the medium of the stage, Tom is willing to die.

Lord Grizzle and the army of rebels he has raised under the banner of democracy and freedom advance to meet Tom Thumb and the giant. In the bloody engagement that ensues, Lord Grizzle kills Queen Glumdalca, and Tom avenges her by killing Lord Grizzle. Once their leader is dead, the rebels disperse. Tom cuts off Lord Grizzle's head and starts a victorious march to the castle.

In the castle, the king, queen, and princess await news of the battle, certain that Tom Thumb will triumph and save them from the rebels. Their hopes are fulfilled when a courtier runs in and tells them of Tom's success, but their happiness is short-lived, for the courtier goes on to tell how, on his march back to the castle, Tom Thumb met a large red cow that swallowed poor Tom at a gulp.

Queen Dollallolla, outraged at the courtier for bringing news of her loved one's death, seizes a sword and kills him. The courtier's mistress then kills the queen. Princess Huncamunca, anxious to avenge her mother's death, slays the courtier's mistress. Another courtier uses the occasion to kill Princess Huncamunca because of a grudge he has long held against her. The princess's maid then avenges her mistress by killing Huncamunca's murderer. The king, dispensing justice, kills the maid. Then the king, with bodies lying all around him, kills himself, with the thought that his only glory is that he is the last to die.

Critical Evaluation:

Although Henry Fielding is chiefly remembered as the author of *The History of the Adventures of Joseph Andrews, and of His Friend Mr. Abraham Adams* (1742; commonly known as *Joseph Andrews*) and *The History of Tom Jones, a Foundling* (1749; commonly known as *Tom Jones*), he achieved his first literary success not as a novelist but as a playwright. In fact, it is fair to say that for roughly eight years between 1730 and 1737, during a particularly exciting era in

the life of the London theater, Fielding was the town's single most popular and most celebrated playwright. In 1730 alone, for example, four of Fielding's plays were produced: *The Temple Beau* at the Goodman's Fields Theater and, at the Little Theatre in the Haymarket, *The Author's Farce, and the Pleasures of the Town, Tom Thumb: A Tragedy*, and *Rape upon Rape: Or, Justice Caught in His Own Trap*.

Two of these early plays, *The Author's Farce* and *Tom Thumb*, are farce burlesques that lampoon a variety of targets ranging from well-known London actors and playwrights to such popular dramatic genres as heroic tragedy. Both plays were initial successes, and *Tom Thumb* in particular achieved enormous popularity, running nearly forty nights over a three-month period between April 24 and June 22 to packed houses, at a time when a nine- or ten-night run was considered a success. It was with this type of dramatic satire—high-spirited, immensely entertaining theatrical "hodgepodges" featuring music, dancing, and scenes of burlesque and parody—that Fielding was to achieve his greatest popular and financial success. Unfortunately, it was also this type of satire that eventually proved to be Fielding's undoing in the theater. The satire of *The Historical Register for the Year 1736* (performed in early 1737) proved so biting that it helped bring about the Licensing Act (June 21, 1737) and, only a few days later, the closing of Fielding's Little Theatre in the Haymarket by order of the British prime minister, Sir Robert Walpole. The closing of Fielding's theater marked the close of his career as a playwright.

Fielding's best-known play, *The Tragedy of Tragedies*, began its theatrical life as a short "afterpiece" titled *Tom Thumb*. In the London of Fielding's day, there were sometimes as many as six theaters open at the same time, all of them energetically competing for the theatergoer's money, and it was common practice for theater managers to attempt to vary their menus to please popular tastes. On a particular evening, for example, a theater might offer a play by William Shakespeare or Ben Jonson as a main piece, followed by a pantomime, a brief comic farce, or even an animal act.

This first version of *The Tragedy of Tragedies* is a very general burlesque that takes as its main target the genre of heroic tragedy. Very popular in the Restoration period, these plays tended to emphasize visual spectacle and verbal bombast at the expense of plot and character. An audience does not need prior knowledge of heroic tragedy to find Fielding's little farce amusing, although a knowledge of the ghosts at the conclusion of Thomas Otway's *Venice Preserved: Or, A Plot Discovered* (pr., pb. 1682) would certainly add to one's appreciation of Tom Thumb's brief return as a ghost just before the multiple deaths that end the play. The deaths themselves suggest the carnage at the conclusion of William Shakespeare's *Hamlet, Prince of Denmark* (pr. c. 1600-1601, pb. 1603). The many wonderful incongruities the play offers—beginning with a tragic hero compared to a "Cock-Sparrow" hopping "at the Head of an huge Flock of Turkeys"—are themselves inherently funny. The expanded version of *Tom Thumb*, first presented in March, 1731, as *The Tragedy of Tragedies*, contains most of the original play's words. It is, however, so very different from the original in many important ways as to make it a totally new work.

In addition to being nearly twice as long as the earlier work, *The Tragedy of Tragedies* is intended as much for readers as for theatergoers. Fielding complicated his plot through the addition of new characters and heightened conflicts, but in the published version he also added a huge array of pseudoscholarly material: a wordy preface and a long series of footnotes, all prepared by the fictional pedant H. Scriblerus Secundus. The result is still satire, but a satire both wider in scope and more focused in its intensity.

In the new play, Fielding widens his attack on heroic tragedy; an early editor of *The Tragedy of Tragedies* counted more than forty specific plays that Fielding attacks, most of them from the late seventeenth century, the heyday of heroic tragedy. As in the original version, Fielding burlesques the pompous, inflated language typical of heroic tragedy. Within the spoken text of the play, the satiric approach is relatively simple: Removed from its ostensibly serious context and relocated into the zany world of Fielding's play, such language virtually satirizes itself. The addition of the "learned" commentary of H. Scriblerus Secundus, however, allows Fielding to expand and complicate the satire.

If there is one common thread running through Fielding's literary career, it is his hatred of pedantry and false learning. The character of H. Scriblerus Secundus, with his verbose style and vast knowledge of theatrical trivia, is itself an effectively comic caricature of the pedant, but the joke goes beyond mere caricature. By annotating one passage after another with further quotations from obscure and forgotten plays, and by missing a long series of very obvious allusions to Shakespeare ("wherefore are thou Tom Thumb" is but one particularly flagrant example), Secundus expands the attack on earlier plays, increases the satire against the kind of false, pedantic learning his own practice so vividly exemplifies, and makes an even bigger fool of himself in the process.

The Tragedy of Tragedies has often been seen as in part politically motivated, but while it is possible to see a few general political references in the play (the descriptions of King Arthur and Queen Dollallolla might, for example, suggest King George II and Queen Caroline) there is simply not enough evidence to support a reading of the play as a coherent political satire.

"Critical Evaluation" by Michael Stuprich

Further Reading

Battestin, Martin C. *A Henry Fielding Companion*. Westport, Conn.: Greenwood Press, 2000. Comprehensive reference book covers many aspects of Fielding's life and work. Includes sections on where he lived, his family, literary influences, his works, themes, and characters.

Hume, Robert D. *Henry Fielding and the London Theatre, 1728-1737*. New York: Oxford University Press, 1988. One of the finest studies available of Fielding's too-often-neglected career as a playwright-manager. Hume, probably the foremost scholar in the field of Restoration and eighteenth century drama, writes lucid, entertaining prose and has marshaled a remarkably impressive array of source materials. Highly recommended.

Hunter, J. Paul. *Occasional Form: Henry Fielding and the Chains of Circumstance*. Baltimore: Johns Hopkins University Press, 1975. A widely respected scholar of eighteenth century British literature provides an excellent literary analysis of *The Tragedy of Tragedies*.

Morrissey, L. J. "Critical Introduction." In *"Tom Thumb" and "The Tragedy of Tragedies,"* edited by L. J. Morrissey. Berkeley: University of California Press, 1970. An excellent resource for readers new to *The Tragedy of Tragedies*. Morrissey's informative introduction is followed by both an excellent text of the full-length play and the earlier, afterpiece version of the play, *Tom Thumb*.

Pagliaro, Harold E. *Henry Fielding: A Literary Life*. New York: St. Martin's Press, 1998. Provides an excellent account of Fielding's life and writings. Chapter 2 is devoted to his plays.

Paulson, Ronald. *The Life of Henry Fielding: A Critical Biography*. Malden, Mass.: Blackwell, 2000. Examines how Fielding's literary works—novels, plays, and essays—all contained autobiographical elements. Each chapter begins with an annotated chronology of the events of Fielding's life.

Rawson, Claude, ed. *The Cambridge Companion to Henry Fielding*. New York: Cambridge University Press, 2007. Collection of essays includes an examination of Fielding's life and discussion of his career in journalism as well as essays on topics such as his writing style and his theatrical career.

_____. *Henry Fielding, 1707-1754: Novelist, Playwright, Journalist, Magistrate—A Double Anniversary Tribute*.

Newark: University of Delaware Press, 2008. Collection of essays by Fielding scholars covers all aspects of Fielding's life and work.

Rivero, Albert J. *The Plays of Henry Fielding: A Critical Study of His Dramatic Career.* Charlottesville: University Press of Virginia, 1989. One of the best purely literary studies of Fielding's plays as a whole. Presents an analysis of *The Tragedy of Tragedies* that lacks any sense of the play's wonderful theatrical potential but is useful for its detailed study of Fielding's language.

The Tragic Muse

Author: Henry James (1843-1916)
First published: serial, 1889-1890; book, 1890
Type of work: Novel
Type of plot: Social realism
Time of plot: 1880's
Locale: Paris and England

Principal characters:
NICHOLAS "NICK" DORMER, a young politician and amateur painter
LADY AGNES DORMER, his mother
GRACE DORMER and BIDDY DORMER, his sisters
JULIA DALLOW, their cousin
PETER SHERRINGHAM, her brother
GABRIEL NASH, a friend of Nicholas
MIRIAM ROOTH, an actor
MRS. ROOTH, her mother
BASIL DASHWOOD, an actor

The Story:

Nicholas Dormer, a handsome young bachelor politician and amateur portrait painter, is vacationing in Paris with his formidable mother, Lady Agnes, the impoverished widow of a Liberal politician, and his two younger sisters, "spinsterish" Grace and lively, lovable Biddy. At an art exhibition, Nick meets an old Oxford friend, Gabriel Nash, an aesthete and dilettante but sufficiently a gentleman to be introduced to the ladies. Another visitor in Paris is the Dormers' cousin, Julia Dallow, a rich and politically minded young widow, whose brother, Peter Sherringham, is at the British Embassy there. Nick's fondness for Julia, her devotion to his political career, Biddy's friendship with Julia and unrequited affection for Peter, and Peter and Nick's congeniality unite the family group with particularly close ties. While they are together in Paris, they hear that the member of Parliament for the constituency where Julia's estate and influence lies died suddenly. Guaranteeing her financial as well as political support, Julia wants Nick to stand for election.

This moment of great promise and family solidarity is threatened unobtrusively by Nash's introduction of Mrs. Rooth and Miriam. They are, respectively, a widow of limited means and vague claims to aristocratic connections in England, and her beautiful daughter, who was brought up in a succession of continental pensions where living is cheap, superficially cultivated, and multilingual. To promote Miriam's aspirations toward the stage, Nash arranges an audition with a notable retired French actor whom Peter knows through his passionate interest in the theater. Peter, also invited to the audition, persuades Nick to join him and suggests that Nick should paint Miriam as the Tragic Muse. Although the audition is a fiasco, Peter is sufficiently intrigued to invite the Rooths to a party at his house. There Miriam recites again, meets the ladies of the family, and makes a bad impression on all but Biddy. Julia, disgusted both with Miriam and with what she considers the frivolousness of Nash, returns to England to organize the election campaign, and the Dormers follow soon after. Peter finds himself increasingly involved with Miriam, to the extent of offering to pay for private lessons with the old French actor. At first, he assumes that his interest is in Miriam's potential as an actor, but he eventually realizes that he was in love with her all along.

At Harsh, Julia's principal estate, where Nick wins the election, he proposes to Julia and is accepted. To their mutual happiness there is added an undercurrent of brewing trouble in his assurance that he will give up his painting, her incomprehension of what this will mean to him, and her refusal to set their wedding date. When Nick next goes to see his father's old friend and political ally, Mr. Carteret, he learns that his prospects of being the rich old bachelor's heir depends on his marriage to Julia.

Peter, meanwhile, returning to Paris after leaving London, finds that Miriam has acquired another patron, an English actor named Basil Dashwood. Peter urges her to give up her theatrical ambition for a greater role as wife of a rising diplomat, but she says that she will accept him only as the husband of an actor. In London, Nick and Julia face similar difficulties as Julia plans to spend the Parliamentary recess on a round of strategic country-house visits, while Nick prefers to use his leisure time painting in his studio. With the wedding date set at last, they separate and Nick retires to his studio, where his first visitor is Nash, whom Nick has not seen since their meeting in Paris. Nash tells Nick that Miriam arrived in London after her first success in Paris and wants Nick to make good his promise to paint her as the Tragic Muse. When Nash brings her to the studio the next day, Nick is excited about her possibilities as a portrait subject. Beginning to paint immediately, he waits until later that night to write Julia about it. Julia fails to get the letter because she returns to London unexpectedly, calls to surprise Nick, and is so stunned to find him with Miriam as a sitter that she leaves without a word and is not at home when he calls that evening. When he finally sees her late at night, she breaks the engagement on the grounds that his preference for the artistic life will never be compatible with her own interest in politics.

The next day, Julia leaves for the Continent. Stopping in Paris to see her brother and tell him what happened, she also urges him to marry Biddy. Although he is determined to forget Miriam, Julia's account makes him more eager to see Miriam than Biddy. He finds a pretext for a journey to London, where he goes straight to Miriam's rented villa. Not finding her at home, he then goes to Nick's studio and there finds Biddy alone. Discussing the break between Nick and Julia with Biddy, who is loyal to and sympathetic with both her brother and her friend, Peter fails to understand either of them; but seeing the portrait of Miriam gives him a deeper understanding of the actor's beauty and of Nick's talent. Peter gives Biddy momentary hope by inviting her to the theater that night to see Miriam act. During the rest of his visit, he spends most of his time with the coterie of Miriam's friends who meet at her house to discuss the theater.

Nick is away from London on a visit to the dying Mr. Carteret, to whom he confesses not only that the engagement is broken but also that he just wrote a letter to his constituency resigning his seat in Parliament. Difficult as it is to disappoint his father's old friend, who treats him like a son, Nick finds it even harder to tell his mother, who believes that the sacrifice of his political career betrays his father's memory,

while the dual sacrifice of Mr. Carteret's and Julia's fortunes betrays his sisters and herself. Only Biddy remains loyal to Nick; she spends more and more time at his studio, where she takes up sculpture.

During Peter's prolonged stay in London, the central characters revolve around one another in a tantalizing minuet: Nick sees his devoted younger sister tortured by the knowledge that Peter, whom she loves, is in love with Miriam, and Peter is tortured by Nash's telling him that Miriam is in love with Nick. For the third time Nash, the detached observer of life, precipitates a crisis in the lives of others. Peter tries to maintain his equilibrium by calling on Lady Agnes and accepting an invitation to dinner, but he cancels it at the last minute when he learns that the first night of Miriam's new play is scheduled. Her superb performance increases his passion so much that he tries again to persuade her to give up the stage to marry him, but she repeats her original terms. Defeated by her determination, Peter accepts promotion to a higher post in some remote country and withdraws.

The next year, while Miriam establishes herself rapidly as a success on the London stage, Nick continues to paint her, although with no interest in her except as a subject. His own artistic career is not successful, and he is worried about debts. Biddy refuses a rich suitor. Julia finally comes back to England accompanied by rumors of romance with a leading politician. At this depressing period, Nash reappears and agrees to sit for a portrait, but after only one sitting he disappears again. His encouragement of Nick's artistic bent has a lasting influence, but the complications he evokes began to disappear when he does. Julia makes overtures through Biddy with the suggestion that she wants to sit for a portrait. While Nick and Biddy are discussing this proposal, they are surprised by the arrival at the studio of Miriam and her new husband, Basil, both excited about Miriam's opening that night as Juliet. Although the house is sold out, they manage to get a seat for Biddy as well as for Nick. At the theater, they see Peter, who returns from abroad in time for the first night but too late to declare again his love for Miriam, who married three days before.

With the Tragic Muse established as a public figure, Nick and Peter bring their private affairs to a swift and easy conclusion. Peter arranges for an extension of his leave in order to return to his post with Biddy as his wife. Nick paints a portrait of Julia that attracts the favorable attention of critics at a private viewing. There are also rumors that Julia's other suitor is worried about her. Whether Nick will ever achieve success in the career for which he sacrificed heavily, as Miriam and Peter achieve it in theirs, remains a provocative question for the future.

Critical Evaluation:

Henry James is generally seen as an American novelist whose theme is innocent Americans confronting the formidable culture of Europe, sometimes to their advantage and sometimes not. James can, however, concentrate his attention on the European scene itself. This novel is an unusual study of British characters, although it commences in Paris. It does, however, return to themes that long interested James and has a particular piquancy in its concern with the theater, since James, at the time the novel was published, was making a concentrated attempt to become a successful playwright, an ambition that was to prove beyond him. James knew personally what it was like to fail in the theater, and more to the point of this novel, he knew what it felt like to want desperately to succeed in an art and to be forced to face the facts not only of success but also of failure.

One of the main ideas pursued in this novel is the need to persist as the first step in the artistic life. Both Miriam Rooth and Nicholas Dormer want to be artists, one on the stage, one as a painter. James is interested in that yearning that refuses to heed advice. Miriam seems to have no real talent when she first auditions for Peter Sherringham and the old French actor, but she refuses to give up and takes their seemingly cruel advice stoically, determined to work at her craft despite the lack of encouragement. Nick is, in some ways, even more courageous. Miriam has little to lose; Nick gives up his promising political career, the woman he loves, and the chance at a considerable fortune promised to him by Mr. Carteret if he shows himself a worthy political commodity. James is interested not only in the artistic drive that overrides all opposition but also in what happens to the aspirant who succeeds, as Miriam does, and the person who discovers that the sacrifice is in vain. The music of success is one thing; to face the music of failure is another, and that is Nick's lot.

There is much talk in the novel about the value of art and of trying to be an artist. When one succeeds, as Miriam does, a further question arises in the form of how one maintains the discipline that will allow the artist to be more than a momentary phenomenon. Some of James's ideas may seem to be out of date, but the question of how one makes the best of oneself, and how to continue at a high level of endeavor, leads to what may seem a surprisingly modern confrontation. When Peter, for all his supposed enthusiasm for the arts, suggests that Miriam could do better marrying him in order to live a life of reflected glory as he rises to social and political honor and celebrity in the world of diplomacy, readers may sense that James was ahead of his time.

The confrontation is not a simple one. It is, in part, the culmination of a battle that begins early in the novel in the relationship between Nick Dormer and Julia Dallow. The quarrel in their case is between the value of art versus the value of politics. This question is visited on them almost by chance by Gabriel Nash, Dormer's old college friend and an avowed follower of the aesthetic life, if only as an enlightened spectator.

When the matter comes up again in the confrontation of Peter and Miriam, it takes an ironic turn, in the first instance, since it is Peter who makes it financially possible for Miriam to pursue her studies, and, more important, to appear in a theatrical production. His confidence and special knowledge of the theater make her career, initially. Afterward, however, he argues, somewhat superciliously, that theater is of less importance than the world of diplomacy, and that Miriam ought to be not only satisfied but also exultant in the idea of being the wife of a distinguished ambassador, a position finer in every way than that of being a fine, even a great, actor. Oddly enough, she is not awed by his reasoning. Julia argues from a position of financial power in attempting to suppress Nick's artistic ambitions, and Peter is guilty of male arrogance in his argument.

There are lesser themes in the novel, which are handled with considerable care. The helplessness, for instance, of women in high society when the social status of their family is considerably higher than its income is seen in the Dormer family. The mother, the daughter, and Nick too are dependent upon the chance of a lucky marriage. Neither of his sisters can support herself, and Nick's decision to become a painter is an act of selfishness that is understandable but harrowing to the women. The way in which they stand helpless, waiting for the good marriage or the chance benefactor to provide money, is an example of the constant theme of money that also pervades James's novels. Miriam finds herself able to make a living, but there is no such relief for the Dormer sisters unless they can make a marriage or Nick can make one for them. James is often defined as a novelist of the comfortable world of wealth and privilege. He was fully aware of that world's limitations and how so much of it depends on money.

James's talent for taking such themes and making drama out of them finds its expression in the novel, the suitable medium for him, given his need and gift for complicated, subtle discourse. His ambitions in theater were, given this need, not surprisingly frustrated. Ideas are the major characters in a James novel; one of the gifts that James possessed was his ability to imagine human situations in which his ideas express themselves with intensity and sensitivity. The confrontation between Miriam and Peter over his proposal of marriage has a freshness and pertinence that goes far beyond the requirements of plot and shows the way in which James recognized how constants of the male-female relationship never change, however enlightened the participants.

"Critical Evaluation" by Charles Pullen

Further Reading

Anderson, Quentin. *The American Henry James*. New Brunswick, N.J.: Rutgers University Press, 1957. Anderson argues that the nature of James's relation to European culture has to be seen in the light of his American lineage. Devotes a chapter to *The Tragic Muse*.

Auchincloss, Louis. *Reading Henry James*. Minneapolis: University of Minnesota Press, 1970. Auchincloss, an American novelist, writes from an author's point of view, with a chapter on the novel.

Coulson, Victoria. *Henry James, Women, and Realism*. New York: Cambridge University Press, 2007. Examines James's important friendships with three women: his sister Alice James and the novelists Constance Fenimore Woolson and Edith Wharton. These three women writers and James shared what Coulson describes as an "ambivalent realism," or a cultural ambivalence about gender identity, and she examines how this idea is manifest in James's works, including *The Tragic Muse*.

Flannery, Denis. *Henry James: A Certain Illusion*. Brookfield, Vt.: Ashgate, 2000. An analysis of the concept of illusion in James's works, including *The Tragic Muse*.

Freedman, Jonathan, ed. *The Cambridge Companion to Henry James*. New York: Cambridge University Press, 1998. A collection of essays that provides extensive information on James's life and literary influences and describes his works and the characters in them.

Gard, Roger, ed. *Henry James: The Critical Heritage*. New York: Barnes & Noble, 1968. A selection of essays on various aspects of James's work, including *The Tragic Muse*.

Lane, Christopher. "The Impossibility of Seduction in James's *Roderick Hudson* and *The Tragic Muse*." In *Mapping Male Sexuality: Nineteenth-Century England*, edited by Jay Losey, Elizabeth J. Dell, and William D. Brewer. Madison, N.J.: Fairleigh Dickinson University Press, 2000. Examines the dynamics of male friendship in the two novels.

Leyburn, Ellen Douglas. *Strange Alloy: The Relation of Comedy to Tragedy in the Fiction of Henry James*. Chapel Hill: University of North Carolina Press, 1968. Focuses on how James manipulates the tone of his fiction, sometimes so subtly that readers have to pay very close attention to not fall victim to his ironies.

Otten, Thomas J. *A Superficial Reading of Henry James: Preoccupations with the Material World*. Columbus: Ohio State University Press, 2006. Otten argues that physical surfaces—such as items of clothing and furniture—are a significant element in James's work, making it impossible to determine "what counts as thematic depth and what counts as physical surface." Chapter 4 provides an analysis of *The Tragic Muse*.

Wilson, Michael L. J. "Gender and Vocation in *The Tragic Muse*." In *Questioning the Master: Gender and Sexuality in Henry James's Writings*, edited by Peggy McCormack. Newark: University of Delaware Press, 2000. Argues that James explores art and economics through the prism of gender.

The Tragic Sense of Life in Men and in Peoples

Author: Miguel de Unamuno y Jugo (1864-1936)
First published: Del sentimiento trágico de la vida en los hombres y en los pueblos, 1913 (English translation, 1921)
Type of work: Philosophy

One of the major original thinkers of the twentieth century, Miguel de Unamuno y Jugo defies clear classification. His book, *The Tragic Sense of Life in Men and in Peoples*, for example, is a remarkably unusual philosophical treatise because in it Unamuno passionately rejects formal logic

and accepts paradox and contradiction as essential to his view of life. Even his style, a rhetoric of passion and intensity, is unlike the calm, detached style of the ordinary philosopher. This passion is a fundamental component of his thought.

A Roman Catholic, Unamuno discarded the Church's view of God; a Spaniard, he denounced the monarchy and the Falangists; a philosopher, he rejected any and all systems. His thinking reflects the movement that was to grow into Christian existentialism, but he preserves the Romantic duality of body and spirit and refuses to discard the mystery of the Catholic Eucharist. He is, in short, an outspoken exponent of confusionism, the philosophical approach to the human predicament that he felt most accurately described the human experience.

Looking back to his own spiritual crisis, Unamuno begins *The Tragic Sense of Life in Men and in Peoples* by stating that the only real person is the affective or feeling one, the one of flesh and bone, not the abstract creature of rationalistic philosophers. This person of flesh and blood has only one problem: the longing never to die. This problem is irrational, so all reason builds upon irrationalities. What intensifies the problem is that the individual wants to be only him- or herself. People want to prolong actual flesh-and-bone existence indefinitely. Reason tells people that this is impossible, despite their feelings. Thus, people are caught in a deadlock between reason, which says that all things must die, and passion, which yearns to live forever. The deadlock is tragic because it has no solution. Unamuno says that disease is anything that disturbs unity; therefore, consciousness itself is a disease, the particular disease that causes people to find some means of self-preservation and self-perpetuation. These two human "instincts"—to survive and to love—are the foundations of the individual and of society.

Through love the imagination creates an ideal world in which it perpetuates itself; this is the realm of knowledge. People seek knowledge only to ascertain whether they are really going to die, because after people become conscious of themselves they do not want to die. This search for knowledge of immortality, the tragic sense of life, is the starting point of philosophy. In a stunning summation, Unamuno alters the Cartesian *Cogito, ergo sum* into *sum, ergo cogito*.

Unamuno points out that all religions have sprung from cults of immortality and that people alone of all the animals know themselves distinct from nature. He further points out that the thirst for immortality always stifles the life that passes and never abides. The affirmation of immortality, furthermore, is based only upon the foundation of the desire for immortality. In short, there is no rational, demonstrable basis for religious faith. People cannot escape their tragic fate. Reason attacks blind faith, and faith that does not feel itself secure has to come to terms with reason, but reason and faith can never reach compromise. Each seeks nothing less than the complete destruction of the other. The only religion to bridge these contradictory states and thus bring them into any kind of harmony is Catholicism, because only Catholicism is a system of contradictions in which the greatest danger is to attempt to rationalize the paradoxical solution symbolized by the Eucharist.

Rationalism in any of its forms—materialism, pragmatism, agnosticism, empiricism, pantheism, or science—cannot explain the soul. Reason deals with dead things but is unable to deal with living things that never remain the same for two moments. People, however, are prisoners of logic, without which they cannot think. Thus, people tend always to make logic subservient to the desire for immortality. This need for logic or reason is always a stumbling block of faith, always ending in skepticism, which is an antivitalism. Thus, the longing never to die finds no consolation in reason; still, people cannot exclude reason because to do so would be to reduce themselves to an irrational animal. The only thing left is to accept both faith and reason as an association of continual struggle—faith to absorb the world into the self and to overcome time and space, reason to absorb the self into the world and perpetuate the self in love. Through this inner struggle people create God, for to believe in God is to long for His existence and to act as if God existed.

Having fully stated the problem of human existence, Unamuno turns from analysis to synthesis after carefully warning that he has no intention to construct a system. He begins with the Pauline triad of faith, hope, and charity. Love personalizes its object; in discovering the suffering in the self and in the universe, it personalizes the universe; that is, love creates God. Faith is the longing for the existence of God, a movement toward a practical truth that lets one live, and the creative power in the individual insofar as the individual creates God through love. Hope is love directed toward the future and growing from the disillusionment of the past; the fundamental hope is the hope for eternal life. Spirit cannot exist without matter and matter always limits spirit, so the inherent state of a person is to suffer. Charity is the impulse to liberate the self, others, and God from matter, from suffering. In the passionate longing not to die, one's instinct of living and instinct of knowing thus come into bitter conflict, all the more so because both absolute certainty (faith) and absolute doubt (reason) are denied. Spiritual love is the result of pity, the awareness of suffering in others caused by the death of carnal love; love cannot, for this reason, exist apart from suffering. The personalization of a suffering universe is the highest view of God attainable. This view is the Christian incarnation. This view is necessarily collective and social, although originally it was the subjectivity of an individual consciousness, projected. Reason attempts to define this God created by faith, hope, and charity and in doing so attempts to kill God.

This deadlock between faith and reason reaches its climax in the apocatastasis (the unification of all things, including sinners—even Satan—with God). The essence of religion is the problem of eternal life. People wish to possess God, not to have God possess them because people do not want to lose the ego or the awareness of self, which a complete union with God implies. What people long for is an eternal prolongation of this life; thus any hypothesis of a heaven without change or without suffering must be false because life necessarily posits change and suffering. Eternity must be unending suffering, unceasing faith, hope, and charity, but the New Testament speaks of the apocatastasis, God's coming to be all in all, and of the anacefaleosis, the gathering together of all things in Christ. Thus, not only must salvation be collective, it must also be the fusion of all things into one person. This is the supreme religious sacrifice, the climax of the human tragedy. People want an eternal Purgatory, however, an ascent that never reaches the climax, an eternity of hope, not of salvation.

Unamuno is not satisfied with speculations upon a mythology of the beyond; he is mainly concerned with life here and now. His system of ethics, however, is ultimately associated to his theology. Good is anything that helps one to satisfy one's longing for immortality. Bad is anything that makes one satisfied with a temporal state. The purpose of ethics is to act in such a way that each person becomes irreplaceable so that no one can fill the person's place. A good life is a vital one centered on action for others; thus the apocatastasis is the supreme rule of ethics. Such a life is symbolized for Unamuno by Miguel de Cervantes' Don Quixote, who represents the vitalist whose faith is based on uncertainty, and by Sancho, the rationalist who doubts his own reason. In these two literary figures he sees the epitome of the tragic sense of life, the desperate, unending struggle between faith and reason.

Further Reading

Baker, Armand F. "The God of Miguel de Unamuno." *Hispania* 74, no. 4 (December, 1991): 824-833. Draws upon *The Tragic Sense of Life in Men and in Peoples* to explicate Unamuno's theology of one deity, a "universal consciousness." Calls attention to similarities of Unamuno's work to Buddhism and to Carl Jung's concept of the collective unconscious.

Callahan, David. "The Early Reception of Miguel de Unamuno in England, 1907-1939." *Modern Language Review* 100 (2005 supplement): 235-243. The publication of *The Tragic Sense of Life in Men and in Peoples* in 1921 brought Unamuno to the attention of English readers for the first time in his career. Callahan describes how the book was denounced by English critics yet it determined the perception of the Spanish author in Britain.

Ellis, Robert R. *The Tragic Pursuit of Being: Unamuno and Sartre*. Tuscaloosa: University of Alabama Press, 1988. A short comparison of the existentialism of Unamuno and French philosopher-writer Jean-Paul Sartre.

Ferrater Mora, José. *Unamuno: A Philosophy of Tragedy*. Translated by Philip Silver. Berkeley: University of California Press, 1962. An excellent, brief survey of Unamuno's philosophy. Ferrater Mora tries to understand Unamuno as the philosopher understood himself.

Ilie, Paul. *Unamuno: An Existentialist View of Self and Society*. Madison: University of Wisconsin Press, 1967. Considers Unamuno's contributions to existentialism in relation to Søren Kierkegaard, Friedrich Nietzsche, Martin Heidegger, Karl Jaspers, and Jean-Paul Sartre.

Luby, Barry J. *The Uncertainties in Twentieth- and Twenty-First Century Analytic Thought: Miguel de Unamuno the Precursor*. Newark, Del.: Juan de la Cuesta, 2008. Explains Unamuno's theories, including his concepts of consciousness, mind and body, language, reality, epistemology, and religion. Describes how his ideas influenced other analytic philosophers and modern scientists.

Nozick, Martin. *Miguel De Unamuno*. New York: Twayne, 1971. An analysis of Unamuno's thought and an evaluation of his literary art. Contains a short biography and a good bibliography.

Wyers, Francis. *Miguel De Unamuno: The Contrary Self*. London: Tamesis Books, 1976. Attempts to make sense of the sometimes violent contradictions in Unamuno's thought, and places him as a precursor to existentialism.

Trainspotting

Author: Irvine Welsh (1958-   )
First published: 1993
Type of work: Novel
Type of plot: Picaresque fiction
Time of plot: Late 1980's-early 1990
Locale: Edinburgh and London

Principal characters:

MARK "RENTS" RENTON, a twenty-five-year-old heroin
    addict and sometime thief; part of a group of friends
    known as the Skag Boys
SIMON "SICK BOY" WILLIAMSON, Mark's friend, a fellow
    heroin addict and Skag Boy
SPUD MURPHY, a heroin addict, thief, and Skag Boy
TOMMY MACKENZIE, a friend of the Skag Boys, an avid
    soccer player who initially strives to avoid drugs
FRANCIS BEGBIE, a violent, alcoholic, chain-smoking
    friend of the Skag Boys
JOHNNY "MOTHER SUPERIOR" SWAN, a well-established
    drug dealer who supplies the Skag Boys with their
    heroin and related equipment
MIKE FORRESTER, a low-level drug dealer and
    acquaintance of the Skag Boys

The Story:

Mark Renton is a heroin addict with a reputation for randomly kicking his habit and relapsing just as suddenly. His propensity to do both is a joke among his friends and acquaintances. Mark prepares to go with his friend Sick Boy to see their dealer, Mother Superior, as Sick Boy is in withdrawal. Mark and Sick Boy belong to a group of heroin addicts known as the Skag Boys, and most people except for their closest associates try to avoid them.

During the Edinburgh Festival, Mark attempts to imitate Sick Boy's method of coming off heroin. He uses one hit of heroin to help him deal with the relative torture of going to the grocery store—a place he typically avoids because it is full of nonaddicts who annoy him. Mark realizes that, at least for the time being, Mother Superior has disappeared, and the only other drug contact he has is Mike Forrester. Mark goes to Mike's place to get a hit, but Mike senses Mark's desperation and makes him suffer through a number of jokes and mind games before he will give Mark anything. Finally, Mike produces opium suppositories, which he claims are the perfect thing to help Mark break his addiction to drugs for good, as they are slow release. Mark declares that he wants a hit of heroin, but he pays for the opium anyway.

Soon, both Sick Boy and Mark are off heroin. Sick Boy is only interested in attracting women, and Mark is concerned about Sick Boy's sexist attitudes, which annoy him. As Sick Boy contemplates which of the young women he has just met will have sex with him, the thought of acquired immuno-

deficiency syndrome (AIDS) courses through his mind. He reasons that if did not contract AIDS by sharing needles with the rest of the Skag Boys, then he could not get it by having intercourse with a woman. He is reminded of a friend of both himself and Mark, Goagsie, who is human immunodeficiency virus (HIV)-positive: It is unclear how Goagsie contracted the virus. Those with HIV and AIDS serve as a warning to others who are at risk, especially heroin addicts. Sick Boy laments that, without heroin or a woman and her money, he has nothing with which to fill himself. Since he has given up heroin as being unsafe, all he has left is women and their money.

The Skag Boys are awakened to the screaming of a woman named Lesley: Dawn, her baby, is dead. Mark notices that the infant resembles Sick Boy; however, he realizes that she could have been the child of any of the Skag Boys.

At night, the Skag Boys and their friends and acquaintances are at a pub. Mark fetches drinks for everyone. When Begbie finishes drinking from a glass pitcher, he throws it over his shoulder and off the balcony. The act creates chaos. The scene is indicative of why Mark has grown tired of Begbie's company. He has been forced to be his friend since elementary school, but, as Begbie's violence has increased, so has Mark's impatience with him.

Tommy, a soccer-playing friend of the Skag Boys, is dumped by his girlfriend Lizzy. He goes to visit Mark while Mark is relapsing and back on heroin. Tommy is curious about heroin and what it does for people. Mark introduces Tommy to heroin.

Without heroin, Mark experiences clarity of thought and an analytic ability that eludes him when he is on drugs. At a nightclub, Mark notices the ease with which Sick Boy and Begbie gain the affection of women. He tries to convince himself that one of the women is unattractive but corrects himself as he realizes that his thoughts are fueled by jealousy. At the end of the night, Mark and Spud take speed and discuss going back on heroin, an idea that Spud does not like.

Before the night is over, Mark meets Dianne. They go to Dianne's place, which turns out to be the house she lives in with her parents. Dianne is not a grown woman but a girl in her first year of high school. Mark finds this out the next morning, and he resolves to avoid future sexual contact with Dianne. Mark's brother, Billy, reenlists in the army and is sent to Belfast.

Mark and Spud return to their heroin habits. To support their habits, they shoplift and are arrested for stealing books. Spud is sentenced to jail immediately, but Mark is released upon the condition that he continue trying to get off drugs. Afterward, Mark, his friends, his parents, and Billy meet at a pub for a celebration of sorts. Spud's mother comes in, accusing the Skag Boys of causing her son's downfall. Begbie informs her that he tried to get Spud off drugs. Although he is surrounded by everyone he knows, Mark feels alone. He goes to see Mother Superior to get heroin, leaving his party behind. He subsequently overdoses. His parents keep him at home to get him clean.

Mark's brother Billy is killed in a bombing in Ireland. Mark giggles at the funeral. The mourners return to the Renton house after the burial. Mark leaves the funeral before his family and gets a ride from Tommy and others, who will not go inside. Once the rest of the family arrives, Mark has sex with his brother's pregnant girlfriend, Sharon. They go to his apartment and talk.

Mark experiences his second funeral after his friend Matty dies of toxoplasmosis. Matty was infected with HIV. He acquired a kitten in an attempt to win back his girlfriend, but she refused the kitten, so he was forced to take it home, where it defecated and urinated as it pleased. The kitten's excrement created a breeding ground for the toxoplasmosis that killed Matty. Mark visits Mother Superior after the dealer has had his leg amputated as a result of injecting heroin into it. Mark marvels that the former drug dealer is still HIV negative. Tommy, however, is HIV positive.

The Skag Boys' last group activity is an accidental opportunity to carry out the largest drug deal of their lives. They acquire almost twenty thousand pounds worth of heroin from Mike Forrester, who is anxious to get rid of it. The group goes to London to carry out the transaction with big-time dealers. Pete Gilbert is the London contact that Sick Boy acquires through an older man, Andreas. When the meeting is set up, Pete offers the group from Edinburgh sixteen thousand pounds for the drugs. They take it, even though they want four thousand more.

After the deal, Spud and Second Prize go to London's SoHo neighborhood to celebrate. Mark is left in charge of the money at Andreas's house. Neither Sick Boy nor Begbie trusts Spud or Second Prize with the money. Begbie and Sick Boy go to play pool. The drug money is in Begbie's athletic bag, and with Andreas distracted by his girlfriend and the Skag Boys out of the way, Mark is free to steal the money and use it to fund a new life in Amsterdam.

Mark decides the only one of his former friends he will try to compensate is Spud, because Spud has always meant well and has never been cared for. Mark reasons that Sick Boy would have stolen the money himself if he had had the chance. Begbie is the excuse Mark gives himself for cheating his entire group of friends. He theorizes that Begbie's psychotic behavior is reason enough to disappoint him. Mark makes his way through London on his way to Amsterdam. He remains hopeful for his future.

Critical Evaluation:

Trainspotting was Irvine Welsh's debut novel. It was published first in the United Kingdom in 1993, and in 1996 an American edition was published. Welsh lives in Edinburgh and London. He held a plethora of jobs before becoming a writer. The groundwork for *Trainspotting* was built in short story collections and novellas, where he told the stories of arguably interesting and disturbed characters.

Trainspotting stands out because of its creation primarily through dialogue. The dialogue consists of the characters' Scottish-dialect conversations both with one another and with readers. Rare passages in the book are written in the traditional third person, in Standard English, easily understood by American readers. A glossary of key terms is provided to inform readers of the definitions of key slang words used throughout.

The use of characters' dialect is an essential tool for immersing readers into Welsh's world of junkies, prostitutes, and those who associate with them. Welsh's plot is full of the philosophies of those on the margins of society, including the rationalizations used to make the most unconventional choices. It also incorporates many references to popular culture. The Skag Boys and their friends are fans of violent martial arts films, and their music consists of Iggy Pop and David

Bowie, not the then-new genre of techno music. The world of working-class Edinburgh is home for the Skag Boys, and it is bleak. It is a world of high unemployment rates and, consequently, widespread drug abuse, prostitution, racism, and violence.

Trainspotting is, in literary terms, a picaresque novel, one that details the life of a rather unsavory male character of low social esteem who serves two masters and, through his experiences, offers a satiric critique of his society. Mark "Rents" Renton emerges as the predominant voice in the novel because his perspective is the one that allows readers the clearest glimpse into the philosophy (albeit troubled), of the heroin addict. At the same time, he points out the disturbing aspects of life in late twentieth century Edinburgh.

Mark's two masters are himself and heroin. Instead of wanting to remain tied to his friends, Mark can think of nothing but ridding himself from them and, hopefully, from his heroin addiction in the process. This is not to say that Mark did not purposefully choose to begin taking heroin, but he maintains that he did so only because, compared to the banal choices around him, heroin was his best option.

The sections and chapters that feature Mark's perspective move the novel. The book is full of characters who have their own dramatic moments, but the key sequences occur when Mark narrates. Welsh sets Mark up to be an unreliable narrator, as his flaws are exposed with unflinching clarity: He is a heroin addict, he hallucinates, he steals, and he is selfish. With this problematic character comes the honesty with which Mark tells his story and that of his friends and environment. Incorporating personal, political, and social perspectives, Mark's narratives are the best-rounded in the novel.

When the story reaches areas Mark is no longer willing to discuss, Welsh inserts a third-person limited narrator to tell readers what is going on as seen through Mark's eyes. Mark, however, is finished with his role in the novel. By the end, he is on his way to Amsterdam and cannot be bothered to comment on the Edinburgh situation further. It is through a Standard English voice that readers can "see" the most developed character in the book walk into the horizon of his own choosing.

Dodie Marie Miller

Further Reading

Blackwell, Bonnie. "The Society for the Prevention of Cruelty to Narrative." *College Literature* 31, no. 4 (Winter, 2004): 1-26. Examines Mark Renton's use of language and his philosophy on verbal speech as one that is less pro-drugs and more antispeech as a means to socialization.

Cardullo, Bert. "Fiction into Film, or Bringing Welsh to a Boyle." *Literature Film Quarterly* 25, no. 3 (1997): 158-163. Discusses the dynamics of adapting *Trainspotting* into a motion picture.

Farred, Grant. "Wankerdom: *Trainspotting* as a Rejection of the Postcolonial?" *South Atlantic Quarterly* 103, no. 1 (Winter, 2004): 215-226. Addresses the social and mythical construction of Scotland, as seen by late twentieth century Scots, particularly the fictional Mark Renton.

Hemingway, Judy. "Contested Cultural Spaces: Exploring Illicit Drug-Using Through *Trainspotting*." *International Research in Geographical and Environmental Education* 15, no. 4 (2006): 324-335. Presents drug use statistics in Britain. *Trainspotting* is used to explore Edinburgh's realms of high and low culture and to discern the role of physical space and culture among drug-using and marginalized populations.

MacLeod, Lewis. "Life Among the Leith Plebs: Of Arseholes, Wankers, and Tourists in Irvine Welsh's *Trainspotting*." *Studies in the Literary Imagination* 41, no. 1 (Spring, 2008): 89-106. Argues that *Trainspotting* is a story of two cities, Leith and Edinburgh, and of those with material wealth and those without. Examines the representation of these contrasts in the novel through dialogue, sense of place, and character philosophy.

The Travels of Lao Ts'an

Author: Liu E (Liu Tieyun, 1857-1909)
First transcribed: Lao Can youji, 1904-1907, serial
  (English translation, 1952; revised, 1990)
Type of work: Novel
Type of plot: Social realism
Time of plot: End of the nineteenth century
Locale: Shandong Province, China

Principal characters:
LAO TS'AN, an itinerant intellectual
SHEN TUNG-TSAO and HUANG JEN-JUI, decent officials
KANG PI and YÜ HSIEN, incorruptible but ruthlessly
  ambitious officials
TS'UI-HUAN and TS'UI-HUA, young women of good family
  who become singsong girls
YELLOW DRAGON, a hermit philosopher

The Story:

Lao Ts'an is an erudite and impoverished scholar who uses his skills in traditional Chinese medicine to earn a modest living in his native homeland of Shandong. Although he is only about thirty years old, his fame begins to grow as more and more people hear about his successful treatment of Huang Jui-ho's running sores, which had long defied the ministrations of many other doctors. After Lao Ts'an adeptly cures a serious throat condition afflicting the concubine of an official named Kao, the official introduces the young man to his colleagues, including the governor of Shandong Province.

Lao Ts'an's conversation with the governor and other officials quickly turns from medicine to current events and politics. Two topics that arise during this conversation are the prosecutorial overzealousness of especially ambitious officials such as Yü Hsien and Kang Pi, who would rather err on the side of punishing many innocent citizens than let a single criminal go unpunished, and the ineffective policies intended to control the Yellow River's flooding. The governor is so impressed by Lao Ts'an's sensible views on these problems that he offers the young man an official post. Lao Ts'an politely declines, insisting that he prefers to offer advice in an informal capacity. Privately, Lao Ts'an realizes that his fondness for frankly expressing his views on controversial topics would be difficult to maintain if he were to become an official. Also, he is not interested in the wealth and power, not to mention the restrictions on his independent way of life, that an official career would bring.

Through various inquiries, Lao Ts'an determines that Yü Hsien's harsh crackdown on banditry in the county of Ch'engwuhsien is resulting in the torture and execution of many innocents while not actually reducing the incidence of banditry in the area. Lao Ts'an thereupon manages to persuade one of Yü Hsien's well-meaning subordinates, Shen Tung-tsao, to take a personal letter from Lao Ts'an to one of his friends in the countryside who is well versed in martial arts and acquainted with many leaders of bandit gangs in the vicinity. As a favor to Lao Ts'an, his friend agrees with Shen Tung-tsao's request to move to Ch'engwuhsien and persuade the bandit gang leaders to stop preying on the county's residents—in other words, to take their business elsewhere. The county's crime rate drops at once, for the only bandit attacks that subsequently occur involve isolated capers undertaken by unskilled local criminal riffraff. These criminals are much easier to apprehend than members of the bandit gangs, and so the county's streets and alleys soon become among the safest in the entire province.

Lao Ts'an subsequently turns his attention to the problem of the prosecutorial fervor of Yü Hsien and Kang Pi, which has resulted in many wrongful convictions and executions of innocent persons. Like a Chinese Sherlock Holmes, the young scholar shrewdly investigates the background of a murder case involving a respectable family in the district. At considerable risk of being arrested and tortured by Kang Pi, Lao Ts'an appears at the latter's court to defend the wrongly accused. He is too late to save all of the family members from torture, but he does manage to uncover damning evidence against the true culprit, whom he orders arrested and brought forth. By doing so, Lao Ts'an spares most of the wrongly accused from further torture and likely execution. The overzealous officials suffer a judicial setback and are transferred to another post.

Lao Ts'an learns that two young women, Ts'ui-huan and Ts'ui-hua, have been sold into a brothel as singsong girls after their families were impoverished in the wake of the Yellow River's flooding. The kindly official Huang Jen-jui eventually convinces Lao Ts'an to redeem Ts'ui-huan from her brothel and take her as his lawfully betrothed concubine. Lao Ts'an subsequently returns the favor by setting up the already married Huang Jen-jui with Ts'ui-hua as his second wife. Premodern China's traditional acceptance of polygamy thus allows the story's loose ends to be tied together.

Critical Evaluation:

It had become a commonplace for Chinese novels of Liu E's day to castigate corrupt officials who would do practically anything in return for a bribe. While Liu E acknowledges the harm done by official malfeasance, he focuses on a less obvious but similarly grave betrayal of the public trust: that of the "honest" official who desires fame and promotion rather than mere profit, and whose conscience remains unruffled while he imposes the most Draconian and indiscriminate crackdowns. As one of the most fascinating late nineteenth century scholarly entrepreneurs, whose achievements ranged from shrewd railway investments to the discovery of the Shang Dynasty oracle bone script, Liu E had his share of run-ins with ruthless officials. Yuan Shih-k'ai, for example, used his influence to get the author arrested on trumped-up charges and exiled to Chinese Turkestan. There Liu E died, a victim of official arrogance, in 1909, a short time after completing his novel satirizing the abuse of power.

In Lao Ts'an, Liu E created a protagonist who embodied many of his own values. These included a conviction that traditional Chinese thought contained many insights that one could combine with aspects of Western thought in formulating ways to deal with the crises that China faced in the modern world. Just as Liu E admired the syncretist teachings of the T'ai-ku school, which combined the Three Teachings (Buddhism, Confucianism, and Daoism), Lao Ts'an finds the same ideas, as voiced by a reclusive scholar nicknamed Yellow Dragon, noteworthy. Yellow Dragon promulgates a middle way between the extremes of Europeanized Chinese revolutionaries, who want to sweep away all traditional Chinese ways, and backward-looking traditionalists such as the Boxers, who categorically reject all ideas from the West. Yellow Dragon argues that while the acceptance of certain Western ideas entails the rejection of negative aspects of traditional Chinese thought, China still needs to base its adaptation to global realities on the foundation of the most workable features of its traditional civilization.

As an example of a negative aspect of traditional Chinese civilization that should be rejected in favor of a Western approach, Lao Ts'an points to a friend's Chinese opium lamp. He does not do so to make the point that Chinese should not let themselves become addicted to drugs such as opium, although he quietly warns his friend of opium's addictive nature and refuses to smoke it whenever some is offered to him; Lao Ts'an instead marvels at the fine workmanship of the opium lamp and laments that China's lack of patent law means that excellent craftsmanship goes mostly unrewarded in China, in contrast to the situation in the West. In his view, China's technological backwardness in comparison with the West is, in considerable part, caused by neglect of the need to reward invention and innovation.

Traditional Chinese thought also holds, in the novel, many answers to China's problems. For example, Lao Ts'an uses his knowledge of the ancient Han Dynasty tracts on flood prevention to persuade key officials to discard the failed river-management policy of widening the Yellow River's channel, which leads to rapid silt buildup on the riverbed, swollen riverbanks, and the subsequent bursting of dikes. He convinces the officials to adopt instead the wise approach of deepening the river channel through dredging, thereby increasing the speed of water flow and decreasing the amount of silt deposited on the river bed.

Perhaps the most striking aesthetic feature of *The Travels of Lao Ts'an* is its density of allegorical motifs. The name of the first patient Lao Ts'an cures, Huang Jui-ho, contains the two Chinese characters used for the "Yellow River," *huang* and *ho*. The sores breaking out all over Huang Jui-ho's body are an allegory for the breaching of the dikes and flooding of the Yellow River valley. The successful healing of the sores is a reference to the decrease of flooding that occurs once the officials take Lao Ts'an's advice to dredge the middle of the Yellow River's channel so as to increase the speed of the water flow. Similarly, a dream that Lao Ts'an has about a huge leaking sailboat on which puzzled helmsmen and a tumultuous crowd are milling about is an allegory for the state of confusion that overcame China in the last years of the Qing Dynasty (1644-1911). The passengers' violent rejection of Lao Ts'an's well-meant advice reflects the despair that Liu E sometimes felt about the possibilities of reform in China—a sadly accurate presentiment.

Philip F. Williams

Further Reading

Holoch, Donald. "*The Travels of Laocan*: Allegorical Narrative." In *The Chinese Novel at the Turn of the Century*, edited by Milena Doleželová-Velingerová. Toronto: University of Toronto Press, 1980. Analyzes the two allegorical incidents in the novel's first chapter and argues that the remainder of the novel can be seen as a structural elaboration of these opening allegories.

Hsia, C. T. *A History of Modern Chinese Fiction*. 3d ed. Bloomington: Indiana University Press, 1999. Appendix 1, "Obsession with China: The Moral Burden of Modern Chinese Literature," includes information on Liu E and *The Travels of Lao Ts'an*.

_____. "*The Travels of Lao Ts'an*: An Exploration of Its Art and Meaning." In *C. T. Hsia on Chinese Literature*.

New York: Columbia University Press, 2004. Combines a thorough analysis of the novel's key aesthetic features with interesting historical research on the pro-Boxer Rebellion officials who served as Liu E's models for Yü Hsien and Kang Pi, who run roughshod over the guilty and the innocent alike in order to garner fame as hanging judges.

Kwong, Luke S. K. "Self and Society in Modern China: Liu E (1857-1909) and *Laocan youji*." *T'oung Pao* 87, nos. 4/5 (2001): 360-392. Examines Liu E's life and career, describing how his experiences provide an idea of the thoughts, feelings, and aspirations of China's educated elite during the last decades of the Qing Dynasty. Includes discussion of *The Travels of Lao Ts'an*.

Lang, D. M., and D. R. Dudley, eds. *The Penguin Companion to Classical, Oriental, and African Literature*. New York: McGraw-Hill, 1969. Includes a section on Liu E that emphasizes the stylistic advance represented by *The Travels of Lao Ts'an* in its highly original prose descriptions of landscape and musical performances.

Lin, Shuen-fu. "The Last Classic Chinese Novel: Vision and Design in *The Travels of Laocan*." *Journal of the American Oriental Society* 121, no. 4 (October-December, 2001): 549-564. Places *The Travels of Lao Ts'an* within the literary and cultural contexts of the last years of the Qing Dynasty. Discusses the structure and "lyric vision" of the novel, its authorial point of view, its juxtaposition of the harsh realities of early twentieth century China with idealized characters and utopian settings, and the protagonist's conflict between his scientific attitude and his traditional Chinese values.

Lu Hsün. *A Brief History of Chinese Fiction*. Translated by Yang Hsien-yi and Gladys Yang. Beijing: Foreign Languages Press, 1976. Includes a section on "novels of exposure" of the Qing Dynasty that contains an analysis of *The Travels of Lao Ts'an*'s portrayal of the official Kang Pi, whose incorruptibility is offset by his autocratic and ruthless ways.

Shadick, Harold. Introduction to *The Travels of Lao Ts'an*, by Liu E. Rev. ed. New York: Columbia University Press, 1990. Informative introduction to the novel provides an excellent starting place for students of the work.

The Travels of Marco Polo

Author: Marco Polo (c. 1254-1324)
First transcribed: Divisament dou monde, fourteenth century (English translation, 1579)
Type of work: Autobiography
Type of plot: Adventure
Time of plot: 1260-1295
Locale: Greater Asia

Principal characters:
NICOLO POLO, a Venetian merchant
MAFFEO POLO, his brother
MARCO POLO, Nicolo's son
KUBLAI KHAN, the emperor of China

The Story:

Nicolo and Maffeo Polo set forth on their first trip to the East in 1260, with a cargo of merchandise for Constantinople. From there, they venture on into the lands of the Tartar princes. Having at last reached the court of Kublai Khan, China's emperor, they manage to ingratiate themselves into his highest favor. During their stay, the khan questions them about the Catholic faith and asks them to return to Europe and ask the pope to send missionaries to his distant land. In the year 1269, the two Polos arrive in Venice. There they learn that Pope Clement is dead, and that Nicolo Polo's wife also died after giving birth to a son, Marco Polo.

There is a long delay in the naming of a new pope. At last, the Polos decide to return to Kublai Khan and to take young Marco with them. Scarcely do they leave Italy, however, when word follows that Gregory the Tenth was elected in Rome. The Polos at once ask the new pope to send missionaries to Kublai Khan, and Gregory appoints two priests to accompany the merchants. Before their arrival at the khan's court, the priests turn back when confronted by strange lands and unknown dangers. Young Marco Polo remembers that the journey to the land of Kublai Khan took three and a half years.

Kublai Khan receives them graciously and appoints Marco one of his attendants. In a short time, Marco learns four different languages, and he is sent by Kublai Khan on various important missions. For seventeen years, the Polos remain at the court of Kublai Khan before they express a desire to return to their own country with their wealth. They feel that if the great khan should die, they will be surrounded by envious princes who might harm them. The khan is unwilling to part with the Polos, but they manage to get his permission by offering to transport some barons to the East Indies. Fourteen ships are made ready for the homeward voyage. The expedition arrives at Java after about three months. Eighteen months more are required for the voyage to the territory of King Argon in the Indian seas. During the voyage, six hundred of the crew are lost as well as two of the barons. From there, the Polos take an overland route to Trebizond. En route, they learn that the great Kublai Khan is dead. The three arrive home safely in 1295, in possession of their wealth and in good health.

When the time comes for him to dictate to the scribe, Rustichello, the story of his travels, Marco remembers that Armenia is divided into two sections, the lesser and the greater. In Armenia Major is the mountain said to have been Mount Ararat, where Noah's ark came to rest. Near this place is a fountain of oil so great that caravans of camels haul away the oil, which is used for an unguent as well as for heat and light.

At the boundaries of the province of Georgiania, Alexander the Great had a gate of iron constructed. This gate, although not all of iron, is commonly said to enclose the Tartars between two mountains.

At Teflis is a fountain wherein hundreds of fish make their appearance from the first day of Lent until Easter Eve. During the remainder of the year, they are not to be seen. Baudas, or Baghdad, known in ancient times as Babylon, lies along the river that opens out upon the Sea of India. The city is one of the great cities of the world and its ruler one of the richest men of all time. He loses his life through his unwillingness to spend a penny of his wealth for its protection. His captor locks him up in his tower, where he starves to death surrounded by gold. In that region, a Christian cobbler causes a mountain to move and, by his miracle, converts many Arabs to Christianity.

In Irak, Marco visits a monastery in which the monks weave woolen girdles said to be good for rheumatic pains. He also visits Saba, from where it is said came the three Magi who adored Christ in Bethlehem. At Kierman, on the eastern confines of Persia, Marco sees the manufacture of steel and products in which steel is used. Much rich embroidery is also found there, as well as splendid turquoises. The Karaunas of the region learn the diabolical art of producing darkness in order to obscure their approach to caravans they intend to rob.

At Ormus, Marco encounters a wind so hot that people exposed to it die. A whole army is once wiped out by the wind, and the inhabitants, seeking to bury the invaders, find the bodies baked so hard that they cannot be moved. Bitter, undrinkable water, the tree of the sun, and the old man of the mountain are all from that region. The old man of the mountain administers drugs to young men to make them think they are truly in paradise. At his orders, they assassinate anyone who is not of the true faith. His followers hold their own lives of little worth, convinced that they will return to Paradise upon their deaths.

On the overland route to Cathay, Marco meets Nestorian Christians as well as people who are part Christian and part Muhammadan. There he finds a miraculous pillar said to remain upright without visible means of support. In Peyn, he discovers chalcedony and jasper as well as peculiar marriage customs. Passing over a desert, he hears strange sounds that are attributed to evil spirits but are later explained as the sounds of shifting sand dunes. At Kamul, he discovers the primitive hospitality of turning over houses and wives for the entertainment of strangers. At Chinchitalas, he discovers the use of material that will not burn, asbestos.

On the borders of the Gobi, the Polos gather supplies for their trip through the desert. They pass close to the land of Prester John and hear the history of the war between Prester John and Genghis Khan. Marco sees the land of Tenduk, governed by the princes of the race of Prester John.

Kublai Khan is a great king who rewards generously those who aid him in the conquest of other nations. Each noble so favored receives a golden tablet inscribed by the khan for the protection of its wearer. Kublai Khan has four principal wives, plus a number of women who are given to him each year. He has some fifty sons, all of whom are appointed to high places in the empire. In the winter, the khan lives in Peking, in a magnificent palace that is eight miles square. His personal bodyguard consists of twelve thousand horsemen.

Greatest in interest among his people are the Tibetans, who produce the scent of musk, use salt for money, and dress in leather. Gold dust is found in their rivers, and among them are said to be sorcerers. Karazan is known for its huge serpents, or crocodiles, which the natives kill for hides and gall. This gall is a medicine for bites from mad dogs.

In Kardandan, Marco observes fathers who take over the nursing of babies. In the city of Mien, he sees two towers, one of silver and one of gold. Bengal he finds rich in cotton, spikenard, galangal, ginger, sugar, and many drugs. The region also supplies many eunuchs.

For a time, Marco holds the government of the city of Yan-Gui upon orders of the khan. Nicolo and Maffeo Polo aid the khan in overcoming the city of Sa-Yan-Fu, the two Venetians having designed a catapult capable of hurling stones weighing as much as three hundred pounds.

Marco thinks the city of Kin-sai, or Hang-chau, so beautiful that the inhabitants might imagine themselves in paradise. There are twelve thousand bridges over the canals and rivers of the city, and the houses are well-built and adorned with carved ornaments. The streets are paved with stone and brick. The people are greatly concerned with astrology. The inhabitants provide for firefighters who keep a constant guard throughout the city. From this city, the khan receives revenue of gold, salt, and sugar.

In the kingdom of Kon-cha, Marco finds people who eat human flesh. He also finds there a kind of chicken covered with black hair instead of feathers. He observes with much interest the manufacture of Chinese porcelain. In his travels, he sees the merchant ships of India, which are large and built in sections so that if one section springs a leak, it can be closed off while repairs are made. On the island of Java he obtains pepper, nutmeg, spikenard, galangal, cubebs, cloves, and gold. Idolators live there as well as cannibals. Elephants, rhinoceroses, monkeys, and vultures are in abundance. He also discovers that the natives pickle certain monkeys so that they resemble dead pygmies. These creatures are then sold as souvenirs to sailors and merchants.

In Lambri, he sees what he thinks are men with tails. He also sees the sago tree, from which the natives make flour. On the island of Nocueran, he visits people living like naked beasts in trees. They possess the red and white sandalwood, coconuts, sapanwood, and cloves. At Angaman, he sees more cannibals. In Ceylon, he finds rubies, sapphires, topazes, amethysts, and garnets. The grave of Adam is believed to be on a high mountain in Ceylon.

Marco thinks India the noblest and richest country in the world. Pearls are found in abundance. The kingdom of Murphili is rich in diamonds. In the province of Lac, he hears that people often live to the age of one hundred fifty years and manage to preserve their teeth by a certain vegetable they chew. In Kael, he finds people chewing a leaf called tembul, sometimes mixed with camphor and other aromatic drugs as well as quicklime. At Cape Comorin, he finds apes of such a size as to appear like men. At Malabar, he finds gold brocades, silk, gauzes, gold, and silver. At Guzzerat, he discovers pirates of the worst character. In Bombay, he buys incense and horses.

Marco visits the island of Madagascar, where the inhabitants report a bird so large it is able to seize an elephant in its talons. He thinks the women of Zanzibar the ugliest in the world. The people do business in elephant teeth and tusks.

Marco recalls how Kublai Khan and his nephew, Kaidu, fought many battles for the possession of Great Turkey. More than a hundred thousand horsemen were brought to fight for each side. At first, Kaidu was victorious. Kaidu had a mannish daughter, Aigiarm, who battled with any man who wanted her for a bride. At last, she seized the man of her choice from the hosts of enemies in battle.

Marco believes that Russia is a region too cold to be pleasant. He speaks of trade in ermine, arcolini, sable, marten, fox, silver, and wax among the natives, who are included in the nation of the king of the Western Tartars. Marco gives thanks to God that the travelers are able to see so much and return to tell about the marvels of many lands.

Critical Evaluation:

The story of Marco Polo's Asiatic journey is one of the most astounding of all travel books of Western civilization. One reason for its popularity is that Marco did not mind mixing fiction and fact. Another is that he possessed in high degree a quality few travelers ever have: the ability to see new things objectively.

The Travels of Marco Polo was passed down in many manuscript versions, none of which is the original. Although it is nearly certain that the scribe Rustichello transcribed the original manuscript in French, manuscripts are extant in almost all of the Western European languages. None of the extant manuscripts is complete; hence, much scholarly attention was focused on speculation about what material was present in the original version and what material was interpolated by later scribes. At least an equal amount of attention is focused on trying to distinguish Marco Polo's observations from the embellishments of Rustichello. To some extent, Chinese historical records are helpful in settling some of these questions. A lesser, although nevertheless vexing, problem arises in attempting to correlate Marco's citation of personal names and place names with their modern-day equivalents and counterparts—a problem stemming from irregular orthography and compounded by transliteration from one alphabet to another as well as by other changes that have occurred, for example, Constantinople becoming Istanbul. The aggregate of these textual difficulties makes analysis and evaluation of Marco's narrative tentative at best.

One matter, however, is considerably less debatable than others: the place of *The Travels of Marco Polo* in literature. Marco Polo's account is, without doubt, soundly within the mainstream of medieval and Renaissance historical-travel literature. Geoffrey of Monmouth's *Historia regum Britan-*

niae (c. 1136; Vulgate version; *History of the Kings of Britain*, 1718), Sir John Mandeville's *The Voyage and Travels of Sir John Mandeville, Knight* (c. 1356), and Richard Hakluyt's sixteenth century books on exploration, among others, join *The Travels of Marco Polo* to form the canon of this literary tradition. These and similar works share certain common features, most of which reflect the attitudes of the age: a mixture of fact and fantasy, a certain cultural ingenuousness, and a rather pervasive credulity about the supernatural. The modern reader is thus entitled to some legitimate skepticism about Marco's report.

This report had the advantage of being designed for a Western readership largely ignorant about the East. Marco's overriding interest was to present the East as something interesting about which the West should learn. His motives were primarily commercial. Marco's access to information was limited by his having had contact exclusively with overlords; his judgments were based largely on mercantile and religious factors. He apparently was impervious to sociopolitical considerations, for his interest was in trade and merchandise, not in ideas. Consequently, the credibility of his eyewitness account was turned toward generating enthusiasm for finding a safe sea route to the East. Much of what Marco had to say, however, provides valuable insight into both Western medieval attitudes and contemporary conditions in the East.

Several significant issues are connected with these insights and attitudes, including the impact of Christianity on the East. Kublai Khan, for example, asked Nicolo and Maffeo Polo, on their earlier journey, to return with one hundred learned Christians (priests and scholars) to discuss Christianity with the wise men of the East. However, Marco records but two priests who come only part of the way with the Polos on their second, more important journey. Kublai Khan made other similar inquiries of Muslim scholars about Islam. One possible implication is that Kublai Khan—and thus the entire Chinese court—was not interested in evangelical Christianity and conversion to Christianity but was intellectually curious about foreign cultures and religions, Marco's Christian biases notwithstanding.

Another issue revolves around Marco's claim that he learned four of the languages of the Tartar nation. Probably he knew Mongol and Turkish—linguistically related languages. It is highly likely that he knew some Persian. The fourth language remains in doubt, but strong evidence suggests that he did not know Chinese. These language skills and limitations most certainly affected Marco's access to information, his perspective on his sources of information, and, as a result, his presentation of information.

Still another issue involves the spurious matter in Marco's account. He confused, for example, the locations of Alexander's barricade and the Great Wall of China with uncharacteristic geographical naïveté. He also included the Prester John legend with no empirical evidence to support it. The narrative refers to several high administrative posts that Marco held under the appointment of Kublai Khan, although meticulously kept records of Chinese administrators and bureaucrats reveal no such appointments. Nevertheless, it is likely that Marco did execute some brief missions for the khan. In addition, while Marco noted the ubiquity of rice in the diet throughout the East, he did not refer to the equally important tea, nor did he mention the well-developed art of Chinese printing—both of which could hardly have escaped his notice. Despite these inaccuracies and inconsistencies, Marco's narrative presented a generally correct picture of conditions in the East as corroborated by other historical records.

Finally, on the issue of cultural judgments Marco categorized people on the basis of religion rather than by ethnic origin or color. Marco distinguished among Jews, Christians, Muslims, and idolatrous heathens (Buddhists and Hindus, for the most part), but he had no patience for intrafaith disputes, even among Christians. As a consequence, he proved a remarkably tolerant person, a good quality for a traveler, for he made no evaluations along racial or cultural lines. Even his judgment that certain African peoples were ugly was an aesthetic pronouncement rather than a racial slur, because he did not consider them inferior. Grouping people according to their religious beliefs was a reasonably typical approach in Marco's day, when religious affiliation was the crux of all matters. Cultural, racial, and ethnic considerations did not emerge as controversial questions until modern times. In this sense, Marco, like his contemporaries, may be considered, in a sense, tolerant.

These aspects of *The Travels of Marco Polo* barely scratch the surface of this remarkable literary document, an extraordinarily rewarding tale that has much to offer, not only for the historian and the student of literature but also for the thoughtful modern citizen.

"Critical Evaluation" by Joanne G. Kashdan

Further Reading

Bergreen, Laurence. *Marco Polo: From Venice to Xanadu.* New York: Alfred A. Knopf, 2007. Lively and well-researched biography. Concludes that even though Polo's book contained some romantic embellishments and outright lies, he was still a perceptive witness to life in the countries in which he traveled.

Cordier, Henri. *The Book of Ser Marco Polo the Venetian Concerning the Kingdoms and Marvels of the East.* Translated and edited by Sir Henry Yule. 3d ed., rev. Amsterdam: Philo Press, 1975. A two-volume scholarly work in the classic tradition, containing comprehensive historical information and striking visual images. Includes extensive footnotes, drawings, engravings, maps, and photographs to illustrate each chapter of Polo's work.

_____. *Ser Marco Polo: Notes and Addenda.* London: John Murray, 1920. Corrections, clarifications, and additions to the 1903 text. Provides further clarification of place names and people named in *The Travels of Marco Polo.*

Haw, Stephen G. *Marco Polo's China: A Venetian in the Realm of Khubilai Khan.* New York: Routledge, 2006. Responds to Wood's theory (below) that Polo never actually traveled to China and to alleged inaccuracies in Polo's account of the trip. Haw maintains that Polo did indeed visit China, and he explains why Polo's travelogue remains an accurate and important source for information about a significant period in Chinese history.

Larner, John. *Marco Polo and the Discovery of the World.* New Haven, Conn.: Yale University Press, 1999. Describes how Polo created his account of his travels and the book's impact on intellectual society in the thirteenth century. Recounts how the book was cowritten by Rustichello da Pisa, a minor author whom Polo met when both men were prisoners in Genoa.

Rugoff, Milton. Introduction to *The Travels of Marco Polo.* New York: The New American Library, 1961. A solid introduction to Polo's life and work. Discusses the influence of the book as the first to "pull the veil off the East."

Wood, Frances. *Did Marco Polo Go to China?* Boulder, Colo.: Westview Press, 1996. Wood argues that Polo did not make the trip to China; she maintains that his travelogue is not an itinerary but a geography book about Asia, containing information from the works of other travelers, including his father and uncle.

Travesties

Author: Tom Stoppard (Tomas Straussler, 1937-   )
First produced: 1974; first published, 1975
Type of work: Drama
Type of plot: Absurdist, problem play, and memory play
Time of plot: 1917 and 1974
Locale: Zurich, Switzerland

Principal characters:

HENRY CARR, a British consulate officer
TRISTAN TZARA, a Dada artist
JAMES JOYCE, an Irish writer
LENIN, a Russian revolutionary
BENNETT, Carr's butler/valet
GWENDOLEN, Carr's sister, and Joyce's secretary
CECILY CARUTHERS, a librarian
NADYA LENIN, Lenin's wife

The Story:

The disjointed, often repetitive plot comes from the mind of Henry Carr, an old British consulate officer reminiscing in 1974 about how his life intersected in 1917 with the Irish writer James Joyce, the Dada artist Tristan Tzara, and the Russian revolutionary Lenin.

The play begins with James Joyce, Tristan Tzara, and Lenin writing in the Zurich library. Tzara is cutting paper and putting the scraps into a hat, pulling out words to read a nonsense poem. Cecily Caruthers, a librarian, tries to silence him. Joyce dictates nonsense poetry to Gwendolen, his secretary, and gives her a folder. Lenin gives a folder to the librarian, but it is switched with Gwendolen's folder. As

Cecily is leaving, she bumps into Nadya Lenin, who enters to converse with her husband. Nadya and Lenin then leave the library.

Old Henry Carr reminisces about the Zurich of 1917. Carr works in the British consulate. Joyce is writing his masterpiece, *Ulysses* (1922). Carr mentions his involvement in writer Oscar Wilde's *The Importance of Being Earnest* (pr. 1895), which Joyce had produced and in which Carr had played Earnest.

Carr talks about two revolutions forming at that time: Lenin's socialist revolution and Tzara's Dada revolution. He discusses Switzerland's potential as a breeding ground for revolution because of the asylum it provides radical thinkers. He becomes his younger self and is served tea by Bennett, his butler/valet. They discuss the war, a war in which Carr had fought.

Carr's memory leads him to repeat bits of dialogue. The characters discuss the tendency of people in Zurich to feign espionage, Tzara's consuming champagne the previous evening, and the abdication of the czar. Carr clearly has problems with socialism, seeing the need for socialists to wait through a period of capitalism.

Carr says that Bolsheviks are violent, telling soldiers to turn against their officers. Lenin wants to return to Russia but is unable to cross international borders. Bennett announces Tzara, who enters and starts speaking nonsense. Gwendolen and Joyce enter. Joyce asks Carr to fund his production of *The Importance of Being Earnest.*

Tzara and Gwendolen leave, and Joyce follows. Tzara and Carr debate the nature of art. Tzara thinks that art should expose society's attempts at creating order, while Carr wants art to portray beauty. Tzara starts repeating the word "dada." Carr and Tzara argue. Carr is offended by Tzara's simplification of war, and Tzara is disgusted with Carr's view of art. The argument climaxes as Tzara continues repeating the word "dada." After some time, Carr offers Tzara a cucumber sandwich. They discuss Cecily and Joyce, and Tzara says he has been in the library admiring Gwendolen, who is Carr's sister. He has come to propose to her.

Carr says he will not give consent to Tzara's marriage proposal and then hands him a library card. It is Tzara's card but has the name "Jack" written on it. Tzara has been pretending to be his own older (fictional) brother. He had come up with the name during a talk with Lenin. Tzara and Carr argue again about art, with Carr saying that artists create the myth that art is important.

Gwendolen raves about Joyce's poems, while Tzara writes a poem of his own, cutting up a Shakespearean sonnet and placing the pieces in a hat. Carr and Joyce discuss the theater that Joyce is running, and Joyce asks Carr to play the lead role in *The Importance of Being Earnest.* The two retire to discuss the play, leaving Gwendolen with Tzara, who has her pull words out of the hat and recite the nonsensical sonnet.

Gwendolen hands Tzara a folder, telling him that she would love him if he would like Joyce. She kisses him as Joyce enters the room. Joyce picks up his hat and leaves as Gwendolen kisses Tzara again. She leaves to talk to Carr, and Joyce reenters the room with pieces of the sonnet all over his shoulders. Joyce asks Tzara about dada and puts the words back in the hat; he then pulls out a paper carnation, and Tzara recounts finding the word "dada."

Joyce and Tzara argue about art: Tzara wants to vandalize art and Joyce believes in the ability of art to make events immortal. Joyce pulls a rabbit out of his hat and leaves. Carr reenters and begins to recall *The Importance of Being Earnest* ordeal, in which Joyce had sued Carr for money for ticket sales and Carr had countersued for what he paid for costumes. Joyce won the suit, and Carr had to pay twenty-five francs. Carr imagines having a retrial and getting Joyce on the witness stand.

Cecily gives a speech about Lenin's exile, implying that Carr is spying on Lenin for the British. Nadya enters the room to talk to Lenin. Cecily translates their conversation, which concerns the revolution. Carr enters the room and talks to Cecily, but she mistakes him for Tzara because she thinks Tzara is Jack.

Cecily and Carr discuss finding some books. They, too, debate the role of art, with Carr defending the apolitical nature of Wilde's play. Cecily hands Carr a folder, which, she says, contains a letter written by Lenin. Carr rebuts some of her Marxist claims, saying that the classes are actually moving closer together.

Cecily accuses Carr of making advances on her. He denies this, but she climbs on the table and starts to chant Marxist gibberish. He yells at her to take off her underwear. He professes his love for her, and they start making love behind a desk as Nadya enters the room.

Nadya talks about Lenin's attempts to reach Russia and that he even wore a wig to get across borders. Tzara argues with Carr over Cecily, and Cecily still thinks Tzara is named Jack. She also thinks Carr is his brother. She runs out of the room crying. He talks about Lenin's plans and his own uncertainty about whether to stop him from reaching Russia. Nadya picks up the story, discussing Lenin's deal with the Germans.

Carr, as a younger man, reenters and stands with Tzara apart from the Lenins. Carr says that Russia will come to socialism with or without Lenin. He and Tzara debate art in history, with Tzara claiming that history also comes out of a hat. Carr resolves to stop Lenin from reaching Russia and sends a telegram to a British officer in Bern, but Lenin has made it into Germany.

Lenin reaches Russia and delivers a speech about the role of art in socialist society. He says that art must support the aims of the revolution and that artists cannot be free until there is a socialist society. Lenin reads a letter that he wrote to Maxim Gorky, responding to accusations of arresting artists. He admits that mistakes were made but that the attitude was correct.

The scene changes to a room where Gwendolen sits. Bennett and Cecily enter, and the scene is written in a musical manner. Cecily and Gwendolen discover they both love Tzara. However, Cecily believes that Carr is Tzara, and when she calls him in, Gwendolen reveals him to be her brother. Tzara enters, and Cecily accuses him of being a Bolshevik. The women ask Tzara and Carr what they thought of what they read in the folders. The men say they were disgusted, and the women exit angrily.

Bennett reads a review of *The Importance of Being Earnest* that praises Carr's performance. Joyce enters and asks Carr for the money for the tickets, which Carr refuses to give because he paid for his costumes. Joyce asks Carr how he got a copy of his manuscript. The women enter and figure out that the folders were switched: Carr got Joyce's chapter and Tzara got Lenin's essay. Everyone reconciles and embraces, dancing offstage. Old Carr and Old Cecily dance. Cecily corrects some parts of Carr's memory and tells the audience that Carr never got close to Lenin and Bennett was in fact the British consul. Cecily and Carr are married.

Critical Evaluation:

Travesties represents one of Tom Stoppard's most intricate and complex statements on the nature of art in society. Stoppard takes an obscure historical incident and turns it into an absurdist circus: Sections of dialogue repeat themselves, the style switches to and from the style of *The Importance of Being Earnest*, and some scenes are performed in song or limerick form. At times it is akin to the Dada anti-art to which Tzara so dearly clings, while at others it burns with the political fire of a speech by Lenin. Through it all, Stoppard presents an important dichotomy in the philosophy of art: its potential for both political propaganda and simple entertainment.

Key themes in the play are revolution and art's role in revolution. Lenin is formulating his ideas and philosophies for the coming socialist revolution in Russia. While he does not figure prominently into the main action of the play, he looms large as a figure who will change the world. His speech about art in act 2 outlines his artistic philosophies, particularly art's subservient role in society. He believes that art should be used as a tool of political systems, rather than as a symptom of them. He also justifies, in his correspondence with Gorky, the state's power over the artist.

Tzara was one of the founders of Dada at the Cabaret Voltaire in 1917. Along with Hugo Ball, Tzara helped formulate Dada's founding principles as an anti-art movement, rejecting the emphasis on logic that had marked previous decades. Nonsense poetry was a key part of performances at Cabaret Voltaire, and so Stoppard's use of it in the play is very typical of Tzara's true artistic expressions. Collage was another ma-

jor outgrowth of the Dada movement, and the play functions as a collage of political and artistic revolutions and personalities populating Zurich at that time. The way Stoppard uses the styles of Wilde and Irish limericks highlights this form.

The play also makes use of the conventions of memory. The repetition of dialogue and the replaying of scenes in different styles mimic a person's processing of the past, reliving certain moments, and forgetting specific details over time. The way in which Cecily corrects Carr at the end reminds the audience of the illusory nature of both theater and memory. Theater performs a similar function for memory: It picks and chooses elements of reality to display on the stage. Stoppard highlights that link through his arrangements of historical elements and stylistic repetition.

Stoppard also makes use of various aesthetic philosophies, particularly those of Wilde. Wilde believed that life should imitate art. Art should be used to represent ideal beauty. Throughout the play, scenes are played in the style of *The Importance of Being Earnest*, and some plot points find their way in, such as the presence of cucumber sandwiches, the Wilde-esque switching of the folders, and the mistaken identities of Tzara and Carr by Cecily and Gwendolen. The names of the women and the identity of Jack are also taken from Wilde's play.

Throughout the play, Stoppard manipulates history and time much as he does in other plays such as *The Invention of Love* (pr. 1997), *Arcadia* (pr. 1993), and *The Coast of Utopia* (pr. 2002). While it deals with major historical figures, like many of his other works Stoppard's play is most rewarding to the historically and culturally literate reader or audience member. A familiarity with Dada and Marxism can help illuminate some of the themes and styles at work in the play.

David Coley

Further Reading

Bloom, Harold, ed. *Modern Critical Views: Tom Stoppard*. New York: Chelsea House, 1986. A selection of essays about Stoppard's major works, including two essays on *Travesties*. Essays also cover Stoppard's general style and philosophy.

Dean, Joan. *Tom Stoppard: Comedy as a Moral Matrix*. Columbia: University of Missouri Press, 1981. Dean explores the way in which Stoppard uses comedy to address both personal and social morality. *Travesties* is discussed with an emphasis on Joyce's and Lenin's competing views of art.

Gabbard, Lucina Paquet. *The Stoppard Plays*. Troy, N.Y.: Whitston, 1982. Gabbard explores several different categories of Stoppard's plays and includes *Travesties* in a section entitled "The Mysteries of Philosophy and Art." Each character and his or her significance are discussed in detail.

Hunter, Jim. *About Stoppard: The Playwright and the Work.* London: Faber and Faber, 2005. Presents a series of later interviews with Stoppard and with those who have staged his work. With a good introduction, this book places Stoppard's plays in context. An indispensable jargon-free guide.

Londré, Felicia Hardison. *Tom Stoppard.* New York: Frederick Ungar, 1981. Londré presents a look at Stoppard's life, major works, and style. Includes a biographical sketch as well as a discussion of *Travesties* as compared with his play *Jumpers.*

Sammells, Neil. *Tom Stoppard: The Artist as Critic.* London: Macmillan, 1988. A look at how Stoppard treats the role of the artist in his plays, particularly in *Travesties.* Sammells looks at how Stoppard works as a critic through his style and his ways of engaging the audience.

Treasure Island

Author: Robert Louis Stevenson (1850-1894)
First published: 1881-1882, serial; 1883, book
Type of work: Novel
Type of plot: Adventure
Time of plot: 1740's
Locale: England and the Spanish Main

Principal characters:
JIM HAWKINS, the cabin boy of the *Hispaniola*
DR. LIVESEY, a physician and Jim's friend
SQUIRE TRELAWNEY, a wealthy landowner
MR. SMOLLETT, the captain of the *Hispaniola*
LONG JOHN SILVER, the leader of the mutineers
BEN GUNN, a pirate

The Story:

One day a strange seaman, Bill Bones, arrives at the Admiral Benbow, the inn owned by young Jim Hawkins's father. Looking for lodgings, Bones comes plodding up to the inn door, where he stands for a time, looking around Black Hill Cove. Jim hears him singing snatches of an old sea song: "Fifteen men on the dead man's chest, Yo-ho-ho, and a bottle of rum." When Bones learns from Jim's father that the inn is a quiet one with little trade, he declares it just the berth for an old seaman. From that time, the strange guest—a retired captain, he calls himself—keeps watch on the coast and the land road by day and drinks freely in the taproom of the inn at night. There he sings and swears great oaths while he tells fearsome tales of the Spanish Main. Bones is wary of all visiting seamen, and he pays Jim to be on the lookout for a one-legged sailor in particular. Bones is so terrible in his speech and manners that Jim's father, a sick man, never has the courage to ask him for payment after the one he made the day he came to the inn. He stays on without ever clinking another coin into the inn's till for his meals and lodging.

The one-legged sailor never comes to the inn, but another seaman named Black Dog does. The two men fight in the inn parlor, to the terror of Jim and his mother, before Bones chases his visitor up the road and out of sight. When he comes back to the inn, he falls down in a fit. Dr. Livesey, who has come to the inn to attend to Jim's father, cautions Bones to contain himself and drink less.

Jim's father dies soon afterward. On the day of the funeral, a deformed blind man named Pew taps his way up to the door of the Admiral Benbow and forces Jim to lead him to the captain. Bill Bones is so terrified when the blind man gives him the Black Spot, the pirates' death notice, that he has a stroke and dies. Because Bones died owing them money, Jim and his mother take the keys to the dead man's sea chest from his pocket and open the chest. As they are examining the contents, they hear the tapping of the blind man's stick as he approaches on the road. Jim quickly pockets an oilskin packet from the chest, and he and his mother leave hurriedly by the back door of the inn as a gang of men breaks in to search for Bones's chest. Mounted revenue officers then arrive and scatter the gang; Pew is trampled to death by the charging horses.

Jim takes the packet from the chest to Dr. Livesey and Squire Trelawney. The three discover that it contains a map locating the hidden treasure of the bloody buccaneer Captain Flint. Squire Trelawney is intrigued and decides to outfit a ship in which to sail after the treasure. The doctor throws in his lot, and they invite Jim to come along as cabin boy. In Bristol, Trelawney purchases a schooner, the *Hispaniola*, and hires Long John Silver to be the ship's cook. Silver promises to supply a crew. When Jim arrives in Bristol and meets Silver, he finds that the sailor has only one leg. He is alarmed when he sees Black Dog again at the inn operated by Silver, but Silver's smooth talk quiets Jim's suspicions.

After the *Hispaniola* sets sail, Captain Smollett, hired by Squire Trelawney to command the ship, expresses his dislike of the first mate and the crew and complains that Silver has more real authority with the crew than he does. One night, Jim, having fallen into a barrel while reaching for an apple, overhears Silver discussing mutiny with members of the crew. Before Jim has a chance to reveal the plot to his friends, the island where the treasure lies is sighted.

The prospects of treasure on the island cause the disloyal members of the crew to pay little attention to Captain Smollett's orders; even the loyal ones are hard to manage. Silver shrewdly keeps his party under control. The captain wisely allows part of the crew to go ashore; Jim smuggles himself along in order to spy on Silver and the men on the island. Ashore, Silver kills two of the crew who refuse to join the mutineers. Jim, alone, meets Ben Gunn, who was with Captain Flint when the treasure was buried. Gunn tells Jim that he has been marooned on the island for three years.

While Jim is ashore, Dr. Livesey goes to the island and finds Captain Flint's stockade. When he hears the scream of one of the crewmen being murdered by Silver, he returns to the *Hispaniola*, where it is decided that the honest men will move to the fort within the stockade. Several dangerous trips in a small, overloaded boat complete the move. During the last trip, the mutineers aboard the ship ready the ship's cannon for action, and Squire Trelawney shoots one seaman from the boat. In the meantime, the mutineers on the island see what is afoot and make efforts to keep Jim's friends from occupying the stockade. Squire Trelawney and his party take their posts in the fort after they have repulsed the enemy. The mutineers on the *Hispaniola* fire one cannon shot into the stockade, but the attack does little damage.

After leaving Ben Gunn, the marooned seaman, Jim makes his way to the stockade. The *Hispaniola* now flies the Jolly Roger, the pirate flag decorated with skull and crossbones. Carrying a flag of truce, Silver approaches the stockade and offers to parley. After he is admitted by the defenders, he demands the treasure map in exchange for the safe return of Squire Trelawney's party to England. Captain Smollett will concede nothing, and Silver returns to his men in a rage as the stockade party prepares for the coming battle. A group of the pirates attacks the stockade from two sides,

swarming over the paling and engaging the defenders in hand-to-hand combat. In the close fighting, the pirates are reduced to one man, who flees back to his gang in the jungle. The loyal party is reduced to Squire Trelawney, Dr. Livesey, Captain Smollett, and Jim.

During the lull after the battle, Jim sneaks off and borrows Ben Gunn's homemade boat. He rows out to the *Hispaniola* under cover of darkness and cuts the anchor line, setting the schooner adrift. In trying to return to the island, he is caught offshore by coastal currents, and when daylight comes, he can see that the *Hispaniola*, like his own small boat, is drifting aimlessly—and the large ship is bearing down on him. Just before Ben Gunn's little boat is smashed, Jim manages to jump from it to the bowsprit of the *Hispaniola*. He finds himself on board alone with one of the pirates, Israel Hands, who has been wounded in a fight with another pirate. Jim takes command and proceeds to beach the ship. Pursued by Hands, he climbs the mast quickly, just avoiding being struck by a knife thrown by the pirate. Jim has time to prime and reload his pistols, and he shoots Hands after being pinned to the mast by another thrown knife that has struck him in the shoulder.

Jim removes the knife from his shoulder, makes the ship safe by removing the sails, and returns to the stockade at night, only to find it abandoned by his friends and now in the hands of the pirates. When Silver's parrot draws attention to the boy's presence, the pirates capture him. Dissatisfied with the buccaneer's methods of gaining the treasure, Silver's men are grumbling. One attempts to kill Jim, who has bragged to them of his exploits on behalf of his friends. Silver, however, for reasons of his own, takes the boy's side and swears that he also would take the part of Squire Trelawney. Silver's disaffected mates give him the Black Spot and depose him as their chief, but the pirate leader talks his way out of his difficulty by showing them, to Jim's amazement and to their delight, Captain Flint's map of Treasure Island.

Dr. Livesey arrives at the stockade under a flag of truce to provide medical care to the wounded pirates. He learns from Jim that Silver saved the boy's life, and Jim hears, to his mystification, that the doctor gave Captain Flint's map to Silver. Following the directions on the map, the pirates go to find the treasure. As they approach the hiding place, they hear a high voice singing the pirate chantey, "Yo-ho-ho, and a bottle of rum." The voice also speaks the last words of Captain Flint. The men are terrified until Silver recognizes Ben Gunn's voice. Then the pirates find the treasure cache opened and the treasure gone. When they uncover only a broken pick and some boards, they turn on Silver and Jim. At that moment, Jim's friends, with Ben Gunn, arrive to rescue the boy.

Jim then learns what has transpired. Early in his stay on the island, Ben Gunn had discovered the treasure and carried it to his cave. After Dr. Livesey learned this from Gunn, Squire Trelawney's party abandoned the stockade, and Dr. Livesey gave the useless map to Silver. Jim's friends moved to Gunn's safe and well-provisioned quarters.

The *Hispaniola* having been floated by a tide, the group is able to leave Treasure Island, abandoning there three escaped pirates. They sail to a West Indies port, where, with the connivance of Ben Gunn, John Silver escapes the ship with a bag of coins. After taking on a full crew, the schooner sails back to Bristol, where the survivors of the adventure divide the treasure among them.

Critical Evaluation:

Although Robert Louis Stevenson produced a large number and variety of writings during his relatively short life and was considered a serious adult author in his own day, he is largely remembered now as the writer of one gothic horror story, *The Strange Case of Dr. Jekyll and Mr. Hyde* (1886), and two boys' books, *Treasure Island* and *Kidnapped: Being Memoirs of the Adventures of David Balfour in the Year 1751* (1886). Such a view is undoubtedly unfair and slights the author's many valuable literary accomplishments, but the fact that these three works have endured not only as citations in literary histories but also as readable, exciting books is a tribute to Stevenson's genius. *Treasure Island* remains the supreme achievement among the three works. Although critics may debate its seriousness, few question its status as the purest of adventure stories. According to Stevenson, the book was born out of his fascination with a watercolor map he himself drew of an imaginary island.

When Jim Hawkins begins by stating that he is telling the story in retrospect, at the request of "Squire Trelawney, Doctor Livesey, and the rest of these gentlemen," readers are assured that all the principals survived the quest successfully, thus giving readers that security necessary in a romantic adventure intended primarily for young people. Although many exciting scenes will ensue and the heroes will face great danger on a number of occasions, readers know that they will overcome all such obstacles. Thus, the suspense centers on how they escape, not on their personal survival as such. At the same time, by denying details of either the precise time of the adventure or the exact location, Stevenson sets readers imaginatively free to enjoy the story unencumbered by the specifics of when or where.

By introducing the mysterious, threatening Bill Bones into the serene atmosphere of the Admiral Benbow Inn, Stevenson immerses readers directly into the story. The strange secret of Bones's background and nature creates the novel's initial excitement, which is then intensified by his apparent fear and subsequent encounters with Black Dog and Blind Pew. In all, the sequence that begins with Billy's arrival and ends with Pew's death serves as an overture to the adventure and sets up most of the important elements in the story, especially Captain Flint's map, which directs the group to Treasure Island, and the warnings to beware of "the seafaring man with one leg," which prepares readers for the archvillain of the tale, Long John Silver.

In the classic adventure story pattern, an ordinary individual, Jim Hawkins, living a normal, routine life, is suddenly thrust into an extraordinary and dangerous situation, which soon gets beyond the control of the individual and his cohorts. Although the hero is involuntarily pressed into danger, he nevertheless can extricate himself and return the situation to normality only through his efforts. The adventure story is, therefore, usually to some extent a coming-of-age novel, whether the hero be fourteen or sixty-four years old.

Near the beginning of the book, the death of Jim's father frees Jim to seek his fortune and places the responsibility on him to find it for the sake of his widowed mother. Without a father of his own, Jim can look to other father figures. He finds two: Dr. Livesey, who represents stability, maturity, and moral responsibility; and John Silver, who suggests imagination, daring, bravado, and energy. Between these two and, more important, through his own actions, Jim finds his own adulthood along with the treasure.

Jim's education begins with the act of searching the belongings of the dead Bill Bones despite the proximity of Pew's pirate band. To accomplish this feat, however, he needs his mother's support. Once the *Hispaniola* sets sail, however, he is on his own. The next stage in his growth occurs when, crouching in the apple barrel, he overhears Silver reveal his plans to his coconspirators. Jim keeps calm, coolly informs his friends, and, with them, devises survival tactics. His initial positive, independent action takes place when they first reach the island and he goes off on his own; he has no specific plan, but he is sure that he can further the cause in some undetermined way. He wanders in the woods and meets Ben Gunn, rejoins his party at the stockade, and engages in his first combat.

When Jim makes his second solo trip, he has a definite course of action in mind; he plans to board the *Hispaniola* and cut it loose to drift with the tide, thus depriving the pirates of a refuge and an escape route. His final test in action comes when he encounters the evil first mate, Israel Hands. When Hands tries to manipulate him, Jim sees through the deception and, acting with considerable courage and dexterity, manages to outmaneuver the experienced pirate. Finally, faced with an enraged adversary, Jim remains calm and, with a knife sticking in his shoulder, still manages to shoot the villain.

His final test of adulthood is not physical, however, but moral. Returning to the stockade, which he still believes to be occupied by his friends, Jim is captured by the pirates. Given the opportunity a short time later to talk privately with Dr. Livesey, Jim refuses to escape: "No . . . you know right well you wouldn't do the thing yourself, neither you, nor squire, nor captain, and no more will I. Silver trusted me, I passed my word, and back I go." Jim puts his word above his life, thus signaling the transition not just from boy to man but, more important to Stevenson, from boy to gentleman.

Although Jim's development is important to the novel, the most vivid and memorable element in the book remains the character of Long John Silver. All critics have noted that he is both bad and good, cruel and generous, despicable and admirable. Some have tried to fuse these elements into a single character "type," a "hero-villain," in which the good and the bad are traced back to a common source. Such an effort is probably wrong. Silver is both good and bad, and his role in the novel demands both kinds of actions. Rather than trying to "explain" Silver psychologically, readers may find it more profitable to analyze the ways in which Stevenson manipulates their feelings toward the character.

In any pirate story, the author faces a moral and artistic dilemma. On one hand, pirates can hardly be presented as moral exemplars or heroes; they must be criminals and cutthroats. On the other hand, pirates are romantically attractive and interesting characters. Enhance their attractiveness, and the book becomes morally distorted; mute it, and the book becomes dull. One solution to this dilemma is to mitigate the pirates' badness by introducing an element of moral ambiguity into the characterization and behavior of some of them without denying the evil effects of their actions, then separate the "good-bad" villains from the "bad-bad" ones. Stevenson uses this technique in *Treasure Island*. Silver is separated from his purely villainous cronies and set against the truly evil figures, Israel Hands and George Merry, with less developed pirate characters remaining in the background.

Stevenson mitigates Silver's evil side with two simple strategies: He presents the ruthless, cruel aspects of Silver's character early in the novel and lets his "better" side reveal itself late in the book, and he keeps the "evil" Silver at a distance and gives readers an intimate view only of the relatively good Long John. Therefore, although readers never forget the viciousness of the character's early words and deeds, these recede into the background as the adventure progresses.

Readers are prepared for the bad Long John Silver by the many early warnings to beware of the "one-legged man." He is then seen manipulating Squire Trelawney and even Jim in their first encounters. Therefore, readers admire his role-playing but fear the conspiratorial evil that obviously lies behind it. Silver's overt treachery is evident in the apple-barrel scene, especially in his callous "vote" to kill all the nonconspirators when the chance arises. Long John reaches the peak of his villainy in the killing of a sailor who refuses to join the mutiny, first stunning the sailor with his crutch and then knifing him to death.

Even these two pieces of evidence of Silver's badness, however, are seen at a distance, from inside an apple barrel and from behind a clump of trees. When Long John moves to the center of the novel and assumes an intimate relationship with Jim, the pirate's character is automatically softened, and by the time Silver and Jim become unwilling partners in survival, the pirate's image and status have considerably changed.

The early view of Silver is that he is not only evil but also invincible. As he becomes less one-dimensionally evil, he becomes progressively more vulnerable, and vulnerability always stimulates sympathy in readers, regardless of the character's moral status. As the tide begins to turn against the pirates, Silver begins to lose control not only of the treasure-hunting expedition but also of his own men. This erosion of power is signaled by an increasing emphasis on his physical disability. The John Silver who must crawl on his hands and knees out of the stockade after the failure of his "embassy" is a far cry from the Silver who can knock down an opponent with a flying crutch and then pounce on him like an animal.

Silver's glibness and adroitness in manipulating the good men of the *Hispaniola* are components of his villainy in the first parts of the book, but when Silver is threatened by a mutiny of his own men and must utilize those same talents to save himself and Jim, they become positive virtues. Although he is obviously motivated by an instinct for self-preservation, Silver does protect Jim from the others and conveys a feeling of honestly liking and wanting to help the lad.

The morally ambiguous ending of the novel is thus the only one artistically possible. John Silver has not been bad enough to hang, and it is hard to imagine his vitality stifled in prison; yet, although he has edged away from the villains, he hardly qualifies as a hero. He is neither punished nor greatly rewarded for his machinations and heroics; rather, he is left to seek another fortune elsewhere.

"Critical Evaluation" by Keith Neilson

Further Reading

Ambrosini, Richard, and Richard Dury, eds. *Robert Louis Stevenson: Writer of Boundaries*. Madison: University of Wisconsin Press, 2006. Collection of essays includes contributions that cover the entire body of Stevenson's work. Divided into four parts: "The Pleasures of Reading, Writing, and Popular Culture," "Scotland and the South Seas," "Evolutionary Psychology, Masculinity, and *Dr. Jekyll and Mr. Hyde*," and "Textural and Cultural Crossings."

Buckton, Oliver S. "'Faithful to His Map': Profit, Desire, and the Ends of Travel in *Treasure Island*." In *Cruising with Robert Louis Stevenson: Travel, Narrative, and the Colonial Body*. Athens: Ohio University Press, 2007. Chapter addressing *Treasure Island* is part of an examination of the importance of travel to Stevenson's life and writing.

Fraser, Robert. *Victorian Quest Romance: Stevenson, Haggard, Kipling, and Conan Doyle*. Plymouth, England: Northcote House/British Council, 1998. Examines *Treasure Island* and other Victorian quest romances within the context of contemporary debates about the nascent sciences of anthropology and archaeology. Describes how the authors of these novels depict encounters with remote places and times in order to ask questions about the institutions and beliefs of their own culture.

Harman, Claire. *Myself and the Other Fellow: A Life of Robert Louis Stevenson*. New York: HarperCollins, 2005.

Substantial biography of Stevenson covers the writer's early family life, his writing and travels, and his curious but successful marriage.

Hellman, George S. *The True Stevenson: A Study in Clarification*. 1925. Reprint. New York: Haskell House, 1972. Draws on Stevenson's letters, conversations with his contemporaries, and his wife's letters to elucidate points about the author and *Treasure Island*.

McLynn, Frank. *Robert Louis Stevenson: A Biography*. London: Hutchinson, 1993. Comprehensive biography considers the impact of the events of Stevenson's childhood and young adulthood on *Treasure Island*. Examines the sources for the story and characters and the immediate success of the work with the public.

Reid, Julia. *Robert Louis Stevenson, Science, and the Fin de Siècle*. New York: Palgrave Macmillan, 2006. Examines the influence of late-Victorian concepts of evolution on *Treasure Island* and other works. Argues that an interest in "primitive" culture is at the heart of Stevenson's writing.

Saposnik, Irving S. *Robert Louis Stevenson*. New York: Twayne, 1974. Solid critical overview of Stevenson's work places *Treasure Island* within the context of his entire canon. Connects the character of Jim Hawkins to other youthful Stevenson heroes in *Kidnapped* and *The Black Arrow* (1888) and offers a useful study of the character Long John Silver.

A Tree Grows in Brooklyn

Author: Betty Smith (1896-1972)
First published: 1943
Type of work: Novel
Type of plot: Bildungsroman
Time of plot: Early twentieth century
Locale: Brooklyn, New York

Principal characters:
FRANCIE NOLAN, a Brooklyn girl
NEELEY NOLAN, her brother
KATIE NOLAN, her mother
JOHNNY NOLAN, her father

The Story:

For their spending money Francie and Neeley Nolan rely on a few pennies they collect from the junk collector every Saturday. Katie, their mother, works as a janitor in a Brooklyn tenement, and the money she and their father earn—he from his Saturday-night jobs as a singing waiter—is barely enough to keep the family alive and clothed.

After their Saturday-morning trips with the rags, metal, and rubber they collect during the week, Francie visits the library. She is methodically going through its contents in alphabetical order by reading a book each day, but on Saturdays she allows herself the luxury of breaking the sequence. At home, sitting on the fire escape, she can look up from her book and watch her neighbors' preparations for Saturday night. A tree grows in the yard; Francie watches it from season to season during her long Saturday afternoons.

At five o'clock, when her father comes home, Francie irons his waiter's apron and then goes to the dry-goods store to buy the paper collar and muslin dickey that will last him for the evening. It is her special Saturday-night privilege to sleep in the front room, and there she can watch the people in the street. She gets up briefly at two in the morning when her father comes home and is given a share of the delicacies he salvages from the wedding or party at which he served. Then, while her parents talk far into the night, Francie fixes Saturday's happenings in her mind and gradually drifts off to sleep.

Johnny Nolan and Katie Rommely meet when he is nineteen and she is seventeen, and they are married four months later. In a year's time, Francie is born. Johnny, unable to bear the sight of Katie in labor, gets drunk, and when the water pipes burst at the school in which he is janitor, he is discharged. Neeley is born soon after Francie's first birthday. By that time, Johnny is drinking so heavily that Katie knows she can no longer rely on him for the family's support. In return for free rent, the Nolans move to a house in which Katie can be janitor.

Francie is not sent to school until she is seven, and Neeley is old enough to go with her. In that way the children are able to protect each other from would-be tormentors. Seated two-at-a-desk among the other poverty-stricken children, Francie soon grows to look forward to the weekly visits of her art and music teachers. They are the sunshine of her school days.

By pretending that Francie goes to live with relatives, Johnny is able to have her transferred to another school that Francie sees on one of her walks. A long way from home, it is, nevertheless, an improvement over the old one. Most of the children are of American parentage and are not exploited by cruel teachers, as are those from immigrant families.

Francie notes time by holidays. Beginning the year with the Fourth of July and its firecrackers, she looks forward next to Halloween. Election Day, with its snake dances and bonfires, comes soon after. Then follows Thanksgiving Day, on which the children disguise themselves with costumes and masks and beg trifles from storekeepers. Soon afterward comes Christmas. The year Francie is ten and Neeley nine, they stand together on Christmas Eve while the biggest tree in the neighborhood is thrown at them. Trees unsold at that time are thrown at anyone who volunteers to stand against the impact. Bruised and scratched, Francie and her brother proudly drag their tree home.

The week before Christmas, when Francie is fourteen, Johnny staggers home drunk. Two days later, he is found, huddled in a doorway, ill with pneumonia. The next day he is dead. After the funeral, Neeley is given his father's ring and Francie his shaving mug, his only keepsakes aside from his two waiter's aprons. To his wife, Johnny leaves a baby, due to be born the following spring.

In March, when their funds are running low, Katie cashes the children's insurance policies. The twenty-five dollars she receives carries them through until the end of April. Then Mr. McGarrity, at whose saloon Johnny does most of his drinking, comes to their rescue. He hires Neeley to help prepare free lunches after school and Francie to do housework, and the money the children earn is enough to tide them over until after Katie's baby is born.

Laurie is born in May. In June, after their graduation from grade school, Francie and Neeley find their first real jobs, Neeley as errand boy for a brokerage house and Francie as a stemmer in a flower factory. Dismissed two weeks later, she becomes a file clerk in a clipping bureau. She is quickly advanced to the position of reader.

In the fall, there is not enough money to send both her children to high school, and Katie decides that the more reluctant Neeley should go. With the money Francie earns and with Neeley's after-school job at McGarrity's saloon, the Nolans have more comforts that Christmas than ever before. The house is warm; there is enough food; and there is money for presents. Fourteen-year-old Neeley receives his first pair of spats, and Francie almost freezes in her new black lace lingerie when they go to church on Christmas morning.

When the clipping bureau closes with the outbreak of the war, Francie gets a job as a teletype operator. By working at night, she is able to take advanced college credits in summer school that year. With the help of a fellow student, Ben Blake, she passes her chemistry and English courses. Francie is eighteen when she has her first real date, with a soldier named Lee Rhynor. The evening he is to leave to say goodbye to his parents before going overseas, Lee asks her to marry him when he returns. Francie promises to write him every day. Three days later, she receives a letter from the girl he married during his trip home.

Katie also has a letter that day. Officer McShane has long been fond of Katie. Now retired, he asks her to marry him. All the Nolans agree to this proposal. As the time approaches for the wedding, Francie resigns her job. With Katie married, she intends to go to Michigan to college, for with Blake's help, she succeeds in passing the entrance exams.

The day before Katie is to be wed, Francie puts the baby in the carriage and walks down the avenue. For a time she watches the children carting their rubbish into the junk shop. She turns in her books at the library for the last time. She sees another little girl, a book in her hand, sitting on a fire escape. In her own yard, the tree was cut down because the tenants complained that it is in the way of their wash, but from its stump a shoot is growing.

Critical Evaluation:

A Tree Grows in Brooklyn was Betty Smith's most popular work. A playwright as well as a novelist, she later adapted *A Tree Grows in Brooklyn* for stage and screen. The novel explores the development of the protagonist, Francis Nolan. Francie is born as the twentieth century begins. Her story mirrors the times. For example, there are advances in medicine and technology (as evidenced by Aunt Sissy's abandoning of the traditional midwife for a hospital birth and Francie's learning to operate teletype machines). When World War I begins, Francie falls in love with a young soldier. These advances and events, however, serve only as a backdrop for the novel. Francie's times are not an essential element of the plot, but a backdrop for Francie's growth.

In *A Tree Grows in Brooklyn*, Smith constructs a type of bildungsroman in which the novel centers on a hero who grows to maturity and finds purpose through experiences. In short, a bildungsroman is about growing up. Smith's novel contains biographical elements. Like her protagonist, she was raised in Brooklyn and struggled to obtain an education. Smith's tale chronicles Francie's development as she learns about life from her mother's family, the Rommelys. Her grandmother, an immigrant from Austria, grieved when her daughters gave birth to daughters because she knew that to be "born a woman meant a life of humble hardship." Smith describes Francie's mother and her aunts (Evy and Sissy) as slender, frail creatures, yet Smith asserts that the women are made of "thin . . . steel."

The women are strong while often the men are weak. For example, Francie's father drinks too much and lacks strength of character. He cannot assume responsibility for himself or for his family. His redeeming qualities are his singing talent and his passion for beauty. These qualities are not enough to sustain him or his family. Similarly, Francie's Aunt Evy is married to Willie Flittman, an unstable, "whimpery" man. His ill-temper creates difficulty for him and his family. Even the horse that pulls Willie's milkcart treats him with disrespect. At the close of the novel, Willie manages to "flit" away, deserting his wife and children to perform as a one-man band.

The female characters are responsible for the successful rearing of the children. Smith asserts that Johnny hailed from a family grown frail. His mother tried to keep her sons for herself. Consequently, all four Nolan boys were dead before they reached thirty-five. Unable to sustain itself, the Nolan family line collapses. In contrast, Francie's mother, Katie, is confident that her son, Neeley, will not become a failure like his father, Johnny. She relies on the contribution of her own character and nurturing to produce a stronger son than her mother-in-law Mrs. Nolan raised. Unlike Mrs. Nolan's, Katie's motives are generous rather than selfish. She attempts to prepare her children for achievement. Francie's grandmother Rommely sent her daughters to grammar school; Katie aims for high school diplomas for her children, knowing that education will provide opportunity for them to achieve a better life. The hope for future generations lies in the influence of the mothers rather than the fathers.

The theme of Smith's novel is survival. Some characters are ill-equipped to overcome poverty and hardship; others thrive. A sense of pride is required for survival and independence, but the story suggests that additional resources are needed. Strength of character and the ability to love and nurture others are critical elements for those characters who succeed. Smith seems to suggest that people cannot prosper unless they are complete emotionally and psychologically, and "love instincts" contribute to making them whole. Consequently, Mr. McShane marries Katie at the close of the novel because he needs someone to love. When Francie ponders her relationship with Ben Blake, she longs for a reciprocal relationship in which she not only needs someone but also someone needs her.

Although generally women in the novel are better than men, women without "love instincts" are portrayed in less than complimentary roles. For example, the narrator comments that in 1908 the school system was a brutal one. Married women were not allowed to teach, leaving only those women made "neurotic by starved love instincts." In addition, the librarian at the local library is characterized as a woman who is indifferent to children. She never learns the patrons' names, never looks a child in the eye, and recommends the same book for eleven-year-old girls year after year. Even Francie's Aunt Sissy does not settle down to "normal" life until she has a family of her own to nurture.

The harsh environment of Brooklyn serves as a crucible that tests the characters. Their neighborhood is a microcosm in which Jewish shopkeepers spit and curse to protest the bargaining of the poor Gentile customers. Irish, German, and Polish immigrants struggle to earn a living among the tenement dwellings. Francie loves Brooklyn, but once she crosses the bridge into New York her world enlarges. She meets a soldier going off to fight in World War I, and he breaks her heart. She learns about life from her job reading newspaper clippings, and she knows that she can never return to the small world she knew as a child. Thus, she attempts to leap from childhood to adulthood by trying to enroll in college without ever having attended high school. At the close of the novel, the family leaves Brooklyn. Francie's mother will live a prosperous life with her second husband, and Francie will attend college in another state, thus expanding her sphere beyond the confines of New York. Francie makes it out of the tenement.

Smith asserts that Brooklyn is where the "Tree of Heaven" grows. The tree sprouts in empty lots, trash heaps, and tenements. When Francie leaves Brooklyn, the tree is still there flourishing—a symbol of the human spirit that continues in the face of adversity. Like Francie, the tree survives in a hostile environment. The novel ends as it began. Another eleven-year-old girl reads from the fire escape, and the young adult Francie sees herself in the girl. Smith closes the novel by emphasizing the universality of existence. Just as the scrubby tree sprouts new shoots, new generations of young girls emerge to learn of life as Francie has.

"Critical Evaluation" by Paula M. Miller

Further Reading

Gelfant, Blanche H. "Sister to Faust: The City's 'Hungry' Woman as Heroine." In *Women Writers and the City: Essays in Feminist Literary Criticism*, edited by Susan Merrill Squier. Knoxville: University of Tennessee Press, 1984. Examines the common attributes of female protagonists such as Francie Nolan, whose physical hunger parallels her longing for knowledge and self-awareness.

Ginsberg, Elaine K. "Betty Wehner Smith." In *American Women Writers: A Critical Reference Guide from Colonial Times to the Present*, edited by Lina Mainiero. 4 vols. New York: Frederick Ungar, 1982. Offers information about Smith's professional career and her works, including a brief assessment of *A Tree Grows in Brooklyn*.

Pearlman, Mickey. "Betty Smith." In *Biographical Dictionary of Contemporary Catholic Writing*, edited by Daniel J. Tynan. Westport, Conn.: Greenwood Press, 1989. Discusses the biographical elements of *A Tree Grows in Brooklyn* and includes background information regarding Smith's similarity to the protagonist Francie Nolan.

Prescott, Orville. "Outstanding Novels." *The Yale Review* 33, no. 1 (Autumn, 1943): 6-12. Provides an assessment of Smith's character development within the novel and examines the elements of local color or regionalism in the work.

Sullivan, Richard. "Brooklyn, Where the Tree Grew." *The New York Times Book Review*, August 22, 1948. A comparison of the common elements in *A Tree Grows in Brooklyn* and Smith's later work. Focuses on related themes, settings, and characters, emphasizing the superiority of the first novel.

Szalay, Michael. "The Vanishing American Father: Sentiment and Labor in *The Grapes of Wrath* and *A Tree Grows in Brooklyn*." In *New Deal Modernism: American Literature and the Invention of the Welfare State*. Durham, N.C.: Duke University Press, 2000. Analyzes literary works that center on the New Deal, demonstrating how the federal government significantly altered the social category of "artist." The chapter on *A Tree Grows in Brooklyn* examines how Smith's novel and *The Grapes of Wrath* express the specifically American conflict between individual freedom and group affiliation, and how this depiction is a response to the changed relationship between the individual, society, and the state.

Yow, Valerie Raleigh. *Betty Smith: Life of the Author of "A Tree Grows in Brooklyn."* Chapel Hill, N.C.: Wolf's Pond Press, 2008. The first published biography of Smith. Recounts the events of her life, describing how her experiences in a blue-collar world influenced her fiction. Analyzes her novels, discussing how Francie and the other protagonists are working-class women who become self-directed and confident.

The Tree of Man

Author: Patrick White (1912-1990)
First published: 1955
Type of work: Novel
Type of plot: Parable
Time of plot: Early twentieth century
Locale: Australia

Principal characters:
STAN PARKER, an Australian farmer
AMY, his wife
THELMA, their daughter
RAY, their son
MRS. O'DOWD, a neighbor

The Story:

Both of young Stan Parker's parents are dead, and Stan has no intention of following in his father's footsteps as a blacksmith or of remaining in the confining atmosphere of the Australian bush town where he grew up. Wanting to start a new life, he leaves his hometown and travels to an unsettled area outside Sydney, where he has inherited some property. He plans to develop the acreage into a farm. He clears the land, plants crops, and builds himself a shack.

Lonely in the wilderness, he visits some relatives in a town, and at a dance there he meets a simple girl named Amy. After a brief courtship, the two are married one morning; they then drive all day in a wagon across the countryside and settle that evening on the primitive farm.

They both work hard and make improvements to their property as the early years of their marriage pass. The major event to take place outside their immediate lives is a great flood, which fortunately does not destroy their farm. Stan joins with other volunteers and assists in rescuing settlers who have been stranded by the flooding. Later, Amy and Mrs. O'Dowd, a neighbor, go to town to meet their husbands after the floodwaters have receded. During this period, Stan and Amy have experiences that will stay with them for the rest of their lives. Stan sees an aged man suspended from a tree above the flooded land; even though the man is dead and Stan can do nothing to help him, the image continues to haunt him. Amy picks up a lost child and takes him home the night after the flood. He disappears the next morning, leaving only a bit of colored glass behind, which she saves (and many years later gives to her grandson).

The Parkers continue to labor, adding to their house, gathering a herd of milk cows, planting and harvesting crops. Other families settle nearby, a village gradually appears, and a wealthy Sydney family constructs a grand country house on adjoining land, naming the estate Glastonbury. Two children are born to the Parkers: a daughter, Thelma, and a son, Ray. Amy develops a fixation on Madeleine, a visitor to Glastonbury, and believes that this elegant woman holds some kind of answer to life's secrets. Later, during a raging bushfire, Stan rescues Madeleine from the burning manor house, and Amy's fantasy crumbles when she sees her idol, her hair burned away, kneeling and retching on the grass.

World War I begins soon after the great fire, and Stan enlists in the army. With Stan away, Amy depends on an elderly German man to help her with the farmwork. The neighbors soon force him to leave, however, because of their hatred for all Germans.

After Stan returns from the battlefields of France, he once more works his farm while his wife carries out her domestic duties faithfully and his children grow into adults. Amy engages in a brief sexual affair with a traveling salesman; Stan knows intuitively that his wife has been unfaithful, but the infatuation passes. Stan and Amy's son, Ray, becomes apprenticed to a saddle maker but decides to leave his old life behind; he wanders across Australia, spends time in prison, and eventually settles in Sydney, where he continues his criminal ways. His sister, Thelma, attends business college in Sydney, goes to work in a lawyers' office, and marries one of the lawyers. Through this marriage, she achieves her dream of living a sophisticated and cultured life, free at last from the dreary farm.

Life continues for Stan and Amy on the farm. They follow a pattern of milking the cows, cooking and eating, sleeping and awakening, dreaming and longing. Amy becomes fatter in her old age, and Stan appears to shrivel. As the years go by, the outside world encroaches more and more on their lives. Their daughter's marriage brings the Parkers into closer contact with Sydney; for the first time in their lives they spend a week in a hotel in the city, where they also attend a stage play. Sydney claims the body of their son Ray, whose life of crime ends with his murder.

The land around the Parker farm, all unsettled in the family's early years, evolves into a suburb. Developers subdivide the neighboring farmland into lots for homes that eventually surround the Parkers' old house, which by this time is almost entirely obscured from view by the plants and trees Amy has planted over half a century. An awareness of mortality enters their lives, first through their son's murder, then through the death from cancer of Amy's longtime friend Mrs. O'Dowd. Finally Stan dies, quickly and simply, in the garden he had carved from the wilderness, with Amy at his side.

Critical Evaluation:

Without question one of Australia's greatest writers, Patrick White received the Nobel Prize in Literature in 1973. By that time he had published eight novels, four plays, and two collections of short stories. Four more novels and plays, along with another collection of short stories and an autobiography, followed. *The Tree of Man*, his fourth novel, holds an important place in the White canon. First, it lays the groundwork for White's imaginary Sydney suburb of Sarsaparilla, which figures prominently in his later fiction and drama. This recurrent setting has often been compared to William Faulkner's Yoknapatawpha County. *The Tree of Man* also brought international attention to White's work, which had earlier gone largely unnoticed both in Australia and abroad. In addition, it marks the first of his books to be written after he returned to Australia following his university years at Oxford, a stint in London as an aspiring writer, extensive travel, and military service during World War II. Of greatest significance, however, is the way this early novel irrevocably altered Australian fiction, which had previously stressed realism and avoided metaphysical speculation. White, fairly or not, once described the typical Australian novel as "the dreary dun-colored offspring of journalistic realism." He set out to change this gloomy assessment of his country's fiction—and did so.

In *The Tree of Man*, White created a parable depicting the contemporary search for meaning. It may appear odd at first to describe the novel in this way. On a simpler level it would be better to classify it as domestic realism. It essentially unfolds the mundane story of Stan and Amy Parker, who marry, work their farm, have children, grow old, and face death. As they carve out their home in the wilderness, they experience flood, fire, dust, and flies—ironically, all of the staples of the very Australian novels White had called "dun-colored." The novel lacks conflict. It moves slowly from one event to another, the years passing almost unnoticed. The narrative fails to build to any kind of climax, and an abundance of domestic details weigh heavily.

What makes *The Tree of Man* a great novel of lasting achievement is that it is a story for all people in all places at all times. It records the history of an Australian family for three generations during the first half of the twentieth century and is quintessentially Australian, but it is finally not only Australian. In 1958, White wrote of the novel in his essay "The Prodigal Son": "I wanted to try to suggest in this book every possible aspect of life, through the lives of an ordinary man and woman. But at the same time I wanted to discover the extraordinary behind the ordinary, the mystery and poetry."

The Tree of Man presents a parable of life's greatest mystery: an individual's understanding of the divine, of God. In White's fictional world, people tend to fall into one of two categories: that of the doers or that of the seekers. Most often only one character acts the role of the seeker or the visionary, with those around him or her concerned more with doing and daily living than with the eternal mystery. Stan Parker is the visionary in *The Tree of Man*, even though he appears to be an ordinary man, as this passage from the novel suggests: "If a poetry sometimes almost formed in his head, or a vision of God, nobody knew, because you did not talk about such things, or, rather, you were not aware of the practice of doing so."

At times Stan's wife, Amy, grapples toward the extraordinary, but "she could not explain that a moment comes when you yourself must produce some tangible evidence of the mystery of life." Neither the Parker children nor any of the other characters in the novel share Stan's "vision of God," which comes to him finally in all its glory at the moment of his death in the garden. Amy, by then a fat, rather disagreeable old woman who neither fully appreciates nor grasps Stan's silent spiritual quest, at times even envies it, walks away from the garden and her husband's body, once more doing the practical thing by calling on those who can help her physically.

The final chapter, only two pages long, is a kind of coda to Stan's quest. His grandson, another visionary, wanders through the garden where Stan died and pledges to put into poetry what his grandfather had known but had been unable to express. It is tempting to see the boy as White himself. In 1956, he had just set out to write a series of powerful novels that were to make brilliant use of the actual Australian garden in a way that far transcends the reality of the setting.

A distinguishing mark of the parable is the simplicity of its story. *The Tree of Man* possesses this quality. The metaphysical implications that stand behind every line do not intrude on the narrative itself, which offers a touching, sometimes comic, account of a family's everyday struggles over a period of fifty years. White's altogether original technique of embedding his ideas into character, narrative, and setting provides a rare, if demanding, reading experience.

Much has been said about the difficulty, at times the inaccessibility, of White's writing style, one critic even dubbing it "illiterate verbal sludge." It would be far more fitting to praise the density of the language, its near poetic qualities, and its appropriateness to the work's purpose. Just as the visionaries yearn to make their realizations known, White, with what he called "the sticks and stones" of language, attempts to express the inexpressible. The structure of the prose generates a nervous energy. This energy strives toward the revelation of the truth, "the extraordinary behind the ordinary, the mystery and poetry."

Robert L. Ross

Further Reading

Bliss, Carolyn. "*The Tree of Man*." In *Patrick White's Fiction: The Paradox of Fortunate Failure*. New York: St. Martin's Press, 1986. Provides a clear analysis of the novel, placing it within the White canon. Part of a larger discussion that argues that all of White's writing stems from a paradox—that is, the failures so often experienced by the characters can in fact lead to their successful redemption.

Bulman-May, James. *Patrick White and Alchemy.* Kew, Vic.: Australian Scholarly Publishing, 2001. Examines the intricate alchemical symbolism in White's work and its connections to Jungian psychology.

Colmer, John. *Patrick White.* New York: Methuen, 1984. Examines the continuity of vision in White's fiction. Discusses and places *The Tree of Man* within that context as an important early work.

During, Simon. *Patrick White.* New York: Oxford University Press, 1996. Examines White's place in Australian history and culture, arguing that his work reflected the end of the country's colonial relationship with Great Britain. Analyzes the connection between White's homosexuality and his writing.

Hewill, Helen Verity. *Patrick White: Painter Manqué— Paintings, Painters, and Their Influence on His Writing.* Carlton, Vic.: Miegunyah Press, 2002. Describes how painting was a source of inspiration for White, addressing specifically the influence of twentieth century Australian art and European modernist and Romantic art on his work.

Hope, A. D. "The Bunyip Stages a Comeback: *The Tree of Man.*" In *Critical Essays on Patrick White*, edited by Peter Wolfe. Boston: G. K. Hall, 1990. Noted review of the novel was written in 1956 by a leading Australian poet. Praises the way White represents "a sense of the mystery of all living" but criticizes his prose style, calling it "pretentious and illiterate verbal sludge."

Kramer, Leonie. "*The Tree of Man*: An Essay in Skepticism." In *Critical Essays on Patrick White*, edited by Peter Wolfe. Boston: G. K. Hall, 1990. Traces Stan Parker's "journey toward enlightenment" by analyzing the formal structure of the novel. Argues that Stan's supposed spiritual illumination has been overestimated by critics and asserts instead that the novel expresses a skeptical "attitude towards metaphysical speculation."

Weigel, John A. *Patrick White.* Boston: Twayne, 1983. Provides a comprehensive introduction to all aspects of White's work and life—an excellent starting point for a study of White's fiction. Includes a well-defined discussion of *The Tree of Man.*

The Tree of the Folkungs

Author: Verner von Heidenstam (1859-1940)

First published: Folkungaträdet, 1905-1907 (English translation, 1925)

Type of work: Novel

Type of plot: Historical

Time of plot: Eleventh and thirteenth centuries

Locale: Sweden

Principal characters:

FOLKE FILBYTER, the founder of the Folkung line

INGEMUND,

HALLSTEN, and

INGEVALD, his sons

FOLKE INGEVALDSSON, his grandson

ULF ULFSSON, a pagan udalman

KING VALDEMAR, a descendant of Folke Filbyter

DUKE MAGNUS, his brother

QUEEN SOPHIA, the wife of Valdemar

LADY JUTTA, her sister

GISTRE HARJANSON, a minstrel

YRSA-LILL, a goatherd

ARCHBISHOP FULCO, the prelate of Upsala

The Story:

Folke Filbyter plants the seed from which grows the mighty Folkung tree. Returning homeward after long sea roving, he brings his ship to shore near a shield maiden's grave ground in the land of Sveas and Goths. Dwarf Jorgrimme, a Finnish sorcerer, prophesies terror will darken the land, and Thor's image will tremble.

Folke tramps inland for two nights, his sack of booty on his back. The third night he comes to Jorgrimme's cave, where the sorcerer gives him drink from the horn Manegarm, treasure of the gods. Then the dwarf cuts the sack so that some of the gold falls out. Discovering the leak, Folke swears he sows the ground with riches he will also reap. There he builds his mighty hall, Folketuna.

Before long Folke has land and thralls but no sons. One

morning his men find Jorgrimme's daughter trapped in a wolf pit, and Folke takes her home to his bed. She has three sons—Ingemund, Hallsten, and Ingevald—but she gets no honor and crouches in the straw like the scurviest thrall. Ingevald stays by his father's side. Ingemund and Hallsten go roving at sea.

Folke, wanting a good marriage for his son, speaks for Holmdis, Ulf Ulfsson's daughter. Meanwhile old Jakob, a begging friar, preaches a new faith in the region. When Ingevald tumbles the dwarfs' one-eyed god, his mother gives him sacred Manegarm, stolen from Jorgrimme's burial cairn. Folke swears blood brotherhood with the king of outlaws and gets great riches. Then Holmdis proudly spurns a match with the thrall woman's son, but Ingevald carries her by force to his father's hall. There, waiting in vain for her kinsmen to rescue her, she brings one son to Folketuna before she dies. After Holmdis's funeral, Folke turns away from Ingevald. Folke Ingevaldsson is his grandfather's heir.

When Jakob comes again, Ingevald, hoping to save his son from the lawless life at Folketuna, gives the child to the priest. For years old Folke rides from hearth to hearth looking for his lost grandchild. Thrall and thane alike know of the grim old man's search.

King Inge travels through the land with his bodyguards, and wherever he stops men either die or are baptized in the new faith. When Ulf Ulfsson speaks for the old gods, the king's earl and chief adviser, a ruthless, priest-trained young man, leaves him bound to perish in the forest. Ingemund and Hallsten, homeward bound, are in Ulf's hall that night and join the king's guard.

Folke is at Upsala when the sacred grove burns and people cry out against Inge and call Blot Sven king. There Folke sees the king's earl, on his hand the star-shaped mark of the child stolen from Folketuna years before. Although the old outlaw offers his riches to help the king's need, young Folke and his uncles are proud men with little wish to have a name as unsavory as Folke Filbyter's associated with them, now that they are counted among the greatest of the king's thanes. They take the treasure he offers to advance themselves, but they seldom visit him in the bare hall where he sits in the dirty straw. At last he opens his veins and dies as unwanted old men did in ancient times.

Two hundred years later, King Holmger lies dead, with the sacred sword Grane on his grave, and Earl Birger of the Folkungs rules in Sweden, although it is his young son Valdemar who wears the crown. Valdemar grows up weak and soft, a lover of pleasure and women. From his far ancestor, Folke Filbyter, he inherits a yeoman's love of the land and a liking for serfs and for outlaws. There are many who

think that his brother, Junker Magnus, should be king, for he is bold and cunning and the better knight. When Magnus unhorses his brother at a great tournament at Belbo and Valdemar laughs at his tumble without shame or regret, Birger is so angry with his son that he collapses from a stroke and dies soon afterward. At the division of the earl's estate, his sons quarrel over a missing drinking horn, Manegarm, an heirloom of the old days.

Valdemar's bride is Sophia, the daughter of Denmark's king. Lady Jutta is her sister. Sometimes Valdemar talks with the maid alone, and she becomes frightened. Valdemar also spends much time in the hut of Yrsa-lill, a woman goatherd, to whom Gistre Harjanson carries Manegarm. The company drinks from it when Valdemar goes to the hut to carouse with herdsmen and outcasts. Meanwhile the land knows confusion. Peasants pay no taxes, and robbers roam the highways. Valdemar will allow no wrongdoer to be punished.

When Jutta wishes to return to Denmark, Magnus and Sir Svantepolk, a worthy knight, set out to escort her. Valdemar overtakes them at the goatherd's hut, where the party stops to rest. After convincing Jutta that Magnus is a trickster, Valdemar accompanies her to the border, and on the way they become lovers. Sir Svantepolk, renouncing his allegiance, rides off to join Duke Magnus. Queen Sophia has Yrsa-lill thrown into a cage filled with snakes. Gistre, the minstrel, rescues her. She afterward lies speechless in the convent at Vreta.

When Jutta has a son beyond the marches, Valdemar gives the child into the keeping of Archbishop Fulco of Upsala. Then the king threatens to take away his brother's titles. Magnus has the sword Grane brought from King Holmger's tomb and fastens it to his own belt. At Vreta, Yrsa-lill regains her speech and prophesies that whoever gets St. Eirik's banner from a man maiden's hands will rule Sweden.

Jutta, now prioress at Roskilde, goes to Upsala for a holy festival honoring St. Eirik. There she finds her son and sees Valdemar surrounded by his wild bodyguard. Moved by her old love, she takes off her religious habit and dresses in the robes of one of the king's favorites. Together she and Valdemar stand on the balcony of the king's house while the people howl disapproval and insults. Queen Sophia orders Jutta sent to a convent in the archbishop's keeping.

Archbishop Fulco gives St. Eirik's banner to some maidens who carry it to Duke Magnus. Afterward there is war between the brothers. Crafty, vain Magnus battles Valdemar and his army of peasants and outlaws. Valdemar, however, seems indifferent to the outcome and sits feasting at Ramundeboda while his army is defeated at Hofva. From that time on Magnus has the crown, but the war does not end with his victory, for Valdemar fights and then flees from lost villages and provinces. At last the outlawed king has nothing left but a jeweled riding whip borrowed from Lady Luitgard, the last friend to share his misfortunes, and he gives that to Gistre and tells the minstrel to go look for Yrsa-lill. Alone and unarmed, Valdemar then surrenders to his brother.

King Magnus, old and sick by that time, gives the country peace. Valdemar lives a prisoner at Nykopingshus, and Luitgard is his only company. Nevertheless, in his captivity he finds such contentment that Magnus dies envying him.

Critical Evaluation:

Like Sigrid Undset in Norway, Verner von Heidenstam drew inspiration from the history of his native Sweden in medieval times. *The Tree of the Folkungs* is a historical novel of imaginative freedom and dramatic vigor. There are two parts to the story. The first deals with the period at the end of the eleventh century—a barbaric, brutal age which in the North saw heathenism and Christianity in conflict. In the second half of the novel, the Folkung family, proud descendants of an ancient peasant freebooter, push their way to the Swedish throne by the middle of the thirteenth century. The pageantry, heroism, humility, superstition, cruelty, and greed of the Middle Ages come alive to the reader. The effect is not one of antiquarianism, however, for Heidenstam is interested in a living past, the growth of a culture, with its mixture of good and evil, nobility and baseness. The writer tells his story with a variety of styles and techniques, mingling myth, legend, history, saga, and fantasy. The result is a literary work of significance and tragic power. The author was awarded the Nobel Prize in Literature in 1916.

The Tree of the Folkungs is romantic with a core of realism. It presents the saga of a great family that held sway in Sweden from the close of the Viking age to the end of the thirteenth century. Written in a style reminiscent of that of ancient legends, this massive novel records the destiny of a nation. In deceptively simple, richly poetic prose, the author vividly brings to life those long-ago times. The primitive religion and lingering superstitions of the people are woven into the narrative, and the close union between these beliefs and the constant struggle of the people with the land and the forces of nature is clearly and dramatically drawn. A deep tranquillity often pervades the exquisite descriptions of the locales; a stolid force suggests throughout the book that the land and the sea are the vital elements in existence, while people come and go, transitory visitors to the scene.

The life of these ancient people is meticulously detailed, their clothes, battle gear, and homes all described with the detail of an anthropological report, yet these details never intrude into the narrative; they give the story a verisimilitude necessary for a modern reader's enjoyment. Perhaps a certain ponderous, humorless quality that exists in the writing was unavoidable, for the people Heidenstam writes about are tough, serious individuals struggling with a world that allows little time for gracious living or humor. The characters strongly believe in the power of fate and possess a great sense of their own destiny. This aspect of the book is both stirring and touching and provides the true emotional impetus to the narrative.

For all of their toughness, these people are essentially innocent, almost childlike. Jealousies, rivalries, hatreds, and primitive passions motivate them. Pride above all rules their lives; loss of pride is more than they can bear. The great Folke Filbyter, the founder of the clan, who weds a dwarf's daughter and lives to see his family great, is memorable, almost superhuman. Over all the family stands the lime tree and the spirit that dwells within it, watching over the family. The branches and spreading roots of the tree provide a rich symbolic framework for the novel equal to the great tree of generations begun by Filbyter.

Further Reading

Brantly, Susan. "Heidenstam's *Karolinerna* and the Fin de Siècle." In *Fin(s) de Siècle in Scandinavian Perspective*, edited by Faith Ingwersen and Mary Kay Norseng. Columbia, S.C.: Camden House, 1993. This critical study of Heidenstam's novel is included in a collection of essays that examine Scandinavian literature and artistic movements that appeared at the end of the last three centuries.

Gustafson, Alrik. *Six Scandinavian Novelists: Lie, Jacobsen, Heidenstam, Selma Lagerlöf, Hamsun, Sigrid Undset.* Princeton, N.J.: Princeton University Press, 1940. Reprint. Minneapolis: University of Minnesota Press, 1966. A chapter on Heidenstam provides biographical information, including the origins of Heidenstam's ideas about depicting the beginnings of his nation.

Warme, Lars G., ed. *A History of Swedish Literature.* Lincoln: University of Nebraska Press, 1996. The chapter "The Aesthetic Revolt of the 1890's" contains several pages of information about Heidenstam, and there are other references to him in this survey.

Zuck, Virpi, ed. *Dictionary of Scandinavian Literature.* Westport, Conn.: Greenwood Press, 1990. Entry on Heidenstam places the poet and writer in his historical and literary contexts. Discusses Heidenstam's nationalistic enthusiasms.

The Trial

Author: Franz Kafka (1883-1924)
First published: Der Prozess, 1925 (English translation, 1937)
Type of work: Novel
Type of plot: Symbolic realism
Time of plot: Early twentieth century
Locale: Germany

Principal characters:
JOSEPH K., a bank employee
FRAU GRUBACH, his landlady
FRÄULEIN BÜRSTNER, his neighbor
ALBERT K., his uncle
HULD, his lawyer
LENI, Huld's servant and mistress
TITORELLI, a painter
THE INSPECTOR,
THE JUDGE,
FRANZ, and
WILLEM, minor officers of the court
THE WASHERWOMAN, befriends K.

The Story:

Perhaps someone has been slandering Joseph K., because one morning, without having done anything wrong, he is arrested. Each morning around eight o'clock the landlady's cook usually brings K., as he is called, his breakfast, and the old woman who lives across the way from him usually stares at him with a curiosity unusual even for her.

This morning, the old woman fails to stare at him, so K. begins to ring her but first hears a knock on his door. Without waiting for a response, a man dressed like a traveler and whom K. does not recognize enters the room. When K. hears a short burst of laughter from another room, he jumps out of bed to investigate. The stranger asks Josef if he would not rather stay in his room, but K. answers that he has no wish to stay in the room nor to be addressed by the stranger, whose name turns out to be Franz. In the next room, K. sees another strange man, whose name is Willem, sitting in front of a window and reading a book. When K. asks to see Frau Grubach, his landlady, Willem puts down his book and informs K. that he is being detained.

Bewildered, K. asks many questions of Franz and his companion, only to find that they can tell him very little about his case. They cannot tell him the reason why he is being held, for they themselves do not know the reason. K. shows these strangers, now his guards, his identification papers. They tell him that they cannot settle his case and that they have been sent to guard him. They also tell K. that they share a similar situation with him because neither of the three knows the intricacies of the law.

The guards think of K. as a reasonable man, and K. is mystified that they are by turn kind to him, yet demanding as well. In a moment of levity, the pair tells K. that he should give them his underwear to hold for him while he undergoes this trial period, and that they will return the underwear to him when he is released. Finally, the inspector arrives; Franz and Willem tell K. that he must wear a black coat before he faces the inspector. K. complies, and then walks into the adjoining room to face his first interrogator.

To his dismay, K. discovers that the inspector is sitting in Fräulein Bürstner's room. Although he seldom speaks to Bürstner because her job as a typist requires that she leave early and return late, K. is protective of her space and offended that the inspector and the other men are using her space as their own. When the inspector asks K. if he is surprised by the morning's events, K. replies that he is surprised but not greatly surprised. The inspector gives no further hint as to the reason for the arrest, and he cannot tell K. whether or not K. has been accused of anything. He advises K. to think more about himself and not about the guards or the inspector, and advises K. not to make such a fuss about his innocence. When K. attempts to reconcile simply with a handshake, the inspector shrugs it off and declares how simple everything seems to K.

The inspector tells K. that he can go to work at the bank as usual, but only if accompanied by K.'s three colleagues, who have been in the interrogation room all along. During the day, several visitors stop by K.'s office with deferential birthday greetings, for it is his thirtieth birthday. Rather than following his usual pattern of arriving at his room around 11 P.M.—after drinks with friends or sometimes a visit to a prostitute—he goes home by 9:30 to talk with Fräulein Bürstner. First, however, K. talks to his landlady and asks her if she knows anything about his situation or about the men in his room earlier in the day. She tells him that she knows he is under arrest, but she knows little more. He then waits for Bürstner to arrive home so that he can apologize to her for the disruption of the proceedings. She finally arrives, and K. tells her his story; she listens with feigned interest only. She has trouble believing that K. has come to her room only to tell her this incredible story. Weary of his presence, she asks K. to leave, but before he does, he seizes her wrist and then kisses her passionately before returning to his room.

A few days later, K. receives a telephone call ordering him to appear before the court for interrogation on Sunday. The authorities tell K. that his hearings will be on Sundays so they do not disrupt his professional life. The hearings take place in a building on a street in a distant district with which K. is unfamiliar. Although the phone call notes the day of the meeting, it does not state a specific time. Recognizing that most such meetings occur at 9 A.M., K. decides to arrive by that time.

K. discovers indistinguishable gray apartment buildings set against industrial buildings; the building to which he proceeds has the look of a warehouse, but it is filled with apartments and activity. Because he does not know the exact room to which he must go, he inquires on several floors before he finally locates the room on the fifth floor; it is filled with old men, most of them with long beards.

The judge asks K. if he is a house painter; K. snappishly replies that he is the junior manager of a bank. The judge then tells K. that K. is one hour and ten minutes late. To this charge, K. replies that he is present now, his appearance in court being the main thing. The crowd applauds. Encouraged, he launches into a harangue damning the court, its methods, the warders who had arrested him, and the meeting time and place. The judge seems taken aback, and the crowd seems to be enjoying this spectacle, often siding with K. The proceedings are then interrupted. At the back of the room, a man, who is a law student, grabs and holds the washerwoman in his arms and then screams, all the while looking at the ceiling. K. dashes from the room, loudly refusing to have any more dealings with the court.

All during the week, K. awaits another summons. When none arrives, he decides to revisit the meeting hall. The washerwoman again meets him kindly and expresses her disappointment that the court was not in session. Because her husband is a court usher, she knows a little bit about the court and its methods. The judge, she tells K., can request at any time that she and her husband move the furniture from their flat so that the court can meet in the rooms. The court is only a lower body that rarely interferes with the freedom of the individuals under investigation. If the court acquits the individual, it means little, for a higher court might arrest the individual again. She shows K. the courtroom and the books on the magistrate's table. K. discovers that the books are dusty and appear never to have been opened; the books, also, are pornographic books, not law books. The woman offers to help K. with his case because she knows that the magistrate likes her. As she and K. are speaking, the law student bursts into the room, seizes her, and carries her up the stairs because the magistrate has called for her.

The woman's husband kindly offers to lead K. up to the law offices, the inner sanctum of the court, located in the attic. Here, K. finds a number of people waiting for answers to petitions. Some of them have been waiting for years, and they are becoming a little anxious about their cases. The hot room under the roof makes K. dizzy, so he sits down. A young woman tries to soothe him, and the information officer applauds K.'s dogged interest in his own case, indicating that many others do not pursue their cases with such care and interest. Suffering from claustrophobia, K. follows the officer's advice and leaves the office for the fresh air of the stairway and the streets and finds himself with renewed energy.

A few evenings later, as K. is walking down a corridor in his office, he hears groans coming from behind a door. Mystified, he opens the door to what he thinks is a utility closet and sees a man with a whip flogging Franz and Willem, the two guards who had originally confronted K. in his own flat. They tell K. they are being punished because of K.'s demand that the court punish the guards. K. replies that he has never reported them, nor does he desire to do so. Haunted by this scene, K. asks his assistants to clean out the closet the next day.

K. and his uncle, Albert K., visit a lawyer named Huld, an old friend of Albert, to whom K. might be able to turn for advice and even defense. While in Huld's office, K. meets Leni, his servant girl whose hand is disfigured by a web between two fingers. She seduces K. with promises that she can help him. All the while, Albert is waiting for him in the car, and upon K.'s return, warns him that his behavior with Leni, who is the lawyer's mistress as well, may have lost K. the case. However, this warning does not stop K. from continuing to employ Huld for a time, realizing that the lawyer understands the labyrinthine nature of the court and its processes. K.'s case does not move very far under Huld's direction, so K. decides that he must handle his own case. He fires Huld.

Titorelli, the court painter, advises K., whom he just met, that he can hope for little with this court. He tells K. that he could receive an actual acquittal, an apparent acquittal, or protraction. No one is ever really acquitted, he says, but sometimes cases can be prolonged indefinitely. In return for Titorelli's advice, K. buys three of his paintings.

Visiting a cathedral, K. is preparing to sit in one of the pews when he hears a priest loudly call his name; the priest then introduces himself as the prison chaplain. K. asks the priest how he is deceiving himself about the nature of the court, and the priest responds by telling K. a parable about a man before the law. This man from the country arrives at the gate to the law, asking to enter; the doorkeeper says that he cannot grant the man admittance just now. The man asks if he can be admitted later, and the doorkeeper replies that it might be possible. The man from the country sits for years waiting to be admitted to the law, entreating the doorkeeper and even the fleas on the doorkeeper's coat to be admitted. Finally, as he is dying, the man asks the doorkeeper why no one else has come over the years to ask about admittance to the law. The doorkeeper replies simply that this entrance to the law is meant solely for the man from the country and for no one else, and he shuts the door. K. and the priest then engage in a long discussion about the nature of the law, and K. leaves the cathedral with little hope about his case.

It is the evening before K.'s thirty-first birthday, and two men in frock coats and top hats arrive at his apartment. K. is sitting in his room in a black coat. He puts on his gloves, seemingly expecting the men. They all leave K.'s building and proceed to an isolated spot in a nearby quarry, where one of the men holds K.'s throat and the other stabs him in the heart. K. dies like a dog.

Critical Evaluation:

Franz Kafka's *The Trial* is one of the most effective and most discussed works to originate in Central Europe in the period between World War I and World War II. Although the complex and ambiguous surface of the novel defies exact interpretation, the plight of Josef K., or K., condemned for some sort of crime by a court with which he cannot communicate, is a profound and disturbing image of humanity in the modern world. To some, the court is a symbol of the Church as an imperfect bridge between a person and God. To others, the symbolism represents rather the search of a sensitive Jew for an elusive homeland, ever denied him. Although unfinished, *The Trial* is a powerful and provocative novel.

The Trial is one of the pillars upon which Kafka's reputation as a major twentieth century writer rests, and it is one of the works he ordered, in his will, to be destroyed. It survives only because his friend Max Brod, who possessed a manuscript of the unfinished novel, dismissed Kafka's request and preserved the manuscript, along with *The Castle* (1926), *Amerika* (1913)—which is available in a translation with the

more correct title *The Man Who Went Missing*—and a host of fragments and shorter works. The salvaging of this novel from the manuscript was not an easy task, however, and controversy still exists regarding the proper order of the chapters and about the placement and interpretation of a number of unfinished segments, which are not included in the usual editions. Fortunately, both the beginning and the end of the novel are extant and, because of the peculiar structure of the work, minor changes in the order of the sections do not alter a reader's understanding of the work.

In the late twentieth century and continuing into the twenty-first century, new translations of Kafka's major works, based on the restored texts in the new German critical edition of the works, began to appear. These translations present Kafka's texts in a form as close as possible to the state in which Kafka left his manuscripts. Breon Mitchell's 1998 translation of *The Trial* makes slight changes in the chapter divisions and in the sequence of chapter fragments; the long first chapter in the Muirs translation has in Mitchell been broken into two chapters. Mitchell's translation illustrates more clearly than ever that Kafka wrote the first and last chapter of the novel simultaneously, and the stylistic and thematic similarities of these chapters become immediately apparent in his translation. For example, in Mitchell, the surprise visit of Franz and Willem, the court's two guards in the first chapter, and their urging that K. put on a black coat to face the inspector are perfectly parallel with the two nameless men in the final chapter who come to retrieve K.—who is dressed in a black coat while waiting for them—to carry out the wishes of the court.

In addition, Mitchell's translation vividly captures the images of humans as animalistic creatures that pervade the novel. The presentation of human traits through animals and the images of humans as animals is a Kafka hallmark. Kafka illustrates the animalistic nature of humans in stories that include *Die Verwandlung* (1915; *The Metamorphosis*, 1936); "Josephine die Sängerin: Oder, Das Volk der äuse" (1924; *Josephine the Singer: Or the Mouse Folk*, 1942); "Ein Bericht für eine Akademie" (1917; "A Report to An Academy," 1946), in which an ape delivers a report; "Der Bau" (1931; "The Burrow," 1946), which features a burrowing creature, perhaps a badger, that obsessively builds and rebuilds its house; and *The Man Who Went Missing*, featuring the protagonist Karl Rossmann, the "horse-man." In *The Trial*, Kafka uses such images to terrific effect. After K. tells Fräulein Bürstner his story, he kisses her all over her face like a thirsty animal lapping at a spring; Leni, lawyer Huld's servant and mistress, has animal-like features, and K. crawls off to embrace this little creature; during the flogging of Franz and Willem, K. compares the cries of the two men being whipped to a dog howling in the courtyard; finally, as the two strangers kill K., he dies like a dog.

Mitchell's translation also makes clear the theatrical nature of *The Trial*. Such theatricality may be found throughout Kafka's writings; his first novel, *The Man Who Went Missing* (also, like *The Trial*, unfinished) concludes with Karl Rossmann's venture to the nature theater of Oklahoma. It is no mistake that the well-known filmmaker Orson Welles directed a 1962 film adaptation of *The Trial* so that its opening scenes reveal the comic nature of the first half of the novel. Some critics have pointed out that *The Trial* begins as a farce and ends as a tragedy. In Mitchell's translation, the first chapter, "Arrest," makes K.'s arrest into a production in which various spectators gaze at his predicament. Almost immediately after he awakes one morning, K. spies the older woman across the way staring at him. As his interrogation before the inspector proceeds, two other people gather with the old woman to watch the proceedings, as do his three colleagues from the bank.

Furthermore, later in the same evening, K. reenacts the interrogation scene for Fräulein Bürstner, playing all the roles in the drama and shouting dramatically. K.'s initial appearance before the magistrate also resembles a stage performance, with K. declaiming his innocence before two galleries of spectators. In the penultimate chapter, the priest in the cathedral performs a scene for K., enacting through his parable the meaning of the law. Finally, K. refers to the two men who come to retrieve him as supporting actors whom the court has sent for him, and he even asks them in what theater they are now playing. As they prepare to kill him in the quarry, a face appears at the window in a nearby building, representing yet another spectator who this time observes not a comedy but a tragedy.

The novel is structured within an exact time frame. Exactly one year elapses between the arrest of K., which takes place on his thirtieth birthday, and his execution, which takes place on the night before his thirty-first birthday. Moreover, the novel tells almost nothing about K.'s past; there are no memories, no flashbacks, no expository passages explaining the background. As in so many of his works, Kafka begins *The Trial* with the incursion of a totally unexpected force into an otherwise uneventful life, and the situation never again returns to normal. Kafka felt that the moment of waking was the most dangerous moment of the day, a time when one was unprotected by the structures of one's life and open to such an incursion.

K., in this vulnerable state, responds to the messengers of the court; from this point, there is no turning back. The court is invisible—a hierarchy in which even the lowest members are somehow beyond K.'s grasp. There are no formal charges, no procedures, and little information to guide the defendant. Indeed, one of the most unsettling aspects of the novel is the constant uncertainty, the juxtaposition of alternative hypotheses, the multiple explanations for events, and the differing interpretations regarding cause and effect. The whole rational structure of the world is undermined, as perceived reality becomes the subject of detailed exegesis such as one might apply to sacred Scripture. Reality itself becomes a vague concept, because the reader is denied the guiding commentary of a narrator and sees everything from K.'s point of view.

The entire work is composed of K.'s experiences; he is present in every scene. Secondary characters appear only as they relate to him, and the reader knows no more than he does. With K., the reader receives information that could be misinformation; experiences bizarre, barely credible incidents; and moves from scene to scene as if in a trance. This narrowness of the point of view becomes oppressive. The reader, in effect, becomes K.

As the German title, *Der Prozess* ("the process") indicates, K.'s story involves a process that includes numerous hearings and investigations; K. experiences a series of trials as he journeys through a legal system that resembles nothing like any legal system with which most people are familiar. As he travels in fits and starts toward a verdict, he meets various people along the way who, like him, are mere puppets of the court. K. is not alone in his inability to comprehend the workings of the court; the others whom he meets cannot comprehend either, for they understand only the little portion of the court with which they are associated. However, by the end of the novel, K. reaches a verdict, and in so doing, he indicates that he understands the court better than most of the workers he has encountered along the way.

In the final lines of the novel, the two men who are executing K. watch him closely to observe the verdict that he will deliver. In the older translation these men are simply watching the final act, while in the new translation it is clear that K.'s verdict demonstrates that he has known all along—or that he has discovered sometime during the process—that he will die.

One is left with the question of what it all means. This is perhaps the wrong question to ask, because it implies that there is a meaning that can be defined, a key to understanding that generally involves assigning some allegorical value to the court: authoritarian society, human alienation from a sense of wholeness and purpose in life, the search for God's grace. Still, it is the genius of Kafka's works that they are inexhaustible and veiled in an ultimately impenetrable mystery. They admit of many interpretations, but the more specific the definition of the meaning of the work, the more inadequate it is to encompass the full amplitude of the novel.

Kafka's works are less allegorical than symbolic; their symbolism lies in the construction of an image or an experience that is analogous to a human experience that lies far deeper than any of the specific problems offered as explanations for the work's meaning. In *The Trial*, K. is confronted with the need to justify his life and to justify it at a metaphysical level deeper than any ex post facto rationalization of his actions. It is a demand he cannot meet, and yet it is inescapable because it arises from within him. He is an Everyman, but he is stripped of his religion and on trial for his life. For Kafka, the trial becomes a metaphor for life itself, and every sentence is a sentence of death.

"Critical Evaluation" by Steven C. Schaber;
revised by Henry L. Carrigan, Jr.

Further Reading

Begley, Louis. *The Tremendous World I Have Inside My Head: Franz Kafka—A Biographical Essay.* New York: Atlas, 2008. Weaving selections from Kafka's letters, journals, novels, and stories into his own biographical narrative, Begley follows Kafka from his early desire to write and his need for quiet to compose and his well-known relationships with Felice Bauer, Milena Jesenkà, and Dora Diamant through his tuberculosis and death.

Bloom, Harold, ed. *Kafka's Novels: An Interpretation.* New York: Rodopi, 2003. A chapter-by-chapter analysis of *The Trial* and two other novels. One essay focuses on Kafka's symbolic language, including his use of metaphors and ambiguous words, describing how he uses this language to visualize "dreams and thoughts on the edge of sleep."

Calasso, Roberto. *K.* New York: Knopf, 2005. A scholarly study in which Calasso seeks to understand what Kafka's fiction is meant to signify. He also examines why K. is so radically different from any other characters in the history of the novel.

Corngold, Stanley. *Lambent Traces: Franz Kafka.* Princeton, N.J.: Princeton University Press, 2004. Argues that Kafka's literary career was an attempt to re-create the ecstasy he felt on the night of September 22, 1912, when he wrote his short story "The Judgment." He describes Kafka's work, including *The Trial*, in terms of this search for personal transcendence.

Gray, Richard T., Ruth V. Gross, Rolf J. Goebel, and Clayton Koelb. *A Franz Kafka Encyclopedia.* Westport, Conn.: Greenwood Press, 2005. A comprehensive volume that contains alphabetized entries on all aspects of Kafka's life and work, including his work's characters, places, and events.

Hayman, Ronald. *K: A Biography of Kafka.* New ed. London: Phoenix, 2001. This book presents a solid and readable account of Kafka's life, intended for the general reader and students. Includes a chronology and an extensive bibliography. First published in 1981.

Liska, Vivian. *When Kafka Says We: Uncommon Communities in German-Jewish Literature.* Bloomington: Indiana University Press, 2009. Liska's brilliant study explores the ways that Kafka presents in his fiction and nonfiction new avenues for creating potential communities.

Preece, Julian, ed. *The Cambridge Companion to Kafka.* New York: Cambridge University Press, 2002. A collection of essays about Kafka, including an analysis of *The Trial* and discussions of Kafka and gender, popular culture, and Jewish folklore.

Rolleston, James, ed. *Twentieth Century Interpretations of "The Trial": A Collection of Critical Essays.* Englewood Cliffs, N.J.: Prentice-Hall, 1976. Ten essays and an introduction offer a wide sampling of critical responses to the "opaqueness" of *The Trial*. Presents Kafka's relationships to psychoanalysis and other modern modes of interpretation. Includes an extensive critical bibliography.

Stach, Reiner. *Kafka: The Decisive Years.* New York: Harcourt, 2005. A now-standard biography that examines Kafka's life and work to 1915 and focuses on the crucial years between 1910 and 1915, years that were, Stach argues, instrumental to Kafka's work as a writer.

The Trickster of Seville

Author: Tirso de Molina (1580?-1648)
First produced: El burlador de Sevilla, c. 1630; first
    published, c. 1630 (English translation, 1923)
Type of work: Drama
Type of plot: Social morality
Time of plot: Seventeenth century
Locale: Naples, Italy; Seville, Spain

Principal characters:
DON JUAN TENORIO, a young man
DON DIEGO TENORIO, his father
CATALINÓN, Don Juan's servant
ISABELA, Duke Octavio's lover
DON PEDRO TENORIO, Don Juan's uncle
MARQUÉS DE LA MOTA, Doña Ana's lover
DON GONZALO DE ULLOA, Doña Ana's father
TISBEA, a fisherwoman
AMINTA, Batricio's betrothed

The Story:

In Naples, Italy, Don Juan Tenorio deceives Isabela by impersonating her lover, Duke Octavio, under the cover of darkness. After Isabela tells Don Juan that she wants to light a lamp, he confesses to her that he is not Duke Octavio. Isabela screams, and Don Juan is apprehended. He is permitted to escape, however, by his uncle Don Pedro Tenorio, the Spanish ambassador.

During a voyage to Spain, Don Juan is shipwrecked on the coast and is rescued by a fisherman's daughter named Tisbea. When Don Juan regains consciousness in Tisbea's arms, he begins to conquer this woman of the lower class. He ardently declares his love, discredits arguments regarding the inequality of their social stations and the responsibilities of marriage vows, and finally obtains her consent to his desires by promising to marry her. Don Juan has ordered his servant, Catalinón, to prepare their horses so that they can escape quickly after he has tricked the young woman. Catalinón repeatedly warns his master that he will some day have to face the consequences of his actions, but Don Juan answers him with the refrain, "That is a long way off." There are also references to fire: the flames of passion and the burning of Tisbea's hut.

Upon arriving in Seville, Don Juan discovers that the king has arranged his marriage to Doña Ana, the daughter of Commander Don Gonzalo de Ulloa. Doña Ana, however, is already in love with her cousin, the Marqués de la Mota, with whom she schedules a nightly meeting. Don Juan intercepts a letter containing a message for the Marqués de la Mota to meet Doña Ana at eleven o'clock, wearing a colored cape. The deceiver changes the hour of the meeting to midnight, trades capes with Mota, and arrives at Doña Ana's at eleven o'clock. Although this rendezvous appears to contain the elements of a master deceit, it causes Don Juan's demise, for Doña Ana becomes aware of the treachery and screams,

alerting her father. The commander fights a duel with Don Juan and is killed. Don Juan departs rapidly from Doña Ana's home and travels to a small village where a peasant woman named Aminta is going to marry a man named Batricio, who thinks that the presence of this nobleman is a bad omen for his wedding.

Batricio laments Don Juan's prominent position at the wedding festivities. That night, when Aminta is expecting Batricio to come to her bed, Don Juan appears. Employing the same techniques he used previously to deceive Tisbea, he persuades Aminta to give in to his desires. As he has done in the past, Catalinón prepares the horses in advance, and both master and servant escape. As the two come to a church, however, Catalinón disturbs Don Juan—who is still amused about how he tricked the gullible peasant woman—with the information that Octavio has learned the identity of Isabela's beguiler and Don Juan is obligated to marry her. Moreover, the Marqués de la Mota is advocating Don Juan's castigation.

At the churchyard, Don Juan and his servant approach Don Gonzalo's tomb, on which stands a statue of the dead commander. The beguiler read the tomb's inscription: "Here the most loyal knight waits for the Lord to wreak vengeance upon a traitor." This inscription insults Don Juan's honor, and he proceeds to mock the statue by pulling its beard and by inviting it to dine with him so that it can retaliate against him. Don Juan is so absorbed in his response to the inscription's affront to his honor that he does not remember his sworn oath of fidelity to Aminta, the oath that led her to give in to him. Don Juan had declared that if he fails to keep his promise to Aminta, God should kill him, by means of a dead man, for treachery and deceit.

Don Juan calmly approaches the hour of his supper engagement with the stone guest. The deceiver even continues to use mocking humor, carelessly entertaining his guest with verses that combine the theme of deceit with that of God's justice being a long time away. In contrast to Don Juan's demeanor, the stone guest is quiet, but then he requests that Don Juan shake hands to seal his agreement to the statue's invitation to join him for supper the next evening. This handshake is the first time Don Juan feels intense fear, and his body drips with a cold sweat.

The final meeting for supper takes place in the chapel where the remains of the commander rest. Don Juan and the statue sit down together to a meal of scorpions and snakes, with wine made of gall and vinegar. Don Juan is the guest, so he is obliged to stay and to listen to mysterious voices that announce the theme of divine justice. When Don Juan again shakes hands with the statue, he feels a fire that begins to burn him. He wants to confess to a priest, but God has already condemned him to the eternal fire of hell.

The king, God's representative on earth, becomes the dispenser of justice. He resolves the marriage problems that Don Juan has created: Octavio marries Isabela, Mota marries Ana, and Batricio marries Aminta. Tisbea, whose cold heart parallels that of the deceiver, is left without a husband.

Critical Evaluation:

Acclaimed by many scholars as having created the first Don Juan in European literature, Tirso de Molina received the honor of accompanying the vicar general to Santo Domingo by way of Seville. Tirso had resided in Toledo, where, under the influence of Lope de Vega Carpio, the creator of the Spanish *comedia* or play, he began to compose theatrical works. Tirso, a Mercederian priest elected to several important positions in the order, prepared himself for writing plays by attending literary academies and participating in poetic competitions. Tirso showed his genius by composing more than three hundred plays—both highly animated and serious *comedias*.

The Trickster of Seville, derived from a libertine story and a Castilian ballad featuring the figure of a stone guest, portrays the theological theme that God punishes blasphemy. Tirso's stylistic procedure involves varying Don Juan's multiple seductions of women by showing the action in the middle of the episodes and then modifying the settings and types of victims. The quantity of seductions provides the rapid pace of the play, and the pace is further supported by the lively dialogue of the verse form, which is varied according to the speaker. The episodic structure of repeated seductions, culminating in Don Juan's encounter with the stone guest, is unified by warnings of tragedy in previous scenes through continual allusions to the finality of death, the judgment of God, and the flames of hell. Don Gonzalo's death resulting

from his attempt to avenge his daughter's lost honor in a duel with the trickster introduces the prime unifying element of the play: the statue erected on Don Gonzalo's tomb that becomes the vehicle of Don Juan's condemnation to hell.

Another unifying factor is Don Juan's *gracioso*, or servant, who emphasizes the theme of procrastination that characterizes the deceiver. Instead of mimicking his master's ideas as a typical *gracioso* would, he cautions Don Juan not to delay his preparation for the Judgment Day. Although the fearful Catalinón underscores Don Juan's courage at the arrival of the stone guest, Catalinón assures the statue that he can trust his master's word as a gentleman, and that Don Juan's dishonesty extends only to his treatment of women. The servant's posture presents an irony that shows his failure to realize that a truly honorable person would behave honestly in dealings with both men and women.

The Spanish honor code serves to define Don Juan's character. Tirso portrays Don Juan's motivation for deceiving his four victims, of both the noble and peasant classes, and robbing them of their worth. Doña Ana, the lover of his friend the Marqués de la Mota, attracts him because she is difficult to possess. The trickster gains access to Doña Ana and another noblewoman, Isabela, by pretending to be another person. Aminta, a peasant whom he lures away from her bridegroom on the day of her marriage ceremony with assurances of wealth and social advancement, attracts Don Juan because she is an unpossessed bride. Tisbea, a fisherwoman, is the only victim who already has a passion that he does little to ignite.

The igniting of Tisbea's hut foreshadows the chapel that threatens Don Juan with hell fire. In this episode, Tirso illustrates the trickster's attitude of mockery by showing him stealing his victim's horses so that he and his servant can quickly escape. The horses, prepared for the escape in advance, symbolize two essential components of the play: speed and urgency. Since Don Juan is onstage for most of the *comedia* in order to unfold the plot, *The Trickster of Seville* contains very few pauses. The playwright's portrayal of the rapid passage of time available for his protagonist to complete his amorous conquests contrasts with the less intense manner of executing death and judgment, producing an effective dramatic tension. Don Juan's repeated declaration that he is going to enjoy his victim intensifies the irony of his assertion, "That is a long way off." The trickster repeats his deceits under the cover of the darkness of night; the protagonist's pronouncement that these are his hours prefigures the lengthy night of his damnation.

The Trickster of Seville served as an admonition to the corrupt nobility of the seventeenth century to act in a more pious manner. Don Juan is not portrayed as a sensual lover who stays to enjoy his conquest; his friend the Marqués de la Mota, who loves Doña Ana, manifests promiscuous behavior by frequenting the brothels of Seville. Don Juan is repeatedly warned to respect women's honor, but his refusal to obey the rules leads to his defying God in his encounter with Don Gonzalo. Tirso, therefore, furnishes a superb illustration of the seventeenth century theological concept that society is basically good, but the individual, endowed by the Creator with the free will to choose between good and evil, often chooses to sin. Because the society's structure is established by God, it is the sinner, such as Don Juan, who makes society the victim of sin. God's representative, the king, restores honor to the victims, resolving the dramatic situation of the *comedia* in a pleasing manner.

The Trickster of Seville introduced a universal type that was later modified by French, German, and English dramatists as well as fashioned into Mozart's famous Italian opera *Don Giovanni*. Tirso's characterization of Don Juan from a Spanish viewpoint has survived its rivals to become one of the great literary creations of all time.

"Critical Evaluation" by Linda Prewett Davis

Further Reading

Albrecht, Jane. *The Playgoing Public of Madrid in the Time of Tirso de Molina*. New Orleans: University Press of the South, 2001. Examines the nature of the audience for Tirso's *comedias*. Describes how the playwright designed his works to please and influence playgoers.

Conlon, Raymond. "The *Burlador* and the *Burlados*: A Sinister Connection." *Bulletin of the Comediantes* 42, no. 1 (Summer, 1990): 5-22. Discusses the symbolic connection between Don Juan and Duke Octavio, examining and comparing their treatment of women.

Simerka, Barbara A. "Eros and Atheism: Providential Ideology in the Don Juan Plays of Tirso de Molina and Thomas Shadwell." In *Echoes and Inscriptions: Comparative Approaches to Early Modern Spanish Literatures*, edited by Barbara A. Simerka and Christopher B. Weimer. Lewisburg, Pa.: Bucknell University Press, 2000. Focuses on elements of atheism and religious skepticism in *The Trickster of Seville* and in an adaptation of the play by British playwright Thomas Shadwell.

Thacker, Jonathan. "Cervantes, Tirso de Molina, and the First Generation." In *A Companion to Golden Age Theatre*. Rochester, N.Y.: Tamesis, 2007. Provides a concise, accessible overview of Tirso de Molina's life and career, with analysis of *The Trickster of Seville* and his other plays.

Weinstein, Leo. *The Metamorphoses of Don Juan*. 1959. Reprint. New York: AMS Press, 1978. Traces the origin of the Don Juan legend to Tirso's *The Trickster of Seville* and explains Don Juan as a practical joker. Shows how various authors have modified the original story.

Wilson, Margaret. *Spanish Drama of the Golden Age*. New York: Pergamon Press, 1969. Provides an excellent summary of the characteristics of the new *comedia* created by Lope de Vega Carpio. Compares Tirso's *comedias* with those of Vega Carpio; chapters and 7 and 8 contain a helpful explanation of *The Trickster of Seville*.

Tristan and Isolde

Author: Gottfried von Strassburg (fl. c. 1210)
First transcribed: Tristan und Isolde, c. 1210 (English translation, 1899)
Type of work: Poetry
Type of plot: Romance
Time of plot: Arthurian age
Locale: Northern continental Europe, Ireland, and England

The Poem:

Rivalin, a lord of Parmenie, tired of baiting Duke Morgan, the wicked ruler, signs a year's truce and sets off for Britain where King Mark of Cornwall is establishing peace and or-

Principal characters:
RIVALIN, a lord of Parmenie
BLANCHEFLEUR, his wife
TRISTAN, their son
RUAL THE FAITHFUL, Tristan's foster father
MARK, king of Cornwall, Tristan's uncle
ISOLDE THE FAIR, King Mark's bride, loved by Tristan
BRANGENE, Isolde's companion
ISOLDE OF THE WHITE HANDS, Tristan's bride

der. Badly wounded while fighting in the defense of Cornwall, Rivalin is pitied and nursed back to health by Mark's sister Blanchefleur, whom he takes back to Parmenie as his bride. Later, hearing of Rivalin's death at Duke Morgan's hand, Blanchefleur goes into labor and dies during the birth of her son. Rual, Rivalin's faithful steward, and his wife rear the boy out of loyalty to their dead lord and mistress and to thwart Duke Morgan's vindictiveness. The boy is named Tristan, in keeping with the sad events preceding his birth and a prophecy of grief to come.

Tristan's education is courtly, both at home and abroad; it includes music, art, literature, languages, falconry, hunting, riding, knightly prowess with sword and spear, and jousting. He uses these accomplishments to great advantage through-out his short life. He is loved deeply by his foster parents, his stepbrothers, and the people of Parmenie.

Kidnapped by Norwegians, Tristan manages to make his way to Cornwall after an eight-day storm at sea. He immediately attaches himself to King Mark's court as a hunter, later the master of the hunt. When his royal lineage is revealed, he becomes his uncle's knight and vassal.

Known far and wide as a doughty knight, Tristan returns to avenge his father's death by defeating and killing Duke Morgan; his lands he gives to Rual and to his sons. Meanwhile, Duke Morolt of Ireland, who exacted tribute from King Mark, demands further payment or a fight to the death in single combat with the Cornish king. Tristan acts as King Mark's emissary to the Irish court, where his efforts to have Duke Morolt recall his demand for tribute are unsuccessful. Duke Morolt does agree, however, to let Tristan fight in King Mark's place. They meet and fight in Cornwall. After wounding Tristan in the hip, Duke Morolt suggests that the young knight yield so that his sister Isolde, queen of Ireland, can nurse him back to health. This offer is refused, and the fight wages fiercely again. Tristan finally slices off Duke Morolt's head and hand.

Tristan, disguised as a beggar, goes to Ireland to be healed. Calling himself Tantris, he ingratiates himself with Queen Isolde, who cures him of his hurt. Afterward, he becomes the tutor in music and in languages to her daughter, Isolde the Fair. When the young Isolde learns that he is the murderer of her uncle, the queen mother forgives him and allows him to return to Cornwall.

In Cornwall, Tristan sings the praises of the Irish princess. Because King Mark makes the young knight his heir, some jealous noblemen, hoping to have Tristan slain, suggest that he return to Ireland and bring Isolde back as King Mark's bride. On his arrival in Ireland, Tristan kills a dragon that long ravished the kingdom. In gratitude, Queen Isolde entrusts her beautiful daughter to Tristan's care.

On the return voyage, Brangene, the faithful companion and cousin of Isolde the Fair, fails to guard carefully the love potion intended by the queen for Isolde and King Mark on their nuptial day. Tristan and the princess drink the potion and are thenceforth enslaved by love for each other. They both experience conflicting duty and desire, turn red and then white, become depressed and exalted, and finally give in to love. To deceive King Mark, Brangene steals into Isolde's bed so that Tristan and Isolde might meet in secret.

After some time passes, Isolde grows apprehensive lest Brangene betray her, and she orders her companion's death. Fortunately, the queen relents before Brangene would die, and all goes on as before until the king is at last informed of Tristan's treachery. King Mark makes many attempts to trap the lovers, vacillating between trust and angry jealousy. Each time a trap is set, Tristan and Isolde prove their false innocence by some cunning ruse.

Finally, the lovers are exiled. The king invites them to return, however, when he discovers them innocently asleep in a cave, a sword between them. Although King Mark urges propriety on their return to court, Tristan and Isolde almost immediately abandon all caution, driven as they are by the caprices of love. Knowing that the king will have them killed if they are discovered, Tristan sets out from Cornwall after accepting a ring from his beloved as a token of fidelity to each other.

During his travels, Tristan performs deeds of knightly valor in Germany, Champagne, and Normandy. In gratitude for his services in Normandy, the duke gives him his daughter Isolde, called Isolde of the White Hands to distinguish her from Isolde the Fair, as his bride. Lovesick and dejected, Tristan accepts his bride in name only—the name Isolde.

(At this point Gottfried's narrative breaks off abruptly. From his source materials and from related versions, the ending that may be constructed is that Tristan is fatally wounded by a poisoned spear and that Isolde the Fair, summoned from Cornwall, arrives after her lover dies. Shock and grief cause her death also. King Mark, learning of the love potion, forgives them and orders the lovers buried side by side in Cornwall.)

Critical Evaluation:

Richard Wagner's opera follows the basic plot of Gottfried von Strassburg's earlier version of this famous tale. The version Wagner chose, nineteen thousand or so lines of which are attributed to Gottfried, is an excellent and extensive telling of one of the most famous love stories of all times. This metrical romance does not follow the line of chivalric romance developed by other writers, and there is no wearisome repetition of knightly deeds of valor in war and tournaments. Instead, Gottfried celebrates romantic love as being greater than chivalric love; his conception of love is more inward, at once enchanting and enthralling, bewildering and ecstatic, one that sways the soul and makes martyrs of those who partake of love's sacrament. The landscape against which Tristan and Isolde move often suggests an inner dreamworld of mysterious compulsion.

Tristan and Isolde is unique in many ways. Although its material is courtly in nature, the poem concludes tragically rather than in the usual redemptive ending, and the sphere of reference is not specifically courtly. In his prologue, Gottfried defines his audience as those "noble hearts" who share the sufferings and joys of love and who are willing to accept the power of love as the central value in life. All other courtly values—honor, religious faith, feudal fidelity—are subordinated to the one overriding force of passion, conceived as an external objective force and symbolized in the magic potion. Even Gottfried's conception of love departs from the courtly pattern, for rather than the usual unfulfilled longing and devoted service of the knight, love in this story is mutual, freely given, and outside the conventions of courtly society. It is a law unto itself and destructive of the social order.

The material of the legend, like that of the Arthurian sagas, may be traced back to Celtic origins, although no versions prior to the twelfth century are extant. In the late twelfth century, the story took shape, and it is the French version by the Anglo-Norman poet Thomas of Brittany or Britain (c. 1160) that provides the direct source for Gottfried—and which enables scholars to construct the probable ending of Gottfried's unfinished work. In Thomas's version, the approach is still distinctly courtly; Gottfried's departures from the norm may be attributed both to his own origin and to his time. Gottfried was most likely not a member of courtly society himself but rather a member of the middle class of the important commercial city of Strassburg. He was wealthy and well educated—as evidenced by his extensive knowledge of theology and law—and familiar with French and German literature, as well as the Latin that was the universal language of higher education at the time. His work shows mastery of formal rhetorical devices and a knowledge of Latin literature remarkable for his time. His literary sophistication is evident in the extended discussion of German authors of his day that he inserts into the story at a point where Tristan's investiture is discussed. It is in this literary excursus that he voices his praise of Hartmann von Aue and castigates Wolfram von Eschenbach for having an excessively difficult and erratic style.

This critical attitude toward his courtly contemporaries is reflected in his approach to the conventions of courtly romance and helps to explain the uniqueness of his work. He is not above mocking even the rituals of the Church, as when Isolde successfully passes a trial by fire through an elaborate ruse that enables her to avoid perjury on a technicality but destroys the intent and integrity of the trial. "Christ," Gottfried says, "is as pliable as a windblown sleeve." One must in fairness point out that by 1210, such a mockery would not be terribly shocking to the educated classes, who would regard the whole idea of trial by fire as rather archaic and superstitious.

Gottfried's discussion of love borrows heavily from the language of mystical writers. In the prologue, the elevating and ennobling qualities generally ascribed to courtly love take on religious significance through the use of specifically religious metaphors; in his imagery and in his presentation of a scale of values, Gottfried stresses the sacred and transfiguring power of love. St. Bernard of Clairvaux has been identified as a source of much of Gottfried's religious love imagery. Scholars are divided on the degree to which one should view this cult of love as an attempt to create a surrogate religion; there is no question, however, that Gottfried viewed love's claims as exerting a powerful counterforce against the social and religious conventions of the time.

The turning away from the public, external values of the courtly epics toward the inner, personal, emotional values of *Tristan and Isolde* is consistent with the wider cultural trends of the time: the new grace and sensitivity evident in the sculptures of the North Portal at Chartres and the break with the conventions of courtly love in the later songs of Walther von der Vogelweide, whose poems develop an ideal of love in which physical consummation replaces the state of prolonged yearning that is the subject of the poetry of the earlier phase of courtly love. The mystical qualities of this love are portrayed in the scene in the Cave of Love, which is an elaborate allegory expressing the ideal state toward which love strives. The sequence of trials and traps surrounding Tristan and Isolde, however, depicts the reality experienced by the "noble hearts" whom Gottfried addresses in his poem when they must live in a world that does not accord to the power of love its due respect.

In this world, the lovers are far from ideal. Isolde uses her servant Brangene shamelessly, and even considers murdering her to prevent possible exposure, while Tristan, banished from the court at last, falls in love with Isolde of the White Hands, lacking the fidelity that Isolde demonstrates. How Gottfried might have resolved this dichotomy can only be guessed, but it is clear that Gottfried sees the company of "noble hearts" as forever torn between love's joy and sorrow, accepting both as equally valid. It is precisely this quality of bitterness that separates love's votaries from the mundane world of pleasure seekers, and it is in relation to this ambivalent state that Gottfried explains the purpose of his work: Sad stories of love increase the pain of a heart that already feels love's sadness, yet the noble heart cannot help but be drawn again and again to the contemplation of love. Like the sacraments of the Church, Gottfried's work is mystical communion: "Their death is the bread of the living." In this insistence upon the centrality of love, Gottfried's romantic tragedy is both the culmination and the turning point of the tradition of courtly love in Germany.

"Critical Evaluation" by Steven C. Schaber

Further Reading

Bromwich, Rachel. "The *Tristan* of the Welsh." In *The Arthur of the Welsh: The Arthurian Legend in Medieval Welsh Literature*, edited by Rachel Bromwich, A. O. H. Jarman, and Brynley F. Roberts. Cardiff: University of Wales Press, 1991. Discusses the Celtic sources of the Tristan legend and argues that they existed mostly in fragments until the fifteenth century.

Chinca, Mark. *Gottfried von Strassburg: "Tristan."* New York: Cambridge University Press, 1997. An overview of the poem with biographical information about Gottfried, a synopsis of the story, a discussion of the Tristan tradition and how Gottfried adapted it, an examination of Gottfried's use of religious analogies and language, and analyses of key passages.

Ferrante, Joan M. "'*Ez ist ein zunge, dunket mich*': Fiction, Deception, and Self-Deception in Gottfried's *Tristan*." In *Gottfried von Strassburg and the Medieval Tristan Legend*, edited by Adrian Stevens and Roy Wisbey. Cambridge, England: D. S. Brewer, 1990. Masterful essay discusses how all the characters perpetrate deceit upon others. Argues that Gottfried implies that emulation of the characters would cause one to be destroyed as the characters are.

Hasty, Will, ed. *A Companion to Gottfried von Strassburg's "Tristan."* Rochester, N.Y.: Camden House, 2003. Collection of essays analyzing the poem, including discussions of humanism in the high Middle Ages, the city of Strasbourg during Gottfried's lifetime, the medieval reception of *Tristan and Isolde*, and the modern conception of Gottfried's work and the Tristan legend. Analyzes the love potion; god, religion, and ambiguity; female figures; and the Isolde of the White Hands sequence in the poem.

Jackson, W. T. H. "Gottfried von Strassburg." In *Arthurian Literature in the Middle Ages*, edited by R. S. Loomis. Oxford, England: Clarendon Press, 1959. Argues that Tristan's sensual love of Isolde is a reflection of the spiritual love they have for each other, and this spirituality excuses their actions.

Jaeger, C. Stephen. *Medieval Humanism in Gottfried von Strassburg's "Tristan und Isolde."* Heidelberg, Germany: C. Winter, 1977. Argues that society is at fault because it cannot cope adequately with the love of Tristan and Isolde.

Rougemont, Denis de. *Love in the Western World.* Translated by Montgomery Belgion. Princeton, N.J.: Princeton University Press, 1983. Describes courtly love, focusing on the lovers' relationship in the Tristan legend; argues the relationship is self-defeating and even masks a death wish.

Sneeringer, Kristine K. *Honor, Love, and Isolde in Gottfried's "Tristan."* New York: Peter Lang, 2002. Analyzes Gottfried's conception of honor in the poem, examining honor in relation to love, sexuality, the role of the artist, and the character of Isolde. Argues that Gottfried's highest notion of honor is when Isolde's sexuality transcends earthly love to join in the mystical union of the soul with Christ.

Tristia

Author: Osip Mandelstam (1891-1938)
First published: 1919 (English translation, 1967)
Type of work: Poetry

Osip Mandelstam's second collection of verses, *Tristia*, was published in 1922 under unusual and intriguing circumstances. The manuscript was taken to Berlin, and the poems were arranged by a fellow poet, Mikhail Kuzmin, who also gave the work its title, after one of the best poems in the collection. Mandelstam borrowed that poem's title from Ovid's work by the same name. Mandelstam was not satisfied, however, with the way the publication was handled. When he published the second edition in 1923, he changed the title to *Vtoraia kniga* (second book) and rearranged the poems. Because the collection was republished as *Tristia*, and because Mandelstam later referred to it as such, *Tristia* is now accepted as its only legitimate title. Perhaps the reason Mandelstam accepted the title was that, like Ovid, he wrote most of the *Tristia* poems on the shores of the Black Sea, and he brought the manuscript from there. Moreover, Mandelstam's life, in which he was frequently on the run, mostly as an internal exile, parallels that of Ovid. His lifelong fascination with classical antiquity also identifies him with Ovid.

The forty-five mostly untitled poems in *Tristia* were written between 1916 and 1920. The poems mark the highest achievements in the early stage of Mandelstam's poetic career, and they represent some of the best poems he wrote. There is no unifying subject in the collection, but several distinct themes can be discerned. What strikes the reader the most are the preponderant references to classical antiquity. The most obvious theme, already familiar from Mandelstam's first collection, *Kamen* (1913; *Stone*, 1981), is the poet's homage to Rome and its civilization. The theme reflects his fascination with the Mediterranean culture and with the unity between cultures that it represents. In a poem of beautiful visual images, "Venetian Life," he uses a Renaissance painting to sing an ode to Rome, the beautiful city on the Adriatic where "jewels are heavy" and where "there is no salvation from love." A Georgian woman who has lost her cameo resembles a beautiful Roman woman ("I've lost a delicate cameo"). Persephone—the Greek goddess of the afterlife and the wife of Hades, but also used by Mandelstam as a Roman goddess—is mentioned in several poems ("I am cold," "Swallow," "As Psyche-Life goes down to the shades"). Mandelstam expresses his greatest veneration of Rome in the short poem "Nature's the same as Rome":

> Nature's the same as Rome, was reflected in it.
> We see images of its civic might
> In the clear air, as in the sky-blue circus,
> In the forum of fields, the colonnades of groves.

Mandelstam asserts that nature has found its most perfect embodiment in Rome, where nature and culture are one and where "stones exist in order to build."

While the references in *Stone* are mostly to Rome, in *Tristia*, Mandelstam dwells on ancient Greece. References to the classical world appear in many of the poems—for example, Phedre (in "No matter how I concealed them"), "the sacred mace of Heracles" (in "The Menagerie"), and the immortal roses of Kypris (in "In Petersburg we'll meet again").

In "The Greeks planned for war," Mandelstam sees Europe as the new Hellas, and he beseeches it to save the Acropolis and Piraeus. The long poem "The thick golden stream of honey took so long" best expresses Mandelstam's love for ancient Greece, where the proverbial golden honey flows in the streets, "the service of Bacchus is everywhere," and "the peaceful days roll by." The poet ends his apotheosis with a mournful cry:

> Golden fleece, where are you, golden fleece?
> The sea's heavy waves roared the whole way.
> Abandoning the ship, its sail worn out,
> Odysseus returned, full with space and time.

This poem, written during World War I and the Russian Revolution, expresses Mandelstam's yearning for more peaceful times and sunny shores. Mandelstam identifies peace, happiness, and plenitude with ancient Greece.

The poem "Tortoise" is another apotheosis of the beauty of ancient Greece. Here "blind lyrists, like bees, give us Ionic honey," "cicadas click like hammers forging out a ring," and "the honeysuckle smells, to the joy of the bees." The poem is an idyll of an arcadian landscape, yet it is an idyll different from that of the Parnassians. Mandelstam felt that the quintessential art in classical Greece was music, not visual arts—hence the metaphor of a tortoise resembling the form of a lyre, an instrument. Moreover, because he wanted to use poetry to reflect the vicissitudes of his own fate—in this instance, the danger of the loss of artistic freedom—Mandelstam wove pictorial and musical images into his own canvas of a land that he placed in the Arcadia and in the islands of the Greek archipelago, the symbol of ancient Hellas.

The third frame of reference in *Tristia* is Jewish culture and history. Though Jewish by origin, Mandelstam was drawn first to Catholicism and then to classical antiquity; he attempted to find in them a sense of his own orientation. He not only preserved his Jewish background but also used his background as a bridge between the Christian and Judaic cultures—a kind of symbiosis that best reflected his own thinking and achieved the unity he desired. In "This night is beyond recall," Mandelstam re-creates the funereal atmosphere shortly after the death of his mother: "And the voices of the Israelites/ Rose above the mother./ I awoke in a cradle, shone upon/ By a black sun." This poem illustrates the poet's ability to use personal experience to transcend a fixed moment in history—in this case, the world war. The fact that the persona awakes in the cradle alone signifies the poet's danger of losing his roots altogether, without finding a new mooring. The foreboding of the potential demise of the ancient and Christian cultures is underscored by the personal tragedy of "the Israelites."

Similar concerns are expressed in "The young Levite among the priests," where the Levite futilely warns his older compatriots of the dangers threatening them all. At the end of the poem, however, Mandelstam sees hope: "We swaddled the Sabbath in precious linen/ With a heavy Menorah lit the night of Jerusalem." The reference to Christ corresponds to the poet's long-harbored desire for a rejuvenation of the two cultures. In "Go back to the tainted lap, Leah," Mandelstam completes his vision of unity by stating that the Hebrew, Leah, must, and will, undergo a change: "You are in love with a Jew,/ You will vanish in him, and/ God will be with you." Finally, Mandelstam combines classical antiquity and its heir, Eastern Orthodoxy, with his Jewish roots and Catholicism in order to express his yearning for unity among all these cultures, as symbolized by a metaphor of the "eternal cathedrals" of Sofia (the East) and Peter (the West) in the final poem of the collection.

Mandelstam did not always seek refuge in antiquity; he was painfully aware of his own time and place. Even when he fled to the past, he used these excursions to fend off the problems besetting him. Nowhere is this more evident than in "Tristia," the title poem of the book. Here, through his knowledge of classical antiquity, the poet foreshadows a separation from his dear ones. The poem parallels the fate of the Roman poet Ovid, who was banished for political reasons to the shores of the Black Sea, where he wrote poetry and where he died. Many of the details in Mandelstam's poem closely follow Ovid's elegy of the same title.

"Tristia" reflects the mood of a man leaving his home, his city, and, possibly, his country—an experience that was always present in the poet's mature life and that turned out to be his final destiny. Stating that he has learned the "science of parting," he gives expression to melancholy mixed with stoicism, even defiance; to hope mixed with latent despair; and to his tacit understanding of what life is about. In this sense, "Tristia" is one of the most essential poems in all of Mandelstam's works. At the time he wrote the poem, he was threatened by numerous dangers, and he had several close calls. The possibility of involuntary parting must have occurred to him often, and his thorough knowledge of classical literature enabled him to give artistic expression to such thoughts and sentiments, using Ovid as a model. The typically Mandelstamian formal aspects—striking images and metaphors, a mixture of lyrical and reflective passages, sporadic departures from the main train of thought, frequent interventions on the part of the poet, and the unique rhythm—all enhance the artistic qualities of "Tristia."

Other references to Mandelstam's own time and place abound. The references concern his beloved city, St. Petersburg, and the looming danger of the Bolsheviks. St. Petersburg is, for Mandelstam, the epitome of an urban society founded on spiritual values. He mentions St. Petersburg again and again, calling it Petropolis as a perfect model of a life-giving city. He is also aware of the dangers of betrayal and decay, as in the poem "At a dreadful height, a wandering fire":

> Above the black Neva, transparent Spring
> Is smashed, the wax of immortality is melting.
> O, if you, star, are Petropolis, your city,
> Your brother, Petropolis, is dying.

The source of this concern is the rise of the Bolshevik menace. In one of his most powerful poems, "The Twilight of Freedom," Mandelstam at first urges his "brothers" to glorify the twilight of freedom, which was one of the first goals and promises of the Bolsheviks. When the ship of the state is set at sea, however, the destination is ambiguous; it could lead to a new dawn or to perdition. Even though the poet urges his countrymen to have courage and try ("We will recall even in Lethe's frost,/ That our land was worth ten heavens"), and even though Mandelstam hints at Lenin taking the nation's helm, the poem has its ambiguities, beginning with the title (the Russian *sumerki*, for example, means either dawn or twilight). Written in 1918, at the beginning of the Russian Revolution, the poem reflects Mandelstam's ambivalence toward that movement.

Among other noteworthy efforts in *Tristia* are the three poems to Olga Arbenina, a woman with whom Mandelstam was briefly in love ("I am cold," "I want to serve you," and "If I am to know how to restrain your hands"). Another oftencited and exquisitely crafted poem is "Solominka" (the straw), about the death of a beautiful woman in love. "Just for joy, take from my palms" is one of the most beautiful poems of the collection; in this work, Mandelstam uses the daring metaphors of bees and honey as symbols of artistic creativity.

Tristia is one of Mandelstam's most important works, and it contains many poems of lasting value. Translations of individual poems collected in *Tristia* have been published in various volumes over the years. The first attempt at publishing most of the poems in one group was made by Bruce McClelland in *The Silver Age of Russian Culture* in 1975; in 1987, McClelland published the entire collection in a bilingual edition.

Vasa D. Mihailovich

Further Reading

Brown, Clarence. *Mandelstam*. New York: Cambridge University Press, 1973. Stresses the artistic merits of Mandelstam's poetry. Chapter 12 analyzes several poems in *Tristia*, and chapter 13 deals with the classical elements of the collection. One of the best studies of Mandelstam's work available in English.

Broyde, Steven. *Osip Mandel'štam and His Age: A Commentary on the Themes of War and Revolution in the Poetry, 1913-1923*. Cambridge, Mass.: Harvard University Press, 1975. Presents detailed analysis of Mandelstam's poems about the Russian Revolution. Includes several poems from *Tristia*.

Cavanagh, Clare. *Osip Mandelstam and the Modernist Creation of Tradition*. Princeton, N.J.: Princeton University Press, 1995. Thorough study focuses on the modernist aspects of Mandelstam's poetry based on classical traditions. Includes discussion of poems contained in *Tristia*.

Loewen, Donald. *The Most Dangerous Art: Poetry, Politics, and Autobiography After the Russian Revolution*. Lanham, Md.: Lexington Books, 2008. Describes how three Russian poets—Mandelstam, Marina Tsvetaeva, and Boris Pasternak—used their autobiographies to defend poets and poetry against the restrictions of the Soviet government in the decades from the 1920's through the 1950's.

Mandelstam, Nadezhda. *Hope Against Hope*. Translated by Max Hayward. New York: Atheneum, 1970.

_____. *Hope Abandoned*. Translated by Max Hayward. New York: Atheneum, 1974. Two-volume memoir by Mandelstam's widow relates the personal circumstances that guided his life and works. Indispensable for an understanding of the poet, the genesis of many of his poems, and efforts to preserve them from destruction.

O'Brien, Kevin J. *Saying Yes at Lightning: Threat and the Provisional Image in Post-Romantic Poetry*. New York: Peter Lang, 2002. Examines poems that were written in response to cataclysmic events. Chapter 4 focuses on Mandelstam's poem "The Horseshoe Finder," which was written after the publication of *Tristia*; the chapter also contains information about *Tristia*.

Vinokur, Val. "Osip Mandelstam's Judaism: Chaos and Cares." In *The Trace of Judaism: Dostoevsky, Babel, Mandelstam, Levinas*. Evanston, Ill.: Northwestern University Press, 2008. Uses the ethical philosophy of Emmanuel Levinas, a Lithuanian-born French Jew, to analyze the relationship of ethics and aesthetics in the works of Mandelstam and other Russian writers.

Tristram

Author: Edwin Arlington Robinson (1869-1935)
First published: 1927
Type of work: Poetry
Type of plot: Arthurian romance
Time of plot: Arthurian period
Locale: England and Brittany

Principal characters:
TRISTRAM, prince of Lyonesse
MARK, his uncle, king of Cornwall
HOWEL, king of Brittany
ISOLT OF THE WHITE HANDS, Howel's daughter
ISOLT, princess of Ireland
GOUVERNAIL, Tristram's friend
ANDRED, Mark's minion
QUEEN MORGAN, the wily queen

The Poem:

Isolt of the White Hands is too pensive and preoccupied for a young woman. She is always looking to the north, toward England. Her father, King Howel of Brittany, loves his daughter too much to let her attitude go unquestioned. Isolt tells her father she is waiting for Tristram, who some time before made a visit to the Breton court. Fond of Isolt as an adult is fond of a child, Tristram gave her on his departure an agate for a keepsake and promised to come back. Now Isolt is a woman of eighteen, and she waits for Tristram as a woman waits for her lover. King Howel tries to tell her that Tristram thinks of her as a child, and that he probably will not return; but Isolt will not be convinced.

In Cornwall it is the wedding day of old, lecherous King Mark and the dark and beautiful Isolt of Ireland, his bride. With the wedding feast in full swing, the wine cup is often passed. Sick of the drunken merriment and sicker with inner torment, Tristram, nephew of the king, leaves the feast and wanders in the fresh night air. King Mark, displeased by his nephew's absence, sends Gouvernail, Tristram's preceptor and friend, to ask him to return. Tristram says only that he is sick. Then Queen Morgan comes to talk to Tristram. She uses all her arts and blandishments on the brooding knight, and they are cunning indeed, for Queen Morgan, much experienced in the arts of love, is more than a little attracted to Tristram. Tristram repeats stubbornly that he is sick.

Then there is a soft step on the stair, as Brangwaine comes, followed a moment later by dark-caped, violet-eyed Isolt of Ireland. She looks at Tristram but says nothing as he takes her in his arms. Memories hang about them like a cloud.

King Mark is old and unattractive, and he wants a young wife in his castle. Yearning for Isolt of Ireland, he sends as emissary his gallant nephew, Tristram, to plead his cause. Tristram has to fight even to get to the Irish court. After he slays the mighty Morhaus, Isolt's uncle, he makes a bargain of state with the Irish king and takes Isolt back to Cornwall in his boat. One night they are alone with only the sea and the stars to look upon them. Isolt waits in vain for Tristram to speak. If he does, she will love him then, and there will be no marriage of convenience with King Mark. Bound by knightly fealty Tristram keeps silent and delivers Isolt to his uncle. Now he looks at her and regrets bitterly that he did not speak on the boat.

Andred steals behind them to spy on them. He is a faithful servitor of King Mark, but jealousy of Tristram and love for Isolt motivate him as well. Tristram sees Andred skulking in the shadow, seizes him, and throws him on the rocks. When King Mark himself comes out to inquire about his absent guests, he stumbles over Andred's unconscious body and stands unseen long enough to hear the passionate avowals of Tristram and Isolt. Since Tristram is his nephew, King Mark does not have him killed, but he banishes Tristram forever from Cornwall on pain of burning at the stake.

The sick Tristram wanders in a fever. When he recovers, he finds himself the captive of Queen Morgan in her castle. Queen Morgan eventually gives up her siege of Tristram's heart and lets him go. Next Tristram goes to Brittany, where a griffin, giant scourge of the Breton land, threatens King Howel and his court. Knightly Tristram, fierce in battle although sick for love, slays the griffin. As a hero, Tristram has a secure place at King Howel's court, and there he marries Isolt of the White Hands. He pities her and she loves him, although she knows of his sorrow. For two years Tristram is a faithful husband and a reigning prince.

Then from the north comes another ship with Gawaine aboard bringing a message from King Arthur. For his deeds Tristram is to become a Knight of the Round Table; hence he is summoned to Camelot. Isolt watches her husband go with quiet despair, for she fears he will not come back. She has little dread of King Mark, for Gawaine tells her in secrecy that King Mark is in prison. The Cornish king forges the pope's signature on a paper ordering Tristram to go fight the Saracens, and his forgery is detected. Isolt nevertheless knows that Tristram's danger lies in Cornwall.

Guinevere, Arthur's queen, and her lover, Lancelot, plot to bring Irish Isolt and Tristram together. Lancelot takes Tristram to Joyous Guard, his trysting castle, and Guinevere brings Isolt of Ireland secretly out of Cornwall. So the lovers are together again, while King Mark is in prison. They have a happy summer together and as autumn draws near Tristram loses a little of his apprehension. Early one morning he goes out on the sea while Isolt sleeps. When he returns, there are strangers in Joyous Guard and Isolt is gone. King Mark, released from prison, has abducted his wife and carried her off to Cornwall.

Tristram mopes in silence until he has a letter from Queen Morgan. She chides him for his lovesickness and urges him to see his Isolt once more. Goaded by the wily queen, Tristram rides to Cornwall prepared to fight and to die for a last look at Isolt. When he arrives at his uncle's castle, he enters easily and in surprised joy seeks out Isolt. She tells him that she is near death. King Mark, in pity for her wasting figure and sick heart, gives her permission to receive her lover. Isolt and Tristram, sad in their love because Isolt is to die, sit on the shore and gaze out at a still ship on the quiet ocean. While they sit thus, the jealous Andred creeps up behind them and stabs Tristram in the back. Tristram, therefore, dies before the ailing Isolt. King Mark finally realizes that Andred is also in love with Isolt, and he regrets that his lecherous lust for a young queen brought sorrow and death.

Gouvernail goes back to Brittany to convey the grievous news of Tristram's death to Isolt of the White Hands, who divines the truth when he disembarks alone. He tells her only part of Tristram's sojourn in England, only that Tristram saw the dying Isolt of Ireland a last time with King Mark's consent, and that Andred killed Tristram by treachery. Isolt is silent in her grief; no one knows what she is thinking, nor how much she divined of Tristram and of the other Isolt. Now Isolt looks no more for a ship from England. On the white sea the white birds and the sunlight are alive. The white birds are always flying and the sunlight flashes on the sea.

Critical Evaluation:

Tristram is the most romantic of Edwin Arlington Robinson's works, in theme, poetic treatment, and philosophy. It is the culmination of a lifetime of interest in the medieval legends surrounding King Arthur. Robinson's interest is reflected in shorter poems ("Miniver Cheevy," 1910) and other long works (*Merlin*, 1917; *Lancelot*, 1920). Although far from light reading, *Tristram* was a success with the American public, and this is only partly to be attributed to the Pulitzer Prize of 1928. Robinson wrote from a deep belief that the love of Tristram and Isolt paralleled the love of many people, even in his own time. In its elimination of some of the traditional colorful details, Robinson's treatment of the story may be considered somewhat stark, although his simpler imagery is beautiful.

The chief element in the original legend that separates the lovers from ordinary human experience is that their love springs from a supernatural potion. Prior to imbibing this potion, Tristram and Isolt are content with fulfilling their obligations: he to provide a bridge for his uncle and she to wed a king. After drinking the brew, they cast their commitments aside. Robinson prefers to motivate the story differently, in order to bring it into the sphere of realism.

The brief journey across the sea from Ireland to Cornwall is, in an example of such a realistic touch, long enough for an attraction between two people to begin but not enough for them to become fully conscious of it. Tristram, already pursued by Queen Morgan and adored by King Howel's daughter, is simply blasé about women finding him attractive. Isolt of Ireland is more aware of her feelings, but she is distracted by wounded pride and by anxiety about her future. Once tender Isolt, with her "dark young majesty," and jaded Mark of the wet mouth and "senile claws" are placed together, the prospect of such an incompatible sexual union jolts Tristram and Isolt awake to their attraction to each other.

The experience of regret after realizing something too late, reflected in the "soul-retching waves" of the ocean, is universally human. In addition, a story has grown up around Robinson regarding his love for his sister-in-law, Emma. The facts are these: When a young man of twenty, a year out of high school, with no particular thought of settling down, Robinson met a charming young woman during a lazy summer vacation. Into this slowly evolving friendship burst Robinson's older brother, Herman, a businessman often on the road, who descended on the vacation resort and wooed and won Emma in the space of few weeks. They were married almost at once. Around the time of this wedding Robinson began a deeply pessimistic work ultimately entitled "The Night Before" (published in 1896 but excluded from his *Collected Works*). Herman's marriage was unhappy and destructive. Robinson is believed to have proposed to Emma after she

was widowed (possibly reflected in his self-mocking poem, *The March of the Cameron Men*, 1932).

Regardless of whether one accepts the romanticizing of Robinson's life, the romanticism of his philosophy is fully a match for the Tristram legend. Robinson grew up in an increasingly materialistic society that seemed on the verge of explaining everything in terms of a mechanized and accidental universe. Robinson opposed this view on many fronts, guided by New England Transcendentalism and other idealistic trends, including Swedenborgianism. His ultimate justification for his views was intuitive. Tristram and Isolt's love, so intense and yet, as Robinson believed, so typical, rules out the possibility of a mechanistically determined universe. His Tristram argues that before human beings were ever created, first such a love had to be conceived. The universe was created in order to bring love about. Love is too much of a marvel to be an accident; therefore, the universe that created it cannot be an accident. Despite the inherent tragedy of the tale, therefore, the reader comes away with a sense of optimism.

Robinson breaks into once-forbidden territory with descriptions of sexuality that are frank and poetic. The poignancy of Isolt as a tragic romantic heroine is elegantly expressed in the same vocabulary that conveys her sexual appeal: She is dark, trembling, and liquefying. The fact that she melts against Tristram, "with the sure surrender of a child," even after the years of her marriage to Mark, is a delicate indication that her feelings for Tristram are in a sense virginal. The ability of both lovers to rise above the jealousy of their rivals evolves into selflessness. This evolution of their love beyond the first romantic impulse into something complex and disciplined, is the modern, rather innovative, and not always welcomed part of Robinson's contribution to the subject.

In their philosophical colloquies, Tristram and Isolt develop Robinson's ideas of the smallness of life and death, which are two "abysmal little words" in the face of love. When Isolt is dragged by force back to Mark, Mark feels the "smallness" of death when she looks at him. Isolt is often described with irony as "small." Another word that the lovers discuss and cut down to size is time. Life is not years, and it is not time that fills life full.

The poem is a model of parallel construction. Episodes alternate until, at the conclusion, the original cast is reassembled. The background of the sea, a timeless symbol of human emotions, pervades the story and provides many of the secondary symbols.

"Critical Evaluation" by D. Gosselin Nakeeb

Further Reading

Anderson, Wallace L. *Edwin Arlington Robinson: A Critical Introduction*. Boston: Houghton Mifflin, 1967. Examines Robinson's life and work, absorbing all preceding scholarship. Includes a bibliography.

Carpenter, Frederick Ives. "Tristram the Transcendent." In *Appreciation of Edwin Arlington Robinson: Twenty-eight Interpretive Essays*, edited by Richard Cary. Waterville, Maine: Colby College Press, 1969. A mature and subtle interpretation of the fates and choices of Robinson's characters. Addresses the theme of time.

Davis, Charles T. "Image Patterns in the Poetry of Edwin Arlington Robinson." In *Appreciation of Edwin Arlington Robinson: Twenty-eight Interpretive Essays*, edited by Richard Cary. Waterville, Maine: Colby College Press, 1969. Guides the reader through the fully developed imagery of *Tristram* as a symbolic system.

Donaldson, Scott. *Edwin Arlington Robinson: A Poet's Life*. New York: Columbia University Press, 2007. Comprehensive critical biography based in part on three thousand previously unavailable personal letters. Analyzes Robinson's poetry and assesses his impact on the development of modern American literature.

Franchere, Hoyt C. *Edwin Arlington Robinson*. New York: Twayne, 1968. A concise and focused study of the life and work, balancing external events with the poet's internal evolution. Franchere's thorough research turns up interesting details not found in other general works.

Gale, Robert L. *An Edwin Arlington Robinson Encyclopedia*. Jefferson, N.C.: McFarland, 2006. Some entries contain information on Robinson's poetry and prose writings, providing the dates of published works, summaries of their content, and critical commentary; other entries discuss his family members, friends, and associates.

Hoffpauir, Richard. "'But This We Know, If We Know Anything': The Conditional Contemplation of Edwin Arlington Robinson." In *The Contemplative Poetry of Edwin Arlington Robinson, Robert Frost, and Yvor Winters*. Lewiston, N.Y.: Edwin Mellen Press, 2002. Analyzes Robinson's poetry and compares his work to that of Frost and of Winters. Describes how the three poets eschewed experimental, modernist verse in favor of more traditional forms of poetry.

Romig, Edna Davis. "Tilbury Town and Camelot." In *Appreciation of Edwin Arlington Robinson: Twenty-eight Interpretive Essays*, edited by Richard Cary. Waterville, Maine: Colby College Press, 1969. Brings out the beauty and poignancy of *Tristram*.

Tristram Shandy

Author: Laurence Sterne (1713-1768)
First published: 1759-1767, as *The Life and Opinions of Tristram Shandy, Gent.*
Type of work: Novel
Type of plot: Satire
Time of plot: 1718-1766
Locale: Shandy Hall in England

Principal characters:
TRISTRAM SHANDY, the narrator
MR. WALTER SHANDY, his father
MR. TOBY SHANDY, his uncle and an old soldier
CORPORAL TRIM, Uncle Toby's servant
MR. YORICK, a parson
DR. SLOP, a medical quack
WIDOW WADMAN, a romantic widow

The Story:

Tristram Shandy, in telling the story of his earliest years, says that he has always believed that most of the problems of his life were brought about by the fact that the moment of his conception was interrupted when his mother asked his father whether he had remembered to wind the clock. Tristram knows the exact date of his conception: the night between the first Sunday and the first Monday of March, 1718. He is certain of this because his father's notebook indicates that before that Monday he had been seriously inconvenienced by an attack of sciatica, and immediately after that day he had set out for London.

Another complication of Tristram's birth was caused by the marriage settlement of his parents. According to this settlement, which Tristram quotes in full, Mrs. Shandy had the privilege of going to London in preparation for childbirth. If Mrs. Shandy were to put Mr. Shandy to the expense of a trip to London on false pretenses, however, then the next child was to be born at Shandy Hall. The circumstance of a needless trip to London had occurred some time before, and Mr. Shandy stoutly insisted that Tristram should be born at Shandy Hall; the birth would be in the hands of a country midwife rather than in those of a London doctor.

As Tristram tells the story, on the night of his birth, his father, Walter Shandy, and Tristram's uncle Toby, Walter's brother, are sitting in the living room engaged in one of their interminable debates. Informed by Susannah, the maid, that Mrs. Shandy is about to deliver her child, they send for the midwife. As an extra measure of safety, they also send for Dr. Slop, a bungling country practitioner whom Mr. Shandy admires because he has written a five-shilling book on the history of midwifery.

Uncle Toby, who has been called the highest compliment ever paid human nature, was a soldier until he was wounded during the siege of Namur in 1695. The wound, the exact position of which is to play a large part in Tristram's story later on, has forced him to retire to the country. At the suggestion of his faithful servant, Corporal Trim, he has built a large and complicated series of model fortifications and military emplacements on a bowling green behind Shandy Hall. Uncle Toby now spends all his time playing soldier and thinking about this miniature battlefield. Mr. Shandy is not impressed with his brother's hobby and keeps him from discussing it by violently interrupting him, so that he can continue, or start, one of his own long and detailed digressions on obscure information.

As the two brothers await the arrival of the midwife and her rival, Dr. Slop, Mr. Shandy asks a rhetorical question on the subject of Mrs. Shandy's preference for a midwife rather than a male doctor. When Uncle Toby suggests naïvely that modesty might explain her choice, Mr. Shandy launches into a long discussion of the nature of women and of the fact that everything has two handles. Given his naïveté, it is impossible for Uncle Toby to understand such affairs.

By the time Dr. Slop finally arrives with his bag of tools, the midwife is already in attendance on Mrs. Shandy; the doctor goes to her room to see about the birth of the child. Meanwhile, Corporal Trim reads a sermon aloud to pass the time. In attending Mrs. Shandy, Dr. Slop unfortunately mistakes Tristram's hip for his head. In probing with his large forceps, he flattens what Tristram always later refers to as his nose. Tristram essentially blames this mistake on the affair of the winding of the clock mentioned earlier. This incident— and a later one concerning the falling of a window sash as

Tristram, still a little boy, relieves himself through a window—brings about a problem in his anatomy that he mentions often.

Between Tristram's birth and almost immediate baptism, Mr. Shandy entertains the company with a long story by the ancient German writer Slawkenbergius, which he has translated from the Latin. The story tells of the adventures of a man with an especially long nose. When Mr. Shandy recovers from hearing the bad news about the accident with the forceps, he is told that his newborn child is very sickly and weak; consequently, he summons Mr. Yorick, the curate, to baptize the child immediately. While rushing to get dressed to attend the ceremony, Mr. Shandy sends word to the parson through the maid, Susannah, to name the child Trismegistus, after an ancient philosopher who is one of his favorites. Susannah forgets the name, however, and tells Mr. Yorick to christen the child Tristram. This name pleases the old man because it happens to be his own as well. By the time Mr. Shandy, still half unbuttoned, reaches the scene, the evil has been done. Despite the fact that Mr. Shandy thinks correct naming most important, his child is Tristram, a name Mr. Shandy believes the worst in the world. He laments that he has lost three-fourths of his son in his unfortunate geniture, nose, and name. There remains only one-fourth: Tristram's education.

Tristram manages to give a partial account of his topsy-turvy boyhood between many digressions on the other members of his family. Uncle Toby continues to answer most of his brother's arguments by softly whistling "Lillibullero," his favorite tune, and by going out to his little battlefield to wage small wars with Corporal Trim. The next important event in the family is the death of Master Bobby, Tristram's older brother, who had been away at Westminster school. Mr. Shandy reacts to this event in his usual way, by calling up all the philosophical ideas of the past on death and discoursing on them until he has adjusted himself to the new situation. When the tragic news reaches the servants, Susannah, despite a desire to show grief, can think of nothing but the wonderful wardrobe of dresses she will inherit when her mistress goes into mourning. Corporal Trim demonstrates the transitory nature of life by dropping his hat, as if it had suddenly died; he then makes an extemporaneous funeral oration.

After many more digressions on war, health, the fashions of ancient Roman dress, and his father's doubts as to whether to get Tristram a tutor and whether to put him into long trousers, Tristram proceeds to tell the history of his Uncle Toby, both in war and in love. Near Shandy Hall lives the Widow Wadman, who, after laying siege to Uncle Toby's affections for a long time, almost gets him to propose marriage to her.

The gentle former soldier, who literally would not kill a fly, finally learns the widow's purpose when she begins to inquire pointedly into the extent and position of his wound. He promises the widow that he will allow her to put her finger on the very spot where he was wounded, and then he brings her a map of Namur and points out the place for her to touch. Uncle Toby's innocence protects him until Corporal Trim finally tells his master that the widow is interested in the spot on his body, not the spot on the surface of the world, where he was wounded. This realization so embarrasses the old man that the idea of marriage disappears from his mind forever. Tristram concludes his story with Parson Yorick's statement that the book has been one of the cock-and-bull variety: The reader has been led on a mad but merry chase through the satirical and witty mind of the author.

Critical Evaluation:

This masterpiece of eighteenth century narrative, *The Life and Opinions of Tristram Shandy, Gent.*, was written by a man who never reconciled his sentimental nature with his roguish tendencies and who never tried to reconcile them. Laurence Sterne was educated at Jesus College, Cambridge, where he met John Hall-Stevenson, a young aristocrat who shared and encouraged his taste for erotic subjects and exaggeration. After taking holy orders, Sterne received an ecclesiastical appointment in Sutton through family connections, but he was temperamentally completely unsuited for the clerical life. In fact, the only part of religion he mastered was sermon writing, but at that he excelled. Eventually, he turned his pen to miscellaneous journalism in York periodicals. In 1759, he published *A Political Romance*, which included many elements that would characterize his masterpiece: allegory, multiple levels of meaning, verbal fanfare, whimsical use of scholastic learning, profanity, and great stylistic versatility.

Nevertheless, it was the appearance of the first two volumes of *The Life and Opinions of Tristram Shandy, Gent.* (commonly known simply as *Tristram Shandy*) that made Sterne an instant celebrity, despite the immediate denunciation of Samuel Johnson, Samuel Richardson, Horace Walpole, Oliver Goldsmith, and other literary establishment figures who condemned Sterne's iconoclastic style and frankly mercenary attitude for both ethical and artistic reasons. Sterne characterized the first part of his life's work as "taking on, not only the weak part of the sciences in which the true part of Ridicule lies, but everything else which I find laugh-at-able." The reader soon discovers that Sterne finds everything laughable, his comic vision as universal and as detailed as that of François Rabelais and Miguel de Cervantes, whose

works strongly influenced Sterne. Like Rabelais's *Gargantua et Pantagruel* (1567; *Gargantua and Pantagruel*, 1653-1694), moreover, Sterne's is a work held together only by the unswerving and exuberant force of the author's own personality. "'Tis a picture of myself," he admitted; indeed, it is impossible to distinguish the profane minister from the alleged narrator, young Tristram—just as Rabelais makes his narrator, Alcofribas, tangible only when it suits him.

Tristram Shandy also has been called "a prolonged conversation" between Sterne and his reader, a conversation in which acquaintance becomes familiarity and then an enduring friendship. For this friendship to occur, however, readers must accept certain ground rules and must be willing to adapt to conventions rarely embraced willingly. In his endless comments to the reader (who is sometimes addressed in the plural, sometimes in the singular, sometimes as "your worship," sometimes as "Madam"), Sterne scolds the reader for wanting to know everything at once (book 1, chapter 4), asks the reader to help him sell his "dedication," assures the reader that the company of the book's readers will swell to include all the world and all time, and dismisses any objections with a mad swirl of his pen. He says that he is quite aware that some readers will understand and others will not; indeed, the varying forms of address to the reader indicate his astute consciousness of the variety of his audience. He states that the "cholerick" reader will toss the book away, the "mercurial will laugh most heartily at it," and the "saturnine" will condemn it as fanciful and extravagant.

Like Cervantes, Sterne is not interested (or so he claims) in apologizing for his work or for himself. Readers must either take him or leave him. At the very beginning, as he embarks on one of his great digressions, he warns readers that to continue may annoy them—only the curious need pass through the narrative line into this first of many excursions with him. "Shut the door," he directs the first kind of reader; if readers pass through it with him, they realize the door is never opened again. Only readers who are willing to let "anything go" will remain on speaking terms with this most quixotic, irrepressible author.

The work itself, alternately characterized by Tristram as "vile" and "rhapsodic," defies structural analysis. Sterne makes his formal principles clear from the beginning: "not to be in a hurry" but to follow every new thought in whatever direction it may beckon until he loses track of his starting point and has to flip back the pages to find his place; "to spend two years discussing one," just as Tristram's mental and emotional autobiography reflects his father's *Tristrapaedia* (the gargantuan work of pedagogy that takes so long in the writing that Tristram grows up before he can start following its directives); and "in writing what I have set about, shall confine myself neither to his [Horace's] rules, nor to any man's rules that ever lived."

Sterne would have understood T. S. Eliot's dictum, "Immature poets borrow, mature poets steal." He not only steals—whether it is the actual music of Uncle Toby's "Lillibullero" or a medieval French theological tract on baptism—but also openly admits and boasts of his thefts. The boasting, however, is itself misleading, because, as William Shakespeare did with Thomas North's translation of Plutarch, Sterne subtly but most effectively alters his thieveries to fit the chaotic image of his own work. At one point, in discussing the nature of digressions, Sterne characterizes that work as "digressive, and . . . progressive too—and at the same time." Digressions, he continues, are "the sunshine" of a writer's art, the very stuff of literary and fictional vitality. Life itself, in the ultimate reading, is nothing but a diverting digression for Sterne; the role of the author, as he embraces it, is to make that essential human digression as diverting, as complicated, and as emotionally and intellectually rich as possible.

The greatness of Sterne's comic wit lies in its indefatigable mastery of making one detail relevant to another, a detail from Tristram's unfortunate life immediately provoking in his father a pointed consideration of Saxo Grammaticus's Danish history or causing Uncle Toby to expound its relationship to the siege of Navarre. Reading *Tristram Shandy* is an education in the esoteric and picayune minutiae of forgotten scholarship, yet at the same time the work shows through parody the irrelevance of scholarship (also following closely in the spirit of Rabelais). By the time readers close even the first volume, they are convinced of the validity of Sterne's point of departure: Epictetus's statement that "not actions but opinions of actions are the concern of men." In other words, it is not what happens to a person that matters but what that individual thinks of what has happened.

The relationship between the Shandean world and the real world is a very close, in fact a promiscuous, one; it is defined by Sterne's deliberate blurring of the line between fictional and real events and by his thematic insistence on the interdependence of thought, feeling, and action. Thought without emotion, Sterne would say, is futile, but feeling without reason is equally sterile. *Tristram Shandy* treats all the elements in human life—love, war, business, theology, religion, science, trade, medicine—with an epic comprehensiveness, and everything is shown to be related to everything else. The texture of the style, however, is not the reassuring predictability of epic; instead, the work is a formal collage of typographical caprice, gestures, dramatic devices, soliloquies, offhand ob-

scenity, and serious and mock-serious treatises—all mixed together extemporaneously and punctuated orally. Sterne is like a magician juggling more balls than anyone can see, but he never loses control because his magic is as unflagging as it is electric. More than any other work of the eighteenth century, Sterne's *Tristram Shandy* is a monument to the complexity, vitality, and *sprezzatura* of the human mind.

"Critical Evaluation" by Kenneth John Atchity

Further Reading

Bowden, Martha F. *Yorick's Congregation: The Church of England in the Time of Laurence Sterne.* Newark: University of Delaware Press, 2007. Examines the religious environment in which Sterne wrote his novels and sermons, explicating passages from his work to demonstrate how his experience of life in rural parishes informed his novels.

Gerard, W. B. *Laurence Sterne and the Visual Imagination.* Burlington, Vt.: Ashgate, 2006. Focuses on the illustrations by William Hogarth and other artists that complemented Sterne's work. Examines the pictorial quality of Sterne's writing, describing how it inspires the visual imagination. Analyzes some of the illustrations for *Tristram Shandy* and *A Sentimental Journey.*

Jefferson, D. W. "*Tristram Shandy* and the Tradition of Learned Wit." In *Laurence Sterne: A Collection of Critical Essays*, edited by John Traugott. Englewood Cliffs, N.J.: Prentice-Hall, 1968. Classic essay, first published in 1951, locates *Tristram Shandy* in the satirical tradition of François Rabelais and Jonathan Swift. Examines how Sterne juxtaposes the discourses of medieval cosmology, medicine, physiology, law, religion, and military science with human folly.

Keymer, Thomas. *Sterne, the Moderns, and the Novel.* New York: Oxford University Press, 2002. Analyzes *Tristram Shandy* in connection with other novels of its time, describing how Sterne retained his popularity by self-consciously playing on his rivals' works.

_____, ed. *The Cambridge Companion to Laurence Sterne.* New York: Cambridge University Press, 2009. Collection of specially commissioned essays presents analyses of all of Sterne's works, with discussion of such key issues as sentimentalism, national identity, and gender. Some of the essays consider Sterne's life and milieu, his literary career, and his subsequent influence on modernism, while several others interpret *Tristram Shandy.*

_____. *Laurence Sterne's "Tristram Shandy": A Casebook.* New York: Oxford University Press, 2006. Reprints some of the essays about the novel that were published in various scholarly journals from the 1990's onward. Includes discussions of narrative and disease in the novel, Sterne as a literary celebrity in 1760, and Sterne, Jonathan Swift, and the skeptical tradition.

Kickel, Katherine E. "Making Sense of Novel Reading: New Curiosity Concerning Synaesthesia in Lawrence Sterne's *Tristram Shandy*." In *Novel Notions: Medical Discourse and the Mapping of the Imagination in Eighteenth-Century English Fiction*. New York: Routledge, 2007. Analysis of Sterne's novel is part of a larger examination of how works of eighteenth century fiction were influenced by medical investigations into the area of the brain that was believed to facilitate imagining. Describes how these novels deal with imagination, creation, and human cognition, expressing both anxiety and excitement about the new medical discoveries.

New, Melvyn. *"Tristram Shandy": A Book for Free Spirits*. New York: Twayne, 1994. Helpful introductory work is designed for students. Provides discussion of the historical milieu, literary importance, and critical reception of *Tristram Shandy* as well as five different, often contradictory, readings of the novel.

_____, ed. *Critical Essays on Laurence Sterne*. New York: G. K. Hall, 1998. Collection of essays includes many that focus on *Tristram Shandy*. Offers comparisons of the novel with *The Poem of Ossian* and the philosophy of John Locke, discussion of narrative representation in the novel, and an examination of the work from a feminist perspective.

The Triumph of Death

Author: Gabriele D'Annunzio (1863-1938)
First published: Il trionfo della morte, 1894 (English translation, 1896)
Type of work: Novel
Type of plot: Psychological realism
Time of plot: Nineteenth century
Locale: Italy

Principal characters:
GIORGIO AURISPA, a young Italian of wealth and family
SIGNOR AURISPA, Giorgio's materialistic father
IPPOLITA, Giorgio's mistress

The Story:

Giorgio Aurispa, a young Italian of old family and sufficient money to enjoy life without working, is in love with a lovely married woman named Ippolita. She lived with her husband for only a few weeks, for she fell ill shortly after they were married. When she began her affair with Giorgio, she left her husband and returned to her family. Marriage is out of the question for the lovers—for religious reasons, they cannot marry as long as one or the other has a living spouse.

Infatuated, both Giorgio and Ippolita often wish they could spend even more time together. On the second anniversary of their first meeting, however, an incident occurs that both regard as an ill omen and that casts a pall over their minds. As they are walking in the gardens of Rome's Pincio, they come to a terrace where a man has just committed suicide. Blood and a lock of blond hair are still in evidence. The suicide of the unknown young man in the Pincio will affect the lovers even more than they realize at the time. Giorgio be-

gins to feel that materialism and sensuality, fostered by his love for Ippolita, have taken too firm a hold on him. Ippolita responds to the suicide as a renewed warning about her own mortality and the fact that she has a tendency toward epilepsy.

Soon after the incident, Giorgio is called home. His father and mother do not live together, and Giorgio has known for some time that his father keeps a mistress. When Giorgio sees his mother, he learns for the first time the full story of his father's conduct. His mother tells him that his father has despoiled the family fortune, refuses a dowry for their daughter, and lives openly with his mistress and two illegitimate children. Giorgio dislikes the financial entanglements of the situation; he has inherited his own money from an uncle. When Giorgio visits his father to intercede for his family, the young man does nothing to help his mother and sister. Instead, he agrees to sign a note as surety for his father, who is trying to borrow money from a bank. Giorgio, however, is struck by the way his father has surrendered completely to a life of gross materialism.

Before he leaves his mother's home to return to Rome, Giorgio visits the apartment in the mansion where his uncle had lived. His uncle had committed suicide, and the realization of his uncle's deed fills Giorgio with curiosity and melancholy. He almost decides to kill himself with the same dueling pistol his uncle used.

Returning to Rome, Giorgio again falls under the spell of Ippolita, even though he is now haunted by his fear of gross sensuality, thoughts of suicide, and a friend's warning that Ippolita is coarse beneath her beauty and will someday find a richer lover. In order to escape his fears, Giorgio searches for a place where he and Ippolita can be away from the world. He thinks that they may be able to live in peace in a small village on the Adriatic coast, where he can work out his emotional and psychological problems.

They begin their new secluded life, but Giorgio finds himself in an even greater quandary. Although at times he feels great happiness in being with his mistress day and night, at other times he sees Ippolita as the embodiment of an animal nature that is slowly but surely ensnaring him as it has ensnared his father. In order to escape, to achieve idealism, Giorgio once more considers taking his own life.

The Church offers no solution to his problem. He and Ippolita are, in their way, devout Catholics. They visit shrines, but the mobs of humanity in these places, the beggars with their sores and ills, only repulse the lovers.

Ippolita's spell continues to work its way with Giorgio. Ippolita is proud of her power to awaken his desires, and she uses this power constantly. Giorgio loves her and hates her at the same time, but he knows that he is not without blame. When their affair began, she was modest and almost frigid. Her husband, to whom she had been married by her family, had been brutal, and she had been ill. Giorgio, the first to stir her emotions, has helped to shape her personality.

As do any two people living together, they discover some irritating traits in each other. Giorgio is displeased with Ippolita's feet, which he regards as too common-looking. Ippolita thinks that Giorgio is often too morbid. Both of them try too hard, as they readily admit, to escape into an idealized world of pleasure.

Trying by all means to keep from antagonizing each other, they continue to make short excursions away from the village. Giorgio has a piano and sheet music sent from Rome to their retreat. Still, however, he finds himself thinking of death—not only his own but Ippolita's as well. He sometimes believes that he can escape from sensuality only through the loss of his beloved. Death is the means he knows he must take to banish her irrevocably. For her part, Ippolita seems to realize what is in his mind. She has dreams in which she sees him dead or taking threatening attitudes toward her. Still, in Giorgio's mind, she is the most beautiful and fascinating of women, and her power over him continues to grow. Often, when he is emotionally distressed, she can draw him from that state of mind with nothing more than a kiss.

One afternoon, while they are swimming, Giorgio has an impulse to drown Ippolita. She seems to sense his mood and refuses to go swimming with him again. One night, after they have shared a pleasant meal, Giorgio persuades his mistress to take a walk with him down to the rocky coast, where fishermen are working at their nets. When they come to a one-plank bridge over which they must walk to reach their destination, Ippolita grows dizzy at the sight of waves and rocks below and refuses to cross. Giorgio, however, feels that he has found the time and place for his despairing deed; he sweeps Ippolita into his arms and plunges both of them to their deaths on the rocks below.

Critical Evaluation:

Gabriele D'Annunzio's early work was written under the influence of French writers, particularly those associated with the Decadent movement. *The Triumph of Death* was published after *Il piacere* (1889; *The Child of Pleasure*, 1898), which follows and analyzes the troubled inner life of a Roman nobleman in a fashion similar to the examination of Giorgio. *The Triumph of Death* is a more sophisticated work than its predecessor, offering a psychological analysis of greater depth, but its power comes from its relentless fascination with mortality.

The story told by the novel is essentially a long explanation of Giorgio's eventual decision to commit suicide and take Ippolita with him. Perhaps it is also a justification of that act, insofar as it might be justified, but D'Annunzio takes care to maintain a distance between himself and his subject. He describes Giorgio's impressions in minute detail, but he refrains from confirming their validity or condoning their morality. It is worth bearing in mind that D'Annunzio went on to write works of a very different nature, forsaking Decadent pessimism to the extent that he became a passionate advocate of mechanical progress, a war hero, and—eventually—a supporter of Benito Mussolini; it would be a mistake to identify him too closely with his protagonist.

Giorgio's disaffection has two root causes. One is his exaggerated distaste for what he considers to be the degradation of his fellow human beings. This reaches a climax in the scenes at the shrine, where the maimed, the mad, and the miserable gather in a vast jostling crowd, competing with animalistic fervor for the privilege of begging the Virgin Mary to grant them release from their suffering. The same distaste is given more intimate expression in the savagely scathing judgment that Giorgio delivers upon his greedy and deceitful father. It is worth noting that his judgment of his whining mother, his corpulent aunt, and his enfeebled sister, Cristina, is no more generous. The people he cannot hate he nevertheless contrives to hold in contempt.

Giorgio frequently disguises his vituperations as attacks on vulgar materialism, but such charges ring true only when they are applied to his father and his sponging friend Exili. What really offends him is infirmity and self-delusion in all their guises. An unsympathetic reader might be tempted to draw the conclusion that Giorgio's greatest fear is that his own strength is insufficient to sustain him against the temptations of self-delusion and the consequent acceptance of weakness. If this is so, the triumph of death to which the title refers might be reckoned a meek surrender to that gnawing anxiety.

The second and more specific cause of Giorgio's morbidity is his love for Ippolita. This may seem paradoxical, in that conventional wisdom asserts that love has an unparalleled power of life enhancement, but in Giorgio's case the magnitude of his love merely intensifies the unbearability of knowing that it cannot endure. Giorgio cannot believe, even for a moment, in the myth of eternal love. He knows, as surely as he knows anything, that passion is transient, that it is by definition something that soars to a peak and then declines. He knows, too, that the higher the peak of ecstasy to which lovers are borne, the further they must descend thereafter; the only question to be settled is how swift the descent will be. In this context, the method of Giorgio's suicide is highly significant. Giorgio chooses the most precipitous of all possible descents.

Readers sympathetic to this kind of extreme gesture might consider that the triumph of death is at least to be credited to Giorgio rather than inflicted on him, although this hardly seems fair to poor Ippolita, who seems utterly guiltless. Although Mario Praz reserves a conspicuous place for her in the long list of Romantic and Decadent femmes fatales, Ippolita makes no active contribution to Giorgio's unbalanced state of mind. Giorgio's abrupt closure of their affair certainly avoids the ignominy of slow decay and degradation, but the decision to take her with him in death serves to undermine rather than to confirm its heroic dimension. In an early scene in the novel, Giorgio studies the audience assembled to hear a concert organized by a famous conductor, marveling at its odd admixture of scientists and followers of un-

orthodox religion: "cold explorers of life and passionate devotees of the cult of dreams." Giorgio is both of these things, and his cold exploration of his own dreams is what will not let him decorate his love or his life with illusions. When he stands witness to the imbecilic hopes and futile desires of those more wretched than himself, he is filled with horror.

In the years between the publication of *The Child of Pleasure* and *The Triumph of Death* D'Annunzio had become fascinated with the philosophy of Friedrich Nietzsche, but *The Triumph of Death* is not a Nietzschean work in any straightforward sense. Were Giorgio an authentic Nietzschean hero, he would have found a way out of his impasse. The Nietzschean will to power would have given Giorgio the energy to rise above his fixation with erotic excitement and make something of himself—preferably an artist. Giorgio does, however, qualify as a Nietzschean character in that he sees through the sham of contemporary ideas and ideals. He has realized that what passes for morality is merely a form of cowardice whose ultimate results are life-denying rather than life-enhancing.

Perhaps Giorgio's philosophy is best regarded as a failed experiment, one that reveals by its failure that the road to a better philosophy leads in another direction—but this does not mean that the novel that tells his story is a failure. On the contrary, the novel achieves perfect unity and a highly effective closure. It is brilliantly detailed and precise. In a world filled with texts that stubbornly maintain that love offers the chance of permanent life enhancement, *The Triumph of Death* is a useful exercise in skepticism with which to balance the argument.

Brian Stableford

Further Reading

Becker, Jared. *Nationalism and Culture: Gabriele D'Annunzio and Italy After the Reisorgimento*. New York: Peter Lang, 1994. Examines Italian nationalist culture before the rise of Fascism by focusing on D'Annunzio's political and literary career. Links the author to proto-Fascist movements in France and Germany, tracing D'Annunzio's impact on racial thinking and the evolution of Italian imperialism.

Duncan, Derek. "Choice Objects: The Bodies of Gabriele D'Annunzio." In *Reading and Writing Italian Homosexuality: A Case of Possible Difference*. Burlington, Vt.: Ashgate, 2006. Explores the representation of male homosexuality in Italian literature from the 1890's through the 1990's, devoting a chapter to the work of D'Annunzio.

Jullian, Philippe. *D'Annunzio*. Translated by Stephen Hardman. London: Pall Mall Press, 1972. Presents a comprehensive examination of D'Annunzio's life and works. *The Triumph of Death* is discussed in chapter 5.

Klopp, Charles. *Gabriele D'Annunzio*. Boston: Twayne, 1988. Provides a concise, thorough overview of the man and his works.

Schoolfield, George C. *A Baedeker of Decadence: Charting a Literary Fashion, 1884-1927*. New Haven, Conn.: Yale University Press, 2003. Discusses thirty-two works written in more than a dozen languages that characterize the literary style of Decadence. Chapter 3 focuses on the writings of D'Annunzio, including discussion of *The Triumph of Death*.

Woodhouse, John Robert. *Gabriele D'Annunzio: Defiant Archangel*. New York: Oxford University Press, 2001. Authoritative biography focuses on D'Annunzio's relationships with the worlds of Italian culture, theater, and politics and evaluates the writer's influence on present-day Italian culture.

Troilus and Cressida

Author: William Shakespeare (1564-1616)
First produced: 1601-1602; first published, 1609
Type of work: Drama
Type of plot: Tragedy
Time of plot: Antiquity
Locale: Troy

Principal characters:
PRIAM, king of Troy
HECTOR and TROILUS, his sons
AGAMEMNON,
ACHILLES,
ULYSSES,
AJAX, and
DIOMEDES, Greek commanders
PANDARUS, a Trojan lord
CRESSIDA, his niece

The Story:

During the Trojan War, Troilus, younger son of Priam, king of Troy, falls in love with the lovely and unapproachable Cressida, daughter of Calchas, a Trojan priest who went over to the side of the Greeks. Troilus, frustrated by his unrequited love, declares to Pandarus, a Trojan lord and uncle of Cressida, that he will refrain from fighting the Greeks as long as there is such turmoil in his heart. Pandarus adds to Troilus's misery by praising the incomparable beauty of Cressida; Troilus impatiently chides Pandarus, who answers that for all it matters to him Cressida can join her father in the Greek camp.

Later, Pandarus overhears Cressida and her servant discussing Hector's anger at receiving a blow in battle from Ajax, a mighty Greek warrior of Trojan blood. Pandarus extols Troilus's virtues to Cressida, who is all but indifferent. As the two discourse, the Trojan forces return from the field. Pandarus praises several Trojan warriors—Aeneas, Antenor, Hector, Paris, Helenus—as they pass by Cressida's window, all the while anticipating, for Cressida's benefit, the passing of young Troilus. When the prince passes, Pandarus is lavish in his praise, but Cressida appears to be bored. As Pandarus leaves her to join Troilus, Cressida soliloquizes that she is charmed, indeed, by Troilus, but that she is in no haste to reveal the state of her affections.

In the Greek camp, meanwhile, Agamemnon, commander of the Greek forces in Ilium, tries to put heart into his demoralized leaders. Old Nestor declares that the seven difficult years of the siege of Troy are a real test of Greek stamina. It is the belief of Ulysses that the difficulties of the Greeks lie in a lack of order and discipline, not in Trojan strength. He reminds his fellow Greek leaders that the disaffection of mighty Achilles and the scurrilous clowning of Patroclus, a Greek leader, provoke disorder in the Greek ranks. Even Ajax, usually dependable, is fractious, and his follower, deformed Thersites, embarrasses the Greeks with his taunts.

As the Greek leaders confer, Aeneas delivers to them a challenge from Hector, who in single combat will defend the beauty and the virtue of his lady against a Greek champion. When the leaders go their several ways to announce the challenge to Achilles and to other Greeks, Ulysses and Nestor decide that the only politic action to take, the pride of Achilles being what it is, is to arrange somehow that Ajax be chosen to fight Hector. Ajax, Achilles, and Patroclus hear of the proclamation but tend to disregard it. Their levity causes the railing Thersites to break with them.

In Troy, meanwhile, Hector is tempted to concede to a Greek offer to end hostilities if the Trojans return Helen to her husband, King Menelaus. Troilus chides his brother and Helenus for their momentary want of resolution. As the brothers and their father, Priam, discuss the reasons for and against continuing the war, Cassandra, prophet and daughter of Priam, predicts that Troy will be burned to the ground by the Greeks. Hector heeds her warning, but Troilus, joined by Paris, persists in the belief that the war, for the sake of honor, must be continued. Hector, although aware of the evil the Trojans are committing in defending Paris's indefensible theft of Helen from her husband, concedes that for reasons of honor the fighting must continue.

The Greek leaders approach Achilles, who keeps to himself since his quarrel with Agamemnon. Refusing to confer with them, Achilles retires into his tent and sends his companion, Patroclus, to make his apologies. Achilles persists in refusing to deal with the Greek commanders, who seek in him their champion against Hector. Ulysses plays on the pride of Ajax with subtle flattery and convinces this Greek of Trojan blood that he should present himself as the Greek champion in place of Achilles.

In the meantime, Pandarus prepares the way for a tryst between Troilus and Cressida by securing the promise of Paris and Helen to make excuses for Troilus's absence. He brings the two young people together in his orchard, where the pair confess to each other their undying love. Cressida declares that if she is ever false, then all falsehood will forever afterward be associated with her name. Pandarus witnesses these sincere avowals of faith and himself declares that if Troilus and Cressida do not remain faithful to each other, then all go-betweens will be associated with his name. These declarations being made, Pandarus leads the young people to a bedchamber in his house.

In the Greek camp, Calchas, Cressida's father, persuades Agamemnon to exchange Antenor, a Trojan prisoner, for Cressida, whose presence he desires. Diomedes, a Greek commander, is appointed to effect the exchange. Planning to ignore Achilles, the Greek leaders pass the warrior with only the briefest recognition. When he demands an explanation of that treatment, Ulysses tells him that fame is ephemeral and that great deeds are soon forgotten. Fearful for his reputation now that Ajax has been appointed Greek champion, Achilles arranges to play host to the unarmed Hector after the contest.

Diomedes returns Antenor to Troy, and, at dawn, he is taken to Pandarus's house to escort Cressida to the Greek camp. When Troilus and Cressida learn of Diomedes' mission, Troilus appeals unsuccessfully to the Trojan leaders to allow Cressida to remain in Troy. Heartbroken, he returns to Cressida and the young couple repeat their vows in their farewells. Troilus then escorts Cressida and Diomedes, who comments on Cressida's beauty, as far as the city gates. When Diomedes and Cressida encounter the Greek leaders outside the walls, Cressida is kissed by Agamemnon, Menelaus, Nestor, Patroclus, and others. Ulysses observes that she appears wanton.

Warriors of both sides assemble to watch Hector and Ajax fight. The two companions clash for only a moment before Hector desists, declaring that he cannot harm Ajax, his cousin. Ajax accepts Hector's magnanimity and invites the Trojan to join, unarmed, the Greek commanders at dinner. Hector, accompanied by Troilus, is welcomed among the Greeks with many warm compliments, but Achilles, meeting Hector, rudely mentions that part of Hector's person in which he will one day inflict a mortal wound. Stung by Achilles' pride and lack of manners, Hector declares hotly that he will destroy all of Achilles at one stroke. The result is an agreement to meet in combat the next day. Ajax manages to calm heated tempers, however, and the feasting begins.

Troilus, anxious to see his beloved Cressida, asks Ulysses where he might find Calchas, and Ulysses promises to be his guide. After the banquet, they follow Diomedes to Calchas's tent, where Cressida meets him and, in affectionate overtures toward Diomedes, reveals to the hidden Troilus that she already has all but forgotten him. As she gives Diomedes, as a token of her love, a sleeve that belongs to Troilus, compunction seizes her for a moment. She quickly succumbs, however, to Diomedes' charms and promises to be his at their next meeting. Diomedes leaves, vowing to kill in combat the Trojan whose sleeve he will be wearing on his helmet. Troilus, unable to believe that Cressida is the woman he loves so passionately, returns to Troy. He vows to take the life of Diomedes.

As the new day approaches, Hector is warned by Andromache, his wife, and by his sister Cassandra not to do battle that day; all portents foretell disaster. When their words prove ineffectual, King Priam tries vainly to persuade Hector to remain within the walls. During the battle, Diomedes unhorses Troilus and sends the horse as a gift to Cressida. Despite his overthrow, Troilus continues to fight heroically. Hector appears to be, for his part, invincible. When Patroclus is severely wounded in the action, Achilles, enraged, orders his followers, the Myrmidons, to stand ready. As the action subsides, and Hector is unarming himself at the end of the day, the Myrmidons, at Achilles' command, close in on brave Hector and fell him with their spears.

Troilus announces to the retiring Trojan forces that Hector was killed by treachery and that his body, tied to the tail of Achilles' horse, is being dragged around the Phrygian plain. As he makes his way to the gates, he predicts general mourning in Troy and expresses his undying hatred for the Greeks. He encounters Pandarus, whom he abruptly dismisses as a cheap panderer, a man whose name will be infamous forever.

Critical Evaluation:

In the Folio of 1623, *Troilus and Cressida* is described as a tragedy; in the Quarto it is called a history; in most structural respects it seems to be a comedy, though a very grim and bitter one. Critics have frequently classified it, with *Measure for Measure* (pr. c. 1604, pb. 1623) and *All's Well That Ends Well* (pr. c. 1602-1603, pb. 1623), as a "problem play," perhaps as much because the play poses a problem in literary taxonomy as because it sets out to examine a problematic thesis. Probably written between *Hamlet, Prince of Denmark* (pr. c. 1600-1601, pb. 1603) and *Othello, the Moor of Venice* (pr. 1604, pb. 1622), during the period of the great tragedies, the play is so full of gloom and venom, so lacking in the playfulness and idealism of the earlier comedies, that critics have attributed its tone and manner either to a period of personal disillusionment in William Shakespeare's life or to his preoccupation at that time with tragic themes.

There is no external and little internal evidence for the biographical conclusion. It may be, however, that, in *Troilus and Cressida*, Shakespeare was affected by the surrounding tragedies. It is as if he took the moral ambiguities and potential chaos of the worlds of the tragedies and ruled out the possibility of redemption and transcendence through heroic suffering. He peoples this tenuous world with blowhards, cynics, and poltroons and ruthlessly lets them muddle through for themselves. The world of *King Lear* (pr. c. 1605-1606, pb. 1608), for example, is on the brink of chaos, but at least there is the sublimity of Lear to salvage it. The world of *Troilus and Cressida* has no one to shore up its structure and challenge disintegration.

Although there were many contemporary versions of the relevant Homeric materials available to Shakespeare, it is clear that he was also familiar with the story as told by Chaucer in *Troilus and Criseyde* (c. 1382). Chaucer's world, however, was full of innocence, brilliance, and hope. If the medieval Criseyde behaves shabbily, it is only the result of feminine weakness and long importuning. If Chaucer's Troilus is naïve and a victim of courtly idealism, at least he

can finally sort things out from an Olympian perspective. Shakespeare does not give his lovers, or the rest of the Greek heroes, this sympathy or opportunity but drags them through a drab and seamy degradation.

Shakespeare begins with characters traditionally honored for their nobility, but he does nothing to develop them even for a fall. He simply betrays them, to show them up, and thereby to represent the extreme precariousness of their world. The bloom of courtly love is gone as is the Christian optimism of the Middle Ages. Shakespeare seems to be reflecting not a personal situation but a late Renaissance malaise as he has his characters impotently preside at the dissolution of the revered old order.

In Chaucer, Troilus's love and woe are instrumental in his maturation and, ultimately, in his salvation. Shakespeare's Troilus is more frankly sensual and his liaison is correspondingly sordid. He does not benefit from an ennobling passion, nor is he allowed to transcend his folly. He is not even accorded the dignity of a significant death. He fights on in pointless, imperceptive frenzy.

Cressida is also debased. She falls from courtly heroine to common whore. Perhaps Shakespeare borrowed her degradation from Robert Henryson's highly moralistic *Testament of Cresseid* (1532), in which the heroine sinks to prostitution. In any case, she does not have the initial austerity and later reserve that dignify the passion and fall of Chaucer's Criseyde. Her language and her every movement suggest that she is more of a slut than a courtly heroine. Even as she enters the Greek camp, her promiscuous behavior betrays her, and her quick submission to Diomedes confirms what is suspected all along. As if the lovers cannot behave foully enough by themselves, Shakespeare provides them with Pandarus, as go-between and commentator, to further sully the relationship.

In Chaucer, the Trojan War provides a fatalistic backdrop that enhances the progress of the tragic love. In Shakespeare, the circumambient Homeric heroes serve only to discredit themselves and to amplify the chaos. Mark Van Doren pointed out that, if Pandarus's role is to degrade the lovers, "the role of Thersites is to cheapen the heroes." They, however, do not need much help from their interlocutor. For example, when Ulysses gives his famous speech on order, one is more struck by the pointless bombast and strangulated rhetoric than by erudition. One is led to suspect that this world is out of touch with its ordering principles and that it is vainly trying to recapture them or to preserve their appearance with tortured language. Similarly, when Achilles delivers his set speech in act 3, it has all of the bitterness but none of the grace of Lear's corresponding speech. This Achilles is a petulant sybarite, and the world is in trouble if he is its hero. The bombast, the irritability, and the inconsequentiality are all-pervasive. Agamemnon and Nestor are nothing more than windbags. When the Greeks meet to discuss plans, or the Trojans meet to discuss returning Helen, the conferences both quickly degenerate into pompous vacuity.

The moral and political disintegration is reflected in the shrill and strident language of the play. The diction, which is jawbreakingly full of inkhornisms, and the rhetorical excesses reinforce the notion that the characters are spinning out of control, no longer able to gain control of their language, no longer able even to give verbal order to their frustrations. The result is a play that can easily seem tedious. Consequently, *Troilus and Cressida* is rarely performed. It has, however, fascinated the critics. What all of this suggests is that the play is more interesting than appealing, more intriguing than satisfying, as it chronicles the demise of a world in which no one is left with the moral stature to make a last stand.

"Critical Evaluation" by Edward E. Foster

Further Reading

Apfelbaum, Roger. *Shakespeare's "Troilus and Cressida": Textual Problems and Performance Solutions*. Newark: University of Delaware Press, 2004. Analyzes the variations and changes in the text of the play and discusses how these alterations affect the play's performance. Describes the difficulties of staging this play and offers performance options.

Barker, Simon, ed. *Shakespeare's Problem Plays: "All's Well That Ends Well," "Measure for Measure," "Troilus and Cressida."* New York: Palgrave Macmillan, 2005. Collection of essays providing a range of late-twentieth century interpretations of the plays. The chapters regarding *Troilus and Cressida* discuss the fragments of nationalism, making history, love, and disease, desire, and representation in the play.

Barroll, J. Leeds, ed. *Shakespeare Studies VI*. Dubuque, Iowa: William C. Brown, 1970. Part of an annual series of Shakespearean review anthologies. "The Traditions of the Troy-Story Heroes and the Problem of Satire in *Troilus and Cressida*," by Mark Sacharoff, considers the story of the play and its earlier sources in light of previous criticism.

_____. *Shakespeare Studies VIII*. New York: Burt Franklin, 1975. A later volume in the above-cited series. In "Cressida and the World of the Play," by Grant L. Voth and Oliver H. Evans, the role of Cressida is considered in terms of her calculating ways, which are seen as a direct response to Troilus's temporary infatuation.

Bullough, Geoffrey, ed. *Narrative and Dramatic Sources of Shakespeare*. Vol. 6. New York: Columbia University Press, 1966. Part of a six-volume series of critical essays concerning the sources of Shakespeare's plays. *Troilus and Cressida* is discussed in a forty-page introduction, which is followed by the actual texts and translations of the sources Shakespeare would have known.

Clark, Ira. *Rhetorical Readings, Dark Comedies, and Shakespeare's Problem Plays*. Gainesville: University Press of Florida, 2007. Examines *Troilus and Cressida* and two other "problem plays," or plays that ostensibly are comedies but lack clear resolutions. Analyzes the most prominent rhetorical features of these plays, including rhetorical devices that were commonly used in Elizabethan literature.

Donaldson, E. Talbot. *The Swan at the Well: Shakespeare Reading Chaucer*. New Haven, Conn.: Yale University Press, 1985. A comparison between several of Shakespeare's plays and their sources in Geoffrey Chaucer's poems. There are two chapters dealing with *Troilus and Cressida*, comparing the play to its literary source, Chaucer's poem *Troilus and Criseyde*.

Elton, W. R. *Shakespeare's "Troilus and Cressida" and the Inns of Court Revels*. Brookfield, Vt.: Ashgate, 2000. Argues that the play was specifically written for an audience of lawyers and law students. Places the play within the context of the Inns of Court revels, or festivities for law students.

Lloyd Evans, Gareth. *The Upstart Crow: An Introduction to Shakespeare's Plays*. London: J. M. Dent and Sons, 1982. A comprehensive discussion of the dramatic works of Shakespeare. Although the major emphasis is on critical reviews of the plays, there are also discussions of sources and the circumstances surrounding the writing of the plays.

Marsh, Nicholas. *Shakespeare: Three Problem Plays*. New York: Palgrave Macmillan, 2003. Examines the unresolved issues in *Troilus and Cressida* and two other plays by analyzing excerpts from their texts, pointing out the multiple interpretations of young men, women, politics and society, and fools. Places the plays in relation to Shakespeare's life and oeuvre, providing historical and cultural context and analyses by five literary critics.

Troilus and Criseyde

Author: Geoffrey Chaucer (c. 1343-1400)
First transcribed: c. 1382
Type of work: Poetry
Type of plot: Love
Time of plot: Antiquity
Locale: Troy

Principal characters:
TROILUS, the young prince of Troy
CRISEYDE, a young widow
PANDARUS, Troilus's friend and Criseyde's uncle
DIOMEDES, a Greek warrior

The Poem:

Calchas, a Trojan prophet who has divined that Troy is doomed to defeat, flees to the Greeks, leaving behind his beautiful daughter, Criseyde, a young widow. One day in April, the citizens of Troy are observing the rites of the spring festival. Among those in the temple is Troilus, a son of King Priam of Troy. Troilus, who has always been scornful of the Trojan swains and their lovesickness, sees Criseyde and falls deeply in love with her at first sight. Himself now sick with the love malady, Troilus invokes the god of love to have pity on him. Because he feels that he has no hope of winning Criseyde, he becomes the scourge of the Greeks on the battlefield.

Pandarus, Troilus's friend, offers his advice and help when he learns that Troilus has lost his heart to a beautiful Trojan. When Troilus at length reveals that his lady is the fair Criseyde, Pandarus, who is Criseyde's uncle, offers to become his mediator. Pandarus thereupon calls on his niece to gossip with her, and in their conversation he brings up the subject of Priam's sons, praising the bravery of Troilus. Gradually he discloses to Criseyde that young Troilus is dying for love of her. Criseyde suspects that the intentions of neither Troilus nor Pandarus are honorable, and she cries out in distress, but Pandarus convinces her that Troilus's love is pure. She feels herself drawn to the prince when she beholds his modesty as he rides past her house after a day of battle outside the walls of Troy. She decides, after much inner turmoil, that it would not be dishonorable to show friendship to Troilus to save the young man's life.

At the suggestion of Pandarus, Troilus writes a letter to Criseyde, to which she responds in a restrained letter of her own. When Troilus, wishing to be with Criseyde, tires of this correspondence, Pandarus arranges a meeting by asking Deiphobus, Troilus's brother, to invite the pair to his house for dinner. After the dinner, Criseyde gives Troilus permission to be in her service and to adore her.

Pandarus, eager to bring about a private meeting of the lovers, studies the stars and decides on a night that will be propitious for a tryst. He invites Criseyde to dine with him on that evening, with Troilus already hidden in his house. After they have dined, as the lady prepares to take her leave, it begins to rain, and Pandarus persuades her to stay. Through Pandarus's wiles, the lovers are brought together. After yielding to Troilus, Criseyde gives him a brooch as a token of their love.

At about this time a great battle is fought between the Greeks and the Trojans, and several of the Trojan leaders are captured. In an exchange of prisoners, Calchas persuades the Greeks to ask for his daughter, Criseyde, in return for Antenor, a Trojan warrior. The Trojan parliament, after much debate, approves the transaction. Hector, another brother of Troilus, is unsuccessful in arguing that Criseyde should remain in Troy. Troilus is in despair.

After plans for the exchange have been made, Pandarus brings the lovers together again secretly. Criseyde, brokenhearted, tells the prince that their separation will not be for long, and that she will remain faithful to him. Troilus and his party accompany Criseyde to the place appointed for the exchange. There they meet Antenor, whom they are to conduct to Troy, and Diomedes, a young Greek warrior, leads Criseyde away to the Greek camp. Troilus returns to Troy to await the passing of ten days, at the end of which time Criseyde has promised she will return. Diomedes manages to seduce Criseyde by the tenth day, however, and she gives him the brooch that Troilus had given her at their parting. In return, Diomedes gives her a horse he had captured from Troilus in battle.

After several weeks of anxious waiting, Troilus writes to Criseyde. She answers him, weakly avowing her love for him and saying that she will return to Troy at the earliest opportunity. Troilus, sensing that something is amiss, grieves. One day, he sees the brooch he had given Criseyde on a piece of armor taken from Diomedes on the battlefield. Knowing that Criseyde has forsaken him for another, Troilus seeks out and fights Diomedes indecisively many times. Eventually the unhappy Troilus is killed by the mighty Achilles.

Critical Evaluation:

Troilus and Criseyde, the only long work completed by Geoffrey Chaucer, is based on the legend of the Trojan War. The characters, however, behave in the best tradition of the medieval romance. Chaucer, an incomparable teller of tales and a great poet, combined his two talents to create this perfectly constructed narrative poem. The effective depiction of character and its development in this work forecasts the shrewd observations of human nature Chaucer would make in the prologue to *The Canterbury Tales* (1387-1400).

Troilus and Criseyde is a paradox of artistic creation. At once both medieval and modern, it holds vast problems of interpretation yet pleases with its wit, style, comedy, and humanity. The work cannot be dated with complete certainty, but certainly by that point in his career, Chaucer—diplomat, man of letters, public official, and onetime prisoner of war—already had a literary reputation, which the appearance of *Troilus and Criseyde* did nothing to diminish. Chaucer's contemporary reputation, in fact, probably rested with this poem at least as much as with the later and much-loved *Canterbury Tales*. It was certainly Chaucer's *Troilus and Criseyde*, more than any other poems that addressed the same subject matter, that later poets used as a source for their own works. The fifteenth century Scottish poet Robert Henryson, for example, wrote of Criseyde's ignoble end in *The Testament of Cresseid* (1532), and William Shakespeare tried his hand at the story with *Troilus and Cressida* (pr. 1601-1602, pb. 1609).

Chaucer himself found the story in Giovanni Boccaccio's *Il filostrato* (c. 1335; *The Filostrato*, 1873); possibly Chaucer was working from an intermediate source—*Le Roman de troyle et de creseida* by Beauvau. The story itself derives from the Trojan legend, but Troilus and Criseyde are such minor figures in Homer's story (and never meet there) that it is apparent that Chaucer had more in mind than the simple retelling of a classical tale.

Much of the discussion in the nineteenth and early twentieth centuries about Chaucer's purpose in writing the poem focused on the palinode, that is, the concluding section of about one hundred lines, in which the narrator repudiates the courtly love that has governed the action of the lovers for more than eight thousand lines. Subsequent criticism has focused on Chaucer's attitude toward love in general, on the poem as tragedy, and on how best to read the poem.

Courtly love was a highly conventionalized, and un-Christian, tradition, dating back at least to Eleanor of Aquitane's court in twelfth century northern France. The courtly love tradition held that love was sensual, illicit, adulterous, secret, and hard to obtain. The lady, the embodiment of virtue who was yet cruel to her lover, granted him her favors only after he had suffered agonies of frustration. Troilus and Criseyde practice courtly love until Criseyde violates one of its prime tenets, loyalty. By defecting from Troilus, she destroys the spell the courtly love tradition casts on the minds of Chaucer's audience. At the very end of the poem, all readers are made to examine the priorities of courtly love and, on a deeper plane, devotion to human love over the love of God. The palinode at the end raises the question of how human beings should live their lives and whether they should desire and want the things of this earth, which can so easily be stripped away. Troilus clearly is the victim of the love of a weak woman, and he discovers that his fate is a tragic one. The narrator at the work's end asks readers to avoid becoming victims of fortune by devoting themselves to God and God's love.

One of the most important aspects of the poem is the elaborate psychological development of its characters. Before Chaucer, the most advanced way of representing psychological states in literature was to abstract feelings and emotions, as well as virtues and vices, embody each in a character, and have these characters contend for possession of the individual. Never before Chaucer had the whole human being been depicted as a feeling, growing person. The tendency in earlier literature was to make the protagonist universal, as is Everyman in the morality play. The characters in Chaucer's poem are in no sense universal. While they are not particularly admirable characters, they share the same psychology with their readers—that is, they show weaknesses and strengths that are very human.

Criseyde's character depends on her situation. In the opening of the poem she is in a dangerous position, afraid of the Trojans, afraid of love, afraid of human involvement—afraid, even, of herself. Her natural inclination is to hold back when Pandarus approaches her on Troilus's behalf, but Pandarus makes a union with Troilus seem desirable, even reasonable. Troilus can protect her socially and politically, and after Pandarus approaches her, she begins to develop complex reactions: fear, resistance, questioning, need, and hope. Troilus and Criseyde are characters who live in a real world of human flaws, vices, joys, hopes, and predicaments. Chaucer's achievement in perfecting psychological realism is of the first magnitude.

Chaucer does not present a consistent view. The narrator in the first eight hundred lines of book 2—up to the point where Criseyde decides to accept Troilus as her lover—is privy to Criseyde's thoughts. After that, the narrator no longer knows what she is thinking but only what she says. Chaucer seems to praise courtly love throughout much of the poem, then suddenly rejects it in the conclusion. Such inconsistencies reflect the medieval aesthetic theory, which holds that art should convey truth. Since the only real truth, in this view, is the permanence of God's laws in God's realm (which is unknowable), humans, who live in their own separate, lower realm, cannot know absolute truth. What they do see is changeable and impermanent. Artists, who try to depict truth as best they can, find that their art becomes as changing and inconsistent as the world they observe. Since they cannot share in God's realm, both artists and audiences must be content with inconsistencies in art.

"Critical Evaluation" by Brian L. Mark

Further Reading

Boitani, Piero, and Jill Mann, eds. *The Cambridge Companion to Chaucer.* 2d ed. New York: Cambridge University Press, 2003. Collection of essays includes discussions of Chaucer's style, the literary structure of his works, the social and literary scene in England during his lifetime, and his French and Italian inheritances. Includes two essays on *Troilus and Criseyde*: "Telling the Story of *Troilus and Criseyde*," by Mark Lambert, and "Chance and Destiny in *Troilus and Criseyde* and the 'Knight's Tale,'" by Jill Mann.

Condren, Edward I. *Chaucer from Prentice to Poet: The Metaphor of Love in Dream Visions and "Troilus and Criseyde."* Gainesville: University Press of Florida, 2008. Presents an in-depth analysis of Chaucer's early poetry in which *Troilus and Criseyde* is compared with his dream visions—*Book of the Duchess* (c. 1370), *House of Fame* (1372-1380), and *Parlement of Foules* (1380).

Donaldson, E. Talbot. *Speaking of Chaucer.* 1970. Reprint. Durham, N.C.: Labyrinth Press, 1983. Includes three chapters devoted to *Troilus and Criseyde*. Explores the connection between Criseyde and the masculine narrator, who is described as loving Criseyde with "avuncular sentimentality," and concludes that the ending of the poem reveals the instability and illusory quality of human love.

Frantzen, Allen J. *"Troilus and Criseyde": The Poem and the Frame.* New York: Twayne, 1993. Discusses the literary and historical context of the poem and provides a reading that focuses on its internal framing devices of social and symbolic orders. Includes a chronology of Chaucer's life and works.

Howard, Donald R. "*Troilus and Criseyde*." In *Chaucer: His Life, His Works, His World.* New York: E. P. Dutton, 1987. Chapter on the poem is part of a masterful biographical, historical, and literary study of Chaucer. Topics addressed include Chaucer's intended audience; his transformation of Boccaccio's *Il filostrato*; the characters of Troilus, Criseyde, and Pandarus; and the achievement of the poem. Concludes that *Troilus and Criseyde* is Chaucer's masterpiece.

Kaminsky, Alice R. *Chaucer's "Troilus and Criseyde" and the Critics.* Athens: Ohio University Press, 1980. Analytical survey of criticism on *Troilus and Criseyde* includes chapters on the philosophy of the poem and on formalistic and psychological approaches to the work.

Knapp, Peggy Ann. *Chaucerian Aesthetics.* New York: Palgrave Macmillan, 2008. Focuses on the aesthetics of *The Canterbury Tales* and *Troilus and Criseyde*, particularly their use of language and representation of games, people, women, humor, and community.

Mieszkowski, Gretchen. *Medieval Go-Betweens and Chaucer's Pandarus.* New York: Palgrave Macmillan, 2006. In medieval literature, two contrasting figures act as go-betweens: the elegant aristocrat, who brings men and women together for consensual romantic love, and the ancient crone, who captures women as prizes. Mieszkowski argues that the character of Pandarus in *Troilus and Criseyde*, who brings the couple together for both lust and romantic love, displays characteristics of both figures.

Pugh, Tison, and Marcia Smith Marzec, eds. *Men and Masculinities in Chaucer's "Troilus and Criseyde."* Woodbridge, England: D. S. Brewer, 2008. Collection of twelve essays offers varying interpretations of the poem's representation of masculinity.

Salu, Mary, ed. *Essays on "Troilus and Criseyde."* 1982. Reprint. Cambridge, England: D. S. Brewer, 1991. Collection of essays addresses such topics as the poem's text, its lessons, its realism, and paganism and comedy in the work.

The Trojan Women

Author: Euripides (c. 485-406 B.C.E.)
First produced: *Trōiades*, 415 B.C.E. (English translation, 1782)
Type of work: Drama
Type of plot: Tragedy
Time of plot: Antiquity
Locale: Outside the ruined walls of Troy

Principal characters:
POSEIDON, the god of the sea and patron of Troy
PALLAS ATHENA, the goddess of wisdom
HECUBA, the queen of Troy
CASSANDRA, her daughter, a prophet
ANDROMACHE, the wife of Hector, prince of Troy
HELEN, the queen of Sparta abducted by Paris
MENELAUS, the king of Sparta
TALTHYBIUS, the herald of the Greeks
CHORUS OF THE CAPTIVE TROJAN WOMEN

The Story:

On the second morning after the fall of Troy and the massacre of all its male inhabitants, Poseidon appears to lament the ruins and vows vengeance against the Greeks. To his surprise, Pallas Athena, the goddess who aided the Greeks, joins him in plotting a disastrous homeward voyage for the victors who despoiled her temple in Troy. They withdraw as Hecuba rises from among the sleeping Trojan women to mourn the burning city and her dead sons and husband. The chorus join her in chanting an anguished lament.

Talthybius, the herald of the Greeks, arrives to announce that Agamemnon chose Cassandra to be his concubine and that the other royal women of Troy were assigned by lot— Polyxena to the tomb of Achilles, Andromache to Achilles' son Neoptolemus, and Hecuba herself to Odysseus, king of Ithaca and conceiver of the wooden horse that led to the fall of the city. Amid the cries of the grieving women, Cassandra appears, bearing a flaming torch in each hand. The chorus is convinced that she is mad as she dances and prays to Hymen, god of marriage, that Agamemnon take her soon to Argos as his bride, for there she will cause his death and the ruin of his entire family. As for Odysseus, she foretells that he will suffer for ten more years on the seas before reaching his homeland. As Talthybius leads her off, he observes that Agamemnon himself must be mad to fall in love with the insane Cassandra.

Hecuba, broken with grief, collapses to the ground. From the city comes a Greek-drawn chariot loaded with the spoils of war and bearing Andromache and her infant son Astyanax. Cursing Helen, the cause of all their woe, Andromache calls upon the dead Hector to come to her and announces enviously that Polyxena was just killed upon the tomb of Achilles as a gift to the dead hero. Drawing upon her last remaining strength, Hecuba tries to comfort the distraught Andromache and urges that instead of mourning for Hector she win the love of Neoptolemus so that her son might grow to adulthood

and perhaps redeem Troy. At this point, the reluctant herald Talthybius announces the Greeks' order that the son of so distinguished a warrior as Hector must not be permitted to reach adulthood but must be killed at once by being hurled from the battlements of Troy. As Talthybius leads away Andromache and her son, a fresh lament and cursing of Helen goes up from the grieving women of Troy.

Suddenly King Menelaus comes striding in the sunlight with his retinue to demand that his faithless wife Helen be dragged to him by her blood-reeking hair. Hecuba pleads with him to slay Helen at once, lest her beauty and feminine wiles soften his will, but Menelaus remains determined to take her back to Greece, where the relatives of those who died for her sake might have the pleasure of stoning her to death. Helen approaches, calm and dignified. Her plea for the right to speak being supported by Hecuba, she argues that she is not responsible for the fall of Troy. The first blame must be attributed to Priam and Hecuba, who refused to kill the infant Paris as the oracle commanded; the second to Aphrodite, who bewitched her into submitting to Paris; the third to Deiphobus and the Trojan guards who prevented her from escaping to the Greeks after she came to her senses. Goaded on by the chorus of Trojan women, Hecuba jeers at these claims, insisting that the gods would not be so foolish as Helen would have them believe, that her own lust drove her into Paris's arms, and that she could always have escaped Troy and her own shame by way of suicide. Helen, falling to her knees, pleads with Menelaus not to kill her. Hecuba also kneels to beg Helen's immediate death and to warn Menelaus against taking her aboard his ship. Menelaus compromises: Helen will return to Greece on another ship and there pay for her shameful life. As Menelaus leads her away, the chorus wails that Zeus forsakes them.

Talthybius then returns, bearing the crushed body of Astyanax on Hector's shield. He tells Hecuba that Andromache, as she was being led aboard Neoptolemus's ship, begged that the infant be given proper burial. The performance of that rite was more than Hecuba could bear, and she was restrained by force from throwing herself into the flames of the city. As the captive women are led to the Greek ships, the great crash of Troy's collapsing walls is heard, and the city is engulfed in smoke and darkness.

Critical Evaluation:

The Trojan Women is a masterpiece of pathos as well as a timeless and chilling indictment of the brutality of war. The circumstances of its composition, and the raging moral indignation behind it, refer to an incident in the Peloponnesian War that occurred a few months before the tragedy was presented in March, 415 B.C.E. The people of Melos tried to remain neutral in the Athenian conflict with Sparta, and Athens responded by massacring the grown males and enslaving the women and children. In *The Trojan Women* Euripides shows Troy after the men were slaughtered, with a handful of women waiting to be taken into bondage. The parallel is clear and painful. Euripides does not stop with that. The women in their anguish show dignity, pride, and compassion, whereas their conquerors are vain, unscrupulous, and empty. Further, the conquering Greeks are shown to be headed for disaster, since the gods have turned against them. When this play was produced, Athens was preparing a large fleet to take over Sicily, an expedition that ended in calamity. The prophecies of sea disasters in the play no doubt made the Athenian audience squirm. Indeed, the whole tragedy seems calculated to sting the consciences of the Athenians. That they allowed it to be produced is amazing. The fact that a nonentity named Xenocles won first prize that year, defeating Euripides, is scarcely surprising.

This play concludes a trilogy of tragedies on the legend of Troy. It was preceded by *Alexandros* (another name for Paris), which dealt with the refusal of Priam and Hecuba to murder their infant Paris, who would eventually bring about the destruction of Troy. This is important because, in *The Trojan Women*, Hecuba sees the full consequences of her choice. *Alexandros* was followed by *Palamedes*, where Odysseus exacts a dire revenge on the clever Palamedes through treachery. *The Trojan Women* merges the Trojan and Greek lines of tragedy, showing them to be complementary aspects of a central agony. This final play presents the culmination of this story of suffering. It is as bleak and agonizing a portrait of war as has ever been shown on the stage.

However, Euripides merely dramatizes a brief portion of the aftermath, about an hour or two the morning after Troy was looted and burned and the Trojan men were put to death.

In that time, one sees enough to realize that war is the most devastating, unheroic activity that humanity has ever devised. No one wins. The Greeks in their swollen vanity commit atrocities against both the gods and human decency, and they are about to receive their just punishment, as Poseidon, Athena, and Cassandra state. The action of the play consists of the revelation of those atrocities, one after the other, as they overwhelm the helpless old queen, Hecuba. It is primarily through Hecuba the enormity of Troy's fall is experienced. The chorus of captive women, Cassandra, Andromache, and Helen serve to balance and to counterpoint Hecuba's anguish as well as to contribute to it.

A brief time before, Hecuba was the proud queen of a great, wealthy city, and within the space of a night she is reduced to a slave. Hecuba witnesses her husband Priam's murder and knows almost all of her children were butchered. Longing for death, she experiences one dreadful thing after another. She learns that she is the prize of Odysseus, the vilest Greek of all, and that her few daughters will be handed out as concubines. She sees her daughter Cassandra madly singing a marriage hymn, and she finally grasps that Cassandra, through prescience, is really singing a death song for herself and for the commander of the Greeks, Agamemnon. Believing her daughter Polyxena to be alive, Hecuba learns from Andromache that the girl had her throat slit. Hecuba, trying to comfort Andromache with the prospect of Astyanax's growing to manhood, sees the little boy taken from Andromache to be executed. Menelaus arrives to drag Helen back to Greece, and Helen, who causes the whole war, calmly faces him down, oblivious of Hecuba's accusations. In this way Hecuba loses the satisfaction of seeing her worst enemy killed, and it is clear that the shallow, worthless Helen will go unpunished. In her final anguish, Hecuba must look upon her poor, mangled grandchild lying on the shield of her dead son, Hector. The last ounce of torment is wrung from her, and she makes an abortive suicide attempt. Hecuba's stark pathos is drawn out to an excruciating dramatic degree.

Yet the play is not a mere shapeless depiction of human pain. Hecuba's suffering is cumulative. There is also a pattern to the appearances of the chorus, Cassandra, Andromache, and Helen. The chorus of captive women serves to generalize Hecuba's grief. If Poseidon will create future misery for the Greeks, the chorus shows the past and present pain of the Trojans on a large canvas. It places Hecuba's agony in perspective as one calamity among many. Moreover, Cassandra, Andromache, and Helen extend the portrayal of the victimization of the women who become the spoils of war: Cassandra, the raped virgin and crazed bride of death; Andromache, the exemplary wife and mother turned into a childless widow and handed over to the son of the man who killed her husband; and brazen Helen, the faithless wife who has the knack of getting her own way in every circumstance. The contrast among these three cannot be more striking.

Euripides takes pains in *The Trojan Women* to show that the only justice in war is punitive and nihilistic. War arises from numerous individual choices and leads to disaster for everyone, the conquered and the victors alike. With Thucydides the historian, Euripides shares the view that power corrupts, promoting arrogance and criminality. His vision of the suffering caused by the war is as valid today as it was when he wrote the play and as it must have been when Troy presumably fell.

"Critical Evaluation" by James Weigel, Jr.

Further Reading

Conacher, D. J. *Euripidean Drama: Myth, Theme, and Structure.* Toronto, Ont.: University of Toronto Press, 1967. Under "War and Its Aftermath," Conacher describes the plot in *The Trojan Women* as "a succession of unrelieved and ever deepening woe" that provides an alternating rhythm of hope and desolation. Presents an introduction to the myth underlying the play.

Croally, N. T. *Euripidean Polemic: "The Trojan Women" and the Function of Tragedy.* New York: Cambridge University Press, 1994. Building on Karl Marx and Michel Foucault, Croally examines the connection between the pleasure of viewing tragedy and the teaching that it conveys, specifically resulting in the questioning of received wisdom.

Euripides. *The Trojan Women.* Translated by Edith Hamilton. New York: Bantam Books, 1971. Hamilton presents the play as the greatest piece of antiwar literature and explores its lack of effect on Athenians' opinions of war. The screenplay included in this volume, written by Michael Cacoyannis, provides insights into the translation of a play into film.

Gregory, Justina. *Euripides and the Instruction of the Athenians.* Ann Arbor: University of Michigan Press, 1991. Gregory examines connections between the words and the deeds of Andromache, Cassandra, Hecuba, and Helen, underscoring that the women had no ability to inspire action. She focuses on tragedy's political contributions in classical Athens and the political elements in Euripides' works.

Morwood, James. *The Plays of Euripides.* Bristol, England: Bristol Classical, 2002. Morwood provides a concise overview of all of Euripides' plays, devoting a separate chapter to each one. He demonstrates how Euripides was constantly reinventing himself in his work.

Scodel, Ruth. *The Trojan Trilogy of Euripides.* Göttingen, Germany: Vandenhjoeck & Ruprecht, 1980. Scodel claims that the dry, analytic rhetoric of *The Trojan Women* balances the emotional pathos. She examines relationships among *Alexandros*, *Palamedes*, *The Trojan Women*, and the satyr play *Sisyphus*.

Stuttard, David, and Tamsin Shasha, eds. *Trojan Women: A Collection of Essays.* York, England: Aod, 2001. Nine essays explore various aspects of the play, including the Cassandra scene, the play as an ancient music drama, and the play's relevance and universality.

Tropic of Cancer

Author: Henry Miller (1891-1980)
First published: 1934
Type of work: Novel
Type of plot: Psychological realism
Time of plot: Late 1930's
Locale: Paris

Principal characters:
NARRATOR
MONA, his wife, who never appears
VAN NORDEN, a friend
CARL, another friend

The Story:

The unnamed narrator, the "I" of the novel, is living at the Villa Borghese with his pal, Boris, during the fall of his second year in Paris. He has no money, no resources, no hopes, and yet is the happiest man alive. A year before he only thought he was an artist; now he is one. All literature has fallen from him, and the book he has written—and that the reader is reading—is not a book; it is a libel, a slander, a defamation of character. The book is a prolonged insult, a gob of spit in the face of Art, and a kick in the pants of God. The narrator promises to sing for his readers—a bit off-key perhaps, but sing nevertheless. The book will be that song.

The villa is about to be rented, and the narrator has to find new lodgings; he begins the narrative as he searches for another place to live in Paris and tries to survive without money. The story follows his wanderings in search of work, friendship, art, and love (both emotional and carnal) as well as lodging and food. The narrator also introduces the reader to an endless list of friends, including Tania, to whom he is singing in the novel; Borowski; Van Norden; the narrator's wife, Mona, who never arrives from home; Boris; Moldorf, who is word-drunk; and finally Irene, who, like Tania, demands that he write fat letters to her. The narrator prowls around Paris, intoxicated by the streets, cafés, and squares— a compendium of Paris place-names and his dreams. Every day he returns to the American Express office on the Place du Opéra to see if he has received letters from home or money from Mona. He remembers his life back in the United States, and the cultural baggage of his past and the freedom he feels in the present merge in his mind and his art.

He concocts a scheme to get food by writing to various acquaintances to beg a meal once a week with each of them. He plans other scams as well. He writes to various women and begs money from them. He scrutinizes his love life and the sexual exploits of his friends. He gets a job proofreading for the Paris edition of an American newspaper published for expatriates and travelers. He works on his book, the book the reader is now reading. Mona writes that she is coming to join him in Paris, and he worries about how his wife will react to his bohemian style of living. Will her presence retard his writing, destroy his freedom to create? He sits in cafés day after day, talking endlessly of art and writing and life.

He meets Carl and Marlowe, neurasthenic American expatriates defeated by their life of exile. He discovers how stifling are the various households he visits. His sense of himself as an artist solidifies amid his wanderings among his friends. He is generous to all the disadvantaged persons he meets, offering them money when he has it, a room when one is available, and food even when he has little himself. Music enthralls him. People become the subject for his musings and the grist for his fiction. The nostalgia that dogs his memories of Mona interrupts his present pleasure with Tania. As time goes on, he becomes the artist/hero of his own creation.

In all of his peregrinations through the netherworld of Paris, he searches for a community, one that can sustain his needs as a man and as an artist. He is constantly frustrated but never disappointed. He travels from Paris to Dijon, a trip that is in itself unsuccessful, but he turns his effort into more material for his thoughts and for his work. At the end of the year, he witnesses the expatriate Fillmore's return to America, and he realizes his own resilience and survival as an artist. Walking back from the railroad station with the cash Fillmore has left for Ginette sagging in his pockets, the narrator takes a cab to the Bois, past the Arc de Triomphe, to the Seine, where he gets out and starts walking toward the Port de Sèvres. Once again free from his entanglements, he realizes that he now has enough money to return to America. He has a vision of New York in the snow, and he wonders what has happened to his wife.

A great peace settles around him as he realizes that he does not want to return—not just yet, anyway. The lazy river, the soil so saturated by history that it cannot be detached from its human background, gives him a golden peace that produces in him the feeling of being on the top of a high mountain. He thinks about how strange humans are, so negligible at a distance and at the same time, close up, so ugly and malicious. They need to be surrounded by sufficient space, space more than time. The river flows through him, the hills gently girdle it about; its course is fixed.

Critical Evaluation:

Tropic of Cancer is without doubt Henry Miller's most famous book. The work is also one of the most notorious novels of the twentieth century and occupies a central place in the legal battle against censorship. Banned from almost the moment it was printed in Paris in 1934, it was not legally available in the United States until Grove Press rather courageously challenged U.S. obscenity laws by openly publishing it in 1961. The book was immediately and widely condemned and suppressed. Grove Press went to court to challenge the statutes used to outlaw the book, and after a protracted and celebrated legal case the U.S. Supreme Court ruled in 1963 that the novel was not obscene. Although similar cases involving D. H. Lawrence's *Lady Chatterley's Lover* (1928) and James Joyce's *Ulysses* (1922) had been brought before the U.S. courts in celebrated attempts to overturn the country's obscenity statutes, it was the *Tropic of Cancer* litigation that finally altered the restrictions on what could be published in the United States.

Miller's first published novel is an episodic tale in fifteen loosely connected sections that reflect the author's indebtedness to, among others, Walt Whitman, another American writer who invented a personal and encyclopedic style. The novel has been called the journal of a "year" in a surreal city and an "eccentric antibook" full of ruminations, anecdotes, rhapsodies, self-promotion, caricatures, and burlesques about art and sex and culture. In any case, *Tropic of Cancer* is a book of large appetites, great ideas, and generous feelings.

Although *Tropic of Cancer* is fiction, it is nevertheless highly autobiographical. Miller has been credited with largely inventing this cross-genre, a fictional type that has become increasingly important as a literary model in contemporary writing. Miller drew heavily on his real-life experiences while living in Paris during the early years of the 1930's to provide him with the raw material for the novel. He mixes detailed examination of both individuals and locale—the environs of Paris are especially important to the flavor and structure of the novel—with a narrative commentary that encompasses a wide range of observations on art and writing. The novel deftly combines these personal reactions with objective descriptions to create a narrative of often hypnotic power.

The book's graphic sexual content—which Miller deliberately used to provoke the reactions that raised all of the legal problems and attracted great public attention—constitutes only a minor portion of the text and, taken in context, proves to be only one of the shocking techniques Miller employs in his assault on the literary establishment. As he states in the opening pages of the novel, he wants his writing to be a "libel, slander, defamation of character"—in short, a prolonged insult to Art and an attack on the conventional notions of what constitutes a novel. This insult has to do as much perhaps with the form of the writing as it does with its subject matter or its "obscene" language. The novel, which is not a novel in the usual sense of the term, is revolutionary, but only partially because of its widely recognized employment of graphic sexuality.

Although much of contemporary cultural and literary criticism has positioned Miller as an important force in the development of literary modernism, modern feminists still largely have focused on the novel's and Miller's obsessive sexism. The lively debate produced by such feminist critiques has generated some provocative readings of the novel, and not all of them have been totally negative: Kate Millet, for example, has defended at least some of Miller's sexual excesses in the novel. Feminist criticism has raised a number of legitimate concerns about Miller's depiction of women in his fiction, which has exposed the patriarchal bias, both individual and cultural, of the novel. It is worth noting, however, that similar charges have been lodged against numerous other works of fiction of the same period. What has become clear from the debate over *Tropic of Cancer* is that the novel,

more than seventy-five years after it was published, is still controversial and capable of stimulating debate about the nature and form of literary art. Miller's "kick in the seat of the pants" remains disturbing today and at times even enrages those who think and write about the place of literature in Western culture. Miller's initial intent to upset conventional notions of the nature of the novel and to extend the boundaries of what fiction legitimately can take for its subject matter remains viable.

Charles L. P. Silet

Further Reading

Balliet, Gay Louise. *Henry Miller and Surrealist Metaphor: "Riding the Ovarian Trolley."* New York: Peter Lang, 1996. Describes the origins, aesthetics, and other characteristics of twentieth century French Surrealism, focusing on how Miller uses Surrealistic images and other techniques in his fiction. Includes analysis of *Tropic of Cancer.*

Blinder, Caroline. *A Self-Made Surrealist: Ideology and Aesthetics in the Work of Henry Miller.* Rochester, N.Y.: Camden House, 2000. Examines how Miller's work was influenced by the French Surrealists and other aspects of French culture. Includes discussion of the "obscene" and sexual nature of Miller's work, but seeks to transcend feminist critiques that define Miller as a male chauvinist, focusing instead on his more general concerns with mass psychology and politics and their relation to art.

Bloshteyn, Maria R. *The Making of a Counter-culture Icon: Henry Miller's Dostoevsky.* Toronto: University of Toronto Press, 2007. Describes the enormous influence of Fyodor Dostoevski on Miller's writing and worldview. Miller and his friends, particularly the writers Lawrence Durrell and Anaïs Nin, were impressed with Dostoevski's psychological treatment of characters, and they sought to depict the characters in their fiction in a similar manner.

Hutchison, E. R. *"Tropic of Cancer" on Trial: A Case History of Censorship.* New York: Grove Press, 1968. Presents a detailed history and analysis of the now infamous obscenity trial that followed the publication of *Tropic of Cancer* in the United States.

Jahshan, Paul. *Henry Miller and the Surrealist Discourse of Excess: A Poststructuralist Reading.* New York: Peter Lang, 2001. Argues that descriptions of Miller's literary style as Surrealist evade a serious analysis of the work. Shows that Miller's texts share with those of the French Surrealists an imagery of excess, but one that is economically and masterfully geared toward readers whose responses help to construct a peculiarly Millerian version of stylistic deviation.

Widmer, Kingsley. *Henry Miller*. Rev. ed. Boston: Twayne, 1990. Brief biographical and critical monograph provides a good overview of both Miller's life and his work.

Williams, Linda R. "Critical Warfare and Henry Miller's *Tropic of Cancer*." In *Feminist Criticism: Theory and Practice*, edited by Susan Sellers. Toronto: University of Toronto Press, 1991. Traces the debates that have arisen in various feminist readings of Miller's depictions of sexuality in *Tropic of Cancer*.

Tropic of Capricorn

Author: Henry Miller (1891-1980)
First published: 1939
Type of work: Novel
Type of plot: Autobiographical
Time of plot: c. 1900-1928
Locale: New York City

Principal characters:
I, HENRY MILLER, the narrator
MONA, or MARA, Miller's lover and obsessive focus
MILLER'S WIFE
HYMIE, a Jewish clerk at the Cosmodemonic Telegraph Company
KRONSKI, a Jewish employee of the Cosmodemonic Telegraph Company
O'ROURKE, a detective at the Cosmodemonic Telegraph Company
VALESKA, a black colleague of Miller and his lover
ROY HAMILTON, a friend of Miller
MAXIE, an acquaintance of Miller

The Story:

In a meditation on his alienation from family and homeland, the narrator reflects that his family is made up of Nordic idiots—clean, tidy, industrious, but unable to live in the present or to open the doors into their souls. Nowhere on earth has he felt so degraded and humiliated as in America, which he envisions as a cesspool of the spirit. Over the cesspool is a shrine to the spirit of work, with its chemical factories, steel mills, prisons, and insane asylums. Miller wishes to see the shrine destroyed, in vengeance for unnamed crimes against him and others.

Miller comments that he had a good time as a child because he did not care about anything—a lesson learned at the age of twelve as a result of the death of a friend. He realized then that things are wrong only when one cares too much. As if to prove that he had learned not to care, he let out a loud fart beside his friend's coffin.

During wartime, Miller has a wife and child and badly needs a job. In a farcical episode involving a clerk named Hymie, office politics, and racism, Miller talks the manager of the Cosmodemonic Telegraph Company into giving him a job hiring and firing messengers. The company is inhumane,

corrupt, and exploitative. After the company decreases the messengers' pay, Miller is forced to be less selective in hiring, which results in a number of grotesque incidents involving epileptic, criminal, and delinquent messengers. In response to the poverty around him, Miller gives all his money away, in turn cadging dollars from acquaintances to buy food for himself. During Miller's time at the Cosmodemonic, he meets an African American woman named Valeska, with whom he has a brief sexual liaison. She commits suicide.

Miller recalls an episode from his childhood in which he and his cousin Gene killed a boy in a gang fight. Miller and Gene hurried home afterward, and Aunt Caroline, Gene's mother, gave them rye bread with butter. Miller remembers this image as particularly potent. In that house, he was never scolded; the image conveys an angelic forgiveness, divine absolution.

Miller describes his friendship with Roy Hamilton, whom he sees as a kind of mystic and prophet. Hamilton is in search of his biological father, who is either Mr. Hamilton or Miller's friend MacGregor. Miller views this quest as futile; he views Hamilton as an emancipated man seeking to establish a biological link for which he has no need. When Hamilton leaves, having renounced both paternal candidates, the MacGregor family is distraught. Miller, in contrast, feels no need of Hamilton's presence after his departure, since Hamilton gave himself completely when he was present. Miller comments that this was his first clean, whole experience of friendship, and his last.

Miller's father falls mortally ill as a result of swearing off alcohol and stopping drinking too abruptly. He makes a miraculous recovery, however, when he makes the acquaintance of a Congregationalist minister. He reads the Bible and attends all the minister's services. He then learns that the minister is leaving town to go to a more advantageous position elsewhere. He tries to persuade the minister to stay, but he fails; this leaves him bitterly disillusioned. He never laughs again, and he takes to sleeping and snoring his life away. Instigated by the image of Hymie's wife's diseased ovaries, Miller goes to a figurative place called The Land of F——k.

One night, Miller is looking for a woman with whom he had a rendezvous. When he fails to find her, he becomes mad with anguish and wants to annihilate the whole earth. Then suddenly he grows calm, light as a feather, and notices the stars. The stars ask him who he is, to think of blowing the earth to smithereens. They have been hanging there for millions of years, and have seen it all, yet still they shine peacefully every night, stilling the heart. The stars point out how in their light, even the garbage lying in the gutter looks beautiful. Miller picks up a cabbage leaf and sees it as absolutely new, a universe in itself. He breaks off a piece and it is still a universe. He knows at that moment that there is a woman waiting for him somewhere and that when they meet, they will recognize each other immediately.

Miller next presents a long hymn to his intense relationship with the Dark Lady, whose name is Mara or Mona. He recalls that the third time he met her she thought he was a dope fiend, the next time she called him a god, and after that she tried to commit suicide, and then he tried, and she tried again. Nothing worked, says Miller, but it did bring them closer together, so close that they interpenetrated. Miller makes the assertion that henceforth he will become hermaphroditic. In a final violent image, he asks the Dark Lady to tack her womb up on his wall, so that he can remember her.

Critical Evaluation:

Tropic of Capricorn is the first of Henry Miller's volumes of autobiographical fantasy. In spite of the title, it is not a sequel to his novel *Tropic of Cancer*, published five years earlier. *Tropic of Capricorn* is less of an attempt at portraying re-

ality than is *Tropic of Cancer*. *Tropic of Capricorn* is more of a free flow of fantastic and subjective associations. It contains more of the ornate, poetic prose that Miller called dictation or cadenza. *Tropic of Capricorn* is a diatribe in which the outraged artist and prophet escapes into grotesque fantasy. It is an account of his alienation within the spiritual dearth of America. Miller's self-proclaimed aim in *Tropic of Capricorn* was to create a monstrous verbal skyscraper that parodied the American consciousness.

Tropic of Capricorn is subtitled *On the Ovarian Trolley*. The metaphor suggests a sexuality that is mechanistic, automatic, not within control of the individual. Certainly the novel, located in Miller's Land of F——k, has a more than usual share of the compulsive pursuit of sex. The ovarian metaphor goes beyond this level. Early in the novel, readers are introduced to Hymie's wife's diseased ovaries. Miller recounts that the image germinated a tropical growth of free associations in him. In particular he mentions that he had never done what he wanted and that out of this frustration had grown an obsessional plant in his psyche, a coral growth that, as it grew, killed all else including life itself. It made life and killed life simultaneously—much as diseased ovaries produce diseased eggs.

The obsessional plant is an image of a destructive growth strangling individual life. This theme of individual spiritual death is expanded to the cosmic level in many references to the spiritual bankruptcy of New York City. The city is described as growing like a cancer; to counterbalance this deadly growth, Miller the artist must grow like the sun. *Tropic of Capricorn* proselytizes against the dehumanizing effect of the industrialized city. Miller says that the smell of a dead horse, although almost unbearable, is preferable to the smell of burning chemicals. The sight of a dead horse with a bullet hole in its temple is better than the sight of a group of men in blue aprons with a truckload of freshly made tin.

Miller is unrivaled in his ability to sum up large truths in colloquial language. For example, he writes that music is the can opener of the soul. When he remarks on the necessity of breaking with one's friends to live creatively, he announces such a time as moving day for the soul. *Tropic of Capricorn* also contains striking examples of Miller's half-serious apocalyptic rantings, such as the declaration that all department stores are symbols of sickness and emptiness, and if all the significance hidden in the miscellany of Bloomingdale's were gathered together on the head of a pin, what would be left is a universe in which the grand constellations would move without the slightest danger of collision.

A more serious apocalyptic treatment is saved for the Dark Lady, or Mona, or Mara, the sexually alluring yet devouring female figure whom Miller identified with his second wife, June Smith. When he meets her, he is as if baptized anew, with his real name: Gottlieb Leberecht Müller. The relationship collapses, and later, when he revisits the place where they met, he realizes that the book that he will write about her has become more important than her. The book becomes a tomb in which to bury her.

Miller surrounds the Dark Lady with paradoxical images of fullness (such as the moon and a ship in full sail) and of death and destruction. Toward the end of the novel, he describes her in terms worthy of the biblical book of Revelation. She is the personification of evil, the destroyer of the soul, the maharani of the night. In the power and intensity of the sexual experience generated by her and Miller, the ovarian trolley image is taken to its furthest extreme. In the final image of the novel, he commands her to tack her womb to the wall, an act of violence and reverence simultaneously.

The novel provides many instances of iconoclastic comedy that challenge hypocrisy. Miller likes to shock, whether it is by copulating with Valeska while his wife is out having an abortion or by asking the grieving Maxie for money in the hushed silence of the funeral parlor over the coffin of their dead friend. Even readers who are appalled at Miller's cynicism cannot fail to relish the sheer theater of such occasions.

Tropic of Capricorn is a flawed work. The fragments of narrative are too slight to support Miller's endless diatribes. His time at the Cosmodemonic Telegraph Company is poorly described. The important character Valeska disappears from the novel without significant comment. The characterization is almost nonexistent, since Miller is too bound up in his own egomania to observe anyone else. One notable exception to Miller's general self-obsession is the account of his father's descent into a sickness caused by too-sudden abstinence from liquor, renaissance via religion, and final disillusionment and retreat into slumber.

Despite its shortcomings, the novel makes glorious reaches into high spiritual realizations, such as the epiphany involving the stars and the cabbage leaf. The possibility of redemption shines through the grim chaos of the city. In one of his most beautiful passages, Miller says that Christ will never more come down to earth, yet he expects something terrifyingly marvelous and absurd, an invention that will bring a shattering calm and void—not the calm and void of the death that infects urban life from the roots up, but of life such as the monks dreamed.

Claire J. Robinson

Further Reading

Balliet, Gay Louise. *Henry Miller and Surrealist Metaphor: "Riding the Ovarian Trolley."* New York: Peter Lang, 1996. Describes the origins, aesthetics, and other characteristics of twentieth century French Surrealism, focusing on how Miller uses Surrealistic images and other techniques in his fiction. Includes analysis of *Tropic of Capricorn*.

Blinder, Caroline. *A Self-Made Surrealist: Ideology and Aesthetics in the Work of Henry Miller.* Rochester, N.Y.: Camden House, 2000. Examines how Miller's work was influenced by the French Surrealists and other aspects of French culture. Includes discussion of the "obscene" and sexual nature of Miller's work, but seeks to transcend feminist critiques that define Miller as a male chauvinist, focusing instead on his more general concerns with mass psychology and politics and their relation to art.

Bloshteyn, Maria R. *The Making of a Counter-culture Icon: Henry Miller's Dostoevsky.* Toronto: University of Toronto Press, 2007. Describes the enormous influence of Fyodor Dostoevski on Miller's writing and worldview. Miller and his friends, particularly the writers Lawrence Durrell and Anaïs Nin, were impressed with Dostoevski's psychological treatment of characters, and they sought to depict the characters in their fiction in a similar manner.

Brown, J. D. *Henry Miller.* New York: Frederick Ungar, 1986. Intersperses biography with criticism of Miller's works, helping to place his writings within the context of the events of his life.

Jahshan, Paul. *Henry Miller and the Surrealist Discourse of Excess: A Poststructuralist Reading.* New York: Peter Lang, 2001. Argues that descriptions of Miller's literary style as Surrealist evade a serious analysis of the work. Shows that Miller's texts share with those of the French Surrealists an imagery of excess, but one that is economically and masterfully geared toward readers whose responses help to construct a peculiarly Millerian version of stylistic deviation.

Lewis, Leon. *Henry Miller: The Major Writings.* New York: Schocken Books, 1986. Intelligently answers those critics who accuse Miller of misogyny and pornography in his novels. Includes a chapter on *Tropic of Capricorn* that focuses on Miller's relationship with June Smith.

Widmer, Kingsley. *Henry Miller.* Rev. ed. Boston: Twayne, 1990. Brief biographical and critical monograph provides a good overview of both Miller's life and his work. Includes a chapter on the main themes of *Tropic of Capricorn*.

Trout Fishing in America

Author: Richard Brautigan (1935-1984)
First published: 1967
Type of work: Novel
Type of plot: Picaresque
Time of plot: Fall, 1960, through fall, 1961, with
    flashbacks to the 1940's
Locale: San Francisco; northern California; Idaho; Tacoma,
    Washington; Portland, Oregon; Great Falls, Idaho

Principal characters:
THE NARRATOR, a married father who takes the persona of
    Trout Fishing in America, a symbolic embodiment of
    the American Dream
TROUT FISHING IN AMERICA SHORTY, a legless, screaming
    middle-age drunk who lives in San Francisco's North
    Beach area
THE KOOL-AID WINO, the narrator's childhood friend

The Story:

Trout Fishing in America begins with a description of the book's cover photograph, a picture of Brautigan and his wife, Virginia "Ginny" Adler, in front of the statue of Benjamin Franklin in San Francisco's Washington Square. The poor gather there around five in the afternoon to eat sandwiches given to them by the church across the street. One of the narrator's friends once unwrapped his sandwich to find only a leaf of spinach inside.

The first time the narrator had heard about trout fishing in America was from a drunken stepfather, and, as a child in Portland, Oregon, he once walked to a street corner and saw a waterfall pouring down from a hill. The next morning, ready to go trout fishing for the first time, he returned to find that the waterfall was only a pair of wooden stairs leading up to a house. Seventeen years later, an actual fisherman, he tried to hitch a ride to go fishing, but no car would pick him up—another disappointment.

Another childhood memory involves the Kool-Aid Wino, a friend who, because of an injury, had to stay home all day. Together, the narrator and the Wino bought grape Kool-Aid and ceremoniously made an entire gallon of it from a nickel package. Ready for a day's drinking, they created their own Kool-Aid reality. Recipes for apple compote, pie crust, "spoonful" pudding, and walnut catsup lead to memories of Mooresville, Indiana, the home of the John Dillinger Museum, where a Mooresville resident once discovered a basement full of rats and, Dillinger-like, bought a revolver to get rid of them. The narrator's memories continue to move back and forth from early recollections to recent ones, and from urban memories to outdoor ones.

In San Francisco (a "Walden Pond for Winos"), the narrator and his friends, unemployed artists, talk of opening a flea circus or committing themselves to a mental asylum, where it would be warm and they would have clean clothes, hot meals, and pretty nurses. At Tom Martin Creek, Graveyard Creek, and other fishing places, the narrator equally fails to find satisfaction, fighting brush, poison oak, and narrow can-

yons to fish. Back in San Francisco, the narrator fantasizes about making love in a bookstore to a woman whose husband owns 3,859 Rolls-Royces. Fishing in Hayman Creek, Owl Snuff Creek, and elsewhere catching great trout equally proves to be a fantasy.

In San Francisco again, the narrator sees Trout Fishing in America Shorty, a legless, screaming middle-aged wino who trundles about in a wheelchair in the North Beach area. When not passed out in the window of a Filipino Laundromat, Shorty wheels through the streets shouting obscenities in fake Italian ("Tra-la-la-la-la-la-Spa-ghet-tiii!"). One day, Shorty passes out in Washington Square in front of the statue of Ben Franklin, and the narrator and a friend think they should crate him up and ship him to American author Nelson Algren, for Shorty is like an Algren character in the books *The Neon Wilderness* (1947) and *A Walk on the Wild Side* (1956). They never get around to shipping Shorty and they soon lose track of him, but Shorty should someday be buried, the narrator concludes, beside the Franklin statue, as he and Franklin are both symbols of America. The narrator fantasizes another symbol of America, the Mayor of the Twentieth Century. Wearing mountains on his elbows and blue jays on his shirt collar, the Mayor is a modern Jack the Ripper, performing deeds of murder at night with a razor, a knife, and a ukelele, the last of these an instrument not even Scotland Yard would suspect.

The narrator continues to fish for trout in places such as Paradise Creek, Salt Creek, Spirit Prison, Duck Lake, and Little Redfish Lake, but he catches very little. He is reminded of a time in Gelatao in southern Mexico when, cleaning an attic for an elderly lady, he came across the trout-fishing diary kept by the lady's brother. It contained a ledger calculating the number of trout he had lost over a seven-year period, more than two thousand.

In another fantasy, at the Cleveland Wrecking Company the narrator inquires about a used trout stream, plus all accessories, for sale at a bargain price. Everything is for sale: land, disassembled waterfalls, trout streams, trees and bushes, animals, birds and insects. He envisions Leonardo da Vinci, on the payroll of the South Bend Tackle Company, inventing a new spinning lure for trout fishing called "The Last Supper." Living, like the Kool-Aid Wino, on invented reality, the narrator takes up residence in a rented cabin above Mill Valley, California, and for no particular reason other than that he had always wanted to, ends his trout-fishing narrative with the word "mayonnaise."

Critical Evaluation:

Richard Brautigan's *Trout Fishing in America*, which appeared in 1967, is actually his first novel (although published after *A Confederate General from Big Sur*, 1964), written in the early 1960's. Its publication was timely: It appeared two years before the famous rock festival at Woodstock, New York, and at the height of the hippie movement. Antiestablishment, ecologically aware, and, simply, hip, it became a national best seller. Its short chapters allow for fast reading and allow readers to skip around, and Brautigan's unconventional wisdom distills much of the thinking of the Woodstock generation.

Readers since the 1960's, however, have had a wider range of reactions to the book. Brautigan's prose often slips into a primerlike flatness, and his messages are sometimes sophomoric and pretentious. *Trout Fishing in America* is a novel in only a very loose sense. It is a collection of random observations and experiences strung together with cute chapter titles. There is, nevertheless, a charm and folk wisdom about the book as well as a concern with the natural world that places it in the serious mainstream of American writing along with works such as Henry David Thoreau's *Walden: Or, Life in the Woods* (1854), Mark Twain's *Adventures of Huckleberry Finn* (1884), and Ernest Hemingway's Nick Adams stories. Brautigan's nature descriptions are often beautiful, and his analysis of the flip side of the American Dream is quite accurate. *Trout Fishing in America* is in many ways the representative novel of Brautigan's generation, as F. Scott Fitzgerald's *The Great Gatsby* (1925) was for his generation.

The title of the novel functions in at least three different ways to unify the varied parts of the book. First, the opening chapter, "The Cover for Trout Fishing in America," not only describes the front photograph but also suggests the author's disguise—his cover—as Trout Fishing in America, a personification of the myth of America as a land of vast open spaces, unlimited resources, and individual opportunity. The chapter describes the statue of Benjamin Franklin in San Francisco's Washington Square; Franklin is the American prototype of the self-made man, the successful Yankee entrepreneur whose rags-to-riches life is the subject of his *Autobiography* (1791). Brautigan's book is Franklin's *Autobiography* turned upside down, a rejection of Franklin's ethic of hard work and the way to wealth.

Early in the book, Brautigan recalls seeing, as a child, fishermen with three-cornered hats. The three-cornered hat, traditionally associated with the early American colonists, reveals these fishermen as typical Americans angling for riches and success, the same kind of "fishing" that was taught to the narrator himself. On his first fishing venture, he sees that what he earlier took to be a beautiful waterfall cascading from a hill is nothing more than a wooden staircase. Like the entire notion of the American Dream, the waterfall is an illusion. In his disguise as Trout Fishing in America, therefore, the narrator presents himself as a true believer in the doctrine of hard work, success, and moneymaking and the myth of the purity of the American landscape. The events throughout the novel undermine that belief.

Second, the title also suggests that the book is about America itself, its vast lands and pure streams that offer unlimited natural riches to all citizens. The novel is a series of disenchantments, some bitter and some sweet. There are the sad dead of Graveyard Creek and the dead fish of Worsewick Hot Springs. There is the inhuman destruction of coyotes at Salt Creek that makes the narrator think of the gas chamber at San Quentin. There is Mooresville, Indiana, home of famous criminal John Dillinger, a town that still features violence, boredom, and anxiety. Most of all, there are the winos, the poor, and the homeless who wait for sandwich time at the church near Washington Square, only to find nothing but a leaf of spinach between two pieces of bread. There are the bums who pick cherries for Rebel Smith and wait like vultures for her discarded half-smoked cigarettes, and the winos and impoverished artists who talk of either opening up a flea circus or committing themselves to an insane asylum for the winter, where there is television and warm beds.

Nowhere is the distance between mythology and actual American experience more evident than in Trout Fishing in America Shorty, a legless one-man riot who appears throughout the novel "in a magnificent chrome-plated steel wheelchair." Shorty is in many ways the quintessential American, a cheerful and energetic rugged individualist, a kind of Rotarian from hell. He thinks he is as good as anybody, drinks in public view, and is a militant patriot, shouting obscenities at the Italians in North Beach. He spends his days passed out in an alcoholic stupor in the front window of a Filipino Laundromat, and the narrator accurately observes that Shorty should someday be buried beside the Benjamin

Franklin statue in Washington Square, for Shorty is the shadow of the Franklin myth of American success.

A third way in which the title functions as the controlling idea of the novel is in its evocation of the agrarian myth of the land and the great outdoors. Throughout the novel is a sense of the purity of nature, of the individualism of those isolated few who have inherited America's pioneer spirit, and of the untapped primal energies that lie beneath the surface of America's eroded landscape. Brautigan's descriptions of natural wildlife and surroundings are done with a loving care that denies cynicism, and his use of American place-names (Owl Snuff Creek, Tom Martin Creek, Big Redfish Lake) suggests a delight in the names that Americans attach to their rivers, lakes, and campsites. Nature is present throughout the book.

In contrast, urban life appears as evil in the novel. Room 208 of a cheap hotel in San Francisco harbors the potential for violence and a prostitute trying to escape from her pimp. The winos and homeless of Washington Square clearly are, even in the glow of the author's sympathetic portrayal, sad, lost souls. The narrator sees his fellow urban apartment dwellers as "dead people." At the end of the book, the narrator rejects urban life and the technology and business ethic that go with it, trudging in the footsteps of Thoreau to his isolated cabin above Mill Valley.

The title, therefore, is what unifies the forty-seven short sections that compose the book, most of them no longer than a page or two. They are largely a series of reminiscences, from the narrator's childhood to the memories of the good places he has fished. Interspersed are glimpses of his present world and life with his wife and daughter. The development in the novel lies in the narrator's increasing disillusionment with the ruins of a corrupt, polluted, and destructive America. The culmination of this disillusionment comes at the Cleveland Wrecking Company. In one of the funniest sequences of the novel, the narrator asks about a used trout stream, plus all accessories, for sale at bargain prices. This is a surreal and miniaturized version of the Franklin business ethic and the modern consumer craze carried to its logical extreme. One more commodity, landscape is portioned out by friendly, affable hustlers to those with a keen eye for bargains. Waterfalls are appropriately stored in the plumbing department, along with toilets and urinals. The Cleveland Wrecking Company has few animals for sale because few are left. The many wild birds, the hundreds of mice, and the millions of insects that are available are the natural inheritors of the future.

At the end of the novel, Trout Fishing in America is seen for the last time, properly enough, near the Big Wood River, ten miles from Ketchum, Idaho, where Ernest Hemingway killed himself. It is Brautigan's farewell to the Hemingway code of masculine endurance and romantic pantheism. In the California bush country, the narrator takes up residence in an isolated cabin above Mill Valley, realizing that he has been angling over a sterile wasteland. He sheds his illusions, discovers his own sexual and creative powers, and creates his own world, like the Kool-Aid Wino from his childhood, who "created his own Kool-Aid reality and was able to illuminate himself by it."

Kenneth Seib

Further Reading

Abbott, Keith. *Downstream from "Trout Fishing in America."* Santa Barbara, Calif.: Capra Press, 1989. Recounts the author's memories of Brautigan from their first meeting in San Francisco in 1966 through the Montana years and back to 1982 in San Francisco. The chapter titled "Shadows and Marble" is a critical essay devoted to Brautigan's language and strategy of fiction.

Barber, John F., ed. *Richard Brautigan: Essays on the Writings and Life.* Jefferson, N.C.: McFarland, 2007. Collection of essays, some written by friends and colleagues of Brautigan, features reminiscences of the man as well as analyses of his writing. Includes previously unpublished photographs and artwork.

Chénetier, Marc. *Richard Brautigan.* London: Methuen, 1983. Introduces all of Brautigan's works, interpreting them from the perspective of Surrealist and deconstructionist fictional theories. Sees *Trout Fishing in America* as a series of images that create a network of narrative meaning.

Foster, Edward Halsey. *Richard Brautigan.* Boston: Twayne, 1983. Provides a good introduction to Brautigan's life and work, showing how Brautigan drew on his own experiences to create his fiction.

Legler, Gretchen. "Brautigan's Waters." *CEA Critic: An Official Journal of the College English Association* 54, no. 1 (Fall, 1991): 67-69. Presents an analysis of Brautigan's treatment of nature and water in *Trout Fishing in America.*

Mills, Joseph. *Reading Richard Brautigan's "Trout Fishing in America."* Boise, Idaho: Boise State University Press, 1998. Offers concise critical analysis of the novel.

Stull, William L. "Richard Brautigan's *Trout Fishing in America*: Notes of a Native Son." *American Literature* 56 (March, 1984): 69-80. Approaches the general themes in *Trout Fishing in America* by examining some of the book's many allusions to other literature and Americana. A good introduction to the novel and to Brautigan.

A True History

Author: Lucian (c. 120-c. 180)
First transcribed: Alēthōn diēgēmatōn, second century
    C.E. (English translation, 1634)
Type of work: Short fiction
Type of plot: Satire
Time of plot: Second century
Locale: The universe

Principal characters:
LUCIAN
ENDYMION, the king of the moon
PHAETHON, the king of the sun
SCINTHARUS, an inhabitant of the whale's belly

The Story:

Heading westward from the Pillars of Hercules, Lucian in his sloop and with a crew of fifty finally reach the Atlantic Ocean. Filled with a thirst for adventure and an intellectual restlessness to see what is on the other side of the world, he finds the first day of the voyage delightful. Then comes a terrible storm that drives the ship before it for seventy-nine days. On the eightieth day, the adventurers come to a lofty wooded island and go ashore.

After resting, twenty sailors accompany Lucian on an exploration of the island. They discover a bronze tablet announcing that Hercules and Dionysus were there, and they see two huge footprints. They also discover that the river has its source in a grapevine and contains Chian wine. Eating the fish that swam in it makes them drunk.

The inhabitants of the island are women, human from the waist up, but growing on vines. Several of the crew, who become too friendly with these creatures, soon find themselves entangled in the vines and taking root. They have to be left behind. The others fill their casks with wine and water and set sail, but they run into a whirlwind that whips the sloop hundreds of miles into the air. A week later, the ship is thrown upon the moon, which is inhabited by men riding vultures. The king of the moon, Endymion, enlists the service of the Greeks in his war against Phaethon and his people of the sun.

The mighty invasion force is made up of eighty thousand vulture-riding cavalry and twenty thousand troops riding birds covered with grass who have lettuce leaves for wings. This vegetarian force has armor of vegetable husks but Greek swords. Among their allies are fighters from other constellations astride monster fleas.

The army of the sun rides flying ants, gnats, and mosquitoes. Some hurl giant radishes; others wield asparagus spears. They are nevertheless no match for the lunar troops until so many centaur reinforcements arrive that the number cannot be set down for fear of creating incredulity. When the moon army is put to flight, Lucian and his friends are captured and bound with spider webs.

To bring the moon people to terms, Phaethon erects a cloud screen, and, cut off from sunlight, the moon troops soon surrender. The terms of capitulation are inscribed on a slab of electrum. With the coming of peace, Lucian has the opportunity to explore the moon and note its wonders.

On the way home, the Greeks pause at Lamptown, which is inhabited by lanterns, and at Cloud-Cuckooland, where Lucian verifies the details of Aristophanes' comedy *Ornithes* (414 B.C.E.; *The Birds*, 1824). Finally the travelers reach the ocean again, only to have their sloop swallowed by a huge whale. In its belly, amid a clutter of wrecked ships, they find Scintharus, who is raising vegetables on an island. He has lived there for twenty-seven years, ever since leaving Cyprus.

There are many other inhabitants, all quarrelsome and unjust. Some have eel eyes and lobster faces; others are half human and half animal. Since their only weapons are fish bones, Lucian decides to attack them. The creatures are all slain in two battles in which the Greeks suffer only one casualty; the sailing master is stabbed with a mullet spine.

One day, after living in the whale for one year and eight months, the Greeks hear a loud uproar in the outside world. Peering between the whale's teeth, they watch a naval battle of giants who man floating islands and fight with oysters and sponges.

At last, the Greeks conceive a scheme to gain their liberty. They set fire to the forest inside the whale; then, as the creature is about to suffocate, they wedge open its jaws and sail out, with Scintharus as pilot. They do not get far, however, for a north wind freezes the ocean. They find refuge in a cave they hollow in the ice until, after a month, it occurs to them to hoist the sails and let the ship glide across the smooth ice to open water.

Sailing in a sea of milk, they take on provisions at a cheese island. They stop at the Isles of the Blessed and watch a lawsuit between Theseus and Menelaus for the custody of Helen. While the hearing is in progress, Helen runs off with a new sweetheart, aided by some of Lucian's crew, and the tourists are deported. Lucian, however, has time to consult Homer on moot points concerning his life and writing and to catalog the famous Greeks who inhabit the isle. Also, he witnesses a prison break by the damned and watches the heroic exploits of Achilles in recapturing them.

On their voyage once again, the travelers pass a place of punishment for liars. Herodotus is there, but Lucian knows that he himself is safe because he never writes anything but the truth. The company spends a month at the Port of Dreams and also pauses briefly to deliver a note to Calypso from Odysseus. Pirates attack them several times and their ship is destroyed, but the travelers finally reach safety in a land that Lucian recognizes as the continent facing his world.

Critical Evaluation:

The point of *A True History*, as Lucian explains in his preface, is to make fun of the extravagant lies put out by poets, philosophers, and historians who write about fantastic creatures and improbable events. Lucian probably has in mind such authors as Antonius Diogenes, whose *Wonders Beyond Thule* appears to have been a particularly notorious example of fictionalizing narrative. *A True History*, the author warns, is nothing of the sort; rather, everything in it is emphatically untrue. The reader, however, should enjoy it as a form of mental relaxation and because it makes fun of such earlier writers as Homer and Plato.

Lucian's narrative of a sea voyage inevitably recalls the journey of Odysseus, and, in fact, there are many allusions to Homer's epics throughout the story. In the second book, when the travelers are in the land of the dead, the narrator actually meets Homer and has the opportunity to ask him some questions. Lucian also frequently parodies philosophers. His description of the descent into the belly of the whale and the eventual reemergence into the open clearly makes fun of Plato's myth of the cave, which elaborated on ideas of knowledge and perception. Throughout *A True History*, there are references to philosophical schools and the quarrels among them. The battle between the forces of the sun and of the moon, with their grotesque armies of hybrid creatures, can, for example, be seen as a satirical depiction of the arguments among philosophers about stars, their size and nature, their inhabitants, and their connections with the earth.

A True History is also a comment on the writing of history, a topic addressed specifically in a treatise entitled *History as It Should Be Written*, which was, however, itself a not entirely serious work. As Lucian outlines, his prime concern is the need for the historian to be truthful and to avoid the excesses of poetry and fiction. In *A True History*, he begins in a

manner that suggests he is following his own precepts and that the narrator will be a careful recorder of facts and figures. Soon, however, the narrative becomes outright fantasy, as the ship of the travelers is carried to the moon in a whirlwind. Much of the humor of the work comes from the matter-of-fact style that is maintained throughout: The narrator presents incredible details in such a way that they become almost believable. Lucian thereby proves his main point: that it is as easy to dress lies up as truth as it is difficult for the hearer to tell the difference between the two.

A True History is a work with overtones of an initiation: The god Dionysus keeps appearing throughout the story, and the first incident in the grapevine arbor has all the elements of an initiation into the Dionysian mysteries. Here, Dionysus and wine appear to represent the excesses of poetic and philosophical fictions; once the travelers become inebriated on the wine of fantasy, they are transported to the moon, into a whale, and to the world of the dead. The narrative also parodies theories of the journey of the soul. According to popular notions, the moon is the first resting place of the soul after death. The descent into the whale is a joke on the traditional descent into the Underworld, while the visit to the land of the dead parodies stock ideas about the Isles of the Blessed.

The journey of the narrator is a search for knowledge. When, at the end of the second book, the travelers reach the "other continent" on the opposite side of the ocean, this is an allusion to Greek speculation about other lands beyond the Atlantic Ocean. Some, however, interpret that other continent as none other than the place from where the narrator started: He returns to it with all the new knowledge gained on the journey, so that it now seems like a strange place. This resembles the situation of a religious or philosophical initiate returning to the "real" world and seeing it now through different eyes.

In *A True History*, Lucian explores the intellectual landscape by blurring and challenging the oppositions and the boundaries on which Greek culture was built. In his fantastic world, the male inhabitants of the moon bear children and play the role of wives for each other; men have cabbage leaves attached to their backsides; and women are half-human, half-donkey. Lucian plays with numbers and dimensions and uses unexpected materials for certain functions, as when his ships have glass anchors and the inhabitants of the moon blow honey from their noses.

A True History partakes of many genres of writing: satire, parody, traveler's tale, romance, and initiation story. It is the first genuine work of science fiction in the Western literary tradition. While it pokes fun at various poets, historians, and philosophers, it rarely does so by name and thus ensures the work's continuing and universal appeal. It was also extremely influential for later works of satire, among them Jonathan Swift's political satire *Gulliver's Travels* (1726) and the science-fiction adventure novels of Jules Verne, which are direct descendants of Lucian's book. Perhaps most important, it was the first work to problematize the issue of truthfulness in literature, provoking many of the same questions about interpretation, authorial reliability, and the nature of fiction that came into the forefront of late twentieth and early twenty-first century analysis of literary texts.

"Critical Evaluation" by David H. J. Larmour

Further Reading

Baldwin, Barry. *Studies in Lucian*. Toronto, Ont.: Hakkert, 1973. An evaluation of Lucian and his works by an expert scholar. Chapter 5 includes comments on Lucian's view of the writing of history. Contains a useful bibliography.

Fredericks, S. C. "Lucian's *True History* as SF." *Science Fiction Studies* 3 (March, 1976): 49-60. Suggests that *A True History* is an early instance of science-fiction writing. The landscape of Lucian's journey can be seen as an "alternative world" through which the author explores the features and problems of the real world.

Georgiadou, Aristoula, and David H. J. Larmour. *Lucian's Science Fiction Novel, "True Histories": Interpretation and Commentary*. Boston: Brill, 1998. Includes an introduction placing *A True History* within the context of Lucian's oeuvre, particularly his concern with distinguishing truth from fiction and exposing philosophers' lies. The commentary traces the sources and meanings of the numerous allusions and parodies of philosophers, poets, historians, and others contained in the text.

Jones, C. P. *Culture and Society in Lucian*. Cambridge, Mass.: Harvard University Press, 1986. A good general study of Lucian's many works. Locates them in the social and intellectual conditions of his time, the Greco-Roman imperial age. Chapters 5 and 6 discuss *A True History* in connection with Lucian's views on truth and lies.

Marsh, David. *Lucian and the Latins: Humor and Humanism in the Early Renaissance*. Ann Arbor: University of Michigan Press, 1998. Describes how European authors in the fifteenth and sixteenth century rediscovered Lucian's comic writings, tracing how the themes and structures of his works were adapted by Renaissance writers. Chapter 6 focuses on *A True History*.

The Truth Suspected

Author: Juan Ruiz de Alarcón (1581-1639)
First published: La verdad sospechosa, 1630 (English translation, 1927)
Type of work: Drama
Type of plot: Comedy
Time of plot: Seventeenth century
Locale: Madrid

Principal characters:
DON GARCÍA, a young man given to lying
DON BELTRÁN, his father
TRISTÁN, his servant
JUAN DE SOSA, a friend, in love with Jacinta
JACINTA, niece of Don Sancho, Don Beltrán's friend
LUCRECIA, her friend

The Story:

When Don García returns home from his studies at the University of Salamanca, he learns that on the death of his brother Gabriel he became the heir to the family estates and fortune. His father, Don Beltrán, also provides him with a shrewd and cynical servant, Tristán. Don García's tutor has already reported that the young man is given to one great vice: lying. Later, his discerning servant agrees. The son's habit naturally worries his father, himself a man of great honor. Though Don Beltrán admits that regard for truth is un-common at the court of Spain, he hates the vice of lying above all others, and he vows to break his son of the habit.

During his first day in Madrid, Don García indulges in his usual practice after meeting two attractive women in the shopping center of the city. Taking his cue from Tristán's remark that the women of Madrid are money-mad, the young gallant tells them that he is a wealthy man from the New World. Though he has been in Madrid hardly a day, he assures one of the women that he has worshiped her from afar for a year. Unfortunately, Don García has misunderstood the information purchased from the women's coachman by Tristán; he thinks that the woman he wants to marry is Lucrecia, but the object of his attentions is really her friend Jacinta.

More lying follows when Don García meets his friend Juan de Sosa, a young man in love with Jacinta but rejected as her suitor by her uncle until he acquires a knighthood. This time, falsely claiming responsibility for a serenade and banquet the preceding night, Don García finds himself challenged to a duel by Juan.

In the meantime, hoping to get his son married off before all of Madrid learns of his habit of lying, Don Beltrán, after giving him a lecture on the value of truth, tells Don García that he has arranged for Don García's marriage to Jacinta, niece of Don Beltrán's old friend Don Sancho. Because Don García thinks that it is Lucrecia whom he loves, he promptly invents a prodigious lie about his marriage to a lady of Salamanca. He declares that while visiting her one night, he was discovered by the lady's father, and so to save her reputation and life, he agreed to marry her.

Lucrecia, to help Jacinta decide which of her suitors she prefers, signs Jacinta's name to a note inviting Don García to wait beneath her balcony. There he talks with both ladies, who are veiled, so he cannot discern their identities. During this talk, his earlier story about a wife in Salamanca and his uncertainty as to which of the women is the one he loves result in the women heaping ridicule and scorn upon him. Rudely dismissed, he receives from Tristán a lecture on the evils of lying.

More lying is necessary when Don Beltrán attempts to send for his son's nonexistent wife. She cannot travel, Don García tells him, because she is going to have a baby. Although Don García laughs at Tristán's warning that "one who lies needs a quick wit and a good memory," his punishment has already begun. When Lucrecia invites him to another meeting at a convent, he finds himself trapped in a mesh of deceit, and the veiled ladies show how unsuccessful his wooing has been. Tristán contributes to his unhappiness by reciting many quotations from Latin and Greek writers. The servant also remarks that he can see no sense to his master's lies when they are so easily discovered.

Even Tristán, however, is fooled by Don García's account of his supposed duel with Juan de Sosa; actually, he placated his former friend by telling more lies. It would have been better had he silenced his challenger on the dueling field, for Juan now appears to tell Don Beltrán that no one with the name of Don García's supposed wife lives in Salamanca. So incensed is the father that he is about to disinherit his son.

Even when he admits the truth, Don García cannot convince his father without corroboration from Tristán. The word of a servant is more trustworthy than the oath of a nobleman, the ashamed father points out.

When Juan's attainment of knighthood clears away that obstruction to his suit, Don Sancho gladly arranges for the young man's marriage to Jacinta; that lady, disillusioned and dubious of a lying suitor, is happy to agree with her uncle's decision. Don Beltrán, too, is won over, and he agrees to arrange for his son's delayed marriage. When the suitors are paired off, Don García sees his lady go to his rival. Even though the whole affair has been based on misunderstanding of identity, it is now too late to correct the mistake. Don García is honor bound to marry Lucrecia.

Tristán again underlines a moral when he assures his master that if he had told the truth instead of lying he would now be happy with Jacinta. Lucrecia, however, is also beautiful.

Critical Evaluation:

Born in what is now Mexico, Juan Ruiz de Alarcón became one of the leading dramatists of the Golden Age in Spain. The twenty-six plays now identified as his are divided into two groups. His early plays, in keeping with the romantic tradition, are marked by complicated plots. His later works are more concerned with the human qualities of his characters and less with dramatic situations. His two best plays belong to his second period. *Las paredes oyen* (pr. 1617; *The Walls Have Ears*, 1942) attacks slander, and *The Truth Suspected* presents an excellent character study of a compulsive liar. The latter play inspired Pierre Corneille's *Le Menteur* (pr. 1643; English translation, 1671).

While lying breaks one of the Ten Commandments, it is not listed among the seven deadly sins, which were central to the imagination of the Middle Ages. Lying as a sin was more fascinating to the minds of the Renaissance. Medieval moralists tended to externalize evil, visualizing it in the forms of assorted evil spirits and human actions, whereas Renaissance moralists were more eager to search for evil within, in emotions and thoughts. Medieval thinkers habitually cited Nero as representative of the worst sinner, while William Shakespeare's Iago is quite possibly the most evil man created by a Renaissance mind. Nero was guilty of such overt crimes as adultery, incest, and wanton slaughter; Iago's most destructive acts were his lies.

It is not surprising, then, that Ruiz de Alarcón should construct one of his best plays with this one vice as its cornerstone. The play deals solely and entirely with that disjunction of reality and human relationships called lying. Don García not only cannot tell the truth, but he also cannot hear it. That is to say, he does not believe the truth when he hears it, even though everyone around him does tell the truth. Lucrecia makes a vain attempt to set straight his identification of the two women, and Don Beltrán forcefully informs him of the disastrous circumstances inevitably resulting from lying, but still the young man persists almost mindlessly in distorting the truth.

Jacinta obviously is meant to be Don García's wife, for not only does he love her at first sight, with her evident approval, but she is also the one young lady of the entire city of Madrid who is chosen by Don Beltrán to become his son's bride. These two events, independent as they are, indicate by their coincidence a kind of providence at work that is subverted by Don García's affliction. In the final analysis, Don García's pathological lying is a disease that results in sterility and death.

This is a departure from the mainstream of sixteenth and seventeenth century comedy, in which societal sterility is threatened by the *senex*, an old man, usually the father of the young man or woman whose love serves as a focal point for the plot. In this play, by contrast, the threat is not a father; it is Don García's debilitating habit. Don Beltrán, far from hindering the love match, exerts himself to aid it. In *The Truth Suspected*, the social evil that needs eradication is lying.

This play departs from most comedies of the period in yet another way. Don García would seem, at first glance, to bear the full brunt of the consequences that result from his lying: He loses the young lady he loves and is forced to marry another whom he does not love. Were these the only results, it could be said that the catastrophe befalls one individual, not a society, but Don Beltrán shares heavily in the disaster. When his first and more virtuous son dies, his hope for retention of honor in his family's future also dies. Don Beltrán is left with an heir who carries a disease fatal to honor. The young lover loses his love; the honorable older man loses his honor. The older man evidently does nothing to deserve his loss of honor.

The question remains, Does Don García deserve his downfall? If this question turns, as often it does, on the motivation for his destructive lying, the question is unanswerable. Other liars lie for pleasure or for profit, but there is no such rationale behind Don García's lying. He lies when the truth would serve his purposes as well or better than his lies, as when he lies about having given the banquet and then lies again in order to extricate himself from the duel. There is no indication that he is too cowardly to fight the duel—there is only the sense that he is driven to lie. Similarly, he lies when the truth is sure to be discovered in a matter of days. When, for example, he tells Jacinta of his wealth, it seems to matter

not at all that his true background is quite adequate to attract her attention.

It is tempting to the modern reader, but probably an error, to psychoanalyze Don García. There is no rationalization provided in the play for Don García's problem. There can be no doubt that his lack of a motive for lying is a part of the playwright's design. Ruiz de Alarcón isolates the central thesis of the play—the evil of lying—so as to present the phenomenon in something very near to its pure form. Certainly the author's method serves to depict the fault as being even more ludicrous and damaging than it usually is in real life, thereby holding it up to ridicule and scorn.

Minor, but telling, similarities can be seen between Don García and that other, more famous hidalgo of Spanish literature, Don Quixote de la Mancha. Don García shares Quixote's addiction to the beautiful lie. García is not in love with the heroic motions of ridding the earth of giants and malevolent knights, but he definitely is enamored of casting himself in the roles of traveler from a mystical land (as Peru was at the time), as silent and adoring lover-from-afar, and as giver of lavish feasts. With both characters, the beautiful lie blinds the liar to the real world. Quixote is morally absolved by his delusion; he believes his lies. Don García is aware of his lies. Another difference between the two is that Quixote's beautiful lie has a form and an ethos of its own (outmoded though it may have been), whereas García's lies are piecemeal and extemporaneous. Quixote's lies lead to insights and revelations; García's lead only to chaos and disappointment.

"Critical Evaluation" by John J. Brugaletta

Further Reading

Brenan, Gerald. *The Literature of the Spanish People.* New York: Cambridge University Press, 1965. Chapter 9 establishes the importance of Lope de Vega Carpio in the development of the new comedy and discusses Ruiz de Alarcón's contribution to this genre.

Claydon, Ellen. *Juan Ruiz de Alarcón, Baroque Dramatist.* Chapel Hill: Department of Romance Languages, University of North Carolina, 1970. Defines the *comedia* in terms of its baroque tendencies and examines the importance of *The Truth Suspected* in literary history.

Halpern, Cynthia Leone. "The Female Voice of Reason in the Plays of Juan Ruiz de Alarcón." *Bulletin of the Comediantes* 57, no. 1 (2005): 61-89. Focuses on the depictions of women in Ruiz de Alarcón's plays, describing how the female characters respond to events strongly and rationally while at the same time entertaining audiences.

Poesse, Walter. *Juan Ruiz de Alarcón.* New York: Twayne,

1972. Provides information about the playwright's life and works and evaluates the techniques he used in composing his plays. Shows the marked difference between Ruiz de Alarcón's plays and those of his contemporaries.

Whicker, Jules. "Lies and Dissimulation: *La verdad sospechosa.*" In *The Plays of Juan Ruiz de Alarcón*. Rochester, N.Y.: Tamesis, 2003. Notes that a preoccupation with deception is a common theme in Ruiz de Alarcón's plays,

reflecting the playwright's fundamental concern that literature tell the truth.

Wilson, Margaret. *Spanish Drama of the Golden Age*. New York: Pergamon Press, 1969. Traces the history of the Spanish theater to the Golden Age of the seventeenth century. Contains a superb explanation of the characteristics of the Spanish *comedia* and discusses Ruiz de Alarcón's contribution to the Spanish theater.

The Turn of the Screw

Author: Henry James (1843-1916)
First published: 1898
Type of work: Novella
Type of plot: Ghost
Time of plot: Mid-nineteenth century
Locale: England

Principal characters:
THE GOVERNESS
MRS. GROSE, housekeeper at Bly
MILES and FLORA, the two children of the house
MR. QUINT and MISS JESSEL, two apparitions

The Story:

It is a pleasant afternoon in June when the governess first arrives at the country estate at Bly, where she is to take charge of Miles, age ten, and Flora, eight. She faces her new position with some trepidation because of the unusual circumstances of her situation. The two children are to be under her complete care, and their uncle, who engaged her, has been explicit in stating that he does not wish to be bothered with his orphaned niece and nephew. Her uneasiness disappears, however, when she sees her charges, for Flora and Miles seem incapable of giving the slightest trouble.

The weeks of June pass uneventfully. Then, one evening, while she is walking in the garden at twilight, the governess is startled to see a strange young man at a distance. The man looks at her in a manner that suggests a challenge and then disappears. The incident angers and distresses the young woman; she decides that the man is a trespasser.

On the following Sunday evening, the governess is again startled to see the same stranger looking in at her through a window. He stares piercingly at her for a few seconds and then disappears. This time the governess realizes that the man had been looking for someone in particular, and she thinks that perhaps he bodes evil for the children in her care. A few minutes later, the governess tells the housekeeper, Mrs. Grose, of the incident and describes the appearance of the man. Mrs. Grose tells her that it is a perfect description of Peter Quint, the valet to the governess's employer—but Mr. Quint is dead.

One afternoon shortly afterward, a second apparition appears. This time Miss Jessel, the former governess, appears in the garden to both the governess and the little girl, Flora. The strange part of the situation is that the little girl refuses to admit to the governess that she sees the figure and knows who it is, though it is obvious that she understands the appearance fully.

The governess learns from the housekeeper that Quint and Miss Jessel had been lovers while alive, though the young woman came from a very fine family and the man had been guilty of drunkenness and worse vices. For what evil purpose these two spirits wish to influence the seemingly innocent children, neither the housekeeper nor the governess can guess.

The secrecy of the children about seeing the ghosts is maddening to the two women. They both feel that the boy is continuing to see the two ghosts in private and conceals that fact, just as he had known of the illicit affair between the valet and the former governess in life and had helped them to conceal it. Yet, when in the presence of the children, the governess sometimes feels that it would be impossible for the two children to be influenced into evil.

The third time the ghost of Quint appears to the governess is inside the house. Unable to sleep, she is reading late at night when she hears someone on the stairs. She goes to investigate and sees the ghost, which disappears when faced by her unflinching gaze. Each night after that, she inspects the stairs, but she never again sees the ghost of the man. Once, she glimpses the apparition of Miss Jessel sitting dejectedly on the lowest stair.

Worse than the appearance of the ghosts is the discovery that the children have been leaving their beds at night to wander on the lawn in communication with the spirits, who are leading them to unknown evil. It becomes apparent to the governess that the children are not good within themselves. In their imaginations, they are living in a world populated by the evil dead restored.

In such an atmosphere, the summer wears away into autumn. In all this time, the children give no sign of awareness of the apparitions. Knowing that her influence with the children is as tenuous as a thread that is likely break at the least stress, the governess does not allude to the ghosts. She herself sees no more manifestations, but she often guesses from the children's attitudes that the apparitions are close at hand. What is worse for the distressed woman is the thought that what Miles and Flora are seeing are things still more terrible than she imagines, visions that sprang from their association with the evil figures in the past.

One day, Miles comes to the governess and announces his desire to go away to school. She realizes that it is only proper that he be sent to school, but she fears the results of ghostly influences on the boy once he is beyond her care. Later, opening the door of the schoolroom, she again sees the ghost of her predecessor, Miss Jessel. As the apparition fades, the governess realizes that her duty is to stay with the children and combat the spirits and their deadly influence. She decides to write immediately to the children's uncle, breaking his injunction against being bothered in their behalf. That night before she writes, she goes into Miles's room and asks the boy to let her help him in his secret troubles. Suddenly a rush of cold air fills the room, as if the window had been blown open. When the governess relights the candle blown out by the draft, the window is still closed, and the drawn curtain has not been disturbed.

The following day, Flora is briefly missing. Mrs. Grose and the governess find her beside the garden pond, and the governess, knowing that the girl had gone there to see the ghost, asks her where Miss Jessel is. The child replies that she only wants to be left alone. The governess can see the apparition of Miss Jessel standing on the opposite side of the pond. The governess, afraid that the evil influence is already dominating the little girl, asks the housekeeper to take Flora to London to request the uncle's aid. In place of the lovable, angelic Flora there has suddenly appeared a little child with a filthy mind and filthy speech, which she uses in denouncing the governess to the housekeeper. That same afternoon,

Mrs. Grose leaves with the child as the governess has requested.

That evening, immediately after dinner, the governess asks Miles to tell her what is on his mind before he leaves the dining room. When he refuses, she asks him if he stole the letter she had written to his uncle. As she asks the question, she realizes that standing outside the window, staring into the room, is the ghost of Peter Quint. She pulls the boy close to her, shielding him from any view of the ghost at the window, while he tells her that he did take the letter. He also informs her that he has already been expelled from one school because of his lewd speech and actions. Noting how close the governess is holding him, he suddenly asks if Miss Jessel is near. The governess, angry and distraught, shrieks at him that the ghost of Peter Quint is just outside the window. When Miles turns around, the apparition is gone. With a scream, he falls into the governess's arms. At first, she does not realize that she has lost him forever—that Miles is dead.

Critical Evaluation:

In 1908, ten years after the first publication of *The Turn of the Screw* as a serial in *Collier's Weekly*, Henry James wrote that he considered the story "least apt to be baited by earnest criticism." His prediction has been shown to be remarkably inaccurate, however, as the decades-long critical debate surrounding *The Turn of the Screw* has proven more vigorous and controversial than that surrounding any of James's other works. It seems that any critic who wishes to do so may find compelling textual evidence that the work is a chilling, straightforward ghost story made all the more horrific by the youthful age of its menaced characters; or that it is a case study of a psychologically disturbed young woman in the grip of a sexually induced hallucinatory neurosis; or that it is an engrossing, powerful moral fable that allegorizes the intertwining of innocence and evil in the human heart; or that it is some combination of all these, despite the fact that the various interpretations are at odds with one another. If nothing else, then, *The Turn of the Screw* is, as James himself called it, "a piece of ingenuity . . . [and] of cold artistic calculation, an *amusette* to catch those not easily caught."

The wealth of contradictory critical evaluations of the work testifies to its complexity and its artistry; the ambiguous overtones of the story readily seem to catch "those not easily caught." For the first several years after the book's publication, most readers seemed to agree with James's appraisal of *The Turn of the Screw* as "a fairy-tale pure and simple," at least in its intent. One early critic for *The New York Times* described the work in 1898 as "a deliberate, powerful, and horribly successful study of the magic of evil," in which the characters of the two children, Miles and Flora, are "accursed, or all but damned, and are shown to have daily, almost hourly, communication with lost souls that formerly inhabited the bodies of a vicious governess and her paramour."

James also described the book as a "trap for the unwary," and the discussion surrounding *The Turn of the Screw* heated considerably with the publication of noted critic Edmund Wilson's essay "The Ambiguity of Henry James" in 1934. Wilson maintains that in the novel "almost everything from beginning to end can be read equally in either of two senses." He considers the governess an unreliable narrator, one whose perception of the events surrounding her stay at Bly is colored and distorted by her own neuroses. He writes, "The governess who is made to tell the story is a neurotic case of sex repression, and . . . the ghosts are not real ghosts but hallucinations of the governess." In taking this position, Wilson is aided by the statement made by James himself, who said that the governess has kept "crystalline" her record of "so many intense anomalies and obscurities—by which I don't of course mean her explanation of them, a different matter."

Proponents of this Freudian reading of *The Turn of the Screw* point to elements of the story that may be read as laden with sexual significance. For example, the governess herself is curiously obsessed with her employer, a handsome young man who does not appear to reciprocate the infatuation. The first appearances of the two evil ghosts, Mr. Quint and Miss Jessel, occur on a tower and beside a lake, respectively, locations that could signify male and female sexuality. At the time of Miss Jessel's appearance, Flora, who is being watched by the governess, is engaged in a game involving joining together two pieces of wood, an activity that could also have sexual overtones to the governess. In this interpretation of the novella as a record of sexual repression, "there is never any reason for supposing that anybody but the governess sees the ghosts," according to Wilson. "She believes that the children see them, but there is never any proof that they do."

Many critics consider this position to be overly rationalistic and materialist, owing more to the philosophical and social climate at the time of the essay's publication (1934) than to elements within the novella itself. Moreover, the Freudian reading, aside from being anachronistic (*The Turn of the Screw* antedates nearly all of Sigmund Freud's publications), does not convincingly explain the governess's detailed description of Quint, a man she has never seen, to Mrs. Grose, the housekeeper, nor does it explain the numerous references made by James himself to *The Turn of the Screw* as a rather conventional ghost story, even to the point of calling it "a shameless pot-boiler" and "grossly apparitional."

One of James's perennial moral themes is the relationship between innocence and experience; he often examines the ideas that innocence itself may involve the provocation of evil elsewhere and that the two are inextricably intertwined within the dual nature, both divine and demonic, of humanity. Along this line, *The Turn of the Screw* may also be interpreted as a subtle but powerful moral allegory, in which Bly becomes a type of the garden of Eden: Evil has entered this Eden with the express purpose of entrapping the souls of Miles and Flora, the archetypal male and female innocents. The governess seeks to "save" the two, and the final words of the novella ("his little heart, dispossessed, had stopped") indicate her dubious victory as the heart of Miles is freed from its "possession" by the evil Quint.

Whatever James's intentions might have been in *The Turn of the Screw*, his public statements regarding it and the textual evidence within the novella itself seem to support both sides of the argument. The modern reader must first consider the novella as a work of immense artistic skill designed to produce horror. Regardless of whether this horror originates in the supernatural or the psychological realm is of little account in assessing its final effect. In the end, all of the book's possible multiple meanings must be taken as parts of a work of art that succeeds or fails on its own terms. This remains true even though readers may not be able to make a final and definitive critical pronouncement regarding its interpretation.

"Critical Evaluation" by Craig Payne

Further Reading

Bailie, Ronnie. *The Fantastic Anatomist: A Psychoanalytic Study of Henry James*. Atlanta: Rodopi, 2000. Approaches James and his works from a psychological perspective, focusing on his unconscious fantasies concerning the human body, primarily the damaged or incomplete human body, and how these fantasies contributed to his creativity. Chapter 4 is devoted to an analysis of *The Turn of the Screw*.

Coulson, Victoria. *Henry James, Women, and Realism*. New York: Cambridge University Press, 2007. Examines James's important friendships with three women: his sister Alice James and the novelists Constance Fenimore Woolson and Edith Wharton. These three women writers and James shared what Coulson describes as an "ambivalent realism," or a cultural ambivalence about gender identity, and she examines how this idea is manifest in James's works, including *The Turn of the Screw*.

Freedman, Jonathan, ed. *The Cambridge Companion to Henry James*. New York: Cambridge University Press, 1998. Collection of essays provides extensive information on James's life and literary influences and describes his works and the characters in them. Robert Weisbuch's essay "Henry James and the Idea of Evil" devotes several pages to a discussion of *The Turn of the Screw.*

James, Henry. *The Turn of the Screw.* Edited by Robert Kimbrough. New York: W. W. Norton, 1966. Offers an excellent collection of source materials, covering James's background sources in his own words and reprinting a number of his letters regarding *The Turn of the Screw.* Includes, in chronological order, reprints of a variety of the critical reactions to the work, from early criticism (1898-1923) through the years of the Freudian controversy (1924-1957) and beyond.

Pippin, Robert B. *Henry James and Modern Moral Life.* New York: Cambridge University Press, 2000. Examines the moral messages that James sought to convey through his writings. Includes analyses of several of James's works, including *The Turn of the Screw.*

Pollak, Vivian R., ed. *New Essays on "Daisy Miller" and "The Turn of the Screw."* New York: Cambridge University Press, 1993. Collection intended for undergraduate students offers feminist and psychological interpretations of the two novels as well as a study of the books within the context of the Victorian period.

Wagenknecht, Edward. *The Tales of Henry James.* New York: Frederick Ungar, 1984. Includes a thorough discussion of the sources and history of *The Turn of the Screw.* Asserts that Freudian readings of the work are serious misinterpretations, arguing that the novella is a straightforward ghost story designed for sophisticated readers.

Twelfth Night
Or, What You Will

Author: William Shakespeare (1564-1616)
First produced: c. 1600-1602; first published, 1623
Type of work: Drama
Type of plot: Comedy
Time of plot: Sixteenth century
Locale: Illyria, a region on the east shore of the Adriatic Sea

Principal characters:
VIOLA (CESARIO), Sebastian's twin sister and Orsino's lover
OLIVIA, a wealthy countess desired by Orsino
MARIA, her maid
SEBASTIAN, Viola's twin brother and Olivia's lover
ANTONIO, Sebastian's friend, a sea captain
ORSINO, the duke of Illyria
SIR TOBY BELCH, Olivia's uncle
SIR ANDREW AGUECHEEK, Olivia's ancient suitor
MALVOLIO, Olivia's steward, a comic villain
FESTE, Olivia's jester

The Story:

Viola and Sebastian, brother and sister twins who closely resemble each other, are separated when the ship on which they are passengers is wrecked during a great storm at sea. Each thinks that the other is dead and sets out alone with no hope of being reunited.

The lovely and charming Viola is cast upon the shores of Illyria, where she is befriended by a kind sea captain. They decide to dress Viola in men's clothing and have her take service as a page in the household of young Duke Orsino. Dressed in man's garb, Viola calls herself Cesario and becomes the duke's personal attendant. Impressed by the youth's good looks and pert but courtly speech, Orsino sends "him" as his envoy of love to woo the Countess Olivia, who is mourning the death of her young brother.

The wealthy Olivia lives in a splendid palace with her maid, Maria; her drunken old uncle, Sir Toby Belch; and her steward, Malvolio. Maria and Sir Toby are a happy-go-lucky pair who drink and carouse with Sir Andrew Aguecheek, an ancient nobleman who is much enamored of Olivia. In return for grog supplied by Sir Andrew, Sir Toby is supposed to press Sir Andrew's suit with Olivia. Actually, however, Sir Toby never stays sober long enough to keep his part of the bargain. All these affairs are observed disapprovingly by Malvolio, Olivia's ambitious, narrow-minded steward, who cannot tolerate jollity in those about him.

When Cesario arrives at the palace, Olivia is instantly attracted to the page—thinking her a man. She pays close attention to Orsino's message, but it is not love for Orsino that causes her to listen so carefully. When Cesario leaves, she sends Malvolio after her with a ring. It is a shock for Viola, who hitherto enjoys playing the part of Cesario, to realize that Olivia fell in love with her in her male clothes.

Meanwhile, Maria, Sir Toby, and Sir Andrew decide to stop Malvolio's constant prying into their affairs and devise a scheme whereby Malvolio will find a note, supposedly written by Olivia, in which she confesses her secret love for him and asks him to wear garish yellow stockings tied with cross garters and to smile continually in her presence. Overjoyed to receive this note, Malvolio soon appears in his strange dress, capering and bowing before the startled countess. Olivia decides that Malvolio lost his wits; to the amusement of the three conspirators, she has him confined to a dark room.

As the days pass, Viola falls in love with the duke, but the latter has eyes only for Olivia, with whom he presses his page to renew his suit. When Cesario delivers another message from Orsino to Olivia, the countess openly declares her love for the young page. Cesario insists, however, that his heart can never belong to any woman. So obvious are Olivia's feelings for Cesario that Sir Andrew becomes jealous. Sir Toby and Maria insist that Sir Andrew's only course is to fight a duel with the page. Sir Toby delivers Sir Andrew's blustering challenge, which Cesario reluctantly accepts.

While these events unfold, Viola's twin brother, Sebastian, is being rescued by another sea captain, named Antonio, and the two become close friends. When Sebastian decides to visit the court of Duke Orsino at Illyria, Antonio decides to accompany him, even though he fears that he might be arrested there because he once dueled with the duke. Upon arriving in Illyria, Antonio gives Sebastian his purse for safekeeping, and the two men separate for several hours.

While wandering about the city, Antonio chances upon the duel between Cesario and Sir Andrew. Mistaking the disguised page for her brother, Antonio immediately goes to the rescue of his supposed friend. When officers arrive on the scene, one of them recognizes Antonio and arrests him in the name of the duke. Thinking that Viola is Sebastian, Antonio asks her to return his purse and is surprised and hurt when she disclaims all knowledge of the captain's money. As Antonio is dragged away, he shouts invectives at "Sebastian" for not returning his purse, thereby alerting Viola to the fact that her brother is still alive.

Meanwhile, the real Sebastian is being followed by Sir Andrew, who never dreamed that this young man is not the same Cesario with whom he just dueled. Prodded by Sir Toby and Maria, Sir Andrew engages Sebastian in a new duel and is promptly wounded, along with Sir Toby. Olivia then interferes and has Sebastian taken to her home, thinking that he is Cesario. After sending for a priest, she marries the surprised—but not unwilling—Sebastian.

As the officers escort Antonio past Olivia's house, Orsino—accompanied by Cesario—appears at her gates. Orsino recognizes Antonio instantly and demands to know why the sailor returned to Illyria—a city filled with his enemies. Antonio explains that he rescued and befriended the duke's present companion, Sebastian, and because of his deep friendship for the lad accompanied him to Illyria despite the danger his visit involves. Pointing to Cesario, he sorrowfully accuses the person he supposes to be Sebastian of violating their friendship by not returning his purse.

The duke is protesting against Antonio's accusation when Olivia appears and salutes Cesario as her husband. Now the duke also begins to think his page ungrateful, especially since he told Cesario to press his own suit with Olivia. Just then Sir Andrew and Sir Toby arrive, looking for a doctor because Sebastian wounded them. Seeing Cesario, Sir Andrew begins to rail at him for his violence until Olivia dismisses the two old men. The real Sebastian then appears and apologizes for having wounded the old men.

Spying Antonio, Sebastian joyfully greets his friend. Antonio and the rest of the amazed group, unable to believe what they see, stare from Cesario to Sebastian. After Viola reveals her true identity and explains how she and her brother became separated, she and Sebastian greet each other warmly. Seeing that the page of whom he grew so fond is a woman, Duke Orsino declares that he will marry her.

After Malvolio is summoned, the plot against him is revealed. As he storms off, vowing revenge, the others begin celebrating the impending marriages of Viola and Orsino and of Sir Toby and Maria. Only Malvolio, unhappy in the happiness of others, remains peevish and disgruntled.

Critical Evaluation:

William Shakespeare wrote *Twelfth Night* apparently to be performed on the twelfth feast day, the joyous climax of the Renaissance Christmas season; however, the feast day itself otherwise has nothing to do with the substance of the play. The play's subtitle suggests that it is a festive bagatelle to be lightly, but artfully, tossed off. Indeed, Shakespeare may have written the play earlier and revised it for the Christmas festival, for it contains many signs of revision.

The tone of *Twelfth Night* is consistently appropriate to high merriment. With nine comedies behind him when he wrote it, Shakespeare was at the height of his comic powers and in an exalted mood to which he never returned. Chronologically, the play immediately precedes Shakespeare's great tragedies and problem plays. *Twelfth Night* recombines many elements and devices from earlier plays—particularly *The Two Gentlemen of Verona* (c. 1594-1595) and *The Comedy of Errors* (pr. c. 1592-1594, pb. 1623)—into a new triumph, unsurpassed in its deft execution.

It is a brilliant irony that Shakespeare's most joyous play should be compounded out of the sadnesses of its principal characters. However, the sadnesses are, for the most part, those mannered sadnesses that the Elizabethans savored. Orsino, for example, particularly revels in a sweet melancholy reminiscent of that which afflicts Antonio at the beginning of *The Merchant of Venice* (pr. c. 1596-1597, pb. 1600). Orsino's opening speech—which has often been taken overly seriously—is not a grief-stricken condemnation of love but rather owes much more to the Italian poet Petrarch. Orsino revels in the longings of love and in the bittersweet satiety of his romantic self-indulgence. He is in love with love.

On the other side of the city is the household of Olivia, which balances Orsino and his establishment. Although Olivia's sadness at her brother's death initially seems more substantial than Orsino's airy romantic fantasies, she, too, is a Renaissance melancholic who is wringing the last ounce of enjoyment out of her grief. Her plan to isolate herself for seven years of mourning is an excess but one that provides an excellent counterbalance to Orsino's fancy; it also sets the plot in motion, since Orsino's love-longing is frustrated by Olivia's decision to be a recluse.

The point of contact between Orsino and Olivia—ferrying back and forth between the two—is Viola. As Cesario, she also is sad, but her sadness, like the rest of her behavior, is more direct and human. The sweet beauty that shines through her male disguise is elevated beyond a vulgar joke by Olivia's immediate, though circumstantially ridiculous, response to her human appeal. Viola's grief is not stylized and her love is for human beings rather than for abstractions. She seems destined to unite the two melancholy dreamers, but what the play instead accomplishes is that Viola, in her own person and in that of her alter ego, her brother, becomes part of both households. The ultimate outcome is a glorious resolution. It is, of course, immaterial to the dreamy Orsino that he gets Viola instead of Olivia—the romantic emotion is more important to him than is the specific person. Olivia, already drawn out of her seclusion by the disguised Viola, gets what is even better for her, Sebastian.

The glittering plot is reinforced by some of Shakespeare's best and most delicate dramatic poetry. Moreover, the drama is suffused with bittersweet music, and the idyllic setting in Illyria blends with language and imagery to create a most delightful atmosphere wholly appropriate to the celebration of love and to the enjoyment of this world.

The one notable briar in the story's rose garden is Malvolio; however, he is easily the play's most interesting character. He is called a Puritan, but although he is not a type, he does betray the characteristics then associated with that austere Anglican sect. He is a self-important, serious-minded person with high ideals who cannot bear the thought of others being happy. As Sir Toby puts it to him, "Dost thou think because thou art virtuous, there shall be no more cakes and ale?" Malvolio suffers within a joyous world; it is against his will that he becomes part of the fun when he is duped and made to appear ridiculous. As a character, he represents a historical group, then growing in power, whose earnestness threatens to take the joy out of life (and, incidentally, to close England's theaters). Yet, Shakespeare does not indulge in a satire on Puritanism. He uses the critical powers of comedy in indirect ways.

Malvolio is ridiculous, but so are the cavaliers who surround him. The absurd Sir Andrew Aguecheek and the usually drunken Sir Toby Belch are the representatives, on the political level, of the old order that Malvolio's counterparts in the real world are soon to topple. While these characters are flawed, they are certainly more engaging than the inflated Malvolio. Shakespeare does not set up the contrast as a political allegory, with right on one side and wrong on the other. Nevertheless, Malvolio is an intrusion into the otherwise idyllic world of the play. He cannot love; his desire for the hand of Olivia is grounded in an earnest will to get ahead. He cannot celebrate; he is too pious and self-involved. Nothing is left for him but to be the butt of a joke—his role in the celebration. Some critics have suggested that Malvolio is treated too harshly, but a Renaissance audience would have understood how ludicrous and indecorous it was for a man of his class to think, even for a moment, of courting Countess Olivia. His pompous and blustery language is the key to how alien he is to this festive context. When he does his bit, Olivia casually mentions that perhaps he is put upon, but this is the only sympathetic gesture he deserves. He is the force that threatens to destroy the celebration of all that is good and refined and joyful in Elizabethan society.

"Critical Evaluation" by Edward E. Foster

Further Reading

Arlidge, Anthony. *Shakespeare and the Prince of Love: The Feast of Misrule in the Middle Temple*. London: Giles de la Mare, 2000. Arlidge, a barrister at the Middle Temple in London, unearthed an archival document revealing that the premiere of *Twelfth Night* was staged at Middle Temple Hall in 1602. He describes the Elizabethan legal community that would have been the audience for this performance at what may be the only surviving building to host the first night of a Shakespearean play.

Atkin, Graham. *"Twelfth Night": Character Studies*. New York: Continuum, 2008. Analyzes the major characters in *Twelfth Night*, using this character study as a means to discuss the play's themes and issues. Describes the general concept of character in English Renaissance plays.

Berry, Ralph. "The Messages of *Twelfth Night*." In *Shakespeare's Comedies: Explorations in Form*. Princeton, N.J.: Princeton University Press, 1972. Discusses the deceits and illusions in the play and concludes that it calls the very nature of reality into question.

Bloom, Harold, ed. *"Twelfth Night."* New York: Bloom's Literary Criticism, 2008. Provides a brief biography of Shakespeare, a summary of the play's plot, discussion of key passages, and a selection of critical essays from the seventeenth through the twenty-first centuries. Includes an entry about the play from Samuel Pepys's diary (1663) as well as essays by Samuel Johnson, William Hazlitt, Charles Lamb, A. C. Bradley, and J. B. Priestley.

Gibson, Rex. *Shakespeare: "Twelfth Night."* New York: Cambridge University Press, 2002. Guidebook designed for advanced-level students of English literature. Provides a commentary on the text; discusses the play's historical, cultural, and social contexts and use of language; offers a survey of critical interpretation.

Levin, Richard A. *Love and Society in Shakespearean Comedy*. Newark: University of Delaware Press, 1985. A critical study of three of Shakespeare's romantic comedies. Two chapters deal with *Twelfth Night*: "Household Politics in Illyria" discusses the acceptance of the various characters into society, while "Feste and the Antiromantic *Twelfth Night*" focuses on the discordant elements of the play.

Lloyd Evans, Gareth. *The Upstart Crow: An Introduction to Shakespeare's Plays*. London: J. M. Dent and Sons, 1982. Focuses mainly on critical reviews of Shakespeare's plays as well as discusses sources, historical context, and background.

Muir, Kenneth, ed. *Shakespeare—The Comedies: A Collection of Critical Essays*. Englewood Cliffs, N.J.: Prentice-Hall, 1965. An anthology of essays that discuss Shakespeare's comedies from various points of view. Harold Jenkins compares *Twelfth Night* with earlier plays by Shakespeare and other playwrights and concludes that it is the greatest of Shakespeare's romantic comedies.

Shakespeare, William. *Twelfth Night*. Edited by J. M. Lothian and T. W. Craik. London: Methuen, 1975. Includes more than eighty pages of introductory material and critical analysis as well as the text of the play itself.

Simpson, Matt. *Shakespeare's "Twelfth Night."* London: Greenwich Exchange, 2006. A student guide that takes a thematic approach to the play, analyzing its issues of wit, madness, gender, love, and deception.

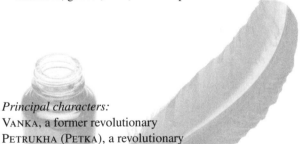

The Twelve

Author: Aleksandr Blok (1880-1921)

First published: Dvenadtsat, 1918 (English translation, 1920)

Type of work: Poetry

Type of plot: Ballad

Time of plot: 1917

Locale: Petrograd, Russia

Principal characters:

VANKA, a former revolutionary

PETRUKHA (PETKA), a revolutionary

KATYA, their girlfriend

The Poem:

On a cold, snowy night, twelve revolutionaries march together down a Petrograd street at the beginning of the Bolshevik Revolution in Russia. A blizzard is blowing at full strength, but it does not slow their advance. As the revolutionaries march in the middle of the street, several bystanders on sidewalks look on with fear and incomprehension etched on their faces. An old woman trembles, afraid of the marchers; she declares that the Bolsheviks will be the death of her and people like her. Looking at the revolutionaries' poster made of canvas, which declares "All the Power to the Constituent Assembly," she complains about waste, noting that all that material could have been used to supply children with foot-clouts. Also watching the marchers are a bourgeois, standing alone with his face buried in the collar of his coat, and a long-haired writer, who curses at the traitors and laments that Russia is dead. A fat "comrade priest" comes slinking through the snow in a black and bulky cassock, with a pendant cross on his belly. A woman wrapped in a Persian fur, confiding to a companion that she has cried and cried, falls flat on her back on the slippery ice. A group of prostitutes at the scene, plying their trade, also look at the canvas poster and declare that they, too, have an assembly that debates how much to charge for their services. All these onlookers are horrified by the uncertainty of the future and by the ferocious looks and behavior of the marching revolutionaries.

The revolutionaries pay little attention to them, however, marching on inexorably, shouting revolutionary slogans, shooting off their guns, singing rowdy revolutionary songs, killing and burning whatever stands in their way, and striking fear into bystanders. Some of them are clad in prison garb. Vanka, a member of the revolutionary group, has run off with Katya, a girlfriend of another revolutionary, Petrukha. In the distance Vanka can still be seen frolicking and dancing with Katya, a woman with a shady past. A shot is heard, and all see Petka shooting at Vanka in a fit of jealousy. He hits Katya instead, killing her, which throws him into inconsolable despair. His comrades try to comfort him, but they also chide him, saying that the times are too serious for little personal matters like that. Petka finds little consolation in their comradely admonition; he tries to explain plaintively to anyone who will listen how good Katya was and how much he loved her.

As the Bolsheviks march on, they suddenly see an apparition in the distance. At first they think it is only a mangy mongrel and they shoot at it, but as they peer into the darkness they see someone with a garland of white roses on his head, waving a red flag. They finally realize that it is Jesus Christ. Immune to their bullets, he seems to take over leadership of the revolutionaries as they continue to march into the snowy night.

Critical Evaluation:

Many critics consider Aleksandr Blok to be the best Russian poet of the twentieth century and one of the best in all of Russian literature. He was a leading representative of the second wave of symbolist poets around the beginning of the twentieth century. His poetry is distinguished by, among other things, a refined taste, which Blok acquired through his aristocratic upbringing, and a pronounced spiritual content. When *The Twelve* first appeared, readers of all kinds were astounded that this work was written by a poet of such credentials.

The action of *The Twelve* takes place in Petrograd (or St. Petersburg, later renamed Leningrad, and now St. Petersburg again), the city known to have provided a spark for the Bolshevik Revolution. The poem also includes a reference to the Neva River, which flows through Petrograd. The behavior of the rowdy marchers resembles that of the Bolshevik revolutionaries as recorded in history. The atmosphere displayed in the poem corresponds to the tumultuous events of 1917 and throughout the revolution and subsequent civil war. Finally, Blok himself confirmed in his diaries and letters that he had the Bolshevik Revolution in mind when he was writing *The Twelve*.

Blok was not a communist or even a communist sympathizer. He supported the February Revolution of 1917, during which the czar was dethroned and a democratic government was installed for the first time in Russian history. As the months wore on, however, and the assembly failed to solve the country's problems, Blok became increasingly disillusioned. When the October (or Bolshevik) Revolution broke out, he lent his support to it even though he was not an advocate of its ideas. As the appearance of Jesus Christ in *The Twelve* would indicate, Blok was no Bolshevik.

Blok had, however, lost faith in the ability of the government to solve the country's problems, which had worsened with the difficulties brought on by World War I. Like the prostitutes in the poem, the parliamentarians debated every issue to death. Like most Russian intellectuals, Blok hoped for reform that would sweep away centuries of injustice, which is exactly what the October Revolution promised to do. Finally, his health was deteriorating during the last years of his life, and he was going through a period of severe stress and fevers. These ailments, it turned out, contributed to his untimely death two years later. The writing of *The Twelve* was a kind of catharsis for Blok.

Most of the first readers of *The Twelve* expressed confusion regarding the poem. The main reason for the negative reaction by both revolutionaries and their opponents was the inclusion of Jesus Christ. The revolutionaries saw the depiction of Jesus as a leader to be a farce; they wanted to have nothing to do with religion. The opponents of revolution also rejected the connection of Jesus with the communist revolution, seeing it as a sacrilege. Blok insisted nevertheless that Jesus was leading the revolutionaries, drawing from an old assertion that Jesus was "the first communist." During this period in his life, Blok was also interested in the historical Christ, and he used the poem to link the two incongruous partners.

Blok himself gave contradictory explanations for his placing Jesus in the poem as a revolutionary leader. Not surprised by the storm of criticism, he said that if the church were real and not merely a class of morally dull functionaries, it would have realized a long time ago that Christ was with the Bolsheviks. Blok believed that all who studied the Bible would see this "obvious" truth. He compounded the confusion the poem had created by saying that sometimes he despised the "womanish phantom" of Christ. The Bolsheviks were right in being afraid of *The Twelve*, he further argued. He did not like the ending of the poem either, saying that he wished it had a different ending. The closer he looked into it, however, the more clearly he saw Christ. Some stylistic devices used by Blok in *The Twelve* tend to confirm its religious underpinnings. Not only does the title recall the twelve apostles, the twelve cantos in the poem reinforce that reference. The question of the poem's religious connotations probably will never be resolved to the satisfaction of all critics.

With *The Twelve*, Blok excels in stylistic matters. A practiced symbolist, he employs many symbols in the poem, although he was no longer writing symbolist poems at the time he wrote *The Twelve*. The symbolism begins with the title as well as with the first words of the poem. The "black night" symbolizes the bleak conditions in which Russia finds itself on the eve of the revolution. The "blizzard" clearly represents the revolution, and the "white snow" stands for the purifying power of the revolution. When he says, "Malice, sorrowful malice/ Bursts the heart. . . ./ Black, holy hate," Blok clearly argues that the destructive fury of the revolution is justified in avenging all the injustices done to the poor.

The onlookers are also symbols. The old woman represents the elderly, who are by nature conservative, cautious, and fearful of losing whatever security they may have, even if it is but little. The bourgeois is a clear target of the communists' animosity, as a representative of the class their struggle is directed against. Other classes are typified by the priest and by a rich woman. The most intriguing symbolic figure is the writer. Blok must have believed that many writers, along with other intellectuals, not only did not understand the revolution but also tried to combat it. The prostitutes serve Blok as a vehicle for ridiculing the efforts of the politicians to solve the society's problems. Ridicule is Blok's strongest weapon against the opponents of the revolution.

Further symbols are the mongrel (standing for the old world, as the poet openly says) and Jesus Christ, who represents the legitimate needs of the downtrodden for justice and love. The poet uses Jesus to remind the revolutionaries not to ignore old verities in their zeal to create a new world. Furthermore, Christ and his teachings can serve as an ameliorating factor in the tendency of the revolutionaries toward brutality. It seems that Blok is reminding the twelve rowdy, murderous marchers of the healing goodness and kindness of the original twelve apostles.

The poem has many other stylistic qualities that, unfortunately, can be appreciated fully only in the original Russian. Its musical quality, expressed in its heavy rhythm (emulating the marching and other dynamic actions, such as shooting), contributes to the dramatic tension the poem creates. A wealth of poetic techniques and a variety of prosodic structures also contribute to the poem's power. In addition, imitations of folk and factory songs and popular jingles appear in cantos dealing with revolutionaries, along with an abundance of common speech; Blok uses these to underscore the folk character of the revolutionaries. Blok was known as a consummate craftsman, and the artistry of *The Twelve*—the next to last poem he wrote—confirms his reputation as one of the best poets in Russian literature.

Vasa D. Mihailovich

Further Reading

Berberova, Nina. *Aleksandr Blok: A Life*. Translated by Robyn Marsack. New York: George Braziller, 1996. Not as comprehensive as Pyman's biography (below), but provides informative firsthand accounts of the poet and the times in which he lived.

Briggs, A. D. P. *A Comparative Study of Pushkin's "The Bronze Horseman," Nekrasov's "Red-Nosed Frost," and Blok's "The Twelve": The Wild World*. Lewiston, N.Y.: Edwin Mellen Press, 1990. Compares three of the best-known Russian long poems, with excerpts in both Russian and English translation. As part of his analysis of *The Twelve*, Briggs demonstrates how rhyme functions as a way to link seemingly unrelated lines.

Hackel, Sergei. *The Poet and the Revolution: Aleksandr Blok's "The Twelve."* New York: Oxford University Press, 1975. Offers one of the best analyses available of the content and the form of *The Twelve*.

Mochulskii, Konstantin. *Aleksandr Blok*. Detroit, Mich.: Wayne State University Press, 1983. Perceptive study of Blok is provided by an émigré critic of spiritual orientation. Emphasizes Blok's relationship to the Bolshevik Revolution.

Pyman, Avril. *The Life of Aleksandr Blok*. 2 vols. New York: Oxford University Press, 1979-1980. One of the most exhaustive treatments available in English of Blok as a man and a writer, written by a prominent former Russian scholar of Russian literature. Includes in-depth discussion of *The Twelve*.

Rylkova, Galina. *The Archaeology of Anxiety: The Russian Silver Age and Its Legacy*. Pittsburgh, Pa.: University of Pittsburgh Press, 2007. Analyzes the work of Blok and other writers of the Silver Age, demonstrating how this literature reflects the social, political, and cultural anxiety that accompanied the Russian Revolution, civil war, and Joseph Stalin's terrorist government.

Vickery, Walter, ed. *Aleksandr Blok Centennial Conference*. Columbus, Ohio: Slavica, 1984. Collection of twenty-one articles addresses various aspects of Blok's life and works. Of special interest regarding *The Twelve* is "The Polyphonic Structure of Blok's *Dvenadtsat*," by Edward Stankiewicz.

Twenty Thousand Leagues Under the Sea

Author: Jules Verne (1828-1905)
First published: Vingt mille lieues sous les mers, serial, 1870; book, 1869-1870 (English translation, 1873)
Type of work: Novel
Type of plot: Science fiction
Time of plot: 1866-1867
Locale: At sea

Principal characters:
PROFESSOR PIERRE ARONNAX, a French scientist
CONSEIL, his servant
NED LAND, his friend and companion
CAPTAIN NEMO, the captain of the *Nautilus*

The Story:

In different parts of the ocean, a number of ships sight a mysterious monster, gleaming with light, such as no man ever saw. After this monster attacks and sinks several vessels, people all over the world are both amazed and alarmed. Finally an American frigate, the *Abraham Lincoln*, is fitted out to find and to destroy the mysterious sea creature. Among its passengers is Pierre Aronnax, professor of natural history in the Museum of Paris, who published his opinion that the monster is a giant narwhal. One of the crew is Ned Land, an expert harpooner. For quite a while, the ship sails without sighting anything even remotely resembling the reported terror of the seas.

The creature is sighted at last. When an opportunity presents itself, Land throws his harpoon, but the monster is uninjured, and Land realizes that it is protected by a thick steel-like armor. During a pursuit in the darkness, a terrific explosion rocks the ship. Aronnax, Land, and Conseil find themselves floundering in the water. Aronnax faints. Regaining consciousness, he discovers that they are aboard some sort of underwater craft. Later, two men come to greet them. The survivors from the ship speak to them in various languages, but the men appear not to understand. Then the captain of the vessel appears and speaks to them in French. He reveals that his name is Nemo, that the vessel is a submarine, and that they are, in effect, prisoners who will have every liberty aboard, except on occasions when they will receive orders to retire to their cabins.

Aronnax learns that the submarine *Nautilus* was built in a complicated manner. Parts of it were secured from various places and secretly assembled on a desert island. Then a fire was set to destroy all traces of the work done there. The ship manufactures its own electricity, has provisions for quantities of oxygen that allow it to remain submerged, and is as comfortable as any home. All food comes from the ocean. There is fish, but fish such as Aronnax never before tasted. There is clothing made from some sort of sea fibers. There are cigars, not of tobacco but of a special seaweed. Captain Nemo shows them air guns that allow him and the crew to go hunting as well as a device that permits the crew to walk the ocean floor.

In the Pacific, Captain Nemo invites the three survivors to a hunt in the marine forest of Crespo, where Land saves Nemo's life by killing a creature that is about to put an end to the captain. Later, the captain saves Land's life. In Ceylon, they watch the pearl divers in the oyster beds. There Nemo saves a native from the jaws of a shark.

Off the coast of Borneo, the three survivors decide to go ashore in the hope of bagging some land game. While they are hunting, they are attacked by natives. Although they manage to get back to the *Nautilus*, the natives remain clustered about the ship. Aronnax is alarmed, certain that the natives will board the submarine when the hatches are opened for oxygen the next morning. He takes his problem to Nemo, who is not at all worried. Instead he tells the professor about a similar experience. Once, when the hatches were opened, natives attempted to come aboard, but the few who touched the rails let out a shriek and retreated in terror. Land touches the rail and is paralyzed with shock; the rail is electrified.

The captain announces suddenly that he will enter the Mediterranean Sea. Aronnax supposes that he will have to circle the Cape of Good Hope. To his astonishment, he learns that the captain discovered a passage under the Isthmus of Suez. The submarine enters the Mediterranean through the underwater passage.

On one occasion, the three companions are ordered to go to their cabins. Some sort of encounter occurs, and Aronnax is later called upon to treat a crew member who is injured. When the sailor dies, he is buried in a coral forest on the ocean floor. By that time, the survivors discover that Nemo has a tremendous fortune in gold salvaged from sunken vessels. Although the captain has some mysterious hatred against society, he nevertheless uses the money to benefit unfortunate people.

Land grows to dislike the captain intensely. He tells Aronnax that he will escape as soon as an opportunity presents itself. They think such an opportunity comes when they round Spain, but their plan does not materialize. When they come close to Long Island, they think the time for escape comes, but a sudden hurricane blows the ship off its course, toward Newfoundland.

On another occasion, the captain astonishes them by heading toward the South Pole. There the ship is endangered by an iceberg, and, for several days, passengers and crew are in danger of being killed. Escaping, they head northward. As the *Nautilus* approaches the coast of Norway, it is suddenly drawn into the notorious maelstrom, the deathtrap for so many ships. Shortly before, the submarine encountered a mysterious ship that attacked it. The submarine succeeds in sinking the unknown vessel. Aronnax believes that in this incident there is a clue to Nemo's hatred of society.

The professor never knows what actually happens after the *Nautilus* is drawn into the maelstrom. When he awakens, he and his companions are safe and sound on a Norwegian island. They also have no idea how they reached the island.

They are the only men who now know the secrets of the ocean—if Nemo and his crew perished.

Critical Evaluation:

Twenty Thousand Leagues Under the Sea was the sixth of Jules Verne's "extraordinary voyages," published in the same year as *De la terre à la lune* (1865; *From the Earth to the Moon*, 1873). Earlier books in the series visited a strange underworld at "the centre of the earth" and the North Pole, unreached at the time, as well as traversing Africa, Australia, and South America. After 1870, Verne began to give more attention to the plots of his novels, but *Twenty Thousand Leagues Under the Sea* belongs to a phase when the joys of imaginary tourism were sufficient in themselves to sustain the production of long and languorous hypothetical travelogues.

Although it is rightly regarded as a classic of science fiction, Verne invented far less than modern readers sometimes realize. The American inventor Robert Fulton had tried to interest Napoleon in his submarine boat—also called the *Nautilus*—in 1800, and Verne had several opportunities to observe submarines being tested in the river Seine. He had certainly seen the model of Charles-Marie Brun's *Le Plongeur* that was displayed at the Paris Exhibition of 1867. Verne's most significant innovations were the powering of the ship by electricity extracted from seawater (a technology that continues to prove elusive) and the diving suits used by Nemo and his crew (which would be fatal to users because of their lack of pressurization).

On the other hand, it is difficult for modern readers to realize how mysterious the undersea world was in Verne's day. Thanks to underwater photography and television there is now a window into that world, but Verne had none at all. The surface of the moon, which the heroes of *From the Earth to the Moon* observed at close quarters, was thoroughly mapped, at least on the side facing the Earth, but the world under the sea was entirely hidden, known only by virtue of what was cast ashore or hauled out by fishermen's nets. Verne's travelers were venturing into an unknown world for the very first time, laying its wonders bare to an audience that had few of the preconceptions that modern readers cannot help but bring to the text. His research was as conscientious as it could possibly be, given the limitations of the available information, and he did an excellent job of weaving a memorable picture around that research. Pedants may complain that he makes seawater far more transparent than it actually is, but he did so with the best possible motives.

In its early phases, *Twenty Thousand Leagues Under the Sea* is a mystery story, and the mystery must have been effective in the early days, when readers of the book did not know that the mysterious "sea beast" pursued by the *Abraham Lincoln* was not a beast at all. To modern readers, the long opening sequence seems like a mere prelude to the real focus of interest, which is the *Nautilus* and its enigmatic captain. Nemo remains a charismatic figure, a perfect incarnation of escapist dreams. Humans are, of course, gregarious beings who cannot live well in the absence of a surrounding society, but that force of necessity inevitably creates tensions and frustrations that lend considerable power to the fantasy of "getting away from it all" and becoming entirely self-sufficient.

Nemo is a strange man, so full of vague hatreds and contempts that he is much less appealing than Ned Land or Professor Aronnax, but that does not make him any less enviable in his splendid isolation. One cannot share his misanthropy wholeheartedly, but it is precisely because it cannot be shared that one is able to understand it and to find something in it to admire. As George Bernard Shaw observed, the fact that reasonable people make every effort to fit in with their surroundings leaves the responsibilities and rewards of progress to unreasonable men. Whatever else he may be, the unreasonable Nemo is certainly a symbol of progress and of enterprise.

Progress has, unfortunately, blurred the effect of the novel's one great dramatic event: the battle with the real sea beast. The creature must have been a giant squid, as must have been the creature that became entangled with the French naval vessel *Alecton* in 1861, which presumably gave Verne the idea. Without the aid of modern information, however, Verne was unable to distinguish between ten-limbed squids and eight-limbed octopodes, and all his translators have hesitated over the choice of an appropriate term, most of them preferring to leave the French word *poulp* unaltered. Filmmakers have understandably made much of this episode but suffered from similar confusions.

There is a nice irony in the fact that the desire to make a better cinematic version of *Twenty Thousand Leagues Under the Sea* was the main inspiration for the development of the first underwater camera by the Williamson brothers in 1916. The story thus became a direct inspiration to the technology that would eventually make a reality of its imaginary quest. That is the true measure of its merit and its worth.

"Critical Evaluation" by Brian Stableford

Further Reading

Butcher, William. *Jules Verne: The Definitive Biography.* New York: Thunder's Mouth Press, 2006. An exhaustive examination of Verne, revealing rich—and sometimes controversial—details of his life. Contradicts some previous biographies, which depict Verne as stodgy and boring.

Butor, Michel. "The Golden Age in Jules Verne." In *Inventory.* London: Cape, 1970. An excellent essay that discusses the symbolic significance of Nemo and his vessel in the context of Verne's oeuvre.

Costello, Peter. *Jules Verne: Inventor of Science Fiction.* London: Hodder and Stoughton, 1978. Chapter 8 of this critical biography deals with *Twenty Thousand Leagues Under the Sea.*

Miller, Walter James. *The Annotated Jules Verne: Twenty Thousand Leagues Under the Sea.* New York: Crowell, 1976. The first full translation of the text, elaborately annotated.

Saint Bris, Gonzague. *The World of Jules Verne.* Translated by Helen Marx, illustrated by Stephane Heuet, foreword by Arthur C. Clarke. New York: Tuttle Point Press, 2006. Collection of anecdotes, extracts from the novels, and illustrations that attempts to re-create the settings and characters of Verne's visionary fiction.

Smyth, Edmund J., ed. *Jules Verne: Narratives of Modernity.* Liverpool, England: Liverpool University Press, 2000. Collection of essays by Verne scholars that examine, among other topics, Verne, science fiction, and modernity; Verne and the French literary canon; and "the fiction of science, and the science of fiction."

Unwin, Timothy. *Jules Verne: Journeys in Writing.* Liverpool, England: Liverpool University Press, 2005. A reexamination of Verne's fiction. Argues that he was a skillful creator of self-conscious, experimental novels. Compares Verne's work to that of Gustave Flaubert and other nineteenth century French authors.

Verne, Jules. *The Complete Twenty Thousand Leagues Under the Sea: A New Translation of Jules Verne's Science Fiction Classic.* Bloomington: Indiana University Press, 1991. Emanuel J. Mickel's introduction offers a comprehensive study of the novel's background and a survey of critical analyses of Verne's work.

Two Essays on Analytical Psychology

Author: Carl Jung (1875-1961)
First published: 1928
Type of work: Psychology

Two Essays on Analytical Psychology has often been called the best student introduction to Carl Jung's work. "The Unconscious in the Normal and Pathological Mind" and "The Relation of the Ego to the Unconscious" are 1928 revisions of essays that Jung wrote earlier. Almost all of Jung's early work was revised extensively before its appearance in the collected edition to which he devoted his last years.

The work begins, as do so many of Jung's writings, with a version of his famous criticism of Sigmund Freud and Alfred Adler. Jung, who was Freud's most famous disciple from 1909 to 1914, held ideas different from Freud's and Adler's that led to personal differences between them, and these differences have been continued with rancor by their followers. One of the crucial points of disagreement is Jung's opinion that Freud's concept of the libido is too narrowly concerned with sexual energy and that Adler's definition of libido as a will to power is also too simplistic. Jung calls the libido, the basic reservoir of human drives, "psychic energy." Jung, however, endorses the cornerstone of Freud's theory, dream analysis, calling this technique "the royal road to the unconscious." Jung advises rising above too exclusive a concern with sexuality or the will to power. These drives are more important to young men than they are to the complete person over a long life span. Jung sees them as partial truths, and he proposes a theory of the psyche that can transcend them.

Undoubtedly there is much to be said for Jung's criticism of Freud and Adler as being concerned too reductively with elective forces in the analysis of human motivation. As time passed, Jung turned more to mythology and folklore for keys to understanding the unconscious, while Freud always stayed within the confines of a patient's personal experience from childhood on. Moreover, no matter how positively one reacts to Jungian theory, one must acknowledge an unrelenting tendency in the Swiss psychologist to schematize. During Freud's productive career, his ideas about the unconscious and its significance changed because of the material presented to him by his patients. In Jung's analysis, however, a few details from dreams led him to set up categories of psychological behavior drawn from his extensive research into primitive religions and the mysticism of Europe and the Near East. This tendency to set up formal patterns of meaning from dream, myth, and legend has led many of Jung's critics to refuse him the name of scientist; they insist that he is a philosopher, and a medieval one at that.

Like many makers of mystical systems, Jung insists that everything within the mind is doubled or paired. Conflict may be destructive to mental health, but it is also necessary to spiritual development. His belief is that energy results from the tension of opposites. According to Jung, for the young the conflicts are outside—with parents, with society—and here, as noted, the analysis of Freud and Adler is most valuable. The conflicts of mature people, however, are within. Many are unable to form significant selves because they are unable or unwilling to come to satisfactory terms with the threatening or "shadow" aspects of the collective unconsciousness.

This last division of the mind is another great distinction between Jungian theory and Freudian. Jung postulates a racial or collective unconsciousness containing what he calls primordial images, figures containing those qualities dramatized in the great myths of past cultures. These images of demoniac power are not inherited in themselves, but the thought patterns that produce them are. For Jung there is a personal unconsciousness such as Freud described, containing one's repressed personal emotions. The collective consciousness, however, is, according to Jung, much more obscure and more powerful, charged with potential for good and evil.

Jung also formulates a distinctive dream analysis. Every interpretation of a dream that equates a dream image with a real object he calls interpretation on the objective level. He contrasts that view with his own subjective interpretation, which brings the dreamer back to the self and is synthetic rather than analytic. This is the point at which the vast store of myth and legend material comes in, as Jung examines dreams in terms of the struggle for mental health and significant life. The archetype of the hero is one of the most famous Jung describes, and he relates how both dreams and legends are parallel in their depiction of the lonely voyage of the hero, beneath or through the sea, to a cave or castle where he must battle a monster for the treasure. The hero image is the health-giving power of the unconscious, Jung says, and the monster is the shadow side—perhaps the dark mother, the feminine image in its nihilistic phase. The treasure the hero can win is life, in the sense of mental balance, a process Jung calls individuation.

For Jung, dreams are another form of the old legends; they are what they say and are not to be translated out of symbolism into psychological motivation (the approach taken by Freud). To analyze dreams, people need to draw parallels from primitive material, because dreams come from the unconsciousness, which contains remnants of human experience in all preceding epochs of evolution. These images are the dominant powers of laws and principles. Prominent in this dark reservoir of the past, aside from the hero, are figures Jung calls the shadows: the wise old man, the mother, the child, and the anima and the animus (images of the feminine and the masculine ideals, respectively). Charged with power that is beyond good or evil, many of these images carry their own shadows or destructive charges. The wise old man in his malevolent role would appear as Satan or some other demon. The mother may be the generous, nurturing aspect of woman or may appear as dark chaos, the chaotic emotion into which the self can sink without a trace.

The all-important process of individuation is achieved, says Jung, through analysis of and compensation for these demoniac powers that threaten psychic stability. The process, involving suffering and action, is often depicted in dreams by rectangles and circles—enclosures of perfection that Jung terms mandalas.

Much of this analysis is like philosophy, Jung admits, but he adds that such must be, for the psyche seeks expression that involves its whole nature, not that merely corrects the minor, irritating obstacles that cause neurosis. One of the essential needs of human, irrational nature is the idea of God, Jung insists. It is necessary for a person's health that the image of the ideal be charged with power and projected outside him- or herself into religious myth. The individual needs a religious figure whose actions may be imitated and whose standards may be upheld.

Jung also describes the function of the persona, that mask the psyche creates to mediate between the desire of the unconscious and the outside world. Individuation consists of the creation of an authentic self, living in dynamic but useful tension between those two forces. If the unconsciousness rides roughshod over the persona, psychosis results. If the unconsciousness is not expressed in some useful way, however, the power from the libido can never be harnessed, and unending psychic paralysis, characterized by unceasing tension and anxiety, results. People must use this dark power, which Jung calls mana, and not be used by it.

It is interesting to observe that many literary people and humanists have become champions of Jung, but few scientists. Although Jung seems so often in his analysis merely to substitute one system of metaphor for another rather than offering any new understanding of mental processes, there can be no denying that, by joining comparative mythology to psychology, Jung has had extraordinary influence on both the reading and the writing of literary works.

Further Reading

Barnaby, Karin, and Pellegrino D'Acierno, eds. *C. G. Jung and the Humanities: Toward a Hermeneutics of Culture.* Princeton, N.J.: Princeton University Press, 1990. Collection of essays from an international conference on the significance of Jung's ideas includes discussions of archetypes and creativity.

Jung, C. G. *Memories, Dreams, Reflections.* Translated by Richard Winston and Clara Winston, edited by Aniela Jaffé. 1963. Reprint. London: Fontana, 1993. Presents Jung's life story as he related it to his secretary. Includes an informative glossary of Jungian terms.

Kerr, John. *A Most Dangerous Method: The Story of Jung, Freud, and Sabina Spielrein.* New York: Alfred A. Knopf, 1993. Study of Jung's intellectual development places emphasis on his relationships with Sigmund Freud and Spielrein, one of the world's first female psychoanalysts. Discusses the early versions of *Two Essays on Analytical Psychology.*

Noll, Richard. *The Jung Cult: Origins of a Charismatic Movement.* Princeton, N.J.: Princeton University Press, 1994. Controversial work suggests that Jung's concept of the collective unconscious, first announced in *Two Essays on Analytical Psychology,* marked a departure from science and a turn to religion.

Stevens, Anthony. *On Jung.* New York: Penguin Books, 1991. Excellent introduction to Jung by a practicing Jungian analyst provides an overview of Jung's theories of the unconscious and personality, followed by an account of Jung's life. Offers a Jungian perspective on the different stages of development.

Tacey, David. *How to Read Jung.* London: Granta, 2006. Presents an accessible explanation of Jung's psychological concepts, including the language of symbols and dreams, the second self, myth consciousness, and the stages of life.

Young-Eisendrath, Polly, and Terence Dawson, eds. *The Cambridge Companion to Jung.* 2d ed. New York: Cambridge University Press, 2008. Collection of essays covers topics such as Jung's ideas and their context, the historical context of analytical psychology, and analytical psychology in practice and in society.

The Two Gentlemen of Verona

Author: William Shakespeare (1564-1616)
First produced: c. 1594-1595; first published, 1623
Type of work: Drama
Type of plot: Comedy
Time of plot: Sixteenth century
Locale: Italy

Principal characters:
VALENTINE and PROTEUS, two young gentlemen
JULIA, the beloved of Proteus
SILVIA, the beloved of Valentine
THURIO, a man in love with Silvia
THE DUKE OF MILAN, Silvia's father

The Story:

Valentine and Proteus, two longtime friends, disagree heartily on whether, as Valentine thinks, the most important thing in life is to travel and to learn the wonders of the world, or whether Proteus is right in believing nothing to be more important than love. The two friends part for a time when Valentine travels to Milan, to seek advancement and honor in the palace of the duke. He pleads with Proteus to join him in the venture, but Proteus is too much in love with Julia to leave her side for even a short time. Julia is a noble and pure young girl, who has many suitors. Proteus at last wins her heart and the two are happy in their love.

Valentine journeys to Milan, and there he learns that his friend is right about the importance of love. Valentine meets the duke's daughter, Silvia, and falls instantly in love with her. Silvia returns his love, but her father wants her to marry Thurio, a foolish man with no personal charms but much land and gold. Valentine longs for Silvia but sees no chance of persuading her father to consent to his suit. Then he learns that Proteus, whose father is ignorant of Proteus's love affair and wishes his son to educate himself by travel, is soon to arrive in Milan.

The two friends have a joyful reunion, and Valentine proudly presents his friend to Silvia. To Proteus he praises the virtue and beauty of his beloved, and when they are alone, Valentine confides to Proteus that, since Sylvia's father refuses to give her to anyone but Thurio, he plans to fashion a rope ladder and steal Silvia from her room and marry her. Valentine, asking his friend to help him in his plan, is too absorbed to notice that Proteus remains strangely silent. The truth is that Proteus, at the first sight of Silvia, forgets his solemn vows to Julia (sealed before he left her with the exchange of rings), forgets his oath of friendship with Valentine, and determines to have Silvia for his own. With protestations of self-hatred for betraying his friend, Proteus tells the duke of Valentine's plan to escape with Silvia from the palace. The duke, forewarned, tricks Valentine into revealing the plot and banishes him from Milan on penalty of his life.

While these events are taking place, Julia, thinking that Proteus still loves her and grieving over his absence, disguises herself as a page and travels to Milan to see her love. She is on her way to Milan when Valentine is forced to leave that city. Valentine, not knowing that his onetime friend betrayed him, believes Proteus's promise that he will carry letters back and forth between him and Silvia.

With Valentine out of the way, Proteus proceeds to get rid of Thurio as a rival. Thurio, foolish and gullible, is an easy man to trick. One night, Proteus and Thurio go to Silvia's window to serenade her in Thurio's name, but Proteus uses the occasion to sing to her and to make protestations of his love for her. Julia, in the disguise of a page, stands in the shadows and hears his betrayal of her as well as Silvia's response that she will love no one but Valentine. She also accuses him of playing false with Julia, for Valentine tells her of his friend's betrothal.

Calling herself Sebastian, Julia, still in the dress of a page, becomes employed by Proteus to carry messages to Silvia. One day, he gives her the ring that Julia herself gave him and tells her to deliver it to Silvia. When Silvia refuses the ring and sends it back to Proteus, Julia loves her rival and blesses her.

Valentine, in the meantime, is captured by outlaws, once honorable men who were banished for petty crimes and took refuge in the woods near Mantua. To save his life, Valentine joins the band and soon becomes their leader. A short time later, Silvia, hoping to find Valentine, escapes from the palace and, with the help of an agent, arrives at an abbey near Milan. There she is captured by the outlaws. When her father hears of her flight, he takes Thurio and Proteus to the abbey to look for her. Julia follows them. Proteus, arriving on the scene first, rescues her from the outlaws before they are able to take her to their leader. Again Proteus proclaims his love for her. When she scornfully berates him, he seizes her and tries to force himself on her. Valentine, who overhears everything, springs upon Proteus and pulls him away from her.

Valentine is more hurt by his friend's duplicity than by anything else, but such is his forgiving nature that when Proteus confessed his guilt and his shame over his betrayal, Valentine forgives him and receives him again as his friend. In proof of his friendship, he is even prepared to give up his claim on Silvia. When she hears that, Julia, still disguised, faints. Reviving, she pretends to hand over to Silvia the ring Proteus ordered her to deliver, but instead she offers the ring Proteus gave her when they parted in Verona. Then Julia is recognized by all, and Proteus admits that he still loves her.

The outlaws appear with the duke and Thurio, whom they captured in the forest. Thurio gives up all claim to Silvia, for he thinks a girl who will run off into the woods to pursue another man much too foolish for him to marry. Her father, convinced at last of Valentine's worth, gives that young man permission to marry Silvia. During the general rejoicing Valentine begs one more boon. He asks the duke to pardon the outlaws, all brave men who will serve the duke faithfully if he will return them from exile. The duke grants the boon, and the whole party makes its way back to Milan. There the two happy couples intend to share their wedding day and be happy in their mutual love and friendship.

Critical Evaluation:

In *The Two Gentlemen of Verona*, William Shakespeare is learning the craft of playwriting, with plot elements, characters, and comic situations that will reappear in later plays. The work also mirrors the literary vogues of its time, particularly the popular prose romances of the day—forerunners of the sentimental novel and the twentieth century psychological novel—that trace the turbulence of adolescence and of youth. Some of Shakespeare's later comedies and his *Romeo and Juliet* (pr. c. 1595-1596, pb. 1597) reflect a similar concern. Himself then the father of a daughter approaching her teens, Shakespeare may have been especially sensitive to the problems of youth.

Proteus and Valentine are Italianates—young gentlemen sent abroad to acquire perfection at a foreign court. Proteus's name, a common Elizabethan label for the Italianate, further establishes that identification. Critics have made much of the geographical "inaccuracy" of Valentine's departure for Milan by boat, ignoring the fact that Shakespeare was too well read and too familiar with the geography of Europe not to know that travel from the real Verona to Milan would have to be land. As in his other plays, Shakespeare uses place names for their connotations. Verona was the home of the lovers Romeo and Juliet, Milan the fashion center of Europe and the seat of the imperial court. With this Verona and this Milan he can retain the three worlds of his source, Jorge de Monte-

mayor's prose romance *Diana* (c. 1559): the world of lovers subject to parental oversight, the sophisticated world of the court, and the green world of the forest.

In the first world, Proteus, like Felis in *Diana* and Euphues in John Lyly's romance of that name (*Euphues, the Anatomy of Wit*, 1578), lives through the wild emotional swings and naïve tentativeness of adolescence, and he submits tamely to his elders. He is in love with love and has an idealized vision of the court, where he hopes to achieve perfection.

In the second world, the world of the court, Proteus is metamorphosed by self-interest and begins to assume poses. His desire for Valentine's Silvia leads him first to disloyalty to both his friend and to Julia and eventually to outright treachery. At the end, rejected by Silvia after his final pose as a knight errant who rescues her from outlaws, Proteus tries to take Silvia by force. Even the more stable Valentine changes at court, becoming adept at exaggerated expression; perfection for him becomes a matter of rhetorical skill—"A man is no man if with his tongue he cannot win a woman"—and a proficiency in conventional formulas and flattery. In fact, as Peter Lindenbaum pointed out, Valentine's love affair is a reaction to his court experience.

Some critics have found fault with the way the play ends in the last of these worlds, the green world. Here, outlaws are readily pardoned, Proteus is forgiven his assault on Silvia, and Valentine temporarily resigns his claim on his beloved in favor of Proteus. Though Proteus's repentance seems sudden, it is plausible because it is preceded by the shock he receives when his villainy is publicly exposed and he recognizes his self-deception. With this recognition, the idealized picture of perfection that the Verona youth envisions for himself—hearing sweet discourse, conversing with noblemen, and being in the eye of every exercise worthy of a nobleman—suddenly gives way to the truth. The court produces this villain, and "shame and guilt confound him." Proteus recognizes not only his own imperfection but that of all humankind: "were man but constant, he were perfect."

To Valentine and to the duke also comes discovery. The duke discovers the true nature of his favorite, Thurio, and of the despised "peasant" Valentine, and he learns to look at Valentine with new eyes and to consider him worthy of his daughter's love. He sees the outlaws as reformed men. The corrupting influence of the court dissolves in the healing of the green forest. Even Julia, who dreams of idealized love at the beginning of the play and then at court learns of the flaws in her beloved Proteus, discovers that she can still love him. Valentine, though he at first reacts with rage, feels the rekindling of his old feelings of friendship. The play thus ends with the regeneration of the protagonists, a conclusion required if the play is to remain faithful to the traditional endings of the prose romances that serve as sources for the play.

Shakespeare does not go into much depth in portraying the characters in this play. In fact, some critics suspected him of writing *The Two Gentlemen of Verona* primarily to mock the idealistic Renaissance romantic codes. It is more likely, however, that he is watching his characters with sympathetic amusement. When Valentine is smitten with Silvia and confides his feelings to Speed, Speed mocks his impassioned behavior and comments, as Silvia enters, that he is now about to witness a puppet show. Even Silvia joins in the mockery, though more gently, when she stops Valentine's exaggerated praise and Petrarchan conventions with "I guess the sequel." Proteus's sentimental gift of a little dog, Jewel, which Launce loses and replaces with the mongrel Crab, is transformed from a gallant gesture into farce when the dog runs under the duke's table and lifts his leg against Silvia's farthingale. Just after Proteus's tender farewell to Julia, Launce parodies lovers' partings with his dog sitting in for the loved one; when Valentine laments his banishment from Silvia, Launce mimics a lover's Petrarchan cataloging of his mistress's physical attributes.

The play also has moments of great charm. Shakespeare offers lyrical passages such as the well-known song "Who Is Silvia?" as well as banter between characters and the lighthearted antics of Speed and Launce.

"Critical Evaluation" by Thomas Amherst Perry

Further Reading

Gay, Penny. "Courtly Lovers and the Real World: *Two Gentlemen of Verona, A Midsummer Night's Dream, The Merchant of Venice.*" In *The Cambridge Introduction to Shakespeare's Comedies.* New York: Cambridge University Press, 2008. Concise, introductory overview of Shakespeare's comic plays. After a discussion of comedy as idea and practice in Shakespeare's time, Gay analyzes the themes of his comedies in their chronological order.

Giese, Loreen L. *Courtships, Marriage Customs, and Shakespeare's Comedies.* New York: Palgrave Macmillan, 2006. Analyzes *The Two Gentlemen of Verona, Twelfth Night,* and lawsuits for matrimonial enforcement filed in London from 1586 to 1611 to understand the era's courtship and marriage practices. Discusses how these plays and lawsuits reflect the expected roles of men and women during courtship and marriage and how people perceived and sometimes challenged these expectations.

Hunt, Maurice. "Catholicism, Protestant Reformation, and *Two Gentlemen of Verona.*" In *Shakespeare's Religious Allusiveness: Its Play and Tolerance.* Burlington, Vt.: Ashgate, 2004. Seeks to determine if Shakespeare's plays were either Protestant or Catholic in sympathy. Argues that Shakespeare syncretized elements of both religions in his plays, a singular achievement during a time when the government and society tolerated Protestanism in drama, while criticizing and stereotyping Catholicism. Demonstrates this religious integration in several plays, including *The Two Gentlemen of Verona.*

Leech, Clifford. Introduction to *The Two Gentlemen of Verona,* by William Shakespeare. London: Methuen, 1969. Concludes that the play is primarily concerned with mocking the idealistic pretensions of Renaissance codes of romantic love and of friendship.

Leggatt, Alexander, ed. *The Cambridge Companion to Shakespearean Comedy.* New York: Cambridge University Press, 2002. Although none of the essays is specifically about *The Two Gentlemen of Verona,* there are numerous references to this play listed in the index.

Lindenbaum, Peter. "Education in *The Two Gentlemen of Verona.*" *Studies in English Literature* 15, no. 2 (Spring, 1975): 229-244. Concludes that the play is about the importance of penitence for past sins. The education of the "perfect man" envisioned at the beginning of the play takes the protagonists to the court and then to the green forest, where they will learn that they are imperfect because they are human.

Schlueter, June, ed. *"Two Gentlemen of Verona": Critical Essays.* New York: Garland, 1996. Compilation of critical essays and reviews of the play dating from the mid-eighteenth through the late twentieth centuries. The essays focus on the play's debate about love and friendship, its low comic characters, and its bewildering conclusion.

The Two Noble Kinsmen

Authors: William Shakespeare (1564-1616) and John
 Fletcher (1579-1625)
First produced: c. 1612-1613; first published, 1634
Type of work: Drama
Type of plot: Romance
Time of plot: Antiquity
Locale: Athens and Thebes

Principal characters:
THESEUS, duke of Athens
HIPPOLYTA, queen of the Amazons, wife of Theseus
EMILIA, Hippolyta's sister
PALAMON and ARCITE, nephews of Creon, the king of
 Thebes
THE JAILER'S DAUGHTER

The Story:

After a witty and informal prologue, the play opens with the wedding procession of Theseus, duke of Athens, and Hippolyta, queen of the Amazons. Before the marriage ceremony can begin, the festivities are interrupted by three queens in black who implore Theseus to come to their aid. Their husbands have been slain fighting against Creon, king of Thebes, and Creon will not permit their bodies to receive a decent burial. Theseus sympathizes with the queens but orders that the nuptial ceremonies proceed. When the queens persist in their pleas, Theseus directs an army to be readied to march against Thebes but makes it clear that he intends to go forward with the marriage. The distracted queens, now aided by both Hippolyta and her sister Emilia, finally persuade Theseus to delay his wedding and wedding night and to move against Creon and Thebes immediately. Theseus asks his lifelong friend Pirithous to act on his behalf and see that the ceremony and festivities proceed, takes leave of his bride with a kiss, and departs with the three queens.

In Thebes, Palamon and Arcite, nephews of Creon, resolve to leave Thebes because they cannot tolerate Creon's cruel tyranny any longer. As they prepare to venture forth on their own, word comes that Theseus is at the gates of Thebes with a mighty army. The cousins, loyal to Thebes if not to Creon, prepare to defend their city against Theseus.

The Athenians are victorious, and Theseus, triumphant, tells the widowed queens that they are free to bury their dead with all due rites and honors. Palamon and Arcite fought bravely, but they have been wounded and captured. As they recover from their wounds in an Athenian prison, they impress the jailer and his daughter with their dignity, grace, and stoic acceptance of their fate: life in prison. The two young men speak eloquently of what their confinement means, of a future without the joys of the hunt or combat, without courtship or marriage, without family. They determine, however, to make their prison a sanctuary remote from the evils that befall men and to be one another's family, to unite their spirits in love through the years to come.

No sooner have the young cousins pledged undying loyalty to one another than Palamon sees Emilia, Hippolyta's beautiful sister, walking in the garden below the prison cell. He falls in love with her at first sight, as does Arcite when he too beholds the young beauty. Palamon asserts that, because he saw her first, Arcite must not love her. Arcite responds that Palamon, who called her a goddess, may love her spiritually; Arcite, on the other hand, will love her as a flesh and blood woman.

In the face of their new passion for Emilia, the cousins' pledge to honor and love one another disintegrates. Palamon rages that, if they were free, he would take Arcite's life for betraying their friendship and his own honor by loving Emilia. Arcite sees no betrayal in his love for Emilia and defies Palamon; consequently, their relationship is transformed from one of love and loyalty to one of rancor and rivalry.

For unrevealed reasons, Arcite is freed by Theseus and banished from Athens, but he takes no pleasure in his freedom because he imagines that Palamon can still see Emilia whenever she visits the garden. Desperate with longing for the sight of Emilia, Arcite assumes a disguise and returns to Athens. He has the good fortune to arrive just when athletic games are being held in honor of Emilia's birthday. Arcite wins virtually every contest, conducts himself with humility and grace, and is rewarded by Theseus, who does not recognize him. The king accepts Arcite into his household and designates him to be a serving man to Emilia.

The jailer's daughter falls madly in love with Palamon and helps him escape. Still manacled, Palamon takes refuge in the forest near Athens. Days later, Arcite—on a spring outing with the court—comes upon the escaped prisoner, who is weak and starving. In spite of Palamon's continued hostility to him, Arcite returns to the forest the next day with a file for his manacles, food, and drink. Palamon is restored to health, and the two cousins agree to resolve their quarrel with swords.

Arcite steals weapons and armor and returns to engage in mortal combat with Palamon. Theseus and his court are also in the forest hunting, and they receive unexpected entertainment from a group of country folk, who perform a lively dance for them. The jailer's daughter, now truly mad with grief at what she imagines to be Palamon's betrayal of her love, is one of the dancers.

Palamon and Arcite arm each other with great courtesy and then struggle violently. Theseus and his party come upon the battling youths, and the king is outraged by their actions; he calls for their immediate execution. In a scene echoing that of the three queens in black, Hippolyta, Emilia, and Pirithous plead with Theseus to be merciful. Reluctantly, he relents and declares that they may live if they renounce their love for Emilia and forget her; both refuse. Theseus then determines that the cousins may go free, but they must return in one month, each accompanied by three knights, and settle their quarrel in the lists. The victor will marry Emilia, and the loser and his companions will be put to death.

As the month passes, the jailer's daughter grows even madder. Her father, a young suitor for her hand, and a doctor all attempt to restore her sanity. Emilia, meanwhile, has expressed no desire to marry either cousin. In fact, she confides to Hippolyta that she does not believe she can ever love anyone as intensely as she did a young female friend who has died. She has no intention of ever marrying. Emilia stoically accepts her fate, however, and struggles in vain to choose one or the other of her suitors as her favorite.

On the night before the appointed battle, Arcite prays to Mars, the god of war, to give him victory; Palamon invokes Venus, the goddess of love, asking her to give him Emilia; and Emilia asks Diana, goddess of chastity, to bring victory to the youth who loves her best. Ironically, all their prayers are answered: Arcite is victorious but dies during the victory parade in a riding accident. Palamon and his companions are spared execution at the last moment, and he is awarded Emilia. Emilia is thus joined to the man who professed to love her most truly. The joy of the couple's union is darkened by the death that made it possible, one love achieved at the cost of another. The subplot is resolved in an equally disturbing and murky manner, as the jailer's daughter, now supposedly recovered, has agreed to marry her young suitor.

Critical Evaluation:

As the prologue acknowledges, the primary source of *The Two Noble Kinsmen* is Geoffrey Chaucer's "The Knight's Tale" (1387-1400), which was itself based on Giovanni Boccaccio's romantic version in the *Teseida* (1340-1341; *The Book of Theseus*, 1974) of a story from Statius's Latin epic *Thebais* (c. 90; *Thebaid*, 1767). Statius, in turn, derived his story from one of the oldest and most tragic Greek legends: the history of Thebes. Although the only book-length study of *The Two Noble Kinsmen*—Paul Bertram's excel-lent *Shakespeare and "The Two Noble Kinsmen"* (1965)—argues that the play is solely the work of William Shakespeare, most scholars agree that John Fletcher collaborated with Shakespeare on the play. Shakespeare is thought to have written act 1, the first scenes of acts 2 and 3, and act 5.

Many scholars have noted the unity of image and purpose throughout the play and argue that the two playwrights collaborated throughout the writing of the script, even if one or the other is primarily responsible for certain parts. The scenes attributed to Shakespeare are generally criticized for their formal, ritualistic quality and lack of concern for character development. Fletcher's scenes are acknowledged to be more dramatically effective but also more melodramatic.

The play revisits themes and concerns of Shakespeare's earlier plays: the nature and influence of the patriarchy, the disruptive power of love, the movement from innocence to experience, and humanity's relationship to fate and the gods. Shakespeare's vision here is darker and more melancholy than in previous plays. Theseus, the champion of patriarchy, is rather cold and remote, and his determination to impose order on the chaotic forces within and without human beings is revealed as successful only in partial ways and only after the destruction or constriction of vital energies and forces. Hippolyta, the Amazon queen, is portrayed as diminished and bound by her marriage to Theseus. The chivalric contest Theseus imposes on Palamon and Arcite results in the failure of one and the death of the other. Order is restored at the end but only at great cost. The justice and civility achieved are not conducive to faith either in humanity's ability to understand and control life or in the beneficent nature of divine providence.

Ostensibly, the play's events enact a conflict between Mars and Venus. Arguably, the forces represented by these gods (male versus female, war versus love) are reconciled in the marriages of Theseus with Hippolyta and Palamon with Emilia. However, the conventional distinctions between masculine and feminine principles are challenged in curious ways. Hippolyta is not merely an elegant and beautiful woman; she is also a ruthless warrior, inured to violence and carnage. Emilia, perhaps the more feminine of the two, is nonetheless a skilled rider and hunter uninterested in marriage. The jailer's daughter is impulsive, resourceful, courageous, and outspoken.

Palamon, once his enmity with Arcite has been established, is consistently associated with the feminine through word and image. Venus seems to be stronger and more disruptive than Mars. The jailer's daughter, who proves to be the play's most dynamic dramatic figure, is driven mad by her love for Palamon, yet her unrestrained passion is perhaps the most positive and selfless energy in the play. Palamon and

Arcite's devoted friendship and youthful innocence is shattered by their competing desire for Emilia.

The loves that the play seems to value without reservation are the youthful, same-sex friendships between Emilia and Flavina, Palamon and Arcite, and Theseus and Pirithous. Only the Theseus-Pirithous relationship has survived youth into maturity, but it is necessarily diminished (or so Hippolyta hopes) by Theseus's marriage. Mature heterosexual love is seen as being an enemy of both innocence and friendship and as requiring the sacrifice of profoundly valuable emotions and relationships.

Chaucer's "Knight's Tale" suggests that one can overcome fortune to a certain extent by accepting whatever happens, by controlling how one responds to life's vagaries rather than attempting to control and order one's life. *The Two Noble Kinsmen*, on the other hand, indicates that love and death are both accidents, that human beings are incapable of understanding not only the workings of providence but also their own inner drives and compulsions. Shakespeare's Theseus is left resigned and melancholy by his flawed efforts to impose order on a world seemingly governed by mere caprice. The three widows in black, although they disappear from the stage after act 1, cast a pall over the entire play. The specter of death interrupts the marriage ceremony in the first act and taints the union of Emilia and Palamon in the final act. *The Two Noble Kinsmen* is flawed dramatically but is nonetheless an interesting and compelling play.

Hal L. Holladay

Further Reading

Bertram, Paul. *Shakespeare and "The Two Noble Kinsmen."* New Brunswick, N.J.: Rutgers University Press, 1965. A rare book-length study of the play. Thorough and excellent analysis both of the play and of previous criticism.

Bloom, Harold. *"The Two Noble Kinsmen."* In *Shakespeare's Romances*, edited by Bloom. Philadelphia: Chelsea House, 2000. A thoughtful and provocative reading of the play; Bloom asserts that the vision of the play is grim but the poetry astonishing.

Donaldson, E. Talbot. *The Swan at the Well: Shakespeare Reading Chaucer.* New Haven, Conn.: Yale University Press, 1985. A comprehensive and highly intelligent comparison of Shakespeare's and Chaucer's versions of the story.

Fletcher, John, and William Shakespeare. *The Two Noble Kinsmen.* Edited by Lois Potter. New York: Routledge, 1997. The definitive edition of the play. The 129-page introduction contains a wealth of material on sources, the history of the collaboration, criticism, intellectual background, and performance.

Frey, Charles H., ed. *Shakespeare, Fletcher, and "The Two Noble Kinsmen."* Columbia: University of Missouri Press, 1989. An excellent resource for study of the play. Contains ten fine essays and an excellent annotated bibliography.

Metz, G. Harold. *"The Two Noble Kinsmen* on the Twentieth Century Stage." *Theatre History Studies* 4 (1984): 63-69. A survey of modern productions of the play.

2001
A Space Odyssey

Author: Arthur C. Clarke (1917-2008)
First published: 1968
Type of work: Novel
Type of plot: Science fiction
Time of plot: 3,000,000 B.C.E. and 2001
Locale: Earth, the moon, Jupiter, Saturn, and deep space

Principal characters:
MOON-WATCHER, a prehistoric man-ape
DR. HEYWOOD FLOYD
DAVID BOWMAN and FRANK POOLE, *Discovery* astronauts
HAL, *Discovery*'s sentient computer

The Story:

Early ancestors of humankind are struggling to survive, and it appears that they will succumb to extinction. Moon-Watcher, who leads a tribe of these primates by virtue of his massive size, encounters a "new rock." The new rock is a

Monolith, a sentient entity in the form of a rectangular block with perfect proportions—the ratio of its depth to width to height is exactly 1 to 4 to 9. The Monolith conducts experiments on Moon-Watcher and his tribe, ultimately providing

Moon-Watcher's people with the ability to utilize and create rudimentary tools. As a result, Moon-Watcher's tribe learns to hunt and defeats a competing tribe, ensuring humanity's eventual existence.

Millions of years later, Dr. Heywood Floyd is sent by the president of the United States to a base on the moon in order to investigate mysterious magnetic fluctuations. The source of the fluctuations is another Monolith found buried in the moon's Tycho crater. Floyd and other scientists refer to the moon's Monolith as Tycho Magnetic Anomaly One (TMA-1) and prepare to conduct experiments on it. Uncovered, the Monolith is exposed to a sunrise on the moon and immediately emits a signal that disrupts almost all nearby electronic equipment. Distant communication satellites record the signal, and its destination is pinpointed.

In 2001, the spaceship *Discovery* travels through space toward Saturn. *Discovery* was initially scheduled to travel only to Jupiter, but its mission was altered shortly before it began, ostensibly for the purpose of surveying Saturn's various moons. Two astronauts, David Bowman and Frank Poole, comprise the ship's crew, while three members of a survey team lie dormant in cryogenic sleep for the journey. Bowman and Poole are accompanied by the ship's advanced computer, the Heuristically programmed ALgorithmic computer (HAL), which is responsible for maintaining the ship's course and systems.

Passing through the asteroid belt and reaching Jupiter, *Discovery* begins a maneuver that slingshots the ship around the gas giant, increasing its speed for the remainder of the journey to Saturn. Following the slingshot maneuver, Bowman and Poole return to their normal duties of caring for the ship. HAL, however, begins to detect various failures in the ship's communications equipment, forcing Poole to conduct repairs on the ship's exterior. Mission control determines that it is HAL, and not the communications equipment, that is malfunctioning. Mission control attempts to brief the astronauts on the procedure to replace HAL's control of *Discovery* with that of a similar computer still on Earth, but communications fail. Indulging HAL, Poole again attempts to conduct repairs on the ship's exterior, but he is killed when Poole's spacepod mysteriously activates and crushes him.

Realizing that HAL is malfunctioning, Bowman demands manual control of the cryogenic chambers and begins the sequence to wake up the survey team. HAL objects and opens the ship's airlock doors, depleting *Discovery*'s atmosphere and killing the survey team in the process. Bowman manages to don a pressure suit and successfully disconnects HAL. Communications are reestablished with Earth and mission control determines that HAL's malfunction was due

to a feeling of guilt caused by the computer's instructions to withhold information from the crew. (Neither Bowman nor Poole was aware of the true objectives of the mission to Saturn, but it was necessary for HAL to know them.) Bowman is finally informed of the Monolith found on the moon and of the signal it sent to Saturn's moon, Japetus (Iapetus).

Once safely in orbit around Saturn, Bowman begins preliminary surveys of Japetus, and it is quickly revealed that another Monolith is located on the satellite's surface. This one, erroneously referred to as TMA-2, is many times larger than the previous Monoliths, but it retains the same extremely precise 1 by 4 by 9 proportions. Aware that no rescue operation can be mounted in time to save him before his oxygen supply runs out, Bowman decides to take a remaining spacepod and travel to TMA-2. As he approaches the Monolith, Bowman notices that it appears to be full of stars and transmits this information to Earth. It is his final transmission, as the Monolith opens, revealing itself to be some sort of portal, or stargate, and sends Bowman to the far reaches of space.

In the stargate, Bowman determines that the gate is fundamentally an interstellar Grand Central Station that connects to other stargates. While traversing its vast expanses, he witnesses ample evidence of other spacefaring races, though it is not evident if those races are still existent or are extinct. Eventually, Bowman is taken to a red giant star and lands on it. To his surprise, he finds himself in a facsimile of a hotel room found on Earth. The room has apparently been constructed based on information sent by the TMA-1 signal. Many of its details are superficial, such as books with no print and a television that shows only programs that are at least two years old. There is air to breathe and food to eat, however, and Bowman eventually succumbs to sleep.

As Bowman sleeps, the hotel room disappears and Bowman begins to live his life backward in his dreams. When he has regressed to infancy, the dream subsides into reality, and Bowman finds himself face to face with another Monolith. The Monolith processes Bowman's thoughts and conducts experiments similar to those conducted on Moon-Watcher millions of years earlier. Bowman experiences a fundamental transformation into a "Star-Child," and he reenters the stargate, this time heading back to Earth. In orbit, Bowman deactivates and detonates the world's nuclear arsenal and with vague intention notes that "history as men knew it would be drawing to a close."

Critical Evaluation:

The evolution for *2001* began in 1948, when Arthur C. Clarke submitted a short story, "The Sentinel," for a competition held by the British Broadcasting Company (BBC). Although the story was rejected, Clarke later proposed it as the basis for filmmaker Stanley Kubrick's *2001: A Space Odyssey* (1968). The two visionaries met following Kubrick's release of *Dr. Strangelove: Or, How I Learned to Stop Worrying and Love the Bomb* (1964) and set out to make a realist science-fiction film. Early in the process, it was decided that the story should be written in novel format and then adapted to a screenplay. Clarke and Kubrick initially worked on the novel together, but Kubrick's need to prepare for film production ultimately left Clarke finishing the novel alone. Still, Kubrick's influence is felt throughout, both in the deliberate pace of the plot and in clearly cinematic descriptive passages. Because of the story's symbiosis, it is nearly impossible to analyze Clarke's novel without acknowledging Kubrick's film and vice versa.

By the time of the film's and book's releases in 1968, Clarke had already established himself as a peer among many of the great scientific minds, including Carl Sagan and Isaac Asimov. Clarke was also heralded as one of the fathers of communications satellites, having proposed geostationary orbits in 1945 to maximize telecommunications coverage. He would later be nominated for the Nobel Peace Prize for this achievement, and he would be knighted in 1998 for services to literature.

The novel *2001* became the first book of a four-book cycle that continued with *2010: Odyssey Two* (1982), *2061: Odyssey Three* (1987), and *3001: The Final Odyssey* (1997). In each novel, Clarke takes great care to adhere to the laws of physics and often successfully predicts future innovations. In *2001*, for instance, Clarke's portrayal of a space-shuttle launch and space-station dock proved to be largely accurate once such technologies came into use, as did Clarke's description of *Discovery*'s slingshot maneuver around Jupiter to gain speed. Politically, Clarke writes of friendly cooperation between U.S. and Russian space agencies, as well as lingering effects of the Cold War.

Presciently realistic and cautionary, *2001*, unlike many science-fiction stories of the era, holds up extremely well under both scientific and literary scrutiny—a testament to Clarke's vision. Written in a simple tone and using straightforward language, the book proceeds at a steady pace. It is neatly divided into six distinct parts, each with its own focus, but tightly woven together into an overarching plot. Nearly the entire novel is narrated from a character's perspective, and, while subtle, the effect of Clarke's brief three-page narration from HAL's point of view is at once alarming and poignant.

The novel deals primarily and unapologetically with general issues of humanity and its interaction with technology. There is little in the novel to suggest that Clarke was concerned with his characters, as he spends very little time providing character histories or exposition. Evolution itself is presented as the result of technological interference at both the beginning and the end of the book. Throughout *2001*, the wonders and dangers of technology are presented side by side, culminating in HAL's murderous rampage in part 4 and Bowman's return to Earth at the conclusion.

Of the six parts, the last four are inhabited by Bowman, who is the story's main protagonist by default. Though he makes no appearance and warrants no mention in parts 1 or 2, he is the sole remaining character in parts 5 and 6. Despite this, his characterization remains primarily that of an observer, in much the same way that Moon-Watcher and Dr. Floyd are the primary observers in parts 1 and 2, respectively. Again, much of Bowman's adventure entails his interaction with technology, first with HAL, then with repairing and operating *Discovery*, and finally with the stargate. It is through his eyes that the bulk of the story is told, but *2001* is very much about the sentient Monoliths and their creation—that is, humanity.

Much has been made of the character of HAL, largely because of the film version's proliferation into pop culture, but in the book HAL is essentially a foil utilized to whittle the crew down to one person. It was because of this whittling that Clarke was subtly able to mirror Bowman's encounter with the Monolith to that of Moon-Watcher's three million years prior. Not so subtle are the near-identical descriptions that Clarke gives to both Bowman and Moon-Watcher's states of mind following each of their encounters with the Monolith: "he was master of the world, and was not quite sure what to do next. But he would think of something."

With these words, Clarke pitches his main theme: that humanity is a great power with a great responsibility. Moon-Watcher's response is decidedly violent, and although it results in the ascension of humankind, it is akin to committing mass murder. Bowman's final act is left untold, but his elimination of nuclear arsenals ends the story on an optimistic note. Clarke was famed for asking, "Is there intelligent life on Earth?" The finale of *2001* seems to answer: If there is not yet, there will be.

Jeffrey K. Golden

Further Reading

Clarke, Arthur C. *The Lost Worlds of "2001."* London: Sidgwick and Jackson, 1972. Clarke's own account concerning the writing and production of Kubrick's *2001*.

Contains early versions of both the novel and the screenplay.

Lewis, C. S., and Arthur C. Clarke. *From Narnia to Space Odyssey: The War of Letters Between Arthur C. Clarke and C. S. Lewis.* Compiled and edited by Ryder W. Miller. New York: iBooks, 2003. A compilation of letters exchanged between Clarke and C. S. Lewis expressing their perspectives concerning technology and its ramifications.

Provides insight into Clarke's defense of technology as a natural aspect of the evolution of humankind.

Wheat, Leonard F. *Kubrick's 2001: A Triple Allegory.* Lanham, Md.: Scarecrow Press, 2001. An unusual attempt at discussing *2001* as pure allegory. Presents Clarke's vision of humankind and technology as an oversimplification of evolution, but provides interesting comparisons to Friedrich Nietzsche and Homer.

The Two Towers

Author: J. R. R. Tolkien (1892-1973)
First published: 1954
Type of work: Novel
Type of plot: Fantasy
Time of plot: The Third Age in a remote legendary past
Locale: Middle-earth, chiefly Rohan, Fangorn, Gondor, and Ithilien

Principal characters:
FRODO BAGGINS, the Ring-bearer
SAMWISE GAMGEE (SAM), his loyal servant
MERIADOC BRANDYBUCK (MERRY) and PEREGRIN TOOK (PIPPIN), young hobbits and Frodo's cousins and friends
GANDALF (MITHRANDIR), a wizard, returned from the depths and transfigured into the White Rider
ARAGORN, the courageous descendant of kings
LEGOLAS, the son of the elven king of Mirkwood
GIMLI, a dwarf and the friend of Legolas
SARUMAN, a wizard, the former leader of the White Council, and now a traitor greedy for power
GOLLUM (SMÉAGOL), a loathsome, corrupted hobbit and once owner of the Ring
THÉODEN, the aged king of Rohan
ÉOMER, his warrior nephew
GRIMA WORMTONGUE, the minister of Théoden but a secret agent of Saruman
TREEBEARD (FANGORN), the leader of the ents, a strange treelike people
SAURON, the Dark Lord of Mordor

The Story:

Immediately after Frodo the Ring-bearer and Sam set off to fulfill their quest for the destruction of the Ring of power, a band of orcs captures the two remaining hobbits, Merry and Pippin. In an attempt to defend them, Boromir of Gondor is mortally wounded. Dying, he confesses to Aragorn that he tried to take the Ring from Frodo, who had put on the Ring and vanished to escape him. Aragorn, Legolas, and Gimli prepare Boromir's body, place it in an elven boat, and send it over the falls down the Great River. They then follow the tracks of the orcs in an attempt to rescue Merry and Pippin. After several days, they meet a company of Riders of Rohan

led by Éomer, the nephew of King Théoden, who reports killing the orcs. The Riders of Rohan did not see the hobbits, but they lend horses to the travelers to follow the trail.

Pippin had tempted an orc to run away with the hobbits for the Ring, which the orc thought was in the hobbits' possession. When a Rider kills the orc, Pippin and Merry escape in the darkness. They enter the mysterious forest Fangorn, where they meet Treebeard, the leader of the ents, who shelters them. After hearing their story, Treebeard calls an Entmoot to decide what action the ents should take against the forces of evil. On the third day, the treelike ents reach their decision and march on Isengard, the traitor Saruman's stronghold.

After the three hunters find hopeful signs that their friends have escaped the orcs, they enter Fangorn. There they meet Gandalf, who has returned from the depths with new power as the result of his ordeal. He calls to Shadowfax, the great horse borrowed from Rohan's king, and the four ride toward Théoden's hall. Théoden, who is bent with age, greets Gandalf inhospitably. His pale, wizened minister Wormtongue, who nourishes the king's infirmities, sits at Théoden's feet and vilifies Gandalf until Gandalf raises his staff, lightning flashes, and Wormtongue is sprawled on the floor. Gandalf leads Théoden from the shadowy hall, and the old king stands erect and returns to manhood. He announces his determination to lead his people against Saruman. To Wormtongue, whose treachery Gandalf has exposed, he offers a choice: Ride into battle against Saruman or accept banishment. Wormtongue spits and rides away to join Saruman. Théoden leaves his niece Éowyn to act as regent in his absence, and Gandalf departs on a secret mission.

The battle of Helm's Deep is fought with great odds favoring Saruman's orcs and wild hillmen. Éomer and Aragorn perform heroic deeds, and Gimli and Legolas compete to see which of them can kill more orcs. With the morning, a strange forest appears on the hills. Théoden leads a gallant charge, and Gandalf returns as the White Rider, striking terror into the enemy. The orcs flee into the forest, but not one comes out.

After the battle, Gandalf leads Théoden and others to Isengard for a parley with Saruman. On the way, they see several ents, and during the night the strange forest strides past them. Arriving at Isengard, they find devastation. The walls are torn down, and the stronghold itself is filled with steaming water; only the ancient impregnable tower, Orthanc, remains undamaged. Seated at the ruined gates are Merry and Pippin. Merry welcomes them in the name of Treebeard and informs them that Saruman is closeted with Wormtongue in Orthanc. The hobbits tell how the ents attacked Isengard, destroyed its walls with their rootlike hands, and diverted the river waters through Saruman's underground domain. Then, to their amazement, Gandalf arrived and asked Treebeard for help against the orcs, and the walking forest moved off toward Helm's Deep. Finally, Wormtongue arrived. Treebeard gave him the choice of joining Saruman or waiting for Théoden and Gandalf; he had chosen Saruman.

Gandalf calls Saruman to the window of Orthanc. The corrupted wizard tries to sway them with his persuasive voice, but this attempt at enchantment fails, and Gandalf offers him freedom to join them against Sauron or to go to Mordor. He refuses to leave Orthanc and turns away, but Gandalf calls him back, casts him from the White Council, and breaks his staff. As Saruman crawls away, Wormtongue flings a heavy crystal ball at Gandalf. It misses its target and Pippin picks it up, but Gandalf quickly retrieves it. The company leaves the ents to keep Saruman from escaping and rides back toward Théoden's hall. Pippin slips the crystal ball away from Gandalf and looks into it. His eye is drawn to the Dark Tower in the crystal, and, confronted by Sauron, he loses consciousness. Gandalf revives him and learns that Sauron had failed to question him about the Ring.

Meanwhile, Frodo and Sam are traveling through barren country, trailed by Gollum. They waylay him but spare his life, and he swears by the Ring to serve Frodo loyally. From this point, he becomes their guide, leading them toward Mordor. During their journey, Ringwraiths sometimes pass overhead, striking terror into their hearts. As they draw nearer to Mordor, the Ring grows heavier, and Frodo feels the constant probing of Sauron's evil Eye. They enter Ithilien, a wooded land with flowing streams. Frodo and Sam are captured by men of Gondor led by Faramir, the son of Denethor and brother of Boromir; Faramir tells the hobbits that he has seen Boromir's body floating in an elven boat. In a rock chamber behind a waterfall, he questions them and learns more about their errand than they intend to divulge; he promises help and gives them provisions. He spares the life of Gollum at Frodo's entreaty, leads them back to the forest, and sends them on their way.

Gollum leads them toward the tower of Minas Morgul, from which an army marches out led by the chief Ringwraith, who stops as if drawn by the power of the Ring but then marches on. Gollum slips away. When he returns and finds Frodo and Sam asleep, a good impulse almost redeems him, but the evil light comes back into his eyes. He leads the hobbits far into a climbing tunnel and there deserts them. They hear a bubbling noise, and Frodo holds up the glass given him by Galadriel, the Elf-Queen. In its piercing light appears Shelob, a huge spidery monster. Blinded temporarily by the light, she retreats. The end of the tunnel is blocked by her web, but Frodo cuts through the cords with his elven sword, Sting, and runs outside. Sam sees that Shelob has used another exit and is pursuing Frodo. As he shouts a warning, Gollum leaps on Sam's back. Driving Gollum off, he turns back to see Shelob winding Frodo in cords. He snatches up Sting and attacks her. As she flings her foul body on him, he holds Sting so that she wounds herself. In agony, she drags herself back to her hole, leaving a trail of slime.

Finding no sign of life in Frodo, Sam decides that he must try to complete the quest alone. When he hears orc voices, he puts on the Ring and vanishes. The orcs discover Frodo's body and carry it toward the tower. Sam learns from their talk that Frodo is not dead but only stunned. Frodo is alive and a captive, and Sam is locked outside.

Critical Evaluation:

The Two Towers is the second volume of the trilogy *The Lord of the Rings*, J. R. R. Tolkien's epic fantasy of war between good and evil. In Tolkien's Middle-earth, good and evil are absolutes, each a recognizable force in the shaping of character and behavior. As the power of evil wielded by the Dark Lord Sauron waxes, diverse peoples are drawn to his banner. Those who would wield the power of good to heal the wounds of Middle-earth—Gandalf, Elrond, Galadriel—find themselves besieged. *The Two Towers* traces the influence and definition of both forces as their great conflict draws once again to a climax.

The narrative of *The Two Towers* is divided into two distinct parts, each addressing the struggle in a separate way. The first portion (book 3) considers the problem in an elemental fashion, exploring the relationship between the natural world and the mechanistic inventions of human beings amid sweeping tales of war involving thousands. Book 4 is set at a far more individual level, examining the effects of good and evil on just three carefully drawn characters.

The critical event of book 3 is the meeting between the young hobbits, Pippin and Merry, and the old ent Treebeard. Newly escaped from the clutches of orcs, the hobbits have suffered a horrifying experience in what seems to be a war among the two-legged sentients who walk the earth. The military situation has become confusing; Sauron and his minions are the obvious enemy of the elves and men of the West, but Saruman the traitor has now set up in competition with both.

Treebeard helps the hobbits see the situation in a simpler and more frightening light: Both Sauron and Saruman are the enemies of nature, as are all who wantonly destroy the forests. Treebeard remembers the vast forests that once covered Middle-earth, now reduced to isolated and dangerous patches of angry trees. Sauron the destroyer had covered the world in darkness once before; even now nothing green grows in the fastness of Mordor. Given the chance, the Dark Lord would reduce the entire earth to heaps of slag and ash.

Saruman is a more immediate enemy in the eyes of Treebeard. The white wizard had once pretended a love for trees, but only mechanical artifice holds true fascination for him. Isengard, Saruman's home, was once a pleasant grove filled with living things, but now it is given over to wheels and rising smokes. All the trees are gone.

To fight evil is to fight the destruction of nature. Evil, however, is a powerful seducer. Wizards, elves, and human beings have all turned their backs on the trees at one time or another. Saddest of all, even some of Treebeard's own kind had once compromised their love of nature, to the sorrow of all. The entwives, rather than sustaining the vigorous wild of the forest, had turned to gardening, ordering nature, forcing plants to grow as they saw fit. They created beautiful gardens, but war destroyed them, and the entwives disappeared. Only wild nature is vigorous enough to survive the changing whims of the peoples of the earth.

Treebeard assists the curse of men, tipping the balance in the defeat of Saruman and destroying the mechanical wizardry of Isengard. The victory destroys an evil danger to his forest while aiding the cause of the West in the great War of the Ring. Treebeard knows better than any that this cooperation between trees and men is temporary, and he foresees that even the free peoples will be increasingly divorced from nature in the future. The destruction of Saruman, or even Sauron, will not destroy all the evil in the world. Nature must look to its own interests as well as it can.

Although the War of the Ring becomes a struggle between nature and artifice on the fields of Rohan, a very different revelation of the relationship between good and evil takes place in the desolate lands east of the River Anduin. Frodo and Sam meet with Gollum, the corrupted creature nearly possessed by the great Ring. What seems at first glance to be a simple confrontation between good and evil becomes something far more subtle.

All three of these hobbits have within themselves a dual capacity for good and evil. A year earlier, in the safety of his living room in the Shire, Frodo had wished Gollum dead, only to be chastised by Gandalf. To deny life is to deny the ability to act, and no one can know what any being's future acts might be. Now, stranded in the wilds on a desperate errand, Frodo finds he must turn to Gollum for help. Gollum knows the way to Mordor, and Frodo must depend on his guidance. He and Gollum complete a bargain to do good, sworn on the Ring—the greatest vessel of evil in all of Middle-earth.

Whereas Frodo is forced to compromise with evil, Gollum is torn in two. Virtually his entire identity has been swallowed by the Ring, and yet he maintains a small kernel of memory of happier times, of green fields and sunlit days. He is two beings in one: a treacherous liar consumed by evil and an ancient and exhausted hobbit possibly capable of decency. The situation dictates that the two halves make a truce to help Frodo, each side hoping to turn the alliance to its advantage.

Sam is not an innocent bystander in the convenient alliance between Gollum and Frodo. Recognizing that the evil side of Gollum is almost certainly dominant, Sam would like nothing better than to kill the treacherous creature. He is stayed from this course by his trust in Frodo's innate goodness as well as by practical considerations: They do need a guide.

Each of the three hobbits has made a compromise; Frodo and Sam have done so in the service of the good quest, and Gollum has done so in the hope of somehow stealing back the Ring of evil. The two forces exist everywhere side by side; remaining pure is practically impossible. The key for each hobbit is to sacrifice the needs of the moment to achieve a greater goal, an ultimate triumph of one force over the other.

Within a narrative devoted to the resolution of a war and the furthering of a quest, Tolkien in *The Two Towers* develops both his definition and his concept of the function of good in its struggle with evil. Identifying evil with the enemies of wild nature, Tolkien elaborates the complexities of the ultimate choice that must be made within each individual mind.

"Critical Evaluation" by Robert Kuhn McGregor

Further Reading

Curry, Patrick. *Defending Middle-earth: Tolkien, Myth, and Modernity.* New York: HarperCollins, 1997. Reprint. Boston: Houghton Mifflin, 2004. Examines the relevance of Tolkien's mythological world for modern readers. Focuses on three aspects of Tolkien's depiction of Middle-earth: its social and political structure, its nature and ecology, and its spirituality and ethics.

Dickerson, Matthew T., and Jonathan Evans. *Ents, Elves, and Eriador: The Environmental Vision of J. R. R. Tolkien.* Lexington: University Press of Kentucky, 2006. Discusses Tolkien's view of the natural world and environmental responsibility, arguing that the lifestyles of his fictional characters anticipate many of the tenets of modern environmentalism and agrarianism.

Drout, Michael D. C., ed. *J. R. R. Tolkien Encyclopedia: Scholarship and Critical Assessment.* New York: Routledge, 2007. Comprehensive reference work contains five hundred entries on a wide range of subjects related to Tolkien's writings and life. Topics covered include characters in Tolkien's fiction, the critical reception of his works, and adaptations of his writing to the screen and other media.

Giddings, Robert, ed. *J. R. R. Tolkien: This Far Land.* Totowa, N.J.: Barnes & Noble, 1983. Collection of essays covers varied topics, including Tolkien's use of humor, his depictions of female characters, and the narrative structure of his novels.

Isaacs, Neil D., and Rose A. Zimbardo, eds. *Tolkien: New Critical Perspectives.* Lexington: University Press of Kentucky, 1981. Offers an introduction to relatively early Tolkien criticism. Includes chapters on Frodo as the old hero and Aragorn as the new, Gandalf's battle with the Balrog, and light and darkness as symbols of Galadriel and Shelob in *The Two Towers.*

Lee, Stuart D., and Elizabeth Solopova. *The Keys of Middle-earth.* New York: Palgrave Macmillan, 2005. Interesting work provides information on Tolkien's medieval sources, featuring modern translations of the original texts.

Lobdell, Jared. *The Rise of Tolkienian Fantasy.* Chicago: Open Court, 2005. Examines Tolkien's fantasy fiction, discussing the writers who influenced him, the elements of his fantasy literature, and his literary heirs, including writers Ursula K. Le Guin, Stephen King, and J. K. Rowling.

_____, ed. *A Tolkien Compass.* LaSalle, Ill.: Open Court, 1975. Collection includes essays on such topics as good and evil in the trilogy, as represented in *The Two Towers* by color symbolism; the corrupting force of power, represented in *The Two Towers* by Gollum; and the spiral narrative structure of *The Two Towers.*

Petty, Anne C. *One Ring to Bind Them All: Tolkien's Mythology.* Tuscaloosa: University of Alabama Press, 1979. Offers a good introduction to the mythology underlying the *Lord of the Rings* trilogy. Includes a structuralist interpretation of the trilogy and traces Frodo's development in *The Two Towers.*

Rosebury, Brian. *Tolkien: A Cultural Phenomenon.* 2d ed. New York: Palgrave Macmillan, 2003. Traces the development of Tolkien's writing over several decades, devoting a lengthy analysis to *The Lord of the Rings.* The revised and expanded edition provides additional information on Tolkien scholarship and discusses director Peter Jackson's film adaptation of *The Lord of the Rings.*

Two Trains Running

Author: August Wilson (1945-2005)
First produced: 1990; first published, 1992
Type of work: Drama
Type of plot: Social realism
Time of plot: 1969
Locale: Pittsburgh, Pennsylvania

Principal characters:
MEMPHIS, a restaurant owner
WOLF, a local numbers runner
RISA, a waitress
HOLLOWAY, a customer and storyteller
STERLING, a customer
HAMBONE, a customer
WEST, a funeral-home director

The Story:

Prophet Samuel is dead. A former reverend, Prophet Samuel became a powerful leader and adviser in the Pittsburgh neighborhood in which Memphis Lee's Restaurant is located, and he amassed both followers and money. Memphis was particularly skeptical of the prophet's virtues even when he was alive, and he continues to express his skepticism. His waitress Risa, who was a devoted follower, defends Prophet Samuel from Memphis's attacks.

Memphis is also troubled by the fate of his restaurant. It has been reasonably successful, but the city has decided to tear it town, along with all the other buildings in the neighborhood. Memphis has accepted the inevitable loss of his restaurant, but he has fixed a price, twenty-five thousand dollars, as the minimum he will accept from the city. West, the local funeral-home director, warns Memphis that he will only receive, at most, twelve thousand dollars, but Memphis remains committed to getting his price before he will agree to the city's demands.

Into this setting comes Sterling, a young man just out of the penitentiary and looking for work. When he asks for advice, Holloway tells him to go see Aunt Ester, a legendary sage who is said to be over three hundred years old and who always tells her visitors to throw twenty dollars into the river. Sterling remains noncommittal, but he is very interested in Risa. Risa, however, is resistant. She once took a razor and scarred her legs in order to avoid being treated as a sex object, and she seems disinterested in Sterling's attentions. However, she does offer Sterling a lucky number to place a bet with Wolf, the neighborhood's numbers runner.

Hambone arrives, much to the displeasure of Memphis, but Risa offers him some food. According to Memphis and Holloway, Hambone painted a fence for the local butcher over nine years ago with the expectation of receiving a ham. The white butcher attempted to pay him a chicken instead, and since that time, Hambone has been unable to complete more than two simple sentences, both of which demand his ham. According to Holloway, Hambone has stood outside the butcher shop every day since then, demanding his ham. Sterling attempts to bond with Hambone and even attempts to teach him a couple of slogans about Malcolm X and the Black Power movement, but Hambone reverts to his obsession with the ham.

The city makes Memphis an offer: It will pay fifteen thousand dollars for his restaurant. Memphis recalls the time he could not raise enough money to see his mother before she died. He vows to keep fighting until he is offered twenty-five thousand dollars.

Memphis and Holloway deliver monologues explaining bits of their past. Memphis reveals why he left his home in Jackson, Mississippi, nearly forty years earlier: He found water on the land he owned, increasing the property's value. As a result, a white man named Stovall and some of his friends took the land, killed his mule, and ran him out of town. Memphis has been vowing to return to Jackson ever since, but he never quite manages to do so. Holloway tells a story about how Aunt Ester cured him of a desire to kill his own grandfather. From that point on, Holloway has been a devout believer in Aunt Ester's ability to help people solve their own problems.

The number Risa gave Sterling to play actually wins, but the people running the game decide to cut the winnings in half. Wolf, who is merely a courier and feels that he is just following orders, dreads telling Sterling that his winnings have been reduced. He fears the former convict's response to the news, worrying that Sterling will blame him and seek to retaliate against him. Wolf talks about getting a pistol for protection.

Holloway informs everyone that Hambone is dead. Both Sterling and Memphis decide separately to go see Aunt Ester for help. When Sterling returns, he dances with Risa and convinces her to go to a birthday rally for Malcolm X. When Memphis returns, he announces that the city has more than met his price, offering him thirty-five thousand dollars. He also repeats Aunt Ester's advice to him. She compared life to a football game and told Memphis that, if you fumble the ball, you must go back for it: If you do not, there is no way to score. She then told him to throw twenty dollars into the river.

Memphis is delighted that he will get more than his asking price, and he starts making plans to return to Jackson and take care of unfinished business there. Meanwhile, Sterling, upon hearing of Hambone's death, breaks into the butcher shop across the street and steals a ham. In the play's final image, Sterling delivers the ham as a gift for Hambone's coffin.

Critical Evaluation:

August Wilson was one of the most celebrated American playwrights since World War II, and he is best remembered for his ten-play history cycle. Each of Wilson's ten plays is set in a different decade of the twentieth century. Together, they form a portrait of the African American experience of the century, in an attempt to demonstrate the ways in which African Americans have suffered, endured, or thrived. *Two Trains Running* won the New York Drama Critics' Circle Award for Best American Play, and it was nominated both for a Tony Award and for the Pulitzer Prize in drama.

In many ways, *Two Trains Running* is the play that offers the clearest insight into Wilson's vision of history. In tackling one of the most tumultuous decades of the twentieth century, the 1960's, Wilson resists most of that decade's iconic reference points. Many reviewers were surprised that the play did not include more recognizable allusions to the period, but for Wilson, the 1960's was not about Vietnam, the Kennedy assassinations, the March on Washington, Stonewall, or Woodstock. Instead, in Wilson's vision, the 1960's are embodied by a group of men hanging out in a diner. Wilson's history is domestic, and his characters' attitudes, struggles, and perceptions communicate the essence of the decade in highly subjective and symbolic ways.

Wilson sees the decade, by its close, as a time of both loss and injustice. Loss comes in the opening stage directions, where Wilson notes that the aptly named West's Funeral Home sits across the street from the restaurant. He reinforces this theme with the news of the death of Prophet Samuel, whose role as a spiritual leader, however dubious, carries echoes of Malcolm X and Martin Luther King, Jr. The characters also speculate in great detail about the practices of burying the dead, and they debate the merits of West's management, professional demeanor, and ethics as a funeral director.

Wilson later intensifies the play's sense of loss with references to the Malcolm X birthday rally and the death of Ham-

bone. Moreover, the neighborhood itself is nearing its end. Sterling even speculates that these events are harbingers of the end of the world. All of these details remind audience members that this play is set at the end of the decade, not in the middle. By 1969, Medgar Evers, Malcolm X, and King were all dead, and the play suggests that the end of the 1960's was a time for confronting loss rather than celebrating victory. The lengthy monologues only add to the feeling that the play is nearly a wake. Wilson suggests, however, that it is not enough to mourn. Instead, he uses the plight of the restaurant and the cutting of Sterling's winnings as reminders that even though the Civil Rights movement is essentially over, the struggles continue. Memphis crystallizes the characters' sense of injustice when he mocks the notion of the blindfolded statue of Justice, suggesting that she of all people should possess clear sight.

The play's title perhaps evokes the fact that, when its characters have faced difficult choices, they have relied on two local advisers: Prophet Samuel and Aunt Ester. Prophet Samuel is largely represented as a fraud, although Risa and the huge crowd across the street clearly believe otherwise. Aunt Ester is a mythical figure and a giver of sage advice. Though she does not appear physically in the play, she is mentioned in other plays from Wilson's history cycle, and she appears as a major character in *Gem of the Ocean* (pr. 2003, pb. 2006), which is set in the first decade of the twentieth century.

For much of *Two Trains Running*, Holloway insists that she is 322 years old. However, Sterling informs everyone that she is actually 349 years old, which is particularly significant when one considers that, if true, she would have been born in either 1619 or 1620, the same time as the arrival of the first Africans in America. In essence, she represents the entirety of the African American experience, and, for Wilson, she serves as an ideal repository of wisdom and dispenser of advice. The message seems fairly clear: If one wants to learn how to deal with injustice and survive, then one must draw from the wisdom of one's elders and heritage.

Aunt Ester's advice to Memphis, the football metaphor of recovering a fumble, repeats a common theme in many of Wilson's plays. His characters are often haunted or burdened by the past, and until they come to terms with it, they can never find any real form of success or contentment. Perhaps the most striking example of this pattern occurs in *The Piano Lesson* (pr. 1987, pb. 1990), when one character must literally wrestle with a ghost.

In the case of Memphis, his dropped ball was his failure to stand up for himself when he was run out of Jackson. Despite his relative financial success and independence in Pittsburgh, he remains highly cynical of other characters' motives, and he remains a potential victim of City Hall, which, in attempting to take his property, is reenacting the abuse Memphis received nearly forty years earlier in Mississippi. However, by fighting for his rights and preparing to return to Jackson, Memphis finally learns to pick up the football. Sterling, too, acts assertively after receiving Aunt Ester's advice, convincing Risa to attend the Malcolm X rally and honoring Hambone, who never stopped fighting for his rights, by stealing the ham.

By the end of the 1960's, African Americans needed to make a choice. Faced with a world where many of their leaders were dead and the Civil Rights movement was in disarray, they could pretend that all was well and try to carry on, or they could recognize injustice, confront the problems from the past, and go back to pick up the football. In Wilson's portrayal, the cultural situation of that moment all comes down to a choice. After all, there are two trains running.

Thomas Gregory Carpenter

Further Reading

Bigsby, Christopher, ed. *The Cambridge Companion to August Wilson.* New York: Cambridge University Press, 2007. This collection features an essay by Stephen Bottoms focusing on *Two Trains Running.* The essays are organized by the chronology of the plays' settings, not by the order in which they were written. The collection is also notable in that most of the authors featured had already published extensively on Wilson.

Elkins, Marilyn. *August Wilson: A Casebook.* New York: Garland, 2000. A very useful collection of essays on Wilson. Rather than focusing on individual plays, most of the essays focus on broader topics such as ideology, aesthetics, and influence. Also features a key interview with Wilson conducted by Richard Pettengill. One of the most useful and wide-ranging books on Wilson.

Herrington, Joan. *I Ain't Sorry for Nothin' I Done: August Wilson's Process of Playwriting.* New York: Limelight, 1998. A unique exploration of Wilson's writing process and its relationship to the theater workshops where he developed his plays.

Nadel, Alan, ed. *May All Your Fences Have Gates: Essays on the Drama of August Wilson.* Iowa City: University of Iowa Press, 1994. An excellent collection of essays covering the first half of Wilson's canon. Of key interest is an essay by Mark William Rocha that uses the concept of "loud talking," a variation on signifyin(g) as explained by Henry Louis Gates, Jr., to highlight Wilson's method of communicating with his audience. Rocha's essay focuses specifically on *Two Trains Running.*

Shannon, Sandra. *The Dramatic Vision of August Wilson.* Washington, D.C.: Howard University Press, 1995. One of the first single-author books on Wilson, and still one of the best. Explores Wilson's development as a playwright from his earliest, unpublished efforts through *Two Trains Running.* Contains one of the best and most broad-ranging interviews conducted with Wilson. An indispensable resource.

Wilson, August. *Conversations with August Wilson.* Edited by Jackson Bryer and Mary C. Hartig. Jackson: University Press of Mississippi, 2006. Reprints some of the most important interviews given by the playwright, in chronological order. Of chief interest are the interviews by Sandra Shannon and Richard Pettengill, since both discuss *Two Trains Running* at some length.

Two Treatises of Government

Author: John Locke (1632-1704)
First published: 1690
Type of work: Politics

John Locke's *Two Treatises of Government* established the author as the intellectual father of the modern constitutional state. The political theories set forth are the foundation for later political philosophers, including Jean-Jacques Rousseau, whose *Du contrat social: Ou, Principes du droit politique* (1762; *The Social Contract*,1764) influenced the beginning of the French Revolution in 1789. Before Thomas Jefferson wrote the Declaration of Independence in 1776, he read and absorbed Locke's *Two Treatises of Government.*

Locke lived during a time of tremendous political upheaval in England, including the Civil War (1642-1646), the beheading of King Charles I (1649), the interregnum (1649-

1660), the Restoration of the Stuart monarchy (1660), and the Glorious Revolution of 1688. These events gave Locke the motivation to advocate the political changes that influenced his and future generations.

In his first treatise, Locke refutes the arguments of Sir Robert Filmer's *Patriarcha: Or, The Natural Power of Kings* (1680), which defends the established order in England. Locke's second treatise, the statement of his own political philosophy, rejects many statements in *Leviathan* (1651) by Thomas Hobbes, which advocates absolute power in the person of the king. The connection between Locke's *Two Treatises of Government* and the Glorious Revolution is also clear. Manuscripts of his work circulated in England for several years prior to 1688, helping to produce the revolution. In the preface to the published version, written in 1689 after William and Mary were given the throne, Locke declared that his treatises "I hope are sufficient to establish the Throne of our Great Restorer, Our present King William."

The major historical impact of Locke's *Two Treatises of Government* is best defined by an analysis of the second treatise (which he subtitled "An Essay Concerning the True Original, Extent, and End of Civil Government"). The content of this essay is best summarized in five major points. The first major point is Locke's definition and discussion of political doctrine. In this point, he declares his belief that government can exist only with the consent of free people. Locke then defines the political power that the government possesses as the power to make laws for the regulation and the preservation of property, to use the collective force of the people to execute the laws, and to protect the people and their property from foreign injury. This summary of the duties of government is notable for what it omits—religion, for example.

The biggest part of Locke's discussion of political doctrine is devoted to the four principles of his philosophy of state. The first principle is that there is a need for a powerful political and social organization. Locke believes that all people are born free; he also believes that the only way free people can protect themselves and their property is to form a community. The second principle is that the only legitimate claim by which a ruler can justify his or her power is by a definite agreement between the ruler and the ruled. Locke uses this contract theory to form the basis for government by consent. The next principle is that different circumstances allow for different degrees of authority being given to the government. A community in need of strong leadership can give near-absolute power to its rulers, but a stable community may severely limit its leaders' authority. In chapter 8 of his second thesis, Locke gives the example of the chiefs of In-

dian tribes in America, who were absolute rulers during times of war, but who exercised very little power during times of peace. The final principle in Locke's philosophy of state is that once a legitimate government is established, the people are bound to obedience. Even if the government proves unsatisfactory, they cannot claim rights not contained in the agreement.

The second major point of Locke's work expands his idea of government by consent into a social contract consisting of two parts. First is a pact of union, in which individuals surrender control over the natural rights to a community, which then acts as a unit to protect the rights of all. Second comes a compact of subjection in which each individual is subject to the will of the community, as long as the community does not violate the individual's rights. Throughout his writings, Locke discusses community by consent but never defines the exact point of origin for that community. He also writes much about the state of nature, which is what exists before the community is formed, but does not precisely describe that state.

Any discussion of Locke's theory of community must include his ideas on how consent is given and what the individual's obligation to the community is afterward. Locke states that before an individual may be bound by community action, there must be solid evidence that he or she gave consent. Direct consent can be given when, upon reaching maturity, he or she takes an oath of allegiance to the government. Tacit consent may be assumed if a person stays in a community for a long period of time without going elsewhere. This tacit consent seems unrealistic, however, because, regardless of an individual's attitude toward the government, he or she may be unable to depart for economic, political, or personal reasons. Even if he or she is able to leave, his or her choices may be so limited that he or she is no more satisfied than before. What Locke apparently means is that any individual living in a community where majority rule prevails is obligated to obey the laws of that community as long as his or her liberty and property are protected. This position establishes a sound moral basis for government, and it is considered one of Locke's major contributions to the modern constitutional state.

The third major point of Locke's second treatise is his discussion of separation of power in government, which can better be understood as a differentiation of power. Locke did not advocate three equal branches of government controlled by a system of checks and balances. Instead, he placed the basic power in the legislative branch, as he declares in chapter 11: "The first and fundamental positive Law of all Commonwealths, is the establishing of the Legislative Power; as the first and fundamental natural law . . . the preservation of the Society, and . . . is . . . sacred and unalterable in the hands where the Community have once placed it."

Legislative supremacy is to be tempered by four limitations. The first is that the legislature cannot have arbitrary power over the lives and property of the people. The legislature has only the power that is transferred to it by consent. People have arbitrary control of their own lives and property, and they have no right to take away the life and property of someone else, so these powers cannot be transferred to the legislature. The second limitation is that the legislature cannot govern by arbitrary decree. It must follow established laws that are interpreted by known and authorized judges. The third limitation is that the legislature cannot take people's property without their consent. Crucial to understanding this limitation is Locke's definition of property, given in chapter 5 of his second treatise. The concept of property consists of two elements: property inherited by all from God and property consisting of one's body and the labor thereof. Locke combined these elements by saying that acorns and apples are given by God to all, but they become the property of those who gather and pick them. That Locke was pleased with his definition of property is proven by a remark in a letter he wrote in 1703: "Property I have nowhere found more clearly explained than in a book entitled *Two Treatises of Government.*" The fourth and last limitation that Locke placed on the legislature is that it cannot transfer its lawmaking power to any other person or organization.

In contrast to legislative supremacy is Locke's concept of executive necessity. The executive is necessary primarily to guarantee the perpetual execution of legislation. He also describes what he calls federative power, by which he means control of foreign policy. Although Locke separates the federative from the executive, he indicates that they are closely related. Conspicuous by its absence in Locke's two treatises is judicial independence, since that concept was long a cornerstone of English constitutional tradition. He seems to include judicial power within the realm of the executive.

The fourth major point of the *Two Treatises of Government*, discussed in chapter 13, consists of the related political principles of popular sovereignty and representative democracy. Locke assigns popular sovereignty (his definition of the term is that the people are the supreme power) to the legislature. That legislature should contain, at least in part, representatives chosen by the people for a specific period of time. When that time is over, the representatives return to their positions as subjects. Locke gives to the executive the power to issue directives regarding the election of the representatives and the assembling of the legislature.

Chapter 19, the last chapter of Locke's second thesis, covers the last major point of Locke's work: the dissolution of government. After he briefly discusses dissolution from without (external force), Locke explains and justifies how a government can be dissolved from within. He describes what is commonly called the right of revolution. One basic reason for this right is if the legislature is altered by an overreaching executive. The alteration could be by the despot's setting up arbitrary will in place of laws, preventing the legislature from assembling, or setting up a legislature of the ruler's own choosing. Revolution would be justified in such cases. It would also be justified if the community is delivered to the subjection of a foreign power. The legislature itself can provoke a justifiable revolution if it breaks its contract, by invading the property of the subjects, for example.

Locke anticipates and answers the charge that his ideas about justifiable dissolution would be foment for revolution. He first states that ill-treated people have a right to seek change. Second, every small problem or abuse of trust does not necessitate a revolution. Finally, Locke indicates that the threat of a revolution may prevent the abuse of power that justifies a real revolution.

Locke's *Two Treatises of Government* contributes at least three basic principles to the modern constitutional state. First, every member of a political society should have an equal voice in governing that society. Second, the idea of social contract helped pave the way for a formal, written constitution. Third, final sovereign power should rest with the people as a whole.

Glenn L. Swygart

Further Reading

Franklin, Julian. *John Locke and the Theory of Sovereignty.* New York: Cambridge University Press, 1978. Emphasizes Locke's role in transforming the theory of sovereignty from a limited concept to a broad principle of the eighteenth century. Includes the influence on Locke of George Lawson and his radical views concerning the dissolution of government and reveals Locke's relationship to the English Whig Party.

Harrison, Ross. *Hobbes, Locke, and Confusion's Masterpiece: An Examination of Seventeenth-Century Political Philosophy.* New York: Cambridge University Press, 2003. Explains and critiques the political ideas of Locke and Thomas Hobbes, placing their philosophies within the context of the political, intellectual, and religious turmoil of seventeenth century Britain. Explores the limits of political authority and the relationship of the government's legitimacy to the will of its people.

Jolley, Nicholas. *Locke: His Philosophical Thought*. New York: Oxford University Press, 1999. A general introduction to Locke's philosophical concepts. Chapter 10, "The Evils of Absolutism," focuses on his political philosophy, including the desire for a more tolerant society expressed in *Two Treatises of Government*.

Lamprecht, Sterling Power. *The Moral and Political Philosophy of John Locke*. New York: Russell and Russell, 1962. Centers on the relationship between Locke and his predecessors and contemporaries. Goes beyond Locke's *Two Treatises of Government* to include his views on human knowledge and understanding.

Locke, John. *Two Treatises of Government*. 2d ed. Edited and with an introduction by Peter Laslett. New York: Cambridge University Press, 1988. Accepted as the standard text for studying Locke's political theories. Contains more than one hundred pages of preliminary material, plus extensively footnoted text and an excellent bibliography.

Sabine, George. *A History of Political Theory*. 4th rev. ed. Hinsdale, Ill.: Dryden Press, 1973. Covers political theory from the ancient Greeks to the twentieth century. Emphasizes Locke's role in developing a theory of the national state.

Tully, James. *A Discourse on Property: John Locke and His Adversaries*. New York: Cambridge University Press, 1980. Locke's theories of property have long caused argument among political thinkers. This book is Tully's attempt to reconsider Locke's ideas.

Zuckert, Michael P. *Launching Liberalism: On Lockean Political Philosophy*. Lawrence: University Press of Kansas, 2002. Zuckert, himself a political theorist, explores the philosophical and theological influences upon Locke's political philosophy, Locke's influence on later liberal thinkers, and his success in transforming the political understanding of Britain and the United States.

_____. *Natural Rights and the New Republicanism*. Princeton, N.J.: Princeton University Press, 1994. Locke was one of many philosophers who wrote about "natural rights." This book about the ideas of a number of philosophers features information about Locke and his influence on the Americans, on questions about natural law, on government, and on property.

Two Women

Author: Alberto Moravia (1907-1990)

First published: La ciociara, 1957 (English translation, 1958)

Type of work: Novel

Type of plot: Social realism

Time of plot: 1943-1944

Locale: Sant'Eufemia, Italy

Principal characters:

CESIRA, a shopkeeper's widow from the Ciociaria hills

ROSETTA, her daughter

CONCETTA, a peasant woman

VINCENZO, her husband

ROSARIO and GIUSEPPE, their sons

FILIPPO, a refugee

MICHELE, his son

PARIDE, a sullen peasant

CLORINDO, a black marketeer

The Story:

Cesira is a peasant woman from the Ciociaria region southeast of Rome. The widow of a Roman shopkeeper, she has continued to run the shop since her husband's death. Selfish, shrewd, and strong-willed, Cesira has concern only for herself and her eighteen-year-old daughter, Rosetta. When the war comes she welcomes it, because in wartime food becomes scarce and expensive. Before long, she and Rosetta are doing a thriving black-market business with the flour, eggs, hams, and potatoes they are able to get from the farmers in her home village and other country places near Rome. Sometimes she says to her daughter that she hopes the war will continue several more years, to provide the young woman with a trousseau and a dowry.

When the Germans occupy Rome and Allied bombing

raids begin to threaten the city, Cesira and Rosetta flee to the Ciociaria hills. At first, they plan to live with Cesira's parents, but then they hear that the village has been evacuated, and they are forced to settle at Fondi, where they live for a time with a slatternly woman named Concetta, her husband, Vincenzo, and their two deserter sons, Rosario and Giuseppe, who are hiding from the patrols that are scouring the countryside for men to be sent off to work in Germany.

This refuge proves unsafe; Cesira overhears Concetta describing her plan to buy her loutish sons' safety by turning Rosetta over to the Fascist bravos. Mother and daughter then flee to Sant'Eufemia, a small village high on the mountain, overlooking the valley. There they live for the next nine months in circumstances of squalor, suspicion, hunger, and fear. They learn what life is like when it is reduced to the essentials of food, clothing, and sleep. At first they have plenty to eat. Filippo, a venal shopkeeper from Fondi, has his hut stuffed with food on which he and his family feast and which he sells to his less fortunate neighbors. Paride, from whom Cesira and Rosetta rent a hut, is grasping and vicious. The wives are no better than their husbands; charity and dignity have been drained out of them. The only person worthy of respect is Michele, Filippo's son; once a student for the priesthood, he has become an embittered existentialist. His belief is that his neighbors have to lose everything before they will understand anything or be able to see themselves and their world. Only then, as in Cesira's case, will they grow in understanding and compassion as well.

As the months pass and Cesira's store of money shrinks, she and Rosetta come to know something of the meaning of suffering, for their life becomes a struggle for survival among the brutal and vicious peasants. Some of their neighbors disappear, taken away by the Germans. Allied bombers raid Fondi. Two English escapees appear; they are fed and sent on their way. The daily acts of living, boredom, small excitements, and details unimportant in themselves show the people of the area as they really are, not in peace but in wartime, when respect for law and order and the fear of God no longer exist.

The liberation, not the war, brings about the ruin of Rosetta, who is raped by a group of French Moroccan troops in a ruined church. Following this experience the young woman becomes promiscuous, causing her mother to lose all belief in decency and goodness. Rosetta takes up with a flashy young black marketeer named Clorindo, Concetta's brutal son Rosario, and others of a gang of young toughs that the war has spawned. Rosetta had been the second victim of the debacle; Michele was killed by fleeing Germans. Out of these terrible events, however, compassion, sorrow, and true

understanding are reborn. Cesira discovers the evil in herself, and, with a sense of renewed hope, mother and daughter return to Rome.

Critical Evaluation:

Alberto Moravia's first novel, *Gli indifferenti* (1929; *The Indifferent Ones*, 1932; also known as *The Time of Indifference*, 1953), published when he was only twenty-one years old, preceded by several years the existential writings of Jean-Paul Sartre. Existentialism, in Sartre's words, is nothing more than an attempt to draw all the consequences of a coherent atheistic position. Existentialism declares that even if God exists, God's existence changes nothing. Existentialism, being a doctrine of action, is basically optimistic. It has frequently been found to be the opposite, however, given its severe and uncompromising bleakness. Existentialism was born of the falling away in Europe from the Christian faith. Philosophers and writers such as Albert Camus and Sartre in France, Martin Heidegger in Germany, and Moravia in Italy, in taking a hard look at the truth of existence in the twentieth century, have been dubbed pessimists. Messengers of a wicked world, they have been mistakenly called wicked themselves.

Existentialism is interested in authentic acts, acts done for their own sake, for the sake of the conscience of the doer, and not to impress others. At times, Moravia takes an extreme view, whereby the authentic can exist only as a dream, fantasy, or thought; any attempt to implement the authentic is bound to degrade it. Throughout *Two Women*, Cesira, the narrator, displays differing qualities of thought. As soon as it enters the world of action, her mental life finds itself compromised. Existence is filled with contradictions; for example, Cesira is forced to depend on the goodwill of people she loathes and despises. People justify even the most barbaric behavior with words. The double role of language is shown clearly in this book: how it is used to cover things up, even to hide the meaning of a person's deeds from the speaker, but how, from time to time, language can speak truth.

Moravia is very skillful at depicting Cesira's inner life through her narration. As the narrator; she is the reader's primary source of information, but her judgment of situations and persons is not necessarily accurate—it is colored by her own biases. She can be admired or deplored according to whether her thought is firsthand and forthright or secondhand and (often) manipulative. The reader's enjoyment of the book lies chiefly in the way Moravia gets in touch with truth.

The reader shares Cesira's innermost registrations; with the rest of the characters, the reader knows only what the characters say and do in the presence of others. It is noteworthy how often their words find no grounding in reality. They speak to make others or themselves feel better (or worse), but seldom to any good purpose or, indeed, to any circumstance capable of realization. Meanwhile, the novel's most significant actions are accompanied by few, if any, words.

Moravia writes of what happens in wartime because of his firsthand experience of it, but also because something of human beings' essential nature can be glimpsed when law and order no longer prevail. Removed from the habits, goals, and insulation of peacetime, human beings find the imminence of death more difficult to ignore, while hunger and dread of the unknown drive them to uncharacteristic deeds—although Moravia might well assert that only under such circumstances are people's deeds truly characteristic. War accelerates change—desperate circumstances call for desperate measures; people are compelled to deeds that they never would have dreamed of doing in peacetime. Apparently insurmountable obstacles are circumvented on occasion through inventiveness.

By the war's end, a new morality—which Cesira, for one, finds to be merely amorality—has come into being. Moravia does not say that this is good or bad, only that it is so, and that, when conditions alter drastically, people need to begin anew by acknowledging these changes rather than by denying them and clinging mindlessly to past codes of conduct. There may be a deplorable decline in values as a result of the war, but what Rosetta and Rosario and Clorindo have to tell Cesira about this postwar world must also be considered. It may be, as Cesira says, that with peacetime many people will gradually return to time-honored standards of decency. What is certain, however, is that not everybody will, and a new strain of thinking has entered the European mind, of which World War II is at once cause and symptom, and of which *Two Women* is an early and gripping analysis.

Two Women concerns death and rebirth, and this is made evident by the importance accorded in the novel to the biblical story of Lazarus. Michele, an intellectual who is sympathetically presented, tells the story and then assures his listeners that it applies to each one of them. They are as good as dead, and until they acknowledge this they stand no chance of being brought back to life—as Lazarus was raised by Christ. Only after Cesira has contemplated and then rejected suicide (upon the advice of Michele's ghost), only after she has dreamed herself as good as dead, and only after she and her daughter feel sorrow stir the pity that was dead in them, can these two women slowly awaken to their new, postwar existence.

This book can be chilling in its implications: Civilization is a thin veneer through which barbarism is always likely to break. There is a relief, even a hope, in this acknowledgment, however, for it shows how words, so often applied to misrepresent and mislead, can occasionally be organized to embody a truth of people's condition. One leaves this novel with a chastened sense of one's ability to control one's fate but also with the feeling that one has been helped to look life full in the face.

"Critical Evaluation" by David Bromige

Further Reading

Dego, Giuliano. *Moravia*. Edinburgh: Oliver & Boyd, 1966. Provides a valuable overview of Moravia's early work, with discussion centering on his naturalistic presentation, his remarkable descriptive ability, his major theme of alienation, and his ceaseless exploration of crises. Includes discussion of *Two Women*.

Heiney, Donald. *Three Italian Novelists*. Ann Arbor: University of Michigan Press, 1968. Examines the novels of Moravia, Cesare Pavese, and Elio Vittorini. Focuses on the technical aspects of the authors' writing and the political and psychosocial aspects of their works.

Lewis, R. W. B. "Alberto Moravia: Eros and Existence." In *From "Verismo" to Experimentalism*, edited by Sergio Pacifici. Bloomington: Indiana University Press, 1969. Describes Moravia as a minor master of the strategy of "artistic conversion, of the transformation of one set of values into another," and succinctly analyzes the "sexualization" of objects, values, and relationships in Moravia's fiction.

Moravia, Alberto, and Alain Elkann. *Life of Moravia*. Translated by William Weaver. South Royalton, Vt.: Steerforth Italia, 2000. Biographical work takes the form of an extended interview of Moravia by his friend Elkann. Moravia discusses his life, his writing, and the events that shaped his imagination, shedding light on the way his experiences influenced his fiction. Weaver, who knew Moravia, provides an introduction in which he discusses the writer.

Peterson, Thomas Erling. *Alberto Moravia*. New York: Twayne, 1996. Provides comprehensive coverage of Moravia's life and works. Includes critical analysis of his major works as well as information on his personal and public activities. Describes the political climate in Italy at the time Moravia was writing and its relevance to Moravia's life.

Ross, Joan, and Donald Freed. *The Existentialism of Alberto*

Moravia. Carbondale: Southern Illinois University Press, 1972. Thorough analysis places Moravia's work within the context of the literature and philosophy of existentialism, underscoring the considerable significance of the concepts of love, suffering, and reality in Moravia's work.

Stella, M. John. *Self and Self-Compromise in the Narratives of Pirandello and Moravia*. New York: Peter Lang, 2000. Analyzes works by Moravia and Luigi Pirandello to examine how they treat issues of identity, focusing on how the two writers' concepts of individual identity were influenced by Buddhist doctrines.

Two Years Before the Mast

Author: Richard Henry Dana, Jr. (1815-1882)
First published: 1840
Type of work: Memoir

Principal personage:
RICHARD HENRY DANA, JR.

The Story:

In August, 1834, Richard Henry Dana, Jr., ships aboard the brig *Pilgrim* out of Boston for a voyage to California as an ordinary seaman. He hopes that the journey will relieve his eye trouble, and upon his return he plans to reenter Harvard College. Since Dana is a greenhorn, he is forced to bunk in the steerage instead of in the forecastle with the other sailors. At first his duties are confusing, doubly so during the first two days, for he is violently seasick. He soon finds his sea legs, however, and quickly learns shipboard routine: During the day, all of the sailors are kept busy cleaning and repairing the ship, and during the night they take turns standing watch.

The voyage is uneventful until October, when the *Pilgrim* passes near the mouth of the River Plate. Here Dana encounters his first real storm at sea. After that, the weather begins to get cold, and the crew prepares to round Cape Horn. The seas there are high, and the crew battles snow and hail. Everyone's clothing is perpetually wet. By mid-November, the ship rounds the Horn and heads north.

The first mishap of the voyage occurs soon after, when a young sailor is swept overboard. A boat lowered to search for him finds no trace of the lost man. In accordance with custom, the captain auctions off the dead man's clothing. Near the end of November the brig makes the island of Juan Fernandez and drops anchor for the first time since departing from Boston. Dana is glad to see land and manages to get on shore for a short time. As soon as the ship takes on fresh water, however, it weighs anchor and heads on for California.

Shortly after Christmas, Dana is acknowledged to be experienced enough to move into the forecastle with the other crew members. Now he is a real seaman. By the middle of

January, the *Pilgrim* makes her first California port at Santa Barbara. Dana learns that his work for the next year will be to load cattle hides into the ship. The sailors carry the stiff, undressed hides out through the surf on their heads and deposit them in a boat, whose crew takes the hides to the ship and stows them away.

Once the hides are on board, the *Pilgrim* takes on some passengers and sails northward to Monterey. There, Mexican customs officers inspect the cargo, after which the company agent aboard the ship sets up a store to trade with the townspeople. The crew is kept busy on a shuttle service between ship and shore. Because he has some knowledge of languages, Dana becomes the interpreter for the *Pilgrim* and is sent ashore on errands that require a knowledge of Spanish. In this way, he becomes acquainted with the town and its people. He finds the Spaniards to be pleasant but lazy; most of the trade is carried out by foreigners. Everyone owns horses, and they are so plentiful that the price of a fine animal is very low.

When business begins to fall off, the *Pilgrim* returns to Santa Barbara to collect more cattle hides from shore. At that time, trouble begins to brew aboard ship. The captain, mates, and crew are at odds. One day, when the captain begins to flog a sailor unjustly, another of the crew remonstrates, whereupon the captain flogs him, too. The sailors are angry, but they have no higher power to which they can appeal, for the captain's word is law. Her hold laden with hides, the *Pilgrim* sails for San Diego.

In San Diego, Dana gets his first shore leave. After drinking for a time with the rest of the crew, he and a friend hire horses and ride to a nearby mission, where they are able to get a good Mexican meal, a welcome change from the salt beef served aboard ship.

The undressed hides are unloaded from the *Pilgrim* and placed in a large shed on the beach, where they are to be dressed and stored until a later time. Just when the ship finishes unloading and is ready to set sail, a man deserts ship. After an unsuccessful search, the brig puts to sea without him.

The *Pilgrim* takes on more hides at San Pedro and then continues on to Santa Barbara. It is the Lenten season, and Dana sees the celebrations ashore. The ship gathers more hides at several places and returns to San Diego. After the hides are unloaded, the captain sends Dana and another man ashore to assist with the dressing of the hides. Then the ship sails north on another coastal voyage.

Dana becomes acquainted with several Sandwich Islanders who live on the beach and work with him; he finds them to be generous men and true friends. Some of his spare time he spends reading books and studying navigation. Each day, he has to take care of a certain number of hides, which have to be cleaned, soaked in brine, scraped, dried, beaten, and stored away.

When the ship *Alert* arrives at San Diego, Dana, anxious to be at sea again, exchanges places with a boy aboard the ship. The *Alert* belongs to the same company as the *Pilgrim* and is to take on the accumulated hides and carry them to Boston. The *Pilgrim* is not scheduled to return to Boston until later. The two vessels exchange captains, and Dana is under the same master as before, but because the first mate of the *Alert* is a good officer, Dana finds conditions much more pleasant in his new berth.

Loading hides, the *Alert* moves up and down the coast for several months. In mid-November, 1835, the ship leaves Santa Barbara with some passengers bound for Monterey. When a terrific gale comes up, however, the ship is unable to put in at Monterey and goes on up the coast to San Francisco. The ship continues working up and down the coast until there are enough hides at San Diego to make a full cargo. In May, the *Alert* heads south for Cape Horn.

Rounding the Horn on the return journey is even worse than on the way out. Just when he is needed most on deck, Dana is laid low with a toothache. For days everyone has to work extra hours because of the danger from icebergs. Finally, the *Alert* gets clear of the ice and runs before a strong wind around Cape Horn.

Once the ship enters the Atlantic tropics, the weather is fair except for occasional violent storms. Some of the men begin to come down with the scurvy, but they are cured after the crew obtains fresh vegetables from a passing ship. On September 21, 1836, the *Alert* anchors in Boston Harbor. Hurriedly the crew performs its last duties in bringing the ship to the wharf. Within five minutes after the last rope is made fast, not one of the crew is left aboard.

Critical Evaluation:

If an attack of measles had not threatened the eyesight of Richard Henry Dana, Jr., and forced his withdrawal from Harvard, the United States would have lost one of the most popular travel adventure books, *Two Years Before the Mast*. Less arduous and unpredictable forms of convalescence certainly were available to a well-born young Bostonian. Dana's physical condition could not have been the only reason for his shipping out as a common sailor; his decision must, to some extent, have represented important psychological and emotional needs—to have an "adventure," to "test" himself and his "manhood," to separate himself, at least temporarily, from the narrow environment and conservative religious atmosphere of his family and social class.

Immediately after returning from his voyage, while finishing his studies at Harvard and then pursuing a law degree, Dana began to record his experiences anew, largely from memory, since his brother Frank lost the log he kept during the voyage. When the book was published in 1840, it became, to everyone's surprise, an instant commercial success. Ten years later, following the discovery of gold in California, it enjoyed a second burst of popularity, for it was almost the only book available that dealt with the early California environment. Dana profited little from the book in a material way; discouraged in his attempts to find a publisher, he sold all rights to the work to *Harper's Magazine* for $250.

Two Years Before the Mast probably remains popular because it combines two of the most popular motifs—those of the travel-adventure romance and the coming-of-age narrative—in a skillful, vivid manner. The genre of travel-adventure romance, which attracted writers as diverse and talented as James Fenimore Cooper, Herman Melville, Henry David Thoreau, Mark Twain, and Ernest Hemingway, was particularly popular in the mid-nineteenth century. Such narratives vicariously fulfill at least two emotional needs of the reader: the glorification of physical hardship and an identification with the overcoming of obstacles, especially nature itself, and an escape from the confines of a narrow, dull environment to a world of sensuous experience. *Two Years Before the Mast* combines much of the former and generous hints of the latter, especially in the description of quaint customs and free lifestyle of the Californians. The secret to the depiction of such an escape vision is to make the exotic, unknown world real to the reader, and this is where Dana succeeds brilliantly.

Although *Two Years Before the Mast* is autobiographical, many readers accepted it as fiction, a tribute to Dana's storytelling abilities. His prose style is direct, concrete, and muted, lacking the rhetorical embellishment so characteristic of most mid-nineteenth century writing but frequently laced with colloquial phraseology. On the whole, the book does not depend on exciting adventures or bizarre situations but rather on careful, restrained descriptions of the seamen's everyday routines and activities, punctuated by periodic crises that Dana renders in vivid, dramatic scenes. The book capitalizes on what has always been one of the primary appeals of "realistic" writing, the intimate description of a profession or activity that seems exotic to the reader.

Moreover, *Two Years Before the Mast* is almost the only nineteenth century narrative of life at sea—Melville not excepted—that does not romanticize the common sailor. Dana likes his mates but presents them as flawed, distinctive human beings, who labor at a very dangerous, difficult job in which they show courage, endurance, and tenacity.

The coming-of-age theme in *Two Years Before the Mast* is given a special twist by the fact that Dana, the initiate, is a young, relatively naïve, religiously conservative Boston aristocrat who thrusts himself into a trial among crude, uneducated, generally amoral sailors. He must not only move from youth to manhood and from innocence to experience but also from outsider to member of a subculture. Throughout the book there is, on his side, a constant tension between his aristocratic inclinations and sensibilities and his democratic convictions and the desire to identify with his cohorts; on the part of the crew, there is a resentment of Dana for his social background and intellectual pretensions coupled with an admiration for his growth and development as an efficient, hardworking seaman.

In the beginning of the book, Dana is obviously a novice, and the crew isolates him in steerage. He learns quickly, however, and gives a good account of himself in the first bad storm. He also establishes the pattern of volunteering for every difficult and dangerous job that comes up, a trait that brings him admiration from the crew as well as a reputation for foolhardiness. When a young sailor is washed overboard, Dana confronts sudden death at sea and comes to learn the superficially joking attitude the men have toward danger and mortality. His view of the basic futility of their lives is crystallized in the summation: "A sailor's life is at best but a mixture of little good with much evil, and a little pleasure with much pain. The beautiful is linked with the revolting, the sublime with the commonplace, and the solemn with the ludicrous."

His initiation into the institutional side of sailing and the justice of the high seas comes when Captain Thompson flogs two men for trivial reasons. Young Dana knew of the captain's absolute power, but not until watching an almost demented, hysterical captain viciously flogging the men did he realize the full meaning of the law. It was at this point that Dana committed himself to fighting for a reform of the maritime laws that allowed such flagrant and arbitrary injustice—a commitment to which he remained true all of his life.

The flogging scene leads directly to his most serious moral dilemma. Throughout the book, Dana tries to identify with the sailors, but, when threatened with a possible disruption of his own career plans, Dana invokes the family name and his place is taken by a less well situated substitute. He tries to mitigate the use of family influence by giving the substitute a handsome share of his pay, but the moral onus remains.

Two Years Before the Mast is an intelligent, exciting, sensitive story of a young man's transition to maturity, a vivid, convincing description of human beings' struggle with the elements and with themselves, an accurate account of life at sea, a colorful portrait of life in California in the early nineteenth century, and a series of colorful, dramatic vignettes. Had Dana decided to devote his life to letters, his writings might very well be today compared to those of his contemporary and friend, Melville. Instead, he chose law, lecturing, and public service, where he had a moderately successful, if unspectacular, career. Although he was proud of its wide appeal, in time Dana came to consider *Two Years Before the Mast* as a boys' book and to recall his maritime adventures almost as a youthful fling. Little did Dana realize, as he stood on the bow of the *Alert* in 1836 pondering what to do with the rest of his life, that he already lived the most important part of it.

"Critical Evaluation" by Keith Neilson

Further Reading

Aaron, Daniel. "Two Boston Fugitives: Dana and Parkman." In *American Literature, Culture, and Ideology: Essays in Memory of Henry Nash Smith*. New York: Peter Lang, 1990. Compares *Two Years Before the Mast* and Francis Parkman's *The California and Oregon Trail* (1849). Though purportedly factual, both incorporate fictive devices, such as psychologically motivated background descriptions and characters whose personalities affect events that are narrated suspensefully. Stresses the authors' family and vocational pressures.

Dana, Richard Henry. *Two Years Before the Mast: A Personal Narrative of Life at Sea*. Introduction by Gary Kinder, notes by Duncan Hasell. New York: Modern Library, 2001. In addition to the text of Dana's book, this edition contains an introduction discussing the book, notes, a glossary, illustrations, and a guide to reading group questions.

Gale, Robert L. *Richard Henry Dana, Jr.* New York: Twayne, 1969. Includes an analysis of the narrative movement, structure, rhetoric, and tone of *Two Years Before the Mast*. Places it in the context of other American journey books.

Lawrence, D. H. *Studies in Classic American Literature*. New York: Seltzer, 1923. This insightful work includes a discussion of the flogging Dana observes and his response to it, his mysterious toothache, and the power of the sea and Dana's descriptions of it.

Peck, John. *Maritime Fiction: Sailors and the Sea in British and American Novels, 1719-1917*. New York: Palgrave, 2001. Analyzes the relationship among fiction, the sea, and national identity in numerous novels, including *Two Years Before the Mast*, which is discussed in chapter 5. Peck describes how these novels express the difference between the sometimes brutal life on the sea and the more civilized values of life on the shore.

Philbrick, Thomas. *James Fenimore Cooper and the Development of American Sea Fiction*. Cambridge, Mass.: Harvard University Press, 1961. Contrasts Dana's realistically accurate depiction of life at sea with Cooper's more romantic treatment in his early sea fiction.

Typee
A Peep at Polynesian Life

Author: Herman Melville (1819-1891)
First published: 1846
Type of work: Novel
Type of plot: Adventure
Time of plot: Mid-nineteenth century
Locale: Marquesas Islands

Principal characters:
HERMAN MELVILLE (TOM), an American sailor
TOBY, his friend
MEHEVI, the chief of the Typees
KORY-KORY, a native servant
FAYAWAY, a native girl
MARNOO, a native taboo man

The Story:

The whaler *Dolly* was long at sea, and the men are discontented and restless when the captain finally gives orders to put in at Nukuheva, one of the Marquesas Islands. This is the chance for which Tom and Toby, two young sailors, are waiting. Even though the natives of the island are known to be cannibals, Tom and Toby desert the ship and flee inland, planning to hide until the *Dolly* sails. They hope to then sign aboard another ship where they would get better treatment.

Tom and Toby begin their flight with only a few biscuits for food. On the first night away from the ship, Tom contracts a disease that causes his leg to swell, and he is in much pain. Nevertheless, he and Toby continue. At last, when their food is all gone, they realize that they can stay alive only by giving themselves up to one of the savage tribes that inhabits the island.

They discover too late that the natives to whom they surrender themselves are the Typee tribe, the most ferocious cannibals on Nukuheva. Tom and Toby are treated with respect, however, and are given food and comfortable quarters. All the natives come to see the strangers. Mehevi, the chief of the

Typees, appoints Kory-Kory as personal servant to Tom. The captives go to live in the home of Tinor, Kory-Kory's mother. Mehevi has a medicine man examine Tom's swollen leg, but the native remedies have no effect on the disease.

Tom, unable to walk, spends most of his time reclining in the house while Kory-Kory attends to his needs. A beautiful young maiden, Fayaway, is also his constant companion. She, among all the Typees, seems to understand the painful situation of the two captives. Toby convinces the Typees that he should be allowed to return to the main harbor on the island to seek medical aid for Tom. On the trail, he is attacked by hostile warriors from a neighboring tribe, and he returns to the Typees with an ugly head wound.

A few days later, Toby discovers a boat offshore. He is allowed to go down by the beach, but Tom is detained in his house. Toby promises to bring medical aid to Tom within three days, but the three days pass without the return of Toby. Tom can learn nothing from the natives; he realizes that now he is the single captive of the Typees. Somewhat recovered, he is allowed to roam almost at will within the country of the

Typees, but he is always accompanied by Kory-Kory, and there is no chance for escape.

As Tom's leg improves, he begins to indulge in the pleasures allowed him and to observe the native life with interest. The Typees seem to exist in a perpetual state of happiness, interrupted only by skirmishes with neighboring tribes. One of Tom's greatest pleasures is to paddle a canoe about a small lake in company with Fayaway. For the privilege of taking Fayaway with him, he has to ask special permission, since entering a canoe is ordinarily taboo for a woman.

One day a handsome stranger appears among the Typees bearing news from other parts of the island. He is Marnoo, a taboo man, who is free to go among all the tribes without harm. When Tom learns that Marnoo knows English, he asks the native to help him escape. This Marnoo cannot do for fear of arousing the anger of the Typees.

The daily life of the natives is extremely regular. Each morning they bathe and eat breakfast. After the meal, they smoke their pipes. The rest of the morning they spend sleeping, conversing, or doing odd jobs about their houses. The men often spend the afternoon in the large meetinghouse of Mehevi; there they relax and joke in a sort of bachelors' club. Before the evening meal, they bathe again. After the meal, the young girls entertain the rest with dancing. Everyone retires at an early hour.

Tom is present at the Feast of the Calabashes. It seems to have some religious significance, but most of the time is spent in eating and drinking. During the two days of the festival, Tom decides that the natives do not take their religion seriously. They possess many idols not treated with any high degree of respect. The most universal religious observance is that of tattooing; everyone is tattooed upon the face, even the women. The bodies of some of the men are completely covered with intricate designs.

Since the men outnumber the women in the tribe, the women often have two or three husbands, but the men never have more than one wife. All in the tribe seem happy with the various aspects of their social organization. Private property is limited to household goods; food is common property. All understand and follow the laws and customs of the tribe; there are never disputes among the Typees.

One day, a battle is fought between the Typees and a neighboring tribe. Afterward, the bodies of the dead enemies are taken to the ceremonial feasting place. For the next day or two, Tom is not allowed to leave the vicinity of his house. He suspects that the Typees are making a meal of their dead enemies. Later he discovers the remains of the meal and finds that he is correct, though the Typees deny that they are cannibals.

A few days later, Marnoo again appears among the Typees. This time he tells Tom to try to escape by means of the same path by which he left. Tom is unable to leave the village, however, for Kory-Kory keeps close watch on him day and night.

Not many days after Marnoo leaves, the Typees excitedly announce the approach of a boat. Tom argues with the natives and finally persuades them to let him go to the beach. He has some difficulty in getting there, since his leg begins to swell again. At the beach, Tom finds a boat from an Australian ship standing just outside the surf. Marnoo tells the Australian captain of Tom's trouble, and he sends a boat loaded with presents to obtain Tom's release. The Typees, however, have no wish to release their captive. In desperation, Tom breaks away from the guard placed around him and plunges into the surf. He manages to reach the boat, and the sailors pull away from shore. Thus ends Tom's captivity among the Typees. His only regret is in leaving the faithful Kory-Kory and the beautiful Fayaway.

Many years later Tom again meets Toby and learns from him that he intended to return to the aid of his injured friend, but he was tricked into boarding a vessel that sailed from Nukuheva the following day. It is only long after Toby gave Tom up for lost that the two friends learn of each other's fate after their separation.

Critical Evaluation:

Herman Melville's assertion in *Moby Dick* (1851) that a whale ship was his Yale and Harvard reminds readers of how central to his development the sea adventures of his youth were and how strongly they would shape his writing. It was from the whaler *Acushnet* that Melville jumped ship in the Marquesas to spend a few weeks among the Nukuheva natives. The episode ended, sooner and less dramatically than in *Typee*, when he departed the island on another whaler, eventually to join the American warship *United States*, for a voyage back to Boston. Though the adventure ended in actuality, it began imaginatively for Melville only when he sought to discover its meaning in the fictionalized account of his sojourn among the cannibals that he called *Typee*. Though actually a novel based upon experience, *Typee* was regarded generally as simply a travel narrative when it appeared, and the work's reputation since has had to fight against that classification. In fact, *Typee* contains more of the basic elements of Melville's later fiction than its detractors have realized, and it deserves a primary place among such other early works as *Redburn* (1849) and *White-Jacket* (1850) that give meaning to the idea of Melville's education on board the ships he sailed as a young man.

The essential facts of *Typee*, except for the time, which Melville considerably exaggerates, are true. He did jump ship in company of a friend named Toby Greene and spent a few weeks among the natives of the Typee valley, where he enjoyed a somewhat ambiguous status as a prisoner-guest. Melville did injure his leg escaping the *Acushnet* and allowed Toby to go for medical supplies. Toby failed to return, having been shanghaied by another whaler, and, after a few weeks Melville was taken off the island by a whaler in search of crewmen. The novel, however, is more than the sum of these few facts, and it cannot be done justice by a reading that regards it as no more than a slightly fictionalized autobiographical narrative. Far from simply recounting his adventures, in *Typee* Melville is examining the fundamental ambiguities in humanity and nature that would characterize his best work as the basis for the unanswerable questions his novels propose.

From its very beginning, the boys' journey into the Typee valley promises to be more than it seems. Running not only from the ship and its cruelly authoritarian master but also from the world of the coast natives, which has been hopelessly corrupted by sailors, administrators, and missionaries, these adventurers make their way down a precipitous route that carries them metaphorically backward in time as it takes them beyond the reach of civilization. Eventually reaching the valley floor, the boys initially encounter Typee (which they still believe to be Happar) as a new paradise. Not only the fecundity and lushness of the rich valley but also the young lovers who are the first inhabitants encountered point to the discovery of a South Seas Eden. This vision of innocence and beauty in the South Seas islands was, to some extent, typical of nineteenth century Romanticism, with its recurrent theme of the noble savage, but Melville, even this early in his career, was no typical Romantic writer.

From the time Tom (now renamed Tommo) settles, albeit unwillingly, into life with the Typees, Melville begins to develop on him a series of symbols that point to the fundamental ambiguity that lies at the heart of the island "paradise." On the one hand, the simplicity, loyalty, and unselfconscious devotion offered by Kory-Kory, and, more particularly, the innocent love and natural sexuality of Fayaway, keep alive the vision of an Edenic garden. On the other hand, Tommo's discovery that he is in the land of the dread Typees rather than among the peaceful Happars leads to his fear of cannibalism, the most dreaded of all humanity's aberrations. Tommo's injured leg, which mysteriously grows worse as his suspicions of cannibalism near confirmation, becomes an objective correlative for his sick spirit, which, cut off from the civilization it sought to escape, languishes. Tattooing also develops a

symbolic value, since it would complete the initiation into the Typean world begun with the ritual name change. Once tattooed, Tommo will never again be able to return to his own world.

The essential ambiguity in *Typee* centers on the prospect of a paradise corrupted at its heart by the horror of cannibalism. In later years, Melville would assert that he could look upon a horror and be familiar with it, but this is not so of Tommo, who cannot reconcile himself to this discovery. More generally, the implications of the innate evil of *Typee* seriously challenge the view of optimistic philosophers of Melville's period who argued that the universe and humanity were essentially good, evil being only an appearance rather than a reality. Tommo might like to think that he, as a civilized human being, somehow transcends the essentially savage nature of humankind, but Melville will not have it so. In the escape scene, Tommo repays the hospitality of his hosts by driving the boat hook into the throat of one of his recent friends. Even as Tommo feels the horror of his violent act, readers feel the horror of Melville's world in which the savage impulse dwells even in the most civilized breast.

Though perhaps less orderly than this reading suggests, Melville's symbols are clearly present, and they serve to put his vision in a direct line of descent from that of his Calvinist forebears who endorsed the doctrine of the essential depravity of humanity. It is only because the symbols are tentative and nascent, rather than fully developed into Melville's mature symbolism, that *Typee* must be seen more as an anticipation of later Melville than as a fully realized work of art in itself. *Typee* does reveal, however, how early Melville began to develop the symbolic mode that would become the hallmark of his greatest novels, and how soon he began to discover those unsolvable questions of the nature of good and evil that would preoccupy him throughout his career.

"Critical Evaluation" by William E. Grant

Further Reading

Bloom, Harold, ed. *Herman Melville.* New ed. New York: Bloom's Literary Criticism, 2008. Collection of critical essays analyzing Melville's work, including Bryan C. Short's piece "'The Author at the Time': Tommo and Melville's Self-Discovery in *Typee.*"

Bryant, John, ed. *Melville Unfolding: Sexuality, Politics, and the Versions of "Typee," a Fluid-Text Analysis, with an Edition of the "Typee" Manuscript.* Ann Arbor: University of Michigan Press, 2008. The manuscript of *Typee,* Melville's most popular novel during his lifetime, was discovered in 1983. Bryant focuses on the "invisible text of revision" in the manuscript, describing how Melville altered his text to create the final version of the novel. This book is linked to an electronic edition of *Typee* to enable readers to chart Melville's process of creating his novel.

Delbanco, Andrew. *Melville: His World and Work.* New York: Knopf, 2005. Delbanco's critically acclaimed biography places Melville in his time, including the debate over slavery and the details of life in 1840's New York. Delbanco also discusses the significance of Melville's works at the time they were published and their reception into the twenty-first century.

Herbert, T. Walter. *Marquesan Encounters: Melville and the Meaning of Civilization.* Cambridge, Mass.: Harvard University Press, 1980. An examination of *Typee* and two other nineteenth century narratives of Americans in the South Seas in the context of how Marquesan societies were irreparably damaged by contacts with white people during this era. Provides excellent readings of the political and the religious dimensions of Melville's book.

Kelley, Wyn. "'Making Literary Use of the Story': *Typee* and *Omoo.*" In *Herman Melville: An Introduction.* Malden, Mass.: Blackwell, 2008. Chronicles Melville's development as a writer, providing analyses of his works.

_____, ed. *A Companion to Herman Melville.* Malden, Mass.: Blackwell, 2006. Collection of thirty-five original essays aimed at twenty-first century readers of Melville's works. Includes discussions of Melville's travels; Melville and religion, slavery, and gender; and the Melville

revival. Also includes the essay "The Motive for Metaphor: *Typee, Omoo,* and *Mardi*" by Geoffrey Sanborn.

Lawrence, D. H. *Studies in Classic American Literature.* New York: Penguin Books, 1978. Lawrence was important in the rediscovery and the reevaluation of Melville in the 1920's. Lawrence's book contains two essays on Melville, including one on *Typee* and *Omoo.*

Levine, Robert S., ed. *The Cambridge Companion to Herman Melville.* New York: Cambridge University Press, 1998. An indispensable tool for the student of Melville, this collection of essays includes discussions of Melville and sexuality, his "traveling god," and "'Race' in *Typee* and *White-Jacket*" by Samuel Otter.

Melville, Herman. *Typee: Complete Text with Introduction, Historical Contexts, Critical Essays.* Edited by Geoffrey Sanborn. Boston: Houghton Mifflin, 2004. In addition to the text of the novel, this volume contains essays written by Melville's predecessors and contemporaries that provide historical context for the depiction of sexuality, tattooing, cannibalism, and taboo in the novel, explaining why the work stirred controversy in its time.

Rogin, Michael Paul. *Subversive Genealogy: The Politics and Art of Herman Melville.* Berkeley: University of California Press, 1985. Incisive psychological and Marxist reading of Melville's life and work, arguing that he is one of the leading thinkers of his age. The book's reading of Melville's family's place in the historical context of the 1840's is unparalleled.

Typical American

Author: Gish Jen (1955-   )
First published: 1991
Type of work: Novel
Type of plot: Tragicomedy and social realism
Time of plot: 1940's-1960's
Locale: China, New York City, and suburban Connecticut

Principal characters:
YIFENG "RALPH" CHANG, a Chinese immigrant
THERESA CHANG, his older sister, also an immigrant
HELEN CHANG, her immigrant friend, later married to Ralph
GROVER DING, a Chinese American businessman
JANIS, Helen's Chinese American friend
OLD CHAO, an engineering professor, who has an affair with Helen
CALLIE and MONA, Helen and Ralph's American-born daughters

The Story:

Yifeng Chang leaves China for the United States and graduate study in engineering. He is given the name Ralph by the foreign affairs secretary of the university he attends in New York City. Ralph, however, cannot return to China because, in 1948, Chinese communists take over Manchuria. U.S. authorities will not allow him to return to his homeland,

and he fails to take their offer to become a U.S. citizen. He soon has visa problems and has to move constantly to avoid immigration authorities. He is forced to drop out of school and ends up with no job, no family, no education, and no visa.

Ralph's older sister, Theresa Chang, is living in China and is engaged to be married. Her fiancé, however, runs off with his father's concubine, so Theresa takes a job with a delicate young woman in Shanghai, who becomes her friend. When the communists take over their homeland, the two women emigrate to the United States, and Theresa renames her new friend Helen. She meets Ralph, who falls in love with her. The two soon marry and move into an apartment, a rundown walk-up in Manhattan, with Theresa.

Helen has a difficult time adjusting to her new life in the United States, even with Ralph and Theresa in her life. She attends English classes, becomes pregnant, and, one day, even manages to fix the apartment-building heater herself. Theresa is in medical school. To motivate Ralph to go back to school, both women soon claim that they have lost their scholarships. Helen becomes friends with Janis, a woman in her English class who is married to a professor, Old Chao. Chao is Ralph's colleague in the university's engineering department.

Helen and Janis plot to fix Theresa up with Grover Ding, a fully assimilated and apparently successful Chinese American businessman. Theresa gets her medical degree, and Ralph finishes his degree and gets a tenure-track job at the university. Ralph and Helen have two daughters, Callie and then Mona.

Time passes, and the three immigrants become U.S. citizens. Ralph gets his driver license and then buys a car. All three adults now feel that they are citizens of the "new world," where dreams do come true. Theresa and Old Chao begin a discreet affair, Helen and Ralph and Theresa buy a house in suburban Connecticut, and Ralph gets tenure in his engineering department.

Soon, the American Dream becomes a disappointment. Ralph finds his job at the university boring, so he joins Grover in a business deal that involves buying a franchise for take-out chicken. Ralph, too, has been "infected" with the American money virus. He takes a leave of absence from the university, takes over the fast-food store, and spends all his time working on increasing the store's success. Ralph and Helen buy new appliances and Ralph cheats a little on his taxes. He also begins drinking beer at dinner with Grover, who hangs around the house, apparently in pursuit of Theresa. The Changs have become almost fully Americanized.

Ralph is cruel to Theresa, taunting her for her affairs, and she moves out and into her own apartment. Grover begins his seduction of Helen. Ralph is now obsessed with his dreams of success and plans to turn his take-out franchise into a sit-down restaurant. Soon after the grand reopening, however, cracks appear in the building because it had been built on unstable land. Ralph and Helen discover that Grover, who has been jailed, apparently for tax evasion, had lured them into the business with full knowledge of its eventual failure.

The Changs buy a dog and call him Grover, in revenge for the man who had cheated them. Ralph gets back his old job at the university, but family tensions continue. Helen, conflicted about telling Ralph the truth about her affair with Grover, calls Ralph a failure. Ralph and Helen get into a fight, and he shoves her through a window, putting her in the hospital. Theresa, believing it is her duty, moves back into the Connecticut house with Ralph and Helen. She continues her affair with Old Chao, which Ralph and Helen come to tolerate. Old Chao lounges around their house as Grover once did.

Grover threatens to buy the woods behind the Changs' house. Ralph confronts him and discovers that he never was jailed for tax evasion, or anything else; Grover had told Ralph and Helen that story only to avoid them, and he also hints at his affair with Helen. Ralph takes Helen for a drive to get her to confess to the affair. When he returns home, he hits Theresa with the car. She is brought to the hospital and remains in a coma. Ralph and Helen are forced to sell their house to pay the hospital bills, and they move into a garden apartment. Sometime later, Theresa miraculously awakens from her coma, and Ralph recalls a final image from the previous summer—of Theresa and Old Chao on twin inflatable rafts in wading pools in their Connecticut backyard, a true American moment of pure pleasure and peace. The Americanization process has ended almost happily.

Critical Evaluation:

Gish Jen's *Typical American* recounts the story of Chinese immigrants in pursuit of the American Dream. It fictionalizes the assimilation process of one Chinese American family after World War II. The novel also is a probing, often comic look at larger issues in mid-twentieth century American society. What happens to the Changs is what happens to many Americans, to some degree—the dreams and the disillusionments, the successes and the failures—but the story illuminates the process from a fresh perspective. Jen's 1996 sequel to this novel, *Mona in the Promised Land*, follows the Changs' younger daughter as she navigates the difficult process of growing up in an upper-middle-class Westchester County community. The novel raises similar issues of ethnicity and assimilation with gentle humor.

Critics often cite Jen's similarities to other well-known Chinese American writers, especially Maxine Hong Kingston and Amy Tan, who also have written assimilation stories of characters with conflicting loyalties to two countries and stories of clashes between generations. A sign of the depth of Jen's fiction lies in her comparison to a broader cross-section of contemporary works and writers. Like these other writers, she clearly represents the strengths and weaknesses of American values and institutions.

The focus in *Typical American* is on the struggles of three Chinese immigrants to become fully American. Jen, though, also focuses on the lure and limitations of American society. All three characters literally think in Chinese—its language, folklore, and maxims—at the same time they are learning to speak English, to become fully American, and to think in English, or American, words. Theresa Chang is perhaps the most successful of the three main characters: She adjusts quickly to life in the United States, achieves status as a medical doctor, and even becomes a "typical" American by having an affair. Helen Chang feels least at home in the United States and has the most difficulty in letting go of traditional Chinese values, like the importance of family. Still, even she becomes resourceful and resilient.

It is Ralph, however, who is at the center of this tragicomedy and who most fully reinvents himself. He is successful in becoming an academic, but he wants money. He breaks up his extended family by forcing his sister, Theresa, to move out of his house, and he is the prime agent of financial loss and of his wife's affair.

Typical American tells the story of the American Dream through Asian eyes. Like European immigrants, who first see the Statue of Liberty, Asian immigrants first see the Golden Gate Bridge in San Francisco Bay as the symbol of passage. The formula for assimilation is the same for all, however.

In *Typical American*, Ralph imitates Benjamin Franklin's first formulation of the self-made man; he also tries to follow the "positive-thinking" advice of Norman Vincent Peale. Ralph's name should remind readers of the founder of the idea of American self-reliance and romantic individualism, Ralph Waldo Emerson. Ralph, too, is duped by a Chinese American (Grover Ding) who has been thoroughly assimilated and who has learned how to cheat others. Ralph's failure is to believe that money means success. He also fails because in believing so, he gives up the values, including his Chinese heritage, that have made him who he is. In the end, he comes to understand that he is not only a man of his dreams but also a man of his limitations. Earlier in the novel,

Ralph and Theresa and Helen criticize "typical American" faults, but by the end, Ralph recognizes that he has become a typical American in his failures as well. True assimilation, he now understands, means having a composite cultural identity of Chinese and American qualities.

Jen's successful literary style is marked by gentle humor and subtle imagery. Buildings, including their first apartment and their restaurant, are falling down around Ralph and his family, just as his own dreams collapse as he heads for his own downfall. The crumbling ceiling of his apartment drops dust all over him, and he becomes "white," a preview of his dreams. Also, Grover appears at the Chang house as a sort of genie with a magic lamp, there to make all of their dreams come true. He turns out, though, to be a trickster who uses his wiles to fool all of them.

David Peck

Further Reading

"About Gish Jen." *Ploughshares* 26, nos. 2/3 (2000): 217-222. A brief but comprehensive and informative profile of Jen and her work in a well-known and respected literary journal.

Lee, Rachel C. *The Americas of Asian American Literature: Gendered Fictions of Nation and Transnation*. Princeton, N.J.: Princeton University Press, 1999. Chapter 2, "Gish Jen and the Gendered Codes of Americanness," is a thorough, detailed analysis of *Typical American* that identifies many of the issues included in the novel, such as gender, class, and race.

Partridge, Jeffrey F. L. *Beyond Literary Chinatown*. Seattle: University of Washington Press, 2007. Chapter 7, "Beyond Multicultural: Cultural Hybridity in the Novels of Gish Jen," includes analysis of both *Typical American* and its sequel, *Mona in the Promised Land*, and argues that cultural assimilation leads to a hybrid sense of Asian American identity.

Xiaojing, Zhou. "Becoming American: Gish Jen's *Typical American*." In *The Immigrant Experience in North American Literature: Carving Out a Niche*, edited by Katherine B. Payant and Toby Rose. Westport, Conn.: Greenwood Press, 1999. Xiaojing charts Jen's differences from an earlier generation of Chinese American writers that includes Maxine Hong Kingston, Amy Tan, and Frank Chin. Characters in *Typical American* make positive changes after they arrive in the United States, exemplifying Jen's theme of the paradox of freedom and freedom's limits.

U

The Ugly American

Authors: William J. Lederer (1912-2009) and Eugene
Burdick (1918-1965)
First published: 1958
Type of work: Novel
Type of plot: Political realism
Time of plot: 1950's
Locale: Sarkhan, Vietnam, Philippines, Cambodia, and
Burma

Principal characters:
Louis Sears, American ambassador to Sarkhan
John Colvin, American entrepreneur
Louis Krupitzyn, Soviet ambassador to Sarkhan
Father John X. Finian, Catholic American priest in
Burma
Joe Bing, U.S. public information officer in Sarkhan
Gilbert MacWhite, American ambassador to Sarkhan
Li Pang, Chinese representative of Chiang Kai-shek
Colonel Edwin B. Hillandale, American in the
Philippines
Major James "Tex" Wolchek, American serving in the
French Foreign Legion
Major Monet, French officer in the Legion
Thomas E. Knox, American poultry expert in Cambodia
Solomon Asch, American negotiator for Asian
Conference on Armaments
Homer Atkins, American engineer in Vietnam
Emma Atkins, Homer's wife
Senator Jonathan Brown, chairman of the Senate
Foreign Affairs Committee

The Story:

Ambassador Lou Sears, a political appointee, is angry at
the Sarkhanese newspaper for printing a defamatory cartoon.
Because he does not know the language, he does not understand the cartoon, but senses the derision that the cartoon expresses. John Colvin, an American businessman, has been
beaten and left for dead at the U.S. embassy's steps; Sears
hears about the incident but dismisses it. Colvin is a former
agent of the Office of Strategic Services (OSS), the World
War II-era precursor of the Central Intelligence Agency
(CIA). He has returned to Sarkhan to help in the fight against
communism and has enlisted the help of a former U.S.
ally, Deong, to sell powdered milk to improve native diets.
Deong, however, is now a communist; he attempted to poison the milk in order to engender anti-American sentiment.
Deong told the Sarkhanese that Colvin was putting aphrodi-
siacs into the milk to make Sarkhanese women sexually com-

pliant. They consequently attacked Colvin and left his body
at the embassy.

Louis Krupitzyn, the Soviet ambassador to Sarkhan, has
spent his life studying communism. He has learned the
Sarkhanese language and religion and molded himself physically and intellectually into the ideal Sarkhanese. As ambassador, he has visited and made friends with local religious
and government leaders. When the United States ships tons
of rice to Sarkhan in foreign aid, Krupitzyn changes the labels on the rice to read "Gift of Russia." The Americans do
not realize the labels have been changed because none of
them have learned Sarkhanese.

Father Finian, an American Catholic priest assigned to
Burma, vows to combat the communist religion. He travels
into the countryside, learning Burmese and enduring months
of dysentery. He then recruits native helpers, notably U Tien,

a jeep driver. They decide to work for freedom of religion, learning why the Burmese like communism and gathering information about the extent of local communist power and spies. They publish a small anticommunist newspaper. Communist publications attack their articles, and the communist faction seeks to locate and kill Finian's volunteers; the anticommunists fight back by broadcasting Russian speeches that belie the communists' propaganda. Despite Finian's success, Sears opposes him for "raising hell" and says his efforts are unnecessary. Sears damages American prestige with wild parties and malicious decisions against people such as Colvin and Finian.

Sears's replacement, Gilbert MacWhite, prepares for his post by studying the Sarkhanese language and culture and preparing to combat communism. However, while entertaining his Chinese friend Li Pang, he foolishly discusses strategy in front of his Chinese servants. Li tests and interrogates the servants, discovering that they have siphoned information to the communists. MacWhite, chagrined at his gullibility, vows to learn more about Southeast Asian politics. He learns that average Americans are good representatives in foreign countries, but bureaucrats are socially destructive. MacWhite hears about Colonel Hillandale, an American liaison officer in Manila who has influenced elections simply by associating and eating with Filipinos in the barrios and playing native tunes on his harmonica.

Major James Wolchek, a former American war hero, is serving with the French Foreign Legion in Vietnam under Major Monet. They lose countless villages to the communists. The communists are following Mao's rules of infiltration and guerilla warfare, while the French adhere to outmoded classical war strategies. After enduring dysentery, fever, parasites, mud, and communist torture, Monet decides to adopt Mao's tactics. He and Wolchek study guerilla warfare, and their first attempt to use it is successful. However, the American general, proud and unwilling to learn from Asians, refuses to change his strategies, and the colonial forces lose Hanoi.

Tom Knox, an Iowan agricultural expert in Cambodia, has learned to love the Cambodian people and their food, and he is liked throughout the country. He recommends better feed and medicine for Cambodia's poultry and wants to import better poultry stock, but his reports to the Foreign Mission are ignored, and the American Aid Mission does not want to hear about chickens. He is angry and vows to publicize his views back in America, but the French treat him to a luxury tour of the world, showering him with gifts, and he forgets about his hurt feelings.

Colonel Hillandale, assisting MacWhite in Sarkhan, learns that the Sarkhanese have great respect for palmistry. He reads palms at a diplomatic function, impressing foreign dignitaries including the prime minister, who follows Hillandale's advice and wants him to advise the king. A diplomatic aide, scornful of palmistry, neglects to inform Hillandale of his appointment with the king, losing an opportunity for positive American influence in the nation.

Solomon Asch, a shrewd union negotiator assigned to mediate an Asian conference on arms, heads the American delegation whose job is to decide what arms the United States will send to its Asian allies. Asch instructs the delegates not to attend drinking parties so they will be alert and arranges for translation into all Asian languages, not just French and English. The French and British want to dominate the conference, but Asch refuses to allow it. Asch is clever and capable, but one of the American delegates acquires a Chinese mistress and stays up nights partying. As a result, he is unprepared and sleepy during the negotiations; he offends the Burmese and the Indians, and the talks fail.

Homer Atkins is a hands-on American engineer in Vietnam who wants to help the people by building a brick factory, quarries, and canneries. Officials and bureaucrats who have never visited the countryside are more interested in building dams and roads for military purposes, and they refuse to listen to his ideas. MacWhite, however, is impressed with Atkins and invites him to Sarkhan. There, Atkins designs bicycle-powered water pumps for the rice paddies with Sarkhanese helpers and starts a mechanics magazine in Sarkhanese. Although the embassy disapproves of their efforts, their business succeeds. Meanwhile, Atkins's wife Emma wonders why all the old people have bent backs. She discovers they use short-handled brooms because they do not want to waste wood on long handles. Emma finds a reed with a longer stalk, plants it in front of her house, and lets neighbors see her making a long-handled broom and using it. Eventually, everyone grows these reeds, makes long-handled brooms, and, years later, they build a shrine to the woman who unbent the backs of the old.

Senator Jonathan Brown, chairman of the Senate Committee on Foreign Affairs, goes on a fact-finding tour of Southeast Asia, determined to find out what the situation really is. Ambassador Gray, in Vietnam, is warned of the senator's visit. Gray and his French counterpart orchestrate a tour, a brochure, an untruthful translator, and parties for the senator that keep Brown away from the Southeast Asian people and their reality, glorifying the status quo. Back in the Senate, Brown refutes all MacWhite's information, saying "I was there." MacWhite's suggestions for saving Sarkhan from the communists are rejected, and his resignation is requested.

Critical Evaluation:

In the prologue and epilogue to *The Ugly American*, William J. Lederer and Eugene Burdick state that their novel is not fiction: The personalities and episodes presented are factual, and only the names have been changed. The country of Sarkhan is fictional, but real countries, such as Laos, Thailand, Vietnam, and Burma, appear in the novel. The purpose of the novel is to bring to light what the authors see as abuses in the foreign service. They plead for diplomats to learn the language of the area in which they serve, read about it, get out of the major cities ("golden ghettoes") and into the countryside, and spend less of their time entertaining rich Americans. They argue that the United States spends too much money on the wrong aid projects while overlooking projects that would cost less and be more helpful. They warn that if members of the foreign service do not learn about communism and changes are not made, Southeast Asia will be lost to communism.

When this angry and cynical novel appeared in the late 1950's, it caused much political reaction. Many were convinced and angered by Lederer and Burdick's contentions; others disagreed. The book was denounced in the U.S. Senate by those whose policies it criticized, and the term "ugly American" became part of the national lexicon, describing Americans abroad who remain ethnocentric and insensitive to other cultures. Characters in the novel were traced by readers to real individuals whose names were only superficially changed. Whereas many at the time discounted the authors' characterizations of American problems in Southeast Asia, their forecasts of the victory of communist tactics in the area were borne out in subsequent decades.

The Ugly American has been criticized for its black-and-white portrayals, drawing lines of good and evil with bureaucrats and elitist European diplomats on one side and "common people," individual working Americans and Asians, on the other. Engineers and hands-on workers of the soil are glorified, even romanticized, in contrast with citified officials who wear suits, never get dirty, and spend all their time eating, drinking, and pursuing other pleasures. The values of the frontier and American principles celebrated by Ralph Waldo Emerson and Walt Whitman are personified in the "good" characters: They are common folk who are not afraid to rub shoulders with indigenous peoples and who respect them enough to learn their language and use their ideas. It is these people, working on their own rather than through government-sanctioned channels, who bring about progress and enhanced relations in Asia.

Whereas unaffected Americans in their "natural," pioneer-like state are glorified, such people are capable of being corrupted by exposure to too many urbanized European gifts, wines, cuisines, and women. Knox, who initially wants to benefit the Asian people with better poultry, is deliberately seduced away from his ideas by the French. The novel achieves an almost archetypal quality: Paradise is lost, as readers see such innocent and well-meaning individuals either lured away from their ideals or crushed by pleasure-loving, self-serving politicians, while the "evil" armies of the Viet Minh and Khmer Rouge lie in wait to swallow the entire region.

The novel's plot is loosely woven, serving merely as a unifying device for the telling of didactic stories, one after another, about well-intentioned projects and people squashed by power politics and the forces of bureaucracy. At the end, the authors present a warning that the Soviet Union will win in Vietnam via many small victories, unless their recommendations are followed. These recommendations include cutting perquisites for American diplomats and their employees abroad and requiring such representatives to learn the languages and cultures of the countries in which they serve, as well as studying the theory and techniques of communism in order to learn how to combat it. They point out that anti-Americanism not only in Southeast Asia but also throughout the world will diminish if these recommendations are adopted.

It is possible to see *The Ugly American* as an allegory of the United States' loss of innocence and the frontier values that made it initially successful against the Old World; thus one may generalize beyond Southeast Asia to discern a global principle. The authors warn against a cultural progression from hardworking poverty through prosperity to decadence, and they criticize the effete generation of pleasure-seekers they see in the United States. They further extol the value of the individual over organizations, physical labor over technology, and diversity over conformity. The populist presentation of the novel itself exemplifies these values, as the authors appeal directly to readers in plain, vivid language and short sentences. They present a series of individual anecdotes of common people, rather than couching their argument in a more logically sequenced genre and aiming it at large organizations such as the government or diplomatic corps.

Sally B. Palmer

Further Reading

Ferrer, Hugh. "Notes on the Connecticut Yankee." *Iowa Review* 36, no. 2 (2006): 168-175. Makes connections between Mark Twain's *A Connecticut Yankee in King Ar-*

thur's Court* (1889) and Lederer and Burdick's *The Ugly American* regarding American imperialism and styles of writing.

Hellmann, John. "Vietnam as Symbolic Landscape: *The Ugly American* and the New Frontier." *Peace and Change* 9, nos. 2/3 (Summer, 1983): 40-54. An insightful analysis that discusses not only the novel's reception and ramifications in American politics and writings but also the authors' literary techniques and ideology.

Trumbull, Robert. "The Ambassador Who Didn't Read Sarkhanese." *The New York Times Book Review*, Octo-

ber 5, 1958. A contemporary description and evaluation of the novel.

Walls, Jim. "A Damning Indictment of Americans Abroad." *San Francisco Chronicle*, October 5, 1958. A review of the plot and implications of the book.

Wilkinson, Rupert. "Connections with Toughness: The Novels of Eugene Burdick." *Journal of American Studies* 11 (1977): 223-239. Discusses Burdick's novels, including *The Ugly American*, providing a context for the novel and a foundation for understanding Burdick's contribution to it.

Ulysses

Author: James Joyce (1882-1941)
First published: 1922
Type of work: Novel
Type of plot: Epic
Time of plot: June 16, 1904
Locale: Dublin

Principal characters:
STEPHEN DEDALUS, a young Irish writer and teacher
BUCK MULLIGAN, a medical student
LEOPOLD BLOOM, a Jewish advertising salesman
MARION "MOLLY" TWEEDY BLOOM, his wife
BLAZES BOYLAN, Molly's lover

The Story:

Buck Mulligan mounts the stairs of the old tower and prepares to shave himself on the morning of June 16, 1904. A moment later, Stephen Dedalus comes to the top of the stairs and stands looking out over Dublin Bay. When Mulligan speaks of the sea glinting in the morning sunlight, Stephen has a sudden vision of his own mother; he had been called back from Paris to her deathbed a year before. He remembers how she begged him to pray for her soul and how he, rebelling against the churchly discipline of his boyhood, refused.

After breakfast, Stephen and Mulligan go off with Haines, a young Englishman who also lives in the old tower. Despite the Englishman's attempts to be friendly, Stephen dislikes Haines, who is given to nightlong drunken sprees. Stephen feels that his own life is growing purposeless and dissolute through his association with Mulligan and other medical students. Stephen is a teacher. It is a half-day holiday at school, and the boys are restless. One of his pupils is unable to do his simple arithmetic problems, and in the boy Stephen sees for a moment an image of his own awkward youth. He is relieved when he can dismiss the class.

Later, Stephen walks alone on the beach. He thinks of literature and his student days, of his unhappiness in Dublin,

his lack of money, his family sinking into poverty while his shabby-genteel father makes his daily round of the Dublin pubs. He sees the carcass of a dead dog rolling in the surf and remembers how a dog had frightened him in his childhood. He is, he thinks wryly, not one of the Irish heroes.

Meanwhile, Leopold Bloom has crawled out of bed to prepare his wife's breakfast. He is a Jewish advertising salesman, for sixteen years the patient, uncomplaining husband of Marion "Molly" Tweedy Bloom, a professional singer of mediocre talent. He is unhappy to know that she is carrying on an affair with Blazes Boylan, a sporting Irishman who is managing the concert tour that she is planning. Bloom munches his own breakfast and reads a letter from his daughter Milly, who works in a photographer's shop in Mullingar. Her letter reminds Bloom of his son Rudy, who died when he was eleven days old. Bloom reads Milly's letter again, wondering about a young student his daughter mentions. For a moment, he is afraid that Milly might grow up to be like her mother.

Bloom sets out on his morning walk. At the post office, he stops to pick up a letter addressed to Henry Flower, Esq., a letter from a woman who signs herself Martha. Bloom, unhappy at home, is carrying on a flirtation by mail under another name. He idly wanders into a church and listens to part of the mass. Later, he joins a party of mourners on their way to the funeral of an old friend, Paddy Dignam, who died suddenly of a stroke. During the service, Bloom watches Father Coffey. He thinks again of little Rudy and of his own father, a suicide. The day's business for Bloom is a call at a newspaper office to arrange for the printing of an advertisement. While he is there, Stephen Dedalus also arrives at the office. The two men see each other, but they do not speak.

Bloom leaves the newspaper building and walks across the O'Connell bridge. He meets Mrs. Breen and gives her an account of Dignam's funeral. She tells him that Mrs. Purefoy is in the maternity hospital in Holles Street. Bloom walks on, watching the sights of Dublin on a summer day. He enters Davy Byrne's pub and orders a cheese sandwich. Later, he goes to the National Library to look at some newspaper files. There Stephen, flushed with the drinks he had at lunch, is expounding to Buck Mulligan and some literary friends his own ingenious theory of William Shakespeare's plays and the second-best bed mentioned in Shakespeare's will. Again, Bloom and Stephen see each other but do not speak.

Bloom goes to the Ormond Hotel for a late lunch. Blazes Boylan comes into the hotel bar before he leaves to keep his appointment with Molly.

Late that afternoon, Bloom gets into a brawl in a pub where the talk is all about the money that Blazes Boylan has won in a boxing match. Bloom escapes from the jeering crowd and walks along the Sandymount shore. In the dimming twilight, he watches young Gertie MacDowell. The moon rises. Bloom decides to stop by the hospital to ask about Mrs. Purefoy. As he walks slowly along the strand, a cuckoo clock strikes nine in a priest's house that he is passing. Bloom considers that he has been cuckolded while he has sat dreaming his amorous fantasies on the Dublin beach, looking at Gertie MacDowell. At the hospital, he learns that Mrs. Purefoy's baby has not yet been born. There he sees Stephen Dedalus again, drinking with Buck Mulligan and a group of medical students. Bloom is disturbed to find the son of his old friend Simon Dedalus in such ribald, dissolute company.

Bloom goes with the medical students to a nearby pub, where Stephen and Buck Mulligan begin a drunken argument over the possession of the key to the old tower. When the group breaks up, Stephen and one of the students go on to a brothel in the Dublin slums; Bloom follows them slowly. All are drunk. Bloom has a distorted, lurid vision of his wife and Blazes Boylan together. Stephen is befuddled and thinks that he sees his dead mother suddenly appearing from the

grave to ask him again to pray for her soul. Running headlong into the street, he is knocked down in a scuffle with two British soldiers.

Bloom takes Stephen home with him. Exhausted by his wild night, Stephen remains silent and glum while Bloom talks about art and science. Bloom begs him to spend the night, to leave Mulligan and his wild friends and come to live with the Blooms, but Stephen refuses. The bells of St. George's Church are ringing as he walks off down the silent street.

Bloom slowly goes to bed. As he drifts off to sleep, he tells Molly firmly that she is to get up and prepare his breakfast in the morning.

Molly Bloom lies awake thinking of Blazes Boylan. She thinks of the mysteries of the human body, of people she has known, of her girlhood at the military post on Gibraltar. She considers the possibility that Stephen Dedalus might come to live with her and her husband. Stephen is a writer—young, refined, not coarse like Boylan. She hears a far-off, shrill train whistle. She recalls all of her past lovers, Bloom's courtship, their years together, the rose she wore in her hair the day Bloom asked her to marry him as they stood close under a Moorish arch. Her thoughts flow on, while her Ulysses, Bloom, the far wanderer of a Dublin day, snores in the darkness by her side.

Critical Evaluation:

On one of its many levels, *Ulysses* is an attempt to recapture completely, so far as it is possible in fiction, the life of a particular time and place. The scene is Dublin—its streets, homes, shops, newspaper offices, pubs, hospitals, brothels, and schools. The time is a single day in 1904. A continuation of the story of Stephen Dedalus as told in *A Portrait of the Artist as a Young Man* (1914-1915, serial; 1916, book), the novel is also a series of remarkable Homeric parallels. The incidents, characters, and scenes of a Dublin day correspond to those of the Odyssean myth. Leopold Bloom is easily recognizable as Ulysses and Molly Bloom, his wife, as Penelope.

The book is written in a variety of styles and techniques; the most significant of which is the stream-of-consciousness method, by which James Joyce attempts to reproduce not only the sights, sounds, and smells of Dublin but also the memories, emotions, and desires of his people in the modern world. This technique—combined with multilayered wordplay, concatenated sentence structures designed to connote as well as denote, and the sheer density and richness of Joyce's allusive language—makes the narrative nonlinear and epic in its proportions. While on the surface *Ulysses* relates one day in the life of its Dubliner characters, Joyce's juxtaposition of his characters' thoughts, descriptions of place, and evocation of history make the book as true an epic as its predecessor by Homer.

Short of Joyce's other great masterwork, *Finnegans Wake* (1939), *Ulysses* is arguably the most "difficult" work in English literature—a work impossible to appreciate fully with only one reading. Readers approaching *Ulysses* for the first time should therefore do so somewhat aggressively. If comprehension lapses—even for pages at a time—it is best to push on. Many elements that appear early in the story make sense only after one has read much further along. Bloom's potato talisman, for example, is mentioned in the fourth episode but remains unexplained until the fifteenth. The novel contains so many such difficulties, and of such variety, that readers sometimes feel lost. Persistent readers, however, will find that the novel is deliberately and intensely structured—Joyce later speculated that he had made it perhaps too structured. Too much or too little, the book's structure helps buoy readers voyaging into the narrative for the first time.

Although he said he did not want them published, Joyce let out two (very similar) schemas of the novel's structure. These charts indicate the following for each of the eighteen episodes: a title referring to the Homeric original, the time of day, a dominant color, a "technic" (the narrative style of the episode), a dominant art (history, literature, philology), an organ of the body, a dominant symbol, and miscellaneous correspondences between Homeric and Joycean characters. The charts have not been an unalloyed blessing to Joyce's readers, because the schemas are sometimes ambiguous and cryptic. Nevertheless, it is difficult to think of another major author whose critics have been so influenced, indeed dominated, by a single piece of text that is external to the work in question. The schemas are at least suggestive with regard to three of the more salient (and problematic) aspects of the book. These three are the Homeric parallels, Stephen's theory about Shakespeare and art, and the episodic structure and use of style.

Shortly after the publication of *Ulysses*, T. S. Eliot applauded the Homeric parallel as having "the importance of a scientific discovery." Ezra Pound thought the parallel was gratuitous, something "which any block-head could trace." The elaborate Homeric correspondence is, however, surely not, as Eliot thought, merely a backdrop to heighten "the immense panorama of futility that is the modern world." Rather, it allows readers an opportunity at faith. One may infer from the novel, if one wishes, that Bloom is a modern reincarnation of Odysseus and that, by extension, the modern age is as heroic as the ancient.

Ulysses was Joyce's favorite hero from his childhood. The quality he was to isolate as unique to the Greek hero was completeness. He observed that Ulysses had been a father, a son, a husband, a lover, and a soldier who was at first a draft dodger and then a hawk. Although this is a rather curious ideal, it suggests what may have been Joyce's purpose. The story of Ulysses constitutes such a full representation of a given complex of attitudes and values that Joyce was able to use it as a paradigm for the structure of a modern story.

The correspondences to Homer are not consistent. Bloom and Stephen are Ulysses and Telemachus, respectively, in only a general way. Correspondences listed on the schema indicate that in the first episode, for example, Stephen is Telemachus but also Hamlet. In the ninth episode, Ulysses is "Jesus, Socrates, Shakespeare." Furthermore, as has been remarked, Stephen is more like a youthful aspect of Ulysses than like Telemachus, who is almost a minor character in Homer's work. There is, then, no one-to-one impersonation of Homeric characters. Rather, there is a play of functions pointing to an essential human, the abstract Ulysses who belongs not exclusively to Homer but to the entire tradition of the Ulysses theme.

The ninth episode, "Scylla and Charybdis," contains Stephen's aesthetic theory. The action is presented as a parable of artistic creation based on Shakespeare's biography. The way the "Ulysses" of the schema functions is rather complex. The schema says that Scylla is "The Rock—Aristotle, Dogma" and Charybdis "The Whirlpool—Plato, Mysticism." "Ulysses," who must sail between these perils, is given as "Socrates, Jesus, Shakespeare." This aspect of Ulysses is manifested in Stephen's discourse; Bloom is not even immediately present. The course is the one the artist must take. It includes going between extremes of the inner and outer worlds of his personal experience. There is a struggle between the flux of everyday life and a permanent, repeated structure in the artist's self. This structure is compared to the mole that remains on Stephen's breast although all the molecules of his body have changed and, in the parable, to a supposed psychological trauma in Shakespeare's youth that determined the structure of his plays and their themes of usurpation, humiliation, and, later, reconciliation. At the level of the individual artistic psyche, the theory recapitulates the determinism treated by the novel as historical and sociological.

As to the individual episodes, the schema names a variety of elements of style that make each unique. Joyce told friends that he intended each to be able to stand on its own. Various episodes are sometimes anthologized and read like short stories. "Circe," episode 15, has been produced as a play many times. Each episode has a limited narrative point of view, but the points of view are clearly never the same. Abundant exegetical literature exists for each episode, treating in detail the unity derived of its tone, style, and themes. For this overview, however, it is more important to note that the various episodic styles are part of a second structural principle in the novel.

Total autonomy and interdependence combine in the episodic structure; Stephen and Bloom, component elements of the "Ulysses" composite, partake of this combination and therefore avoid becoming mere allegorical types. They are, in fact, complete individuals. This pattern suggests the paradoxical doctrine of the Trinity, in which three complete and equal Persons have one Essence. Of the Trinity, Joyce once said that when one is contemplating one Person, the others slip from view. So it is with Stephen and Bloom; for that matter, any individual episode in *Ulysses* seems capable of absorbing the reader's whole attention. It is, therefore, the overview that leads the reader best through the myriad captivations of Joyce's odyssey.

"Critical Evaluation" by James Marc Hovde

Further Reading

Arnold, Bruce. *The Scandal of "Ulysses": The Life and Afterlife of a Twentieth Century Masterpiece.* Rev. ed. Dublin: Liffey Press, 2004. Focuses on the many publication and copyright problems that have plagued the novel since its creation.

Benstock, Bernard, ed. *Critical Essays on James Joyce's "Ulysses."* Boston: G. K. Hall, 1989. Collection contains a cross-section of contemporary and later criticism on the work. Special emphasis is given to the "Nausicaa" episode.

Brown, Richard, ed. *A Companion to James Joyce.* Malden, Mass.: Blackwell, 2008. Collection of essays includes discussion of the worldwide influence of Joyce's work, with specific analysis of its impacts on the literature of Ireland, Germany, Japan, India, New Zealand, and France. *Ulysses* is examined in Richard Brown's essay "Molly's Gibraltar: The Other Location in *Ulysses*" and Maud Ellmann's "*Ulysses*: The Epic of the Human Body."

Bulson, Eric. *The Cambridge Introduction to James Joyce.* New York: Cambridge University Press, 2006. Provides an introductory overview of Joyce's life and work, addressing Joyce as a modernist, a journalist, a translator, a lecturer, and a lover. Chapter 3 analyzes five of Joyce's works, including *Ulysses*, and chapter 4 chronicles his works' critical reception from 1914 through 2005.

Ellman, Richard. *James Joyce.* 2d ed. New York: Oxford University Press, 1982. Biographical work is widely considered one of the finest literary biographies of the twentieth century. Contains extensive discussion and analysis of *Ulysses*. Highly recommended.

Emig, Rainer, ed. *"Ulysses": James Joyce.* New York: Palgrave Macmillan, 2004. Collection of analytical essays approaches the novel from various perspectives, including gender studies, postcolonial studies, and deconstructivist theory.

Gilbert, Stuart. *James Joyce's "Ulysses": A Study.* 1930. Reprint. New York: Vintage Books, 1955. Classic work is still highly valuable. Covers the novel chapter by chapter and discusses in useful outlines many of the schemas underlying the work. A good starting point.

Gillespie, Michael Patrick, and Paula F. Gillespie. *Recent Criticism of James Joyce's "Ulysses": An Analytical Review.* Rochester, N.Y.: Camden House, 2000. Survey of *Ulysses* scholarship focuses on criticism written since 1970. Organized by topics, including the novel's narrative thread; gender, sex, and sexuality; and cultural identity and the new nationalism.

Kenner, Hugh. *"Ulysses": A Study.* Baltimore: Johns Hopkins University Press, 1987. Discusses the plot of the novel thoroughly, in a manner equally useful for beginning and repeat readers. A substantial contribution from a preeminent literary critic.

Pierce, David. *Reading Joyce.* New York: Pearson Longman, 2008. A longtime teacher and scholar of Joyce provides a framework for Joyce's work. Devotes three chapters to an explication of *Ulysses* as well as analysis of its characters Leopold and Molly Bloom.

Thornton, Weldon. *Voices and Values in Joyce's "Ulysses."* Gainesville: University Press of Florida, 2000. Analysis attempts to answer a long-standing question about the novel: Why does Joyce use a different style for each of its last ten episodes?

Wilson, Edmund. *Axel's Castle: A Study of the Imaginative Literature of 1870-1930.* 1931. Reprint. New York: Farrar, Straus and Giroux, 2004. Wilson, an eminent literary critic, discusses modernist writers. The chapter on Joyce contains an excellent summary of *Ulysses* and places Joyce's artistic and technical achievement in a historical context.

Ulysses

Author: Alfred, Lord Tennyson (1809-1892)
First published: 1842
Type of work: Poetry
Type of plot: Dramatic monologue

When Alfred, Lord Tennyson, published "Ulysses" in 1842, his contemporaries tended to read the poem straightforwardly, as a speech given by a heroic figure who asserts that there is value in learning, in doing, and in taking risks. Later critics, however, have read it as the almost unconscious confession of a failed king trying to assert himself even as he reveals himself. Such later treatments, intelligent and insightful as they are, still tend to make the poem into a case study. It is true that Tennyson's Ulysses is not a perfect man: He proposes to give up his duties, abandon his wife, and risk the lives of his companions, but his search is his reason for living, and Tennyson makes this need to go on searching the central theme of his poem.

"Ulysses" in form is a dramatic monologue—that is, it is delivered as a speech by a particular figure to a particular understood audience (not just the poem's readers); in a sense, it is a scene from a play but nevertheless entire in itself. The poem's title character and speaker, Ulysses (the Roman name of the Greek hero Odysseus), is best known from Homer's *Odyssey* (c. 725 B.C.E.; English translation, 1614). In this monologue, he addresses the crew of his ship, men with whom he has had many adventures. (According to *Odyssey*, Odysseus was the only survivor of his ill-fated voyages, so his current crew is likely made up of men who have shared in his adventures after his return from the war.) Thus, the quest he proposes to his men is not new.

The work is in blank verse, unrhymed iambic pentameter—the verse form of most of William Shakespeare's plays. Iambic pentameter can be readily spoken but is nevertheless rhythmic and, so, elevated in tone. Besides the effect of the verse form, the poem is filled with images and sounds that suggest the emotional state of the speaker. For instance, "the long day wanes, the slow moon climbs, the deep/ Moans round with many voices." One should note the repetition of vowel sounds in "day" and "wane," the alliteration of "moon" and "Moans," and the slow, humming murmur of all those *m*'s and *n*'s. These aural components of the poem produce a musical effect that is melancholy but not, in the end, the voice of a man trying simply to escape: Ulysses follows these words with the harsher sounds of command: "Push off, and sitting well in order smite/ The sounding furrows." These

lines employ explosive sounds generated by the initial *p* and several *t*'s and a final hard *d*.

Some critics have held that the speaker is talking to himself in the first part of the poem, only later addressing his men, but the poem is better understood as a single long speech to an actual audience, even if the speaker sometimes does think aloud. In a way, there are three parts to the work. In the first part, Ulysses gives his reasons for setting off on a new journey. In the second part, he speaks about the situation in Ithaca and says that, by choosing his son as his successor, he has ensured that his people will be taken care of in his absence, so that leaving on a new quest is not an abandonment of his duty. In the third part, Ulysses encourages his men (he himself has no need of encouragement).

Because Odysseus (Ulysses) also appears in other works, Tennyson's poem contains echoes of those variants, especially of the Ulisse (the Italian version of the name) portrayed by the medieval Italian poet Dante. Ulisse appears in the third volume of Dante's *La divina commedia* (c. 1320; *The Divine Comedy*, 1802), *Inferno* (Hell). He has been consigned to Hell as a false counselor, having lied at various times and devised stratagems that brought about the destruction of Troy. He is also there because he went beyond the proper bounds of human existence, according to the standard Christian beliefs of Dante's time, by seeking knowledge and experiences that are forbidden to humans. The arguments of Tennyson's Ulysses suggest his motives for setting off on such a voyage, but Tennyson's evaluation of the voyage and motives was very different from that of Dante. Indeed, in the nineteenth century, imperial European powers such as Great Britain would have encouraged such a voyage. Moreover, the fact that the ancient Roman orator Cicero praised Ulysses as a model of wisdom represented a significant stamp of approval to the educated English social classes of Tennyson's era.

Tennyson wrote "Ulysses" in part to expresses his grief and to cope with the death of his friend, Arthur Henry Hallam, to whose memory Tennyson would dedicate his long series of poems, *In Memoriam* (1850). Tennyson held that "Ulysses" expressed his feelings about Hallam's death, as well as asserting "the need for going forward, and braving the struggle of life." A writer's intent is not always what he succeeds in presenting, so a reader should not automatically think that a poem is simply an emotional statement about the poet's life or a direct expression of his emotions, but there is little doubt that Tennyson intended Ulysses, in a sense, to be the bearer of his own emotions.

In the beginning of the poem, Ulysses speaks of being an idle king, "match'd with an aged wife," performing the duties of kingship, but obviously regarding them as an inferior way of living. These lines have been read as suggesting that Ulysses is egoistically revealing his own incompetence as king, as well as being a misogynist. His words about his wife are not flattering to himself, an old man wanting to escape his marriage, but in a sense he is speaking a truth. Tennyson is not being ironic here: Ulysses should be taken at his word. He expresses his true wish for the freedom to discover, for it is action, discovery, and learning that give meaning to his life. It is in action that he has really, intensely lived.

When Ulysses suggests that his son Telemachus is better fitted than he himself for the kingship role, he neither seeks to insult Telemachus nor to excuse himself. Telemachus does fit his role—he is not driven to be something he is not; he has prudence—a virtue but also a certain lack of spirit. He is unlikely to take chances. Ulysses sees his son as a creator of order, which makes him a valuable figure, but Telemachus is not a discoverer. He will find nothing new. He is a necessary figure in the world, the steady man who brings about structure—indeed, without such men, Ulysses himself could never set out. Ulysses, by contrast, is not suited to be an administrator, giving "Unequal laws" to a people who are not very civilized. He follows his true role, which is to take risks, to seek out the unknown, not just for egoistic pleasure but because he seeks the intensity of life.

Even the poem's imagery, powerful and positive, suggests delight in action as well as in gaining knowledge. Again, images reinforce such a reading, as when Ulysses compares himself to a tool that rusts when it is not burnished after use. This "tool" is almost surely a sword, but it may symbolize bold action of any sort, not necessarily war. However, Ulysses does admit a certain pleasure in war when he speaks later of his own reputation. Warfare involves action at

the peak of risk, so for Ulysses it is of great value. For Ulysses, then, one is not here simply to exist, to serve, or to carry on the ordinary duties of citizenship. Indeed, there is an egoism there, but "Life piled on life/ Were all too little, and of one to me/ Little remains."

L. L. Lee

Further Reading

Culler, A. Dwight. *The Poetry of Tennyson*. New Haven, Conn.: Yale University Press, 1977. A discussion of the major poems up to *Idylls of the King* (1859-1885).

Francis, Elizabeth A., ed. *Tennyson: A Collection of Critical Essays*. Englewood Cliffs, N.J.: Prentice Hall, 1980. Excellent and insightful collection of essays reflecting trends in critical thought.

Jump, John D., ed. *Tennyson: The Critical Heritage*. 1967. Reprint. New York: Barnes & Noble, 1986. Collects a range of essays that provide older interpretations and discussions of the major poems.

Killham, John, ed. *Critical Essays on the Poetry of Tennyson*. New York: Barnes & Noble, 1960. This collection includes E. J. Chiasson's "Tennyson: A Re-Interpretation," a reading that discusses the idea that Tennyson's Ulysses may not be the admirable figure seen in earlier criticism.

Kissane, James D. *Alfred Tennyson*. New York: Twayne, 1970. A useful and well-written introduction to Tennyson's works.

Nohrnberg, James. "Eight Reflections of Tennyson's 'Ulysses.'" *Victorian Poetry* 47, no. 1 (2009): 101-150. Major essay discussing the relationship of the poem to other texts, such as Arthur Hallam's "Timbuctoo" (1829).

Painter, Megan Gribskov. *The Aesthetic of the Victorian Dramatic Monologue*. Lewiston, N.Y.: Edwin Mellen Press, 2000. "Ulysses" is the major example text in this study of the poetics of dramatic monologues in the Victorian era.

Tennyson, Charles. *Alfred Tennyson*. 1950. Reprint. New York: Macmillan, 1969. A biography by the poet's grandson. Useful for its accounts of Tennyson's own thoughts on his works.

The Unbearable Bassington

Author: Saki (Hector Hugo Munro, 1870-1916)
First published: 1912
Type of work: Novel
Type of plot: Satire
Time of plot: Early twentieth century
Locale: London

Principal characters:
COMUS BASSINGTON, the "unbearable" Bassington
FRANCESCA BASSINGTON, his mother
ELAINE DE FREY, an heir
COURTNEY YOUGHAL, a young member of Parliament
HENRY GREECH, Mrs. Bassington's brother

The Story:

Francesca Bassington is a successful member of London society who is able to make a little money go a long way. Her greatest interest in life is the drawing room in her small, perfect house on Blue Street. Foremost among her treasures is a famous Van der Meulen masterpiece, which hangs in the paneled place of honor in that charming room. She also has a son, Comus, who presents a serious problem to his mother because of his casual attitude toward life. Francesca comes to the conclusion that there is only one solution for her son's future. He must marry a wealthy young woman. Her first choice is Emmeline Chetrof, who will eventually come into a comfortable fortune and, most important of all, will upon her marriage inherit the house in which Francesca lives.

During the time Comus is at school, Francesca writes her son, asking him to show special kindness to Emmeline's brother Lancelot. This suggestion causes Comus to treat the child even more cruelly, and her plans for a match between Comus and Emmeline end dismally. Two years later, when Comus is turned loose in his mother's fashionable world of Mayfair and Ascot, she persuades her brother, Henry Greech, to secure a position for the young man as a secretary to Sir John Jull, the governor of an island in the West Indies. Not wanting to leave England, Comus sends to a newspaper an article criticizing Sir John. This scurrilous attack is written by Courtney Youghal, a young politician whom Comus knows and admires. Printed over Comus's signature, it has the desired result. Comus loses the position Sir John promised.

At a dinner given by Lady Caroline Benaresq, Francesca first learns that her son is interested in Elaine de Frey, a wealthy young woman who resembles a painting by Leonardo da Vinci. At the same party, Francesca learns that Courtney is also interested in the young heir.

One summer afternoon, Elaine entertains her two suitors, Comus and Courtney, at tea in her garden. Elaine, an earnest and practical young lady, analyzes her suitors carefully; although she realizes that Comus is both frivolous and undependable, she finds herself falling in love with him and making excuses for his shortcomings. Courtney, a rising member of Parliament, also interests her and seems to her practical mind a better risk than Comus. When the tea is served, Comus snatches up a silver basket containing the only bread and butter sandwiches and dashes off to feed the swans. Returning with the basket, an heirloom of the de Frey family, Comus asks permission to keep it as a souvenir of the delightful tea party. Elaine does not wish to part with the piece of silver, but Comus makes such a scene that she finally concedes to his wishes.

One fine June morning, all of London society turns out to ride, to walk, or to sit in the chairs along the Row. Courtney is there discussing the theater with Lady Veula Croot. In a secluded part of the Row, Elaine and Comus rent chairs. The two drifted apart slightly because of small unrepaid loans, which Comus requested, and because of the affair of the silver basket. That morning, Comus again asks Elaine to lend him money—five pounds to pay a gambling debt. She promises to send him two pounds by messenger and curtly asks to be excused. He hurts her pride and alarms her practical sense of caution. As she is leaving the Row, she meets Courtney. Over the luncheon table, they become engaged.

At an exhibition at the Rutland Galleries, Comus learns of Elaine's engagement. Elaine intends to write Comus a gracious but final note, but instead she goes to visit her cousin Suzette to break the news of her engagement. When Elaine returns home after her call, she finds a letter from Comus awaiting her. In the letter, he thanks her for the loan, returns the money, and promises to return the silver basket in lieu of a wedding gift.

Francesca learns of the engagement, a blow to her elaborate plans, from the inveterate gossip, George St. Michael. She informs Comus that he must take a position in West Africa, for which Henry made arrangements. With his eyes on the Van der Meulen masterpiece, Comus asks his mother if she could not sell something. Francesca is fiercely angry at such a suggestion and scolds him severely.

That night, lonely Comus watches the play from the stalls of the Straw Exchange Theatre. He envies Courtney and

Elaine and their circle of friends. Francesca learns from St. Michael, her usual source, that Emmeline is to be married but only after a long engagement. Therefore, her beloved house on Blue Street is safe for a time. Francesca entertains at a dull dinner party in honor of her son's departure—a party to which none of Comus's friends is invited.

In the meantime, Courtney and Elaine take their wedding trip on the Continent. During their honeymoon, they soon discover that neither loves the other and that the marriage is not likely to be successful. Comus is exiled to West Africa and is bored and unhappy. Shortly before Christmas, Francesca receives a cablegram saying that Comus is dangerously ill. To calm herself, she walks in the park; for the first time, she realizes how selfish her love for her possessions, especially the Van der Meulen, is. During the time she is walking, her brother brings an eminent critic to inspect the masterpiece. She returns to the house and finds a cablegram announcing the death of Comus. A few minutes later, Henry arrives to inform her that the Van der Meulen masterpiece is not an original but only a good copy. While his voice buzzes on and on, Francesca sits stricken among her prized pieces of silver, bronze, and porcelain—all of them as beautiful and soulless as Francesca herself.

Critical Evaluation:

The Unbearable Bassington synthesizes the attitudes, ideas, techniques, stylistic mannerisms, and narrative quirks that made Saki one of the most entertaining and provocative writers in Edwardian England. It was also his first novel and represents his most serious attempt to gain recognition as an important literary artist. The great artistic merit of *The Unbearable Bassington* suggests that, had Saki not been killed in World War I, he might well have ranked with Aldous Huxley as a satirical chronicler of the disillusioned, disintegrating British upper class in the years following the war.

The Unbearable Bassington immediately impresses the reader as a vivid, brilliant, amusing, ironical portrait of pre-World War I upper-class English society. As a member of that group, Saki knows it intimately and, although he never seriously questions the social and political institutions that support it—the rigid class system, economic and social injustice, and imperialism—he sees its brittleness, shallowness, frivolity, and materialism, and he describes it with a deft and bitter wit that is as provoking as it is amusing. If most of the personages are more caricature than character, they are a colorful crew, in constant motion and conflict. The dialogue is made up of a steady stream of acute observations, sharp, witty exchanges, and brilliant epigrams. The social rituals, subtle class distinctions, and special mannerisms of

the group are sketched with both careful precision and ironical understatement.

There is more to *The Unbearable Bassington* than a witty description of a superficial social stratum. The real importance of the novel depends on the seriousness of the action and the fates of the primary characters. Saki reveals his true feelings about not only his own social grouping but also life in general. At the center of *The Unbearable Bassington* is the tragicomic mother-son relationship of the two "unbearable" Bassingtons, Comus and Francesca.

Comus's unbearableness is mitigated by his wit, his liveliness, and his honest awareness of, and ironical attitude toward, the self-destructive streak that guarantees he will do precisely the wrong thing at exactly the wrong time to destroy any chance he may have for success or happiness. He is frustrated by his Edwardian society and alienated from it. He desperately wants to belong to it, yet he systematically botches every opportunity he has to consolidate his position in it, first in driving off Emmeline Chetrof and then, more important, in alienating himself from Elaine de Frey. It is impossible to say whether these impulsive, apparently subconscious, self-defeating actions are the result of a curious integrity or a weak perversity.

The love-hate relationship Comus feels toward his social milieu is most intensely focused in his feelings toward his mother. When Comus systematically ruins his chances for "good" marriages, does he do it to upset his mother's plans? If so, is it hostility? Or perhaps resentment at being "used" to assure her financial security? Or love—an attempt to force her to come out of her materialistic shell and behave toward him as a real mother?

The climax of the relationship comes when, after Comus loses Elaine to Courtney Youghal, they discuss his future. He suggests they "sell something"—meaning the "Van der Meulen" painting—to give him the capital to go into business. She refuses and so, discouraged, Comus agrees to try West Africa, where he withers and dies.

In view of the close identification of Comus's fate with the picture, it is difficult to understand the critical objections to the final revelation that the "Van der Meulen" is, in fact, a fake. The pathos and bitterness that emerge from *The Unbearable Bassington* come from Francesca having chosen her material objects over her son; she discovers, too late, how much she really loves and needs him and how little her possessions really matter. Thus, Henry's final revelation that the picture is phony, told to Francesca as she sits clutching the cablegram informing her of Comus's death, brings together the book's thematic and emotional elements into a bitterly ironic and dramatically potent conclusion. Without it, the book's ending would be merely sad; with it, the finale touches the fringes of tragedy—but only the fringes.

Neither Comus nor his mother is the stuff of which real tragedy can be made. Their lives are too artificial, their preoccupations too trivial, their values too frivolous, and their flaws too venal to be taken too seriously. Nevertheless, the antiheroic view of life that developed and flourished since Saki's time makes the poignancy and absurdity of their final situation most vivid and acceptable to the modern reader. If Saki is the chronicler of a society and world that vanished with World War I, his attitude toward that world seems especially valid for the complex, ambiguous world that succeeded it.

Further Reading

Baring, Maurice. Introduction to *The Unbearable Bassington*, by Saki. New York: Viking Press, 1928. Thematic analysis of the novel, which Baring calls "an ironic tragedy on a high level." Argues that Saki possessed a stoic view of life, recognizing the fragility of human relationships but resigned to struggle for the preservation of a civilized society.

Bloom, Harold, ed. *Twentieth Century British Literature*. Vol. 4. New York: Chelsea House, 1987. Collection of excerpts from reviews by eminent literary critics of the early twentieth century. Allows readers to place *The Unbearable Bassington* in the context of Saki's career, and relates it to his short stories; also comments on the quality of satire in the novel.

Byrne, Sandie. *The Unbearable Saki: The Work of H. H. Munro*. New York: Oxford University Press, 2007. A comprehensive critical biography. Byrne describes his preoccupations with England, the values of the British Empire, and gay young men.

Cavaliero, Glen. "Juvenile Delinquents: Stalky and Saki." In *The Alchemy of Laughter: Comedy in English Fiction*. New York: St. Martin's Press, 2000. Saki's writing is included in this examination of comedy in English fiction, in which Cavaliero discusses how parody, irony, satire, and other types of humor are evident in these works.

Gillen, Charles H. *H. H. Munro (Saki)*. New York: Twayne, 1969. General survey of Saki's career as a historian, journalist, short-story writer, novelist, and playwright. Surveys the critical reception of *The Unbearable Bassington*; explains how the novel summarizes themes present throughout Saki's writings and discusses his handling of issues involving sexuality.

Langguth, A. J. *Saki: A Life of Hector Hugh Munro*. New York: Simon & Schuster, 1981. Well-researched and well-written biography integrating literary analysis with details of Saki's life. A chapter on *The Unbearable Bassington* reviews the biographical genesis of the work and comments on characterization. Judges the novel a mixed success.

Spears, George James. *The Satire of Saki*. New York: Exposition Press, 1963. Demonstrates how Saki uses a number of satiric techniques in the novel to explore the "will to destruction" residing in humankind; notes how he manages to evoke sympathy for the mother in the story.

The Unbearable Lightness of Being

Author: Milan Kundera (1929-   )
First published: L'Insoutenable Légèreté de l'être, 1984 (English translation, 1984; in Czech as *Nesnesitelná lehkost bytí*, 1985)
Type of work: Novel
Type of plot: Philosophical
Time of plot: 1960's and 1970's
Locale: Czechoslovakia and Switzerland

Principal characters:
TOMAS, a surgeon
TEREZA, Tomas's wife
SABINA, an artist, Tomas's mistress
FRANZ, a university lecturer, Sabina's lover

The Story:

Tomas is visiting a provincial town in Czechoslovakia to perform surgery when he meets Tereza in a café, where she works as a waitress. Shortly after he returns home to Prague, she turns up at his apartment with a heavy suitcase. They make love immediately. She then comes down with flu, and he is unable to make her leave his apartment for a week afterward. Even when he has installed her in an apartment of her own, he is unable to leave her.

Although Tomas loves Tereza as he has loved no other woman, he is unable to give up seeing other women. Chief among these is the artist Sabina. Sabina resembles Tomas in her wish not to be weighed down by the heavy burden of love and in her tendency to betray those who threaten her freedom. At Tomas's request, Sabina finds work for Tereza in a photographic darkroom and encourages her to develop her talent for photography. The two women become friends, though their relationship is affected by Tereza's awareness of Sabina's continuing relationship with Tomas.

Tomas marries Tereza and buys her a dog, which they name Karenin. Both actions are partly motivated by Tomas's desire to try to make amends for his womanizing. Tereza's efforts to tolerate Tomas's lifestyle are undermined by her recurring dreams that reveal her inability to accept his infidelities. When he recognizes the suffering his actions cause Tereza, Tomas is racked with guilt, but he is still unable to stop seeing other women.

Following the liberalization of Czechoslovakia under the leadership of Alexander Dubček (the Prague Spring), Soviet tanks roll into Prague and a military occupation begins. Tereza roams the streets with her camera, capturing the horrors of the occupation on film. She gives the film to foreign visitors to smuggle out of the country and publish abroad. When Tomas is offered a job in Zurich, Switzerland, he and Tereza move there. His passport is taken as he crosses the border, so he knows that if he ever goes back to Czechoslovakia, it will be for the rest of his life.

Sabina is already living in Switzerland, in Geneva. She becomes involved with Franz, a university lecturer. Franz is married to Marie-Claude, but he leaves his wife to be with Sabina. One day when he turns up at Sabina's apartment, however, she has gone, leaving no forwarding address.

Tereza, worn down by Tomas's infidelities, flees back to Prague, to what she has dubbed the country of the weak. Tomas cannot resist the pull of Tereza and follows her, knowing that they cannot escape again.

Tomas writes a piece for a newspaper commenting on the guilt of the Soviet authorities, and the piece is interpreted as subversive. When he refuses to sign a retraction proposed by the secret police, he has to resign from his job as a surgeon (since he is an employee of the state). He takes a job as a window cleaner.

In an ironic twist, Tomas and Tereza learn that when they believed they had been acting to oppose the regime, they may actually have helped it. Tereza discovers that her photographs could have been used by the secret police to identify opponents of the occupation. When Tomas was interrogated by the secret police, he had lied about the appearance of the editor who commissioned his article, only to unwittingly implicate another editor who, unknown to him, resembles his made-up description.

Tomas's work as a window cleaner gives him plenty of opportunities for assignations with women. He is something of a hero to his clients, who know that he must have refused to cooperate with the regime to have been hounded out of medical practice. Tereza, in an attempt to understand Tomas's appetite for extramarital sex, turns the tables on him and has sex with another man, someone who had protected her from some abuse in the bar where she works. When it is suggested to her that the whole scene may have been set up by the secret police as a blackmailing device, she develops a strong desire to leave Prague.

She and Tomas go to live and work on a farm in the country, he as a driver and she as a cowherd. Their dog, Karenin, develops cancer and dies. Tereza reflects that her love for Karenin is in a sense superior to her love for Tomas, since she has never asked the dog for anything in return, whereas she always wants Tomas not to cheat on her. Tomas, however, tells her that he is happy in the countryside, where he does not carry on affairs, presumably from lack of opportunity.

One day, a farmworker dislocates his shoulder, and Tomas has to put it back in place. The worker, feeling happy, suggests that they all drive to a nearby town to go dancing. On the way back, the truck they are riding in gets a flat tire. When Tomas and Tereza set about changing the tire, they are accidentally crushed to death. Sabina, in Paris, learns of their deaths. She moves to California, where she enjoys considerable success selling her paintings. She continues to live in avoidance of the weight of love and commitment, such weight having killed Tomas and Tereza.

Critical Evaluation:

The Czech writer Milan Kundera is widely considered one of Europe's most outstanding novelists. In 1975, his books were denounced as counterrevolutionary and banned by the Czech Communist government. Partly as a result of this, he is often labeled a dissident, in spite of his conviction that his works are not political. His characters are not representatives of any ideology, but unique individuals whose viewpoints are challenged and developed by personal and social dilemmas. Kundera's works offended the Czech Communist government because they are emphatically apolitical; they insist on the primacy of the individual. Kundera's novels do not assert opinions; rather, they pose questions and search for answers: He never knows which of his characters are right.

In line with this stance, his novels, *The Unbearable Lightness of Being* included, show the influence of writers such as

Miguel de Cervantes, Franz Kafka, and Denis Diderot, in that the novels dismiss conventional novelistic structures in favor of parallel explorations of related themes, multiple standpoints represented by different characters, and integration of dreams, fantasy, and philosophical contemplation with realistic narrative. *The Unbearable Lightness of Being* was published in 1984 to great critical acclaim. This novel is notable for its bold juxtapositions: an intimate love story set against the backdrop of the Prague invasion, the subtle workings of human relationships set against larger metaphysical truths. Kundera views his characters with a sharp ironic insight balanced by immense compassion and humor. Among twentieth century novelists, he is arguably one of the wisest observers of the pathos and paradoxes of adult love.

The Unbearable Lightness of Being develops a theme that recurs in a minor way in all of Kundera's earlier novels and in some of his poetry: the opposition between heaviness and lightness. Tomas espouses the philosophy of lightness, which for him means the pursuit of many sexual liaisons without the burden of love and commitment. As the narrator comments, however, the heavier the burden, the more real one's life becomes; the absence of a burden makes one take leave of the earth and become as insignificant as one is free. Tomas's opposite is Tereza, who arrives with her heavy suitcase and cannot be brushed off. His commitment to lightness and consequent resistance to fidelity to Tereza is counterbalanced throughout the novel by a highly significant metaphor: Tereza seen by Tomas as an abandoned child sent downstream in a bulrush basket and washed up against his bed. The narrator repeatedly insists on the power of this metaphor over Tomas: How can he resist such an image? Tereza's fidelity to Tomas is described as the one pillar that anchors their relationship to the ground. As he becomes more closely involved with her, her grief over his womanizing weighs heavily on both of them. Tomas eventually embraces the burden of this heavy relationship, choosing to be with Tereza over a new job, a home, and freedom in Switzerland.

Sabina's devotion to lightness is more complete. She maintains lightness by betraying every expectation placed upon her: by the Communists in her youth; by those who wish her to denounce the Soviet regime; by her lover, Franz. Franz is somewhat of a parallel character with Tereza in that he favors commitment over levity. He is committed to the political ideal of the Grand March. Sabina, in contrast, had trouble with the political parades of her youth. She could never keep in step or remember the songs.

Significantly, Sabina, with her horror of being weighed down by love, by kitsch, and by heavy tombstones, is the only one of the four main characters who survives. The others are literally and metaphorically crushed to death by heavy weights: Tomas and Tereza are crushed by their truck, and Franz dies in pursuit of his earnest commitment to the Grand March, killed by a heavy blow. Tomas and Tereza's love and Franz's commitment, however, lend their lives significance and weight.

Related to the theme of lightness and weight is the "*Es muss sein!*" ("It must be!") motif, taken from a weighty musical phrase in a Beethoven quartet. When Tomas leaves Zurich to rejoin Tereza in Prague, he says to himself, "*Es muss sein!*" Almost immediately, a paradox strikes him: His relationship with Tereza was in fact born of a chain of laughable coincidences, such as his going to a particular town to do a surgery and his stopping in a particular café. The narrator comments that perhaps Tomas's real "*Es muss sein!*," the overriding necessity of his existence, is his profession as a surgeon. That assumption is called into question when Tomas takes a certain joy in losing his profession and becoming a window cleaner. He is able to forget his work as soon as he goes home; he has found lightness and freedom from the vampire "*Es muss sein!*" that had sucked his blood. Finally, Tomas is left with the "*Es muss sein!*" of his womanizing. This weighty compulsion also drops away during his time with Tereza on the farm. The narrator notes Tomas's curiosity to discover what lies beyond "*Es muss sein!*" The outcome of the novel suggests that perhaps it is death.

Kundera often uses musical structures and themes in his work, and this novel is no exception. Its structure has been called symphonic, in the sense that the first part presents the basic theme, the middle parts are explorations of the theme from the points of view of different characters, and the final part is the resolution of the theme. Kundera even uses musical terminology to describe the last two parts: "The Grand March" is *fortissimo* and *prestissimo*, loud, fast, and cynical in mood, with lots of events; "Karenin's Smile" is *pianissimo* and *adagio*, very soft, with few events.

Claire J. Robinson

Further Reading

Aji, Aron, ed. *Milan Kundera and the Art of Fiction: Critical Essays*. New York: Garland, 1992. Collection of critical essays addresses such topics as Kundera and the eighteenth century English novel, the narrative technique and characterization of *The Unbearable Lightness of Being*, and Kundera's contribution to the novel form.

Banerjee, Maria Nemcová. *Terminal Paradox: The Novels of Milan Kundera*. New York: Grove Weidenfeld, 1990. Presents philosophical and psychological analysis of Kundera's long fiction, including a comprehensive chapter on *The Unbearable Lightness of Being*. Well worth reading for its insights into Kundera's techniques and characters.

Bloom, Harold, ed. *Milan Kundera*. Philadelphia: Chelsea House, 2003. Collection of essays offers discussion of topics such as Kundera's use of sexuality in his writings and estrangement and irony in his work. Includes an informative introductory overview.

Frank, Søren. *Migration and Literature: Günter Grass, Milan Kundera, Salman Rushdie, and Jan Kjærstad*. New York: Palgrave Macmillan, 2008. Examines works by Kundera and three other authors, focusing on the theme of migration and the various strategies these writers use to describe the experience of exile and homelessness.

Hruby, Peter. *Daydreams and Nightmares: Czech Communist and Ex-Communist Literature, 1917-1987*. Boulder, Colo.: East European Monographs, 1990. Contains a lucid chapter on Kundera's life and his political and literary development. Briefly discusses individual works, including *The Unbearable Lightness of Being*.

Miletic, Tijana. *European Literary Immigration into the French Language: Readings of Gary, Kristof, Kundera, and Semprun*. New York: Rodopi, 2008. Kundera, Romain Gary, Agota Kristof, and Jorge Semprun are twentieth century writers whose native language was not French, but who chose to write in this language. Examines the common elements in their work from linguistic, sociological, and psychoanalytic perspectives.

Petro, Peter, ed. *Critical Essays on Milan Kundera*. New York: G. K. Hall, 1999. Includes a review of *The Unbearable Lightness of Being* by novelist E. L. Doctorow, several interviews with Kundera, and essays that address topics such as the use of commedia dell'arte style in his novels and the slow pace of his works. Essays of particular interest are "Kundera's Quartet (On *The Unbearable Lightness of Being*)," by Guy Scarpetta, and "A Body of One's Own: The Body as Sanctum of Individual Integrity in Kundera's *The Unbearable Lightness of Being*," by Marjorie E. Rhine.

Uncle Silas
A Tale of Bartram-Haugh

Author: Joseph Sheridan Le Fanu (1814-1873)
First published: 1864
Type of work: Novel
Type of plot: Gothic
Time of plot: Nineteenth century
Locale: England

Principal characters:
MAUD RUTHYN, an English heir
AUSTIN RUTHYN, her father
SILAS RUTHYN, her uncle and guardian
MILLY, Silas's daughter
DUDLEY, Silas's son
LADY MONICA KNOLLYS, Maud's cousin
DR. BRYERLY and LORD ILBURY, trustees of the Ruthyn estate
MADAME DE LA ROUGIERRE, a governess
MEG HAWKES, a servant

The Story:

Maud Ruthyn spends a lonely childhood in the great old house at Knowl. Her mother dies when she is very young, and her father, Austin Ruthyn, becomes a recluse who seldom leaves the grounds of his estate. Disappointed in Parliament many years earlier, he retires from public life to devote himself to scientific and literary studies. These lead him to Swedenborgianism, a doctrine suited to his eccentric and moral tastes. Maud knows him as a kindly but solitary and taciturn man.

For this reason, she never questions him about her uncle Silas, her father's younger brother, who lives at Bartram-Haugh, a Derbyshire estate owned by Austin. His portrait as a handsome young man hangs in the oak room at Knowl, but from vague hints and whispers of the servants, she knows that there is a mystery surrounding this relative whom she never met, and that the scandal clouds her father's life as well.

One of the few visitors at Knowl is Dr. Bryerly, a tall, ungainly man who always dresses in black and wears an untidy scratch wig. Like Maud's father, he is a Swedenborgian. The girl is greatly in awe of him, but she knows that he has her father's confidence. One day, Austin shows her the key to a locked cabinet in his study. He is soon to go on a journey, he says, and after his departure she is to give the key to Dr. Bryerly.

Maud is a little past seventeen years old when her father employs a new governess, Madame de la Rougierre, a tall, masculine-looking woman with sly, smirking manners. Maud dislikes her from the start. On every possible occasion, the governess questions her charge about Austin's will and business affairs; sometimes Maud thinks the woman is deliberately spying on the household. One day, Madame de la Rougierre and her pupil walk to a ruined abbey near Knowl, where a strange young man accosts Maud. The girl is frightened by his coarse appearance and offensive manner, but Madame de la Rougierre ignores the incident.

Maud forgets the whole affair in her excitement over the arrival of Lady Monica Knollys, her father's cousin from Derbyshire and a brisk, sensible noblewoman. During the visit, Madame de la Rougierre pretends to be ill, and it turns out that she and Lady Monica knew each other in the past. When Lady Monica tells Austin that the governess is not a suitable companion for his daughter, he accuses her of prejudice, and they have a terrible argument, as a result of which Lady Monica leaves Knowl abruptly. Before leaving, she warns Maud against Madame de la Rougierre and cautions her always to be on guard against her. Lady Monica also tells Maud that at one time her uncle Silas, whom she clearly does not like, was suspected of murder, but that nothing was charged. Later, Silas becomes interested in religion.

A short time later, while Maud is walking with Madame de la Rougierre in the park, they see on an unfrequented road a carriage with one woman as its only passenger. They continue on their way and meet three men, among them the coarse young stranger who approached Maud near the ruins of the abbey. All are tipsy and address the governess with rough familiarity. When one of the men tries to seize Maud, her screams attract two gamekeepers. In a scuffle with the intruders, one of the gamekeepers is shot. Austin and the servants try to intercept the strangers at the park gates, but the men and their woman companion disappear.

Madame de la Rougierre is given notice not long afterward. One night, Maud falls asleep in her father's study. She awakens to find the governess going through his private papers. Informed of the midnight search, Austin discharges the woman immediately.

When Austin dies suddenly of a heart attack, Maud understands at last to which journey he was referring. She also learns that Dr. Bryerly was her father's physician as well as his friend. With the key she gives him, the doctor unlocks the cabinet that contains Austin's will. Its provisions disturb Dr. Bryerly and fill Lady Monica with dismay. After varying bequests to relatives, friends, and servants, the remainder of Austin's great estate is given to Maud, under the trusteeship of Dr. Bryerly, Lord Ilbury, Sir William Aylmer, and Mr. Penrose Cresswell. Silas Ruthyn is appointed Maud's guardian, with the stipulation that the girl is to live with him at Bartram-Haugh until her twenty-first birthday. Lady Monica immediately recalls the strange circumstances under which Mr. Charke, a turfman to whom Silas owed large gambling debts, was found dead at Bartram-Haugh; only the fact that the body was discovered in a bedroom locked from the inside kept Silas from being charged with murder. In turn, Dr. Bryerly is disturbed by the knowledge that Silas would inherit her fortune if Maud dies before her majority, and he advises that an attempt be made to have the provisions of the wardship put aside. Silas, however, refuses to relinquish his guardianship. Maud, who interprets the will as her father's wish that she vindicate her uncle's name by becoming his ward, announces that she will go to live with Silas in Derbyshire.

With her maid, Mary Quince, Maud travels by carriage to Bartram-Haugh, where she finds the house to be old and rambling; many of the rooms are closed and locked, and the grounds are wild and neglected. Although Silas welcomes his niece courteously and with many pious sentiments, it seems to Maud that at times he is secretly laughing at her. His own rooms are furnished in great luxury. The quarters Maud shares with her cousin Milly, however, are shabby and bare. Milly is a loud, good-humored girl at whom her father sneers because of her hoydenish manners. Maud takes an immediate liking to her young relative. There is also a son, Dudley, but Milly says that her brother is seldom at home.

When Maud and her cousin go for a walk the next morning, they find the gate leading into Bartram Close locked and guarded by Meg Hawkes, the miller's rough-tongued daughter, who refuses to let them pass. The girls enter the park by a seldom-traveled path that Milly knows, and there they meet a pleasant young gentleman who introduces himself as Mr. Carysbrook, a tenant at the nearby Grange.

Maud's only companion is Milly, and she sees very little of her uncle, who is addicted to laudanum and passes many of his days in a coma. Sometimes, the girls are summoned to sit in his room while he lies quietly in bed. One day, Dr. Bryerly appears unexpectedly to transact some business with Silas. When the doctor questions her, Maud replies that she is happy at Bartram-Haugh. Dr. Bryerly gives her his address in

London and tells her to communicate with him if the need should ever arise.

Early in December, Lady Monica opens her house at nearby Elverston and invites Maud and Milly to visit her. Among the guests at dinner is Mr. Carysbrook. Lady Monica tells Maud that he is really Lord Ilbury, one of her trustees.

When Maud returns to Bartram-Haugh, she meets Dudley Ruthyn, who is the same vulgar young man she encountered twice before at Knowl. When she mentions those meetings, Silas brushes the matter aside. He declares that the spirits of youth run high at times, but that Dudley is a gentleman. Maud is relieved to learn that Milly dislikes and fears her brother, and the girls avoid him as much as possible. When Meg Hawkes becomes ill, Maud brings her medicines and delicacies and wins the strange girl's devotion.

Lord Ilbury calls at Bartram-Haugh and expresses the hope that Maud will be allowed to visit his sister at the Grange, but Silas refuses his consent. Dr. Bryerly also comes and accuses Silas of misusing his ward's property. Infuriated, Silas orders him out of the house. A short time later, Milly is sent to study in a French convent. Maud misses her company, but her situation becomes even more unbearable when Dudley begins to persecute her with proposals of marriage. Silas tells her she should consider the matter seriously for a fortnight. Before that time passes, however, Dudley's unwelcome attentions abruptly end when his secret marriage to Sarah Mangles, a barmaid, is revealed. Sarah is the woman Maud saw in the carriage at Knowl. Silas is furious and sends Dudley and his bride away. Before his departure, Dudley offers to conduct Maud safely to Lady Monica for twenty thousand pounds. Convinced that this is another of his schemes, she refuses. A few days later, she sees in the paper an announcement stating that Dudley and his wife sailed for Melbourne.

Silas confesses to his ward that he faces final and complete ruin. To elude his creditors, he will be forced to send Maud to join Milly in France; he himself will travel by another route to join them there. Maud grows apprehensive, however, when she learns that her companion on the journey is to be Madame de la Rougierre, her former governess. Confined like a prisoner, she tries to communicate her plight to Lady Monica, but the servant she bribes to carry her letter returns the message to his master. With reproaches for her ingratitude and accusations against him, Silas tells her that she is to leave for France immediately with Madame de la Rougierre; Mary Quince, the maid, will follow with him in a few days.

Guarded by her grim companion, Maud is taken to London and spends the night in an obscure hotel. The next night,

they take a train to Dover, so Madame de la Rougierre informs her, but when she awakens the next morning, she finds herself in one of the upper chambers at Bartram-Haugh. Madame de la Rougierre says only that there was a change in plans. Maud realizes that her only hope lies in Meg, who unexpectedly appears.

That night, Madame de la Rougierre drinks some drugged wine intended for Maud and falls asleep on the girl's bed. Crouched in the shadows of an old press, Maud is surprised to see the window of the room swing inward and a man suspended by a rope clamber over the sill. The intruder is Dudley; the announcement of his departure for Australia was another of Silas's fabrications. Dazed, she sees him raise a spiked hammer and strike at the figure on the bed. When old Silas enters by the doorway and the two begin to open a trunk containing the girl's jewelry, she takes advantage of the noise and runs from the room. As she leaves the house, she encounters Tom Brice, a servant who is in love with Meg. The man curses his master's villainy and drives Maud to safety at Elverston.

She is so shaken by her experience that Lady Monica hurries her off to France at once, and two years pass before she learns what happened after her flight. Silas killed himself with an overdose of opium; Dudley disappeared; and Madame de la Rougierre's body was found buried in the courtyard, its whereabouts disclosed by Meg's old father. Subsequent investigation revealed that Maud's room was the chamber in which Charke was found dead; the peculiar construction of the window frame explained how his murderer was able to enter a room locked from the inside.

Eventually, Milly becomes the wife of a worthy clergyman. Meg marries Brice and the two emigrate with money given them by Maud. Dr. Bryerly gives up his practice and undertakes the management of the Ruthyn estates. Maud marries Lord Ilbury and finds new happiness as a wife and mother.

Critical Evaluation:

Uncle Silas is more than a sentimental, nineteenth century story of the designing uncle and the lovely heir driven nearly insane by terror. It is a well-constructed novel, rambling in the Victorian fashion but highly effective in the mechanics of atmosphere and of suspense. In fact, Joseph Sheridan Le Fanu protested against his novels being labeled as examples of the sensational school of fiction popularized by Wilkie Collins and Charles Reade. In his view, his fiction was a continuation of the type of tragic romance exemplified in *The Bride of Lammermoor* (1819) and other novels by Sir Walter Scott. The fact remains that readers have never deserted Le

Fanu, and this novel represents his fiction at its best. Most notable is his handling of character and scene as they are sometimes seen in old Dutch paintings, with certain figures prominently in the foreground, others in the middle distance, and still others in the background. All are clearly visualized, however, and busy with whatever happens to be at hand. Uncle Silas and Madame de la Rougierre are creatures of terror in the foreground, but equally relevant are Dudley Ruthyn, Dr. Bryerly, Lady Monica, Milly, and Meg Hawkes, figures successively removed from the center of the action but no less necessary for the atmosphere and plot.

Uncle Silas may well represent the supreme achievement in the development of the gothic novel of terror. In the leisurely pace of its early chapters, the careful, thorough delineation of the setting and the atmosphere, the ornate, sensuous prose style, the use of traditional gothic devices, and the creation of a sinister larger-than-life villain, *Uncle Silas* resembles the earlier masterpieces of "Monk" Lewis, Ann Radcliffe, and Charles Maturin. Nevertheless, the directness and the simplicity of the action; the sharpness, the subtlety, and the psychological accuracy of the characterizations; and the carefully controlled first-person point of view all point to the sophisticated, economical modern suspense or crime novel.

The heroine of the book, Maud Ruthyn, is not particularly sympathetic; she is intellectually unimpressive, emotionally erratic, frequently snobbish, and occasionally haughty. She is, however, an excellent narrator. The reader sees everything through her eyes, and her fears become the reader's fears, but since her judgments are frequently inaccurate or incorrect, readers often see her danger and understand her mistakes long before she does. Like many gothic heroines, Maud realizes her precarious situation only after she misses the opportunity to escape from it. It is primarily through her growing sense of desperation and panic, accompanied by a gradual, belated understanding of her plight, that Le Fanu develops the reader's own sense of impending doom.

As is often the case with gothic novels, the bad characters are more impressive than the good ones. The conspirators complement one another's particular villainies. Even the minor scoundrels, Dudley Ruthyn and "Pegtop" Hawkes, are sharply defined individually, whereas the major villains, Madame de la Rougierre and Uncle Silas, are two of the most memorable characters in the entire genre.

From the start, the governess is a dominating, grotesque, and foreboding presence. While Silas remains in the background, Madame de la Rougierre hovers over Maud, "gobbling and cackling shrilly" with her exaggerated French manners, her crude physical gestures, her effusive expressions of concern, all performed in such an overwrought and clearly hypocritical fashion that even Maud detects the conspiracy behind her actions. Her sudden reappearance in the secret room at Bartram-Haugh is one of the novel's greatest shocks.

It is, however, Silas Ruthyn who remains the novel's most vivid image. Even before Silas appears in person, Le Fanu arouses curiosity about him through sinister hints, Austin Ruthyn's mysterious references, and Lady Monica's revelations. When Silas becomes an active character, he appears frightening and puzzling. He is associated, above all, with death. His health is precarious, and the atmosphere he projects, the objects with which he surrounds himself, the habits in which he indulges, all give off suggestions of mortality and impending doom. In him, the lines between reality and illusion and between life and death are blurred.

The conspirators, however, are not simply evil incarnate. While they have all the trappings of typical gothic villains, they are pathetic and even comic when their villainy is seen to be more the result of frustration and desperation than of outright evil. Dudley is a wastrel; he possesses good looks but neither the intellectual capacity nor the emotional stability necessary to make anything of himself. Madame de la Rougierre, despite her sinister behavior and grotesque looks, is revealed, in the end, to be weak and pitiable. She is, as Lady Monica suggests early in the book, nothing more than a crude, petty thief, mixed up in a conspiracy she only half understands and suffering from a weakness for alcohol that finally costs her her life.

Even Silas is almost as much to be pitied as condemned. A man of obvious talent and intellect, he becomes dissipated and perverted by weakness of character. All of his life he makes the wrong decisions, bets on the wrong horses, and sees his efforts turn out badly. To a man as firmly committed to the idea of hereditary aristocracy as Silas, the spectacle of his son Dudley is the final disillusionment. Pressed by creditors, weakened by drug addiction, unsatisfied by his religious speculations, and painfully aware of his own worthlessness, Silas persecutes Maud as a last desperate attempt to salvage something out of his wasted life.

Further Reading

Bowen, Elizabeth. "*Uncle Silas*." In *Collected Impressions*. New York: Knopf, 1950. An incisive and appreciative analysis of *Uncle Silas* that places the novel on the same plane as Emily Brontë's *Wuthering Heights*.

Howes, Marjorie. "Misalliance and Anglo-Irish Tradition in Le Fanu's *Uncle Silas*." *Nineteenth-Century Literature* 47, no. 2 (September, 1992): 164-186. Analyzes themes of heritage and inheritance in *Uncle Silas*. Focusing on the character of Maud Ruthyn, Howes develops a feminist critique of the problematic status of the Anglo-Irish. An informed and lucid use of literary theory enhances the critical discussion.

Le Fanu, Joseph. *Uncle Silas*. Edited by W. J. McCormack. New York: Oxford University Press, 1981. A scholarly edition, containing a corrected text, a Le Fanu chronology, a bibliography, and a lengthy critical introduction that stresses connections with themes that emerged in later Irish writers, such as William Butler Yeats and James Joyce. Provides a comprehensive critical appraisal of the novel based on a sense of the central significance of deception in its formal design and complex plot.

McCormack, W. J. *Sheridan Le Fanu and Victorian Ireland*. New York: Oxford University Press, 1980. At the center of this definitive study of Le Fanu's life and times is an elaborate and sophisticated reading of *Uncle Silas*. Drawing on Le Fanu family papers and his intellectual and cultural background, McCormack acknowledges *Uncle Silas*'s place both as one of the landmark achievements of the gothic genre in English and as a revealing commentary on the mind-set of the Anglo-Irish class to which Le Fanu belonged.

Milbank, Alison. *Daughters of the House: Modes of the Gothic in Victorian Fiction*. New York: St. Martin's Press, 1992. Of the two chapters devoted to Le Fanu, one deals with *Uncle Silas* and offers an analysis of the interlinking of gothic, feminist, and Swedenborgian elements in the novel. The protagonist, Maud Ruthyn, is the focus of this critique.

Sage, Victor. *Le Fanu's Gothic: The Rhetoric of Darkness*. New York: Palgrave Macmillan, 2004. Examines Le Fanu's stylistic development and narrative methods, placing his work within the context of the cultural politics of his era. Includes an analysis of *Uncle Silas*.

Walton, James. *Vision and Vacancy: The Fictions of J. S. Le Fanu*. Dublin: University College Dublin Press, 2007. An examination of all of Le Fanu's fiction, discussing his philosophy and literary influences. Places Le Fanu's work within the context of Victorian English and Continental novels. Demonstrates how his horror writing stands apart from traditional ghost stories of the Victorian era.

Uncle Tom's Cabin
Or, Life Among the Lowly

Author: Harriet Beecher Stowe (1811-1896)
First published: 1851-1852, serial; 1852, book
Type of work: Novel
Type of plot: Social realism
Time of plot: Mid-nineteenth century
Locale: Kentucky and Mississippi

Principal characters:
UNCLE TOM, a slave
MR. SHELBY, a plantation owner
GEORGE SHELBY, his son
HALEY, a slave dealer
EVA ST. CLARE, the daughter of a wealthy southerner
SIMON LEGREE, a planter
ELIZA, a runaway slave
HARRY, her son
TOPSY, a young slave

The Story:

Because his Kentucky plantation is encumbered by debt, Mr. Shelby makes plans to sell one of his slaves to his chief creditor, a New Orleans slave dealer named Haley. The dealer shrewdly selects Uncle Tom as partial payment on Shelby's debt. While Haley and Shelby are discussing the transaction, Harry, the son of another slave, Eliza, comes into the room. Haley wants to buy Harry too, but at first Shelby is unwilling to part with the child. Eliza hears enough of the conversation to be frightened. She confides her fears to George Harris, her husband, a slave on an adjoining plantation. George, who is already bitter because his master has put him to work in the fields when he is capable of doing better work, promises that someday he will have his revenge on his hard masters. Eliza has been brought up more indulgently by the Shelbys, and she begs George not to try anything rash.

After supper, the Shelby slaves gather for a meeting in the

cabin of Uncle Tom and his wife, Aunt Chloe. They sing songs, and young George Shelby, who has eaten his supper there, reads from the Bible. In the big house, Mr. Shelby signs the papers making Uncle Tom and little Harry the property of Haley. Eliza, upon learning her child's fate from some remarks made by Mr. Shelby to his wife, flees with Harry, hoping to reach Canada and safety. Uncle Tom, hearing that he has been sold, resigns himself to the wisdom of Providence.

The next day, after Haley discovers his loss, he sets out to capture Eliza. She has a good head start, however, and Mrs. Shelby purposely delays Haley's pursuit by serving a late breakfast. When Eliza catches sight of her pursuers, she escapes across the partially frozen Ohio River by jumping from one piece of floating ice to another, with young Harry in her arms. Haley hires two slave catchers, Marks and Loker, to track Eliza and Harry through Ohio. If they catch her and her son, they are to be given Eliza as payment for their work. They set off that night.

Eliza and Harry, on the run, find shelter in the home of Senator and Mrs. Bird. The senator takes them to the house of a man known to aid fugitive slaves. Uncle Tom, however, is not so lucky. Haley makes sure that Tom will not escape by shackling his ankles before taking him to the boat bound for New Orleans. When young George Shelby hears that Tom has been sold, he follows Haley on his horse. George gives Tom a dollar as a token of his sympathy and tells the slave that he will buy him back one day.

At the same time, George Harris begins his escape. Light-skinned enough to pass as a Spaniard, he appears at a tavern as a gentleman and takes a room there, hoping to find help through the Underground Railroad before too long. Eliza is resting at the home of Rachel and Simeon Halliday when George Harris arrives in the same Quaker settlement.

On board the boat bound for New Orleans, Uncle Tom saves the life of young Eva St. Clare, and in gratitude Eva's father purchases the slave from Haley. Eva tells Tom that he will now have a happy life, for her father is kind to everyone. Augustine St. Clare is married to a woman who imagines herself sick and therefore takes no interest in her daughter, Eva. St. Clare had gone north to bring his cousin, Miss Ophelia, back to the South to provide care for the neglected and delicate Eva. When they arrive at the St. Clare plantation, Tom is made head coachman.

Meanwhile, Loker and Marks are on the trail of Eliza, George, and Harry. They catch up with the fugitives, and in a fight George wounds Loker. Marks flees, and the Quakers who have been protecting the runaways take Loker along with them and give him medical treatment.

Unused to lavish southern customs, Miss Ophelia tries to understand the South. Shocked at the extravagance of St. Clare's household, she attempts to bring order out of the chaos, but she receives no encouragement. Indulgent in all things, St. Clare is indifferent to the affairs of his family and his property. Uncle Tom lives an easy life in the loft over the stable. He and little Eva become close friends, with St. Clare's approval. Sometimes St. Clare has doubts regarding the morality of the institution of slavery, and, in one of these moods, he buys an odd, pixielike slave child, named Topsy, for his prim and proper New England cousin to educate.

Eva grows increasingly frail. Knowing that she is about to die, she asks her father to free his slaves, as he has so often promised he will one day do. After Eva's death, St. Clare begins to read his Bible and to make plans to free all his slaves. He gives Topsy to Miss Ophelia legally, so that the spinster might rear the child as she wishes. Then, one evening, while trying to separate two quarreling men, he receives a knife wound in the side and dies shortly afterward. Mrs. St. Clare, who inherits all his property, has no intention of freeing the slaves, and she orders that Tom be sent to the slave market. At a public auction, Tom is sold to a brutal plantation owner named Simon Legree.

Legree drinks heavily, and his plantation house has fallen into ruin. He keeps dogs for the purpose of tracking runaway slaves. At the plantation's slave quarters, Tom is given a sack of corn for the week; he is told to grind it himself and bake the meal into cakes for his supper. At the mill where he goes to grind the corn, Tom aids two women, and in return, they bake his cakes for him. He read selections from the Bible to them.

For a few weeks, Tom quietly tries to please his harsh master. One day, while picking cotton, he helps another slave, a woman who is sick, by putting cotton into her basket. For this act, Legree orders him to flog the woman. When Tom refuses, Legree has him flogged until he faints. A slave named Cassy comes to Tom's aid. She tells Tom the story of her life with Legree and of a young daughter who had been sold years before. Then she goes to Legree's apartment and torments him. She hates her master, and she has power over him. Legree is superstitious, and when Cassy talks, flashing her eyes at him, he feels as though she is casting an evil spell. Haunted by the secrets of his guilty past, he drinks until he falls asleep. By the next morning, however, he has forgotten his fears, and he knocks Tom to the ground with his fist. Meanwhile, far to the north, George and Eliza and young Harry are making their way slowly through the stations on the Underground Railroad toward Canada.

Cassy and Emmeline, another slave, are determined to make their escape. Knowing the consequences if they should be caught, they trick Legree into thinking they are hiding in the swamp. When Legree sends dogs and men after them, they sneak back into the house and hide in the garret. Legree suspects that Tom knows where the women have gone and decides to beat the truth out of him. He has Tom beaten until the slave can neither speak nor stand. Two days later, George Shelby arrives to buy Tom back, but he is too late—Tom is dying. When George threatens to have Legree tried for murder, Legree mocks him. George strikes Legree in the face and knocks him down.

Still hiding in the attic, Cassy and Emmeline masquerade as ghosts. Frightened, Legree drinks harder than ever, and George Shelby is able to help them escape. Later, on a riverboat headed north, the two women meet a lady named Madame de Thoux, who says that she is George Harris's sister. With this disclosure, Cassy learns also that Eliza, her daughter who had been sold years before, is the Eliza who married George and, with him and her child, has escaped safely to Canada. These relatives are reunited in Canada after many years. In Kentucky, George Shelby frees all of his slaves in the name of Uncle Tom.

Critical Evaluation:

In Harriet Beecher Stowe's view, slavery was an evil against which anyone professing Christianity must protest. *Uncle Tom's Cabin* was precisely such a protest. Stowe believed that the debate over slavery often missed or minimized the essential point that the families of slaves were torn apart by the institution. Her own strong family orientation informs the novel throughout, even as her unconventional pursuit of a career as a professional writer gave her the means of conveying her thoughts to the wider world.

Writing this novel gave Stowe a professional outlet. Like many educated nineteenth century American women, she experienced frustration because there was little opportunity for educated women to use their voices to influence the course of American life. Like her father, husband, and brothers, Stowe felt called to preach. Denied a pulpit, she used *Uncle Tom's Cabin* as her sermon, her means of educating the world about a system that she was convinced was evil and must be stopped.

As a professional writer of the nineteenth century, Stowe knew that there was a large female reading public. Consequently, much of the novel is designed to appeal to those readers as it paints slavery as a male-devised system that women are called upon to correct. The novel features several strong female characters whose common sense and strong human sympathy recoil from slavery's inhumanity. Throughout the novel, human feeling is raised above the eco-

nomics of self-interest and the expediency of laws. Moreover, Stowe "feminized" the slave narrative, stressing Eliza's heroic escape from bondage with her son as well as the ingenious plan used by Cassy to free herself from Simon Legree. Prior to her novel, most accounts of slavery, such as Frederick Douglass's *Narrative of the Life of Frederick Douglass, an American Slave* (1845), were told from the male perspective and celebrated male courage and resourcefulness.

Uncle Tom's Cabin provides a panorama of nineteenth century American culture, which suggests that its author was a precursor of the realistic writers who dominated the literary scene after the Civil War. The novel contains innumerable characters of all types and backgrounds: slaves and slave catchers, slave owners and Quakers, a self-pitying southern belle and an unsympathetic New Englander, mothers and children, unprincipled politicians and slovenly cooks, the careless and the deeply caring, the sexually exploited and the sadistic, the angelic and the impish. It includes scenes along the shores of Lake Erie and in the currents of the Mississippi River, in Ohio and in Kentucky, in Arkansas and in Canada. Using a broad canvas as she did, Stowe hoped to show that slavery, far from an isolated and temporary problem, was institutionalized and nationalized and affected not only slaves and slave owners but the entire country. Moreover, she showed that persons of all types, from the good to the evil, were caught in the power of the institution.

Uncle Tom's Cabin has been criticized on several grounds. It is said to lack form and control; its social purpose is sometimes seen as incompatible with fine aesthetic qualities. However, the moralism and didacticism displayed in the novel were, in a sense, part of Stowe's aesthetic. That is, she believed that art was not above morality but was activated by it. She did not believe in art for art's sake, but rather in the power of art to do good.

The novel's titular hero has been criticized for his willingness to submit to white men's arbitrary power and physical abuse. One must remember, however, that Stowe was influenced by her Christian faith when she created Tom and his actions. To her, Tom's submission was not to tyranny but to Christian principle, and in that submission lay his power to change the world for the better. Stowe created Tom in the image of Jesus Christ.

"Critical Evaluation" by William L. Howard

Further Reading

Adams, John R. *Harriet Beecher Stowe*. Rev. ed. Boston: G. K. Hall, 1989. Provides biographical information about Stowe and about the Beecher family as well as critical examinations of Stowe's writings. Connects *Uncle Tom's Cabin* to Stowe's religious ideas and personal experiences.

Allen, William. *Rethinking "Uncle Tom": The Political Philosophy of Harriet Beecher Stowe.* Lanham, Md.: Lexington Books, 2009. Analyzes how *Uncle Tom's Cabin* depicts the conditions of democratic life and the nature of modern humanism. Places this novel and Stowe's other work within the context of nineteenth century abolitionism and reformism.

Ammons, Elizabeth, ed. *Harriet Beecher Stowe's "Uncle Tom's Cabin": A Casebook.* New York: Oxford University Press, 2007. Includes several of Stowe's letters and other writings dealing with the abolition of slavery as well as twentieth century critiques of the novel by James Baldwin, Leslie Fiedler, and others.

Crozier, Alice C. *The Novels of Harriet Beecher Stowe.* New York: Oxford University Press, 1969. Notes that Stowe was less interested in the novel as art than in the novel as history. Traces the influence of the British writers Sir Walter Scott and Lord Byron on her work. Comments on the cultural context in which the novels were written, which accounts not only for the Victorian sentimentality of *Uncle Tom's Cabin* but also for a distinctively American realism that anticipates Mark Twain.

Foster, Charles H. *The Rungless Ladder: Harriet Beecher Stowe and New England Puritanism.* New York: Cooper Square, 1970. Focuses on Stowe's inner struggle with New England Puritanism, identifying what she read and how that affected her life and writings. Demonstrates how *Uncle Tom's Cabin* was a product of her religious thinking and personal anguish, and argues that Stowe projects herself and her own struggles, particularly her attempt to reconcile herself with the death of one of her children, onto the novel's characters.

Gossett, Thomas F. *Uncle Tom's Cabin and American Culture.* Dallas, Tex.: Southern Methodist University Press, 1985. Excellent, detailed study shows why *Uncle Tom's Cabin* was the most widely read American novel of its time. Describes the conditions that led to the creation of the book and then analyzes the work both as fiction and as social criticism. Also discusses the reception the novel received upon its publication in the American North and South and in Europe.

Hedrick, Joan D. *Harriet Beecher Stowe: A Life.* New York: Oxford University Press, 1994. This biography is a good source of information about Stowe's career as a writer. Traces her writing of *Uncle Tom's Cabin* from her initial resolve, through her decision to address the sexual exploitation of female slaves, to her effort to substantiate the events depicted in the novel with facts collected in *A Key to Uncle Tom's Cabin.*

Meer, Sarah. *Uncle Tom Mania: Slavery, Minstrelsy, and Transatlantic Culture in the 1850's.* Athens: University of Georgia Press, 2005. Examines how blackface minstrelsy, the debate about slavery, and America's emerging cultural identity in the nineteenth century affected how *Uncle Tom's Cabin* was read, discussed, dramatized, sold, and politicized in the United States and abroad. Examines the novel itself and the sketches, songs, plays, and translations it inspired.

Parfait, Claire. *The Publishing History of "Uncle Tom's Cabin," 1852-2002.* Burlington, Vt.: Ashgate, 2007. Chronicles the publication history of the novel, including discussion of female authorship, copyright issues, and author-publisher relations. Describes how various editions of the novel reflect changes in American culture.

Rosenthal, Debra J. *A Routledge Literary Sourcebook on Harriet Beecher Stowe's "Uncle Tom's Cabin."* New York: Routledge, 2004. Includes primary documents placing the novel within the context of nineteenth century American history, reviews of the novel from the 1850's, and a selection of twentieth century critiques. Provides analyses of key passages.

Uncle Vanya

Author: Anton Chekhov (1860-1904)
First produced: Dyadya Vanya, 1899; first published, 1897
   (English translation, 1914)
Type of work: Drama
Type of plot: Impressionistic realism
Time of plot: Nineteenth century
Locale: Russia

Principal characters:
ALEXANDR SEREBRYAKOV, a retired professor
YELENA ANDREYEVNA, his twenty-seven-year-old wife
SONYA ALEXANDROVNA, his daughter by his first wife
MARYA VOYNITSKY, the widow of a privy councillor and
   mother of his first wife
IVAN VOYNITSKY, her son
MIHAIL ASTROV, a doctor
MARINA, an old nurse

The Story:

Astrov, the doctor, calls to attend the retired Professor Serebryakov, who complained all night of pains in his legs. To the doctor's annoyance, the professor leaves for a long walk with his wife, Yelena, and his daughter, Sonya. Astrov tells the old nurse, Marina, that he is so overworked he feels a hundred years old. He also feels that, having worked with weak, discontented people for years, he became as strange as they. Caring for nothing and no one, he wonders if people living a hundred years hence will remember men like him who struggled to beat out the road for them.

Marina explains that the professor completely changed the routine of the house, so that everyone waits on him and routine work is fitted in where possible. Ivan Voynitsky enviously describes the fortunate life the professor has. The professor lives on the estate of his first wife, whose mother dotes on his every word. He is retired now and writing as he pleases; he has a new and beautiful young wife to cater to him. It is, however, Ivan, Sonya's Uncle Vanya, who blindly follows his mother's ideals and makes the estate a splendidly productive place that can supply all the professor's needs. Only recently did Ivan realize how selfish the professor is. Ivan tells his mother that he can no longer bear to hear of the pamphlets that were her life for the last fifty years.

When the professor comes in, he immediately excuses himself to return to his writing. Yelena, apologizing to the doctor, says that her husband is well again. Both Ivan and the doctor admire her extravagantly, and the doctor invites her and Sonya to come to his estate to see his trees. A crank on the subject of trees, the doctor wants to restore the countryside to its state before the peasants indiscriminately cut down the forests. Yelena realizes Sonya is attracted to the doctor. Yelena is bored with everything, even Ivan's love for her.

When the professor again complains of pains in his legs, he keeps his wife awake for two nights. Believing that he earned the right to be disagreeable and tyrannical at his age,

and feeling that he is in a vault with stupid people who make foolish conversation, he refuses to see the doctor he summoned. He begs not to be left with Ivan, who will talk him to death. Only Marina seems to be able to handle him; she leads him away so that the others can rest.

Yelena asks Ivan to try to reconcile everyone. When Ivan declares his love to her again, she leaves him. Ivan realizes he could have fallen in love with her ten years before and might even have married her if he had not been wrapped up in the ideal of fulfilling the professor's wishes. He feels cheated in the realization that the retired professor is a nonentity.

Ivan and the doctor continue the drinking they start while the doctor waits to see the professor. Sonya asks them both to stop, Ivan because he is living on illusions, the doctor because she does not want him to destroy himself. She tries to tell him obliquely that she loves him, but he feels that his reactions are blunted. He will never be able to love anyone, though Yelena might be able to turn his head.

Yelena and Sonya effect a reconciliation when Yelena explains that she married Sonya's father in the belief that she loved him, only to find she was in love with an ideal. Having lost that illusion, she finds herself very unhappy. Sonya, glad to make friends with her, is happy about everything; she speaks at last to the doctor, even if he does not understand her.

While waiting for the hour at which the professor asks all the family to join him, Yelena complains of being bored. Sonya suggests that she help on the estate. When Yelena declines all suggestions, Ivan tells her she is too indolent to do anything. To make matters worse, her indolence is catching, for he stopped work to follow her, as did Sonya and the doctor, who used to come once a month but now comes daily. Since Yelena seems to have mermaid blood in her veins, he says, she should let herself go for once and fall in love with a water sprite. Yelena is indignant. Ivan, as a peace offering, goes to get her some autumn roses.

Sonya asks Yelena's help. She knows the doctor comes to see Yelena, not even realizing Sonya is there. Yelena decides to speak to him in Sonya's behalf. When she does, he laughs at her for pretending she does not know why he comes. Then he kisses her. Yelena halfheartedly holds him off until she sees Ivan returning with the roses.

The professor, not content with country living but unable to live in the city on the income from the estate, suggests that they sell the estate, invest most of the money, and buy a small place in Finland with the remainder. His plan is greeted with horror, particularly by Ivan, who is driven almost mad as he feels the estate slipping away from Sonya, the work of twenty-five years undone. He explains how the estate was bought for Sonya's mother and handed on to Sonya; how he paid off the mortgage and made the place productive; how Sonya and he slaved on the property by day and over books by night with only the professor in mind. Feeling cheated, he rushes away while the professor declares that he can no longer live under the same roof with Ivan. Yelena begs him to leave the place immediately, but to apologize to Ivan before they leave. When the professor tries to make amends, Ivan shoots at him twice, missing both times.

Marina, pleased with the arrangement, hopes that matters will settle down after the professor and his wife leave. Astrov refuses to go home before Ivan gives back the morphia he took from the doctor's bag. Ivan, saying he is a madman, begs for a way out, but the doctor laughs and says that the two of them, the only well-educated men in the district, are swamped in the trivialities of country life and that they are both eccentric, a very normal human condition. After reconciliations all around, the professor and Yelena leave, followed by Astrov. Marina rocks away with satisfaction, Ivan's mother goes back to her pamphlets, and Sonya assures Ivan that they completed their lives' work and will find rest in heaven.

Critical Evaluation:

Anton Chekhov's oeuvre opened Russian literature and world drama to the art of everyday trifles and occurrences. In exploring Russian society, Chekhov questioned the purpose of life, but he was less interested in finding an answer than in posing the right questions.

To understand Chekhov's drama, it is necessary to understand the milieu in which he wrote, the innovations that were changing Western theater practices, and the stance of the dramatist himself. Russia in the 1880's and 1890's was experiencing the erosion of rigid class distinctions that had characterized the *ancien régime*. Much of the landowning gentry was impoverished and under the necessity of selling off parcels of their large estates to the rising mercantile and industrial class. Serfdom had finally been abolished, and the enormous peasant class was faced with both displacement and new opportunities. The age of those great Russian novelists Fyodor Dostoevski and Leo Tolstoy was coming to a close, and as it did it was opening the way for a new kind of art. Throughout Western civilization, science and technology were modifying the lenses through which artists and philosophers looked at the world and humanity's place within it.

This was the age of literary realism and naturalism, and writers began to focus on the lives and problems of ordinary people. On the stage, the theater of social consciousness pioneered by Henrik Ibsen and August Strindberg gave rise to a new kind of dramaturgy and stagecraft. Chekhov took the realistic innovations of the Scandinavians one step further in creating his kind of naturalistic drama, a drama with no real beginnings or endings, and one that recognizes the complexities and continuities of life.

Chekhov, trained as a physician, was eminently suited for this kind of examination. His practice had carried him to all the levels of Russian society and intensified his objective observational powers. Initially acclaimed as a short story writer, he began to write for the theater in the early 1880's. The four plays considered his masterpieces—*Uncle Vanya*, *Chayka* (1896; *The Seagull*, 1909), *Tri sestry* (1901; *The Three Sisters*, 1920), and *Vishnyovy sad* (1904; *The Cherry Orchard*, 1908)—emerged from the period during which Konstantin Stanislavsky and Nemirovich-Danchenko founded the Moscow Art Theatre, where Chekhov's plays first found successful productions. Chekhov did not, however, approve of the highly realistic and tragically inclined interpretations that the first productions of the Moscow Art Theatre gave to his plays. Until his death in 1904, he insisted that he had written comedies of Russian life.

Uncle Vanya, the second of Chekhov's plays produced by the Moscow Art Theatre, is a reworking of an earlier play from 1889 entitled *The Wood Demon (Leshy)*. *Uncle Vanya* eliminates many of the more romantic elements and rambling aspects of the earlier version and shifts some of the focus from the physician character (the wood demon of the 1889 play) to the new title character. Indeed, it has been argued that *Uncle Vanya* has no single protagonist but rather four major characters, Ivan (Uncle Vanya), Dr. Astrov, Sonya, and Yelena. The critic Philip Bodinat went so far as to declare that the protagonist of the play is "the individual" as embodied by each of the four major characters in conflict with the stifling environment of provincial Russian life.

Certainly, *Uncle Vanya* depicts characters who have the potential to live fuller lives but who cannot escape from the rut of societal expectations and self-imposed restrictions. Chekhov draws these individuals sympathetically but critically. Ultimately, they are all frustrated in their attempts to embrace a more meaningful existence. They are offered the possibility of art, but this opportunity is repeatedly devalued. When Sonya pleads with Yelena to play the piano to celebrate their reconciliation, Yelena must first secure the permission of her husband, who is disturbed by the music when he is not feeling well; he refuses, and the two women must do without the music. Later, it is Yelena who is the agent obstructing the artistic impulse. She asks to see Astrov's drawings of the forest, intending to sound him out about his feelings for Sonya. He spreads them out before her and explains how they depict the destruction of the area, but when he realizes that she is bored by his passion, he whisks them out of sight.

Serebryakov, the retired professor, embodies a withered academic view of art as described in Vanya's angry outburst:

A person lectures and writes about art for precisely twenty-five years, but he understands precisely nothing about art. For twenty-five years he's gone on chewing up and spitting out everyone else's ideas about realism, naturalism, and every other kind of nonsense. For twenty-five years he's been lecturing and writing about what intelligent people have known for a long time and what stupid people have no interest in. To put it bluntly, for twenty-five years he has been pouring from one empty pot into the next.

Vanya's anger and frustration stem from his long-held delusion that he is contributing to the world's knowledge by working to secure the means for the professor to carry on his writing.

Love, another means for rising above the mundane, is also thwarted throughout the play. Vanya's unrequited passion for Yelena is doubly painful because he realizes that he might have won her devotion had he wooed her when she was younger. Yelena confesses to Sonya that she once thought she loved her husband because of her fascination with his fame, but it was a hollow passion that could not endure. The attraction between Astrov and Yelena is thwarted by social and moral conventions, yet it also destroys any hope of Astrov's ever reciprocating Sonya's devotion.

The close of the play finds all of the characters in the same situation they occupied before Serebryakov and Yelena descended on the estate. The one difference is that now they must live without the illusions of their hopes. Each must once again take up the stifling trifles of daily life to distract themselves from their lives of quiet desperation. However, Chekhov also reveals that what transpires on stage is not the only conclusion to the dilemmas the characters face. In essence, what Chekhov does is to throw out a challenge to the members of the audience to examine their own lives and expectations.

Jane Anderson Jones

Further Reading

Bentley, Eric. "Craftsmanship in *Uncle Vanya*." In *Anton Chekhov's Plays*, translated and edited by Eugene K. Bristow. New York: Norton, 1977. Bentley explains how Chekhov's naturalism in *Uncle Vanya* is grounded in his mature psychological vision that life has no real endings.

Bordinat, Philip. "Dramatic Structure in Chekhov's *Uncle Vanya*." In *Chekhov's Great Plays: A Critical Anthology*, edited with an introduction by Jean-Pierre Barricelli. New York: New York University Press, 1981. Bordinat argues that *Uncle Vanya* follows classical dramatic construction if the protagonist is seen as "the individual" embodied in the four major characters. The conflict then becomes the individual's desire for happiness in the face of the provincial Russian "wasteland."

Bunin, Ivan. *About Chekhov: The Unfinished Symphony*. Edited and translated by Thomas Gaiton Marullo. Evanston, Ill.: Northwestern University Press, 2007. Bunin, a writer and Nobel laureate, began a biography of Chekhov but did not complete it before he died in 1953. Although incomplete, the book provides intimate details of Chekhov at work, in love, and in relationships with other Russian writers.

Gottlieb, Vera, and Paul Allain, eds. *The Cambridge Companion to Chekhov*. New York: Cambridge University Press, 2000. Collection of essays about Chekhov, including a biography, an essay placing his life and his work within the context of Russia, and a discussion of the playwright at the Moscow Art Theatre. Also includes director Leonid Heifetz's notes about staging *Uncle Vanya*.

Kataev, Vladimir. *If Only We Could Know: An Interpretation of Chekhov*. Edited and translated by Harvey Pitcher. Chicago: Ivan R. Dee, 2002. Kataev, a Russian scholar, offers interpretations of Chekhov's works, emphasizing the uniqueness and specificity of each character and incident. Includes the essay "Wasted Lives: *Uncle Vanya*."

Peace, Richard. "*Uncle Vanya*." In *Chekhov: A Study of the Four Major Plays*. New Haven, Conn.: Yale University Press, 1983. Peace focuses on the symbolism of *Uncle Vanya* and discusses the significance in the play of tea drinking, the forest, the storm, birds and animals, and work.

Rayfield, Donald. *Anton Chekhov: A Life*. New York: Henry Holt, 1998. Comprehensive biography, offering a wealth of detail about Chekhov's life and work.

_____. *Chekhov's "Uncle Vania" and "The Wood Demon."* London: Bristol Classical Press, 1995. A close reading and interpretation of *Uncle Vanya*. Rayfield describes how the play evolved from Chekhov's unsuccessful comedy *The Wood Demon*.

Yermilov, V. "*Uncle Vanya*: The Play's Movement." In *Chekhov: A Collection of Critical Essays*, edited by Robert Louis Jackson. Englewood Cliffs, N.J.: Prentice-Hall, 1967. Discusses the use of musical and weather imagery in the play. Yermilov points out the cyclical movement of the play: The external situation at the end replicates the situation at the beginning, but internally everyone has changed.

Under Fire
The Story of a Squad

Author: Henri Barbusse (1873-1935)
First published: Le Feu: Journal d'une escouade, 1916 (English translation, 1917)
Type of work: Novel
Type of plot: Political
Time of plot: 1914-1915
Locale: France

Principal characters:
VOLPATTE,
EUDORE,
POTERLOO, and
JOSEPH MESNIL, French soldiers

The Story:

High up in the mountains, the rich old men have every type of medical care at their sanatorium. When an obsequious servant softly tells them that war has begun, they take the news in various ways. One says that France must win; another thinks it will be the last war. Far down on the plain, they can see specks, like ants, hurrying to and fro. Those thirty million men, in their common misery, hold great power in their hands. When they become miserable enough, they will stop wars.

The soldiers come out of the dugouts in the morning to the sound of rifle fire and cannonading. They wear fantastic dress against the cold, the damp, and the mud, and all are incredibly dirty. As they stumble out into the trenches, they reach inside their clothes to scratch their bare skins. As they walk along the trench, the oozy mud releases each foot with a sticky sigh. Bertrand's squad, holding a secondary trench in the reserve line, is getting ready for another day. Lamuse, the ox man, is puffy around the eyes; he had been on fatigue duty during the night.

Three breathless fatigue men bring up the breakfast. One of the squad, Paradis, asks what is in the cans. When the mess man merely shrugs, Paradis looks in the cans and sees that they hold kidney beans in oil, bully beef, pudding, and coffee.

One man explains to his neighbor the arrangement of the trenches, for he has seen a military map and has made calculations. There are more than six thousand miles of trenches on the French side and as many more on the German side. The French front is only an eighth of the total world front. Just to think about it makes one feel more insignificant, and it is terrible to imagine so much mud. The only possible way to look at the whole matter is to concentrate on dislodging the Germans in the opposite lines.

One man, a private, once saw a captured Prussian colonel who was being led along the communication trench. When the private kicked him, the officer nearly had a seizure to think that a subordinate had touched him. The squad agrees that the German officers are the real evil.

There is a disturbance just ahead; several important people are coming to visit. From their oaths and grunts, it is clear that they are civilians. One of the visitors is so bold as to ask whether the coffee is good. The squad remembers the saying that a war can be won if the civilians can hold out.

When the mail comes, rumors fly fast. Many are sure that their squad is soon to be sent to the Riviera for a long rest; one man has heard that they are going to Egypt. The troops stop gossiping when a company of African soldiers moves by; they conclude that an attack has been planned, for the Africans are notoriously ferocious fighters.

During a sharp attack, both of Volpatte's ears are almost

severed. At the dressing station, the doctors bandage his head. Volpatte is happy to be going to the rear, where at last he will be able to rest. After a long while, he returns to the trenches with his ears nicely sewed. When his comrades ask him about the hospital, he becomes so angry he can scarcely speak. Then it all comes out: The hospital is swarming with malcontents, malingerers, and general shirkers. The worst are those assigned to the hospital for duty; they seem to think they run the whole war. The squad soothes Volpatte, saying, let those who can, get by easily.

When the squad retires for a brief rest, they are billeted in a village where, for an outrageous sum, they rent a cowshed without walls. They use a door set up on boxes as a table and a plank as a bench, but they find it a wonderful experience to be aboveground once more. The woman who runs the house sells them wine for twenty-two sous, although the established price is fifteen sous a bottle. Everywhere they go they hear the same story: The civilians are enduring all the hardships.

Eudore gets a fourteen-day leave. His wife, a practical person, has applied well in advance for a permit to go to the village of her husband's people. She runs a tiny inn with only one room, where she would have no privacy to entertain her man, whereas Eudore's people have a big house. Eudore arrives in his village after much delay with only seven days left of his furlough, but his wife is not there; her permit has not arrived. Fearing that he will miss her, he stays with his parents and waits. Then she writes to say that no permits are allowed for civilian travel. Eudore goes to the mayor and gets permission to go to his wife. It is raining very hard when he gets off the train to walk the several additional miles to his home. On the way, he falls in with four other soldiers returning from leave. They tramp along together in the rain until they come to the inn. Eudore and his wife cannot turn the four soldiers out in the rain, and so all six of them spend the night sitting in chairs in the tiny room. Early in the morning Eudore must leave, as his furlough is over.

Fraternization with the enemy is strictly forbidden. While out looking for bodies, Poterloo takes a chance and falls in with some German privates, jolly fellows who offer to go with Poterloo to a nearby Alsatian village so that he can see his wife. Poterloo puts on some great boots and a German coat and follows his new friends behind the German lines. They reach the village safely, and that night, Poterloo walks twice past the house where his wife is staying with relatives. Through the lighted window, he can see his wife and her sister at dinner with a group of German noncommissioned officers. They are eating well and enjoying themselves. Poterloo carries back to the trenches a disheartening image in his mind: his wife laughing up into the face of a German sergeant.

Of the six Mesnil brothers, four have been killed by 1915, and the survivors, Joseph and André, have been pessimistic about their own chances. On reconnaissance, one of Bertrand's squad discovers André, dead, propped upright in a shell crater. At first they are afraid to tell Joseph, but when they tell him he does not seem much affected by the news. Bertrand is killed, and Joseph is wounded in the leg. He is taken to the dismal dressing station, a large dugout. There are many men in the dugout, most of them resigned to death, all of them given to spiritless discussion. They agree that to stop war, one has to kill the spirit of war, and that appears to be a difficult job. It comes as a new thought to some of them that they are the masses, and the masses have the power to stop war, but it is too big a job. Many men think only in terms of killing the enemy. It hardly matters anyway, as nearly all of them will be dead soon. The war goes on.

Critical Evaluation:

World War I was the first conflict to produce a major body of literature written by men who had actually been involved in the fighting. Among the poets, novelists, and memoirists who recorded their experiences in the trenches of the western front, many strove to voice protests equal to the enormities that they had suffered and witnessed. Henri Barbusse was one of the first of these, and *Under Fire* was one of the few World War I novels that was written and published before the war ended. It furnished a model for later writers. Barbusse composed the book in the hospital from diaries he had written at the front in 1914-1915, and he published it in both serial and novel forms late in 1916. *Under Fire* proved an immediate success. In France, it won the prestigious Goncourt Prize, and by the end of the war it was a worldwide best seller, having sold almost a quarter of a million copies.

The novel's critical reception was mixed. Early reviewers tended to judge it according to whether they believed that life at the front was as wretched as Barbusse depicted it to be. Some were outraged by what they felt to be seditious political views expressed in the work, but many critics greeted its graphic descriptions almost with relief: Here at last, they felt, was the truth about the war. At the time *Under Fire* reached the public, a time when the cost in human life continued to mount without any visible impact on the stalemate in France and Belgium, attitudes toward the war had begun to shift away from the enthusiasm and idealism of the war's first year. Those critical of the war considered the raw immediacy of *Under Fire* to be its chief virtue; if the characters seemed less carefully drawn and the story line less tightly constructed than in more polished literary works, this only lent it greater plausibility as a documentary.

Under Fire came to be less widely read after the late 1920's, when it was supplanted by a deluge of war writing. By the late twentieth century, however, many critics considered the novel an important milestone and a work exemplifying some of the difficulties of the protest novel, among them that of reconciling realism and prophetic vision. Although the most gripping chapters in *Under Fire* ("Of Burdens," "The Portal," "Under Fire," and "The Fatigue-Party") present a convincing picture of day-to-day survival in the trenches and of the chaos of battle, these sections are mixed with the kind of earnest political invective and dogma that can become tedious, as it does in the last chapter, "The Dawn." Barbusse had joined the army with mixed impulses; as a committed socialist and pacifist, he supported the war because he believed he would be serving the socialist cause and fighting German militarism in pursuit of a new and peaceful Europe. Yet in *Under Fire* he argued that the war must be abandoned after all, for the enemy was not Germany but the profiteers and "sword-wavers" in the rear on both sides. The collapse of the trenches into mud and water during the final bombardment described in the book effects a kind of cosmic cataclysm, a dissolution of earth, water, fire, and air into a single muddy element that apocalyptically heralds the "new heaven and new earth" glimpsed by the soldiers in the last chapter. Here, however, the sudden transformation of Barbusse's simple and unaffected comrades into unanimous spokesmen for socialist dogma strains the reader's credulity.

Barbusse's chief interest was not in his work's qualities as fiction but in its power as protest—its ability to communicate the almost unspeakable facts about the experience of his fellow soldiers as a corrective to the heart-cheering, idealistic accounts in the newspapers. As fiction, it could be published without interference from the official censors. Whatever its shortcomings as literature, *Under Fire* filled an urgent need, the thirst of both civilians and soldiers for an unrestrained firsthand depiction of the front lines.

Barbusse's novel was an important influence on the war poetry of Siegfried Sassoon (1886-1967) and Wilfred Owen (1893-1918) and—perhaps partly by way of their poems— on the war prose of the late 1920's and early 1930's. Such later classics of the war as Erich Maria Remarque's novel *Im Westen nichts Neues* (1928, serial; 1929, book; *All Quiet on the Western Front*, 1929) and Robert Graves's autobiography *Goodbye to All That* (1929) employ a similarly episodic and graphic style but forgo the political didacticism, allowing themes to emerge from parallels among the episodes. *Under Fire* thus constitutes an important source of the enduring

myth of World War I, which presents soldiers as the innocent victims of a belligerent and bloodthirsty older generation of politicians, generals, and profiteers.

Barbusse's narrative strategy was influenced by naturalism, especially by novels of Émile Zola such as *Germinal* (1885; English translation, 1885) and *La Débâcle* (1892; *The Downfall*, 1892). Such novels strove, with almost scientific accuracy, to document the life of the working classes yet also to show how all life is subject to natural laws, just as science produces general theories from minute observations. Naturalist authors urge reform by demonstrating that individual lives are determined by social and economic forces greater than the individuals. Jonathan King argues that the strengths and weaknesses of *Under Fire* cannot be appreciated without reference to the risk inherent in social realism of submerging the author's visionary purpose under the mass of detail. In *Under Fire*, it is where Barbusse abandons documentation that the writing become implausible and ineffective.

The disconnected vignettes that constitute the narrative of *Under Fire* were meant to acquire coherence from the novel's prophetic purpose; from another perspective, however, they anticipated the discontinuous, juxtaposed scenes of the great works of the 1920's. Perhaps both the strengths and weaknesses of *Under Fire* argue the impossibility of grasping the enormities of World War I, or of making coherent sense out of its wastefulness. It is as though the war had inaugurated the fragmentation that convinced such early twentieth century writers as Virginia Woolf, James Joyce, and T. S. Eliot that traditional narrative continuity was no longer appropriate.

"Critical Evaluation" by Matthew Parfitt

Further Reading

Cruickshank, John. *Variations on Catastrophe: Some French Responses to the Great War.* New York: Oxford University Press, 1982. Informative study is chiefly concerned with the problems that the protest novel entails for authors and critics. Attempts to account for the uneasy combination of realism and political prophecy in *Under Fire*.

Field, Frank. *Three French Writers and the Great War: Studies in the Rise of Communism and Fascism.* 1975. Reprint. New York: Cambridge University Press, 2008. Pays scant attention to *Under Fire*'s literary qualities but provides extensive discussion of its place in the development of Barbusse's political commitments.

Harris, Frank. "Henri Barbusse." In *Latest Contemporary Portraits.* 1927. Reprint. New York: Johnson Reprint, 1968. Early appreciation of Barbusse focuses on *Under Fire*.

Jones, Tobin H. "Mythic Vision and Ironic Allusion: Barbusse's *Le Feu* and Zola's *Germinal*." *Modern Fiction Studies* 28, no. 2 (Summer, 1982): 215-228. Comparison of the uses of mythic patterns and social vision in the two works is illuminating, although occasionally overburdened with literary theory.

King, Jonathan. "Henri Barbusse: *Le Feu* and the Crisis of Social Realism." In *The First World War in Fiction: A Collection of Critical Essays*, edited by Holger Klein. New York: Barnes & Noble, 1977. Helpful study of *Under Fire* places the novel in historical context, demonstrating how the literary and political movements of its time explain many of its problems and peculiarities.

Smith, Leonard V. "Masculinity, Memory, and the French World War I Novel: Henri Barbusse and Roland Dorgeles." In *Authority, Identity, and the Social History of the Great War*, edited by Frans Coetzee and Marilyn Shevin-Coetzee. Providence, R.I.: Berghahn Books, 1995. Explores the representation of soldiers in war novels by the two French authors. Smith has written extensively about the roles of France and French soldiers in World War I.

Sturrock, John. *The Word from Paris: Essays on Modern French Thinkers and Writers*. London: Verso, 1998. Survey of twentieth century French literature and philosophy presents profiles of significant writers and thinkers. Devotes a chapter to Barbusse that includes discussion of *Under Fire*.

Under Milk Wood
A Play for Voices

Author: Dylan Thomas (1914-1953)
First produced: 1953, public reading; first published, 1954; first staged, 1956
Type of work: Drama
Type of plot: Domestic realism
Time of plot: Indeterminate
Locale: Llareggub, Wales

Principal characters:
CAPTAIN CAT, a blind, retired sea captain
THE REVEREND ELI JENKINS, one of God's innocents
POLLY GARTER, the village wanton
MOG EDWARDS, a draper
MYFANWY PRICE, a dressmaker and sweetshop proprietor
MR. PUGH, a schoolmaster
MRS. PUGH, his wife, a shrew
MR. WALDO, a barber, herbalist, and lecher
MRS. OGMORE-PRITCHARD, the twice-widowed owner of Bay View, a house for paying guests
BUTCHER BEYNON
MRS. BEYNON, his wife
GOSSAMER BEYNON, their daughter, a schoolteacher
ORGAN MORGAN, a musician
CHERRY OWEN, a tippler
MRS. OWEN, his wife
WILLY NILLY, the postman
MRS. WILLY NILLY, his wife, who reads all the mail before her husband delivers it
SINBAD SAILORS, a young pub keeper
MARY ANN SAILORS, his grandmother
LORD CUT-GLASS, an eccentric recluse
NOGOOD BOYO, a fisherman
OCKY MILKMAN

The Story:

Night's deep shadows lie over sleeping Llareggub, a small, decayed seaside resort village—so a guidebook might describe the town, a place of no particular interest to the sportsman, the health seeker, or the tourist. Under the black, moonless sky, the cobblestone streets are silent, and Milk Wood is empty of lovers, the darkness disturbed only by the secret, rustling animal life. In their darkened houses the people of Llareggub sleep, their dreams filled with love or hate, desire or dismay.

Captain Cat is a retired, blind sea captain. Through his dreams echo the voices of sailor friends lost long ago, with whom he shared the same girl, Rosie Probert. Mog Edwards, the draper, in sleep loves Myfanwy Price more than all the cloths and weaves in the great Cloth Hall of the world. Myfanwy, secretly in love with Mog, promises in her sleep to warm his heart beside the fire so that he can wear it under his vest after he closes his shop. Mr. Waldo lies in a drunken slumber beside his unhappy, unloved wife; other women he has known pass through his dreams. Mrs. Ogmore-Pritchard gives orders to the two husbands she has bossed into their graves. Inspectors fly into the dreams of Mrs. Beynon, the butcher's wife, to persecute her husband for selling the meat of cats and owls. Her daughter, Gossamer, a schoolteacher, dreams of her lover, a small, rough man with a bright bushy tail like a fox's. Sinbad Sailors hugs his pillow and imagines that he is embracing Gossamer Beynon. His grandmother dreams of the Garden of Eden. Willy Nilly, the postman, walks fourteen miles in his sleep. Polly Garter dreams of babies.

Day breaks, and the people arise and go about their business. The Reverend Eli Jenkins, whose God is a God of innocence and wonder, goes to his door and, in the bright sunshine, sings his morning service, a lyric that might have come out of Robert Herrick. Mrs. Ogmore-Pritchard, whose god is cleanliness, does not care to have boarders in her clean rooms and starched beds, their breath all over the furniture, their feet trampling her carpets. Ocky Milkman puts water in the milk before he delivers it. Mr. Pugh, the schoolmaster, daydreams of feeding his wife an arsenic-and-weed-killer biscuit; at breakfast he reads *Lives of the Great Poisoners*, the title of his book concealed by a brown paper wrapper. Polly Garter nurses the youngest of her brood. Sinbad Sailors opens his pub, the Sailors Arms, and drinks a pint of beer. (The hands of the ship's clock in the pub have stood at half past eleven for half a century, so that it is always opening time.) Mr. Cherry Owen hears how, while drunk, he hurled sago at the wall, just missing his wife and the picture of Auntie Blossom, and danced on the table. Mrs. Willy Nilly,

the postman's wife, steams open letters and reads them aloud. Nogood Boyo, lying on his back among crabs' legs and tangled lines in the unbailed bottom of his dinghy, looks at the sky and says that he does not know or care who might be up there looking down. Sinbad Sailors continues to dote on Gossamer Beynon. Lord Cut-Glass, in his kitchen filled with clocks, one for each of his sixty-six years, squats to eat from a dish marked "Fido." Captain Cat remembers the rowdy long ago of his youth.

Night falls, and Llareggub prepares to return to sleep. Mog Edwards and Myfanwy Price, a town's length between them, write to each other the daily love letters that they never mail. Mrs. Ogmore-Pritchard seals her house against the night air and the damp from the sea. The Reverend Eli Jenkins recites his sunset poem, asking God to look after and bless the people of Llareggub, a town where no one is wholly good or wholly bad. Mr. Cherry Owen goes off to get drunk at the Sailors Arms; his wife has two husbands, one drunk, one sober, and she loves them both. Captain Cat, secure in his bunk, goes voyaging in his dreams. In Milk Wood, where lovers stray, drunken Mr. Waldo hugs Polly Garter in the warm silence under the trees, but it is not Mr. Waldo or any of her lusty, six-foot lovers Polly is thinking of, but Willy Weazel—little Willy Wee—who is dead and six feet underground.

Critical Evaluation:

As a human being, Dylan Thomas had many failings, but he possessed one quality that redeemed him: He was a dedicated craftsman and devoted to his art. A like claim may be made for his radio play *Under Milk Wood*, which Thomas subtitled *A Play for Voices*. Completed shortly before his death, this rich and earthy prose drama testifies to his scrupulous craftsmanship, his delight in character, his humorous apprehension of experience, and his talent for re-creating the sounds of nature. In addition, the play marks a stage in the development of his career, presenting the world without rather than a world within, for it was written at a time when Thomas seemed to be turning away from a highly personal poetry and the exploration of his own private sensibility to a wider view of society.

The work has a history stretching over more than a decade. In one of his early stories, Thomas first used the invented place-name Llareggub, but the idea of writing a drama with this imaginary setting did not come to him, apparently, until approximately 1944. Following the suggestion that his material deserved more extended treatment, he first planned a play to be called "The Town Was Mad," its theme the ironic contrast between individuality and innocence on one hand and prejudice and social conformity on the other. As originally planned, the story was to deal with a government commission sent to investigate a community of eccentrics. The indignant citizens insist that a trial be held and their case heard. When the prosecution describes a town that is ideally sane, the people of the village decide that they want no part of the sane world and beg to be cut off from it as quickly as possible. Later, however, Thomas decided to let his story grow more naturally out of the personalities and everyday involvements of his people. When he died suddenly in November, 1953, three separate versions of his play existed in manuscript. The version finally decided on for presentation and publication was that accepted by his executors as the final work.

It is easy to understand the appeal that *Under Milk Wood* holds for the radio audience and the general reader. The true quality of Thomas's verse was always more auditory than visual, so the poems that frequently look odd or complicated on the printed page often make marvelous sense when they are read aloud. Then the poet's cumulative and indirect imagery creates a tonal effect of movement between line and line. In radio presentation, in which understanding is by the ear alone, the auditory richness of Thomas's work is unhampered. The town and its people come vividly to life within the imagination of the hearer. The play relies almost entirely on the spoken word, not on visual effects. Furthermore, despite its verbal sophistication, the play is democratic—rambunctious, impassioned, ribald, lyric, funny, tender.

To Thomas, Milk Wood is a place of wonder and love. To old Mary Ann Sailors, humble in her faith, it is God's garden, the proof of Eden, a heaven on earth, and her belief is that Llareggub is the Chosen Land. To the restless, night-haunted village boys and girls it is the bridal bed of secret love. To the Reverend Eli Jenkins it is a sermon in green, wind-shaken leaves on the innocence and goodness of humanity.

No conflict develops; no problems are resolved. The material of the play is as impressive as it is simple, for the author's chief concern was to convey a sense of the life that underlies the complicated business of living, even in commonplace lives and among people who are no better and no worse than they are in most places. *Under Milk Wood*, for all its brevity, is a play of subtly mixed effects. As an attempt to capture life at its source, it joins reality and fantasy as closely as humor and tragedy blend in the lives of its characters. Dylan Thomas in this drama presents a picture of ordinary life, but one universalized by insight and imagination. The innocence of art adds as much to his picture of life as do the compassion and tolerance that come with experience.

Further Reading

Davies, Peter. *Student Guide to Dylan Thomas*. London: Greenwich Exchange, 2005. Biographical and critical study of Thomas provides background useful to readers of *Under Milk Wood*. Disagrees with critics who charge that Thomas's poetry is merely a "careless outpouring of incoherent feeling" and demonstrates how he was a dedicated craftsman who struggled to make his works communicate his beliefs.

Goodby, John, and Chris Wigginton, eds. *Dylan Thomas*. New York: Palgrave, 2001. Collection of essays presents discussion of topics such as Thomas's celebration of the female, Welsh contexts in his poetry, and his depiction of "radical morbidity." *Under Milk Wood* is discussed in John Goodby's essay "'Very Profound and Very Box-Office': The Later Poems and *Under Milk Wood*."

Holbrook, David. "'A Place of Love': *Under Milk Wood*." In *Dylan Thomas: A Collection of Critical Essays*, edited by C. B. Cox. Englewood Cliffs, N.J.: Prentice-Hall, 1966. Views the play as the romanticized "toy town" of Thomas's childhood. Asserts that the play is trivial when contrasted with James Joyce's work.

Korg, Jacob. *Dylan Thomas*. New York: Twayne, 1965. Devotes a chapter to Thomas's prose, including *Under Milk Wood*. Sees the work as lacking the substance of Thomas's poetry, but praises its comic vitality, its humor, and its theme of "the sacredness of human attachments."

Lycett, Andrew. *Dylan Thomas: A New Life*. London: Weidenfeld & Nicolson, 2003. Candid biography presents a wealth of detail about Thomas's life. Examines the contradiction between the man who lived like the devil and the poet who wrote like an angel.

Moynihan, William T. *The Craft and Art of Dylan Thomas*. Ithaca, N.Y.: Cornell University Press, 1966. Discusses *Under Milk Wood*, in particular its humor, its idealized characters, and its theme of the importance of asserting beauty in an imperfect world.

Rea, J. "Topographical Guide to *Under Milk Wood*." *College English* 25, no. 7 (April, 1964): 535-542. Describes Llareggub to help students visualize the play's action and comments on the sources of some place-names. Includes a map of the village.

Williams, Raymond. "Dylan Thomas's Play for Voices." In *Dylan Thomas: A Collection of Critical Essays*, edited by C. B. Cox. Englewood Cliffs, N.J.: Prentice-Hall, 1966. Summarizes the play's acting history and examines Thomas's use of narrative, dialogue, and song. Compares the play to the "Circe" episode of James Joyce's *Ulysses* (1922).

Under the Greenwood Tree

Author: Thomas Hardy (1840-1928)
First published: 1872
Type of work: Novel
Type of plot: Pastoral
Time of plot: Nineteenth century
Locale: Rural England

Principal characters:
DICK DEWY, a passenger carrier
REUBEN DEWY, his father, also a passenger carrier
MR. SHINER, a wealthy farmer
MR. MAYBOLD, the vicar
FANCY DAY, a schoolteacher and organist

The Story:

On Christmas Eve, the Mellstock Choir prepares to set out for its annual caroling venture. In fine voice, mellowed by generous mugs of cider, the men and boys gather at the home of Reuben Dewy. Then, with their fiddles and the cello of Grandfather Dewy, they depart on their rounds. After calling at outlying farms and houses, they arrive at the schoolhouse to serenade the new schoolmistress, Fancy Day. At first, there is no indication that she has heard them; but at last, she appears, framed, picture-like, in a window. Later, the men miss young Dick Dewy. When they find him, he is leaning against the school, staring up listlessly at the now-darkened window.

At church the following morning, Fancy Day causes a stir of excitement. She is the main attraction for Dick Dewy, Farmer Shiner, and the new vicar, Mr. Maybold, but she does not endear herself to a number of other men in the congregation because she commits what they regard almost as blasphemy. For as long as anyone can remember, the male choir has provided music for the service, but the young woman, on her first day in church, leads the young girls in singing along with the men. Some of the older and wiser ones foresee trouble from a woman who is so forward.

Dick gives his annual party on the afternoon and evening of Christmas Day. When Dick can claim Fancy for a dance, he is transported with joy; but when she dances with Shiner, a more handsome and more wealthy man, Dick is downcast. When Shiner escorts the lady home, the evening is ruined for young Dick.

Using a handkerchief left behind by Fancy as his excuse, Dick finds the courage to call at the schoolhouse a few days later. A very inexperienced lover, he simply returns the handkerchief, stammers a "good day," and departs. It is not until spring that he makes any real progress in his love affair. By that time, Dick is a wan and shadowy figure of a man. He speaks to no one of his love, but it is obvious to all but Fancy and her other two admirers that Dick is not himself.

Before Dick can declare himself, however, a delegation from the choir waits on Vicar Maybold. The delegation has been made uneasy by a rumor that the group is to be displaced by organ music played by Fancy Day; soon, the choir learns that the rumor is true. The vicar has brought an organ to the church because he prefers that instrument to a choir. To spare the feelings of the faithful choir members, however, he agrees to wait before deposing them. They are to have the dignity of leaving on a special day, not on an ordinary Sunday.

Dick's big day comes when he is allowed to bring Fancy and some of her belongings from the home of her father. He is dismayed to find Farmer Shiner also present, but when Fancy allows him to touch her hand at the dinner table, Dick's spirits rise perceptibly. On the ride home, he cannot find the words that are in his heart; he feels, nevertheless, that he has made some progress. In the weeks that follow, rumors of Fancy's friendliness with Maybold and with Shiner drive Dick to desperation. One day, he writes Fancy a letter in which he bluntly asks whether he means anything to her. When he receives no answer from Fancy, he resolves that he will talk to her next Sunday.

Before Sunday comes, however, Dick has to go on an errand for Maybold's mother, taking him to a neighboring town. He is preparing to leave for home again when he sees Fancy waiting for the carrier. Seizing the opportunity, Dick helps her into his cart and triumphantly carries her off. On the drive home, he finally finds the courage to propose to her and is as much surprised as overjoyed to hear her acceptance.

Because they will not be able to marry for some time, Dick and Fancy keep their betrothal a secret. Furthermore, Fancy's father has told her that he hopes she will accept Shiner for a husband. One trait of Fancy's character troubles Dick. She seems to take undue pleasure in dressing to please others, but whenever he prepares to punish her by letting her worry about him for a change, Fancy apologizes for her vanity. Unable to resist her tears, the young lover takes her back into his heart before she knows there has been a problem.

On the day Dick is at last to meet Fancy's father to ask for her hand, Dick prepares himself carefully. Fancy's father tells him bluntly that he is not good enough for Fancy and that she is too cultured, too well educated, and too wealthy for a plain carrier. Sadly, Dick agrees, and he turns toward home.

Fancy, however, is not so easily defeated. When tears fail to move her father, she resorts to the age-old trick of languishing away for love. She does not eat, at least not so that her father notices; she merely pines and sighs. The ruse works, and her father reluctantly finds himself begging her to marry her young lover. The date is set for the coming midsummer.

On the day Fancy is installed at the organ and the choir is discontinued, Dick can not attend church because he has to serve at the funeral of a friend. Fancy has put her hair in curls and in other ways dresses more lavishly than usual. Dick is sorry to see her dress so beautifully, especially given that she knows he will not be present to see her. Still, she puts him off brusquely. On his way home that night, Dick walks through the rain to get one last glimpse of his love before he retires for the night. She refuses to lean far enough out her window to give him a kiss. Later, when she sees Vicar Maybold approaching through the rain, she greets him warmly. The vicar, who had been enchanted with her appearance that morning and knows nothing of her betrothal to Dick, has decided to ask for her hand in marriage. Surprising even herself, Fancy accepts him.

The next morning, Maybold meets Dick on the road. Still thinking himself betrothed, Dick shyly tells Maybold of his coming marriage to Fancy. Shocked, Maybold keeps silent, leaving Dick ignorant of Fancy's faithlessness. Maybold then sends a note to the young lady, telling her that she must not forsake Dick. Before his note can be delivered, Maybold receives a note from Fancy, in which she writes that she had been momentarily swayed by the prospect of a more cultured, elegant life; she begs to withdraw her acceptance of his proposal because she has loved and still loves another.

The wedding takes place that summer. It is a great celebration, marred only by Maybold's refusal to perform the ceremony. Dick is puzzled and cannot think of any way in which he might have offended the vicar. After the ceremony, Dick tells his bride that they will never have a secret between them; Fancy replies that they never will, beginning from that day forth.

Critical Evaluation:

Under the Greenwood Tree is the novel that confirmed Thomas Hardy in his profession as a writer. His first novel, an unpublished work called "The Poor Man and the Lady (wr. 1867), had been suppressed at his own request, while *Desperate Remedies* (1871), a novel of sensation, was, he felt, poor stuff by comparison, although it was successful.

Under the Greenwood Tree is the creation of person who had served his apprenticeship as a writer, during which time he found his voice and, most important, his subject. Although gentler in tone than many of his later novels, a pastoral idyll rather than a full-blown tragedy, *Under the Greenwood Tree* nonetheless establishes the distinctive characters of the Wessex countryside and people that will permeate Hardy's later novels. To create his particular version of Wessex, Hardy draws heavily on memories of his own childhood and the characters, customs, and music that he recalls from that time. This is further underlined by the book's structure, which sets the courtship and marriage within the space of one year that is punctuated with country festivals. Consequently, the portrait of Reuben Dewy and his family and friends is heavily tinged with nostalgia for a time now past; one might argue that Hardy is alert already to the need to record these customs before they are irrevocably lost.

At the same time, however, while critics have argued that Hardy is lamenting the loss of the old ways, a close reading of *Under the Greenwood Tree* would suggest that Hardy also knows that times change; while he would not necessarily support change for change's sake, he nonetheless recognizes that without change, a culture will ossify. Thus, in *Under the Greenwood Tree*, Fancy Day personifies the spirit of modernity. Quite apart from being a spirited and independent young woman, who also is well educated and now taking up the role of schoolteacher in Mellstock, she also brings with her such newfangled notions as the idea that the women within the congregation should also participate in the singing, rather than simply leaving it to the men of the Mellstock Quire (choir). This, in turn, prompts the new and progressive vicar, Maybold, to consider replacing the choir with an organ, which Fancy will then play. Whether Maybold is driven by the desire to encourage female emancipation, as Fancy desires, is debatable.

When he formally proposes to Fancy, Maybold's desire is to see her as an ornament to his drawing room, where she will sing and play and hold court. Attractive as that at first seems to Fancy, her true mettle is shown when she subsequently rejects his proposal in favor of that of Dick Dewy. She turns down a passive female role for something more dynamic as the wife of the oldest son of a local businessman, but a son who is now branching out into business in partnership with his father. It seems doubtful that Fancy will sit quietly at home in the drawing room. She has, in effect, rejected an old-fashioned clerical lifestyle for a more contemporary role as a country businessman's wife, in the same way that she demurred when her father insisted that she should allow Farmer Shiner, a prosperous local landowner, to pay her court.

Fancy's father, head keeper on an estate, sees marrying into the gentry as the way forward, but it is as though Hardy has already realized that the clergy and the landowner are already outmoded country figures. The motif of the triangle of suitors is one that Hardy will return to most notably, and with more tragic results, in *Far from the Madding Crowd* (1874). In this famous novel, Bathsheba Everdene takes on the role of a more wilful Fancy and rejects modernity in the shape of Gabriel Oak, a working farmer, before discovering the weaknesses of the more traditional country figures of the soldier and the landowner.

Much of *Under the Greenwood Tree* is focused on the business of keeping up appearances, and no one seems to be immune to this occupation, with perhaps the exception of Shiner. As his name implies, however, he already is so well polished that he draws criticism for being too immaculate. Hardy often uses the maintaining of appearances as a way of extracting a little gentle comedy from situations. In one scene, Dick visits the Day family and stays for a meal. Mrs. Day gradually strips the table service around them and replaces the "everyday" table setting with her best setting, normally reserved for special guests. Likewise, Mrs. Dewy is concerned to put on a good show for her neighbors on high days and holidays, although appearances slip as, in one case, evening wears on and the men and women begin to dance.

Furthermore, Dick is a little anxious that Fancy devotes a good deal of attention to her appearance and is deeply vexed when, for her first performance as organist at church, she dresses her hair in curls, although he will not be there to see her; those same curls, of course, are what convince Maybold that she will make a perfect wife. While attempting to court Fancy, Dick, too, is not immune to making the best of his own appearance. He participates in a long discussion about what will be most suitable for him to wear when he approaches Fancy's father. Throughout the novel, Hardy underlines how conscious the families are of how they appear to others, and how they want themselves to be seen. Again, modernity is knocking at the door.

Revised by Maureen Kincaid Speller

Further Reading

Daleski, H. M. *Thomas Hardy and Paradoxes of Love.* Columbia: University of Missouri Press, 1997. Daleski reevaluates the treatment of gender in Hardy's novels, defending the author from charges of sexism and maintaining that some of Hardy's female characters are depicted sympathetically. Argues that Hardy is the premodern precursor of sexual failures and catastrophic ends.

Gatrell, Simon. *Thomas Hardy and the Proper Study of Mankind.* Charlottesville: University Press of Virginia, 1993. Notes that *Under the Greenwood Tree* asserts an air of social harmony, albeit with an odd, discordant voice. Concludes that the marriage of Fancy Day and Dick Dewy symbolizes a renewal of village life.

Kramer, Dale, ed. *The Cambridge Companion to Thomas Hardy.* New York: Cambridge University Press, 1999. An introduction and general overview of Hardy's work, ideas, and literary skills. Essays explore Hardy's biography, aesthetics, and the impact of his work on developments in science, religion, and philosophy in the late nineteenth century. Also contains a detailed chronology of Hardy's life and the essay "The Patriarchy of Class: *Under the Greenwood Tree, Far from the Madding Crowd, The Woodlanders.*"

Mallett, Phillip, ed. *The Achievement of Thomas Hardy.* New York: St. Martin's Press, 2000. A collection of essays analyzing select Hardy novels and other works. Examines Hardy and nature, Hardy and architecture, and the presence of poets in his novels, among other topics. Includes a bibliography and an index.

Millgate, Michael. *Thomas Hardy: A Biography Revisited.* New York: Oxford University Press, 2004. This biography enhances and replaces Millgate's 1982 biography, considered to be one of the best and most scholarly Hardy biographies available. Includes a bibliography and an index.

_____. *Thomas Hardy: His Career as a Novelist.* New York: Random House, 1971. Considers *Under the Greenwood Tree* to be a kind of woodland pastoral or novel of rural manners. Concludes that Hardy's novel, though an idyll, contains many elements that are less than idyllic.

Page, Norman, ed. *Oxford Reader's Companion to Hardy.* New York: Oxford University Press, 2000. Three hundred alphabetically arranged entries examine Hardy's work and discuss his family and friends, important places in his life and work, and his influences. Also examines critical approaches to his writings and provides a history of his works' publication. Also includes a chronology of his life, lists of places and characters in his fiction, a glossary, and a bibliography.

Tomalin, Claire. *Thomas Hardy.* New York: Penguin, 2007. This thorough and finely written biography by a respected Hardy scholar illuminates the novelist's efforts to indict the malice, neglect, and ignorance of his fellow humans. Tomalin also discusses aspects of his life that are apparent in his literary works.

Vigar, Penelope. *The Novels of Thomas Hardy: Illusion and*

Reality. New York: Humanities Press, 1978. Argues that *Under the Greenwood Tree* is a light, often humorous, pastoral tale, one barely touched by extravagances of coincidence and melodrama and one that seldom strays into the realms of passion and tragedy.

Under the Net

Author: Iris Murdoch (1919-1999)
First published: 1954
Type of work: Novel
Type of plot: Comic and philosophical
Time of plot: Early 1950's
Locale: London and Paris

Principal characters:
JAKE DONAGHUE, the protagonist
FINN, his close friend
MADGE, his landlady
DAVE GELLMAN, a philosopher and teacher
SAMMY STARFIELD, a bookie
ANNA QUENTIN, Jake's former girlfriend
SADIE QUENTIN, her sister
HUGO BELFOUNDER, Jake's former roommate
LEFTY TODD, a labor leader
MRS. TINCKHAM, a shop owner
MISTER MARS, a dog
JEAN PIERRE, a novelist

The Story:

Returning to London from France, Jake Donaghue learns that he and his friend, Finn, are being evicted from their free lodgings with their landlady, Madge. The two friends ask Dave Gellman, a teacher and philosopher, if they can stay with him, but Dave will only agree to allow Finn, and his and Jake's baggage, to remain. Jake, Dave says snidely, has to make other arrangements with a lady friend. Finn suggests Jake ask Anna Quentin, Jake's former girlfriend.

Though Jake has not seen or heard from Anna in years, he finds her easily once he starts looking. However, Anna will only let him stay one night, but suggests that he contact her sister, Sadie, who is looking for a caretaker for her place while she is away. Anna promises to contact Jake if she should need him.

The next day, Sadie agrees to let Jake watch her flat. She is especially concerned about the unwanted attentions of Hugo Belfounder, Jake's former roommate. As roommates, the two had had many philosophical discussions, one of which Jake turned into a not-very-successful novel, *The Silencer*. In the novel, Jake had attempted to replicate one particular conversation with Hugo that dealt with language as the falsifier of experience. Jake feared his novel had betrayed Hugo's

ideas, so he ended their friendship by not meeting him one night as planned.

Reminded of all this, Jake returns to Madge's to pick up her copy of *The Silencer.* Instead, he runs into Sammy Starfield, a bookie who thinks he has stolen Madge from Jake. He offers Jake money as compensation, but Jake refuses. Instead, he allows Sammy to bet money on the horses and, should they win, give the winnings to Jake.

On Tuesday, Jake reports to Sadie's flat. As soon as she leaves, the phone rings. The caller is Hugo. Jake identifies himself, but Hugo hangs up. Jake decides to track Hugo down, even though Sadie had told him not to leave the flat. Jake finds that he is locked in. Luckily, Dave and Finn are walking down the street. They find Jake's situation hilarious, but agree to get him out.

Finn picks the lock, and the three set off to find Hugo at the address Sadie had for him. There they find a note saying Hugo is at a nearby pub—but the note does not say which pub. They never find Hugo, but they do find Lefty Todd, leader of the Independent Socialists. Lefty and Jake have a political discussion until the pub closes. The group walks to the Thames River, and everyone but Dave strips for a swim. More drinking follows. Finally, Lefty leaves, and Finn passes out. Suddenly, Dave remembers that he has a note for Jake. The note, a couple days old now, is from Anna, asking Jake to see her at once. Afraid he is too late, Jake hurries to Anna's mime theater.

Finding the theater empty, Jake spots a truck containing Anna's things. A note attached to the neck of a rocking horse has Jake's initial on it. Anna has had an offer and could wait no longer for Jake. At this upsetting news, Jake jumps from the truck and goes to Hyde Park, where he passes out in the grass.

Jake wakes up and returns to Sadie's to retrieve her copy of his novel. There, he eavesdrops on Sadie and Sammy, who are plotting to sell Jake's translation of novelist Jean Pierre's book *The Wooden Butterfly* to Hugo's film company. Jake decides he must go to Sammy's flat to retrieve his translation. He calls Finn to help him. At Sammy's place, they find Mister Mars, a movie dog, but not Jake's translation. Jake decides to kidnap the dog to exchange him for the translation.

Finn returns to Dave's place, and Jake sets off for the Bounty Belfounder film studio with Mister Mars, intending to find Hugo and warn him about Sadie and Sammy's plot. Jake tricks his way into the well-guarded studio, where a labor rally led by Lefty Todd is in progress. Hugo is listening to Lefty and will not talk to Jake. A riot ensues, and the police show up. Worried that he will be arrested for stealing Mister Mars, Jake gets the dog to play dead and then uses the sympathy of the crowd for the poor limp dog and his owner to escape the scene.

Back at Dave's flat, Jake finds several letters that have arrived for him. One contains money from Sammy for the bets he had placed a few days earlier. In the face of Sammy's honorable act, Jake decides to contact him about the dog. However, Dave and Finn have already contacted Sammy to protect themselves from implication after seeing a picture of Jake and Mister Mars in a newspaper article about the riot. Dave accuses Jake of impulsive behavior but is interrupted when a telegram arrives for Jake from Madge with money and directions to meet her in Paris. Jake leaves Mister Mars with Dave and leaves immediately.

Once in Paris, Jake learns Madge has purchased all of Jean Pierre's works for film, including the book that Sammy and Sadie had been eager to purchase after reading Jake's translation. Madge wants to put Hugo's film studio out of business and wants to hire Jake as her script writer. She claims to love Jake and says she wants to help him have what he has always wanted: "money for doing nothing." Jake turns her down, and the offer leaves him depressed.

Outside, Jake gets caught up in national celebrations. Re-membering the times he and Anna had shared in Paris, he suddenly thinks he sees her and then follows her. He finally catches up to the woman but finds she is not Anna after all. His entire life seems to be an illusion.

Back in London, Jake returns to Dave's flat and goes to bed. In Jake's absence, Finn has disappeared. Dave leaves Jake alone and even continues to take care of Mister Mars. Jake gets a job as an orderly at the hospital across the street from Dave's place. One afternoon, Hugo is brought in my ambulance after getting hit on the head with a brick at a Lefty Todd rally. Jake believes that fate has brought Hugo to him and is determined to take the opportunity to talk to him.

From Hugo, Jake learns that Hugo loves Sadie but Sadie does not love him in return. Instead, it is Anna who loves Hugo. Also, though Sadie might love Jake, Jake loves Anna. Hugo declares the situation hopeless and demands that Jake help him escape immediately from the hospital. Jake warns Hugo about the plot on his studio, but Hugo does not care about that. He is giving up the studio to become a watchmaker, a job for which he says he has a talent. As they escape, Jake is spotted by his supervisor and knows he will be fired.

Once Jake and Hugo part ways, Jake realizes that everything has changed for him because all his assumptions have been false. Jake ends up back at Mrs. Tinckham's shop with Mister Mars. Here he opens the mail that had again been collecting for him at Dave's flat. The letters and packages help to clear things up for Jake, giving him an unobstructed view of reality. He now wants to buy Mister Mars and to get another job in a hospital, a job that he can do well and a job he enjoys. He plans to write at night. Though Jake takes this as revelation, it is just what Dave has been telling him to do with his life.

Critical Evaluation:

Under the Net was Iris Murdoch's debut as a novelist. Her philosophical concerns are apparent in this earliest novel, as is the humor for which she became well known. As in her later works, much of the humor in *Under the Net* is derived from its complex plot centered on a few midsummer weeks in the life of protagonist Jake Donaghue, a loner with a nose for trouble. Jake speaks dismissively about his relationship with the people closest to him, Madge and Finn in particular. Meanwhile, he has totally unrealistic fantasies about those he has lost touch with through his own neglect: Hugo and Anna. The goal of the novel is to transform Jake from the shallow person he is to the artist he has the potential to be.

Dave Gellman, the philosopher, is the one character who sees through Jake. Jake dislikes Dave's honesty; however, he relies on Dave, who takes care of Finn, Mister Mars, and

Jake's mail without demanding compensation for these services. Dave tells Jake at the outset of the novel, "Society should take you by the neck and shake you and make you do a sensible job. Then in your evenings you would have the possibility to write a great book." In the end, this is just what Jake decides he must do.

In this moral fable, Jake has the potential to be an artist but has been misusing this potential to write a bad novel, *The Silencer*, and to translate bad fiction—the novels of Jean Pierre—from French to English. He refuses to believe that he is capable of achieving his own redemption. Because of this, Jake chases after illusory relationships, only to find that they are not at all what he had imagined. Though Jake cannot see it clearly, most of the people he knows seem to be avoiding him.

When Jake is finally able to confront Hugo, the veil of self-deception is lifted from his eyes. Their conversation and subsequent escape provides the novel's climax. As Jake says, "He wanted to be rid of me. I wanted to be rid of him." Hugo, the saint, has provided Jake, the artist, with the ability to finally see reality and do as Dave suggested he do: work during the day and write a real novel at night. At least this is what Jake tells Mrs. Tinckham—the unbiased collector of everyone's tales—to whom he has gone to restart his life. That he is unwilling to tell her what he does not really understand about the genetics of her kittens is a sign that he is ready for the real world.

Though Jake is an unreliable narrator, and doubts linger about his ability to follow through with his plan, the success of novelist Jean Pierre suggests that Jake might be able to succeed, too. Furthermore, the inventiveness Jake has shown in imagining the unreality of his own life shows his creative potential.

Murdoch has loosely used elements of William Shakespeare's *A Midsummer Night's Dream* (pr. c. 1595-1596, pb. 1600) in *Under the Net*. The action takes place entirely during July—at midsummer. In a letter from Lefty Todd that Jake opens at Mrs. Tinckham's shop at the novel's close, this reference is made directly. Lefty hopes he was not the ass of the play. However, Jake was meant to be Bottom, under enchantment throughout the novel but freed from that enchantment at the end.

Publishing regularly for more than forty years, Murdoch produced twenty-six novels, several plays, and several philosophical treatises. Though born in Dublin, Ireland, on July 15, 1919, Murdoch grew up in London. Her Irish mother was an opera singer, and her English father was a civil servant who had served with the cavalry during World War I. After attending Somerville College, Oxford, she had government jobs and also had a year of unemployment. She was then elected a fellow at St. Anne's College, Oxford, where she lectured in philosophy for fifteen years before leaving to write full-time. The allegedly great love of Murdoch's life—Franz Steiner—died of a heart attack in 1952. In 1956, she married John Bayley, seven years her junior. Bayley became a professor of English at Oxford and also published fiction. The childless couple remained married until Murdoch's death from complications due to Alzheimer's disease in 1999.

In addition to philosophy, Murdoch studied the classics and also ancient history. She was influenced by philosopher Ludwig Wittgenstein, with whom she studied before St. Anne's, and by philosopher-novelist Jean-Paul Sartre, whom she had met in the 1940's and about whom she wrote her first published, book-length work—*Sartre, Romantic Rationalist* (1953). Plato's writings on beauty, art, and the real world are at the center of Murdoch's moralistic philosophy, and she had used her novels to apply this philosophy. Her fiction tends to be optimistic about the ability to see life as it really is. Her fiction also has a comic edge, though at times that comedy is dark. Many of her novels contain allusions to the plays of Shakespeare.

Laurie Lykken

Further Reading

Bove, Cheryl K. *Understanding Iris Murdoch*. Columbia: University of South Carolina Press, 1993. A lucid and valuable handbook for college students that separates Murdoch's works into two broad categories—the ironic tragedy and the bittersweet comedy—to explain how the writings express her philosophy, depict human relationships, and handle plot and theme.

Conradi, Peter J. *Iris Murdoch*. New York: W. W. Norton, 2001. A biography of the novelist that examines her early life as an imaginative only-child, through the trauma of World War II, up to her final years. Describes Murdoch's life as a search for good in a particularly evil century.

Grimshaw, Tammy. *Sexuality, Gender, and Power in Iris Murdoch's Fiction*. Madison, N.J.: Fairleigh Dickinson University Press, 2005. Examines representations of power, sexuality, and gender in Murdoch's fiction, providing a feminist reading of the work and describing how Murdoch's treatment of homosexuality, bisexuality, cross-dressing, and related issues reflect her preoccupations with reality and morality.

Nolan, Bran. *Iris Murdoch: The Retrospective Fiction*. 2d ed. New York: Palgrave Macmillan, 2004. Takes a psychological approach to Murdoch's work, focusing on how she represents past events and their effects on her characters. Includes analysis of novels that were not discussed in the first edition, published in 1999; also includes a new preface, an updated bibliography, and three additional chapters covering Murdoch's most important and popular novels.

Rowe, Anne, ed. *Iris Murdoch: A Reassessment*. New York: Palgrave Macmillan, 2007. A collection of essays that reinterprets Murdoch's work in terms of twenty-first cen-

tury debates about the aesthetic impulse, moral philosophy, gender and sexuality, literature, and authorship. Includes comparisons of Murdoch's work with works by other authors.

Spear, Hilda D. *Iris Murdoch*. New York: Palgrave Macmillan, 2007. Provides an introduction to Murdoch's novels, tracing how she progressively uses the plots of her books to address philosophical issues such as the nature of reality as well as good and evil.

Under the Volcano

Author: Malcolm Lowry (1909-1957)
First published: 1947
Type of work: Novel
Type of plot: Psychological realism
Time of plot: November 1, 1939
Locale: Quauhnahuac (Cuernavaca), Mexico

Principal characters:
GEOFFREY FIRMIN, the British consul at Quauhnahuac
YVONNE CONSTABLE, his former wife
HUGH FIRMIN, his half brother
JACQUES LARUELLE, a French film director
DR. ARTURO DÍAZ VIGIL, Geoffrey Firmin's doctor

The Story:

On November 2, 1939, the Mexican Day of the Dead, Jacques Laruelle, a French film producer, is ready to leave Quauhnahuac, Mexico. Before leaving, Laruelle joins his friend Dr. Vigil, and the two talk about their common acquaintance, Geoffrey Firmin, former British consul to Quauhnahuac, who was murdered exactly one year earlier.

After his visit with Dr. Vigil, Laruelle walks toward the Casino de Silva and recalls that day a year before. His recollections lead Laruelle to remember the time he spent with Geoffrey and his half brother, Hugh, at the Taskersons's home when all three were youngsters. One memory moves to another, and the story of Geoffrey and Hugh's childhood is told.

Laruelle stops at the Cervecería XX, where he chats with Señor Bustamente, owner of the bar and neighboring cinema. Bustamente tells Laruelle that he suspects that the dead consul might have been a spy, or "spider." At the end of their conversation, Bustamente gives Laruelle the copy of Elizabethan plays that Laruelle borrowed from Geoffrey. Laruelle intended to create a French version of the Faustus story. As he thumbs through the book, Laruelle finds a letter that Geoffrey wrote to his estranged wife, Yvonne, attempting to talk her into returning to him. Geoffrey never mailed the letter. When Laruelle leaves the bar, he walks up the Calle Nicaragua and remembers the day when Geoffrey was murdered and Yvonne was trampled to death by a horse.

On the morning of the 1938 Day of the Dead, Geoffrey did not sleep and sat in the cantina drinking. Unexpectedly, Yvonne, the consul's former wife, appeared. She left Quauhnahuac the year before for America, where she secured a divorce from Geoffrey. Almost as unexpected was the return of the consul's half brother and Yvonne's lover, Hugh. Hugh returned because he felt that he could not stay away without suffering the pains of guilt that Yvonne suffered.

After their reunion, Geoffrey, Yvonne, and Hugh left on a trip to Tomalín. Their trip was interrupted when they stopped by the home of Laruelle. Laruelle was one of Yvonne's former lovers, and the stopover caused much distress for Geoffrey because of Yvonne and Hugh's new closeness. Geoffrey drank several tequilas. Hugh and Yvonne went to a fiesta.

When the consul awakened from his drunken sleep, he was addressed by two beings. An evil angel urged him to drink rather than think of Yvonne. At the same time, a good angel made threats about his drinking. This was the first connection between Geoffrey and the Faustus story that Laruelle proposed. The evil angel won when Geoffrey turned to drink because he felt that he could not successfully perform his duties as a husband.

When Hugh and Yvonne returned from the fiesta, Hugh joked that perhaps his brother was a black magician. Hugh acted as a deterrent to any chances of Yvonne and Geoffrey ever getting back together. Hugh took Yvonne for a horse-back ride. On the ride, Hugh identified himself with Judas because he felt that he betrayed his brother. When Hugh and Yvonne returned, they found Geoffrey awake, and the three continued their journey.

The trip to Tomalín was interrupted when the travelers noticed a wounded Indian. Mexican law and possible repercussions influenced the group not to make an effort to assist the wounded man. Geoffrey saw a fellow traveler rob the dying man. Geoffrey and Hugh argued about the rationality of not helping the man. None of the three travelers was decisive. Hugh and Yvonne were indecisive because of the law, and Geoffrey was indecisive because he was more concerned about finding the next cantina for a drink.

The travelers stopped and went to the Salon Ofelia for a drink. In the salon, Geoffrey's feelings erupted into a storm of violent words thrown at Yvonne and Hugh, accusing them of crimes against marriage and against brotherhood. Geoffrey drank mescal, which he earlier associated with his demise. While drinking the mescal, Geoffrey remembered a similar time when he drank all night and was supposed to meet a lady, Lee Maitland, who failed to arrive. To his surprise, he could not remember exactly who this lady was. Geoffrey was losing control of his perception of reality.

Geoffrey saw his doom symbolized in the nearby volcano. He showed himself to be a Faustian character by broadcasting that he loved hell and could not wait to return there. He then rushed out of the Salon Ofelia as if in pain. Yvonne and Hugh rushed after him and tried to catch up with him. Although Geoffrey had damned them for their adultery, Yvonne and Hugh knew that they had to get him back to Quauhnahuac. They took the wrong path.

As they pursued Geoffrey, Hugh and Yvonne visited several cantinas, looking for him. At each cantina they had a drink before going on. They eventually found themselves wandering around in the forest. As they wandered around, they heard a distant shot, not knowing that it was the sound of Geoffrey's execution by Mexican officials. Drunk, Yvonne tripped and fell over a log, and she was trampled by a horse that escaped from Geoffrey. Hugh wandered through the woods singing a revolutionary song and accompanying himself on a guitar.

As he lay dying, Geoffrey imagined that he heard Laruelle and Dr. Vigil back in Quauhnahuac trying to comfort the grieving Yvonne and Hugh. When his hallucination was complete, Geoffrey screamed and died. Someone threw a dead dog into the ravine with the dead Englishman.

"The Story" by Thomas B. Frazier

Critical Evaluation:

Although *Under the Volcano* was well received on first publication, the novel did not sell well and was not reprinted for many years. Since 1958, however, it has shared in the growing appreciation of Malcolm Lowry that followed his death in 1957 and the publication of his third volume, *Hear Us O Lord from Heaven Thy Dwelling Place*, in 1961. Lowry would have appreciated the irony of late acclaim. In the first chapter of *Under the Volcano*, Jacques Laruelle receives two messages from Geoffrey Firmin, the protagonist of the novel, who died the year before. The doomed, damned, and dead Geoffrey still manages to communicate with the living, and they possibly pay more attention to his words now than they did when he was alive. The posthumous publications of Lowry serve much the same purpose; readers and critics are paying more attention to what Lowry has to say now that he is dead.

His message is summed up in one word: doom. His characters feel they cannot escape their fate; it is as if the volcano in whose shadow Geoffrey lives was also Lowry's imaginative projection of the crises and the violence of his time. The sense of doom is the central feature of Lowry's vision and work, and an English reviewer, noting that James Joyce in *Ulysses* (1922) and Lowry in *Under the Volcano* use one day for the action, suggests that the time of Lowry's novel is simply "Doomsday." Undoubtedly, the sense of doom, intensified by waste and exile so prevalent in Lowry's life, is a response to the mid-1930's, the time when Lowry began to write the novel. Such a sense of doom has not lost its relevance. In *Under the Volcano*, doom is presented as accident; Hugh Firmin causes the death of Geoffrey, his half brother, by leaving an incriminating cable message in the jacket he borrows from Geoffrey; in turn, Geoffrey releases the horse that later kills Yvonne Constable, his former wife.

The novel tends to move on an allegorical level into a consideration of human destiny. This idea is important, for the novel would be a failure if it were considered only on its realistic level. The action relates very little to any moral. The qualities that tend to be presented as enduring and worthy of regard are compassion for the individual and the sense of doom that looms over the alcoholic. Geoffrey's death is not seen as a punishment for his weaknesses; it is simply the culmination of the series of tragic events that take place in the consul's soul that day—his death merely ends the series of spiritual defeats he succumbs to during his fall.

This idea must have been unpalatable in the late 1940's and in part could account for the lack of continuing interest in Lowry. Furthermore, the difficulty of estimating the true standing of *Under the Volcano* was due to a lack of enough writing by Lowry to place the novel in a context. Readers may see that the novel is probably the center not only of Lowry's projected sequence of six novels, ending with *Hear Us O Lord from Heaven Thy Dwelling Place*, but also the center of all of his work, particularly his poetry.

Lowry's work is a continuous whole, with its central novel representing hell or the point of lowest descent. The covert references to his first novel, *Ultramarine* (1933), in the sixth chapter of *Under the Volcano* are balanced by references to Dollarton, Lowry's residence near Vancouver, in the fourth and ninth chapters. Dollarton is the setting of much of *Hear Us O Lord from Heaven Thy Dwelling Place* and of his last poems. Similarly, *Under the Volcano* is echoed in his poems, including one entitled "For *Under the Volcano*," and in his shorter fiction.

Recognition of the midway position of the Mexican novel indicates three features of Lowry's work: its painfully autobiographical sources; its unity or continuity; and its close texture and highly symbolic content, an indirect product of the first two features.

The general features of Lowry's writings are shown in four aspects of *Under the Volcano*, two of which are immediately apparent. The novel is very specifically placed in time and space; the events of the first chapter occur on November 1, 1939, exactly a year after the events of the remaining eleven chapters, which in turn are clearly timed as occurring at stated intervals throughout the eleven hours of the action. The geographical placing of the novel in Quauhnahuac, Mexico, for the first seven chapters and in nearby Tomalín and Parián for the last four affords Lowry an opportunity to use his flair for symbolism. The principal geographical feature of the area is the *barranca*, or ravine, which local legend says opened on the day of the Crucifixion. The unity of Lowry's vision, or rather possibly his single-minded view of the world, enables him to fix the novel firmly in space and time and to range rapidly over them, giving a sense of cosmic urgency to the most innocent description. For example, the first paragraph mentions the Tropic of Cancer and the Juggernaut of India. Furthermore, Lowry's delight in symbolism is evident in the apparently innocuous introduction and juxtaposition of the terms "Crucifixion," "Cancer," and "Juggernaut."

As one reads further, however, two other aspects of the novel may strike one as severe disadvantages: one is the nature of the protagonist, the other the play of allusion. Both, however, are necessary to Lowry's serious intention. The allusions are part of the web of symbols constructed of reiterated references, for example, those to a film poster advertising "Las Manos de Orlac con Peter Lorre," the Great Wheel at the fiesta (the "Maquina Infernal"), Maximilian

and Carlotta, a dying turtle, shrieking fawns, a pariah dog that follows Geoffrey through the day and down into the *barranca*, the madman with the bicycle tire, and especially three signs: a fingerpost "To Parián"; the inscription, to the effect that life without love is impossible, over the door of Laruelle's house; and, most important, the sign in the public garden warning that those who destroy will be evicted. At a glance, it will be seen that these are susceptible to symbolic interpretation, but Lowry uses them both in complicated sets and at crucial moments of the action to increase their power enormously. Two instances show this usage. When Yvonne meets Geoffrey again, it is the morning after the night of the Red Cross Ball, held on All Hallows' Eve in the Hotel Bella Vista. The year is 1938, and the first words of the consul are the statement that a corpse will be transported by express. The time, place, occasion, and message all combine in gruesome congruity, especially if one is aware, as on a second reading, that the corpse is Geoffrey himself. In chapter 7, Geoffrey contemplates the view across the *barranca* from the top of Laruelle's house and remembers how they used to play golf together as boys, having especial difficulty with what they called Hell Bunker and retiring to the nineteenth hole in a pub called the Case Is Altered. In his present changed circumstances, Geoffrey visualizes a golf shot across the *barranca* to what he terms the Golgotha Hole, leading to his present refuge and the scene of his death, the tavern "The Farolito" ("The Little Lighthouse") at Parián, where the fingerpost points him.

The irony of these sets of symbols is made more effective because Geoffrey knows what they presage but cannot communicate his knowledge to Yvonne, Laruelle, Hugh, or Dr. Vigil, all of whom are trying to help him escape. This lack of communication leads to what appears to be the second disadvantageous aspect of the novel, the character of the protagonist. At first sight, Geoffrey resembles the feckless drunkard of some of Lowry's short stories. The point is whether he is drinking mescal to drown his sorrows or, since he calls it the "nectar of immortality," to avoid his fate; in either case, it both enables him to recognize the signs of doom and renders him incapable of showing their meaning to others, even when he, Hugh, and Yvonne see the dying Indian.

The explanation is that Geoffrey, as British consul, is not so much a character as a type. He is deliberately isolated from his native land, from the Mexicans around him, and from Hugh, Yvonne, and the others. The reader may see him as Everyman. Within narrow limits, he exemplifies the crisis of the liberals in the 1930's when they realized that the world was heading toward violence and disorder, that liberalism could not stop the march of history.

Such was Lowry's conviction when he wrote *Under the Volcano*, and it forms part of the autobiographical base of the novel. Lowry wrote in exile, in Cuernavaca; he was divorced in 1939. The conditions of the novel's composition and its Everyman character place it in the mainstream of great modern novels. The play of symbolism is intended to raise the novel from the level of plot and action to the level of universal applicability and ritual.

Geoffrey is in a "damnable" situation: He is divorced; his consulate is closed; he cannot stop drinking. He is also damned by his own past actions: his inability to answer Yvonne's letters and the murder of German officers during an engagement. He is also doomed by the actions of those around him: the affair between Laruelle and Yvonne and the hopeless dreams of Hugh. Every stage of his progress on the Day of the Dead—his reunion with Yvonne, his visit with Laruelle, the bus ride to Tomalín, his final encounter with the secret police at Parián—is an inexorable step in the chain of circumstances that draws him to the *barranca* and to his death.

If these steps are viewed as part of the elaborate ritual of preparing a victim for sacrifice, the ritual itself is an attempt to purge the awareness of disaster with the acceptance of love. The ritual fails to avert Geoffrey's fate, making *Under the Volcano* a compelling record of disaster and doom.

Further Reading

Asals, Frederick. *The Making of Malcolm Lowry's "Under the Volcano."* Athens: University of Georgia Press, 1997. Asals charts the slow development of the novel, studying the various manuscripts Lowry produced between 1940 and 1947 and analyzing the implications of the novel's revisions. Includes bibliography and index.

Asals, Frederick, and Paul Tiessen, eds. *A Darkness That Murmured: Essays on Malcolm Lowry and the Twentieth Century.* Toronto, Ont.: University of Toronto Press, 2000. Essays are provided by the best-known Lowry scholars, people who knew him, and his first wife. They cover biographical material as well as criticism and interpretation of his work. Includes bibliography and index.

Bowker, Gordon. *Pursued by Furies: A Life of Malcolm Lowry.* New York: St. Martin's Press, 1995. A comprehensive, scholarly biography; the preface provides pithy comments on the relationship between Lowry's life and fiction. Bowker argues that Lowry's life after the publication of *Under the Volcano* grew so chaotic that he was unable to devote his attention to writing a comparable novel.

Day, Douglas. *Malcolm Lowry: A Biography.* New York: Oxford University Press, 1973. Demonstrates how the novel is intent on making a moral statement, which is achieved by Lowry's presentation of the four major characters.

Epstein, Perle E. *The Private Labyrinth of Malcolm Lowry: "Under the Volcano" and the Cabbala.* New York: Henry Holt, 1969. Examines Lowry's use of myths and symbols for conveying the theme of *Under the Volcano*. Likens Lowry's use of Mexican folklore to the Cabbala.

Gass, William H. "In Terms of the Toenail: Fiction and the Figures of Life." In *Fiction and the Figures of Life.* New York: Alfred A. Knopf, 1970. Argues that *Under the Volcano* is a day-in-the-life story of British consul Geoffrey Firmin.

Markson, David. *Malcolm Lowry's "Volcano": Myth, Symbol, Meaning.* New York: Times Books, 1978. Probably the most thorough investigation of *Under the Volcano*. Explains Lowry's use of symbols, allusions, and themes.

Spender, Stephen. Introduction to *Under the Volcano* by Malcolm Lowry. New York: New American Library, 1971. Spender's introduction is a must for anyone reading *Under the Volcano* for the first time. Puts the novel into its context in Lowry's canon.

Woodcock, George, ed. *Malcolm Lowry: The Man and His Work.* Tonawanda, N.Y.: Black Rose Books, 2007. A collection of essays analyzing Lowry's life and work. The first section provides analysis of all of Lowry's fiction, while the second section examines the influences on Lowry's writings, including his life experiences and his love of jazz and films.

Under the Yoke

Author: Ivan Vazov (1850-1921)
First published: Pod igoto, serial, 1889-1890; book,
    1893 (English translation, 1894)
Type of work: Novel
Type of plot: Historical
Time of plot: 1875-1876
Locale: Bulgaria

Principal characters:
KRALICH, a revolutionary
RADA, his sweetheart
SOKOLOV, a doctor
MARIKA, a girl

The Story:

One day Marko, a substantial family man, sits down to his evening meal. His children and his relatives are a noisy crowd, but over the din they hear an alarming noise in the yard. The women all shriek, because they are afraid of robbers. Marko takes a pistol and goes to investigate. In the stable, he finds an exhausted and furtive man cowering in the dark.

Ivan Kralich, the fugitive, returns to the village of Bela Cherkva after escaping from a Turkish prison. The Turks are harsh rulers of Bulgaria, and anyone suspected of revolutionary tendencies is either killed outright or imprisoned. Nevertheless, eight years of confinement failed to quench Kralich's spirit. Making his getaway, he asks for sanctuary because the Turks are on his trail. Marko, a patriot who knew Kralich's family, tells the fugitive to remain in hiding in his stable. As he returns to the house, however, Turkish policemen knock at the door. They heard the women shrieking and come to see what the trouble is.

As soon as Marko can get rid of the Turks, he hurries back to the stable, but Kralich disappears. Hearing the police, he climbed the wall and ran. Unfortunately, he runs into a patrol and escapes them only after leaving his coat in the hands of the Turks. They shoot at him, but the fugitive escapes into the countryside. It is raining, and at last he takes refuge in a mill. As he crouches in a dark corner, the miller comes in with his innocent fourteen-year-old daughter, Marika. Kralich watches unobserved as they make beds on the floor. Then two Turkish policemen knock and force their way into the mill. One of them is a notorious lame man who cut off a girl's head a short while before. The miller is terror stricken when the Turks order him to get them some raki.

Knowing that they want Marika, the miller bravely refuses to leave. Throwing aside all pretense, the Turks seize him and start to bind him. Kralich is moved to action when the despairing miller calls to Marika for help. He takes an ax and after a brief struggle kills the Turks. After Kralich and the miller bury the bodies, the grateful miller leads Kralich to a good hiding place in a nearby monastery.

While Kralich is resting, Sokolov, the village doctor, finds himself in trouble. Although Sokolov is called a doctor, he received no training and prescribes few medicines; he is regarded with suspicion by the Turks because he is a patriotic Bulgarian and because his peculiar habits include keeping a pet bear. That night, as he is playing with the bear, the Turks arrest him on a charge of treason.

What happened was that Kralich asked Sokolov the way to Marko's house, and the compassionate doctor gave Kralich his coat. When Kralich loses the coat during his escape from the patrol, the police recognize Sokolov's garment. In the pockets they find revolutionary documents. The arrest creates a sensation in the district. Kralich, hearing of Sokolov's trouble, starts to the village to clear him. Marko, however, cleverly fools the police by substituting a harmless newspaper for the incriminating documents when the official messenger stops for a drink in a tavern. The evidence disappears, so the easygoing Turkish bey releases Sokolov.

Kralich changes his name and finds a job teaching school. He maintains contact with the revolutionaries, however, and soon welcomes to the cause his friend Mouratliski, who also fled from the Turks. Mouratliski, passing as an Austrian photographer, soon becomes a familiar figure in the village. Kralich continues to discuss the cause of liberty and wins many converts. He also falls in love with Rada, a gentle orphan who teaches in the girls' school.

Once the townspeople give a play in which Kralich takes a leading role. The bey, who understands no Bulgarian, is an honored guest. At the end of the play Kralich leads the cast in singing patriotic and revolutionary songs. The audience is much moved. The quick-witted Bulgarian translating for the bey assures the Turkish official that the songs are part of the drama.

Kralich finally comes under suspicion when a spy informs the Turks that the schoolmaster is working for Bulgarian independence. A detachment of police surround the church while the villagers are at worship, but Kralich gets through the cordon by assuming a disguise. He then flees to the mountains and the woods and for months leads a wandering life sheltered by patriotic Bulgars. He preaches continually the need for revolution. One day, when he attends a party in a small village, Turks come and beat an old man to death. Kralich leads a small group, including the giant Ivan Kill-the-Bear, out along a trail, and they wait in ambush. The Bulgars succeed in killing the Turks and leave their bodies to be eaten by wolves.

Meanwhile, in Bela Cherkva, Rada leads an uneasy life. The village knows of her love for Kralich and twits her on her hopeless affair after his disappearance. In particular, a student named Kandov makes her life miserable by following her about. At last Kralich slips into the village to visit her. Rada, overjoyed, is reluctant to part from him again, and Kralich invites her to go to Klissoura, a nearby village, where he is busy organizing a revolt. Soon afterward she sets out, but Kandov follows her and finds the house where she is staying. When Kralich appears, he is already a little jealous because he received an anonymous letter accusing Rada of intimacies with Kandov. As soon as he sees Kandov with her, Kralich becomes angry and leaves.

Under the fiery leadership of Kralich, the inhabitants of Klissoura prepare to revolt. On the day for the rising, the little garrison proclaims its independence of Turkey, and the citizen soldiers, after setting their wooden cannon on the trail, prepare to battle the Turks. Bela Cherkva does not revolt as planned, however, and the whole Turkish strength is concentrated on Klissoura. The Bulgarians are quickly overwhelmed. When the victors begin pillaging the town, Rada is lucky enough to get back to Bela Cherkva with the help of Ivan and his wife.

A fugitive once more, Kralich wanders hungry and cold through the Balkans. At last, he takes shelter in the mill and sends the faithful Marika into town with a letter asking Sokolov to bring him clothes. Marika cannot find the doctor, who also becomes a fugitive, but by chance the letter falls into Rada's hands. She makes up a bundle of clothing and starts off to the mill.

Sokolov, meanwhile, joins Kralich. When Rada arrives, the lovers have a brief and tearful reunion before pursuing Turks attack the mill. Kralich and Sokolov are both armed, and for a time, they hold their own against the enemy. Rada is the first to be killed by gunfire. Kralich kisses her cold lips and returns to the battle. The Turks quickly close in on the two Bulgarians when the defenders' ammunition gives out. Kralich's head is mounted on a pole and carried in triumph back to the village.

Critical Evaluation:

Under the Yoke was published after Bulgaria won independence from Turkish rule. Translated, the novel brought to Western readers a fresh and vivid insight into the affairs of that troubled country. Although the story is tragic, the treatment of the theme is romantic in the manner of Sir Walter Scott; and through fictitious characters and events, the trials of the Bulgarians are faithfully re-created. *Under the Yoke* is a competently written political novel that glorifies Bulgarian independence through the story of a young revolutionary and his struggles. Although melodramatic and unrealistic in parts, the novel is very effective in presenting a picture of life in Bulgaria in the years of Turkish domination.

Under the Yoke reflects Ivan Vazov's keen interest in the details of the Bulgarian nationalist movement's activities. He himself participated in the independence movement, and many of the novel's memorable scenes owe their vividness to the fact that when he wrote them Vazov was relying heavily on deeply felt personal experiences. His hometown of Sopot is the model for Bela Cherkva in the novel and is the town where he was involved in preparations for what turned out to be an unsuccessful uprising, much like that led by Kralich in Klissoura. Unlike Bela Cherkva, however, which in the novel escapes harm by backing out of the planned rebellion, Sopot was attacked by the Turks; when Vazov returned there in 1878 after independence was won, he found the town destroyed and his father among those murdered.

Vazov is at his best in the political scenes, at the school where Kralich teaches or at the theater, and in his scenes of domestic life. The opening scene in the book, for example, in which the reader sees the Marko family at dinner and gets a vivid description of their table manners and conversation, immediately provides a realistic setting for the story. Likewise, Vazov skillfully handles the scenes at the school, with his portrayals of Rada and Kralich and their students. He shows how many of the underlying political and social problems in Bulgaria's history are crucially related to the education of the young. At the same time, on a more personal level, he weaves in the love story of Kralich and Rada. There are weaknesses in the plot, however, such as Vazov's tendency to use action scenes, such as police searches and murders, to fill in between the much more central political scenes. These episodes occur so frequently and are over so quickly that they become almost mechanical; they seem to be tools used to hurry the narrative forward to the next key event.

The ending of *Under the Yoke* is melodramatic and bitter and reflects the author's romantic conception of revolution and his depression over the failure of the movement. It also dramatizes his basic distrust of the masses and his feelings that the common people are in some way responsible for their own oppression. It is clear, too, that the author believes that small-group terrorist acts are the only truly effective revolutionary device. In Rada's and Kralich's death scene, the author's romanticism and his cynicism about human nature can be seen simultaneously.

Further Reading

Choice. Review of *Under the Yoke*, by Ivan Vazov. 9 (June, 1972): 514. Hails the publication in English of this important work. Praises the work of the translators and editor in making the work accessible to English readers.

Gyllin, Roger. "Iván Vazov: A National Monument's Development as a Writer and Personality." In *Snorri Sturluson and the Roots of Nordic Literature / Snori Sturluson i korenite na nordskata knižovnost*, edited by Vladimir Stariradev. Sofia, Bulgaria: Department of German and Scandinavian Studies, University of Sofia, 2004. This article may be difficult to find, as not many libraries have books from Bulgaria. It is one of the few English-language discussions of Vazov's life and literary career, describing the conditions under which he wrote *Under the Yoke*. Compares Vazov's literary production to August Strindberg's "both quantitatively and in the richness of genres," but argues that Vazov is to a much higher degree than Strindberg a "national writer and patriot."

Haffner, Susanne A. Review of *Under the Yoke*, by Ivan Vazov. *Library Journal* 97 (January, 1972): 86. Describes the importance of the novel in the context of Bulgarian history. Cites some weakness in characterization and the strength of the novel's largely accurate account of a revolution.

Mihailovich, Vasa D., ed. *South Slavic Writers Before World War II*. Vol. 147 in *Dictionary of Literary Biography*. New York: Gale Research, 1995. Introductory overview, providing a biography of Vazov and a critique of his work.

Under Two Flags

Author: Ouida (1839-1908)
First published: 1867
Type of work: Novel
Type of plot: Sentimental
Time of plot: Mid-nineteenth century
Locale: London and environs, continental Europe, and Algeria

Principal characters:
THE HONORABLE BERTIE CECIL, a young guardsman
BERKELEY, his younger brother
LORD ROCKINGHAM, "THE SERAPH," Bertie's friend
RAKE, Bertie's servant
LADY GUINEVERE, Bertie's married lover in London
CIGARETTE, a Frenchwoman patriot
COLONEL CHATEAUROY, Bertie's enemy
PRINCESS CORONA D'AMAGÜE, the Seraph's sister

The Story:

Although a fashionable member of his London set and an admirable fellow in every other respect, the Honorable Bertie Cecil of the First Life Guards is uncommonly low on credit. No moneylender in London will accept his note after he has mortgaged his whole inheritance. In these circumstances, he stakes everything on winning a race with his six-year-old horse, Forest King. With good-humored generosity, he nevertheless lends his younger brother, Berkeley, fifty pounds. The following day, he rides Forest King to victory over a difficult course and receives the praise of his Lady Guinevere, a fashionable peeress.

His father, Lord Royallieu, lives in the same mortgaged splendor that he has taught his three sons to enjoy. Lord Royallieu loves two of his sons but not Bertie, who looks too much like his dead wife's lover and, to the old viscount's detestation, carries the dead lover's name. The old man takes every occasion to sneer at Bertie's extravagance, and one day, he reveals his suspicion that Bertie is really the son of Alan Bertie.

Bertie is otherwise lucky in the world. Sought after by half the women in London, he carries on flirtations with many. Lady Guinevere is one of his conquests. Rake, his valet, is devoted to him. Bertie salvaged Rake from a bad scrape in the army and has always treated him with friendly decency.

Bertie is disturbed by his financial affairs, so his head

groom promises to drug Forest King for a fee. When it is learned that Forest King was drugged before a race in Baden, Bertie's friends, far from blaming him, pretend to agree that the horse was merely ill; nevertheless, Bertie feels disgraced.

Bertie's best friend, Lord Rockingham, is known to his comrades of the Guards as the Seraph. While Lord Rockingham is attempting to discover the mystery of Forest King's condition, he receives a report that Bertie Cecil has forged the Seraph's name to a note. Bertie cannot deny the charge, for the note was presented at a time when he was dining with Lady Guinevere. Wishing to protect her name from scandal, Bertie allows himself to be accused. He knows that his brother forged the note, and he hopes to protect Berkeley's name as well; consequently, Bertie leaves Europe suddenly to escape arrest.

Accompanied by Rake, Bertie makes his escape on Forest King. Rake discovered that the groom had drugged Forest King, and he has pummeled him for it. He and his master ride to a place of safety, and then Bertie orders Rake to take Forest King to Lord Rockingham. He waits in hiding for a time, hoping Lady Guinevere will save him by telling of his whereabouts when the forged note was presented. She chooses to keep silent, however, holding her reputation at greater worth than Bertie's name.

At last, by a mere throw of the dice in Algeria, Bertie decides to cast his lot with the French Foreign Legion instead of with the Arab cause. The faithful Rake accompanies him. Back in England, it is believed that Bertie has died in a French train wreck. Rockingham has Forest King; the old viscount burns Bertie's picture.

Using the name Louis Victor, Bertie makes his mark with his new companions in the Foreign Legion. They marvel at his skill with horses, at his bravery, and at his brilliance in conversation. Bertie is a twelve-year veteran Legionnaire when he receives, six months late, the news that his father has died at the age of ninety. His older brother has inherited the viscount's title.

Cigarette, a woman of independent spirit and a dancer and singer for the troops, comes to understand and admire Bertie. She warns him against Colonel Chateauroy, who hates Bertie because of his gallant record and popularity, and asks him never to disobey any of the colonel's unreasonable commands. Partly because he pities her, Bertie promises. Shortly afterward, Cigarette saves Bertie's life when he is in danger from some drunken Arabs. She adores him, but he is indifferent toward her.

Bertie spends his spare time carving chessmen of ivory and walnut. Through this occupation, he meets the lovely Princess Corona d'Amagüe, a woman who had been unhappily married to a man injured while saving her brother's life. Her husband died soon after, and the princess has felt responsible for his death. Bertie soon falls in love with Princess Corona.

Colonel Chateauroy makes it clear that he will never permit Bertie to be promoted above the rank of corporal. Bertie learns that Rake has purposely been getting himself into trouble to prevent his own promotion, for he does not wish to outrank his master. One day, Bertie reads in an old English journal that his older brother has died suddenly and that Berkeley has become Viscount Royallieu.

The regiment is ordered out. In the gory fighting that follows, Cigarette saves the day when she arrives at the head of a fresh squadron of cavalry. She finds Bertie on the battlefield; he has been badly wounded. In the tent to which she has him carried, Bertie begins to talk incoherently while Cigarette sits beside him. Everything she hears him say makes her more jealous of the princess. She also learns that Bertie is English. No French person ever hated the English more than she. At her request, Bertie is not told who brought him back from the battlefield and cared for him during his sick ravings.

Three weeks later, Bertie is startled when the Seraph comes as an English tourist to visit the Legion camp. Bertie does not wish to encounter his former friend, so he asks for and receives permission to carry dispatches through hostile territory to another Legion post. With the faithful Rake, he rides away on a mission that means almost certain death. Rake is killed in an Arab ambush, but Bertie delivers his dispatches safely. On his return trip, he stops at an inn and there sees his brother Berkeley, who is one of a party of tourists traveling with Princess Corona. Bertie gives no sign of recognition; he merely spurs his horse and continues on.

Berkeley follows Bertie, however, and catches up with his older brother. Berkeley reveals his fear that Bertie might claim the title. Indifferent to all except Berkeley's selfishness, Bertie asks his brother to leave Algeria at once. Shortly afterward, Bertie discovers that Princess Corona is really the younger sister of the Seraph. She also becomes aware of Bertie's real name and insists that he make himself known to her brother. She begs him to claim his title, but he refuses.

Princess Corona asks Cigarette to tell Bertie that the Seraph is looking for his former friend. In another interview with Bertie, the princess asks him to tell his story and let the world be the judge. As Bertie leaves her tent, he is intercepted by Colonel Chateauroy, who insults the princess. In a sudden rage, Bertie strikes his superior officer. He is subsequently arrested and sentenced to death.

When Cigarette hears about Bertie's fate, she forces

Berkeley, whom she has met accidentally, to acknowledge that Bertie is in reality his brother, an exile for Berkeley's crime and the true heir to the estate of Royallieu. She carries her story to a marshal of France and demands that Bertie's honor be saved although his life is already to be forfeited. With a stay of execution signed by the marshal, Cigarette rides at full speed to reach the Legion camp before the hour set for Bertie's execution.

The Seraph, not Cigarette, reaches Bertie first. Despite the Seraph's entreaties, Colonel Chateauroy refuses to delay the time of execution. Cigarette reaches the spot just as the firing squad fires its volley, and with her own body, she takes the bullets intended for Bertie. She dies, but the marshal's order is safely delivered. A child of the army and a soldier of France, Cigarette has given her life to save a comrade. It is a sacrifice that Bertie and Princess Corona, happily reunited, are never to forget. In the end, Bertie is even reunited with Forest King.

Critical Evaluation:

Under Two Flags is a rollicking and absorbing, if flawed, masterpiece. It combines breathless action, preposterous situations, flashbacks, short stories, prolix and stilted dialogue, and almost interminable and often repetitious psychological analysis. It was first published serially, which may account for the regularly spaced end-of-chapter climaxes and for Ouida's frequent recapitulations of past events as reminders to her readers.

The thirty-eight chapters of *Under Two Flags* fall into almost exactly equal thirds. Chapter 12 ends with the escape of Bertie and Rake. In chapter 24, the hero learns that his elder brother's death should give him the title of Lord Royallieu. By the end of chapter 36, which is devoted to Bertie's court-martial, readers have had sufficient foreshadowing hints to be assured that Cigarette will save the day—for Bertie's honor, his love of Princess Corona, and Cigarette's own glory. Chapters 37-38 make up a denouement and coda. Interestingly, the conclusive action of the entire novel begins in chapter 19 with the revelation that Bertie carves chessmen.

Ouida adopts an omniscient, cinematic point of view and places and moves her characters like actors. She is always telling readers about one person's actions or thoughts to which other people are not privy, sometimes by being nearby, but out of earshot. This device can become awkward, as when the Seraph is kept almost fatally unaware that Corporal Victor is actually Bertie. Related is Ouida's use of coincidence. To begin with, the appearance of Berkeley, the Seraph, and Corona in Algeria is unrealistic; even more incredible is Bertie's wandering bemused outside Corona's rooms,

rescuing a goat from drowning, and, in the process, chancing to find Corona's broken necklace nearby—naturally, he must return it to her later. Ouida manages splendid visual effects, not only through innumerable scenic descriptions but also through quick, cinematic shifts to action scenes. In chapter 36 alone, images include the divisional encampment bathed in autumnal noon light, Bertie being dramatically court-martialed, Cigarette sulking in her room, a carrier pigeon flying through Cigarette's oval window with a letter, and Cigarette's fortuitous encounter with Berkeley in the crowded street.

Ouida handles time well. She intriguingly avoids dating the action of her novel, but when she briefly mentions Alexandre Dumas, *fils*, Jean Léon Gérôme, John Tenniel, and, especially, Napoleon III and Abd-el-Kader, readers can place the major African episodes in the 1850's. Ouida varies her generally chronological story line with short flashbacks (for an awkward example, Bertie's escape from Baden to Marseilles, which is tardily detailed in chapter 18), protracted narrations of earlier action (the peculiar marriage of Princess Corona, whose husband's quick death makes her a rich, virgin widow, in chapter 22; Léon Ramon's joining the Foreign Legion because his girlfriend has spurned him, in chapter 23), and occasional almost Homeric lists of fellow soldiers (for example, thumbnail sketches of seven men, some with marvelous nicknames, in chapter 16). One flashback—involving Marquise, who, when insulted by his adjutant, bayonets him to death and is executed by a firing squad (chapter 20)—is an example of Ouida's foreshadowing skill. Later, Bertie is condemned to an identical death for striking his colonel. Ouida cleverly keeps the reader in suspense by using unfulfilled foreshadowing. In one dramatic example, when Bertie learns that Forest King was drugged, he wants the culprit left to him to deal with (chapter 10); the reader eagerly awaits this scene of revenge, but in vain.

Ouida, intoxicated by words, serves them up lavishly. Her style is a unique combination of often unusual diction, syntax habitually tortured, quaint and courtly speech, snippets of French (not always translated), and spectacular figures of speech. Words such as "acquirements," "excitation," "flissa," "insouciance," "lentiscus," "rataplan," "sabretache," and "yawner"—among others equally obscure—challenge the reader's attention. Ouida describes almost everything, including food both dainty and coarse, tempting drinks, opulent clothes and stained uniforms, living quarters (boudoirs, hotel rooms, barracks, desert tents), weapons, dances, jewelry, dice and cards, and animals—especially horses, both racing and in combat. Her similes and metaphors often derive from water, flowers, storms, weapons, art objects, and animals. Cigarette alone is likened to a kitten, chamois, a light-winged bird, and a menacing little leopard; in turn, she derogates Corona by repeatedly labeling her a silver pheasant. Ouida names animals so delightfully that anyone in search of a moniker for a pet should consult *Under Two Flags*. Readers might consider Bay Regent, Blue Ruin, Etoile Filante, Irish Roan, Pas de Charge, Wild Geranium, or Vivandière. Lady Guinevere's horse is Vivandière, whose name prefigures the advent of Cigarette, world literature's most heroic *vivandière*.

Under Two Flags is ridiculous if read with the expectation that a novel should be realistic. It contains, however, beautifully sketched natural scenery and descriptions of the accoutrements of mid-nineteenth century men and women. It remains a very exciting book for all its sometimes wearying length, and its moral messages—concerning such matters as unrewarded work, hiding one's good deeds, honor, loyalty, discipline, promises kept, developing endurance, and unselfish love—should be inspiring to young and old alike.

Ouida reveals much of herself, as well as her times, in this rousing romance. Her father was French, and her mother was English; Ouida, whose real name was Maria Louisa de la Ramée, therefore lived, in a sense, under two flags. She criticizes effete English aristocracy (especially the women) and pigheaded French militaristic colonialism alike in *Under Two Flags*, her fourth novel. As soon as it was published, she became immensely popular. The book eventually went into sixty-three editions in English. She was also controversial, being allegedly too intimate with talkative guardsmen both during and after smoky dinners. She traveled restlessly, wrote forty-seven books in all, spent her considerable royalties foolishly, and came to prefer her many dogs to friends. She died lonely and poverty-stricken in Italy. In *Under Two Flags* two of her most memorable generalizations concern loneliness and old age. She says that "loneliness in the midst of numbers . . . [is] the most painful of all solitude" (chapter 22), and she calls old age "nothing else but death that is *conscious*" (chapter 21). Like Cigarette, Ouida would have wished to die young, full of vigor, and surrounded by virile soldiers.

"Critical Evaluation" by Robert L. Gale

Further Reading

Beerbohm, Max. "Ouida." In *More*. London: John Lane, 1899. Still one of the finest essays available on Ouida. Praises her energy, her love of beauty in nature and art, the fascination of her discursive plots, her characters, and her scenic range and store of information.

Benchérif, Osman. *The Image of Algeria in Anglo-American Writings, 1785-1962*. Lanham, Md.: University Press of America, 1997. Examines how American and British writers in the period discussed experienced and represented Algeria, and how Algerians responded to these literary images. Includes a chapter discussing perception and depiction of the French conquest of Algeria in *Under Two Flags*.

Bigland, Eileen. *Ouida: The Passionate Victorian*. London: Jarrolds, 1950. Praises *Under Two Flags* as Ouida's deservedly most famous romantic extravaganza, noting in particular her description of desert action. Argues that Cigarette is hauntingly vital and lovable, especially when compared with Guinevere and Corona.

Gilbert, Pamela K. "Ouida: Romantic Exchange." In *Disease, Desire, and the Body in Victorian Women's Popular Novels*. New York: Cambridge University Press, 1997. Chapter focusing on Ouida is part of a larger work that analyzes her works, including *Under Two Flags*, as well as the works of other Victorian popular novelists. Argues that these works were regarded as a feminine disease infecting the healthy, male, imperial culture.

Porch, Douglas. *The French Foreign Legion: A Complete History of the Legendary Fighting Force*. New York: HarperCollins, 1991. Discusses the maneuvers of the Emir Abd el-Kader, Arab resistance leader, against the French near Oran. In criticizing novels and films that have been produced about the Foreign Legion, approvingly quotes one commentator who calls *Under Two Flags* "giddy [and] romantic."

Schaffer, Talia. "The Dandy in the House: Ouida and the Origin of the Aesthetic Novel." In *The Forgotten Female Aesthetes: Literary Culture in Late-Victorian England*. Charlottesville: University Press of Virginia, 2000. Chapter on Ouida is part of an examination of the work of several nineteenth century women writers, "the female aesthetes." Describes how Oscar Wilde and other male writers adapted these women's plots, ideas, and literary styles.

Schroeder, Natalie, and Shari Hodges Holt. *Ouida the Phenomenon: Evolving Social, Political, and Gender Concerns in Her Fiction*. Newark: University of Delaware Press, 2008. Analyzes Ouida's life and work as a complex reflection of Victorian cultural paradoxes, including debates about the New Woman and aestheticism.

Stirling, Monica. *The Fine and the Wicked: The Life and Times of Ouida*. New York: Coward-McCann, 1958. Biography includes high praise for *Under Two Flags*. Relates several elements in the work to the events of Ouida's personal life and to contemporary society, art, and literature.

Under Western Eyes

Author: Joseph Conrad (1857-1924)
First published: 1911
Type of work: Novel
Type of plot: Psychological realism
Time of plot: Early twentieth century
Locale: St. Petersburg, Russia; Geneva, Switzerland

Principal characters:
RAZUMOV, a Russian student
VICTOR HALDIN, a revolutionist
NATHALIE HALDIN, his sister
MRS. HALDIN, the mother of Victor and Nathalie
THE ENGLISH PROFESSOR, a friend of the Haldins

The Story:

A student at the St. Petersburg University, Razumov, while not talkative or gregarious, is generally respected by the other students. His silences are attributed to profundity of thought, and his behavior inspires confidence and good opinion. Absorbed in his studies, Razumov remains largely indifferent to the impression he makes on his fellow students. He dreams of winning scholarly honors, and he has no wish to become involved in the revolutionary activities that occupy the minds of such acquaintances as Victor Haldin, a youth in whose company he occasionally spends some time. Razumov's mother is dead; his father, Prince K——, acknowledges his illegitimate son only to the extent of sending him money secretly, through an intermediary. As a result, the unspent feeling that Razumov is unable to direct toward parents or toward family finds its way into other channels. He lavishes much of it on his country and feels, in his loneliness, that if he were not a Russian, he would not be anything.

The pattern of Razumov's life is abruptly altered by a strange turn of circumstances. On a snowy morning in St. Petersburg, a sensational event occurs—a political terrorist assassinates a prominent government official and then escapes. An hour or two later, the unsuspecting Razumov returns to his apartment to find a visitor awaiting him. The guest is Victor Haldin. Presuming on his casual acquaintance with Razumov, Haldin selects the latter's quarters as a place of temporary refuge. When pressed for an explanation, he confesses that he is the killer sought by the police. He asks Razumov to help him in making his escape from the city.

Razumov is dismayed and knows he will be compromised and ruined by Haldin's visit if it ever becomes known. He goes, nevertheless, in search of a driver who might spirit Haldin away, but he finds one helplessly drunk. His dismay and despair deepen; finally, Razumov decides that he cannot continue to shield Haldin. In his extremity, he breaks an unwritten rule by calling on Prince K—— to ask his advice and beg his protection. Prince K—— immediately contacts the authorities, and Haldin is promptly apprehended and executed. After an extended interrogation by General T—— and

Councilor Mikulin, Razumov is released, but not before he is marked down by the councilor's sharp eyes as a tool of great potential usefulness to the government.

Meanwhile, in Geneva, Haldin's mother and sister wait anxiously for news of him. When word of his execution arrives, they are grief-stricken and bewildered. Their efforts to find out the exact circumstances of his end are blocked by the mystery and vagueness that shroud the whole affair. Nathalie, Victor's sister, is relieved when she hears that a Russian named Razumov arrived in Geneva. According to rumors that were circulating, this man is an escaped colleague of her brother, a fellow conspirator and revolutionist. Surely he, better than any other, will be able to solve the puzzle of her brother's arrest and execution.

To the Haldins, Razumov proves to be an elusive and an enigmatic quarry. He loses himself at once in a circle of revolutionists in exile, including the celebrated Peter Ivanovitch, the legendary Madame de S——, and the sinister Nikita. Among them, he is admired as a hero. Razumov finds this role increasingly difficult to maintain, especially after he meets Nathalie and falls in love with her. Razumov finally breaks under the strain of maintaining his deception. Through his journal, which he sends to Nathalie, she learns his true relationship to her brother. On an impulse, he then confesses to the revolutionists the fact that he is a government spy. He is brutally beaten by Nikita, and his hearing is destroyed. Stumbling in front of a tramcar, he suffers from two broken limbs and a crushed side and is picked up by passersby and carried to a hospital.

The tragic story of Razumov might end there, but his will to live proves too strong. Nursed back to partial health by a motherly revolutionist, he eventually returns to his homeland. There, in the south of Russia, he shares a two-room cottage with his Good Samaritan friend, the devoted Tekla. Some of the revolutionists come to regret the cruel treatment Razumov received at their hands. Periodically, they visit his cottage to be stimulated by his intelligent and original views on politics, on society, and on morality.

Critical Evaluation:

Under Western Eyes was written during a time when Joseph Conrad was making great strides forward in his achievement as a writer but was not yet receiving widespread attention. When it was first released, the novel was criticized for its remote and somber subject matter, which took Conrad further away from general public reception, especially since it followed so closely on the heels of *Nostromo* (1904) and *The Secret Agent* (1907), two other books that had garnered much critical acclaim but little public reception. Since then, critical reception of the novel has developed to the point where the novel is now considered to be one of Conrad's greatest achievements.

One of Conrad's aims in writing the book was to attempt to make the Russian character comprehensible to a Western reader, whose only prior experience with Russian themes, perhaps in a cheap novel or popular magazine, might have created a stereotyped impression. The novel is a terrible indictment of Russia, suggesting that Conrad may have been moved to write about what he saw as the truth of the Russian mind-set, which differed little before and after the revolution. Critics have noted the Dostoevskian nature of the novel, but it must be noted that Conrad detested Fyodor Dostoevski, so the novel may be considered a reaction against Dostoevski rather than a tribute to him.

Appearances and their deceptive nature are important themes in the book. Razumov's quiet and solitary nature leads his fellow students to assume that he is a deep thinker, a strong character, and politically committed, while in reality he is none of these. He is more of a blank page on which others project their hopes, desires, and emotions. Haldin comes to Razumov because of his confidence in Razumov's character. He is the first of many characters to misperceive the actual nature of Razumov's character. Haldin is also blind to the true nature of many other things. He misperceives the nature of Ziemianitch and the inhabitants of the inn where he resides. When Razumov actually goes to the inn and comes upon the people Haldin described so glowingly, only to find them all shabby and drunk, this provides a humorous, ironic counterpoint. Even when Razumov tries to explain himself to Haldin after the betrayal is arranged, Haldin never truly understands what Razumov is trying to tell him and goes to his death still blind to Razumov's character. He continually misinterprets Razumov's actions, emotions, and expressions as being favorable, instead of the threats to him that they actually represent.

Haldin is the victim of his own vision, which blinds him to reality. Razumov and even Ziemianitch become victims of Haldin's ideas, as do Nathalie and her mother, who come to believe his deed not worth the sacrifice. Razumov, ironically, does come to accept that Haldin's goal—revolution—is the way of the future. He, however, cannot bring himself to adopt a cause or to lose himself in a communal effort. Razumov, unlike the revolutionists, is a man without illusions. He is condemned by his lack of illusions to remain cut off from life. Razumov even comes to embrace this isolation, since to be alone is to be free of others' misinterpretations of one's conduct and, especially, of one's words. Razumov illustrates Conrad's idea of the dangers of nonsolidarity.

Coupled with the idea of the nature of appearances, another major theme in the novel is the power of words, for destructive and for constructive purposes. For the narrator, the most striking feature of the Russian national character is its loquacity. Razumov's habit of silence sets him apart and causes his fellow students to consider him "a strong nature—and altogether trustworthy man," a man to whom Haldin unhesitatingly and wrongly entrusts his life.

In the novel, words are either incomprehensible or deliberately concealing. For example, the narrator can never quite grasp what Nathalie means when she talks of ideas, because their "enigmatical prolongations vanish somewhere beyond my reach." For the Russian, silence is dangerous—something Haldin never realizes when placing his trust in Razumov.

Razumov comes to know the awful power of words: "words . . . are the great foes of reality." He notes, "Speech has been given to us for the purpose of concealing our thoughts." Early in the novel, Razumov takes great delight in "deceiving people out of their own mouths," as he takes people's words and uses them in continuing his deception. He is always misinterpreted and begins to take a perverse delight in fostering this, putting it to his own use. Razumov, continually on the verge of confession, is clearly a poor candidate for a life of intrigue, which makes it strange that the astute Mikulin did not observe this. In his confrontations with the revolutionaries in Geneva, Razumov is compelled to play dangerously with lies and double meanings. He is still under the suspicion that he is being watched and judged and is seized by a spirit of perversity that, together with his hatred of lying and deception, causes him to confess, as he had earlier been driven to confess to Haldin.

Ultimately, his confession to the revolutionaries is motivated by a wish to "escape from the prison of lies." In escaping from lies, Razumov escapes from words. Razumov thinks that silence and invisibility are things to be envied: "The people that are neither seen nor heard are the lucky ones—in Russia," he tells Nathalie. What makes Haldin's crime so unforgivable to Razumov is that "he went around talking of me," thus creating the suspicion in the minds of the police and his fellow students that he had something to do with the assassination plot.

Razumov's habit of silence is a cause of his original misunderstanding with Haldin and, much later, it is Mrs. Haldin's silence during Razumov's interview with her that is a precipitating factor in his confession to Nathalie. Razumov's silence ultimately destroys him. Ironically, his power lies in silence. His taciturnity inspires confidence. His silence also leads to the misinterpretations of his character that lead to his downfall.

"Critical Evaluation" by Craig A. Larson

Further Reading

Carabine, Keith. *The Life and the Art: A Study of Conrad's "Under Western Eyes."* New York: Rodopi, 1996. A study of the relationship between Conrad's life and his art as demonstrated in *Under Western Eyes*. Focuses on Conrad's creation of the novel he described as "without doubt" the "most deeply meditated novel that came from under my pen."

Hay, Eloise Knapp. *The Political Novels of Joseph Conrad.* Chicago: University of Chicago Press, 1963. Studies the variety of political thought and themes in Conrad's work. The chapter on *Under Western Eyes* calls it Conrad's "last great political novel."

Kaplan, Carola M., Peter Mallios, and Andrea White, eds. *Conrad in the Twenty-first Century: Contemporary Approaches and Perspectives.* New York: Routledge, 2005. Collection of essays that analyze Conrad's depiction of postcolonialism, empire, imperialism, and modernism. Includes two essays focusing on *Under Western Eyes*.

Peters, John G. *The Cambridge Introduction to Joseph Conrad.* New York: Cambridge University Press, 2006. An introductory overview of Conrad, with information on his life, all of his works, and his critical reception.

Rieselbach, Helen Funk. *Conrad's Rebels: The Psychology of Revolution in the Novels from "Nostromo" to "Victory."* Ann Arbor: University of Michigan Press, 1985. Discusses the consequences of Razumov's speech and silence. Calls the novel "Conrad's most extensive treatment of the theme of betrayal—the psychological motivations behind it and its consequences."

Robert, Andrew Michael. *Conrad and Masculinity.* New York: St. Martin's Press, 2000. Uses modern theories about masculinity to analyze Conrad's work and explore the relationship of masculinity to imperialism and modernity. *Under Western Eyes* is discussed in the chapter entitled "Masculinity, 'Woman' and Truth: *The Secret Agent, Under Western Eyes, Chance*."

Schwarz, Daniel R. *Conrad: "Almayer's Folly" to "Under Western Eyes."* Ithaca, N.Y.: Cornell University Press, 1980. Contains an excellent chapter on *Under Western Eyes*, focusing on the novel's "rejection of political commitment in favor of personal relationships and private commitments."

Smith, David R., ed. *Joseph Conrad's "Under Western Eyes": Beginnings, Revisions, Final Forms.* Hamden, Conn.: Archon Books, 1991. Five essays by Conrad specialists trace the development of the novel from manuscript to finished work and cover a variety of topics related to the book.

Stape, J. H., ed. *The Cambridge Companion to Joseph Conrad.* New York: Cambridge University Press, 1996. Collection of essays discussing Conrad's life and analyzing his work, including discussions of the Conradian narrative, Conrad and imperialism, Conrad and modernism, and Conrad's literary influence. Keith Carabine's essay focuses on *Under Western Eyes*.

Watts, Cedric. *A Preface to Conrad.* 2d ed. New York: Longman, 1993. A good starting point for Conrad scholarship, with general biographical and cultural background on the writer.

The Underdogs
A Novel of the Mexican Revolution

Author: Mariano Azuela (1873-1952)
First published: Los de abajo, 1915, serial; 1916, book,
    1916; revised, 1920 (English translation, 1929)
Type of work: Novel
Type of plot: Historical
Time of plot: 1914-1915
Locale: Zacatecas and Jalisco, Mexico

Principal characters:
DEMETRIO MACÍAS, a poor Indian of Jalisco
LUIS CERVANTES, an opportunistic journalist and political
    turncoat
CAMILA, a villager
LA PINTADA, "The Painted Lady," a prostitute and camp
    follower
WHITEY MARGARITO, a sadistic soldier

The Story:

Demetrio Macías is a peaceful Indian who knows nothing about revolutions. When, as a follower of Francisco Indalécio Madero, he is hounded by the political leader of Jalisco, he flees with his wife and child to the mountains. There, federal soldiers come upon the fugitives at breakfast, and Demetrio runs off. He returns with a gun, however, to prevent the wild and lawless soldiers from raping his wife. Being no killer, Demetrio lets them go free, only to have them come back with reinforcements and burn his fields. Demetrio then joins a band of sixty sharpshooting rebel outlaws and helps them to drive off twice that many soldiers. During the fighting, two of the rebels are killed, and Demetrio is shot in the leg.

For two weeks, the outlaws remain hidden in a native village, looked after by Indians who hate the government. Venancio, a barber-surgeon, tends to Demetrio's wound, and the village women use poultices of laurel and fresh pigeon blood to heal him. An attractive young woman named Camila is his nurse.

One day, the pseudointellectual Luis Cervantes blunders into the village and explains that he has deserted the government forces because his commanding officer assigned him to menial duty. Distrusting Cervantes' glib tongue and big words, the rebels pretend to condemn him to death. One outlaw dresses in a priest's robes and pretends to hear the deserter's last confession to determine whether he is a spy. Accepted eventually as a revolutionist, Cervantes then urges the rebels to join the great revolutionary leaders of Mexico. Camila falls in love with him. Although she makes her feelings evident, Cervantes never encourages her, not even on the night of the outlaws' departure. Camila has never responded to Demetrio's lovemaking—Demetrio is only an Indian.

Hearing from messengers that Victoriano Huerta's *federales* have fortified the city of Zacatecas, Cervantes urges the band to hurry to join the besiegers and take part in

the capture. He flatters Demetrio by telling the Indian that he is more than a common rebel, that he is a tool of destiny to win back the rights of the people.

Demetrio plans a surprise attack on one of the towns along their march, but an Indian guide betrays the scheme, and the *federales* are prepared to resist. A friendly citizen shows the rebels a back way into the town, however, and the garrison is overwhelmed. The rebels find and stab the treacherous guard and kill the federal soldiers who survived the attack.

By the time General Natera arrives in the district, Demetrio's reputation has grown so great that he is made a colonel in the revolutionary army. Failing to take Zacatecas, the rebels are forced to retreat, discarding their booty along the road. Demetrio thinks of going back to Camila, until news of General Pancho Villa's coming excites the rebels and gives them fresh incentive.

During the next battle, Cervantes and Solis, an idealist, take refuge in a place where they think they will be safe. While they discuss the significance of the revolution, Solis is struck and killed by a stray bullet. Demetrio's gallant charge turns the tide of battle for Villa and wins Demetrio promotion to the rank of general.

While drinking and boasting in a tavern after the battle, Demetrio meets Whitey Margarito, a vicious soldier, and La Pintada, a prostitute with whom Demetrio goes looking for a hotel room. Her insistence that, as a general, he should occupy a house of his own makes him decide to commandeer a fine residence.

During the ransacking, Cervantes finds a valuable diamond ring and the soldiers tear the pictures from books in the library. Whitey, joining Demetrio's forces, runs off with Cervantes' woman companion while Demetrio is arguing the matter of taking her instead of La Pintada, of whom he has tired.

Soon afterward, the rebels raid the house of Don Monico, Demetrio's landowning enemy, and burn the estate. Cervantes, having collected much loot, suggests that he and Demetrio hide it in case they are forced to leave the country. Demetrio wishes to share it with the others. Still an idealist, he believes the rebel cause will triumph. Cervantes promises to get Camila for his leader, as Demetrio still wants her above all.

Cervantes goes to the village and persuades Camila to return with him. Believing that Cervantes is in love with her, she is surprised to find herself in Demetrio's bed. The next morning, La Pintada discovers Camila and offers to help her escape. Camila refuses. She has found that she likes Demetrio, and she decides to stay with him and the rebel army.

During the march against General Orozco at Jalisco, Whitey shows his cruelty when he tortures a prisoner by tightening a rope around the man's neck until his eyes bulge. Later, when kindhearted Camila persuades Demetrio to return ten bushels of confiscated corn to a starving villager, Whitey gives the man ten lashes instead. Camila's protests at the incident win her the enmity of La Pintada, who has taken up with Whitey since Demetrio and Cervantes discarded her. When Demetrio, siding with Camila, orders La Pintada away from the camp, she becomes enraged and stabs Camila.

When Demetrio and his men reach Aguascalientes, they find Villa and Venustiano Carranza, once allies, fighting each other. The federal forces, taking advantage of the disunity among the rebel generals, defeat Villa at Celaya. The defeat is a terrible shock to Demetrio's followers, who cannot bring themselves to believe that their idol has been beaten. The rebels are forced to retreat.

Cervantes escapes safely across the border. From El Paso, he writes to Venancio, the barber-surgeon, telling him that Whitey has shot himself. Cervantes invites Venancio to join him in Texas, where, with the barber's money, they can open a restaurant.

After Villa's defeat, Demetrio finds the villagers no longer willing to help the rebels. To them, he and his followers have become outlaws once more. Somewhat discouraged, he decides to return home. He has been away two years and has seen much, but he cannot answer his wife's questions when she asks him why he kept on fighting. He lacks Cervantes' glib tongue to put his true feelings into words.

Trying to pacify the landowners of the region, the government sends troops into the uplands after the outlaw band. Once more the rebels and the federal troops clash. Outnumbered, the outlaws perish on the spot where two years before they had won their first victory. After the fighting has ended, the soldiers find the body of Demetrio Macías, his dead eyes still sighted along the barrel of his gun.

Critical Evaluation:

Mariano Azuela knew firsthand the materials of this novel, for he had served as a military doctor with Pancho Villa's Golden Boys. His vivid account of revolutionary Mexico was first published serially in a small El Paso newspaper. Almost forgotten, it was revived in 1924 and won immediate fame for its author. Pessimism marks this story of "those below"—*los de abajo*—at the beginning of the Mexican Revolution. This is no overall picture of the revolution but rather a blending of excitement, cruelty, and beauty as seen through the eyes of a man practically pushed into the struggle, a soldier who fought because the enemy was in front of him. Best known of Azuela's sixteen novels, *The Underdogs* has appeared in dozens of Spanish editions and has been translated into many languages.

This favorite story about the Mexican Revolution still merits its international fame. It has both literary and sociological worth. Azuela's honesty glitters in it because he does not overly caricature the Porfirista enemy even while lampooning him. Neither does Azuela spare the hypocrisies of his own side. His characterization is true to life, and his action scenes are fast and clear. Violence, pathos, beauty, and tragedy are etched against Jalisco's night-blackened hills, so that the reader receives an indelible image of revolutionary pageantry, with its women *soldaderas*, bandoliered rebels, uniformed *federales*, and greedy nouveau riche who muddy the pond of revolutionary ideals. While painting only local vignettes of a nationwide holocaust, *The Underdogs* presents both the seedy and the inspiring aspects of the entire event.

The genuine worth of this novel was not recognized until almost a decade after its publication. By the mid-1920's, however, it had been translated into various languages and was considered both a Latin American and a Mexican classic. It was written almost literally amid powder smoke, when Azuela was in despair because he saw that the revolution was drowning some injustices in blood only to spawn others as bad and as self-perpetuating. The virtue of the novel thus lies in its eyewitness impressions of intense, futile events. Azuela captures the excitement of times when bandoliered peons rode and marched off to war to the strains of the "Zacatecas March" or "La Cucaracha," when the Victorian, Bourbonic, ordered age of Porfirio Díaz was dying. Lamentably, it was being supplanted by a violently conceived but stillborn new order that was not even to attempt many of its reforms until many dismal years later.

Ranked internationally as the best novel of the Mexican

Revolution, *The Underdogs* helped transform the novel into the most important literary genre of Latin America. (Before 1910, novels by Latin American authors had inspired few translations and little fame beyond the local regions in which the individual novels were produced.) *The Underdogs* may also be the first Latin American novel whose singular literary style was shaped by the subject matter rather than by academic tradition. For example, in this work, time is telescoped to reflect the rapidity of events, and linguistic nuances tinge different aspects of the novel, including characters, scenes, and episodes. Individual members of Demetrio's command symbolize certain features of Mexican society—one soldier is a former barber, others are peons, both poor and prosperous, and there are also prostitutes, virtuous countrywomen, a former waiter, and many other types. Although the venal characters are city dwellers and never country folk, the latter are sometimes ignorant.

Using an elliptical style, Azuela selects and spotlights a few specific characteristics of a person, a scene, or a situation so as to describe it deftly. He thus uses disjointed scenes, rather than systematic chapters, to strengthen the overtone of violent eruption. Selfishness wins, idealism is crucified, and the novel's true protagonist—Mexico's poor—does not march out of misery.

Although fragmented into many swift scenes, the novel is divided into three basic sections. The first section has twenty-one chapters and reflects hope; the last two sections have a total of twenty-one chapters and reflect failure. It is in the latter two portions of the novel that the filth, nastiness, and lewdness of war are best painted, when persons such as Cervantes realize that the revolutionary issues will not be decided by logic or delicacy but by brute power, as symbolized by self-made, upstart generals who care little for ideals.

Azuela uses colors and details well. The natural dialogue is regionalistic but not difficult and, although each personality uses special shades of language that subtly characterize him or her, a high percentage of the characters speak in standard Spanish.

The revolution ultimately disappeared without having helped the common people who needed help; rather, it had made their lives more difficult. Azuela's sympathy in *The Underdogs* is thus always with the poor, whom he neither idealizes nor attacks. For the opportunists who betrayed the revolutionary ideals, he reserves a special sarcasm.

Azuela's masterpiece became the standard novel of the revolution, which was the first significant socioeconomic upheaval in Latin America. Most other revolutionary movements of the preceding years had not sought to aid the submerged masses, the mestizo, the Indian, the laborer, the underdog in general. Following Azuela's example, many Mexican and other Latin American novelists took up the fight for reform, denouncing tyranny and championing the cause of the forgotten. Since 1916, numerous starkly realistic novels have been published throughout Latin America that defend the underdog.

William Freitas

Further Reading

Azuela, Mariano. *"The Underdogs": Pictures and Scenes from the Present Revolution—A Translation of Mariano Azuela's "Los de abajo" with Related Texts.* Translated by Gustavo Pellón. Indianapolis, Ind.: Hackett, 2006. In addition to the text of the novel, this volume contains chronologies of Azuela's life and the Mexican Revolution, a map showing the itinerary of Macías's band, and several essays placing the novel in its historical and literary context. These essays include discussions of Azuela's views of the Mexican Revolution and the place of *The Underdogs* in Mexican culture.

Brushwood, John S. *The Spanish American Novel: A Twentieth-Century Survey.* Austin: University of Texas Press, 1975. Scholarly examination of Latin American works devotes a chapter to Azuela's best-known novel, comparing and contrasting it with other novels produced in 1916.

Canfield, J. Douglas. "Monsters from Below: *Los de abajo.*" In *Mavericks on the Border: The Early Southwest in Historical Fiction and Film.* Lexington: University Press of Kentucky, 2001. Chapter on *The Underdogs* is part of a larger study of novels and films in which maverick protagonists cross metaphorical boundaries as well as the actual southwestern boundaries dividing Anglo, Mexican, and Native American cultures.

Dabove, Juan Pablo. "*Los de abajo*: The Feast, the Bandit Gang, the Bola (Revolution and Its Metaphors)." In *Nightmares of the Lettered City: Banditry and Literature in Latin America, 1816-1929.* Pittsburgh, Pa.: University of Pittsburgh Press, 2007. Chapter on *The Underdogs* is part of an analysis of the theme of banditry in works of Latin American literature. Argues that the literary representation of the bandit is essential to an understanding the development of Mexico and other Latin American nations in the nineteenth and early twentieth centuries.

Griffin, Clive. *Azuela: "Los de abajo."* London: Grant & Cutler, 1993. Excellent study of Azuela's masterpiece presents information on the historical backdrop of the Mexican Revolution and discussion of realism in the novel, its characterization, and its structure.

Leal, Luis. *Mariano Azuela*. New York: Twayne, 1971. Provides information on Azuela's life and works. Asserts that Azuela's novels, especially *The Underdogs*, offer some of the best depictions in literature of Mexico's transition from the past to the present.

Parra, Max. *Writing Pancho Villa's Revolution: Rebels in the Literary Imagination of Mexico*. Austin: University of Texas Press, 2005. Examines *The Underdogs* as well as novels by other authors, chronicles, and testimonials written from 1925 to 1940 to examine how these works depict Pancho Villa's rebellion, either praising or condemning his style of leadership.

Schwartz, Kessel. *A New History of Spanish American Fiction*. Coral Gables, Fla.: University of Miami Press, 1972. Presents close analysis of the novels of the Mexican Revolution, with an extensive discussion of *The Underdogs*. Describes the novel as Azuela's masterpiece and possibly the definitive novel of the Mexican Revolution.

Understanding Media
The Extensions of Man

Author: Marshall McLuhan (1911-1980)
First published: 1964
Type of work: Media criticism

Marshall McLuhan, in *Understanding Media*, argues that a medium is best understood, from a functional perspective, as a technological "extension" of a human sense. Thus, the medium of radio extends the sense of hearing, and the medium of the printed book extends the visual sense into the once predominantly oral-aural realm of language. For McLuhan, even clothing (or fashion) becomes a medium, extending the tactile sense of the skin. Even a light bulb is a medium: a technological advancement upon the candle, which is itself a medium or tool that extends human vision into the dark.

From this functional premise comes a second: The medium itself constitutes its own primary content or message. As media interact with one another, they influence human perceptions and alter the balance of a person's senses (vision, hearing, taste, touch, smell). These changes in a person correspond with larger social changes and usually are rooted in the introduction of new media that significantly change not only what society perceives but also, more important, how society perceives.

Understanding Media expands upon the argument made in McLuhan's previous work *The Gutenberg Galaxy: The Making of Typographic Man* (1962). The earlier book studies how the introduction of typography at the beginning of the European Renaissance supplanted the predominantly oral-aural culture of medieval Europe and increased the importance of the visual sense at the expense of the oral-aural. The cool, detached visual sense helped nurture a rational Humanism that replaced the hot, engaged, oral-aural-dominated world of medieval Europe; in medieval times, truth was a matter of religious revelation. By providing a uniform system of printing and the verbatim repeatability of written works, the medium of typography also informed "messages" that ranged from the scientific method and individual rights to democracy and nationalism.

Understanding Media broadens *The Gutenberg Galaxy*'s distinction between Europe's medieval "tribal" culture and an industrialized, modern Western culture. At the same time, McLuhan argues that the introduction of electronic media (including radio, television, and computer-based communication) is "retribalizing" modern culture into postliterate social organizations based on a new balance of the senses (with less dominance of the detached visual sense). McLuhan argues that tribal societies are relationship-intensive and have little industrial specialization. For example, in addressing the medium of games, he argues that baseball epitomizes nineteenth century industrialization with its specific roles for each player, whereas football and ice hockey (with roles supposedly less specialized than baseball) are tribal sports indicative of postindustrial electronic culture. As the baseball-football example suggests, McLuhan is quick to make general observations that may not stand up to specialist scrutiny.

One of McLuhan's motifs in *Understanding Media* is the limitation of specialist research and scholarship. Trained as a literary critic, he makes ample use of literary allusions, ranging from Andrew Marvell and John Milton to T. S. Eliot and

James Joyce, to demonstrate the influence of book and print technology on the themes and psyche of literary artists. However, he also relies heavily on cultural historians such as Arnold Toynbee and Lewis Mumford to document the effects of media such as the wheel, roads, and towns on cultural evolution.

Perhaps the essay form of Michel de Montaigne had been McLuhan's primary model for his thirty-three chapter book. McLuhan decries academic specialism, both in theme and form. Each essay in *Understanding Media* (on topics ranging from roads and housing to radio, the telegraph, and automation) passes easily from general to particular without documentation and support for lofty generalizations. For example, the chapter "Games" moves from a discussion of tribal ritual and the founding of the Greek Olympics to observations on baseball and football in less than three pages. At times, intriguing ideas that might form the topic of an entire book-length study are raised in one paragraph, only to be dropped in the next. For instance, McLuhan comments that the social customs of one generation become the games of the next—those games then can become the jokes of the succeeding generation. However, he provides no examples and moves on to his next point. Likewise, McLuhan aims for a popular audience beyond the specialist realms of academia by incorporating informal language and slang into his arguments. He uses terms such as "fun," "puny," and "flunky" as well as phrases such as "global village" and "an eye for an ear."

McLuhan is most prescient in his analysis of the effects of electronic media on language, communication, and social patterns. For McLuhan, the repeatability of print typography altered the balance of the human senses to favor the visual, therefore underscoring the values of uniformity and equality. These values, in turn, led to the development of industrialization by specialists in production and to the invention of mass-manufactured interchangeable parts. The influence of the electronic media of the nineteenth and twentieth centuries, he continues, is only beginning to be felt; electronic media, he argues, will have the same transformative power that typography had exerted in the Renaissance. While *Understanding Media* is a product of the 1960's, and McLuhan had died in 1980, the book nevertheless anticipates the rise of the Internet and the World Wide Web in the late twentieth century. With the Web, especially, came new forms of instantaneous, global, emotionally intensive, and interactive forms of communication, such as blogging and social networking.

Perhaps the most audacious claim of *Understanding Media* is that "electronic circuitry" (his term for digital media, including the Internet and Web) serves not only as an extension of a person's central nervous system but also as a means of developing a global collective consciousness. At this point in his argument, McLuhan appears to be departing from social science and entering the realm of science fiction—or its progenitor, mythology. He seems to be envisioning a universal self, fragmented in a primordial fall into individual beings connected and disconnected by a variety of communication media that will one day become reintegrated into wholeness and unity. In his work, he acknowledges his debt to the myth of a universal self delineated in James Joyce's *Finnegans Wake* (1939) and to William Blake's prophecies of the fall and rise of the universal human being in *Jerusalem: The Emanation of the Giant Albion* (1804-1820).

It remains to be seen how digital media will furhter influence the human senses (or nurture new combinations into being) and possibly speed civilization's evolution or decay, but it is clear that McLuhan's interest in these possibilities show him to be an ambitious thinker willing to take on the mantle of prophet rather than submit to the humble role of social critic.

Luke Powers

Further Reading

Cavell, Richard. *McLuhan in Space: A Cultural Geography.* Toronto, Ont.: University of Toronto Press, 2002. Analyzes McLuhan's ideas about space and spatial form (as defined by either the visual or aural senses) as the foundation of his media theory.

Gordon, W. Terrence. *McLuhan: A Guide for the Perplexed.* New York: Continuum, 2010. Offers a close reading of McLuhan's work, including *Understanding Media*. Focuses on tracing the development of his thought and ensuring his ideas are not misinterpreted. An excellent source for students and general readers needing clarification of McLuhan's thinking.

Griffin, Em. *A First Look at Communication Theory.* 7th ed. New York: McGraw-Hill, 2008. A primary textbook for university courses in communication theory. The text places McLuhan in the context of the development of media analysis and communication theories of his contemporaries Roland Barthes and Stuart Hall.

Levinson, Paul. *Digital McLuhan: A Guide to the Information Millennium.* New York: Routledge, 1999. Examines the legacy of McLuhan's media theory in the digital age. Levinson evaluates the accuracy of McLuhan's predictions of an "electronic culture" in *Understanding Media* as well as his other works.

McLuhan, Marshall, and Quentin Fiore. *The Medium Is*

the *Massage: An Inventory of Effects.* 1967. Reprint. Corte Madera, Calif.: Ginkgo Press, 2005. This expanded edition combines McLuhan's text (much of it from *Understanding Media*) with Fiore's dynamic graphic design. The graphical nature of the book, with its photographs, illustrations, and variety of fonts and type sizes, as well as McLuhan's provocative quotations, well-illustrates his theories about the strengths and limitations of print media.

Marquand, Phillip. *Marshall McLuhan: The Medium and the Messenger.* Rev. ed. Boston: MIT Press, 1998. Foreword by Neil Postman. A biography of McLuhan that analyzes his work as well as his role as a public intellectual. Devotes several key chapters to the mid-1960's, during which *Understanding Media* transformed McLuhan from provocative academic to social sage.

Theall, Donald, and Edmund Carpenter. *The Virtual McLuhan.* Montreal: McGill-Queen's University Press, 2001. Theall, a former student of McLuhan, offers personal insight into the man and his ideas. With Carpenter, Theall focuses on the influence of maverick literary figures such as James Joyce and William Blake on McLuhan's thought and on McLuhan's own maverick approach to academic writing.

Undine

Author: Friedrich de la Motte-Fouqué (1777-1843)
First published: 1811 (English translation, 1818)
Type of work: Novel
Type of plot: Symbolism
Time of plot: Middle Ages
Locale: Austria

Principal characters:
UNDINE, a water spirit
SIR HULDBRAND, a knight
KÜHLEBORN, Undine's uncle
BERTALDA, Sir Huldbrand's beloved

The Story:

Near a forest in Austria there lives an old fisherman, his wife, and their foster daughter, Undine. The nearby wood is said to be inhabited by spirits who are enemies of the mortal human beings living outside the forest.

One day, the young knight Sir Huldbrand of Ringstetten is traveling through the forest when a storm breaks. As he rides through the gloomy wood, he is pursued and tormented by manifestations of unearthly folk. At last he comes to the edge of the forest and takes refuge in the fisherman's cottage, where he is given food and shelter.

Sir Huldbrand is amazed by the beauty of young Undine, who asks him to tell the story of his adventures in the forest. The fisherman, however, forbids the telling and cautions that it is unwise to talk of spirits at night. Undine—rebellious, mischievous, and untamed—disappears into the night when her foster father reproves her.

The fisherman and the knight call for her to return, but their voices are lost in the noise of the wind and of the rain. As the storm increases, they become more worried and finally set out in search of her. It is Sir Huldbrand who finds her, safe and sound in the leafy bower where she is hiding. When he returns with her to the fisherman's cottage, he tells her of his adventures in the forest. The storm rages so furiously that the cottage and its four inhabitants become cut off by encircling floods.

Sir Huldbrand relates how it came about that he traveled through the forest. He fell in love with Bertalda, a haughty lady who insisted that he prove his love and courage by a journey through the dreadful wood. At that point in his tale, Undine becomes jealous of the lady and bites the knight's hand. A few days later, a priest, who loses his boat in the swirling stream, takes refuge on the island. That night he marries Undine and Sir Huldbrand. The marriage changes the girl completely. She becomes submissive, considerate, and full of affection. She gains a soul.

After the floodwaters subside, the couple leave for the knight's home, Castle Ringstetten. On the way, they go to pay homage to the duke of the domain, and in his hall they met Bertalda. Undine takes Bertalda to her bosom and announces that she has a surprise for her. Shortly before, Undine told her husband that she really is a water spirit, and that she can live on earth only until he rejects her love; then Kühleborn, who rules the waters, will call her back to her water home. She lived with the fisherman and his wife since she was a child, having appeared at their cottage on the evening of the day when their own child had, apparently, been drowned.

Undine's surprise, which she arranges with the help of Kühleborn, is to reveal that Bertalda is the long-lost child of the fisherman and his wife. At first the proud lady refuses to accept them as her true parents. When she demands proof of the story, she is identified by a birthmark on her body. Bertalda's foster parents are disgusted with her and cast her off. The next day, Bertalda accosts Undine and Sir Huldbrand outside the duke's castle. Dressed as a poor fishing girl, she is ordered to sell food to learn humility and the dignity of toil before being allowed to rejoin her real parents. Pitying her, Undine and Sir Huldbrand insist that she live with them at Castle Ringstetten.

Life does not always go smoothly at the castle. One day, Undine, who is loved by the servants, orders the well to be sealed. Bertalda wants the water from it to remove her freckles, and she orders the seal removed, but Sir Huldbrand insists that Undine is mistress of the castle and the well remain sealed. Bertalda then decides to go to the fisherman's cottage. She goes through the Black Valley, where Kühleborn, who hates her, puts all sorts of difficulties in her way. She is finally rescued by Sir Huldbrand and Undine, who follow her flight.

Later, the three start down the Danube to visit Vienna. Everything goes wrong, and the sailors think the boat is bewitched. Finally, in exasperation, Sir Huldbrand forgets Undine's advice not to remonstrate with her whenever they are close to water. He tells her that he is tired of her and her spirit relatives and orders her to return to her watery home. Although he is sorry as soon as he speaks the words, he cannot recall them; Undine already disappears beneath the waves.

Sir Huldbrand grieves at first, but as time passes, he thinks less often of Undine. At length he and Bertalda decide to be married. The priest who married Sir Huldbrand to Undine refuses to perform the ceremony, and so they are married by another. Bertalda then commands the workmen to remove the stone from the well that Undine ordered sealed. All are terrified when a white figure emerges from the well. It is Undine. She goes into the castle and tells Sir Huldbrand that he must die.

Sir Huldbrand expires while he looks upon her face, and Undine vanishes. There are some who say that she reentered the well. At the funeral, Undine joins the mourners kneeling by the grave, but by the end of the service she disappears. Then water springs forth on the spot where she knelt, and a stream appears to flow about the knight's grave. It is Undine surrounding her lover in death.

Critical Evaluation:

Undine appeared in print the year before Jacob and Wilhelm Grimm published the first volume of their classic collection of tales drawn from local oral traditions, *Kinder- und Hausmärchen* (1812, 1815; *Grimm's Fairy Tales*, 1823-1826). The German Romantic movement helped to create an intense interest in the past and the presumably obsolete beliefs preserved in folklore. Proponents of German nationalism, who supported the notion of a German nation, believed that the many small principalities and city-states shared a common German heritage that was reflected and embodied in the ideas and images in Teutonic folklore. While the Grimm brothers were preserving and repackaging authentic folklore, Romantic writers such as Friedrich de la Motte-Fouqué set out to write *Kunstmärchen*, or "art folktales," that would not merely capture but refine the essence of the Germanic soul.

In *Undine*, la Motte-Fouqué employs one of the most frequently repeated folkloristic motifs: that of the mortal man who marries a supernatural female but loses her when he breaks some significant condition imposed on the union. In his 1891 *The Science of Fairy Tales*, Edward Hartland calls such tales "swan-maiden" stories after one of the several examples of the motif collected by the Grimm brothers. Another famous version is the story of Melusine, whose husband was forbidden to look upon her naked body on certain days—a tale that was ironically reworked by the greatest of all German Romantics, Johann Wolfgang von Goethe, in "The New Melusine." Later literary versions, written with *Undine* in mind, include Hans Christian Andersen's "The Little Mermaid" and Oscar Wilde's "The Fisherman and His Soul."

The supernatural world of Teutonic mythology is more closely connected with the world of nature than the French world of faerie, which was exported into Britain by the Norman conquest. Teutonic spirit inhabitants are "elementals" associated with the four elements of Classical belief: kobolds with the earth; sylphs with the air; salamanders with fire, and undines with water. In Austria, where la Motte-Fouqué's story is set, undines were inevitably associated with the river Danube. The passage from past to future, from wilderness to civilization, is symbolically embodied in the course of the Danube as it descends from the heavily forested mountains to the agricultural plain and to the great city of Vienna. This is the journey that Huldbrand, Undine, and Bertalda eventually undertake, which is beset by trouble and brings the fatal moment when Huldbrand's fit of temper allows the waters to reclaim their own. In another kind of story, this banishment of the wild past might have been a merciful release allowing

Huldbrand and Bertalda to get on with their lives, safe in the ideological fortress of civilization, but in a *Kunstmärchen* the severance is fatal.

Huldbrand is the story's primary representative of civilized values—values the Romantics were more than happy to link to the chivalric code allegedly observed by the legendary knights who secured the empire of Christendom and brought Europe out of the Dark Ages. In first abandoning Bertalda in favor of the less-demanding Undine, Huldbrand yields to seduction, but not as straightforward a seduction as that featured in many folkloristic versions of the motif. Because Undine is a changeling who was already traded for Bertalda in infancy, Huldbrand is in a sense falling in love with Bertalda as she ought to have been: poor, humble, and innocent. Unfortunately, although her marriage to Huldbrand makes Undine fully human—which means that she forsakes the values of her own kind for his—what Huldbrand ends up with is a convincing fake rather than the real thing.

When Bertalda tries to make her own journey through the Black Valley to recover her allotted place in the scheme of things, Kühleborn, the supreme spirit of the waters, puts obstacles in her way. Huldbrand and Undine come to her aid and give her the opportunity to continue pursuing her claim. While they live in secure isolation in his castle, Huldbrand prefers Undine to Bertalda and decides in her favor in the matter of sealing the well. Once they are on the Danube, however, the balance of power changes. It is inevitable that Huldbrand must pay the price for his confusion. Having betrayed the innocently deceptive Undine, he cannot thereafter forge a lasting union with the chastened and enlightened Bertalda. The soul that Undine acquired by virtue of their union was his, and the ghost of Undine reemerges from the well whose spring nourishes the soil of his estates to claim his life in forfeit.

On the most obvious level, *Undine* offers an allegory of the relationship between nature and humankind, in which nature can never quite be subjugated to the authority of human use because it always retains the final sanction of death. As a wholehearted Romantic, la Motte-Fouqué is entirely sympathetic to Undine; it is tragic that Huldbrand is unable to be faithful to her and thus unable to secure their harmonious union. Even a wholehearted Romantic has to concede, however, that the forces of nature that produce Undine, and to whom she remains inextricably linked in spite of her temporary domestication, are not nearly as sweet as she seems to be. The story acknowledges that there is a fundamental contest between nature and humankind, one that humankind cannot ever win; the spirits that harass Huldbrand at the beginning of the story cannot prevail by storm and stress because he is a brave young knight, but they have other ways of forcing his capitulation. His bravery cannot withstand subtle seduction, his chivalric values cannot shelter him forever against attacks of bad temper, and—perhaps most important of all, for all its understatement in the text—he cannot remain forever young. In the end, nature wins because the processes of aging are irresistible.

"Critical Evaluation" by Brian Stableford

Further Reading

Gosse, Edmund. "La Motte-Fouqué: A Critical Study." In *Undine*, by Friedrich de la Motte-Fouqué. London: Lawrence and Bullen, 1896. Gosse's translation is one of the best of several English versions; his prefatory essay discusses the sources and the reception of the work.

Green, David. "Keats and la Motte-Fouqué's *Undine*." *Delaware Notes* 27 (1954): 34-48. Discusses the influence of *Undine* on John Keats's *Lamia* (1820) and other poems involving supernatural women.

Hoppe, Manfred K. E. "Friedrich de la Motte-Fouqué." In *Supernatural Fiction Writers: Fantasy and Horror*, edited by Everett F. Bleiler. New York: Scribner's, 1985. The essay contains an elaborate discussion of *Undine*, connecting its *femme fatale* theme to Fouqué's own experiences.

Mornin, Edward. "Some Patriotic Novels and Tales by de la Motte-Fouqué." *Seminar* 11 (1975): 141-156. Places *Undine* and other works by Fouqué in the political context of German Romanticism and German nationalism.

The Unfortunate Traveller
Or, The Life of Jack Wilton

Author: Thomas Nashe (1567-c. 1601)
First published: 1594
Type of work: Novel
Type of plot: Picaresque
Time of plot: Mid-sixteenth century
Locale: England and continental Europe

Principal characters:
JACK WILTON, a page for King Henry VIII and a soldier of
  fortune
DIAMANTE, a rich widow and later Jack's wife
THE EARL OF SURREY, Jack's friend and benefactor
HERACLIDE DE IMOLA, the host of Jack and Diamante in
  Rome

The Story:

Jack Wilton is a page serving in the army of King Henry VIII of England when his adventures begin. While the English troops are encamped near Turwin in France, Jack pretends that he has overheard the king and his council planning to do away with a certain sutler, or civilian provisioner, and he convinces the sutler that he ought to give away all of his supplies to the soldiers and then throw himself on the king's mercy. Completely fooled, the sutler does just that. The king, enjoying the prank, gives the sutler a pension and forgives Jack.

Shortly after this escapade, Jack befriends a captain who forces Jack to help him get rich by throwing dice. Jack tires of his subservience to the captain and persuades the officer that the best means of getting ahead in the army is to turn spy and seek out information valuable to the king. The gullible captain enters the French lines and is discovered by the French and almost killed before he is hustled back to the English camp.

The campaign over, Jack finds himself back in England once more. When the peacetime duties of a page begin to pall, he leaves the king's household and turns soldier of fortune. After crossing the English Channel to find a means of making a livelihood, he reaches the French king too late to enter that monarch's service against the Swiss. He travels on to Münster, Germany, where he finds John Leiden leading the Baptists against the duke of Saxony. He observes a notorious massacre in which the Baptists are annihilated because they refuse to carry the weapons of war into battle.

After the battle, Jack meets the earl of Surrey, who is on the Continent at the time. Surrey was acquainted with Jack at King Henry's court and is glad to see him again. He confides to Jack his love for Geraldine, a lovely Florentine woman. Surrey proposes that Jack travel with him to Italy to find her. Since Jack has no other immediate plans, he readily consents to accompany the earl.

Jack and Surrey proceed southward into Italy. As they travel, Surrey proposes to Jack that they exchange identities for a time, so that the nobleman can behave in a less seemly fashion. Pleased at the prospect of being an earl, even temporarily, Jack agrees.

Upon their arrival in Venice, the two are taken up by a courtesan named Tabitha, who tries to kill the man she thinks is the earl of Surrey, using the true earl as her accomplice. Surrey and Jack turn the tables on her, however, and cause her and her pander to be executed for attempting to conspire against a life. In the process, however, Jack unknowingly comes into possession of some counterfeit coins. When they use the money, Jack and the earl are seized as counterfeiters and are sentenced to death.

While in prison awaiting execution, Jack meets Diamante, the wife of a goldsmith; her husband has imprisoned her because he suspects her of infidelity. Jack has sex with Diamante after assuring her that by doing so she is avenging herself on a husband who does not believe in her chastity.

After a few weeks in prison, Jack and the earl are released; an English gentleman who had heard of their plight had secured the efforts of the poet Aretine to prove to the court that Tabitha and her procurer were the counterfeiters. Aretine also sees to it that Diamante is released from prison. She continues to be Jack's mistress, and within a few weeks, after her husband dies of the plague, Jack marries her.

Jack decides to travel, and he and Diamante leave the earl of Surrey in Venice. Jack takes such pleasure from bearing the nobleman's title, however, that he continues to do so. After some time, Surrey hears that there is another earl by the same name and goes to investigate. Learning that the double is Jack, Surrey forgives him, and they once again resume their interrupted trip to Florence. Upon arriving there, the earl issues a challenge to all the knights and gentlemen of the city; he hopes thereby to prove his love for Geraldine. The tournament is a great success, and Surrey carries off all the honors of the day. After that, Surrey and Jack part company, and Jack, still accompanied by Diamante, goes on to Rome.

In Rome, Jack and Diamante live with Johannes and Heraclide de Imola. During the summer, Signor de Imola dies of the plague. Shortly after his death, and before his corpse can be removed from the house, bandits break in and rape Heraclide de Imola and Diamante. Jack is overpowered by the bandits and unable to help the women. Heraclide kills herself after the attack. When police arrive at the house, they blame Jack for what has happened. He is unable to clear himself because the only other witness is Diamante, whom the bandits have kidnapped.

A banished English earl appears in time to save Jack from the hangman's noose by producing witnesses to a deathbed confession made by one of the bandits. Jack is released and goes in search of Diamante. While searching for her, he falls through an unbarred cellar door into the house of a Jew, where he finds Diamante making love to an apprentice. The Jew, roused by the noise of the fall and Jack's angry shouting at Diamante, comes into the cellar and accuses them both of breaking into his house and corrupting his apprentice. Under the law, they become the Jew's bond servants. Jack is turned over to another Jew, the pope's physician, to be used in a vivisection.

He is saved from this horrid death when one of the pope's mistresses falls in love with him and uses her influence to secure him for herself. Diamante also falls into the woman's hands. Jack and Diamante keep their previous relations a secret and wait for a chance to escape from the woman's house. One day, while the woman is away at a religious festival, they run off, taking with them as much loot as they can carry.

Traveling northward, Jack goes to Bologna. There he witnesses the execution of a famous criminal, Cutwolfe, who had confessed to murdering the bandit who led the assault on Heraclide de Imola and Diamante months before. Moving on into France, Jack finds the English armies once again in the field, and he returns to King Henry's service.

Critical Evaluation:

Following the example of Robert Greene, one of his predecessors at St. John's College, Cambridge, Thomas Nashe overcame whatever religious scruples might have been bred into him as a preacher's son and set out with profane determination to become one of the first professional writers in England and one of the most controversial. As a member of the University Wits, he distinguished himself with the diversity of his authorial talents, unashamedly plying the writer's trade as polemical pamphleteer, poet, dramatist, and re-

porter. He said of himself, "I have written in all sorts of humours more than any young man of my age in England."

When he died, still a young man in his thirties, Nashe left behind a veritable grab bag of miscellaneous literary pieces. Later critics have often concluded that Nashe's explosive productivity was more comparable with the effect of a scattergun than with that of the big cannons wielded by such contemporaries as William Shakespeare, Ben Jonson, and Philip Marlowe. Nashe has been accused of superficiality, of both thought and style, and he richly merits the accusation. Nevertheless, all would agree that at least two of his works deserve the continued attention of all those interested in the development of English literary style: *The Unfortunate Traveller: Or, The Life of Jack Wilton* and *Pierce Penilesse, His Supplication to the Divell* (1592), which received three editions in the first year of publication alone.

Pierce Penilesse, Nashe's most popular and wide-ranging satirical pamphlet, is a harsh, graphic indictment of the follies and vices of contemporary England, seen from the perspective of one of the first indisputable forerunners of yellow journalism. Nashe's ready talent for immediately distilling the fruits of his observation and experience into gripping firsthand reports served him well in the complicated narrative of Jack Wilton.

The Unfortunate Traveller was written almost one hundred and fifty years too early to be classified as a novel. It is, however, an important forerunner of the English novel as it was to develop in the eighteenth century. *The Unfortunate Traveller*, along with Sir Philip Sidney's *Arcadia* (1590), was one of the high points of the literature of the last years of the sixteenth century. The level of realism is high in this work, yet Nashe also catered to the Elizabethan taste for the romantic and farfetched, especially in dealing with Italy and the Italians. Seldom has a work, even in later centuries, described in such detail the horrors of public torture and execution and incidents of rape and looting.

Rambling narrative, travelogue, earthy memoir, diary, tavern yarn, picaresque adventure, and political, nationalistic, and religious diatribe, *The Unfortunate Traveller*, although impossible to classify generically, is nevertheless clearly one of the seminal starting points in the development of the English novel. The critics are in general agreement with H. G. Wells, who declared that the work "has no organic principle; it is not a unified work of art," yet it definitely has an organic wholeness. That wholeness is as much external as internal, provided more by the author's pen than by the ephemeral events in the life of the main character.

The lack of unity in the work accurately reflects the mind of its author, who had a mind as chaotically diverse as the narrative it produced. The structure of the book, a recounting of Jack's travels through Great Britain, the Low Countries, Germany, France, and Italy, seems entirely arbitrary. It is a structure ideally suited to Nashe's always changeable purpose and varying interests. The reader will look in vain for a balance between one part of Jack's travels and another; there is none, since Nashe sees contemporary life as completely unbalanced. Like Jack, the author stays where he likes as long as he likes and especially as long as he senses the reader can still be interested. Nashe's sense of his audience is one of his most charming assets, and it is highly appropriate that this tale is set up in the guise of a barroom brag on the part of Jack, lately returned from Bologna. Nashe's structural nonchalance almost certainly influenced Laurence Sterne's *Tristram Shandy* (1759-1767).

Sterne also must have been intrigued by the ambiguity of viewpoint found in *The Unfortunate Traveller*. At times in the book it appears almost certain that the author has forgotten about Jack entirely, setting off on his own to denounce, castigate, ridicule, or expound on one thing or another. At other times, Nashe can be most subtle in his handling of the complicated relationship between narrator and fictive reader, as when Jack quotes a Latin phrase to justify his actions, mistranslating it for his ignorant victims and leading readers to wonder whether the mistranslation is also intended to poke fun at them ("Tendit ad sydera virtus," for example, which Jack renders as "There's great virtue belongs, I can tell you, to a cup of cider"). If Sterne in *Tristram Shandy* overlooked the neat narrative distinctions that Dante and Geoffrey Chaucer had drawn between the naïve pilgrim and the narrator-pilgrim, he was able to do so with the comfortable knowledge that Nashe had done it first and had succeeded brilliantly.

Nashe's style reaches its finest and most characteristic expression in this book: with the vivacity of an undiminishing *sprezzatura*, brilliantly uneven, uncontrolled, and disorganized. *The Unfortunate Traveller* walks a precarious line between the realistic and romantic perspectives and frequently, as Nashe did in his own mind and life, gains its appeal from its inability to prevent one aspect from overflowing into the other. The journalistic nature of Nashe's prose is marked both positively and negatively: positively for its unprecedented precision of detail, proving the author's considerable powers of observation (equaled only by his lack of discipline), and negatively for his inability to separate objective narration from personal viewpoint—indeed, his unwillingness to see the value of such a separation. The result is a work as prodigious for its literary faults as it is for its virtues.

The reason this work continues to be read lies to some extent in the character of Jack Wilton himself, the semifictional counterpart of Nashe's own personality. Jack is an earthy Everyman with whom every new reader can identify—in his ambivalence between ambition and cowardice, between the desire for adventure and the need for security, between aggressiveness and passivity; in his switch from awestruck observer to cantankerous prankster, from innocent victim to devious culprit; in his love of acting and enjoyment of performance; in his passionate enthusiasms and vicious hatreds. He is as typical of the Renaissance English spirit as he is universal. In him, Nashe depicts brilliantly what is so rarely successful, a mixture of opposites. *The Unfortunate Traveller* is a mixture of the devout and the debauched, the sacred and the profane, the scholarly and the vulgar, the delicate and the brutal, the aristocratic and the common, the explorer and the patriot that made Elizabethan and Tudor England quite different from any other English era before or since. The singularity of an age, after all, can be found only in its tensions, in the peculiar coupling of opposing forces. *The Unfortunate Traveller*, in the unforgettable crudity and refinement of its humor, and in its instantaneous leaps from highly serious didacticism to profoundly trivial farce, is a kind of template both shaped by and reproducing the shape of its times.

"Critical Evaluation" by Kenneth John Atchity

Further Reading

Barbour, Reid. *Deciphering Elizabethan Fiction*. Newark, N.J.: University of Delaware Press, 1993. Summarizes the narrative action of *The Unfortunate Traveller* and examines the motif of decipherment in the work. Argues that Jack Wilton's world cannot be explained simply, for chaos rules it.

Brown, Georgia. "Generating Waste: Thomas Nashe and the Production of Professional Authorship." In *Redefining Elizabethan Literature*. New York: Cambridge University Press, 2004. Discusses Nashe's era's preoccupation with shame as both a literary theme and an authorial stance, and includes analysis of *The Unfortunate Traveller*. Part of a larger work that explores the new definitions of literature and authorship that emerged in England during the 1590's.

Fleck, Andrew. "Anatomizing the Body Politic: The Nation and the Renaissance Body in Thomas Nashe's *The Unfortunate Traveller*." *Modern Philology* 104, no. 3 (February, 2007): 295-328. Examines Nashe's use of anatomical imagery in the book, relating it to the new understanding of human physiology that emerged during the Renaissance.

Liebler, Naomi Conn, ed. *Early Modern Prose Fiction: The Cultural Politics of Reading*. New York: Routledge,

2007. Collection of essays analyzes prose fiction in early modern England, assessing the impact of this genre on society and literature. Three of the essays focus on Nashe: "Day Labor: Thomas Nashe and the Practice of Prose in Early Modern England," by Stephen Mentz; "How to Turn Prose into Literature: The Case of Thomas Nashe," by Stephen Guy-Bray; and "Counterfeiting Sovereignty, Mocking Mastery: Trickster Poetics and the Critique of Romance in Nashe's *Unfortunate Traveller*," by Joan Pong Linton.

McGinn, Donald J. *Thomas Nashe.* Boston: Twayne, 1981. Provides an introduction to Nashe's life and art. Includes a meaty chapter on *The Unfortunate Traveller* that summarizes the work's complicated plot and then examines critics' estimation of its place in the history of the novel.

Relihan, Constance C. "Rhetoric, Gender, and Audience Construction in Thomas Nashe's *The Unfortunate Traveller.*" In *Framing Elizabethan Fictions: Contemporary Approaches to Early Modern Narrative Prose*, edited by Constance C. Relihan. Kent, Ohio: Kent State University Press, 1996. Presents an in-depth analysis of the book.

Simons, Louise. "Rerouting *The Unfortunate Traveller*: Strategies for Coherence and Direction." *Studies in English Literature, 1500-1900* 28, no. 1 (Winter, 1988): 17-38. Argues that the work has a "novelistic coherence" in its plot and rhetoric, noting that the plot shows the education of Jack Wilton, and the work's images reinforce that theme.

The Unnamable

Author: Samuel Beckett (1906-1989)
First published: L'Innommable, 1953 (English translation, 1958)
Type of work: Novel
Type of plot: Absurdist
Time of plot: Mid-twentieth century
Locale: Unnamed

Principal characters:
THE UNNAMABLE
MAHOOD, an Irishman
WORM

The Story:

The Unnamable, although he never calls himself that, seems to be an old male who is not certain of where he is, who he is, or if, in fact, he actually exists. Intelligent, loquacious, and sometimes very funny, he constantly bemoans his odd situation. He believes that he has been used for some unknown reason by some unknown persons who put words in his mouth, although he is not sure that he has a mouth. He is certain that the constant talk that flows through him is, in part, some kind of punishment. He believes that until he does his "pensum" (a term for a school assignment for misbehavior), he cannot get on to his lesson and satisfy his tormentors, who he hopes will let him go so that he can fall silent and cease to exist. However, he has no idea what his pensum is or what his lesson is. Instead, he presumes that in time, in constant babbling, he will by chance utter the right words or phrases and be allowed his freedom. He has trouble trying not to give in to his urge to talk about things about which he knows little or nothing.

All that he actually is prepared to accept as true is the fact that he is sitting in some unknown, dim place; he can feel the pressure on his backside from some kind of seat without a back, and he can feel the pressure of his arms resting on his thighs. He also thinks that certain male figures are passing in front of him on a kind of circular path, but since he can look only forward, he is not certain where they are coming from.

An early tale initially concerns a character named Mahood but then slides into being a tale about the Unnamable himself, who has returned from a long trip abroad and is trying to get back to his family. He is disabled and having difficulty in reaching them. He takes so long, in fact, that they are all dead when he enters their home, and he has to be content to stamp about on their putrid corpses. The Unnamable habitually rejects the possibility of these incidents being true or having anything to do with him. A later tale again involves Mahood. On that occasion, legless, armless, and speechless, he is living in a large jar across from a small restaurant in a Paris side street close to the slaughterhouse. The proprietor of the restaurant takes some desultory care of him, feeding him scraps, cleaning out his jar, covering his head in inclement weather, and using the surface of the huge jar to display her menus. She does not speak to him, and no one looking at the menu seems to notice him, although his rigidly clamped head protrudes over the lip of the jar. It is a kind of life, but the Unnamable is not fooled: It is not his life.

Later on, another character appears, since Mahood seems to have exhausted his power to convince. This one, called Worm, is less than human; it has a single, unlidded eye but no other physical features, save for the coiled body of a serpent. It never manages to become anything more than a failed attempt to exist in any active manner. The Unnamable suspects that it is just another attempt to convince him that he has a life.

These bizarre tales are interspersed among the Unnamable's long, sometimes confused but always lively considerations of his situation. Ultimately, the Unnamable is where he started, with tears running down his face and a constant flow of grotesque, sometimes offensively vulgar ideas running unbidden through his mind. Occasionally, it seems that he just might have escaped the clutches of his tormentors. There are occasional moments of silence, but inevitably the babble begins anew, and the Unnamable knows that the misery will continue, perhaps forever.

Critical Evaluation:

Samuel Beckett's *The Unnamable* can be read in at least three different ways or combinations of ways. The work is the final volume of a trilogy of novels beginning with *Molloy* (1951; English translation, 1955) and *Malone meurt* (1951; *Malone Dies*, 1956), and it can be read in conjunction with those texts. It might be suggested that the character in *The Unnamable* is, in fact, Malone, who apparently dies in the second novel. It might be that the complaining voice of this novel is all that is left of Malone after death—a cruel joke of continuing existence after departure from the corporeal world. This might go some way toward explaining why the character has no body but is living in a kind of miserable limbo. The matter of interpretation is complicated by the fact that so many of the names of supposed imaginary characters mentioned by the speaker are, in fact, characters in previous Beckett novels, and not only those of the trilogy. The possibility therefore arises that the novel is autobiographical, above all because there is considerable talk about the Unnamable having invented these characters.

The best way to deal with the novel is to take it at face value as a factual account of an absurd experience in the late

twentieth century. The idea of the absurd is, quite simply, that something means what it says. Beckett's work in general is a literary representation of the proposition that life is meaningless and absurd in the sense of not making any sense, a conclusion reached on the basis of the twentieth century loss of social, political, and religious certainties. The novel may thus be read as a metaphor for the chaotic nature of the human condition during that time. The work can also be interpreted philosophically, given Beckett's interest in the problem of how human beings know not only themselves but others and their relations with those others. How do people know things? It is an old problem for philosophers, and it is a question that shows up regularly in Beckett's work.

The Unnamable is a long account narrated in the first person by someone, supposedly a man, who does not know who or where he is but has strong suspicions that he is being manipulated. He is prepared to talk about this situation and complain about it in terms not only of the past but of the present. The complaints make sense as a psychological representation of that sort of problem, and there is considerable credibility in how the narrator acts and reacts. There is further confirmation of reality in the way Beckett explores how a person's mind goes on and on even when the individual might want to stop that mind, particularly in times of stress. In that sense, *The Unnamable* is a sensible study of an odd but not uncommon human predicament.

The narrative voice in the novel is subject to quick changes, not only of subject but also of opinion, and a fact established at one moment is denied in the next. The form of the work is, in fact, a dramatic monologue in prose form. The dramatic monologue as a poetic form was perfected by Robert Browning, but it was already used in William Shakespeare's soliloquies and later with considerable success by poets such as T. S. Eliot and W. H. Auden. In all these cases, the narrator has a problem—sometimes trivial, sometimes very serious—and his or her speaking about it usually leads to some sort of solution that is apparent either in a new understanding or in action. Sometimes, however, the act of consideration leads to failure, as it does in T. S. Eliot's "The Love Song of J. Alfred Prufrock" (1915). Much the same thing happens in *The Unnamable*. The speaker neither learns the truth of his situation nor is able to escape from it, despite his determined attempts to consider the matter from all angles.

However odd or absurd the situation may be, it has its basis in the human condition. This is particularly true in the twentieth century, a time characterized by skepticism, disbelief, and sheer destructiveness. Beckett's characters may be physically impoverished, but intellectually they are formidable, sometimes foul-mouthed but astringently clever and blessed with the gift of saying things wittily and with flashes of graveyard humor. It is possible to read the novel as a realistic representation of a man who has lost touch with reality and is living within his own mind in paranoid terror. Certainly, there is a gritty reality about him, despite his denial of corporeal proportion. A more valid reading, however, interprets the novel as absurdist. The absurd is, in fact, not simply content that does not make ordinary sense; it is a literary genre that demands to be accepted as it is presented. Like many of the arts, literature in the twentieth century occasionally attempted to disassociate itself from meaning in the realistic sense. Music and the visual arts were often successful in this endeavor. Literature, however, wedded as it is to words that have fixed meanings, a fixed form in sentences and paragraphs, has been hard-pressed to become "meaningless" in the artistic sense. Beckett made this attempt. His greatest ambition was to write on nothing, and in later works he goes even further in his attempt to get beyond sense. *The Unnamable* can be considered to represent the midpoint of this development.

Charles Pullen

Further Reading

Alvarez, Alfred. *Beckett*. 2d ed. London: Fontana, 1992. A short, lively, and sometimes opinionated discussion of Beckett by a critic who does not altogether trust the author and who knows how to argue not only for his strengths but also against his limitations. Contains a good short discussion of the intellectual climate that precipitated absurdist literature.

Cousineau, Thomas. *After the Final No: Samuel Beckett's Trilogy*. Newark: University of Delaware Press, 1999. Analyzes the three books in order of publication, describing how in the course of the work Beckett demystifies each of the principal authority figures from whom Molloy has sought protection and guidance.

Esslin, Martin, ed. *Samuel Beckett: A Collection of Critical Essays*. Englewood Cliffs, N.J.: Prentice Hall, 1965. Collection of essays includes important commentary by some of the most widely respected Beckett critics. Covers all phases of Beckett's work, including his novels.

Kenner, Hugh. *A Reader's Guide to Samuel Beckett*. London: Thames and Hudson, 1973. An essential resource for anyone determined to understand the works of Beckett. Comments clearly and simply on the individual texts, including *The Unnamable*.

_____. *Samuel Beckett: A Critical Study*. Berkeley: University of California Press, 1968. Work by probably the best commentator on Beckett is lively, imaginative, and extremely good at placing Beckett in the Irish tradition as well as assessing his part in the movement of experimental literature.

McDonald, Rónán. *The Cambridge Introduction to Samuel Beckett*. New York: Cambridge University Press, 2006. Chapter 4 of this concise overview of Beckett's life and work includes a discussion of the trilogy.

Mercier, Vivian. *Beckett/Beckett*. New York: Oxford University Press, 1977. An Irish scholar with understanding of the Irish mind, absurdist literature, and Beckett offers helpful insights into all the novels, particularly into the trilogy ending with *The Unnamable*.

Pultar, Gönül. *Technique and Tradition in Beckett's Trilogy of Novels*. Lanham, Md.: University Press of America, 1996. Devotes a chapter to each of the three books in the order of their publication. The chapter on *The Unnamable* discusses its mix of fact and fiction along with other elements of the novel. Other chapters compare the three novels to other works of European literature and philosophy.

An Unsuitable Job for a Woman

Author: P. D. James (1920-   )
First published: 1972
Type of work: Novel
Type of plot: Detective and mystery
Time of plot: 1972
Locale: Cambridge and London, England

Principal characters:
CORDELIA GRAY, a novice private detective
BERNIE PRYDE, owner of a detective agency, and
    Cordelia's boss
SIR RONALD CALLENDAR, a noted scientist, and Cordelia's
    first client
MARK CALLENDAR, Sir Ronald's son
EVELYN BOTTLEY CALLENDAR, Mark's mother
ELIZABETH LEAMING, Sir Ronald's business manager
MAJOR MARKLAND, Mark Callendar's former employer
SERGEANT MASKELL, local police investigator
SOPHIA TILLING, Mark's girlfriend
HUGO TILLING, her brother, and Mark's close friend

The Story:

Private detective Cordelia Gray is on her way to work, not knowing that her boss, Bernie Pryde, had died the night before. Upon arriving at the office, Gray discovers his body and a suicide note that outlines his terminal illness. She subsequently learns she has inherited the firm, his gun, and his debts. Given Great Britain's handgun laws, the inheritance of the gun is a tricky matter.

Elizabeth Leaming, the business manager for Gray's first client, Sir Ronald Callendar, is waiting at the office when Gray returns from the cremation. Leaming chides her for being late, noting that it is eighteen minutes past 4 P.M., the stated return time posted on the door, and then expresses her wish to speak to Mr. Pryde. Surprised at the news of his death, Leaming then begins to taker her leave, but Gray enthusiastically sells her own skills in hopes of keeping the client. After a phone call consultation with her employer, Leaming hires Gray and asks her to come immediately to meet Sir Ronald and learn about the case.

On the train journey to Cambridge, Leaming quizzes Gray on her training. Gray learns that Leaming and Sir Ronald were referred to Pryde by a former client, whom Pryde always predicted would send them an important referral. Gray reminisces about Pryde and also thinks of her own past as she compares herself to Leaming. Gray's mother had died when she was an infant and her father was not always able to take proper care of her. Although strongly not religious himself, he entrusted young Cordelia to the nuns; Gray, during her formative years, had lived at a convent school.

Gray is uncomfortable in the luxury and formality of the Callendar residence, but is rejuvenated when given information about the case. She is also given a photograph of Mark

Callendar, Sir Ronald's son, whose death sparked the investigation. Gray sleeps with the photo at night, with her hands "closed protectively" over the envelope. The next morning, Gray assembles her supplies, including a new notebook labeled with the case name, and begins her investigation.

Gray learns that Mark had taken his job as a gardener for Major Markland quite recently, after giving up his place at Cambridge University abruptly, in the middle of the term. In speaking with the major, his wife, and his sister, Gray learns a number of details—and opinions—about Mark, who did not disclose his parentage to his new employer, had no real experience with gardening, and had the bad manners to kill himself in his lodgings on their grounds. Armed with more details about Mark's time at Cambridge, Gray heads off to the university to meet with his former tutor and to track down Mark's girlfriend and other friends. Gray also speaks with the local police officer, Sergeant Maskell, who had investigated the incident at Mark's cottage on the Markland property.

Gray's initial inquiries convince her that Mark had been murdered and his supposed suicide had been faked. Gray learns more about Mark and the relationship he had with his father, which had been affected by the death of Mark's mother when he was a baby. This link bonds Gray even more closely to Mark.

Gray is soon pulled into the world of Sophia and Hugo Tilling. Sophia was Mark's girlfriend and her brother Hugo was one of Mark's closest friends. They try to include Gray in their world, but she is wary of the overtures, and there is clearly a socioeconomic gap between them. Their friendliness makes Gray suspicious, and as she continues to become strongly bonded with Mark, or at least the version of Mark she is constructing, Gray begins to believe the Tillings had played a part in Mark's death.

Later, Gray locates a woman named Nanny Pilbeam, who had sent flowers to Mark's funeral. Gray assumes this woman had been Mark's nursemaid from childhood and learns that the nanny's real name is Annie Goddard. She also learns that Goddard had been Mark's mother's nurse. Goddard provides many details about Sir Ronald, whom Goddard had known as Ronny. Ronny had been the gardener's son and had married the boss's daughter, Evelyn.

Goddard had visited Mark because she had been entrusted with one of his mother's prayer books, which she Goddard to give to Mark after his twenty-first birthday. A curious inscription provides a major clue to the mystery. Goddard points Gray to Dr. Gladwin, who had treated Mark's mother, leading Gray to uncover the key to the case.

Gray also learns during the final stages of her investigation that someone else has been a step ahead of her, making similar inquiries into the case. She is attacked by Chris Lunn, Sir Ronald's laboratory assistant. Although she threatens Lunn with a gun, she does not shoot him. As he flees the scene, he is killed in a car wreck. Gray makes her report to Sir Ronald. In the report she outlines her theory about the case.

Gray's report reveals that Sir Ronald had Mark killed to avoid the truth coming out about Mark's real mother and to avoid losing the fortune that he was counting on Mark inheriting from her family upon his twenty-fifth birthday. To make Mark's death look like an accident, Sir Ronald's minions strangled Mark and then dressed his body in women's lingerie and applied makeup to suggest an accidental death or suicide by erotic asphyxiation. Gray surmises that Mark's friend Hugo and the others had discovered the body and, to spare Mark's reputation and because of their own beliefs that his death had been engineered, removed the makeup and clothing so that Mark would appear to be an ordinary suicide. Knowing that someone else had been involved in some way, Sir Ronald had hired an investigator to look into who that person might be and to deflect any potential suspicion that he himself had been involved.

After Gray confronts Sir Ronald, his business manager, Leaming, enters the room and shoots him, later explaining to Gray that Mark had been her son and that she had been the one who tampered with the scene, removing the makeup and clothing. Gray chooses to help Leaming cover up the incident. She recalls some of her training from Pryde and arranges the scene to suggest that Sir Ronald had committed suicide.

Although some of the police remain suspicious, Gray's account of the events eventually is accepted as truth. She talks to several of the detectives about Pryde, who had left the police force after a brief stint and had always regretted his lack of success there.

Critical Evaluation:

P. D. James, dubbed the queen of crime by critic Julian Symons, has contributed extensively to the mystery genre since her first novel, *Cover Her Face* (1962). Many critics, scholars, and fans lament, however, that James wrote only two novels featuring Cordelia Gray. Gray was one of the first female private-investigator protagonists to appear in literature, and the first British example, which makes *An Unsuitable Job for a Woman* the most-studied novel of James's oeuvre.

Feminist critics in particular have paid attention to the differences between the two Gray novels and have theorized about why the series did not continue. There may certainly be other reasons, but James wrote in her autobiography that she quit writing about Gray because a British television adaptation took too many liberties with the character. Responding to reader queries and pleas, James wrote in the essay "Ought Adam to Marry Cordelia?" (1977) that the answer is no: Gray should not marry Adam Dalgliesh, another of James's popular protagonists. James may have decided that Gray was just too much trouble.

Gray also provides an interesting subject for critics and scholars because of the ethical issues involved in the cases and because of the choices she makes. While private investigators are not above breaking the law, it is rarer to see a detective put his or her own life and liberty at stake to protect a killer. In *An Unsuitable Job for a Woman*, Gray embraces the role of judge and jury in shaping the outcome of the Callendar case, and she does it for emotional reasons. She seems different in the second Gray novel, *The Skull Beneath the Skin* (1982); this issue of character development may also provide a clue to the cessation of the novel's with Gray as protagonist.

Although this novel is groundbreaking in many ways, it is good to remember that it is one of James's earlier works and its plot is less complex and more linear than her later works. Gray jumps to conclusions about a number of things throughout the investigation, leading her through a quick succession of suspects, and she is often intensely involved in the case. In *An Unsuitable Job for a Woman*, she feels connected to Mark and even comes into possession of some of his belongings, including the belt that had been found around his neck. She begins wearing the belt herself as a symbol of her connection. In some ways, this scene may reflect an honest portrayal of a novice investigator (as well as an honest portrayal of a sensitive young woman during a formative experience), but her sudden and exact realization that Evelyn Bottley Callendar's cryptic note refers to her blood type may seem contrived. There novel also includes a number of convenient coincidences that wrap up loose ends quickly and tightly, such as Leaming dying in a car accident.

These minor criticisms are common to new writers of mystery and detective fiction. The fact remains that James became a master of the genre and became one of the best writers of the twentieth century, of any genre. *An Unsuitable Job for a Woman* also paved the way for a number of women to write mysteries and, importantly, to write mysteries with female protagonists.

Elizabeth Blakesley Lindsay

Further Reading

Bakerman, Jane S. "Cordelia Gray: Apprentice and Archetype." *Clues* 5, no. 1 (1984): 101-114. Bakerman asserts that *An Unsuitable Job for a Woman* is particularly notable for developing new models in detective fiction, including the early portrayal of a professional female detective and its unique application of the bildungsroman motif to the genre.

Kotker, Joan G. "The Re-imagining of Cordelia Gray." In *Women Times Three*, edited by Kathleen Gregory Klein. Bowling Green, Ohio: Bowling Green State University Popular Press, 1995. Kotker compares and contrasts the portrayal of Gray in the two novels that feature her. In terms of *An Unsuitable Job for a Woman*, Kotker provides numerous insights into Gray's psychological motivations.

Macdonald, Andrew. "P. D. James." In *British Mystery and Thriller Writers Since 1960*, edited by Gina Macdonald. Farmington Hills, Mich.: Bruccoli Press, 2003. A thorough biographical study of James's life and works, including her novels through *Death in Holy Orders*.

Maxfield, James F. "The Unfinished Detective: The Work of P. D. James." *Critique* 28 (Summer, 1987): 211-223. Maxfield analyzes Gray's affinity with the victim, Mark, delving into Gray's connection to and juxtaposition with Mark as James develops the story.

Nelson, Eric. "P. D. James and the Dissociation of Sensibility." In *British Women Writing Fiction*, edited by Abby H. P. Werlock. Tuscaloosa: University of Alabama Press, 2000. Nelson offers an interesting discussion of James's use of Shakespearean allusions and the connections he sees between James and T. S. Eliot's *The Waste Land*.

Nixon, Nicola. "Gray Areas: P. D. James's Unsuiting of Cordelia." In *Feminism in Women's Detective Fiction*, edited by Glenwood Irons. Toronto, Ont.: University of Toronto Press, 1995. Nixon offers a feminist analysis of *An Unsuitable Job for a Woman* and compares the work to the second Gray novel as well as James's other works.

Porter, Dennis. "Detection and Ethics: The Case of P. D. James." In *The Sleuth and the Scholar: Origins, Evolution, and Current Trends in Detective Fiction*, edited by Barbara A. Rader and Howard G. Zettler. Westport, Conn.: Greenwood Press, 1988. Porter notes that Gray's character "suggests the form that heroism in the modern world might take" and dissects the ironies and ethical dilemmas that James weaves through *An Unsuitable Job for a Woman*.

Priestman, Martin. "P. D. James and the Distinguished Thing." In *On Modern British Fiction*, edited by Zachary Leader. New York: Oxford University Press, 2002. Priestman endorses James as a literary novelist, providing an interesting defense of the mystery genre in a collection of essays that focus on a broad range of British writers.

Rowland, Susan. *From Agatha Christie to Ruth Rendell: British Women Writers in Detective and Crime Fiction*. New York: Palgrave Macmillan, 2003. A general study of detective and crime fiction written by women, with a section on the life and work of James. Also includes an interview with the novelist.

The Unvanquished

Author: William Faulkner (1897-1962)
First published: 1938
Type of work: Novel
Type of plot: Bildungsroman
Time of plot: Mid-1860's
Locale: Mississippi and Alabama

Principal characters:
JOHN SARTORIS, a colonel in the Confederacy
ROSA MILLARD (GRANNY), his mother-in-law
BAYARD SARTORIS, his son
RINGO, Bayard's companion, a young slave on the Sartoris plantation
DRUSILLA HAWK, Colonel Sartoris's second wife
AB SNOPES, a neighbor of the Sartoris family

The Story:

During the Civil War, Colonel Sartoris comes home for a day to warn his family that Yankee soldiers are nearby and to help build a stock pen to hide his animals from the Yankees. A few days later, a Yankee soldier rides onto Sartoris land. The colonel's twelve-year-old son Bayard and his companion Ringo, a slave on the plantation, shoot at the soldier. The boys hide under Granny's skirts when more soldiers come to search the property for them. Granny denies that any children live on the property, and a colonel orders the rest of the men off the land while eyeing Granny's skirts. A family man himself, he leaves after telling Granny his name—Colonel Dick—and saying he hopes she will suffer nothing worse from the Northerners.

Later, advised by Colonel Sartoris, Granny leaves for Memphis because of the dangers of the war. Joby, the Colonel's servant, drives a wagon carrying Granny, Ringo, Bayard, and a trunk filled with silver that was buried in the yard for safekeeping. During the journey, Yankee soldiers steal their mules and Bayard and Ringo chase them unsuccessfully on a "borrowed" horse. Colonel Sartoris finds the boys and takes them home, capturing a Yankee camp on the way. Joby and Granny also make it back home with the help of "borrowed" horses, and the trunk containing the silver is again buried in the yard. Yankee soldiers come to capture Colonel Sartoris. True to a dream of Granny's, Loosh, Ringo's father, shows the Yankee soldiers where the trunk is buried. They take it and burn the house, but Sartoris escapes. Loosh and his wife Philadelphy leave because the Yankee soldiers tell them they are free.

Granny, Ringo, and Bayard drive six days to Hawkhurst, Alabama, to recover their trunk, their mules, and the runaway slaves. On the journey, they pass hundreds of former slaves who are following the Yankee troops to freedom. At Hawkhurst, Granny's niece, Drusilla Hawk, joins the group, and the four of them travel to the river, where Yankee soldiers have built a bridge. After crossing, the soldiers hurry to destroy the bridge so the people who have followed them

to freedom will be unable cross. The Sartoris wagon gets pushed into the river, and the four travelers make it to the other side, where the Yankee troops are now stationed.

Granny asks to speak with Colonel Dick. She asks for the return of her mules, her trunk, and Loosh and Philadelphy. Colonel Dick gives Granny a written statement from the commanding general dated August 14, 1863, that validates the return of 10 chests, 110 mules, and 110 former slaves who are following the troops. The document allows them to pass safely through any Yankee troops they might encounter and also to petition them for food during the journey home.

Once home, Granny, with the aid of Ringo and Ab Snopes, forges papers similar to the document given to her by Colonel Dick to requisition mules from various Yankee regiments in the area. She keeps the mules in the hidden pen on Sartoris property until she either sells them to other Yankee units or gives them to neighbors impoverished by the war. Near the end of the war, just before the Yankee troops leave the South, they discover Granny's activities. The Yankees, acting on information from Ab Snopes, take back all the mules still in the Sartoris pen. Snopes then talks Granny into one last deal, getting valuable horses from Southern raiders. Although Ringo and Bayard try to stop Granny, she goes to the raiders and is killed. After Granny's funeral, Uncle Buck McCaslin rides with Ringo and Bayard to find Grumby, the man responsible for Granny's death. For months, they track the raiders. When they are close, Uncle Buck leaves the boys because of a gunshot wound he has suffered during the chase. In a fight, the boys kill Grumby; they then nail his body to the compress where Granny was killed and bring Grumby's right hand back to place on Granny's grave.

Drusilla, having fought alongside Sartoris and his troops, returns from the war with the colonel and works with Ringo, Bayard, and Joby to regenerate the land while Sartoris works in Jefferson, four miles away. Drusilla's mother and the women of Jefferson are outraged that Drusilla camped with the widower Sartoris during the war and has now returned to live on his land. They insist that Drusilla and Sartoris marry and unknowingly set election day as the day of the wedding. Drusilla sets out for Jefferson to meet Sartoris and marry him but gets involved in the politics of election day. Sartoris kills two men who are trying to get an African American elected marshall; he appoints Drusilla voting commissioner, and the white men return with Drusilla to the Sartoris land to vote against the African American candidate. In the excitement, Drusilla forgets to get married.

About eight years later, Bayard is in his third year studying law in Oxford, Mississippi. Ringo comes to him to report that John Sartoris has been killed by his rival, Ben Redmond. On the forty-mile ride home, Bayard reflects on the last few years: his father's marriage to Drusilla and the code of violence to which they adhere, his father's railroad venture with Redmond, their run against each other for political office, his father's humiliating taunting of Redmond, and his father's recent decision to turn against killing and meet Redmond unarmed. Bayard knows Drusilla and the men in Jefferson will expect him to avenge his father's death. Bayard, who cannot forget the death of Grumby, realizes that killing is not a satisfactory solution. Determined neither to kill again nor to be a coward, he goes to Jefferson the next day to meet Redmond unarmed. Redmond shoots twice, intentionally missing Bayard, and leaves town. Bayard returns home and finds that Drusilla has gone to live with her brother but has left behind a sprig of verbena for him.

Critical Evaluation:

One of America's greatest writers, William Faulkner was awarded the Nobel Prize in Literature in 1949. A prolific writer, he published through five decades, from the 1920's into the 1960's. Faulkner's major subject matter was the complicated history of the American South, and his fiction deals with it with humor, irony, and sympathy. Fifteen of his twenty novels are set in Yoknapatawpha County, a fictionalized version of the land around Oxford, Mississippi, where Faulkner lived. His novels and short stories reverberate so that it is not only the South or the United States about which Faulkner writes but also all people concerned with what he called in his Nobel Prize acceptance speech the "old verities and truths of the heart . . . courage and honor and hope and pride and compassion and pity and sacrifice."

Faulkner's tenth novel, *The Unvanquished*, is set in Yoknapatawpha County and deals with the Civil War and Reconstruction. The novel comprises seven titled chapters, six of which were published in magazines as independent stories before being revised for publication in the novel. The last chapter, "An Odor of Verbena," was written specifically

for the novel. Although the same themes, setting, characters, and some stylistic devices of this novel appear in other Faulkner works, *The Unvanquished* highlights adventure, sacrificing some of the complexity of Faulkner's greater novels.

The style of *The Unvanquished* makes it one of the least difficult of Faulkner's novels to read. Known for their complicated shifts in point of view and chronology, Faulkner's novels are often demanding. *The Unvanquished*, on the other hand, is narrated by a single character, Bayard Sartoris. A bright twelve-year-old when the novel begins, Bayard's age and intelligence also simplify the novel for readers. The plot is presented almost entirely in chronological order, so readers are able to follow the life of the Sartoris family during the Civil War and through the months following the South's surrender. The last chapter jumps ahead about eight years into Reconstruction. Only the last chapter uses extended flashbacks that break the chronological order of the narrative. In the first six stories, Bayard ages from twelve to his midteens; the last chapter, covering two days, begins and ends with him aged twenty-four, but flashbacks present him at twenty and again at twenty-three.

Two rather typical Faulknerian stylistic devices, delayed information and repetition with variation, allow the narrative to function well as a novel despite comprising seven separate stories. Delayed information connects chapters while adding suspense to the novel. In the first chapter, the Yankee colonel who allows Granny to hide Bayard and Ringo tells her his name, but that name is not revealed to readers until chapter 3. Climactic scenes are sometimes recounted obscurely at first, only to be revealed in more detail later. For example, readers are left uncertain at first as to the fate of the ambushed Yankee in chapter 1 and of Grumby in chapter 5. Later passages clarify that the Yankee was not hit but that Grumby was killed and mutilated.

Repetition with variation also helps connect the different chapters. The stock pen built in the first chapter plays a crucial role in a number of the other chapters. The prayer and the soap used by Granny as an antidote for sin and swearing help provide humor and continuity of character throughout the novel. The odor of the Civil War soldier, perceived as "powder and glory" in the first chapter, is transformed in the fifth chapter into the odor of the raider Grumby, perceived as "sweat" and "grease," and in the final chapter into the odor of verbena, a symbol of victory and peace. Parallel scenes help knit the novel and develop characterization. Bayard, the narrator, eagerly shoots at—but misses—a Yankee soldier in the first chapter, feels confused when he kills Grumby in the fifth chapter, and refuses to kill in the last chapter. The development of the novel parallels this character development, as readers see the society of the South changing through the character of Bayard, who moves beyond the violence of the past to break the chain of killing.

The Unvanquished is populated by a number of singular and powerful characters. As it is narrated by Bayard Sartoris as he grows into manhood, his experiences educate him by repeatedly testing his courage, judgment, and burgeoning maturity. He and Ringo, as young men, romanticize the struggles and especially the exploits of Bayard's father, John Sartoris. The colonel's own character is revealed with increasing accuracy through Bayard's changing perspective.

Colonel Sartoris, to whom is attached a large degree of myth, is a reader of Sir Walter Scott, an author favored by defenders of the Old South. Even as *The Unvanquished* begins, the South is defeated, disintegrating at the end of a war Rosa Millard considers the foolishness of men. She too, however, represents the old ways, braving Union soldiers to fetch her property, dressed in her best, carrying cuttings of ancient roses. She approaches her task with courage but also with the decorum of her station in a lost South.

Bayard's and Ringo's adventures vacillate between accompanying this woman on her civilized mission to regain her property, and conspiring with her and Ab Snopes against the Union Army to steal and resell to them their own mules— dividing the booty among those in their community who have been devastated by the war. Finally, the boys respond with vengeance to the violence that takes Rosa's life. In a war-torn South, then, they move from scratching out the movements of the Confederate Army in the dirt, to helping Rosa maintain some of the decorum expected of her station as a genteel, Southern matriarch, to outlawry and murder.

In the "reconstructed South" of the final chapter, when Colonel Sartoris is killed by his rival Redmond, Bayard has become a university student of twenty-four. He finds that it is not so easy to avenge his father's death, even though Drusilla, with whom he is nearly in love, hands him dueling pistols and fully expects that he will act according to the old codes. The community, including some of the colonel's own former soldiers, think that Sartoris was partly to blame for his own death, having pushed Redmond to desperation.

Bayard's choice to confront Remond but not to shoot him—in fact, to allow Redmond to fire two shots at him—is his way of both acknowledging the codes of the past and showing that their absolutes are no longer viable. He has learned to abhor violence and to look at the world in a way that now acknowledges its complexities and moral ambiguities, even when it concerns his own father, whom he once considered the bravest and most daring of men. By aiming wide and allowing Bayard to live, Redmond demonstrates that this embrace of complexity is valid.

Powerful women also people the novel. Ultimately, all of them, in one way or another, reestablish the claims of community and social expectation. While Rosa has violated these in her outlawry, she has done so primarily for the welfare of her neighbors. Drusilla is among Faulkner's women characters who dare to cross rigidly established gender lines, dressing as a man and finally riding with Colonel Sartoris as one of his "men." When she returns, the women of the community insist that she dress like a woman and that she marry the colonel, having ridden and camped with him, to reclaim her respectability. The colonel agrees to marry Drusilla, even though he is not in love with her, acceding himself to the women's insistence. These women repair at least this small tear in the social fabric, as is the case in so many of Faulkner's novels, in which women decry and then fix what the menfolk have foolishly destroyed.

The Unvanquished grapples as a novel with the painful transition from the old way of life—however stained by the horror of slavery, however elevated as myth, however beautiful in some ways—to the new South, which must face defeat, deal with Reconstruction, and learn what to salvage from the past and what to let go. Ab Snopes, a thief and a man of so little honor he betrays Rosa, is a key to this transition. He and his values will become part of the new South, and the Snopeses will bring with them to town the kind of grasping and crass commercialism that represents the worst of progress. *The Unvanquished* presents the last moments of the crisis through the consciousness of a young man whose moral journey is representative of the journey that all those who wish to survive with honor in the new South must take.

Marion Petrillo; revised by Susie Paul

Further Reading

Brooks, Cleanth. *William Faulkner: The Yoknapatawpha Country*. New Haven, Conn.: Yale University Press, 1963. Presents a favorable discussion of the novel, remarking on its strong characterization and the importance of the female characters. Finds the last chapter a strong coda for the novel's themes.

Hoffman, Daniel. *Faulkner's Country Matters: Folklore and Fable in Yoknapatawpha*. Baton Rouge: Louisiana State University Press, 1989. Contains a clear synopsis of the novel's plot, as well as discussions of Bayard's maturity and his relationship with Ringo.

Marius, Richard. *Reading Faulkner: Introduction to the First Thirteen Novels*. Compiled and edited by Nancy Grisham

Anderson. Knoxville: University of Tennessee Press, 2006. A collection of the lectures that Marius—a novelist, biographer, and Faulkner scholar—presented during an undergraduate course. Provides a friendly and approachable introduction to Faulkner. Includes a chapter on *The Unvanquished*.

Roberts, Diane. "A Precarious Pedestal: The Confederate Woman in Faulkner's *Unvanquished*." *Journal of American Studies* 26, no. 2 (August, 1992): 233-246. Notes that the novel does not endorse the more masculine roles of Granny or Drusilla.

Taylor, Nancy Dew. "'Moral Housecleaning' and Colonel Sartoris's Dream." *Mississippi Quarterly* 37, no. 3 (Summer, 1984): 353-364. Concentrates on the last speech between the colonel and Bayard; believes that only the methods, not the aggressive nature and goals, of the colonel change.

Towner, Theresa M. *The Cambridge Introduction to William Faulkner.* New York: Cambridge University Press, 2008. An accessible book aimed at students and general readers. Focusing on Faulkner's work, the book provides detailed analyses of his nineteen novels, discussion of his other works, and information about the critical reception of his fiction.

Walker, William E. "*The Unvanquished*: The Restoration of Tradition." In *Reality and Myth*, edited by William E. Walker and Robert L. Welker. Nashville, Tenn.: Vanderbilt University Press, 1964. Deals with the maturation of Bayard Sartoris, the theme of the novel. Suggests that Bayard restores the southern tradition by eschewing violence. Explores the different ways Bayard is influenced by Granny, Colonel Sartoris, Drusilla, and other characters.

Up from Slavery

Author: Booker T. Washington (1856-1915)
First published: 1901
Type of work: Autobiography

Booker Taliaferro Washington's best-selling autobiography, *Up from Slavery*, has been translated into more than one dozen languages and is part of an African American literary tradition that has found its place among the American classics. The book's fifteen chapters give a progressive historical account of the author's life as it began on a plantation in Franklin County, Virginia, in 1858. The poverty and human misery of Washington's early years are documented with unusual candor in the first two chapters. He did not know his father, had very little recollection of his extended family, never slept in a bed before the Emancipation Proclamation was issued, never ate a family meal with knives and forks around a table as a child, and had a trying ordeal wearing his first pair of heavy and hard wooden "brogans" on his feet. After his family moved to Malden, West Virginia, to work at the salt furnace and coal mine, they lived in the most derelict of conditions, surrounded by unreconstructed African Americans who were given over to excessive "drinking, gambling, quarrels, fights, and shockingly immoral practices." Washington worked very long, hard, and lonely hours, and was exploited by his stepfather, but he never lost the "intense longing to learn to read and write."

Washington learned to read from an old copy of Webster's spelling book that his mother got for him. Since African American teachers were rare, any black person who could read and write almost always became an educator. After a young black soldier from Ohio moved into Malden, he was immediately pressed into establishing "the first school for Negroes." The people were so poor, the teacher got his support from "boarding around"—sleeping and eating with a different family each day. Washington comments: "Few people who were not right in the midst of the scenes can form any exact idea of the intense desire which the people of my race showed for education. . . . It was a whole race trying to go to school. Few were too young, and none too old, to make the attempt to learn."

When Booker himself went to register at his first school, he chose the name Washington so he could have two names like the other students. He had such a passion for education, no obstacle could deter him from going to college. He traveled over eighty miles on foot, slept under (wooden) sidewalks, and worked on a shipping dock just to earn enough to buy breakfast and pay his way to Hampton, five hundred miles from home. Matriculation at Hampton was the dream of a lifetime. There, Washington met General Samuel C. Armstrong, who had a great impact on Washington's life. The ideology of industrial education taught at Hampton fashioned Washington's career.

Following his graduation from Hampton in 1875, Washington assisted in a successful campaign to move the capital of West Virginia from Wheeling to Charlestown. His rhetorical ability in the campaign brought him many speaking engagements, and he seriously considered a career in public service. He also taught for a year in West Virginia before spending a year as a student at Wayland Seminary in Washington, D.C. In 1878, Armstrong recruited him to teach Native Americans in Indian territory, and he won the complete confidence of his students there. Washington noted that Indians were served at restaurants and admitted to hotels, but he was not.

Chapter 7 begins the epoch in Washington's life for which he is best known. In the spring of 1881, General Armstrong called him to Alabama, where he would begin his life's work building Tuskegee Institute. There, Washington said he found "hundreds of ignorant" and uncultured "hungry, earnest black souls who wanted to secure knowledge" and who had not "degraded and weakened their bodies by vices such as are common to the lower class of people in the large cities." Encouraged by local blacks and an allocation of two thousand dollars from the state legislature to pay a teacher to start a college, Washington opened the institute in an "old dilapidated shanty near the colored Methodist church" in June, 1881. The building was in such deplorable disrepair that a student had to hold an umbrella over Washington's head as he taught in the leaking, unheated shack. For the first few months, Washington supported himself by "boarding around." Often the people had nothing to eat except "slave food"—fat pork, corn bread, and black-eyed peas. The poor people of the area were so anxious to demonstrate their freedom and to share in the "American culture" that they allowed plantation owners to dupe them into buying expensive furniture on credit with extremely heavy premiums.

Against all odds, Washington pursued his goal of establishing industrial education for blacks. Desperate for funds and proper support, he found his task as hard as that of the early Israelites who had to "make bricks without straw." On one occasion, he pawned his ring to obtain fifteen dollars to purchase supplies to make bricks. He was convinced, however, that the students who were involved in brick making and building construction were not only getting practical education but also building moral character. Brick making was inseparably tied to morality and became a required course on the curriculum for all students. In return, the institute's brick industry encouraged whites to do business with blacks at Tuskegee and provided much-needed patronage.

Chapters 13 and 14 narrate some personal as well as nationally significant events in Washington's life. He mentions his marriage to Olivia Davidson only as an afterthought. As if the romantic was forbidden territory for this black industrial educator, the only paragraph in the book in which he gives a hint that he was interested in companionship is used to discuss "Miss Davidson's" untiring work at Tuskegee and their sons' early mastery of brick making. Washington was accepted on the popular lecture circuit because "there was no word of abuse" of the South in any of his addresses, and they rarely dealt with the question of race. He states, "I determined never to say anything in a public address in the North that I would not be willing to say in the South." Hence in his address to the National Education Association at Madison, Wisconsin, Washington argued that "the policy to be pursued with reference to the races was, by every honorable means, to bring them together and to encourage the cultivation of friendly relations, instead of doing that which would embitter." Washington contended that African Americans must put the interests of their community over individual voting rights.

The Madison speech to the National Education Association introduced him to a very wide audience in other cities of the North. In 1893, he gave a five-minute address to about two thousand southern and northern whites of the Christian Workers in Atlanta, Georgia, and was hailed a "friend of the white race." The speech that really catapulted Washington into the national spotlight, however, was his address to the Atlanta Cotton States and International Exposition on September 18, 1895. In his autobiography he states, "I knew . . . that this was the first time . . . a member of my race had been asked to speak from the same platform with white Southern men and women on any important national occasion." Washington's speech lasted only twenty minutes but sent ripples throughout the continental United States and around the world, and its impact was felt in America for almost a century.

Washington used the speech to show that white-black cooperation could be of concrete (or brick) benefit, increasing production. He appealed to Congress to support the rebuilding of the South in the interests of both ethnic groups. He argued that "while the Negro should not be deprived by unfair means of the franchise, political agitation alone would not save him, and that back of the ballot he must have property, industry, skill, economy, intelligence, and character." Washington told African Americans to cast down their buckets in agriculture, mechanics, commerce, and domestic service in the South. He said the greatest danger for his people was that they would despise manual labor and misuse freedom. Washington also told whites to cast down their buckets among the eight million blacks in the South "without strikes and labor wars, tilling your fields, clearing your forest, building your railroads and cities." Whites should cast down their buckets in African American education for the benefit of the nation.

Many whites did not hear his plea to them to cast down their buckets of opportunity among black people. Most whites saw the speech as primarily a call for African Americans to remain subservient to whites. Governor Bullock of Atlanta ran out to congratulate Washington, and the media said that Washington was profound. President Grover Cleveland received a copy of the speech with delight and opened a line of communication from the White House to Washington. President D. C. Gilman of Johns Hopkins University in Baltimore invited Washington to serve on the "Judges of Award in the Department of Education at Atlanta."

As far as African Americans were concerned Washington's view that "the agitation of questions of social equality is the extremist folly" was preposterous. They felt that the idea of sacrificing civil rights for supposed good relations and meager wages was untenable. Months after the speech, black ministers and religious bodies continued their condemnation of the Tuskegee president. W. E. B. Du Bois labeled the speech the "Atlanta Compromise" and saw it as another sellout to the white community at the expense of justice, freedom, equality, and integration.

Washington's fame spread in Europe, Africa, Canada, and the Caribbean. Letters poured in from Paris and London with both praise and condemnation. Washington received many honorary degrees and awards. He was regarded as the spokesman for black America, and financial support for Tuskegee flowed in with the letters of congratulation and recognition.

The autobiography ends with Washington's descriptions of various events. He discusses the work of his second wife, Margaret James Murray, and their children. He recounts his meeting in Boston with Du Bois, Paul Lawrence Dunbar, and other prominent African Americans when he went to give a speech. Washington describes his successful tour of Europe and especially his experiences in England. The last chapter chronicles the complimentary correspondence that Washington received.

The book offers several surprises. Washington claims that "the ten million Negroes inhabiting this country . . . are in a stronger and more hopeful condition, materially, intellectually, morally, and religiously, than is true of an equal number of black people in any portion of the globe." Paradoxically,

he constantly portrays African Americans as primitive and lacking the "good morals and culture" found among whites. He even claims that the black teachers in the South were just as miserably poor in their preparation for teaching as they were in moral character. For Washington, good relations between the black and white races were more desirable for African Americans than civil rights and justice. These controversial ideas continue to generate condemnation and praise every time Booker T. Washington's name is mentioned.

N. Samuel Murrell

Further Reading

Brundage, W. Fitzhugh, ed. *Booker T. Washington and Black Progress: "Up from Slavery" One Hundred Years Later.* Gainesville: University Press of Florida, 2003. Collection of ten essays reconsiders *Up from Slavery.* Includes discussions of the book as history, as biography, and as legend; its historical and economic contexts; its depictions of women and masculinity; and its significance for South Africans.

Cain, William E. "Forms of Self-Representation in Booker T. Washington's *Up from Slavery.*" *Prospects* 12 (1987): 201-222. Deals effectively with an often-neglected aspect of *Up from Slavery*—its literary style. Notes that Washington deliberately and carefully crafted the wording of his book in a conscious attempt to avoid seeming egocentric and argues that Washington consciously created a literary counterpart to the typical self-effacement used by black people of that period to avoid clashes with white people.

Carroll, Rebecca, ed. *Uncle Tom or New Negro? African Americans Reflect on Booker T. Washington and "Up from Slavery" One Hundred Years Later.* New York: Broadway Books/Harlem Moon, 2006. In addition to the text of *Up from Slavery,* this edition contains commentary by twenty scholars, writers, business executives, and others who provide disparate opinions of Washington and his legacy for African Americans.

Fitzgerald, Charlotte D. "The Story of My Life and Work: Booker T. Washington's Other Autobiography." *Black Scholar* 21 (Fall, 1991): 35-40. Unknown to many people is an earlier version of *Up from Slavery,* published a year earlier. Fitzgerald reveals that it was poorly written by an incompetent ghostwriter. The original version said more about self-help and less about those things that make Washington appear accommodationist; Fitzgerald suggests that Washington tried in his second edition to avoid offending former slaveholders.

Howard-Pitney, David. "The Jeremiads of Frederick Doug-lass, Booker T. Washington, and W. E. B. Du Bois and Changing Patterns of Black Messianic Rhetoric, 1841-1920." *Journal of American Ethnic History* 6 (Fall, 1986): 47-61. Presents a valuable discussion of the messianic-prophetic dimension of black leadership in the late nine-teenth and early twentieth centuries. Although more ac-commodationist than Douglass or Du Bois, Washington appears as a genuinely prophetic voice in the black quest for liberation.

James, Jacqueline. "Uncle Tom? Not Booker T." *American Heritage* 19 (1968): 50-63, 95-100. Takes a fresh ap-proach to a traditional theme. Shows that "Uncle Tom" is an inappropriate rubric to define Washington, since he was always fighting in his own way for racial equal-ity; Washington realized, however, that an overt chal-lenge to the system would only result in worsened condi-tions.

Norrell, Robert J. *Up from History: The Life of Booker T. Washington*. Cambridge, Mass.: Belknap Press, 2009. Critically acclaimed biography argues that Washington is a victim of "presentism," or the tendency to see the past in terms of present assumptions. Explains how activists in the Civil Rights era dismissed Washington as an "an un-worthy hero, one who had sold out his people to racist white power," and maintains that these critics failed to un-derstand the era in which Washington lived. Places Wash-ington's life within the context of his own times, demon-strating how, by those standards, he was a great African American leader.

U.S.A.

Author: John Dos Passos (1896-1970)
First published: 1930-1936; includes *The 42nd Parallel*, 1930; *1919*, 1932; *The Big Money*, 1936
Type of work: Novels
Type of plot: Historical
Time of plot: 1900-1935
Locale: United States

Principal characters:
FAINY "MAC" McCREARY, a labor organizer
JANEY WILLIAMS, a private secretary
JOE WILLIAMS, her brother
J. WARD MOOREHOUSE, a public relations executive
ELEANOR STODDARD, an interior decorator
CHARLEY ANDERSON, an airplane manufacturer
RICHARD ELLSWORTH SAVAGE, Moorehouse's assistant
EVELINE HUTCHINS, Eleanor Stoddard's partner
ANNE ELIZABETH "DAUGHTER" TRENT, a relief worker
BEN COMPTON, a radical
MARY FRENCH, a labor worker
MARGO DOWLING, a film star

The Story:

The Spanish-American War is over. Politicians with mus-taches say that America is now ready to lead the world. Mac McCreary is a printer for a fly-by-night publisher in Chi-cago. Later he works his way to the West Coast, where he gets work as a printer in Sacramento and marries Maisie Spencer, who can never understand his radical views. They quarrel, and he leaves for Mexico to work in the revolution-ary movement there.

Janey Williams, who has grown up in Washington, D.C., becomes a stenographer. She is always ashamed when her sailor brother, Joe, appears in her life, and she is even more ashamed of him after she becomes secretary to J. Ward Moorehouse. Of all Moorehouse's female acquaintances, she is the only one who never becomes his mistress. Moore-house's boyish manner and blue eyes are the secrets of his success. They attract Annabelle Strang, a wealthy nympho-maniac whom he marries and later divorces. Gertrude Staple, his second wife, helps to make him a prominent public rela-tions expert. His shrewdness makes him an ideal man for government service in France during World War I. After the war, he becomes one of the leading advertising executives in the United States.

Eleanor Stoddard hates the sordid environment of her childhood, and her delicate, arty tastes lead her naturally into partnership with Eveline Hutchins in the decorating business and eventually to New York and acquaintanceship with J. Ward Moorehouse. In Europe with the Red Cross during the war, she lives with Moorehouse. Back in New York in the 1920's she uses her connections in fashion and becomes engaged to a member of the Russian nobility.

Charley Anderson, who had been an aviator in the war, becomes a wealthy airplane manufacturer thanks to a successful invention and astute opportunism. He marries a woman who has little sympathy for his interest in mechanics. In Florida, after a plane crash, he meets Margo Dowling, a young woman actor. Anderson's series of drunken escapades ends in a grade-crossing accident.

Joe Williams, a sailor, meets Della in Norfolk, and she urges him to give up seafaring and settle down. Unable to hold a job, he ships out again and almost loses his life when the ship he is on is sunk by a German submarine. When Joe gets his third mate's license, he and Della are married. Over the course of time he suffers illness in the East Indies, is arrested in New York for not carrying a draft card, and is torpedoed once more off the coast of Spain. Della is unfaithful to him. Treated coldly the few times he looks up his sister Janey, he ships for Europe once more. One night in St. Nazaire he attacks a huge Senegalese who is dancing with a girl he knows. His skull is crushed when he is hit over the head with a bottle.

Teachers encourage Dick Savage in his literary talents. During his teens, he works at a summer hotel, and there he sleeps with a minister's wife who shares his taste in poetry. A government official pays Dick's way through Harvard, where Dick cultivates his aestheticism and mild snobbery before he joins the Norton-Harjes ambulance service and goes to Europe. There some of his letters about the war come to the attention of censorship officials, and he is shipped back to the United States. His former sponsor gets him an officer's commission, and he returns to France. In Italy, he meets a relief worker named Anne Elizabeth Trent, who is his mistress for a time. When he returns to the United States, he becomes an idea man for Moorehouse's advertising agency.

Eveline Hutchins, who has a small artistic talent, becomes Eleanor Stoddard's partner in a decorating establishment in New York. All her life she has tried to escape from boredom through sensation. Beginning with the Mexican artist who was her first lover, she has had a succession of affairs. In France, where she is Eleanor's assistant in the Red Cross, she marries a shy young soldier named Paul Johnson. Later she has a brief affair with Charley Anderson. Dissatis-

fied, she decides at last that life is too dull to be endured, and she dies from an overdose of sleeping pills.

Anne Elizabeth Trent, known as Daughter, is the child of moderately wealthy Texans. In New York, she meets Webb Cruthers, a young anarchist. One day, seeing a police officer kick a woman picketer in the face, Daughter attacks the officer with her fists. Her night in jail disturbs her father so much that he makes her return to Texas, where she works in Red Cross canteens. Later she goes overseas, meets Dick Savage, becomes pregnant by him, and learns that he has no intention of marrying her. In Paris, she goes on a drunken spree with a French aviator and dies with him in a plane crash.

Benny Compton is the son of Jewish immigrants. After six months in jail for making radical speeches, he works his way West through Canada. In Seattle, he and other agitators are beaten by deputies. Benny returns to the East, where one day police break up a meeting where he is speaking. On his twenty-third birthday, Benny goes to Atlanta to begin serving a ten-year sentence. Released after the war, he lives for a time with Mary French, who is also politically active.

Mary French spent her childhood in Trinidad, where her father, a physician, did charity work among the native miners. Mary, planning to become a social worker, spends her summers at Jane Addams's Hull House in Chicago. She goes to Washington as secretary to a union official and later works as a union organizer in New York City. There she takes care of Ben Compton after his release from prison in Atlanta. While working with the Sacco-Vanzetti Committee, Mary falls in love with Don Stevens, a fellow Communist Party member. After he is summoned to Moscow with a group of party leaders, Stevens returns to New York with a wife assigned to him by the party. Mary goes back to her committee work for laboring men's relief.

Margo Dowling has grown up in a run-down house in Rockaway, Long Island, with her drunken father and Agnes, her father's mistress. At last, Agnes leaves her lover and takes Margo with her. In New York, Agnes becomes the common-law wife of an actor named Frank Mandeville. One day, while drunk, Mandeville rapes Margo. Margo then runs off to Cuba with Tony, an effeminate Cuban guitar player whom she later deserts. She is a cheerful companion for Charley Anderson, who gives her a check for five thousand dollars on his deathbed. In Hollywood, she meets Sam Margolies, a successful producer, who makes a star of her.

Jobless and hungry, a young hitchhiker stands by the roadside. Overhead drones a plane in which people with big money ride the skyways. Below, the hitchhiker, with empty belly, holds his thumb up as cars speed by. The haves and the have-nots—this is America in the Depression-era 1930's.

Critical Evaluation:

John Dos Passos's statement at the beginning of *U.S.A.*—that America is, more than anything else, the sounds of its many voices—offers several insights into the style and content of the trilogy. The style, for example, reflects the author's attempt to capture some sense of characteristically American voices, not only in the narration but also in what are called the "Newsreel," "Biography," and "Camera Eye" modes. These last three narrative modes reflect, respectively, the public voice of the media and popular culture, the oratorical and eulogistic voice of the biographies, and the personal and private voice of the artist. The most important voices in the trilogy, however, are those of the chronicles in which Dos Passos introduces a cross section of American voices ranging from the blue-collar worker to members of the professional and managerial classes and representing a variety of regional and ethnic backgrounds. Like the poet Walt Whitman, whose work profoundly influenced Dos Passos, Dos Passos takes all America as his subject matter as he tries to capture the sounds of the many voices that characterize its people.

Many scholars have associated the social, political, and economic views expressed in *U.S.A.* with Marxism. Leftists in the 1930's liked to believe this important author had a common cause with them. It is the American economist Thorstein Veblen, however, rather than Karl Marx, who seems to have shaped Dos Passos's thinking about the economic and political situation in the United States during the first part of the twentieth century. Dos Passos had read Veblen's *The Theory of the Leisure Class* (1899), *The Theory of Business Enterprise* (1904), and other writings, and it was from these sources that his attack on the American business economy stemmed. *The Big Money* offers a biography of Veblen in which Dos Passos summarizes the economist's theories of the domination of society by monopoly capitalism and the sabotage of workers' human rights by business interests that are dominated by the profit motive. According to Dos Passos, Veblen saw two alternatives: a society strangled and its workers destroyed by the capitalists' insatiable greed for profit or a society in which the needs of those who do the work is the prime consideration. Veblen held out hope that the workers might yet take control of the means of production before monopoly capitalism could plunge the world into a new dark age. Dos Passos further developed the idea that any such hope died with World War I and that the American dream of democracy was dead from that time forward.

Against the background of Veblen's ideas, *U.S.A.* can be seen as a documentary chronicling the growing exploitation of the American worker by the capitalist system and a lamentation for the lost hope of Veblen's dream of a society that would make the producer the prime beneficiary of the producer's own labor. The best characterization of the blue-collar worker in the trilogy is Mac McCreary—a rootless laborer constantly searching for some outlet for his idealistic hope of restoring power to the worker. Certainly one of the most sympathetic characters in *U.S.A.*, Mac dramatizes the isolation and frustration of the modern worker, who is only a human cog in the industrial machine, unable either to take pride in his work or to profit by it. Other characters as well fit within the pattern of the capitalist system as Veblen described it or else, like Mac, revolt against the injustice of the system. There are the exploiters and the exploited, and there are some few, like Mary French and Ben Compton, who make opposition to the system a way of life. Equally prevalent are those characters who dramatize Veblen's theory of conspicuous consumption by serving as playthings (Margo Dowling), lackeys (Dick Savage), or promoters (J. Ward Moorehouse) for those who control the wealth and power.

Throughout the trilogy, the essential conflict is that between the business interests who control the wealth and the workers who produce it. Dos Passos is almost equally concerned with the way in which the system of monopoly capitalism exploits and destroys even those of the managerial class who seem to profit most immediately from it. Dick Savage, for example, starts out as a talented young writer only to be corrupted by the system. Charley Anderson, who early could be seen as typifying the American Dream of success through ingenuity and imagination, dies as much a victim of the system as any of its workers. J. Ward Moorehouse, in contrast, makes nothing and produces nothing, but his is the talent that can parlay nothing into a fortune and the mentality that can survive in the world of *U.S.A.*

The two national historical events to which Dos Passos gives most attention are World War I and the execution of the anarchists Nicola Sacco and Bartolomeo Vanzetti. The war, as Dos Passos saw it, under the pretense of making the world safe for democracy, gave the capitalists the opportunity they needed to solidify their power. For Dos Passos, democracy was dead in America from World War I, and the Sacco and Vanzetti case proved it. The deaths of these two immigrant Italian radicals on a trumped-up charge of murder was, in Dos Passos's eyes, the ultimate demonstration of the fact that traditional freedoms were lost and that monopoly capitalism had usurped power in America. When, in his later and more conservative years, Dos Passos was accused of having deserted the liberal positions of his youth, he maintained that his views had not shifted from those he argued in *U.S.A.* The evidence of the novel would seem to bear him out. The *U.S.A.*

trilogy is a more nostalgic than revolutionary work. It looks back to that point in American history before the options were lost rather than forward to a socialist revolution. Dos Passos's finest work shows him as a democratic idealist rather than as a socialist revolutionary.

"Critical Evaluation" by William E. Grant

Further Reading

Casey, Janet Galligani. *Dos Passos and the Ideology of the Feminine.* New York: Cambridge University Press, 1998. Discusses Dos Passos's female characters, placing them within the context of the gender representations and ideas about gender that were prevalent in the 1920's and 1930's. Chapter 4 is devoted to an analysis of *U.S.A.*

Hook, Andrew, comp. *Dos Passos: A Collection of Critical Essays.* Englewood Cliffs, N.J.: Prentice-Hall, 1974. Explores the trilogy's political and social influences, themes, techniques, and Dos Passos's contradictory stylistic blend of romantic individualism and radical history.

Landsberg, Melvin. *Dos Passos' Path to "U.S.A.": A Political Biography, 1912-1936.* Boulder, Colo.: Associated University Press, 1972. Traces the development of Dos Passos's political and social attitudes and his literary influences.

Ludington, Townsend. *John Dos Passos: A Twentieth Century Odyssey.* Rev. ed. New York: Carroll & Graf, 1998. Standard biography connects contradictions in Dos Passos's personality and writings to his illegitimacy and to his role as an outsider. Includes Dos Passos's planning notes for *U.S.A.*, which show the work's historical influences.

McGlamery, Tom. *Protest and the Body in Melville, Dos Passos, and Hurston.* New York: Routledge, 2004. Focuses on the ways in which the three authors' "bodies manifest in their texts." Chapter 2, "Producing Remembrance: John Dos Passos's Body in the Text," provides biographical information and an analysis of *U.S.A.*

Moglen, Seth. *Mourning Modernity: Literary Modernism and the Injuries of American Capitalism.* Stanford, Calif.: Stanford University Press, 2007. Argues that American literary modernism was a psychological and political response to the evils of capitalism and demonstrates this thesis through an examination of *U.S.A.*

Nanney, Lisa. *John Dos Passos Revisited.* New York: Twayne, 1998. Excellent introductory study of Dos Passos's life and works draws on previously untapped sources to describe how Dos Passos's own paintings, his interest in the visual arts, and his friendships with artists affected his development as a modernist.

Pizer, Donald. *Dos Passos' "U.S.A.": A Critical Study.* Charlottesville: University Press of Virginia, 1988. Relates the trilogy to Dos Passos's life and times. Examines themes and techniques, using work plans, character lists, tables, and typescripts. Offers detailed analysis of the four modes of narration: camera eye, biography, newsreel, and narrative.

Strychacz, Thomas. "Reading John Dos Passos Reading Mass Culture in *U.S.A.*" In *Modernism, Mass Culture, and Professionalism.* New York: Cambridge University Press, 1993. Examination of *U.S.A.* is part of a larger study of Dos Passos and three other modernist writers in the period from 1880 to 1940. Argues that these writers were influenced by, and not opposed to, mass culture, although they sought to create works that were more esoteric than the popular fiction of their times.

Wagner-Martin, Linda. *Dos Passos: Artist as American.* Austin: University of Texas Press, 1979. Discusses Dos Passos's use of a shifting panoramic view to re-create history and evaluates the effect of this technique on characterization. Traces the effects of American mythology and American political and economic realities on *U.S.A.*

The Use of Force

Author: William Carlos Williams (1883-1963)
First published: 1938
Type of work: Short fiction
Type of plot: Psychological realism
Time of plot: Early twentieth century
Locale: A home in the United States

Principal characters:
THE DOCTOR, the narrator
MATHILDA OLSON, the doctor's young patient
MR. and MRS. OLSON, her parents

The Story:

A doctor makes a house call to the Olson family because the daughter is very ill. When the doctor arrives, he sees the little girl sitting in her father's lap in the kitchen; the parents, who are new patients to the doctor, are distrustful and do not tell him more than they have to. The doctor knows that since they are paying him to tell them what is wrong with the child, the parents feel no responsibility to assist him.

The child is particularly attractive, with magnificent blond hair. The doctor says she looks like one of those pictures of children often reproduced in advertising leaflets or in the photogravure section of the Sunday newspaper. The doctor can tell immediately from her flushed face that she has a high fever, which her parents say she has had for three days. The doctor, suspecting diphtheria, which has broken out in the school where the child attends, asks if the little girl has had a sore throat. The parents say she does not seem to have a sore throat, but that she has refused to let them look to see if she has. The doctor tries to examine the little girl, but she will not open her mouth. Strong and silent, she only stares at him coldly.

When the parents try to reassure the child that the doctor is a nice man who will not hurt her, he grinds his teeth in disgust at their use of the word "hurt," which he knows only further frightens her. When he moves his chair closer, the child claws at his eyes and knocks his glasses to the floor. Embarrassed, the parents once again call him a nice man. The doctor, angry, tells them not to call him that—that he is not a nice man, that he is here to see if she has diphtheria, which might kill her. The battle has just begun.

The doctor insists on getting a throat culture, for the girl's own protection. The father tries to hold the little girl, but his shame at her behavior and his fear of hurting her makes him let her go at the crucial moment. The doctor, meanwhile, thinks to himself how he has fallen in love with the "savage brat," whereas her parents are contemptible to him. During the struggle, while the doctor and her parents have become crushed and exhausted, the girl rises to magnificent heights of insane fury.

The child screams that the doctor is hurting her, that he is killing her, and the mother becomes upset; she asks if the little girl can stand all this. The husband tells the wife to get out of the room, that the child might indeed have diphtheria. He holds her down, and the doctor grasps her head and tries to get the wooden tongue depressor in her mouth. When he finally gets it behind the girl's back teeth, she bites down and shatters the depressor to splinters. Determined, the doctor asks for a spoon. Although the child's mouth is bleeding and she is screaming hysterically, the doctor persists with his examination, for he says to himself that it is for her own good. He says he has seen two children lying dead because their parents had neglected the disease.

The doctor says to himself that he is now getting beyond reason, that he could have torn the child apart, and would have enjoyed doing so. His face is burning with pleasure at attacking her. He rationalizes that she must be protected from her own idiocy and that others must be protected from her, but he knows that what he feels is a longing for muscular release.

The doctor finally forces open the girl's mouth and sees that both tonsils are covered with membrane. He knows now that she has been hiding her sore throat for days, lying to her parents to avoid the discovery of her secret. At the end, the child is so furious she tries to get off her father's lap to attack the doctor, while her eyes fill with tears of defeat.

Critical Evaluation:

Although William Carlos Williams spent much of his life as a pediatrician, and perhaps had actually experienced more than one difficult encounter with a sick child, "The Use of Force" is not simply a story about one doctor's admirable efforts to save a child from her own stubborn self, nor is it a story about one doctor's attacking a child with sadistic cruelty. If the event were described in a novel about the experiences of a small-town doctor, it might be merely an example of one such encounter among many others. However, the story suggests a more universal and general meaning because it is a short story, leading the reader to presume it will have some central significance; because the encounter is told in such violent, seemingly symbolic terms; and because it includes the doctor's philosophic conclusion about what drives him to force the child's mouth open.

The use of force is a legal concept, a principle that allows authorities to exercise physical force against another person if such force is deemed justifiable to protect the individual or to protect society from the individual. The principle is not without controversy. For example, sometimes police are accused of an unjustified use of force to subdue a suspected criminal or to quell protesters. Whereas law enforcement argues that such use of force is necessary to protect others or itself, critics often argue that law enforcement is sadistic and cruel, that it uses force to attack an individual or a group of which they disapprove.

The doctor in this story, a professional healer who epitomizes rational control and embodies a basic human desire to help others, knows the meaning of his actions when he says he has gone beyond reason in his struggle with the child. Although he has society on his side—as he says, the child must be protected from herself, and others must be protected from her spreading the disease—he knows that what drives him at the moment he tries to get the tongue depressor in her mouth is unthinking fury, what he calls a longing for muscular release. These thoughts lead to his shame.

The story does not suggest that this particular doctor is evil or sadistic, or that humankind is basically cruel. Rather, the story suggests that there is a dark human need in all of us to use force. The doctor becomes so caught up in his use of force, which ironically his profession as a helper permits in this story, that he persists even when reason tells him he should desist. Just as the little girl has a secret hidden deep within her, which the doctor's use of force exposes, so also does the doctor, as a representative of civilized humanity, have his own hidden secret—the irresistible drive toward physical violence that only social mores hold in abeyance. The story suggests that when society gives permission to exercise this physical force against another, it is hard to resist.

The doctor's secret in this story is similar to that embodied in Robert Louis Stevenson's famous tale *Dr. Jekyll and Mr. Hyde* (1886). The dark impulse laid bare by Williams is the same force embodied when the civilized Dr. Jekyll drinks the potion and becomes the vicious Mr. Hyde. A much more complex exploration of this secret can be seen in Joseph Conrad's *Heart of Darkness* (1899, serial; 1902, book). It is what Kurtz discovers in the jungle when he cries out, "the horror, the horror."

Two linguistic aspects of this seemingly straightforward story further suggest it is more than merely a realistic anecdote of a doctor's visit to examine a sick child. First, there is Williams's technique of conveying the dialogue without quotation marks. This lack tends to blur what otherwise would have been merely a realistic scene, creating instead the effect of a dreamlike, universally symbolic action. This sense of the event being more important for what it represents than for what it is on a surface level is further emphasized by the repetition of language that suggests extreme physical violence, which makes the encounter seem more like a battle than an examination. The doctor says he becomes so exasperated with the father he could kill him; the girl screams, "You're killing me"; the doctor says he could have torn the child apart in his fury and that it was a pleasure to attack her. To one critic, this language of violence is a symbolic enactment of a rape, suggesting a close link between sex and violence in civilized society.

Finally, the doctor's philosophical generalizations about the motivation for his violence suggests that the story has some universal significance about human nature. Although the story recounts the doctor's winning the battle with the little girl, the story is really about his losing the battle that all civilized human beings wage to subdue their violent physical natures.

Williams's story has become a classic in American literature. Its universal meaning about dark secrets hidden in all human begins is explored also in such great works as *Dr. Jekyll and Mr. Hyde*, *Heart of Darkness*, and Fyodor Dostoevski's *Prestupleniye i nakazaniye* (1866; *Crime and Punishment*, 1886).

Charles E. May

Further Reading

Baker, William. "Williams' 'The Use of Force.'" *Explicator* 37 (Fall, 1978): 7-8. Argues that the sick girl believes that if evil is not discovered it does not exist. Also argues that the doctor is angry with himself because he is required to use force even for a noble purpose.

Baldwin, Neil. *To all Gentleness: William Carlos Williams, the Doctor Poet.* Baltimore: Black Classic Press, 2008. An intimate biographical portrait of Williams, the doctor, poet, and writer who was driven to caring and creating. Based on author Baldwin's extensive archival study.

Dietrich, R. F. "Connotations of Rape in 'The Use of Force.'" *Studies in Short Fiction* 3 (Summer, 1966): 446-450. Claims that the language of the story suggests a sexual violation: The tongue depressor is a phallic symbol, and the girl's bleeding symbolizes the loss of virginity. Argues that the sexual connotations of rape suggest the savagery of human nature that lies just beneath the surface of civilized society.

Jones, Anne Hudson. "Literature and Medicine: An Evolving Canon." *Lancet* 348 (November 16, 1996): 1360-1362. A general discussion of "The Use of Force" within the context of other works of literature with themes of medicine and the medical profession.

Wagner, Linda W. "Williams' 'The Use of Force': An Expansion." *Studies in Short Fiction* 4 (Summer, 1967): 351-353. Disagrees with R. F. Dietrich's argument that the en-

counter between the sick child and the doctor is symbolic of rape. Argues that the use of force can be explained by other reasons.

Watson, James G. "The American Short Story: 1930-1945." In *The American Short Story: 1900-1945*, edited by Philip Stevick. Boston: Twayne, 1984. A brief general discussion of the themes of Williams's short stories, suggesting that "The Use of Force," like many of his stories, is concerned with obstacles to communication.

Whitaker, Thomas R. *William Carlos Williams.* Rev. ed. Boston: Twayne, 1989. General introduction to Williams's writing, including brief discussions of his short stories.

Utilitarianism

Author: John Stuart Mill (1806-1873)
First published: 1861, serial; 1863, book
Type of work: Philosophy

One of the geniuses of the modern era, John Stuart Mill coined the term "utilitarianism," the subject of this brief, five-part essay. By doing so, he reaffirmed and redefined the philosophical doctrine espousing the practical, useful idea that the rightness of an action may be measured by whether it achieves the greatest possible good for the greatest possible number. It was a doctrine around which a small but influential group of English radical reformers—utilitarians—rallied, Mill among them. All of Mill's intellectual activities were calculated to effect changes in British society. When *Utilitarianism* was published in 1863, Mill already enjoyed international recognition as a distinguished political economist. He was a precocious polymath, however, and his fame rested equally on his contributions to political theory and to political philosophy. *On Liberty*, for example, which he published in 1859, just a few years before *Utilitarianism*, stands as one of the greatest expositions on civil liberty ever written and endures as an assertion of cultural freedom.

John Stuart Mill imbibed his utilitarian philosophy and his extraordinary education from his father, James Mill. James Mill, in turn, had been a companion to, and a devoted disciple of, Jeremy Bentham. Although Bentham acknowledged intellectual debts to various European thinkers, including Claude-Adrien Helvétius, Cesare Beccaria, Voltaire, and Jean le Rond d'Alembert, he nevertheless rightly has

been considered the founder of the British utilitarian movement.

Britain's utilitarians premised their philosophy on Bentham's remarkable work *An Introduction to the Principles of Morals and Legislation* (1789), a reformist document that sought to bring scientific analysis to bear on ethics, legislation, and law. The opening chapter of Bentham's landmark work furnishes utilitarians with the basis of their beliefs, namely, that humanity is the servant of two absolute masters that govern all of its actions: pleasure and pain. The principle of utility, therefore, lies in approving or disapproving of every action according to its tendency to augment or to diminish the individual's, or society's, happiness. Utility itself Bentham identifies as "that property in any object" that tends to produce "benefit, advantage, pleasure, good, or happiness" or, conversely, that prevents "mischief, pain, evil, or unhappiness." Around such principles and definitions, Bentham elaborates the philosophy to which John Stuart Mill adhered for many years.

By the 1860's, however, reassessments of utilitarian philosophy seemed in order. Previously the beneficiary of wide exposure among educated people in Great Britain as well as in Europe, utilitarianism had lost its original force. Utilitarians were disturbed that their precepts were being confused with the merely expedient behavior by which they often characterized a flourishing new generation of industrialists and entrepreneurs. They worried that the literature about utilitarian doctrines had become so abundant that understanding of them was being diluted. In addition, John Stuart Mill had begun a reevaluation of his own thought, and thus of Bentham's ethical concepts. James Mill's death made John Stuart's work easier; the elder Mill had censored his son's writings, particularly those dealing with utilitarian beliefs. The importance of *Utilitarianism* thus lay in its reflections of changes in John Stuart Mill's intellectual position. While the essay does not rank among Mill's greatest works, it nonetheless became the best-known essay on the subject.

The "General Remarks" with which Mill prefaces his essay are significant chiefly because Mill, unlike Bentham, makes no pretense of using the scientific method to justify his principles. Bentham and Mill alike employed deductive reasoning. Each based his discussions on assumptions, or first principles, that were not susceptible to scientific proof. It may be true intuitively, for instance, that all humanity acts to maximize pleasure and to minimize pain. It is a matter of common sense. It cannot be proven, however. Scientific reasoning, in contrast, draws no conclusions from intuition, common sense, innate ideas, or first principles premised on assumptions. Science has general laws, to be sure, but they are arrived at through step-by-step proof, generally mathematical. Mill insists that the morality of individual actions is not solely a question of commonsensical observation. The morality of individual actions also can be tested through the application of moral laws to those actions and to their consequences. Mill, in short, tries to demonstrate how close together those who reason inductively are to the utilitarian position arrived at deductively.

Explaining in chapter 2 "what utilitarianism is," Mill introduces his famous qualitative distinctions to the orthodox Benthamite position. Mill departs from Bentham's view that the superiority of mental over physical pleasures is due to the greater permanence, safety, and uncostliness of mental activity over the physical. For Bentham the differences are merely quantitative. Mill also derides prevalent depictions of utilitarian ideas as vulgarly hedonistic. It is absurd, for example, to say that the pleasure that a drunk derives from breaking crockery is equal to the pleasure an individual derives from listening to Mozart. Mill argues that there are qualitative distinctions between, say, the drunk's pleasure and the intellectual's pleasure drawn from thought, from feelings, and from play of the imagination as well as from the moral sentiments. In fact, he reminds readers that every Epicurean or hedonistic theory of life has assigned higher values to the more enduring pleasures attending the cultivation of the mind or efforts to

ennoble the character. Even if it were demonstrable that noble persons are not invariably happier because of their nobility, still, Mill declares, the world in general benefits immensely from the example of noble and virtuous character.

Friends and critics alike note Mill's inconsistency in taking this position. The inconsistency is as follows: If good things are good in proportion to the amount of pleasure they bring, one cannot add that pleasure itself is more or less desirable in terms of something else—say, of human dignity—that is not pleasure. Mill, however, is not primarily concerned about remaining logical. Rather, he is interested in adding Stoic and Christian elements to utilitarianism to transform what many people considered a barren, godless, and inhumane philosophy into a humane one that agrees with the ethics of their religions or other ethical systems.

While addressing further critical attacks on utilitarian beliefs, Mill proceeds in his third chapter to explain the "ultimate sanction" of utilitarian ethics. Bentham and early utilitarians had taken an extreme dualistic approach. They viewed as different the result of an individual's action and the motive that informed that action. After all, an individual can only will his or her own happiness, not ensure it. Subsequently, critics had complained that utilitarian standards were too demanding, that people cannot be expected always to act so as to promote society's general interest—that is, to act out of a sense of duty.

In rejoinder, Mill points to the mistake of confusing a standard of morals, which furnishes a test of what one's duties are, with the requirement that a sense of duty must always inform one's actions. Once the general happiness principle is recognized as the ethical standard, Mill explains, the sanction for an individual to act in accordance with that standard arises from the "natural" or "social feelings of mankind." Another natural motivator would be the pain produced in the individual's conscience when that person's actions contravene such natural, social feelings. The ultimate sanction, therefore, lies with an individual's subjective desire to see that his or her duty and the "conscientious feelings of mankind" are in harmony.

In the fourth chapter Mill seeks to demonstrate "of what sort of proof the principle of utility is susceptible." He acknowledges that questions of ultimate ends—the greatest good, for example—cannot be proved in the ordinary sense. He argues, however, that while no reason can be given as to why the general happiness is desirable, it is still a fact that all people desire their own happiness. Since each person's happiness is good to that person, the general happiness therefore is a good to the aggregate of all persons. To explain why virtuous people might not will happiness for themselves—that is, to show why the desire for happiness is not the sole canon of morality—Mill draws a psychological distinction between will and desire. Will, he suggests, is amenable to habit, and out of habit individuals might will something they do not desire or, conversely, might desire something because they will it. Since on historical grounds Mill locates the source of will in desire for happiness, it seems clear to him that the Benthamite pleasure-pain criterion is still valid. That pleasure and pain, from the beginning of one's life experiences, respectively act in accord with, or against, tendencies of the will, regardless of how they are explained, Mill simply declares to be fact.

Mill's final chapter, the lengthiest portion of *Utilitarianism*, originally was written, according to his stepdaughter, as a separate essay that, with cosmetic changes, he appended to the book. The argument Mill presents, while conventional in utilitarian terms, nevertheless became familiar to a large audience and was cited frequently. This was chiefly because, from Bentham's day onward, one of the major goals of the utilitarians was to banish the outworn traditions and fictions that cloud understanding of British law. The utilitarians sought to supplant them with scientific definitions and classifications of the entire body of law. An important objection to such utilitarian efforts, and to the approach to law that was associated with them, stemmed from popular impressions that justice was something absolute, immutable, and independent of public or private opinions and influences.

Responding to the charge that utilitarians perceive justice as a matter of expediency, not as an absolute, Mill denies that utilitarian sentiments have their origins in any ideas of expediency. He declares boldly that while utilitarian sentiments about justice are not founded in expediency, whatever is moral in those sentiments is. Justice, in sum, is not an absolute. After defining attributes ordinarily attached to justice, he proceeds to demonstrate, by evoking specific cases, that in actuality the concept of justice historically not only has been filled with ambiguities but also has been the subject of constant disagreement.

The nature of justice being thus controverted, what is required, Mill asserts, is some practical, external, or objective standard by which to measure it. That standard, he suggests, is to be found in the utilitarian concept of "social utility." Justice, from his utilitarian perspective, is another name for certain social utilities continuously reassessed in the light of what produces the most good for the largest number of people within a community or society. Such social utilities, he acknowledges, are far more important, absolute, and imperative than others as a class. Furthermore, they are distinguishable from the "milder feeling which attaches to the mere idea of promoting human pleasures or conveniences" by the definite nature of their commands and the sterner character of their sanctions.

The logical inconsistencies in *Utilitarianism* have long been recognized. Blending elements of older utilitarian precepts with his new ones—and not ignoring difficult philosophical problems along the way—Mill humanizes hedonistic utilitarianism and lends impetus to its modernization.

Clifton K. Yearley

Further Reading

Berger, Fred R. *Happiness, Justice, and Freedom: The Moral and Political Philosophy of John Stuart Mill.* Berkeley: University of California Press, 1984. Provides a thorough evaluation of the moral and political contributions and implications of John Stuart Mill's utilitarianism.

Carlisle, Janice. *John Stuart Mill and the Writing of Character.* Athens: University of Georgia Press, 1991. Presents an examination of Mill's life and thought in relation to his ideas about virtue and character.

Crisp, Roger, ed. *Routledge Philosophy Guidebook to Mill on Utilitarianism.* New York: Routledge, 1997. Collection of essays is helpful in clarifying Mill's understanding of utilitarian philosophy.

Donner, Wendy. *The Liberal Self: John Stuart Mill's Moral and Political Philosophy.* Ithaca, N.Y.: Cornell University Press, 1991. Offers a carefully developed interpretation of the basic themes and arguments in Mill's political philosophy and ethics.

Lyons, David. *Rights, Welfare, and Mill's Moral Theory.* New York: Oxford University Press, 1994. Interprets how Mill understood human rights and responsible public policy within the framework of his utilitarianism.

Reeves, Richard. *John Stuart Mill: Victorian Firebrand.* London: Atlantic Books, 2007. Authoritative and well-received biography recounts the events of Mill's life and discusses his philosophy and his pursuit of truth and liberty for all.

Riley, Jonathan. *Liberal Utilitarianism: Social Choice Theory and J. S. Mill's Philosophy.* New York: Cambridge University Press, 1988. Presents thoughtful discussion of Mill's philosophy and its relationship to late twentieth century political and economic policy.

Skompski, John, ed. *The Cambridge Companion to Mill.* New York: Cambridge University Press, 1998. Collection of essays updates the scholarship on Mill's writings, exploring the wide variety of themes that they contain.

West, Henry R. *Mill's "Utilitarianism": A Reader's Guide.*

London: Continuum, 2007. Places the work within the context of Mill's life and Jeremy Bentham's philosophy, provides a chapter-by-chapter explanation of the text, and discusses the work's themes, reception, and influence.

_____, ed. *The Blackwell Guide to Mill's "Utilitarianism."* Malden, Mass.: Blackwell, 2006. In addition to the complete text of *Utilitarianism*, this edition includes numerous essays about the work. Some place the work within the context of Mill's life and total philosophy and Bentham's ideas about utilitarianism; others discuss the theories contained in the text, including its ideas about value, rights, and sanctions; and still others assess the work's influence and its relationship to twenty-first century issues.

Utopia

Author: Thomas More (1478-1535)
First published: De Optimo Reipublicae Statu, deque Nova Insula Utopia, 1516 (English translation, 1551)
Type of work: Long fiction
Type of plot: Utopian
Time of plot: Mid-fifteenth century

How to make a better world in which to live has fascinated the minds of thinkers in every age. From Plato to the present, people have been thinking and writing about what the world would be like if people could create an earthly paradise. One of the most famous pieces of such thought and writing is Thomas More's *Utopia*, a work so famous that its title has come to mean an ideal state. Originally written in Latin, the international language of medieval and Renaissance Europe, the book was widely read, and as early as 1551 a translation into English was made by Ralph Robinson, a London goldsmith.

The book is in two parts, with the second part (curiously enough) written first, in 1515, and the introductory half written in the following year. The book begins with a fictional frame story in which More tells how he traveled to Antwerp on a royal mission and there met Peter Giles, a worthy citizen of Antwerp, who in turn introduced him to Raphael Hythloday, whose name means in Greek "a talker of nonsense."

Hythloday proves to be more than a mariner, for in his conversation he appears to More to be a man of ripe wisdom and rare experience. Hythloday was supposedly a companion of Amerigo Vespucci when that worthy was supposed to have made his voyages to America. It was on one of his voyages with Vespucci that Hythloday, according to his own account, discovered the fabled land of Utopia, somewhere in the oceans near the Western Hemisphere.

The first part of *Utopia* does not deal with the legendary island; rather, Hythloday visits England, converses with Cardinal Morton, and suggests to that churchman (who was Henry VII's chancellor) some reforms that might benefit England. Among the reforms the fictional Hythloday suggests are the abolition of the death penalty for theft, the prevention of gambling, less dependence upon the raising of sheep for wool, discontinuance of use of mercenary soldiers, cheaper prices for all commodities, and an end to the enclosure of the common lands for the benefit of great and wealthy landlords. Although Cardinal Morton listens intently to Hythloday's suggestions, a lawyer objects that Hythloday's reforms cannot be undertaken and that they would not be deemed desirable by anyone who knows the history and customs of England.

In this first part of *Utopia*, More is pointing out some of the social and economic evils of sixteenth century European life. More than that, he is suggesting that only an outsider can see the faults with an objective eye. The introduction of the lawyer's objections, which are cut short by Cardinal Morton, suggests also that More discerned in sixteenth century society persons who opposed reform and who had reasons—not necessarily edifying ones—for doing so. Part 1 of *Utopia* is More's way of preparing the reader, through contrast, for the section in which his ideal realm is delineated.

In the second part, Hythloday expounds at length about

the culture of the land of Utopia (Latin for "nowhere"), which he visited during his travels. Hythloday describes Utopia as an island kingdom that is crescent shaped and about five hundred miles in perimeter, separated from other lands by a channel constructed by its founder, the fabulous King Utopus, who saw that the Utopian experiment, if it were to succeed, must be isolated and protected from the encroachments of warlike and predatory neighbors. The island is divided into fifty-four shires, or counties, each with its own town, no town more than a day's walking journey from its neighbors. The central city, Amaurote, is the capital, the seat of the prince who is the island's nominal ruler.

The government of Utopia is relatively simple and largely vested in older men, in patriarchal fashion. Each unit of thirty families is ruled by one man chosen by election every year. Each ten groups of families elects a member of the island council. This council in turn elects the prince, who serves throughout his lifetime unless deposed because of tyranny. The council meets every three days to take up matters of consequence to the people, and no decision is made on the same day the problem is advanced, lest undue haste cause mistakes.

It is not in government alone that More introduces suggestions for reform in his *Utopia*. In this ideal state everyone works, each man having a trade or craft, except the unusually talented, who are selected for training and service in the academy of learning. The workday is six hours long, with the time divided equally between the morning and the afternoon. Each man spends a two-year period working as a farmer in the shire outside the city in which he resides. Since everyone works, there is more than enough food and all other commodities for the inhabitants. All goods are community-owned, with each person guarding what is given him for the benefit of the commonwealth. The tastes of the people are simple; having enough individually, no one desires to have more than others. Even the prince of Utopia is designated only by the symbol of a sheaf of grain, a symbol of plenty. Each person is garbed in durable clothing of leather, linen, or wool. Jewelry is given to children to play with, so that everyone associates such baubles with childishness. Gold and silver are despised, being used for chamber pots, chains for slaves, and the marks of criminal conviction.

In the dialogue, More interjects some objections to the communal idea, but this is the only point on which he seems to have reservations. However, even on this point Hythloday's answers to his objections satisfy him.

Violence, bloodshed, and vice, says Hythloday, have been done away with in Utopia. Lest bloodshed of any kind corrupt the people, slaves are required to slaughter the cattle.

Dicing and other forms of gambling are unknown. The people choose instead to labor for recreation in their gardens, improve their homes, attend humanistic lectures, enjoy music, and converse profitably with one another. The sick are provided for in spacious hospitals erected in each quarter of each city. In the event of a painful and incurable illness, the priests consult with the patient and encourage him or her to choose death administered painlessly by the authorities. Although no one is required to do so, everyone eats in mess halls, where slaves prepare the meals under the supervision of the wives of the family group. At mealtime, young and old eat together, except for children under five, and enlightening, pleasant conversation is encouraged.

The Utopian criminal is enslaved, rather than put to death, as he was in sixteenth century England. Adultery is regarded as a crime and punished by slavery. Marriage for love is encouraged, but also prudence in selecting a mate. Males must be twenty-two and women eighteen before marriage is permitted. The welfare of the family is a state matter, since the family is the basic unit of the Utopian state. The people are anxious for the commonwealth to be rich, for the Utopians buy off their enemies and use their wealth to hire foreign mercenary soldiers; they hope in this manner to encourage potential enemies to murder one another instead of attacking Utopia.

The Utopians are described as a religious people who practice toleration, which was almost unknown in Tudor England. Some are Christians; others worship God in other ways. Atheism and militant sectarianism alike are forbidden.

If to a contemporary reader much of what More cites as an ideal to be reached seems not idealistic enough, then such a reaction may be considered a sign of great hope, in that people have improved over time and that they may continue to do so. Two additional points should be made in connection with More's work. One is that his borrowings from Plato and other earlier authors did not prevent him from adding much that was his own in theory and practice. The second point is that, in the time since the writing of *Utopia*, some of the author's ideas have been, in England and elsewhere, put into effect—unlikely as they may have appeared to his contemporaries. Human society may never come to the utopian ideal, but some credit should go to More for urging improvement in the human condition.

Further Reading

Ackroyd, Peter. *The Life of Thomas More*. London: Chatto & Windus, 1998. A helpful biographical study of More's life and times, which explores the ideas he developed and the difficult personal decisions he faced.

Baker-Smith, Dominic. *More's "Utopia."* Toronto, Ont.: University of Toronto Press in association with the Renaissance Society of America, 2000. A complete study of *Utopia* that places the book within the context of early sixteenth century Europe and More's humanism. Traces the book's sources in classical and Christian political thought, surveys its critical reception during the last four centuries, and assesses its role in cultural history.

Fox, Alistair. *Thomas More: History and Providence.* New Haven, Conn.: Yale University Press, 1983. An intellectual biography tracing the evolution of More's thought, delving deep into his views about God and humanity.

_____. *"Utopia": An Elusive Vision.* New York: Twayne, 1993. A veteran More scholar offers an interpretation of More's aims in the writing and vision of *Utopia*.

Guy, John. *Thomas More.* London: Arnold, 2000. A study of More's life and thought written by a leading historian of Tudor England.

Hexter, J. H. *More's "Utopia": The Biography of an Idea.* New York: Harper & Row, 1965. Examines *Utopia* for evidence of its stages of composition. This sequence forms the basis for analyzing More's intentions in writing *Utopia* and the ideas he wanted to express in his work.

Johnson, Robbin S. *More's "Utopia": Ideal and Illusion.* New Haven, Conn.: Yale University Press, 1969. An essay interpreting *Utopia* based on an honors thesis by a Yale undergraduate. Presents More's *Utopia* as a continuing discourse on the balance between ideal and reality in society and government.

Majeske, Andrew J. *Equity in English Renaissance Literature: Thomas More and Edmund Spenser.* New York: Routledge, 2006. Examines *Utopia* and Spenser's *The Faerie Queene* to describe how the ancient Greek concept of equity took on a new meaning in sixteenth century England.

Marius, Richard. *Thomas More.* New York: Alfred A. Knopf, 1984. A well-crafted biography that analyzes a man torn between the medieval world of faith and the modern world of reason and who ultimately chose the spirit over the flesh.

Martz, Louis L. *Thomas More: The Search for the Inner Man.* New Haven, Conn.: Yale University Press, 1990. An effort to interpret the complexities of More's life, which involved politics, philosophy, and religion.

Monti, James. *The King's Good Servant but God's First: The Life and Writing of Saint Thomas More.* San Francisco: Ignatius Press, 1997. A biographical study that explores the clash of politics and religion in More's life.

Olin, John C., ed. *Interpreting Thomas More's "Utopia."* New York: Fordham University Press, 1989. Helpful essays by important More scholars who explore and assess the meaning and significance of More's classic work on the ideal human society.

V

V.

Author: Thomas Pynchon (1937-   )
First published: 1963
Type of work: Novel
Type of plot: Satire
Time of plot: 1898-1956
Locale: Europe, United States, and Africa

Principal characters:
BENNY PROFANE, a schlemiel
HERBERT STENCIL, an adventurer
SIDNEY STENCIL, Herbert's father, a spy
PAOLA MAIJSTRAL, the wife of Profane's former shipmate
FAUSTO MAIJSTRAL, her father, a Maltese poet
HUGH GODOLPHIN, an explorer
EVAN GODOLPHIN, his son, a World War I pilot
THE WHOLE SICK CREW, a group of decadents in New York
RACHEL OWLGLASS, Paola's roommate and Profane's sometime girlfriend
McCLINTIC SPHERE, a jazz saxophonist
V., the object of Herbert Stencil's quest

The Story:

At the end of 1955, Benny Profane drifts off the street and into the Sailor's Grave, a Norfolk tavern, and finds his old shipmate Pig Bodine. Pig had abandoned his military duty. He had abandoned ship, driven crazy by Pappy Hod, whose wife, Paola, had left him to become a barmaid at the Sailor's Grave.

After a wild New Year's Eve party, Profane and Paola take a bus to New York. Profane begins to worry that Paola is becoming dependent on him, so he dumps her off on Rachel Owlglass, his occasional girlfriend. Freed of Paola, he travels across town on the subway until he meets the Mendoza family, who helps him get a job hunting albino alligators under the streets in New York's sewer system.

Meanwhile, Rachel pays her roommate Esther's financial debt to Dr. Schoenmaker, the plastic surgeon who had performed Esther's nose job. Esther's surgery had reminded the doctor of his original motivation to practice reconstructive surgery. As a mechanic in World War I, Schoenmaker's hero, the ace aviator Evan Godolphin, had a horribly disfiguring accident. A quack surgeon experimented with grafting ivory, silver, and other inert matter into Evan's face. This material later decayed and destroyed the young, once-handsome Godolphin's appearance.

Haunted by his father's death in Valletta in 1919, Herbert

Stencil materializes in New York in 1956 at a party thrown by the Whole Sick Crew. He is tormented by a passage in his father's diary that refers to a mysterious "V." When he reads this passage, Stencil begins his quest for V.

It is now 1898. Sidney Stencil, Herbert's father, is in Cairo when British spy, Porpentine, is assassinated here. Sidney soon encounters Victoria Wren, a beautiful young tourist with a penchant for espionage. They are both in Florence one year later when Hugh Godolphin and his son, Evan, are drawn into a revolutionary conspiracy and an absurd plot to steal painter Sandro Botticelli's *Venus*.

The theft fails, but the enigmatic figure resurfaces in a story Herbert hears in the Rusty Spoon, a place frequented by the Crew. According to Stencil, Vera Meroving is a guest at Foppl's Siege Party, a depraved romp in the African fortress of a German official who fondly recalls Luther von Trotha's annihilation of the native population. Later, in New York, Paola gives Stencil a copy of her father's "Confessions," which document the appearance of V. in Valletta during World War II. V., who is disguised as the Bad Priest, is attacked by the local children, who disassemble her. They remove her glass eye, her artificial foot, and other inanimate parts her body has accumulated. She then dies. Finally, Stencil receives information about a lesbian relationship between an unnamed woman, possibly V., and a young ballerina in 1913 Paris. After the dancer's onstage death, the mysterious woman is rumored to have fled to Valletta.

In New York, Profane avoids making any commitment to his adopted family and returns to Rachel. He reminds Rachel that he is a schlemiel, incapable of living in peace with inanimate objects. Still, she finds him a night watchman's job at Anthroresearch Associates, where he has imaginary conversations with SHOCK (Synthetic Human Object, Casualty Kinematics) and SHROUD (Synthetic Human, Radiation Output Determined), two test dummies.

Esther gets pregnant by her plastic surgeon, and the Whole Sick Crew hosts a party to raise money to send her to Cuba for an abortion. Profane and Rachel, who sees herself as Esther's protector, follow her to the airport, but Profane literally trips over the Mendoza family and allows Esther to escape. Dejected because he thinks he has lost two women, Profane decides to leave Rachel. He blames his schlemiel-hood for their doomed relationship and thus evades responsibility for his inability to care.

At the same time, McClintic Sphere, a jazz musician, visits a prostitute. They go for a drive outside the city. Paola, who has been impersonating a prostitute, confesses her identity to Sphere. She also announces her intention to return home to Malta. Outside New York, Sphere arrives at the conclusion that a person must learn to "keep cool, but care."

Stencil knows he, too, must return to Valletta. Apprehensive about his visit to the country where his father had died and afraid that his quest is ending, Stencil invites Profane to accompany him to Malta.

Paola, Stencil, and Profane sail to Valletta. When they arrive, Paola sees Pappy Hod and tells him that she is going to wait for him in Norfolk. Stencil meets Fausto but chooses not to believe the story about the death of the Bad Priest. He follows a clue to Stockholm, where his quest continues. Alone, Profane falls in with Brenda Wigglesworth, an American tourist. He admits he has not learned anything, and they disappear together into the night.

During Malta's June Disturbances of 1919, Sidney Stencil has an affair with Veronica Manganese, a fascist spy, who is accompanied by Evan Godolphin. After the violence, V. abandons Sidney. As he departs the island, a random waterspout capsizes his boat and kills him. From the shore, the mutilated Evan watches as the small boat vanishes beneath the surface of the sea.

Critical Evaluation:

The publication of *V.*, winner of the prestigious William Faulkner Foundation's award for the year's best first novel (1963), signaled the arrival of a major American novelist. While a few readers find Thomas Pynchon's work to be as elusive as the author himself (an intensely private person who has allowed little biographical information to surface), others marvel at his labyrinthine plots and astounding erudition. The range of Pynchon's writing, including *The Crying of Lot 49* (1966), *Gravity's Rainbow* (1973), the short-story collection *Slow Learner* (1984), and *Vineland* (1989), invites inevitable comparisons to François Rabelais, Laurence Sterne, James Joyce, Edgar Allan Poe, Herman Melville, Walt Whitman, T. S. Eliot, William Faulkner, and Vladimir Nabokov, securing Pynchon's place among the top echelon of contemporary male writers.

A common criticism of Pynchon is that he is a difficult writer. It is this difficulty, however, which makes novels like *V.* and *Gravity's Rainbow* so rewarding to read and reread. Pynchon's texts are not easily comprehensible, because he intends to do nothing short of reinventing the way people interpret their experiences.

Much of the difficulty of *V.* stems from Pynchon's focus on the epistemological uncertainty of human experience in modern times. His character, Antarctic explorer Hugh Godolphin, laments his inability to penetrate the surface of Vheissu, describing the unknown land as a tattooed woman whose skin "would begin to get between you and whatever it was in her that you thought you loved." Tourists, he feels, only want the surface of a strange land, while an explorer wants to reach its heart. Godolphin's revelation that he has been to the South Pole and has witnessed "Nothing" echoes Marlowe's discovery in Joseph Conrad's *Heart of Darkness* (1899, serial; 1902, book) and reflects Sidney Stencil's view of the "Situation." For Stencil, "no Situation had any objective reality: it only existed in the minds of those who happened to be in on it at any specific moment . . . a sum total or complex more mongrel than homogeneous."

In the novel's present time, Benny Profane, the "human yo-yo," moves around like a tourist, finally admitting at the end of the book that he never learned "a goddamn thing." On the other hand, Herbert Stencil diligently pursues traces of V. as they appear around the world, but it is impossible to know whether the plots he detects are real or if he is projecting "cabals" onto "the world's random caries." Pynchon's sophisticated narrative technique subtly displays how the events of the past are "Stencilized." The Egyptian episode is generated from "veiled references to Porpentine" in his father's journals, alluding to an incident that occurred before Stencil was born. "Mondaugen's Story," the reader is told, took "no more than thirty minutes" when Stencil heard it in the Rusty Spoon, but when he retold it to Dudley Eigenvalue "the yarn had undergone considerable change." The section "V. in love" is told to Stencil secondhand by the composer Porcepic. All of Stencil's information, in fact, comes to him secondhand. Because Stencil is not present at any of the events he recounts, the reader must ask if these are caries or cabals. To his credit, Pynchon does not afford the reader any solid ground from which to survey what is real and what is illusion.

Stencil's sections reproduce V.'s "obsession with bodily incorporating little bits of inert matter" as he incorporates people into his narrative of the quest for V. The theme of the inanimate asserts Pynchon's distress at the progressive dehumanization of contemporary life, whereby people are becoming more like objects every day. Profane turns himself into an object by retreating into his role as a schlemiel, which lets him experience only the "cool" surface of life while he avoids any of the potential dangers involved in caring about another person. Rachel Owlglass, who is overly fond of her car when Profane meets her, begins to act overprotective of people she imagines as victims. The jazz player McClintic Sphere offers a third possibility that is "the only way clear of the cool/crazy flipflop": "Love with your mouth shut, help without breaking your ass or publicizing it: keep cool, but care. . . . There's no magic words."

Sphere's philosophy cannot sum up that of Pynchon; however, it offers a reference point in the text from which the reader can examine Pynchon's analysis of history and imperialism, his use of entropy and other scientific metaphors, and his original moral vision for the twentieth and twenty-first centuries. In any case, readers should be able to agree with the elder Stencil that "there is more behind and inside V. [and *V.*] than any of us had suspected."

Trey Strecker

Further Reading

Bloom, Harold, ed. *Thomas Pynchon: Modern Critical Views*. Philadelphia: Chelsea House, 2003. A collection of critical essays, including discussions of Pynchon's literary significance; the themes of anarchy and possibility in his fiction; and Pynchon in the context of paranoia and literature.

Brownlie, Alan W. *Thomas Pynchon's Narratives: Subjectivity and Problems of Knowing*. New York: Peter Lang, 2000. Analysis of three early novels, including *V.*, focusing on their characters' inability to attain reliable knowledge of the self and the world. Examines Pynchon's ideas about history and science and how he uses these ideas to prod readers to take the political and personal actions that his characters cannot.

Grant, J. Kerry. *A Companion to "V."* Athens: University of Georgia Press, 2001. A chapter-by-chapter explication of the novel, summarizing its events, clarifying its allusions, and offering various interpretations.

Herman, Luc, and John M. Kraft. "Fast Learner: The Typescript of Pynchon's *V.* at the Harry Ransom Center in Austin." *Texas Studies in Literature and Language* 49, no. 1 (2007): 1-20. This journal article reveals and analyzes fascinating details about the writing and editing of Pynchon's first novel

Hite, Molly. "Duplicity and Duplication in *V.*" In *Ideas of Order in the Novels of Thomas Pynchon*. Columbus: Ohio State University Press, 1983. Challenges the view of V.'s intrusive, enigmatic recurrence as a puzzle. Argues that metaphoric relations or repetition replace conventional linear narration.

Levine, George, and David Leverenz, eds. *Mindful Pleasures: Essays on Thomas Pynchon*. Boston: Little, Brown, 1976. An essential work of Pynchon criticism. Analyzes problems of identity that center on the desire to avoid randomness and the paranoid tendency to create order. Includes essays on women, apocalypse, language, and entropy in *V.*, and an appendix with useful biographical data.

New, Melvyn. "Profaned and Stenciled Texts: In Search of Pynchon's *V.*" In *Thomas Pynchon: Modern Critical Views*, edited by Harold Bloom. Philadelphia: Chelsea House, 2003. Notes the reader's role in creating systems of organization in artistic texts. Employs a generic distinction between the romance and the novel to examine how Pynchon's text defies closure.

Slade, Joseph W. *Thomas Pynchon*. 2d ed. New York: Peter Lang, 1990. The first book-length discussion of Pynchon's fiction serves as an excellent introduction to his complex work. Traces dominant themes, motifs, allusions, and tensions in *V.* A helpful chronological approach unravels the novel's time scheme.

Thomas, Samuel. *Pynchon and the Political*. New York: Routledge, 2007. Examines the radical political elements of Pynchon's work, describing how the novel creates a new relationship between the political and the aesthetic. Chapters 3 and 4 focus on *V.* and on *Gravity's Rainbow*.

Witzling, David. *Everybody's America: Thomas Pynchon, Race, and the Cultures of Postmodernism*. New York: Routledge, 2008. Examines the relationship between Pynchon's experimental style and his interest in race relations in *V.* and other novels. Argues that Pynchon is ambivalent about the emergence of identity politics and multiculturalism.

The Vagabond

Author: Colette (1873-1954)
First published: La Vagabonde, 1911 (English
    translation, 1954)
Type of work: Novel
Type of plot: Psychological realism
Time of plot: Early twentieth century
Locale: France

Principal characters:
RENÉE NÉRÉ, a music-hall mime
MAXIME DUFFEREIN-CHAUTEL, an admirer
BRAGUE, a mime
HAMOND, a friend of Renée
ADOLPHE TAILLANDY, Renée's former husband

The Story:

Renée Néré muses as she applies makeup to her face in her dressing room at a French music hall. She looks into the mirror at her own reflection, and it begins to speak to her. Her image asks her why she is seated there, all alone. Renée waits to go onstage to perform and listens to the voice of her double in the mirror, all the while wondering who or what might appear at her dressing-room door to change her state of solitude. Renée wishes for something that will release her from the solitary life she has created for herself, but she also fears any change.

She performs her act and returns to her dressing room to find a note from Maxime Dufferein-Chautel, the marquis de Fontanges. The marquis expresses his admiration for her talents on the stage and inquires whether Renée has other talents. He invites her to dine with him that evening, but Renée refuses.

Alone again in her dressing room, she reviews her eight years of marriage and three years of separation from Adolphe Taillandy, a pastelist. He had lied to her and had been a womanizer. Renée had been a jealous and tormented young wife, and she turned to literature as an outlet. She has written four books that attained varying levels of success, but once she separated from Taillandy, she was shunned by their middle-class friends. That was when she took a ground-floor flat for herself in Paris and turned to the music hall to earn her living.

Meanwhile, Brague, another mime, has set up an evening performance by the two of them at a private home. Renée arrives at the residence of a wealthy Parisian to dance before an assembled audience, and she spies several of her former husband's mistresses in the audience. Aware of the shock in their eyes, she dances before them unabashed but aware of the pain of her past. It is not she, Renée reflects, who has done any wrong.

The winter progresses, and one night Renée's friend Hamond brings Maxime, uninvited, to dinner at Renée's flat. She is not impressed with him as a suitor and laughs him off.

When the show at the music hall closes, Renée wonders what she will do next. Maxime continues to visit Renée, which causes her to acknowledge her desire for companionship. When Maxime tells her that he loves her, she does not respond. She tells Hamond, however, that she will never love anyone again after the devastating experience of her marriage to a liar and a cheat.

Renée signs a contract to leave Paris for a forty-day tour of provincial theaters with Brague, and she happily tells Maxime and Hamond about her forthcoming tour. Maxime visits her at her apartment to ask her to stay in Paris, and while there, he approaches her and kisses her. Renée resists, but then she gives in to the kiss and experiences a sensual reawakening. This causes a conflict in her mind—she feels that to give in to sexual impulses means a return to the kind of humiliation she experienced with her unfaithful husband, a reenactment of the painful state of submission to a man.

She refuses to give herself to Maxime, as her unhappy past keeps her from trusting him or her own impulses. By the time she embarks on her tour, however, her love for Maxime has blossomed. They come to an understanding that they will live together as a couple when she returns; she will give herself to him fully. Renée leaves Paris in high spirits, looking forward to coming back to Maxime. She leaves him a love letter upon her departure in which she proclaims that she will return tired of solitude and ready to begin her life with him fully and completely.

While Renée is away from Paris, she and Maxime exchange passionate letters. Gradually, however, as she travels by train further away from Paris, into the regions of her childhood, during the following days and nights, doubts assail her and grow until a letter arrives for her in Avignon. Maxime, afraid of losing her, has sensed that Renée is drifting away from him emotionally during her extended tour of provincial France, so he has written to her with a proposal of marriage. Renée's conflict increases. She reflects that marriage is a form of confinement, although it has its positive sides, while her vagabond existence, although lonely and hard, allows her to live as an independent soul.

As she embarks on the return leg of her trip, Renée begins to separate herself from Maxime psychologically. Once back in Paris, she furtively enters her apartment alone. In the early-morning light, she leaves a note for Maxime, telling him that she will not see him again. She returns to her life as the traveling artist, on her way to perform in a tour of South America.

Critical Evaluation:

Considered by many critics to be one of the greatest of French fiction writers, Colette was the first woman member of the Académie Goncourt. The author of more than fifty books, she began her writing career at the insistence of her first husband, Henri Gauthier-Villars, known as Willy. She was twenty-seven years old when her first novel, *Claudine à l'école* (1900; *Claudine at School*, 1956), was published under her husband's name. That novel was the beginning of the highly popular Claudine series. After her divorce from Willy, Colette supported herself as a music-hall mime and continued to write, publishing the acclaimed novels *The Vagabond*, *Chéri* (1920; English translation, 1929), and *La Fin de Chéri* (1926; *The Last of Chéri*, 1932). Many more novels followed, and Colette became widely celebrated.

In *The Vagabond*, Colette treats the theme of a woman's conflicts between love and independence. Her probing analysis of the psychological states that give power to these conflicts and her lyrical, rhythmic prose style give voice to the struggles women have with society and with their own desires. Analytical, harsh, lyrical, and honest in its examination of a woman's choices, *The Vagabond* is one of Colette's most important novels.

The novel's theme may be stated as a woman's difficulty in reconciling sensual love with the need for independence. This dilemma is posed by Renée, who, wounded by the memory of her past with her former husband, cannot give in to her temptation for a physical and emotional relationship with a man. Rather, she must choose a life of independence and solitude, marked by hardship and freedom.

The novel is divided into three parts and is told in the first person. In the arena of the music hall, individuals—though facing difficult, lonely lives—reach out to help one another. Renée, however, must choose between a relationship with a man and her own freedom in negotiating the world on her own terms. There is, it seems, no other choice. For the heroine, there is the individual female life, fraught with solitude and hardship but with a degree of freedom, or there is the life

in relationship to a man, which may bring fulfillment but is confining.

Renée Néré is thought to be the most autobiographical of Colette's heroines. Colette had suffered from the infidelities of her first husband, and she portrays the emotional effects of betrayal through Renée. Colette's earlier works, especially those of the Claudine series, portray young women who settle for love as a state of physical desire and a social and psychological state of submission to men. Colette's later, more mature heroines ask, as did Colette, for a love that can encompass more than just the physical. Renée is an example. A thirty-three-year-old divorcée who supports herself as a music-hall artist, she parallels many aspects of Colette's earlier years. Unlike Colette, Renée is unable to break away from the effects of her past. When she does become involved with Maxime, she is hindered by her lack of trust and preoccupied with thoughts of aging.

The effect of the past on the present is an underlying motif in *The Vagabond*. In the opening paragraph, the heroine faces herself in a mirror and holds a conversation with herself. Her reflection prompts Renée to examine where she is and where she has been. The heroine's consciousness is also a mirror that reflects her past in such a way that Renée cannot embrace a life that holds sensuality, a relationship with a man, and freedom all at once. The mirror held up to the past reveals the heroine's struggle against society, which demands the submission of women to men. Renée's struggle is also with herself. Through the conflicted Renée, Colette poses the question of whether it is possible for woman to accept her natural desires while remaining independent. This masterfully written novel can be seen as an extended conversation that Colette had with herself on the themes of sexuality and freedom.

Further Reading

Cottrell, Robert D. *Colette*. New York: Frederick Ungar, 1974. Basic overview provides a good starting place for students of Colette's works. Discusses and evaluates *The Vagabond* with emphasis on the themes of freedom and sexuality.

Crosland, Margaret. *Colette: The Difficulty of Loving*. Indianapolis: Bobbs-Merrill, 1973. Critical biography analyzes the subject's work as well as her life. Janet Flanner, long a commentator on the French scene, contributes an interesting introduction. Supplemented with a chronology of the events of Colette's life.

Francis, Claude, and Fernande Gontier. *Creating Colette*. 2 vols. South Royalton, Vt.: Steerforth Press, 1998-1999. Worthwhile and comprehensive biography of Colette.

The first volume chronicles the first forty years of her life and stresses the importance of her African ancestry and maternal family background in understanding her work. The second volume covers the years from 1912 to her death in 1954.

Holmes, Diana. *Colette*. New York: St. Martin's Press, 1991. Notes how Colette's fiction deals with female sexuality, domestic life, and the problems of working women in a man's world. Argues that Colette's stories need to be judged by female critics and asserts that the stories are open-ended and thus innovative for their time.

Sarde, Michèle. *Colette: Free and Fettered*. Translated by Richard Miller. New York: William Morrow, 1980. Study of Colette's life and work is one of the most informative books on the author available. It has not been superseded by subsequent studies and profits from a Gallic stamp and mood that non-French commentators have not yet begun to match. Uses quotations from *The Vagabond* to illuminate Colette's life.

Southworth, Helen. *The Intersecting Realities and Fictions of Virginia Woolf and Colette*. Columbus: Ohio State University Press, 2004. Argues that although the two authors lived in different countries, there were similarities in their lives, literary styles, and the themes of their works. Places the two subjects within the context of a group of early twentieth century artists and writers and describes Woolf's contacts with France and Colette's connections with British and American writers. *The Vagabond* is one of the novels discussed in chapter 3.

Stewart, Joan Hinde. *Colette*. Updated ed. New York: Twayne, 1996. Provides discussion of how Colette emerged as a writer, her apprenticeship years, the erotic nature of her novels, and her use of dialogue. Places *The Vagabond* in the context of Colette's career.

Ward, Nicole Jouve. *Colette*. Bloomington: Indiana University Press, 1987. Analyzes structures, tropes, themes, and characters in Colette's work. Includes illuminating discussion of *The Vagabond*.

Vanity Fair
A Novel Without a Hero

Author: William Makepeace Thackeray (1811-1863)
First published: serial, 1847-1848; book, 1848
Type of work: Novel
Type of plot: Social satire
Time of plot: Early nineteenth century
Locale: England and Europe

Principal characters:
BECKY SHARP, an adventuress
AMELIA SEDLEY, her friend
JOSEPH SEDLEY (JOS), Amelia's brother
RAWDON CRAWLEY, Becky's husband
MISS CRAWLEY, Rawdon's wealthy aunt
OLD SIR PITT CRAWLEY, Rawdon's father
YOUNG SIR PITT CRAWLEY, Rawdon's brother
GEORGE OSBORNE, Amelia's husband
CAPTAIN WILLIAM DOBBIN, Amelia's friend

The Story:

Becky Sharp and Amelia Sedley become good friends while they are students at Miss Pinkerton's School for girls. It is proof of Amelia's good, gentle nature that she takes as kindly as she does to her friend, who is generally disliked by all the other girls. Amelia overlooks the indications of Becky's selfishness as much as she can. After the two girls finish their education at the school, Becky accompanies her friend to her home for a short visit. There she first meets Joseph Sedley, Amelia's older brother, called Jos, who is home on leave from military service in India. Jos is shy, unused to women, and certainly to women as designing and flir-

tatious as Becky. His blundering and awkward manners do not appeal to many women, but Becky is happy to overlook these faults when she compares them with his wealth and his social position. Amelia innocently believes that her friend fell in love with her brother, and she discreetly tries to further the romance.

To this end, she arranges a party at Vauxhall. Becky and Jos, along with Amelia and her admirer, George Osborne, are present. There is a fifth member of the group, Captain Dobbin, a tall, lumbering fellow, also in service in India. He was in love with Amelia for a long time, but he recognizes that dashing George is much more suitable for her. All the maneuvering of the flirtatious Becky and the amiable Amelia, however, is not sufficient to corner Jos, who drinks too much punch and believes that he made a silly figure of himself at the party. A day or so later, a letter delivered to the Sedley household announces that Jos is ill and plans to return to India as soon as possible.

Since there is no longer any reason for Becky to remain with the Sedleys, she leaves Amelia, after many tears and kisses, to take a position as governess to two young girls at Queen's Crawley. The head of the household is Sir Pitt Crawley, a cantankerous old man renowned for his miserliness. Lady Crawley is an apathetic soul who lives in fear of her husband's unreasonable outbursts. Becky decides that she has nothing to fear from her timid mistress and spends most of her time ingratiating herself with Sir Pitt and ignoring her pupils. Becky also shows great interest in Miss Crawley, a spinster aunt of the family, who is exceedingly wealthy. Miss Crawley pays little attention to Sir Pitt and his children, but she is fond of Rawdon Crawley, a captain in the army and a son of Sir Pitt by a previous marriage. She is so fond of her dashing young nephew that she supports him through school and pays all of his gambling debts with only a murmur.

During Becky's stay, Miss Crawley visits Sir Pitt only once, at a time when Rawdon is also present. The handsome young dragoon soon falls prey to Becky's wiles and follows her about devotedly. Becky also takes care to ingratiate herself with the holder of the purse strings. Miss Crawley finds Becky witty and charming and does not attempt to disguise her opinion that the little governess is worth all the rest of the Crawley household put together. Becky, therefore, finds herself in a very enviable position. Both Sir Pitt and his handsome son are obviously interested in her. Miss Crawley insists that Becky accompany her back to London.

Becky is expected to return to her pupils after only a short stay with Miss Crawley; but Miss Crawley takes ill and refuses to allow anyone but her dear Becky to nurse her. Afterward, there are numerous other excuses to prevent the governess from returning to her duties. Certainly, Becky is not unhappy. Rawdon is a constant caller and a devoted suitor for Becky's hand. When the news arrives that Lady Crawley died, no great concern is felt by anyone. A few days later, however, Sir Pitt himself appears, asking to see Miss Sharp. Much to Becky's surprise, the baronet throws himself at her feet and asks her to marry him. Regretfully, she refuses his offer. She is already secretly married to Rawdon.

Following this disclosure, Rawdon and his bride leave for a honeymoon at Brighton. Chagrined and angry, old Miss Crawley takes to her bed, changes her will, and cuts off her nephew without a shilling. Sir Pitt raves with anger. Amelia's marriage also precipitates a family crisis. Her romance with George proceeds with good wishes on both sides until Mr. Sedley loses most of his money through some unfortunate business deals. Then George's snobbish father orders his son to break his engagement to a penniless woman. George, whose affection for Amelia was never stable, is inclined to accept this parental command; but Captain Dobbin, who sees with distress that Amelia is breaking her heart over George, finally prevails upon the young man to go through with the marriage, regardless of his father's wishes. When the couple arrive in Brighton for their honeymoon, they find Rawdon and Becky living there happily in penniless extravagance.

Captain Dobbin also arrives in Brighton. He agrees to act as intercessor with Mr. Osborne. Nevertheless, his hopes of reconciling father and son are shattered when Mr. Osborne furiously dismisses Captain Dobbin and takes immediate steps to disown George. Captain Dobbin also brings the news that the army is ordered to Belgium. Napoleon landed from Elba. The Hundred Days begins.

In Brussels, the two couples meet again. George is infatuated with Becky. Jos, now returned from India, and Captain Dobbin are also stationed in that city; Captain Dobbin is in faithful attendance upon neglected Amelia. Everyone is waiting for the next move that Napoleon will make; but in the meantime, the gaiety of the duke of Wellington's forces is widespread. The Osbornes and Crawleys attend numerous balls. Becky, especially, makes an impression upon military society, and her coquetry extends with equal effect from general to private. June 15, 1815, is a famous night in Brussels, for on that evening the duchess of Richmond gives a tremendous ball. Amelia leaves the party early, brokenhearted at the attentions her husband shows Becky. Shortly after she leaves, the men are given orders to march to meet the enemy. Napoleon entered Belgium, and a great battle is impending.

As Napoleon's forces approach, fear and confusion spread throughout Brussels, and many of the civilians flee the city, but Amelia and Becky do not. Becky is not alarmed, and Amelia refuses to leave while George is in danger. She remains in the city some days before she hears that her husband was killed. Rawdon returns safely from the Battle of Waterloo. He and Becky spend a merry and triumphant season in Paris, where Becky's beauty and wit gain her a host of admirers. Rawdon is very proud of their son.

Amelia also has a child. She returned to London almost out of her mind with grief, and only after her son is born does she show any signs of rallying. When Becky grows bored with the pleasures of Paris, the Crawleys return to London. There they rent a large home and proceed to live well with little money. By this time, Becky is a master at this art, and so they live on a grander scale than Rawdon's small winnings at cards would warrant. Becky becomes acquainted with the nobility of England and makes a particular impression on rich old Lord Steyne. At last, all society begins to talk about young Mrs. Crawley and her elderly admirer. Fortunately, Rawdon hears nothing of this ballroom and coffeehouse gossip.

Through the efforts of Lord Steyne, Becky eventually achieves her dearest wish, presentation at Court. Presented along with her is the wife of the new Sir Pitt Crawley. The old man died, and young Sir Pitt, his oldest son and Rawdon's brother, inherited the title. Since then, friendly relations were established between the two brothers. If Rawdon realizes that his brother also fell in love with Becky, he gives no sign, and he accepts the money his brother gives him with good grace; but more and more, he feels himself shut out from the happy life that Becky enjoys. He spends much time with his son, for he realizes that the child is neglected. Once or twice he sees young George Osborne, Amelia's son.

Amelia struggles to keep her son with her, but her pitiful financial status makes it difficult to support him. Her parents grow garrulous and morose with disappointment over their reduced circumstances. At length, Amelia sorrowfully agrees to let Mr. Osborne take the child and rear him as his own. Mr. Osborne still refuses to recognize the woman his son married against his wishes, however, and Amelia rarely sees the boy.

Rawdon is now deeply in debt. When he appeals to Becky for money, she tells him that she has none to spare. She makes no attempt to explain the jewelry and other trinkets she buys. When Rawdon is imprisoned for a debt, he writes and asks Becky to take care of the matter. She answers that she cannot get the money until the following day. An appeal to Sir Pitt, however, brings about Rawdon's release, and he returns to his home to find Becky entertaining Lord Steyne. Not long afterward, Rawdon accepts a post abroad, and he never returns to his unfaithful, scheming wife.

Amelia's fortunes now improve. When Jos returns home, he establishes his sister and father in a more pleasant home. Mrs. Sedley dies, and Jos resolves to do as much as he can to make his father's last days happy. Captain Dobbin returns from India and confesses his love for Amelia. Although she acknowledges him as a friend, she is not yet ready to accept his love. It is Captain Dobbin who goes to Mr. Osborne and gradually succeeds in reconciling him to his son's wife. When Mr. Osborne dies, he leaves a good part of his fortune to his grandson and appoints Amelia as the boy's guardian.

Amelia, her son, Captain Dobbin, and Jos took a short trip to the Continent. This visit is perhaps the happiest time in Amelia's life. Her son is with her constantly, and Captain Dobbin is a devoted attendant. Eventually, his devotion overcomes her hesitation and they are to be married. At a small German resort, they encounter Becky once more. After Rawdon left her, Becky was unable to live down the scandal of their separation. Leaving her child with Sir Pitt and his wife, she crossed to the Continent. Since then, she was living with first one considerate gentleman and then another. When she sees the prosperous Jos, she vows not to let him escape as he did before. Amelia and Jos greet her in a friendly manner, and only Captain Dobbin seems to regard her with distrust. He tries to warn Jos about Becky, but Jos is a willing victim of her charms.

Becky travels with Jos wherever he goes. Although she cannot get a divorce from Rawdon, Jos treats her as his wife, and despite Captain Dobbin's protests, he takes out a large insurance policy in her name. A few months later, his family learns that he died while staying with Becky at Aix-la-Chapelle. The full circumstances of his death are never established, but Becky comes into a large sum of money from his insurance. She spends the rest of her life on the Continent, where she assumes the role of the virtuous widow and wins a reputation for benevolence and generosity.

Critical Evaluation:

When critics call William Makepeace Thackeray's characters in *Vanity Fair* lifelike, they are using that term for a subtler meaning than it usually conveys. His people are not true to life in the sense of being fully rounded or drawn with psychological depth. On the contrary, readers sometimes find their actions too farcical to be human, as in Jos Sedley's ignominious flight from Brussels after the battle of Waterloo, or too sinister to be credible, as in the implication that Becky poisons Jos to collect his insurance—totally out of keeping with what readers learn about her in the previous sixty-six chapters. She may be a selfish opportunist, but she is not a murderer. Thackeray's characters are lifelike if "life" is defined as a typological phenomenon; when readers shrug their shoulders and say, "that's life," readers are indulging in a kind of judgment on the human race that is based on types, not individuals, on the common failings of all men and women, not on the unique goodness or evil of some. Insofar as all people share one another's weaknesses, everyone is represented in *Vanity Fair*. Human banality levels all. That is the satirical revelation that *Vanity Fair* provides—that is the way in which its characters are lifelike.

Thackeray's general approach is comic satire; his method is that of the theatrical producer, specifically, the puppeteer. In his prologue, he calls himself the "Manager of the Performance" and refers to Becky, Amelia, and Dobbin as puppets of varying "flexibility . . . and liveliness." Critics usually interpret this offhanded way of referring to his principal characters as a vindication of his own intrusions and asides; as a reminder to the reader that he, the author, is as much involved in the action as any of his characters. Nevertheless, readers should probably take a harder look at Thackeray's metaphor: He is a puppeteer because he must be one; because his people are puppets, someone must pull the strings. The dehumanized state of Regency and early Victorian society comes to accurate life through the cynical vehicle of Thackeray's puppeteering. Sentimentality and hypocrisy, closely related social vices, seem interchangeable at the end of the novel when Thackeray gathers all the remaining puppets: Amelia and Dobbin, a "tender little parasite" clinging to her "rugged old oak," and Becky, acting out her newfound saintliness by burying herself "in works of piety" and "having stalls at Fancy Fairs" for the benefit of the poor. "Let us shut up the box and the puppets," concludes Thackeray, "for our play is played out."

Despite the predictability of all the characters' puppetlike behavior, they often exhibit just enough humanity to make their dehumanization painful. Thackeray wants readers to feel uncomfortable over the waste of human potential in the vulgar concerns of *Vanity Fair*. George Osborne lives like a cad, is arrogant about his spendthrift ways, is unfaithful to his wife, and dies a hero, leading a charge against the retreating French at Waterloo. The reader is left with the impression that the heroism of his death is rendered irrelevant by the example of his life. Such satire is demanding in its moral vision precisely because it underscores the price of corruption: Honor becomes absurd.

Rawdon Crawley's love for his little son slowly endows the father with a touch of decency, but he is exiled by the "Manager of the Performance" to Coventry Island where he dies of yellow fever "most deeply beloved and deplored." Presumably the wastrel, separated from his son, dies in a position of duty. Are readers to pity him for having been forced, by his financial situation, to accept the position at Coventry as a bribe from Lord Steyne? Thackeray is elusive; again, the suggestions of pathos are touched on so lightly that they hardly matter. The indifference itself is *Vanity Fair*'s reward. For all of his jocularity and beef-eating familiarity, the "Manager of the Performance" sets a dark stage. *Vanity Fair* is colorful enough: the excitement at Brussels over Waterloo, the gardens at Vauxhall, the Rhine journey; but it is a panoply of meretricious and wasteful human endeavor. Readers really do not need Thackeray's moralizing to convince them of the shabbiness of it all.

Astonishing is the fact that, despite the novel's cynicism, it also has immense vitality. Readers sense the very essence of worldliness in its pages. It is difficult to deny the attractiveness of *Vanity Fair*. John Bunyan made that perfectly clear in *The Pilgrim's Progress* (1678, 1684), and Thackeray simply updates the vision. What was allegory in Bunyan becomes realism in Thackeray; the modern writer's objectivity in no way detracts from the alluring effect achieved by Bunyan's imaginary Vanity Fair. Bunyan still operates in the Renaissance tradition of Spenserian facade; evil traps man through illusion, as exemplified in the trials of the Knight of the Red Crosse. Thackeray drops the metaphor of illusion and shows corruption bared—and still it is attractive.

Becky Sharp is described as "worldliness incarnate" by Louis Kronenberger, but the reader cannot deny her charms. Thackeray calls his book "A Novel Without a Hero," but readers and Thackeray know better. Becky's pluck and ambition are extraordinary; her triumph is even more impressive because of the formidable barriers of class and poverty she scales. When she throws the Johnson dictionary out of the coach window as she leaves Miss Pinkerton's academy, readers are thrilled by her refusal to be patronized; her destructive and cruel manipulations of the Crawleys have all the implications of a revolutionary act. Thackeray actually emphasizes Becky's spirit and power by making virtuous Amelia weak and sentimental. Although readers are tempted to see this as a contradiction of Thackeray's moral intention, they must remember that he understood very clearly that true goodness must be built on strength: "Clumsy Dobbin" is Thackeray's somewhat sentimental example of this point. The human tragedy is that most men and women cannot reconcile their energies with their ideals and that in a fallen world of social injustices, people must all sin to survive. It is ironic that precisely because Becky is such an energetic opportunist, readers almost believe her when she says, "I think I could have been a good woman if I had 5000 a year."

"Critical Evaluation" by Peter A. Brier

Further Reading

Bloom, Harold, ed. *William Makepeace Thackeray*. New York: Chelsea House, 1987. Anthology of critical essays on important Thackeray novels. An excellent starting place for discussion of his major works.

Clarke, Micael M. *Thackeray and Women*. DeKalb: Northern Illinois University Press, 1995. Examines Thackeray's life, novels, and other works from a feminist-sociological perspective to analyze his treatment of female characters, demonstrating how his writings critique the position of women in Western culture. Includes bibliographical references and an index.

Fisher, Judith L. *Thackeray's Skeptical Narrative and the "Perilous Trade" of Authorship*. Burlington, Vt.: Ashgate, 2002. An analysis of Thackeray's narrative techniques, describing how he sought to create a "kind of poised reading which enables his readers to integrate his fiction into their life."

Harden, Edgar F. *The Emergence of Thackeray's Serial Fiction*. Athens: University of Georgia Press, 1979. Discussion of the serial structure of five novels, including *Vanity Fair*, with focus upon the manuscripts and process of composition as the novels evolved. Explains how the fact that the novel was written in serial installments shaped its form.

_____. *Thackeray the Writer: From Journalism to "Vanity Fair."* New York: St. Martin's Press, 1998.

_____. *Thackeray the Writer: From "Pendennis" to "Denis Duval."* New York: Macmillan, 2000. Two-volume biography chronicling Thackeray's development as a writer, beginning with his experiences as a book reviewer and culminating in the creation of *Vanity Fair*. Traces how Thackeray became an increasingly perceptive social observer.

Ray, Gordon N. *Thackeray: The Age of Wisdom, 1847-1863*. New York: McGraw-Hill, 1958. The second volume in the authoritative two-volume biography of Thackeray, authorized by the Thackeray family. Provides a good study of Thackeray as well as an excellent study of *Vanity Fair*.

Shillingsburg, Peter. *William Makepeace Thackeray: A Literary Life*. New York: Palgrave, 2001. An excellent introduction to the life of the novelist, thorough and scholarly, but accessible. Includes a chapter on reading *Vanity Fair*, notes, and index.

Sundell, M. G., ed. *Twentieth Century Interpretations of "Vanity Fair."* Englewood Cliffs, N.J.: Prentice-Hall, 1969. Comprehensive collection of six essays on such topics as characters, form, theme, and content. Eight short viewpoints give concise focus to various elements of the novel.

Taylor, D. J. *Thackeray: The Life of a Literary Man*. New York: Carroll and Graf, 2001. A lengthy biography that argues for Thackeray's preeminence among nineteenth century English novelists. A generally comprehensive study that sheds much light on his work.

Tillotson, Kathleen. "*Vanity Fair*." In *Thackeray: A Collection of Critical Essays*, edited by Alexander Welsh. Englewood Cliffs, N.J.: Prentice-Hall, 1968. Discusses Thackeray's plan and purpose. The book contains two other excellent essays: "On the Style of *Vanity Fair*" by G. A. Craig and "Neoclassical Conventions" by John Loofbourow.

The Varieties of Religious Experience
A Study in Human Nature

Author: William James (1842-1910)
First published: 1902
Type of work: Religious philosophy

Philosopher William James's *The Varieties of Religious Experience* is based on a series of twenty Gifford lectures he delivered at the University of Edinburgh in Scotland, beginning in May, 1901. James was asked to discuss natural religion, which traditionally had been conceived as a discipline on the border between philosophy and theology. As such, natural religion was thought to exclude both the notion of divine revelation and any claim of tangible religious experience. James's own concept differed in looking not at God as an object of devotion but at human attitudes toward God, including belief, supplication, direct experience, and doubt and disbelief. The word "varieties" in the book's title indicates James's intention to catalog and evaluate the range of religious experiences accessible to different human faculties. Indeed, James denies that there is only one "religious sentiment."

The invitation to lecture in Edinburgh left James both exultant and humbled, as he admitted in his first address: "It is with no small amount of trepidation that I take my place behind this desk, and face this learned audience." James's characteristic modesty aside, the magnitude of the subject, even in a twenty-lecture format, was daunting. His initial plan was to devote ten lectures to descriptive, or psychological, examination and the remaining ten lectures to metaphysical considerations based on his philosophical studies. Though a professor of philosophy at Harvard University, James had studied psychology and had also earned a medical degree. He had spent so much time on the psychological aspects of religious experience that he had little time left for the metaphysical, aside from his brief conclusions about the distinctive qualities of the religious life.

James begins his study by examining testimony about religious experience. He thinks his investigation would be most fruitful if confined to religious pioneers rather than to those who have followed their teachings. James identifies two different questions one must ask about the articulation of religious experience: What is its origin, and what is its significance or value? For example, while affirming that the Bible has great spiritual value, one might ask under what "biographic conditions" and states of mind its authors contributed to it. James attacks the common failure to make this distinction, a failure that can lead some to dismiss the value of religious thinking because of a thinker's flaws. Similarly, he notes that Quakerism is a highly admirable faith, but quotes at length from the journal of its founder, George Fox, to show "pathological aspects" in Fox's thinking. However, declares James, Fox's mental instability should not negate the significance of the Quaker faith, which, indeed, "is impossible to overpraise." James also points out that one can just as readily find mental and physical defects among atheists and agnostics, for example.

James then questions the meaning of the divine, as conceived by human beings, and asks what constitutes a religious experience. He wishes to avoid an excessively narrow definition, for "There are systems of thought which the world usually calls religious, and yet which do not positively assume a God." Buddhism, for example, has been called a "hopeless" or "atheistic" religion; and the Transcendental philosophy of Ralph Waldo Emerson "seems to let God evaporate into abstract Ideality." For James, the divine is "the first and last thing in the way of power and truth. Whatever then were most primal and enveloping and deeply true."

On the question of what makes a religious experience, James asserts that the religious attitude is a "solemn and serious reaction" to the divine as he defines it. The religious attitude can engender a happy state of mind that does not, however, represent an escape from the pain of life but embraces and overmatches the sense of tragedy. Moreover, the religious attitude is far stronger than any "moral" determination to resist the pain of mortality through sheer willpower.

Further delineating his subject, James says the life of religion "consists of the belief that there is an unseen order, and that our supreme good consists in harmoniously adjusting ourselves thereto. This belief and this adjustment are the religious attitude." James notes that philosopher Immanuel Kant had believed that objects of belief such as god, the design of freedom, the soul, and the afterlife are concepts and not capable of sensory apprehension; thus, they are not properly objects of knowledge at all. "Yet strangely enough," James writes, these objects of belief "have a definite meaning *for our practice*. We can act *as if* there were a God."

The major portion of James's study concerns personal testimony of religious experience, culled from literature and from correspondence with friends or acquaintances. He augments the huge volume and range of examples with a balanced perspective and eloquent commentary. The "varieties of religious experience" reported in these lectures lead James to conclude—in keeping with his own pluralistic philosophy—that "Men's religions need not be identical." Thus, he devotes lectures (and pages) to such religious qualities as "healthy-mindedness," "the sick soul" (which can be healed by spiritual conversion), saintliness, mysticism, and the philosophical approach.

In contrasting healthy-minded people with sick souls, James notes that even in hardship, some individuals—Walt Whitman, for example—appear to have an innate sense of life's goodness and to believe in a beneficent God rather than a God of wrath. Sick souls, on the other hand, harbor profound depression and a sense of evil. However, James sees sick souls as potentially deriving the greatest benefit from religious conversion, in that they have the greatest capacity for a fully balanced view of good and evil.

James next catalogs aspects of conversion, drawing from many personal descriptions. Conversion may be "sudden," "prolonged," "unconscious and involuntary," or "conscious and voluntary." He finds that truly converted people relinquish all worries and adopt the belief that all is well, have a sense of truths they were not previously aware of, and perceive the world as if it were completely new.

Turning to mystical states, James describes the characteristics that give these states an unassailable validity: Mystical states defy rational explanation, provide a sense of luminous insight, have only fleeting duration, and cause the mystic to feel "as if his own will were in abeyance." The nonmystic is not in any way subject to the mystical experience.

Nearing the end of the work, James addresses the function of philosophy with respect to religion. Although he notes that some people are temperamentally inclined to consider religion from a philosophical perspective, he warns against attempting philosophical proofs of religion's validity. Philosophy must not encourage inappropriate endeavors to escape the perfectly valid "subjective standards" of religious experience or lead to "dogmatic theology." In James's view, God's metaphysical attributes can have "no practical validity."

James does, however, see a use for philosophy in religion if transformed into a science of religions. This could include eliminating "doctrines that are now known to be scientifically absurd or incongruous" and "[s]ifting out unworthy formulations." This methodological enterprise would put the philosophy of religion on a par with the objective physical sciences. Just as the physical science of optics, for example, is based on observable facts that are continually verified, so too would a science of religions "depend for its original material on facts of personal experience, and would have to square itself with personal experience through all its critical reconstructions."

In "Conclusions," James broadly summarizes the distinctive qualities of the religious life, finding that it includes the following beliefs:

That the visible world is part of a more spiritual universe from which it draws its chief significance;

That [a] union or harmonious relation with that higher universe is our true end;

That prayer or inner communion with the spirit thereof—be that spirit "God" or "law"—is a process wherein work is really done, and spiritual energy flows in and produces effects, psychological or material, within the phenomenal world.

James's lecture transcription has a distinctive literary quality. His science of religions had barely begun to develop a vocabulary of its own, leaving the author, a brother of novelist Henry James, relatively free to employ his own characteristic mode of expression. Religious scholar Jaroslav Pelikan remarked,

The old cliché that Henry James wrote novels as though they were philosophical treatises whereas William James wrote philosophical treatises as though they were novels, while unfair to Henry, [well] describes William, including the William James of *Varieties of Religious Experience*.

James's wide range of informants, including literary sources, and his generous presentation of anecdotal evidence sometimes make the book read like a sprawling novel. James himself, acting as a sort of moral guide, can deliver observations like the following to deflate the vainly ambitious in a manner worthy of the ending of, for example, novelist F. Scott Fitzgerald's *The Great Gatsby* (1925):

Well, we are all such helpless failures in the last resort. The sanest and best of us are of one clay with lunatics and prison inmates, and death finally runs the robustest of us down. And whenever we feel this, such a sense of the vanity and provisionality of our voluntary career comes over us that all our morality appears but as a plaster hiding a sore it can never cure, and all our well-doing as the hollowest substitute for that well-*being* that our lives ought to be grounded in, but, alas! are not.

Thomas Rankin

Further Reading
Carmody, Denise Lardner, et al. *The Republic of Many Mansions: Foundations of American Religious Thought*. St. Paul, Minn.: Paragon House, 1998. A study of American religious thought from the eighteenth to the twentieth centuries. Centers on the ideas of William James as a philosophical pragmatist, Jonathan Edwards as a Puritan thinker, and Thomas Jefferson as an Enlightenment secularist.

Carrette, Jeremy, ed. *William James and "The Varieties of Religious Experience": A Centenary Celebration*. New York: Routledge, 2004. Designed as a companion book, this volume collects essays that examine *The Varieties of Religious Experience* in the context of James's other works, describe contemporary responses to James's book, and assess its historical importance and significance to the twenty-first century.

Gale, Richard M. *The Philosophy of William James: An Introduction*. New York: Cambridge University Press, 2005. Considers James's theory of belief in the context of his ethics, metaphysics, logic, and pragmatism. Also examines his theory of belief as it relates to mysticism, selfhood, and the wider issues of religious experience and philosophical inquiry.

James, William. *The Will to Believe, and Other Essays in Popular Philosophy*. 1956. Reprint. New York: Dover, 1990. A collection of essays by James that first appeared between 1896 and 1903. The first several chapters defend the legitimacy of religious faith, thus constituting a supplement, in a way, to *The Varieties of Religious Experience*.

Richardson, Robert D. *William James: In the Maelstrom of American Modernism.* Boston: Houghton Mifflin, 2006. An exhaustive 622-page biography of James as a prominent member of an extraordinary family. Several chapters address James's religious thought, with a particular focus on the psychology of faith—balanced with philosophical pragmatism—in *The Varieties of Religious Experience.*

Taylor, Charles: *Varieties of Religion Today: William James Revisited.* Cambridge, Mass.: Harvard University Press, 2002. Transcript of lectures by scholar Charles Taylor in Vienna in 2000. Taylor assesses the religious thought of James as he considers the place of religion in the present secular age.

Vathek
An Arabian Tale

Author: William Beckford (1760-1844)
First published: 1786
Type of work: Novel
Type of plot: Gothic
Time of plot: The past
Locale: Arabia

Principal characters:
VATHEK, an Arabian sultan
THE GIAOUR, a magician and a prince of darkness
CARATHIS, Vathek's mother
EMIR FAKREDDIN, a noble prince
NOURONIHAR, his daughter
GULCHENROUZ, her betrothed

The Story:

Vathek is an Arabian caliph whose reign is marked by turbulence and unrest. A sensuous person, he builds five palaces, each devoted to the enjoyment of one of the five senses, and his fondness for food and women consumes much of his time. In addition to the gratification he finds in the life of the senses, he also tries to master the sciences and the deep, unfathomable secrets of the world beyond. To this end, he builds a huge tower where he pursues his studies in astronomy and astrology. There Carathis, his mother, burns refuse and live bodies to appease the dark powers.

One day, Vathek obtains several mysterious sabers from a hideous, repulsive stranger. These sabers bear letters the caliph is unable to decipher. He offers great rewards to anyone who can read them; but because the punishment for failure is also great, few accept the offer. At last, an old man appears to read the inscriptions. The next morning, however, Vathek discovers that the inscriptions changed. From that time on, the letters on the sabers change daily.

Vathek is in despair. He begs the stranger to return and explain the inscription to him, for he is sure that the letters are the key to the dark kingdom and the riches Vathek hopes to find there. The stranger, who is the Giaour, finally reappears and tells Vathek that only a sacrifice will put the powers in a receptive mood. On a journey with his court, Vathek throws fifty children into a chasm as a sacrifice for the bloodthirsty

Giaour. The people are angered by his cruelty and begin to hurl execrations at Vathek, but his guards return him safely to his palace.

Carathis continues her own sacrifices in the tower, to the disgust and anger of the people, who increasingly object to Vathek's defiance of Mahomet and the Muslim creed. Obeying a message written on a mysterious piece of parchment, Vathek and his court set out on a pilgrimage in search of the mountains of Istakhar, where the secrets of the dark world are to be revealed to him. On the way, they meet the messengers of Emir Fakreddin, a deeply religious prince. For some time, Vathek is Fakreddin's guest. Although he loathes the prayers and the religious ceremonies observed by his host, he is attracted to Fakreddin's daughter, the lovely Nouronihar. She is long betrothed to her cousin Gulchenrouz, and their mutual devotion has the approval of the emir and of his people.

Nouronihar so attracts Vathek that he plots to seize her by force. Fakreddin, already scandalized by Vathek's behavior, is informed of the plot. He and his court determine to outwit Vathek. He administers a drug to the young lovers, and when Vathek sees them in their deathlike trance, he is convinced they are dead. Nouronihar and Gulchenrouz are secretly taken to a safe retreat and looked after by Fakreddin's servants. When the young people awaken they believe that they really died and that they are now in Paradise.

One day, however, Nouronihar strays from the hidden retreat and is discovered by Vathek. She finally yields to his entreaties and becomes the favorite of his harem. After Vathek and his wives and followers continue their journey, Nouronihar comes to share her lord's ambition; she, too, wishes to enjoy the pleasures of that strange other world and, like Vathek, she is willing to resort to the most unscrupulous behavior to realize those desires.

At last, after a long journey, the entourage arrives at the mountains of Istakhar and enters the secret retreat of Eblis, dread lord of darkness. There they find all the beautiful and strange wealth they desire. They are given permission to roam through the palace and to enjoy its treasures to their hearts' content. In the vast domed hall of the palace, they see creatures whose hearts are continually devoured by fire, and they learn that a like fate is to be theirs, for they seek knowledge that no mortal should know.

Carathis is also summoned to the abode of Eblis. Transported on the back of an evil monster, she comes at once to the mysterious palace and is overjoyed to view its secrets at last. Then, before the eyes of Vathek and Nouronihar, her heart catches fire and a consuming flame bursts forth to punish her eternally for her crimes. A moment later, flames begin to burn in the hearts of Vathek and Nouronihar. The fifty children whom Vathek sacrificed are miraculously returned from death and, along with Gulchenrouz, are carried to an earthly paradise. For them, life is perpetual happiness. Not having sought evil, they achieve goodness.

Critical Evaluation:

William Beckford's *Vathek* is usually classified as a gothic novel, and it does indeed contain many of the same elements as the gothic novels more typically set in Europe, including a defiant and charismatic villain, a submerged but obsessive interest in perverse sexuality, and a diabolical bargain that ultimately leads to damnation. *Vathek* is, however, a highly idiosyncratic example of the gothic genre, not only in the overblown exoticism of its Eastern setting but also in its near-comedic grotesquerie. As if the text's inherent eccentricities were not enough, the familiar English version of it is an unauthorized translation of an unpublished manuscript of Beckford's text, which he wrote in French, by a clergyman named Samuel Henley. Beckford seems to have disapproved of the translation beyond the fact that it preceded publication of his original version.

The most obvious debt *Vathek* owes is to *The Arabian Nights' Entertainments* (fifteenth century), which was translated into French by Antoine Galland 1704-1717. A more direct influence, however, was Voltaire, whom Beckford met in Paris in 1777, the year before Voltaire's death. Voltaire borrowed materials from Galland to construct a series of extended satirical works he called *contes philosophiques* (philosophical tales); these included *Zadig* (1747) and *La Princesse de Babylone* (1768; *The Princess of Babylon*, 1769), as well as *Candide: Ou, L'Optimisme* (1759; *Candide: Or, All for the Best*, 1759). It was probably the rumor that Voltaire composed *Candide* at a single sitting that prompted Beckford to boast (falsely, according to his biographers) that he wrote *Vathek* in a single session of something less than seventy-two hours.

If *Vathek* was intended to be a *conte philosophique*, it is a peculiar example. Such tales are supposed to have clear and explicit morals, though philosophical reasoning often proceeds doggedly to dreadful inconclusiveness. As *Candide* demonstrates—the philosophical tale can be more a powerful devastator of hopeful systems than a supporter of them. Voltaire, however, subjects his corrosive skepticism, mocking sarcasm, and phantasmagorical imagination to a strict discipline, whereas Beckford plainly sees no reason not to give free rein to imagination, which is what he allows his character Vathek to do. Five years before the publication of the first of the Marquis de Sade's elaborately extended *conte philosophique*—which proposes that morality is an arbitrary and hollow sham, and that nothing in nature can deny the powerful the right to indulge to the full in perverse pleasures—Beckford's Caliph Vathek had gone forth in search of similar extremes.

That great figure of diabolical bargains, Doctor Faust, negotiates with the devil for enlightenment, pleasure, and profit, but Vathek desires what is beyond mere pleasure and profit, some final and absolute evil. The dreadful fate that claims him at the end is not the kind of trivial damnation that later claims such gothic villains as Matthew Gregory Lewis's monk. Instead, Beckford devises the awful revelation that the archfiend Eblis has no absolute to offer. Vathek's hell is the realization that his boundless desires must remain forever unsatisfied. One of the great triumphs of the text is the image that encapsulates this fate: the limited hellfire that cages but never consumes the heart. This fire does not merely singe the flesh and rack the body with pain; it is a metaphysical flame that leaves all the yearnings of the flesh intact while mocking all ambition, emotion, and enlightenment. The image of the eternally burning heart remains unsurpassed throughout the subsequent centuries when legions of writers delved in search of the ultimate horror.

Beckford inherited an immense fortune from his erratic father, which included the neo-Gothic monstrosity of Fonthill Abbey, which was repeatedly burned to the ground and rebuilt at vast expense and ever greater expansiveness. Beckford turned the abbey into a fabulous palace, fully equipped for the contemplation of absolutes. The life he led there was rumored to be debauched, at least in its latter phases. Certainly he was well-placed to dream of such desires as those that consume Vathek.

Beckford seems to bow to conventional morality in his novel's last paragraph, in which he describes the fate of "the humble and despised Gulchenrouz" as that of passing "whole ages in the undisturbed tranquillity and the pure happiness of childhood." He must have known (through Galland if not otherwise) that the paradise promised by the Qur'an to the faithful followers of Allah bears no more resemblance to this imagined fate than do orthodox visions of hell to the novel's Halls of Eblis. It can be assumed that, as a loyal follower of Voltaire, Beckford means his concluding observation sarcastically, and that he intends to imply that paradise is a place fit only for children, bliss fit only for the ignorant, and peace fit only for the mindless. The final irony of Vathek's paradoxical damnation is that there is no alternative that anyone blessed with freedom of desire could possibly want. That conclusion entitles *Vathek* to be considered an authentic *conte philosophique*, for it represents a braver display of authentic horrors than all the gothic novels that trailed in its wake.

Brian Stableford

Further Reading

Alexander, Boyd. *England's Wealthiest Son: A Study of William Beckford*. London: Centaur Press, 1962. Includes chapters on the origins of *Vathek* and its connection with the three supplemental episodes that Beckford wrote in the 1820's, which did not appear in print until 1912.

Cass, Jeffrey. "Homoerotics and Orientalism in William Beckford's *Vathek*: Liberalism and the Problem of Pederasty." In *Interrogating Orientalism: Contextual Approaches and Pedagogical Practices*, edited by Diane Long Hoeveler and Jeffrey Cass. Columbus: Ohio State University Press, 2006. Cass's study of the novel is included in a collection of essays about Orientalism. The essays demonstrate Great Britain's condescending attitude toward the Near East in the eighteenth and nineteenth centuries.

Day, William Patrick. *In the Circles of Fear and Desire: A Study of Gothic Fantasy*. Chicago: University of Chicago Press, 1985. One of many studies of gothic fiction that include a discussion of *Vathek*. Links the work to the "apocalyptic vision" of literary modernism.

Frank, Frederick. "*Vathek: An Arabian Tale*." In *Survey of Modern Fantasy Literature*, edited by Frank N. Magill. Englewood Cliffs, N.J.: Salem Press, 1983. A useful essay on the work, which draws interesting comparisons between *Vathek* and the works of Edgar Allan Poe.

Graham, Kenneth W., ed. *"Vathek" and the Escape from Time: Bicentenary Revaluations*. New York: AMS Press, 1990. Collection of essays interpreting the novel from a variety of perspectives, including discussions of the influence of landscape and architecture on the book; *Vathek* and Orientalism, fantasy, the gothic, Persian Sufism, and decadence; and the book's influence on Edgar Allan Poe.

Mahmoud, Fatma Moussa, ed. *William Beckford of Fonthill 1760-1844: Bicentenary Essays*. Port Washington, N.Y.: Kennikat Press, 1972. Includes Mahmoud's essay, "Beckford, *Vathek* and the Oriental Tale," which offers a comprehensive analysis of *Vathek*, and Mahmoud Manzalaoui's "Pseudo-Orientalism in Transition: The Age of *Vathek*," a useful account of the work's literary-historical context.

Richardson, Alan, ed. *Three Oriental Tales*. Boston: Houghton Mifflin, 2002. *Vathek* is one of the three stories contained in this collection and examination of the Oriental-tale genre. In addition to the text of the novel, this edition contains an introduction with Richardson's comments about the genre, samples of Orientalist writing that appeared in eighteenth century British journals, and modern critical essays analyzing the three works.

Varma, Devendra P. "William Beckford." In *Supernatural Fiction Writers: Fantasy and Horror*, edited by Everett F. Bleiler. New York: Scribner's, 1985. A brief essay that provides information and interesting speculations about the origins of *Vathek* and its connections to Beckford's own life.

Venice Preserved
Or, A Plot Discovered

Author: Thomas Otway (1652-1685)
First produced: 1682; first published, 1682
Type of work: Drama
Type of plot: Tragedy
Time of plot: Renaissance
Locale: Venice

Principal characters:
JAFFEIR, a young Venetian, formerly Priuli's servant
PRIULI, Jaffeir's father-in-law, a senator
BELVIDERA, Priuli's daughter and Jaffeir's wife
PIERRE, the friend and fellow conspirator of Jaffeir
RENAULT, another conspirator
ANTONIO, a senator
AQUILINA, a courtesan

The Story:

Jaffeir, formerly the servant of Priuli, a senator of Venice, secretly woos and marries Belvidera, Priuli's daughter. For three years the couple live comfortably and blissfully, despite the father's antagonism; then Jaffeir loses his fortune. When he goes to ask Priuli for aid, in the name of Belvidera, the old senator refuses to help in any way, and he swears that his ungrateful daughter and her equally ungrateful husband will have to make their way as best they can. Jaffeir, after reminding Priuli that it is he who saved Belvidera from a shipwreck after which she fell in love with him, leaves the senator's home in a most unhappy frame of mind.

Soon afterward Jaffeir meets Pierre, a friend who gave long and faithful, though unrewarded, service to Venice. Pierre, sympathizing with Jaffeir, offers him the means of getting revenge on Priuli and striking, as he put it, a blow for liberty against the bad government of the senate. Jaffeir agrees to meet Pierre that night and to become a member of the band of conspirators. When he arrives home, Jaffeir is also comforted by Belvidera, who claims that she is rich as long as she has his love, no matter how little fortune they possess.

Meanwhile Pierre goes to visit Aquilina, a courtesan whom he loves. He is extremely incensed with the woman because she gave herself for money to old Antonio, a senator. Antonio's theft of his mistress makes Pierre more eager than ever for revenge. He makes Aquilina, who loves him, swear to extract all the information she can from Antonio and pass it on to the conspirators, who are meeting that night in Aquilina's house.

When midnight comes, Jaffeir is sadly bewailing his fate on the Rialto. There Pierre meets him and conducts him to the conspirators' meeting place. Because the plotters are unwilling to take Jaffeir into their number, he brings Belvidera and offers her as hostage for his honesty. The leader of the plotters, Renault, and the Spanish ambassador, who also have a hand in the plot to ruin the government, accept her as hostage. She is to be killed if Jaffeir fails them in any way.

The next day Jaffeir's hopes for revenge and his confidence in his fellow conspirators are shaken when he learns that Renault offered violence to Belvidera and was driven off only by her screams. Belvidera swears that she will bear anything, if only she knows why she was offered as a hostage. Jaffeir, seeing her predicament, and thinking it only fair that she know the truth, reveals the plot to assassinate the senate and take over the city. Because the mass assassination will include her father, Belvidera, greatly shocked, tries to convince her husband that terrible wrongs will be committed against innocent people in the mass slaughter that is planned.

In the evening, the conspirators meet to complete plans for the uprising, which is to take place that same night. At the meeting Jaffeir is seized with revulsion for the plot and the conspirators; he slips away from the meeting and goes to Belvidera. The two start toward the chamber where the senate council is meeting. On the way they are taken prisoners by the ducal guard and escorted to the council. To the senators and the duke Jaffeir admits his part in the plot and prevails on their fear to gain a general amnesty for his friends in exchange for information preventing the overthrow of the government. Within a matter of minutes, the other conspirators are brought in as prisoners. They, including Pierre, are furious with Jaffeir for revealing the plot. Pierre, refusing to listen to Jaffeir, much less to forgive him, slaps Jaffeir's face.

The senators, although they gave their word that the conspirators would be permitted to live, break their promise and sentence the prisoners, including Pierre, to death on the wheel. Jaffeir's rage knows no bounds when he learns of that perfidy. He offers to stab Belvidera, who is pledged as hostage for his faithfulness to the plot. When his love prevents his actually killing her, he persuades her to go to her father and seek his aid in rescuing the conspirators, lest her own life be forfeit for their deaths. Priuli, overcome at last by his love for his daughter, agrees to help Belvidera. His promise, however, is made too late.

When Jaffeir arrives at the scene of execution, he learns that all of the conspirators except Pierre have already been killed by the public executioner. Pierre had been saved until last because his request to speak to Jaffeir was granted. On the scaffold Pierre apologizes for slapping Jaffeir's face and asks him a boon. Jaffeir readily assents and Pierre whispers to him. He asks that Jaffeir save him from an ignominious death by stabbing him instead. Jaffeir immediately complies and then turns his dagger into his own breast. He dies within seconds of his friend.

Aquilina, hoping to save Pierre's life, went to seek the aid of Antonio. When the senator refused to help her, she stabbed him and left him to die. In the meantime Belvidera, overcome by her fears, becomes distraught in her father's house. In spite of Priuli's efforts and those of his servants, she becomes steadily worse. She quickly goes mad, even before she knows of her husband's death by his own hand; he tells her when she sees him last that they will never meet again. Before the messenger arrives to tell of Jaffeir's death, her husband's ghost appears before her. Shortly after the messenger comes and leaves, the ghosts of Jaffeir and Pierre appear briefly. Following their appearance she goes into a frenzy and dies. Her father, sick of the bloodshed, plotting, and violent death, begs his attendants to take him away to a lonely place where the sun never shines, so that he might mourn in solitude and darkness the loss of his daughter and her unhappy fate.

Critical Evaluation:

Thomas Otway's career as a dramatist lasted only eight years (his first play, *Alcibiades*, was performed in 1675; his last, *The Atheist*, in 1683), but during that brief period he was able to establish himself as one of the leading playwrights of his day. *Venice Preserved* secured Otway a more lasting reputation. Acted 337 times during the eighteenth century, it continued to be popular during the nineteenth century and remains one of the more frequently anthologized plays from the period.

Otway lived and wrote during the turbulent reign of Charles II (1600-1685). A popular but troubled monarch, Charles was plagued by a long series of political crises. One such crisis, known as the Popish Plot, involved an alleged attempt by the Catholic Church to overthrow the English government. Though a hoax, the Popish Plot played on deep-seated national fears, inciting considerable furor and helping bring to a head the long-standing conflict between the king's supporters (the Tory party) and his opponents (the Whig party). Otway's loyalty lay staunchly with the king, and *Venice Preserved*, his best-known play, with its portrait of a Venice racked by political strife and double-dealing, can be seen in part as a celebration of Charles's political victory over the Whig opposition.

How appreciative the initial audience of *Venice Preserved* was of its political dimension is amply suggested by the extent of royal patronage: King Charles attended the play's third night (the profits of which traditionally went to the author), and two months later the king's brother, James, duke of York (later King James II), and James's wife, the duchess of York, attended special performances. The royal brothers no doubt took particular relish in the savage personal satire against their foremost political opponent, Anthony Ashley Cooper, first earl of Shaftesbury, portrayed by Otway in the characters of Antonio and Renault as a corrupt, debauched sensualist without moral or political principles. (Soundly defeated and in fear for his life, Shaftesbury fled England several months before the play opened.) It is unlikely, however, that either Charles or James was able to discern any grander satirical scheme at work. Though clearly anti-Whig in its sentiments, *Venice Preserved* does not effectively "reduce" to a coherent political allegory, and no historical counterparts exist for the three lead characters, Jaffeir, Pierre, and Belvidera. In fact, except for the personal attack against Shaftesbury and a general parallel between the murky world of Venetian politics and the conspiracy-laden England of Otway's day, *Venice Preserved* can best be viewed not as a political satire at all but rather as an especially effective example of the serious Restoration drama known as pathetic tragedy.

In pathetic tragedy, the playwright is most concerned with fashioning a dramatic vehicle that will arouse powerful emotions in his audience. Pity, not surprisingly, is the principal emotion targeted, and the elements of plot, character, and theme are arranged in ways that will help maximize an emotional response. In *The Orphan* (1680), Otway already proved himself something of a master in this form, and *Venice Preserved*, with its loftier theme of the conflicts between love and honor, personal loyalty and public duty, set against the background of Europe's most notoriously decadent and corrupt city, was a hit with audiences, critics, and actors alike.

If one sets aside one's modern prejudices against overblown, bombastic melodrama, one can readily see what made *Venice Preserved* such a long-lived, popular entertainment. First, and perhaps most important, from an acting perspective, there is the play's "openness" to dramatic interpretations. The three lead roles (Jaffeir, Pierre, and Belvidera) permit a wide range of equally valid interpretive choices. Pierre, for example, has been variously portrayed as a heroic idealist and as a Machiavellian schemer, while one noted eighteenth century actor (Susanna Cibber) played Belvidera as delicate and passive, and another (the beautiful and gifted

Sarah Siddons) made her the virtual center of the play. Against earlier interpretations of Jaffeir as a pathetic weakling, the great David Garrick offered an interpretation of Jaffeir marked by a violent and stormy nature. Important staging considerations also include the notorious "Nicky-Nacky" scenes between Aquilina and Antonio. They have been presented in some productions as almost farcical in tone and in others as sordid and repulsive. Rather than confront the problem of which presentation to choose, most eighteenth century acting companies simply cut out the scenes altogether. On a performance level, then, *Venice Preserved* is truly protean, open to any number of staging and interpretive possibilities.

This openness, taken together with the play's obvious "pathetic" objectives, creates problems for the critic who would like to treat *Venice Preserved* principally as a literary text. Even the major elements of character and theme are difficult to interpret. Any reasonable analysis, for example, must take Jaffeir as the play's central character—his two decisions, after all, first to join the conspiracy and second to betray it, provide what little plot there is. Neither decision, however, seems either intelligently or nobly motivated. He joins the conspirators mainly to seek revenge against his father-in-law for denying him financial assistance and then betrays them to the Venetian senate after one of the conspiracy leaders sexually assaults his wife. Both moves are dramatically plausible, of course, but neither seems likely to increase Jaffeir's heroic stature. The disaster that ensues therefore seems thematically opaque. The conclusions one can legitimately draw from Jaffeir's plight are that it is bad to join conspiracies but even worse to betray them. Even Jaffeir's arguably authentic heroic acts—killing Pierre and then turning the dagger upon himself—though undoubtedly impressive theater, seem in retrospect to suggest pathetic desperation more than heroic defiance.

Equally problematic is Otway's portrayal of the Venetian senate and the conspirators who plot against it. The senators are venal and unscrupulous; the conspirators, with the exception of Pierre, are no better. Certainly Otway means to place Jaffeir within a classic "double-bind" situation, caught between what appear to be equally compelling demands (friendship and loyalty to one's country). When the choice is between two evils, however, rather than two "goods," one is led inevitably to question the hero's intelligence rather than to admire his heroism. Perhaps, as several critics have suggested, Otway's ultimate intention is to reveal not humanity's potential nobility but its tragic inadequacy.

"Critical Evaluation" by Michael Stuprich

Further Reading

Brown, Laura. *English Dramatic Form, 1660-1760: An Essay in Generic History.* New Haven, Conn.: Yale University Press, 1981. An interesting discussion, within the context of "affective" tragedy, of Otway's two best-known plays, *The Orphan* and *Venice Preserved.*

Kelsall, Malcolm. Introduction to *Venice Preserved*, edited by Malcolm Kelsall. Lincoln: University of Nebraska Press, 1969. Kelsall's is one of the best modern editions of *Venice Preserved.* His introduction is first-rate in its discussion of Otway's main source, the many problems attendant upon viewing the play as a political satire, and its long life on the English stage.

Leissner, Debra. "Divided Nation, Divided Self: The Language of Capitalism and Madness in Otway's *Venice Preserv'd.*" *Studies in the Literary Imagination* 32, no. 2 (Fall, 1999): 19. Argues that the play "dramatizes a national neurosis" that was created by the social and political turmoil in England in the years from 1678 to 1682, and that this neurosis affects Jaffeir.

Milhous, Judith, and Robert D. Hume. *Producible Interpretation: Eight English Plays, 1675-1707.* Carbondale: Southern Illinois University Press, 1985. Highly recommended for anyone interested in Restoration drama. The chapter on *Venice Preserved* provides a lucid and interesting introduction to the play as well as a fascinating history of the many different stagings Otway's play received over the course of the eighteenth and nineteenth centuries.

Munns, Jessica. *Restoration Politics and Drama: The Plays of Thomas Otway, 1675-1683.* Newark: University of Delaware Press, 1995. Argues that *Venice Preserved* reflects the private and public paranoia generated by political conditions in Restoration England, particularly the Popish Plot.

Stroup, Thomas B. "Otway's Bitter Pessimism." In *Essays in English Literature of the Classical Period Presented to Dougald MacMillan.* Chapel Hill: University of North Carolina Press, 1967. A classic general study of Otway. Stroup sees all of Otway's dramatic works as cynical and frustrating and finds *Venice Preserved* to be a moral chaos marked by "broken oaths and curses."

Taylor, Aline MacKenzie. *Next to Shakespeare: Otway's "Venice Preserv'd" and "The Orphan" and Their History on the London Stage.* New York: AMS Press, 1966. Though originally published in 1950, this remains one of the most exhaustive and reliable accounts of *Venice Preserved* and its stage history.

Venus and Adonis

Author: William Shakespeare (1564-1616)
First published: 1593
Type of work: Poetry
Type of plot: Erotic
Time of plot: Antiquity
Locale: Greece

Principal characters:
VENUS, goddess of love
ADONIS, a handsome youth loved by Venus

The Poem:

In all the world there is no more beautiful figure, no more perfectly made creature, than young Adonis. Although his beauty is a delight to the sun and to the winds, he has no interest in love. His only joy is in hunting and riding over the hills and fields after the deer and the fox. When Venus, the goddess of love, sees the beauty of young Adonis, she comes down to Earth because she is filled with love for him.

Meeting him one morning in the fields as he rides out to the hunt, she urges him to dismount, tie his horse to a tree, and talk with her. Adonis has no desire to talk to any woman, even the goddess, but she forces him to do as she wishes. Reclining by his side, she looks at him with caressing glances and talks passionately of the wonder and glory of love. The more she talks, the more she begs him for a kind look, a kiss, the more anxious he becomes to leave her and go on with his hunting. Venus is not easily repulsed, however; she tells him how even the god of war was a willing prisoner of her charms. She numbers all the pleasures she can offer him if he will accept her love. Blushing, Adonis finally breaks from her arms and goes to get his horse.

At that moment, his stallion hears the call of a jennet in a field nearby. Aroused, he breaks the leather thong that holds him and gallops to her. At first the jennet pretends to be cold to the stallion's advances, but when she perceives that Adonis is about to overtake his mount, she gives a neigh of affection and the two horses gallop away to another field. Adonis is left behind.

Dejected, he stands thinking of the hunt that he is missing because his horse ran away. Venus comes up to him again and continues her pleas of love. For a while he listens to her, but in disgust he turns finally and gives her such a look of scorn that the lovesick goddess faints and falls to the ground. Thinking he killed her with his unkind look, Adonis kneels beside her, rubs her wrists, and kisses her in hope of forgiveness. Venus, recovering from her swoon, asks him for one last kiss. He grudgingly consents before turning to leave. When Venus asks when they can meet the next day. Adonis replies that he will not see her, for he is to go boar hunting. Struck with a vi-

sion, the goddess warns the youth that he will be killed by a boar if he hunts the next day, and she begs him to meet her instead. She throws herself on the boy and carries him to the Earth in her arms in a last attempt to gain his love, Adonis admonishes the goddess on the difference between heavenly love and earthly lust. He leaves her alone and weeping.

The next morning finds Venus wandering through the woods in search of Adonis. In the distance, she can hear the noise of the dogs and the voices of the hunters. Frantic because of her vision of the dead Adonis, she rushes through the forest trying to follow the sounds of the hunt. When she sees a wounded and bleeding dog, the fear she feels for Adonis becomes almost overpowering. Suddenly she comes upon Adonis lying dead, killed by the fierce wild boar he hunted. Venus's grief knows no bounds. If this love is taken from her, then never again should man love happily. Where love is, there also will mistrust, fear, and grief be found.

The body of Adonis lies white and cold on the ground, his blood coloring the soil and plants about him. From this soil grows a flower, white and purple like the blood that spots his skin. With a broken heart, Venus leaves Earth to hide her sorrow in the dwelling place of the gods.

Critical Evaluation:

Venus and Adonis and *The Rape of Lucrece* (1594), two of William Shakespeare's most famous nondramatic works, were probably composed during the period between June, 1592, and May, 1594, while the theaters were temporarily closed because of the plague. *Venus and Adonis*, the earlier of the two poems, was entered at the Stationers' Register on April 18, 1593, and was printed shortly thereafter by Richard Field, who, incidentally, had originally come from Stratford-on-Avon. *Venus and Adonis* was the first work of Shakespeare ever to be printed.

It should not be supposed from the date of composition that *Venus and Adonis* was merely a way of passing time while the theaters were closed. All indications are that Shakespeare thought of this poem as the public commencement of his serious literary work as distinct from his quotidian employment as a dramatist. Indeed, Shakespeare never bothered to see his plays into print, a fact that has proved the bane of editors ever since. *Venus and Adonis*, however, was handsomely printed with an ornate dedication to the earl of Southampton in which Shakespeare speaks of the poem as his first serious literary effort. In subject and style, it is a kind of poetry that occupied most of Shakespeare's serious contemporaries.

Although the poem has been transmitted in only a few manuscripts, there is ample evidence that it was extremely popular in its own day. By 1600, it had become one of the most frequently quoted poems of the period, and many of Shakespeare's contemporaries referred to it with admiration. Even Gabriel Harvey, fellow of Cambridge and stern arbiter of critical taste, noted the great fame that the poem enjoyed among undergraduates, although he did add reservations about the erotic nature of the poem. In that eroticism, *Venus and Adonis* reflected a vogue for such poetry, which appeared in profusion in the 1590's. Like Shakespeare's, these narrative or reflective poems generally drew on classical or pseudoclassical sources.

Shakespeare derived the story of *Venus and Adonis* from Ovid's *Metamorphoses* (c. 8 C.E.; English translation, 1567), the main difference being that in his poem Adonis becomes a coy and reluctant lover. This variation may be the result of accidental or intentional conflation of the tale with Ovid's story of Hermaphroditus and Salmacis or that of Narcissus. It could also be the result of the influence of stories in book 3 of Edmund Spenser's *Faerie Queene* (1590, 1596), in Thomas Lodge's *Scillaes Metamorphosis* (1589), or in Christopher Marlowe's *Hero and Leander* (1598). In any case, the change brings it in line with other late sixteenth century poems that stress male beauty. Regardless of the source, the substance of the poem is almost entirely conventional.

The few original additions that Shakespeare seems to have made—the digressive episode of the jennet and the stallion and the descriptions of the hunting of the fox and the hare, for example—are notable more for the conventional beauty of their style than for their narrative power. The entire poem is, in fact, an excellent example of stylistic decoration, an ornate work for a sophisticated audience more interested in execution than originality. The poetry is on the surface, in the ingenious handling of commonplaces and in the brilliant flourishes of image and phrase.

Virtually nothing happens in the poem. The bulk of it is taken up with the amorous arguments of Venus interspersed with objections from Adonis. There is no forward movement, merely a debate that results in no conclusion. The characters do not develop; they simply are what they are and speak in accord with their stylized roles. The plot does not move from event to event by means of internal causality. Indeed, the only movement, that from the debate to the final scene in which Venus comes upon Adonis's body, is occasioned more by the emotional necessities of the poem than by demands of plot.

It is tempting to see the poem, especially the debate, as a moral allegory in which Adonis represents rational control over sensual excess, while Venus represents not only passion but also the enduring love that can triumph over mutability. It is hard, however, to support this interpretation very far. Neither view prevails, and the interdeterminacy suggests that the allegory is merely another ornament, not the heart of the poem. Moreover, the tone of the speeches and the tone of the narrator's commentary do not support moral earnestness. The many puns and erotic innuendos provide a suave distance, true both to Ovid and to Elizabethan taste.

The poem is a compendium of the themes that recur in the amatory poems and sonnet sequences of the age. The arguments proposed by Venus, for example, are familiar appeals to the desire for immortality. *Carpe diem* is prominent, as is the appeal to survival through procreation, and both are themes that Shakespeare exploited in his sonnets. Similarly, Adonis's rationalistic view of sex is reminiscent of Shakespeare's Sonnet 129 and many poems by Sir Philip Sidney.

The poem is also a storehouse of the rhetorical figures and imagistic techniques of Elizabethan lyric style. Balance and antithesis, alliteration and assonance, produce a pleasing aural effect not so much to underline the meaning as to call attention to their own beauty. The imagery is sharply and brilliantly visual with bright reds and whites being the dominant, and highly conventional, colors. Images are there to embellish, not to explain, and even Adonis's fatal wound is gorgeous. The six-line stanza provides a supple medium for the gentle rhythms and sound patterns. The whole is an elegantly decorated blend of common themes into a pathetic-ironic showpiece.

"Critical Evaluation" by Edward E. Foster

Further Reading

Beauregard, David N. *"Venus and Adonis."* Shakespeare Studies 8. Edited by J. Leeds Barroll. New York: Burt Franklin, 1975. Considers critical studies of the story that range from classical interpretations of the original myth to twentieth century analyses of Shakespeare's poem.

Bullough, Geoffrey, ed. *Narrative and Dramatic Sources of Shakespeare.* New York: Columbia University Press, 1966. Part of a six-volume series of critical essays on the sources of Shakespeare's works. Included in the discussion of *Venus and Adonis* is a 1575 translation of Ovid's *Metamorphoses* by Arthur Golding.

Cheney, Patrick, ed. *The Cambridge Companion to Shakespeare's Poetry.* New York: Cambridge University Press, 2007. Includes essays discussing Shakespeare and the development of English poetry; rhetoric, style, and form in his verse; the poetry in his plays; and his poetry as viewed from a twenty-first century perspective. "*Venus and Adonis*" by Coppélia Kahn analyzes this poem.

Cousins, A. D. *Shakespeare's Sonnets and Narrative Poems.* New York: Longman, 2000. Chapter 1 focuses on *Venus and Adonis*, including discussions of the poem's narrator, Venus and metamorphosis, and Adonis the rhetorician.

Hyland, Peter. *An Introduction to Shakespeare's Poems.* New York: Palgrave Macmillan, 2003. Discusses the sources of Shakespeare's poetry. Analyzes *Venus and Adonis* and other nondramatic verse. Places Shakespeare's poetry within the context of the politics, values, and tastes of Elizabethan England, arguing that he was a skeptical voice during this socially turbulent era.

Jahn, J. D. *The Lamb of Lust: The Role of Adonis in Shakespeare's "Venus and Adonis."* Shakespeare Studies 6. Edited by J. Leeds Barroll. Dubuque, Iowa: William C. Brown, 1970. An intense study of the personality of Adonis that Shakespeare creates in his poem.

Mortimer, Anthony Robert. *Variable Passions: A Reading of Shakespeare's "Venus and Adonis."* New York: AMS Press, 2000. Detailed analysis of the poem, examining its shifts in tone, means of continuity, and inversion of gender roles. Places the poem within the context of its Ovidian source and within the continental tradition of poems about Venus and Adonis.

Muir, Kenneth. "*Venus and Adonis*: Comedy or Tragedy?" In *Shakespearean Essays*, vol. 2. Edited by Alwin Thaler and Norman Sanders. Knoxville: University of Tennessee Press, 1974. Considers how the myth of Venus and Adonis has been interpreted by various authors and how Shakespeare's audience might have interpreted the poem.

Prince, Frank Templeton. Introduction to *The Poems*, by William Shakespeare. New York: Routledge, 1990. Provides more than forty pages of introductory material in which Prince discusses the text and provides critical interpretations of the works. Includes appendixes with information about the sources of Shakespeare's poems, with particular emphasis on *Venus and Adonis*.

The Vicar of Wakefield

Author: Oliver Goldsmith (1728/1730-1774)
First published: 1766
Type of work: Novel
Type of plot: Domestic realism
Time of plot: Eighteenth century
Locale: Rural England

Principal characters:
DR. PRIMROSE, the vicar of Wakefield
DEBORAH, his wife
GEORGE, the oldest son
SOPHIA, the younger daughter
OLIVIA, the older daughter
MR. BURCHELL, in reality, Sir William Thornhill
SQUIRE THORNHILL, Dr. Primrose's landlord and Olivia's betrayer
ARABELLA WILMOT, George's fiancé

The Story:

Dr. Primrose and his wife, Deborah, are blessed with five fine children. The two daughters, Olivia and Sophia, are remarkable for their beauty. The Primrose family lives in a quiet rural community, where they enjoy both wealth and good reputation. The oldest son, George, falls in love with Arabella Wilmot, the daughter of a neighbor, and the two families make mutual preparations for the wedding. Before the wedding, however, Dr. Primrose and Miss Wilmot's father quarrel over the question of a man's remarrying after the death of his wife. Dr. Primrose stoutly upholds the doctrine of absolute monogamy. Mr. Wilmot, who is about to take his fourth wife, is insulted. The rift between the two families widens when news comes that Dr. Primrose's broker has run off with all of his money. Mr. Wilmot breaks off the wedding plans, for the vicar is now a poor man.

George departs for London to make his fortune, and the

rest of the family prepares to go to another part of the country, where Dr. Primrose finds a more modest living. On the way, they meet a man who wins the admiration of Dr. Primrose by a deed of charity to a fellow traveler. The man, Mr. Burchell, rides along with them. Suddenly, Sophia is thrown from her horse into a stream, from which Mr. Burchell is able to save her. The gratitude of Deborah assures Mr. Burchell of a warm welcome whenever he should choose to call on them.

Their new home is on the estate of wealthy Squire Thornhill, a young man known for his attentions to all the young ladies in the neighborhood. Deborah thinks that either of her daughters would make a good match for the young squire. Soon afterward, a fortunate meeting draws the squire's attention toward Olivia, and her mother's scheming makes Squire Thornhill a steady caller at the Primrose home, where Olivia blushingly protests that she thinks him both bold and rude. Mr. Burchell also calls frequently, but his interest seems to center upon Sophia, who does not deny her pleasure at his attention. Dr. Primrose, however, cannot approve of Mr. Burchell, for he lost all of his fortune and seems to live in relative poverty, which reveals an indifference to his fallen condition.

Two noble ladies from the city meet the Primrose family in their rustic retreat, and Sophia and Olivia become charmed by talk of city ways. When the women speak of their need for companions in their households, Deborah immediately suggests that Olivia and Sophia be selected. The two daughters are pleased at the thought of going to the city, despite Mr. Burchell's vigorous objections. All is set for the journey, however, when Deborah receives a letter stating that a secret informant so slandered Olivia and Sophia that the city ladies will not consider them fit companions. At first, Deborah and her husband cannot imagine who the slanderer could be. When they learn that Mr. Burchell is the informant, Dr. Primrose orders him from the house. Mr. Burchell leaves with no signs of remorse or shame.

Olivia begins to insist that Squire Thornhill's repeated visits mean that he intends to marry her. Dr. Primrose does not believe that the squire really would marry Olivia and suggests to his daughter that she consider the offer of a neighboring farmer, Mr. Williams. When the squire still fails to ask for her hand, Olivia agrees to marry the young farmer, and the wedding date is set. Four days before her wedding, Olivia runs away. With the help of Squire Thornhill, Dr. Primrose learns that Mr. Burchell carried away the girl.

Saddened by his daughter's indiscretion, the resolute father sets out to find her and to help her. On his journey, he becomes ill and lies in bed in an inn for three weeks. On his recovery, he gives up all hope of finding Olivia and starts home. On the way, he meets Arabella, who inquires about George.

Dr. Primrose assures her that George has not been heard from since he left his family to go to London. Squire Thornhill, who is courting Arabella, asks about Olivia, but the father can give him no news. Fortune brings George, impoverished and in ill luck, back to his father at that time. Pitying the bad fortune of the young boy, Squire Thornhill gives him a commission in the army and sends him away. Arabella promises to wait for her former sweetheart to make his fortune and to return to her.

Dr. Primrose starts for home once more. At a roadside inn, he finds his dear Olivia, who tells him her terrible story. The villain with whom she ran away was not Mr. Burchell. It was Squire Thornhill, who seduced her after a mock ceremony by a false priest. The squire then grew tired of her and left her. Dr. Primrose takes the girl home with him. Bad luck, however, has not forsaken the vicar. As he approaches his house, he sees it catch fire and burn to the ground. His family escapes, but all of their belongings are destroyed.

Kindly neighbors help the penniless Primroses to set up living quarters in an outbuilding on the estate. News comes that Squire Thornhill intends to marry Arabella. This report angers Dr. Primrose; to add to his indignation, Squire Thornhill comes to see him and offers to find a husband for Olivia so that she can stay near the squire. The doctor is enraged at this offer and orders him away. The squire then demands Dr. Primrose's quarterly rent payment which, since the disaster of losing his home, the vicar cannot pay.

Squire Thornhill has Dr. Primrose sent to debtors' prison. Soon after being lodged in prison, the vicar encounters his son, George, who, learning of the squire's cruelty, attacked him and is sentenced to hang for attempted murder. Dr. Primrose feels that the happiness of his life is completely shattered. Next, he learns that Sophia has been kidnapped.

Nevertheless, virtue and honesty are soon rewarded. Sophia is rescued by Mr. Burchell, who turns out to be the squire's uncle, Sir William Thornhill. With the squire's treachery exposed, the Primrose family is released from its misery. Arabella and George are reunited. Even Olivia is saved from shame, for she learns that the priest who married her to the squire was a genuine priest. Sophia marries Sir William, and Arabella marries George. Dr. Primrose looks forward to his old age with happiness and joy in the good fortune of his children. In the end, even he is rewarded for his virtue. The broker who ran away with his money is apprehended, and Dr. Primrose is once again a wealthy man.

Critical Evaluation:

Two themes dominate Oliver Goldsmith's story of domestic tragedy and joy: The first is a satiric look at the insidious workings of vanity, even on such unpretentious people as Dr. Primrose and his family; the second is the instability of fortune, which ensures that happy people must expect disaster and miserable people may expect relief.

The first theme is the more significant. As the novel's narrator, Dr. Primrose portrays himself as a man committed to intellectual pursuits and charitable actions, one who rejects the world's vanities. His self-evaluation is not inaccurate. He assigns his income to the relief of the poor (although he does so unwisely, as he learns), and he certainly commits himself to rarefied intellectual activities, although his subjects—specifically his promotion of a religious dogma of monogamy that disallows second marriages even on the death of one's spouse—are of only minor interest to the world.

What Dr. Primrose does not understand, however, is his own naïveté, and that blindness is the source of the novel's ironic humor. While Primrose tells his story through the filter of his own innocence, Goldsmith arranges that the reader will understand—or at least suspect—the things that Primrose ignores. This disparity between the narrator's limited vision and the reader's insight creates an ironic point of view that allows the reader to laugh at Dr. Primrose even while sympathizing with him.

The irony of Primrose's limited self-understanding colors much of what he does. He fails to imagine that his family might come to need the income he signs over to charity. He fails to imagine that financial advisers might be dishonest. Importantly, he fails to recognize the difference between the honest values of Mr. Burchell and the false values of the attractive Squire Thornhill and his flashy companions.

As a result of the vicar's limited understanding of the world, his responses to it are frequently wrong. They are often the result of his own vanity, particularly of his intellectual capabilities, which are not nearly so penetrating as he imagines. These limitations lead him to various errors. His intense commitment to the minor doctrine of monogamy leads him to offend his son George's future father-in-law and thus to spoil the prospects for his son's marriage. His reverence for the classics and the limitations of his ability in disputation lead him to confuse the flimflam of the deceitful Jenkinson for real learning, again with disastrous results for his family.

It would be wrong simply to dismiss Primrose as a fool, however, for Goldsmith underscores that Primrose's understanding may be limited, but his heart is golden. Primrose is quick to offer aid to those who need it; he is quick to forgive Olivia in her disgrace and devastated at the news of her death; he is genuinely devoted to his family and finds their presence enough to give him courage even in debtors' prison. Gold-

smith never suggests that shrewdness is to be preferred to love as a value by which to live.

Primrose's innocence and his vanities are shared by his family; they, too, mistake things that glitter for true gold. No one in the family seems able to see beyond the glamorous clothes and pretentious talk of the town ladies whom Thornhill brings to the house. No one recognizes the virtue of Burchell's offering unpopular opinions about the family's actions. No one suspects that his damning letter might be interpreted as a condemnation of the town ladies rather than of the Primrose daughters. Olivia is quick to be attracted to Thornhill, even though she has every reason to believe in his reputation as a rake.

Olivia's situation demands closer examination. Her elopement with Thornhill on his false promises of marriage, his betrayal of her with what seems to be a fraudulent wedding ceremony, and her subsequent decline because of her shame—all are common elements of eighteenth and early nineteenth century fiction. Similar events occur in Samuel Richardson's *Pamela* (1740-1741) and *Clarissa* (1747-1748), and in Jane Austen's *Pride and Prejudice* (1813). The values of the age demanded that respectable women be virgins when they married, and custom assumed that any woman who eloped surely was involved in sexual relations with her partner. The rakehell young man who would go to any lengths to seduce women who attracted him—even arranging false marriages—is another conventional character in fiction of the period. Goldsmith never challenges these conventions; like the Primroses, he assumes that marriage, even to one who proves himself to be a scoundrel, is a satisfactory solution to Olivia's disgrace.

The eighteenth century saw a vogue for sentimental fiction, and *The Vicar of Wakefield* is an example of that fashion. It is characterized by the idealized pictures of rural family life that appear throughout this novel as well as in the pathos of the disasters that befall Primrose and his family. The family's lost income, the fire, the disgraced daughter, Primrose's unjust imprisonment, all exemplify the taste of the age for exercising one's tender emotions. Olivia's sad song, which asserts that "when lovely woman stoops to folly" the only fate appropriate to her is to die, offers another example of this sentimentality. That such fiction is not intended to be realistic can be seen from this novel's use of coincidences and disguise.

Through all the family's disasters, however, Dr. Primrose remains faithful in his belief that better things are surely in store for them all, just as he continues to assert that the loving presence of his family can make up for any losses. Along with its gentle humor, this theme must be the source of much of this novel's appeal. For all of their follies, the Primrose family clings to love as a main strength for enduring adversity, feeling certain that the fortunes of the miserable must surely rise if they only endure.

"Critical Evaluation" by Ann D. Garbett

Further Reading

Adelstein, Michael E. "Duality of Theme in *The Vicar of Wakefield*." *College English* 22 (February, 1961): 315-321. Argues that Goldsmith changed his theme in the course of writing this novel, shifting from the theme of providence to that of fortitude, thus changing Dr. Primrose from an innocent simpleton to a resolute hero.

Bellamy, Liz. *Commerce, Morality, and the Eighteenth-Century Novel*. New York: Cambridge University Press, 1998. Describes how eighteenth century economic discourse was reflected in the fiction of that period, including *The Vicar of Wakefield* and other sentimental novels.

Church, Richard. *The Growth of the English Novel*. New York: Barnes & Noble, 1961. Analyzes the novel and sees its tone as characteristic of the national style, praising particularly the ease of Goldsmith's writing.

Harkin, Maureen. "Goldsmith on Authorship in *The Vicar of Wakefield*." *Eighteenth Century Fiction* 14, no. 3/4 (April-July, 2002): 325. An analysis of the novel focusing on what Harkin describes as Goldsmith's "uncertainties about what the character and possibilities of his age are, especially for the writer and literary intellectual."

Jeffares, A. Norman. *Oliver Goldsmith*. London: Longmans, Green, 1965. Discusses how the novel's theme of Primrose's submission to adversity joins with Goldsmith's gentle irony, which emerges from the straight-faced style of the vicar-narrator. Notes the similarity between Goldsmith's vicar and Henry Fielding's Parson Adams.

Nünning, Vera. "Unreliable Narration and the Historical Variability of Values and Norms: *The Vicar of Wakefield* as a Test Case of a Cultural-Historical Narratology." *Style* 38, no. 2 (Summer, 2004): 236-252. Focuses on what Nünning maintains is the "unreliable narration" in the novel, discussing the questions the book raises about unreliability.

Phelps, Gilbert. *A Reader's Guide to Fifty British Novels, 1600-1900*. New York: Barnes & Noble, 1979. Offers a brief biography, a summary of the novel's plot, and a section of critical commentary. Faults the novel's proportions but praises its clarity of style.

Skinner, Gillian. *Sensibility and Economics in the Novel, 1740-1800: The Price of a Tear*. New York: St. Martin's Press, 1999. Skinner contradicts the traditional belief that *The Vicar of Wakefield* and other eighteenth century sentimental novels are a "feminine" genre, maintaining that these books actively engage in contemporary economic and political debates.

Victory
An Island Tale

Author: Joseph Conrad (1857-1924)
First published: 1915
Type of work: Novel
Type of plot: Psychological realism
Time of plot: Early twentieth century
Locale: East Indies

Principal characters:
AXEL HEYST, an idealist
LENA, a woman whom Axel befriends
MR. SCHOMBERG, a hotel owner
MR. JONES and MARTIN RICARDO, gamblers
PEDRO, their servant
DAVIDSON, a sea captain
WANG, Heyst's servant

The Story:

After the Tropical Belt Coal Company goes into liquidation, Axel Heyst continues to live at the No. 1 coaling station on Samburan. Strange in his manners and desires, he is a legend among the islanders; they call him a Utopist. The coal company came into existence after Heyst met an Englishman named Morrison in a Portuguese seaport, where the man was about to lose his trading ship, *Capricorn*, because of an unpaid debt. Heyst was sympathetic and offered him a loan. Because Heyst was anxious to keep his generosity a secret and Morrison eager to conceal his shaky finances, the two men pledged secrecy, with the understanding that Heyst would thereafter have a share of the *Capricorn*'s shipping business.

Schomberg, the owner of a hotel in Sourabaya, heard of the partnership and discovered that Heyst maintained some kind of hold over Morrison. Morrison established the coal company and then died in England. After that, Schomberg, who hated Heyst, constructed a mysterious kind of villainy around him and was gleeful when the coal company liquidated.

After Heyst retires from the human society of the islands, Davidson, a ship's captain, comes upon him living alone on Samburan. Worrying over Heyst's welfare, Davidson adopts the habit of sailing ten miles out of his way around the north side of Samburan in case Heyst is in need of aid. At one point, Davidson brings Heyst to Sourabaya, where he stays at Schomberg's hotel. Later, Davidson hears bits of a story that Heyst ran off with a girl who was at the hotel with a troupe of entertainers. He is baffled that the shy, quiet Heyst would take a girl back to Samburan with him. Mrs. Schomberg pities the girl and helps Heyst escape with her. The affair causes quite a bit of gossip on the island because it concerns Heyst.

When Heyst came to the hotel, he was unaware of Schomberg's hatred. The entertainers were not very attractive to Heyst's fastidious mind, but one girl wearing white muslin seemed younger than the others. Noticing her distress at being ordered to join a guest at a table, Heyst was prompted by the same instinct that led him to help Morrison. He invited the girl to sit with him. The girl, Lena, told Heyst about herself. While she was growing up in England, her father taught her to play the violin. After his death, she joined the group of entertainers with whom she now worked. Schomberg had been stalking her ever since the troupe came to the hotel. The contrast between Heyst and the other men she met was enough to cause the girl to be attracted to her new friend, and she welcomed his promise of help. After Heyst took Lena away, Schomberg's hatred was tremendous.

Three strangers then come to Schomberg's hotel: Mr. Jones, Martin Ricardo, and a beastlike, hairy creature whom they call Pedro. Before long, these men transform Schomberg's hotel into a professional gambling house. Schomberg's obsession for Lena is increased by his belief that, if he has her at his side, he can rid his hotel of the gamblers. One afternoon, Ricardo tells Schomberg that he was employed on a yacht where he was first attracted by Jones's polished manners. The two stole the captain's cash box and jumped ship. Later, Pedro became attached to them. Schomberg decides that these thieves might leave his hotel if he can arouse their greed by the prospect of richer plunder. He offhandedly tells the men of Heyst's alleged wealth and mentions that Heyst lives on a lonely island with a girl and a hoard of money.

Together, Ricardo and Schomberg begin to plan their pillage of the island on which Heyst lives.

On his island, Heyst lives with his Chinese servant, Wang, until Lena joins him. She tells him that he saved her from more than misery and despair. Heyst tells her the story of his own background. His father was a cynical, domineering man whom he disliked. After his death, Heyst drifts, searching for some meaning in life, a meaning never glimpsed until he meets Lena.

One evening, Wang announces that he saw a boat drifting offshore; Heyst goes to investigate. He discovers Ricardo, Jones, and the beastlike Pedro perishing of thirst in a boat moored beside a small jetty. Heyst helps the men to shore and takes them to an abandoned bungalow for temporary quarters. That night, Heyst finds that his gun is missing from his desk; Wang, frightened, took it. Meanwhile, Ricardo and Jones speculate about locating Heyst's money.

Early in the morning, Ricardo steals into Heyst's bungalow and sees Lena combing her hair. He jumps at her hungrily, but she is able to defend herself. When the struggle is over and the repulsed man sees that she raises no outcry, his admiration for her increases. She asks him what the men want on the island. Surprised that they came for money that she knows Heyst does not possess, she is determined to protect Heyst from Schomberg's evil plan. She loves Heyst and knows she can repay his kindness by leading Ricardo and his partners on to their destruction.

Observing Ricardo's attack on Lena, Wang decides to withdraw from this confusion of white people's affairs; he flees to the forest. When Heyst reports the loss of his servant to Jones and Ricardo, they offer him the service of Pedro. Because their manner makes it impossible for him to refuse, Lena and Heyst know that they are lost. Davidson will not sail past the island for three more weeks. Their only weapon was stolen, and they are left defenseless. When Heyst mentions their helpless position without a weapon of defense, Lena recalls that, during their scuffle, she glimpsed the knife Ricardo wears under his trouser leg.

That night, Ricardo comes to the bungalow for dinner with Heyst and Lena. During the evening, Ricardo indicates that Jones wants Heyst to visit him. Before he leaves, Heyst insists that Pedro be sent out of the way, and Ricardo orders the brute to go down to the jetty. After Heyst leaves, Lena allows Ricardo to make love to her so that she can take possession of his knife. Meanwhile, Heyst mentions Lena's presence to Jones. Jones, who suffers a pathological hatred for women, did not even know of Lena's existence. Heyst convinces him that Schomberg lied about the existence of a cache of money on the island to get rid of the gamblers and to inflict revenge upon Heyst, a revenge that Schomberg is too cowardly to inflict himself. Enraged by what he considers a conspiracy on the part of Ricardo and Schomberg, Jones suggests that they go to Heyst's bungalow.

Meanwhile, Lena takes Ricardo's knife. As the two men enter the bungalow, Jones fires over Heyst's shoulder, and the bullet pierces Lena's breast. Ricardo springs through the doorway. Jones follows his partner outside and shoots him in the darkness. Heyst carries Lena to the bed, and, as she lies there, deathly pale in the candlelight, she demands the knife, her symbol of victory. She dies as Heyst takes her in his arms, speaking, for the first time, words that come from the depths of his heart.

Critical Evaluation:

It is tempting but potentially incorrect to see *Victory* as a melodramatic morality play in which good battles evil and love wins in the end. For one thing, all the kind and compassionate characters are killed by story's end. If death is "the wages of sin," then Joseph Conrad seems to be suggesting that death is the wages of virtue and loyalty as well—hardly the makings of a very convincing morality play. Conrad is a master of relating ambiguous motives and moral choices. In other stories, such as *Heart of Darkness* (1899), *Lord Jim* (1900), *The Secret Agent* (1907), and *The Secret Sharer* (1910), the propriety of an action is all too often based on one's point of view, and Conrad's narrative techniques frequently make the moral parameters of an event very unclear.

In *Victory*, for example, much of Heyst's story is told by, or at least seen through, the eyes of Davidson. This distancing technique, whereby one slowly learns the truth of a story, makes it impossible to read *Victory* as a simple commentary on love, embodied in Lena and represented by the otherwise ineffectual Heyst. These two are present in a world that is dominated by scoundrels such as Ricardo and Schomberg, brutes such as Pedro, and irredeemably sinister figures such as "plain Mr. Jones." A sentimental and allegorical reading will render meaning, but that meaning will not admit the moral complexities that Conrad builds into the novel through the characterization of his protagonist, Axel Heyst.

Those complexities are best represented in Heyst's relationship not so much with his father as with his father's ideas. The younger Heyst has been "passing through life without suffering . . . invulnerable because elusive," having made himself strictly a spectator, an astute but aloof observer of the human scene. Surely, this is Conrad's Heyst, and, despite a critical tradition to the contrary, this Heyst is no Christ figure; if anything, he is more of an Antichrist, a person convinced after the fiasco of his involvement with Morrison that

"all action is bound to be harmful . . . devilish. That is why this world is evil upon the whole." He will tell the stunned Davidson, who could never fathom the real reason behind Heyst's beliefs, "now I have done with observation, too."

When Conrad reveals how much the elder Heyst's ideas shaped his son, his point becomes clear. Heyst's father had been "the most uneasy soul that civilization had ever fashioned to its ends of disillusion and regret . . . unhappy in a way unknown to mediocre souls," the narrator reveals early on, and Heyst himself will later confess to Lena, "after listening to him, I could not take my soul down into the street to fight there. I started off to wander about, an independent spectator—if that is possible." This is the very point Conrad is making; this isolated observation is not possible. Heyst, self-described as "a man of universal scorn and unbelief," is, rather than a positive foil to Jones's evil, very much the same kind of character as Jones, for both imagine that there is no worthwhile human action. The only difference is, instead of taking advantage of people as Jones and his sort do, Heyst removes himself from all human company, too scornful, disdainful, and disillusioned to be bothered—but too much a gentleman to say so.

It is no more possible, however, for Heyst to avoid the dilemma of making a moral choice than it is for anyone else, and it is not a melodramatic touch on Conrad's part, given the extent to which he establishes and exposes Heyst's philosophical underpinnings, to present love as the force that draws Heyst not only out of his isolation but also out of his inaction as well. That the choice ends tragically is hardly proof that Heyst's earlier detached cynicism is the more correct attitude. The real lesson that he learns from the experience, as Davidson later reports, is "woe to the man whose heart has not learned while young to hope, to love—and to put its trust in life!" The tragedy for Heyst is that he learns this too late. Because this bold statement of the novel's theme comes at the end of Conrad's long process of meticulously working out the details of this philosophical and ethical struggle, he earns the right to be so bold.

Victory is not a melodrama, or a morality play, or a psychological thriller, but it is, in the best sense of the phrase, a philosophical novel that explores the theme of human moral involvement in an indifferent, if not outrightly absurd, universe. Conrad achieves this in an entertainingly suspenseful story that does not preach but does state its case in clear and obvious terms expressing Conrad's view that action is always morally ambiguous, even though human beings are always called upon to act.

"Critical Evaluation" by Russell Elliott Murphy

Further Reading

Gillon, Adam. *The Eternal Solitary: A Study of Joseph Conrad*. New York: Bookman, 1960. Explores the key role that isolation played in Conrad's life and work. Presents *Victory* as a melodrama that effectively discusses, in symbolic terms, the nature of solitude and its consequences.

Johnson, Bruce. *Conrad's Models of Mind*. Minneapolis: University of Minnesota Press, 1971. Explores Conrad's continual readjustment of his fictions to fit changing philosophical models of human behavior and motivation. Discusses the way *Victory* reassesses the individual's need for human solidarity and community.

Meyers, Jeffrey. *Joseph Conrad: A Biography*. New York: Charles Scribner's Sons, 1991. A highly readable critical biography. Discusses *Victory* as Conrad's most misunderstood, underrated, and controversial novel, its theme being the failure of love in an idyllic setting.

Moser, Thomas. "Conrad's 'Later Affirmation.'" In *Conrad: A Collection of Critical Essays*, edited by Marvin Mudrick. Englewood Cliffs, N.J.: Prentice-Hall, 1966. Explores the role chance plays in Conrad's later novels, particularly *Victory*, and how it makes the novels' apparent affirmations more evasive.

Peters, John G. *The Cambridge Introduction to Joseph Conrad*. New York: Cambridge University Press, 2006. An introductory overview of Conrad, with information on his life, all of his works, and his critical reception.

Robert, Andrew Michael. *Conrad and Masculinity*. New York: St. Martin's Press, 2000. Uses modern theories about masculinity to analyze Conrad's work and explore the relationship of masculinity to imperialism and modernity. *Victory* is discussed in the chapter entitled "Vision and the Economies of Empire and Masculinity: *Victory*."

Sherry, Norman, ed. *Conrad: The Critical Heritage*. Boston: Routledge & Kegan Paul, 1973. An impressive collection of responses to Conrad's work at the time it first appeared. The section devoted to *Victory* gives insight into Conrad's critical reputation and the novel's reception in the midst of World War I.

Stape, J. H., ed. *The Cambridge Companion to Joseph Conrad*. New York: Cambridge University Press, 1996. Collection of essays discussing Conrad's life and analyzing his work, including discussions of the Conradian narrative, Conrad and imperialism, Conrad and modernism, and Conrad's literary influence. The many references to *Victory* are listed in the index.

A View from the Bridge

Author: Arthur Miller (1915-2005)
First produced: 1955, as a one-act play (first published, 1955); 1956, as a two-act play (first published, 1957)
Type of work: Drama
Type of plot: Tragedy and psychological realism
Time of plot: Early 1950's
Locale: Brooklyn, New York

Principal characters:
EDDIE CARBONE, a longshoreman
BEATRICE CARBONE, his wife
CATHERINE, his seventeen-year-old niece
RODOLPHO, Beatrice's cousin, an illegal immigrant from Italy
MARCO, Rodolpho's older brother, also an illegal immigrant
LOUIS, a longshoreman
MIKE, a longshoreman
ALFIERI, a lawyer
MR. LIPARI, a neighbor of the Carbones
MRS. LIPARI, his wife
TWO IMMIGRATION OFFICERS
TWO "SUBMARINES," illegal immigrants

The Story:

Eddie, a middle-aged longshoreman, works the docks in the Red Hook district of Brooklyn in the mid-1950's. Alfieri, a first-generation Italian immigrant, practices law in the neighborhood. Eddie lives with his wife Beatrice and his seventeen-year-old niece Catherine. Both have open affection for Eddie.

It becomes almost immediately clear that the affection between Eddie and his niece may be unhealthy, planting the seeds for discontent. This relationship is quickly demonstrated when Catherine decides to leave secretarial school early in order to accept a lucrative job, one that Eddie fears will expose her to untrustworthy men. His desire at first appears to be to protect her. It quickly becomes clear, however, that Eddie has unarticulated and perhaps unconscious desires to possess Catherine himself. Eddie's wife, Beatrice, sees the situation clearly, but she lacks the ability to confront her husband with her concerns. Instead, she becomes Catherine's primary supporter, urging her to take the job, to accept her emerging maturity, and to enter the world as an adult. All these urgings are made in spite of Eddie and his adamant protestations to the contrary.

Beatrice's two cousins, Marco and Rodolpho, are on their way to Brooklyn from Italy, and they plan to stay in the Carbone apartment until better accommodations can be arranged. They arrive, two illegal immigrants, and their impact on the Carbone household is felt immediately. Eddie experiences an instant dislike for Rodolpho, who sings in a high tenor voice and welcomes traditionally female tasks. In addition, Rodolpho is blond, evoking tales of Danes who came to Italy in the ancient past and left their legacy in the form of pale hair and skin. To make matters worse, the immigrant, who has difficulties at work with the other longshoremen because he is too effeminate, is attracted to Catherine, and she returns his feelings.

In Eddie's assessment, something is wrong with Rodolpho. Eddie's desire for his niece is exacerbated by her growing affection for her second cousin. Eddie visits Alfieri, the lawyer, seeking some legal protection for his family. Eddie believes that Rodolpho is after his niece for one reason only: to gain American citizenship through marriage. Alfieri relates to Eddie that the only legal matter at hand is the fact that Rodolpho and his brother Marco are in the country illegally. To report the two to the immigration office may be the legal recourse, but, as Eddie knows, it is not the moral choice. It would violate the values of Italian American culture to take such a step.

As a result, Eddie chooses to prove to his niece how ineffectual Rodolpho is as a man. After a tense dinner, Eddie challenges the younger man to a boxing match that turns instead into a lesson, humiliating Rodolpho. Marco, the silent one, sees what is happening to his brother and challenges Eddie to a test of strength. In the test that follows, Eddie proves unable to lift a chair from the floor by the lower part of the chair's leg. Marco then proceeds not only to lift the chair but also to raise it over his head, revealing himself as a hidden threat. The stage is thus set for a confrontation between the two strong and viral men.

Rodolpho and Catherine are in the apartment alone. He responds to her questions, which have been motivated by Eddie's distrust, with respect and honor. She believes and accepts him, and they retire to the bedroom. An inebriated Eddie appears on the scene, as Rodolpho emerges from the bedroom. In outrage, the drunken Eddie orders the young man out of his home. Catherine responds that if Rodolpho leaves, she will leave as well. Eddie grabs his niece and kisses her on the mouth, his deeply hidden need for possession coming to the fore. When Rodolpho protests, Eddie, desperate to prove the man's lack of manliness, kisses his adversary on the mouth as well. As a result of this confrontation, the two immigrants move into another apartment in the same complex, and Rodolpho and Catherine set the date for their marriage. In desperation, Eddie places the call to the immigration office, an act he soon comes to regret.

Rodolpho and Marco are taken into custody, along with two other illegal immigrants, members of the Lipari family. All of them know that it was Eddie who served as informant, even though he protests his innocence vehemently. As Marco is being led away by the officers, he confronts Eddie with his charges of treachery and spits in his face in front of Eddie's neighbors and family. Alfieri arranges for the brothers to be released on bail with the agreement that Marco will stay away from Eddie.

The marriage of Rodolpho and Catherine is set. Eddie refuses to attend the ceremony and demands that Beatrice do the same: If she goes to the wedding, Eddie declares, she is not to return home. Rodolpho appears and strives to make amends. He accepts the fact that he has inadvertently been the cause of the problems and asks Eddie for forgiveness. Eddie does not want apologies; he wants his reputation back. When Marco arrives to collect his brother for the wedding, a fight breaks out. Eddie is no match for the younger, stronger man, and, in desperation, he pulls a knife. Marco succeeds in turning the knife against Eddie, who is subsequently killed. All the final actions occur in front of the entire neighborhood, as the spectators become a silent chorus and Alfieri serves as spokesperson for all as he delivers the final monologue, bringing the tragic tale to a close.

Critical Evaluation:

Arthur Miller modeled *A View from the Bridge* after Greek tragedy: He made the lawyer, Alfieri, the leader of a dramatic chorus, mimicking the ancient Greek dramas of Sophocles and Euripides. As a result, it is Alfieri's view that defines the action of the play and its unfolding. He remains the play's narrator throughout, even as he relates scenes to which he was not a witness, and he warns the audience from the beginning that he is powerless to divert the action from its anticipated bloody course. In addition to the chorus, the play incorporates a classical Greek temporal structure: The narrative unfolds at an unusually rapid pace within the conventions of mid-twentieth century American drama. It incorporates few frills; instead, the action of the play is rapid and unrelenting.

Much has been written about the impact upon Miller of the anticommunist witch hunt led by Senator Joseph McCarthy and the hearings conducted by the House Committee on Un-American Activities (also known as HUAC). It is well known that Miller was responding to these events when he wrote *The Crucible* (pr., pb. 1953), which allegorized the hunt for communists in its tale of the witch trials conducted in Massachusetts in the seventeenth century. It could be argued, however, that *A View from the Bridge* was an even more important play for Miller in his quest to understand and respond to McCarthyism. In fact, Miller used the character of Eddie Carbone as a reference in his statements to HUAC when he was called to testify and name associates known to him to be communists. Unlike the central character of his drama, Miller did not point his finger at anyone, and he consequently remained on the high moral ground that Eddie Carbone forfeits by his actions in the play.

Miller notes in his writings about *A View from the Bridge* that he had been told a story about a longshoreman who turned two illegal Italian immigrants into the authorities and about the impact that act had on the surrounding community. He states that the shape of the story reminded him of a Greek myth, but he was unable to find any similar tale in ancient sources. Regardless, he decided to create an American myth using many of the structural devices found in the works of the Greek masters. As is true of the chorus in *Oidipous Tyrannos* (c. 429 B.C.E.; *Oedipus Tyrannus*, 1715), Miller's chorus (represented by Alfieri backed by the residents of the Red Hood area) can only report what is happening; it cannot change the course of events. Alfieri even states near the end of act 1 that he can see exactly what is going to happen, but he is powerless to influence matters. True to Greek structure, what happens must happen; there is no denying it. When deeply felt passions are in play and out of control, horrible things will emerge.

Miller originally titled the work, which began as a one-act play, *An Italian Tragedy*. He writes in *Echoes Down the Corridor: Collected Essays, 1947-2000* (2000) of encountering the phrase "Where is Pete Panto" etched on the Brooklyn Bridge in the early 1950's. He became obsessed with the story of Panto, a strong voice against union corruption who mysteriously disappeared. With the aid of his friend, stage and film director Elia Kazan, Miller researched the story and wrote a screenplay based on it called *The Hook*. The work was considered too inflammatory for the times, however, and was denied production. In a way, *A View from the Bridge* is Miller's return, if not to Panto and union discontent, then to the Red Hook area and the lifestyle he had researched. When it was produced on Broadway in 1955 along with *A Memory of Two Mondays* (pr., pb. 1955), it was not well received. It was seen as being too close to the McCarthy era and the sensitive matters that were under scrutiny at that time. It was not until ten years later, as a full-length play, that the work found an American audience, this time produced Off-Broadway with a young Robert Duvall in the central role.

It seems that Miller was unable to avoid controversy. He sought to stage a production of *A View from the Bridge* in London in 1956, directed by Peter Brook. The Lord Chamberlain's Office, which had to approve all plays before they could be produced in Great Britain, declared that the play's insinuations of homosexuality were too blatant and refused to approve the production. To circumvent the decision, Brook moved the production to a private club, and Miller's important play finally achieved its most impactful hearing. It was Brook who encouraged Miller to expand the work to two acts. In London, theater-goers were not concerned with un-American activities, and, as a result, the tragedy was viewed, accepted, and admired for its theatrical merits. It is the two-act version of the play that has survived and become one of Miller's most important contributions to Western drama.

Kenneth Robbins

Further Reading

Brater, Enoch, ed. *Arthur Miller's America: Theater and Culture in a Time of Change.* Ann Arbor: University of Michigan Press, 2005. Contains a valuable section on *A View from the Bridge* and its place within the culture of its development.

Epstein, Arthur D. "A Look at *A View from the Bridge.*" In *Critical Essays on Arthur Miller*, edited by James J. Martine. Boston: G. K. Hall, 1979. Provides valuable insight into the play, with emphasis on characterization.

Miller, Arthur. *Arthur Miller: Eight Plays.* Garden City, N.Y.: Nelson Doubleday, 1981. This collection contains, among seven other works, *A View from the Bridge*, as well as a valuable introduction by the author that addresses many aspects of his dramaturgy.

_____. *Echoes Down the Corridor.* New York: Viking

Press, 2000. In his second autobiography, Miller offers insights into his thinking as he approached the writing of such dramas as *A View from the Bridge*.

_____. *The Theater Essays of Arthur Miller*. Edited by Robert A. Martin. New York: Viking Press, 1978. This collection contains many of Miller's writings on the theater in general, most notably "On Social Plays," an essay that clearly identifies the author's commitment to works of social importance.

Otten, Terry. *The Temptation of Innocence in the Dramas of Arthur Miller*. Columbia: University of Missouri Press, 2002. Provides insights into the world of Miller's dramatic works, exploring particularly the playwright's representations of innocence and its tragic fall.

View with a Grain of Sand

Author: Wisława Szymborska (1923-   )
First published: "Widek z ziarnkiem piasku," 1986 (English translation, 1995, in *View with a Grain of Sand: Selected Poems*)
Type of work: Poetry

Wisława Szymborska's "View with a Grain of Sand" is a thirty-seven-line metaphysical and existential poem comprising seven irregular stanzas that vary between four and seven lines. The poem has no regular meter or rhyme scheme. Poetic meaning often does not survive translation, given that it is difficult to translate the rhythms, rhyme, tone, idioms, and puns created in another language. However, because Szymborska writes with clear, straightforward language, English translations of her poetry tend to be faithful to the original.

The poem is told from the point of view of an anonymous speaker using the familiar and inclusive "we" and "our" and "us." The reader and speaker are experiencing the same scene together.

As with most of Szymborska's poems, "View with a Grain of Sand" examines and undermines common, everyday perceptions. Szymborska looks at the ordinary and taken for granted and shows how they are astonishing as well. She embraces the Pascalian notion of human consciousness—that consciousness is what defines humans and separates humans from not only the inanimate universe but also other life forms. As Blaise Pascal's universe remains "unaware," so does that of Szymborska. All awareness lies with the human observer. In Pascal's view of consciousness, dignity and higher nobility are found in this human awareness.

The poem begins with a falling grain of sand, echoing William Blake's "Auguries of Innocence" (wr. 1803; pb. 1863), which also famously begins with a grain of sand.

Here, Blake is showing how something seemingly insignificant can actually be infinite, and that the unimportant can be more significant than what is normally considered important or significant. While Szymborska agrees with Blake—that nothing is simply ordinary—she examines the ordinary from the perspective of human perception and expression. One might look at that grain of sand as Blake does, and see a "world" in it, but Szymborska insists that perception is just an illusion. The grain of sand does not "know" that it is this thing called sand: It does not need a name and can exist without "knowing" it has a name. The grain of sand, also, does not know whether it is falling or motionless, or that it is "somewhere." Naming and placing are human conventions—they mean nothing to an inanimate object and do not affect its existence. It does not care, because it does not know to care.

The poem continues as the speaker sees the grain of sand falling (unknowingly) upon a windowsill. Through the window the speaker has a wonderful view of a nearby lake. However, the view does not know it is a view. It is a wonderful view only to a human observer. Next comes a description of four of the five human senses—sight ("colorless, shapeless"), hearing ("soundless"), smell ("odorless"), and touch ("pain"). The view from the window exists without feeling; hence, it exists without pain. Singling out pain here is deliberate, for if Szymborska had said, for example, that the view does not know its own "beauty" and exists "joylessly," readers simply might have felt sorry for the view. That it exists painlessly, instead, implies that there could be an upside to not having awareness. The line reminds readers that perceived pain is actually an illusion, formed by consciousness creating its own awareness.

Next, the speaker contemplates the lake itself. The lake also does not know it exists as a particular, unique thing. It does not know it has dimensions, that it is wet, or that its waves make sounds. All the defining properties assigned to the lake by humans have no meaning to the lake itself; they only have meaning to the human mind. Likewise, the sky above is inherently "skyless"; there is no sky for the lake. The speaker discusses how in the skyless sky the sun does not really set; it is human perception that sees a setting sun. The skyless sky, too, does not knowingly hide behind unaware clouds, and the wind blows with no consciousness of its blowing.

Szymborska shows that the metaphors humans apply to inanimate objects can be misleading. This is even truer when applied to intangible things such as time. "One second" is an arbitrary unit of time, created by humans. Time has no awareness of its own passing; it has no "inner" units of measurement. "Time," too, is often spoken of in anthropomorphic terms. However, those terms are merely human creations. Time is not a conscious being; that it "rushes by," for example, is only perceived by humans.

One reason for Szymborska's influence and popularity is her ability to tackle existential puzzles masterfully in concise, straightforward, and accessible language. In "View with a Grain of Sand," the puzzle she examines is human perception and communication, especially the making of metaphors. Metaphors are central to reasoning, and essential to the language of poetry.

David Michael Merchant

Further Reading

Baranczak, Stanisław. "The Szymborska Phenomenon." *Salmagundi*, no. 103 (Summer, 1994): 252-265. Baranczak, who translated "View with a Grain of Sand" into English, discusses the difficulties of translation, as well as Szymborska's skillful use of language, the questioning nature of her poems, and her popularity as a poet.

Bojanowska, Edyta M. "Wisława Szymborska: Naturalist and Humanist." *Slavic and East European Journal* 41, no. 2 (Summer, 1997): 199-223. Examines Szymborska's views of nature and humankind, including humankind's place in nature. Looks at the four major themes found in her nature poems: consciousness, perfection, evolution, and death. Discusses "View with a Grain of Sand."

Carpenter, Bogdana. "Wisława Szymborska and the Importance of the Unimportant." *World Literature Today* 71, no. 1 (Winter, 1997): 8-12. This brief article examines Szymborska's belief in the significance of the common and the everyday. Also looks at Szymborska's popularity.

Carpenter, John R. "Three Polish Poets, Two Nobel Prizes." *Kenyon Review* 20, no. 1 (Winter, 1998): 153-156. A brief article that examines themes in Szymborska's poetry. Also reviews the different English translations of her poetry.

Karasek, Krzysztof. "Mozartian Joy: The Poetry of Wisława Szymborska." In *The Mature Laurel: Essays on Modern Polish Poetry*, edited by Adam Czerniawski. Chester Springs, Pa.: Seren Books/Dufour, 1991. In this collection of essays on modern Polish poetry, Karasek's essay explores how each of Szymborska's poems makes up an autonomous world. Includes a short discussion of "View with a Grain of Sand."

Kostkawska, Justyna. "'To Persistently Not Know Something Important.'" *Feminist Theory* 5, no. 2 (2004): 185-203. Argues that Szymborska's poetic concerns for the ordinary, the unknown, the particular, and the insignificant are common to the practice of feminist science, which also, like Szymborska, values questioning and process over absolute knowledge and finality.

Szymborska, Wisława. "I Don't Know: The 1996 Nobel Lecture." *World Literature Today* 71, no. 1 (Winter, 1997): 5-7. The transcript of Szymborska's lecture upon receiving the 1996 Nobel Prize in Literature. She discusses her views of poets and poetry.

Vile Bodies

Author: Evelyn Waugh (1903-1966)
First published: 1930
Type of work: Novel
Type of plot: Satire
Time of plot: Between World War I and World War II
Locale: England

Principal characters:
ADAM FENWICK-SYMES, a young writer
NINA BLOUNT, his fiancé
COLONEL BLOUNT, her eccentric father
AGATHA RUNCIBLE, one of the Bright Young People
MILES MALPRACTICE, another of the Bright Young People
LOTTIE CRUMP, the proprietor of Shepheard's Hotel
CAPTAIN EDDY (GINGER) LITTLEJOHN, Nina's beloved
MRS. MELROSE APE, a female evangelist
FATHER ROTHSCHILD, a Jesuit
A DRUNKEN MAJOR

The Story:

During the rough English Channel crossing, almost everyone is in some stage of seasickness. Some become tipsy and take to their berths. The Bright Young People, led by Agatha Runcible and effeminate Miles Malpractice, strap themselves with sticking plaster and hope for the best. A few hardy souls gather in the smoking room where Mrs. Melrose Ape, a famous female evangelist traveling with her troupe of singing angels, bullies them into singing hymns. Father Rothschild, S.J., contemplates the sufferings of the saints.

Adam Fenwick-Symes, a young writer, is hurrying home to marry Nina Blount. To his dismay, the Dover customs authorities confiscate and burn the manuscript of the autobiography he wrote while in Paris. Almost as bad is the case of Agatha, who is stripped and searched after being mistaken for a notorious jewel smuggler.

In London, Adam's publisher offers him a contract to write a novel, but with no advance in royalties. With only ten shillings to his name, Adam wonders how he is going to get married. Luckily, he is staying at Shepheard's Hotel. Lottie Crump, the proprietress, who bullies kings and advises members of Parliament, is careless about bills if she likes her guests. Most of her guests are drunk. One young man makes a foolish bet with Adam and loses a thousand pounds. Adam calls Nina and tells her they can get married immediately, but before he leaves the hotel a drunken major persuades him to put the money on the horse, Indian Runner, in the November Handicap. Then the major disappears, and Adam is forced to call Nina again and tell her that their marriage will be postponed.

Adam and Nina go to Archie Schwert's costume party. Finding the affair dull, some of the Bright Young People go off to Lottie's for a drink. Judge Skimp, an American guest, is entertaining. One young woman, who fell while swinging on a chandelier, dies, despite the champagne used to bathe her forehead.

The party is about to break up when Miss Brown invites the group to her house, which happens to be No. 10 Downing Street, for her father is Sir James Brown, the prime minister. Agatha stays all night because she had forgotten the key to her own house. The next morning, still in her Hawaiian grass skirt, she finds reporters and photographers waiting when she goes out the front door. Reports of midnight orgies at No. 10 Downing Street cause a change of government, and Mr. Outrage, whose dreams are filled with visions of nude Japanese ladies, becomes the new prime minister.

On Nina's advice, Adam calls on Colonel Blount to ask if the eccentric gentleman can finance his daughter's wedding. The colonel generously gives him a check for a thousand pounds. Adam is jubilant and takes Nina to a country hotel where they stay overnight. He is so happy that she waits until the next morning to tell him that her father, an absentminded movie fan, signed Charlie Chaplin's name to the worthless check. The wedding is postponed once more.

At Lady Metroland's party for Mrs. Ape, Baron Balcairn, a gossip columnist known as Mr. Chatterbox, shows up in disguise after the host refuses to send him an invitation. Suspected of spying on a secret political conference among Lord Metroland, Father Rothschild, and Mr. Outrage, he is exposed. Deciding to give his paper the scoop of scoops, he reports a sensational but false account of indiscreet confessions made by aristocrats whom the evangelist converted. Then he goes home, turns on the gas, puts his head into the oven, and quietly dies.

Adam becomes Mr. Chatterbox. In the meantime, Balcairn's hoax swamps the courts with libel suits against the *Daily Excess*. Mrs. Ape confirms the story in a special interview and then departs with her angels to pep up religion at Oberammergau, Germany. Because Adam is forbidden to mention the names of those suing the paper, he is forced to invent fictitious people for his column. Among his creations is a man named Ginger, a model of fashion and a popular figure in society.

He is rather surprised when he finally encounters Captain Eddy Littlejohn, a man whom everyone calls Ginger. Adam and Nina meet him at the November Handicap, where Indian Runner comes in first, paying thirty-five to one. A few minutes after the race, Adam spies the drunken major, but he disappears before Adam can push his way through the crowd to collect his winnings.

Adam promises Nina that he will speak to her father again. He finds the colonel making a film based on the life of John Wesley and too busy to pay any attention to Adam. During his absence, Nina writes his column and mentions green bowlers, a fashion item that is taboo in the *Daily Excess*. As a result, Adam loses his job, and Miles becomes Mr. Chatterbox. Miles takes the post because he needs the money. His brother, Lord Throbbing, returns unexpectedly from Canada and throws Miles, along with his disreputable boxing and racing friends, out of Throbbing House.

Adam, Agatha, Miles, and Archie Schwert go to the auto races where, to get into the pits, they wear brassards indicating that they belong to the crew of car 13. Between heats, Adam again meets the drunken major, who, after assuring him that his thirty-five thousand pounds are safe in the bank, borrows five pounds to make a bet.

When the driver of car 13 is disabled by an Italian rival, Agatha, who wears a brassard designating her as a spare driver, takes the wheel. Careening madly, she establishes a course record for the lap before she leaves the track and drives across country until she crashes the car into a monument. She is found wandering about in a dazed condition and dies in a nursing home, still thinking that she is driving in a spinning world of speed and sound.

Adam has no money to pay Lottie's bill for seventy-eight pounds sixteen and twopence. Meeting Ginger Littlejohn, he borrows that amount and promises in return that Ginger can marry Nina. Shortly after Ginger and Nina return from their honeymoon, Ginger is called up for military service. Adam and Nina spend Christmas with Colonel Blount. The Wesley film is finished, and the colonel, planning to show it as a Christmas treat, is too preoccupied to notice that his supposed son-in-law is a writer he met previously as Fenwick-Symes. On Christmas night, they hear that war was declared.

Adam meets his drunken major again on a blasted battlefield during a lull in the fighting. The officer, who insists that he is now a general, announces that he lost his division. Adam is not quite so badly off; he loses only one platoon. The general offers to pay the thirty-five thousand pounds on the spot, but Adam thinks the money will be useless. They do find the general's car and in it are a case of champagne and Chastity, one of Mrs. Ape's singing angels. Adam drinks some of the wine and falls asleep, leaving the general and Chastity to entertain each other.

Critical Evaluation:

The element of roman à clef is much stronger in Evelyn Waugh's first novel, *Decline and Fall* (1928), than in his second, *Vile Bodies*. A few characters reappear in the second novel but very briefly, and none is crucial to the plot or theme. The supposed similarity of *Vile Bodies* to *Decline and Fall* is, upon close examination, found to be somewhat superficial and based mostly on the reappearance of the victim as hero.

Adam Fenwick-Symes, the protagonist of *Vile Bodies*, is in a sense a man of the world: a novelist, recently returned from Paris, and one of the Bright Young People. Yet during much of the novel he is a passive figure, an antihero, a man to whom things happen. Because the world in which he moves is one lacking order and stability, the things that happen to him often make no sense. Before the novel ends, however, Adam changes from victim to trickster and turns Ginger into the clown of the piece. When Adam sells Nina to Ginger and carries off the Great Christmas Imposture at Doubting Hall, some critics see him as a precursor to Basil Seal, the rogue of later novels.

In *Vile Bodies*, the narrator frequently becomes a sort of camera's eye, which cuts from scene to scene, revealing dialogue and external behavior only, and often leaving Adam to wander about. The result is a collection of many short scenes, snatches of conversation, and bits of farce, all of which combine to create a pastiche effect. Since the narrator, during these montage passages, does not go inside the minds of any of the characters, he seems very distant from them. Events that should strike the reader as horrible are thus rendered merely funny.

There are three deaths in the novel. During a drunken party at Shepheard's Hotel, Miss Florence (Flossie) Ducane is killed when she falls from a chandelier, which, as the *Evening Standard* delicately puts it, "she was attempting to mend." Simon Balcairn, who is both the last Earl of Balcairn and Mr. Chatterbox of the *Daily Excess*, sticks his head in the oven after Margot Metroland blackballs him from society.

Agatha Runcible never comes out of shock following a mis-adventure in a runaway racing car; from her bed in the nursing home to which she has been taken, she says portentously, "How people are *disappearing*, Adam."

These deaths elicit no sympathy from the reader, not because the reader (or Waugh) is a monster but because the characters are. They are grotesqueries. Cruel and terrible things do indeed happen to them, yet they are like circus performers called out by the ringmaster, Evelyn Waugh, to run through their paces. Their various acts may contain a latent tragedy, but it is well disguised behind the gaudy costumes and painted faces.

Waugh is always interested in religion, and the religious element is prominent in *Vile Bodies*, although it serves to furnish the subject matter for burlesque. The action of the novel occurs primarily during a Christmas season (between November 10 and Christmas Day) in the "near future," as the author is at some pains to point out in his foreword. The first character to appear is Father Rothschild, S.J. This ubiquitous Jesuit possesses in profusion those qualities that most excite British prejudice: He is a plotter in international affairs; he knows everything about everybody, even the location of the prime minister's love nest in Shepheard's Hotel; and he is of the fabulously wealthy banking family, thus exuding the double menace of wily Jesuit and crafty Jewish financier. Another ecclesiastic, a rector, plays a small comic role as Colonel Blount's neighbor and reluctant chauffeur. The second half of the novel features the making of a bogus film of the life of John Wesley at Doubting Hall, known to the locals as "Doubting 'All."

The embodiment of "modern" religion in the novel is the rum-drinking revivalist, Mrs. Melrose Ape. She is clearly a caricature of Aimee Semple McPherson and is one of only two characters in the novel whose models can be definitely identified (the other being Lottie Crump, the champagne-swigging proprietor of Shepheard's Hotel in Dover Street, who is the famous Mrs. Lewis of the Cavendish Hotel in Jermyn Street). The lesbianic Mrs. Ape is accompanied by a band of angels, who carry their wings in violin cases and sing her famous hymn "There Ain't No Flies on the Lamb of God." The irrepressible Margot Metroland proselytizes two of the proselytizer's angels, Chastity and Divine Discontent, for her Latin American Entertainment Company, a white slavery ring.

The slippery Mr. Isaacs and the Wonderfilm Company of Great Britain demean Doubting Hall at the behest of the dotty Colonel Blount. In the film, Wesley is wounded in a duel, nursed back to health by his lover, Selina, Countess of Huntingdon (played by Effie La Touche), and later, in America, rescued from Red Indians by the same Lady Huntingdon disguised as a cowboy.

The novel is highly episodic; what plot movement there is emanates from two rather mild conflicts: establishment disapproval of the Younger Generation and Adam's desultory quest for the means to marry Nina. The plot is both less fantastic and less skillfully constructed than that of Waugh's first novel, *Decline and Fall*, an opinion with which Waugh himself agreed.

Some critics have compared Waugh's early novels, especially *Vile Bodies*, to the work of the American novelist F. Scott Fitzgerald. After all, Waugh was writing about the Bright Young People not long after Fitzgerald wrote about the flappers of the Jazz Age. However, when an American cinema agent suggested in 1946 that Waugh must have been greatly influenced by Fitzgerald, Waugh responded that he "had not then read a word of his."

"Critical Evaluation" by Patrick Adcock

Further Reading

Davis, Robert Murray. "Title, Theme, and Structure in *Vile Bodies*." *Southern Humanities Review* 11 (Winter, 1977): 21-27. Argues that both the structure and the theme of *Vile Bodies* is written from a Christian perspective. Maintains that Waugh's novels were "religious" long before they became "Catholic" with the publication of *Brideshead Revisited* (1945).

Jervis, Steven A. "Evelyn Waugh, *Vile Bodies* and the Younger Generation." *South Atlantic Quarterly* 66 (Summer, 1967): 440-448. Examines Waugh's portrayal of the Bright Young People, Britain's equivalent of the Jazz Age flappers, and argues that Waugh's disgust with their chaotic and pointless lives helped turn him toward Roman Catholicism.

Kleine, Don W. "The Cosmic Comedies of Evelyn Waugh." *South Atlantic Quarterly* 61 (Autumn, 1962): 533-539. Focuses on Waugh's early comedies, *Decline and Fall* and *Vile Bodies*, and the fact that many critics have ignored Waugh's essential seriousness of purpose.

Patey, Douglas Lane. *The Life of Evelyn Waugh: A Critical Biography*. Malden, Mass.: Blackwell, 1998. Examines Waugh's life within the context of his work, providing critical assessments of his novels and other writings. Chapter 2 includes a discussion of *Vile Bodies*.

Phillips, Gene D. *Evelyn Waugh's Officers, Gentlemen, and Rogues: The Fact Behind His Fiction*. Chicago: Nelson-Hall, 1975. Chapter 2, "Exile from Eden: The Early Satires," connects the escapades in *Vile Bodies* with Waugh's own experiences as a Bright Young Person. Cites Waugh's diaries, his nonfiction travel books, and newspaper accounts of the period.

Villa Flor, Carlos, and Robert Murray Davis, eds. *Waugh Without End: New Trends in Evelyn Waugh Studies.* New York: Peter Lang, 2005. Collection of papers presented at a 2003 symposium during the centenary of Waugh's birth. Includes discussions of Waugh and Catholicism, his depiction of the English gentleman, and homosexual themes in works by Waugh and E. M. Forster.

Walker, Julia M. "Being and Becoming: A Comment on Religion in *Vile Bodies* and *Brideshead Revisited.*" *Evelyn Waugh Newsletter* 16, no. 2 (Autumn, 1982): 4-5. Discusses the fact that *Vile Bodies* was published in the year of Waugh's conversion to Roman Catholicism and that the book to some extent reflects this. Argues that Waugh the satirist approaches religion obliquely in *Vile Bodies*, exposing its gross vulgarization in the modern world, whereas in *Brideshead Revisited* he affirms his belief in the religious life more directly.

Waugh, Alexander. *Fathers and Sons: The Autobiography of a Family.* London: Headline, 2004. Alexander Waugh, the grandson of Evelyn, chronicles four generations of his family, focusing on its father-son conflicts and its literary achievements. Includes illustrations, bibliography, and index.

The Village

Author: Ivan Bunin (1870-1953)
First published: Derevnya, 1910 (English translation, 1923)
Type of work: Novel
Type of plot: Social criticism
Time of plot: Early twentieth century
Locale: Russia

Principal characters:
TIKHON ILITCH KRASOFF, a self-made landowner
KUZMA ILITCH KRASOFF, his imaginative brother
THE BRIDE, a peasant woman employed by Tikhon
RODKA, a peasant and the husband of the Bride

The Story:

The ancestors of Tikhon and Kuzma Ilitch Krasoff are nothing to be proud of: Their great-grandfather had been hunted from Durnovka with wolfhounds, their grandfather had distinguished himself by becoming a thief, and their father, a petty huckster, had died early in life as a result of his drinking. The sons, after serving for a time as clerks in town stores, take to the road as itinerant peddlers. After they travel together for many years, their partnership is mutually dissolved during an argument over the division of profits. The two part very bitterly.

After the partnership is broken, Tikhon takes over a posting station a few miles from Durnovka, the little village where his family has lived for many generations. Along with the station, he operates a liquor dispensary and general mercantile establishment. Determined to become a man of some consequence, he begins to build up his fortune although he is already in his forties. He decides to follow the tax collectors and buy land at forced sales, and he pays the lowest possible prices for what he purchases.

Tikhon's private life is anything but rich. He lives with his cook, a mute woman, who becomes the mother of his child. The child, however, is accidentally smothered, and soon afterward Tikhon sends the woman away and marries a noblewoman, by whom he tries to have children. His efforts, however, are fruitless, for the children are always born premature and dead. As if to make up, temporarily at least, for his wife's failure to present him with children, fate gives Tikhon the opportunity of finishing off, economically speaking, the last member of the family that had held his own ancestors in serfdom through the previous centuries.

Life is not easy for Tikhon. A government order closes all the dramshops, including his, and makes liquor a state monopoly. Tikhon also continues to be disturbed by the fact that he has no children, as he believes this indicates his failure in life.

The summer following the government order closing his liquor business proves to be a bad one. There is no rain and it is very hot, so the grain harvest on his lands is only a fraction of what it should have been. During the fall, Tikhon goes to a fair to do some horse-trading, and while he is there he becomes disgusted with himself and with life in general, which suddenly seems pointless to him. He begins drinking heavily, downing immense quantities of vodka, although not enough to interfere with the conduct of his business.

Tikhon's life is little affected by the war with Japan that breaks out soon afterward; he is more affected by persistent rumors of an attempt at a socialist revolution in the Russian legislative body. When he learns that the great landowners—those who own more than a thousand acres—are likely to have their estates taken from them for redistribution, he even begins to agitate a little for the new laws. Soon, however, he changes his mind when he discovers that the peasants on his own land are plotting against him. One Sunday, he hears that they are meeting at Durnovka to rise in rebellion against him. He immediately goes to the village, but the peasants refuse to listen to him and drive him away with force. The uprising is short-lived, and within a few days the peasants are back to deal with him again, but Tikhon no longer trusts them—he thinks of them as little better than treacherous animals.

One of the workers on Tikhon's land is a young peasant named Rodka, who is married to a young girl of some beauty who is always called the Bride. The girl is a source of annoyance to Tikhon because she arouses him sexually. On several occasions she resists his unwelcome attentions, but finally he has his way with her. The Bride does not complain; she simply endures, much as she endures the terrible beatings that her husband administers to her with a whip. The beatings make Tikhon afraid of Rodka, and so he plots to do away with the peasant. Such scheming, however, proves unnecessary, for the Bride herself poisons her husband. Tikhon, at least, is sure that she has poisoned her husband, although no one else thinks so.

Chance brings to Tikhon's attention a volume of poems written by his brother, Kuzma. Stirred by the knowledge that his brother is still alive and also an author, Tikhon writes him a letter, telling him that it is high time they buried their past differences and became friends again. Kuzma comes to Durnovka, and the two brothers become, at least on the surface, friendly. Tikhon offers his brother the overseership of the estate at Durnovka, and Kuzma accepts because he has no other prospects for earning a living.

Kuzma Krasoff has done nothing with his life. Following the dissolution of his partnership with Tikhon years before, he worked here and there, as a drover, a teamster, a general worker. Then he fell in love with a woman at Voronezh and lived with her for ten years, until she died. In that decade, he busied himself by trading in grain and horses and by writing occasionally for the local newspaper. All of his life he has wanted to become a writer. He received no education, except

for short periods of instruction at the hands of an unemployed shoemaker and from books he borrowed occasionally. He considers his life a complete waste, for he has never been able to settle down to writing seriously.

In his maturity Kuzma blames all of his troubles, and the troubles of Russians in general, on a lack of education. He believes that education is the answer to every problem confronting him and his country, and he asserts that the Russians, whom he regards as little better than barbarians with a wide streak of hatred in their makeup, would be better folk if they were educated.

Kuzma's life as overseer on his brother's estate is not a happy one. He feels that the position is a last resort, and he dislikes the people with whom he has to deal, including Tikhon. He is also perturbed by the Bride, whom Tikhon has sent to cook and keep house for him. She does not arouse him as she had aroused Tikhon, but Kuzma is bothered by her presence, and he feels extremely sorry for her because, a few years before, a group of men had raped her. That incident, Kuzma feels, lingers like a cloud over her existence. When at last he speaks to Tikhon about the matter, Tikhon, supposing that Kuzma has been sampling the same favors that he himself had enjoyed in the past, laughs at his brother's scruples. Nevertheless, he does arrange to marry off the woman, and the Bride becomes the wife of a peasant on the estate. On the wedding day, only Kuzma realizes that the prospect of a husband brings no joy to the Bride and that she, like himself, will never really be happy.

Critical Evaluation:

Born of a noble though impoverished family in 1870, Ivan Bunin was reared on his father's country estate and educated by tutors. After a time at the University of Moscow, he traveled as a journalist and began writing poetry. By 1901, his poetry received some acclaim, and in 1903 his translations of Lord Byron and Henry Wadsworth Longfellow brought him the Pushkin Prize. His stories also brought him wide attention. *The Village*, in 1910, made him internationally famous.

In the years preceding World War I, Bunin traveled widely, especially in the Middle East. At the time of the Russian Revolution, Bunin sided with reactionary groups. He left Moscow in May, 1918, and the following February he fled the country; he spent most of the rest of his life in France. His literary output, never large, maintained a high quality, and in 1933 he was awarded the Nobel Prize in Literature. In 1941, the seventy-year-old Bunin and his ailing wife fled Paris after the Nazi conquest and lived destitute in unoccupied France. The Tolstoy Foundation solicited funds for their relief. Later, it was revealed that Bunin had sheltered a Jewish journalist for the length of the Occupation. In 1950, he published *Vospominaniya* (*Memories and Portraits*, 1951), a brief autobiography that included reminiscences on his relationships with such friends as Ivan Turgenev and Leo Tolstoy. He died in semiobscurity, at the age of eighty-three, at his home in Paris.

Bunin, in an autobiographical introduction to the American edition of *The Village*, stated that it was one of a series of novels written to portray the character of the Russian people. In the series, said Bunin, he attempted to lay bare the Russian soul in all of its complexity and depth and in its invariably tragic state. Bunin also stated that no one who knew the Russian people as he did could have been surprised by the beastliness of the Russian Revolution and its effects on Russia. Some critics have called Bunin cruel in his portrayal of the Russian people, for he shows them as vicious, egocentric, hatred-filled individuals who care little for anyone but themselves. Bunin himself stated that he was content to have painted a more realistic picture of the Russian people than the idealized conception usually given in the literature of his land, a land from which he was an exile after the revolution.

The Village presents a grim picture of life in pre-Soviet Russia. It is a world in which people are known by nicknames or crude labels: the Bride, the Goat, Duckhead, the Fool. The villagers do not even know how to acknowledge one another's humanity. These country folk, uneducated and brutalized by hard lives, are stimulated only by disasters; they revel in wife beating and the thrashing of small children, and they gather around to watch fights or fires. Violence provides their only entertainment, their only break in the monotony of living. The Russia of this novel is a violent, primitive land, where poor men lash their beasts and women equally.

Bunin wrote with the care of a historian or a sociologist describing a kind of life doomed to extinction because of its rottenness. Dirt, filth, and manure seem to cling to everything and everyone in the village. At times, it is difficult to distinguish the human beings from the animals. Bunin does not romanticize the old ways or the country life. His precise, elegant prose pictures—with vivid images and skillful, merciless irony—portray the truth as he sees it.

The superstitious peasants lead wretched lives, struggling merely to subsist. People who have to struggle to exist get into the habit, so that even after the need ceases, they continue struggling, and their lives become bounded by possessions and prices. Tikhon Ilitch (known as Stiff-Leg) tries vainly to find salvation in "business," but neither busy-ness nor business can bring him happiness. After decades of labor, Tikhon can only reflect: How brief, how devoid of meaning, is life!

Deniska, with his short legs, mouse-colored hair, and earth-hued skin, is one character who might offer hope for the future. He is bright and self-educated and is known as an agitator. Nevertheless, it is Kuzma Krasoff, Tikhon's younger brother, who represents the aspirations of the self-educated poor man. His life, despite his efforts, has come to nothing, and he is reduced to working for his brother and to vague desires to write about how he came to be a failure. True, he was born in a country with more than one hundred million illiterates, but he had hoped to make something of himself. He reads, he writes, he studies, but all to no avail. He despairs of both himself and his country. What kind of nation, his friend Balashkin cries, would seek to destroy all its best writers? They killed Alexander Pushkin and Mikhail Lermontov, imprisoned Taras Shevchenko for ten years, dragged Fyodor Dostoevski out to be shot. Nikolai Gogol went mad. Balashkin recounts the destruction of many other writers as well. Kuzma, however, clings to the belief that Russia is a great nation—that it must be great, and so must he.

Kuzma is the kind of man who rushes from enthusiasm to enthusiasm, embracing the philosophy of Tolstoy, then patriotism, then something else. Perhaps, Bunin seems to suggest, his shallow idealism and lack of tenacity are characteristic of the Russia of that day. "All Russia is nothing but village," remarks one of the characters. Kuzma also quotes Gogol: "Russia! Russia! Wither art thou dashing?" and "Vain Babblers, you stick at nothing!"

Like most of the greater Russian novelists who preceded him, Bunin was a craftsman who set forth the incidents in his narratives with an ease that adds to the lifelike quality of his characters. Also like most Russian writers, he threads a somber symbolism through this and his other novels. At times, Bunin's prose possesses the sadness and poetic enchantment of Anton Chekhov's stories; his realism is tempered with an aristocratic dedication to art and style. There are moments when Russian village life seems almost too terrible to bear, yet it all rings true. Beneath the hues of gray and the careful objectivity, a deep understanding seems to radiate through, almost like a touch of sympathy.

Bunin's art was rooted in Turgenev, Chekhov, and Tolstoy; the author always had an aversion to Dostoevski's work. Bunin did not, however, attempt the psychological novel, which dominated nineteenth century Russian fiction. Some readers might even hesitate to call *The Village* a novel. When the book first appeared in Russia, many critics condemned its bleak vision even while admiring its art and its blending of realism with poetry. Most readers even now prefer Bunin's short stories, especially the famous long tale

"The Gentleman from San Francisco" (1922), certainly the writer's masterpiece. Nevertheless, *The Village* presents a memorable picture of a place and a time, an invective against the cruelty and stupidity of Russian peasant life.

"Critical Evaluation" by Bruce D. Reeves

Further Reading

Connolly, Julian. *Ivan Bunin*. Boston: Twayne, 1982. Presents an analytical survey of Bunin's major works, with a special emphasis on the evolution of Bunin's views on human existence. Examines the treatment of Russian society in *The Village* against the background of Bunin's perceptions of the inevitable decline and fall of major cultures and civilizations.

Kryzytski, Serge. *The Works of Ivan Bunin*. The Hague, the Netherlands: Mouton, 1971. The first monograph on Bunin published in English contains a detailed description of Bunin's work and its critical reception. Compares Bunin's treatment of Russian peasant life in *The Village* to that found in the works of his contemporaries.

Marullo, Thomas Gaiton. *If You See the Buddha: Studies in the Fiction of Ivan Bunin*. Evanston, Ill.: Northwestern University Press, 1998. Examines the influence of Buddhism on Bunin's writing, focusing on six of his works; chapter 2 is devoted to a discussion of *The Village*. Points out how these works express Buddhist concepts of self, craving, enlightenment, regression, and rebirth, and how these ideas helped Bunin make sense of his world.

_____, ed. *Ivan Bunin: Russian Requiem, 1885-1920—A Portrait from Letters, Diaries, and Fiction*. Chicago: Ivan R. Dee, 1993.

_____. *Ivan Bunin: From the Other Shore, 1920-1933—A Portrait from Letters, Diaries, and Fiction*. Chicago: Ivan R. Dee, 1995.

_____. *Ivan Bunin: The Twilight of Emigré Russia, 1934-1953—A Portrait from Letters, Diaries, and Memoirs*. Chicago: Ivan R. Dee, 2002. Three-volume compilation of letters, diary and memoir excerpts, and stories—along with comments from Bunin's family, friends, and others who knew him—chronicles the author's life. Marullo's introduction and commentary in each volume place the compiled materials within the context of Bunin's life and times.

Woodward, James B. *Ivan Bunin: A Study of His Fiction*. Chapel Hill: University of North Carolina Press, 1980. Stimulating discussion of Bunin's work analyzes the role that nature plays in his fiction. Also focuses on the way that human attitudes toward nature shape the experiences of Bunin's characters.

The Villagers

Author: Jorge Icaza (1906-1978)
First published: Huasipungo, 1934; revised, 1951 (English translation, 1964)
Type of work: Novel
Type of plot: Social realism
Time of plot: Twentieth century
Locale: Ecuador

Principal characters:
ALFONSO PEREIRA, a debt-ridden landowner
BLANCA PEREIRA, his wife
LOLITA, their daughter
DON JULIO, his uncle
POLICARPIO, an overseer
ANDRES CHILIQUINGA, an Indian laborer
CUNSHI CHILIQUINGA, his wife
PADRE LOMAS, the village priest
JUANCHO CABASCANGO, a well-to-do Indian tenant farmer

The Story:

Alfonso Pereira is an Ecuadoran landowner plagued by domestic and financial troubles. His wife, Blanca, nags him, and he is worried about his seventeen-year-old daughter, Lolita, who wants to marry a man who is part Indian. Don Julio, his uncle, adds to his difficulties by demanding repayment of a loan of ten thousand sucre, a debt already three months overdue.

When Pereira confesses that he is unable to pay the loan, Don Julio suggests that his nephew try to interest Mr. Chapy, a North American promoter, in a timber concession on Pereira's mountain estate. Privately, the old man suspects that Mr. Chapy and his associates are on the lookout for oil and use their lumber-cutting activities in the region as a cover. To interest the North Americans, however, it will be necessary to build fifteen miles of road and to get possession of two forest tracts. Also, the Indians have to be driven off their *huasipungos*, the lands supplied to them in return for working on the estate.

Pereira assures his uncle that such a course will be difficult. The Indians, having a deep affection for their lands along both sides of the river, will never willingly relinquish them. Old Julio ridicules Pereira's sentimentality and tells him to return to the estate at Tomachi and build the road. Back home, Pereira discusses his problem with Padre Lomas, the village priest. The padre agrees to persuade the Indians to work on the road: He will tell them that the labor is the will of God. They also try to determine how many *mingas*, parties in which Indians are plied with drinks to make them willing to work, will be necessary before the road can be completed. Jacinto Quintana, proprietor of the village store and saloon, promises that he and his wife, Juana, will make the home brew for the first of the *mingas*.

Andres Chiliquinga, an Indian worker, is unhappy because Pereira has returned. Andres had gone against his master's and the priest's wishes by marrying Cunshi. Andres is one of thirty Indians sent to start cutting wood and clearing the roadbed.

To find a wet nurse for her baby, Blanca Pereira examines some of the Indian mothers. Their undernourished babies are diseased, some with malaria or dysentery; others are epileptic or mentally disabled. Policarpio, the overseer, finally chooses Cunshi, mother of the healthiest child in the village, and takes her to the Pereira house. The master, seeing the young Indian woman, forces her to bed with him and then rapes her.

One night, Andres makes the long trip home to see his wife. Finding no one in their hillside shack, he becomes suspicious and angry. The next day, he deliberately lets his ax fall on his foot. The Indians treat the cut with spider webs and mud, but when the bandage is removed, three days later, the foot is so badly infected that Andres is sent home. A medicine man who poulticed the sore saved Andres's life, but the wound leaves Andres disabled.

One day, while Pereira and the priest are at the Quintana store discussing the building of the road, they send Jacinto on an errand. After his departure, both men force themselves upon Juana and rape her.

Pereira gives Padre Lomas one hundred sucre for a big Mass. Then he holds a *minga*, and work on the road is accelerated. Storms make life miserable for the Indian workers, unprotected as they are in their camps. Some die when they try to drain a swamp. Others perish in quicksand. Pereira, choosing to risk the lives of the Indians rather than follow a

longer, safer route, keeps the workers drunk and entertains them with cockfights. The laborers continue to toil.

The priest visits Juancho Cabascango, an Indian with a prosperous *huasipungo* beside the river, and asks for one hundred sucre to pay for another Mass. When the Indian refuses, Padre Lomas curses him. A short time later, a flash flood drowns some of the Indians and their cattle. Blaming the disaster on Juancho, his superstitious neighbors beat him to death. The priest declares the affair the will of God and easily collects several hundred sucre for his Mass.

At last, the road is completed, but the Indians receive none of the benefits Padre Lomas had promised. He, however, buys a bus and two trucks, which take all transportation work from those who used to drive mule teams into Quito with the products of the region. Young Indians now ride the bus to the city and, there, become criminals and prostitutes.

As a result of easy transportation and the possibility of a profitable sale in Quito, Pereira decides not to give the Indians their customary grain from his plentiful harvest. Policarpio's protests do no good. When the hungry Indians go to Pereira's patio and beg their master to relieve the hunger of their families, he tells them that their daily pay of fifty centavos is generous enough. Besides, the ton and a half of corn needed to feed the Indians will help considerably in reducing his debts. He does, however, heed his overseer's warning and asks that guards for his estate be sent from Quito.

Hunger stalks the region and babies and old people perish. When one of Pereira's cows dies, the famished Indians beg for the carcass. He refuses, thinking they might be tempted to kill other cows, and orders Policarpio to bury the dead animal. Desperate, Andres uncovers it; after he and his family eat some of the meat, the tainted flesh kills Cunshi. Padre Lomas demands twenty-five sucre, more than the Indian could ever earn, in payment for burying the dead woman. That same night, Andres steals one of his master's cows and sells it to a nearby butcher. Tracked down by dogs, Andres is captured and flogged in Pereira's patio. There is no one to protest except his small son, who is almost killed by the white men when he tries to help his father.

A score of foreigners arrives in Tomachi. The Indians welcome them timorously, thinking that these new white men could certainly be no more cruel than their Spanish masters. Mr. Chapy's first act, however, is to order the Indians driven from their *huasipungos* to make room for company houses and a sawmill.

When Andres's son brings news of the order, the Indians rebel. They had stoically accepted the cruelty of the whites, even the lechery of the white men toward the Indian women, but the Indians feel that the land is theirs. Jacinto vainly tries to stop them when they march on the village. The enraged Indians kill six of the white men. The others, including Mr. Chapy, flee in their automobiles.

They return, over the road the Indians had built, with three hundred soldiers under a leader who had killed two thousand Indians in a similar rebellion near Cuenca. Troops hunt down and machine-gun Indians of all ages, male and female. The few survivors, taking refuge in Andres's hillside shack, roll rocks down on the soldiers and shoot at them with birdguns. Finally, the soldiers set fire to the thatched roof. When the Indians run from the burning house, the troops shoot them without mercy.

Critical Evaluation:

The brutal novel *The Villagers* flows swiftly. Technically, it is one of the better Spanish American novels. Its virtues are legion, as are its defects, and among the former are interesting dialogue, bitter irony, sardonic humor, interesting plot, effective use of detail, exposure of social injustice, and crispness of style with short sentences that get to the point. *The Villagers* presents the Ecuadoran Andes so clearly that readers see them in stark detail, hear the sounds of the sierra, and experience the odors, temperature changes, and direction of the night wind. *The Villagers*' crowning virtue is its defense of Ecuador's oppressed Indians. For this reason the novel has been considered Jorge Icaza's most significant novel. It helped launch the cycle of *indianista* novels, which are devoted to telling the story of the Indians. The novel's protagonist is not only an Indian but also *the* Indian, who is characterized collectively but clearly, even to the peculiar flavor of his Spanish.

Decay is a prominent and depressing note in *The Villagers*, with its frequent images of garbage, filth, mold, slime, and rotten meat. Trash, dirt, and profanity are always present; everything is sloppy and unkempt, reflecting life's hopelessness. Depression is thus a constant note, accentuated by dismal mountain fogs, clammy cold, foul speech, and superstition. *Soroche* (altitude sickness) occasionally strikes, as do other afflictions. Alcoholism is the Indian's bane, for the *huasipunguero* abandons everything—chickens, corn, potatoes, children—for alcohol.

The characters in the novel generally fail to change or develop. At the novel's end, they are almost the same personalities and characters that they were at its start. The principal exception is the Indian community itself, for "from all corners of the soul, from every pore, grow the secret rebellions of a slave." Icaza also implies that the mestizo or mulatto in Ecuador suffers from a psychological inferiority complex.

The latter villains, unfortunately, are crudely drawn. Don Alfonso Pereira is a second-rate Simon Legree, a consistent rascal, self-server, hypocrite, and uncomplicated brute from start to finish. He snarls, curses, and brutalizes Indians but cringes from those above him. The priest is worse; he is so utterly depraved as to be comical. He extorts money from hungry Indians, sells passages out of Purgatory or burial plots "close to Heaven" at alarming prices, builds a lucrative trucking business on ill-gotten money, and commits ridiculous rascalities too numerous to mention, including the drunken rape of Juana. Referred to as the Cassocked One, the priest is a symbol of Icaza's disenchantment with religion, and it is puzzling that this caricature has not aroused disdain or even criticism from many generations of students, professors, and other readers.

Other ogres in *The Villagers* are wealthy people, businessmen, whites, property owners, and gringo capitalists. The gringos career about in Cadillacs, oblivious to Indians; they relish money and lack human feelings. It is possible that they were grotesquely overdrawn by Icaza to appeal only to readers blinded by prejudice, but it should also be recalled that the novel was intended as a tirade against the social injustice that then blighted Ecuador. Icaza possibly had the illusion that his novel would bring a better life to the Indians, but initially his work was better received and lauded abroad than it was in his own country. In any event, Icaza exposed the plight of Ecuador's peons and also the decay of the rural aristocrats, who had left the work of their ancestors to live luxuriously in the city. The novel also promotes the conflict of the races, namely the indigenous peoples against the whites. White aristocrats are portrayed as hard, unfeeling, and cruel. They are contemptuous of Indians and exploit the poor. Some critics feel that Icaza's work had political motivations; others compare him to John Steinbeck and consider him a social reformer.

No one in *The Villagers* apparently wishes to live in the country, since life in Quito is much richer. The countryside is backward, isolated, and uncomfortable; the city is cultured and far superior. Nature is unattractive; its beauties are not mentioned and not extolled. Nature's dangers are stressed, however, such as the scene in which a man dies horribly by drowning in mud. Little interest is shown in animals, birds, and plants. The novel is almost devoid of color. Tints of sunrises, sunsets, mountains, skies, fields, or towns are generally lacking, and even the grayness of the constant mountain mist is assumed rather than described. The author's treatment of color is a deliberate stylistic device to increase the feeling of dismal hopelessness.

Although of Spanish origin and comfortable background,

Icaza decided as a youth to champion Ecuador's poor of all races. Having attracted international attention, his novel eventually won acceptance in Ecuador and undoubtedly helped the Indian. It has therefore helped to implement some social reform and to attract attention to the cause of the indigenous peoples of the region. Thus, as have other novels written with the intention of provoking reform, the novel has succeeded, through its literary readability, in making considerable impact on its society.

"Critical Evaluation" by William Freitas

Further Reading

Flores, Angel. "Jorge Icaza." In *Spanish American Authors: The Twentieth Century*. New York: H. W. Wilson, 1992. A survey of Icaza's works. Stresses Icaza's contributions to modern Ecuadoran literature.

Foster, David William, and Virginia Ramos Foster, eds. "Icaza, Jorge." In *Modern Latin American Literature*. New York: Frederick Ungar, 1975. Excerpts from critical studies. An excellent starting point to Icaza's works.

Gonzälez-Pérez, Armando. *Social Protest and Literary Merit in "Huasipungo" and "El mundo es ancho y ajeno."* Milwaukee: Center for Latin America, University of Wisconsin, 1988. Indicates that Icaza is an important pro-Indian spokesperson in Ecuadoran political circles. Describes how his works often explore themes pertaining to economic exploitation of native populations.

Kristal, Efraín, ed. *The Cambridge Companion to the Latin American Novel*. New York: Cambridge University Press, 2005. This overview of Latin American fiction includes a chapter about Andean novels, in which *The Villagers* is examined and placed within the wider context of the region's literature.

Vetrano, Anthony Joseph. *Imagery in Two of Jorge Icaza's Novels: "Huasipungo" and "Huairapamushcas."* Tuscaloosa: University of Alabama Press, 1972. Icaza's social concerns for the indigenous Ecuadoran population inspired realistic scenes well-known for their portrayal of the physical abuse of the Indian worker. Vetrano analyzes such images in Icaza's two best-known novels.

Villette

Author: Charlotte Brontë (1816-1855)
First published: 1853
Type of work: Novel
Type of plot: Bildungsroman
Time of plot: Nineteenth century
Locale: Belgium

Principal characters:
LUCY SNOWE, a young teacher
JOHN GRAHAM BRETTON, a physician
MRS. BRETTON, his mother
POLLY HOME, Bretton's beloved
GINEVRA FANSHAWE, a schoolgirl
MONSIEUR PAUL EMANUEL, a teacher of literature
MADAME BECK, the mistress of a girls' school

The Story:

As a young girl, Lucy Snowe visits her godmother, Mrs. Bretton, about twice each year. It is a warm, active household, and Lucy loves Mrs. Bretton. During one of Lucy's visits, young Polly Home, whose widowed father is leaving England for the Continent, comes to stay with the Brettons. Polly is mature and worldly for her years, and she develops a tender, almost maternal, fondness for Mrs. Bretton's son, Graham. Because Lucy shares a room with the young visitor, she becomes the recipient of her confidences. Polly's father had originally intended to send his daughter to Mrs. Bretton's home for an extended stay, but he becomes lonely for her and returns to take his daughter back to Europe with him. Lucy's

visits with the Brettons come to an end when they lose their property and move away. After that, Lucy loses track of her godmother.

As a grown woman, Lucy earns her living by acting as a companion to elderly women. Tiring of her humdrum existence, she travels to France. There an unusual chain of circumstances leads her to the city of Villette and to a school run by Madame Beck and her kinsman, Monsieur Paul Emanuel. Owing to Lucy's calm disposition, ready wit, firm character, and cultivated intellect, she soon receives an appointment as instructor of English at the school.

Attending the school is Ginevra Fanshawe, a pretty but

flighty and selfish girl whose relationship with Lucy takes the form of a scornful friendship. Madame Beck is a clever schoolmistress. She conducts her school, which has both day students and boarders, through a system of spying that includes occasional furtive searches among the personal possessions of others and also a constant stealthy watching from her window. Despite Madame Beck's behavior, Lucy feels a firm respect for her. Her system is steady and unflagging. Monsieur Paul is a voluble and brilliant instructor. He always seems to be at Lucy's elbow admonishing her, tantalizing her intellect, attempting to lead her. Often, Lucy attributes the peculiar notions of the pair to their Catholicism, which Lucy abhors. Dr. John, a handsome, generous young practitioner who attends the school's students, is a general favorite at the institution. Although she does not betray her knowledge, Lucy recognizes him as the John Graham Bretton, whom she had known as a child.

In her characteristically scornful and triumphant manner, Ginevra Fanshawe confides to Lucy that she has a pair of ardent suitors: Isidore, who, according to Ginevra, is madly in love with her, and Colonel de Hamal, whom Ginevra herself prefers. One night in the garden, Lucy finds a letter intended for someone at the school. Dr. John appears in time to assist Lucy in disposing of the missive before the spying Madame Beck can interfere. The young doctor apparently knows the person for whom the letter is intended. Some time later, Lucy learns that Ginevra's Isidore is Dr. John himself, and that the nocturnal letter had been sent by de Hamal; Dr. John had been trying to protect his beloved. Dr. John confesses that he hopes to marry the schoolgirl.

Alone at the school's dormitory during a vacation, Lucy is overcome by depression. She has been haunted in the past by the apparition of a nun, and the reappearance of this specter so exacerbates the already turbulent emotions of the young teacher that she flees into the streets of the town. There she wanders, driven to despair by her inner conflicts, until she comes to a Catholic church. Under a strange compulsion, she is led to make a confession to the priest, but she later regrets her action. While trying to find her way back to the school, she faints. Upon regaining consciousness, she finds herself in a room with familiar furnishings. She is in a Villette chateau occupied by her godmother, Mrs. Bretton, and Graham Bretton—the man known at the school as Dr. John. Graham, who is giving Lucy medical attention, for the first time recognizes her as the young girl who had so often stayed at his home in England.

Lucy becomes a frequent visitor in the Bretton home. Before long, she realizes that she is in love with Dr. John. The warm friendship between the two young people is the subject of constant raillery by the sarcastic Monsieur Paul. While at a concert one evening with Dr. John and Mrs. Bretton, Lucy notices Ginevra in the audience. The schoolgirl begins to mimic Mrs. Bretton, and although the older woman is unaware of her actions, Dr. John is not. Quite suddenly, seeing how irreverently Ginevra can behave toward a woman as good as his mother, he realizes how weak and selfish the girl is, and his infatuation with her ends in disgust.

At another concert he attends with Lucy, Dr. John rescues a young girl named Paulina Bassompierre from a rough crowd. Upon bringing her home, he discovers that she is in reality Polly Home. Repeated meetings between Polly, who is now called Paulina, and Dr. John foster the doctor's love for the girl who has loved him since childhood. Lucy, closing her eyes and ears to this grief, believes that Dr. John is lost to her. Fortunately, a new phase of life begins for her at the school. Madame Beck gives her greater freedom in her work, and Monsieur Paul shows a sincere interest in her mind and heart. The only flaw in Lucy's tranquillity is the reappearance of the apparition of the nun.

One day, Madame Beck sends Lucy on an errand to the home of Madame Walravens. There Lucy is told a touching story about Monsieur Paul. In his youth, he loved a girl, Justine Marie, but her cruel relatives refused his suit and Justine subsequently died. Filled with remorse, Monsieur Paul undertook to care for Justine Marie's relatives. There survive old Madame Walravens and a priest, Father Silas, the same man to whom Lucy had confessed. The priest had been Monsieur Paul's tutor, and he is anxious to keep his former pupil from succumbing to the influence of Lucy, a heretic. Lucy's affection for Monsieur Paul grows, but her hopes are suddenly dashed when the truculent professor announces that he is leaving France for the West Indies. Madame Beck, always present when Monsieur Paul and Lucy meet, keeps the distraught young woman from talking to him. Ginevra Fanshawe has meanwhile eloped with de Hamal. A letter from the runaway girl explains Lucy's ghostly nun—de Hamal had thus attired himself when making nocturnal visits to Ginevra.

On the eve of his sailing, Monsieur Paul arranges a meeting with Lucy to explain his sudden forced departure and recent silence. Surrounded by his possessive relatives, he has occupied his time with secret arrangements to make Lucy mistress of the school. To avoid the temptation of telling Lucy about his plans before they were consummated, he has remained apart from her. He promises that upon his return, in three years, he will rid himself of all his encumbrances so that he will be free to marry her.

Margaret McFadden-Gerber

Critical Evaluation:

Charlotte Brontë's *Villette*, which is loosely based on the author's time as a student in Brussels, Belgium, is a first-person narrative of development, with Lucy Snowe at its center, both as protagonist and as a sometimes unreliable narrator. In the course of the novel, Lucy grows from a shadowy, self-effacing adolescent into an independent, self-possessed woman, learning to live her own life and tell her own story. She narrates that story from within the framework of the conventions of the female narrative of domestic or romantic love even while the story critiques those conventions.

The novel's first two scenes, which are centered on other characters, reveal Lucy as passive, virtually invisible, and cynical. At the Bretton home, Lucy exists on the margin, and she observes and describes the household's domestic activities rather than participating in them herself. The lives and loves of Mrs. Bretton, her son Graham, and little Polly Home are the central focus. After Lucy leaves the Brettons and is orphaned by the deaths of her own family, she again experiences life vicariously through Miss Marchmont, a wasted woman for whom Lucy is a companion and nursemaid. In neither place does Lucy feel a part of the scene, and in both places she is treated as little more than a hand to serve and an ear to listen. Lucy is defined, and she defines herself, within the narrow confines of her duties to others.

It is at Madame Beck's school in Villette that Lucy's struggle for independence and self-definition begins. Here, despite the restrictions of being female, she first encounters the opportunity to distinguish herself in opposition to those conventional restrictions. Adamantly Protestant and unable to speak French, Lucy is isolated in the bustling, strange world of foreign Catholics, under the supervision of a woman who silently patrols her school and searches its inmates' possessions. Lucy is appalled by this "woman's world" of well-tended but lazy, cunning females, and to some extent she keeps herself separate from that world. She is, however, also attracted to these women, who represent dimensions of Lucy's own characteristics and desires—Madame Beck with her independence and authority, Paulina with her magnetic delicacy, and Ginevra with her narcissistic beauty. Lucy experiences contradictory impulses. Proud of her calm detachment, she is also pained by being deprived of the traditionally feminine joys of motherhood and romance. Lucy is caught in the conflict between her desire to stand outside conventional feminine roles and her attraction to those same roles.

The men in the novel play an important part in Lucy's struggle for self-definition as a woman. Lucy at first cherishes a strong, and secret, passion for Graham Bretton and hopes that he will someday return her love. Graham, how-

ever, views her as an "inoffensive shadow," and, blithely telling her to "cultivate happiness," he unknowingly tortures her by confessing to his love first for Ginevra and then for Paulina. In contrast to Graham, who sees Lucy as devoid of passion, Monsieur Paul sees Lucy as a woman of just barely contained emotions. He reprimands her for her "finery" when she wears a simple pink dress and for her "flirtatiousness" when she jokes with Graham. On the other hand, Monsieur Paul encourages her to cultivate her intellect and her emotions, and as their friendship (and later romance) ripens, she becomes more assured and self-confident.

From the moment that Madame Beck commands Monsieur Paul to define Lucy's character by "reading" her face when she arrives, those around Lucy attempt to interpret exactly who she is. Much of what they do is to misread her, for Lucy leads a double life: the constrictive life of the body and the free life of the intellect and imagination. In the former, she is limited by her social position and her physical appearance. In the latter, she is free to explore her desires for love and independence. Her letters to Dr. John reveal this dichotomy: She begins by writing letters full of passion, which she destroys, and only then writes the calm, friendly notes that give nothing away, which she sends. When she receives letters from him, however, she buries them under a tree so that no one else will find them.

Brontë's imagery and symbolism reflect this doubleness in the descriptions of Lucy's narrow bed, her visits to the attic, and her buried letters. The nun who haunts her solitude is also emblematic of passions buried in an appearance of cold hauteur (hence the name Lucy Snowe, fire and ice). We see images of Lucy's passion in the novel's frequent storms and in her enjoyment at playing and acting during Madame Beck's birthday celebration. The frequent but private tears that she sheds further show her pent-up emotions. The scene at the citywide celebration brings together these images, for here is a microcosm in which she encounters virtually all of the significant people in her life and experiences the various emotions that have accompanied her life until then, including feelings of detachment, love, jealousy, contempt, and anger. In releasing, exploring, and finally accommodating herself to these emotions, she becomes a whole woman.

Lucy's story recounts her attempts to find a place for herself within the limited and constrictive range of acceptable Victorian womanhood that she encounters, from the heartless flirt or domestic homebody to the sexless schoolmistress or self-sacrificing nun. Even as she rejects each of those in turn, she learns to adapt parts of the roles to fit her own desires. She wants for herself the peaceful domesticity of Mrs. Bretton and Polly Home, the romantic adventures of

Ginevra Fanshawe, and the power of Madame Beck. In the end, she does get this combination when Monsieur Paul gives her a little school of her own (combining the world of domesticity and the world of work). Brontë creates domestic bliss for Lucy without domestic responsibilities, for Monsieur Paul leaves immediately after having declared his love and given Lucy her school. Lucy is thus able to live and work in an atmosphere combining romantic anticipation and independence. These years are, as she says, the happiest of her life. In *Villette*, Brontë thus rewrites the typical woman's story and the typical romance ending, and the novel concludes ambiguously as Lucy, again the unreliable narrator, refuses to give a definitive account of her and Monsieur Paul's fate.

Judith Burdan

Further Reading

Allott, Miriam, ed. *The Brontës: The Critical Heritage*. London: Routledge & Kegan Paul, 1974. Fascinating collection reprints sixteen reviews and comments from 1853, the year of *Villette*'s publication. William Makepeace Thackeray is admiring, if condescending, whereas Matthew Arnold finds the novel "disagreeable."

_____. *Charlotte Brontë: "Jane Eyre" and "Villette"—A Casebook*. 1973. Reprint. London: Macmillan, 1993. Contains various writings about *Villette*, including several opinions from the year the novel was published as well as later Victorian assessments and critical views from the 1950's and 1960's. An informative introduction includes biographical information and a brief review of Brontë's critical reception.

Edwards, Mike. *Charlotte Brontë: The Novels*. New York: St. Martin's Press, 1999. Extracts sections from *Jane Eyre* (1847), *Shirley* (1849), and *Villette* to analyze the layers of meaning and the combination of realism and fantasy in these texts.

Glen, Heather. *Charlotte Brontë: The Imagination in History*. New York: Oxford University Press, 2002. Presents analysis of all of Brontë's novels and contradicts previous biographical works with evidence that Brontë was more artistically sophisticated and more engaged in contemporary social issues than many scholars have asserted. Devotes two chapters to *Villette*.

_____, ed. *The Cambridge Companion to the Brontës*. New York: Cambridge University Press, 2002. Collection of essays examines the lives and works of the three sisters. Includes analysis of all of Charlotte's novels, a feminist perspective on the sisters' work, and a discussion of the Brontës and religion.

Keefe, Robert. *Charlotte Brontë's World of Death*. Austin: University of Texas Press, 1979. Offers a reading of the novels based on the premise that all of Brontë's works are influenced by the death of her mother and siblings. Includes a lengthy chapter on *Villette*, which is judged the finest of her works.

Linder, Cynthia A. *Romantic Imagery in the Novels of Charlotte Brontë*. London: Methuen, 1978. Examines Brontë's reliance on Romantic ideology for the construction of her novels. A chapter on *Villette* analyzes the complex structure of the work to show how the author effectively dramatizes the effects of Lucy's abortive love affairs.

Menon, Patricia. *Austen, Eliot, Charlotte Brontë, and the Mentor-Lover*. New York: Palgrave Macmillan, 2003. Examines how Brontë, Jane Austen, and George Eliot handled matters of gender, sexuality, family, behavior, and freedom in their work.

Nestor, Pauline. *Charlotte Brontë*. Totowa, N.J.: Barnes & Noble, 1987. Examines Brontë's life and fiction from a feminist perspective and devotes one chapter to each of the novels. Asserts that *Villette* is the story of a woman's development from weakness to strength, from dependence to self-sufficiency.

_____, ed. *"Villette."* New York: St. Martin's Press, 1992. Collection of nine essays includes sophisticated yet accessible feminist interpretations of the novel. Includes an informative editor's introduction.

Plasa, Carl. *Charlotte Brontë*. New York: Palgrave Macmillan, 2004. Assesses Brontë's writings by viewing them from a postcolonial perspective. A chapter focusing on *Villette* is titled "'A Thing Double-Existent': Foreigners and Slaves in *Villette*."

A Vindication of the Rights of Woman, with Strictures on Political and Moral Subjects

Author: Mary Wollstonecraft (1759-1797)
First published: 1792
Type of work: Social criticism

Mary Wollstonecraft's *A Vindication of the Rights of Woman, with Strictures on Political and Moral Subjects* is considered by many to be the manifesto of feminism and one of the first written expressions of feminist ideas. Although others before Wollstonecraft had written about the need for women's rights, *A Vindication of the Rights of Woman* (as the work is best known) is the first comprehensive statement about the need for women to be educated and for philosophical treatises on the nature of gender differences.

Like many late eighteenth century essays, this text may seem to later readers to ramble and repeat ideas when the point has already been made. Wollstonecraft is expressing new and radical concepts that shocked many, and which were connected to the ideas fueling the French Revolution, an event that so frightened the English government that it suspended most political and many civil liberties during this time. Wollstonecraft's repetitions and careful, sometimes overstated, logic can be explained as the natural reflex of anyone who introduces revolutionary notions to a culture.

Wollstonecraft's primary concern is the education of women. *A Vindication of the Rights of Woman* is, in large part, a rebuttal to Jean-Jacques Rousseau's ideas, expressed primarily in his book *Émile: Ou, De l'éducation* (1762; *Emilius and Sophia: Or, A New System of Education*, 1762-1763; better known as *Émile: Or, Education*, 1911) concerning the proper education of men and women. Rousseau contends that civilization has debased humanity, which would be better off in what he calls the state of nature. He argues that women should be educated to be the solace and companions of men when men wish to turn from serious pursuits and be entertained and refreshed. Accordingly, the guiding principles of a woman's education should be to teach her to obey and to please.

The title of Wollstonecraft's collection also reflects that of another work, *A Vindication of the Rights of Man, in a Letter to the Right Honourable Edmund Burke* (1790), which Wollstonecraft wrote in response to English conservative philosopher Edmund Burke's criticisms of the French Revolution, which he expressed in *Reflections on the Revolution in France* (1790). Burke rejects not only the revolution's

violence, but also the premise that all men could and should govern themselves. Wollstonecraft's critique points out the flagrant problems among the working classes in England, effectively disputing Burke's claims.

Wollstonecraft bases much of her argument in favor of women's education on the fact, which had only recently been agreed on, that women do have souls. She asserts that because women are immortal beings who have a relationship to their creator, they must be educated in the proper use of reason. She believes that the quality that sets humans apart from animals is reason, and the quality that sets one human apart from another is virtue. Rousseau argues that emotion is the preeminent human quality; Wollstonecraft contends that humans have passions so they can struggle against them and thereby gain self-knowledge. From God's perspective, the present evil of the passions leads to a future good from the struggle to overcome them. The purpose of life for all humans, not just men, is to perfect one's nature through the exercise of reason. This leads to knowledge and virtue, the qualities God wishes each person to gain. It is, therefore, immoral to leave women in ignorance or to be formed merely by the prejudices of society. An education that develops the mind is essential for any mortal creature.

The essay argues that both wealth and gender roles create major problems in society, because both tend to create unequal relationships among humans. Inequality leads either to slavery or to despotism, both of which warp the human character. Wollstonecraft contends that all humans have a will to exert themselves, and that they will do so. Dependence on a father or husband, which was woman's lot at the time in which Wollstonecraft wrote, creates cunning and deceit just as slavery did. Wollstonecraft argues that women's typical education in the home is a common knowledge of human nature, the use of power in indirect ways (cunning), a soft temper, outward obedience, a "puerile propriety," and an overemphasis on beauty. This type of education does not develop a good person, but one who is immature; incapable of sustained, orderly thought; and, therefore, easily influenced. However, this person will still exert her will indirectly. Such an education does not produce a good citizen, Wollstonecraft argues, and it would be for the good of society to educate women's reason.

This type of domestic education does not produce good wives or mothers either, she argues, and these are the primary human (not female) duties of women. A woman is taught to earn her way by charming and flirting, fascinating a man. Wollstonecraft is quick to point out that love does not last: The cornerstone of any good marriage is friendship. A woman would do better to inspire respect rather than sensual fascination. Furthermore, a woman who is constantly concerned with pleasing men does not make a good mother. She does not have the character to guide her own children, and sometimes views her daughters as rivals rather than becoming their mentor and friend. This can be damaging to the family, particularly if she is left a widow, and, in turn, damages society. Here, Wollstonecraft employs her most famous image, stating that this current miseducation produces women much like hothouse flowers, which are artificially induced to bloom too early and, therefore, become weak.

Wollstonecraft argues that having too much power over another person also damages human character. Monarchs, she points out, are frequently put on the throne through treachery and crime. How can a person be properly educated in reason and morality when that person is surrounded by such activity? Wealth, in fact the entire aristocratic system, produces abuses of power and cripples the human character, she contends. All military branches are based on inequality, on obeying without understanding. Not only the monarch, the aristocracy, and the military, but also priests and husbands rely on blind obedience for their power. She contends that as the divine right of kings has been rejected through reason, the divine right of husbands over their wives should end as well. Society should work to develop well-educated, moral citizens. To that end, society would do well not to develop professions that produce warped human beings, since all human character, not just of women, is formed by the habits of one's occupation and society at large.

Wollstonecraft's views show the influence of the Enlightenment. Enlightenment philosophy developed alongside the scientific revolution that followed the Spanish Inquisition, witch burnings, and the Protestant Reformation. The Inquisition and witch burnings came from a worldview based on tradition and dogma. Persons who did not obey the Catholic Church or the king without question were tortured and murdered; many women who were burned were accused of disobeying their husbands, the Church, or the monarch. The Reformation, and the subsequent period now called the Enlightenment, can be viewed as a reaction against the extremes of this time. Reason was emphasized above dogma; the Ref-

ormation gave each individual direct access to God, whereas earlier one had to approach the divine through the priesthood. The structure of European government, the divine right of kings, was also called into question. If individuals could approach God themselves, they could also govern themselves. These ideas, in addition to the Iroquois Federation system of government found among Native Americans, fueled the American and French revolutions and subsequently spread until the United States and most of Europe adopted forms of democracy as the primary system of government.

Wollstonecraft concedes that men are superior to women in physical strength, but writes that this is a superiority of degree, not kind. Women and men are similar in the kind of virtues they should and do possess, if not in the amount. Therefore, women should be educated in a manner similar to that of men and be treated as human beings, not as a special subspecies called feminine. Having made this concession, Wollstonecraft states that since a natural physical superiority exists, men should feel no need to produce unnatural weakness in women. She argues for natural exercise for girls, rejects feminine garments that restrict and damage the body, and encourages girls to express themselves naturally rather than developing simpering, weak ways to entice men.

This essay often argues directly with Rousseau, John Milton, and other poets and philosophers. It also addresses itself to a variety of books and manuals written as advice on how women should conduct themselves and raise young girls. The same points underlie these direct critiques: Women should be encouraged to be reasonable, not simply feminine; girls should be allowed healthy exercise and play; an overemphasis on being feminine rather than human is harmful not only to women but also to men and society in general.

Wollstonecraft anticipates psychological models of human development in her discussion of the source of gender differences. While the authors she critiques argue that girls naturally have a fondness for dress and appearance, or love to play with dolls or listen to gossip because it is their nature, Wollstonecraft points to the everyday circumstances of little girls' lives to explain their predilections. She also points out, anticipating novelist-critic Virginia Woolf in her feminist essays, that men also have a fondness for dress: One could simply observe military men, judges, or priests. In this same vein, in her critique of some male professions, Wollstonecraft argues that miseducation can produce foolish men. The foolishness of women that men often criticize has been produced by society through women's miseducation. Foolishness is not a gender characteristic, but a trait that comes from miseducation, a condition that can be remedied.

The essay concludes with recommendations on how to correct the problems it has outlined. First, women should be properly educated. Women must be able to support themselves in case a husband or family member cannot do so. Giving women access to the professions will reduce prostitution and social problems. Women also should have the legal rights of citizens—the rights to own property, have custody of their children, and participate in government.

Wollstonecraft's essay produced a great stir, both critical and favorable. Public opinion, however, was scandalized after her death when her husband, William Godwin, published the frank facts of her life—sex outside marriage, an illegitimate child, and a suicide attempt. Feminist ideas were branded as immoral and dangerous, apt to lead other women to live such a life. Nevertheless, whenever concerns for women's rights rise in the public consciousness, *A Vindication of the Rights of Woman* is pulled from the shelf, dusted off, reread, republished, and discussed with a great stir, both critical and favorable.

Theresa L. Crater

Further Reading

Craciun, Adriana, ed. *Mary Wollstonecraft's "A Vindication of the Rights of Woman": A Sourcebook*. New York: Routledge, 2002. Includes analyses of key passages, a contextual overview of the work, Wollstonecraft's letters and other contemporary documents about women and education, and responses to the work dating from Wollstonecraft's time to the late twentieth century.

Falco, Maria J., ed. *Feminist Interpretations of Mary Wollstonecraft*. University Park: Pennsylvania State University Press, 1996. A collection of twelve essays on a variety of political issues. Contains two essays that compare the thought of Jean-Jacques Rousseau and Wollstonecraft, including one that is a fictional dialogue composed of passages from their works to illustrate how these two champions of human rights disagreed on women's rights. Other essays deal with liberalism, slavery, the evolution of women's rights since the time of Wollstonecraft, and the changing reactions to Wollstonecraft since her death.

Ferguson, Moira, and Janet M. Todd. *Mary Wollstonecraft*. Boston: Twayne, 1984. A volume in the Twayne authors series providing concise, scholarly, and well-documented accounts of both Wollstonecraft's life and her literary career. Includes an assessment of her ideas, style, and influence. Stresses her professional achievements more than her personal experience.

Jacobs, Diane. *Her Own Woman: The Life of Mary Wollstonecraft*. New York: Simon & Schuster, 2001. A lively, well-researched biography that includes previously unavailable material from the letters of Joseph Johnson, Wollstonecraft's publisher.

Johnson, Claudia L., ed. *The Cambridge Companion to Mary Wollstonecraft*. New York: Cambridge University Press, 2002. Collection of essays providing numerous interpretations of Wollstonecraft's work and influence. Three of the essays deal with *A Vindication of the Rights of Woman*: "Mary Wollstonecraft's *Vindications* and Their Political Tradition" by Chris Jones, "The Religious Foundations of Mary Wollstonecraft's Feminism" by Barbara Taylor, and "Mary Wollstonecraft's *A Vindication of the Rights of Woman* and the Women Writers of Her Day" by Anne K. Mellor.

Kramnik, Miriam Brody. Introduction to *A Vindication of the Rights of Woman*, by Mary Wollstonecraft. New York: Penguin Books, 1975. This lengthy introduction to Wollstonecraft's work surveys her life and literary contributions. It discusses her within the framework of the history of feminism and compares her approach with the piecemeal efforts of nineteenth century feminists.

Sapiro, Virginia. *A Vindication of Political Virtue: The Political Theory of Mary Wollstonecraft*. Chicago: University of Chicago Press, 1992. An excellent analysis of Wollstonecraft's contribution to both feminism and Western political thought.

Taylor, Natalie Fuehrer. *The Rights of Woman as Chimera: The Political Philosophy of Mary Wollstonecraft*. New York: Routledge, 2007. Focuses on Wollstonecraft's political ideas, particularly her concept of the nature of woman. Compares her ideas to those of Aristotle, John Locke, and Jean-Jacques Rousseau, demonstrating how she critiqued her male predecessors and created her own philosophy.

Todd, Janet. *Mary Wollstonecraft: A Revolutionary Life*. New York: Columbia University Press, 2000. A close biographical examination of Wollstonecraft's life and work.

The Violent Bear It Away

Author: Flannery O'Connor (1925-1964)
First published: 1960
Type of work: Novel
Type of plot: Psychological realism
Time of plot: 1952
Locale: Tennessee

Principal characters:
FRANCIS MARION TARWATER, a fourteen-year-old boy
 trained to be a prophet
GEORGE F. RAYBER, his uncle
MASON TARWATER, Francis's great-uncle
BISHOP RAYBER, Francis's cousin
BERNICE BISHOP RAYBER, Francis's aunt, George's wife
BUFORD MUNSON, a neighbor
T. FAWCETT MEEKS, a traveling salesman
LUCETTE CARMODY, a child evangelist

The Story:

Mason Tarwater, great-uncle of Francis Marion Tarwater, has died at the breakfast table one morning. The old man had spent years training his nephew, with whom he lived in a backwoods spot called Powderhead, how to bury him properly. As young Francis Tarwater begins to prepare for the burial, he recalls events from his life with Old Tarwater and the various reasons he does not want to follow in the old man's footsteps. Young Tarwater recalls that the old man had kidnapped him from the home of his uncle, George F. Rayber, and provided a fundamentalist education quite different from the education the boy would have received in public school. Young Tarwater also recalls the old man's stories about his life as a prophet and his failed attempts to save relatives other than his great-nephew, notably Rayber, whom Old Tarwater kidnapped at age seven; Rayber rejected the old man's preaching and later tried to get young Tarwater back. Old Tarwater would tell his great-nephew that he shot Rayber in the leg and ear to prevent the boy's being taken away by Rayber and the woman who became his wife, Bernice Bishop.

Old Tarwater was pleased that Rayber and Bernice had only one child and that the child, Bishop Rayber, was an idiot, for idiocy would protect the boy from Rayber's foolish ideas. Young Tarwater remembers that he had been ordered by Old Tarwater to accept the mission of baptizing little Bishop. He also remembers a trip to the city with Old Tarwater, who found out from lawyers that he could not take Powderhead from Rayber and give it to young Tarwater; it was on this day that young Tarwater got the only glimpse of both Rayber and Bishop that he could remember while living with Old Tarwater.

As Tarwater starts to dig the old man's grave, he hears a stranger's voice. When two black people, a woman and Buford Munson, interrupt Tarwater's digging to have him

fill their jugs with liquor, Tarwater goes to Old Tarwater's still and gets drunk. The stranger's voice encourages young Tarwater to go his own way. After being scolded by Buford, Tarwater falls asleep, and Buford buries Old Tarwater in accordance with the old man's wishes. When young Tarwater awakes, he burns down the house, thinking Old Tarwater's body is still in it, and runs off toward the city.

A traveling salesman, T. Fawcett Meeks, picks up the hitchhiking Tarwater on the highway, lectures him about loving customers, hard work, and machines, and delivers him to the home of Rayber. While being transported by Meeks, Tarwater remembers Old Tarwater's stories of Rayber's life, especially how Rayber arranged for his sister to take a lover and give birth to Tarwater and how Rayber once betrayed Old Tarwater by writing up their conversations as a case study for a magazine. Old Tarwater's kidnapping of Francis Tarwater followed his reading of Rayber's article.

When Rayber takes young Tarwater into his home, they seem very strange to each other. Tarwater sees Rayber's hearing aid as a sign that Rayber is a mechanical man; Rayber sees the old man's influence all over young Tarwater. Rayber's son, Bishop, is immediately friendly, but Tarwater rejects the little boy. Rayber sets out on a campaign to introduce Tarwater to the city and the modern world. Tarwater is thoroughly unimpressed with the modern world, but he does sneak out of the house one night, and Rayber follows to find out what Tarwater likes. They end up at a Pentecostal church, where a child evangelist, Lucette Carmody, starts to direct her sermon at the astonished Rayber. The next day, Rayber tries taking Tarwater to the city park. While there, Rayber remembers how he had once tried to drown Bishop. Then Rayber notices Tarwater is about to baptize Bishop in the park's fountain and stops him. Later, Tarwater's memory of the park trip reveals that Tarwater's stranger/friend had encouraged him to drown Bishop.

After the trip to the park, Rayber next tries to get through to Tarwater by taking him fishing. While the two are out on the lake in a boat, Rayber's analysis of Tarwater's mind causes Tarwater to vomit, jump from the boat, and swim to shore. Rayber plans to surprise Tarwater with a visit to Powderhead to make him confront feelings about his past, but when Rayber goes to Powderhead in advance to prepare, he realizes that he cannot bear to return with Tarwater. Back at the lake, Rayber allows Tarwater to take Bishop out in a boat; in his cabin, Rayber collapses as he senses that Tarwater is drowning his son. Fleeing from the lake, Tarwater plans to take possession of Powderhead, as he tells the sleepy truck driver who gives him a ride. Tarwater admits to baptizing Bishop but denies that the act has any significance. After being dropped off, Tarwater is picked up by a man who gives him a smoke, drugs him to sleep with liquor, and rapes him.

When Tarwater awakes, he burns the woods around where the rape occurred, then heads toward Powderhead. He burns more woods when he hears his stranger/friend's voice again. When he reaches Powderhead, he encounters Buford, who explains that Old Tarwater was properly buried after all. Now Tarwater has a vision of his own role as a prophet, and instead of remaining at Powderhead, he heads back toward the city.

Critical Evaluation:

Flannery O'Connor is widely considered one of America's greatest short-story writers as well as one of the best religious writers of the modern era. Although her collected works comprise little more than two dozen stories and two novels, and although many of her works replay similar plots using similar sets of characters, she did a masterful job of investigating the specific issues that obsessed her. O'Connor's fictions are filled with humor as well as with profound insights into the eccentric, sometimes tortured strategies human beings use to create meaning.

O'Connor's people are sometimes considered flat, almost cartoonish, but *The Violent Bear It Away* uses several devices to emphasize the complexities of psychology. For example, the conflicting sides to Francis Marion Tarwater's mind are given voices in the form of strangers and friends who talk to him. Although Tarwater consistently refuses to confess his thoughts to other, real characters, he does carry on conversations with parts of himself, allowing O'Connor to analyze his simultaneous attraction to and rejection of the religious and nonreligious paths his various parental figures have planned for him. In addition, O'Connor draws numerous parallels among Old Tarwater, Rayber, Francis Tarwater, and even

Bishop, encouraging the reader to assume that what one character thinks or feels, the others might experience in some form.

Each of the characters arguably contains parts of the others. Although Old Tarwater is dead when the novel begins, the reader receives so much information about the old man's stories and opinions, and the other characters are so haunted by him, that Old Tarwater seems clearly alive. When Tarwater marches off toward the city at the novel's end, the reader knows that he carries the other characters with him. Even at times when O'Connor's intent may seem to be to distinguish between characters, as when Rayber and Tarwater remember in separate chapters their trip to the city park, the reader can assume that each character feels much of what the other feels. In general, the novel's numerous flashbacks leave the reader with the impression that at least three characters are here collaborating on the creation of a family mythology and that they all exist beyond time, whether alive or dead.

One of O'Connor's major themes is the power of mystery. The kind of rationality promoted by such characters as Rayber and Meeks, with its intelligence testing, its laws, and its economy tied to the machine, is consistently ridiculed by the novel. In O'Connor's world, almost anything is valuable if it turns off the common sense of the brain. Idiocy is good as a protection from education. Liquor may be endorsed as a way to shut down consciousness. Violent acts are essentially unreasonable, but they may be necessary to break through the mind's reasonable defenses.

O'Connor's love of mystery also relates to the religious themes in the novel. Tarwater and Old Tarwater both have problems with forming overly sensible expectations about what a moment of religious insight would be. They expect elaborate visions of exotic divinity; what they get is much more homespun—revelation through images of water and fire, fish and bread. One of the major tasks O'Connor sets for herself in this novel is to make interesting for the modern reader the sacrament of baptism, a ritual in danger of becoming boring through familiarity. To force the reader to investigate the meaning of baptism, she makes it new by having it performed on an idiot by an unenthusiastic Tarwater, who kills at the same time he baptizes. O'Connor makes religion intellectually interesting by making it painful rather than comforting. Old Tarwater says, "The world was made for the dead," a sentiment O'Connor seems to endorse. O'Connor is also interested in making fresh for modern readers the idea of the prophet. Her prophets are individualistic, anti-intellectual, destructive, and suicidal—so driven by unconscious forces as to seem insane.

One of the paradoxes of the novel is that while the characters pursue intensely eccentric personal paths, they ultimately seem remarkably similar. For all its rejection of the city, O'Connor's novel hints at the possibility of building a good community. Although the four main characters are white, there are indications that Tarwater at the end of the novel will also minister to African Americans, and Buford Munson, a black man, is arguably the novel's most religious character. There may be less reason to be confident that Tarwater will someday bring women into his community; he has been taught to consider women whores, and the acquaintance of Lucette Carmody, the female who most fascinates Tarwater, may do little to move Tarwater out of his adolescence. Another of the novel's surprises is how little family seems to have to do with the building of community. Relations between parents and children are always strained and sometimes violent in O'Connor's work, and the conscious rejection of family often seems necessary for an O'Connor character to find the right path.

Marshall Bruce Gentry

Further Reading

Asals, Frederick. *Flannery O'Connor: The Imagination of Extremity.* Athens: University of Georgia Press, 1982. Examines O'Connor's attraction to polar oppositions. Emphasizes the Christian sacramentalism, psychology, and use of doubles in *The Violent Bear It Away* as well as the differences between O'Connor's two novels.

Bacon, Jon Lance. *Flannery O'Connor and Cold War Culture.* New York: Cambridge University Press, 1993. Treats O'Connor as a southern critic of nationalistic Cold War culture in the United States. Asserts that *The Violent Bear It Away* represents a rejection of cultural pressures to conform in terms of politics, public education, consumerism, and religion.

Cash, Jean W. *Flannery O'Connor: A Life.* University of Tennessee, 2002. Painstakingly researched chronicle of O'Connor's life depicts her as a very private, odd, and self-contained woman, devoted to Catholicism and to her writing.

Darretta, John. *Before the Sun Has Set: Retribution in the Fiction of Flannery O'Connor.* New York: Peter Lang, 2006. Focuses on the biblical ideas of retribution, salvation, and grace in O'Connor's fiction, including *The Violent Bear It Away.*

Gentry, Marshall Bruce. *Flannery O'Connor's Religion of the Grotesque.* Jackson: University Press of Mississippi, 1986. Distinguishes between O'Connor and her narrator in *The Violent Bear It Away* in an effort to answer the claim that O'Connor wrote from the devil's point of view. Discusses O'Connor's typescripts and emphasizes Rayber's similarity to other characters.

Gooch, Brad. *Flannery: A Life of Flannery O'Connor.* New York: Little, Brown, 2008. Biography provides much critical analysis of O'Connor's fiction, both the individual works and the scope of the author's career. Argues that despite the fact that she wrote two novels, O'Connor was not really a novelist but was perhaps the greatest twentieth century American short-story writer.

Hendin, Josephine. *The World of Flannery O'Connor.* Bloomington: Indiana University Press, 1970. Controversial but important early study generally downplays religious explanations of O'Connor's works. Treats *The Violent Bear It Away* as an examination of a failed initiation into manhood in which the protagonist finally reverts to a painfully childish role.

Johansen, Ruthann Knechel. *The Narrative Secret of Flannery O'Connor: The Trickster as Interpreter.* Tuscaloosa: University of Alabama Press, 1994. Emphasizes the structures in O'Connor's texts and examines the apocalyptic nature of those texts as well as the role of the trickster figures. Compares O'Connor's two novels to each other and to biblical narratives.

Kirk, Connie Ann. *Critical Companion to Flannery O'Connor.* New York: Facts On File, 2008. Provides a good introduction to O'Connor's fiction. Includes a concise biography, entries on O'Connor's two novels and other works, with subentries on her characters, and entries about her friends, literary influences, and the places and themes of her fiction.

The Violent Land

Author: Jorge Amado (1912-2001)
First published: Terras do sem fin, 1942 (English
    translation, 1945)
Type of work: Novel
Type of plot: Social realism
Time of plot: Late nineteenth century
Locale: Bahia, Brazil

Principal characters:
COLONEL HORACIO DA SILVEIRA, a cacao planter
COLONEL SINHÔ BADARÓ, another planter
DOÑA ESTER DA SILVEIRA, Colonel da Silveira's wife
DOÑA ANA BADARÓ, Colonel Badaró's daughter
CAPTAIN JOÃO MAGALHÃES, in love with Doña Ana
DR. VIRGILIO CABRAL, Doña Ester's lover and da Silveira's
    lawyer
MARGOT, a prostitute
JUCA BADARÓ, Colonel Badaró's younger brother

The Story:

In the minds of most Brazilians, the São Jorge dos Ilhéus is a semibarbarous country ruled by a handful of rich planters who style themselves colonels. These men rose, almost without exception, from humble origins by means of courage, bravado, and murder. The two most important planters are Colonel Horacio da Silveira and Colonel Sinhô Badaró. Between their lands lies a large forest, upon which both men have long cast covetous eyes. The forest, actually a jungle, could be cleared to uncover almost fabulous cacao-growing soil.

Among the strangers who pour into the region in search of wealth at the time are several people who are to range themselves on one side or the other in the coming struggle. Dr. Virgilio Cabral, a cultured and talented lawyer, allies himself with da Silveira. With the lawyer comes Margot, a beautiful prostitute who fell in love with him and became his mistress while he was a student. Another arrival is Captain João Magalhães, a professional gambler and a courageous opportunist who calls himself a military engineer. Among his admirers are Juca Badaró, Colonel Badaró's younger brother, and Doña Ana Badaró, the colonel's daughter, who is also the heir to the Badaró fortunes.

Soon after his arrival, Cabral falls in love with Ester, da Silveira's beautiful wife. The woman, who hates her semibarbarous husband, quickly returns the affection of the more cultured man. When she becomes his mistress, both know that they will be killed if the husband finds them out. As his ardor for Ester increases, the lawyer's affection for his former mistress wanes, and soon Margot finds herself unwanted by her lover. In retaliation, and because she needs someone to support her, Margot becomes the mistress of Juca. Out of spite, she also furnishes him with scandal about the opposition, gossip that he turns to account in the newspaper that favors the Badarós.

Professionally, as well as amorously, Cabral is a success, for he finds an old survey of the contested lands and registers the title in da Silveira's name after he bribes the registry officials. The Badaró family quickly retaliates by burning the registry office and all the records on file. In addition, the Badarós hire Magalhães to run a survey for them. He makes the survey, even though he lacks the proper knowledge to do so. His presence at the Badaró plantation earns him the respect of the Badaró brothers and the love of Doña Ana Badaró. The self-styled captain, always an opportunist, permits himself to fall in love with the woman and pay court to her.

The Badaró family is the more powerful of the two factions, so da Silveira goes to several small planters and promises to let them divide half of the forest land if they, as a group, will help him hold it against the Badarós. There is bloody fighting on both sides of the forest and within it, for both factions hire many assassins and bodyguards to back up their interests with bullets. The Badarós control the local government, and the state government is in opposition to the federal government of Brazil.

Juca is assassinated by a hired gunman after he insults Cabral. Juca found the lawyer dancing—at the woman's request—with Margot and insulted the lawyer for daring to do so. On the other side, too, there are disappointments and deaths. Cabral and da Silveira are deterred in their plans when the colonel falls ill with a fever. The planter recovers, but his wife, the lawyer's mistress, becomes ill as a result of nursing her husband. Her death removes one incentive in the efforts of both her husband and her lover, but they stubbornly continue the fight.

As the struggle in the courts and in the fields continues, the Badarós spend more and more money. They not only sell their current crop of cacao pods but also sell their next year's crop to raise funds. Before his assassination, Juca saw to it that his niece, Doña Ana, was married to the gambler, for he saw in Magalhães an ambitious man willing to fight for money and power. The proposal the Badarós make is so tempting that the captain agrees to take his wife's name, her father insisting that he do so to carry on the Badaró line.

At first, by tacit consent, the contending parties do no damage to one another's cacao trees, but as the Badarós become desperate, they instruct their desperadoes to burn the cacao groves. Their opponents see that the matter has to be settled at once, lest both parties be irretrievably ruined and become victims of someone stronger than they. Colonel da Silveira and his henchman, along with their paid gunmen, attack the Badaró plantation in force and drive off the family, after killing all the men except a handful led by Magalhães.

Da Silveira and his men think that the women of the Badaró household were sent away, but the attackers are greeted by gunfire from Doña Ana herself as they enter the house. When she runs out of ammunition, she gives up, expecting to be killed. The attackers let her go, however, because she is a woman. The Badaró rout is completed by an announcement from the Brazilian capital that the political party favoring da Silveira is in power and is sending troops and government agents to the district to quiet the violence. The jungle lands are ceded to the da Silveira faction by the government's action. Da Silveira is forced to stand trial for the murder of Juca, but the trial, staged more to clear the colonel than to find him guilty, is a mere formality.

The district quickly settles down after the great feud ends and the new government starts its operations, but there is to be one more assassination. While going through his dead wife's effects, da Silveira discovers the letters Cabral wrote to her. He is horrified and embarrassed to learn of her infidelity, which he did not suspect, and his lawyer's duplicity. After thinking about the matter for some time, he sends a gunman to clear his honor by killing the man who made him a cuckold.

To symbolize the new peace that comes into the frontier district, the Church makes the city of Ilhéus the seat of a newly created diocese and sends a bishop to officiate as its representative there. As if to show the value of the former jungle land, the cacao trees planted there produce a crop in the fourth year, a full twelve months earlier than usual.

Critical Evaluation:

Jorge Amado's novel is titled *Terras do sem fin* (the endless lands) in Portuguese. This story is the standard-bearer of the cacao cycle in Brazilian literature, a series of novels exposing exploitation of cacao workers. Brazilian novelists have long been making a huge mosaic of Brazil with their novels, each novel being a tiny stone in the literary mosaic of that subcontinent, and Amado's work is a worthy contribution and his masterpiece.

The Violent Land (first published in English in 1945) is the story of Bahia's Panhandle, where a balmy climate, fertile soil, and lack of high winds make it one of the few areas on earth well suited for chocolate trees, whose weak stems and heavy pods need heat but cannot stand strong winds. Amado's characterization is particularly representative of the raw frontier that the Panhandle of Bahia (a narrow strip stretching southward toward the mountains of Espirito Santo) has been for so long. The reader thus sees not only an area where the "colonels" and their heavily armed cohorts oppress the weak but also the Bahian *sertão* (backlands) in general, brimming with blood, old feuds, religious messianism, and fanaticism. Amado's characters are thus not larger-than-life but authentic, flesh-and-blood realities from rural Bahia. His principal characterization flaw is an error of omission, for the warmly human types so common everywhere in Brazil, including Bahia, are lacking in the pages of *The Violent Land*.

This novel refreshingly explodes the oft-heard myth that Brazil, unlike Spanish America, is a bland and frivolous land not given to violence. Amado's novel bristles with the violence and mystery endemic to the *sertão*, and it is for this reason that Amado's title of *The Endless Lands* has been changed for the book's English translation into *The Violent Land*. Amado paints a land fertile with blood, as his preface indicates. Set at about the end of the nineteenth century, when cacao was power, wealth, and life, the novel's action portrays the enslavement of everything and everyone to the cacao pod. The shadow of cacao darkens every heart. It smothers finer instincts and levels all characters from aristocratic Colonel Horacio da Silveira to the more common Badarós. Nothing washes away the cacao stain. Workers in the orchards have a thick crust of cacao slime on their boots, and the colonels, lawyers, merchants, and *jaguncos* (hired killers) have cacao slime in their hearts.

The Violent Land reflects progress, however, for the colonels are drawn as a crude but civilizing force in Brazil's historic "march to the west" that opened up the once trackless *sertão*. Amado was born on a cacao plantation in 1912 and admired the *fazendeiros* (ranchers), such as his own father, who settled the raw Panhandle, crossed lands, built roads, and founded towns, all this through heroic strength and what Amado terms "the poetry of their lives." The novel's first scene, symbolically enough, is aboard a ship drawing away from the black-tile roofs of the baroque city of São Salvador de Bahia. The passengers aboard are immigrants to the rich but violent lands of the Panhandle and are discussing property, money, cacao, and death. They sing a sad song that presages disaster, but that night, in their staterooms and steerage quarters, they dream of laden cacao trees.

Landscape is an important factor in *The Violent Land* and reflects Brazil's intrinsic beauty. Amado paints the golden mornings dawning over green palms, the red soil under the cacao trees, the blue-green waves of the sea, and indigo skies. One also sees stormy nights, wild Brahma cattle, birds, and snakes. Trees are almost idolized, especially the cacao. Above all, Amado lyrically paints the forest in the uninterrupted sleep that it enjoyed before the colonels came. Days and nights pass over the virginal expanses of trees, along with winter rains and summer suns. The waiting forest is like an unexplored sea, locked in its own mystery: virginal, lovely, and radiant. Amado also presents the varied Bahian racial types, from Scandinavian-like blonds to Latin brunettes and Hamitic blacks. One also sees the colonels in khaki trousers, white hats, and gun belts as well as the leather-clad *jaguncos*, legendarily ferocious *oncas* (wild cats), ranch tools, and folklore.

Fear is an additional element in the story. The forest's mysteries incite fear—Ester hysterically fears snakes and is haunted by the phobia that they will one night invade her house en masse. The backlanders tell many snake stories, while dogs howl at night, rain clouds are dark, and nights are jet-black; but the violent Badaró family and the *jaguncos* do not know fear. The Badarós even read the Bible daily for they, like the endless lands that they so ruthlessly penetrate, are many-sided.

Lamentably, the storied and colorful old city of São Salvador de Bahia does not loom in *The Violent Land*. Little, pastel São Jorge dos Ilhéus, "a city of palms in the wind," is, however, well depicted. Its streets are lined by palms, but it is dominated by the cacao tree, for the scent of chocolate is in every conversation, and each colonel's fortune can be measured by the size of his mansion. Inland from the pastel town, on every red-dirt road leading into the cacao lands, are crosses without names.

Brazilian novelists complained for decades that the harsh, nasal, Germanic-sounding Portuguese language in which they wrote was "the Graveyard of Literature," a literary cul-de-sac. *The Violent Land*, however, was translated into more than twenty languages, and translations of other novels into foreign languages have since been opening Brazilian literature to the world. Amado's masterwork also helps reveal that the key to Brazilian literature is not chronology, or style, or study of influences, but geography. *The Violent Land* is to be read and regarded as a work of the land of Bahia.

"Critical Evaluation" by William Freitas

Further Reading

Brower, Keith H., Earl E. Fitz, and Enrique Martínez-Vidal, eds. *Jorge Amado: New Critical Essays*. New York: Routledge, 2001. One of the essays, "Bitter Harvest: Violent Oppression in *Cacau* and *Terras do sem fin*" by Sandra L. Dixon, focuses on *The Violent Land*. Other essays analyze Amado's early work, his critical reputation, and Brazilian popular music in his fiction.

Chamberlain, Bobby J. *Jorge Amado*. Boston: Twayne, 1990. A study of Amado's major novels. Chamberlain places the author's fiction in a biographical and bibliographic context, offers critical analysis, and lays the groundwork for a reevaluation of the author's novelistic output. Discusses *The Violent Land* as the forerunner of the later novels. Includes chronology and annotated bibliography.

Ellison, Fred P. *Brazil's New Novel: Four Northeastern Masters*. Berkeley: University of California Press, 1954. An insightful study examining style, theme, and characterization in Amado's early fiction. Includes a discussion of *The Violent Land*. One of the earliest studies in English of Amado.

Lowe, Elizabeth. *The City in Brazilian Literature*. Madison, N.J.: Fairleigh Dickinson University Press, 1982. Characterizes Amado's depiction of Salvador, Bahia, as "picturesque exoticism," and his portrayal of the urban poor as "carnivalization."

Pescatello, Ann, ed. "The Braziliera: Images and Realities in Writings of Machado de Assis and Jorge Amado." In *Female and Male in Latin America: Essays*. Pittsburgh, Pa.: University of Pittsburgh Press, 1973. Compares Amado's female characters (including those in *The Violent Land*) with those of Machado de Assis. Detects a preoccupation with class and race in both writers' characterizations of women.

Schade, George D. "Three Contemporary Brazilian Novels: Some Comparisons and Contrasts." *Hispania* 39, no. 4 (December, 1956): 391-396. Compares the structure, theme, and characterization in *The Violent Land* with Graciliano Ramos's *Ang stia* (1936; *Anguish*, 1946) and Rachel de Queiroz's *As três Marias* (1939; *The Three Marias*, 1963).

The Virginian
A Horseman of the Plains

Author: Owen Wister (1860-1938)
First published: 1902
Type of work: Novel
Type of plot: Western
Time of plot: Late nineteenth century
Locale: Wyoming

Principal characters:
THE VIRGINIAN, a cowboy
JUDGE HENRY, the Virginian's employer
TRAMPAS, a cowboy and the Virginian's enemy
STEVE, a cowboy friend of the Virginian
SHORTY, a cowboy at Judge Henry's ranch
MOLLY WOOD, a young schoolteacher at Bear Creek,
    Wyoming

The Story:

The Virginian is sent by his employer, the owner of the Sunk Creek Ranch, to meet an Eastern guest at Medicine Bow and escort him 260 miles from the town to the ranch. While the Virginian and the guest await the arrival of the Easterner's trunk on the next train, the cowboy enters into a poker game. One of the players, a cowboy named Trampas, accuses the Virginian of cheating. The man backs down before the Virginian's gun, but it is clear to everyone that the Virginian has made an implacable enemy.

A few months later, in the fall, a schoolmistress comes West from Vermont to teach in the new school at Bear Creek, Wyoming. All the single men—and there are many of them in the territory—eagerly await the arrival of the new teacher, Molly Wood. The Virginian is fortunate in his first meeting with her. A drunken stage driver tries to ford a creek in high water and maroons his coach and passenger. The Virginian, who is just passing, lifts the young woman out of the stage and deposits her safely on the bank of the stream. After he rides away, Molly misses her handkerchief and realizes that the young cowboy somehow contrived to take it.

The next time the Virginian sees Molly, she is a guest at a barbecue. He rides his horse for two days for the opportunity to see her, but she coquettishly refuses to notice him. Piqued, the Virginian and another cowboy get drunk and play a prank on all the people who brought babies to the barbecue; they switch the babies' clothing, so that many of the mothers carry off the wrong children. Before returning to Sunk Creek, the Virginian warns Molly that she is going to love him eventually, no matter what she thinks of him now.

During the next year, the Virginian begins to read books for the first time since he left school in the sixth grade. He borrows the books from Molly, which gives him the opportunity to ride to Bear Creek to see her at intervals. In the meantime, he rises high in the estimation of his employer. Judge Henry puts him in charge of a party of men who are to escort two trainloads of steers to the Chicago market.

On the trip back to the ranch, the Virginian's men threaten to desert the train to go prospecting for gold that was discovered in the Black Hills. The ringleader of the insurgents is Trampas. The Virginian sees that the best way to win over the men is to make a fool of Trampas. His chance comes when the train stops near a bridge that is being repaired. Since there is no food on the train, the Virginian goes out and gathers a sackful of frogs to cook. Then he begins to tell a tall story about frogs that completely takes in Trampas. When the other cowboys see how foolish Trampas appears, they are willing to return to the ranch, much to the discomfiture of their ringleader.

The Virginian returns to Sunk Creek to find a pleasant surprise awaiting him: The ranch foreman leaves because of his disabled wife, whereupon the judge makes the Virginian his foreman. Trampas expects to be discharged from his job as soon as the Virginian becomes foreman, but the Virginian decides it is better to have his enemy in sight, so Trampas stays on, sullen and defiant.

The following spring, the Virginian makes a trip to a neighboring ranch. On the way back, he is attacked by Indians and severely wounded. He manages to escape from the Indians and make his way to a spring. There he is found, half dead, by Molly. The Indians are still in the vicinity, but the young woman stays with him at the risk of her life. She binds his wounds, takes him back to her cabin, and calls a doctor.

Molly, who is preparing to return to her home in the East, has already packed her possessions. She postpones her return to care for the Virginian, and by the time he recovers sufficiently to go back to work, she changes her mind. She is sure by then that she is in love with the cowboy foreman, and when the Virginian leaves her cabin for Sunk Creek, Molly promises to marry him.

Upon returning to work, the Virginian finds that his enemy, Trampas, has disappeared, taking another of the cowboys, Shorty, with him. About the same time, the ranches in that territory begin to lose cattle to rustlers. A posse is formed to track down the cattle thieves. After several weeks of searching, two of the thieves are caught. Since the rustlers somehow managed to gain control of the local courts and were already freed on one charge, the posse hanged both of them. It is a terrible experience for the Virginian, especially since one of the men, Steve, was a close friend. The Virginian hates to think he hanged his friend, and the hurt is worse because the condemned man refused to say a word to his former companion. On his way back to Sunk Creek, the Virginian comes across the trail of the remaining two rustlers, Trampas and Shorty. Because they have only one horse between them with which to escape, Trampas murders Shorty.

When Molly hears of the lynching and of the Virginian's part in it, she at first refuses to marry him. After a conversation with Judge Henry, however, she realizes that the Virginian did no more than his duty. She and the Virginian are reconciled, and a date is set for their wedding.

On the day before their wedding, Molly and the Virginian start to ride to Medicine Bow. On the way, they meet Trampas, who gallops ahead of them into the town. Molly questions the Virginian about the man and discovers the enmity between the two. When they arrive in town, they are warned that Trampas said he would shoot the Virginian if he were not out of town by sunset. Molly tells him that she can never marry him if he fights with Trampas and kills him. The Virginian, knowing that his honor is at stake, leaves her in the hotel and goes out to face his enemy. Trampas fires first and misses. Then the Virginian fires and kills Trampas.

When the Virginian returns to the hotel, Molly is too glad to see him alive to remember her threat. Hearing the shots, she was afraid that the Virginian was killed. They are married the following day, as they planned, and spend two months of their honeymoon high in the Rocky Mountains.

Critical Evaluation:

The Virginian is based on Owen Wister's experiences in the cattle country of Wyoming during the 1880's and 1890's, and he used that personal knowledge to create the model for all future Western novels. The setting for the story is the cattle business of the Wyoming Territory, when tension grew between large cattle ranchers and smaller stock raisers. In April, 1892, wealthy cattlemen organized an expedition to arrest or kill all those in northern Wyoming who were suspected of being rustlers. The Johnson County War that ensued became one of the most notorious episodes of fron-

tier violence. As an aristocratic visitor from Pennsylvania, Wister knew many of the men who were involved on the side of the large ranchers, and he used the people and events of the range war as a backdrop for the rivalry between the Virginian and his enemy, the rustler Trampas. He modeled Judge Henry on Frank Wolcott, a leading participant in the Johnson County violence.

Beyond describing the frontier situation, the novel had a larger artistic purpose. Wister traveled to the West to recuperate after a nervous breakdown and to experience a change from the spreading industrialism and social tension of the Eastern United States where he grew up. In *The Virginian*, Wister deals with the way the Eastern narrator and the Virginian's future bride respond to the rough life in the West during the heyday of the range cattle industry. By the time Wister wrote his novel two decades later, the open range and the free life that the cowboys and ranchers knew was already vanishing. *The Virginian* reflects his sense that something valuable was lost with the spread of civilization, a feeling shared by many Americans in the early part of the twentieth century. Wister's book evokes the spirit of the West and laments the passing of that spirit in the face of modern progress and economic development. In novel form, Wister expresses many of the same ideas that Frederick Jackson Turner discusses in his 1894 essay "The Significance of the Frontier in American History" and his 1920 book *The Frontier in American History*.

The Virginian is actually more a series of separate episodes and encounters than a fully realized novel. Some of these moments became classics of the Western genre. The first confrontation, for example, between the Virginian and Trampas—including the response "When you call me that, smile"—was based on an actual encounter Wister had seen, which with his skill as a writer he transformed into so memorable a moment that it has been duplicated on motion picture screens and television programs ever since. The final shootout between hero and villain in town just after sunset likewise became the model for countless repetitions of that confrontation in other Western novels, motion pictures, and television episodes.

What gave *The Virginian* its classic status in the literature of the American West were the larger themes Wister developed within the framework of the novel. With his ability to handle all the challenges he encounters in his rugged environment, the Virginian represents the strength and power of the frontier. He emerges as a true gentleman because of the instinctive rightness of his behavior. He only kills Trampas after giving him the first shot. In his depiction of the Virginian's courtship of Molly Wood, Wister depicts the underlying virtues of the West and its codes of manliness, honor, and self-reliance. In his depiction of the Virginian's confrontation with Trampas and the practice of cattle rustling, Wister even manages in Judge Henry's words to Molly to make an argument for frontier lawlessness and lynching as a necessary response to the untamed conditions of the West.

At the same time, the East and its values are shown to have a civilizing effect on the Virginian and his world. He responds to Molly's gentility and learning by beginning to read books and extend his rudimentary education. He forsakes the lonely and doomed life of the average young cowhand to become a trusted foreman and eventually a prosperous ranch owner in partnership with his patron. At the end of the book, he evolves into a model of the frontier capitalist supervising many businesses. The Virginian is shown to be equally at his ease in the East with Molly's straitlaced relatives and in the West as an honest man who succeeds in the individualistic world of the frontier.

The Virginian achieved instant best-seller status when it was published in 1902 because it captured so well the American fascination with the frontier and with the people who tamed the West in the nineteenth century. Readers responded to the laconic competence of the hero, the implicit violence of the rivalry with Trampas, and the romantic love story with the Eastern schoolteacher. The book also struck a chord because of Wister's skill in evoking an era that was so recently past.

Wister never repeated the popular success of *The Virginian* with any of his other works. The character he created went on to be the subject of four motion pictures and a long-running television series. While Wister knew that he touched a chord in the national psyche with his fictional creation, he did not succumb to the temptation to exploit his book's success with a sequel or related novels. The Virginian remains what he was in Wister's book. He is the Western hero with an obscure past that prepared him for the dangers he had to face. He passes through the story, righting wrongs, illuminating character, and doing justice. At the end, he finds happiness and personal fulfillment as do, vicariously, Wister's readers.

"Critical Evaluation" by Lewis L. Gould

Further Reading

Cobbs, John L. *Owen Wister.* Boston: Twayne, 1984. Argues that Wister was a good writer whose works deserve more attention. Devotes one chapter to a discussion of *The Vir-*

ginian and provides a good survey of other secondary sources on the book through the early 1980's.

Etulain, Richard W. *Owen Wister.* Boise, Idaho: Boise State College, 1973. A brief survey of Wister's career and a good introduction to his writings. Includes some perceptive comments about *The Virginian.*

Graulich, Melody, and Stephen Tatum, eds. *Reading "The Virginian" in the New West.* Lincoln: University of Nebraska Press, 2003. Collection of novels reexamining the novel and using the book as a means of studying twenty-first century writing about the region. Includes discussions of Wister's life and travels, his handling of gender and race in *The Virginian*, the novel's role in American literary and cultural history, and adaptations of the novel for film, stage, and television.

Lambert, Neal. "Owen Wister's Virginian: The Genesis of a Cultural Hero." *Western American Literature* 6 (Summer, 1971): 99-107. A perceptive analysis of the development and meaning of the central figure of Wister's novel by one of the leading students of his work.

Payne, Darwin. *Owen Wister: Chronicler of the West, Gentleman of the East.* Dallas, Tex.: Southern Methodist University Press, 1985. One of the best available biographies of Wister, which draws on extensive research in his papers at the Library of Congress and other manuscript collections. Contains an abundance of material on the history of *The Virginian* and the response it evoked during Wister's lifetime.

Reid, Margaret. "'Traces of a Vanished World' in Owen Wister's *The Virginian.*" In *Cultural Secrets as Narrative Form: Storytelling in Nineteenth-Century America.* Columbus: Ohio State University Press, 2004. Devotes three chapters to the novel, discussing its genesis, influence on subsequent literature, romance and nostalgia in the work, and the book's depiction of frontier heroes. Argues that the Western frontier has taken on a "mythic force" in the creation of America's national identity.

White, G. Edward. *The Eastern Establishment and the Western Experience: The West of Frederic Remington, Theodore Roosevelt, and Owen Wister.* New Haven, Conn.: Yale University Press, 1968. Examines the way in which Wister interacted with the West and the historical circumstances that led him to write *The Virginian.* Considers Wister's links with participants in the Johnson County War of April, 1892.

The Virginians
A Tale of the Last Century

Author: William Makepeace Thackeray (1811-1863)
First published: 1857-1859, serial; 1858, 1859, book
Type of work: Novel
Type of plot: Historical
Time of plot: Late eighteenth century
Locale: England and the colony of Virginia

Principal characters:
GEORGE and HARRY WARRINGTON, the Virginians
RACHEL ESMOND WARRINGTON, their mother
GEORGE WASHINGTON, a family friend
LORD CASTLEWOOD, an English kinsman
MARIA ESMOND, Lord Castlewood's sister
BARONESS BERNSTEIN, Rachel Warrington's half sister and formerly Beatrix Esmond
COLONEL LAMBERT, a friend
THEO LAMBERT, Colonel Lambert's daughter and George's wife
HETTY LAMBERT, Colonel Lambert's other daughter
FANNY MOUNTAIN WARRINGTON, Harry's wife

The Story:

Although Harry and George Warrington are twins, George is declared the heir to their father's estate by virtue of having been born half an hour before his brother. Both are headstrong lads, greatly pampered by their widowed mother, Rachel Esmond Warrington, who manages her Virginia estate, Castlewood, much as she managed the mansion in the old country. She never lets her sons forget their high birth, and she herself had dropped the name of Warrington in favor of her birth name, Esmond, so that everyone would remember her noble rank. Rachel is a dictator on her plantation, and although she is respected by many, she is loved by few.

Harry and George are trained according to the place and the time. They learn to ride, to shoot, and to gamble like gentlemen, but they have little formal education other than a small knowledge of Latin and French. Their mother hopes they might pattern themselves after Colonel George Washington, who is their neighbor and her close friend. Harry worships Washington from his youth to his death, but George and Colonel Washington are never to be friends.

When General Braddock arrives from England to command the English troops in the war against the French, Washington and George join his forces. Although Harry is a better soldier, George represents the family because of his position as elder son. Braddock is defeated, and George is reported captured and killed by the French. George's mother blames Washington for not guarding her son, and Washington is no longer welcome at Castlewood.

Upon George's death, Harry becomes the heir, and his mother sends him to visit his relatives in England. There he meets his mother's kinsman, Lord Castlewood; her half sister, Baroness Bernstein; and Will, Maria, and Fanny Esmond, his cousins. Of all of his relatives, only Baroness Bernstein is fond of him. Harry and Will are enemies from their first meeting, and the rest of the family thinks him a savage and tolerate him only because he will some day inherit the estate in Virginia. Harry thinks he is in love with Maria, who is his mother's age, and sends her many gifts and passionate letters declaring himself hers and asking for her hand in marriage.

Harry is the toast of the country. He spends money lavishly on fine clothes and horses and at first wins thousands of pounds at cards; but when his luck turns and he loses all of his money, most of his former friends have only unkind words for him. Matters become so desperate that he is jailed for his debts, and Baroness Bernstein is the only one of his relatives who offers to help him. Nevertheless, there is a string attached to her offer. She is violently opposed to his intended marriage to Maria and will pay his debts only if he promises to break his word to that lady. Although Harry is tired of Maria, he feels it beneath a gentleman of his position to break his word, and he refuses the Baroness's help under her conditions. He would rather remain in prison.

There his brother George finds him. George escaped from the French after eighteen months in prison and returned to his home in Virginia, where he and his mother decided that he, too, should visit England. He pays his brother's debts, and the two boys have a joyful reunion. Harry now has to return to his status as younger brother, and George assumes his place as heir to Castlewood in Virginia.

Before Harry's imprisonment and George's arrival in England, Harry made the acquaintance of Colonel Lambert and his family. There were two daughters, Theo and Hetty, whom the twin brothers found charming. Theo and George fell in love, and after overcoming her father's objections, they were married. At first, they lived in poverty, for George spent all of his money to rescue Harry from debtors' prison and to buy for him a commission in the army. For a time, George's only income is from two tragedies he wrote, one a success and the other a failure.

Shortly after Harry receives his commission, he joins General Wolfe and sails for America to fight the French in the colonies. Maria releases him from his promise to her, and he gladly takes leave of his English relatives. About this time, George inherits a title and an estate from an unexpected source. Sir Miles Warrington, his father's brother, dies; and young Miles Warrington, the only male heir, is killed in an accident; therefore, the title and the estate fall to George. He and Theo now live in comparative luxury. They travel extensively, and one day they decide to visit George's mother and brother in Virginia.

When they arrive in America, they find the colonies to be in a state of unrest. The colonists are determined not to pay all the taxes that the British Crown levied against them, and there is much talk of war. There is also trouble at Castlewood. Harry marries Fanny Mountain, the daughter of his mother's housekeeper, and his mother refuses to accept the girl. Harry moves to his own smaller estate, but there is a great tension among the members of the family. George and Theo and their mother are loyal to the king. Harry becomes a true Virginian and follows General Washington into battle. Despite their different loyalties, the brothers remain friends.

Shortly before the end of the war, George and Theo return to England. Although they are grieved at the outcome of the war, it makes little difference in their lives. Harry visits them in England after the death of his wife, but their mother never again leaves Virginia. George and Theo try to persuade Hetty to marry Harry, whom she once loved deeply, but she refuses to leave her widowed father. The only departure from their quiet life comes when Lord Castlewood tries to steal Castlewood in Virginia from their mother after her deed and title are burned during the war. George, however, is able to prevent the fraud and save the estate. Intending never to leave England again, he renounces his right to the Virginia land. Harry returns to Virginia, where he is made a general, to live out his life at Castlewood in the company of his mother. The brothers are destined never to meet again, but their love for each other goes with them throughout their lives.

Critical Evaluation:

William Makepeace Thackeray is popularly believed to have conceived the idea for *The Virginians* after seeing two swords, mementos of the Battle of Bunker Hill, mounted in the manner described in the opening of the novel in the library of a contemporary historian named Prescott. While such anecdotes are often false, Thackeray did visit Prescott and later outlined to American novelist John Esten Cooke a plan for the novel that is, indeed, strongly suggested by the opening of the work. The story was to take place during the American Revolution and was to include two brothers as the predominant characters who would take different sides in the conflict and who would be in love with the same woman. The war itself was to be given major emphasis. Obviously, Thackeray failed to adhere very closely to this plan, and the significant shortcomings of the work are probably chargeable to that regrettable fact. Thackeray faced two problems in the writing of *The Virginians* that well may have been responsible for his seemingly pointless deviation from a sound, organized plan. One of the problems is inherent in the writing of a sequel novel: The author is faced with the twin constraints of fidelity to previous characterizations and compatibility with an established history. Such constraints, as other authors have proved, are almost invariably detrimental to artistic achievement. The second problem arises from Thackeray's commitment to write the novel in serial form, which placed him under a compulsion to provide regular monthly installments that could wait neither for adequate historical research nor for proper artistic attention. Whether these problems were, in fact, the cause of Thackeray's abandoning many of the details of his original plan is, of course, mere speculation and is deserving of no more consideration than speculation warrants. What is clear, however, is that the compelling opening of the work suggests a promising study in comparative values and conflicting loyalties in a novel of epic scope. This promise is in no way delivered. What readers are given instead is a largely shapeless work that begins promisingly enough but dawdles through stretches of irresolute composition and culminates in a series of major events that are crammed into a hasty denouement.

In *The Virginians*, as in most of Thackeray's works, readers must bestow what critical acclaim they might feel inclined to give it principally on the artful characterizations it contains and on the value of its social commentary. Thackeray's settings somehow never quite emerge as definitive places, in marked contrast to later Victorians Thomas Hardy and Joseph Conrad, whose settings are so powerfully conceived that they become virtual characters in their own right and often influence events directly. Thackeray's descriptions of physical environment seem somehow deficient, as if he painted with temperas diluted with too much water. He succeeds in rendering only a faint impression of the precincts in which his characters move. Furthermore, the scantly defined settings cannot be well defended by the argument that the environment in which Thackeray's characters pursue their thoughts and actions is of significantly less importance to his purpose than are the motivations and the social interfaces of those characters. In a novel titled *The Virginians*, character and setting ought to be inextricably bound. The central theme of the work—insofar as one can be said to exist—is the contrast between the innocence and simplicity of the New World and the corruption and sophistication of the Old World. This contrast was, ultimately, the cause of the revolt in the colonies and no small contributor to the success of that revolt. Furthermore, it is the very hub about which the central conflict was surely intended to revolve; it, however, does not achieve this function. Included among the reasons why must be the lack of delineation of a physical as well as a societal identity, for the New Eden engendered the altered values that finally made the separation of England and the colonies a matter of more than mere distance.

The Virginians, however, does contain a relatively effective contrast of social life in England and in Virginia, but the predominance given to English society is excessive and at the expense of a complete treatment of plantation life in America. Furthermore, the effectiveness of the contrast is frustrated by Thackeray's failure to provide a parallel contrast between the twins. An attempt is apparent, but it is ineffectual because of the lack of structure of the work. The novel becomes not so much a story of conflict between brothers who respond to the sound of different drums but separate stories of characters who only incidentally are twins. The motivations are not fully developed; the brothers seem to move independently rather than in opposition to each other, and, as a consequence, the conflict that should have been the very core of the novel is essentially nonexistent.

If there are major failures in the work, there are major triumphs as well. Numbered among the foremost of these is the singular and fascinating portrait of the Baroness Bernstein, the former Beatrix of *The History of Henry Esmond, Esquire* (1852), now an old woman. The Baroness is a minor masterpiece of characterization in a period of literature when authors did not yet consciously employ the subtlety of psychological motivation. Sapped by satiety of all interest and emotion except a single passion for cards, the Baroness's capacity for humanity appears to be as shriveled as her body. Nevertheless, under the stimulus of Harry and George Warrington and the memories of their grandfather that they invoke in her, the Baroness briefly regains the capacity for human feeling with which she was endowed before a life of decadence and wealth displaced it with selfishness and callous indifference. The Baroness's final scene, in which she

falls asleep over her cards during a visit of George and rouses to a lost contact with reality, possesses a vivid reality and an impressively dramatic impact.

The secret of Thackeray's most successful characterizations seems to lie in the deft and subtle touches of inner conflict with which he invests them, and this is true of the better-drawn members of the cast of *The Virginians*. Beatrix displays a strength of character that is less incipient than it is suppressed by the society in which she moves. Parson Sampson's betting, card playing, dicing, drinking, and telling of "lively" jokes, despite his moral convictions, "humanize" the unreverent reverend and serve to suggest that all men are susceptible to corruption, regardless of calling.

Although less captivating than the Baroness and less skillfully drawn than either she or Parson Sampson, Mrs. Esmond Warrington nevertheless stands out as a notable characterization as well. What makes her role in the novel significant, however, is the careful juxtaposition of her and the Baroness, her half sister. The effectiveness of the contrast points to the intended but unachieved parallel effect with George and Harry. Additionally, the central protagonists are emphatic failures. Harry's weaknesses do not fit him either for sympathy or for the interest a villain would generate, and George's benevolent nature is of the smug, self-satisfied kind that alienates rather than endears.

The novel contains much that is interesting, much that is delightful, and some social comment worthy of the making. The novel offers as much or more to the social historian of Thackeray's era as it does to the reader who wishes to know about Virginia in the eighteenth century.

"Critical Evaluation" by Terrence R. Doyle

Further Reading

Clarke, Micael M. *Thackeray and Women*. DeKalb: Northern Illinois University Press, 1995. Examines Thackeray's life, novels, and other works from a feminist-sociological perspective to analyze his treatment of female characters, demonstrating how his writings critique the position of women in Western culture. Includes bibliographical references and an index.

Colby, Robert Alan. "*The Virginians*: The Old World and the New." In *Thackeray's Canvass of Humanity*. Columbus: Ohio State University Press, 1979. Contextual analysis of the novel focusing on its origin and the stage it represents in Thackeray's development as a writer. Includes an interesting discussion of Thackeray's portrayal of George Washington.

Fisher, Judith L. *Thackeray's Skeptical Narrative and the*

"Perilous Trade" of Authorship. Burlington, Vt.: Ashgate, 2002. An analysis of Thackeray's narrative techniques, describing how he sought to create a "kind of poised reading which enables his readers to integrate his fiction into their life."

Harden, Edgar F. *The Emergence of Thackeray's Serial Fiction*. Athens: University of Georgia Press, 1979. Discusses the serial structure of five novels, including *The Virginians*, with focus upon manuscripts and the composition process. Explains how the novels were shaped in view of the fact that they were written in serial installments.

_____. *Thackeray the Writer: From Journalism to "Vanity Fair."* New York: St. Martin's Press, 1998.

_____. *Thackeray the Writer: From "Pendennis" to "Denis Duval."* New York: Macmillan, 2000. Two-volume biography chronicling Thackeray's development as a writer, beginning with his experiences as a book reviewer and culminating in the creation of *Vanity Fair*. Traces how Thackeray became an increasingly perceptive social observer.

Monsarrat, Ann. *"The Virginians."* In *An Uneasy Victorian: Thackeray the Man*. New York: Dodd, Mead, 1980. Engaging and lucid account of Thackeray's painstaking work to bring back heroes of his previous novels in *The Virginians*. Recommended for the researcher who already has some knowledge of Thackeray's works.

Ray, Gordon. *Thackeray*. 2 vols. New York: McGraw-Hill, 1955-1958. Biography of Thackeray includes thoughtful essays on the novels. The era and background of the author also are discussed.

Williams, Joan M. *Thackeray*. New York: Arco, 1969. Brief but lucid exposition of the novel. Excellent starting point for a beginning study of Thackeray's writings.

The Visit

Author: Friedrich Dürrenmatt (1921-1990)
First produced: Der Besuch der alten Dame: Eine tragische Komödie, 1956; first published, 1956 (English translation, 1958)
Type of work: Drama
Type of plot: Tragicomedy
Time of plot: Mid-twentieth century
Locale: Güllen, Central Europe

Principal characters:
CLAIRE ZACHANASSIAN, a former local girl, now a multimillionaire
TOBY and ROBY, gum-chewers, part of Claire's retinue
KOBY and LOBY, both blind, part of Claire's retinue
ALFRED ILL, Claire's former lover
TOWNSPEOPLE, identified by occupation or number
MISS LOUISA, the only townsperson identified by name

The Story:

Claire Wascher leaves Güllen in disgrace forty-five years before the action begins. Now rich, she announces her intention to return to her impoverished native town. The townspeople, who hope that she might wish to help them out of the poverty they have endured for years, await her return with considerable anticipation. They hope that Claire's emotional tie to Alfred Ill, her former lover, will induce her to be financially generous to her former town; Alfred Ill knows that if she makes the expected gift he will be a sure victor in the next mayoral contest. As the townspeople, who serve the function the chorus does in classical Greek plays, await Claire's arrival, they are a model of community cohesiveness and congeniality. Poor as they are, they are united by the seemingly indestructible bonds that traditionally hold tightly knit communities together.

Claire arrives amid much celebration. She greets the townspeople and Alfred Ill, amused by their transparent cordiality. At a festive banquet she makes it clear that they are correct in their assumption: She is prepared to give the town a gift of 500 million marks. As with most large gifts, however, this one carries a stipulation.

Claire left Güllen forty-five years earlier after naming Alfred Ill in a paternity suit; he denied responsibility for her pregnancy and prevailed by bribing two witnesses to give false evidence. Claire was driven out of Güllen by its upstanding, self-righteous citizens, and after she left, Alfred Ill married a well-to-do woman who set him up in a business. Claire went to Hamburg, where she was forced to become a prostitute before eventually marrying the multimillionaire Armenian oil tycoon Zachanassian and becoming rich.

Zachanassian, whose name she keeps despite many subsequent marriages, left her the bulk of her fortune.

Claire now dangles the dazzling prospect of the huge sum of money before the townspeople on the condition that they right the wrong they and Alfred Ill inflicted on her and her child, who lived for only one year: She will make the gift in return for the murder of her former lover. She wants, as she put it, to purchase justice. She introduces to the townspeople her butler, who was the former magistrate of Güllen who decided the paternity case against her, and two blind, castrated old men in her retinue, who are the two perjuring witnesses. Alfred Ill tries to assure her that the past is forgotten and forgiven, but Claire insists that nothing is forgotten, and that she will await the town's decision.

During the weeks that Claire waits she marries three more times. She watches grimly as the insidiousness of her offer becomes increasingly apparent. Before long, the townspeople begin to buy things on credit. At first, when Alfred Ill thanks them for standing by him, they respond loyally. Then it occurs to him that they would not be buying expensive things on credit if they were not expecting their financial position to change. Gradually, attitudes toward him change. Those who supported him now begin to blame him for his indiscretion with Claire and revile him for the way he handled the paternity suit.

Alfred Ill vainly seeks protection from the mayor, the police, and the church. When he tries to flee Güllen, he is detained by the townspeople. Finally, he faces up to his guilt and publicly accepts responsibility for his misdeeds. The townspeople call for his suicide, but he refuses to give them this satisfaction. If they want Claire's money, they will have to kill him and bear the guilt that comes with his murder. In a somber assembly, a group of townspeople murder him collectively so that no one person will have to bear the guilt. The doctor pronounces death by heart failure. Claire collects the corpse, presents the check, and leaves the town with her full retinue. At the newly refurbished train station, the prosperous townspeople silently watch Claire leave.

Critical Evaluation:

In *The Visit*, Friedrich Dürrenmatt poses the basic question of what inroads money, or the promise of it, makes upon the morality of people who are not inherently bad. The citizens of Güllen are average, with average strengths, weaknesses, and foibles. Claire has early been made aware of the consequences of greed, since Alfred Ill's two bribes determined the outcome of her paternity suit.

On the surface, *The Visit* is a play about vengeance, but beyond that it is a tragicomedy that explores human motivation and morality. In the play, Dürrenmatt examines the dark underside of a community unified in its poverty that disintegrates with the prospect of riches. Claire's plan of vengeance is not only directed against the man who had dishonored her but against the community that also defined her disgrace.

Dürrenmatt's sparing use of names helps his audience realize that the community is an aggregation of types rather than individuals. Only Claire and Alfred Ill emerge as individuals. The rest of the townspeople act as a chorus and come to represent the collective ideals of the community. Among those who are identified by occupation rather than number, the priest, the schoolmaster, the police officer, and the physician come in for particularly harsh treatment. They are respected members of the community who should fight to uphold its highest ideals but do not.

As is typical in Dürrenmatt's works, the antihero, Alfred Ill, comes from a low societal class. As the play progresses, however, it is Alfred Ill who finds some degree of salvation, achieving a separate peace with himself before his neighbors succumb to Claire's temptation and murder him.

As the townspeople gradually become aware of how money can change their lives, they increasingly begin to use language more to conceal than to express their thoughts. Claire stands in sharp contrast to this. She is Medea-like in her furious outbursts against the professional people in town who fail to offer the sort of moral leadership that might have saved Güllen from its own nightmarish avarice.

The play opens and concludes with a chorus, giving it a symmetry that serves to heighten the irony of what transpires during the three acts. By play's end, Güllen is much improved materially, but the price is a collective guilt that will plague them in the years to come. Dürrenmatt's audiences easily grasp the message that Güllen is a kind of Everytown meant to represent the twentieth century materialistic dilemma in the starkest terms.

As Dürrenmatt presents her, Claire, who suffered from an unjust society, permits the injustice to consume her utterly. Her emotions were long ago snuffed out to the point that she is unable to grow, whereas Alfred Ill, the small-time, petty, unimportant man, undergoes a transformation that allows him to face his fate with composure and equanimity.

It is not surprising that *The Visit* is Dürrenmatt's most enduringly popular and successful play and that it has been translated into most major languages. The work is appropriate to its time, striking a responsive chord in those who struggle with the question of how to achieve an equilibrium between the material and the ideal in society.

R. Baird Shuman

Further Reading

Bogard, Travis, and William Oliver, eds. *Modern Drama: Essays in Criticism.* New York: Oxford University Press, 1965. Adolf D. Klarmann's contribution, "Friedrich Dürrenmatt and the Tragic Sense of Comedy," remains one of the most significant appraisals of the playwright.

Crockett, Roger A. *Understanding Friedrich Dürrenmatt.* Columbia: University of South Carolina Press, 1998. An introductory overview, examining *The Visit* and other works by Dürrenmatt. Crockett describes the playwright's view of a chaotic, Godless universe, while also pointing out the many elements of comedy in his work.

Donald, Sydney G. *Dürrenmatt: Der Besuch der alten Dame.* Rev. ed. Glasgow: University of Glasgow, 1993. An eighty-page study guide to the play, designed for high school and undergraduate students.

Hammer, Carl, ed. *Studies in German Literature.* Baton Rouge: Louisiana State University Press, 1963. Includes F. E. Coenen's extended essay on modern German theater, which makes interesting observations about Dürrenmatt and places him within the broad context of German drama.

Peppard, Murray B. *Friedrich Dürrenmatt.* New York: Twayne, 1969. Peppard's analysis of *The Visit* is penetrating and sensitive. He provides an excellent overview of the play, comments on elements of its composition, and interprets it in understandable terms. One of the best sources for those just beginning to read Dürrenmatt.

Price, David W. "The Political Economy of Sacrifice in Dürrenmatt's *The Visit*." *Southern Humanities Review* 35, no. 2 (Spring, 2001): 109. Analyzes *The Visit* by using the contemporary literary theories of René Girard and Roberto Calasso about the concepts of ritual, sacrifice, and economy in the modern world.

Shaw, LeRoy, ed. *The German Theater Today.* Austin: University of Texas Press, 1963. A valuable collection of essays drawn from a symposium on modern German theater. The material on Dürrenmatt's early plays provides useful background to those unfamiliar with the playwright.

Whitton, Kenneth S. *Dürrenmatt: Reinterpretation in Retrospect.* Providence, R.I.: Berg, 1990. Whitton's understanding of Dürrenmatt is impressive. His material on *The Visit* brings together a considerable amount of interpretive theory on the play.

Volpone
Or, The Fox

Author: Ben Jonson (1573-1637)
First produced: 1605; first published, 1607
Type of work: Drama
Type of plot: Social satire
Time of plot: Sixteenth century
Locale: Venice

Principal characters:
VOLPONE, a knave
MOSCA, his servant
CORBACCIO, an old gentleman
CORVINO, a merchant
VOLTORE, an advocate
LORD POLITIC WOULD-BE, a knight
LADY POLITIC WOULD-BE, his wife
BONARIO, Corbaccio's son
CELIA, Corvino's wife
PEREGRINE, a gentleman traveler

The Story:

Volpone and his servant, Mosca, are playing a cunning game with all who profess to be Volpone's friends, and the two conspirators boast to themselves that Volpone acquired his riches not by the common means of trade but by a method that cheated no one in a commercial sense. Volpone has no heirs. Since it is believed he possesses a large fortune, many people are courting his favor in the hope of rich rewards after his death.

For three years, while Volpone feigns gout, catarrh, palsy, and consumption, valuable gifts are given to him. Volpone is in truth quite healthy and able to enjoy various vices. Mosca's role in the grand deception is to assure each hopeful, would-be friend that he is the one whom Volpone honored in an alleged will.

To Voltore, one of the dupes, Mosca (which means "fly") boasts that particular attention is being paid to Voltore's interests. When Voltore ("vulture") leaves, Corbaccio ("crow") follows. He brings a potion to help Volpone ("fox"), or so he claims. Mosca knows better than to give his master medicine from those who are awaiting the fox's death. Mosca suggests that to influence Volpone, Corbaccio should go home, disinherit his own son, and leave his fortune to Volpone. In return for this generous deed, Volpone, soon to die, will leave his fortune to Corbaccio, whose son will benefit eventually.

Next comes Corvino, who is assured by Mosca that Volpone, now near death, named him in a will. After the merchant goes, Mosca tells Volpone that Corvino has a beautiful wife whom he guards at all times. Volpone resolves to go in disguise to see this woman.

Sir Politic Would-Be and his wife are traveling in Venice. Another English visitor, Peregrine, meets Sir Politic on the street and gives him news from home. While the two Englishmen are trying to impress each other, Mosca and a servant come to the street and erect a stage for a medicine vendor to display his wares. Volpone, disguised as a mountebank, mounts the platform. While he haggles with Sir Politic and Peregrine over the price of his medicine, Celia appears at her window and tosses down her handkerchief. Struck by Celia's beauty, Volpone resolves to possess her. Meanwhile Corvino brutally scolds Celia and tells her that henceforth he will confine her to her room.

Mosca goes to Corvino with news that physicians recommended that a healthy young girl sleep by Volpone's side and that other men are striving to be the first to win Volpone's gratitude in this manner. Not to be outdone, Corvino promises that Celia will be sent to Volpone.

Mosca also tells Bonario, Corbaccio's son, that his father is about to disinherit him. He promises to lead Bonario to a place where he can witness his father's betrayal.

When Lady Politic Would-Be comes to visit Volpone, she is so talkative Volpone fears she will make him sick in truth. To relieve Volpone's distress, the servant tells the lady that Sir Politic is in a gondola with a young girl. Lady Would-Be hurries off in pursuit of her husband. Volpone retires to a private closet while Mosca leads Bonario behind a curtain so the young man can spy on Corbaccio. At that moment, eager to win favor with Volpone, Corvino arrives with Celia, and Mosca sends Bonario off to another room so he will not know of her presence. Meanwhile Corvino, who intends to deceive Celia about what he thinks is the true purpose of

her lying with Volpone, tells Celia what she has to do to prove her chastity. To quiet her fears, and to guarantee the inheritance from Volpone, Corvino assures his distressed wife that Volpone is so decrepit he cannot harm her.

When they are alone, Volpone leaps from his couch and displays himself as an ardent lover. As he is about to rape Celia, Bonario appears from his hiding place and saves her. While Mosca and Volpone, in terror of exposure, bewail their ruined plot, Corbaccio knocks. Volpone dashes back to his couch to assume his role of an invalid. As Mosca assures Corbaccio of Volpone's forthcoming death, Voltore enters the room and overhears the discussion. Mosca draws Voltore aside and assures the lawyer that he is attempting to get possession of Corbaccio's money so that Voltore will inherit more from Volpone. Mosca further explains that Bonario mistook Celia's visit and burst upon Volpone and threatened to kill him. Taken in by Mosca's lies, Voltore promises to keep Bonario from accusing Volpone of attempted rape and Corvino of villainy; he orders Bonario (who, unlike Volpone, Mosca, Corvino, Corbaccio, and Voltore, is innocent) arrested.

Mosca proceeds with his case against Celia and Bonario. He assured Corvino, Corbaccio, and Voltore, independently, that each would be the sole heir of Volpone. He added Lady Would-Be as a witness against Celia. In court Voltore presents Celia and Bonario as schemers against Corvino, and he further shows that Bonario's father disinherited his son and that Bonario dragged Volpone out of bed and attacked him. Corvino and Corbaccio testify against Celia and Bonario, while Mosca whispers to the avaricious old gentlemen that they are helping justice. To add to the testimony, Mosca presents Lady Would-Be, who tells the court she saw Celia beguiling Sir Politic in a gondola. Mosca promises Lady Would-Be that as a reward for her testimony her name will stand first on Volpone's list of heirs.

When the trial is over, Volpone sends his servants to announce that he is dead and that Mosca is his heir. While Volpone hides behind a curtain, Mosca sits at a desk taking an inventory of the inheritance as the hopefuls arrive. The next step in Volpone's plan is to escape from Venice with his loot. Mosca helps him disguise himself as a commodore. Mosca also puts on a disguise.

Having lost his hopes for the inheritance, Voltore withdraws his false testimony at the trial, and Corbaccio and Corvino tremble lest their own cowardly acts be revealed. The court orders Mosca to appear. Suspecting that Mosca plans to keep the fortune for himself, the disguised Volpone goes to the court. When the dupes, learning that Volpone is still alive, begin to bargain for the wealth Mosca holds,

Volpone throws off his disguise and exposes to the court the foolish behavior of Corbaccio, Corvino, and Voltore, and the innocence of Celia and Bonario. The court then sentences each conspirator according to the severity of his crime. Bonario is restored to his father's inheritance, and Celia is allowed to return to her father because Corvino attempted to barter her honor for wealth. The court announces that evil can go only so far before it kills itself.

Critical Evaluation:

Written during a period in which Ben Jonson had turned his hand largely to the making of entertaining masques and satirical antimasques, *Volpone*'s success did something to make up for the failure of his tragedy, *Sejanus His Fall* (1603). *Volpone* was performed by the King's Men in London, and at the two universities to which Jonson later dedicated the play in his prologue. The play also led to Jonson's most fertile dramatic period, that of the great comedies, which include *Epicœne: Or, The Silent Woman* (1609), *The Alchemist* (1610), *Bartholomew Fair* (1614), and *The Devil Is an Ass* (1616). Jonson was preeminent among the Elizabethans and the Jacobeans as that rare combination of the academic and the creative genius. He was a serious classicist who criticized William Shakespeare's "little Latin and less Greek," modeling his own plays on the Romans. As a humanist he brought classical control and purity to English forms. More than anyone else at the time, Jonson followed critical prescriptions of his own time and of the classical era. Jonson believed that the poet had a moral function in society; he viewed drama as a means of social education. This attitude paved the way for the great English satirists of the eighteenth century. His diverse artistic character makes Jonson both representative of his own age and a predecessor of the more rigorous classicism of the Augustans.

Jonson's style, as might be expected, is disciplined, formal, balanced, classically simple, and unembellished—a style that foreshadows the Cavalier School (who called themselves the sons of Ben). His dramatic verse is highly stylized, vibrant, and fast-moving; readers are hardly aware they are reading poetry. Rarely does Jonson allow himself the lyrical excursions of Shakespeare or the rhetorical complexity of Christopher Marlowe, although he was capable of both. There is a solidity, firmness, and straightforward clarity in his comedies equaled only by the classical French comic theater of Molière. In *Volpone* Jonson follows the Aristotelian unities of time, place, and action. The action of the play takes only one day (the unity of time); it occurs entirely in Venice (place); and, with the exception of some of the exchanges between Peregrine and Sir Politic Would-Be, the action is unified structurally, all centered on the machinations of Volpone, his follower, and the greedy dupes.

The theme of the play is greed, the vice that dominates the actions of all the characters. Family bonds, marriage, and legal justice are not merely disregarded by Corbaccio, Corvino, and Voltore; they are also made the means by which the characters' inhuman avarice destroys them. Jonson implies that their greed is all too human; these characters may be exaggerations but they are not aberrations. It is ironic that the Politic Would-Bes, though they, too, want Volpone's money, seem less offensive and morally corrupt simply because they do not sell their souls for a hope of lucre. They are idiotic but they are not vicious. The passages in which they appear are a kind of relief. Although *Volpone* is a comedy, it is so serious that it is almost equally tragic; as a satire, it accomplishes the difficult feat of being funny and morally incisive at the same time. *Volpone* may be a comedy insofar as it deals with particular figures in a particular situation, but its social moral is earnest. Jonson succeeds brilliantly in combining the stereotyped characters of Latin comedy, the Renaissance characters of humors (which he himself used in his first comedy, *Every Man in His Humour*, 1598), the popular tradition of beast fables (from which he derived the names of his characters), and astute psychological insight to make them all come alive onstage. Although the plot of *Volpone* is original, it is based on a common Roman fortune-hunting theme dealt with by Horace, Juvenal, Pliny, Lucian, and Petronius. Jonson turns his fortune hunters loose in contemporary Venice—chosen, no doubt, because the English of the time regarded Italy as a country of crime and rampant passions. By using a setting roughly contemporary to that of his original audience, Jonson makes the point that con artists and greedy dupes are part of every age. Such is the high moral purpose of comic satire, which Jonson points out in his preface to the play.

Another important theme is that of imitation, as a distortion of normal reality. Sir Politic Would-Be seeks to ape Volpone, an imitation of a dying man. Characters are constantly assuming either literal or figurative disguises; Mosca, for example, fascinates the audience with his ability to make what his dupes see before their eyes conform to whatever fabrication he leads them to accept. Lady Would-Be attempts to cover her mental deformities with physical cosmetics, and her dressing scene is one of the most pathetic in the play. Carrying imitation even further, Volpone pretends to be a mountebank (something he actually is) in a complicated and convincing scene that leads to the question of how one can distinguish between a real imitator and an imitation imitator. Volpone and Mosca are actors throughout. They are also directors, leading the fortune hunters, one by one, to give their best performances; in the process, they reveal how close to the surface lies the actor's instinct in all people. Any strong desire, such as greed, can activate the attempt at deception. Gilded lies and rampant desires create chaos, confusing notions of species, class, sex, and morals.

Volpone is the exuberant guiding spirit of misrule who takes constant pleasure in his mental agility and showmanship. Mosca is equally forceful; his only motive seems to be a delight in perpetrating perversities, and he accepts his inheritance only because it allows him to continue to be perverse. The three birds of prey, Corbaccio, Corvino, and Voltore, stumble over one another in their haste to devour the supposed carcass. They are hideous caricatures, and they are, ironically, caricatures of themselves—as the development of the play from the first scene demonstrates. Mosca and Volpone simply bring out the worst in them; they do not plant it. The sham trial in act 4 is the dramatic triumph of Jonson's career. When Corvino calls Voltore "mad" at the very point at which the old man becomes sane again, the audience sees that it, too, was beguiled by the terrible logic of greed.

"Critical Evaluation" by Kenneth John Atchity

Further Reading

Bowers, Rick. *Radical Comedy in Early Modern England: Contexts, Cultures, Performances*. Burlington, Vt.: Ashgate, 2008. Applies the theories of Mikhail Bakhtin and other philosophers to analyze early modern English comedies, describing the types of humor employed in these plays and how they satirize political, religious, and medical authority. Chapter 8 discusses *Volpone* and several of Jonson's other plays.

Cave, Richard Allen. *Ben Jonson*. New York: St. Martin's Press, 1991. Devotes a chapter of analysis to the play's plot, themes, and characters. Includes some discussion of the play's production history.

Dessen, Alan C. *Jonson's Moral Comedy*. Evanston, Ill.: Northwestern University Press, 1971. Dessen devotes one chapter to a discussion of *Volpone*, which he sees as pivotal, marking a shift in Jonson's perceptions away from the influences of the old morality plays such as *Everyman* and toward a satiric comedy that examines the moral implications of human failings.

Donaldson, Ian. *Jonson's Magic Houses: Essays in Interpretation*. New York: Oxford University Press, 1997. Donaldson, a Jonson scholar, provides new interpretations of Jonson's personality, work, and literary legacy. Chapter 7 focuses on *Volpone*.

Dutton, Richard. *Ben Jonson, "Volpone," and the Gunpowder Plot*. New York: Cambridge University Press, 2008. Describes the circumstances of Jonson's creation of *Volpone*, which he began writing shortly after he took part in the 1605 Gunpowder Plot. Dutton demonstrates how the play uses a form of beast fable to allude to the plot.

Harp, Richard, and Stanley Stewart, eds. *The Cambridge Companion to Ben Jonson*. New York: Cambridge University Press, 2000. Collection of essays about Jonson's life and career, including analyses of his comedies and late plays, a description of London and its theaters during Jonson's lifetime, and an evaluation of his critical heritage.

Loxley, James. *A Sourcebook*. New York: Routledge, 2002. An introductory overview of Jonson's life and work, particularly useful for students. Part 1 provides biographical information and places Jonson's life and work within the context of his times; part 2 discusses several works, including *Volpone*; part 3 offers critical analysis of the themes in his plays, the style of his writing, and a comparison of his work to that of William Shakespeare.

McEvoy, Sean. *Ben Jonson, Renaissance Dramatist*. Edinburgh: Edinburgh University Press, 2008. McEvoy analyzes all of Jonson's plays, attributing their greatness to the playwright's commitment to the ideals of humanism during a time of authoritarianism and rampant capitalism in England. Chapter 4 focuses on *Volpone*.

Martin, Mathew R. *Between Theater and Philosophy: Skepticism in the Major City Comedies of Ben Jonson and Thomas Middleton*. Newark: University of Delaware Press, 2001. Martin provides deconstructionist and other modern critical interpretations of *Volpone* and several other Jonson plays.

Miles, Rosalind. *Ben Jonson: His Craft and Art*. New York: Barnes & Noble, 1990. Discusses *Volpone* with particular attention to the techniques of Jonson's satire, noting that nothing is exempt from his dark vision of human beings as jungle animals, quick to prey on one another.

Summers, Claude J., and Ted-Larry Pebworth. *Ben Jonson*. Boston: Twayne, 1979. A general introduction to Jonson and his work. Includes a discussion of *Volpone* that concentrates on the play's satiric themes and structure.

Volupté
The Sensual Man

Author: Charles-Augustin Sainte-Beuve (1804-1869)
First published: 1834 (English translation, 1995)
Type of work: Novel
Type of plot: Psychological
Time of plot: Early nineteenth century
Locale: France

Principal characters:
AMAURY, the narrator and a man of sensibility
THE MARQUIS DE COUAËN, a royalist
MADAME DE COUAËN, his wife
AMÉLIE DE LINIERS, a woman in love with Amaury
MADAME R., the wife of a royalist sympathizer

The Story:

On the ship that takes him to the United States, probably forever, Amaury undertakes to tell the story of his life to a young friend. Having renounced his past life to live a new one abroad, he is afraid that he might find more pleasure than he should in those past memories; but he feels that his experience can prove useful to the young man, in whom he recognizes so many of his own tendencies.

Amaury, losing his parents, was reared by an uncle in Brittany. In his youth he was sheltered from the world outside his house, which at that time was slowly recovering from the effects of the French Revolution. He spent most of his time studying, and, prone to dreaming, he was actually more concerned with the adventures of Cyrus, Alexander, and Constantine than he was with the men and events of his own day. His Latin teacher was Monsieur Ploa, a man absolutely devoid of personal ambition; only a misinterpretation of Vergil or Cicero could momentarily get him excited. Monsieur Ploa had Amaury translate the voluptuous passages of the *Aeneid* (c. 29-19 B.C.E.; English translation, 1553) or the *Odes* (23 B.C.E., 13 B.C.E.; English translation, 1621) of Horace with a complete candor that his disciple did not share.

When Amaury was about fifteen years old, he spent six weeks at a neighboring castle. His life there, no longer checked by his regular schedule, helped to develop his tendency to melancholy; he would disappear into the woods reciting poetry with tears in his eyes, and he would forget to come back for meals.

At the age of eighteen, he began visiting friends in the neighborhood. He would often visit Monsieur and Madame de Greneuc, in whose household lived two granddaughters orphaned during the revolution. The older, Amélie de Liniers, was a charming woman who soon considered herself engaged to him. Amaury, however, did not feel like settling down in life without first learning something of the world.

During a hunting party, Amaury met the Marquis de Couaën, an influential figure in royalist circles, who invited the young man to his castle. There Amaury met Madame de Couaën, the Irish wife of the marquis. One day, Amaury wandered in the woods, lost in his thoughts. As he emerged from the woods, Madame de Couaën called to him from the window and asked him to pick up an ivory needle she lost. When he took it up to her, she asked him if he would, in the absence of her husband, accompany her to the little chapel of Saint-Pierre-de-Mer before the sun set. As they were walking along, she explained to Amaury that she was making a pilgrimage for her mother in Ireland, from whom she received bad news.

That walk was more or less the beginning of a hopeless love relationship between Amaury and Madame de Couaën, an affair in which his respect for the marquis and the true love of Madame de Couaën for her husband left him with the sole possibility of platonic adoration. To escape such a situation, he attempted to retire as a hermit on a nearby deserted island once inhabited by Druids, but after spending only one night there, he abandoned that project. He then decided to go to Ireland on a boat that brought the marquis some secret dispatches; he would see Madame de Couaën's mother and possibly establish some useful political connections for the marquis. As he embarked, after leaving a letter of explanation in his room, Madame de Couaën came running to the beach with word that her mother just died. While he tried to comfort her she tearfully begged him never to get married but to stay with them, help her husband, and understand her as no one else can.

The Marquis de Couaën went to Paris for some political meetings and took his wife, son, and daughter with him to avoid raising suspicions. Amaury accompanied them to Paris. When they returned to Couaën, they found the coast occupied by soldiers.

Amaury went to see Amélie, who was preparing to follow her grandmother to Normandy. When he insisted that they ought to delay for two years before making a decision concerning their future, Amélie simply asked him to be prudent.

On his way home, Amaury learned that the marquis was arrested in Paris; he rushed immediately to Couaën to destroy some papers before the police officers would arrive there. Without objection or thanks, Madame de Couaën accepted his help, and the next day they left for Paris with the two children. There Amaury communicated with Monsieur D. and Monsieur R. in an effort to secure their help.

Meanwhile, the marquis was allowed to receive visitors, and his wife went to see him every day. Amaury spent every evening with her. At the same time, he was beginning to feel attracted to Madame R., a lonely and disillusioned woman who often visited Madame de Couaën. Amaury also decided to experience physical love with a prostitute, but he accomplished his purpose with no real pleasure.

In the midst of these circumstances, Amaury could see no future for himself. He became involved in a royalist conspiracy, more in an effort to find self-fulfillment in a chivalric cause than to satisfy any political convictions. Faced with imminent action, he realized that his position might endanger the future of the marquis, bring grief to Madame de Couaën, and show ingratitude toward Monsieur R. and Monsieur D. Fortunately, his secret political involvement was never disclosed.

When the marquis was sent to Blois, Amaury did not accompany his friends, although they wanted him to come with them. Left in Paris, he visited Madame R. and wrote to Blois, where the royalist political leaders were being tried. Madame R., while refusing to become his mistress, liked to be seen with him in public and demanded the most foolish proofs of his attachment. They never really trusted each other, and she was always jealous of his love for Madame de Couaën.

A letter from the marquis arrived, announcing the death of his son and the alarming state of his wife's health; the nobleman further asked for a two-week pass to bring her to Paris for medical attention. Madame de Couaën, who considered the death of her son a punishment for her own weakness, was unhappy to discover the relationship between Amaury and Madame R.

On a day when Amélie came to visit Madame de Couaën, Madame R. was also present, and Amaury realized that his instability caused the unhappiness of three women. Caught in his youth in the web of illegitimate love, he was unable to choose either true virtue or carefree disorder. He never saw Amélie again.

Back in Blois, Madame de Couaën sent him a medallion of her mother and a souvenir of her son. Shortly afterward, he ended his affair with Madame R. Years later he heard that Monsieur R. received a post of importance and that Madame R. became the mother of a son. Thus reaching the bottom of a moral abyss, Amaury enlisted in the army with the idea of finding death on the battlefield; he arrived at Austerlitz only after the battle was won. Convinced that there was no place for him in society, he decided to become a priest.

Several years later, after he took holy orders, he decided to visit again his uncle's farm and the castle at Couaën. He received no news from Blois for several weeks, and he was afraid that Madame de Couaën's health had not improved. On his arrival at Couaën he was surprised to find a flurry of activity; his friends had returned the day before. Although Madame de Couaën was very weak, she welcomed him warmly, adding that someone might soon need his assistance. As her condition became worse, Amaury administered the rites of absolution and extreme unction. Madame de Couaën died soon afterward and was buried in the chapel of Saint-Pierre-de-Mer.

This experience and the emotions it called forth proved extremely trying to Amaury, who immediately left Brittany and, a short time later, France. He hoped to find abroad some peace in obscure but useful activities.

Critical Evaluation:

The fame of *Volupté* is the result, in part, of its transposition of real events to the fictional plane. The relationship between Amaury and Madame de Couaën depicts some elements of the affair between Charles-Augustin Sainte-Beuve and Victor Hugo's wife, Adèle. In the novel, however, their relationship is purely platonic. The admiration, friendship, and subsequent enmity of Sainte-Beuve and Hugo appear in the relationship of Amaury and the Marquis de Couaën. The fictional characters reconcile; however, Sainte-Beuve and Hugo did not reconcile. Sainte-Beuve's childhood in Picardy becomes Amaury's in the poetically appropriate Brittany, a land of strong religious traditions, a mythic aura, and a history of royalist conspiracies. Although Sainte-Beuve made his novel credible by basing it on actual events, the themes generated from the story are larger in scope. Through the interaction of spiritual, erotic, and political intrigue, Sainte-Beuve explores the various nuances of memory, the struggle between the spirit and the flesh, divine and human love, the role of the great individual in history, and the conflict between fame and obscurity.

The main plotline traces Amaury's moral disarray and spiritual strivings and, generally, the moral duality of all people. Amaury's spirit is dominated by *volupté*, or a combination of indolence, apathy, self-indulgence, and indecisiveness. Amaury seeks sensual gratification, and he repudiates his responsibilities as a member of the community. The cult of sensuality reveals itself as a stage in the development of every generation. In youth, desire is confused with sacred love. Later, sublime love separates from sensual pleasure. With age, humans realize that without love for the soul or the intellect, beauty and pleasure are impermanent. Without this realization, sensual diversion replaces moral solicitude and intellectual lucidity. Amaury takes pride in his own fall, out of a sense of revolt against God. When he realizes that he sacrificed the happiness of others in the process of his own spiritual disintegration, he turns inward and replaces idle dreaming with prayer. Since Amaury examines his own emotional and intellectual states with such exhaustiveness and subtlety, and since he takes pleasure in recalling his debauchery, his conversion seems incomplete.

Most of the major characters are presented as mysteries. Madame R. personifies passionate love. Like Amaury, she pursues appearance rather than interior depth. Madame de Couaën represents sublime love, ironically out of her indifference and her inability to understand Amaury's advances. She does not have an affair with Amaury, but she nevertheless views the death of her son as divine punishment. She seeks spiritual solace from Amaury. Madame de Couaën inspires intellectual infidelity, and she motivates Amaury's turn against the marquis. The Marquis de Couaën represents the proud, ambitious people who shape history. His frustrated political ambition, like the repressed physical desire between Amaury and Madame de Couaën, drives him to self-destruction. Despite the differences of the Marquis and Amaury, they reconcile after the death of Madame de Couaën. Sainte-Beuve's humbling of Victor Hugo in the character of the marquis was likely the product of envy, even though the proud conspirator finally emerges as a figure of considerable tragic stature.

For the most part, the story is told chronologically, with occasional flashbacks. Only at the beginning of part 2 does the narrator reflect on his current circumstances. The novel's disorganization conveys the aimlessness of the hero. The theme of flight predominates, and it is expressed through continual changes of scene. The idyllic charm of Amélie's home and Madame de Couaën's chateau are contrasted to the corruption of Paris. The narrator also moves easily between real and imaginary—or metaphorical—landscapes, such as paths of salvation and stormy seas of the soul. Despite the haphazard action, the exploration of ambition, love, and faith from a single point of view provides thematic unity. Amaury's continual wanderings and self-exile suggest an allegory of humanity's estrangement from God; however, Amaury's complex quest does not have a clear goal, and it does not result in a simple truth.

Like Amaury, Sainte-Beuve, who projects his present circumstances thirty years into the past, emphasizes memory over currency. Since the novel concerns events from memory, it examines the inner truth of emotional and intellectual perception rather than external events. Even though dialogue is rare, and conversations are related secondhand, the interaction of viewpoints plays a decisive role in the action. Speech hides as much as it reveals. The profusion of subordinate and parenthetical clauses and the deliberate interruption of syntactic flow are suited to the narrator's own indecision. Silences, or long-delayed responses, instead, communicate more effectively.

Beneath apparent motives and outward events of the novel lie the secret impulses of the subconscious. Throughout the novel, desire conflicts with performance. Amaury dreams of ideal love, but he pursues promiscuous satisfaction, instead. Madame de Couaën's forgetfulness and anxieties cloud her perception. The dreamlike atmosphere of the novel simulates the thin veil separating conscious from unconscious perception. The vague descriptive passages, filled with mirrors, water, and reflections, are flavored by memory. Physical appearances are merely sketched in, and images of erosion dominate the novel. The ornamental style, complete with archaic words, extended and often outrageous metaphors, incomplete sentences, and breaks in logical sequence, veils the narrative in unreality. Sainte-Beuve prefers to suggest meaning rather than expound.

Critics recognized that the prolix language of the novel departed radically from the established traditions of French prose. The majority of Sainte-Beuve's contemporaries found the language needlessly obtuse and the episodic nature of the plot and the moralizing passages clumsy. The experimental qualities of Sainte-Beuve's novel, however, inspired several famous contemporaries. Charles Baudelaire defended the attempt to communicate through association rather than through direct statement. Gustave Flaubert found inspiration in the attempt to render boredom and futility, and Honoré de Balzac continued to explore the theme of dissolution. Sainte-Beuve, on the other hand, never again wrote fiction; he turned, instead, to literary criticism.

"Critical Evaluation" by Pamela Pavliscak

Further Reading

Barlow, Norman. *Sainte-Beuve to Baudelaire: A Poetic Legacy.* Durham, N.C.: Duke University Press, 1964. Analyzes the influence of Sainte-Beuve's elaborate style and thematic preoccupations on Charles Baudelaire's poetry. The chapter on *Volupté* examines Amaury's exploration of sensual and spiritual love. Although Barlow traces the spiritual journey, his didacticism is distracting.

Chadbourne, Richard. *Charles-Augustin Sainte-Beuve*. Boston: Twayne, 1977. A survey of Sainte-Beuve's life and works, reappraising his fiction and poetry and discussing his literary criticism. The chapter on *Volupté* analyzes innovations in narrative technique and genre.

Finn, Michael R. "The Language Hysteria of Sainte-Beuve." In *Proust, the Body, and Literary Form*. New York: Cambridge University Press, 1999. Analyzes nineteenth century French literature about hysteria and other nervous afflictions, much of it written by writers suffering from these conditions. Compares Marcel Proust's anxieties about writing *Remembrances of Things Past* to these earlier writers. In addition to the chapter about Sainte-Beuve, there are many other references to him throughout the book that are listed in the index.

Lehmann, A. G. *Sainte-Beuve: A Portrait of the Critic, 1804-1842*. Oxford, England: Clarendon Press, 1962. Overview of the novel, emphasizing its failure to create convincing characters or to use dialogue effectively. The criticism is unbalanced, however, since Lehmann judges *Volupté* as a realist novel rather than as a Romantic confession.

Mulhauser, Ruth. *Sainte-Beuve and Greco-Roman Antiquity*. Cleveland, Ohio: Press of Case Western Reserve University, 1969. Traces the classical sources of Sainte-Beuve's literature and criticism: Greek and Roman culture combined with Romantic reverie and intellectual curiosity. Discusses Sainte-Beuve's Hellenism, or love of physical beauty.

Nelles, Paul. "Sainte-Beuve Between Renaissance and Enlightenment." *Journal of the History of Ideas* 61, no. 3 (July, 2000): 473. Focuses on Sainte-Beuve's literary criticism. Describes how he legitimized literary history as a French academic discipline and discusses some of his ideas about literature.

Nicolson, Harold. *Sainte-Beuve*. London: Constable, 1957. Surveys Sainte-Beuve's work. The chapter on *Volupté* considers the novel as a representation of the love triangle of Sainte-Beuve, Adèle Hugo, and Victor Hugo and also analyzes the prose style and thematic unity of the work.

The Voyage of the Beagle

Author: Charles Darwin (1809-1882)
First published: 1839
Type of work: Nature writing

The Voyage of the Beagle shows the English naturalist Charles Darwin's brilliant mind already at work on the problems that led to his seminal theory of evolution. The work's title is somewhat misleading, for the author actually has little to say about the voyage. The original full title—*Journal of Researches into the Geology and Natural History of the Various Countries Visited by H.M.S. Beagle, Under the Command of Captain FitzRoy, R.N., from 1832 to 1836*—is a better reflection of the scope of the work.

The Voyage of the Beagle is not only an important book in the history of modern thought but also a highly significant one in the life of Darwin. As a young man, Darwin had little sense of vocation or direction. When he was sixteen, he began a career of medicine at Edinburgh University. Discovering, however, that he was unfit for the profession, he entered Christ College, Cambridge, three years later in 1828 to prepare himself to be a clergyman. Failing to take honors or to distinguish himself in any way, he accepted the offer of Captain Fitz Roy of the *Beagle* to sign on as a naturalist on a voyage around the world that eventually took five years. During that time, Darwin not only discovered himself and his career but also began making those observations that he later developed into the theory of evolution expounded in *On the Origin of Species* (1859). This work, together with the works of Karl Marx and of Sigmund Freud, constituted a powerful influence on twentieth century scientific thought and values.

In December, 1831, the brig *Beagle* of the Royal Navy set sail from Devonport, England, to begin a series of surveys of Patagonia, Tierra del Fuego, Chile, Peru, some of the islands of the Pacific, and Australia. In addition, chronometric measurements were to be made while the ship circumnavigated the earth. Darwin kept a detailed record of the journey that included observations in natural history and geology. It was in particular his observations on the relationships between animals segregated geographically (those living on islands and those on the mainland) and on the relationships between species separated by time (those living forms and those recently extinct ones) that forced him to reconsider the standard, scientific view of the fixity of species. He was also impressed by "the manner in which closely allied animals replace one another in proceeding southwards" in South America.

The *Beagle* began the voyage by sailing to the coast of South America by way of the Canary Islands, the Cape Verde Islands, and the island of St. Paul's Rocks. From the first American seaport the ship touched, Rio de Janeiro, Darwin went on an inland excursion, and upon his return he made natural history observations near Botofogo Bay. From there the expedition went southward to the mouth of the River Plate, where Darwin remained several weeks collecting animals, birds, and reptiles. On his journeys to the interior, he met gauchos and witnessed their skill with the lasso and the bolas in capturing horses and cattle.

From the next anchorage at Rio Negro, Darwin decided to go to Buenos Aires by land under the protection of the Spanish army, who had declared war on various Indian tribes. On this journey, he was able to observe the habits of the South American ostrich.

After a stop in Buenos Aires, Darwin set out for Santa Fe by means of a slow bullock wagon. He returned by boat down the Parana River to the seacoast and joined the *Beagle* at Montevideo. On an excursion inland from that seaport, Darwin observed herds of sheep that were watched only by dogs who had been brought up with the flocks. On the coast of Patagonia, a land where Spanish settlement was unsuccessful, Darwin observed the guanaco, or wild llama, which he found to be extremely wary but easily domesticated after capture. From Patagonia, the *Beagle* went to the Falkland Islands, where Darwin found horses, cattle, and rabbits thriving on the seemingly desolate land. In Tierra del Fuego, the natives existed in an utterly savage state, with barely enough food and clothing to maintain a miserable existence.

On board the *Beagle* were three Fuegians, who had been taken to England to be educated and taught the Christian religion and who were now to be returned to their own tribes, accompanied by a missionary. The ship anchored in Ponsonby Sound, and four boats set out to carry the Fuegians home. All the natives gathered on shore wherever they landed and asked for gifts. When their wants were not entirely satisfied,

they became hostile. The missionary decided that it would be useless for him to stay among them.

Once the *Beagle* arrived in Valparaiso, Chile, Darwin set out to observe the geological formations of the base of the Andes Mountains. On that journey he saw copper and gold mines.

While at anchor in a harbor of the island of Chiloe, all aboard were able to observe the eruption of a volcano on the Chilean mainland. About a month after the *Beagle* sailed north again, a great earthquake shook parts of the coast and the nearby islands. Darwin saw the damage caused by the earthquake in the harbor city of Concepción, where almost every building was demolished. Part of the town also was swept by a tremendous tidal wave.

After the *Beagle* returned to Valparaiso, Darwin procured guides and mules and set out to cross the Andes to Mendoza. Proceeding eastward through the Portillo Pass and returning through the Uspallata Pass, he reported beautiful scenery and collected much interesting geological and natural history data. When the *Beagle* sailed up the coast of northern Chile and continued northward to Peru, Darwin saw a saltpeter works and visited Lima. The city did not impress him, for it was dirty and ugly, suffering from many revolutions and an almost continual state of anarchy.

Lima was the last point at which the *Beagle* touched on the western coast of South America. The ship proceeded next to the Galápagos archipelago, where the most interesting feature was the prevalence of great tortoises. The inhabitants often killed these reptiles for their meat. Most of the birds on the islands were completely tame, for they had not yet learned to regard man as their enemy. The ship proceeded on to Tahiti, where Darwin was impressed by the swimming ability of the Polynesians. He explored the mountains of the island with the help of guides.

From Tahiti, the *Beagle* went south to New Zealand, New South Wales, and Australia. There Darwin first saw the aborigines' social greeting of rubbing noses, the equivalent of the European custom of shaking hands.

After leaving this group of islands, the ship headed back to Brazil to complete chronometric measurements. On the way, Darwin visited the island of St. Helena. It was on this last part of the journey that Darwin began to record in his journal his theories about the formation of coral reefs, many of which he observed during his stay in the South Seas. Darwin was glad to leave Brazil for the second time, for the practice of slavery in that country sickened him. In October, 1836, the *Beagle* returned to England.

As important as *The Voyage of the Beagle* is to the understanding of the genesis of Darwin's theory of evolution and of an appreciation of his own struggle for self-discovery, the book's most significant aspect is the insight it provides into the Victorian mind. Darwin shared many characteristics with other Victorian intellectuals of his generation, among them Thomas Carlyle, John Stuart Mill, John Henry Newman, and Alfred, Lord Tennyson. Principally, this generation of the 1830's was motivated by a conviction of personal destiny and a sense of being at the beginning of a new era in which the old ways of viewing matters would no longer apply. With the exception of Newman, they all came to embrace an idea of progress, either spiritual or social. Darwin found in nature a reason to assert that there was biological progress. Indeed, he provided Tennyson, for example, with metaphoric proof, in his theory of natural selection, of the poet's own concept of ethical evolution. *The Voyage of the Beagle* reflects the combination of zest for adventure and sense of mission that identifies Darwin clearly with his age and generation.

Most impressive perhaps about Darwin was his capacity for experiences of all kinds. From the start, he exhibited immense energy and thoroughness. Despite his commitment to naturalistic data, he remained responsive to the human dimension, and his observations were touched by sentiment and, at times, outrage. His description of the sheepdogs could be written only by an animal lover, and he did not hold back his outrage and disgust when he saw the conditions of anarchy and poverty in Lima.

One of the most salient aspects of nature, which Darwin faced with unceasing honesty, particularly in the Galápagos islands, was that of cruelty. About twenty years after the return of the *Beagle*, he wrote, "What a book a devil's chaplain might write on the clumsy, wasteful, blundering, low, and horribly cruel works of nature." In a sense, it is the other side of the coin of natural selection. If Darwin's theory of evolution pointed to a general progress of a species, it also revealed the indifference of nature to individuals within the species. It is precisely Darwin's openness to nature that allowed him to perceive this duality, and it was his scientific honesty—which necessitated his acceptance of his observation—that supported the final development of his thought. Both of these attributes are already reflected in Darwin's first book, *The Voyage of the Beagle*.

David L. Kubal

Further Reading

Colley, Ann C. "Nostalgia and *The Voyage of the Beagle*." In *Nostalgia and Recollection in Victorian Culture*. New York: St. Martin's Press, 1998. Colley argues that *The Voyage of the Beagle* and works by other British Victorians emanated from their personal recollections and reflect their feelings of nostalgia.

Farrington, Benjamin. *What Darwin Really Said*. New York: Schocken Books, 1982. A basic elucidation and analysis of Darwin's achievement, with a chapter devoted to discussion of Darwin's composition of *The Voyage of the Beagle*.

Keynes, Richard Darwin, ed. *Charles Darwin's "Beagle" Diary*. New York: Cambridge University Press, 1988. Provides the raw material that Darwin used for his narrative. Also includes a useful biographical glossary of persons referred to in the work and connected with it.

Moorehead, Alan. *Darwin and the "Beagle."* London: Hamish Hamilton, 1969. An illustrated and well-detailed introduction to the historical details of Darwin's voyage, including information about his contemporaries and companions, where he went, and what he saw.

Nichols, Peter. *Evolution's Captain: The Tragic Fate of Robert FitzRoy, the Man Who Sailed Charles Darwin Around the World*. London: Profile, 2003. Tells about the voyage from the perspective of FitzRoy, the ship's captain, who spent five years circling the globe with Darwin. The voyage led to Darwin's theories of natural selection—theories that horrified the religious FitzRoy and ultimately led to his suicide.

Porter, Duncan M. "The *Beagle* Collector and His Collections." In *The Darwinian Heritage*, edited by David Kohn. Princeton, N.J.: Princeton University Press, 1985. A historical discussion of the notebooks Darwin kept on the voyage and of his intellectual preparation for accompanying the *Beagle* as the ship's naturalist and for writing his work.

Sulloway, Frank J. "Darwin's Early Intellectual Development: An Overview of the *Beagle* Voyage." In *The Darwinian Heritage*, edited by David Kohn. Princeton, N.J.: Princeton University Press, 1985. A thorough, critical analysis of all the documents—including notebooks and sketches—from which Darwin composed his narrative.

The Voyage Out

Author: Virginia Woolf (1882-1941)
First published: 1915
Type of work: Novel
Type of plot: Bildungsroman
Time of plot: Early twentieth century
Locale: London, the mid-Atlantic, and South America

Principal characters:
RACHEL VINRACE, an inexperienced young woman of twenty-four
HELEN AMBROSE, Rachel's aunt
RIDLEY AMBROSE, Rachel's uncle, a scholar
WILLOUGHBY VINRACE, Rachel's father and owner of the *Euphrosyne*
MR. PEPPER, an old friend of Willoughby Vinrace
RICHARD DALLOWAY, a wealthy gentleman and former parliamentarian
CLARISSA DALLOWAY, Richard's wife
TERENCE HEWET, a novelist, twenty-seven years old
ST. JOHN HIRST, a brilliant twenty-four-year-old intellectual
SUSAN WARRINGTON, a companion to her elderly aunt
ARTHUR VENNING, a barrister with a passion for airplanes
MRS. THORNBURY, the consummate matron
EVELYN MURGATROYD, an impassioned, straightforward young woman
MR. FLUSHING and MRS. FLUSHING, buyers and sellers of native artifacts for great profit

The Story:

In London, Helen and Ridley Ambrose board the *Euphrosyne*, which will take them to Santa Marina in South America, where they plan to vacation. On board the ship, the Ambroses meet their niece, Rachel, whose father owns the ship and whom they have not seen in several years, and Mr. Pepper, an old family friend. The ship is soon under way, and as they sail, Helen studies her companions. She judges Rachel to be unformed, a character defect she attributes to her sheltered existence; Pepper she considers somewhat of a bore.

Rachel is indeed an unformed young woman. Her mother is dead, and she lives with her aunts and is seldom in society. She knows virtually nothing of the relations between men and women and has no confidants; her questions such as "Are you fond of your sister?" are judged inappropriate by her aunts and left unanswered. The things she does hear her aunts discuss seem to Rachel to have nothing to do with life. She deduces that no one ever says anything they mean or talks about anything they have felt. By the age of twenty-four, Rachel is confused but wondering and inarticulate about her feelings and observations. Unable to express her inner life through language, she instead plays the piano, believing that music expresses all the things one means and feels but cannot talk about.

While the ship is in port at Lisbon, Willoughby Vinrace, ashore on business, learns that an English couple have over-whelmed his clerk with their persistence and won a short passage aboard the *Euphrosyne*. The presence of the Dalloways introduces quite a change into the group. Clarissa energetically and skillfully fosters conversations and shows interest in everyone; Richard enthusiastically and sincerely discusses his political ideals.

The short time spent with the Dalloways affects Rachel profoundly. The couple talk with her about art, sexism, suffering, and making the world better for the poor. One day, during a storm, Richard kisses Rachel while they are alone together. Rachel has never been kissed, and the experience bewilders and terrifies her. Soon after this incident, the Dalloways depart. Helen perceives a change in her niece and is determined to learn the cause, suspecting that it has something to do with the Dalloways. When Rachel blurts out that Richard kissed her and tells the effect the kiss had on her, Helen realizes the depth of Rachel's ignorance about sexual matters and attempts to illuminate her.

In her new, self-appointed role as Rachel's mentor, Helen asks Willoughby to leave Rachel with her and Ridley in Santa Marina rather than take her with him. He consents, and shortly afterward he leaves them and Mr. Pepper at their destination.

Helen and Rachel develop a ritual they call seeing life, an evening walk through Santa Marina. On one of these walks, they find themselves at a hotel that houses foreign travelers, among them two young Englishmen named Terence Hewet and St. John Hirst, who befriend Rachel and Helen. Helen is glad of this connection and hopes that the young men will contribute to Rachel's education. Hirst's prejudices against women lead him to offend Rachel, but Terence believes that people can break through divisive boundaries, and he and Rachel quickly form a solid friendship. Rachel is encouraged to inquire, speculate, and articulate her thoughts and feelings. She ponders existence, self, and truth.

When Susan Warrington and Arthur Venning, two of the other English travelers at the hotel, become engaged, Rachel wonders what it is to be in love. She and Terence talk at great length about the subject and about men and women in general: their separate spheres, their respective perceptions and powers, woman suffrage, and the changes marriage brings to people, creating wives and husbands where once there had been individuals. They watch such changes come over Arthur and Susan.

Rachel and Terence wonder about their own relationship and whether they feel love for each other. With Hirst, Helen, and Mr. and Mrs. Flushing, the two take an excursion up the river, away from civilization and toward remote villages. Having disembarked to explore the terrain, all but Rachel and Terence are too oppressed by the heat to do so. Leaving the others, they follow a trail into the growth, and while they walk, they talk about their feelings and decide that they do love each other. Significantly, at this moment they become uncertain of the way back to their friends, although they are sure of the direction in which the river lies. They eventually find their way back to the others.

The couple dream of a unique marriage, but Helen has a presentiment of disaster that is realized when Rachel becomes ill shortly after the river expedition. Her illness diminishes her memory and separates her from the ordinary world, and as the fever worsens this distance widens, until she is unable to bridge it. She seems to be at the bottom of the sea. After many days of fever, she dies. Terence, who is with her when she dies, perceives for an instant that in death they have achieved perfect union. Then he realizes that he will never see Rachel again and becomes distraught, crying out her name.

As news of Rachel's death spreads at the hotel, the people who have known her respond variously. Some wonder whether there is any reason or meaning to her death. Mrs. Thornbury wonders whether there is order, equating it, characteristically, with happiness. Mrs. Flushing is furious with death, refusing to submit. Arthur and Susan do not wish to discuss death and try to steer the conversation in a different direction, while Evelyn Murgatroyd can talk of nothing else. Some wonder what caused Rachel's illness and how it might have been prevented. Some ponder the immortality of the soul. Life quickly returns to normal, however. People make plans to leave for home, and there are good-byes to be said and packing to be done. While Hirst lies back in a chair in the hotel's large common room and listens to their noise, the hotel guests pick up their books and their knitting and climb the stairs to bed.

Critical Evaluation:

The Voyage Out is Virginia Woolf's first novel. It is also one of her more accessible novels, as it employs a fairly traditional structure and narrative style and very little of the sometimes difficult, lyric, and highly idiosyncratic style that marks her other novels. In this work, Woolf explores questions about sex and gender, human relationships, civilization and social convention, class and power, social responsibility, existence, reality, and knowledge. This exploration takes place within the structure of a bildungsroman, a work that recounts the education of a single character, in this case, Rachel. Significantly, Rachel learns her lessons through a series of relationships with and observations of a diverse lot of human beings that includes Clarissa and Richard Dalloway, Helen Ambrose, Terence Hewet, St. John Hirst, Susan Warrington and Arthur Venning, Mr. and Mrs. Flushing, Evelyn Murgatroyd, and Mrs. Thornbury.

Each of these characters represents a type of human being, a point Hirst makes early in the novel. He believes that certain types of people find themselves sharing the same inscribed circles and are therefore capable of enjoying relationships with only those people. Different types find themselves within different circles, inhabiting space with others who are like them. There is no fraternizing among different types, and for this reason, he believes, men and women cannot have real relationships. They are simply too different from each other.

Hewet, in contrast, represents the desire to connect with others, and he argues about this with Hirst. It appears that Hewet achieves some success in his belief that people can cross boundaries and connect: It is he who organizes the picnic that brings together disparate groups, "putting virgins among matrons," and it is he who provides Susan and Arthur the opportunity to become engaged and plans the successful ball in honor of the engaged couple. He is also able to establish an easy dialogue with the reticent Rachel. The tragic outcome of their relationship, however, casts a shadow on such optimism. Some critics interpret Rachel's death as possibly an allegorical dictate that all attempts at authentic human connection are doomed.

Woolf's use of the powerful symbol of water—as embodied in the ocean, in a young woman's embarking on an adventure aboard her father's ship, and in a river excursion away from civilization and toward the primitive—also enriches the novel's statements about human relationships. It is little wonder that Woolf's first female protagonist, Rachel Vinrace, can begin her education and growth toward self-knowledge and articulation only after separating herself from her father's sphere of control, for the author had a problematic relationship with her own overbearing father. Rachel must learn to navigate and stay afloat on her own. Indeed, throughout the novel, Woolf describes Rachel and her inner processes in terms of water, rivers, streams, and the sea. When she and Terence first meet, Rachel is stooping to put her hands in a stream; she does not shake hands with him because hers are wet. This detail not only illustrates Rachel's preoccupation with water and self-knowledge but also suggests that, because of the rules of social decorum, immersion in the self can make people unfit for human interaction.

The Voyage Out suggests that Rachel is ultimately unable to negotiate between her inner world, represented in terms of water, and the outer world of social convention and relationships. Seduced by her own inner life, she retreats further from others, deeper into the water, until, during her illness, there is such a "gulf between her world and the ordinary world [that] she could not bridge" it. Rachel has achieved the total embrace of the self, leaving the others behind to make what sense they can of her death.

Julie Thompson

Further Reading

Adams, David. "Shadows of a 'Silver Globe': Woolf's Reconfiguration of the Darkness." In *Colonial Odysseys: Empire and Epic in the Modernist Novel*. Ithaca, N.Y.: Cornell University Press, 2003. Analyzes *The Voyage Out* and other British novels that examine the relationship between Britain and its colonies. Argues that the structures and literary allusions of these novels place them in the epic tradition, in which the protagonist journeys away from a familiar world and into an alien society.

Barrett, Eileen, and Patricia Cramer, eds. *Virginia Woolf: Lesbian Readings*. New York: New York University Press, 1997. Part 2 of this collection of conference papers focuses on Woolf's novels, with lesbian interpretations of *The Voyage Out* and six other books.

Briggs, Julia. *Virginia Woolf: An Inner Life*. Orlando, Fla: Harcourt, 2005. Biography focuses on Woolf's work in relation to her fascination with the workings of the mind. Traces the creation of each of Woolf's books, from *The Voyage Out* through *Between the Acts* (1941), combining literary analysis with details of Woolf's life.

De Gay, Jane. "From Woman Reader to Woman Writer: *The Voyage Out.*" In *Virginia Woolf's Novels and the Literary Past*. Edinburgh: Edinburgh University Press, 2006. Chapter focusing on The Voyage Out is part of a study that analyzes Woolf's novels and other works to explore her allusions to and revisions of the plots and motifs of earlier fiction.

DeSalvo, Louise A. *Virginia Woolf's First Voyage: A Novel in the Making*. Totowa, N.J.: Rowman & Littlefield, 1980. Discusses the novel's inception, inspirations for characters and events, and themes. Detailed comparisons of the drafts of the work offer insight into Woolf's creative process.

Goldman, Jane. *The Cambridge Introduction to Virginia Woolf*. New York: Cambridge University Press, 2006. Provides a wealth of information designed to help students and other readers better understand Woolf's writings, including biographical details and discussions of the novels. One section places Woolf's life and work within historical, political, and cultural context, including information about the Bloomsbury Group; another section focuses on critical reception of the works from the 1940's through the 1990's and includes contemporary reviews.

McDowell, Frederick P. W. "'Surely Order Did Prevail': Virginia Woolf and *The Voyage Out.*" In *Virginia Woolf: Revaluation and Continuity*, edited by Ralph Freedman. Berkeley: University of California Press, 1980. Clearly explicates the novel's psychological complexity, darkness, and questioning of meaning and reality.

Paul, Janis M. *The Victorian Heritage of Virginia Woolf: The External World in Her Novels*. Norman, Okla.: Pilgrim Books, 1986. Includes a chapter on *The Voyage Out* that considers the novel within its aesthetic and historical context and pays particular attention to Woolf's struggle between Victorian and modernist conventions, both in life and in literature. Discusses Woolf's experimentation with form.

Roe, Sue, and Susan Sellers, eds. *The Cambridge Companion to Virginia Woolf*. New York: Cambridge University Press, 2000. Collection of essays by leading scholars addresses Woolf's life and work from a wide range of intellectual perspectives. Includes analyses of her novels and discussions of Woolf in relation to modernism, feminism, and psychoanalysis.

Rose, Phyllis. *Woman of Letters: A Life of Virginia Woolf*. 1978. Reprint. San Diego, Calif.: Harcourt Brace Jovanovich, 1987. Biographical work includes a chapter on *The Voyage Out* that offers a compelling discussion focusing on Woolf's use of character to explore social and philosophical issues.

W

Waiting

Author: Ha Jin (1956-   )
First published: 1999
Type of work: Novel
Type of plot: Historical realism
Time of plot: 1963-1983
Locale: Muji City and Goose Village, China

Principal characters:
LIN KONG, an army doctor
SHUYU, his wife
HUA, their daughter
MANNA WU, Lin's girlfriend, a head nurse
HAIYAN NIU, Manna's friend, a nurse
BENSHENG, Shuyu's brother

The Story:

Every summer for the past eighteen years, army doctor Lin Kong has returned to his house in Goose Village to try to divorce his wife, Shuyu, whom he had married by arrangement. Like years before, the separated couple travels to the court of Wujia Town to initiate the divorce, but Shuyu always changes her mind. On occasion, Shuyu's brother, Bensheng, a greedy and simple-minded peasant, travels with the couple. In front of others, he shames his brother-in-law, Lin. He reminds him of Shuyu's loyalty and her sacrificial care for his parents prior to their deaths. Defeated once again, Lin returns to his job at the hospital in Muji City and delivers the disappointing news to his girlfriend, Manna Wu, a nurse.

It is now 1964, and Manna enrolls at the hospital for studies in nursing. She is in her mid-twenties. During her studies, she gets romantically involved with a lieutenant from Shanghai. After a brief courtship based on camaraderie and celibacy, they two are engaged; but the affair suffers when they are separated by duty. Upon her graduation, Manna is assigned to stay at the army hospital, while her fiancé is transferred to a regiment on the Russian border. A correspondence ensues, during which Manna's fiancé eventually breaks their engagement and marries his cousin in Shanghai. By that time, Manna is twenty-six years old, and because she is quite a plain woman, her chances of marriage are slim. In addition, the rules of conduct forbid the hospital's doctors to date or marry their coworkers, so they seek their partners elsewhere.

In her first—and failed—relationship, Manna confides in Lin, her teacher and a married man of good reputation. At first, the two are no more than comrades, and she has helped him make dust jackets for his multiple books. One day,

Manna's feet are brutally blistered in a long-distance training march, so Lin takes care of her at a rest stop at a farmhouse. Because of his kindness, the young woman develops a crush on him. As a gift, she gives him a ticket to an opera of a patriotic theme, and on the day of the event, Lin is surprised to find Manna sitting in the seat next to his. Her affection for him becomes obvious: During the performance she touches his hand, a gesture, albeit bold and inappropriate, that inspires Lin to dream of the young woman that same night. The comrades begin spending more time together, but their friendship is strictly platonic.

As gossip at the hospital insinuates their affair, Lin is called into a meeting with Ran Su, the vice director of the political department at the hospital. Lin promises to maintain the propriety of their relationship until he can legally divorce his wife. Encouraged by her girlfriend, Haiyan Niu, Manna arranges for a place where she and Lin can be intimate. Lin rejects the idea, leaving Manna wondering about the nature of his affection for her. Lin is indeed uncertain about his love for Manna. The two go through a brief breakup, but after reconciliation, Lin seriously considers the option of divorce.

Lin and Shuyu's marriage was never based on physical or intellectual intimacy. Still, he enjoys returning to Goose Village, where he finds comfort and peace in the old, simpler ways of living. Shuyu's love for Lin is sacrificial. She is a simple woman, an obliging wife, a good homemaker and cook; she never nags him for money despite a very modest lifestyle that she and her daughter can afford on Lin's allowance. However, she is a woman of the old ways. To Lin's embarrassment, her feet are bound according to custom; and although never an attractive woman in the first place, years of hard work have taken a toll on her appearance. Only a year his junior, she looks much older than he. Lin decides that the only basis for his divorce could be the lack of love in his marriage, but in truth, he is unable to feel love toward either Shuyu or Manna.

During the next eighteen years, Manna is presented with a couple of opportunities for marriage. The first candidate is Lin's cousin Liang Meng, a teacher and a widower with three children. He writes a letter to Lin about the hardships of raising his children alone, and Lin agrees to set him up with Manna. She agrees to a date, but chooses at this time to compare the two men; she dismisses Liang Meng as bookish.

Another opportunity arrives from the higher powers at the hospital. Vice Commissar Wei, whose wife has been sent to a labor camp for writing a counter-revolutionary booklet, is in search of her replacement among the hospital staff. Despite his jealousy, Lin agrees to let Manna meet him. On the second date, the vice commissar lends Manna a copy of poet Walt Whitman's *Leaves of Grass* (1855), about which she agrees to write him a letter. Unable to understand the book, Manna asks for Lin's assistance, and Lin takes on the task. Although Manna's essay impresses the vice commissar, he rejects Manna's candidacy based on the letter's poor handwriting. In truth, he has been dating several women at once, eventually hiring a young teacher for the job. The rejection spurs more gossip at the hospital, and with time, it turns Manna more bitter; she becomes hopeless about her future.

One spring, Lin contracts tuberculosis and is quarantined at the hospital. Rooming with him is Geng Yang, an officer to whom Manna had been introduced at the movie theater on her date with the vice commissar. Manna visits Lin, who introduces her as his girlfriend. Later, when the two patients are alone, Lin confides in Geng Yang about his failed attempts to divorce his wife. He also confesses about the strictly platonic nature of his relationship with Manna and about her virginity.

After his recovery, Lin departs for Shenyang City to attend a program for officers. With the excuse of having some of Lin's books in his possession, Geng Yang lures Manna into his hospital room and rapes her. Although Manna does not tell authorities, she confides in her friend Haiyan, who then tells her husband. The gossip travels quickly, and although there is no dishonorable pregnancy after the rape, Manna's reputation worsens even more. Lin learns of the rape from Manna upon his return six weeks later. By this time, Geng Yang has fully recovered and is discharged from the army.

It is now 1983, and Lin has been separated from Shuyu for eighteen years, long enough to acquit the marriage without a partner's consent. They go to the People's Court in Muji City, and the divorce is settled peacefully. Lin goes on to arrange for Shuyu's permit to live and work in the city and later finds a city job for his daughter, Hua. He sells the house in Goose Village and, against all objections by his brother, Bensheng, leaves the stock to his older brother. For reasons of propriety, Lin and Manna wait before applying for their marriage license, after which preparations for the wedding take a full course. They have a traditional communist wedding ceremony, at which homage is paid to Chairman Mao Zedong, and the two are finally married; but the groom is bored, and the bride leaves the ceremony in tears after Ran Su calls their love bitter.

In marriage, Manna turns out to be a passionate lover, which leaves her new husband exhausted; when it begins to affect his job, he asks her to take it easier on him. Soon, Manna is pregnant with twins. Lin first attempts to persuade her to have an abortion, but she is determined. By now, she is forty-four years old. The pregnancy is difficult, and Lin realizes that the years of waiting have turned Manna into a bitter, boring woman. The birth of their sons, River and Lake, strains the marriage even more. The babies are born sickly and recover only because of an old remedy from Hua, who visits her father often to help out with the chores that Manna barely fulfills.

The pregnancy has worsened Manna's heart, and according to the doctors, she does not have long to live. Domestic fights continue, and Manna grows jealous. Disillusioned and disappointed by his second marriage, Lin seeks refuge from his problems at the apartment of his former wife and daughter. There, he asks for forgiveness and asks them to wait for his return.

Critical Evaluation:

Waiting, Ha Jin's second novel, has received much critical acclaim, including the 1999 National Book Award and a 2000 PEN/Faulkner Award. Harnessed on cultural, political, and personal themes from the home country of the writer—from which he had escaped in 1985—*Waiting* is a history lesson on the People's Republic of China before and after the Cultural Revolution (1966-1976).

The novel examines a dual split in culture through the protagonist's journeys between Goose Village and Muji City. The character of Lin Kong is conflicted between the restrictions that exist in the old and new cultures of his contemporary China. In the agricultural suburbs, Lin encounters the ways of the old country, ways that existed prior to the Cultural Revolution. In these suburbs, he finds certain comfort, but also is frustrated by the narrow-minded traditions, such as the customs of arranged marriages and of binding women's feet, and the preference for boys over girls. The never-ending intrusion of his greedy brother-in-law in the matters of his family also belongs to the old ways.

The urban ways, in some contrast, are influenced by the teachings of the Chinese Communist Party, but they, too, have ideology-driven rules of conduct that constrict a person's liberties. For example, celibacy and lack of privacy are imposed upon Lin's relationship with Manna, eventually suffocating their emotional lives and eliminating all dignity in their courtship. A lifetime of following the rules turns Lin into a dispassionate person. Seemingly lacking any drive or ability to make a decision, he goes along with orders and rules no matter their ridiculousness.

Dreams, which repeat as a literary device in the novel, are the only truthful expressions of the story's characters' needs and wants. Critic Louis J. Parascandola, in his article "Love and Sex in Totalitarian Society" (2005), compares *Waiting* to George Orwell's famous futuristic novel *Nineteen-Eighty Four* (1949). In both novels, totalitarian regimes are criticized for ridding their citizens of personal liberties, including their freedom to love or to pursue sexual pleasure. Lin experiences love and passion neither in his arranged marriage to Shuyu nor in his obliged courtship of Manna; the only outlet for his urges is his dream life. Only when asleep or daydreaming can Lin experience love or sexual desire toward Manna. In real life, however, he continues to carry on with the expected protocol, following the rules that contribute to his indecisiveness. In the end, he robs both women—his wife and his girlfriend—of time, which they waste waiting for a resolution of their triangular relationship.

The female characters of both Jin's and Orwell's novels suffer firsthand from the rules imposed on them by totalitarianism. The women are pegs in the hands of men—their husbands or their political leaders—and are dispensable and unappreciated. Through the introduction of secondary female characters, Jin tells the tragic tales of their destinies—from the numerous women who suffer from the insatiable sexual appetite of an army official; to the imprisoned wife of Vice Commissar Wei; to the woman who arrives at Lin's hospital with a charged battery inside her body, lodged there by a husband who wants to prevent the birth of a daughter. The primary women in Lin's life also suffer at the hands of men, either by destructive intention or, as in the case of Lin, a lack of any intention. Although Lin is not an abusive man, his biggest fault is his inability to love.

Lin's first wife, Shuyu, leads a life of isolation and servitude. Only Lin can better her living situation. However, he takes her for granted, having no awareness of the scarcity of her living conditions. Manna, an orphan from an early age, has opportunities, too, but they are different and limited. Because of the rules imposed by the party, Manna and Lin cannot leave the grounds of the hospital together, but neither are they allowed to be left alone without a chaperone. The party's rules against divorce, and the expectations of women's virginity before marriage, are meant to protect them; instead, they ruin their lives.

Women's sexuality is another leading theme of the novel. According to tradition, men seek virgins to be their wives. Celibacy is expected in courtship, yet even in marriage, sex is permitted for procreation, not pleasure. When Shuyu's wish for a son brings her to Lin's bedroom, she is rejected and shamed by her husband. In their eighteen-year marriage, they sleep separately, even when in the same house. Manna's protection of her virginity not only turns her into an old maid; Geng Yang rapes her. For fear of being considered promiscuous, Manna cannot turn to the authorities. (As mundane a task as Manna learning to ride a bicycle is judged as promiscuous as well.) There seems to be no outlet to women's sexuality, and yet women are the only characters capable of expressing their desires and passions.

As Jin examines in her *The Writer as Migrant* (2008), "the writer should be not just a chronicler but also a shaper, an alchemist, of historical experiences." *Waiting* is an accomplishment of historical value. It portrays the Communist society of China with detail and precision, but it also paints the smaller personal tragedies under a regime of restriction and control. It is not an epic novel: The span of the characters' journeys is narrow, and their lives are extremely simple. Still, it is impossible not to find Jin's characters sympathetic, because the writer himself invests in a nonjudgmental understanding of their humanity.

Vera Chernysheva

Further Reading

Hsia, C. T. "Obsession with China: The Moral Burden of Modern Chinese Literature." In *A History of Modern Chinese Fiction*. 2d ed. New Haven, Conn.: Yale University Press, 1971. Hsia's brilliant essay examines the modern Chinese literary tradition that Jin, in large part, is reacting against in his novels, including *Waiting*.

Jin, Ha. *The Writer as Migrant*. Chicago: University of Chicago Press, 2008. Jin presents his thoughts and observations on the idea of the migrant writer—the exiles, refugees, immigrants, and emigrants writing about topics such as nostalgia, homeland, and memory. Also discusses their choice to write in the language of either their native or their adopted cultures.

Kinkley, Jeffrey C. "*Waiting*." *World Literature Today* 74, no. 3 (Summer, 2000): 579-580. In this brief review of *Waiting*, Kinkley points out the main theme of the novel: Jin's representation of the old country, the China that Kinkley himself left behind in 1985.

Parascandola, Louis J. "Love and Sex in Totalitarian Society: An Exploration of Ha Jin and George Orwell." *Studies in the Humanities* 33, no. 1 (June, 2005): 38-49. Parascan-
dola's comparison of Jin's *Waiting* to George Orwell's *Nineteen-Eighty Four* examines the effects of totalitarian regimes on human emotions, love and sex in particular. He summarizes Lin Kong's self-denial of love and pleasure as masochistic and inhuman, which is the novel's main warning against regimes such as that of China.

Prose, Francine. "The Eighteen-Year Itch." *The New York Times Book Review*, October 24, 1999, p. 9. Through the leading themes of sexuality and relationships, Prose examines the implications of China's regime to the personal lives of Jin's characters in *Waiting*.

Waiting for Godot

Author: Samuel Beckett (1906-1989)
First produced: En attendant Godot, 1953; first published, 1952 (English translation, 1954)
Type of work: Drama
Type of plot: Absurdist
Time of plot: Indeterminate
Locale: A country road

Principal characters:
VLADIMIR, a tramp
ESTRAGON, another tramp
POZZO, a success-blinded materialist
LUCKY, Pozzo's servant
A BOY, a messenger from Godot

The Story:

Estragon tries to take off his boot but fails. Vladimir agrees with him that it sometimes appears that there is nothing one could do. They are glad to be reunited after a night apart. With Vladimir's help, Estragon succeeds in removing his boot, which was causing him pain. Vladimir, also in pain, cannot laugh in comfort; he tries smiling instead, but it is not satisfactory.

Vladimir muses on the one Gospel account that says Christ saved one of the thieves. Estragon wants to leave, but they cannot leave because they are waiting for Godot. They become confused about the arrangements and wonder if they are waiting at the right time, in the right place, and on the right day. They quarrel briefly but then, as always, they reconcile.

Estragon and Vladimir consider hanging themselves from the nearby tree but decide that it would be safer to do nothing until they hear what Godot says. They do not know what they have asked Godot for. They conclude that they have forgone their rights. Vladimir gives Estragon a carrot, which he eats hungrily. They decide that although they are not bound to Godot, they are in fact unable to act.

Pozzo enters, driving Lucky, who is laden with luggage, by a rope around his neck. Estragon and Vladimir mistake Pozzo for Godot but accept him as Pozzo. Although he attempts to intimidate them, he is glad of their company. After ordering Lucky to bring him his stool and his coat, Pozzo gives Lucky the whip. Lucky obeys automatically. Vladimir and Estragon protest violently against Pozzo's treatment of Lucky, but Pozzo deflects their outburst and the subject is dropped.

After smoking a pipe, Pozzo rises. He then decides he does not want to leave, but his pride almost prevents him from reseating himself. The tramps want to know why Lucky never puts down the luggage. Pozzo says that Lucky is trying to make Pozzo keep him. When Pozzo adds that he would sell Lucky rather than throw him out, Lucky weeps. Estragon tries to dry the servant's tears, but Lucky kicks him away; Estragon then weeps. Pozzo philosophizes on this and says that Lucky has taught him all the beautiful things he knows but that the fellow has now become unbearable and is driving him mad. Estragon and Vladimir then abuse Lucky for mistreating his master.

Pozzo breaks into a monologue on the twilight, alternating between the lyrical and the commonplace and ending with the bitter thought that everything happens in the world when one is least prepared. He decides to reward Estragon and Vladimir for praising him by making Lucky entertain them. Lucky executes a feeble dance that Estragon mocks but fails to imitate.

Estragon states that there have been no arrivals, no departures, and no action, and that everything is terrible. Pozzo next decides that Lucky should think for them. For this Vladimir replaces Lucky's derby hat. Lucky's thoughts are an incoherent flood of words resembling a dissertation on the possible goodness of God, the tortures of hellfire, the prevalence of sport, and the vacuity of suburbs. The words desperately upset Lucky's listeners, who attack him and silence him by seizing his hat. Having restored Lucky to his position as carrier, Pozzo and the tramps say many farewells before Pozzo and Lucky finally leave.

The Boy calls to Vladimir and Estragon. He brings a message from Godot, who will come the next evening. The Boy, a goatherd, says that Godot is kind to him, but he beats the Boy's brother, a shepherd. Vladimir asks the Boy to tell Godot only that he has seen them.

By the time the Boy leaves, night has fallen. Estragon decides to abandon his boots to someone else. Vladimir protests, and Estragon says that Christ went barefoot. Once again they consider and reject the idea of separating. They decide to leave for the night, but they stay where they are.

The following evening, the boots are still there and the tree has grown some leaves. The tramps have spent the night separately. Vladimir returns first. When Estragon comes back, he says that he has been beaten again, and Vladimir feels that he could have prevented such cruelty. Vladimir begins to talk of the previous day, but Estragon can remember nothing about it except for his being kicked. They are then overwhelmed by the thought of the whispering voices of the dead around them. They try to break their silence but succeed only in part. By a great effort, Estragon recalls that he and the others spent the previous day chattering inanities. He reflects that they have spent fifty years doing no more than that.

They discover that the boots left behind by Estragon have been exchanged for another old pair. After finding Lucky's hat, which assures them that they have returned to the right place, they start a wild exchange of that hat and their two hats, shifting them from hand to hand. Finally Vladimir keeps Lucky's hat and Estragon keeps his own.

Once more Estragon decides to leave. To distract him, Vladimir suggests that they "play" Pozzo and Lucky. Puzzled, Estragon leaves, but he returns almost immediately be-cause some people are coming. Vladimir is jubilant, convinced that Godot is arriving. They try to hide, but there is nowhere for them to go. Finally Lucky enters with Pozzo, who is now blind. Lucky falls and drags Pozzo down with him. Pozzo cries for help, and Vladimir passionately wishes to act while he has the opportunity to do one good thing as a member of the human race, a species that appalls him. Pozzo is terrified, and Vladimir also falls in his attempts to raise him. Estragon falls too while trying to lift Vladimir. As Estragon and Vladimir fight and argue on the ground, they call Pozzo "Cain" and "Abel." When he responds to both names they conclude that he is all of humanity. Suddenly they get up without difficulty.

Pozzo prepares to leave, but Vladimir wants Lucky to sing first. Pozzo explains that Lucky is dumb. Estragon and Vladimir want to know when he was afflicted, and Pozzo, angry, says that all their lives are merely momentary and time does not matter. He leaves with Lucky.

While Estragon sleeps, the Boy enters to say that Godot will come, not that night but the next. The message for Godot is that the Boy has seen Vladimir. The Boy leaves, and Estragon awakes. He immediately wants to leave, but Vladimir insists that they cannot go far because they must return the next night in order to wait for Godot, who will punish them if they do not wait.

Estragon and Vladimir remark that only the tree in the landscape is alive, and they consider hanging themselves again. Instead, they decide that if Godot does not come to save them the next night, they will hang themselves. At last the tramps decide to go, but they remain immobile.

Critical Evaluation:

Waiting for Godot is a landmark in modern drama. When it premiered in Paris, its originality stunned audiences. No one had seen or heard anything like it before. Initially, some were disgusted, some were puzzled, and some were wildly enthusiastic. Within a short time, however, audiences came to the theater prepared for a wholly new dramatic experience and went away with praises for Samuel Beckett. The play ran for more than three hundred performances in Paris, and other productions were mounted in London and major cities on the Continent. The play was soon widely translated and performed around the world. After a disastrous U.S. premiere in Miami, Florida, *Waiting for Godot* went on to a successful New York run, suggesting that the play was best received by audiences made up of sophisticated intellectuals.

Nevertheless, audience enthusiasm for *Waiting for Godot* has not been matched by unalloyed critical acclaim. To be sure, many critics as well as eminent playwrights have paid high tribute to the play, but several other critics have been repelled or baffled by it, their reactions most often stemming from misunderstanding of the play. In order to avert such misunderstanding, it is necessary to examine two crucial aspects of the play: its language and its philosophical orientation.

First of all, the language of the play is intimately connected to Beckett's own background in language studies and literary influences. Beckett was born in Dublin, Ireland, and took his bachelor's degree in French and Italian at Trinity College. After teaching English in Paris for two years, he returned to Trinity to teach and complete his master's degree in French. Next, he traveled in England and on the Continent, and he wrote poems, short stories, and novels in English. He at last settled permanently in Paris, except for a brief hiatus during World War II, and began writing in French in the late 1940's. *Waiting for Godot* was originally written in French and then translated into English by Beckett himself. The play is full of verbal and linguistic play; it is the work of a master of words and wordplay.

Second, during Beckett's first sojourn in Paris, from 1928 to 1930, he met James Joyce, a meeting that launched a long and mutually satisfying friendship between the two Irish expatriates and language experts. The philosophical influence of Joyce on Beckett's work is evident in the language play in *Waiting for Godot*. Puns, allusions, and linguistic tricks abound. Joyce and Beckett had little respect for literary convention, including, to an extent, the convention that everything in a book should make perfect sense or be perfectly clear.

Critics have expended great effort, for example, in trying to decipher the word "Godot." Beckett himself declined to explain, but critics, undeterred, continue to speculate. The most common view is that Godot is God, with the "ot" as a diminutive suffix. The French title, *En attendant Godot*, seems to lend support to this interpretation. Another suggestion is the analogy between Godot and Charlot (both utilizing the diminutive suffix), the latter being the French name for silent-film star Charles Chaplin's famous character the Little Tramp. The kind of hat that the Little Tramp wears, a derby, plays a significant part in the stage business of *Waiting for Godot*. Some readings inevitably deteriorate into the preposterous—that Godot represents Charles de Gaulle, for example. A much more likely explanation involves an allusion to a highly obscure source: Honoré de Balzac's comedy *Le Faiseur* (pr. 1849; also known as *Mercadet*; English translation, 1901). Balzac's play revolves around a character named Godeau who strongly influences the action of the play but never appears onstage. The parallels between the Balzac

work and *Waiting for Godot* are too close to attribute to mere coincidence. Beckett, like Joyce, had a marked fondness for the esoteric literary allusion. It is possible, of course, to circumvent these literary contortions and simply view Godot as a state of being: the waiting, bracketed by birth and death, that we call life.

In addition, Beckett plays other word games in *Waiting for Godot*. Estragon, for instance, begins a sentence that Vladimir then finishes. The overwhelming monotony of the dialogue, reflecting the monotony in the characters' lives, is reminiscent of the exercise drills in old language texts of the "*La plume de ma tante est sur la table*" variety, further suggesting the debasement of language and the consequent breakdown of communication. The non sequiturs that emerge from rapid-fire exchanges in the dialogue echo the music-hall comedians of Beckett's youth. Beckett's penchant for wordplay reveals the influence of his language training and of his friend James Joyce.

The philosophical orientation of *Waiting for Godot* is another matter, however, for the years of Beckett's residence in France coincided with a period of great ferment in existential philosophy, most of it centered in Paris. Beckett is not a formal or doctrinaire existentialist, but he could hardly avoid being affected by existentialism, for such ideas were part of his cultural milieu. There is no systematically existential point of view in *Waiting for Godot*—as there is in, for example, the plays of Jean-Paul Sartre and the novels of Albert Camus—but a generally existential and absurdist view of the human condition comes through very clearly in the play. Vladimir and Estragon, and Lucky and Pozzo, are psychically isolated from one another; despite physical proximity, they are alienated and lonely, as indicated by their failure to communicate meaningfully. In that state of mind, each despairs, feeling helpless in the face of an immutable destiny. Unlike the formal existentialists, however, Estragon and Vladimir hope, and it is that hope that sustains them through their monotonous and immobile existence. They wait. They wait for Godot, who will surely bring them words of comfort and advice, and who will intervene to alter their destinies. By maintaining this hope, by waiting for Godot to come, Vladimir and Estragon avoid facing the logic of existential philosophy, which postulates hopelessness followed by a sense of futility, reducing humankind to absurdity. In this way, Vladimir and Estragon attain truly heroic proportions; they endure.

Beckett's play has been criticized, even by Estragon, because, as the tramp puts it, "Nothing happens." In fact, however, a great deal does happen: There is a lot of action, much coming and going. However, action in this sense is quite superficial, for all of it is meaningless. That very action assumes a rhythm and a pattern that constitute the structure of the play. The repetitious movements and dialogue reinforce the existential theme of the play: that life is a meaningless and monotonous performance of endlessly repeated routine. The pattern established in the first act is recapitulated in the second act, with only slight variation. Obviously the action in *Waiting for Godot* is not the action of conventional drama, but it is this unique fusion of theme and structure that accounts for the startling originality of the play and that rightly earns Beckett a place as one of the few genuine innovators in modern drama.

"Critical Evaluation" by Joanne G. Kashdan

Further Reading

Bair, Deirdre. *Samuel Beckett.* 1978. Reprint. New York: Simon & Schuster, 1993. Comprehensive biography draws on hundreds of interviews with Beckett's friends and acquaintances. Provides much interesting circumstantial information on the genesis of *Waiting for Godot*, its controversial early productions, and its translations.

Bloom, Harold, ed. *Samuel Beckett's "Waiting for Godot."* New ed. New York: Bloom's Literary Criticism, 2008. A "sequel" to the collection of essays Bloom published on the play in 1987, containing essays that did not appear in the previous book. Prominent Beckett scholars, including Martin Esslin, Ruby Cohn, Michael Worton, Lois Gordon, and Rónán McDonald, examine the play's absurdity and its existential dimension and discuss the "Godot phenomenon."

_____. *"Waiting for Godot": Modern Critical Interpretations.* New York: Chelsea House, 1987. Eight representative selections by leading interpreters of Beckett's work (including Ruby Cohn, Martin Esslin, John Fletcher, and Hugh Kenner) consider the theatrical, religious, and philosophical implications of *Waiting for Godot*.

Connor, Steven, ed. *"Waiting for Godot" and "Endgame."* New York: St. Martin's Press, 1992. Four of the eleven interrelated essays in this collection deal with *Waiting for Godot* in terms drawn from contemporary theory. They range from the liberal humanist reading of Andrew Kennedy on action and theatricality to Jeffrey Nealon's definition of a postmodernist culture that validates the self through the playing of serious games.

Esslin, Martin. *The Theatre of the Absurd.* 3d ed. New York: Penguin Books, 1980. Highly influential for its famous definition and its lucid study of the movement of which *Waiting for Godot* is a classic part. Focusing on existential elements, the analysis attempts to account for the complexity of the effect of the play.

Gordon, Lois. *Reading Godot.* New Haven, Conn.: Yale University Press, 2002. Provides in-depth analysis of the play, interpreting it from linguistic, philosophical, critical, and biographical perspectives. Demonstrates how the play dramatizes Beckett's insights into human nature and the emotional lives of individuals.

Graver, Lawrence. *Samuel Beckett, "Waiting for Godot."* 2d ed. New York: Cambridge University Press, 2004. Comprehensive critical study of the play includes information on its genesis and reception, a comparison of the English and French versions, and discussion of its influence and place in the contemporary theater.

Hutchings, William. *Samuel Beckett's "Waiting for Godot": A Reference Guide.* Westport, Conn.: Praeger, 2005. Resource designed for college students provides a plot summary, bibliographic essays, and chapters discussing the play's origins, its various editions, and its performance history as well as the cultural, historical, and intellectual contexts within which it was written.

Karic, Pol Popovic. *Ironic Samuel Beckett: Samuel Beckett's Life and Drama—"Waiting for Godot," "Endgame," and "Happy Days."* Lanham, Md.: University Press of America, 2007. Analyzes the three plays with a focus on Beckett's use of irony as a means of communication, catharsis, and freedom for characters living in a world of permanent chaos.

Lawley, Paul. *"Waiting for Godot": Character Studies.* London: Continuum, 2008. Focuses on the four main characters in the play, discussing the pairings they form and what these pairings mean. Also seeks to unravel the difficulties inherent in interpreting the work.

Waiting for Lefty

Author: Clifford Odets (1906-1963)
First produced: 1935; first published, 1935
Type of work: Drama
Type of plot: Social criticism
Time of plot: Mid-1930's
Locale: New York City

Principal characters:
LEFTY COSTELLO, the chairman of a taxi-driver union's
    strike committee
HARRY FATT, a corrupt union official
JOE MITCHELL, a taxi driver
EDNA MITCHELL, his wife
MILLER, an industrial lab assistant, later a cabbie
FAYETTE, an industrialist
SID, a taxi driver
FLORENCE, a woman in love Sid
IRV, Florrie's brother
"CLAYTON," a company spy
AGATE KELLER, a taxi driver
HENCHMAN, a gunman who backs up Fatt
DR. BARNES, chief of medicine at a hospital
DR. BENJAMIN, a surgeon at the hospital, then a cabbie

The Story:

At a meeting of taxi drivers, a union official urges a committee of six men not to call a strike. Voices from the audience call out for Lefty, who was elected chairman of this strike committee, but Lefty has mysteriously disappeared. The union official, Fatt, and his Henchman threaten the union members and call those urging a strike "reds" (that is, communists). One of the committee members, Joe Mitchell, gets up and makes an impassioned plea for the strike. He starts to describe an encounter with his wife, Edna, which is then enacted onstage. The committee remains onstage in the background, where it comments as a chorus on the action it observes.

Joe comes home from a hard day driving a cab to find that the furniture he and Edna have been buying on installment has been repossessed and that Edna has had to put their two children to bed hungry. Edna accuses Joe of belonging to a union that is run by racketeers, urges him to start his own honest union, and threatens to go back to her old boyfriend. The chorus of committee members in the darkened semicircle beyond Joe and Edna comments that she will. Joe exits, saying he is going to look for another taxi driver, Lefty Costello, who was recently making statements similar to Edna's.

In a flashback, Miller, another one of the committee members, encounters Mr. Fayette, an industrialist. Fayette gives a raise to Miller, then a lab assistant, and moves him to a new project, working with a Dr. Brenner to manufacture poison gas. Fayette also asks Miller to send him secret weekly reports on Dr. Brenner. Miller balks at what he calls spying, but Fayette warns him to think of the consequences of refusing—the chorus comments that he will lose his job. Fayette then fires Miller, and Miller punches Fayette in the mouth.

Florence is at home with her brother Irv. She is waiting for another member of the strike committee, Sid Stein, to pick her up and take her to a dance. Irv argues that Florence should stop seeing Sid, because his job as a taxi driver does not pay him enough to support them. Florence insists that she loves Sid, but she promises her brother she will talk to him about his prospects. Sid and Florence have been engaged for three years, unable to marry because of their financial commitments to their families. When he arrives, Sid tells Florence that the deck is stacked against people like them in the current depression. Sid tells Florence goodbye, but the scene ends with Florence burying her face in her hands and Sid on his knees with his face in her lap.

At the union meeting, Fatt is still berating the strike committee. He calls up a member of the audience, Tom Clayton, who Fatt says comes from Philadelphia, where the union recently attempted a strike. Fatt asks Clayton to tell the committee what happened as a result. Clayton claims that the union should listen to Fatt, that the time is wrong for a strike. Suddenly, a voice from the audience shouts out for Clayton to sit down, and, after a brief struggle, the heckler rushes onstage to announce that Clayton is an imposter: His real name is Clancy, and he is a company spy. Fatt tries to have the accuser thrown out, but he continues his accusations: Clayton has been a company spy for years, breaking up unions across the country. When Clayton denies these accusations, the accuser says that he knows the truth because Clayton is his own brother. Clayton escapes down the center aisle.

One of the committee members, Benjamin, helped the man from the audience make his case. He enacts an incident from his earlier career as a surgeon. Benjamin has been removed from an operation at the last minute by a Dr. Leeds. He comes into the office of Dr. Barnes to complain that Leeds is incompetent. Barnes explains the switch by telling Benjamin that Leeds is the nephew of a powerful senator. Moreover, the woman Benjamin was to have operated on is a charity case, and they are about to close the charity ward entirely to save money. Worse, Benjamin himself is going to be let go. Benjamin knows why: He is Jewish, and he has met this prejudice before. The phone rings, and Barnes announces that the woman has died on the operating table. Benjamin says he will get a job driving a cab and help change the United States. He raises his clenched fist.

Back at the strike committee meeting, another member, Agate Keller, has risen to speak, Despite Fatt and his henchman's attempts to silence him, the audience urges him on. Agate's weapon is sarcasm: He knows their union is fine, he says, but when he tried to put on his coat today, he discovered his union button was on fire for shame. Fatt and his gunman try to remove Agate physically, but other committee members intervene, and Agate continues. It is a question of class warfare, Agate says: The bosses will do anything to deflate wages and prevent strikes. Joe and the others from earlier scenes—Edna, Sid, Florrie, and Doc Barnes—need to join the struggle. Suddenly, a man dashes up the center aisle to announce that Lefty has been found with a bullet in his head. The play ends with triumphant calls for a strike.

Critical Evaluation:

Waiting for Lefty is the best strike play to come out of the Great Depression. Basing his work on a 1934 taxi strike in New York, Clifford Odets wrote the play in three days for a contest of one-act plays that workers could stage at their own meeting places, and soon it was being performed everywhere. The action takes place within the semicircle defined by the members of the strike committee, and scene changes are defined largely by lighting. The lights on the committee are darkened when they become a chorus commenting on action in other times and places, and the lights come back up when the action returns to the committee's meeting. The audience of the play represents the union membership, and characters attending the meeting are seated among audience members. Those who attended early performances of the play streamed out of the theatre chanting "Strike! Strike!" as if they had been caught up in a strike vote themselves.

The play was produced by the Group Theatre, a left-wing theater company organized by Harold Clurman, Cheryl Crawford, and Lee Strasberg. The production was the closest thing to agitprop (agitation propaganda—a work intended to incite its audience to political action) to come out of the 1930's—a decade that produced a great deal of social fiction and drama. The ideas in the play—including class warfare and exploitation of workers by corrupt companies—are vaguely Marxist, but the force of the drama comes through its stories of human suffering. The conflicts within the play are linked: Fatt is like Fayette (hence their similar names), who is like the medical establishment in scene five. They are all arrayed against honest men and women struggling to build decent lives, such as the workers on stage trying to take over a corrupt union (a story that would be retold a few years later in the 1954 film *On the Waterfront*).

Characterization tends to be flat in this short play: Fatt and his henchman are stereotypes of corrupt union officials, while the strike committee's members are noble and self-sacrificing. These relatively simplistic characterizations work, however, in this modern morality play, whose aim is not to achieve aesthetic sophistication but to move the audience to action. Supporting the effectiveness of the play's message are its language and stagecraft. The dialogue reflects contemporary life, and characters talk as they would be expected to—Sid and Florrie even greet each other in a mock parody of contemporary Hollywood romances. Similarly, the lack of separation between stage and audience means that theatergoers are immediately caught up in the drama: audience members shout out, rush the stage, or flee it down the aisles.

Waiting for Lefty was a landmark in the social theater and radical literature of the 1930's, "the birth cry of the thirties," as Harold Clurman wrote in his memoir of the period, *The Fervent Years* (1945) that somehow caught and crystallized the emotional sympathies of audiences like no other play of the decade. Theatergoers found a dramatic, cathartic vehicle for their Depression-era frustrations. *Waiting for Lefty* was only the first of five plays Odets saw produced in 1935, and he had later successes in the theater, including *Golden Boy* (pr., pb. 1937) and *The Country Girl* (pr. 1950, pb. 1951), as well as a parallel career as a screenwriter in Hollywood.

Like much of the radical literature that came out of the 1930's, *Waiting for Lefty* was ignored or attacked in the Cold War culture that permeated the United States in the decades after the 1930's, but starting in the 1960's and 1970's the literature and legacy of the 1930's were rediscovered. Odets—like John Steinbeck, Lillian Hellman, and other leftwing writers of the 1930's—was reevaluated, and plays such as *Waiting for Lefty* were reexamined. In that process, it was discovered that the play is a stirring piece of theater that captured human emotions at the bottom of America's worst economic crisis.

Odets's revolutionary sympathies are as much for the individual as for any social class; the two most affecting scenes in the play focus on couples. As the political and cultural pendulum has swung back toward the middle following the Cold War, critics and historians have discovered other ideas in Odets to discuss, such his dynamic feeling for the American family, his dramatic sense of the socioeconomic forces stifling the American Dream during the Great Depression, and his compassion for the characters trapped by those forces. *Waiting for Lefty* is now seen as a vital work of theater that emerged in a unique moment in American history and as a play that speaks out for essential American values.

David Peck

Further Reading

Brenman-Gibson, Margaret. *Clifford Odets, American Playwright: The Years from 1906 to 1940.* New York: Atheneum, 1981. This comprehensive biography of the playwright includes detailed background to the Group Theater and the opening night of *Waiting for Lefty.*

Cooperman, Robert. *Clifford Odets: An Annotated Bibliography, 1935-1989.* Westport, Conn.: Meckler, 1990. Exhaustive overview; includes a bibliographic essay surveying Odets scholarship and annotated entries for both Odets's own works and works of scholarship about the playwright.

Demastes, William W. "Clifford Odets." *American Playwrights, 1880-1945: A Research and Production Sourcebook.* Westport, Conn.: Greenwood Press, 1994. Provides a great deal of useful information about the playwright and the play, *Waiting for Lefty.*

Herr, Christopher. *Clifford Odets and American Political Theatre.* Westport, Conn.: Praeger, 2003. Herr's biography is useful in describing the political content and context of Odets's plays, the background to Odets's work in the 1930's and 1940's, and his associations with both the Group Theatre and Hollywood.

Weales, Gerald. *Clifford Odets: Playwright.* New York: Pegasus, 1971. The standard study of Odets; includes a detailed analysis of *Waiting for Lefty* that outlines the impressive ways in which Odets built the brief scenes of this short play.

Waiting for the Barbarians

Author: J. M. Coetzee (1940-   )
First published: 1980
Type of work: Novel
Type of plot: Allegory
Time of plot: Nineteenth or twentieth century
Locale: A colonial settlement and the surrounding wilderness in an unnamed country

Principal characters:
THE MAGISTRATE, the narrator, the administrator of a frontier settlement
COLONEL JOLL, officer of the Third Bureau of the Civil Guard
GIRL, a prostitute
BARBARIAN GIRL
MANDEL, warrant officer under Colonel Joll's command

The Story:

The narrator, the Magistrate, administrates a town on the frontier of an unnamed empire. He looks forward to a quiet retirement and spends some of his free time excavating the site of an old town buried in the dunes, where he has found a cache of wooden slips covered with mysterious writing. Colonel Joll travels to the Magistrate's town from the imperial capital to investigate attacks by indigenous people whom the empire calls "barbarians." Joll interrogates and tortures two prisoners captured on the road, a boy and his grandfather. After killing the grandfather, he continues the torture until the boy confesses that his people, the barbarians, are preparing an attack against the empire. Troubled by these acts of torture and skeptical about the barbarian threat, the Magistrate gives Joll supplies, men, and horses to conduct a raid on the nomadic barbarians.

Joll returns with more prisoners, whom he interrogates

over five days. The Magistrate spends his nights with a prostitute, but he is troubled by dreams. Joll eventually returns to the capital, and the Magistrate releases and feeds the brutalized captives.

The Magistrate takes in a young barbarian woman who was maimed and partially blinded by the interrogators, then left behind by the surviving barbarians. He initiates a nightly ritual in which he rubs her body with oil until he falls asleep. The girl works as a kitchen maid in the Magistrate's house during the day and comes to his rooms every night. The Magistrate is fascinated by the scars left by the torturers.

The Magistrate begins to have a dream that recurs later, in which he approaches a group of children playing in the snow. He associates one of the children with the barbarian girl. In waking life, he finds the barbarian girl impenetrable—a blank surface—and wonders if that is what the torturers felt as well. Through the girl, he begins to discover his complicity with the torturers. Failing to find the desire to have intercourse with the barbarian girl, he resumes his visits to the prostitute. The Magistrate learns that the government plans to launch an offensive against the barbarians in the spring.

In early March, the Magistrate sets out with three men to return the girl to the barbarians. On the journey, they suffer from treacherous terrain and bad weather. They finally encounter a group of barbarian men. The Magistrate asks the girl to return to the town with him, but she refuses and leaves with the barbarians.

Upon his return, the Magistrate is met by an officer named Mandel who accuses him of treason and imprisons him in the building where the other prisoners were tortured. The Magistrate feels that he is becoming like an animal. Escaping, he eventually wanders out to the excavation site in the dunes, but since he will die if he remains outside the walls of the settlement, he finally returns to his cell on his own.

Joll returns with a group of barbarian prisoners who are tethered together with a wire that runs through holes in their hands and cheeks. As the townspeople crowd around the spectacle of torture, the Magistrate comes forward and yells, "No!" Soldiers strike him to the ground, breaking his arm.

The next day, Joll summons the Magistrate and asks him to read the slips of wood. The Magistrate pretends to read the slips, making up a story that indicts the Empire. Then, he says that the slips are a kind of allegory; they can be read in many ways. Joll mockingly calls him the "One Just Man" and turns him over to Mandel, who tortures and humiliates him over a period of weeks. Finally, Mandel forces the Magistrate to wear a woman's dress and hangs him from a tree, stopping just short of execution. One day, Mandel unexpectedly tells the Magistrate that he is a free man.

Rumors circulate about the second expeditionary force, which has failed to return. Many townspeople are leaving. Resentful soldiers are breaking into the empty houses and looting them. In time, two soldiers from the expedition are seen to approach the settlement, but they are corpses that have been braced upright in their saddles. At nightfall, the remaining soldiers flee the town with horses and as much loot as they can carry.

The Magistrate returns to his old apartment. The townspeople, still anticipating a barbarian attack, prepare as well as they can for winter. One night, Joll returns seeking horses and supplies. The Magistrate and Joll stare at each other through the glass. The men start to leave, but the Magistrate detains one man, who tells him that the army was not beaten by force. The barbarians simply led them out into the desert and then disappeared.

The Magistrate returns to his old hobbies. He attempts to write a history of the place but fails. He decides instead to wrap the slips of barbarian writing in oilcloth and rebury them at the excavation site.

Critical Evaluation:

J. M. Coetzee was born and raised in South Africa, a descendent of the Dutch colonists called Afrikaners. A linguist and literary scholar, he is one of the most highly honored contemporary writers. Among his many awards, Coetzee has twice received the prestigious Man Booker Prize. He received the Nobel Prize in Literature in 2003.

Waiting for the Barbarians, Coetzee's third novel, explores themes such as self-knowledge, the causes of inhumanity, and the difference between historical time and natural time. The Magistrate comes to understand his own role in the oppression of the native people as "the lie that Empire tells itself when times are easy." He also muses that the Empire, which is obsessed with its own preservation, forces people to live by historical time rather than by the seasonal rhythms of natural time. Children symbolize the ability to live in natural time. The novel's final image of the town's children building a snowman represents a return to life in harmony with nature.

The image of the children working on the snowman evokes another major theme: the body as a site of power. The Magistrate at first believes that Colonel Joll's torture techniques are intended to uncover the truth. After he himself is tortured, he realizes that the torturer's main goal is not to elicit a confession, truthful or otherwise, but simply to reduce the subject to a hurt body that can no longer resist through reasoning or language. While the body is vulnerable, however, it also resists in its own way, as the Magistrate learns when his sex drive and appetite reassert themselves as he recovers from his injuries.

Much of the critical discussion of *Waiting for the Barbarians* has focused on its historical and political context. Specifically, critics have examined how the nameless empire in *Waiting for the Barbarians* relates to the brutal policies of racial segregation in South Africa. These policies, collectively called apartheid, were maintained by the Afrikaner-led government from 1948 until 1994, when the democratically elected African National Congress took power. The novel, though, could be set in any country terrorized by an oppressive regime, or it could be viewed even more broadly as a critique of the effects of civilization. Coetzee has expressed ambivalence about the fact that he has been primarily identified as a South African writer.

Waiting for the Barbarians can also be viewed within the context of the development of literary allegory from the Middle Ages onward. In traditional allegory, such as the anonymous medieval play *Everyman* (late fifteenth century), characters do not possess psychological depth. They are types that stand for ideas such as Death, Knowledge, and Beauty. As a modern political allegory, *Waiting for the Barbarians* is more closely related to Franz Kafka's story "In the Penal Colony" (1914), in which names such as The Explorer and The Officer reflect the roles that the characters play within an unidentified colonial regime. The characters of Kafka are certainly more psychologically complex than are the characters in *Everyman*; however, because "In the Penal Colony" is written in the third person, character development is limited to what can be revealed through dialogue and action. The first-person narration of *Waiting for the Barbarians* creates a more intimate interior world. Full of self-doubt and shame, the Magistrate seeks to understand the most painful aspects of physical existence. He is at once an individual and an allegorical idea.

Coetzee's use of the continuous present tense, a stylistic technique characteristic of some postmodern literature, also affects the novel's perspective. Instead of recounting the events of the novel, the Magistrate narrates them as they occur. Dominic Head argues that the present tense forces readers to share the limited perspective of the Magistrate and thus implicates them in the Magistrate's guilt. On a more visceral level, the present tense intensifies readers' bodily identification with the Magistrate, particularly the horror of his torture.

The allegorical and psychological elements of the novel raise questions that might be difficult to broach in realist fiction. While the word "barbarians" is used by the colonists to refer to actual people, the idea that the word represents is elusive. By the end of the novel, it is clear that Joll and his men are the true "barbarians." At the same time, the barbarians are merely a mirage within the minds of the imperialists. Empire both preserves and destroys itself in the pursuit of this mirage.

Sheli Ayers

Further Reading

Attridge, Derek. *J. M. Coetzee and the Ethics of Reading: Literature in the Event.* Chicago: University of Chicago Press, 2005. Attridge examines the ethical significance of Coetzee's work. Good introduction to the themes prevalent in Coetzee's fiction.

Attwell, David. *J. M. Coetzee: South Africa and the Politics of Writing.* Berkeley: University of California Press, 1993. Explains how Coetzee's fiction is related to the political and cultural context of South Africa. Chapter 3 is about *Waiting for the Barbarians.*

Gallagher, Susan. *A Story of South Africa: J. M. Coetzee's Fiction in Context.* Cambridge, Mass.: Harvard University Press, 1991. Provides a detailed reading of Coetzee's novels in their historical context while defending the author's nonrealist style.

Head, Dominic. *The Cambridge Introduction to J. M. Coetzee.* New York: Cambridge University Press, 2009. Provides a chapter on Coetzee's life, a critical overview of each of his novels, and a chapter on his works' critical receptions.

_____. *J. M. Coetzee.* New York: Cambridge University Press, 1998. Chapter 4 offers a thematic analysis of *Waiting for the Barbarians*, including an interpretation of the Magistrate's recurrent dream.

Huggan, Graham, and Stephen Watson, eds. *Critical Perspectives on J. M. Coetzee.* New York: St. Martin's Press, 1996. Includes essays by various critics and a preface by Nadine Gordimer.

Post, Robert M. "Oppression in the Fiction of J. M. Coetzee." *Critique* 27, no. 2 (Winter, 1986): 67-77. Compares *Waiting for the Barbarians* to "The Narrative of Jacobus Coetzee," which appears in *Dusklands* (1974), in order to identify elements of *Waiting for the Barbarians* within the context of South African history.

Waiting to Exhale

Author: Terry McMillan (1951-   )
First published: 1992
Type of work: Novel
Type of plot: Social realism
Time of plot: 1990
Locale: Denver, Colorado; Phoenix, Arizona

Principal characters:
SAVANNAH JACKSON, a thirty-six-year-old woman who
    hopes to succeed in the television industry
BERNADINE HARRIS, a thirty-six-year-old divorced mother
JOHN, Bernadine's former husband
JOHN JUNIOR and ONIKA, their children
GLORIA MATTHEWS, a hair-salon owner
TARIK, Gloria's teenage son
ROBIN STOKES, a thirty-five-year-old underwriter
RUSSELL, Robin's married lover
MICHAEL, a colleague whom Robin dates
DR. KENNETH DAWKINS, Savannah's married lover
MARVIN KING, Gloria's neighbor and love interest
JAMES WHEELER, a civil rights attorney who befriends
    Bernadine

The Story:

Savannah Jackson's sister Sheila tells Savannah about a business owner named Lionel, and Lionel invites Savannah to attend a New Year's Eve party. As Savannah gets ready to ring in 1990, she reflects on her annoyance with Sheila and their mother, who have suggested that Savannah is miserable because she does not have a husband and does not live closer to her family. She realizes she does not need a man to validate her but admits that, as she broke up with Kenneth Dawkins four years ago, she wants to be in love again.

Even though she has already moved four times in fifteen years, Savannah is about to move again because she finds Denver, particularly the men, boring. The only person she knows in Phoenix is her college roommate, Bernadine Harris, but this does not prevent her from interviewing for a job there after visiting and learning about an opening in the publicity department at a local television station. Savannah is excited about securing the job since it will help her get closer to her dream of producing television programs. However, her new job will pay twelve thousand dollars per year less than her old job.

The prospect of a pay cut worries Savannah because it could interfere with her ability to take care of her mother. Her mother receives Social Security benefits and food stamps, but her monthly income is so low that she has difficulty taking care of her financial obligations in Pittsburgh, where she lives in a Section 8 apartment. At the New Year's Eve party, Savannah sees Lionel and is attracted to him, but she becomes annoyed and leaves when she discovers he has a date.

Bernadine Harris has been married for eleven years. She is stunned when her husband John tells her he wants a divorce because he intends to marry Kathleen, his twenty-four-year-old white bookkeeper. Bernadine knew that their relationship was disintegrating and even wanted to end it herself, but she is still unprepared for the anger and dismay she feels when John tells her he has filed for divorce. At first, she feels betrayed because John has chosen to leave her for a white woman, but then she realizes that the real betrayal stems from John's attempt to control her.

Bernadine looks back on her marriage and realizes that, at John's insistence, she delayed beginning a catering business so they could develop his computer software company. After John Junior and Onika were born, John insisted that Bernadine stay home with the children. A few years later, Bernadine grew tired of being a stay-at-home mother and took a job as a controller at a real estate agency. She planned to save enough money to fund a catering business, but she never followed through on this plan. Now an angry Bernadine takes Xanax to try to cope with the pain of a failed marriage.

Robin Stokes is just as unhappy as Bernadine but for different reasons. She depends on psychics, numerologists, and astrologers to determine the course of her personal life, but nothing has prepared her for the disappointing relationship she has with Russell. She tries to convince him to marry her, but he marries someone else instead. When Russell stops living with her for a while, she gets involved with a coworker named Michael, whom she describes as overweight and uninteresting.

Gloria Matthews has decided that relationships with men are not worth the trouble they cause and has settled into a life of single motherhood, running her hair salon, watching prime-time television, and overeating. Her morning begins with an argument with her seventeen-year-old son, Tarik. Tarik does not want to be home when his father David comes for a rare visit because he realizes David is coming only out of obligation. Gloria became pregnant with Tarik during her senior year of college. As a Catholic, Gloria felt that having an abortion would be unbearable, so she gave birth to Tarik and asked only that David visit him sporadically.

Bernadine, one of Gloria's clients, is the topic of morning gossip at Oasis Hair when Gloria enters the salon. Gloria is alarmed to learn that Bernadine—distraught after John left her—shopped at Circle K in her bathrobe while her children were home alone. Gloria tries to telephone Bernadine but cannot reach her. Later that evening, Tarik is not home when David visits. The teen calls Gloria to ask for permission to spend the night at a friend's house. Reluctantly, Gloria acquiesces. David prepares to leave, but Gloria attempts to convince him to spend the night with her. She stops when David announces he is gay.

Bernadine takes John Junior and Onika to her mother's house. Later, she throws John's clothes in the front yard and sets fire to his BMW. She spends the rest of the week in a depressed stupor that gives her the strength to go back to Sun City to pick up her children. On Saturday, Bernadine and the children watch as neighbors purchase John's antique car and other possessions for a dollar.

The next day, Gloria waits anxiously for Tarik to come home; when he does, she discovers that he has been sexually active. As she asks more questions about who he is sleeping with, she notices he prefers white and light-skinned girls. She tries to discuss the issue of color with him, but sharp pains in her chest make it difficult.

Savannah is disappointed because her friend cannot help her drive to Phoenix. She mentions the situation to Lionel, who offers to take the trip with her. While on the trip, Savannah has sex with Lionel but realizes he is not the kind of man with whom she would like to be involved.

John is concealing his income and other assets from Bernadine, so she hires a lawyer to uncover his actual worth. When her divorce is final, she celebrates at a hotel, where she meets and falls in love with James Wheeler, a civil rights attorney. James is married to a white woman who is dying of cancer.

Savannah's mother gives Savannah's telephone number to Kenneth, who is supposedly unhappily married. He visits Savannah, and they rekindle their relationship. Gloria develops a friendship with her new neighbor, Marvin. He helps her accept that Tarik is capable of making his own decisions, even decisions she questions, such as traveling around the world performing with the service organization Up With People. When Gloria is hospitalized and told she has a clogged artery, Marvin tells her doctor he is her husband and pledges to be supportive during her recovery.

Just when Bernadine feels that she is settling into her new life, the children tell her that John has remarried and Kathleen is pregnant. Similarly, Robin gets a jolt when things do not work out with Michael, and she meets Troy, a drug user who rarely goes to work. When Robin is not distracted by men, she is devoted to helping her mother take care of her father, who has Alzheimer's disease. Robin writes a successful proposal for a ten million dollar account, gets a raise, and is promised a significant bonus. She plans to use the money to pay off her debts and help her parents. She is hurt when her father dies, but relieved that her mother will not have to continue to put her own health in jeopardy. Bernadine's case is finally settled, and she is awarded nearly one million dollars. She decides to abandon her dream of starting a catering business. She will open a store instead and call it Bernadine's Sweet Tooth.

At the end of 1990, each woman has grown in some way. Savannah is finally given an opportunity to compete for a position as an assistant producer. She stands up to her mother and tells Kenneth she is no longer interested in him. Bernadine learns she is strong enough to fight for her own happiness. Gloria finds the courage to love someone other than Tarik. Robin realizes that Russell will not support her or the baby she is carrying, but she finds comfort in her friendships, and this assurance is all she needs.

Critical Evaluation:

Waiting to Exhale offers a realist depiction of African American women's romantic, platonic, and familial relationships. Written in both the first person and the third person, each of the twenty-eight chapters alternates between the perspectives of the four main characters. In the beginning of the novel, each of the women believes she will exhale once she has found the man who complements her, but by the novel's end the women realize they will exhale when they love themselves, their families, and their community.

Terry McMillan uses each character's life as an opportunity to highlight health and social issues prevalent in African American communities. For example, Robin's mother has had a double mastectomy, and Gloria suffers from hypertension. Tarik's father confides in Gloria about his sexuality, and one of her employees contracts AIDS, providing a forum for discussions about homophobia, bisexuality, and sexually transmitted diseases. Black Women on the Move, an organization committed to serving the community, is reminiscent of historic social clubs made up of African American women. The group raises money for scholarships and various service projects that will address social issues.

Waiting to Exhale was the first of McMillan's novels to achieve "cross-over" success beyond an African American readership. Professional women were intrigued by McMillan's depiction of female characters in their thirties who seem to be succeeding in every area of their lives except in relationships with men. McMillan has been criticized for her depiction of African American men, as most of the male characters are unemployed, irresponsible, and dishonest. The novel, however, includes honest and admirable men such as James, Michael, and Marvin.

Shortly after the novel's release, it was placed on the *New York Times* best-seller list, alongside the works of notable writers such as Toni Morrison and Alice Walker. Audrey Edwards noted that three weeks after its release the novel went into a tenth printing, and three weeks after that, paperback rights were auctioned for $2.64 million.

Waiting to Exhale is noteworthy because when it was published few books depicted self-empowered African American women who were not primarily victims of racism, classism, and sexism. There were also few contemporary books that posed questions about African American male and female relationships, the African American middle class, and the strength of African American female friendship.

McMillan has been credited with paving the way for similar novels to be published.

KaaVonia Hinton

Further Reading

Canty, Donnella. "McMillan Arrives." *English Journal* 85, no. 4 (April, 1996): 86-87. Praises McMillan's storytelling and voice.

Edwards, Audrey. "Waiting To Inhale." *Essence* 23, no. 6 (October, 1992): 77-80. Explains the success of the novel in terms of book sales and bids for paperback rights.

Ellerby, Janet Mason. "Deposing the Man of the House: Terry McMillan Rewrites the Family." *MELUS* 22, no. 2 (Summer, 1997): 105-117. Looks closely at McMillan's depiction of family in *Waiting to Exhale* and other novels.

Larson, Charles R. "The Comic Unlikelihood of Finding Mr. Right." *Chicago Tribune*, May 31, 1992, p. 6. Suggests that McMillan wrote *Waiting to Exhale* with hopes of selling the movie rights.

Mitchell, Carmen Rose. "Re-thinking Agency in *Waiting to Exhale*." In *Black Professional Women in Recent American Fiction*. Jefferson, N.C.: McFarland, 2004. Argues that McMillan provides a unique view of professional African American women in the workplace.

Reid, E. Shelley. "Beyond Morrison and Walker: Looking Good and Looking Forward in Contemporary Black Women's Stories." *African American Review* 34, no. 2 (Summer, 2000): 313-328. Suggests that McMillan and other African American women writers are writing books that are in the tradition of those written by celebrated writers such as Alice Walker and Toni Morrison.

Walden
Or, Life in the Woods

Author: Henry David Thoreau (1817-1862)
First published: 1854
Type of work: Essays

Early in the summer of 1845, Henry David Thoreau left his family home in the village of Concord, Massachusetts, to live for two years by himself in a rude house that he had constructed beside Walden Pond in a far corner of Concord township. While there, he wrote in his journal about many of the things he did and thought. Thoreau was not the owner of the land on which he settled, but he had received the owner's permission to build his house and to live there. His objective was really to live simply and think and write; in addition, he proved to himself that the necessities of food, clothing, shelter, and fuel could be obtained rather simply for a man who desired only what he needed.

As early as March, 1845, Thoreau went out to Walden Pond and cut the timber he needed for the framework of his house, doing all the labor himself. When that was done and the framing was in place, Thoreau bought a shanty from an Irish railroad worker. He then tore down the shanty and used the boards for the sidings of his house, even making use of many of the nails already in the boards. By July, the house was ready for his occupancy. Before the advent of cold weather the following fall, Thoreau built himself a fireplace and a chimney for cooking and heating purposes. He also lathed and plastered the interior of the one-room house so that it would be warm and comfortable during the cold New England winter.

Having done all the work himself, and having used native materials wherever possible, Thoreau had built the house for the absurdly low cost of twenty-eight dollars. In addition to providing himself with a place to live, he believed he had taught himself a great lesson in the art of living. He was also vastly pleased that he had provided himself with a place to live for less than a year's lodging had cost him as a student at Harvard College.

In order to get the money he needed to build the house, Thoreau had planted about two and one-half acres of beans, peas, potatoes, corn, and turnips, which he sold at harvest time. The land on which they were grown was lent by a neighbor who believed, along with everyone else, that the land was good for nothing. In addition to selling enough produce to pay his building expenses, Thoreau had enough yield left from his gardening to provide himself with food. He did not spend all of his time, however, working on the house or in the garden. One of his purposes in living at Walden Pond was to live so simply that he might have plenty of time to think, to write, and to observe nature, and so he spent only as much time in other labors as was needed. He had little respect for possessions and material things. He believed, for example, that most people are really possessed by their belongings, and that literary works such as the *Bhagavadgītā* (c. fifth century B.C.E.) are worth more than all the towers and temples of the Orient.

Thoreau was quite proud of how little money he needed to live comfortably while at Walden Pond. The first eight months he was there, he spent only slightly more than one dollar per month for food. In addition to some twenty-odd dollars he received for vegetables that he had raised, his income, within which he lived, was slightly more than thirteen dollars. His food consisted almost entirely of rye and Indian-meal bread, potatoes, rice, a little salt pork, molasses, and salt. His drink was water. Seldom did he eat large portions of meat, and he never hunted. His interest in the animals that lived in the woods and fields near Walden Pond was the interest of a naturalist. Although he spent some time fishing, he felt that the time he had was too valuable to spend in catching fish to feed himself. For the small amounts of cash he needed, Thoreau worked with his hands at many occupations, working only as long as was necessary to provide himself with the money required to fulfill his meager wants. He kept as much time as possible free for thinking and studying. He studied people and nature more than he studied using books, although he kept a few well-selected volumes around him at all times.

While at Walden Pond, summer and winter, Thoreau lived independent of time. He refused to acknowledge days of the week or month. When he wished to spend some time observing certain birds or animals, or even the progress of the weather, he felt free to do so. Almost the only thing that reminded him that other people were rushing chaotically to keep their schedules was the whistling of the Fitchburg Railway trains, which passed within a mile or so of his dwelling. Not that he disliked the railroad; he thought it, in fact, a marvel of human ingenuity, and he was fascinated by the cargoes that the trains carried from place to place. He was glad, however, that he was not chained to the commerce those cargoes represented. As much as he sometimes enjoyed the sounds of the trains, he enjoyed far more the sounds of the birds and animals, most species of which he could recognize, not only as a country dweller knows them but also as the naturalist knows them. The loons, the owls, the squirrels, the various kinds of fish in Walden Pond, the migratory birds—all of these were part of his conscious existence and environment.

People often dropped in to visit with Thoreau, who frankly confessed that he did not consider people very important. In *Walden* he fails, in fact, to tell who his most frequent visitors were. He preferred only one visitor—a thinking one—at a time. Whenever he had more visitors than could be accommodated by his small house and its three chairs, he took them into his larger drawing room, the pine wood that surrounded his home. From what he wrote about his treatment of all but a very few of the people who came to visit him, it is very probable that he was an unfriendly kind of host, one who, if he had nothing better to do, was willing to talk, but who usually had more to occupy him than simple conversation.

During the winter months, Thoreau continued to live comfortably at Walden Pond, though his activities changed. He spent more time at the pond itself, making a survey of its bottom, studying the ice conditions, and observing the animal life that centered on the pond, which had some open water throughout the year.

After two years of life at Walden, Thoreau left his house there. He felt no regret for having stayed, or for leaving; his attitude was that he had many lives to live and that he had finished with living at the pond. He had learned many lessons, had had time to think and study, and had proved what he had set out to prove twenty-six months before, that living can be extremely simple and yet highly fulfilling to the individual.

Critical Evaluation:

Few contemporaries of Henry David Thoreau would have predicted the enormous popularity his small volume *Walden* would eventually win. Author and work were virtually neglected during Thoreau's lifetime. Locally, he was considered the village eccentric; even his great friend and mentor, Ralph Waldo Emerson, was disappointed because his young disciple seemingly frittered away his talent instead of "engineering for all America." After Thoreau's death in 1862, his works attracted serious critical attention, but unfavorable reviews by James Russell Lowell and Robert Louis Stevenson severely damaged his reputation. Toward the end of the nineteenth century he began to win favorable attention again, mainly in Britain. During the Great Depression of the 1930's, when most people were forced to cut the frills from their lives, *Walden*, which admonishes readers to "Simplify, simplify, simplify!" became something of a fad. In the 1960's, with new awareness of environmental issues and emphasis on nonconformity, Thoreau was exalted as a prophet and *Walden* as the individualist's bible.

Walden can be approached in several different ways. It can be viewed as an excellent nature book. During the Romantic era, many writers, such as William Wordsworth, Percy Bysshe Shelley, Ralph Waldo Emerson, and Walt Whitman, paid tribute to nature. Thoreau, however, went beyond simply rhapsodizing natural wonders. He was a serious student of the natural world, one who would spend hours observing a woodchuck or tribes of battling ants, who meticulously sounded and mapped Walden Pond, who enjoyed a hilarious game of tag with a loon. Like Emerson, he saw nature as a master teacher. In his observations of nature, Thoreau was a scientist; in his descriptions, a poet; in his interpretations, a philosopher and psychologist. Certainly he was an ecologist in his insistence on humanity's place in (not power over) the natural universe and on the need for daily contact with the earth.

Walden may also be considered as a handbook for the simplification of life. As such, it becomes a commentary on the sophistication, "refinement," frequently distorted values,

and devotion to things of civilized society. Thoreau admits the necessities of food, shelter, clothing, and fuel, "for not till we have secured these are we prepared to entertain the true problems of life with freedom and a prospect of success." He then illustrates how people may strip these necessities to essentials for survival and health, ignoring the dictates of fashion or the yearning for luxury. "Most of the luxuries, and many of the so called comforts of life," he asserts, "are not only not indispensable, but positive hindrances to the elevation of mankind." With relentless logic he points out how making a living has come to take precedence over living itself; how people mortgage themselves to pay for more land and fancier clothing and food than they really require; how they refuse to walk to a neighboring city because it will take too long, but then must work longer than the walk would take in order to pay for a train ticket. He questions the dedication to "progress," noting that it is technological, not spiritual. "We are in great haste to construct a magnetic telegraph from Maine to Texas; but Maine and Texas, it may be, have nothing important to communicate."

Perhaps the most serious purpose of *Walden*, and its most powerful message, is to call people to freedom as individuals. One looks at nature in order to learn about oneself; one simplifies one's life in order to have time to develop the self fully; one must honor one's uniqueness if one is to know full self-realization. It is this emphasis on nonconformity that has so endeared Thoreau to the young over successive generations; many young readers have adopted as their call to life these words from the final chapter of *Walden*: "If a man does not keep pace with his companions, perhaps it is because he hears a different drummer. Let him step to the music which he hears, however measured or far away."

Thoreau's prose exhibits an ease, a clarity, and a concreteness that separate it from the more abstract, eloquent, and frequently involuted styles of his contemporaries. The ease and seeming spontaneity are deceptive. Thoreau revised the book meticulously during the five years it took to find a publisher; five complete drafts demonstrate how consciously he organized not only the general outline but also every chapter and paragraph. For an overall pattern, he condensed the two years of his actual Walden experience into one fictional year, beginning and concluding with spring—the time of rebirth.

The pace and tone of *Walden* are also carefully controlled. Thoreau's sentences and paragraphs flow smoothly. The reader is frequently surprised to discover that sentences occasionally run to more than half a page, paragraphs to a page or more; the syntax is so skillfully handled that one never feels tangled in verbiage. The tone varies from matter-of-fact to poetic to inspirational and is spiced with humor—usually some well-placed satire—at all levels. Even the most abstract topics are handled in concrete terms; Thoreau's ready use of images and figurative language prepares one for twentieth century Imagist poetry.

Taken as a whole, *Walden* is a first-rate example of organic writing, with organization, style, and content fused to form a work that, more than 150 years after its publication, is as readable as and perhaps even more timely than when it was written. In *Walden*, Thoreau reaches across the years to continue to "brag as lustily as Chanticleer . . . to wake my neighbors up."

"Critical Evaluation" by Sally Buckner

Further Reading

Bloom, Harold, ed. *Henry David Thoreau's "Walden."* New York: Chelsea House, 1987. Collection offers a representative selection of some of the best criticism of *Walden* published since Cavell's *The Senses of "Walden"* (cited below). Although primarily a celebration of Thoreau, includes some essays that question his solipsism and his debt to Emerson.

Cafaro, Philip. *Thoreau's Living Ethics: "Walden" and the Pursuit of Virtue.* Athens: University of Georgia Press, 2004. Examines Thoreau's ethical philosophy, focusing on *Walden* but also considering his other works. Explains how Thoreau's ideas are part of a tradition of ethical thinking that dates from the ancients to the present day.

Cavell, Stanley. *The Senses of "Walden."* New York: Viking Press, 1972. Classic work represents a prelude to later readings of Thoreau's masterpiece. Argues that readers can uncover *Walden*'s mysteries by giving the fullest attention to all that Thoreau says in the work.

Myerson, Joel, ed. *The Cambridge Companion to Henry David Thoreau.* New York: Cambridge University Press, 1995. Collection of essays includes discussions of Thoreau's reputation, Thoreau and Concord, Thoreau and Emerson, and Thoreau and reform. An essay by Richard J. Schneider provides an analysis of *Walden*.

_____. *Critical Essays on Henry David Thoreau's "Walden."* Boston: G. K. Hall, 1988. Collection contains a complete record of critical reaction to *Walden* beginning with early reviews by Horace Greeley, George Eliot, and several anonymous reviewers of Thoreau's day. Includes reprints of more than a dozen twentieth century essays examining such topics as the structure of *Walden* and its language.

Petrulionis, Sandra Herbert, and Laura Dassow Walls, eds. *More Day to Dawn: Thoreau's "Walden" for the Twenty-first Century.* Amherst: University of Massachusetts Press, 2007. Collection of essays focuses on Thoreau's continued relevance, including discussions of modes of representation in *Walden*, *Walden* and the Georgic mode, and Thoreau's materialism and idealism.

Ruland, Richard, ed. *Twentieth Century Interpretations of "Walden": A Collection of Critical Essays.* Englewood Cliffs, N.J.: Prentice-Hall, 1968. Excellent resource presents nine short essays and twelve shorter viewpoint articles that offer a coherent reading of Thoreau's book. Includes a brief chronology of Thoreau's life.

Shanley, J. Lyndon. *The Making of "Walden."* Chicago: University of Chicago Press, 1957. Detailed study examines how Thoreau wrote the first version of *Walden* while living at Walden Pond and how he rewrote it between 1848 and 1854. Contains the text of the first edition of *Walden*.

Thoreau, Henry David. *Walden: A Fully Annotated Edition.* Edited by Jeffrey S. Cramer. New Haven, Conn.: Yale University Press, 2004. Authoritative version of the text provides extensive annotation as an aid to twenty-first century readers. Includes Thoreau's notes and corrections to the text.

Walden Two

Author: B. F. Skinner (1904-1990)
First published: 1948
Type of work: Novel
Type of plot: Utopian
Time of plot: 1940's
Locale: Walden Two farm, thirty miles from the largest
city in an unnamed midwestern state

Principal characters:
T. E. FRAZIER, founder, leader, and chief behaviorist of the
Walden Two experimental community
PROFESSOR BURRIS, psychologist
PROFESSOR CASTLE, philosopher
ROGERS, recently demobilized soldier
STEVE JAMNIK, his friend
BARBARA MACKLIN, Rogers's girlfriend
MARY GROVE, Jamnik's girlfriend
MRS. NASH, Walden Two nurse

The Story:

Professor Burris, a senior psychologist, attended graduate school with a brilliant maverick scholar named T. E. Frazier. Two recently discharged soldiers approach Burris, fascinated by rumors of an experimental community run by Frazier. The men ask Burris to help them reach the community.

Soon, a party of six embarks on a short bus ride to the Walden Two farm, which is located about a hundred miles from the university in a neighboring midwestern state. Joining Burris, the two young men, and their two girlfriends is Professor Castle from the philosophy department. They reach the farm and begin to learn about it.

Over the course of a few days, the two academics tour the farm; try their hand at physical labor; meet and talk to some of the Waldenites; absorb the rudiments of the social, political, and cultural life in the compound; and debate the pros and cons of social engineering with Frazier. In the end, both professors and one of the couples return home, while the other soldier and his girl settle at the farm. Back at the university, Burris feels increasingly restless and dissatisfied with the American way of life. Eventually, he submits a letter of resignation and, liberated, rejoins the Walden Two community. There, encouraged by Frazier, he writes an account of his earlier visit that, on the last pages, is revealed to have been the text of the novel.

Critical Evaluation:

B. F. Skinner was the twentieth century's most influential advocate—not to say ideologue—of behavioral engineering. When in 1971 he made the cover of *Time* magazine, applauded as the greatest living American psychologist, it was a culmination of his quest to bring his controversial message into the American sociocultural mainstream.

In his student years, Skinner was drawn to the fiction and nonfiction of the science-fiction legend and unapologetic eugenicist H. G. Wells. As a young man, before he ever penned his first psychology paper, Skinner determined he would be a writer, buoyed by praise from poet Robert Frost. However, the rejection letters he received from the publishing houses to which he submitted the typescript of *Walden Two* (the only book of his not written in longhand) unanimously censured the novel's static plot, one-dimensional characters, and ham-fisted style. Indeed, the bulk of the story consists of a series of lectures and harangues given by Frazier to the visiting group, punctuated only by the querulous Castle. This dogged adversary of the novel's behaviorist character was modeled on Alburey Castell, a philosopher who was engaged in a running verbal feud with Skinner about the merits of behavioral engineering.

Skinner himself conceded that the closest thing to a protagonist in his novel, T. E. Frazier, was an ill-concealed incarnation of his own views. To be precise, the author partitioned himself narratively in the manner of Thomas Moore in *De Optimo Reipublicae Statu, deque Nova Insula Utopia* (1516; *Utopia*, 1551). In this classic of the genre, Moore cast himself as a sympathetic but uninformed listener, while voicing many of his actual opinions through Hythloday, the bearer of news from nowhere. Skinner, whose first name was Burrhus, named his narrator Burris, readily conceding in subsequent interviews and publications that Burris and Frazier were different parts of himself.

Given that *Walden Two* is essentially an expression of Skinner's ideas on how to apply behavioral conditioning to human affairs, the plot is thin and derivative. It follows the conventions of utopian fiction established in such seminal novels as *Utopia*, Edward Bellamy's *Looking Backward:*

2000-1887 (1888), and William Morris's *News From Nowhere* (1890). *Walden Two* would go on to become the most influential and the most vilified utopian work of the century.

Few could have guessed from its humble beginnings that the novel would achieve such fame and infamy. For more than a decade, it sold only a few hundred copies per year. The advent of the radical 1960's, however, plucked it out of obscurity—so much so that by the early 1970's the book's sales exceeded 100,000 copies annually. Skinner's utopia became a literary byword, as it went on to sell more than 2.5 million copies in all the major and most minor languages of the world and to receive more condemnations than any other work of utopian fiction.

Many readers, in fact, took *Walden Two* to be a satire of utopian fiction, if not an outright dystopia. The editors of the 1952 anthology *The Quest for Utopia* even denied it an entry, claiming that it violated the utopian spirit. By then, reviewers had attacked Skinner's recipe for a good life. The *Journal of Philosophy* led the assault, flaying Skinner's model as horrible and predicting that it would produce nothing but contented nonpolitical robots. The *Philosophical Review* put Skinner on par with the Nazis, declaring that his views on American democracy and capitalism were not very different from the attacks of the National Socialists.

If Skinner's new republic, governed by benevolent behaviorist-kings, did nothing to impress philosophers, cultural critics were even less amused. The normally restrained *New York Review of Books* called it sadistic and fascistic. *Fortune* saw in the novel a vicious miniature of Aldous Huxley's dystopian *Brave New World* (1932). More than two decades later, Ayn Rand's attack on Skinner's *Beyond Freedom and Dignity* (1971)—commonly regarded as a nonfiction version of *Walden Two*—was, if anything, even more hysterical. Her reference to a Frankensteinian monster typified the rhetoric of the countless political, scientific, and cultural heavyweights who rallied against behaviorism and Skinner.

Walden Two is, in its structure, quite typical of utopian fiction: A visitor to an experimental community learns its ways accompanied by a local guide. Its form is also conventional, weaving the classical unities of time, place, and action out of discrete, dialogue-driven scenes. The novel embraces many traditional utopian ends such as egalitarianism, classlessness, and social welfare. It emphasizes the cultivation of human potential in a manner indebted to nineteenth century American Transcendentalism and to the entire nineteenth century European tradition of bildungsroman (although, interestingly, Skinner depicts the development, not of an individual, but of a community).

The innovation of *Walden Two* is to be found in the fact that it is a utopia of means—an embodiment of an ongoing scientific research program. As such, in defiance of the convention of placing utopias in distant, mythical, or idealized locations, Skinner placed his fictive community squarely in mid-twentieth-century United States and in the American Midwest. No matter that, in *Beyond Freedom and Dignity*, Skinner debunked what most citizens of the United States took to be the essence of being an American: His utopia, in the heart of America's heartland, is a very American better place. The Walden Two community is an American small town writ large, reprising the myth of a country born in the countryside, where regular folks practice liberty, equality, and the pursuit of happiness. Framed by Thomas Jefferson at the cradle of the new republic, this Virginian landowner's vision of agrarian simplicity underwrites *Walden Two*, augmented by Henry David Thoreau's distrust of large-scale social institutions.

Like the Amish or the Hutterite communes, Skinner's community prospers in happy mediocrity, practicing the "have not, want not" ethic of sustainability and self-sufficiency. Skinner almost certainly had the Hutterites in mind when composing *Walden Two* (his biographer documents his youthful readings about the Shakers and the Mormons and a visit to Oneida, the site of one of the more successful American utopian communities). The community's strong work ethic, their collective spirit whereby members see themselves as serving the whole social organism, their tradition of strong leadership (exemplified by the sect's mid-seventeenth century founder, Andreas Ehrenpreis), their self-sufficiency, and their high birthrate—all are mirrored in Skinner's fiction, down to the injunction that they must divide down the middle and settle new lands when their numbers swell past a certain point.

Significantly, the story of *Walden Two* does not end in 1948 but continues into the twenty-first century. Like many other revolutionary works of fiction, *Walden Two* transcended the confines of literary fiction and inspired a wave of social transformations. Beginning in the late 1960's, no less than three dozen experimental communities sprang into existence in order to put Skinner's social-engineering blueprint to the test. Although most of them quickly succumbed to a range of behavioral problems that were supposed to have been solved by Skinner's techniques, two of these self-styled Walden Two-type communities, the Twin Oaks in Virginia and Los Horcones in Mexico, remain in operation.

Originally, Skinner wanted to call his utopia *The Sun Is but a Morning Star*, an allusion to the concluding line of Thoreau's *Walden: Or, Life in the Woods* (1854). *Walden* in many ways parallels Skinner's own exploration of the relation between literature and science, or fiction and life. The parallels between these two literary and philosophical classics go far beyond their titles. Like *Walden*, aside from the spell it cast on the millions who read it and the thousands who lived by it, the conceptual repercussions of *Walden Two* remain as urgent today as ever. Indeed, to the extent that utopias reflect the times in which they are written and the times in which they are read, they are never obsolete.

Peter Swirski

Further Reading

Bjork, Daniel W. *B. F. Skinner: A Life*. New York: HarperCollins, 1993. An excellent and sympathetic biography that focuses in equal proportions on Skinner the man, Skinner the scientist, and Skinner the writer.

Kuhlmann, Hilke. *Living Walden Two: B. F. Skinner's Behaviorist Utopia and Experimental Communes*. Champaign: University of Illinois Press, 2005. An outstanding study of the social repercussions of the experimental communes inspired by the novel; begins with a useful discussion of *Walden Two*.

Kumar, Krishan. "The Utopia of 'Behavioral Engineering': B. F. Skinner and *Walden Two*." In *Utopia and Anti-Utopia in Modern Times*. Malden, Mass.: Blackwell, 1991. A lengthy article that traces a number of the traditional utopian themes in Skinner's book.

Skinner, B. F. "Walden Two Revisited." Preface to *Walden Two*, by Skinner. Indianapolis, Ind.: Hackett, 2005. The author's preface to his novel, written twenty-eight years after the original publication. Skinner comments on the necessity of social engineering in view of the contemporary environmental and social problems besetting American society.

Thoreau, Henry David, and Jeffrey S. Kramer. *Walden: A Fully Annotated Edition*. New Haven, Conn.: Yale University Press, 2004. A classic autobiographical account of Thoreau's two-year sojourn in nature; a direct literary and in some ways behavioral inspiration for Skinner's experimental farm.

Wolfe, Peter. "*Walden Two* Twenty-five Years Later: A Retrospective Look." *Studies in the Literary Imagination* 6, no. 2 (1973): 11-26. A critical, though at times overly laudatory, reading of stylistic and structural elements in the novel.

A Walk on the Wild Side

Author: Nelson Algren (1909-1981)
First published: 1956
Type of work: Novel
Type of plot: Picaresque
Time of plot: 1930's
Locale: Texas; New Orleans, Louisiana

Principal characters:
DOVE LINKHORN, a hobo, con artist, and sexual athlete
TERASINA VIDAVARRI, owner of the café in Arroyo, Texas, and Dove's lover
KITTY TWIST, Dove's hobo companion and later a prostitute in the whorehouse in New Orleans where he works
OLIVER FINNERTY, a New Orleans whorehouse operator
ACHILLES SCHMIDT, a legless strongman
HALLIE BREEDLOVE, a classy prostitute who is in love with him

The Story:

Fitz Linkhorn barely manages to make a living pumping out cesspools, but his consuming vocation is preaching from the courthouse steps in Arroyo, a small town in the Rio Grande Valley of Texas. He denounces all sins except drinking, because he is drunk as often as possible. Fitz has two sons: Byron, who is weak and sickly, and Dove. Dove has had no education because his father does not want to send him to a school with a Catholic principal. Instead, Dove is supposed to see movies with Byron to learn about life, but he never gets to go because his brother does not have the price of a ticket. Dove gets his education from the hoboes who hang around the Santa Fe tracks, telling one another what towns, lawmen, jails, and railroad bulls to avoid.

Dove begins hanging around the La Fe en Dios chili parlor in the ruins of the Hotel Crockett on the other side of town. The hotel is the place where Fitz had met the mother of his sons. The hotel is closed, but the seldom-visited café is not; it is run by Terasina Vidavarri, a wary woman who had been raped by a soldier. She continues Dove's education by teaching him how to read from two books: a children's story-book and a book about how to write business letters. Dove and Terasina eventually become lovers, and at one point Dove takes Terasina by force.

Byron steals from the café, and Terasina mistakenly blames Dove for the crime. She is so angered that she throws him out, and Dove leaves Arroyo on a freight train. He takes up with a girl named Kitty Twist, a runaway from a children's home, and saves her life when she is about to fall under the wheels of a train. When the two attempt a burglary in Houston, Kitty is caught. Dove gets away on a freight train to New Orleans, and one of the first things he sees after he arrives there is a man cutting the heads off turtles that are to be made into turtle soup. The man throws the turtle bodies into a pile, and, even with the heads cut off, the bodies try to climb to the top of the pile. One is able to reach the top of the pile before it slides back to the bottom.

In the port city, with its many different influences and cultures, Dove experiences his most interesting adventures. He works as a painter on a steamship (but does not paint anything), fools a prostitute who tries to rob him, sells coffeepots and "beauty certificates" (which supposedly entitle the bearer to a treatment at a beauty shop) while seducing the women to whom he is selling, and, in his most memorable escapade, works in a condom factory. The condoms, which are called O-Daddies and bear interesting names and colors, are made in a house by a mom-and-pop firm run by Velma and Rhino Gross.

Dove's lengthiest stay is with the people who inhabit the twin worlds of Oliver Finnerty's brothel and Doc Dockery's speakeasy. In the brothel he finds—in addition to his old friend Kitty Twist, who has become a prostitute—Hallie Breedlove, a onetime schoolteacher who is the star of Finnerty's string of girls. Hallie is in love with Achilles Schmidt, a former circus strongman whose legs have been cut off by a train. Schmidt's upper body is still powerful, and every day he surges into Dockery's bar with the air of one who could beat up anyone there—and he could. Dove's main job at Finnerty's is to couple with the girls in the place, who pretend to be virgins being deflowered, while customers watch through peepholes.

Hallie, who still retains vestiges of her former life as a teacher, is interested in Dove's mind and helps him to continue to learn to read. Dove's closeness to Hallie angers Schmidt, however, and Schmidt assaults Dove in Dockery's bar. He beats Dove so badly that Dove is blinded, and then a gang of people descend on Schmidt and kill him. Dove manages to make his way back to Texas and Terasina's cafe.

Critical Evaluation:

Nelson Algren, all of whose works are about characters from the lower levels of life—tramps, con artists, prostitutes, petty criminals, and drug addicts—is often considered to be a naturalistic novelist in terms of both philosophy and style. Literary naturalism is a viewpoint that emphasizes that human life is materialistic (based on the struggle for the acquisition of money, prestige, and property and without a spiritual component). Naturalistic novelists concentrate on earthy, even sordid subjects; their style involves the presentation of many physical details. *A Walk on the Wild Side* is so full of physical details that it appears to have no plot at all. The reader is deep into the novel before he or she realizes that there is no specific conflict, and no challenges to be met other than the conflict and challenge of life itself. Although it appears at first glance that Algren's works fit neatly into the naturalistic pattern, in actuality Algren uses the naturalistic elements of his works to make points about the spiritual nature of his characters. Algren signals to the reader that he is not concerned exclusively with material existence. One way in which he does so is through his use of a lyrical, almost rhapsodic, style.

The scene in which the beheaded turtle crawls to the top of the pile of other decapitated creatures is central to an understanding of Algren's outlook. The turtle is slow and odd-looking, hardly a likely animal to be chosen as a symbol of indomitability, as an eagle or a lion might be. Through his use of the turtle, Algren reminds the reader that even the lowly people he writes about have dreams and higher yearnings. A horrible death is the turtle's fate, but even after death it keeps going, straining to reach the top of the pile, like Schmidt after his mutilation and Dove after his blinding. The dead turtle finally falls back to the bottom of the pile, however; in this way Algren reminds the reader that the ultimate fate is defeat—at least in this life and in this world.

Algren presents many other clues in *A Walk on the Wild Side* that he is concerned with the spirit and not simply the body. Dove Linkhorn's father, Fitz, insists on presenting his own religious view of life regardless of who is listening and regardless of the consequences. The name of his son, Dove, is associated with peace, and Dove never loses his self-possession and control even when he does not understand the crazy world through which he wanders. The café that Terasina operates is called the La Fe en Dios (faith in God), and the characters move about on a railroad called the Santa Fe (holy faith). Finnerty's brothel and Dockery's bar are located on Perdido (lost) Street.

Algren believes that the place to look for spiritual richness is among the downtrodden and the poor. A life in which one is obliged to do without leads one, sometimes without one's knowledge, to a life within, a life of the spirit. It is a spiritual verity that the less one has, the better-off one is spiritually, because material possessions tend to tie one down to a life centered on the pointless acquisition of more possessions. Algren implies that if one is to keep one's soul, one must walk through the wild side of human behavior. Algren also draws on another ancient spiritual lesson: From pain and suffering comes the growth of the spirit.

As well as exploring spiritual development, Algren draws heavily on two literary traditions, those of the picaresque and the innocent. The picaresque story, which originated in Spain in the sixteenth century, tells the story of a rogue (*pícaro*) who moves from place to place, living by his wits, conning people, and staying one step ahead of the law. Dove is a picaro, and the relative formlessness of the novel is an inheritance from the picaresque tradition. At the same time, he is an innocent, a person whose naïveté and wonder about life serve as foils to the corruption and venality of those around him. Even after he is beaten blind by Achilles Schmidt (himself an icon of spiritual triumph), Dove returns, still himself and still ultimately unbroken, to Terasina Vidavarri, who operates the café and whose name means "true life."

A Walk on the Wild Side differs from most of Algren's other work, which also features low characters caught in desperate circumstances, because in those other works the characters are finally defeated and even destroyed by a world in which everything works against them. In *A Walk on the Wild Side*, however, although the usual collection of grotesque characters, wild settings, and violent actions appears, everyone, good and bad, keeps bouncing back. Dove, for example, seems to take his beating from Schmidt and his blindness as simply another condition with which he must live. He does not descend into despair or self-pity. Algren is too familiar with life's wild side, however, to give his novel a happy ending. At the end of the novel, Dove stands in front of Terasina's café, but he has not gone inside, and it is not clear whether Terasina will accept him. The novel's conclusion is not happy, but it is hopeful.

Jim Baird

Further Reading

Algren, Nelson. *Conversations with Nelson Algren.* Interviews by H. E. F. Donohue. New York: Hill & Wang, 1964. In a series of interviews, Algren discusses his life and his writings, including *A Walk on the Wild Side.*

Bluestone, George. "Nelson Algren." *Western Review* 22 (Autumn, 1957): 27-44. Bluestone was the first to identify Algren as not only a naturalistic writer but also one with broader themes than tragic realism. Includes some discussion of *A Walk on the Wild Side.*

Cox, Martha Heasley, and Wayne Chatterton. *Nelson Algren.* Boston: Twayne, 1975. Provides discussion of all of Algren's work up to 1975, with a chapter on *A Walk on the Wild Side.* Includes biographical information and bibliographies.

Giles, James R. *Confronting the Horror: The Novels of Nelson Algren.* Kent, Ohio: Kent State University Press, 1989. Discusses *A Walk on the Wild Side* as an example of absurdist comedy and notes the influence on Algren of the works of Louis-Ferdinand Céline.

Horvath, Brooke. *Understanding Nelson Algren.* Columbia: University of South Carolina Press, 2005. Examination of Algren's work features a brief overview of his life and detailed analysis of *A Walk on the Wild Side* and other writings. Describes Algren's literary style and the social and political concerns expressed in his work.

Lipton, Lawrence. "A Voyeur's View of the Wild Side: Nelson Algren and His Reviewers." In *The Man with the Golden Arm,* by Nelson Algren. 50th anniversary critical ed. Edited by William J. Savage, Jr., and Daniel Simon. New York: Seven Stories Press, 1999. Lipton's article, originally published in 1957 in the *Chicago Review,* evaluates the early critical commentary on *A Walk on the Wild Side* and offers further critical observations.

Ward, Robert, ed. *Nelson Algren: A Collection of Critical Essays.* Madison, N.J.: Fairleigh Dickinson University Press, 2007. Collection presents analyses of some of Algren's novels as well as studies of Algren as an American outsider, the paperback revolution's effect on Algren's reputation, and Algren's relationship to post-World War II Chicago.

Wallenstein

Author: Friedrich Schiller (1759-1805)
First produced: Wallensteins Lager, 1798 (*The Camp of
Wallenstein*, 1846); *Die Piccolomini*, 1799 (*The
Piccolominis*, 1800); *Wallensteins Tod*, 1799 (*The
Death of Wallenstein*, 1800); first published, 1800
Type of work: Drama
Type of plot: Historical
Time of plot: Thirty Years' War (1618-1648)
Locale: Germany

Principal characters:
WALLENSTEIN, the duke of Friedland, generalissimo of the
imperial forces in the Thirty Years' War
OCTAVIO PICCOLOMINI, a lieutenant general
MAX PICCOLOMINI, the general's son, a colonel
COUNT TERZKY, Wallenstein's brother-in-law
BUTLER, an Irish soldier of fortune
THEKLA, Wallenstein's daughter

The Story:

Wallenstein, the duke of Friedland, was once dismissed from the service of Emperor Ferdinand, but during the Thirty Years' War, in which the countries of central Europe are battling to prevent their annihilation by the forces of Gustavus Adolphus of Sweden, the emperor recalls Wallenstein and gives him extraordinary powers to create an army to drive the Swedes out of central Europe. Wallenstein raises such a powerful army, but both its leaders and the rank-and-file soldiers feel that they owe allegiance to their commander rather than to the emperor.

Wallenstein's army achieves many victories, and the situation in central Europe becomes less tense. The threat to his dominions having decreased, the emperor wishes to curtail Wallenstein's power, lest the conquering hero attempt to dictate to the crown. Wallenstein in turn becomes suspicious of the emperor and his government, and he wavers on the verge of declaring himself for the Swedes.

The emperor makes arrangements to have Wallenstein removed from his post, and as a first step he sends a war commissioner, Von Questenberg, to Wallenstein's camp. The commissioner finds the soldiers so sensitive to their leader's wishes that they are ready to follow him should he turn traitor. The commissioner shares his fears with Lieutenant General Octavio Piccolomini and gives him the emperor's secret commission to take over the army and to arrest Wallenstein. Wallenstein, who believes that General Piccolomini is his trusted friend and brother officer, does not suspect that Piccolomini is more loyal to his monarch than to Wallenstein.

General Piccolomini wishes to have the help of his son, Colonel Max Piccolomini, in his plans, but the son, who has grown up under Wallenstein's tutelage, refuses to believe that Wallenstein could ever be anything but virtuous. Moreover, Max is in love with Wallenstein's daughter, Thekla, and has high hopes that the great general-duke will permit them to marry. Young Piccolomini does not know that Wallenstein, fired with ambition and filled with suspicion of the emperor, is actually plotting to go over to the Swedes with his army in return for being made king of Hungary. Wallenstein regards his daughter as a future queen, not as the wife of a colonel.

Worried by the arrival of Von Questenberg, Wallenstein gives one of his trusted henchmen the task of seeing to it that all his great leaders sign an oath to follow him wherever he might lead, even if he leads them away from the emperor. The henchman plans a great banquet to accomplish the deed. Before the banquet, he shows the officers a document that he refuses to let them sign. After the banquet, when the men are drunk, he substitutes another document containing a pledge of loyalty to Wallenstein. All the leaders sign except Max Piccolomini, who has remained sober and realizes that he cannot take a vow against the emperor without forfeiting his honor.

Wallenstein believes that the leaders will be compelled to follow him after they sign the document, a paper that will compromise them in the emperor's eyes regardless of how the signatures were obtained. General Piccolomini has signed the document, wishing to let Wallenstein proceed far enough with his plan to expose his traitorous intent. The general knows it will be easier to turn the army away from Wallenstein after it becomes clear that he is a traitor.

A crisis arises when Wallenstein receives orders to send a large part of his army to a distant point under the command of another leader. The same messenger also brings news that an army from Spain, not under Wallenstein's command, is due to arrive in a matter of days. Seeing that his power is threatened, Wallenstein refuses to break up his army and begins to push forward his negotiations with the Swedes in the hope that he can complete his arrangements within a few hours. While Wallenstein prepares to move his army, General Piccolomini sets his own plan in motion. First he goes to all the officers and convinces them, with the exception of the colonels of two regiments, one of them his own son, that Wallenstein is ambitious and a traitor. The commanders agree to move their troops and, under General Piccolomini, remain loyal to the emperor.

The Swedes, through their envoy, are making inordinate demands on Wallenstein. Among other things, they wish to have control of Prague and the fortress at Egra, to ensure that Wallenstein will not turn traitor against them. At first Wallenstein refuses to turn over the fortifications, but at last he agrees. Shortly afterward, his brother-in-law, Count Terzky, informs him that various regiments have marched away. Wallenstein realizes what has happened when the count tells him about General Piccolomini's negotiations with Von Questenberg and the emperor's commission authorizing the general to relieve Wallenstein of his command.

Although his grand design is collapsing, Wallenstein resolves to go ahead with his plan to join the Swedes. He is still busy with his preparations when his daughter comes to him with Colonel Max Piccolomini, who is still loyal to his commander. The couple ask to be allowed to marry, but Wallenstein refuses. During the interview, Max Piccolomini realizes the extent of Wallenstein's ambitions for himself and his daughter and the fact that the duke intends to turn traitor. The young officer thereupon decides to join his father in the plan to arrest Wallenstein. When Wallenstein tries to keep Max Piccolomini prisoner, the colonel's regiment rescues him from Wallenstein's soldiers.

Wallenstein flees with his few remaining troops and his family to Egra, where he had planned to meet the Swedish forces. With him is Colonel Butler, an Irish soldier of fortune. Because Wallenstein had dissuaded the emperor from making Butler a count, the Irish adventurer takes revenge by contriving Wallenstein's murder at Egra. Word comes to Egra, shortly before Wallenstein's assassination, that Max Piccolomini has met his death in a wild attack on the Swedish forces. Shocked by these events, Thekla flees from Egra.

When General Piccolomini arrives at Egra, he is horrified to learn that Wallenstein had been murdered just moments previously. Butler, confused by this turn of events, flees to the emperor to explain his actions. After his departure, a messenger arrives at Egra to inform General Piccolomini that the emperor has elevated him to the rank of prince.

Critical Evaluation:

On February 25, 1634, Albrecht Wallenstein, the duke of Friedland, was murdered in Eger (also known as Egra). He had had an astonishing career, rising to power first as the sav-

ior of the Holy Roman Emperor. The emperor had, after initial success in putting down a Protestant uprising, found himself facing an army led by King Christian IV of Denmark and financed by England and the Netherlands. This was the second stage in the Thirty Years' War, which would sap the strength of the empire in a series of confrontations between 1618 and 1648. Wallenstein offered the emperor nothing less than an army—twenty thousand men, raised at his own expense—and his success was stupendous. He pursued the enemy across Europe and finally defeated Christian IV in his own kingdom.

The forces of Wallenstein's jealous rivals, however, succeeded in persuading the emperor, who was in fact alarmed by the extent of Wallenstein's success and power, to dismiss the duke. Wallenstein retired quietly, knowing that he would again be needed. In 1630, Sweden entered the war and decisively defeated the imperial forces. At that point Wallenstein was recalled to service. He accepted, but on his own terms, and he led an army of about forty thousand men with virtual autonomy. After initial victories, his thoughts turned to a negotiated peace, and again the emperor began to entertain fears. Friedrich Schiller's great trilogy is the record of the downfall of a man who created history and seemed above petty intrigue, a man who could have been the harbinger of a new era of peace.

Schiller knew well that the historical Wallenstein was not a suitable figure for tragedy. As a professor of history at Jena, Schiller had written a history of the Thirty Years' War in the early 1790's, and he had at that time pointed out that the duke was in fact an unsympathetic character. It was less his personal magnetism than his money that had held the army together, as well as the prospect of the spoils to come with success. Wallenstein's fall was a product of his own miscalculations, and he lacked nobility of character. As a dramatist, however, Schiller saw the possibility of creating a tragedy that would rival those of William Shakespeare and the Greeks. He developed the characters of Wallenstein and of his principal associates, invented the idealized figures of Max and Thekla, and shaped the events to create a coherent vision of conflicting loyalties, duty, guilt, and tragic expiation. All the while, he yet remained remarkably faithful to the historic events.

In the first section of the trilogy, *The Camp of Wallenstein*, Schiller creates the milieu of the time and presents both the visible signs of the general's greatness and an intimation of the divisions within his army, divisions that reflect the tensions that will destroy Wallenstein himself. In a prologue, Schiller explains that this portrait of the camp is an essential part of the work: It is Wallenstein's power that misleads his heart; his camp alone explains his crime. This symbolic representation is meant to place the individual Wallenstein in the nexus created by the diverse forces at play: the expectations of his soldiers, Wallenstein's own power and its limits, and the potential for its misuse. The army is his creation, but it had also come to have its own independent existence. Wallenstein may be the creator of historical forces, but he is also carried by those forces and ultimately becomes their victim.

The second section of the trilogy, *The Piccolominis*, presents the political intrigue that precipitates the tragedy. When Wallenstein first appears, the movement against him has already begun and the forces leading to his destruction have been set in motion. He is unaware of this, however, and imagines himself still to be a free agent. Indeed, one of his main characteristics is that of keeping his options open, putting off decisions, as though he were the sole factor involved in directing the course of history. He has breadth of vision and ranks far above his less imaginative subordinates, and yet he is guilty of a kind of hubris, expressed primarily in his readiness to betray his emperor.

Octavio Piccolomini, whom Schiller elevates to a major role in the plot, is unswervingly loyal to the emperor but betrays his commander. Schiller thus establishes a field of tension in which each figure in the plot experiences divided loyalties and is forced to make a choice. The agony of decision is intensified through the addition of the character of Max—Octavio was actually childless—a young man who, in the midst of mutual betrayals, insists on honesty and the authority of the heart over pragmatism. His father argues necessity, but Max argues simple right and wrong. He is one of the most radiant of Schiller's creations, an idealist who cannot accept a breach of honor and who is torn between his loyalty to his father and his loyalty to Wallenstein, whom he regards as a second father. Schiller realized that this figure might well become the central focus of the play, and in fact for some readers this interpretation seems natural. However, in the last section, *The Death of Wallenstein*, Schiller passes from a focus on the conflict of those around Wallenstein and from details of plot to focus on Wallenstein himself. Johann Wolfgang von Goethe observed that in this last section the purely human aspects are dominant. Wallenstein becomes an increasingly tragic figure as the plot against him moves inexorably forward.

The tragedy is more than that of Wallenstein alone, however; all the figures are caught in a movement of history that is in part Wallenstein's own creation and yet also something independent that moves by its own laws. Insofar as he is a creator, Wallenstein is responsible for his own destruction; yet every character is forced by history to make a choice that compromises his integrity. All are stricken. Even Max, the only pure soul, is destroyed by the intolerable conflict in which the net of betrayals has placed him, and for Octavio, the bereaved victor, it must be a hollow triumph when he is elevated to the rank of prince.

"Critical Evaluation" by Steven C. Schaber

Further Reading

Garland, H. B. *Schiller.* Westport, Conn.: Greenwood Press, 1976. Contains biographical information and interpretation of Schiller's major plays. Explains the construction of *Wallenstein* and mentions Johann Wolfgang von Goethe's suggestions. Provides interpretation and criticism of the characters and plot, with many quotations in German.

Graham, Ilse. *Schiller's Drama: Talent and Integrity.* New York: Barnes & Noble, 1974. Provides readings of many of Schiller's plays. Discusses special issues of *Wallenstein* and includes a chapter about the connections between *Wallenstein* and Goethe's *Über Laokoon.*

Hammer, Stephanie Barbé. *Schiller's Wound: The Theater of Trauma from Crisis to Commodity.* Detroit, Mich.: Wayne State University Press, 2001. Argues that Schiller was one of the first playwrights to explore the topic of psychological trauma. Analyzes how his plays depict the relationships among pain, spectacle, and money. *Wallenstein* is discussed in chapter 3.

Kerry, Paul E., ed. *Friedrich Schiller: Playwright, Poet, Philosopher, Historian.* New York: Peter Lang, 2007. Collection of essays examines Schiller's various vocations—such as a poet, dramatist, historian, prose writer, and philosopher—and discusses the status of his work two hundred years after his death. Includes an essay analyzing *Wallenstein.*

Martinson, Steven D., ed. *A Companion to the Works of Friedrich Schiller.* Rochester, N.Y.: Camden House, 2005. Collection of essays includes discussions of Schiller's philosophical aesthetics, his lyric poetry, the reception of his works in the twentieth century, and the works' relevance to the twenty-first century, as well as analyses of specific works. An essay by Dieter Borchmeyer examines *Wallenstein.*

Saranpa, Kathy. *Schiller's "Wallenstein," "Maria Stuart," and "Die Jungfrau von Orleans": The Critical Legacy.* Rochester, N.Y.: Camden House, 2002. Traces the critical reaction to Schiller's late historical dramas, from his own time until postreunification Germany, including examinations of the responses to these plays in Nazi Germany and in the former German Democratic Republic.

Sharpe, Lesley. *Friedrich Schiller: Drama, Thought, and Politics*. New York: Cambridge University Press, 1991. Devotes a full chapter to *Wallenstein*, examining Schiller's sense of tragedy, melancholia, charisma, characterization, and style. Includes extensive chronology, bibliography, notes, and index to Schiller's works

_____. *A National Repertoire: Schiller, Iffland, and the German Stage*. New York: Peter Lang, 2007. Examines Schiller's influence on the German theater of his time by analyzing his plays' impact on the Mannheim National and Weimar Court theaters, with which he was closely associated. Places his theatrical career in parallel with that of August Wilhelm Iffland, an actor and playwright who eventually produced Schiller's plays at the Berlin National Theatre. Describes the relationship between Schiller and Goethe as playwrights.

Simons, John D. *Friedrich Schiller*. Boston: Twayne, 1981. Discusses Schiller's aesthetics and examines his poetry and dramatic works. Analyzes *Wallenstein*, with emphasis on historical background and the political, social, economic, and military situation of the time. Includes chronology and bibliography.

Thomas, Calvin. *The Life and Works of Friedrich Schiller*. 1901. Reprint. New York: AMS Press, 1970. Examines the works of Schiller in remarkable detail. Gives commentary on *Wallenstein* and compares it to Schiller's earlier works. Includes biographical information and an examination of the characters in the works as well as Schiller's method.

The Wanderer

Author: Alain-Fournier (1886-1914)
First published: Le Grand Meaulnes, 1913 (English translation, 1928)
Type of work: Novel
Type of plot: Psychological
Time of plot: Nineteenth century
Locale: France

Principal characters:
AUGUSTIN MEAULNES, the wanderer
FRANÇOIS SEUREL, his friend
FRANTZ DE GALAIS, a young aristocrat
YVONNE DE GALAIS, his sister
VALENTINE BLONDEAU, Frantz's fiancé

The Story:

François Seurel's father is head of the middle school and one of the higher elementary classes at the Sainte-Agathe village school, and his wife teaches the younger children. François lives in the school with his parents and his sister Millie and attends classes with the other pupils. He never plays much with the village boys, however, because of an infection in his hip.

When François Seurel is fifteen years old, Augustin Meaulnes enters the school. With his arrival, a new life begins for Seurel, for Meaulnes banishes his contentment with his family and his love for staying home. As his hip continues to improve, Seurel begins to spend more time with Meaulnes in the village. Even life at the school becomes livelier, for Meaulnes always draws a crowd of people around him in the evenings.

The adventure begins one Christmas Day, when Meaulnes sets out for the railroad station to meet Seurel's grandparents, Monsieur and Madame Charpentier. When the grandparents arrive, Meaulnes has disappeared. Three days later, he casually takes his seat in the classroom where Monsieur Seurel is conducting a lesson. No one knows where he has been, and he claims when questioned that he himself does not know. Sometimes at night, in the attic room they share, Seurel awakens to find Meaulnes pacing the floor, fully clothed, eager to reenter a mysterious world he had once glimpsed briefly. Meaulnes promises to take Seurel along the next time he leaves on a journey.

At last, Meaulnes tells Seurel the story of the adventure he had when he ran off from the school. It had been a very cold December day, and Meaulnes had lost his way; with darkness falling, he found that his horse was lame. He wandered to a cottage, where he was fed, and then he stumbled on until he found a barn in which, cold and lost, he fell asleep. The next day he wandered a long distance, until that night he came to a manor where small children and old people were merrily planning a wedding feast. Tired and cold, Meaulnes crawled through a window and climbed into a bed, where he slept all night. The next day, thinking that he was one of the wedding guests, some strolling players invited him to eat with them. Then Meaulnes discovered the reason for the feast. Frantz de Galais, the son of the man who owned the manor, had gone off to fetch his fiancé for their wedding.

All that first day, Meaulnes danced and played with the other guests. The next day, he met a beautiful girl with whom he fell in love. Although she declined to see him again, she promised to wait for his return to the manor. Inquiring about the strange girl, Meaulnes learned that she was Yvonne de Galais, Frantz's sister. Frantz returned to the manor without his bride, and he dismissed all the guests. Meaulnes joined the crowd of children and old people as they dejectedly walked and rode away from the manor. He fell asleep in a cart, and when he awoke he found himself near the Sainte-Agathe school.

Meaulnes's story seems unreal to young Seurel, but the arrival of a strange boy at the school brings the story to reality. The boy, who is dressed as a gypsy and who reminds Meaulnes of the Bohemians he saw at the manor, steals the map Meaulnes has been making to find his way back to the manor. Meaulnes and Seurel learn that the boy is young Frantz de Galais, who in a fit of despair after losing his sweetheart has run away with a band of gypsies. The boys promise that they will help Frantz if they can, but one night Frantz disappears. Meaulnes finally goes to live in Paris; after he leaves the school he writes only three letters to Seurel.

Months pass. Seurel finishes his school days and goes to visit relatives in another village. There he hears that a mysterious manor is not far off. Seurel eagerly takes up his friend's quest. His cousins, he learns, know Yvonne. The manor was razed after Frantz's disappearance, but his sister often comes to visit Seurel's cousins. One night, she arrives, and Seurel tells her that Meaulnes hopes someday to find her again. Seurel learns from his aunt that Frantz's fiancé was afraid to marry him because, as the daughter of peasants, she was certain that such great happiness could not come to her. She is now in Paris, working as a dressmaker. Seurel recalls his promise to help Frantz if he can. First, however, he intends to find Meaulnes and bring him to Yvonne de Galais.

When Seurel finds Meaulnes, the adventurer is packing his clothes to go on a journey. He abandons his plans, and he and Yvonne are married, but there is something mysterious in their lives that keeps them from being as happy as Seurel had expected them to be. One night, Frantz appears near the village. Seurel meets with him and listens to his complaints

of loneliness and sorrow. The following morning, Meaulnes leaves Yvonne, who is pregnant, to go on another adventure.

Seurel is now a teacher at the Sainte-Agathe school. For months he and Yvonne await Meaulnes's return. After her baby is born, Yvonne dies, leaving Seurel with an untold sadness. He searches through his friend's old papers and finds a diary that tells him why Meaulnes was so troubled before his disappearance. While Meaulnes was living in Paris, he had met Valentine Blondeau, who became his mistress. Valentine often spoke of her former lover, whom she had deserted because she feared to marry him. When she showed Meaulnes her lover's letters, he realized that Valentine was the fiancé for whom Frantz de Galais had never stopped searching. In anger, Meaulnes told her that he would leave her, and Valentine cried that she would then return to Paris to become a streetwalker. After returning to his mother's home, where Seurel had found him, Meaulnes began to feel remorse for his treatment of Valentine.

Seurel, reading the diary, realizes that Meaulnes must have been packing to go in search of Valentine when Seurel brought the news that Yvonne had been found. He decides that Meaulnes deserted Yvonne to go on the same quest.

As Yvonne's daughter grows into a lovable, pretty child, Seurel often visits to play with her, but she does not allow him to possess her affections completely. She always seems to be waiting for someone. One afternoon, while playing with the little girl, Seurel notices a burly stranger approaching. As the man comes nearer, Seurel recognizes Meaulnes. He tells Seurel that he has brought Valentine and Frantz together at last. With tears in his eyes at the news of his wife's death, Meaulnes takes his daughter into his arms. Seurel watches the father and daughter play together, and the schoolmaster smilingly imagines that he can envision Meaulnes arising in the middle of the night, wrapping his daughter in a cloak, and silently slipping off with her on some new adventure.

Critical Evaluation:

"The novel that I have carried in my head for three years," Alain-Fournier wrote in 1905, "was at first only me, me, and me, but it has gradually been depersonalized and enlarged and is no longer the novel that everybody plans at eighteen." That novel, *The Wanderer*, written and revised over a period of six more years, is the major work of the author, who fell in battle at Saint-Remy in 1914. Although *The Wanderer* is surely more than a romantic autobiography, aspects of the author appear in the three important male characters: the meditative, passive François Seurel, the adventurer Augustin Meaulnes, and the despairing lover Frantz de Galais. Like each of them, Alain-Fournier was a romantic idealist, a dreamer, a child-man not entirely able to come to terms with adult responsibilities. Precisely for this reason, his childlike vision of reality gives the story a psychological dimension beyond its trappings of sentimental fantasy.

Seurel, the narrator, is the most timorous of the three heroes; he experiences life vicariously through the more intense activities of the others. When he must act to assist his beloved friend Meaulnes, however, he does so decisively. "Admiral" Meaulnes is bold in dreams but indecisive when he needs to act, and his will is paralyzed by guilt. While living in Paris, he betrays Valentine Blondeau (as in real life Alain-Fournier deceived Jeanne B.), and for that reason—and because he has betrayed Yvonne's brother, who truly loves Valentine—he cannot accept the pure love of Yvonne de Galais. Toward the end of the novel, after reconciling Frantz with Valentine, Meaulnes partly eases his own guilt feelings and becomes free to accept the love of his young daughter. It is questionable, however, whether there is happiness in store for Frantz, the most idealistic and shadowy of the three hero-wanderers, for he is pursued by a child's dream of perfection that he cannot possibly realize. For Seurel, the passive sympathizer, love is a dream that only other, stronger souls can hope to attain; for Meaulnes, the adventurer, love is a quest, never a conquest; for Frantz, the hopeless searcher, love may be the final tragic deception.

As for Yvonne and Valentine, they are merely projections of the idealized dreams, or guilty passions, of the male child-heroes. Apart from their lovers, they have no lives of their own. Indeed, it is the heroes' peculiar childlike fantasy concerning women and love that unifies the novel and provides its psychological insights. The three male heroes are drawn to one another in a friendship so devoted that it resembles a ritual of brotherhood: protective, empathetic, nearly mystical. At the same time, they are half-maddened by love for "pure" women. This love is overpoweringly sudden, threatening (even when the object is as frail and delicate as Yvonne), and absolute. Once they have fallen in love, the child-heroes are victims of their fate: Their bond of brotherhood is shattered, their lives fragmented.

To express this story of a child's fascination with, and fear of, love and sexuality, Alain-Fournier effectively uses a Symbolist-impressionist style. Like Maurice Maeterlinck, he is a master of pauses and sudden breaks in the narrative that underscore the sense of tension and menace. He subtly shifts between scenes of realistic detail presented with perfect clarity (the wedding feast, for example) and scenes of haunting, ambiguous, hallucinatory mystery (Meaulnes's meeting with Yvonne). At his best, Alain-Fournier writes passages of touching simplicity. At other times, he loses artistic restraint and allows his characters to declaim romantically bombastic speeches. Some of his symbolic passages, too, tend to be murky, the prose childish instead of childlike. Such lapses are rare, however. Alain-Fournier is justified in saying of his one great novel, "If I have been childish and weak and foolish, at least I have, at moments, had the strength in this infamous city to create my life, like a marvelous fairy-tale."

Further Reading

Blair, Fredrika. Introduction to *The Wanderer*. Translated by Françoise Delisle. Garden City, N.Y.: Doubleday, 1953. Presents an analysis of Alain-Fournier's style that connects it to the impressionist and Symbolist movements in art and literature. (This edition's translation of the work has been superseded by later ones.)

Ford, Edward. *Alain-Fournier and "Le Grand Meaulnes" ("The Wanderer")*. Lewiston, N.Y.: Edwin Mellen Press, 1999. Discusses Fournier's life and his interest in primitivism, arguing that *The Wanderer* is a primitivist novel. Explains the novel's structure, the literary influences that shaped Alain-Fournier's work, and the novel's influence on other writers.

Fowles, John. Afterword to *The Wanderer*. Translated by Lowell Bair. New York: New American Library, 1971. A well-known British novelist explains his enthusiasm for the novel and shows why he thinks the work must be read on its own terms and why it resists conventional critical analysis.

Gibson, Robert. *The End of Youth: The Life and Work of Alain-Fournier*. Exeter, England: Impress, 2005. Gibson, who published his first biography of Alain-Fournier in 1953, reassesses Alain-Fournier's life and work based on newly discovered information. Includes new material about the two great loves of Fournier's life, Yvonne de Quivrecourt and "Simone," the leading boulevard actress of her day, as well as many letters from Fournier's friends and fellow writers, a compilation of his work as a literary gossip columnist, the complete drafts of his second novel, and the plays left unfinished when he went off to war in 1914.

_____. *The Land Without a Name: Alain-Fournier and His World*. London: Paul Elek, 1975. Thorough, dense, yet accessible study reviews all previous scholarship on Alain-Fournier as well as his posthumously published correspondence. Uses the theme of the lost paradise as its organizing principle.

Gurney, Stephen. *Alain-Fournier*. Boston: Twayne, 1987.

Provides a complete introduction to the writer and his work. Relates *The Wanderer* to Alain-Fournier's poems and letters, especially the ones he wrote to his brother-in-law, who was a literary and psychological soul mate. Contains a good selected bibliography.

Jones, Marian Giles. *A Critical Commentary on Alain-Fournier's "Le Grand Meaulnes."* New York: St. Martin's Press, 1968. Reviews many important themes of the novel in detail and provides a good starting point for further discussion.

The Wandering Jew

Author: Eugène Sue (1804-1857)
First published: Le Juif errant, 1844-1845 (English translation, 1868)
Type of work: Novel
Type of plot: Melodrama
Time of plot: 1831-1832
Locale: France

Principal characters:
RODIN, an ambitious Jesuit
MONSIEUR L'ABBE D'AIGRIGNY, the provincial of the Jesuits
BLANCHE SIMON,
ROSE SIMON,
FRANÇOIS HARDY,
PRINCE DJALMA,
JACQUES DE RENNEPONT or COUCHE-TOUT-NUD,
GABRIEL DE RENNEPONT, and
ADRIENNE DE CARDOVILLE, the descendants of Marius de Rennepont and the heirs to his legacy
SAMUEL, the Wandering Jew
HERODIAS, a woman who demanded the head of John the Baptist

The Story:

A solitary figure stalks down a bleak hill in Poland. He is an old man, his face gentle and sad. His footsteps leave in the soil imprints of a cross made by the several large nails in his shoes. He is hurrying, for he has to be in Paris on the thirteenth of February, 1832, when the surviving descendants of his sister will gather in that city—the last members of that family over whom he watched for eighteen centuries. The lonely traveler is the Wandering Jew, that artisan of Jerusalem who mocks Christ on the day of the Crucifixion, the sinner condemned to wander undying through the centuries over all the world. Far in the wilds of America a woman also turns toward Paris, driven by that same power that guides the Wandering Jew. She is Herodias, who demanded the head of John the Baptist on a charger, also condemned to live through the centuries of sorrow.

François Baudoin, called Dagobert, a faithful friend of Marshal Simon and an old Bonapartist hero, never falters in his loyalty toward the Simon family. Years before, he followed the marshal's Polish wife into Siberia, where she was exiled, and after her death he set out with her twin daughters,

Blanche and Rose, for Paris, where, on a certain day in February, 1832, a legacy awaits the two girls. This is the legacy of Marius de Rennepont, an ancestor who, despoiled by the Jesuits, salvaged out of his ruined estate a house and a small sum of money. He placed the money in the hands of a faithful Jewish friend named Samuel, who promised to invest it profitably. One hundred fifty years later the descendants of this ancestor are to gather at a house where each is to receive a share of the legacy. Blanche and Rose Simon are only half-aware of the fortune awaiting them, for they were too young to understand what Dagobert told them about their inheritance.

If these heirs of Marius de Rennepont do not know of the legacy, others nevertheless do. For many years the Jesuits, masters of an intricate and diabolical conspiracy, plot to prevent the descendants from acquiring the money. They are responsible for Marshal Simon's exile and for his wife's banishment to Siberia.

The plotters are so meticulous and so thorough in their scheming that they persuade young Gabriel de Rennepont to become a priest and a member of the Society of Jesus. Through Gabriel they hope to acquire the tremendous fortune, for by preventing the other heirs from reaching Paris—and the society has agents all over the world who will do its bidding under any conditions—they can ensure that Gabriel will inherit the legacy. Then, since he is forbidden by his vow of poverty to possess money, the funds will revert to the society. With that money the Jesuits will be able to reestablish their supremacy over the French people and will be able once more to govern countries and guide the destiny of Europe.

As soon as Dagobert and the two girls arrive in Paris, the Jesuits arrange to have them spirited away to a convent. Adrienne de Cardoville, another descendant of the de Rennepont family, is declared insane and committed to an asylum. Jacques de Rennepont, a good-hearted sensualist named Couche-tout-Nud, is jailed for debt. Prince Djalma, who left India despite the efforts of the Jesuits, is drugged. François Hardy, a benevolent manufacturer, is sent out of town through the treachery of a friend who is a Jesuit spy.

As a result of that Jesuit conspiracy, on that fateful day in February, 1832, only the priest, Gabriel de Rennepont, goes to claim the legacy at the house of an old Jew known as Samuel. With Gabriel are Monsieur l'Abbe d'Aigrigny, Provincial of the Jesuits, and Rodin, his secretary. Before the reading of the will, Gabriel is persuaded to sign a paper in which he renounces all claims to the legacy. When the bequest is announced, the Jesuits are astounded at the incredible sum of the inheritance, which grew from 150,000 francs to a fortune of 212,175,000 francs. Just as the money is being handed over to the priests, however, a strange woman appears and produces a codicil to the will, a document suspending its execution for three months. The woman is Herodias, but none then call her by that name. The priests are enraged, and they fear that their conspiracy will be exposed. Adrienne de Cardoville is certain to be released from the asylum. General Simon is reported to be on his way back to France to claim his daughters. Couche-tout-Nud will borrow money from his friends to pay his debts. Prince Djalma will soon awaken. Hardy will return to Paris from his fruitless errand.

Rodin immediately produces a paper that places him in complete charge of the Jesuit cabal. He proclaims that they did not lose, that they can and will win by employing psychological methods instead of violence. He will let each heir destroy himself or herself by his or her own desires, passions, or vices.

During the following three months, Rodin pretends that he leaves the service of the Abbe d'Aigrigny and passes himself off as a friend of the de Rennepont heirs. He secures the release of the Simon girls and Adrienne, and by those acts he becomes known as a good, unselfish man. Shortly before her death, one of Adrienne's servants confesses that she was blackmailed into spying for the Jesuits, and she reveals the whole sordid, brutal, unprincipled conspiracy. Rodin, however, is not yet willing to accept defeat. At his direction, Hardy's factory is burned to the ground, his best friend's treachery is revealed, and his beautiful young mistress is spirited away. A broken man, Hardy is taken to a Jesuit retreat, where he accepts the doctrines of the order and dies as the result of the penances and fasts imposed upon him. Couche-tout-Nud, separated from his mistress, dies a miserable death after an orgy arranged by another Jesuit agent. The Simon girls are taken to a hospital during a cholera epidemic and die there of the disease. Prince Djalma, led to believe that Adrienne has become the mistress of Agricola Baudoin, Dagobert's son, attacks Agricola and kills a girl whom he mistakes for Adrienne. He discovers his error too late, for in his remorse he already swallowed poison. Adrienne chooses to die with him.

When the time comes for the final disposition of the de Rennepont legacy, Gabriel is the only survivor. Just as Rodin is about to claim the inheritance in the name of his churchly office, the casket containing the money and securities bursts into flames and the fortune is lost forever. A moment later Rodin falls to the floor and writhes in agony. As he left a church, shortly before claiming the legacy, he took holy water from the fingers of an Indian who accompanied Prince Djalma from India and who became a lay member of the Jesuits. Too late, Rodin realizes that he was poisoned in some manner by the Indian. He dies a few minutes later.

Gabriel de Rennepont, shocked when he realizes the crimes of greed and lust for power that the lost fortune caused, retires to live out the rest of his brief life with his friends, the Baudoin family. After Gabriel's body is laid in the de Rennepont tomb, old Samuel goes to a secret spot where a great cross is set upon a lonely hill. There Herodias finds him. In the dawn's light each sees upon the face of the other the marks that age put upon them, but they find peace and happiness at last. Samuel—for he is the Wandering Jew—gives praise that their long punishment is ended, and Herodias echoes his words.

Critical Evaluation:

The Wandering Jew is an enormous novel. It touches several continents and the worlds of religion, economics, the supernatural, politics, medicine, and social protest. There are hundreds of characters on this vast stage and dozens of plots, subplots, and plots within subplots. The novel is in that tradition of French literary Romanticism that mixes the supernatural with politics and social commentary. Its vast scale, reminiscent of Victor Hugo's *Les Misérables* (1862; English translation, 1862), also is mindful of the large social tapestry of eighteenth century novels. Further, Eugène Sue loves melodrama. He attempts, at every juncture, to induce the extremes of horror, anticipation, and suspense in his readers through a variety of well-tested literary techniques. The novel is also of interest for the study of genre: It is a precursor of the mystery-detective novel as well as being an example of the Romantic novel.

It must be said that *The Wandering Jew* is not a successful novel. In terms of theme, action, character, and style, it must be classified as a magnificent, towering failure. Central to the novel's difficulties is Sue's inability to connect and unify the vast and complicated action of the work. The intrigues and schemes of the Jesuits and the problem of the legacy, although convenient, simply cannot sustain the ambitious weight of this novel. The world of *The Wandering Jew* is overflowing, without sufficient discipline imposed on the material. Indeed, Sue's Romanticism carries him quite far away from the discipline of some sort of unity, be it of place, of time, or of structure.

In *Voyna i mir* (1865-1869; *War and Peace*, 1886), another very large novel, the scope is also enormous and the characters and motives are extremely various, but Leo Tolstoy has a firm grasp of his war-and-peace theme and the processes of history. At the same time, he is able to offer vivid and accurate psychological and moral descriptions. The thematic content of *The Wandering Jew* is clouded by Romanticism and idealization, and, in addition to superficial and melodramatic characterizations, Sue offers large doses of the supernatural and mysticism. Weaknesses of characterization, action, and theme are, naturally, reinforced and magnified as the scope of the work increases. Sue's attempt itself, however, is impressive, and there are frequent artistically valid and touching individual scenes. The novel retains its place in the canon of Western literature by virtue of its great accomplishments in the areas of exploration of genre (the mystery-detective novel, the Romantic novel) and engrossing plot.

Further Reading

Murch, Alma Elizabeth. *The Development of the Detective Novel.* New York: Philosophical Library, 1958. Offers a historical context for considering *The Wandering Jew* as an early detective novel.

Pickup, Ian. "Eugène Sue." In *Nineteenth Century French Fiction Writers: Romanticism and Realism, 1800-1860,* edited by Catharine Savage Brosman. Vol. 119 in *Dictionary of Literary Biography.* Detroit, Mich.: Gale Research, 1992. Provides basic facts about Sue's life and works. Places his distinctive realism in relation to that of other nineteenth century French realist authors, as well as to the Romanticism against which they were rebelling.

Rye, Marilyn. "Eugène Sue." In Vol. 4 of *Critical Survey of Mystery and Detective Fiction*, edited by Carl Rollyson. Rev. ed. Pasadena, Calif.: Salem Press, 2008. Provides a brief overview of Sue's life, work, and contribution to world literature. Focuses on his novel *The Mysteries of Paris.*

The Wandering Scholar from Paradise

Author: Hans Sachs (1494-1576)
First produced: Der fahrende Schüler im Paradies, 1550; first published, 1880 (English translation, 1910)
Type of work: Drama
Type of plot: Farce
Time of plot: Sixteenth century
Locale: Nuremberg, Germany

Principal characters:
THE FARMER, a crude peasant
HIS WIFE, an ignorant, dreaming housewife
THE STUDENT, a quick-witted young man, more adventurer than scholar

The Story:

A Nuremberg woman claims to all and sundry that her deceased first husband is still her true love. She dismisses her second husband as being no lover at all and describes him as scrimpy, mean, and sour of disposition. One day, while she is voicing her complaints, the wandering Student comes by, doffs his hat in a polite gesture, and begs for alms. Rightly guessing that boasts about his successes in Paris will impress the woman, he immediately uses the advantage it gives him when the Wife misunderstands him to say that he has come from Paradise.

The Wife's mind is still lost in dreams of her first husband when she asks the Student if he knows the departed one. The Student allows that he does not, but he thinks that on his return to Paradise the acquaintance can perhaps be effected. The Student goes on to tell her how ill-clothed, ill-fed, and completely destitute her late husband is, whereupon the Wife accepts his offer to take gifts back to her husband.

As the Student prepares to leave, the Wife inquires when he might come again to bring word of her first love. He assures her that the road is long and difficult and that he will not be likely to pass her way again. Without delay and with a minimum of ceremony, the Student takes her gifts and strides off—and none too soon, for the Farmer appears just as the young man is taking his departure.

The Wife continues to sing the love song that she had been singing just before meeting the Student, but now, as her husband notices, she sings happily. Naïvely, she tells him of the visitor who has brought her happiness and of her having sent gifts to her first love. Craftily concealing his anger at her simplicity, the Farmer sarcastically orders her to prepare more gifts that he might take them to the Student as additional presents to the man who, though dead, retains her devotion. Then, laden with the gifts, he goes off in search of the Student.

In a rough slough the Student is stuffing his booty into bushes when he hears the Farmer approaching. With cunning and a veil of innocent helpfulness, he directs the Farmer deeper into the furze, where he claims the culprit is hiding. He also offers to help the Farmer by holding his horse while he goes on his search. When the Farmer is out of sight, the Student rides off on the horse, with the Farmer's and the Wife's contributions across the saddle. Meanwhile, the Farmer stumbles through the slough, getting muddier and more scratched with each step in his vain effort to find the offending traveler from Paradise.

At their cottage, the Wife is peering into the distance for some sign of the Farmer. Her chief concern is that her husband might be lost in the mist on the moor and unable to overtake the Student to add to her gifts. Her doubts vanish when she sees the Farmer trudging in slowly and wearily, hoping against hope that his horse has come home on its own. Not seeing the animal, he accepts the fact that he has been duped. What can he do or say to the Wife—the stupid one, the gullible one—whom he had intended to beat for giving away a few farthings and some worn-out clothes? She is indeed a lesser fool than he, who has lost his swiftest horse.

Stirred to activity in an effort to ease her husband's anger,

the Wife carries in the milk pails and asks about the success of his search. The Farmer mumbles a halting explanation of his altruism; he decided, he says, to make a gift of his horse to the Student, since the young man was tired and had far to go. The Wife is overwhelmed by her husband's unexpected kindness. For his thoughtfulness in behalf of her first husband, she promises that were he to die that night, she would send him all manner of presents in Paradise. Such a generous husband should have the goodwill of his neighbors, she declares, and she proceeds to circulate the story of her husband's generosity throughout the parish. The angry Farmer decides that it is bad enough to be burdened with such a fool of a wife; it is unbearable to think that his neighbors consider him the same kind of fool. The moral is that if married people are to get along, they must cover for each other's weaknesses and not let others see the flaws in their bonds of wedlock.

Critical Evaluation:

Hans Sachs gained international fame as the central figure of Richard Wagner's opera *Die Meistersinger von Nürnberg* (1867). Sachs was a *Meistersinger*, or master singer, who plied his trade as a shoemaker in the city of Nuremberg, where he was also the leader and a creative innovator in the local *Singschule*, the guild of poets and musicians. The guild members were mostly artisans, skilled in the composition and singing of rigid technical formulas, who claimed descent from the medieval *Minnesänger*, or courtly poets. To gain the rank of *Meister*, a candidate had to compete in a public contest in which he created and performed a new melody and a new stanzaic form.

Between 1511 and 1516, during the prescribed *Wanderjahre* that completed a craftsman's professional and general education, Sachs the journeyman shoemaker and poet traveled throughout Germany and Austria. An eager student and accomplished writer, he had gained a reputation as a poet before he returned to Nuremberg at the age of twenty-two to marry and settle down. A prolific poet for the rest of his eighty-two years, he left more than two hundred plays; countless fables, epic poems, and anecdotal stories; and more than four thousand master songs. In addition to his writing, he was influential in the stagecraft of his day both as an actor and as a theatrical manager. There was no theater that could be termed professional in Nuremberg, but the Nuremberg *Meistersinger* guild carried on a lively amateur theatrical tradition and performed plays in churches, convents, and inn yards. The performances were so popular that playgoers were sometimes known to interrupt the church's afternoon religious service in order to obtain seats for an evening's theater performance.

Sachs classified his dramatic works as tragedies, comedies, *Fastnachtspiele* (Shrovetide plays), and, quite simply, plays. Critics are in general agreement that the tragedies and comedies, while exhibiting a wide range of subjects from biblical material to medieval legends and classical mythology, are often plodding in style and technique. It is with his innovations and skill in the Shrovetide plays that Sachs achieved mastery.

The Shrovetide play, essentially a farcical dialogue written in verse and centered on a humorous incident, was meant to amuse theatergoers during carnival time. It generally reflects the lives of the peasants and burghers among whom Sachs lived. The early Shrovetide plays were rather formless and full of coarse and obscene humor. Sachs made the humor gentler, tightened the form, and created a theatrical piece that delivered satire and wit together with a moral lesson. His moral stance reflects his vigorous Protestantism; his championship of Martin Luther in 1523 inspired him to compose a poem titled "Die Wittembergerisch Nachtigall" ("The Wittenburg Nightingale") that praised the reformer's efforts.

Sachs was a genial storyteller who delighted in human foibles and avoided the pitfalls of cynicism or bitterness; his usual satiric targets were boorish simpletons or shrews. *The Wandering Scholar from Paradise* exhibits much of the best that appears in Sachs's Shrovetide plays. The play pokes good-humored fun at a simple, gullible woman and her more cunning but no less easily fooled husband. As is often the case, the clever trickster in the play is an itinerant student, lacking in goods but not in wit. No doubt Sachs's five years as a wandering journeyman contributed to his knowledge of such characters.

Critics have praised Sachs's ear for the language of the commoner and for achieving harmony between subject and style in plays such as *The Wandering Scholar from Paradise*. He is also credited with imposing solid construction and unity on the typical rambling structure of the Shrovetide play. One technique he employs is to limit settings. Early plays wandered from locale to locale, making little distinction between them. In his play, Sachs uses only two locales—the farmhouse and the bog—and he indicates in the stage directions that a curtain with a slough painted on it be drawn to mark the change of scene. Sachs also provides precise stage directions for the actors, instructing them in how to portray certain actions.

Most significant is the way in which Sachs achieves unity through his characterization. The Wife in *The Wandering Scholar from Paradise* reveals her naïveté from the very opening of the play as she sings a romantic ballad and laments the loss of her first husband. Sachs directs the actor to sob and sigh deeply during the speech. Her excited mistaking of the word Paris for Paradise reveals to the Student, as well as to the audience, not only that she is ingenuous but also that she will be gullible. It is important to note in addition, however, that she is duped because of her kindheartedness and generosity. She is genuinely concerned for the well-being of her former husband.

When the Farmer realizes how his simpleton wife has been tricked by the Student, he is determined to get revenge and immediately goes after him, not bothering to enlighten his wife as to her witless behavior. There is time enough to box her ears when he returns with the goods she has given to the Student. His determined haste leads to his downfall, for he is so intent on capturing the Student that he follows the directions given to him by that very Student pretending to be a doltish peasant. Chagrined by his own gullibility, the Farmer returns home unable to chastise the Wife for her stupidity. To make matters worse, he learns that she has boasted of his generosity to the whole parish, and his neighbors are vastly amused by the tale.

Although the Farmer has lost his goods and his reputation for cunning tightfistedness in the community, he has gained some humanity and understanding of marital relationships. This is pointed out in Sachs's traditional moral observation at the close of the play:

> Folly in folly must find excuse
> If married folks are to live in truce
> And the bonds of wedlock not show cracks—
> Which is the warning and wish, of Hans Sachs.

It is a temperate warning that has been delivered with humor and good grace.

Hans Sachs's Shrovetide plays represent the pinnacle of sixteenth century German dramatic activity. Sachs's achievement, however, must be considered the climax of medieval amateur theater rather than the harbinger of a new form.

"Critical Evaluation" by Jane Anderson Jones

Further Reading

Aylett, Robert, and Peter Skrine, eds. *Hans Sachs and Folk Theatre in the Late Middle Ages: Studies in the History of Popular Culture.* Lewiston, N.Y.: Edwin Mellen Press, 1995. Collection of essays presents analysis of Sachs's theater works, including discussions of comedy, satire, realism, and victim heroines in his plays. Also included are essays comparing Sachs and Giovanni Boccaccio and addressing word formation in works by Sachs and his contemporaries.

Garland, H. B. "The Sixteenth Century." In *A Concise Survey of German Literature*. Coral Gables, Fla.: University of Miami Press, 1971. Places Sachs in the context of the contemporary Protestant burghers of Nuremberg and Augsburg and discusses the prominence given the poet by Richard Wagner's opera. Claims that Sachs's influence has less to do with his writing than with Wagner's famous portrayal.

Liptzin, Sol. "Early German Literature." In *Historical Survey of German Literature*. New York: Prentice-Hall, 1936. Discusses the *Meistersinger* guilds of sixteenth century Germany and points out Sachs's mastery in such Shrovetide plays as *The Wandering Scholar from Paradise*.

Merkel, Ingrid. "Literature of the Sixteenth and Seventeenth Century." In *The Challenge of German Literature*, edited by Horst S. Daemmrich and Dieter H. Haenicke. Detroit, Mich.: Wayne State University Press, 1971. Discusses Sachs's regeneration of the Shrovetide play, claiming that his structure, lively dialogue, and realistic characterizations might have laid the groundwork for German comedy but that he had no successors.

Robertson, J. G., and Dorothy Reich. "The Drama in the Sixteenth Century." In *A History of German Literature*, edited by Dorothy Reich with W. I. Lucas et al. 6th ed. Elmsford, N.Y.: London House and Maxwell, 1970. Asserts that Sachs was the most prolific humanist dramatist and created new forms. Concludes that *The Wandering Scholar from Paradise* is one of the best extant Shrovetide plays.

Rose, Ernest. "The Parabolic and Didactic Style: Middle Class Literature." In *A History of German Literature*. New York: New York University Press, 1960. Discusses the strengths and limitations of Sachs's verse and dramas, and concedes that his Shrovetide plays were lively and amusing to contemporary audiences and are similarly well received by modern audiences.

The Wapshot Chronicle

Author: John Cheever (1912-1982)
First published: 1957
Type of work: Novel
Type of plot: Satire
Time of plot: 1890's-1950's
Locale: St. Botolphs, Massachusetts; Washington, D.C.; New York City; a rocket-launching station

Principal characters:
LEANDER WAPSHOT, a Yankee skeptic, philosopher, and skipper of the launch *Topaze*
SARAH WAPSHOT, his brisk, practical wife
MOSES and COVERLY, their sons
MELISSA, Moses' wife
BETSEY, Coverly's wife
HONORA WAPSHOT, a wealthy cousin and the family matriarch
JUSTINA WAPSHOT MOLESWORTH SCADDON, another wealthy cousin
ROSALIE YOUNG

The Story:

St. Botolphs had been a bustling, prosperous river port in the days of the Massachusetts clipper fleets. It is currently, however, kept alive by a few small industries and by summer visitors. It is a moribund port town with a tourist center of antique stores, gift shops, and tearooms quaintly decorated with the handcrafted artifacts of an older seafaring and agricultural United States.

Leander Wapshot's home, West Farm, cluttered with the memories and the possessions of dead and gone Wapshots, is an image of a good past and an uncertain present. The Wapshots, like the village, have come down in the world. The older generations of the family's men were seafaring wanderers in their youth, and they came back to St. Botolphs with their manhood seasoned by the hardships and perils of their calling and with their wits sharpened by the strategies of trade in foreign ports. The ancestral Wapshot men had memories of lovely, naked brown women in the islands of the Pacific. Leander has never known adventure in far places or a sultry paradise of love. Failing fortunes and changing times have beached him inland; he is a spiritual castaway on the shores of Wapshot tradition and dependent on Cousin Honora's charity.

Nominally, Leander is the head of the family, but the real power is Cousin Honora, a matriarch who speaks and acts with the authority of one who holds the purse strings. In her eccentric way, she regards Leander and herself as the holders of a family trust, Leander because he has fathered two sons, herself because she controls the fortune, which she intends to pass on to the boys when they marry and produce sons of their own. Meanwhile, she pays the bills and bullies Leander. He has never been provident, and now he is old. A man should be useful for something, however, so Cousin Honora bought the *Topaze*, a battered old launch that Leander ferries daily between Travertine and the amusement park at Nangasakit across the bay. In Honora's opinion, the *Topaze* keeps Leander out of other mischief and satisfies his taste for romance and nonsense. Leander's wife, Sarah, is a brisk, practical woman who indulges her husband, looks after her sons, and, as president of the Women's Club, works energetically for the civic improvement of St. Botolphs.

In spite of his failings, old Leander, with his regard for ceremony and for the idea of life as a process of excellence and continuity, dominates the family's consciousness. In his zest for life, he is the guardian of tribal rituals and of masculine skills that he hopes to pass on to his sons, Moses and Coverly. What the sons absorb from his examples of parental love and wisdom shows them to be true Wapshots. Although the family fortunes depend on proof of their virility, they cannot take ordinary mortals as wives after they have heard of the pagan sirens, singing on distant beaches, of the Wapshot past.

Rosalie, for example, although catapulted into the Wapshot household from a blazing car in which her lover dies, is not romantic enough. Rosalie's giving herself to Moses is a gesture of her inner despair. Her brief passage through Leander's world serves chiefly as an excuse for Cousin Honora's decision that the time has come for Moses to go out into the world to seek his fortune in the approved Wapshot manner.

When Moses leaves home, Coverly also runs away. First a government employee in Washington, Moses later finds his place in a New York fiduciary house. Coverly's adventures are more varied and include failure to get a job in a carpet factory because the company psychiatrists decide he is psychologically unstable. Coverly finds work as a department store clerk, goes to night school, has civilian status in a secret government project in the South Pacific, and finds a position on a rocket-launching project in the West. Both brothers, in the end, find what they are seeking. Moses chooses Melissa, the

penniless ward of another Wapshot cousin who is the parsimonious widow of a five-and-dime-store tycoon. This rich widow, Justina Wapshot Molesworth Scaddon, lives in ugly baroque discomfort on the Hudson. For Melissa's sake, Moses put up with Cousin Justina's penny-pinching and nagging. Coverly's fate comes to him in the person of Betsey, a lonely, unpretentious southern woman. So the Wapshot fortunes are made secure, for with the births of sons to Melissa and Betsey, Cousin Honora proves as good as her word and turns her money over to Moses and Coverly.

Meanwhile, Leander's world has fallen apart. He has wrecked the *Topaze*, and Cousin Honora refuses to pay for the repairs. When Sarah Wapshot converts the old craft into "The Only Floating Gift Shoppe in New England" and opens the establishment with a gala tea and a sale of Italian pottery, Leander is heartbroken. At first he tries to keep busy writing his memoirs, but remembrance proves too painful for him to continue. Finally, disgusted with the ugliness of life, he drowns himself. Moses and Coverly, returning to St. Botolphs to buy their father a new boat, instead hear the burial service for those who have perished at sea. On a later visit home, Coverly finds in a book of Shakespeare a note of advice bequeathed by Leander to his sons, a litany of idiosyncratic personal belief and homely folk wisdom.

Critical Evaluation:

The first thing the reader notices in *The Wapshot Chronicle* is the novel's paradoxical tone, a mix of comedy and tragedy, darkness and light. John Cheever is intent on imitating the richness and the paradoxical, unpredictable nature of life, full of joy, silliness, humor, love, hate, pain, and frustration in combination.

The lack of structure and logic in people's lives is reflected in the structure of the novel, where narrative coherence, cause and effect, and meaning are subservient to the anecdotal. Just as in real life the significance of events is not always immediately clear or indeed remains obscure forever, the interpretation of what befalls Cheever's characters is often left to the reader. The narrator's whimsical, capricious, and arbitrary presence may be seen as analogous to God's role in people's lives—if one thinks of the deity as one who determines the flow of events without reference to justice, logic, or clarity. The narrator in *The Wapshot Chronicle* reports, sometimes with tongue in cheek; the narrator does not steer the characters from one well-structured event to the next.

A central theme of the novel is what life may mean—what people are to learn from the sum of their experiences and how they are to react to turns of events that they do not expect and over which they have no control. *The Wapshot Chronicle* ends with the touching description of Leander's funeral, to which his sons have returned to honor him in his hometown of St. Botolphs. Amid his tears, Coverly reads the passage from William Shakespeare's *The Tempest* (pr. 1611, pb. 1623) that Leander wanted read at his funeral. The passage from Shakespeare emphasizes fragility—that people are all actors in some grand drama, actors made only of dreams. If there is a fundamental message in the novel, it is what Leander affirms in the notes he made in a book of Shakespeare's work that Coverly finds while going through his father's things after the funeral. These rules to live by, the final words in the novel and apparently the sum of Leander's experience, are simple, very practical guides for the most part: Never sleep in the moonlight, never make love with one's pants on, and take a cold bath every morning.

The list of rules ends with more general affirmations—that the world is to be admired, that the love of a good woman is to be relished, and that people should trust in God, after all. Hence the novel ends on a note of positive closure: Moses and Coverly have come home, and Honora has honored her promise to endow them as her heirs, now that they have produced sons. Moses and Coverly have evidently weathered their trials and learned their own lessons.

The Wapshot Chronicle is presumably a parody of histories, as suggested by the word "chronicle." The novel tells about the distinction between what is apparent and what lies beneath the surface of personalities and events. In this regard, the novel's narrative mocks the stature and dignity of New England and its figures (Honora, for example, is often seen in public in a three-cornered hat). The narrator also remarks that the ladies of the Wapshot clan always eat daintily in public but stuff themselves like animals at home. The history of St. Botolphs is less a story of continuous prosperity than one of decadence. In an image that illustrates the novel's skewed tone, Honora heads for Boston shortly after Leander's funeral to take in a Red Sox baseball game. The narrator describes her, in her three-cornered hat, as a pilgrim, gallant and absurd, who is nonetheless confident of her country's noble power and endurance.

"Critical Evaluation" by Gordon Walters

Further Reading

Bailey, Blake. *Cheever: A Life*. New York: Alfred A. Knopf, 2009. Presents a thoroughly researched account of Cheever's life and paradoxical character.

Bosha, Francis J., comp. *John Cheever: A Reference Guide*. Boston: G. K. Hall, 1981. Offers excellent discussion of the inconsistent critical response to Cheever's fiction. Provides a comprehensive, fully annotated listing of works about Cheever, including reviews, articles, and interviews.

_____, ed. *The Critical Response to John Cheever*. Westport, Conn.: Greenwood Press, 1994. Presents a sampler of reviews and critical essays on all of Cheever's publications. Reprints five reviews of *The Wapshot Chronicle* and includes a new essay by Kenneth C. Mason on "tradition and desecration" in the two Wapshot books.

Collins, R. G., ed. *Critical Essays on John Cheever*. Boston: G. K. Hall, 1982. Collection of essays provides a good overview of the critical reception of Cheever's fiction. Reprints many of the most important and influential reviews and essays, some in revised form. A new essay by Samuel Coale on Cheever's "romancer's art" is especially noteworthy.

Donaldson, Scott. *John Cheever: A Biography*. New York: Random House, 1988. Presents a richly detailed, objective, sympathetic account of Cheever's life and work. Discusses the publication and reception of *The Wapshot Chronicle*, in which, Donaldson asserts, "Cheever distilled in one book the accumulated vitality of two decades."

Hunt, George W. *John Cheever: The Hobgoblin Company of Love*. Grand Rapids, Mich.: Wm. B. Eerdmans, 1983. Provides informative summaries of the plots of Cheever's novels and examines the works in terms of Cheever's Christian perspective.

Meanor, Patrick. *John Cheever Revisited*. New York: Twayne, 1995. The first book-length study of Cheever to make use of his journals and letters published in the late 1980's and early 1990's. Focuses on how Cheever created a mythopoeic world in his novels and stories. Includes three chapters analyzing the Wapshot novels, *Bullet Park*, and Cheever's other novels.

Simon, Linda. "Bewildering Love: John Cheever and the Legacy of Abandonment." In *Naming the Father: Legacies, Genealogies, and Explorations of Fatherhood in Modern and Contemporary Literature*, edited by Eva Paulino Bueno, Terry Caesar, and William Hummel. Lanham, Md.: Lexington Books, 2000. Discusses how Cheever's poor relationship with his father influenced his concept of fatherhood and the representation of fatherhood in his fiction. Discusses Leander Wapshot as a portrait of Cheever's father.

The Wapshot Scandal

Author: John Cheever (1912-1982)
First published: 1964
Type of work: Novel
Type of plot: Satire
Time of plot: Early 1960's
Locale: St. Botolphs, Massachusetts; Proxmire Manor, a Westchester suburb; Talifer, a missile research base

Principal characters:
HONORA WAPSHOT, matriarch of the Wapshot clan, a Yankee individualist, and an anachronism in the modern world
COVERLY WAPSHOT, her good-hearted, well-meaning cousin, a public relations worker at the Talifer Missile Site
BETSEY WAPSHOT, his wife, a woman of whims
MOSES WAPSHOT, another cousin, a stockholder and an alcoholic
MELISSA WAPSHOT, his wife, a modern Circe disguised as a suburban matron
EMILE CRANMER, the grocery boy who becomes Melissa's lover
DR. LEMUEL CAMERON, the atomic scientist in charge of the Talifer Missile Site
MR. APPLEGATE, the rector of Christ Church in St. Botolphs, also an alcoholic
GERTRUDE LOCKHART, a Proxmire Manor matron driven to drunkenness, promiscuity, and suicide by the failure of her household appliances
NORMAN JOHNSON, an agent of the Internal Revenue Service

The Story:

Honora Wapshot is an eccentric spinster and the septuagenarian guardian of the Wapshot treasure trove, oldest living descendant of a family that settled in the town of St. Botolphs, Massachusetts, in the seventeenth century. Honora supervises—but mainly underwrites with quarterly checks from a trust fund—the lives of her two young cousins, Moses and Coverly Wapshot. The two brothers have lost both their mother, Sarah, and their father, Leander, who drowned while swimming.

After a Christmas visit to Honora during which he is haunted by the ghost of his high-minded father, Coverly travels west. He returns to a world that would have baffled his father—the Talifer Missile Site. At this top-secret complex of experimental laboratories and space-travel equipment, some irrevocable error by a personnel-selecting machine has recently placed Coverly in the department of public relations, although he was trained for computer programming. He lives in Talifer with his wife, Betsey, and their son, Binxey, but their social life in the community is a little bleak. One day Betsey, after watching with bland indifference as a neighbor falls to his death on a cement terrace, neglects to notify any-

one because of her vague fear that she might violate security regulations. Coming home one day, Coverly learns that their garbage pail has been taken by a neighbor, and Coverly and the neighbor's husband come to blows and bites over the incident. Shortly afterward, Betsey and Coverly attempt to meet their neighbors (who have never called on them since their arrival) by inviting twenty-five people to a cocktail party; the plan is aborted, however, when no one appears. Betsey is shattered, and her reaction takes the form of a lasting resentment of Coverly, whom she blames for making her live in Talifer.

Through a strange accident of circumstance, Coverly is offered a position on the personal staff of Dr. Lemuel Cameron, the egomaniacal titan of the missile complex. Coverly, however, is entirely at the mercy of Cameron's caprice and soon discovers that he is nothing more than a chauffeur for the great man. Also, beneath the surface of Cameron's brilliance and cultural pretensions (he is capable of quoting a little poetry) lies the viciousness of a man who professes a belief in the blessedness of the universe but who talks with perfect equanimity of the destruction of the world. Cameron also suffers agonies of lust that can be satisfied only by a mistress in Rome, beats his subordinates in ferocious outbursts of temper, and has driven his son to insanity by practicing hideous extremes of cruelty in the name of discipline. In a short time, therefore, Coverly finds that he has hitched his wagon to a rather sinister star.

When Coverly's security clearance at the missile site is withdrawn because of Honora's delinquency on her federal income tax, he expects that Cameron will get him reinstated. When he goes for that purpose to Washington, where Cameron is being questioned by a congressional committee, Coverly witnesses a rather startling phenomenon: As a result of Cameron's savage temperament, his own security clearance is withdrawn.

Moses Wapshot has trouble with his work but far more trouble with his wife, Melissa. He works at a brokerage house (presumably in New York City), and the couple lives with their son in an affluent suburban cocoon called Proxmire Manor, where the only thing that occupies the police is the memory that once, several years prior to the time of the novel, a woman was arrested for tearing up a parking ticket. The community makes a pretense of maintaining rigid moral standards. Melissa quickly learns, for example, that a certain couple is being expelled from Proxmire Manor because the wife has been flagrantly promiscuous, notably with grocery boys and deliverymen. Melissa is bored with such standards, and she becomes a little unhinged when she stumbles across "evidence" of lesbianism at a local dance that evening. Shortly thereafter, she develops a fondness and then a passion for Emile Cranmer, the boy who delivers her groceries. She seduces him without much difficulty. They begin with a weekend at her house in Nantucket, followed by rendezvous in Boston, in New York, and, eventually, in a little shack outside the town of Proxmire Manor.

Emile engages in the affair with little compunction; Melissa's money buys him food to satisfy an insatiable appetite and supplies him with expensive baubles, such as an eight-hundred-dollar sapphire ring. Melissa pays much more than money to maintain the affair. After meeting Emile for the third time, she is tortured with remorse and seeks release in drunkenness. When she goes to a doctor for a physical examination, she becomes so aroused that she ends up having sex with him. As a last resort, she seeks the counsel of the minister, who does nothing but refer her to the town psychiatrist. Melissa, however, will not settle for the explanation that she is simply sick (and therefore irresponsible). She has only one place left to go—back to Emile.

Moses learns of his wife's infidelity from Emile's mother. The impact of the news is explosive: He nearly strangles his wife, then he leaves his home and turns to drink and dissipation. Through a series of bizarre and elaborate maneuvers, Melissa manages to meet Emile in Italy, where she has gone with her son. She buys Emile at an auction in Ladros for a hundred thousand lire; they retire to her luxurious villa, and they are last seen together in Rome. For his part, Moses abandons himself completely to sex and alcohol. On Christmas Eve, at the end of the novel, Coverly finds him in the upstairs room of the St. Botolphs hotel drunkenly wallowing in the embrace of an equally inebriated widow. Moses goes home with Coverly to Honora's house, but the next morning he shuts himself in a closet full of bourbon.

During all of this, Honora has been steadily losing her grip. She seems at first incapable of any serious wrong, but then she learns that because she has never paid any federal income tax, she faces a criminal indictment. Her friend Judge Beasley recommends that she take her money out of the bank and leave the country. She follows his advice and decides on a ship to Europe, but this move is scarcely the end of her troubles. On the ship she is flattered by the attentions of a nice-mannered young man who helps her to get around the decks; when he tells her that he is a stowaway, she arranges for him to be fed regularly in her cabin, and she develops enough interest in him to be capable of jealousy when she sees him in the company of another woman. One morning, however, in the early hours, he attempts to steal her money belt, and she strikes him over the head with a brass lamp. She thinks at first that he is dead, but he survives the blow and pursues his calling elsewhere. Before the ship docks at Naples, Honora sees him strolling by with another aging victim on his arm. Her only way of releasing her fury is by striking out at the entire ship, which she does through the simple expedient of plugging her curling iron into an outlet in the bathroom of her cabin. This, as she has already discovered, has the effect of blowing out the ship's generators.

Honora enters the Bay of Naples, therefore, on a ship in darkness. In Italy, she finds little to brighten her world. She visits the pope in the Vatican, but his rather precarious command of the English language frustrates communication between them and only sharpens her nostalgic yearning for the familiar territory of St. Botolphs. A short time later, her wish to return is satisfied, but in a cruelly unexpected way. Norman Johnson, an agent of the Internal Revenue Service who had visited her first in St. Botolphs, now comes to her calmly and politely with extradition papers, a criminal indictment, and an order for the confiscation of all her property. She returns to St. Botolphs immediately and spends the last of her days immured in her old house, consuming nothing but bourbon. Shortly before Christmas, she is pronounced dead of starvation. She leaves Coverly with the command to hold a Christmas dinner in her house for the inmates of the local institute for the blind. Coverly executes her wish.

Critical Evaluation:

In *The Wapshot Chronicle*, John Cheever tells the story of the eccentric Wapshot clan from the once-prosperous seaport town of St. Botolphs, modeled on Quincy, Massachusetts, where Cheever grew up. Autobiographical to a degree, the novel traces the coming-of-age of the two sons against the many blows their father suffers to his self-esteem in his relations with his wife, who starts her own business, and his cousin Honora, the spinster-matriarch who controls the Wapshot inheritance. *The Wapshot Scandal* takes up the sons' and their elderly cousin's fortunes some years later. Both novels were generally well received; *The Wapshot Chronicle* earned for its author a National Book Award, and *The Wapshot Scandal* received a Howells Medal. Reviewers and critics, however, continued to wonder whether Cheever the short-story writer possessed the right temperament and talent to write a novel that was more coherent and less episodic. His reputation as a writer of short, relatively realistic fiction depicting generally middle-class, often suburban characters seemed sufficient reason to judge his work according to such standards.

Cheever, however, was not trying to write according to such standards; he was adapting the conventions of nineteenth century novels such as George Eliot's *Middlemarch* (1871-1872), Sarah Wapshot's favorite reading, to meet the demands of life in the mid-twentieth century. Far from proving narrative mismanagement on Cheever's part, the multiple plots of both Wapshot books, *The Wapshot Scandal* in particular, suggest the psychological restlessness of his nomadic characters. Even as Cheever creates a soothing, nostalgic sense of distance and wholeness (for example, by using the phrase "at the time of which I am writing"), he undercuts it by making this distant past closely resemble the reader's own present and by deploying transitional phrases ("in the meantime" and "at about this time") that suggest randomness rather than causality, comic coincidences rather than cosmic connections. As Cheever undercuts the novel's seeming realism by interjecting elements of farce and fantasy, he undermines the ceremoniousness that figures so importantly in *The Wapshot Chronicle*, which begins with an Independence Day parade and ends with Leander's funeral. Cheever's choosing to frame *The Wapshot Scandal* with two ambivalently described Christmas scenes makes the book's ceremoniousness seem a little too pat, too self-consciously

contrived, leaving the novel poised between celebration and satire. Haunted at the beginning by Leander's ghost and sounding more hollow than hallowed at the end, *The Wapshot Scandal* winds down in three progressively shorter parts of 160, 100, and 47 pages.

"Oh Father, Father, Father, why have you come back?" Coverly asks early in the novel. Although this comic Hamlet is not charged with avenging a father's murder most foul, there is something rotten nevertheless. *The Wapshot Chronicle* ends with Leander's "Advice to My Sons," but *The Wapshot Scandal* begins with Coverly wondering whether he has any counsel to give his son at a time when the world is "changing with incomprehensible velocity" and "total disaster seemed to be [so much a] part of the universal imagination" that even the Vatican wants a missile. As in Cheever's 1961 story "The Brigadier and the Golf Widow," fears about nuclear destruction are the outward manifestation of fears of a more inward kind, fears that the modern condition does not so much evoke as exacerbate. No longer a moral touchstone, the old river town of St. Botolphs (the first of Cheever's novelistic metaphors for confinement) has been supplanted by suburban life (his second). Suburbia is represented by Talifer, a security-conscious residential development for twenty thousand people attached to a missile site and research center, and Proxmire Manor, an upscale New York suburb where putting up a for-sale sign is considered a subversive act. Cheever's rendering of American social practices is cartoonish yet full of insights into the mid-twentieth century epidemic of social and psychological malaise.

"Loneliness was one thing, and she knew how sweet it could make light and company seem, but boredom was something else, and why, in this most prosperous and equitable land, should everyone seem so bored and disappointed?" Melissa's question is at the heart of this novel and much of Cheever's fiction as well as his life. Part of the reason for this disappointment is that the world has grown not only more prosperous but "more and more preposterous," artificial and alienating. Another part of the reason is the immense chasm separating the characters' dreams and their actual existences. Emile, for example, "wanted something that would correspond to his sense that life was imposing; something that would confirm his feeling that, as he stood at the window of Narobi's grocery store watching the men and women on the sidewalk and the stream of clouds in the sky, the procession he saw was a majestic one." Melissa "had wanted to bring into her life the freshness of a journey," but early in her affair with Emile she realizes that she "had achieved nothing but a galling sense of moral shabbiness." What Melissa experiences so acutely Cheever often records in a comically deflating language targeted not at the characters' aspirations per se but at the ways they seek to realize or articulate those aspirations.

Spiritual striving takes various, generally unsatisfying, often debased forms: sex, suburban living, decorum (which can be either a mode of hope or a form of hypocrisy), and shopping. The supermarkets in *The Wapshot Scandal* may not be as Dantesque as the one in "The Death of Justina" (1961) or as massive as the Buy Brite in *Oh, What a Paradise It Seems* (1982), but they are pervasive and serve an important thematic function. Melissa figuratively shops for love at the family-owned Narobi's, soon to be driven out of business by "the new market on the hill" (a description that ironically echoes John Winthrop's admonition to his fellow Puritans in 1630 to be "as a city on a hill," "a model of Christian charity"). In Italy, Melissa, "grieving, bewildered by the blows life has dealt her," tries to fight off the "Roman blues" by shopping at the Supra-Marketto Americano. If this modern Ophelia appears "no less dignified a figure of grief than any other," as the narrator contends (only half-facetiously, one suspects), it is because she is engaged in her own oddly angled way in "the engulfing struggle with good and evil." She intuitively understands, as do the other characters in this richly comic yet strangely disturbing novel, what a certain old senator means when he says to Dr. Cameron, "We possess Promethean powers but don't we lack the awe, but humility, that primitive man brought to the sacred fire?"

"Critical Evaluation" by Robert A. Morace

Further Reading

Bosha, Francis J., comp. *John Cheever: A Reference Guide.* Boston: G. K. Hall, 1981. Presents excellent discussion of the inconsistent critical response to Cheever's fiction. Provides a comprehensive, fully annotated listing of works about Cheever, including reviews, articles, and interviews.

_____, ed. *The Critical Response to John Cheever.* Westport, Conn.: Greenwood Press, 1994. Sampler of reviews and critical essays on all of Cheever's publications includes five reprinted reviews of *The Wapshot Scandal* as well as a new essay by Kenneth C. Mason on "tradition and desecration" in the two Wapshot books.

Collins, R. G., ed. *Critical Essays on John Cheever.* Boston: G. K. Hall, 1982. Offers a good overview of the critical reception of Cheever's fiction. Reprints many of the most important and influential reviews and essays, some in revised form, including Frederick Karl on pastoral, Beatrice Greene on Cheever's vision as an effect of style, and Frederick Bracher on comedy. A new essay by Samuel Coale on Cheever's "romancer's art" is especially noteworthy.

Donaldson, Scott. *John Cheever: A Biography.* New York: Random House, 1988. Fair-minded and richly detailed biography offers one of the fullest and most objective, but nevertheless sympathetic, accounts of Cheever's life and work available. Includes information on the publication and reception of *The Wapshot Scandal.*

Hunt, George W. *John Cheever: The Hobgoblin Company of Love.* Grand Rapids, Mich.: Wm. B. Eerdmans, 1983. Provides informative summaries of Cheever's plots and criticism of his works before offering critical readings in terms of Cheever's Christian perspective.

Meanor, Patrick. *John Cheever Revisited.* New York: Twayne, 1995. The first book-length study of Cheever to make use of his journals and letters published in the late 1980's and early 1990's. Focuses on how Cheever created a mythopoeic world in his novels and stories. Includes three chapters analyzing the Wapshot novels, *Bullet Park,* and Cheever's other novels.

Simon, Linda. "Bewildering Love: John Cheever and the Legacy of Abandonment." In *Naming the Father: Legacies, Genealogies, and Explorations of Fatherhood in Modern and Contemporary Literature,* edited by Eva Paulino Bueno, Terry Caesar, and William Hummel. Lanham, Md.: Lexington Books, 2000. Discusses how Cheever's poor relationship with his father influenced his concept of fatherhood and the representation of fatherhood in his fiction. Discusses Leander Wapshot as a portrait of Cheever's father.

War and Peace

Author: Leo Tolstoy (1828-1910)
First published: Voyna i mir, 1865-1869 (English
    translation, 1886)
Type of work: Novel
Type of plot: Historical
Time of plot: 1805-1813
Locale: Russia

Principal characters:
PIERRE BEZUHOV, the illegitimate son of a wealthy count
NATASHA ROSTOVA, the beautiful daughter of a well-to-do
    Moscow family
NIKOLAY ROSTOV, Natasha's older brother
ANDREY BOLKONSKY, a wealthy Russian prince
HÉLÈNE KURAGINA BEZUHOVA, Pierre's beautiful and
    immoral wife
ANATOLE KURAGIN, Hélène's brother
PRINCESS MARYA BOLKONSKAYA, Andrey's sister
OLD PRINCE BOLKONSKY, Andrey's tyrannical father
KUTUZOV, commander in chief of the Russian Army,
    appointed in August, 1812
NAPOLEON BONAPARTE, emperor of the French

The Story:

In 1805, it is evident to most well-informed Russians that war with Napoleon is inevitable. Austria and Russia join forces at the Battle of Austerlitz, where they are soundly defeated by the French. In the highest Russian society, however, life goes on as though nothing of tremendous import were impending. After all, it is really only by a political formality that Russia has joined with Austria. The fact that one day Napoleon might threaten the gates of Russia seems ridiculous. Soirees and balls are held, old women gossip, and young women fall in love. War, though inevitable, is being waged on foreign soil and is, therefore, of little importance.

The attraction that military service holds for the young noblemen of Russia is understandable enough, for the Russian army has always offered excellent opportunities for ambitious, politically inclined young men. The army provides a wholesome release for their energies. Young Nikolay Rostov, for example, joins the hussars simply because he feels drawn to that way of life. His family idolizes him because of his loyalty to the czar, because of his courage, and because he is so handsome in his uniform. Natasha, his sister, weeps over him, and Sonya, his cousin, promptly falls in love with him.

By contrast, Pierre Bezuhov, a friend of the Rostov family, is looked upon as somewhat of a boor. He has just returned from Paris, where he studied at the university, and he has not yet made up his mind what to do with his life. He will not join the army, for he sees no sense in a military career. His father gives him a liberal allowance, and he spends it frivolously at gambling. In truth, he seems like a lost man. He starts long arguments, shouting loudly in quiet drawing rooms, and then suddenly lapses into sullen silence. He is barely tolerated at soirees until his father dies and leaves him a fortune; then, suddenly, he becomes popular. He attributes his rise to some new personality development of his own, and he is no longer sullen; rather, he loves everyone, and it is quite clear that everyone loves him. His most dogged follower is Prince Vassily Kuragin, the father of a beautiful, unmarried daughter, Hélène, who is recognized everywhere as a prospective leader of St. Petersburg society. Pierre is forced into marrying her by the crafty prince, who knows a good catch when he sees one. The marriage, however, is not a success.

Pierre Bezuhov's closest friend is Prince Andrey Bolkonsky, an arrogant, somewhat cynical man who despises his wife, Lise. The "Little Princess," as Lise is called, is pregnant, but Prince Andrey can endure the bondage of domesticity no longer. When he receives a commission in the army, he leaves Lise at the family estate, Bleak Hills, in the care of his sister Marya and his tyrannical old father and goes off to war. During his absence, Princess Lise gives birth to a son but dies during childbirth. Prince Andrey returns after the Battle of Austerlitz to find himself free once more, but he enjoys no feeling of satisfaction in his freedom. He seeks out Pierre and turns to his friend for answers to some of the eternal questions of loneliness and despair that torture him.

Pierre has joined the brotherhood of freemasons and, through his association with the group, has arrived at a philosophy of life that he sincerely believes to be the only true philosophy. Had Pierre realized that the order initiated him solely because of his wealth, he would never have adopted the members' ideals. Pierre restores some of Prince Andrey's lost courage, however, by means of his wild if unreasoning enthusiasm. In the belief that he is now an unselfish, free individual, Pierre frees his peasants and sets about improving his estate; having absolutely no sense of business administration, he loses a great deal of money. Finally, with his affairs in hopeless disorder, he leaves an overseer in charge and retires to Bleak Hills and Prince Andrey's sane company.

Nikolay Rostov is in the thick of the fighting. Napoleon overcame the Prussian forces at Jena and reached Berlin in October, 1806. The Russians once more go to the assistance of their neighbors, and the two opposing armies meet in a terrible battle at Eylau in February, 1807. In June, Nikolay enters the campaign at Friedland, and when the Russians are beaten, he naïvely thinks the war is over. Napoleon and Czar Alexander sign the Peace of Tilsit, and Napoleon, who possesses a remarkable gift for flattery, promises, with no intention of keeping his word, that Russia will be given a free hand with Turkey and Finland. For two years, Nikolay enjoys all the privileges of his post in the army without having to endure any of the risks. Napoleon has gone to Spain.

After having served in minor skirmishes as an adjutant under General Kutuzov, leader of the Russian forces, Prince Andrey returns to the country. He has some business affairs to straighten out with Count Rostov, marshal of his district, and so he goes to the Rostov estate at Otradnoe. There Andrey almost immediately falls under the spell of Count Rostov's lovely young daughter, Natasha. He fancies himself in love as he has never loved before. Once again, he turns to Pierre for advice. Pierre, however, has experienced an unfortunate quarrel with his wife, Hélène. They are now separated, and Pierre has fought a senseless duel with an innocent man because he suspected his wife of being unfaithful. At the sight of Prince Andrey so hopelessly in love, Pierre's great heart is touched. He has always been fond of Natasha, whom he has known since childhood, and the match seems to him ideal. With love once more flowing through his heart, he takes his wife back, feeling very virtuous at his own generosity, and he encourages Prince Andrey in his suit.

Natasha has ignored previous offers of marriage, but when the dashing and wealthy Prince Andrey comes on the scene, she loses her heart to him instantly. He asks her parents for her hand, and they immediately consent to the match, an excellent one from their point of view. When Prince Andrey breaks the news to his quarrelsome and dictatorial old father, however, the ancient prince says that he will not give his blessing until a year has elapsed. He feels that Natasha has too little money and is much too young to take charge of Prince Andrey's home and his son. Marya, Prince

Andrey's sister, also disapproves of the match, for she is jealous of her brother's fiancé.

Natasha is heartbroken but agrees to wait a year; Prince Andrey keeps their betrothal a secret, in order, as he says, to let her have complete freedom. Natasha goes to Moscow to visit a family friend, and there her freedom is too complete. One night she attends the opera with Pierre's wife, Hélène, who is now recognized as an important social leader; there she meets Hélène's disreputable brother, Anatole. Unknown to Natasha, Anatole had been forced to marry a peasant girl whom he had ruined. The young rake now determines to conquer Natasha. Aided by his unscrupulous sister, he forces his suit, and Natasha becomes confused. She loves Prince Andrey, but he has joined the army again and she never sees him; she also loves Anatole, who is becoming more insistent every day. At last, she agrees to run away with Anatole and marry him. Anatole arranges with a defrocked priest to have a mock ceremony performed. On the night set for the elopement, however, Natasha's host discovers the plan, and Natasha is confined to her room. Unfortunately, she has already written to Prince Andrey's sister to ask to be relieved of her betrothal vows.

When Pierre hears of the scandal, he forces Anatole to leave town. He then goes to see Natasha. Strangely, he is the only person whom she trusts and to whom she can speak freely. She looks upon him as if he were an older uncle, and she is charmed with his gruff friendliness. Pierre feels attracted to Natasha in a way he knows he should not be, as he is not free, but he manages to let her know that he will be a friend to her, and she is pleased by his attentions. She soon begins to recover from her misfortune, but she will never again be the lively, frivolous girl whom Prince Andrey had loved.

Natasha's actions have dealt Prince Andrey a terrible blow to his pride, but in the army there are many engrossing matters to take his attention away from himself. By 1810, the Franco-Russian alliance has gradually dissolved. When France threatens to free Russia of responsibility for Poland, the czar finally understands that Napoleon's promises meant little. The dapper little French emperor has forsaken Russia in favor of Austria as the center of his European domination. He marries Marie Louise, and, in 1812, with his eyes unmistakably fixed on Moscow, he crosses the Nieman River. From June to August, Napoleon enjoys an almost uninterrupted march to Smolensk.

In Smolensk, he finds burned and wrecked houses. The city is deserted. This marks the beginning of fierce opposition. Old General Kutuzov, former leader of the army of the East and now in complete charge of the Russian forces, is determined to halt the French advance. His tactics, however, are the very reason the Russians fail to win a decisive victory. Instead of attempting to halt the French, he might have succeeded by drawing them deeper and deeper into the country, lengthening their lines of communication and cutting them off in the rear. It is odd, too, that Napoleon, in attempting to complete his march, also lessens his chances for victory.

Battle succeeds battle, with heavy losses on both sides, before Napoleon finally leads his forces to Borodino. There the most senseless battle in the whole campaign is fought. The Russians, determined to hold Moscow, which is only a short distance away, lose nearly their whole army. The French forces dwindle in proportion, but it is clear that the Russians have gotten the worst of the battle. General Kutuzov, bitter and war-weary, decides, against his will, that the army cannot hold Moscow. Again a triumphant Napoleon marches into a deserted city.

Prince Andrey has been gravely wounded at Borodino. The Rostovs are already abandoning their estate to move into the interior when many wagons loaded with wounded soldiers are brought to the house for shelter. Among these is Prince Andrey himself. Natasha nurses him and sends for Marya, his sister, and his son, Nikolushka. Old Prince Bolkonsky, suffering from the shock of having French soldiers almost upon his doorstep, dies of a stroke. Nikolay manages to move Marya and the boy to safer quarters. Although Prince Andrey welcomes his sister, it is evident that he no longer expects to recover. Natasha nurses him tenderly, and they once more declare their love for each other. When his wound festers, Prince Andrey knows that the end is near; soon after, he dies in his sleep. United in tragedy, Marya and Natasha become close friends; young Nikolay finds Prince Andrey's sister attractive.

Pierre Bezuhov decides to remain in Moscow. Fired with thoughts of becoming a national hero, he hits upon the plan of assassinating Napoleon. He is captured as a prisoner of war, however, when he attempts to rescue a Russian woman who is being molested by French soldiers.

Napoleon's army completely disintegrates in Moscow. After waiting in vain for peace terms from the czar, Napoleon decides to abandon Moscow and head back to France. His soldiers—a ragged, irresponsible, pillaging group, once part of the most powerful army in the world—gather up their booty, throw away their supplies, and start off on the road back to Smolensk as winter comes on, taking prisoners with them. Pierre Bezuhov, luckily, is at the outset robust and healthy. Traveling with the other prisoners, he learns from experience that happiness can consist of merely being warm and having enough to eat. His privations age and mature him.

He learns responsibility and gains courage, and he develops a sense of humor at the irony of his plight. His simplicity and even temperament make him a favorite with the French and the Russians alike.

On the road to Smolensk, the French forces become completely demoralized. Cossacks charge out of the forests and cut the lines, taking countless French prisoners and rescuing the Russian captives. Many Frenchmen desert; others fall ill and die on the road. Pierre is freed at last, and he returns to Orel, where he falls ill with fever. Later he learns of the deaths of Prince Andrey and his own wife. Hélène had died in St. Petersburg after a short illness. These shocks, coupled with the news of the defeat of the French, seem to deprive him of all feeling. When he finally recovers, he is overwhelmed with a joyous sense of freedom of soul, a sense that he has at last found himself, that he knows himself for what he really is. He knows the sheer joy of being alive, and he is humble and grateful. He has discovered a faith in God that he never knew before.

Pierre returns to Moscow and renews his friendships with Marya Bolkonskaya and the Rostovs. Once more Natasha charms him, and Pierre suddenly realizes that she is no longer a child. He loves her now, as always, and so when the opportunity presents itself, he dutifully asks Natasha's parents for her hand in marriage. The two marry and go on to be very happy together. Natasha is an efficient wife who dominates her husband, much to the amusement of their friends; Pierre loves her and respects her because she knows how to take charge of everything. She manages his estates as well as their household.

Nikolay, though not entirely sure that he loves Marya, knows that to marry her would be a wise thing. The Rostovs are poor now, and the old count has left his affairs in a deplorable state. At the insistence of his mother, Nikolay finally proposes to Marya, and the two families are joined. The union proves happier than Nikolay had expected, and he and Marya adopt Prince Andrey's son, Nikolushka.

Pierre and Natasha eventually have four fine children of whom they are very proud. Although society thinks that Natasha carries her devotion to her husband and children to an extreme, Natasha and Pierre are happier than they have ever been before, and they find their life together to be a fulfillment of all their dreams.

Critical Evaluation:

Leo Tolstoy's *War and Peace* is a panorama of Russian life in that active period of history known as the Napoleonic era. The structure of the novel indicates that Tolstoy was not concerned with plot, setting, or even individual people, as such; rather, his purpose was to show that the continuity of life in history is eternal. Each human life has its influence on history, and the developments of youth and age, and war and peace, are so interrelated that in the simplest patterns of social behavior vast implications are recognizable. Tolstoy wanted to present history as it is influenced by every conceivable human force. To do this, he needed to create not a series of simple, well-linked incidents but an evolution of events and personalities. Each character changes and affects others; these others influence yet others, and gradually, imperceptibly, the historical framework of the nation changes.

War and Peace is a moving record of historical progress, and the dual themes of this vast novel—age and youth, war and peace—are shown as simultaneous developments of history. Tolstoy wrote both this novel and *Anna Karenina* (1875-1877; English translation, 1886), two of the greatest works of fiction in Russian literature, when he was at the height of his powers as a writer. He enjoyed a happy marriage, and he was busy managing his country estate as well as writing. His life had a healthy, even exuberant, balance between physical and intellectual activities. *War and Peace*, in particular, reflects the passionate and wide-ranging tastes and energies of this period of his life—before domestic strife and profound spiritual conversion led him to turn away from the world as well as from art. The novel is huge in size and scope; it presents a long list of characters and covers a splendid variety of scenes and settings. At the same time, however, it is carefully organized and controlled.

The basic controlling device involves movement between clusters of characters surrounding the major characters Natasha, Kutuzov, Andrey, and Pierre. The second ordering device is thematic and involves Tolstoy's lifelong investigation of the question, What is natural? This theme is offered in the first chapter at Anna Scherer's party, where readers encounter the artificiality of St. Petersburg society and meet the two chief seekers of the natural, Andrey and Pierre. Both Andrey and Pierre love Natasha, who is an instinctive embodiment of the natural in particularly Russian terms. Kutuzov is also an embodiment of Russian naturalness; only he can lead the Russian soldiers in a successful war against the French. The Russian character of Tolstoy's investigation of the natural, or the essential, is the main reason *War and Peace* is referred to as a national epic. Tolstoy's characters, however, also represent all people.

Natasha's group of characters centers on the Rostov family, and the novel is, among many things, a searching study of family life. Count Ilya Rostov, a landowning nobleman, is a sympathetic portrait of a carefree, warmhearted, wealthy man. His wife is somewhat anxious and less generous in spirit, but they are happily married, and the family as a whole is harmonious. Natasha's brothers and sisters are rendered with great vividness: the passionate, energetic Nikolay; the cold, formal Vera; the youthful Petya; the sweet, compliant Sonya, cousin to Natasha and used by Tolstoy as a foil to her. Natasha herself is bursting with life. She is willful, passionate, proud, humorous, and capable of great growth and change. Like all the major characters, she seeks the natural. She is the natural; her instincts are right and true. All of book 7, particularly chapter 7, when she sings and dances, dramatizes the essential Russianness of Natasha's nature. Her nearly consummated love affair with Anatole Kuragin, her loss of Andrey, and her final happy marriage to Pierre show how intensely life-giving she is. One of the great experiences of reading *War and Peace* is found in witnessing her slow transition from slim, exuberant youth to thick-waisted motherhood. For Tolstoy, Natasha can do nothing that is not natural and right.

Kutuzov stands above the generals who cluster about him. Forgotten at the start of the war, he is called into action when all else seems to have failed. Unlike the other generals, many of them German, Kutuzov knows that battles are not won in the staff room by virtue of elaborate planning but by the spirit of the soldiers who actually do the fighting. Kutuzov alone knows that one must wait for that moment when the soldiers' spirits are totally committed to the battle. He knows that the forces of war are greater than any one man can control and that one must wait upon events and know when not to act as well as when to act. His naturalness is opposed to Napoleon's artificiality. A brilliant strategist and planner, Napoleon believes that he controls events. His pride and vanity are self-blinding; he cannot see that if he invades Russia, he is doomed. Kutuzov's victory over Napoleon is a victory of the natural and the humble, for he is, after all, a man of the people. Furthermore, the figure of Kutuzov is very closely related to Tolstoy's philosophy of historical change and necessity.

The characters of Andrey and Pierre probably represent two sides of Tolstoy, the rational-spiritual and the passionate-mystical, although these labels are far too simple. Andrey's group of characters centers on the Bolkonsky family: the merciless, autocratic, but brilliant General Bolkonsky, Andrey's father, and his sister Princess Marya, who is obedient, pious, and loving and who blossoms when she marries Nikolay Rostov. When readers first see Andrey, he is bored and even appears cynical; yet, like Pierre, he is searching for an answer to life, and he undergoes a series of awakenings that bring him closer to the natural. The first awakening occurs when he is wounded at Austerlitz and glimpses infinity beyond the blue sky; the second, at his wife's death; the third, when he falls in love with Natasha; and the last, when he dies. In all of these instances, Andrey moves closer to what he conceives of as the essential. This state of mind involves a repudiation of the world and its petty concerns and passions. In all but one of these instances, death is involved. Indeed, Andrey's perception of the natural is closely related to his acceptance of death. He comes to see death as the doorway to infinity and glory and not as a fearful black hole. Death becomes part of the natural rhythm, a cycle that promises spiritual rebirth.

Pierre's group is composed of St. Petersburg socialites and decadents: the Kuragin family, comprising the smooth, devious Prince Vassily; his son, the rake Anatole, and daughter, the beautiful, corrupt Hélène, Pierre's first wife; the rake Dolokhov; and finally, in Pierre's third or fourth transformation, the peasant Platon Karataev. Unlike Andrey, Pierre takes an approach to life that seems almost strategically disordered and open—he embraces all forms of life passionately and hungrily. Compared to Andrey, with his rigorous and discriminating mind, Pierre seems hopelessly naïve and chaotic.

Pierre, however, even more than Natasha, is capable of vital and creative change. As Andrey seems fitted to perceive intimations of essences beyond the world, Pierre seems fitted to find his essences in the world. He shucks off his mistaken connection with Hélène and her family and experiences the first of his own awakenings in the conversion to freemasonry (one of several interesting "false" conversions in the novel, one other being Natasha's after she is rejected by Andrey). Pierre, too, learns from death, both in his duel with Dolokhov and in his observations of the battle of Borodino. His two most important awakenings, however, occur in his love for Natasha and in his experience as a prisoner of the French. In the latter instance, he encounters the harmonious, perfectly round (whole) peasant Karataev, who teaches him to accept all things—even death—in good grace and composure of spirit. When Natasha encounters Pierre after he has had this experience, she rightly recognizes that he has been transformed. All that is superficial and nonessential is gone from him. Their eventual marriage is a union of two vital human beings tempered by suffering. At the end, there is more than a hint that Pierre is involved in efforts on the part of the aristocracy to modify the ossified system of government under the czars. Life and change go on.

War and Peace, perhaps beyond any other work, shows the advantages of the long novel. Readers of *War and Peace* feel a sense of space and a sense of change through the passage of time that are impossible to transmit so vividly in shorter fiction. This great novel reveals the beauty and injustice, the size and complexity, of life itself.

"Critical Evaluation" by Benjamin Nyce

Further Reading

Citati, Pietro. *Tolstoy*. Translated by Raymond Rosenthal. New York: Schocken Books, 1986. Gives a full explanation of Tolstoy's youth and background that led to the writing of his novels. A huge section is devoted to *War and Peace*, with attention to the work's portrayal of historical Russia. Provides sketches of the novel's major characters.

Clay, George R. *Tolstoy's Phoenix: From Method to Meaning in "War and Peace."* Evanston, Ill.: Northwestern University Press, 1998. Initially focuses on the literary techniques and structure of the novel, then demonstrates how these elements support the book's larger thematic meaning.

De Courcel, Martine. *Tolstoy: The Ultimate Reconciliation*. Translated by Peter Levi. New York: Charles Scribner's Sons, 1988. Comprehensive study explains the research Tolstoy conducted in order to write the historical novel *War and Peace* and his marital situation at the time he was writing it.

Feuer, Kathryn B. *Tolstoy and the Genesis of "War and Peace."* Edited by Robin Feuer Miller and Donna Tussing Orwin. Ithaca, N.Y.: Cornell University Press, 1996. Analyzes the numerous drafts of *War and Peace*, tracing the novel's development and the evolution of its characters. Discusses Tolstoy's original intention to make *War and Peace* the first volume in a trilogy of novels about the Decembrist movement.

Love, Jeff. *The Overcoming of History in "War and Peace."* New York: Rodopi, 2004. Argues that the novel is a great experiment in which Tolstoy deliberately "stretches the boundaries of narrative" because he is striving to "take up the infinite whole" and "subject it to human mastery."

Orwin, Donna Tussig, ed. *The Cambridge Companion to Tolstoy*. New York: Cambridge University Press, 2002. Collection of essays includes discussions of Tolstoy as a writer of popular literature, the development of his style and themes, his aesthetics, and the reception of his works in the twentieth century. Gary Morson provides an analysis of *War and Peace*.

Shklovsky, Viktor. *Energy of Delusion: A Book on Plot*. Translated by Shushan Avagyan. Champaign, Ill.: Dalkey Archive Press, 2007. English-language translation of the book that some scholars have called the greatest critical work on *War and Peace*. Shklovsky, a prominent Soviet literary critic who died in 1984, examines the form of the novel, what it was like to read the book in the 1980's, and many other aspects of the epic work.

Simmons, Ernest J. *Tolstoy.* London: Routledge & Kegan Paul, 1973. Focuses on Tolstoy as a major thinker of his time, a religious, social, and political reformer. Describes Tolstoy's childhood and his life as a writer and discusses the reception of *War and Peace* and its early criticism. Includes notes from Tolstoy's diary during the time he wrote *War and Peace.*

The War of the Mice and the Crabs

Author: Giacomo Leopardi (1798-1837)
First published: I paralipomeni della
batracomiomachia, 1842 (English translation, 1976)
Type of work: Poetry
Type of plot: Mock epic

Italians consider Giacomo Leopardi one of the great poets of the nineteenth century, although his work is relatively unknown in the English-speaking world. His life was short and bitter, and he was crippled by disease, usually in need of money, and cut off from the world around him. Most of the poetry for which he is praised is his lyric poetry, which is marked by the beauty, concreteness, and exactness of its language. Leopardi's language is, in itself, an assertion and creation of human value, yet in all of his work, both prose and poetry, he expresses a realistic, pessimistic view of human existence. Leopardi believed that human belief in happiness is an illusion: Happiness is not now, but always to come. This illusion of happiness and good applies not only to individual lives but also to human institutions.

Leopardi, a great scholar, wrote not only lyric poetry but also remarkable philosophic essays and political satires, one of which is the narrative poem *The War of the Mice and the Crabs.* This work came late in Leopardi's career, and originally even some of his closest supporters disapproved of it; one of them called it "a terrible book." It was so widely criticized because it is a scathing satire not only of the European intellectual and political world of the early nineteenth century but also of the rhetoric, pretensions, and posturings of those Italian patriots who wanted an independent, unified Italy. Italy at that time was a collection of small, often mutually antagonistic, states; most of the north, including Milan and Venice, was directly or indirectly controlled by the Austro-Hungarian Empire, which many Italians considered alien and uncivilized.

Leopardi was an Italian patriot, and two of his earliest poems were patriotic. He believed that Italy had been a leader in civilizing the world and perhaps could be again. He hated the emptiness of bluster, however, and thought that certain kinds of patriotism were simply refusals to face reality. He also believed that most political and social theories were intellectual daydreams.

The War of the Mice and the Crabs builds on the ancient Greek poem *The Batrachomyomachia,* once attributed to the poet Homer. The poem—the title literally means "the war of the frogs and the mice"—is a mock epic in the form of a beast fable, using animals in order to satirize the heroic values of the Homeric poems *Iliad* (c. 750 B.C.E.; English translation, 1611) and *Odyssey* (c. 725 B.C.E.; English translation, 1614). Leopardi's Italian title can be translated as "the additions to" (or "the things left out of") "the war of the frogs and the mice." He modernizes the satire in order to speak of Italy, its warring factions, and the overriding power of the intruding Austro-Hungarian Empire. At the same time, he comments on the political, historical, and universal theorizing that asserts order. The political world that Leopardi's poem depicts is essentially chaotic; the only thing that matters in the end is brute force. The natural world is also chaotic, purposeless, leading only to motionless death.

Leopardi's satire is found not solely in subject matter but also in form. For example, *The War of the Mice and the Crabs* is in cantos (longer divisions) and octaves (eight-line stanzas)—divisions and stanzas used by the Renaissance Italian writers of romantic epics, such as Ludovico Ariosto's *Orlando furioso* (1516, 1521, 1532; English translation, 1591). A number of later mock-epic poems deliberately used the same form in order to satirize the elevated tone of the standard romantic epic. Leopardi chose the form in order to emphasize the satirical note.

In the Greek poem, the mice attack the frogs to get revenge for the accidental drowning of their prince; they are winning the war when the gods decide that they do not want the frogs to be destroyed and so send an army of crabs to help the frogs. Leopardi's poem begins with the mice in frightened retreat from the terrible crabs. The king of the mice has been killed, and the mice are utterly demoralized.

The mice obviously represent the Italians, and the crabs represent the armies sent by the Austro-Hungarians, but there is no straightforward allegory here. The history is generalized, and only rarely can the reader identify what exact historical figures Leopardi had in mind in his leaders of the mice and the crabs. This is deliberate, for he is commenting on the political oppression and the foolish hopes common to many eras.

The mice finally notice that the crab army has stopped pursuing them. They regroup, elect a new leader, Rubatocchi (Chunk-Stealer), and decide to send an envoy to the crabs, choosing Count Leccafondi (Bottom-Licker) to ask why they have been attacked. There is a long characterization of Leccafondi, who represents the best of progressive thought but is essentially shallow because that thought is shallow. He arrives at the camp of the crabs, is taken to the headquarters of General Brancaforte (Strong-Claw), and tries to soothe the cruel crabs with his diplomatic skills. Brancaforte consults with his king, Senzacapo (Without-Head, or Headless)—representing Emperor Francis I of Austria-Hungary—who dictates harsh terms, including stationing troops in Rat City, the mice's capital. Indeed, the Austrians had troops in all of the major cities they had occupied. Brancaforte defends the crabs' actions by arguing that the crabs are right because they have power, although he seems to think that this is natural law.

Rat City is based on Naples, a city that Leopardi despised as corrupt and vicious. Here the poet digresses to a savage attack on the decay of European civilization. Meanwhile, the mice have elected a new king. Surprisingly, Rubatocchi had refused the throne, so the mice turn to Rodipane (Bread-Muncher), the son-in-law of the old king. This is acceptable to the crabs because the new king belongs to an established royal family. Here Leopardi mocks the readiness to believe that virtue resides in certain families.

Rodipane agrees to a constitution, but this is repellent to the crabs. The Austrian emperor and the other rulers of Europe had rejected the idea that a people have the right to elect their king. More important, they thought no king should agree to a constitution. Such acts imply that rulers can be enthroned and dethroned by the people, that they have no absolute right to their power.

In the opening of canto 4, Leopardi digresses again with an attack on a priori theories of human behavior, mocking romantic ideas of the natural human being destroyed by civilization and conservative ideas that a golden age was lost through human sinfulness. Leccafondi returns with the crabs' terms, which the mice reluctantly accept. Rodipane gives free cheese and polenta—bread and circuses—to the mice and gains popularity. The crabs set up their garrison, but the mice revive their prosperity and recover their courage. Leccafondi is named minister of the interior, and all seems well. The crabs, however, feel threatened. Emperor Senzacapo sends orders to the head of his garrison, Boccaferrato (Iron-Mouth), to order the mice to abrogate the constitution.

The mice resist and decide to fight, but as soon as the crab army appears, they run away. Leopardi is mocking what he regarded as the Italian impulse to swagger but not to fight. Only Rubatocchi is brave, and he dies slaughtering crabs.

The crabs seize Rat City with the help of their garrison there. They keep Rodipane as puppet king; their envoy, Camminatorto (Crooked-Walker), rearranges the government in the image of the crab world. Camminatorto is based on a number of people, but in particular Prince Klemens von Metternich (1773-1859), the powerful Austrian minister who led the European reactionaries against all democratic ideas after the final defeat of Napoleon I of France.

Leccafondi, although hardly a revolutionary, is caught up in intrigues. The crabs exile him, and he wanders the world looking for help for the mice, getting promises but no real help, just as happened to the Italian exiles of the time. One night, he takes refuge in the house of a man named Daedalus. This Daedalus may not be the Daedalus of Greek legend, but he is a great inventor. Wishing to help the mice, he suggests that he and Leccafondi visit the residence of the dead animals. There Leccafondi can consult the dead mice, who are reputed to know more than the living. Daedalus makes wings for Leccafondi, and the two of them fly around the globe until they come to their destination, an island in the Pacific. Leccafondi goes alone to the underground abode of the dead mice and finds them staring silently and blankly ahead: Death itself is neither reward nor punishment for one's actions in this world; religious beliefs concerning the afterlife are false. The dead mice are apparently emotionless, forbidden to laugh. When Leccafondi asks if the mice will get the promised help, there is a great stir as the dead mice repress their laughter.

For the moment they speak, telling him that upon his return he should consult a general named Taster. Taster will tell the mice how to recover their lost honor. Most commentators consider Taster to be Leopardi's image of himself. Leccafondi and Daedalus return to Rat City, where the mouse immediately visits Taster. Taster at first refuses to give advice because he has no stomach for vain plots. At last he speaks, but the reader never hears his good advice. Leopardi ends his poem with the excuse that the ancient manuscripts he has been "translating" ran out here and that he cannot finish his story. No doubt Leopardi himself had no real solution to the Italian problem. The very abruptness of the poem's ending emphasizes the major themes: The natural and human worlds are morally purposeless, and people must not rely on empty words.

L. L. Lee

Further Reading

Barricelli, Gian Piero. *Giacomo Leopardi*. Boston: Twayne, 1986. Provides complete and intelligent discussion of Leopardi's work, with detailed treatment of individual poems and prose works. Includes a short but informative section on *The War of the Mice and the Crabs*. Supplemented with notes, references, selected bibliography, and index.

Bloom, Harold. *Genius: A Mosaic of One Hundred Exemplary Creative Minds*. New York: Warner Books, 2002. Leopardi is one of the literary "geniuses" whose work is discussed in this volume. Provides a brief introductory overview of his life, his major works, and his significant literary achievements.

Caserta, Ernesto G. Introduction to *The War of the Mice and the Crabs*. Chapel Hill: University of North Carolina, Department of Romance Languages, 1976. Caserta's introduction to his prose translation of the poem and his presentation of the historical situation of the time are useful for helping readers understand *The War of the Mice and the Crabs* and Leopardi's achievement as more than a lyric poet. Includes selected bibliography.

Origo, Iris. *Leopardi: A Study in Solitude*. 2d ed. 1953. Reprint. New York: Helen Marx Books, 1999. Standard introduction to Leopardi includes discussion of his life and his works.

Perella, Nicolas James. *Night and the Sublime in Giacomo Leopardi*. Berkeley: University of California Press, 1970. Presents superb discussion of Leopardi the poet. A three-stanza quotation from *The War of the Mice and the Crabs* in the original Italian may be informative for readers with some knowledge of the language. The quotation is offered as part of an analysis of Leopardi's use of the sublime. Includes notes.

Press, Lynne, and Pamela Williams. *Women and Feminine Images in Giacomo Leopardi, 1798-1837: Bicentenary Essays*. Lewiston, N.Y.: Edwin Mellen Press, 1999. Examines the role of female characters and feminine imagery in Leopardi's work, focusing on his cantos. Discusses the influence of contemporary women writers on Leopardi's literary and intellectual development.

Singh, Ghan Shyam. *Leopardi and the Theory of Poetry*. Lexington: University Press of Kentucky, 1964. Provides thorough discussion of Leopardi's aesthetic ideas and practices, including the influence of the ideas of the English Romantics on his work.

Veronese, Cosetta. *The Reception of Giacomo Leopardi in the Nineteenth Century: Italy's Greatest Poet After Dante?* Lewiston, N.Y.: Edwin Mellen Press, 2008. Examines the reception for Leopardi's work within the context of the Risorgimento, the movement for Italian unification, and the context of nineteenth century European culture generally.

The War of the Worlds

Author: H. G. Wells (1866-1946)
First published: 1898
Type of work: Novel
Type of plot: Science fiction
Time of plot: Late nineteenth century
Locale: Woking and London, England

Principal characters:
THE ANONYMOUS NARRATOR, also the story's main character
OGILVY, the first to discover a Martian cylinder
THE ARTILLERYMAN, the only survivor of an assault on the Martians
THE CURATE, the anonymous narrator's companion and victim

The Story:

Although scientists have speculated about intelligent life on Mars, it comes as a complete surprise to England when Martians land, having been shot to Earth in flaming cylinders. At first the projectiles are mistaken for shooting stars or meteors. Then Ogilvy, the first to discover one of the cylinders that has landed, realizes that it is hollow; as it cools, he can hear something inside unscrewing the cylinder's top. Ogilvy informs a local journalist, Henderson, and soon a crowd, including the narrator, gathers around the cylinder. The narrator suspects the object has come from Mars, but he does not think that it contains a living being. He and the crowd are shocked when grayish tentacles emerge from the cylinder. The crowd flees as the huge creature appears; it is the size of a bear, with a sheen like wet leather, two large, dark eyes, and a lipless mouth, heaving and pulsating. Just before the narrator runs away he catches sight of the monster's large inhuman eyes and fungoid mass, which he finds disgusting and terrifying.

The humans decide to send a deputation (including Ogilvy and Henderson) to parlay with the Martians, since it seems that the Martians are intelligent even if human beings find them repulsive. The deputation, however, is wiped out in a blinding flash of fire and smoke, which the narrator later learns was the Martians' heat ray. People panic; the narrator is stunned by the swiftness of the destruction.

The Martians begin to terrorize the cities and the countryside, dealing a silent and quick death to anyone in their way. For the first time it occurs to the narrator that the Martians mean to rule Earth, although he assures his wife that it seems unlikely that they will prevail, given that Earth's gravitational pull on their bodies is three times that of Mars. Returning home, the narrator regains some of his confidence.

In London, the news from Woking seems so incredible that it is deemed a ruse. Even at Woking junction, where the trains still run, the Martian invasion is treated as a rumor and a curiosity, not a cause for evacuation. The narrator can hear the Martians hammering and stirring, making some sort of preparations. A company of soldiers is dispatched to form a cordon around the pit where the Martians' cylinders landed. The Martians stay in the pit, but then the narrator, at home, sees one of his chimneys crack, and he realizes the power of the heat ray. He sends his terrified wife away to the town of Leatherhead. Out on the road, the narrator meets people escaping from the area of the pit. The Martians have set fire to everything within range of their heat ray.

The narrator then gets his first full view of a walking Martian or Martian machine of glittery metal, swinging its long, flexible tentacles. It has come out of the third of the ten Mar-

tian cylinders that landed on Earth. On the road the narrator encounters an artilleryman, the only survivor of an artillery clash with the Martians, who describes his fallen comrades as burnt meat. The destruction wrought by the Martians has been indiscriminate and universal, unprecedented in the history of warfare on Earth. The artilleryman decides to try to get to London to join the horse artillery there; the narrator opts to return to Leatherhead. The third cylinder blocks their way, however. Although the artillery does destroy one Martian, it proves ineffective against the heat ray, which obliterates everything in its path. The narrator just misses being killed as the foot of a Martian machine comes within yards of his head.

The narrator then realizes that the Martians are methodically destroying the country. Every twenty-four hours, another cylinder arrives to strengthen and consolidate their power. Although England sends all of its heavy guns and warships against the Martians, this firepower is destroyed as soon as it comes within range of the heat ray.

Unable to return to Leatherhead, the narrator takes refuge in a house occupied by a curate who is devastated and depressed by the invasion, believing it to be a sign of God's judgment. Soon it becomes clear to the narrator that the curate has gone insane. Talking to himself, refusing to listen to the narrator's pleas that they must ration their food and make no noise, the curate puts both his own life and the narrator's life in jeopardy. Martian tentacles have already invaded the house and have just missed detecting the narrator's presence. When the curate announces that he is going out to preach the word of God that sanctions this destruction of the world, the desperate narrator feels he has no choice but to kill the curate to keep him from exposing them both; he bashes the curate in the head with the back of a meat cleaver.

After more than two weeks, his food supply exhausted, the ravenous narrator decides to leave the house and take his chances on the streets, where he once again encounters the artilleryman. It now seems clear to the artilleryman that there is no way of defeating the Martians. He plans an underground life; he will live in the city's sewers and try to find ways to accommodate himself to the Martian rulers. The narrator rebels against the idea of such a subhuman existence, but he also thinks that the rule of human beings on Earth is over. Humans have become merely food for Martians, who feed by injecting themselves with human blood.

To the narrator's astonishment, however, he soon comes across the rotting bodies of Martians, and it suddenly occurs to him that they have been destroyed by the lowliest of life-forms: bacteria. Mars does not have the bacteria found on

Earth, and so the Martians have no immunity to these tiny organisms, which the human body has learned to tolerate over thousands of years. The narrator sees the destruction of the Martians as only a reprieve for humankind, however. Although he has been incredibly fortunate in that he has survived and has been able to reunite with his wife, he now lives with a sense of insecurity, no longer certain of Earth's invulnerability.

Critical Evaluation:

The War of the Worlds is one of H. G. Wells's most riveting stories. Much of its power stems from its first-person narrator. He is a learned man, a writer on scientific subjects, equipped with a precise mind and a formidable ability to describe what he sees. He begins his story calmly, rehearsing the evidence for life on Mars and explaining the investigations of his contemporaries. At the same time, he brings to his opening words a tone of foreboding, a sense of someone who has been through an ordeal—even though he does not explain what has happened to him. Instead, he re-creates events as he experienced them, enhancing the drama and suspense of the novel.

The narrator intensifies the interest of his story by releasing details about the Martians gradually. This steady but well-paced dispensing of information whets the curiosity, but it is also a realistic device, since the point of the story is that it takes the world some time to understand the ramifications of the invasion. At first, the Martians stay in their pit, a mystery until they begin to range across the country. Their heat ray is not well understood because from a distance it is obscured by the smoke of the destruction it causes. Only when the narrator gets uncomfortably close to the line of fire does he realize what sort of destructive instrument humans are confronting.

Much of the gripping narration centers on the sheer struggle to survive. As the narrator learns about the Martians' awesome power, he must also adapt to the destruction of civilization. He never loses his intelligent and resilient manner, but he does become increasingly desperate. The curate, an irrational man, has to be killed if the narrator is to survive. The narrator shows no remorse for his act, only pity, because the insane curate had become a danger to himself and to the narrator. Also, the narrator seems to hold little tolerance for the religious point of view. Several critics have commented on Wells's hostility toward organized religion in his other works.

If the narrator does not lose his humanity, the artilleryman nearly does. When they meet a second time, the artilleryman is guarding his ground and tells the narrator that he must look to some other part of England for food. After the artilleryman recognizes the narrator, he relaxes his guard and tries to persuade the narrator that the human race is beaten. Although he dreams of somehow outlasting the Martians—or at least coming to some sort of compromise with them—he is a defeated man who will settle for living on a level so subhuman that it appalls the narrator.

In addition to the brilliant evocation of the Martian invasion, Wells provides the first description in English literature of modern, mechanized warfare. The images of cities and countryside wiped out with weapons of mass destruction were startling and prophetic. Wells's vision challenged the complacency of the English regarding their secure and commonsense life. His science-fiction novels heralded a century of unprecedented destruction, the displacement of whole human populations, and the use of technology as a tool of dehumanization.

Wells enhances the effectiveness of his first-person narrator by including in the novel accounts of how the Martian invasion is reported in the press. Another theme of the novel is how mass populations get their news and how a modern society copes with disruptions in communications networks and transportation. Few people actually witness the events of the novel; many more react to what they read in newspapers, which sometimes contain inaccurate reports or only partial accounts.

It is quite extraordinary the way Wells provides both the immediacy of firsthand experience and a sense of a whole society mobilizing to comprehend and to defend itself against a foreign menace. Parts of the Martian invasion that the narrator has not witnessed and that are not clarified in the newspapers are supplied by the narrator's relating of his brother's experiences during the invasion. His brother's reports not only help to put the narrator's experiences into a context and to fill in gaps but also provide another voice that the narrator must absorb and factor into his own account. Consequently, the novel captures a sense of both the immediate events and a retrospective account of them. The novel becomes both the narrator's autobiography and an objective historical account.

The novel's ending, although it includes the narrator's sentimental reunion with his wife, is anything but optimistic. Wells conveys an extraordinary feeling of loss—not merely of lives and homes and institutions but also of confidence in the human spirit. It is a sobering conclusion, marking an end to the ebullience of the nineteenth century faith in science and human progress, to the idea that human beings were unlocking the secrets of nature. Wells believed, certainly, that twentieth century science and technology would make remarkable discoveries, but he was shortly to write a series of novels predicting devastating warfare as well. *The War of the Worlds* is a warning, probing, brooding look at humankind's place in the universe and a counsel against smugness.

Carl Rollyson

Further Reading

Costa, Richard Hauer. *H. G. Wells*. Rev. ed. Boston: Twayne, 1985. Praises *The War of the Worlds* for its vivid imagery, its superb characterizations, and its antiutopian theme. Notes Wells's extraordinary grasp of his own times from a sociological standpoint.

Hammond, J. R. *An H. G. Wells Companion: A Guide to the Novels, Romances, and Short Stories*. New York: Barnes & Noble, 1979. Examines Wells's ability to describe startling events happening to ordinary people, his remarkable anticipation of how crowds react to events of mass destruction, his superb evocation of actual settings, and his literary style. Includes a map showing the sites of the Martian invasion.

_____. *A Preface to H. G. Wells*. New York: Longman, 2001. Provides information on Wells's life and cultural background as well as the important people and places in his life. Also offers critical commentary on Wells's works and a discussion of his literary reputation.

McConnell, Frank. *The Science Fiction of H. G. Wells*. New York: Oxford University Press, 1981. Compares the themes of *The War of the Worlds* to Wells's work as a scientific journalist. Contrasts the novel with other tales of invasion and discusses the narrative's image patterns, the uniqueness of Wells's description of the Martians, the role of the curate, and the relationship between realism and fantasy in Wells's fiction.

Mackenzie, Norman, and Jeanne MacKenzie. *The Life of H. G. Wells: The Time Traveller*. Rev. ed. London: Hogarth Press, 1987. Compares the novel to scientific theories of catastrophe and stories of the apocalypse. Emphasizes the moral tone of the novel, which was written at a time when there was much discussion of a decadent England.

McLean, Steven, ed. *H. G. Wells: Interdisciplinary Essays*. Newcastle, England: Cambridge Scholars, 2008. Collection of essays analyzes individual novels and discusses general characteristics of Wells's work. Keith Williams's essay "Alien Gaze: Postcolonial Vision in *The War of the Worlds*" focuses on this novel.

Wagar, W. Warren. *H. G. Wells: Traversing Time*. Middletown, Conn.: Wesleyan University Press, 2004. Analyzes all of Wells's work, focusing on the author's preoccupation with the unfolding of public time and the history and future of humankind. Demonstrates how Wells's writings remain relevant in the twenty-first century.

Wells, H. G. *"The War of the Worlds." Fresh Perspectives on the H. G. Wells Classic*. Essays edited by Glenn Yeffeth. Dallas, Tex.: BenBella Books, 2005. In addition to the text of the novel, this edition features essays by scientists, science-fiction writers, and social commentators that discuss the novel's social and historical influences and its continuing relevance.

War Trash

Author: Ha Jin (1956-   )
First published: 2004
Type of work: Novel
Type of plot: Historical realism
Time of plot: 1951-1953 and early twenty-first century
Locale: Korean Peninsula and China

Principal characters:
YU YUAN, a Chinese army officer
TAO JULAN, his fiancé
PEI SHAN, commissar of Yuan's army unit
CHANG MING, a divisional clerical officer
DR. GREENE, a U.S. Army medical officer
WANG YONG, the leader of the Chinese Nationalist POWs
GENERAL BELL, the U.S. Army commandant of the POW camp
MR. PARK, the leader of the North Korean POWs

The Story:

Yu Yuan, now seventy-three years old, is visiting his son's family in the United States and is completing his documentary-style memoir in English about his experiences as a Chinese prisoner of war, or POW, during the Korean War. He hopes that someday his grandchildren will read his memoir and fully understand the meaning of the long tattoo on his belly that reads "F——k . . . . U . . S ." (the mutilated outcome of having removed part of the tattoo).

Yuan's story begins in 1949, when the Communists come to power in China. Yuan is a sophomore at the elite Huanpu Military Academy in the southern city of Chengdu. This academy, the equivalent of West Point in the United States, had played an important role in the Chinese Nationalist regime, so its students are viewed with suspicion by the new regime. Consequently, Yuan is required to take special courses in Marxism and undergo mutual and self-criticism. After graduation, he is assigned as an officer with the People's Liberation Army (PLA).

The Korean War breaks out, and he tells his mother and his fiancé, Tao Julan, a student at a teacher's college, that he will return home in one or two years. After traveling for four days, Yuan's division arrives at the North Korean border. Before the trip, the division's commissar, Pei Shan, orders him to bring along an English-Chinese dictionary, explaining that it will serve as a special weapon. Yuan is assigned to help Chang Ming, a divisional clerical officer, edit the unit's bulletin.

On April 22, 1951, Chinese and North Korean forces launch a major offensive. The offensive is initially successful, but Yuan's unit is eventually pushed back and his squad separated from the main force. After three months of guerrilla life, Yuan is shot in the left thigh, which fractures his leg; he is soon captured by U.S. forces. He is transferred to a camp in Pusan, South Korea. Surgery is successfully performed on his leg by Dr. Greene, a young female surgeon and U.S. Army officer. They become friends, and Yuan teaches her Chinese characters.

Yuan is next sent to compound 72 on Koje Island. Americans guard the camp but do not go inside. Yuan's compound is under the direct control of the Taiwanese Nationalist Party. He is assigned to a company overseen by Wang Yong, a former Nationalist army corporal. Mainland Chinese POWs in this compound are constantly intimidated, cajoled, beaten, and bribed by the Nationalists to get them to sign up for repatriation to Taiwan. Yuan is given special attention because he is a graduate of the Huanpu Military Academy. He soon has to confront a horrible dilemma: If he refuses to go to Taiwan, the Nationalists will assume that he is a Communist and, hence, their enemy; his life will be in danger, and he will be prevented from seeing his family. If he elects to return to the mainland, he will be treated as a criminal by the government because he had allowed himself to be captured.

Yuan, like many of the mainland Chinese prisoners, wants to return to the mainland not for political reasons but because his family is there. Meanwhile, he has established contact with Ming, who is in compound 71, which is under the control of the PLA. Ming tells him to keep him informed about what happens in his compound, number 72. One day, Yong invites Yuan to dinner. During the dinner, he actively courts Yuan to go to Taiwan. Yuan gets drunk, and when he wakes up the next day he discovers that his belly has a tattoo that reads "F——k COMMUNISM." He immediately informs Ming what had happened so that he will not get into trouble. To protect himself from Yong, Yuan declares he is willing to be repatriated to Taiwan.

On the day Chinese POWs have to inform the camp authorities what country they want to be returned to, Yuan outsmarts his Nationalist captors and says he wants to return to the mainland. He is then transferred to compound 602, which is controlled by the Communists, and is happily reunited with his comrades. He realizes that he can no longer stand aloof from politics. Yuan soon applies for membership in the United Communist Association, but his request is refused and he has to do a public self-criticism because he is still viewed with suspicion by the party.

To draw world attention to the plight of POWs and to embarrass the U.S. authorities, Mr. Park, the head of the Korean POWs, decides to kidnap General Bell, the U.S. commandant of the camp at Koje Island. The mainland Chinese prisoners resolve to help. Bell is abducted and forced to sign a document promising better treatment for the prisoners. After he is released, U.S. forces launch a massive attack on the Korean and Chinese compounds; many prisoners are killed or wounded, and Yuan is temporally put into a special prison. After his release, he is sent to a camp on Jeju Island. At the camp, Yuan meets Shanmin, a sixteen-year-old soldier, and starts to teach him Chinese. Division commissar Pei Shan next orders the Chinese POWs to raise the mainland's flag on National Day to draw the attention of the Chinese government, and a bloody fight ensues between the Americans and the Chinese.

Yuan is given a final test by Shan. He is ordered to impersonate his assistant Feng Wen and travel to Pusan to register again. Yuan soon realizes he had been picked to impersonate Wen because he is not a party member and therefore is expendable; Wen is not expendable. The authorities quickly find out that Yuan is not Wen—his fingerprints do not match those in the records. Yuan quickly tells them that he hates Communism, and then he shows them his tattoo. They send him to camp 8 on Cheju Island, which is under the command of Yong, who warmly welcomes him back and forgives his previous behavior. Yuan again tells him he wants to go to Taiwan.

In 1953, the camp is moved to the demilitarized zone for

the final step of the repatriation process. Several days later, Yuan enters the repatriation tent and informs the authorities that he wants to return to the mainland. He is reunited with his comrades, who are initially treated well by the government. Yuan has his tattoo changed to "F——k . . . . U . . S ." (removing most of the letters in "COMMUNISM"), but soon they all have to undergo terrifying study sessions. Yuan learns that his mother had died and that his fiancé now refuses to marry him because of his status as a former POW. Because Yuan is not a party member, he is treated better than most of his comrades. He is given the job of teaching Chinese, geography, and English at a middle school.

Critical Evaluation:

Ha Jin, the most critically successful native Chinese writer in the United States, was born in 1956 in Liaoning, China. He came to the United States in 1985 for graduate study at Brandeis University. When the Tiananmen massacre occurred in 1989, Jin decided to emigrate to the United States. He also is the author of books of poetry. All of his writings were first written in English, in large part, according to Jin, because he considers English much more flexible than written Chinese in terms of expression and diction.

Jin's writing style is noted for its clarity, straightforwardness, and simplicity, and for its accurate depiction of complex emotions. His close attention to the minute details of everyday life has been frequently compared to the attention of nineteenth century novelists Charles Dickens and Honoré de Balzac. Jin's works also show the strong stylistic and thematic influences of Russian writers Isaac Babel, Anton Chekhov, Nikolai Gogol, and Leo Tolstoy.

War Trash is a rare, historically accurate depiction of the lives of a group of Chinese POWs and their treatment by U.S. forces from 1951 to 1953 in the Korean War. The POW experience is shown through the perspective of Yu Yuan, a young soldier in the Chinese army. The novel is heavily researched, and Jin also relied upon his father's memories of the war as well as his own experiences living for six months in a Korean village while serving in the People's Liberation Army.

War Trash, however, is more than an account of a little-known chapter of an often-forgotten war. All of Jin's fictional writings about China are political because he considers Chinese society to be one that is managed by the Chinese government. Therefore, his overarching theme has always been the conflict between ideological thinking and basic human drives and aspirations. In *War Trash*, this conflict is given a tight focus because of the political nature of war and the repatriation dilemma faced by Chinese POWs. In this extreme environment, core ideological and national allegiances play an all-determining role in relationships among people.

Jin has stated that he initially intended this novel to be a novella, but he could not stop writing because of fear, the same fear Chinese POWs had as captives, who knew they would be treated as major criminals when they returned home. *War Trash* accurately captures this profound and abiding fear among the prisoners. On a deeper level, the work is a careful exploration of conventional notions of nationality, belief, and identity. Jin raises fundamental questions via Yuan about the validity of these ideas.

Yuan, an objective observer and perennial outsider throughout the story, soon realizes that unbridled abstraction is "the crime of war: it reduces real human beings to abstract numbers." Later, he understands that certain political creeds, like communism, also are grounded in abstractions and thus reduce persons to statistics. Yuan strenuously tries to think by himself in an environment in which reflection and reason are repressed. As he asks early in the book, "Why couldn't I remain alone without following anyone else?" He also is skeptical about the motivation and methodology used by his superiors, like Commissar Pei Shan. The title of the novel, *War Trash*, concisely captures one of the story's central themes: the inhumane ways in which overtly abstract and self-serving political and national ideologies lead to the treatment of human beings as disposable items—trash.

Yuan ultimately represents the benevolent and equalitarian impulses of human nature. This is shown by his frequently expressed wish to become a physician like Dr. Greene, "who dealt with individual patients in a war and didn't have to relish any victory other than the success of saving a limb or a life." Yuan's dogged disregard of conventional categories regarding people and their beliefs is revealed in his easily made friendships with such varied individuals as Dr. Greene, the outcast Bai Dajian, the lovesick U.S. corporal Richard, the black U.S. private Frank Holeman, and the sixteen-year-old illiterate infantryman Shanmin.

Furthermore, *War Trash* is an atypical Chinese novel, for it powerfully critiques the idea of Chineseness. The noted literary critic and historian C. T. Hsia in 1961 wrote a now-famous essay criticizing modern Chinese writers of being so obsessed with the problematic condition of China and the issue of Chinese identity. He argues that these writers have become restricted in their ability to explore the modern human condition because of this obsession. This obsession remains true of most contemporary Chinese writers; Jin is a rare exception.

In *War Trash*, Jin brilliantly transcends Chinese history and demonstrates how Chinese identity can be rendered more substantial when mixed with universal conceptions of human nature. By firmly grounding the novel not just in Chinese experience but also in human experience, Jin transforms the work into a telling story about humanity as reflected in the travails of one person in a time of war.

Ronald Gray

Further Reading

Banks, Russell. "View from the Prison Camp." *The New York Times*, October 10, 2004. Banks, a well-known American writer and critic, examines *War Trash* in this lengthy, readable review of Jin's novel.
Buruma, Ian. "Chinese Shadows." *The New York Review of Books* 52, no. 5 (2005): 14-15. A noted writer on East Asia examines Chinese identity in this review of Jin's *War Trash*.
Hsia, C. T. "Obsession with China: The Moral Burden of Modern Chinese Literature." In *A History of Modern Chinese Fiction*. 2d ed. New Haven, Conn.: Yale University Press, 1971. Hsia's brilliant essay examines the modern Chinese literary tradition that Jin, in large part, is reacting against in *War Trash*.
Jin, Ha. *The Writer as Migrant*. Chicago: University of Chicago Press, 2008. Jin presents his thoughts and observations on the idea of the "migrant" writer, the exiles, refugees, immigrants, and emigrants writing about topics such as nostalgia, homeland, and memory.

The Warden

Author: Anthony Trollope (1815-1882)
First published: 1855
Type of work: Novel
Type of plot: Social realism
Time of plot: Mid-nineteenth century
Locale: London and Barchester, England

Principal characters:
THE REVEREND SEPTIMUS HARDING, the warden of Hiram's Hospital
ELEANOR HARDING, his young daughter
JOHN BOLD, a young physician
DR. GRANTLY, the husband of Mr. Harding's older daughter
TOM TOWERS, a newspaperman
SIR ABRAHAM HAPHAZARD, Mr. Harding's counsel

The Story:

At the age of fifty, the Reverend Septimus Harding is appointed precentor of Barchester Cathedral, a position that carries with it the wardenship of Hiram's Hospital. For more than four hundred years, this institution has provided a home for twelve men in their old age; because the institution's income has grown to a considerable size, both the warden and the steward receive substantial yearly salaries. With his income of eight hundred pounds a year, Mr. Harding is able to provide comfortably for his younger daughter, Eleanor. His older daughter, Susan, is married to Dr. Grantly, the archdeacon of the cathedral.

John Bold, a young physician with a small practice, turns his energies to reform. On investigation, he discovers that the will of John Hiram, the donor of the hospital, made no stipulation that would result in such a discrepancy as exists between the incomes of the warden and the steward and the incomes of the twelve residents. Bold decides that it is his duty to bring the discrepancy to light. He engages the interest of a newspaperman friend, Tom Towers, and the services of a solicitor named Finney, who explains the situation to the residents and encourages them to think in terms of an annual income of as much as one hundred pounds a year. Most of them sign a petition addressed to the bishop, asking that justice be done.

When *The Jupiter*, the newspaper for which Towers works, begins to publish editorials about the greediness of the Church and unscrupulous clergymen, Mr. Harding is distressed. It has never entered his head that he is living on an income not his by rights, and he begins to talk of resigning. Eleanor agrees that if her father is unhappy at Hiram's Hospital, they would be better off at Crabtree Parva, a small parish that belongs to Mr. Harding and that pays an annual income of fifty pounds.

Dr. Grantly, a worldly man, will not hear of Mr. Harding's

resignation. He insists that the warden has an obligation to the Church and to his fellow members of the clergy that requires a firm stand against the laity and the press. Besides, as he points out, the living Mr. Harding would receive at Crabtree Parva would not enable Eleanor to make a suitable marriage.

Dr. Grantly comes to the hospital and addresses the residents. He tells them that John Hiram had intended simply to provide comfortable quarters for old single men who have no other homes. Dr. Grantly's speech has little effect on anyone except John Bunce and two of his cronies. John Bunce, who is especially close to Mr. Harding, serves as the old men's subwarden. The others feel they have a right to a hundred pounds a year.

When Eleanor sees how unhappy the whole affair has made her father, she begs him to resign. She also goes to John Bold and begs him to give up the suit. After promising to do anything he can for her, Bold declares his love. Eleanor, who had not meant to let matters go so far, confesses that she loves him in return.

Bold goes to see Dr. Grantly and tells him that, for reasons best known to himself, he is withdrawing the charges he had made. Dr. Grantly replies that he does not think the defendants wish to have the suit withdrawn. He has been advised that Mr. Harding and the steward are, in effect, servants, and therefore are not responsible and cannot be defendants in a suit.

Mr. Harding decides to go to London for a conference with Sir Abraham Haphazard, the counsel for the defense. Eleanor has come home expecting to tell her father all that Bold has told her, but she cannot bring herself to discuss her own affairs before those of the wardenship are settled. Mr. Harding has decided that he has no right to the income from Hiram's Hospital.

Bold also is going to London. When he arrives there, he meets with Tom Towers and asks him not to print any more editorials about the Barchester situation. Towers says that he cannot be responsible for the attitude of *The Jupiter*. Bold then goes to the offices of his lawyer and tells him to drop the suit. The lawyer sends word to Sir Abraham.

Mr. Harding arrives in London and is given an appointment with Sir Abraham the next night at ten o'clock. He has explained his intention in a note to Dr. Grantly and now is afraid that Dr. Grantly will arrive in London before he has a chance to carry out his plan. He leaves his hotel at ten in the morning and spends most of the day in Westminster Abbey in order to avoid Dr. Grantly. That night, he tells Sir Abraham that he must in all conscience resign his post as warden. When he returns to his hotel, he finds Dr. and Mrs. Grantly

waiting for him, but their arguments cannot sway the warden. Back in Barchester, he writes a formal letter of resignation to the bishop and sends a copy to Dr. Grantly.

The bishop offers Mr. Harding a position as chaplain in his household, but he declines the offer. Then it is suggested that a trade be effected between Mr. Harding and Mr. Quiverful of Puddingdale. Mr. Quiverful, who has twelve children, would be glad to double his annual income and would be impervious to any attacks from the press. Nevertheless, this arrangement also meets with opposition, for Puddingdale is too far from Barchester for Mr. Harding to attend to his duties as precentor at the cathedral.

As the time for Mr. Harding's departure from Hiram's Hospital draws near, he calls in all the residents and has a last talk with them. They are disturbed—even those who petitioned the bishop—for they know that they are being deprived of a friendly and sympathetic warden.

Mr. Harding takes lodgings and is given a tiny parish at the entrance to the cathedral close. His daughter Eleanor marries John Bold. Mr. Harding's income continues to be ample for his needs. He dines frequently with the bishop and keeps his violoncello at Eleanor's house, where he often goes to make music. In short, Mr. Harding is not an unhappy man.

Critical Evaluation:

Anthony Trollope, one of the most prolific and popular Victorian novelists, began his successful Barchester series of six novels with *The Warden*, which was published in 1855. Trollope spent many years working for the civil service in the post office division and only gradually made enough money by his writing to retire and write full time. *The Warden* brought him his first financial success as an author. Trollope owes his success with readers and critics alike in part to his knowledge of ecclesiastical and political mores, his clever writing style, and the sympathy he shows for his characters and, indeed, for the human condition.

The story of *The Warden* is based very loosely on several ecclesiastical inquiries of Trollope's era in which the Anglican Church was accused of diverting monies from ancient endowments to the pockets of idle clergymen, thereby stinting the charitable purposes for which the endowments had been intended. Trollope's novel raises just such an ethical question, then complicates the issue by making the benefiting clergyman, Mr. Harding, the most honest and decent of men. Trollope states his own view of the matter through his narrator when he says, "In this world no good is unalloyed, and . . . there is but little evil that has not in it some seed of what is goodly."

Most of the characters in *The Warden* display this mixed

quality. John Bold, the reformer, is zealous to do good but inadvertently injures Mr. Harding, whom he respects, whereas Archdeacon Grantly bullies and insults Mr. Harding, whom he purports to defend. Eleanor Harding assiduously defends her father to John Bold while furthering her own romance. The warden himself, in his humility and honesty, is the most consistent character. Harding, a cello-playing church mouse, ultimately faces down his church-militant son-in-law Grantly and resigns as warden of Hiram's Hospital, but, as Trollope had predicted through his narrator, the twelve bedesmen who were his charges are worse off and no one has gained anything.

Trollope uses his knowledge of ecclesiastical minutiae, Church and English politics, and journalism to good advantage in *The Warden*, bringing the reader to see that seemingly small points of dispute can matter more and affect more lives than such large events as wars and international intrigue.

Trollope employs several chapters of *The Warden* to satirize fellow writers in the figures of Dr. Pessimist Anticant, who is intended to represent Thomas Carlyle, and Mr. Popular Sentiment, who represents Charles Dickens. He criticizes Dr. Anticant for instituting himself "censor of things in general" and being too hard on others, while noting that Mr. Sentiment fights an incredible number of evil practices by making "his good poor people . . . so very good [and] his hard rich people so very hard." He also takes a swipe at the Pre-Raphaelite painters for depicting overly ethereal subjects. Obviously these allusions to well-known figures of Trollope's own time were more easily understood and popular in Victorian England than they have been in subsequent eras.

The Warden is written from a third-person, omniscient point of view that includes many authorial asides to the reader in which Trollope asks the reader's opinion, chides the reader for a probable uncharitable response to happenings in his story, and makes whimsical comments. Trollope also employs a number of rhetorical devices to ironic or comic effect, including euphemism, oxymoron, and grotesque or startling anticlimax. The names of his characters are likewise a source of delight, ranging from Mr. Quiverful, father of twelve, to Sir Abraham Haphazard, Mr. Harding's fancy London lawyer. Like Trollope's other works, *The Warden* also contains many allusions to authors such as William Shakespeare, Dickens, and John Milton.

Trollope's narrator often writes with a divided voice in *The Warden*: He assumes a pseudonaïve tone in describing one character or situation, then turns the tables by employing a worldly-wise phrase or two to describe the same subject, thereby letting the reader know he is not so naïve as he first appeared. The stylistic, rhetorical, and narrative techniques in the novel create comedy and irony as well as insight into character.

Trollope's interest in character transcended his concern for plot, descriptive detail, and locale, although he was quite adept in establishing those as well. *The Warden* actually includes very few descriptive details of places and things, yet the reader has a vivid mental picture of the Barchester milieu. Trollope achieves this through his use of characterization. Archdeacon Grantly could expound his Tory, High Church convictions nowhere as well as in Plumstead Episcopi, and Mr. Harding lends descriptive presence to the rectory of Hiram's Hospital.

By studying the environs of Barchester and its denizens, Trollope invests *The Warden* with his central insight and theme, the mixed quality of most human endeavors and choices. Overfunded ecclesiastical preferments are irresponsible on the part of the Anglican Church, yet Mr. Harding, who holds one of these sinecures, is a good and honest man. John Bold, Tom Towers, the newspaperman, and Hiram's bedesmen are zealous reformers, yet their reforms serve no useful end and in fact do harm. Dr. Grantly maintains the prerogatives of the Anglican Church, but he is little interested in justice within the Church. Trollope looks at these creatures he has devised with amused tolerance and, through them, warns his readers not to judge their fellows too hastily. *The Warden* instructs and gives insight into the human condition as it delights.

"Critical Evaluation" by Isabel B. Stanley

Further Reading

Bridgham, Elizabeth A. *Spaces of the Sacred and Profane: Dickens, Trollope, and the Victorian Cathedral Town.* New York: Routledge, 2008. Describes how Trollope and Charles Dickens use Victorian cathedral towns as settings within which to critique religious attitudes, business practices, aesthetic ideas, and other aspects of nineteenth century English life.

Bury, Laurent. *Seductive Strategies in the Novels of Anthony Trollope, 1815-1882.* Lewiston, N.Y.: Edwin Mellen Press, 2004. Focuses on seduction in all of Trollope's novels, arguing that seduction was a survival skill for both men and women in the Victorian era. Demonstrates how Trollope depicted the era's sexual politics.

Cockshut, A. O. J. *Anthony Trollope: A Critical Study.* New York: New York University Press, 1968. Discusses Trollope's views on human nature, property and rank, families, religion and the clergy, death, politics, and love—

all subjects that inform *The Warden*, the first of his Barchester novels.

Glendinning, Victoria. *Anthony Trollope*. New York: Alfred A. Knopf, 1993. Considered the standard late twentieth century biography of Trollope. Provides insight into the characters of Mr. Septimus Harding and Archdeacon Grantly. Connects the plot of *The Warden* to actual ecclesiastical scandals in the Anglican Church in the Victorian era.

Markwick, Margaret. *New Men in Trollope's Novels: Rewriting the Victorian Male*. Burlington, Vt.: Ashgate, 2007. Examines Trollope's novels to trace the development of his ideas about masculinity. Argues that the novels' male characters are not conventional Victorian patriarchs and demonstrates how Trollope's works promoted a "startlingly modern model of manhood."

_____. *Trollope and Women*. London: Hambledon Press, 1997. Examines how Trollope could simultaneously accept conventional Victorian ideas about women and sympathize with women's difficult situations. Demonstrates the individuality of his female characters. Includes discussion of Trollope's depictions of both happy and un-happy marriages, male-female relationships, bigamy, and scandal.

Mullen, Richard, and James Munson. *The Penguin Companion to Trollope*. New York: Penguin, 1996. Comprehensive guide describes all of Trollope's novels, short stories, travel books, and other works; discusses plots, characters, background, allusions, and contemporary references; and places the works in their historical context.

Sadleir, Michael. *Trollope: A Commentary*. New York: Farrar, Straus, 1947. Sadleir and Frederick Page produced the uncorrupted Oxford edition of *The Warden*. In this study, Sadleir uses Trollope family papers and letters as well as contemporary reviews of *The Warden* to elucidate some of Trollope's sources and the initial reception of the book.

Skilton, David. *Anthony Trollope and His Contemporaries: A Study in the Theory and Conventions of Mid-Victorian Fiction*. New York: St. Martin's Press, 1972. Situates Trollope and *The Warden* in the context of the mid-Victorian world. Shows Trollope's work in relation to that of other authors of the period, such as Charles Dickens and William Makepeace Thackeray.

Washington Square

Author: Henry James (1843-1916)
First published: 1880
Type of work: Novel
Type of plot: Psychological realism
Time of plot: c. 1850
Locale: New York City

Principal characters:
DR. AUSTIN SLOPER, a prominent New York physician
CATHERINE SLOPER, his daughter
MRS. LAVINIA PENNIMAN, his sister
MORRIS TOWNSEND, Catherine's suitor

The Story:

Peace, especially of the domestic variety, becomes increasingly important to Dr. Sloper when he enters his fifties. Intelligent, poised, and distinguished in his profession, he is accustomed to meeting life on his terms. He suffers the loss of his wife and a young son many years before, but the passage of time softens this blow. Now he dwells quietly and comfortably in his mansion on Washington Square with his only remaining child, Catherine, and his widowed sister, Mrs. Penniman.

Neither of his companions inspires the doctor with great fondness. His sister has just the sort of nature, incurably romantic, devious, and feminine, to set his teeth on edge; he sees her presence in his establishment as merely a necessary inconvenience to provide female supervision for his growing daughter. As to his daughter, Dr. Sloper thinks Catherine is a good girl but incurably dull. By her twenties, she never has a romantic interest or even the prospect of such. She is shyly fond of her father and very much afraid of him, especially when an ironical tone creeps into his voice. He is, however, generally kind and courteous to her, though more self-contained than an adoring daughter might wish.

Catherine's taste for ornate dress is one of the characteristics that her father finds especially trying. She long cherishes this taste without venturing to express it, but when she reaches the age of twenty, she buys herself a red satin gown trimmed with gold fringe. Her father inwardly grimaces at the thought that a child of his should be both ugly and over-dressed.

Catherine wears her red gown on the evening when she first meets Morris Townsend. The occasion is a party, given by her aunt, Mrs. Almond. Catherine quickly becomes convinced that she never met a young man so handsome, clever, and attentive. When his absorption with Catherine attracts notice, Townsend shifts his attentions to Mrs. Penniman, whose romantic sensibilities are soon aflutter with delight and anticipation. Before the evening ends, she manages to intimate to this agreeable young man that he is welcome to call in Washington Square.

Soon Townsend is in regular attendance on Catherine. Mrs. Penniman, undertaking the role of a middle-aged Cupid, presses Townsend's claims and assists his cause as ardently as she dares. Dr. Sloper, on the other hand, is at first skeptical and then becomes concerned. An interview with the young man strengthens his conviction that Townsend's charming manner is a mask for irresponsibility and selfishness. He suspects that Townsend is living off the meager resources of his sister, a widow with five children, and the doctor determines to investigate the matter. Before he can do so, however, Catherine tells him that Townsend proposed to her and that she is anxious to accept him.

When his suspicions are confirmed by a talk with Townsend's sister, the doctor is more than ever convinced that Catherine's suitor is a fortune hunter. For once, however, his objections fail to sway the infatuated girl. As a last resort, Dr. Sloper declares that if Catherine marries Townsend he will disinherit her. This measure will not leave her penniless by any means, since an inheritance from her mother will provide her a comfortable income, but it will reduce by two-thirds the amount Catherine would otherwise be able to expect.

Mrs. Penniman, alarmed, counsels delay, and Townsend agrees to part with Catherine while she accompanies her father to Europe. Both Townsend and Mrs. Penniman hope that time will soften the doctor's obdurate opposition to the match. Catherine, while agreeing to make the trip, cherishes no such illusions. When she and her father return several months later, the situation remains unchanged. Catherine is determined to go ahead with the marriage, but Townsend keeps putting her off. One day, he vanishes from New York altogether.

Years pass before she sees him again. By that time, Dr. Sloper is dead; fearful to the end that Townsend might reenter Catherine's life, he left his fortune to charity. One night, while Catherine is sitting quietly at home, there is a ring at the door. Townsend comes back, secretly encouraged by the unwearying Mrs. Penniman. Bearded, heavier, and now

forty-five years old, he is still personable; his manner makes it clear that he expects a warm welcome in Washington Square. The lapse of twenty years might have taken much from him, including the European wife of whom Catherine vaguely heard, but he did not lose the bright assurance with which he now waits for his words to work their old magic on Catherine's heart.

He stands, hat in hand, murmuring warm phrases, but Catherine does not ask him to sit down. She looks at him as if he is a stranger, repelling all advances and brushing off all explanations with a cool imperturbability worthy of the old doctor himself. For Catherine there is no longer any question of yielding to his charm: She suffered too much. This time it will be she who sends him away. She dismisses him with a finality he has no choice but to accept and to understand.

Critical Evaluation:

Henry James, discussing his novel *Washington Square* in a letter to his brother, stated that "the only good thing about the story is the girl." James, however, underestimated his book. The novel is a masterpiece in the interweaving of the moral and the psychological dimensions with the influence of an economy-oriented society on the different characters. Catherine Sloper emerges as a woman who defies her overprotective father, who is a pillar of society, but her victory is a small one, for which she must pay a great price. Dr. Austin Sloper regards his daughter as a dull and unattractive heir whose major function is to see to his welfare. She, however, awakens to the father's tyranny, to the fortune-hunting motives of her suitor, and to the meddling of her aunt, the three people she loves and trusts. Catherine moves from her unthinking acceptance of the idea that as a woman she is inferior to a sense of self-worth that challenges the rigid value system of Washington Square.

Sloper, a scholarly doctor who lives and works in the best society of New York City, is a local celebrity whose path to prosperity is made easier by his marriage. When after the death of his wealthy wife and young son Sloper is left with a disappointing daughter, he leaves her to the care of his widowed sister, Lavinia Penniman, whom he considers to be of "foolish indirectness and obliquity of character." He does not expect much from Catherine except devotion, but his intellectual pride makes him incapable of loving her. His own devotion to business leads him to think of Catherine as a marketable product, which means that she need only be "clever" in womanly ways—knowing how to dress and how to talk to gentlemen, and how to be efficient in knitting or embroidering.

Sloper is obsessed with his powerful social position and convinced of his intellect. He is proud of his ability to judge and categorize people, and he is convinced that Catherine, whom he considers "abnormally deficient" in intelligence, must be protected from fortune hunters. When Morris Townsend starts calling on her, Sloper is suspicious. His investigation reveals that Townsend is not a gentleman. He lives off his sister and has no money or prospects. Catherine, however, is not led by her father's warnings. Instead, encouraged by Mrs. Penniman, Townsend becomes for her the embodiment of romance. Her infatuation is stronger than her sense of duty to her father, and although Townsend is not romantically sincere, he awakens in Catherine her father's own selfishness. She begins to see that he does not treat her well, especially during the European tour that Sloper intends as a means of cooling her relationship with Townsend. When he abandons his daughter in the Alps, after she refuses to give up her suitor, the doctor goes too far. According to Sloper's economic view, the trip should make Catherine more valuable in the marketplace, but since she insists that Townsend be the buyer, he changes his will to make her less of a financial asset.

When Catherine observes that her father is a cold man of business and intellectual pride, she accepts her economic loss without regret and resolves to marry Townsend immediately. When Townsend reneges on his promises, Catherine refuses to give her father the satisfaction of knowing that she was jilted. She also refuses to promise Sloper that she will never marry Townsend, but when Mrs. Penniman, not understanding the change in her surrogate daughter, brings Townsend back years later for another chance at marriage, Catherine is morally outraged.

Catherine wins the battle of money and sex, but it kills her ability to love. Betrayed by the three people she loves, she learns merely to "fill the void." She becomes a "kindly maiden-aunt" to girls who confide in her, and she is an "inevitable figure at all respectable entertainments." She tolerates her meddling aunt, who continues to live with her in the fashionable house in Washington Square. Catherine grows from what her father considers a dull girl into a perceptive woman who does what she thinks is right. Yet, she feels that the "great facts" of her career are that Townsend trifled with her affection, and that her father broke its spring. Catherine is not able to separate entirely from the confinements of her world, but she does confront the wrongdoings of her father and her suitor. She does not yield to the hypocrisy of society. Though she does not change that society, she is aware of the inner transformation that gives her a sense of accomplishment.

Sloper is right about Townsend, but he is a victim of his pride. He is so obsessed with his sense of power, including his assumed rationality, that he is able to love only himself. He labels his daughter an inferior product and exults in dominating her. Her rebellion becomes an entertainment for him, but he underestimates her. His confidence in himself and in socioeconomic prevalence blinds him to the change in Catherine, and he is unaware of the prejudices that limit him and make him morally inferior to Catherine.

In *Washington Square*, James focuses on Catherine's efforts to attain an identity in an environment dominated by men such as her father. By challenging a value system that protects and promotes male superiority, she proves Sloper wrong.

"Critical Evaluation" by Noel Schraufnagel

Further Reading

Coulson, Victoria. *Henry James, Women, and Realism*. New York: Cambridge University Press, 2007. Examines James's important friendships with three women: his sister Alice James and the novelists Constance Fenimore Woolson and Edith Wharton. These three women writers and James shared what Coulson describes as an "ambivalent realism," or a cultural ambivalence about gender identity, and she examines how this idea is manifest in James's works, including *Washington Square*.

Fisher, James. "On the Ladder of Social Observation: Images of Decadence and Morality in James's *Washington Square* and Wilde's *An Ideal Husband*." In *Henry James Against the Aesthetic Movement: Essays on the Middle and Late Fiction*, edited by David Garrett Izzo and Daniel T. O'Hara. Jefferson, N.C.: McFarland, 2006. A comparison of James's novel and Oscar Wilde's play.

Freedman, Jonathan, ed. *The Cambridge Companion to Henry James*. New York: Cambridge University Press, 1998. A collection of essays that provide extensive information on James's life and literary influences and describe his works and the characters in them.

Hall, Donald. "Afterword." In *Washington Square*, by Henry James. New York: New American Library, 1980. Stresses the moral dilemma represented by Dr. Sloper's role as both protector and antagonist of his daughter.

Hoffman, Charles G. *The Short Novels of Henry James*. New York: Bookman, 1957. Discusses the dramatic structure of the book, which was influenced by its serial publication in *Cornhill Magazine* and *Harper's New Monthly Magazine*.

Hutchinson, Stuart. *Henry James: An American as Modernist*. London: Vision Press, 1983. Treats the book as James's attempt to discover a historical tradition for American literature, which he thought did not share the European sense of belonging to a civilized order.

Samuels, Charles Thomas. *The Ambiguity of Henry James*. Urbana: University of Illinois Press, 1971. An analysis of James's use of irony to illustrate Catherine Sloper's integrity. Compares Dr. Sloper's fascination with observing innocence to that of the governess in James's *The Turn of the Screw* (1898).

Willen, Gerald, ed. *"Washington Square": The Crowell Critical Library*. New York: Thomas Y. Crowell, 1970. A casebook with fourteen critical entries, including excerpts from books on James by Joseph Warren Beach, Edwin T. Bowden, Richard Poirier, Leon Edell, and Maxwell Geismar. Also includes four previously unpublished essays, the most enlightening being Leo Gurko's analysis of the distortion of personality by a dominant trait.

The Wasps

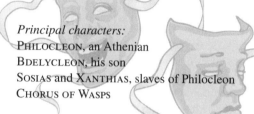

Author: Aristophanes (c. 450-c. 385 B.C.E.)
First produced: *Sphēkes*, 422 B.C.E. (English translation, 1812)
Type of work: Drama
Type of plot: Satire
Time of plot: Fifth century B.C.E.
Locale: Athens

Principal characters:
PHILOCLEON, an Athenian
BDELYCLEON, his son
SOSIAS and XANTHIAS, slaves of Philocleon
CHORUS OF WASPS

The Story:

Afflicted with a constant desire to judge and to convict the people brought before the courts of Athens, Philocleon is locked up in his own house by his son, Bdelycleon, who previously tried all rational means of persuading his father to give up his mania and become a gentleman. Bdelycleon even resorts to a net cast around the house in order to keep his father from leaving. Two slaves, Sosias and Xanthias, are set to guard the house, and Bdelycleon, as an added precaution, watches from the roof.

The three men are kept busy thwarting Philocleon's attempts to escape. He tries to crawl out through the chimney, threatens to chew his way through the net, and, at last, is almost successful when he crawls beneath the belly of his ass, in the manner of Odysseus, and then insists that the beast be taken out and sold. The ass moans and groans so intently, however, that Xanthias notices the concealed burden. Philocleon is caught and thrust back into the house just before the other jurymen, the Wasps, arrive to escort him to the courts.

When the Wasps arrive, Philocleon appears at an upper window, tells them of his plight, and begs them to help him find some means of escape. Between them they decide that his only hope is to gnaw through the net and then lower himself to the ground. In this manner Philocleon all but regains his freedom when Bdelycleon, who, worn out with watching,

fell asleep, awakens and again detains him. Although the Wasps quickly come to the aid of their friend, they are no match for the stones and clubs used against them by Bdelycleon and the two slaves, and they are soon driven back.

In the argument that follows, Bdelycleon explains that he simply wants his father to lead the joyous, easy life of an old man rather than concern himself constantly with the tyranny and conspiracy of the courts. He argues convincingly enough to force Philocleon into a debate on the merits of his occupation. Philocleon agrees that if Bdelycleon can convince the Wasps, who are to act as judges, that a public career is disreputable, then he will give it up. The old man, speaking first, defends the jury system on the basis of the pleasures and the benefits that he personally derives from it. Bdelycleon, on the other hand, proves that the jurists are no more than the slaves of the rulers, who themselves receive the bulk of the revenue that should go to feed the hungry people.

Philocleon, along with the Chorus, is converted by Bdelycleon's persuasive argument. Philocleon thinks that he cannot live without judging, however, so Bdelycleon consents to allow him to hold court at their home. Philocleon is to be allowed to judge the slaves and all other things about the house. This solution has the added advantage, as Bdelycleon carefully points out, of allowing Philocleon to eat and to drink and to enjoy all the comforts of home at the same time that he is following his profession.

Philocleon agrees to this solution. All the paraphernalia of a court are quickly assembled, and the first case is called. Labes, one of the household dogs, is accused of stealing and devouring a Sicilian cheese all by himself, having refused to share it with any other animal. Bdelycleon himself undertakes the defense of Labes and pleads for mercy, but Philocleon feels it his duty as a judge to convict everyone and everything that is brought into his court. His son, however, tricks his father into acquitting the dog, an act that is foreign to Philocleon's nature.

Philocleon then concludes that he betrayed the one thing sacred to him—reaching a guilty verdict—and that he is, therefore, no longer capable of judging. Bdelycleon's problems are apparently solved at this point, for his father agrees to live a happy and carefree life. Such a plan, however, entails changing Philocleon's whole mode of being. His manner of dress, his speech—everything about him has to change; in short, he needs to acquire at least some of the elementary social skills. He is to learn how to walk, how to recline at dinner, and what to talk about in order to appear a gentleman of leisure.

After a short period of training Bdelycleon takes his father to a dinner party, where Philocleon quickly proves that he is as much a hardheaded old man as ever. He drinks and eats too much, he insults both his host and the other guests, he beats the slaves who wait on him, and, finally, he runs off with a nude flute girl. On his way home with the girl he strikes everyone that he encounters.

By the time Philocleon arrives home, he has a large following, all anxious to accuse him and to bring him before those courts he so recently abandoned. He tries to appease the people by telling them stories that he just learned and by using his other social skills, but to no avail; everyone clamors for justice. Philocleon, paying no attention to their cries, continues to talk and to act as if he is far above such plebeian concerns. Bdelycleon, who hurries after his father, finally catches up with him and again uses force to get him into the house. This time Bdelycleon is unable to keep the old man there. Philocleon immediately returns to the streets, now determined to prove his dancing skill, and leads off the Chorus in a licentious, drunken dance.

Critical Evaluation:

The Wasps is a brilliant combination of political and social satire. Produced in 422 B.C.E., this play, like Aristophanes' earlier work, is an attack on Aristophanes' personal enemy Cleon, who in Aristophanes' plays is a demagogue

and a manipulator of the Athenian people. In this play Aristophanes does not criticize Cleon for advocating continuation of the Peloponnesian War (431-404 B.C.E.), which was in a temporary lull at the time the play was presented. Instead, Cleon's supposed control of the democratic juries is the focus of the playwright's scorn. The poet's criticism reaches beyond the person of Cleon to the whole institution of popular juries, making *The Wasps* an important historical document regarding contemporary attitudes toward this Athenian institution. *The Wasps* is, however, more than a political critique. Its plot revolves around a single elderly juror whose son wishes to cure the old man's addiction to jury service. *The Wasps* is a brilliant social satire, partly as a result of its clever depiction of tensions between young and old and between rich and poor in Athenian society.

The system of trial by popular jury was a hallmark of Athenian democracy and one of Athens's unique contributions to the world. Most lawsuits were heard by large juries, sometimes composed of more than five hundred volunteers, whose only qualifications were to possess Athenian citizenship and to be over thirty years of age. For their service on juries participants received a small sum, too small to make jury service attractive to most, but enough to enlist the very indigent, infirm, and elderly. Juries were therefore largely peopled by such individuals. The Athenians stubbornly maintained the fiction that the popular juries were representative of the people as a whole. The continuing relevance of this issue is clear. From their verdicts there was no appeal, no matter how capricious or unjust the decision. This background is necessary for understanding the thrust of Aristophanes' comedy. The play suggests that Cleon, by promising greater pay or otherwise manipulating the verdicts of popular juries, exercised undue influence over the courts. Cleon claimed that he was merely acting as the watchdog of Athens, but others, like Aristophanes, apparently saw his activities as another aspect of his vulgar and dangerous political ambition.

One way that Aristophanes makes his topical political satire explicit is by naming his crazed juryman Philocleon ("Cleon-lover") and his son Bdelycleon ("Cleon-hater"). Philocleon, who retired from working his farm and handed over his estate to his son, is in some respects a stereotype of the kind of juryman whom Cleon supposedly could control: He is elderly, he counts on his small income from jury service, and most of all he is drunk with the power he possesses as a jury member over rich and poor alike. All the same, Aristophanes does not depict Philocleon, who is the protagonist of the play, as a mindless stooge. He is extremely clever in frustrating the efforts of his son to curb his appetite for jury duty, and as he articulates the pleasures of sitting in judgment, one is inclined to sympathize with him. On the other hand, although Bdelycleon seems perfectly justified in trying to free his father from his unusual obsession, he appears as a staid, personality free, and generally much less sympathetic character than his father. That Aristophanes probably shared the political views of the less-attractive character is testimony to his outstanding ability as a comic writer.

The Wasps is unique among the surviving plays of Aristophanes in that it contains all of the formal parts of a Greek comedy that scholars consider to be the traditional constituents of the genre. In particular, the play contains a fully developed contest (*agon*) in which the merits and defects of the Athenian jury system are debated. The appearance of the chorus, dressed as wasps equipped with a fearsome sting with which to strike at litigants, means that Philocleon will have support in his advocacy of the joys of jury service. Like Philocleon, the chorus is composed of poor, elderly men who enjoy the feeling of power that comes with passing judgment over those who stand before them as litigants or defendants. In taking the opposite side in the debate, Bdelycleon can only argue that they are duped by individuals such as Cleon. Bdelycleon then openly appeals to their greed and barely manages to win the debate by persuading Philocleon and the chorus that they are poorly compensated for their heroic efforts.

The purpose of the formal debate is to free Philocleon from his obsession, but interestingly enough this object is not accomplished by the end of the contest. Philocleon agrees only to transfer the apparatus of the court to his own home. This is indicative of the strong and stubborn character of Philocleon. At his home the mock trial of the dog by Cuon (Greek for "dog"; the word also sounds like "Cleon") takes place, recalling Cleon's statement that he is the watchdog of Athens and incidentally revealing in the middle of the parody little-known aspects of the workings of the Athenian system of justice. The dog is acquitted of the crime because Bdelycleon sophistically marshals all the manipulative power of oratory in defense of his client, who can only bark. The outcome—it is implied that Philocleon never before voted for acquittal—is a disturbing revelation. Philocleon is free to give himself to new pleasures that are supposedly more appropriate to his age and status. A rejuvenated Philocleon leaves jury duty behind and indulges in food, drink, and sex to his heart's content. *The Wasps* ends with such a burst of riotous celebration that one may suspect, in the view of the proper Bdelycleon, his father's cure is perhaps worse than the original disease.

"Critical Evaluation" by John M. Lawless

Further Reading

Aristophanes. *Wasps*. Edited and translated by Alan H. Sommerstein. Warminster, England: Aris and Phillips, 1983. Provides scholarly introduction, bibliography, Greek text, facing English translation, and commentary keyed to the translation. Sommerstein's translation supersedes most earlier versions.

Dover, K. J. *Aristophanic Comedy*. Berkeley: University of California Press, 1972. Useful and authoritative study of the plays of Aristophanes. Chapter 9 provides a synopsis of the play, discussion of problems with theatrical production, examination of the character of Philocleon, and relevant information on the Athenian courts. An essential starting point for study of the play.

Freydberg, Bernard. "*Wasps* and the Limits of Logos." In *Philosophy and Comedy: Aristophanes, Logos, and Eros*. Bloomington: Indiana University Press, 2008. Freydberg analyzes the philosophical concepts in *The Wasps* and several other plays by Aristophanes

Harriott, Rosemary M. *Aristophanes: Poet and Dramatist*. Baltimore: Johns Hopkins University Press, 1986. In this study of all of Aristophanes' plays, the plays are not discussed in individual chapters but as each illustrates the central themes and techniques of his work.

Rothwell, Kenneth S., Jr. "The Literary Fragments of Aristophanes' *Knights, Wasps*, and *Frogs*." In *Nature, Culture, and the Origins of Greek Comedy: A Study of Animal Choruses*. New York: Cambridge University Press, 2007. Rothwell analyzes *The Wasps* and other comedies in which Aristophanes featured animal choruses. He maintains that these animal characters may be a conscious revival of an earlier Greek tradition of animal representation.

Silk, M. S. *Aristophanes and the Definition of Comedy*. New York: Oxford University Press, 2002. Silk looks at Aristophanes not merely as an ancient Greek dramatist but as one of the world's great poets. He analyzes *The Wasps* and the other plays to examine their language, style, lyric poetry, character, and structure.

Spatz, Lois. *Aristophanes*. Boston: Twayne, 1978. A reliable introduction to the comedy of Aristophanes for the general reader. Chapter 4 summarizes the play and offers discussion of the plot and the major themes.

Whitman, Cedric. *Aristophanes and the Comic Hero*. Cambridge, Mass.: Harvard University Press, 1964. A standard work on the characterization of the Aristophanic protagonist. Chapter 4 discusses *The Wasps*, with special emphasis on the generational conflict depicted by the play.

The Waste Land

Author: T. S. Eliot (1888-1965)
First published: 1922
Type of work: Poetry

T. S. Eliot, together with Ezra Pound, revolutionized the style and structure of poetry in the early twentieth century. Eliot was a modernist poet who, as Pound claimed, modernized himself. His reading of the French Symbolists, especially Jules Laforgue, and such seventeenth century metaphysical poets as John Donne, gave him models for the use of precise imagery and complex structures that contrasted with the softness of late Romantic poetry. With his first book of poems, *Prufrock, and Other Observations* (1917), a new voice appeared in poetry.

Eliot was very successful as a poet and critic in his early years in London. He completed a doctoral dissertation on F. H. Bradley, the philosopher (though he never returned to Harvard to defend it), and in 1915 he married Vivienne Haig Wood. The marriage was unhappy, however, and in 1921 Eliot entered a sanatorium in Switzerland to recover from an emotional breakdown. It was during this disturbed period of his life that he wrote *The Waste Land*. Later that year, Eliot gave the poem to Pound, who cut it by half into its latest form. Eliot's original title for the poem was "He Do the Police in Different Voices," but Pound preferred emphasizing the mythic structure and cut the social satire. Upon publication in 1922, the poem was immediately recognized as a major if very difficult creation. The poet later described *The Waste Land* as "the relief of a personal and wholly insignificant grouse against life; it is just a piece of rhythmical grumbling." It was read by most critics, however, as a social indictment rather than as a personal utterance.

The poem begins with an epigraph from Petronius and a dedication to Ezra Pound as *il miglior fabbro* (the better maker), the tribute paid by Arnaut Daniel to Dante in *Purgatory* of *La divina commedia* (c. 1320; *The Divine Comedy*, 1802). The epigraph portrays the Cumean Sibyl responding to the question "Sibyl, what do you want?" with the answer "I want to die." This sets the mood of despair and hopeless resignation. In portraying the spiritual, sexual, and social emptiness of the post-World War I world, Eliot drew on Jessie L. Weston's *From Ritual to Romance* (1920), on the medieval quest for the Grail, and on James Frazer's *The Golden Bough* (1890-1915), especially the sections on a dying god who is resurrected. From its inception, the poem was centrally concerned with the myth of a dead land that needs to be renewed by a quester or a sacrificial god.

The first section of the poem, "The Burial of the Dead," is a reference to the burial service in the Anglican Church. The time is April, but instead of being a period of renewal it is "the cruelest month." The outer renewal of the seasons is not matched by that within the speakers and characters in the poem. The imagery shifts to the dryness of the wasteland, a place "where the sun beats,/ And the dead tree gives no shelter, the cricket no relief,/ And the dry stone no sound of water." The imagery of dryness becomes a central motif in the poem and is used to define the spiritual and social aridity of the time.

Knowledge and authority in this decayed world are found in "Madame Sosostris, famous clairvoyante" and her pack of tarot cards rather than in the church or state. One of the cards in that deck, "the man with three staves," represents the Fisher King, the wounded ruler whose disease causes the wasteland; the disease can be relieved only by the quester for the Holy Grail who successfully answers ritual questions at the Chapel Perilous. His answers complete the quest and bring fertility to the land. In the last part of this section, Eliot portrays the "Unreal City," an allusion to Charles Baudelaire, with a crowd of dead crossing London Bridge and a corpse that is planted, which will not bloom or provide relief—a parody of renewal. The world of the wasteland is dominated by the living dead.

In the next section, "A Game of Chess," Eliot explores the social world of the wasteland. First, he shows a nervous society woman who isolates herself among the "glitter of jewels" and "synthetic perfumes." Her social life is a substitute for a meaningful one; her routine consists of "The hot water at ten./ And if it rains, a closed car at four." The social world depicted here is similar to the fearful and frustrated world of "The Love Song of J. Alfred Prufrock."

The section ends with a descent into a London pub where two women from the lower class discuss the return of Lil's husband, Albert, from the war. He "wants a good time" upon his return, but Lil has no teeth, and she is a wreck since she took "them pills to bring it off," a reference to her abortion. The sordid scene of sexual and personal sterility is presented in counterpoint with allusions to Ophelia's farewell in William Shakespeare's *Hamlet, Prince of Denmark* (pr. c. 1600-1601, pb. 1603). Eliot consistently juxtaposes the decayed present with the heroic past, using allusions to the Bible, Shakespeare, Richard Wagner, and other great sources of the past.

"The Fire Sermon," the third section, is an allusion to the sermon preached by the Buddha against the fires of lust. Here, Eliot continues his analysis of the arid, meaningless sexuality that fails to bring life or renewal. He begins with negative images of the river Thames: "The river bears no empty bottles, sandwich papers,/ silk handkerchiefs, cardboard boxes, cigarette ends/ Or other testimony of summer nights. The nymphs are departed."

Eliot juxtaposes the sordid modern river with Edmund Spenser's marriage song, "Prothalamion." He also refers to the Fisher King, who is "fishing in the dull canal" and whom he merges with an allusion to the passage in Shakespeare's *The Tempest* (pr. 1611, pb. 1623) in which Ferdinand mourns the supposed death of his father. The song by Ariel to Ferdinand suggests a process in which the bones of his father are metamorphosed into beautiful objects such as "pearls." Eliot contrasts these positive images of metamorphosis with the death-in-life of his world.

Positive allusions are also contrasted with the gay-sex proposal of Mr. Eugenides and the mechanical sexual scene between the carbuncular clerk and the typist. The sexual scene is mediated by Eliot's use of Tiresias, the blind Greek prophet. Eliot claimed that "Tiresias, although a mere spectator and not indeed a 'character,' is yet the most important personage in the poem, uniting all the rest. . . . What Tiresias *sees*, in fact, is the substance of the poem." What Tiresias sees in that passage is the clerk engaging a "bored and tired" young typist in a sexual liaison that she neither desires nor resists. "His vanity requires no response." At the completion of the meaningless, mechanical act, she says, "Well now that's done: and I'm glad its over."

These scenes are followed by one of the most positive images in the poem: There is music in a bar on Lower Thames Street "where fishmen lounge at noon." Eliot expands the allusion to the Fisher King with a reference to a London church, Magnus Martyr, where the walls "hold/ Inexplicable splendor of Ionian white and gold." This is then contrasted with the recurring images of the river that "sweats oil and tar." Another sexual interlude is contrasted with the glorious past, this time with an allusion to Queen Elizabeth sailing on the Thames with her favorite, Essex. After the sexual act, "He wept. He promised 'a new start.' I made no comment. What should I resent." The section ends with images of burn-

ing and of the fires of lust not purged in the poem, slightly mitigated by an allusion to Saint Augustine, who achieved a purgation of these fires by asking God to deliver him from its ravages.

The fourth section of the poem is as brief as it became controversial. It deals with the death of "Phlebas the Phoenician," who drowns in water rather than being renewed by it, and ends with a warning of the transitoriness of life: "Gentile or Jew/ O you who turn the wheel to winward,/ Consider Phlebas, who was once handsome and tall as you." This passage resembles the burial of the body earlier, for this death, too, even though it is by water, brings no renewal.

The last section of the poem, "What the Thunder Said," begins with imagery associated with the Passion of Christ. Eliot chooses to show the death of Christ rather than his resurrection, but even that is preferable to death-in-life: "He who was living is now dead/ We who were living are now dying/ With a little patience." This is followed by images of dryness and an allusion to the appearance of Christ to the disciples at Emmaus.

After a reference to Hermann Hesse's *Blick ins Chaos* (1920; *In Sight of Chaos*, 1923), which portrays the situation of Eastern Europe, the poem moves to the "empty chapel" where the quester passes the last test in the search for the Grail. This leads to the change to which the poem is pointing from the beginning: "Only a cock stood on the rooftree/ Co rico co rico/ In a flash of lightning. Then a damp gust/ Bringing rain." The imagery of rain presumably renews the wasteland. Eliot then turns to the renewal of the individual, using allusions from yet another tradition, the Indian *Upanishads*. He cites the three principles of renewal from that text: give, control, and sympathize. Control can be achieved, but the other principles are yet to become a part of the individual's life. Each individual remains locked within himself, unable to give to others or to sympathize with their plight.

The poem ends with images of leaving the wasteland behind: "I sat upon the shore/ Fishing, with the arid plain behind me/ Shall I at least set my lands in order?" The only order that can be brought about is through a baffling series of allusions and the limited assent: "These fragments I have shored against my ruins." The last lines again refer to the principles of individual renewal from the *Upanishads* and to the work's ending, "Shantih," which Eliot translates in a footnote as "The Peace that passeth understanding." This blessing expresses a desire for enlightenment and peace, but in the poem it is only cited, not achieved.

The Waste Land was recognized soon after its publication as a tremendously important work, one that both defined an attitude toward the period and established a model for other poets to follow. It was believed at the time that poetry needed to be complex, difficult, and filled with allusions to earlier writers, that its structure needed to be mythic and its style a dazzling juxtaposition of elements. The expectations and social role of poetry continually change, but *The Waste Land* continues to be regarded as a monumental achievement that challenges and rewards its readers.

James Sullivan

Further Reading

Beasley, Rebecca. *Theorists of Modernist Poetry: T. S. Eliot, T. E. Hulme, Ezra Pound.* New York: Routledge, 2007. An overview of the origins, aesthetics, and theories of modernist poetry as exemplified by the work of Eliot and his two contemporaries. In addition to analyzing individual poems, Beasley discusses the modernist critique of democracy, the importance of World War I in the development of the new poetics, and the modernist conception of an ideal society.

Bloom, Harold, ed. *T. S. Eliot's "The Waste Land."* Updated ed. New York: Chelsea House, 2007. Collection of essays providing a range of interpretations of the poem.

Brooks, Cleanth, Jr. "*The Waste Land*: An Analysis." *Southern Review* 3, no. 1 (1937-1938): 106-136. Despite its age, this reading by one of the most influential practitioners of the New Criticism remains relevant for its ability to draw out the poem's complexities and ironic structure.

Cooper, John Xiros. *The Cambridge Introduction to T. S. Eliot.* New York: Cambridge University Press, 2006. An introductory overview to Eliot's life and work, focusing on his poetry. Chapter 3 includes an eighteen-page discussion of *The Waste Land*.

Eliot, T. S. *The Annotated "Waste Land" with Eliot's Contemporary Prose.* Edited, with annotations and introduction, by Lawrence Rainey. 2d ed. New Haven, Conn.: Yale University Press, 2006. In addition to the text of the poem, this edition contains extensive annotations, which explain the work's ambiguities and complexities. Rainey's introduction describes the poem's origins and printing history. This volume also contains some of Eliot's correspondence and his essays about the function of criticism and

the poetry of Charles Baudelaire, Andrew Marvel, John Dryden, and the Metaphysical poets.

Frye, Northrop. *T. S. Eliot.* New York: Grove Press, 1963. A prominent literary critic provides an analysis of Eliot's works, focusing on the critical perspective of myth. Frye draws excellent conclusions on the archetypal aspects of *The Waste Land*.

Kenner, Hugh, ed. *T. S. Eliot: A Collection of Critical Essays.* Englewood Cliffs, N.J.: Prentice-Hall, 1962. A useful collection of essays, including three pieces on *The Waste Land*.

Moody, A. David, ed. *The Cambridge Companion to T. S. Eliot.* New York: Cambridge University Press, 1994. Collection of essays, including discussions of Eliot's life; Eliot as a philosopher, a social critic, and a product of America; and religion, literature, and society in Eliot's work. Also features the essay "Improper Desire: Reading *The Waste Land*" by Harriet Davidson.

Raine, Craig. *T. S. Eliot.* New York: Oxford University Press, 2006. In this examination of Eliot's work, Raine maintains that "the buried life," or the failure of feeling, is a consistent theme in the poetry and the plays. Chapter 3 contains an explication of *The Waste Land*.

Rainey, Lawrence. *Revisiting "The Waste Land."* New Haven, Conn.: Yale University Press, 2005. Rainey, who compiled an annotated edition of *The Waste Land* (above), provides a detailed interpretation of the poem. He reveals new information about Eliot's methods of writing the poem and the sequence in which he composed its parts.

Selby, Nick, ed. *T. S. Eliot: "The Waste Land."* New York: Columbia University Press, 2001. A history of the poem's critical reception, beginning with the earliest reviews and critiques in the 1920's and 1930's and proceeding to interpretations written from the perspectives of the New Criticism, Marxism, feminism, modernism, and other approaches to the work.

Williamson, George. *A Reader's Guide to T. S. Eliot: A Poem-by-Poem Analysis.* New York: Noonday Press, 1953. Reprinted. Syracuse, N.Y.: Syracuse University Press, 1998. A close reading of all of Eliot's poems, with a useful introduction to the interpretative problems of *The Waste Land*.

Watch on the Rhine

Author: Lillian Hellman (1905-1984)
First produced: 1941; first published, 1941
Type of work: Drama
Type of plot: Melodrama
Time of plot: Late spring, 1940
Locale: Near Washington, D.C.

Principal characters:
FANNY FARRELLY, a dowager matriarch
DAVID FARRELLY, her son, a lawyer
SARA MULLER, her daughter
KURT MULLER, Sara's German husband, an anti-Nazi
   resistance fighter
JOSHUA,
BABETTE, and
BODO, their children
COUNT TECK DE BRANCOVIS, a ne'er-do-well European
   refugee
COUNTESS MARTHE DE BRANCOVIS, his wife, and a
   daughter of Fanny's childhood friend
ANISE, Fanny's French housekeeper
JOSEPH, Fanny's African American butler

The Story:

In the aristocratic Farrelly home outside Washington, D.C., Fanny Farrelly, with the assistance of her two servants, Anise and Joseph, prepares for the arrival of her daughter, Sara, and her husband and children. Sara has not visited her mother for twenty years, and Fanny has never met her three grandchildren. Nervous about the visit, Fanny tries to get her son, David, and her house guests, Count Teck de Brancovis and Countess Marthe de Brancovis, to breakfast by 9 A.M., as her late husband had decreed.

To her housekeeper, Anise, Fanny reveals that the count and countess are heavily in debt and that she is concerned about David's attraction to the countess. As Fanny and David breakfast on the terrace, Teck and Marthe argue about money, including his gambling with the Nazis at the German embassy, and about Marthe's attraction to David.

After the count and countess retire to the terrace, the Mullers arrive and are impressed with the spacious living room. Sara, poorly dressed, delights in the beautiful things she could not remember. The family discusses Sara's childhood and her memories of unlocked doors, plentiful food, and beautiful clothes—such a contrast to her own family's bleak existence.

Pleased with Sara's mature children, Fanny asks her, "Are these your *children*? Or are they dressed up midgets?" Responding to Fanny's and David's questions, Kurt, Sara's husband, talks about his family's travels and admits that he has not worked at his profession as an engineer for several years, since 1933. He also confesses that his family has not had ade-

quate breakfasts because his new occupation, which he identifies as "anti-fascist," does not pay well. Earlier in his work as an engineer his life was normal. Married to Sara for twelve quiet years, their lives changed when a festival in his hometown ended with a street fight and the murder of twenty-seven men by Nazis.

Kurt and Teck are wary of each other. Kurt recognizes the count's name, and Teck probes to find out more about Kurt. While the family breakfasts on the terrace, Teck examines their luggage. When Marthe tries to interfere, Teck threatens her, warning her not to make plans with David.

Ten days pass, and everyone is now comfortable in the house. Sara is crocheting, Fanny and Teck play cribbage, Bodo "repairs" a heating pad for an anxious Anise, Joseph teaches Joshua to play baseball, and Babette makes potato pancakes for dinner. When Teck questions the children in an obvious attempt to learn more about their father, Sara cuts him off, saying, "It's an indulgence to sit in a room and discuss your beliefs as if they were a juicy piece of gossip."

Teck announces that he and Marthe plan to leave in a few days and suggests that the nature of Kurt's work means that the Mullers will also be moving on. Fanny objects, joking that she plans to keep her family with her for several years because she will take a long time to die. David and Kurt return from assisting a local farmer, and talk turns to Babette's birthday party and to presents for the whole family. Teck becomes angry at the suggestion that David has bought jewelry for Marthe, so Fanny tries to distract him by confronting him with the rumor that he has won a great deal of money in a card game with Nazis.

Kurt and Teck spar about Germany, and Kurt sings "Watch on the Rhine," a song about Germans returning home from World War I. Kurt also sings lyrics made up by Germans, with whom he has fought against the fascists in Spain. Teck again questions the children about their father's activities. Kurt responds, telling Teck to address his questions directly to him.

The atmosphere is temporarily lightened when Marthe enters with dresses that Fanny has bought for Sara and Babette. The pleasant scene is interrupted by a long-distance phone call for Kurt. Teck, Marthe, and David argue about David's gift to Marthe. She declares she will not leave with Teck, insisting David does not have much to do with her situation. When Fanny objects to her staying, Marthe informs her that she had been forced by her mother into the marriage with Teck when she was only seventeen years old and that it had always been an unhappy relationship.

Kurt returns from the call, saying he must leave for California. Teck confronts him with a news story on the capture of three of Kurt's resistance colleagues in Germany. Teck had learned of the capture at the German embassy the previous evening, and upon reviewing a list of resistance fighters, a list the Nazis had given him, he made the connection between Kurt and a man called Gotter, whom the Nazis want. Revealing that he has broken into Kurt's briefcase and had found $23,000 in cash, Teck demands $10,000.

David and Fanny insist that Kurt not submit to the blackmail because they do not believe Teck could harm anyone in their safe American home. Kurt, however, explains that he belongs to an organization the Nazis have outlawed, and they have placed a price on his head. Consequently, he has had problems with his passport and cannot go to the American authorities. Sara realizes that Kurt has to return to Germany to buy friends out of the German prisons, though this would involve great risks for him. She comforts Kurt, clearly supporting his decision.

A half hour later, Kurt, Sara, Fanny, and David are waiting anxiously for Teck to return. Kurt uses the opportunity to dispute the idea that Nazis are supermen. He talks about his imprisoned friend Max, who had saved his life. Teck returns with Kurt's briefcase, but when Kurt refuses to pay the blackmail money, Fanny and David decide they will do so. With them out of the way, Kurt overpowers Teck and kills him.

Kurt justifies his actions to David and Fanny, who accept the violence as necessary and admire Kurt's struggle and sac-

rifices. Emotion-laden farewells follow. Kurt's farewell to his children is especially moving as he speaks of men who love children and fight to make a "good world" for them. Fanny and David are left alone, "shaken out of the magnolias," and bracing for the trouble they know will come when Teck's body is discovered.

"The Story" by Elsie Galbreath Haley

Critical Evaluation:

When Lillian Hellman began writing *Watch on the Rhine* in 1939, the United States had not yet entered World War II, although the playwright was among those urging the U.S. government to commit itself to resisting the Nazi drive to conquer Europe and, perhaps, the United States as well. By the time the play was produced, the Soviet Union had renounced its anti-Nazi policies and had formed a pact with Adolf Hitler. Even though Hellman had supported Joseph Stalin's antifascist line earlier, she refused to endorse the American Communist Party's allegiance to the Hitler-Stalin pact. Indeed, her play renews her commitment to the antifascist cause.

Hellman's aim, however, is not merely to expose the work of Nazi agents in the United States, nor is it to celebrate the heroism of antifascists such as Kurt Muller. She wants, rather, to destroy American complacency—the idea that those like Fanny are safe at home. Evil lurks in Fanny's home precisely because she has provided it with a domicile. Not until Americans like Fanny become aware of America's role in the world, and realize that the country cannot remain isolationist—and keep itself from evil—will the United States be safe and sound.

In early drafts of the play, Hellman identifies Kurt as a communist, thus honoring her belief that the communists are owed a tribute for their early and stalwart opposition to fascism. However, Kurt's communist beliefs become a liability as soon as Stalin forms his partnership with Hitler. Gradually, through many drafts, she drops Kurt's party affiliation, deciding it is more important to make him a universal figure of resistance, a common man called to do extraordinary feats to help restore sanity and order to society.

It had been very important for Hellman to present Kurt as not only a family man but also a vulnerable hero. He detests the need to murder Teck. Such brutality cannot be reconciled with civilized values, and yet the play offers Kurt no other choice. Fanny and David recognize this; that they are willing to become implicated in Kurt's crime is Hellman's signal to her American audience that they, too, will have to become involved in evil to expunge it.

Watch on the Rhine is generally considered the best of the anti-Nazi plays of the 1930's and 1940's, primarily because Hellman wraps her political message in a character drama that focuses on several positive and likable characters. Hellman has been praised for making her protagonist a German, allowing for Muller to assess the Nazis from the point of view of another German.

"Critical Evaluation" by Carl Rollyson

Further Reading

Austenfeld, Thomas Carl. "The Moral Act: Lillian Hellman Fights Fascists in the Parlor." In *American Women Writers and the Nazis: Ethics and Politics in Boyle, Porter, Stafford, and Hellman.* Charlottesville: University Press of Virginia, 2001. An analysis of *Watch on the Rhine*, describing how the play reflects Hellman's political and ethical convictions against fascism and her travels to fascist Spain and Nazi Germany.

Estrin, Mark W. *Critical Essays on Lillian Hellman.* Boston: G. K. Hall, 1989. Contains twenty-three essays discussing three main topics—Hellman's plays, her memoirs, and the Hellman persona. Of special interest are Jacob H. Adler's essay, in which he discusses blackmail in *Watch on the Rhine* and other Hellman plays, and Timothy J. Wills's article, which examines Hellman's political plays and her perspective on war.

Griffin, Alice, and Geraldine Thorsten. *Understanding Lillian Hellman.* Columbia: University of South Carolina Press, 1999. Examination of Hellman's major plays, discussing her style, concern for moral issues, and influence on other American playwrights, including Tennessee Wil-

liams, Arthur Miller, and Marsha Norman. Chapter 4 focuses on *Watch on the Rhine*.

Holman, Lorena Ross. *The Dramatic Works of Lillian Hellman.* Stockholm: Uppsala University Press, 1973. An accessible source for beginners, this book contains a chapter on *Watch on the Rhine* that analyzes characters and structure in detail. Includes an extensive bibliography with journal and newspaper articles and reviews.

Horn, Barbara Lee. *Lillian Hellman: A Research and Production Sourcebook.* Westport, Conn.: Greenwood Press, 1998. Provides an overview of Hellman's life and a plot summary, history, and critical overview of *Watch on the Rhine*. Includes bibliographies of works by and about Hellman.

Lederer, Katherine. *Lillian Hellman.* Boston: Twayne, 1979. A detailed overview of Hellman's life, plays, and nonfiction. Includes a selected bibliography of Hellman's works and secondary sources about the writer. In the discussion of *Watch on the Rhine*, Lederer takes issue with those who see its importance primarily in the character of Kurt Muller, arguing instead that the play concerns multiple characters and as such will remain relevant.

Martinson, Deborah. *Lillian Hellman: A Life with Foxes and Scoundrels.* New York: Counterpoint, 2005. Martinson recounts the events of Hellman's life, describes her galvanic and often acerbic personality, and provides information about the composition and production of her plays.

Rollyson, Carl. *Lillian Hellman: Her Legend and Her Legacy.* New York: St. Martin's Press, 1988. A comprehensive biography of the complex Hellman. Also includes an analysis of *Watch on the Rhine*.

Water Music

Author: T. Coraghessan Boyle (1948-   )
First published: 1981
Type of work: Novel
Type of plot: Picaresque
Time of plot: 1795-1806
Locale: Africa, England, Scotland, and Germany

Principal characters:
MUNGO PARK, a Scottish explorer and author
NED RISE, a con man
JOHNSON (KATUNGA OYO), Mungo's friend and adviser in Africa
AILIE ANDERSON PARK, Mungo's wife
ALEXANDER "ZANDER" ANDERSON, her brother
GEORGIE GLEG, Ailie's persistent suitor
FANNY BRUNCH, Ned's beloved
BILLY BOYLES, Ned's accomplice
ALI, a Moorish potentate
DASSOUD, Ali's henchman
SARAH COLQUHOUN, Ned's mother
EDWARD PIN, her lover
PRENTISS BARRENBOYNE, Ned's benefactor
NELSON SMIRKE, Ned's relentless enemy
SIR REGINALD DURFEYS, Johnson's former owner
SIR JOSEPH BANKS, director of the African Association
LORD TWIT, member of the African Association and Ned's enemy
ADONAIS BROOKS, Fanny's admirer
KARFA TAURA, an African who helps Mungo
D. W. DELP, a surgeon
THE BARONESS, Mungo's lover
THOMAS PARK, Mungo's eldest son

The Story:

In 1795, Scottish explorer Mungo Park is sent to western Africa to find the Niger River, which no European has ever seen. Mungo is the fourth adventurer dispatched by the African Association for Promoting Exploration, a group of wealthy Englishmen intent upon expanding knowledge of uncharted regions. His task is made difficult by geography, climate, and the frequent hostility of the Africans. Captured by the Moorish potentate Ali, Mungo is about to be blinded by Dassoud, Ali's henchman, when he is saved by Johnson, his guide and interpreter. Born Katunga Oyo, Johnson is a former South Carolina slave who became the London valet to Sir Reginald Durfeys and learned to love the world of English writers such as John Milton and Alexander Pope. After killing a gentleman in a duel, Johnson was transported back to Africa, where he escaped and joined up with Mungo.

Back in London, Ned Rise, a lowborn Londoner, survives by his wits, and Ailie Anderson, Mungo's longtime fiancé, waits for Mungo to return from Africa. Ned earns money in a tavern by staging a show featuring a black servant having sex with two prostitutes. Ailie, the daughter of a physician in

Selkirk, Scotland, longs for Mungo's return and must resist the attentions of Georgie Gleg, her father's assistant.

Ned is the illegitimate son of Sarah Colquhoun, an alcoholic. As a youth, he was tortured by Edward Pin, Sarah's lover, who cut off the boy's fingertips to make him a better street beggar. After Pin was killed, Ned lived on the streets. At twelve, he was taken in by Prentiss Barrenboyne, a wealthy bachelor who taught him to play the clarinet. Ned lived with Barrenboyne for seven years, until his benefactor was killed in a duel with Johnson. A life of living by his wits has led to the sex show. When police raid it, Ned plunges into the icy Thames River, the first of two times he will be assumed to be dead.

Rescued from the river by two fishermen, Ned begins selling what he passes off as authentic Russian caviar. He must assume disguises to hide from those arrested in or socially embarrassed by the sex-show raid. Ned especially wants to avoid Smirke, the landlord of the tavern, who would kill him without hesitation. When he is recognized by Billy Boyles, he enlists his old friend in the caviar scam.

In Africa, Johnson and Mungo are taken on a journey into the desert. They escape and make their way to Segu, which sits on the west bank of the Niger. Because the African Association, directed by Sir Joseph Banks, knows Africa only from sixteenth century maps, Mungo's discovery of the river will change the European perception of the continent. During his London days, Johnson told several members of the association about Africa, but they have no faith in the words of their racial "inferior." Even Mungo cannot shake his view of Johnson as a savage because his guide rejects the Bible.

Back in Scotland, Gleg gives Ailie a microscope, stimulating her enthusiasm for making scientific sketches of minutia. Mungo grows weary of exploring and of Africa. When Johnson is apparently eaten by a crocodile, Mungo continues his journey alone. His supporters are beginning to believe that the explorer will not return, and Ailie agrees to marry Gleg if she has not heard from Mungo in a year.

Ned meets and falls in love with Fanny Brunch, Sir Joseph's parlormaid. The two plan to elope to the Hague, but his enemies track him down and beat him. In the melee, Lord Twit is killed, and Ned is blamed for murder.

Mungo is captured by Dassoud's men but escapes, only to be overcome by fever. He is taken in by Karfa Taura, who admires his literacy. Mungo then joins some slave traders and becomes surgeon on a slave ship to South Carolina before making his way back to England. Ailie walks out on Gleg on the day of their wedding; she learns later that Mungo has returned but resents his decision to stay in London to write *Travel in the Interior Districts of Africa* (1799). Humiliated, Gleg leaves Selkirk. Mungo becomes caught up in his own celebrity and is seduced by the baroness. When he finally returns to Selkirk, Ailie demands he court her again from the beginning, and they soon marry.

With Ned imprisoned and awaiting execution, Fanny despairs for her future and agrees to become the mistress of the lustful Adonais Brooks in exchange for the aristocrat's assistance to Ned. Nevertheless, Ned is hanged, only to regain consciousness while his body is about to be dissected during a medical lecture. He and Boyles become body snatchers so that the surgeon, Delp, will keep quiet about Ned's miraculous survival. When one of their thefts is discovered, a reward is offered for the capture of the grave robbers. Ned leaves for Hertford, hoping to find word of Fanny, who has been taken to Germany by Brooks. In Germany, Fanny discovers that she is pregnant with Ned's child and escapes. Later, in London, her son is snatched, and she commits suicide by jumping off Blackfriars Bridge.

Now the father of three, Mungo settles in Peebles, Scotland, as a physician but finds the work tedious and longs for more adventures. Ned meets his son in Hertford, but he does not know the boy's identity. Ned is convicted of trespassing and sentenced to twenty years at hard labor. He and Boyles volunteer to join Mungo's next expedition in exchange for pardons. The famous explorer leaves Scotland and Ailie, who is pregnant with their fourth child, without telling her his destination. She decides they are finished when she learns that Mungo and Zander, her beloved brother, have abandoned her. Gleg returns after an absence of seven years.

In Africa, Ned considers Mungo foolish but brave and tries to ingratiate himself to the explorer. He is appalled to see his enemy Smirke among the explorer's men. Mungo is unable to recruit many Africans because they perceive him as a bad risk. Other inhabitants are even less friendly: They kill Boyles. Ned decides he must somehow take charge of the expedition, or all its members will be doomed.

Mungo stumbles into Johnson's village and finds his old friend alive. Calling himself Isaaco, Johnson refuses to acknowledge his identity. He is disheartened to see that Mungo has not learned from his past mistakes. Smirke attacks Ned, who overpowers his adversary and sells him to cannibals. The men contract fevers, and Zander dies.

Ailie becomes bored waiting for her life to resume and soon starts acting like a widow. She goes boating with Gleg, who seduces her. The Loch Ness monster appears, and she takes its manifestation as a signal of her waywardness.

Mungo builds a boat to sail down the Niger, but Johnson refuses to go. While launching his boat, Mungo narrowly escapes shots fired by the relentless Dassoud. On the river, Mungo finds himself constantly surrounded by hostile peoples. Each time, he escapes his aggressors only after losing men and supplies. Ned admires Mungo for having a purpose in his life and decides not to go back to England. Dassoud catches up with Mungo and fires at him again just as the boat crashes into the rocks of the Niger. Only Ned survives. Ailie establishes a shrine to the fallen hero and refuses to respond to Gleg's proposal. Years later, Thomas, the son of Mungo who is most like his father, disappears into Africa and is never heard from again.

Critical Evaluation:

Water Music announced the arrival of a fresh voice in American fiction. T. Coraghessan Boyle's debut novel established a pattern that he would follow in subsequent works such as *World's End* (1987), *The Road to Wellville* (1993), and *The Women* (2009). In these novels, Boyle uses the past, often incorporating historical figures and events, to examine the foibles of his own time.

While working on a doctorate at the University of Iowa in

the 1970's, Boyle emphasized nineteenth century English literature in his studies, though a collection of short stories served as his dissertation. *Water Music* shows the influence of works by Charles Dickens such as *Oliver Twist: Or, The Parish Boy's Progress* (serial, 1837-1839; book, 1838; originally pb. as *The Adventures of Oliver Twist*) and *David Copperfield* (serial, 1849-1850; book, 1850; originally pb. as *The Personal History of David Copperfield*), but it also has much in common with earlier English novels. With the constant ups and downs of its characters; its reliance on coincidence; and its treatment of poverty, greed, crime, bawdy sex, and bodily functions, *Water Music* recalls such picaresque novels as Henry Fielding's *The History of the Life of the Late Mr. Jonathan Wild the Great* (1743; revised, 1754), Tobias Smollett's *The Advertures of Roderick Random* (1748), and Daniel Defoe's *The Fortunes and Misfortunes of the Famous Moll Flanders, Written from Her Own Memorandums* (1722; commonly known as *Moll Flanders*).

Like John Barth's *The Sot-Weed Factor* (1960; revised, 1967) and Thomas Berger's *Little Big Man* (1964), *Water Music* offers a loving perspective on the conventions of the picaresque novel. The novel is full of colorful characters, improbable situations, and numerous cliffhangers. Though Boyle visited London and Selkirk, he did not know Africa at first hand. He acknowledges in the "Apologia" that he is not interested in historical accuracy and that he sprinkled *Water Music* with deliberate anachronisms to call attention to the artifice of his narrative; these anachronisms include such slang expressions as "tell it like it is." The novel is crammed with allusions to works created after Park's time by writers, poets, filmmakers, and musicians including Dickens, Anthony Trollope, Edward Lear, Thomas Hardy, Joseph Conrad, George Bernard Shaw, Robert Frost, Nikolai Gogol, Mikhail Sholokhov, Flannery O'Connor, Luis Bunuel, Muddy Waters, Bob Dylan, and Arlo Guthrie. Boyle keeps his readers aware that they are in the midst of an imaginative act, not historical fact.

Boyle considers serious topics, such as racism, imperialism, and the societal inequities embodied by Ned and Fanny. The powerful ignore the poverty of London. The members of the African Association seek to exploit Africa without regard for its inhabitants, whom they regard as backward. Mungo is a benign racist, interpreting his travels as something no one else ever experienced and ignoring the inhabitants he encounters. Ailie refuses to accept reports of her husband's death because they originate with people she regards as racial inferiors.

The Mungo-Johnson relationship satirizes the standard treatment in American fiction of the strong white hero and his loyal nonwhite sidekick, as in James Fenimore Cooper's *The Last of the Mohicans* (1826) and Mark Twain's *Adventures of Huckleberry Finn* (1885). Johnson is infinitely wiser and more resilient than Mungo. Ailie is an intelligent, resourceful woman whose ambitions are restrained by the strictures of her society, which insists on seeing her only as a wife and mother. Likewise, Fanny has only two choices in life: She can be a servant or a whore.

Ned becomes the hero of *Water Music* by refusing to remain a victim. While he and Mungo share many characteristics, Ned is much more adaptable. He is more realistic than Mungo, and he grows to appreciate Africa for what it has to offer his soul. The novel's title refers to the 1717 orchestral movements by George Frideric Handel, and *Water Music* is filled with references to music and to water. The Niger remains only a destination for Mungo, and he pays for ignoring its dangerous beauty with his life. Ned will thrive in Africa because he hears the river's music.

Water Music offers considerable entertainment value. Boyle has fun with his narrative by using unusual words—especially those related to food—offering overripe passages to call attention to his self-mocking style, and injecting oddities such as an elaborate recipe for baked stuffed camel. Boyle epitomizes the vitality of the storyteller.

Water Music celebrates the power of the written word. Johnson sees it as a source of everything from wisdom to sexual potency. Mungo repays a Muslim for his hospitality by scribbling the Lord's Prayer on a slate. The man wipes the slate clean with a wet cloth, squeezes the residue into a cup, and drinks it to derive maximum benefit of the words. *Water Music* is a testament to the joys of language and literary style.

Michael Adams

Further Reading

Boyle, T. Coraghessan. "An Interview with T. Coraghessan Boyle." Interview by Elizabeth Adams. *Chicago Review* 37, nos. 2/3 (Summer, 1991): 51-63. The author briefly discusses the influence of nineteenth century British fiction on his work.

_____. "T. Coraghessan Boyle: The Art of Fiction CLXI." Interview by George Plimpton and Elizabeth Adams. *Paris Review* 42 (Summer, 2000): 100-126. Boyle discusses the impact of reading more than one hundred nineteenth century novels before writing *Water Music* and how Dickens inspired him to be a popular entertainer through his fiction.

Gleason, William Paul. *Understanding T. C. Boyle*. Columbia: University of South Carolina Press, 2009. Excellent overview of *Water Music*. Discusses its factual sources and literary inspirations

Howe, Nicholas. "Looking for a River: Or, Travelers in Africa." *Research in African Literatures* 32, no. 3 (Autumn, 2001): 229-241. Places Park's writings in the context of other writing about African exploration. Discusses Boyle's depiction of Park as a geographical missionary.

Law, Danielle. "Caught in the Current: Plotting History in *Water Music*." *Inbetween* 5, no. 1 (March, 1995): 41-50. Examines Boyle's use of historical fact in his fiction.

Waverley
Or, 'Tis Sixty Years Since

Author: Sir Walter Scott (1771-1832)
First published: 1814
Type of work: Novel
Type of plot: Historical
Time of plot: 1745
Locale: England and Scotland

Principal characters:
EDWARD WAVERLEY, a young English officer
BARON BRADWARDINE, a Scottish nobleman
ROSE BRADWARDINE, the baron's daughter
EVAN DHU MACCOMBICH, a follower of Fergus Mac Ivor
DONALD BEAN LEAN, a Highland bandit
FERGUS MAC IVOR VICH IAN VOHR, the leader of the clan of Mac Ivor
FLORA MAC IVOR, Fergus's sister
PRINCE CHARLES EDWARD STUART, the Young Pretender

The Story:

The English family of Waverley is long known for its Jacobite sympathies. In 1745, Waverley-Honour, the ancestral home of the family, is a quiet retreat for Sir Everard Waverley, an elderly Jacobite. In an attempt to seek political advantage in London, his brother, Richard Waverley, swears loyalty to the king.

Edward Waverley, the son of Whig Richard, divides his time between his father and his Uncle Everard at Waverley-Honour. On that great estate, Edward is free to come and to go as he pleases, for his tutor Pembroke, a devout dissenter, is often too busy writing religious pamphlets to spend much time with the education of his young charge. When Edward becomes old enough, his father obtains a commission in the army for him. Shortly afterward, he is ordered to Scotland to join the dragoons of Colonel Gardiner. Equipped with the necessary articles of dress, accompanied by a retinue of men selected by Sir Everard, and weighed down by the dissenting tomes of Pembroke, Edward leaves Waverley-Honour in quixotic fashion to conquer his world.

He is instructed by Sir Everard to visit an old friend, Sir Cosmo Comyne Bradwardine, whose estate is near the village of Tully-Veolan in the Scottish Lowlands. Soon after his arrival at the post of Colonel Gardiner, Edward obtains leave to go to Tully-Veolan. There he finds Sir Everard's friend both cordial and happy to see him. The few days spent at Tully-Veolan convince Edward that Scotland is a wilder and a more romantic land than his native England. He pays little attention to Rose Bradwardine, the baron's daughter, his youthful imagination being fired instead by the songs and dances of Davie Gellatley, the baron's servant, and by tales about the Scottish Highlanders and their rude ways. At Tully-Veolan, he is also confronted by a political issue that was but an idealistic quarrel in his former existence; these Scottish people are Jacobites, and because of his father's politics and his own rank in the army of Hanoverian George II of England Edward ostensibly is a Whig Royalist.

During his stay at Tully-Veolan, an event occurs that changes Edward's life. It begins with the unexpected arrival of Evan Dhu Maccombich, a Highlander in the service of the renowned clan chieftain Fergus Mac Ivor Vich Ian Vohr, a friend of the baron. Since his taste for romantic adventure is aroused, Edward begs another extension of his leave in order to accompany Evan Dhu into the Highlands. In those rugged hills, Edward is led to the cave that shelters the band of Donald Bean Lean, an outlaw who robs and plunders the wealthy Lowlanders. Staying with the bandit only long enough to discover the romantic attachment between Donald's daughter Alice and Evan Dhu, Edward again sets out into the hills with his cheerful young guide. His curiosity is sufficiently whetted by Evan's descriptions of Fergus Mac Ivor and his ancient castle deep in the Highland hills at Glennaquoich.

The welcome Mac Ivor extends to Edward is openhanded and hearty. No less warm is the quiet greeting that Flora, Mac Ivor's sister, has for the English soldier. Flora is a beautiful woman of romantic, poetic nature, and Edward soon finds himself deeply in love with the chieftain's sister. Mac Ivor seems to sanction the idea of a marriage. That union can never be, however, for Flora vows her life to another cause—that of placing Charles, the young Stuart prince, on the throne of England. When Edward proposes marriage, Flora advises him to seek a woman who can attach herself wholeheartedly to his happiness; Flora claims that she cannot divide her attentions between the Jacobite cause and marriage to one who is not an ardent supporter of Charles Edward Stuart.

Edward's stay at Glennaquoich is interrupted by letters carried to him by Davie Gellatley from Tully-Veolan. The first is from Rose, who advises him that the Lowlands are in a state of revolt. Since her father is absent, she warns Edward not to return to Tully-Veolan. The other letters inform him that Richard Waverley engaged in some unfortunate political maneuvers that caused his political downfall. On the heels of this news come orders from Colonel Gardiner, who, having heard reports of Edward's association with traitors, is relieving the young officer of his command. Repulsed by Flora and disgraced in his army career, Edward resolves to return to Waverley-Honour. He equips himself suitably for the dangerous journey and sets out toward the Lowlands.

Because of armed revolt in Scotland and the linking of the Waverley name with the Jacobite cause, Edward finds himself under arrest for treason against King George. The dissenting pamphlets of Pembroke that he carries, his stay in the Highlands, and the company he keeps there are suspicious circumstances that make it impossible for him to prove his innocence. He is captured by some of the king's troops and turned over to an armed guard with orders to take him to Stirling Castle for trial on a charge of treason.

Because he is a friend of Mac Ivor, however, a quick ambush rescues Edward from his captors, and he finds himself once again in the hands of Highlanders. He recognizes them as a party of Donald Bean Lean's followers. Indeed, Alice once appears among the men to slip a packet of letters to him, but at the time, he has no opportunity to read the papers she gives him so secretively.

A few days' journey brings Edward to the center of Jacobite activities at Holyrood, the temporary court of Charles Edward Stuart, who secretly crosses the channel from France.

There Edward finds Mac Ivor awaiting him. When the Highlander presents Edward to Charles, the Pretender welcomes the English youth because of the name he bears. The prince, trained in French courts, is a model of refinement and courtesy. His heartfelt trust gives Edward a feeling of belonging, particularly because he lost his commission, his cause unheard, in the English army. When Charles asks him to join in the Scottish uprising, Edward assents. Mac Ivor seems quite happy about Edward's new allegiance. When the young Englishman asks about Flora, Mac Ivor explains that he brought her along to the prince's court so that she can help him gain a political foothold once the battle is won. Edward resents this manner of using Flora as bait, but soon he perceives that the court of the Pretender functions very much like the French court where Charles and his followers learned statecraft. Mac Ivor presses Edward to continue his courtship of Flora. The sister of Mac Ivor, however, meets his advances coldly. In the company of the Highland beauty is Rose, whose father also joins the Stuart cause.

Edward is accepted as a cavalier by the women who cluster around Charles. Under the influence of the Pretender's courtly manners, Edward soon becomes a favorite, but Mac Ivor's sister persists in ignoring him. He begins to compare the two women, Rose and Flora, and Rose gains favor in his eyes as he watches them together.

The expedition of the Pretender and his Highlanders is doomed to failure. As they march southward to England, they begin to lose hope. The prince orders a retreat to Scotland. Many of the clansmen are killed at the disastrous Battle of Culloden. The survivors escape to the Highlands to spend their days in hiding from troops sent to track them down. A few are fortunate enough to make their way in safety to France.

Edward manages to get away and to find a friend who helps him to steal back to Scotland, where he hopes to find Rose. By now, Edward clears himself of the earlier charges of treachery and desertion, which were the initial cause of his joining the Pretender. It is Donald Bean Lean who deceives Colonel Gardiner with a false report of Edward's activities. The letters Alice slips to him convey that information to Edward. Now he hopes to escape to France with Rose and wait for a pardon from England. Richard Waverley dies, and Edward inherits his fortune.

Mac Ivor and Evan Dhu are executed for their crimes against the Crown, and the power of the Highland clan is broken. Flora enters a Catholic convent in France, the country in which she was reared. Edward and Rose are married once Edward makes certain of his pardon. They return to Tully-Veolan, where the baron's estate awaits its heirs.

Critical Evaluation:

Regarded as the first historical novel, Sir Walter Scott's *Waverley* is a striking representative of literature about the Highlanders and Lowlanders of pre-nineteenth century Scotland. Like Maria Edgeworth in her *Castle Rackrent* (1800), Scott intended his novel to be a romanticized sketch of a people and their customs during a time that had faded into history by the time he wrote *Waverley*. A tension exists in the novel between Scott's romanticized description of the Highlanders who fought in the Stuart uprising of 1745 and a story based on historical fact and eyewitness accounts.

Scott romanticizes the story by including various vivid, poetic descriptions of the eerie, rugged Highland terrain to elicit a sense of awe in his readers. Inspired by the success of his long poem *Lady of the Lake* (1810), Scott intended *Waverley* as a piece of poetic prose. Scott also romanticizes the novel through the plot. Typical of heroes of romances, Edward overcomes many obstacles in pursuit of a valued object. In the course of the novel, a young man whose perceptions were clouded by the romantic tales of English chivalry and Highland nobility that he read as a child experiences disillusionment and education. An introvert who needs someone to care for him, Edward finds a companion in Rose Bradwardine, a gentlewoman more inclined to domestic pleasures than to Highland heroics. At one significant point, Rose proves to be Edward's rescuer; gaining the support of Prince Charles, she has Edward rescued from his Lowland captors and returned to the forces of Fergus Mac Ivor. When Edward learns that it is Rose who rescued him, he pledges to marry her.

Edward's romance is made interesting by the nature of his conflict: He is torn in his allegiance between the old Jacobite order, represented by Prince Charles Edward Stuart and Fergus and Flora Mac Ivor, and the new Hanoverian order represented by Colonel Talbut, who ventures into the battle between the Scots and the English to rescue Waverley. Fiercely loyal, the Highlanders supporting Charles Stuart's claim to the English throne are holding on to a way of life that, to Scott, has become archaic. On the other hand, the Hanoverians—and Edward is initially a part of this order as a young British recruit—are more rational, more benevolent. To Edward, this conflict is intensified by Flora, sister of Highland prince Mac Ivor. Although Edward falls in love with Flora, he finally accepts that this woman, as politically fanatical as her brother, is not the companion he seeks. Edward's conflict is resolved when he concludes that the warring life of the Highlander is not for him, and Scott creates a traditional ending: Edward marries Rose, characters that become estranged from the Crown are forgiven, and enmities are placed aside.

A possible contradiction of Scott's romanticizing of the Highlanders is his device of intermingling historical narratives from individuals who witnessed the Highland uprising of 1745. In the final chapter of *Waverley*, Scott asserts that this work is historically accurate: "The accounts of the battle at Preston, and the skirmish at Clifton, are taken from the narrative of intelligent eye-witnesses, and corrected from the History of the Rebellion by the late venerable author of Douglas." In his preface to the third edition, Scott defends the character of the ruthless Highlander Callum Beg as being "that of a spirit naturally turned to daring evil and determined, by the circumstances of his situation, to a particular species of mischief." Following the defeat of the Highlanders and the trial and execution of Mac Ivor, the romantic ending is somewhat anticlimactic.

The one element that most contributes to the success of *Waverley* is the character of Mac Ivor, who is not only the novel's most realistic character but also its one true hero. Mac Ivor is an intensely loyal man who is true to his word and incapable of understanding Edward's doubts about joining the Highland cause. Mac Ivor is a tragic hero, however, because his steadfastness is also his flaw. He remains intensely, even blindly, loyal to the Stuarts, and in the most powerful scene of the novel, he proclaims his loyalty to Scotland and the Stuart cause as he is condemned to execution for his role in the uprising.

The other characters must be judged in relation to Mac Ivor. Edward Waverley, as his name suggests, is not capable of Fergus's unwavering devotion to a political cause. Because of his friendship with Mac Ivor, Edward learns that his is not to be a life of military endeavor. Mac Ivor makes the point to Edward, completely taken by Charles's charisma, that the prince mingles foolish words with his military talk and that he is not the gallant, heroic figure that he might seem to be. The Pretender ultimately abandons his Highland supporters and flees to the Continent, but Mac Ivor remains and is finally beheaded. Even Baron Bradwardine, representative of a heroic past that Scott tries to capture, is pedantic, pretentious, and ridiculous when measured by the realistic and heroic standard of Mac Ivor. The only character who is a match for Mac Ivor's heroism is Colonel Talbut, who also represents the benevolence and rationality of the new Hanoverian order.

The novel's vivid descriptions and high adventure support Scott's purpose in writing this novel. Although not born a Highlander, Scott wrote *Waverley* for "the purpose of preserving some of the ancient manners, of which I have witnessed the almost total extinction."

"Critical Evaluation" by Richard Logsdon

Further Reading

D'Arcy, Julian Meldon. *Subversive Scott: The Waverley Novels and Scottish Nationalism*. Reykjavík, Iceland: Vigdís Finnbogadóttir Institute of Foreign Languages, University of Iceland, 2005. Demonstrates how the novels contain dissonant elements, undetected manifestations of Scottish nationalism, and criticism of the United Kingdom and its imperial policy. Chapter 1 examines *Waverley*.

Davie, Donald. *The Heyday of Sir Walter Scott*. London: Routledge & Kegan Paul, 1961. Considers some of the factors contributing to the enormous popularity of Scott's novels in the nineteenth century.

Hillhouse, James Theodore. *The Waverley Novels and Their Critics*. New York: Octagon Books, 1968. Contains critical reviews of Scott's novels.

Humphrey, Richard. *"Waverley."* New York: Cambridge University Press, 1993. Concise, useful introduction to the novel. Humphrey divides his analysis into four parts: "Scott's changing world and the making of *Waverley*," "*Waverley* as story," "*Waverley* as history," and "*Waverley* as initiator"—by which he means that the novel provided a model not only for subsequent Scott works but also for novels written by many other writers. An interesting appendix contains contemporary accounts of the Battle of Prestonpans.

Irvine, Robert P. "The State, the Domestic, and National Culture in the Waverley Novels." In *Enlightenment and Romance: Gender and Agency in Smollett and Scott*. New York: Peter Lang, 2000. Analyzes the fiction of Scott and of Tobias Smollett within the context of the emergence of social sciences and the dominance of novels written by female writers in the eighteenth century. Describes how the authors adapted the feminine romance and the domestic novel to assert control over the narrative structure of their novels.

Lincoln, Andrew. "Towards the Modern Nation: *The Lay of the Last Minstrel, Marmion, The Lady of the Lake*, and *Waverley*." In *Walter Scott and Modernity*. Edinburgh: Edinburgh University Press, 2007. In his examination of Scott's novels and poems, Lincoln argues that these were not works of nostalgia; instead, Scott used the past as a means of exploring modernist moral, political, and social issues.

Scott, Sir Walter. *Waverley: Or, 'Tis Sixty Years Since*. Edited by Claire Lamont. New York: Oxford University Press, 1986. Contains an excellent introduction to the historical and narrative background of *Waverley*, as well as Scott's notes and prefaces to the novel.

Shaw, Harry E., ed. *Critical Essays on Sir Walter Scott: The Waverley Novels*. New York: G. K. Hall, 1996. Collection of essays published between 1858 and 1996 about Scott's series of novels. Includes journalist Walter Bagehot's 1858 article about the Waverley novels and discussions of Scott's rationalism, storytelling and subversion of the literary form in his fiction, and what his work meant to Victorian readers. Marilyn Orr's essay "Real and Narrative Time: *Waverley* and the Education of Memory" analyzes this novel.

Welsh, Alexander. *The Hero of the Waverley Novels*. New Haven, Conn.: Yale University Press, 1963. An interpretation of Scott's hero, whose behavior is determined by class and who is acted upon by outside forces.

The Waves

Author: Virginia Woolf (1882-1941)
First published: 1931
Type of work: Novel
Type of plot: Psychological realism
Time of plot: Between World War I and World War II
Locale: England

Principal characters:
BERNARD, a phrase maker
NEVILLE, a poet
SUSAN, an elemental woman
RHODA, a plain, clumsy misfit
JINNY, a hedonist
LOUIS, a self-conscious outcast of his social group
PERCIVAL, a symbol of the ordinary person

The Story:

The waves roll shoreward, and at daybreak the children awake. Watching the sunrise, Bernard, maker of phrases and seeker of causes, sees a loop of light—he will always think of it as a ring, the circle of experience giving life pattern and meaning. Shy, passionate Neville imagines a globe dangling against the flank of day. Susan, who loves fields and seasons, sees a slab of yellow, the crusted loaf, the buttered slice, of teatime in the country. Rhoda, awkward and timid, hears wild cries of startled birds. Sensuous, pleasure-loving Jinny sees a tassel of gold and crimson. Louis, of a race that had seen women carry red pitchers to the Nile, hears a chained beast stamping on the sands.

While the others play, Louis hides among the currants. Jinny, finding him there and pitying his loneliness, kisses him. Suddenly jealous, Susan runs away, and Bernard follows to comfort her. They walk across fields to Elvedon, where they see a woman writing at a window. Later, in the schoolroom, Louis refuses to recite because he is ashamed of his Australian accent. Rhoda is unable to do her sums and has to stay in. Louis pities her, for she is the one he does not fear.

The day brightens. Bernard, older now, yawns through the headmaster's speech in chapel. Neville leans sideways to watch Percival, who sits flicking the back of his neck. A glance, a gesture, Neville realizes, and one could fall in love forever. Louis, liking order, sits quietly. As long as the headmaster talks, Louis forgets the snickers at his accent and memories of kisses underneath a hedge. Susan, Jinny, and Rhoda are in a school where they sit primly under a portrait of Queen Alexandra. Susan thinks of hay waving in the meadows at home. Jinny pictures a gold and crimson party dress. Rhoda dreams of picking flowers and offering them to someone whose face she has never seen.

Time passes, and the last day of the term arrives. Louis goes to work in London after his father, a Brisbane banker, had failed. In his attic room, Louis sometimes hears the great beast stamping in the dark, but now the noise is that of city crowds and traffic. At Cambridge, Neville reads Catullus and waits with uneasy eagerness for Percival's smile or nod. Bernard is Byron's young man one day, Shelley's or Dostoevski's the next. One day, Neville brings him a poem. Reading it, Bernard feels that Neville will succeed and that he will fail. Neville is in love with Percival. In his phrase making, Bernard becomes many people—a plumber, a horse breeder, an old woman on the street. In Switzerland, Susan dreams of newborn lambs in baskets, of marsh mist and autumn rains, of the lover who will walk with her beside dusty hollyhocks. At a ball in London, Jinny, dancing, feels as if her body glows with inner fire. Rhoda, at the same ball, sits and stares across the rooftops.

They all love Percival. Before he leaves for India, they meet at a dinner party in London to bid him good-bye. Bernard, not knowing that Susan loves him, is already engaged. Louis is learning to cover his shyness with brisk assurance; the poet has become a businessman. Rhoda is frightened by life. Waiters and diners look up when Jinny enters, lovely and poised. Susan arrives looking dowdy, hating London. Neville, loving Percival in secret, dreads the moment of parting that will carry him away. Here, thinks Bernard, is the ring he had seen long ago. Youth is friendship and a stirring in the blood, like the notes of Percival's wild hunting song.

The sun passes the zenith, and shadows lengthen. When word comes that Percival has been killed in India, Neville feels as if that doom has been his own. He will go on to become a famous poet and scholar, always a lonely man waiting in his rooms for the footstep on the stair of this young man or that whom he will love in place of Percival. Bernard is married by now, and his son has been born. He thinks of Susan, whom Percival had loved. Rhoda also thinks of Susan, engaged to her farmer in the country. She remembers the dream in which she had offered flowers to a man whose face had been hidden from her, and she knows at last that the man had been Percival.

Shadows grow longer over country and town. Louis, a wealthy, successful businessman, plans a place in Surrey with greenhouses and rare gardens. He still keeps his attic room, though, where Rhoda often visits; they have become lovers. Susan walks in the fields with her children or sits sewing by the firelight in a quiet room. Jinny grooms a body shaped for gaiety and pleasure. Neville measures time by the hours he spends waiting for the footstep on the stair, the young face at the door. Bernard tries to snare in phrases the old man on the train, the lovers in the park. The only realities, he thinks, are in common things. He realizes that he has lost friends by death—Percival for one—and others because he had not wished to cross the street. After Louis and Rhoda part, Louis gets a new mistress: a vulgar cockney actor. Rhoda, always in flight, goes to Spain. Climbing a hill to look across the sea toward Africa, she thinks of rest and longs for death.

Slowly, the sun sets. At Hampton Court, the six friends meet again for dinner. They are old now, and each had gone a different way after Percival had died in India years before. Bernard feels that he has failed. He had wrapped himself in phrases; he had sons and daughters, but he had ventured no farther than Rome. He had not become rich, like Louis, or famous, like Neville. Jinny had lived only for pleasure, little enough, as she was learning. After dinner, Bernard and Susan walk by the lake. There is little of their true thoughts they can say to each other. Bernard, however, is still a maker of phrases. Percival, he says, had become like the flower on the table where they ate—six-sided, made from their six lives.

So it seems to Bernard years later, after Rhoda had jumped to her death and the rest are even older. He wonders what the real truth had been beneath Louis's middle-class respectability, Rhoda's haunted imagination, Neville's passion for one love, Susan's primitivism, Jinny's sensuous pleasures, his own attempt to catch reality in a phrase. He had been Byron's young man and Dostoevski's and also the hairy old savage in the blood. Once he had seen a loop of light, a ring, but he had found no pattern and no meaning, only the knowledge that death is the great adversary against whom humans ride in the darkness where the waves break on the shore.

Critical Evaluation:

In *The Waves*, Virginia Woolf explores the fictional representation of the unconscious and the connection between the unconscious and fluidity, the interplay of which permeates the text. Images and suggestions of fluid elements permeate the text and extend from the book's title through its closing line, "The waves broke on the shore." Bernard invites Susan to explore a new idyllic world of fluid, unshackled communication where "the lady sits between the two long windows, writing."

Woolf expresses this idea of fluidity most purely in the interludes. In the first interlude, "Everything became softly amorphous, as if the china of the plate flowed and the steel of the knife were liquid." The fluidity of formerly concrete objects, the liquidity of formerly blunt or sharp ones, constitutes a metamorphosis metaphor throughout the novel, as in the interlude "A plate was like a white lake." When the sun sinks, in a later interlude, the iron black boot becomes "a pool of deep blue," and the rocks "lose their hardness."

Tellingly, Neville, who hates "dangling" or "dampish things," is the most resistant to the disruption caused by such fluidity. He insists on order. Somewhat ironically, he is the spokesperson for the powerless frustration of being appropriated by someone else's language when he says, "We are all phrases in Bernard's story." Neville alludes to the illusory nature of linguistic mastery and critiques allegedly guaranteed meanings: "Nothing should be named lest by so doing we change it."

Bernard, the discriminating phrase maker, uses language in ways that satisfy his ego. When describing how and what he will write to impress his woman friend with his profundity, he acknowledges his ability to appropriate events. After his discussion with Neville, Bernard alludes to the power to create and re-create the self, or selves, that constitutes a presence: "I am Bernard; I am Byron; I am this, that and the other. . . . For I am more selves than Neville thinks."

Woolf's idealistic vision of the emerging self is possible only when the feminine and masculine permeate each other. This androgyny is given its most physical manifestation in the most body-oriented of the characters, Jinny, who describes many experiences in terms of fluid interaction between men and women. Jinny, who objectifies herself in the looking glass, reflects both literally and figuratively on the limitations of language for her. To experience the warmth and privacy of another soul, Jinny must first be fluid. She claims in the passage immediately preceding a dance with a melancholy romantic man, "I flutter. I ripple. I stream like a plant in the river, flowing this way, flowing that way."

Conversely, Rhoda expresses, indeed exemplifies, what happens to those who are not fluid or permeable: "What I say is perpetually contradicted. I am to be broken. I am to be derided all my life. . . . The wave breaks. I am also a girl, here in this room." As a girl confined to a certain definable space, both her speech and her very existence are subject to contradiction.

Confined in a way different from Rhoda, Susan makes it her ambition to "have more" than either Rhoda or Jinny has, and she will do so through her children. She personifies the cyclic nature of women's lives and realities: childbearing and rearing, about which she is strangely ambivalent when she declares that "I shall be debased and hide-bound by the bestial and beautiful passion of maternity." Though relegated to this sphere by the dictates of biology, Susan at least imagines an odd sort of self-determination, a self-willed denial and isolation, which Woolf indicates with the repeated phrase "I shall."

Louis, on the other hand, voices the orderly hyperlinear reality of men's lives: "This is life; Mr. Prentice at four; Mr. Eyres at four-thirty." He repeatedly refers to the stability and satisfaction he receives from having this definite schedule, while Susan regards such regularity as insufferable tedium. Though multisensory in her descriptions of this ennui, Susan's senses are muted.

Regulation holds even more complex ramifications for Neville. Even though being a poet places him in a position to order or not to order life's elements as he sees fit, he feels beset by the gravest responsibilities. He echoes the burden of duties, weights, and obligations until it subsides after middle age. Just as Neville acknowledges that they are scarcely to be distinguished from the river—the life-source of creation—Woolf writes in the interlude immediately following that "sky and sea are themselves indistinguishable." This expresses the ultimate permeability of boundaries between human existence and nature. Significantly, this climactic anticlimax occurs only after the "sun had sunk" and thus when darkness (a metaphor for the unconscious) is able to flow: It washes down streets, rolls its waves along grass, blows along slopes, envelops, and engulfs.

Woolf's awareness of unconscious forces becomes clear in her portrayal of inherent contradictions, for this covering darkness must come before humans can be enlightened. Bernard's summation soliloquy epitomizes the eternal struggle of the mind to bring ideas to light and sift the elements of life. Sensation, the subconscious, self-consciousness, sex, and guilt all lead to a sustained inquiry into selfhood. Woolf uncovers the insufferable pain of denying permeability, that is, claiming boundaries, as when the bodies of the novel's six characters become separated. Only among themselves, Bernard reflects, is there a "body of the complete human being." Thus can he speak of them in the first person plural (yet singular) and collective (yet individual): "our life . . . our identity."

The blurring of separateness manifests itself when Bernard contemplates the suicide of one of this body's parts. As he imagines his own attempt to convince Rhoda to wait and not to kill herself, he realizes he is also persuading his own soul: "For this is not one life; nor do I always know if I am man or woman, Bernard or Neville, Louis, Susan, Jinny or Rhoda—so strange is the contact of one with another." Woolf projects her own worldview through Bernard, who sees wholes and unity as illusions. He seeks throughout his life to find something unbroken through language—a perfect unity among phrases and fragments.

At several moments throughout this soliloquy, Bernard is able to see clearly what it is that differentiates the emanations, which Woolf did not intend or perceive as individual characters; what they all have is a "rapture; their common feeling with death." Indeed, *The Waves* is Woolf's elegy to her deceased brother, Thoby. Percival is Woolf's creation of a rare complete person who, though a victim of senseless death, is the prime antagonist. Percival's death is a rupture in the lives and sensibilities of the six other parentless peers who make up one whole identity. At the same time, that death functions as their unifying core or nucleus. Death is both a victory and a defeat, a loss of self but at the same time an ecstatic embrace. Percival's death, the novel's transition and transformation point, occurs in the center of the book. The movement is from diffusion in the first half of the book (covering early childhood, school, and separate paths taken according to gender and class) to emergence in the second half, which includes their reactions to Percival's death, middle age and the solidifying or coalescing of identities, nostalgia, the reunion dinner at court, and Bernard's soliloquy.

Bernard defies death, which he deems the enemy, but he is able to do so only by his acceptance of and belief in the "eternal renewal, the incessant rise and fall and fall and rise again." The oscillating waves suggest the undercurrents of Woolf's novel, the undertow that pulls humans into the extension of their selves, the quickening of memory and deepening of perception, and, intermittently, allows them to surface. Given that the early titles for this novel included "The Life of Anybody" or "Life in General," part of Woolf's search may have been for a voiceless, characterless form of expression that could contribute to the work's profoundly surreal quality. A complex part of that quest is, inevitably, an ongoing individuation of self while that self is almost antithetically in communion with the other (or, in this case, others). Rhoda achieves this—as Woolf herself would later—in the ultimate isolation of suicide.

The Waves represents the refinement of Woolf's subjective novels and possibly an attempt to transform the genre. The writing in *The Waves* is generative rather than conclusive, recursive rather than discursive. Woolf demonstrates that, like waves, the experience of being in the world constitutes a fluid, perpetual process of reconstruction.

"Critical Evaluation" by Roseanne L. Hoefel

Further Reading

Barrett, Eileen, and Patricia Cramer, eds. *Virginia Woolf: Lesbian Readings*. New York: New York University Press, 1997. Part 2 of this collection of conference papers focuses on Woolf's novels, including *The Waves*, through the lens of lesbian literary criticism.

Briggs, Julia. *Virginia Woolf: An Inner Life*. Orlando, Fla: Harcourt, 2005. Biography focusing on Woolf's work and her fascination with the workings of the mind. Briggs traces the creation of each of Woolf's books, from *The Voyage Out* through *Between the Acts*, combining literary analysis with details of Woolf's life.

Caughie, Pamela. *Virginia Woolf and Postmodernism*. Urbana: University of Illinois Press, 1991. Discusses the artist figure in *The Waves*, using sources from later Woolf criticism to discuss this novel.

De Gay, Jane. "'Lives Together': Literary and Spiritual Autobiographies in *The Waves*." In *Virginia Woolf's Novels and the Literary Past*. Edinburgh: Edinburgh University Press, 2006. Examines Woolf's preoccupation with the fiction of her predecessors. Analyzes eight novels and other works to explore her allusions to and revisions of the plots and motifs of earlier fiction.

Goldman, Jane, ed. *Virginia Woolf: "To the Lighthouse," "The Waves."* New York: Columbia University Press, 1998. Surveys the changing critical reception of the two novels from the earliest contemporary reviews through critiques published in the 1990's.

Kaivola, Karen. *All Contraries Confounded: The Lyrical Fiction of Virginia Woolf, Djuna Barnes, and Marguerite Duras.* Iowa City: University of Iowa Press, 1991. A discussion that focuses on Rhoda's relations to language and culture in *The Waves*. Rhoda's exclusion from language suggests the restricted ways women can participate in culture. She has no place, no identity, nothing is fixed for her; she is equally alienated from her body.

Kostkowska, Justyna. *Virginia Woolf's Experiment in Genre and Politics, 1926-1931: Visioning and Versioning "The Waves."* Lewiston, N.Y.: Edwin Mellen Press, 2005. Chronicles the longest creative period in Woolf's career, culminating in the publication of *The Waves*. Examines impersonality, censorship, and other historical and personal factors that led her to experiment with genre and the depiction of the feminine in this novel.

Lee, Hermione. *The Novels of Virginia Woolf.* New York: Holmes & Meier, 1977. Includes a thirty-page chapter analyzing *The Waves* and comparing its stream-of-consciousness technique with those employed by Marcel Proust and James Joyce. Contrasts the lack of social realism in this novel with Woolf's other novels.

Marcus, Jane. "Britannia Rules *The Waves*." In *Hearts of Darkness: White Women Write Race.* New Brunswick, N.J.: Rutgers University Press, 2004. Argues, among other topics, that *The Waves* strongly conveys Woolf's indictment of imperialism.

The Way of All Flesh

Author: Samuel Butler (1835-1902)
First published: 1903
Type of work: Novel
Type of plot: Social realism
Time of plot: Nineteenth century
Locale: England

Principal characters:
GEORGE PONTIFEX, a publisher of religious books
THEOBALD, George's son
ALETHEA, George's daughter
CHRISTINA, Theobald's wife
ERNEST, Theobald's oldest son
MR. OVERTON, Ernest's friend
ELLEN, Ernest's wife

The Story:

Mr. and Mrs. Pontifex are middle-aged when their son George is born. When the time comes for George to learn a trade, they accept the offer of Mr. Pontifex's brother-in-law to take George with him to London as an apprentice in his printing shop. George learns his trade well, and when the uncle dies he wills the shop to his nephew.

George marries, and five children are born to him and his wife: John, Theobald, Eliza, Maria, and Alethea, at whose birth Mrs. Pontifex dies. George considers himself a parent motivated only by the desire to do the right thing for his children. When Theobald proves himself not as quick as John but more persistent, George picks the clergy as Theobald's profession. Shortly before his ordination, Theobald writes to his father that he does not wish to become a minister. In reply, George threatens to disinherit him. Theobald submits and is ordained. He then has to wait for an older member of the clergy to die so that he can be given a living.

The Allabys have three daughters, all of marriageable age. After selecting Theobald as a possible husband for one of the daughters, Mr. Allaby suggests to his daughters that they play a game of cards to decide who will become Theobald's wife. Christina wins. Without knowing of this, Theobald obligingly courts Christina until he wins her promise to marry him. George writes to Theobald that he objects to his son's marriage into the impoverished Allaby family, but Theobald is too deeply committed to release himself. Five years later, he obtains a decent living in a community called Battersby, where he and Christina settle. Because their first child is a son and the first new male Pontifex, George is pleased. For the first time in his life, Theobald feels that he has done something to satisfy his father. After Ernest comes Joseph and then Charlotte. Theobald and Christina rear their children with strict adherence to principles that they believe will mold fine character. The children are disciplined rigorously and beaten when their parents deem it appropriate. When George dies, he leaves 17,500 pounds to Theobald and 2,500 pounds to the oldest son, Ernest.

From the oppressive existence at home under the almost

obsessive rule of his parents, Ernest is sent to Roughborough to be educated under Dr. Skinner, as strict a disciplinarian as Theobald. Ernest is physically weak and mentally morose. He might have succumbed completely to his overpowering environment had he not been rescued by an understanding and loving relative. Alethea Pontifex, Theobald's sister, retired to London, where she lives comfortably on an inheritance that was wisely invested. Looking about for someone to whom she can leave her money when she dies, Alethea hits upon Ernest. Because she does not wish to bestow her fortune blindly, however, she determines to learn more about the boy. She moves to Roughborough so that she can spend time with him.

From the first, she endears herself to the lonely youngster. She encourages him to develop his own talents, and when she learns that he has a passion for music, she suggests that he learn how to build an organ. Enthusiastically, he sets about to learn wood construction and harmony. Theobald disapproves, but he does not forbid Ernest's activities because he and Christina are eager that Ernest inherit Alethea's money. Ernest's shrinking personality changes under the benevolent influence of his aunt. When Alethea dies, she leaves her money in the hands of her best friend, Mr. Overton, whom she appoints to administer the estate that will go to Ernest on his twenty-eighth birthday.

After Ernest completes his course at Roughborough, Theobald sends him to Cambridge to study for the ministry. At Cambridge, Ernest makes a few friends and takes part in athletics. He is ordained soon after he receives his degree and then goes to London. Still innocent and unworldly, he entrusts the inheritance he receives from his grandfather to his friend Pryer, who cheats him out of it. Because he cannot differentiate between good and evil people, Ernest also becomes entangled in a charge of assault and battery and is sentenced to a term in the workhouse. Theobald sends word that henceforth Ernest is to consider himself an orphan.

Ernest is twenty-three years old at the time. Unknown to Ernest, Mr. Overton is still holding the estate Alethea left for him. Mr. Overton begins to take an interest in Ernest's affairs. When Ernest is released from prison, he goes to Mr. Overton for advice concerning his future, since it is no longer possible for him to be a clergyman.

While Ernest was at Roughborough, Christina hired a young girl named Ellen as a maid. She and Ernest become good friends simply because Ellen is kinder to him than anyone else at home. When she becomes pregnant and Christina learns of her condition, she sends Ellen away. Fearing that the girl might starve, Ernest follows her and gives her all the money he has. Theobald learns about this from John, the coachman, whom Theobald thereupon dismisses.

Soon after his release from prison, Ernest meets Ellen again by chance in a London street. Because both are lonely, they marry and set up a secondhand shop selling clothing and books with the help of Mr. Overton, who deplores the idea of their marriage. Unknown to Ernest, Ellen is a habitual drunkard. Before long, she so impoverishes him with her drinking and her foul ways that he dislikes her intensely. He cannot leave her, however, because of the two children she bore him.

One day, Ernest again meets John, his father's former coachman, who reveals that he is the father of Ellen's illegitimate child and that he married Ellen shortly after she left Theobald's home in disgrace. Acting on this information, Mr. Overton arranges matters for Ernest. Ellen is promised an income of a pound a week if she will leave Ernest, and she readily accepts the proposal. The children are sent to live in a family of happy, healthy children, for Ernest fears that his own upbringing will make him as bad a parent as Theobald was.

When Ernest reaches the age of twenty-eight, he inherits Alethea's trust fund of seventy thousand pounds. By that time, Ernest is a writer. With a part of his inheritance, he travels abroad for a few years and then returns to England with material for a book he plans to write. He goes on to publish many successful books, but he never tells his own story. Mr. Overton, who has access to all the Pontifex papers and who knows Ernest well, writes the history of the Pontifex family.

Critical Evaluation:

Aside from many essays and articles, Samuel Butler wrote fifteen books, among them several travel books and five on science. He was strongly influenced by Charles Darwin's *On the Origin of Species by Means of Natural Selection* (1859), an influence that is reflected in the substance and style of *The Way of All Flesh*. That influence, however, is revealed only gradually in the philosophizing of Mr. Overton and Ernest Pontifex. Butler began the novel in 1873 but interrupted its composition several times to do scientific writing; he finally completed it in 1885. In chapters 8 and 25, for letters from Theobald and Christina to their son Ernest, Butler used letters that had actually been written to him by his parents. Because he so caustically satirized members of his family, he refused to publish *The Way of All Flesh* so long as any of them were living. It was his literary executor who arranged publication in 1903 despite the fact that Butler's two sisters were still alive.

Those family letters are among the various bits of evidence in *The Way of All Flesh* that Butler uses wittily but relentlessly to persuade the reader that the central character, Ernest, is fortunate to survive, much less surmount, his parents' mid-Victorian Christian tutelage and his formal schooling. Ernest slowly and unsteadily begins to overcome the narrow, stupid, and often cruel values imposed upon him. At last, he dimly perceives what Butler believed human beings would instinctively remember had it not been for the restrictions of Victorianism. Ernest learns mostly by hindsight, in the wake of disastrous involvements with such supposed friends as Pryer and Ellen. Nevertheless, he also learns by naïvely and tortuously sifting through the controversial and fashionable religious and scientific issues of his time. Butler gently satirizes Ernest's pursuit of "first causes" or other abstractions, and his fortunes take a decided change for the better when he gives up "abstractions" for the most part, sheds his alcoholic wife, and realizes that because he is the child of his parents he will be unable to be a good father himself. He therefore places his children with good, simple people who can love them and make them happy adults. Like Butler, Ernest at the age of thirty settles into bachelor quarters in London, where until his death he contentedly writes, paints, enjoys music, and reflects upon the folly of much that transpires in the world.

Butler did not go to prison; instead, he went to New Zealand, where between 1858 and 1864 he raised sheep profitably. The earlier circumstances of Ernest's life, however, closely parallel those of Butler's through the Cambridge period and, to a lesser extent, following that period. Much of the critical discussion of the novel has, as a result, centered on the author's personal life. Some critics have thought that Butler treats Theobald and Christina unfairly and thereby alienates the reader. Other critics have said of Butler, as Overton says of Ernest in contrasting him with Othello, "he hates not wisely but too well."

Critical comment also addresses the quantity of coincidences in the novel. Of perhaps the greatest consequence is Ernest's encounter with John, from whom he learns that John and Ellen are legally husband and wife; this leads to Ernest's being freed from a dreadful marriage. It may also be considered implausible that Overton is so successful in investing Ernest's inheritance that it increases fivefold and allows Ernest to live comfortably for the rest of his life.

Many critics interpret the autobiographical dimension in *The Way of All Flesh* as a literary precedent for parent-son and self-discovery novels such as Somerset Maugham's *Of Human Bondage* (1915), D. H. Lawrence's *Sons and Lovers* (1913), and James Joyce's *A Portrait of the Artist as a Young Man* (1914-1915). Other perspectives, however, are possible, particularly for readers long familiar with Freudian and post-Freudian psychological approaches to the novel. Readers of Norman Mailer's autobiographical works, for example, may view Butler's work as more than either personal

diatribe or overreaction to the excesses of Victorianism. Novelists now thread through mazes of neuroses and attempt to expose the origins of neurotic and self-destructive behavior such as that practiced by Ernest; often, they propose therapeutic solutions to the protagonists' problems. However imperfectly Butler integrated the autobiographical or personal and the theories that underlie his novel, he was doubtless trying to show the causes of Ernest's stunted personality and his path to relative self-respect and happiness.

The narrative of the novel proceeds slowly because only in the course of thirty years of painful experience can Ernest achieve some intellectual objectivity and degree of self-knowledge. He learns that he must totally reject his self-centered parents' pious domination. He learns, according to Mr. Overton, that virtue springs from experience of personal well-being—the "least fallible thing we have." When meditating in prison, Ernest decides that a true Christian takes the "highest and most self-respecting view of his own welfare which is in his power to conceive, and adheres to it in spite of conventionality." Nevertheless, circumstances change, as Mr. Overton informs the reader, and the self is always changing: Life is nothing but the "process of accommodation," and a life will be successful or not according to the individual's power of accommodation. Mr. Overton is doubtless Butler's alter ego, and his detached view of Ernest reveals that "smug hedonism" is more accurately seen as less than a perfect resolution: Ernest is somewhat withdrawn and lonely, bearing ineradicable marks of his heredity and environment.

Butler explores the themes of heredity and environment plurally through telling the histories of several generations of Pontifexes: Only Ernest's great-grandparents led happy, instinctual lives. The title of the novel gives a summarized version of Butler's judgment, that it is the way of all flesh to learn, if at all, by rejecting convention and dogma and to live by self-direction.

"Critical Evaluation" by Mary H. Hayden

Further Reading

Cavaliero, Glen. "Godliness and Good Behaviour: *The Way of All Flesh*." In *The Alchemy of Laughter: Comedy in English Fiction*. New York: St. Martin's Press, 2000. Analyzes numerous English novels, including *The Way of All Flesh*, to demonstrate how their authors make use of various forms of comedy.

Daniels, Anthony. "Butler's Unhappy Youth." *New Criterion*, January, 2005. Daniels analyzes *The Way of All Flesh*, arguing that it may be the most devastating literary assault upon a father written by a son. Describes how Butler's father, Thomas, and the father in the novel, Theobald Pontifex, stand accused of committing odious acts.

Ganz, Margaret. "Samuel Butler: Ironic Abdication and the Way to the Unconscious." *English Literature in Transition (1880-1920)* 28, no. 4 (1985): 366-394. Charts the novel's many ironic twists of sentimental phrases to show Butler's abrogation of familiar assurances and his anticipation of twentieth century uncertainty.

Guest, David. "Acquired Characters: Cultural vs. Biological Determinism in Butler's *The Way of All Flesh*." *English Literature in Transition (1880-1920)* 34, no. 3 (1991): 283-292. Discusses Butler's understanding of Darwin; emphasizes the novel's anticipation of pessimistic cultural determinism.

Holt, Lee E. *Samuel Butler.* Rev. ed. Boston: Twayne, 1989. Asserts the book's challenge was to show the near-destruction of a young man by the stupidity of his parents while describing a new type of human fulfillment not reflected in traditional terms of success. To this were added Butler's theories of inherited evolutionary forces.

Paradis, James G., ed. *Samuel Butler, Victorian Against the Grain: A Critical Overview.* Toronto, Ont.: University of Toronto Press, 2007. Collection of essays, including discussions of Butler's views on evolution, evolutionary psychology and *The Way of All Flesh*, his bachelorhood, his travel writing, and his photography

Rosenman, John B. "Evangelicalism in *The Way of All Flesh*." *College Language Association Journal* 26 (September, 1982): 76-97. Rosenman argues that the novel charts the history of the influence of Evangelicalism in four generations of English society. Asserts that Butler's use of Scripture surpasses that of any other writer in English, suggesting that, although he criticizes the practices of Christians, he writes from a deep moral earnestness.

Sieminski, Greg. "Suited for Satire: Butler's Re-tailoring of *Sartor Resartus* in *The Way of All Flesh*." *English Literature in Transition (1880-1920)* 31, no. 1 (1988): 29-37. Demonstrates how Butler composed his novel as a satirical response to Thomas Carlyle, whom he hated. Ernest does not seek action, but the humiliation of others.

The Way of the World

Author: William Congreve (1670-1729)
First produced: 1700; first published, 1700
Type of work: Drama
Type of plot: Comedy of manners
Time of plot: Seventeenth century
Locale: London

Principal characters:
LADY WISHFORT, an aged coquette
MRS. FAINALL, her daughter
MRS. MILLAMANT, Lady Wishfort's niece
FOIBLE, a servant
SIR WILFULL WITWOUD, Lady Wishfort's nephew
WITWOUD, his half brother
MIRABELL, a gentleman of fashion
WAITWELL, his servant
FAINALL, Lady Wishfort's son-in-law
MRS. MARWOOD, Fainall's mistress

The Story:

Mrs. Millamant, by far the most beautiful and wittiest of all the fine ladies in London, is sought after by all the beaux in town. The niece of the rich Lady Wishfort, she is also an heir in her own right and is looked upon with great favor by Witwoud, a kinsman of Lady Wishfort. Millamant's acknowledged preference among her suitors, however, is for young Mirabell, who is the only man in London who can match that lady's devastating wit.

Mirabell is as great a favorite among the ladies in the town as Millamant is among the beaux. He is the perfect gallant; she is the perfect coquette. Among Mirabell's jealous admirers is Mrs. Marwood, the mistress of Fainall, Lady Wishfort's son-in-law. In fact, Mirabell has but one real enemy among the ladies, and that is Lady Wishfort herself. On one occasion, to further his suit with Millamant, Mirabell falsely made love to the old lady. Discovering his subterfuge later, she never forgave him. She determines that he will never marry her niece so long as she controls Millamant's fortune. In consequence, Mirabell is hard put to devise a scheme whereby he might convince Lady Wishfort to consent to the marriage.

The plan he devises is an ingenious one. Realizing that Lady Wishfort will respond to anything that even resembles a man, he promptly invents an imaginary uncle, Sir Rowland, who, he says, has fallen madly in love with Lady Wishfort and wants to marry her. He forces his servant, Waitwell, to impersonate this fictitious uncle. To placate Waitwell and further ensure the success of his plan, he contrives his servant's marriage to Lady Wishfort's maid, Foible.

His scheme might have worked were it not for the counterplans of the designing Mrs. Marwood and her unscrupulous lover, Fainall. Although she pretends to despise all men, Mrs. Marwood is secretly in love with Mirabell and has no intention of allowing him to marry Millamant. Fainall, although he detests his wife heartily, realizes that he is dependent upon her and her mother's fortune for his well-being, and he resolves to stop at nothing to make sure that fortune is in his control.

While these plans proceed, Millamant gives little thought to plots or counterplots. She has not the slightest intention of compromising with life but insists that the world's way must somehow be made to conform to her own desires. She has little use for the life around her, seeing through its shallow pretenses and its falsity, and yet she knows that it is the world in which she has to live. She realizes that any attempt to escape from it into some idyllic pastoral existence, as her aunt often suggests, will be folly.

Millamant tells Mirabell the conditions under which she will marry him, and they are stringent conditions, not at all in conformity with the average wife's idea of her lot. She will have in her marriage no place for the ridiculous codes and conventions that govern the behavior of the people around her. She will be entirely free of the cant and the hypocrisy of married life, which are only a cloak for the corruption or misery hidden underneath social custom. In short, she refuses to be merely a married woman in her husband's or society's eyes. Mirabell, likewise, has certain conditions that must be fulfilled before he turns from bachelor into husband. When his demands prove reasonable, both lovers realize that they see life through much the same eyes. They decide that they are probably made for each other.

However, the world does not come to the same conclusion. Lady Wishfort, still embittered against Mirabell for his gross deception, resolves that Millamant is to marry a cousin, Sir Wilfull Witwoud, a country lout many years her senior, who has just arrived in London. Fortunately for Millamant, Sir Wilfull turns out to be a harmless booby who, when drunk, becomes the most understanding of men.

There is a greater obstacle, however, in the scheme that Mirabell himself plans. Waitwell, disguised as Mirabell's imaginary uncle, Sir Rowland, pays ardent court to Lady Wishfort and would have been successful in inveigling her into marriage were it not for a letter from Mrs. Marwood exposing the whole scheme. Lady Wishfort's maid, Foible, succeeds in intercepting the letter, but Mrs. Marwood appears at Lady Wishfort's in person and discloses the deception.

Lady Wishfort is furious, and more determined than ever to prevent any marriage between her niece and Mirabell. She angrily discharges Foible from her employ. Mrs. Fainall, Lady Wishfort's daughter, is on the side of the two lovers. When Foible informs her that she has tangible proof of the relationship between Fainall and Mrs. Marwood, Mrs. Fainall resolves to prosecute her husband to the limit. Meanwhile, the wily Fainall takes pains to have all of his wife's property transferred to his name by means of trumped-up evidence of an affair between his wife and Mirabell.

In this act, Lady Wishfort begins to see for the first time the scheming villainy of her daughter's husband. Mirabell, with the aid of Foible and Millamant's servant, Mincing, exposes the double-dealing Mrs. Marwood and her lover and further proves that, while she is yet a widow, Mrs. Fainall conveyed her whole estate in trust to Mirabell. Lady Wishfort is so delighted that she forgives Mirabell all of his deceptions and consents to his marriage to Millamant.

Critical Evaluation:

Although born in England, William Congreve was reared and educated in Ireland, thus joining the procession of great Irish comic writers that includes Richard Sheridan, Oliver Goldsmith, Jonathan Swift, Oscar Wilde, and George Bernard Shaw. Returning to England as a young man, Congreve studied at law briefly, wrote a novel, and joined with John Dryden in a translation of some works of Juvenal. His literary rise was rapid, and his first comedies, *The Old Bachelor* (1693) and *Love for Love* (1695), were highly successful. His sole tragedy, *The Mourning Bride* (1697), acclaimed by Samuel Johnson a generation later, was widely applauded. However, *The Way of the World*, now considered the masterpiece of all Restoration comedies, was coolly received. Congreve became involved in a notorious controversy over the morality of the stage and had to defend his plays strenuously from what he felt was misrepresentation. Despite this, he held honorary posts under King William and Queen Anne and was associated with Sir John Vanbrugh in the direction of the Queen's Theatre in Haymarket. He was one of the most admired literary figures during the reign of Queen Anne; the duchess of Marlborough was his patron, and Alexander Pope, John Gay, Swift, Richard Steele, and Voltaire were his friends. When Congreve died in 1729, he was buried with much pomp and ceremony in Westminster Abbey.

Restoration comedy was critical comedy, bringing "the sword of common sense" to bear upon the extravagances of the period. Congreve's works are perhaps as close to those of Molière as the English theater ever came; his plays brought an ironic scrutiny to the affectations of his age, with a style and a perfection of phrase that still dazzle audiences. He has been called the wittiest man who ever wrote the English language in the theater; certainly, his characters speak some of the wittiest dialogue. Without question, *The Way of the World* introduced a new standard of wit and polish to the theater. In Millamant, Congreve created one of the great characters of English drama, a comic heroine at once lovable and laughable. The poetry of the courtly life of the Restoration is summed up in the duet between these two brilliant lovers, Mirabell and Millamant.

The Way of the World is carried forward by the witty speeches of the characters rather than by dramatic reversals. The play is all of one piece, a world of wit and pleasure inhabited only by persons of quality and "deformed neither by realism nor by farce." The plot is confusing but almost irrelevant, and the situations exist really only for the conversation. Although Congreve seems almost above such concerns as careful plotting, he is surprisingly artful in some of his stage effects. By delaying the entrance of Millamant until the second act, he arouses intense anticipation in the audience. The fifth act, crowded as it is with activity, flows with continual surprises.

Some critics have held that *The Way of the World* is marred by the artificial contrivances of the plot, but most audiences pay no attention to the complications, relishing instead the characters and the dialogue. The design of the play is to ridicule affected, or false, wit. Possibly, the play's original lukewarm reception was a result of its coming too close to the faults of the courtly audience to be wholly agreeable to them. The dialogue is, also, closely woven, and the repartee demands such close attention that it might have exhausted its listeners. *The Way of the World* is now one of the most frequently revived and enjoyed of all of the Restoration comedies.

Apart from the presentation of incidental wit, Restoration comedy had two main interests: the behavior of polite society and of pretenders to polite society, and particular aspects of sexual relationships. The wit varied from a hard, metallic kind that seemed to exist for its own sake, with no relation to anything, to subtle satire. Occasionally, even Congreve falls into a pattern of easy antitheses, monotonously repeated until the sting of surprise is lost. His wit is never as blunt or as ruthless as that of William Wycherley. Considered fairly outspoken for many generations, the comedy seems primarily to consist of titillation, to suggest more than it delivers. However, the best of the Restoration playwrights, such as Congreve, did not rely entirely on titillation to get their laughs. There is also much feeling present in *The Way of the World*, particularly in the battle of the sexes. Congreve could not view love merely as a gratification of lust, as some of the Restoration playwrights seemed to think of it.

The characters in *The Way of the World* are among the best drawn in any Restoration comedy—or perhaps in any play of the period, comic or tragic. Besides Mirabell and Millamant, one of the most perfect pairs of lovers in any comedy, the play boasts a parade of such personalities as Foible, Witwoud, Petulant, and particularly Lady Wishfort, who approaches the tragic in her desperate attempt to preserve her youth. No character in the play, not even Fainall, fails to surprise the audience with witty observations. In *The Way of the World*, Congreve penetrates deeper than any of his contemporaries into the mysteries of human nature; he possesses more feeling for the individual and is subtler in his treatment of human idiosyncrasies.

The Way of the World reflects attitudes concerning sexuality that prevailed for centuries; above all, the play suggests, the most fascinating aspect of sexual relations is that of the chase. The pursuit, usually of the male for the female, although sometimes reversed, dominates Restoration comedy and is both glorified and satirized in *The Way of the World*. The lovely and intelligent Millamant herself expresses her belief in the necessity for a period devoted to such pursuit if a woman is to attract and to keep her lover. By playing hard to get, a woman proves her eventual worth. Congreve takes these conventional attitudes and fabricates his comedy from them, weaving a complicated and fascinating satire that continues to delight audiences and readers after two centuries.

"Critical Evaluation" by Bruce D. Reeves

Further Reading

Holland, Norman. *The First Modern Comedies*. Cambridge, Mass.: Harvard University Press, 1959. This remains required reading for any student of English comedy written between the Restoration and the eighteenth century. Holland's discussion of *The Way of the World* does justice to the play's many complexities. Highly recommended.

Muir, Kenneth. *The Comedy of Manners*. London: Hutchinson University Library, 1970. A handy little book that provides an overview of the principal writers of stage comedy in England between the Restoration and the early eighteenth century. The chapter on Congreve contains a fine discussion of *The Way of the World*.

Novak, Maximillian E. *William Congreve*. New York: Twayne, 1971. One of the best general introductions to Congreve, with an act-by-act discussion of *The Way of the World* and an extensive annotated bibliography.

Owen, Susan J., ed. *A Companion to Restoration Drama*. Malden, Mass.: Blackwell, 2001. Collection of essays discussing the types of Restoration drama, placing these plays within the context of their times, and analyzing works by individual playwrights. There are numerous references to Congreve and his plays that are listed in the index. His work is also considered in Miriam Handley's essay "William Congreve and Thomas Southerne."

Powell, Jocelyn. *Restoration Theatre Production*. London: Routledge & Kegan Paul, 1984. A delightful and very readable account of Restoration drama. Powell discusses music, acting styles, and scenery; provides many wonderful illustrations; and concludes with a particularly sensitive and informed discussion of *The Way of the World*.

Sieber, Anita. *Character Portrayal in Congreve's Comedies "The Old Batchelour," "Love for Love," and "The Way of the World."* Lewiston, N.Y.: Edwin Mellen Press, 1996. Focuses on the numerous types of characters in the comedies, including some who are placed in opposition to each other, such as wits versus fools and fops, country characters versus urban gallants and ladies, and old people versus young people. Sieber also discusses Congreve's use of historical characters and his themes of love and marriage.

Williams, Aubrey L. *An Approach to Congreve*. New Haven, Conn.: Yale University Press, 1979. Williams stresses the "common ground" of Christian belief shared by Congreve and his audience. Controversial, but clearly and persuasively written. The chapter on *The Way of the World* focuses on Mirabell, the play's hero, whom Williams would exonerate of the charges of Machiavellianism so often brought against him.

Young, Douglas M. *The Feminist Voices in Restoration Comedy: The Virtuous Women in the Play-Worlds of Etherege, Wycherley, and Congreve*. Lanham, Md.: University Press of America, 1997. Focuses on the female characters in Congreve's plays who demand independence from and equality with men before they commit to courtship or marriage. Devotes a chapter to *The Way of the World*.

The Way We Live Now

Author: Anthony Trollope (1815-1882)
First published: 1874-1875, serial; 1875, book
Type of work: Novel
Type of plot: Social realism
Time of plot: February to August, 1873
Locale: London and Suffolk, England

Principal characters:
LADY CARBURY, a writer
SIR FELIX CARBURY, her son
HETTA CARBURY, her daughter
ROGER CARBURY, the squire of Carbury Hall, in love with his cousin Hetta
PAUL MONTAGUE, also in love with Hetta
MRS. WINIFRED HURTLE, an American, formerly Paul Montague's fiancé
AUGUSTUS MELMOTTE, a financier
MARIE MELMOTTE, his daughter
LORD NIDDERDALE, Marie's suitor
MR. ADOLPHUS LONGSTAFFE, the squire of Caversham Hall
DOLLY LONGSTAFFE, his son
GEORGIANA LONGSTAFFE, his daughter
EZEKIAL BREHGERT, a Jewish banker and Georgiana's suitor
MR. BROUNE, a newspaper editor
RUBY RUGGLES, in love with Sir Felix Carbury
JOHN CRUMB, Ruby's fiancé
MRS. PIPKIN, Ruby's aunt and Mrs. Hurtle's landlady

The Story:

Lady Carbury is beset by worries about her career and the futures of her son and daughter. She tries to flatter editors into reviewing her new book favorably; she tries to persuade her daughter Hetta to marry her cousin Roger Carbury; and she hopes to find an heir to marry her wastrel son, Sir Felix.

Roger Carbury is deeply in love with Hetta, but Hetta loves Roger's friend, Paul Montague. Roger earlier persuaded Paul to break with his American fiancé, Mrs. Hurtle, arguing that her vagueness about her past, coupled with rumors that she fought a duel with her husband and shot a man, make her an unsuitable wife for an English gentleman. When Paul falls in love with Hetta, however, Roger feels betrayed.

Sir Felix is a financial drain on his mother; his chief pastime is gambling with other dissolute young gentlemen at their club, the Beargarden. He reluctantly agrees to his mother's plan that he court Marie Melmotte, the only child of the arrogant financier Augustus Melmotte. Melmotte is in London only for a short time and is dogged by rumors of past shady dealings, but he establishes himself as London's leading financial genius. Felix's wooing of Marie lacks spirit, but Marie thinks him beautiful and determines to marry him despite her father's opposition and preference for another suitor, Lord Nidderdale, whose family connections are superior to those of Sir Felix. Marie, who knows she has control over money that her father settled on her in order to make it secure if his speculations fail, devises a plan whereby she and Sir Felix will elope to New York. Melmotte's men seize Marie in Liverpool before her ship sails, however, and Sir Felix does not leave London at all, instead spending the night gambling away the money provided him by Marie and his mother. Lady Carbury, in anguish over her son's behavior, turns for help to Mr. Broune, an editor with whom she flirted and whose marriage proposal she rejected, but with whom she begins to develop a more honest intimacy.

Melmotte skillfully draws members of the British upper classes into his financial schemes, the biggest of which involves selling shares in a projected railroad from Utah to Mexico. Montague is made a partner in the scheme through his association in California with Hamilton Fisker, a wheeler-dealer who originates the railroad plan. Melmotte organizes a toothless board of directors, including English aristocrats with no financial expertise, among them Sir Felix Carbury and Adolphus Longstaffe. Longstaffe is a Suffolk squire; unlike Roger, Longstaffe has social ambitions that lead him to live far beyond his means.

Longstaffe's financial straits lead him to sell one of his properties, Pickering, to Melmotte (and foolishly to give Melmotte the title deeds before Melmotte pays him) and to suggest that his daughter Georgiana stay with the Melmottes in London. Georgiana despises the Melmottes but thinks her only hope of finding a husband is to spend the social season in London. When Georgiana becomes engaged to the banker Mr. Brehgert, her family is outraged that she would marry a Jew. Her father orders her to return to Caversham, and she writes Brehgert such an insensitive letter that he breaks off the engagement.

Melmotte's aura of astounding wealth and his businsses' ever-increasing profits move political leaders to sponsor his candidacy for Parliament. The climax of the political campaign coincides with a magnificent dinner Melmotte gives for the visiting emperor of China. Melmotte is elected, but many of the social and political elite of London who vied for tickets to the dinner fail to attend when rumors arise that Melmotte committed forgery. Melmotte indeed forged the signature of Longstaffe's son on a document giving Melmotte title to Pickering. Melmotte enters Parliament but knows he has little chance of saving his reputation and his fortune.

While he courts Marie, Sir Felix also arouses the interest of Ruby Ruggles, a Suffolk farm woman who deserted her fiancé, the meal and pollard dealer John Crumb, to run away to London, where she stays with her aunt, Mrs. Pipkin, and goes out to music halls with Sir Felix. Boarding with Mrs. Pipkin is Mrs. Hurtle, who came to London hoping to resume her engagement to Paul. Paul loves Hetta, but he so hates causing pain to Mrs. Hurtle that he agrees to call on her and even to spend a weekend with her in a seaside hotel. After Roger encounters them on the beach, Paul finally makes a firm break with Mrs. Hurtle (he also withdraws from the Railroad Board) and becomes engaged to Hetta. Sir Felix, coming to Mrs. Pipkin's house in search of Ruby, finds Mrs. Hurtle there and tells Hetta about Mrs. Hurtle's entanglement with Paul. Hetta, distraught, breaks off her engagement.

Mrs. Pipkin and Mrs. Hurtle persuade Ruby to marry Crumb after Crumb gives Sir Felix a beating. Marie, no longer caring whom she marries, becomes engaged to Lord Nidderdale, but the engagement collapses when Melmotte, having again committed forgery, is found out and kills himself with prussic acid. Marie still has the money her father settled on her, and she goes to California with Mrs. Hurtle, whose former husband now claims their divorce is invalid, and with Fisker, whom Marie marries.

At Paul's request, Hetta goes to Mrs. Hurtle to inquire about her relationship with Paul. Mrs. Hurtle, resisting her desire for revenge, convinces Hetta that Paul was faithful to her. Hetta and Paul marry, and Roger, knowing he will never love anyone else, invites them to live at Carbury Hall and promises to make their son his heir. Georgiana settles for marriage to a curate. Lady Carbury marries Mr. Broune, and Sir Felix is sent to Germany under the care of a clergyman.

Critical Evaluation:

Although some critics regard *The Way We Live Now* as Anthony Trollope's masterpiece, the novel was greeted with disappointment by its first readers. Trollope came to see it as an aberration, going too far in its satirical disgust with the corruption of upper-class British society. His earlier novels strive for a balance between belief in the virtuous stability of British institutions and the viability of the British class structure, and skepticism about their defects. In *The Way We Live Now*, moral concerns seem nearly to disappear from the lives of upper-class characters, who give themselves over to greed and ostentation.

A key figure in the novel is an outsider of murky origins and shady financial dealings, Augustus Melmotte, whose rapid rise in English society, even to the point of election to Parliament, is supported by members of the ruling class. Those who support him are aware that Melmotte is a fraud but are cynically eager to attach themselves to his power to make money. He represents "the way we live now." The central figure for "the better way we lived in the past" is Roger Carbury, one of the model English gentlemen who appear in many of Trollope's novels. Roger is an ideal. His modest country estate has been in his family for centuries. He lives within his income, without ostentation, as did his forefathers; he believes "a man's standing in the world should not depend at all upon his wealth" (though it certainly is connected to inherited social standing—Trollope is no democrat). He is absolutely trustworthy, and he "would have felt himself disgraced to enter the house of such a one as Augustus Melmotte."

The Way We Live Now presents Roger as an anachronism. His social standing in the general estimation—though not in his own—is eclipsed by that of more ambitious neighboring families such as the Longstaffes, who live beyond their means and are easy prey for Melmotte's investment schemes. Roger is nearly alone in the world: He never marries, and his sisters go off to India and the American West with their husbands. His cousin Hetta, whom he wants to marry, prefers Paul Montague, who, although not despicable, is morally and socially unanchored. Demonstration of this is his becoming one of the members of the board of directors of Melmotte's railroad scheme. Without a son of his own, Roger fears his heir will have to be Hetta's wastrel brother, Sir Felix.

Roger lacks an immediate family and seems unlikely to acquire one, but many other characters in the novel have dys-functional families. One of these is Lady Carbury and her two children: Lady Carbury spoils her son, who is incapable of caring for anyone and who threatens to bankrupt her. Lady Carbury seems to have little feeling for her daughter other than anger that Hetta refuses to be married off safely to Roger. Family relations are even worse among the Longstaffes, the Melmottes, and, Trollope leads readers to assume, myriad other upper-class families of the 1870's.

The dominant symbol of the loss of traditional moral values is gambling. The novel parallels a general upper-class eagerness to buy shares in Melmotte's railroad speculation with the nightly card games enjoyed by Sir Felix, the Longstaffes's son Dolly, and other dissolute young gentlemen. The IOUs they exchange when they run out of cash are the equivalent of the worthless pieces of paper representing shares in Melmotte's yet-to-be-built railroad. When it is discovered that one of the young gentlemen habitually cheats, the others are at first shocked but quickly absorb cheating as yet another category of behavior one might as well accept.

Trollope's idealization of Roger makes it clear that *The Way We Live Now*'s critique of a money-oriented capitalistic world comes from a conservative, aristocratic perspective. Unlike Charles Dickens's *Little Dorrit* (1855-1857), for example, which has a predecessor of Melmotte in the financial schemer Merdle, Trollope's novel is not concerned with the exploitation of the poor.

Despite its stolid conservatism, *The Way We Live Now* becomes in its later sections more complex and open-ended in its depiction of the dilemmas facing Trollope's society. One example of this development is the way in which Trollope's characterization of Melmotte shifts from caricature to a moving, if also horrifying, psychological portrait of a man caught up in a game he can no longer control. A second example is the novel's treatment of its more independent female characters. Lady Carbury, Marie Melmotte, and Mrs. Hurtle all serve Trollope as examples of what is going wrong with London society, but they also emerge as women doing their best to free themselves from the abusive situations life gives them. In the second half of the novel, Roger, who has no use at all for Mrs. Hurtle and little for Lady Carbury, seems increasingly irrelevant. The novel's broad satire diminishes, and Trollope seems to become increasingly engaged with the emotional complexities of his characters.

Anne Howells

Further Reading

Barickman, Richard, Susan MacDonald, and Myra Stark. *Corrupt Relations: Dickens, Thackeray, Trollope, Col-*

lins, and the Victorian Sexual System. New York: Columbia University Press, 1982. Explores the extent to which Trollope's fiction, like that of some of his contemporaries, moves beyond the sexual stereotypes of its time to recognize how these stereotypes damage the lives of women and men.

Bridgham, Elizabeth A. *Spaces of the Sacred and Profane: Dickens, Trollope, and the Victorian Cathedral Town.* New York: Routledge, 2008. Describes how Trollope and Charles Dickens use the setting of Victorian cathedral towns to critique religious attitudes, business practices, aesthetic ideas, and other aspects of nineteenth century English life.

Bury, Laurent. *Seductive Strategies in the Novels of Anthony Trollope, 1815-1882.* Lewiston, N.Y.: Edwin Mellen Press, 2004. A study of seduction in all of Trollope's novels. Argues that seduction was a survival skill for both men and women in the Victorian era and demonstrates how Trollope depicted the era's sexual politics.

Gilmour, Robin. *The Idea of the Gentleman in the Victorian Novel.* Winchester, Mass.: Allen & Unwin, 1981. Sets Trollope's gentlemanly ideal in its historical context.

Harvey, Geoffrey. *The Art of Anthony Trollope.* New York: St. Martin's Press, 1980. Thoughtful discussion of *The Way We Live Now*, praising Trollope's combination of "an absolutist moral stance and a high degree of moral relativism."

Levine, George. *The Realistic Imagination: English Fiction from Frankenstein to Lady Chatterley.* Chicago: University of Chicago Press, 1981. One of the best discussions of Trollope's modes of representation, emphasizing the dependence of Trollope's realism on "an almost cynical acceptance of the necessity for arbitrary and traditional rules."

MacDonald, Susan Peck. *Anthony Trollope.* Boston: Twayne, 1987. Excellent introduction to the complexities of Trollope's fiction. Includes an annotated bibliography.

Markwick, Margaret. *New Men in Trollope's Novels: Rewriting the Victorian Male.* Burlington, Vt.: Ashgate, 2007. Examines Trollope's novels, tracing the development of his ideas about masculinity. Argues that Trollope's male characters are not the conventional Victorian patriarchs and demonstrates how his works promote a "startlingly modern model of manhood."

_____. *Trollope and Women.* London: Hambledon Press, 1997. Examines how Trollope could simultaneously accept the conventional Victorian ideas about women while also sympathizing with women's difficult situations. Demonstrates the individuality of his female characters. Discusses his depiction of both happy and unhappy marriages, male-female relationships, bigamy, and scandal.

Mullen, Richard, and James Munson. *The Penguin Companion to Trollope.* New York: Penguin Books, 1996. A comprehensive guide that describes all of Trollope's novels, short stories, travel books, and other works; discusses plot, characters, background, tone, allusions, and contemporary references; and places the works in their historical context.

The Wealth of Nations

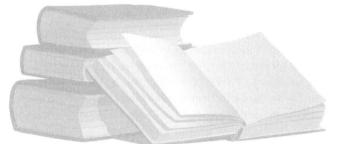

Author: Adam Smith (1723-1790)
First published: 1776, as *An Inquiry into the Nature and Causes of the Wealth of Nations*
Type of work: Economics

The classic statement of economic liberalism, the policy of laissez-faire, was written during a ten-year period by Adam Smith, a Scottish professor of moral philosophy. The book's ideas were useful in encouraging the rise of new business enterprise in Europe, but the ideas could not have taken hold so readily had it not been for the scope of Smith's work and the effectiveness of his style.

As a philosopher, Smith was interested in finding intellectual justification for certain economic principles that he came to believe, but as an economist and writer, he was interested in making his ideas prevail in the world of business. He was reacting against oppressive systems of economic control that were restricting the growth of business, but although he concerned himself with general principles and their practical application, he was aware of the value of the individual, whether employer or laborer. There is no reason to believe

Smith would have sanctioned monopolistic excesses of business or any unprincipled use of the free enterprise philosophy. To cite him in reverential tones is not to gain his sanction.

Smith begins his work with the assumption that whatever a nation consumes either is the product of the annual labor of that nation or is purchased with the products of labor. The wealth of the nation depends upon the proportion of the produce that goes to the consumers, and that proportion depends partly upon the proportion of those who are employed to those who are not, but even more on the skill of the workers and the efficiency of the means of distribution.

Book 1 of *The Wealth of Nations* considers the question of how the skill of the laborers can best be increased. Book 2 is a study of capital stock, since it is argued that the proportion of workers to nonlaborers is a function of the amount of capital stock available. In book 3 Smith explains how Europe came to emphasize the industry of the towns at the expense of agriculture. Various economic theories are presented in book 4, some stressing the importance of industry in the town, others the importance of agriculture. Book 5 considers the revenue of the sovereign, or commonwealth, with particular attention paid to the sources of that revenue and the consequences of governmental debt.

In Smith's view, the productive power of labor is increased most readily by the division of labor: If each worker is given a specific job, the worker becomes more skillful, time is saved, and machinery will be invented that further speeds the rate of production. Smith believes that, as a result of the increase in production that followed the division of labor, a well-governed community would enjoy a "universal opulence which extends itself to the lowest ranks of people."

Smith regards the division of labor as a necessary consequence of the human propensity to trade or to exchange one thing for another. He believes that the propensity to trade is a consequence of a more fundamental human trait: self-love. Thus, for Smith, the basic motivating force of any economic system is the self-interest of each person involved in the system.

Money originated as a means of facilitating exchange when the products of those who wish to barter are not desired by those with whom they choose to trade. To use Smith's example, a butcher who has all the bread and beer he or she needs will not accept more bread or beer in exchange for meat. If the person with bread or beer can exchange it elsewhere for "money"—whether it be shells, tobacco, salt, cattle, or, the most favored medium of exchange, metal—the money can be used to buy meat from the butcher.

Among the most important ideas in *The Wealth of Nations* is Smith's claim that labor is the real measure of the exchangeable value of commodities. Commodities have a value in use, but this value is unimportant to the producer, who seeks to exchange what was made for something that is needed. The amount of work that can be purchased with a commodity is the real exchangeable value of that commodity. Thus, Smith defines wealth as the power of purchasing labor. The nominal, as distinguished from the real, price of commodities is their money value.

Smith defines the natural price as the average price of a commodity in a community and the market price as the actual selling price. He presents the familiar principle of supply and demand by stating that market price increases when the quantity of a commodity brought to market falls short of the demand.

Wherever there is perfect liberty, the advantages and disadvantages of different uses of labor and stock must be either equal or tending to equality, according to Smith. There are counterbalancing circumstances that affect equality: the agreeableness of the job, the cost of learning the business, the constancy of employment, the amount of trust that must be put in the employee, and the probability of success.

Smith makes a distinction between productive and unproductive labor. Labor is productive when it adds to the value of something, unproductive when it does not. The labor of a manufacturer adds to the value of the material that is used, but the labor of a menial servant adds nothing to the value of the employer who is served. This distinction is important, because capital is explained by reference to the proportion of productive to unproductive labor. Capital can be used for purchasing raw materials, for manufacturing, for transportation, and for distribution.

Smith was confident that he could discover the natural order of economic matters. To later critics, however, it appeared that he was mistaking his own preferred kind of economic situation for that which would prevail if economic relations among people were in no way affected by social habit. His inclination is to regard what would prevail in a civilized community free from governmental restraint as the natural state of affairs. This view is acceptable when he says, for example, "According to the natural course of things, therefore, the greater part of the capital of every growing society is, first, directed to agriculture, afterwards to manufactures, and last of all to foreign commerce"; however, the following account of rent is more provocative: "Rent, considered as the price paid for the use of land, is naturally the highest which the tenant can afford to pay in the actual circumstances of the land." Smith appears to have written without obvious interest in supporting one economic class against another, and his definitions of "natural" price, rent, and other economic factors are couched in neutral terms.

Smith's experiences as a teacher and philosopher are reflected most clearly in his account "Of the Expence of the Institutions for the Education of Youth." He is rather bitter about the quality of education that results when the teacher is not driven by economic necessity to do his or her best. He asserts that professors who are responsible only to their colleagues are likely to allow one another to neglect their duties as teachers. The result is that "In the university of Oxford, the greater part of the public professors have, for these many years, given up altogether even the pretense of teaching." Smith favors giving students a considerable part to play in the selection and retention of teachers, and he warns that if this is not done, the professors would devise ways of giving "sham-lectures" and would force their students to attend regularly and keep silent.

Smith thinks that the wealthy and wellborn can see to the education of their young, but that the state should support education for those who cannot otherwise afford it. He argues that it is important, particularly in free countries, that the public be educated to exercise good judgment.

In considering the revenue of the state, Smith proceeds on the principle that whatever expense is beneficial to the whole society can justly be defrayed by the general contribution of the whole society. Thus, defending the society, supporting the chief magistrate, administering justice, maintaining good roads and communications, supporting state institutions or public works, and, under certain circumstances, defraying the expenses of educational institutions and institutions for religious instruction are all properly supported by general contribution of the whole society.

Support of the institutions and activities of the state must come either from some fund belonging to the state or from the revenue of the people. Smith considers three sources of the revenue of individuals: rent, profit, and wages. His discussion of taxes is based upon four maxims: The taxpayer ought to be taxed according to ability to pay, as determined by revenue; the tax should be certain in the sense that there should be no question as to the time, manner, or quantity of payment; taxes should be levied in a convenient manner, for example with taxes on consumer goods paid when the goods are bought; and the tax should be economical in the sense that it should not be expensive to collect.

Smith's *The Wealth of Nations* is a temperate, thorough, engrossing analysis of the economic facts of life in a free industrial society. Insofar as it is, to some extent, a proposal, it is not surprising that it has not won universal approval; but it is a masterpiece of its kind, and its influence on modern thought and practice has been significant.

Further Reading

Brown, Vivienne. *Adam Smith's Discourse: Canonicity, Commerce, and Conscience*. London: Routledge & Kegan Paul, 1994. Discusses the attack on mercantilism in *The Wealth of Nations* and reveals problems with Smith's theories. Examines these theories from political, moral, and economic viewpoints. Discusses inconsistency between *The Wealth of Nations* and Smith's *The Theory of Moral Sentiments* (1759).

Evensky, Jerry. *Adam Smith's Moral Philosophy: A Historical and Contemporary Perspective on Markets, Law, Ethics, and Culture*. New York: Cambridge University Press, 2005. Focuses on Smith's ideas about morality as expressed in *The Wealth of Nations* and other works. Draws on the analyses of modern economists to examine Smith's economic concepts. Chapters 5 through 9 focus on books 1 through 5, respectively, of *The Wealth of Nations*.

Fay, Charles R. *The World of Adam Smith*. New York: A. M. Kelley, 1965. Classic work on the philosopher. Presents a historical, economical, and philosophical overview of Scotland and England in the eighteenth century, providing insight into the development of Smith's philosophy and his disdain for mercantilism.

Fleischacker, Samuel. *On Adam Smith's "Wealth of Nations": A Philosophical Companion*. Princeton, N.J.: Princeton University Press, 2004. Explains the book in terms of Smith's philosophical ideas about science, morality, and knowledge. Argues that Smith has moral as well as pragmatic reasons for endorsing capitalism and discusses his strong belief in human equality.

Heilbroner, Robert. *The Nature and Logic of Capitalism*. New York: W. W. Norton, 1985. Well-recognized authority on Smith dissects the philosopher's works, in particular *The Wealth of Nations*, to indisputably establish Smith as a predominant figure in the rise of capitalism and of a free market economy.

Henderson, Willie. *Evaluating Adam Smith: Creating "The Wealth of Nations."* New York: Routledge, 2006. Analyzes *The Wealth of Nations* as a cultural document, created with eighteenth century ideas about human nature, economy, and argument. Describes Smith's rhetorical strategies, his relationship with his readers, and how he constructed his economic visions.

Hollander, Samuel. *The Economics of Adam Smith*. Toronto, Ont.: University of Toronto Press, 1973. One of the best surveys of Smith's ideas on economics.

Muller, Jerry. *Adam Smith in His Time and Ours*. New York: Free Press, 1993. Describes the basic economic theories in *The Wealth of Nations*. Examines the effect of those theories on the mercantilism of Smith's time, on the growth of capitalism, and on the late twentieth century.

Pack, Spencer J. *Capitalism as a Moral System: Adam Smith's Critique of the Free Market Economy*. Brookfield, Vt.:
Edward Elgar, 1991. Draws out Smith's criticisms of laissez-faire and of capitalism.

Rashid, Salim. *The Myth of Adam Smith*. Lyme, N.H.: Edward Elgar, 1998. Argues that Smith's economic analysis is greatly overrated; finds inaccuracies in factual data and inconsistencies and fallacies in Smith's analysis.

The Weary Blues

Author: Langston Hughes (1902-1967)
First published: 1926
Type of work: Poetry

The Weary Blues, Langston Hughes's first published volume of poetry, is grounded in a blues aesthetic. Hughes, one of the younger writers of the Harlem Renaissance, had begun publishing his verse in such journals as *The Crisis*, *Opportunity*, and *Survey Graphic*, and his landmark poem "The Negro Speaks of Rivers" appeared in *The Crisis* in 1921. His work, as well as that of fellow Harlem Renaissance poets such as Countée Cullen, Claude McKay, and Gwendolyn Bennett, was also published in the short-lived journal *Fire!!* (1926), edited by Wallace Thurman. *The Weary Blues*, which contains an introduction by the respected writer and photographer Carl Van Vechten, was published during the height of the Jazz Age, when the blues recordings of Mamie Smith, Ma Rainey, and Bessie Smith were in vogue.

Jazz and blues themes underlie Hughes's presentation of Harlem nightlife. Jazz, which provided a stimulus for poets such as Carl Sandburg and Vachel Lindsay, was more than an incidental subject for Hughes. Although the *aab* rhyme pattern of traditional blues songs is not pronounced in *The Weary Blues*, Hughes structured a number of his poems on blueslike formats, and he used vernacular to replicate the vocal patterns of black speech.

The collection of poems treats a primary blues theme, that of the problems encountered in personal relationships. At the time the work first appeared, many critics did not appreciate the blues elements that Hughes explored because they thought these elements represented an area of African American life that was not socially uplifting. *The Weary Blues* shows Hughes's determination to present the many sides of African American life. The poems address romantic love, African heritage, and the social aspects of race and color. In doing so, they raise the experiences of the common people to the level of art. The poems distill Hughes's own experiences in locations as varied as Mexico, West Africa, and Harlem.

The collection contains seven sections: "The Weary Blues," "Dream Variations," "The Negro Speaks of Rivers," "Black Pierrot," "Water-Front Streets," "Shadows in the Sun," and "Our Land." Each section is named for the first poem of the group. The book opens with "Proem," in which Hughes defines "Negro" with references to African heritage, slavery, musical contributions, and oppression.

The "Weary Blues" section consists of fifteen poems that depict Harlem nightlife through images of cabarets, performing artists, and personal relationships. Structured in free-verse form, the single poem "The Weary Blues" contains a blues lyric from an actual blues composition. The poem depicts the jazz life through the observations of a persona sensitive to the conditions of performance, who comments:

> Droning a drowsy syncopated tune,
> Rocking back and forth to a mellow croon,
>   I heard a Negro play.
> Down on Lenox Avenue the other night
> By the pale dull pallor of an old gas light.

In these lines, syncopation, the defining rhythmic quality of jazz, is characterized by the word "rocking." The nightclub is the setting in which musicians labor to the point of weariness, and the act of performance is equated with race in the image of "ebony hands." The observer also notes "the sad raggy tune," a reference to ragtime and to the sadness and despair implicit in the blues performance.

"Jazzonia," the second poem in this section, describes an

uptown nightclub where jazz artists are accompanied by a sensuous dancer whose movements imply seduction, which is signified by "Eve" or "Cleopatra." Another poem depicting dance, "Negro Dancers," contains black vernacular and representations of jazz rhythms in syllables that suggest future motifs of bebop. The closing line of the poem, "Two mo' ways to do de Charleston!," refers to the highly popular dance style associated with James P. Johnson.

In "The Cat and the Saxophone (2 A.M.)," the lyrics to a popular song—"Everybody loves my baby but my baby don't love nobody but me"—are used to form a call-and-response pattern that parallels the conversation in a cabaret. "Young Singer" and "Cabaret" are other poems depicting jazz venues. In "Cabaret," the persona asks, "Does a jazz-band ever sob?"—a question that implies that the observer is somewhat distanced from the blues experience. In "To Midnight Nan at Leroy's," the persona speaks in syncopated black vernacular. The poem portrays African American women and the problematic love relationships often depicted in blues songs.

Using jazz performance as a backdrop, "Harlem Night Club" explores interracial socializing. The poem suggests that nightlife integration does not signify social equality. African American women performers are the subject of "Nude Young Dancer," and in "Young Prostitute" sexual exploitation is suggested in the line "like a withered flower." The withering of the prostitute contrasts with the exotic sensuousness of the dancer in "To a Black Dancer in 'The Little Savoy.'"

The black woman dancer is also portrayed in "Song for a Banjo Dance," which is set in a rural folk context, whereas the ability of the blues to provide a transcendent experience is exemplified in "Blues Fantasy." The closing poem of the section, "Lenox Avenue: Midnight," restates nightlife themes and evokes the cabaret atmosphere.

"Dream Variations," the second section of *The Weary Blues*, presents nature and romantic themes. Though these lyric poems focus primarily on such images of nature as the moon and autumn, they include references to racial themes as well. The dream metaphor, central to Hughes's poetic concept, is evident in the title poem, in which black liberation is equated to the end of "the white day." In "Winter Moon," the moon is described as "thin and sharp and ghostly white." "Fantasy in Purple" contrasts musical images of African American culture with those of European culture. The drum signifies African American culture and announces tragic social circumstances. The "white violins" are contrasted with the "blaring trumpet" and "darkness." "March Moon" is an ironic lyric poem that personifies the moon as a naked woman "undressed" by the wind. The closing poem, "Joy," uses personification to locate joy in an urban situation.

The third section, "The Negro Speaks of Rivers," contains one of Hughes's best-known poems. Dedicated to W. E. B. Du Bois, "The Negro Speaks of Rivers" traces African heritage from the perspective of a universal black persona who compares the black legacy with certain major rivers of the world. These rivers, which form the structure of the poem, represent locations where people of African descent have lived: "I've known rivers ancient as the world and older than the/ flow of human blood in human veins." The Euphrates, the Congo, and the Nile represent ancient heritage; slavery in the Americas is symbolized by the Mississippi. The poem also uses "soul" to identify sources of being and spirituality.

"Cross," the second poem in this section, deals with race mixture and the uncertain identity of the mulatto, who is "neither white nor black." "The Jester" questions the dual mask of comedy and tragedy. In "The South," the speaker, angry and embittered by racial persecution, describes the South as "Beast-strong" and "Idiot-brained." Personified as a woman, the South rejects the love of black people. By contrast, the North, although cold, is a "kinder mistress." In "Aunt Sue's Stories," Hughes examines oppression in the South and the legacy of slavery through the oral tradition, and he praises blackness in "Poem," which counters the negative stereotypes of darkness: "The night is beautiful/ So the faces of my people."

In the fourth section, "Black Pierrot," Hughes addresses romantic love and images of black women. In the signature poem, the speaker is troubled by unrequited love. "Color" is used to identify the night, the soul, and hope in "a new brown love." In "Harlem Night Song," cabaret and jazz are the backdrop for a declaration of love. In "Poem," a lyrical praise to black beauty, the black woman becomes a symbolic figure of adoration and "black" is a positive: "My black one,/ Thou art not beautiful/ Yet thou hast/ A loveliness/ Surpassing beauty." Using biblical pronouns, the persona redefines beauty through the negative stereotype of darkness. "Songs to the Dark Virgin" and "When Sue Wears Red" elevate black women as timeless representatives of ancestral queenliness. Susanna Jones appears like "an ancient cameo/ turned brown by the ages."

"Water-Front Streets," the fifth section, draws on Hughes's experience as a seaman. The title poem uses the dream motif and traditional British poetic language to suggest the romantic hopes of a sailor destined for places "where the spring is wondrous rare." Other poems in this section, such as "A Farewell" and "Long Trip," use water imagery and the journey motif to portray separation and isolation. "Caribbean Sunset," a four-line poem, describes the sun in startling images of blood. "Natcha" addresses the theme of love for sale, and "Death of an Old Seaman" considers the seaman's soul and afterlife.

In the sixth section, "Shadows in the Sun," Hughes focuses primarily on women. Isolation, suicide, illness, labor, and alienation are among the themes he covers. "Beggar Boy" describes a lad whose flute song contrasts with his bare existence. "Troubled Woman" presents an image of despair and fatigue by portraying a woman who is "Like a/ Wind-blown autumn flower." "Suicide's Note," a three-line piece, implies death by drowning. "To the Dark Mercedes of 'El Palacio De Amor'" and "Mexican Market Woman" depict, respectively, the young beautiful prostitute and the aged vendor whose labor is timeless. These poems, along with "Soledad: A Cuban Portrait," reflect the poet's treatment of women in the Spanish-speaking world of the Americas. "Young Bride" also deals with a woman's tragic circumstances. The dream motif is developed in "The Dream Keeper," in which the poet sees the escape of dreaming as an alternative to life's realities: "Bring me all your dreams,/ You dreamers."

In "Our Land," the final section, the title poem calls for a natural world of "gorgeous sun" and "tall thick trees" as opposed to a "land where life is cold." Other poems return to political and race-conscious themes. "Lament for Dark Peoples" describes the disruption of Native American and African cultures by European "civilization." The "red" and "black" people are "caged" in "the circus of civilization." "Poem" treats the clash of African and Western civilizations, and "Danse Africaine" shows the connection between African dance and a heritage of rhythm. "Summer Night" considers jazz images and musical life. In "The White Ones," the poet uses whiteness to address ambivalent feelings and relative beauty: "I do not hate you,/ For your faces are beautiful, too." Two of Hughes's best-known poems close the collection: "Mother to Son," which develops the metaphor of life as "no crystal stair," and "Epilogue," also known as "I, Too," which describes the "darker brother" and his resolve to declare his beauty and his rightful place at the "table" of equality.

Joseph McLaren

Further Reading

Bloom, Harold, ed. *Langston Hughes.* New ed. New York: Chelsea House, 2008. Collection of critical essays examines Hughes's life and work. Includes a discussion of Hughes, primitivism, and jazz.

Cullen, Countée. Review of *The Weary Blues*, by Langston Hughes. In *Langston Hughes: Critical Perspectives Past and Present*, edited by Henry Louis Gates, Jr., and K. A. Appiah. New York: Amistad, 1993. A fellow Harlem Renaissance poet questions the merit of Hughes's jazz and blues poems but praises his more traditional lyrical verse.

Feinstein, Sasha. "Weary Blues, Harlem Galleries, and Southern Roads." In *Jazz Poetry: From the 1920's to the Present.* Westport, Conn.: Greenwood Press, 1997. Examination of the history of jazz poetry cites the publication of Hughes's *The Weary Blues* as the first time the genre became "fully embraced." Includes discussion of this collection.

Jemie, Onwuchekwa. *Langston Hughes: An Introduction to the Poetry.* New York: Columbia University Press, 1976. One of the first full-length treatments of Hughes's poetry remains useful for students. Discusses both jazz and blues themes and treats *The Weary Blues* in chapter 2, "Shadow of the Blues."

Miller, R. Baxter. *The Art and Imagination of Langston Hughes.* 1989. Reprint. Lexington: University Press of Kentucky, 2006. Examines Hughes's poetry by focusing on the imaginative process. *The Weary Blues* is interpreted in chapter 3, "'Deep like the Rivers': The Lyrical Imagination," as a work that reveals a diversity of techniques.

Nardi, Steven A. "'By the Pale Dull Pallor of an Old Gas Light': Technology and Vision in Langston Hughes's *The Weary Blues.*" In *New Voices on the Harlem Renaissance: Essays on Race, Gender, and Literary Discourse*, edited by Australia Tarver and Paula C. Barnes. Madison, N.J.: Fairleigh Dickinson University Press, 2006. Presents an analysis of the collection, which is described as a "central text" in the development of Hughes's poetics, as in this work Hughes moved beyond his earlier Carl Sandburg-influenced verse to create poetry drawing on African American folk culture and music.

Rampersad, Arnold. *1902-1941: I, Too, Sing America.* Vol. 1 in *The Life of Langston Hughes.* 2d ed. New York: Oxford University Press, 2002. First volume in a definitive biography of Hughes addresses the literary history of *The Weary Blues* in the context of Hughes's relationship to other literary figures of the 1920's.

Tracy, Steven C. *Langston Hughes and the Blues.* 1988. Reprint. Urbana: University of Illinois Press, 2001. Provides a comprehensive treatment of the blues influences in Hughes's poetry. Includes a substantial definition of the structures of blues songs and corresponding patterns in Hughes's poetry. Examines *The Weary Blues* in chapter 3, "Creating the Blues."

The Web and the Rock

Author: Thomas Wolfe (1900-1938)
First published: 1939
Type of work: Novel
Type of plot: Impressionistic realism
Time of plot: 1900-1928
Locale: North Carolina, New York, and Europe

Principal characters:
GEORGE WEBBER, a young writer
ESTHER JACK, his beloved

The Story:

George Webber's childhood is one of bleakness and misery. He is a charity ward who lives with his aunt and uncle. George's father deserted him and his mother and went off to live with another woman. After the death of George's mother, her Joyner relatives take George into their home, where the boy is never allowed to forget that he has Webber blood mixed in with his Joyner blood. Strangely, all of his good and beautiful dreams are dreams of his father, and often he hotly and passionately defends his father to the Joyners. His love for his father makes his childhood a divided one. George hates the people his aunt and uncle call good, and those they call bad, he loves. A lonely child, George keeps his thoughts and dreams to himself rather than expose them to the ridicule of the Joyners, but the picture of that happy, joyful world of his father, and others like him, stays with him during those bleak years of his childhood.

When George is sixteen years of age, his father dies, leaving the boy a small inheritance. With that money, George leaves the little southern town of Libya Hill and goes to college. There he finds knowledge, freedom, and life. Like many other young men, George wastes some of that freedom in sprees of riotous and loose living, but he also reads everything he can get his hands on, and he is deeply impressed with the power of great writers. George is beginning to feel the need to put some of his thoughts and memories down on paper. He wants to write of the two sides of the world—the bright, happy world of the people who have everything and the horrible, dreary world of the derelicts and the poor. His college years end, and George fulfills the dream of every country boy in the nation; he goes to the city, to the beautiful, wonderful "rock," as he calls New York.

The city is as great and as marvelous as George knew it would be. He shares an apartment with four other young men; it is a dingy, cheap place, but it is their own apartment, where they can do as they please. George, however, finds the city to be a lonely place in spite of its millions of people and its bright lights. There is no one to whom he is responsible or to whom he belongs. He thinks he will burst with what he knows about people and about life, and, because there is no one he can talk to about those things, he tries to write them down. He begins his first novel.

The next year is the loneliest one George ever knew. He drives himself mercilessly. He is wretched, for the words torturing his mind will not go on the paper as he wants. At the end of a year, he takes the last of his inheritance and goes to Europe. He hopes to find there the peace of mind he needs to finish his book. The cities of Europe do not hold his salvation. He is still lonely and bitter, because he cannot find the answer to the riddle of life. He goes back to New York, and the city is no longer an unfriendly enemy, for George finds Esther.

They meet on the ship bound for New York. Esther is Mrs. Esther Jack, a well-known and successful stage-set designer. She is fifteen or twenty years older than George, but she is also younger in many ways, for Esther loves people and believes in them. Where George is silent and distrustful, Esther is open and trusting. George sometimes feels that theirs is the greatest love of all times, at once brutal and tender, passionate and friendly, so deep that it cannot last. For the next three years, however, he is the king of the world. To Esther, George tells all of his dreams, all of his memories, and all of his formerly wordless thoughts about life and people.

At first, George fails to realize that Esther means more to him than just a lover. Gradually, he comes to know that through her he is becoming a new person, a man who loves everyone. For the first time in his life, George belongs to someone. Since he is no longer lonely, the torture and the torment leave him. At last, his book begins to take shape, to become a reality. George is happy.

Slowly, however, the magic of his affair with Esther begins to disappear. He still loves her more than he believes possible and knows that he will always love her, but they begin to quarrel, to have horrible, name-calling scenes that leave them both exhausted and empty, even the quarrels that end with passionate lovemaking. At first, George does not know the reason for those scenes, although he always knows that it is he who starts them. Slowly, he begins to realize that he quarrels with Esther because she possesses him so completely; he gave her his pride, his individuality, his dreams, and his manhood. Unknowingly, Esther is also a factor in his disillusionment, for through her he meets the great people of the world—the artists, the writers, the actors—and he finds those people disgusting and cheap. They destroy his childhood illusions of fame and greatness, and he hates them for it.

When George's novel is finished, Esther sends the manuscript to several publishers she knows. After months pass without his hearing that it is accepted, George turns on Esther in one final burst of savage abuse and tells her to leave him and to never return. Then he goes to Europe again.

Although he goes to Europe to forget Esther, he does nothing without thinking of her and longing for her. Esther writes to him regularly, and he paces the floor if the expected letter does not arrive; but he is still determined to be himself, and, to accomplish his purpose, he must not see Esther again.

One night in a German beer hall, George gets into a drunken brawl and is badly beaten. While he is in the hospital, a feeling of peace comes over him for the first time in ten years. He looks into a mirror and sees his body as a thing apart from the rest of him. He knows that his body was true to him, that it took the abuse he heaped upon it for almost thirty years. Often he was almost mad, and he drove that body beyond endurance in his insane quest—for what, he does not know. Now he is ready to go home again. If his first novel is not published, he will write another. He still has much to say. The next time he will put it down correctly, and then he will be at peace with himself. At last, George is beginning to find himself.

Critical Evaluation:

In *The Story of a Novel* (1936), Thomas Wolfe responded to critics' complaints that he could write only about his own life, and that his Scribner's editor, Maxwell Perkins, was responsible for organizing the material of his first two novels, *Look Homeward, Angel* (1929) and *Of Time and the River* (1935). He promised to write in a more objective, disciplined style, and, to prove that he could structure his sprawling fiction without assistance, he severed his professional association with Perkins. In July, 1938, two months before he died following a brain operation, Wolfe submitted to his new editor, Edward C. Aswell, the manuscript from which his last two novels, *The Web and the Rock* and *You Can't Go Home Again* (1940), were assembled. Although somewhat more objective and more finely controlled than his earlier fiction, the novels continue the supreme subject of all of his work: the story of his own life reshaped into myth.

Critics have said that *The Web and the Rock* is at once the best and the worst novel written by Wolfe. Certainly the first part of the book, that describing George Webber's childhood in a southern town, is an excellent regional chronicle. Here Wolfe's genius with words reaches new heights. The rest of the novel, however, drags somewhat from overdone treatment of a love story in which similar scenes are repeated until they become monotonous.

George Webber, described as monkeylike, with long arms and an awkward, ambling gait, scarcely resembles the tall, hawklike Eugene Gant of *Look Homeward, Angel*. Nevertheless, he is surely another psychological portrait of Wolfe, the tormented artist among Philistines. In the first part of *The Web and the Rock*, the author attempts to provide for his hero a new family and social background, but the Joyners, despite their vitality, are mere copies of the Pentlands; Libya Hill resembles Altamont; and the moody, romantic Webber recalls the young Eugene. Some of the minor characters, notably the baseball hero Nebraska Crane and Aunt Maw, are brilliantly drawn. The chapter "The Child by Tiger," originally published as a short story, reveals Wolfe's great power to create tragic myth. Above all, the strength of the first part of the book rests upon the author's heroic vision of the townspeople and the mountain folk of North Carolina—a stock of enterprising, stubborn, passionately independent souls. They represent the mysterious web of the earth. Like George, a child of the mountain folk, they are tied by threads of destiny not only to the land but also to the seasons, the workings of time. As an artist, Webber understands intuitively the heart of things, the patterns of life and of dreams.

In roughly the second half of the novel, Wolfe contrasts the web of the earth with the rock of the city of New York. At this point in his writing, he abandons, for the most part, his scheme of objectivity and deals with the experiences of his own life. George meets and falls in love with Esther Jack (the same Esther who first appears to Eugene Gant in the "Faust and Helen" chapter of *Of Time and the River*)—in real life, the stage designer and artist Aline Bernstein. With remarkable frankness, Wolfe describes the tragic course of the affair between these markedly different personalities: the egotistic, brilliant, despotic provincial genius and his mistress, a sophisticated, sensitive, upper-middle-class Jewish wife and mother. As a realist, Wolfe is at his best detailing scenes of lovemaking and eating, of tempestuous quarrels and passionate reconciliations. Throughout the extended part of the book that deals with the love affair—for all of its excesses and absurdities—Wolfe is able to touch the reader: George and Esther truly care about each other and try desperately to make their fragile relationship endure.

The theme of *The Web and the Rock* is the fragility of all dreams. The rock of New York, which George loves as well as fears, begins to crumble in this novel. The city, founded upon greed and selfish power, has no soul. To escape from his own sense of ruin, George visits pre-Nazi Germany, already ripe for the advent of Adolf Hitler. George hopes to recapture, among the drunken revelers at a Munich Oktoberfest, the sense of joy of his own manhood; however, he becomes violent, engages in a savage fight with the beer-hall swaggerers, and is terribly beaten. By the end of the novel, he wishes to return to the United States so that he might establish his dreams once again upon a foundation that will endure: upon the web of his failing sense of the earth and the rock of an already insecure civilization. In the last chapter, "The Looking Glass," Webber comes to understand the futility of these dreams.

Further Reading

Bloom, Harold, ed. *Thomas Wolfe.* New York: Chelsea House, 1987. A collection of eight essays by seven writers, including a general overview of Wolfe's fiction, an examination of his treatment of the South, and "*The Web and the Rock*" by Leo Gurko.

Ensign, Robert Taylor. *Lean Down Your Ear upon the Earth, and Listen: Thomas Wolfe's Greener Modernism.* Columbia: University of South Carolina Press, 2003. An ecocritical interpretation of Wolfe's work, examining his depiction of the natural world and his characters' connection with it. The references to *The Web and the Rock* are listed in the index.

Evans, Elizabeth. *Thomas Wolfe.* New York: Frederick Ungar, 1984. An excellent introduction to *The Web and the Rock.* Analytically summarizes its episodes and discusses Wolfe's narrative devices.

Holliday, Shawn. *Thomas Wolfe and the Politics of Modernism.* New York: Peter Lang, 2001. A reevaluation of Wolfe, describing how the experimental nature of his fiction and other aspects of his work and life define him as a modernist writer.

Idol, John Lane, Jr. *A Thomas Wolfe Companion.* Westport, Conn.: Greenwood Press, 1987. Explains how Wolfe's editor became virtually his coauthor. Identifies as major themes an artist's problems in a hostile environment; loneliness; and personal, social, and religious conflicts. Presents a book-by-book plot summary, an explication of symbols, and analyses of characters, all of whom are identified in a glossary.

Johnston, Carol Ingalls. *Of Time and the Artist: Thomas Wolfe, His Novels, and the Critics.* Columbia, S.C.: Camden House, 1996. Examines the bitter relationship between Wolfe and the literary critics, and how he responded to their critiques in his fiction and letters. The section on *The Web and the Rock* and *You Can't Go Home Again* provides information about the initial American and German reviews and later reviews from the 1940's until after the 1960's.

Kennedy, Richard S. *The Window of Memory: The Literary Career of Thomas Wolfe.* Chapel Hill: University of North Carolina Press, 1962. Definitively combines biographical data and critical perceptions to fit *The Web and the Rock* into the evolution of Wolfe's career.

Ryssel, Fritz Heinrich. *Thomas Wolfe.* Translated by Helen Sebba. New York: Frederick Ungar, 1972. Shows how Wolfe confronted and partially solved technical and thematic problems resulting from his turning to less autobiographical writing in *The Web and the Rock.*

A Week on the Concord and Merrimack Rivers

Author: Henry David Thoreau (1817-1862)
First published: 1849
Type of work: Memoir

In 1839, two years after his graduation from Harvard College, Henry David Thoreau and his brother John built a riverboat with their own hands and took the leisurely trip that provides the framework for Thoreau's *A Week on the Concord and Merrimack Rivers.* Although the work is based on a real experience, Thoreau molded his material to fit his artistic requirements. Thus the actual time of the trip is reduced to seven days, each represented by a chapter in the work. The author does not hesitate to introduce observations and references to literary works that occur in his journals years after the actual journey. It is a mistake, then, to consider this work as a travel journal, just as it is a mistake to consider Thoreau's *Walden: Or, Life in the Woods* (1854) as merely a treatise on domestic economy.

A Week on the Concord and Merrimack Rivers includes both prose and poetry and often provides meticulous observations about the flora, fauna, and geography of the areas through which the boat passes. For instance, the sight of a fisherman leads the author early in the work to discuss at length the fish in shoals in the stream and the "fish principle in nature" that disseminates the seeds of life everywhere so that wherever there is a fluid medium, there are fish. In this respect, the work is somewhat like the scientific data gathering in nineteenth century works such as Charles Darwin's *The Voyage of the Beagle* (1839). The work, however, is neither a naturalist's handbook nor a traveler's guide.

Actually, the geographical journey down the rivers is a metaphor for the reader's journey into the mind of the author. As Thoreau relates what he saw and thought as he drifted down the river, the reader enters the flow of ideas in the writer's mind. Just as the current of the stream bears along the boat with Thoreau and his brother, so the current of ideas in Thoreau's mind bears along the reader by evoking the joy and nostalgia that the author feels for those lost, golden days. As Thoreau says, human life is very much like a river running always downward to the sea, and, in this book, the reader enters for a moment the flow of Thoreau's unique existence.

One must remember that the circumstances of Thoreau's life provide an undercurrent of emotion in this apparently tranquil holiday as he recalled it in the solitude of Walden Pond. Both Henry and his brother John had been deeply in love with the same girl, Ellen Sewall, the daughter of a prominent New England family. John had first proposed marriage to her and had been refused; Henry fared no better. Perhaps their relative poverty was a contributing factor in their rejection. The two brothers were therefore friendly rivals, and their relationship occasions a long discussion of the nature of friendship. When one says that someone is a friend, one commonly means only that he or she is not an enemy. The true friend, however, will say, "Consent only to be what you are. I alone will never stand in your way." The violence of love is dangerous; durable friendship is serene and equable. The only danger of friendship is that it will end. Such was the emotional relationship of the two brothers.

Yet their friendship was to end. Within a year after their trip, John died suddenly and horribly. Thoreau could not look back to their vacation on the rivers without realizing that the happiness of those times could never be repeated. In a very real sense, the work is a prose elegy for his dead brother, the true friend, the rival in love. As in all elegies, the reader follows the progress of the mourner's soul as it seeks consolation for the loss, and the consolation comes from the passage of the seasons and the observation of the natural processes of death and regeneration. This unstated elegiac element is the main motive for the composition. Why grieve for a particular lost friend when all the world is subject to decay and change? Every natural object when carefully observed shows the natural process of death and rebirth. If one must grieve, one should therefore grieve for the sadness of all things and the transitory nature of all beauty found in the material world. So if one were to go to a New England village such as Sudbury, one would see in great detail the teeming activity there, but one must not forget that it was settled by people who were once as much alive as the people there now, but who are all gone, their places taken by new people. The Indians are replaced by the white settlers and the settlers in turn by their children. The Concord and Merrimack rivers flow timelessly into the sea; every individual life flows to its conclusion. The passage of the seasons is cyclical in that every autumn implies a future springtime. The voyage on the rivers is circular, and the two brothers return to their point of departure; thus life must pass back into the great body from which it was first drawn.

Thoreau's thinking is strongly conditioned by Romantic ideas. The whole book represents a return to nature. The author sees an accord between nature and the human spirit. He observes that he has a singular yearning for all wildness. He values cultural primitivism. He says that gardening is civil and social, but it wants the vigor and freedom of the forest and the outlaw. In fact, there may be an excess of cultivation that makes civilization pathetic. Thoreau's poetry is plainly in the style of the English Romantics, written in ballad measure and celebrating nature and primitive heroes:

> Some hero of the ancient mold,
> Some arm of knightly worth,
> Of strength unbought, and faith unsold,
> Honored this spot of earth.

Among poets, Thoreau praises Homer because he lived in an age when emotions flowed uncorrupted by excessive cultivation. Like William Wordsworth, he has a theory that the world is but a canvas to human imagination. He says that surely there is a life of the mind above the wants of the body and independent of it and that this life is expressed through cultivation of the capacity of the imagination. Like many Romantic writers, Thoreau seems to exalt the emotions at the expense of the rational faculty. He says that people have a respect for scholarship and learning that is out of proportion to the uses these commonly serve and that the scholar has not the skill to emulate the propriety and emphasis of the farmer's call to his team. For Thoreau, act and feeling should be valued above abstract thought.

Thoreau's work constitutes a major document in Transcendentalist thought. His observation that a farmer directing his team of horses is as important as a scholar's thought is connected to the theological notion that every person is called to perform a peculiar activity, to fill a particular place in life. This view—that life presents a duty for everyone, that music is the sound of universal laws promulgated, and that marching is set to the pulse of the hero beating in unison with the pulse of nature and stepping to the measure of the universe—is characteristic of the pervasive moralism in Transcendentalist thought. When Thoreau looks at a sunset, he records that he is grateful to be reminded by interior evidence of the permanence of universal laws. In other words, by personal intuition a person watching a sunset is aware of an immanent deity presiding over the universe and providing people with an ethical imperative, a duty to do.

At the end of the week, Thoreau's boat grates once more on the bulrushes of its native port. The trip provides a framework to support a vast weight of Thoreau's thought—direct observation of nature, elegiac sentiment, Romantic and Transcendentalist notions—all flowing naturally across the mind of a young man as he drifts through the pastoral countryside of nineteenth century New England.

Further Reading

Cafaro, Philip. *Thoreau's Living Ethics: "Walden" and the Pursuit of Virtue.* Athens: University of Georgia Press, 2004. Examines Thoreau's ethical philosophy, focusing on *Walden* but also considering his other works, including *A Week on the Concord and Merrimack Rivers.* Explains how Thoreau's ideas are part of a tradition of ethical thinking that dates from the ancients to the present day.

Drake, William. "*A Week on the Concord and Merrimack Rivers.*" In *Thoreau: A Collection of Critical Essays*, edited by Sherman Paul. Englewood Cliffs, N.J.: Prentice-Hall, 1962. Easily accessible essay argues that Thoreau's trip on the Concord and Merrimack rivers is an exploratory journey into thought.

Fink, Steven. *Prophet in the Marketplace: Thoreau's Development as a Professional Writer.* Princeton, N.J.: Princeton University Press, 1992. Contains a detailed discussion of the structure of *A Week on the Concord and Merrimack Rivers* and how Thoreau composed the book.

Johnson, Linck C. *Thoreau's Complex Weave: The Writing of "A Week on the Concord and Merrimack Rivers."* Charlottesville: University of Virginia Press, 1986. Extensive study focuses on both the complete version of the book and its first draft, which is included in its entirety.

Myerson, Joel, ed. *The Cambridge Companion to Henry David Thoreau.* New York: Cambridge University Press, 1995. Collection of essays includes discussions of Thoreau's reputation, Thoreau and Concord, Thoreau and Emerson, and Thoreau and reform. An essay by Linck C. Johnson provides an analysis of *A Week on the Concord and Merrimack Rivers.*

Thoreau, Henry David. *The Illustrated "A Week on the Concord and Merrimack Rivers."* Edited by Carl F. Hovde, William L. Howarth, and Elizabeth Hall Witherell. Princeton, N.J.: Princeton University Press, 1983. The text of *A Week on the Concord and Merrimack Rivers* is accompanied by photographs by Herbert Wendell Gleason that visually document Thoreau's rivers. Includes an informative historical introduction to the book.

The Well

Author: Elizabeth Jolley (1923-2007)
First published: 1986
Type of work: Novel
Type of plot: Psychological realism
Time of plot: Six years during the 1980's
Locale: Rural Western Australia

Principal characters:
HESTER HARPER, an emotionally starved middle-age woman
KATHERINE, a teenage orphan taken in by Hester
MR. BIRD, manager of Hester's finances
MR. HARPER, Hester's father
MR. and MRS. BORDEN, buyers of Hester's farm
HILDE HERZFELD, young Hester's governess
JOANNA, Katherine's friend

The Story:

A young Katherine is driving home with Hester Harper after a party. They hit something on the road, but Hester says it is not a kangaroo. They dispose of the dead thing in their well at home.

Six years earlier, Hester, who is respected in town for her farming knowledge and her business acumen, brings fifteen-year-old Katherine home to the wealthy Harper farm. The orphan girl, living with Mrs. Grossman, a local shop owner, had faced return to the convent orphanage, but Hester had stepped in before she was brought there.

After her own father's death, Hester increasingly neglects the business of farming and concentrates on pleasurable domestic, creative, and expensive activities with Katherine. Hester ignores the sound advice of her father's friend, Mr. Bird, and continues to spend money. Four years after bringing Katherine home, she has to send her farm workers away and rent the farm to the Bordens, a fecund young couple with a healthy family of boys. Hester retreats to a few isolated acres at the corner of the property and lives with Katherine in an old shepherd's hut that has a disused well in the yard. She is still a relatively wealthy woman.

Hester is infatuated with Katherine. Their days are filled with music and dancing, inventing stories, dressing up in their new clothes, intricate sewing, and cooking increasingly elaborate meals. The two often picnic on the edge of the well and hear its murmurs and sighs, brought on by the wind. When the two women do not feel like washing up, they throw their dirty dishes into the well. They also fantasize about a princess or a prince and a troll living in the well.

Katherine regularly writes to her friend Joanna, whom she knows from the orphanage. Joanna writes that she has served her time in remand and is now free, leading Katherine to yearn more and more for her friend. Hester sees Joanna as an intruder in the idyllic world she and Katherine have created. She feels that Joanna may threaten her life with Katherine and entice her to leave. However, despite her misgivings, she allows Katherine to have Joanna visit for a week.

Mr. Bird makes an occasional visit to the farm. On one visit, he tells Hester that the Bordens want to buy the farm. He advises Hester that she would be wise to do so, and she eventually agrees, keeping a large amount of cash on the isolated property. Hester plans to take Katherine on a trip to Europe, just like the trip the young Hester took with her German governess, Hilde Herzfeld. First, however, Joanna is coming for a visit. Katherine begins to learn to drive so that she and Joanna will be able to go into town without Hester.

Hester and Katherine attend a party to celebrate the Bordens' purchase of the farm. Hester takes great pleasure in watching Katherine dance. Mrs. Borden tells Hester that she dresses Katherine in a way that is too young for her. Hester is disturbed by the suggestion that she is dressing Katherine childishly. She also is troubled by her own loss of status with the townspeople, given that she is no longer a landowner. She also is disturbed by Joanna's impending visit.

Katherine insists on driving home from the party. She hits something with the car on the road near Hester's house. Hester claims they hit a man and that he is now dead. She urges Katherine to drive close to the well so that she can heave the body into it. She soon discovers that her house has been burglarized and thinks that the dead man may have the money on him. Hester insists that Katherine will have to climb down the well to retrieve the money. In the morning, she leaves Katherine alone as she drives to the store to buy a long rope.

Hester returns with the rope. Katherine tells her that she has been talking to the man in the well and has given him some bedding and food. He wants to marry her, she claims. Hester thinks Katherine is ill; she apparently is fantasizing about the man, whom she calls Jacob. Katherine hands Hester a one-hundred-pound note, which she says she received from Jacob to buy more food. Hester now believes that Katherine had stolen her money, and she thinks that if Katherine is allowed the key to the car, she will rescue the man and leave with him.

Later at night, Hester guards the car keys while both women sleep in the kitchen. Rain breaks the drought. Hester, troubled by her dreams, reveals the next day that when she was fourteen years old, she had discovered Hilde bleeding profusely in the bathroom. Hilde had told Hester to go away and to call her father, but Hester, not wishing to acknowledge that Hilde was miscarrying Mr. Harper's child, had instead retreated to her bedroom to hide under the covers. This was the last time she saw Hilde, who was driven away early the next morning by her father.

Before dawn, Hester approaches the well and finds that it is filling with water. She thinks she sees a sleek head and also a hand on the final ladder rung. She is inclined to get the rope to try to rescue the man, but Mr. Borden comes by, which stops her. He says that he will have his men put a cover on the well. Hester agrees to the job, and the well is soon covered tightly.

Hester goes to town to see Mr. Bird about her finances. She is shocked to find that he has been ill for some time and is now in a city hospital. His secretary hands her several books with all her financial dealings meticulously recorded. The books include instructions for Hester, should she wish to withdraw her money. Mr. Bird soon dies in the hospital.

Hester and Katherine are getting ready to pick up Joanna from the train station. Hester, still terrified that Katherine will leave with Joanna, uncharacteristically runs out of gasoline and begins to walk to the gas station for more. She leaves Katherine, who is sewing a costume for herself, in the car. Hester is picked up by Mrs. Borden, and one of the Borden children begs to be told a story about a monster. Hester begins her story of the night she and Katherine hit something in the road.

Critical Evaluation:

Elizabeth Jolley's novel, *The Well*, tells the story of Hester Harper, who has never known her mother, had been cared for by her grandmother, and, later, had been cared for by a governess named Hilde Herzfeld. Hilde had cherished the girl, teaching her to sing, dance, sew, and cook. She helped Hester overcome her self-consciousness, and she involved her in romantic dreams. Hilde and young Hester also took a tour of Europe together.

Once Hilde had been ignobly bundled from the house after a miscarriage, Hester realized that she shared her only friend with a rival, her father. Hester was sent to boarding school for two years. Her grandmother died while she was at the school. Emotionally, Hester seems arrested by Hilde's departure and her grandmother's death. As an adult, she still does not speak of Hilde, until she meets Katherine. She remains unmarried and has no children. She is determined that Katherine will remain innocent despite the girl's fascination with romance, magazines, and films and film stars.

Katherine is full of energy, and it becomes clear that as she gets older, from fifteen to twenty-one, she becomes more interested in marriage and longs to reestablish her friendship with Joanna. The two young women are the same age and share similar interests. Some of the novel's black humor stems from the differences in age, education, and cultural interests between the older Hester and the younger Katherine.

Jolley, in having Hester bring the orphan Katherine to her own home, is suggesting that Hester is trying to re-create the nurturing relationship she had with Hilde. Hester plans a trip to Europe with Katherine and teaches her in the same way she had been taught by Hilde. Hester ends up obsessively infantilizing, manipulating, and possessing Katherine, and she does not recognize Katherine as a sexual being. This obsession also leads Hester to keep Katherine from others as much as possible, leaving her isolated with the teenager in a shepherd's hut on the farm, an ideal place for their fantasy life. Hester is able to freeze time until intruders, such as Joanna and the "something" in the well, threaten to disrupt her plans.

A number of critics have argued that the well symbolizes repressed female sexuality. The stories that Katherine and Hester imagine about who lives in the well (Katherine thinks of a princess or prince and Hester thinks of an antisocial troll) suggest Katherine's naïve romanticism and Hester's fear of men as beasts. Hilde's miscarriage and Mr. Harper's sexual involvement with the governess means that an intruder (Mr. Harper) had destroyed Hester and Hilde's relationship. Hester cannot bear to think of Katherine being possessed by a rival or of her reproducing. Once the body is thrown into the well, various desires are released. Katherine expects to marry the man, but Hester faces repressed memories of Hilde's plight.

Given Hester's obsessive intent to keep Katherine to herself, the "something" they hit on the road may indeed have been a kangaroo rather than a man. Hester may be lying to Katherine to bind them more tightly. Once the well is covered, neither woman refers to it again. Hester later remembers a doll that became wedged in the well of a doll's pram at Mr. Bird's house. The imagery used is similar to the description of a sleek head Hester thought she saw in the well, suggesting she now understands her fear of reproduction.

At the end of the novel, Hester is inspired by the liveliness of the numerous Borden children to begin a frightening tale of a monster she had met on the road one dark night. Perhaps Jolley is taking the reader back to the very beginning of the novel, and the story of the accident. Hester is inventive, and she finds herself wanting to speak again with an author—a woman closer to her own age—she has met a few times at Grossman's store.

The Well, Jolley's seventh novel, won the Miles Franklin Award in 1987. The book was adapted to a film of the same name and released in 1997.

Christine Ferrari

Further Reading

Bird, Delys, and Brenda Walker, eds. *Elizabeth Jolley: New Critical Essays*. North Ryde, N.S.W.: HarperCollins, 1991. This study of Jolley's life and works includes many references to *The Well* from various theoretical perspectives.

Dibble, Brian. *Doing Life: A Biography of Elizabeth Jolley*. Crawley: University of Western Australia Press, 2008. This biography contains a wealth of information on Jolley and her writing. Dibble was given complete access to Jolley's private papers and spent a decade producing the work.

Gilbert, Pam. *Coming Out from Under: Contemporary Australian Women Writers*. Sydney: Pandora Press, 1988.

Chapter 3 summarizes early interviews with Jolley and analyzes the novels up to and including *The Well*.

Ittner, Julia. "Home-Breaking and Making in the Novels of Elizabeth Jolley." In *Homemaking: Women Writers and the Politics and Poetics of Home*, edited by Catherine Wiley and Fiona R. Barnes. New York: Garland, 1996. Argues that, like many women writers, Jolley shows how a woman's ties to home and family can be crippling or liberating.

Jolley, Elizabeth. "Elizabeth Jolley." Interview by Ray Willbanks. In *Australian Voices: Writers and Their Work*. Austin: University of Texas Press, 1991. Focuses on Jolley's fiction, including characters, themes, and development, but includes some interesting information on the author's personal background and how the events of her life influenced her writing.

Lindsay, Elaine. "Elizabeth Jolley's Catalogue of Consolation." *Southerly* 66 (2006): 52-66. Explains the optimistic tone of Jolley's writings as the product of her belief in the possibility of transformation.

Lurie, Caroline, ed. *Central Mischief: Elizabeth Jolley on Writing, Her Past, and Herself*. New York: Penguin, 1992. This is an eclectic collection of essays, articles, and talks by Jolley.

McCowan, Sandra. *Reading and Writing Elizabeth Jolley: Contemporary Approaches*. South Freemantle, W.A.: Freemantle Arts Centre Press, 1995. Examines Jolley's work, including *The Well*, from a variety of critical perspectives.

Salzman, Paul. *Hopelessly Tangled in Female Arms and Legs: Elizabeth Jolley's Fiction*. St Lucia: University of Queensland Press, 1993. Chapter 2 focuses on the complex symbolism of the well in the novel as a space of repressed desires and female creativity.

The Well of Loneliness

Author: Radclyffe Hall (1880-1943)
First published: 1928
Type of work: Novel
Type of plot: Social realism
Time of plot: Early twentieth century
Locale: England and France

Principal characters:
STEPHEN GORDON, a young lesbian
COLLINS, a housemaid
MISS PUDDLETON, Stephen's governess
ANGELA CROSSBY, Stephen's first lover
MARY LLEWELLYN, Stephen's principal lover
JONATHAN BROCKETT, a gay playwright and Stephen's friend
VALÉRIE SEYMOUR, an author and a salon host
MARTIN HALLAM, Stephen's friend

The Story:

Sir Philip and Lady Anna Gordon assume that their first-born will be a boy, so when Anna gives birth to a girl, they name her Stephen. Schooled happily at Morton, the family's country estate, daughter Stephen endears herself to her father with her boyish demeanor, which troubles her mother and confuses the children of the local gentry. The first sign of her sexuality emerges at the age of seven, when she becomes infatuated with a housemaid named Collins; Stephen is enraged one day to find a footman kissing Collins in a garden shed. Given a new pony, which swiftly replaces the housemaid in her affections, Stephen names it Collins. Riding with her father and hunting with the gentry becomes Stephen's great passion; her skill wins respect despite her unladylike manners, and soon her father presents her with a fine hunting horse, Raftery.

A tall, athletic teenager, Stephen learns to ride, fence, and speak fluent French, but her father wants to enlarge her learning and so hires Miss Puddleton, or Puddle, to be her governess. Under Puddle's exacting tutelage, Stephen resolves to become a writer. At a Christmas party, she at last finds a companion, Martin Hallam, her equal in imagination and love for nature, and he soon becomes her first close friend. On the eve of his return to Canada, he proposes marriage, and Stephen flees from him in horror. Only Sir Philip—and perhaps Puddle—recognizes Stephen's true nature, but he proves unable to speak of it, even when, in confusion, Stephen seeks his aid.

With mother, father, and daughter each concealing a private torment, the sudden death of Sir Philip brings what little remains of Morton's former joy to an abrupt end. A final deathbed struggle to explain Stephen's nature to his wife and daughter comes too late.

In town one day in her twenty-first year, Stephen encounters Angela, the discontented American wife of a humorless businessman. Friendship soon ripens into a passionate affair, although it is displayed with strictly "schoolgirl kisses." Stephen's conscience regarding Angela's happiness forces her to urge Angela to leave her husband and follow Stephen to Paris. Angela immediately refuses, demanding, "Could you marry me, Stephen?" Month after month, the affair limps on, until one night Stephen spies Angela and Ralph in their garden tenderly embracing. Mortified, Stephen pours her soul into a long, explicit letter, but Angela, affronted by this indiscretion, shows it to Ralph, who in turn sends a copy to Lady Anna. Shocked and disgusted, Anna confronts Stephen and refuses to share a home with her: One of them must leave. Stephen withdraws to her father's study and there discovers a hidden shelf of books about homosexuality by a German psychiatrist, annotated in her father's handwriting. Praying for a sign, she lets a Bible fall open; the page reads, "And the Lord set a mark upon Cain." The choice seems clear; Puddle pledges to stand by Stephen in her exile.

Two years later, Stephen achieves overnight success with her first novel, but her second novel is a disappointment, even to its solitary and workaholic author. At a literary lunch, she renews an acquaintance with Jonathan Brockett, a gay playwright who secretly recognizes in Stephen a fellow "invert." Eventually, Brockett persuades Stephen that she can revive her creative energy, evidently flagging in the second novel, only if she sees more of the world, starting with Paris. Stephen cuts her remaining ties with her mother and Morton and moves to Paris with Puddle. There, Brockett introduces Stephen to a circle of sexually ambiguous writers surrounding Valérie Seymour, proving that Stephen's exile need not be utterly lonely.

World War I breaks out, and during two years with the London Ambulance Column, Stephen notices other lesbians fitting comfortably into the new roles that war opened to them. Longing to serve her country near the front lines, she joins a unit of Englishwomen in a French Ambulance Corps, who drive wounded soldiers to the field hospital. There, Stephen falls in love with Mary Llewellyn, a young and equally brave volunteer. After the armistice, Stephen, scarred (an indication of the mark of Cain) and decorated, takes Mary into her Parisian home. The young couple spends the winter in Orotava, Spain, but they become increasingly despondent and uneasy as Stephen tries to protect Mary from the consequences that Mary will suffer if she commits herself to Stephen. At a point of crisis, however, they declare a love that would withstand the world's judgment: "and that night they were not divided."

Now utterly in love, Stephen and Mary return to Paris and establish a household with Stephen as husband and Mary as wife. Their social isolation deepens, however, and while Stephen turns obsessively to writing, her only "weapon," Mary grows bored and unhappy. Brockett persuades them to use Valérie Seymour's salon to extend their circle, and they find consolation in new friends, including courageous lesbians, however tormented and damaged. Stephen and Mary's glimpse of the seedy nightlife of Paris demoralizes them, however, and after the sudden death of their friend, Barbara, and the suicide of her lover, Mary becomes too vulnerable for Stephen to confide in with the old frankness.

When Martin Hallam, living temporarily in Paris, reappears, the three become fast friends. Stephen gradually realizes that Martin and Mary are becoming romantically attached, and at last Martin challenges Stephen to let Mary go, insisting that Mary will prove unable to survive the trials of the taboo "marriage" with Stephen. A contest for Mary's heart ensues, although neither Martin nor Stephen reveals it to Mary, and at last Martin concedes defeat. Stephen, however, has already decided that Martin is right after all, that all her love is not enough to bring Mary true happiness. At last, Stephen's devotion makes her lie to Mary, saying she has been unfaithful, and thus she drives Mary into Martin's arms. Together, Mary and Martin depart; alone, Stephen prays for all sexual inverts, "Give us also the right to our existence!"

Critical Evaluation:

The Well of Loneliness is the first novel in English to make an unabashed plea for an understanding of lesbians, or "female sexual inverts," the term used in Radclyffe Hall's time. In many respects the novel falls short of literary greatness—its heavy-handed moralizing, scenes of exaggerated melodrama, and frequently ponderous diction dull its effectiveness. It remains unique, however, in its era as a wholly sympathetic story of a lesbian's struggle to forge her identity. It stands first in a long succession of "coming out" novels, and continues to inform and inspire readers. If Hall's principal purpose was to persuade her readers that a lesbian minority not only exists but should be permitted to participate in society and contribute to its welfare, there can be little doubt that she has achieved considerable success through the years.

At the time *The Well of Loneliness* came out in both England and the United States in 1928, publishers of novels that portrayed homosexuals faced charges in these two countries of violating laws against obscenity. Hall's publisher was brought to trial, in both England and the United States. The British judge, who refused either to read the book or hear from the notable authors, including Virginia Woolf and E. M. Forster, who came to testify on its behalf, considered the work's literary merit irrelevant to the question of whether it was obscene, and banned it. The U.S. court, however, after a heated trial, refused to deem the book obscene.

The portrayal of the character of Stephen Gordon is colored by the psychological thinking of Hall's day, particularly by the work of Havelock Ellis, who insisted that sexual inverts, far from being sociopaths who posed a danger to society, were capable of leading useful and honorable lives. Ellis's comments on *The Well of Loneliness* may be found as a preface to some editions.

The novel, however, does not propose that lesbians could lead happy, normal lives in the world as Hall knew it, but rather that inverts represent a distinct group who merit sympathy, perhaps even pity. Stephen is pictured as possessing the soul of a man in the body of a woman; in dress and manner she resembles a man, and Hall is less concerned to make her "normal" than sympathetic. In today's terms, Stephen could be considered transgender, and certainly gender ambiguous. Others argue Stephen is a traditional "butch" lesbian. Hall's depiction is only partly attributable to the assumptions of her time: Deeply traditional ideas of society and nature underpin the novel, and they make Stephen's martyrdom heroic and, ironically, stigmatizing. Stephen is an aristocrat with a deep faith in the values of her class, but her journey is one of renunciation: She renounces Mary as she renounced Morton, but she rejects neither. The rootedness that Morton gave her becomes her gift for Mary when she "delivers" her to Martin and a conventional heterosexual life. Hall's portraits of homosexuals can be difficult to distinguish from ones meant to condemn: Other than Stephen, her inverts are casualties of the world's unkindness, and in the bar scenes their infirmity might be easy to mistake for depravity.

Stephen's virility is not merely the product of psychological theorizing, however, but rather the expression of the author's idealism and theological purpose. Religious conviction plays a crucial and frequently overlooked role in *The Well of Loneliness*; indeed, the novel amounts to a hagiography. Stephen's separation from Mary at the novel's end, although disappointing to some readers, expresses Stephen's commitment to an absolute good rather than to a personal one—to what is truly best rather than merely what she wants for herself. Hall, a Roman Catholic convert, saw a vast divide between the truth of the world and the truth of God. As Christ-figure and saint, Stephen makes the disapproval of mortals irrelevant. She acts out her sexual desire while others (such as Puddle) remain hypocritically silent because she possesses inner strength to match her outer strength. Stephen possesses a strength that enables her to forge sanctity out of persecution, while other inverts must sooner or later crumble under the weight. This strength, moreover, enables her to become a war hero, and so prove the value of lesbians to a nation in need. Her victimization is transformed by a moral idealism that, while fruitless in the eyes of this world, owes allegiance to God.

Matthew Parfitt

Further Reading

Baker, Michael. *Our Three Selves: The Life of Radclyffe Hall*. New York: William Morrow, 1985. A comprehensive biography of Hall that examines the publication and reception of *The Well of Loneliness*. Several chapters deal with the trial and publicity surrounding the banning of the book in England. The discussion connecting *The Well of Loneliness* to Hall's other novels also is helpful. Includes photographs of Hall, her family, and lovers.

D'Cruz, Doreen. "Miming the Masculine: Radclyffe Hall's *The Well of Loneliness*." In *Loving Subjects: Narratives of Female Desire*. New York: Peter Lang, 2002. D'Cruz examines various forms of female desire, including lesbian sexuality, in *The Well of Loneliness* and other literary works.

Doan, Laura, and Jay Prosser, eds. *Palatable Poison: Critical Perspectives on "The Well of Loneliness."* New York: Columbia University Press, 2001. Collection of early reviews and critical essays dating from 1928 through the end of the twentieth century that examine numerous aspects of the novel. Includes discussions of the depiction of the "mannish lesbian," the book as a war novel, and Hall and lesbian modernists.

Faderman, Lillian. *Odd Girls and Twilight Lovers*. New York: Penguin Books, 1991. This history of lesbians in twentieth century America provides a historical framework for understanding the experiences of women who love women and includes a discussion of the role of *The Well of Loneliness* in providing women with knowledge of lesbian sexuality.

Franks, Claudia Stillman. *Beyond "The Well of Loneliness."* Aldershot, England: Avebury, 1984. A thorough critical treatment of Hall's controversial novel.

Jay, Karla, and Joanne Glasgow, eds. *Lesbian Texts and Con-*

texts: *Radical Revisions*. New York: New York University Press, 1990. A collection of critical essays on lesbian fiction and literature, a number of which discuss Hall and her work. A selective bibliography lists numerous fiction, nonfiction, and critical works by and about lesbians and lesbian literature.

Love, Heather. "Spoiled Identity: Radclyffe Hall's Unwanted Being." *Feeling Backward: Loss and the Politics of Queer History*. Cambridge, Mass.: Harvard University Press, 2007. Focuses on Hall's novel and other literary works that were written before the modern gay and lesbian rights movement, describing how these books reflect their society's homophobia and heterosexism and their authors' resulting pain, anger, and isolation.

McPike, Loralee. "A Geography of Radclyffe Hall's Lesbian Country." *Historical Reflections/Reflexions Historiques* 20, no. 2 (1994): 217-242. Argues that lesbian sexuality is only one focus of the novel. The novel also concerns the human condition in general.

Noble, Jean Bobby. "Passionate Fictions: Radclyffe Hall's *The Well of Loneliness*." In *Masculinities Without Men? Female Masculinity in Twentieth-Century Fictions*. Vancouver: University of British Columbia Press, 2004. Chronicles the emergence of the masculine female figure and how this figure is represented in twentieth century literature, including *The Well of Loneliness*.

O'Rourke, Rebecca. *Reflecting on "The Well of Loneliness."* New York: Routledge, 1989. A critical examination of *The Well of Loneliness* with a selected bibliography of books and articles by and about Hall. Especially interesting is the author's discussion of the reactions to the novel from readers of all sexualities.

Souhami, Diana. *The Trials of Radclyffe Hall*. New York: Doubleday, 1999. A respected biography of Hall, with a focus not only on the moral and legal fights over the publication of *The Well of Loneliness* but also on Hall's long-time relationship with artist Una Troubridge and Hall's controversial life.

Westward Ho!

Author: Charles Kingsley (1819-1875)
First published: 1855
Type of work: Novel
Type of plot: Historical
Time of plot: Sixteenth century
Locale: England and South America

Principal characters:
AMYAS LEIGH, an adventurer
FRANK LEIGH, his brother
SIR RICHARD GRENVILE, Amyas's godfather
EUSTACE LEIGH, Amyas's and Frank's cousin
ROSE SALTERNE, the beloved of Amyas and Frank
SALVATION YEO, Amyas's friend
DON GUZMAN DE SOTO, a treacherous Spaniard
AYACANORA, an Indian maiden
MRS. LEIGH, the mother of Amyas and Frank

The Story:

Amyas Leigh has a secret longing to go to sea, but he never speaks of it because he knows his parents think him too young for such a rough, hard life. When he meets John Oxenham and Salvation Yeo, who are recruiting a crew to sail to the New World after Spanish treasure, he begs to be allowed to join them, but his parents and Sir Richard Grenvile, his godfather, persuade him to wait a while. The next year, his father dies of fever, and his brother Frank goes to the court of Queen Elizabeth. Then Sir Richard persuades Amyas's mother to let the boy accompany Sir Francis Drake on the

first English voyage around the world. Finally, Drake and his adventurers return, and Amyas, no longer a boy but a blond young giant, comes back to his home at Bideford, in Devon.

He remembers one face in the village better than any other: Rose Salterne, the mayor's daughter. All the young men love and honor her, including Amyas and his brother Frank, who returns from court. She is also loved by Eustace Leigh, the cousin of Amyas and Frank. Eustace is a Catholic. His cousins distrust him because they suspect he is in league with the Jesuit priests. When Rose spurns his love, he vows revenge. The other young men who love Rose form the Brotherhood of the Rose, and all swear to protect her always and to remain friends, no matter who should win her.

Shortly after Amyas returns from his voyage with Drake, Yeo comes to him and Sir Richard with a strange and horrible tale. The voyage that he made with Oxenham was ill-fated, and Oxenham and most of the crew were captured by the Spanish Inquisition. Oxenham had a child by a Spanish lady, and before they were separated, Yeo vowed that he would protect the child. Yeo did his best, but the child was lost, and now Yeo begs that he might attach himself to Amyas and go wherever Amyas goes. In his travels, he thinks that he might someday find the little maid again. Amyas and Sir Richard are touched by the story, and Amyas promises to keep Yeo with him. Before long, the two sail with Sir Walter Raleigh for Ireland, where they will fight the Spaniards.

In Ireland, Raleigh defeats the Spaniards, and Amyas takes Don Guzman de Soto, a Spanish nobleman, as hostage. Don Guzman accompanies him back to Bideford, to wait for his ransom from Spain. Don Guzman is a charming gentleman, and it is not long before he catches the eye of Rose. After his ransom is paid, he leaves England; then it is learned that Rose also disappeared in the company of Lucy the witch. Her father, Amyas, Frank, and the other young men of the Brotherhood of the Rose are wild with grief. All vow to sail to La Guayra in Caracas, where Don Guzman went to be governor and where they feel Rose fled to join him.

Their voyage is an eventful one. When they near La Guayra, they are seen by the Spaniards, and they fight many times before they reach the shore. Amyas and Frank go ashore with a few men to try to rescue Rose. There they learn that Eustace knew of their voyage and beat them to their destination to warn Don Guzman of their approach. Frank and Amyas hear Rose tell Eustace that she is happily married to Don Guzman, so they know she will never leave with them. Nevertheless, they also hear Eustace beg her to run away with him, threatening to turn her over to the Inquisition if she refuses. At that threat, Frank and Amyas attack Eustace, but he escapes and is never heard of again. Rose flees into the fort. As they make their way back to their ship, Frank is captured by Don Guzman's men. Amyas is knocked unconscious, but his men carry him back to the ship.

When the ship is damaged in a later encounter with the Spaniards, the crew beaches her and begins a march toward the fabled city of Manoa. It is a long and hazardous journey over high mountains and through a land of hostile Indians. They find no El Dorado, but a young priest of one of the tribes falls in love with Amyas and follows him the rest of the journey. She is called Ayacanora, and, although she is

of an Indian tribe, she seems to have the look of a white woman.

After more than three years, the little band reaches the shore of New Granada. There, after a furious fight, they capture a Spanish galleon. After they secure her and set sail, they go into the hold and release the prisoners the Spaniards have aboard. One of them is Lucy the witch, who tells them of the horrible fate of Rose and Frank. Before Eustace disappeared from La Guayra, he reported to the Inquisition that Rose kept her Protestant faith. She and Lucy were taken before the terrible tribunal, where Frank was also turned over to the torturers. Lucy confessed that she accepted the Catholic faith, but Frank and Rose, refusing to yield to the Inquisitors, were tortured for many days before they were burned at the stake. When Amyas hears this story, he is like a madman, vowing never to rest until he kills every Spaniard he sees. Two Spanish dignitaries on the ship witnessed the burning of Frank and Rose, and Amyas has them hanged immediately.

At last, the ship reaches Devon, and Amyas takes Ayacanora to his home, where his mother welcomes her and treats her as a daughter. During the voyage, Yeo discovers that she is the little maid he promised Oxenham to protect, and he becomes a father to her. Amyas treats her as he might a sister, but Ayacanora is not happy at this treatment.

After a time, Amyas fits out a ship and prepares to go with Drake to Virginia, but before they sail, the Spanish Armada arrives off English shores. Amyas, with his ship, joins the rest of the fleet in that famous battle. After twelve terrible days, the Armada is defeated and almost every Spanish ship destroyed. Amyas, however, is not satisfied. Don Guzman is aboard one of the Spanish ships, and although Amyas pursues him relentlessly, he has to sit by and watch a storm tear the Spaniard's ship apart. Amyas curses that he himself was not able to kill Don Guzman and thus avenge his brother's death.

As Don Guzman's ship breaks apart, a bolt of lightning strikes Amyas's ship, blinding him and killing Yeo. At first, Amyas is full of despair. One day, he has a vision. He sees Rose and Don Guzman together and knows that the Spaniard really loved her and mourned her until his death. Then he sees himself with Don Guzman, acknowledging their sins to each other and asking forgiveness. After that, he feels at peace with himself.

Amyas returns to his mother's home, and there she and Ayacanora care for him. Realizing how much the girl loves him, he is so grateful for the tenderness she shows him that he gives her his heart. In Bideford, the blind hero spends his remaining days dreaming of his past deeds and of the great glory to come for his country and his queen.

Critical Evaluation:

Charles Kingsley, the son of a clergyman of the Church of England, studied at Cambridge University and was the parish priest for the Anglican parish in Eversley, Hampshire, from 1842 until his death. Interested especially in historical subjects, his wide reading brought him the appointment of Regius Professor of Modern History at Cambridge University. He was known as a Christian Socialist because of his pamphlets in support of improving the social and economic life of the working classes. He also wrote poetry and novels.

Kingsley was perhaps best known for espousing what came to be called Muscular Christianity. He believed that Christianity involved the warfare of the forces of good against the forces of evil and held up as role models figures such as Joshua and David from the Old Testament and Alfred the Great and Sir Philip Sidney from English history. He believed that the proper Christian life was one of action rather than of contemplation, of physical exertion rather than of mental exertion, of moral certitude rather than of ambiguity, and of bluster rather than of meekness.

Kingsley wrote three other novels before *Westward Ho!* Two of them, *Yeast* (1848) and *Alton Locke* (1850), were problem novels that dealt with the political and social conditions of the Victorian working classes; the third, *Hypatia* (1853), was a historical romance set in the fifth century, which attacked indirectly the spread of rationalism and Catholicism in the nineteenth century. *Alton Locke* was moderately successful, with sales stimulated by the book's reputation for socialism. The other two did not sell well. Always short of money, Kingsley wanted a story that would both be a good vehicle for his ideas and bring in some income. In February, 1854, just as Britain became involved in the Crimean War, a conflict to prevent Russian expansion in the eastern Mediterranean, he began thinking of a historical romance set during the days of the Elizabethan sea dogs. Kingsley paused to write a patriotic pamphlet, *Brave Words for Brave Soldiers*, which exhorted the British to believe that they were God's army fighting for God's cause, and then returned to his novel.

Westward Ho! reflects Kingsley's deep opposition to the growth of Catholicism in British society, a growth that took the forms of an invigorated Roman Catholic Church and the appearance of a movement that emphasized a more Catholic style of worship in the Church of England, the Oxford Movement. A staunch Protestant, Kingsley criticized Catholic practices in his earlier novels. The novel also reflects his belief that Britain's imperial expansion was God's way of spreading Protestantism throughout the world; he thus chose to dedicate *Westward Ho!* to Sir James Brooke, an adventurer

who carved out of the island of Borneo a territory that he ruled as "white rajah," and George Augustus Selwyn, Anglican missionary bishop of New Zealand. These men, he wrote in his dedication, exhibited the same "manful and godly, practical and enthusiastic, prudent and self-sacrificing" English virtues that characterized the Elizabethan sea dogs. Finally, *Westward Ho!* is an example of war propaganda; reviewers and readers at the time knew that the novel's Spaniards stood for the Russians with whom their country was locked in combat.

The themes of *Westward Ho!* include patriotism to Great Britain, anti-Catholicism, violence, and Muscular Christianity. Patriotism and anti-Catholicism are linked in Kingsley's mind because he shared the common beliefs that Protestantism is the basis of the British constitution, that Protestant Britain is God's chosen country, and that Catholicism leads to despotism. Thus, British institutions are superior to those of other countries because they are godly; they are godly because they are Protestant; and they are Protestant because they are British. Kingsley contrasts British manliness, good humor, simple Christian piety, and devotion to duty with Spanish effeminacy, deceit, semipagan worship of idols, and greed. The most clear-cut contrast is that between two female figures: the Virgin Queen Elizabeth I of England and the Spanish vision of the Virgin Mary. The English Virgin Queen possesses all the English virtues, while the Spaniards endow the Virgin Mary with all their vices. Kingsley was strongly influenced in these views by the nationalist historian J. A. Froude.

Violence and Muscular Christianity are also linked in the novel. Kingsley presents violence as the appropriate response to dilemmas. Because one's enemies are evil, violence is the best, perhaps the only, godly response, whether it be Israelites smiting Canaanites and Philistines or Englishmen smiting Spaniards and Russians. On the personal level, Kingsley also sees violence as an appropriate way of solving problems. In the novel's opening, Amyas Leigh, tired of being intimidated by the priest-schoolmaster John Brimblecombe, breaks his slate over the bumbling man's head. Muscular Christians thus deal and receive blows in the service of good against evil. The Elizabethan sea dog, who combines athletic and military prowess in the service of Protestant England, thus is the model Muscular Christian.

Kingsley allows some ambiguity in his depiction of the ungodly enemy, an ambiguity that reflects his own uncertainty at Britain's incompetent conduct of the Crimean War. He remains certain, however, that the English are good and that their enemies are bad. Hence, although he gives virtues to a few Spanish characters, such as Don Guzman, he makes them virtuous in spite of their religion and nationality. At the end of the book, Kingsley writes a powerful scene in which Don Guzman and his ship sink into the waves, denying Amyas his revenge; disappointed, Amyas hurls his sword into the sea and criticizes God for having cheated him of vengeance. A bolt of lightning strikes him blind. Kingsley's message is that Amyas's error lies in letting his revenge become personal rather than national and religious; it is for this he is punished, not for seeking vengeance itself.

Westward Ho! was Kingsley's most successful novel. It sold well throughout the English-speaking world, securing the finances of the newly established Macmillan publishers. The book remained in print for more than a century and entered the canon of boys' literature. Its greatest cultural influence was on the generations of British and American boys who imbibed the novel's messages of ultra-nationalism, religious crusading, and lighthearted violence.

"Critical Evaluation" by D. G. Paz

Further Reading

Beeson, Trevor. "The Novelist: Charles Kingsley, Chester and Westminster." In *The Canons: Cathedral Close Encounters*. London: SCM Press, 2006. An account of Kingsley's life, ecclesiastical career, and social and religious significance.

Chitty, Susan. *The Beast and the Monk: A Life of Charles Kingsley*. London: Hodder and Stoughton, 1974. Using confidential papers that had been closed to researchers for more than a century, Chitty attempts to link Kingsley's writings with his erotic sensibilities, especially his enjoyment of conjugal love. Chitty includes a chapter that discusses Kingsley's financial difficulties at the time of writing *Westward Ho!*, difficulties that influenced his choice of theme.

Collums, Brenda. *Charles Kingsley: The Lion of Eversley*. New York: Barnes & Noble, 1975. This more conventional biographical approach is a useful introduction to Kingsley's public life. It includes substantial extracts from *Westward Ho!* as part of its investigation of the background to Kingsley's writing.

Dodd, Philip. "Gender and Cornwall: Charles Kingsley to Daphne du Maurier." In *The Regional Novel in Britain and Ireland, 1800-1990*, edited by K. D. M. Snell. New York: Cambridge University Press, 1998. Focuses on the depiction of Cornwall in novels by Kingsley and other writers. Dodd maintains that, for Kingsley, Cornwall was the "site of a forward-looking, confident masculinity."

John, Juliet, and Alice Jenkins, ed. *Rethinking Victorian Culture*. New York: St. Martin's Press, 2000. This reassessment of nineteenth century British culture includes two essays about Kingsley: "Purging Christianity of Its Semitic Origins: Kingsley, Arnold, and the Bible" by Stephen Prickett and "'More Interesting than All the Books, Save One': Charles Kingsley's Construction of Natural History" by Frances O'Gorman.

Klaver, J. M. I. *The Apostle of the Flesh: A Critical Life of Charles Kingsley*. Boston: Brill, 2006. Comprehensive intellectual biography of Kingsley, placing his life and work within the broader context of the social, religious, and historical developments that occurred during his lifetime.

Martin, Robert Bernard. *The Dust of Combat: A Life of Charles Kingsley*. New York: W. W. Norton, 1960. A well-balanced biography of Kingsley. The author has an excellent analysis of Muscular Christianity.

Rapple, Brendan A. *The Rev. Charles Kingsley: An Annotated Bibliography of Secondary Criticism, 1900-2006*. Lanham, Md.: Scarecrow Press, 2008. An annotated bibliography of selected works about Kingsley's writings, life, and activities.

Sutherland, J. A. *Victorian Novelists and Publishers*. Chicago: University of Chicago Press, 1976. This study of the relationship between writers and their publishers argues that financial considerations sometimes determined writers' choices of form, style, and subject matter. The chapter on *Westward Ho!* describes the artistic, financial, and personal factors that shaped the process of writing the book. Kingsley worked with his publishers to produce a spectacularly successful book that was distributed with a view to capitalizing on the Crimean War.

What Maisie Knew

Author: Henry James (1843-1916)
First published: 1897
Type of work: Novel
Type of plot: Psychological realism
Time of plot: 1890's
Locale: London, Folkestone, and Boulogne, England

Principal characters:
MAISIE FARANGE, the daughter of divorced parents
IDA FARANGE, her mother
BEALE FARANGE, her father
MISS OVERMORE, a governess and, later, the second Mrs. Beale Farange
MRS. WIX, a governess
SIR CLAUDE, Ida Farange's second husband

The Story:

Beale and Ida Farange are divorced with much publicity. At first, each fights to keep their daughter Maisie, but at last it is arranged that the girl should spend six months with each. The first period is to be spent with her father. Maisie is confused by the divorce. At first, she truthfully reports to her parents what each says about the other, but finding that her candor leads to furious outbursts and that she is being used as an innocent messenger, she soon becomes silent on the subject of the absent parent and appears to absorb no knowledge during her visits.

Ida engages Miss Overmore, a pretty governess, whom Maisie is unhappy to leave when it is time to return to her father. Soon, however, to Ida's fury, Miss Overmore is engaged to be Maisie's governess at Beale Farange's house. Upon her subsequent return to Ida, Maisie is placed in the care of Mrs. Wix. She learns no lessons from Mrs. Wix but adores her conversation and feels comfortable and secure with her.

During Maisie's next stay with Beale, he goes to Brighton for a few days together with Miss Overmore. When the governess returns, she finds Mrs. Wix waiting for her. Mrs. Wix alone is concerned for Maisie's welfare, and she is outraged by the child's environment. She announces that Ida is about to remarry, and she gives Maisie a photograph of Sir Claude, her future stepfather. Miss Overmore thereupon announces that she just married Beale.

Some time after his marriage, Sir Claude calls and is received by the new Mrs. Beale Farange. Maisie is delighted by their apparent understanding and declares that she brought them together. Sir Claude wins Maisie's love by being gentle with her and by declaring that he intends to make her his responsibility. In spite of the pain of leaving the new Mrs. Farange, the girl is pleased to go home with him. Ida's love for her new husband, however, soon wanes, and she has several lovers. When she accuses Sir Claude of basely stealing Maisie's affections and threatens to drive Mrs. Wix out of the house for supporting him, Maisie feels that she belongs nowhere. Mrs. Wix is determined to meet her responsibility for

Maisie, and she desires to "save" Sir Claude from Mrs. Beale Farange, whom he frequently visits. Fearing for the loss of her livelihood, she wishes that Sir Claude would take a house for himself where she and Maisie will also live.

On one outing, Sir Claude takes Maisie to her father's new house, which she is afraid to enter for fear of losing him if she remains there. Once in the house, however, she is again enthralled by Mrs. Farange's beauty and is interested to learn that Beale matters no more to his wife than Sir Claude does to Ida. Maisie remains happily with her stepmother after Sir Claude assures her that he will provide for Mrs. Wix and visit her frequently.

After a long absence, Sir Claude visits Maisie again. While they are walking in the park, they meet Ida with an unknown, military-looking man. Both Ida and Sir Claude become terribly angry, and Maisie is sent to talk with Ida's escort, whom her mother calls the Captain. Maisie, who is by that time thoroughly aware that neither parent loves her, weeps when the Captain praises her mother highly and is eager to agree that she is "good." Sir Claude, unable to learn from Maisie what the Captain said to her, sends her home alone in a cab.

Mrs. Farange tells Maisie that she meets Sir Claude away from her home but that he is reluctant to visit them and thus compromise Maisie. The three hope to meet at a London exhibition; instead, they unexpectedly encounter Beale. After a subdued but violent quarrel, Maisie is whisked away by her father to the house of his mistress. In a way that is intended to elicit Maisie's refusal, he offers to take her to America with him.

Encouraged by Mrs. Wix, Sir Claude takes Maisie to Folkestone as the first step toward making a home for them in France. There Ida arrives suddenly and surrenders Maisie to Sir Claude's guardianship. The following day, they cross to France, where Mrs. Wix joins them. Sir Claude intends to return to England and to Mrs. Beale Farange once Maisie's father finally leaves. Sir Claude confesses that he fears Mrs. Farange as he formerly feared Ida. Mrs. Wix, still strongly opposed to Mrs. Farange, asks to be sent to England to sever their relationship. Sir Claude refuses this request and goes off to England alone.

While he is away, Mrs. Wix explains to the bewildered Maisie that she refuses to condone the immorality of Mrs. Farange and Sir Claude in living together with them. Also, she declares that she will never again leave Maisie. After several walks and much thought, the full implications of what this situation might mean becomes apparent to Maisie. She realizes, too, that she has no moral "sense," and having rapidly absorbed the idea of such a sense from vague but emphatic conversations with Mrs. Wix, she decides to show in her future responses that she does indeed possess it.

When they return to their hotel after a morning walk, Maisie is unexpectedly greeted by her stepmother. Mrs. Wix's own "moral sense" is nearly destroyed by Mrs. Farange's charm and determination to have the governess-companion as an ally. According to Mrs. Farange, now that the girl's father has left, Maisie is her own daughter. In this way, she intends to hold Sir Claude through his devotion to the girl. Mrs. Wix wavers, but Maisie declares that she will stay with Sir Claude only if he is alone.

The next morning, Mrs. Wix awakens Maisie with the news that Sir Claude has arrived. When Maisie breakfasts alone with him, he asks her if she will leave Mrs. Wix and live with him and Mrs. Farange. She asks to see Mrs. Wix before deciding. Later, while walking with Sir Claude, she says she will give up Mrs. Wix only if he will give up Mrs. Farange. Maisie makes her decision when the four people confront one another in a final struggle at the hotel. When she fails in her appeal that Mrs. Farange give up Sir Claude, Maisie decides to stay with Mrs. Wix.

Critical Evaluation:

Readers and critics alike at times feel frustrated with Henry James's *What Maisie Knew*, the careful, detailed record of the emergence of a young girl's consciousness. James scholars are still puzzled over why the artist turned a serious novel over to such an apparently unsophisticated protagonist, and some have wondered whether a complex, realistic social satire can be communicated through a medium who does not understand much of what she sees. Critics are equally perplexed at the moral ambiguity around which the plot of the novel revolves, an uncertainty the novel's disturbing conclusion does nothing to dispel. Such responses are probably inevitable, for *What Maisie Knew* seems to have escaped even the control of its author.

Written during a period of artistic transition for James, the novel is a strange mixture of the kind of masterful story-telling that characterizes such early works as *Washington Square* (1880) and the psychological complexity of later masterworks such as *The Golden Bowl* (1904). Perhaps the transitional aspect of the novel is best illustrated by the fact that James himself was not sure how long the manuscript should be. He originally conceived the work as a short story in which a young innocent is victimized by adults whose motives she cannot hope to fathom. The detailed notebooks James kept during the process of planning the story show that the idea grew steadily in James's imagination. Maisie's case became compelling for the writer, and he worked on the book with the kind of curiosity associated more with a reader than with an author. This sense of an outcome beyond anyone's control finds its way into the finished version of the novel in the form of the narrator's frequent admissions that, since what Maisie knows is so often more than she can put into thoughts or words, it is all one can do to follow the child's development, let alone interpret or control it. When even an author cannot make complete sense of a novel's events, a reader must expect some degree of uncertainty. Some aspects of the paradoxical nature of *What Maisie Knew* seem destined to remain unresolved.

From the outset, the novel is calculated to test the moral stance of its readers. James presents an abundance of low behavior but does not balance the text by providing high ground to which the heroine or the reader might escape. While the fact that the novel begins with a divorce was not enough to offend their sense of propriety, readers at the end of the nineteenth century were still unused to the practice. The hint of scandal surrounding Beale and Ida Farange's divorce would probably have been palpable even if James had not emphasized the "bespattered" and "damaged" condition in which Maisie's parents emerged from their ordeal. The undercurrent of dishonesty and adultery accompanying the divorce foreshadows not only the new lovers that both Beale and Ida take thereafter but also the irresponsible behavior of Maisie's estranged parents in communicating their hostilities through their daughter. The hateful words Beale and Ida send each other on the lips of their young daughter become "an epitaph for the tomb of Maisie's childhood." This mistreatment is compounded in the course of the novel in further examples of neglect and emotional cruelty suffered by the likable child, in whose confused thoughts it becomes increasingly uncomfortable to dwell.

The characters who might improve Maisie's lot, Miss Overmore, Sir Claude, and Mrs. Wix, each with whom Maisie falls in love, all fall short. They all use their bond with Maisie in attempts to forge or secure their relationships with each other or with Beale and Ida. The caretaking love of an adult that should surround and protect a child is invariably corrupted in the novel by the adults' sexual love for each other. By making sexual or romantic attachment the barrier to the nurturing that Maisie needs, James makes the traditional solution to Maisie's problems, a new mother and father, impossible to attain. Any pair that might emerge from the chaotic nexus of relations—Beale and Miss Overmore, Ida and Sir Claude, or Sir Claude and Mrs. Wix—would necessarily be lovers first and surrogate parents second. Because their relationships are based on sex, they are morally inappropriate guardians for Maisie. James's complex moral scheme weaves an insoluble paradox. In fact, he mocks the very possibility of a moral solution to the problems of the novel.

Mrs. Wix continually browbeats Maisie with the concept of moral correctness. She teaches the child disgust for the sexual relationships of the other adults (while secretly coveting just such a bond with Sir Claude). James makes Mrs. Wix the emblem of moral perspective by using the term "straighteners" for the woman's eyeglasses. As Mrs. Wix confronts the possibility of losing Maisie and Sir Claude forever, she becomes furious with moral outrage. The innocent Maisie watches as the governess's "straighteners . . . seemed to crack with the explosion of their wearer's honesty." Here it becomes clear that hypocrisy is the cause of the moral disintegration of the novel's perspective.

James seems to be declaring that it is precisely in those moments of ethical and emotional dilemmas when good judgment is most urgently required that good judgment breaks down and solutions become impossible. Because the adults who are attracted to each other (although Sir Claude does not desire Mrs. Wix) cannot pair off without continuing the cycle of scandal, Maisie's options eventually dwindle down to the hope that one of her caretakers will forsake sexual desires and commit exclusively to her. The novel's most poignant scene occurs in a provincial French train station, when Sir Claude appears to be considering the possibility of escaping to Paris with the little girl. The prose in this passage is full of pseudoromantic tension, and it may be that Sir Claude himself senses that, for he lets the train to Paris go and thus renounces both his claim on and responsibility for the pathetic little girl. Maisie's return trip across the Atlantic with Mrs. Wix is a typically Jamesian solution to an ethical muddle. In the works of James, life's complexities do not yield to simple solutions, nor do misdeeds result in happy endings. This lesson is particularly painful in *What Maisie Knew* because an innocent child is the victim.

"Critical Evaluation" by Nick David Smart

Further Reading

Cargill, Oscar. *The Novels of Henry James*. New York: Macmillan, 1961. A vigorous study of all of James's novels. Cargill draws on the observation of several prominent literary critics and discusses James in the light of English and American literary history. Evaluates moral and artistic aspects of James's work.

Coulson, Victoria. *Henry James, Women, and Realism*. New York: Cambridge University Press, 2007. Examines James's important friendships with three women: his sister Alice James and the novelists Constance Fenimore Woolson and Edith Wharton. These three women writers and James shared what Coulson describes as an "ambivalent realism," or a cultural ambivalence about gender identity, and she examines how this idea is manifest in James's works, including *What Maisie Knew*.

Freedman, Jonathan, ed. *The Cambridge Companion to Henry James*. New York: Cambridge University Press, 1998. A collection of essays that provide extensive information on James's life and literary influences and describe his works and the characters in them.

Kaplan, Fred. *Henry James: The Imagination of Genius*. New York: William Morrow, 1992. A thorough narrative account of the life of Henry James. Kaplan considers American and English political history, literary history, and the personal life of James, while discussing the writer's complete oeuvre.

Miller, J. Hillis. *Versions of Pygmalion*. Cambridge, Mass.: Harvard University Press, 1990. Miller's work on the ethics of narration is difficult, but his chapter on *What Maisie Knew* is valuable both for its background information on the social climate in which the novel was written and for its clearly written examination of the complexity of the ethical dilemma in which James places his characters and readers.

Mitchell, Juliet. "*What Maisie Knew*: Portrait of the Artist as a Young Girl." In *The Air of Reality: New Essays on Henry James*, edited by John Goode. London: Methuen, 1972. A complete examination of the pressures that shape Maisie's consciousness. Mitchell argues against reading a sexual undercurrent into the relationship between Maisie and Sir Claude.

Pifer, Ellen. "Innocence on the Brink: James's *What Maisie Knew*." In *Demon or Doll: Images of the Child in Contemporary Writing and Culture*. Charlottesville: University Press of Virginia, 2000. Examines the ambiguous and contradictory conceptions of childhood in the twentieth century and how the period's fiction reflects this confusion. Describes how James's depiction of children anticipated post-Freudian ideas of childhood.

What the Butler Saw

Author: Joe Orton (1933-1967)
First produced: 1969; first published, 1969
Type of work: Drama
Type of plot: Farce
Time of plot: 1960's
Locale: England

Principal characters:
DR. PRENTICE, the head of a psychiatric clinic
MRS. PRENTICE, his wife
GERALDINE BARCLAY, a secretarial applicant
NICHOLAS BECKETT, a hotel page
DR. RANCE, an inspector of psychiatric clinics
SERGEANT MATCH, a police officer

The Story:

Geraldine Barclay, an attractive young woman in search of her first job, appears at Dr. Prentice's clinic one day to be interviewed for a secretarial position. Under interrogation from Prentice, she tells him that her father deserted her mother many years ago when the latter was a chambermaid at the Station Hotel. She herself did not see her mother for a long time, and her stepmother, Mrs. Barclay, died recently from being penetrated with a certain part of a statue of Sir Winston Churchill that was destroyed in a gas-main explosion. Geraldine's legacy from her stepmother is that part of the Churchillian statue, which she carries with her in a box to the interview.

Prentice orders Geraldine to undress for a physical examination and asks her to cooperate in the testing of a new contraceptive device. She agrees. His plan is foiled suddenly by the entrance of a disheveled Mrs. Prentice, who spent the night at the Station Hotel with the hotel page after attending a lesbian meeting. With Geraldine naked behind a screen, Prentice makes frantic attempts to hide Geraldine's clothes. His wife sees Geraldine's dress, however, and, arriving wearing only a fur coat with a slip underneath, puts on the dress.

Nicholas Beckett, the young hotel page, arrives to check Mrs. Prentice's bag for missing articles and to bribe her to let him sell pictures taken during their tryst at the hotel. Like Geraldine, Nick comes from a broken family. He asks for the job in Prentice's office and leaves only when Prentice hurriedly gives him some money.

A third intrusion into Prentice's plans occurs in the person of Dr. Rance, an inspector of psychiatric clinics. Discovering the naked Geraldine, he immediately proclaims her insane, the first of many similar proclamations. His habit is to question patients only after he issues insanity verdicts. He then interrogates Prentice about his background and follows with questions to Mrs. Prentice about her husband. He notes Prentice's apparent obsession with women's clothes. A fourth intruder, Inspector Match, arrives on a matter of national importance having to do with Sir Winston Churchill's statue.

Nick conveniently reappears with Mrs. Prentice's freshly cleaned dress and wig. Prentice, desperate to find attire for Geraldine, orders Nick to undress and Geraldine to put on his uniform. Nick is then asked to wear Mrs. Prentice's leopard-spotted dress and to impersonate Geraldine in a subsequent interrogation by Match. At the end of the first act, in the interest of professional correctness, it is agreed that Mrs. Prentice will examine Geraldine (actually Nick in disguise) and that Match will examine Nick (actually Geraldine in disguise).

At the start of the second act, the desperation of Geraldine and Nick to unravel what is so obvious that it needs no unraveling leads Geraldine to insist on being arrested. Meanwhile, at the same time that Prentice rapidly loses control of events, Rance gains control by his obsessive insistence on giving Freudian interpretations of everything having the slightest appearance of a sexual nuance: bisexuality, transvestism, incest, nymphomania, sadomasochism, and the like. Even Match falls victim to Rance's freewheeling accusations, namely, that he, too, may be a victim of a sexual assault by Prentice. When Rance insists on examining Match and orders him to undress, Nick is able to put on the police officer's uniform so as to arrest himself.

To ensure his ability to safely straitjacket Prentice, Rance asks Mrs. Prentice for a gun. She produces two, one for herself and another for Rance. As variously disguised persons flee out one door and in another, shots are fired that result in wounds to Match and Nick. By this time, Match finds himself attired in Mrs. Prentice's leopard dress, and the confusion seems total.

Geraldine is finally given a chance to tell her story, and when her lost brooch is produced Nick says he has one just like it. Mrs. Prentice then begins her own story of having broken a brooch in two, pinning one half to the clothing of each of her twins, a boy and a girl. The Prentice family reunion is made complete with Mrs. Prentice's confession that the brooch was given her in partial payment by an unknown man (who turns out to be Prentice) with whom she enjoyed a liaison during a power outage at the Station Hotel, the result of which was the birth of twins. Mrs. Prentice's story concludes with an account of her tryst with Nick in the same room in which she conceived him.

The revelations about the Prentice family, however, solve only one of the farce's two mysteries. Geraldine clears up the mystery of Match's investigation when she opens the box she brought with her to the interview, containing her stepmother's legacy to her, the lost part of Churchill's statue, a phallus.

In the final scene, all embrace. A skylight opens, a rope ladder lowers, and a bloodied Match descends, announcing that the great man, Churchill, "can once more take up his place in the High Street as an example to us all of the spirit that won the Battle of Britain." Bedraggled, all pick up their clothes and follow Match back up the ladder.

Critical Evaluation:

Joe Orton's farcical world is diminished, at worst distorted, by a mere summary of the story. Although he follows the oldest of farce conventions—including the plot device of twins separated at birth, a situation that necessitates the use of disguises so as eventually to reveal true identities—he changes the very nature of farce by adapting those conventions in his own inimitable way. All farce depends on social satire as a main theme, and in this respect Orton is a traditional satirist. As farce conventions demand, Orton's characters are flat and represent the excesses of his age's vices. Tradition also dictates a happy ending in which families are reunited and social norms, purified of wrongdoings, restored.

It is in this restoration that Orton makes a clean break with tradition. At the end of the play, nothing has changed. Mrs. Prentice's incest will not be punished. Dr. Rance will profit financially from the best seller he envisions about sexual perversions. Dr. and Mrs. Prentice will continue in their customary sexual pursuits. Match will go on championing an England that is no more. Geraldine and Nick will look for jobs.

The basis for Orton's reputation is his probing of the difference between behavior and the language used to make that behavior appear respectable. The physical disguises are a mere structural underpinning for the characters' linguistic disguises, which they use to justify their actions. Orton's language is that of the accepted idioms of the time, understood by all, yet ingeniously alien to the context in which they are used.

The basic elements of a job interview rise to heights of absurdity when, in response to Geraldine's confession that she has no idea who her father was, Prentice replies that he can-

not hire her if her birth was in any way miraculous; he adds "You did have a father?" He abuses professional ethics when he convinces Geraldine to test a new contraceptive device, at the same time asking her not to mention it to his nymphomaniacal wife, whom he confesses he married for her money and whose sexual pursuits he likens to the search for the Holy Grail. Two lies, then, begin a long procession of lies and disguises. All stem, as Prentice at one point tells Geraldine, from his misguided attempt to seduce her. Mrs. Prentice joins in the absurdity when she reminds Nick, who tells her that he has an offer for an option on the pictures, that her contract with him does not include "cinematic rights."

It is Rance, however, who raises Prentice's charade to the level of burlesque. Without analysis, he immediately interprets Geraldine's nakedness as her attempt to "re-enact her initial experience with her parent." The result, he says, is madness. When Prentice attempts to convince Rance that Geraldine is no more mad than he (Prentice) is, Rance replies that "no madman accepts his madness. Only the sane do that." Rance, in fact, introduces himself to Prentice as the representative of "Her Majesty's government" and his "superior in madness." He fails to realize that he speaks of himself when he says that the sane seem as strange to the madmen as the madmen seem to the sane. Under questioning, Prentice confesses to Rance that his tutor, unable to reach madness, taught it to others, and that it is those students who now run the mental institutions. Orton considers the clinic a microcosm of modern England.

The farce is more than a satire on psychiatry, however. It enters new territory when Rance claims to be the representative of order while Prentice is the representative of chaos. The real Orton emerges in this line, which is at the center of his life and plays. Orton had a stultifyingly lower-middle-class upbringing in Leicester, after which he spent ten years in London unsuccessfully trying to act and write and six months in an English prison. Above all, Orton was gay in a society in which homosexuality was illegal. His idea of chaos challenged existing sexual mores and, in a perverse way, liberated the characters temporarily to indulge in sexual identities that could exist only in fantasies or in the dreamworld.

The only characters who want to tell the truth but are denied the opportunity until the very end are Geraldine and Nick. By the time they can tell the truth, it is too late to have any influence. Geraldine and Nick, by being propelled from one disguise to another, also experience a kind of Alice-in-Wonderland adventure denied them in real life. In the end, both return to a world in which the job for which they search may continue to evade them.

Ronald Bryden's designation of Orton as the dramatist of welfare-state gentility is apt, for whether riding on a London bus listening to average people engaged in everyday conversation or while indulging in his own sexual proclivities, Orton experienced the life about which he wrote. He already had dealt with the shibboleths of small-town hypocrisies in *Entertaining Mr. Sloane* (1964), police dishonesty in *Loot* (1965), religious corruption in *Funeral Games* (1968), and corporate slavery in *The Erpingham Camp* (1966). In *What the Butler Saw*, he pulled out all stops in an uproarious farce in which the axioms of the new religion, psychiatry, are bared with ferocious hilarity. His insistence on truth, especially in his alteration of the traditional farce ending, freed him from the dishonesty that not only would have made him the kind of hypocrite he denounces in his farce but would have kept him imprisoned in a society whose law against homosexuality was not repealed until 1968, a year after his death. Despite the fact that Orton wrote only three long stage plays and four short plays for radio and television, he has been accorded a place with Harold Pinter and Tom Stoppard, two other major dramatists known for their innovative use of language.

Susan Rusinko

Further Reading

Bigsby, C. W. E. *Joe Orton*. London: Methuen, 1982. Deals with Orton's stylistic and thematic qualities in the context of contemporary European drama.

Burke, Arthur. *Laughter in the Dark: The Plays of Joe Orton*. London: Greenwich Exchange, 2001. Analyzes Orton's comedies and traces the connections between his work and his life.

Charney, Maurice. *Joe Orton*. London: Macmillan, 1984. Places Orton's work in the farcical tradition that goes back to origins in Greece and Rome.

Coppa, Francesca, ed. *Joe Orton: A Casebook*. New York: Routledge, 2003. Collection of essays analyzing Orton's work and controversial life. Some of the essays compare his plays with those of Oscar Wilde and Caryl Churchill, while others discuss his black camp humor and Orton as a gay rebel.

Innes, Christopher. "Joe Orton: Farce as Confrontation." In *Modern British Drama, 1890-1990*. New York: Cambridge University Press, 1992. Introduces Orton as a playwright of his time.

Lahr, John. *Prick up Your Ears*. New York: Alfred A. Knopf, 1978. Reprint. Berkeley: University of California Press, 2000. Traces the influences on Orton's development as a dramatist.

Orton, Joe. *The Orton Diaries*. Edited by John Lahr. London: Methuen, 1986. An entertaining account by Orton about himself, written during the last year of his life.

Rusinko, Susan. *Joe Orton*. New York: Twayne, 1995. Introductory overview containing a biography and analysis of Orton's career and individual plays, with one chapter devoted to *What the Butler Saw*.

When Rain Clouds Gather

Author: Bessie Head (1937-1986)
First published: 1968
Type of work: Novel
Type of plot: Social realism
Time of plot: 1964
Locale: Golema Mmidi, Botswana

Principal characters:
MAKHAYA, a South African refugee
PAULINA SEBESO, a single mother
GILBERT, an agricultural specialist from England
MMA MILLIPEDE, the aging village matriarch
DINOREGO, her longtime friend
PARAMOUNT CHIEF SEKOTO, the tribal chief over Golema Mmidi
CHIEF MATENGE, his brother

The Story:

Makhaya has fled South Africa because of his involvement in a bomb plot. He crosses the border into Botswana, and after being befriended by Dinorego, he decides to stay in the village of Golema Mmidi. Dinorego immediately introduces him to Gilbert, a British agricultural specialist who has also made the village of Golema Mmidi his home. Dinorego calls Gilbert his son, and explains to Makhaya that Gilbert is a giving person, always wanting to help people become more prosperous. He tells him that Gilbert can even eat the local food—sour milk porridge and goat meat—which has turned European stomachs in the past.

Gilbert has been working diligently on a cattle cooperative in Botswana for three years, and everyone has been looking forward to reaping its benefits except Chief Matenge. Matenge, who is a spoiled and authoritarian troublemaker, has been dispatched by his brother Sekoto to Golema Mmidi to keep Gilbert from becoming a nuisance. Matenge and Gilbert have been at loggerheads for many months over the cooperative, and every advance that Gilbert makes in the project results in two steps back because of Matenge's intrusions.

Dinorego refers Makhaya to Gilbert, believing the newcomer can assist the Englishman in his agricultural undertakings. Gilbert invites Makhaya to share a meal with him at his house, and he is amazed when Makhaya explains the simple tribal name that he was given. Gilbert decides that Makhaya is not interested in tribalism and decides to take him on as a worker on his farm. He teaches Makhaya how to drive a tractor and gives him lessons in agriculture; Makhaya then utilizes his knowledge of the Tswana language to pass on the European's agricultural information to the women of the village.

Golema Mmidi has suffered a drought, and without cultivation the land and streams were taken over by dry grass. Gilbert sees that fencing the area would prevent the livestock from freely grazing and would prevent desertification, but Matenge tells people that Gilbert wants to enslave them by putting up fences on their land. Gilbert wins the elders over by showing them the progress made by fencing his own land. Soon, everyone is interested in the changes that Gilbert initiates, but their interest only serves to infuriate Matenge. When Matenge finds out that Gilbert has hired a refugee on his farm, he approaches his brother Sekoto, who informs him that he will have to speak to the police.

Despite being burdened with the anger he carries as a result of living as a second-class citizen in apartheid-era South Africa, Makhaya succeeds in winning over everyone he meets, including the police constable, George Appleby-Smith. George agrees to support Makhaya after questioning him. The constable believes that Makhaya's quiet and respectful deameanor underscores his past, which at times makes him indignant over situations that he cannot control. Makhaya also meets Mma Millipede, who takes an instant liking to him based on his vulnerable state. Without realizing it, Makhaya has also made an admirer of Paulina Sebeso, who is attracted to Makhaya's good looks. Unaware of her interest, however, Makhaya unintentionally spurns Paulina's

advances. When Gilbert undertakes a large-scale millet plantation project, he puts Makhaya in charge of instructing the women of the village. It is only after the millet project begins that Makhaya starts to realize Paulina's feelings.

Paulina is a single mother to two children. Her eight-year-old son works at the cattle post for most of the year, in return for which Paulina receives payments that help her and her daughter subsist. When a famine strikes the cattle post, many cattle die, and the men who have been at the post return to their villages. Paulina asks Rankoane, one of the ranchers, why he did not send her son home. He responds that he expected her son to have arrived two weeks ago, as he had sent him home with a severe cough. Distraught, Paulina decides to go into the bush to find him. Makhaya accompanies her, and they find the bones of her son huddled in an empty mud hut. After returning to Golema Mmidi, Paulina holds a funeral service for her son that the whole village attends. A week passes, and Paulina receives a visit from one of Matenge's servants, who tells her that she has offended the chief and must report to the court.

Paulina's offense to the chief is her failure to report her son's death. A crowd of Paulina's friends has gathered at her house, expecting to report for work to begin planting millet. The women accompany Paulina to Chief Matenge's house, and on the way they draw a large crowd of other villagers, including Dinorego, Makhaya, and Gilbert. The crowd waits, unsure of what to expect, until George Appleby-Smith arrives. Makhaya tires of waiting and breaks down the door; he finds the body of Matenge waiting, hanging from a rope. George determines that Matenge was fearful of the crowd and decided to take his own life; he phones Sekoto to explain that his brother has killed himself.

Makhaya is haunted by the vision of vultures surrounding the body of Paulina's son. He struggles to come to terms with the idea of a world where children can face such a wretched end. He finds comfort in his ability to create a new beginning with Paulina, to whom he proposes marriage; she happily agrees.

Critical Evaluation:

Bessie Head was born in a mental hospital in 1937 to a white mother from a rich family. Head's father was a black stable hand (at a time when interracial relationships were illegal in South Africa). After her birth, Head was put into foster care. She never knew her parents or her grandparents; her only family was the son to whom she gave birth. Because of her own fragmented, racialized sense of identity and her lack of all family ties, Head's work frequently focuses on issues of isolation, land, and race, while her characters often struggle with tribalism, feelings of outsiderness, and frustration over political stagnation.

Head's first novel, *When Rain Clouds Gather*, is used by the Peace Corps, where it is required reading for members serving as agricultural volunteers in Botswana. Like many of Head's novels, it is based on her own life experiences. The cattle cooperative that Head writes about is based on the Bamangwato Development Farm cooperative, where she worked in 1966. The character of Makhaya is based on the author herself—both were South African refugees living in Botswana. Makhaya is driven by the desire to find peace after abandoning the dangerous life of a political freedom fighter. He wants to settle into a simple life with a wife and children.

Makhaya's exposure to Gilbert and the cattle cooperative gives him something positive to strive toward: The cultivation of the land into something to be shared by everyone, for the prosperity of all, fits with Makhaya's need to see beauty in humanity. Gilbert's ability to live among the people of Botswana and to work toward the success of Golema Mmidi is enough to make Makhaya believe in people again. Likewise, just as Gilbert is the first white person that Makhaya has met who has good intentions toward Africans, so too is Makhaya one of the first Africans Gilbert has met who is not hindered by tribalist ties. The two figures are able to work together toward a community that benefits black people and white people—something unheard of in a country so close to apartheid-era South Africa. Makhaya, like the author he is based on, searches for simple connections to the world in order to make sense of the tragedies and traumas he has experienced.

As in many of her novels, Head showcases the role of women in the task of bettering communities. Paulina Sebeso leads the women to build a plantation of tobacco that will not only provide monetary relief for them all but will also turn their land from desert to pasture. In the heavily patriarchal society that predominates in southern Africa, Paulina's group has been able to surpass the definition placed on them by their society and make an astounding contribution toward their own livelihood. In this way, the land and the women who cultivate it serve as a metaphor for the rebirth of the community, which, if neglected, can lead to a severe drought of the human spirit. Moreover, working together on the land, they work toward reconciliation between men and women, Africans and Europeans, and the past and the present. They thereby forge a new national identity out of the colonial past. As a land so close to the racial stratification of South Africa, Botswana struggles in Head's work for an identity separate from colonialism and the racism that remains in the nation of which it was once a protectorate. Written in 1966, *When Rain*

Clouds Gather portrays a country at the hopeful beginning of what it later blossomed into—the Botswana that would come to be known as Africa's "success story."

Shannon Oxley

Further Reading

Abrahams, Cecil, ed. *The Tragic Life: Bessie Head and Literature in Southern Africa.* Trenton, N.J.: Africa World Press, 1990. The essays in this collection discuss the themes commonly found within Head's work, as well as the author's imagery, narrative strategies, feminist discourses, and representations of madness.

Brown, Coreen. *The Creative Vision of Bessie Head.* Flushing, N.Y.: Fairleigh Dickinson University Press, 2003. Discusses Head's life and the ways in which her novels reflect the personal struggles she faced in her lifetime. Provides a good critical interpretation of each text and addresses the importance of each one within Head's oeuvre.

Eilersen, Gillian Stead. *Bessie Head: Thunder Behind Her Ears—Her Life and Writing.* Portsmouth, N.H.: Heinemann, 1995. A basic biography; provides useful background to the author's work by recounting her life and exile.

Head, Bessie. *A Woman Alone.* Portsmouth, N.H.: Heinemann, 1990. Collection of Head's essays, in which she writes about her troubled beginnings as a "colored" woman growing up in South Africa and about her migration to Botswana. She also discusses the process of writing and how her life experiences have informed her fiction.

Ibrahim, Huma, ed. *Emerging Perspectives on Bessie Head.* Trenton, N.J.: Africa World Press, 2006. This collection of commentary from scholars around the globe constitutes a detailed and comprehensive critical work on Head. Evaluates Head's contribution to the canon of African literature, as well as the range and scope of her fiction and nonfiction.

Johnson, Joyce. *Bessie Head: The Road of Peace of Mind—A Critical Appreciation.* Newark: University of Delaware Press, 2008. Focuses on Head's creative process; seeks to detect and analyze the author's use of oral traditions in her written work.

Sample, Maxine, ed. *Critical Essays on Bessie Head.* Santa Barbara, Calif.: Greenwood Press, 2003. A collection of scholarly essays that focus on themes commonly found in Head's work. Maureen Fielding's essay focusing on agriculture and healing and Maxine Sample's commentary on space and perspective are both equally imperative to anyone interested in *When Rain Clouds Gather.*